Financial Accounting

Financial Accounting:

An Introduction to Concepts, Methods, and Uses

Fourth Canadian Edition

Sidney Davidson, Ph.D., C.P.A.
University of Chicago

Brian G. Gaber, Ph.D., C.A.
University of Waterloo

C. L. Mitchell, M.B.A., F.C.A.
University of British Columbia

Clyde P. Stickney, D.B.A., C.P.A.
Dartmouth College

Roman L. Weil, Ph.D., C.P.A., C.M.A.
University of Chicago

Holt, Rinehart and Winston of Canada, Limited
Toronto

Canadian Cataloguing in Publication Data

Main entry under title:
Financial accounting : an introduction to
concepts, methods, and uses

4th Canadian ed.
Includes index.
ISBN 0-03-922603-4

1. Accounting.   I. Davidson, Sidney, 1919–

HF5635.F53 1989   657'.044   C89-093288-3

Publisher: David Collinge
Editor: Rachel Campbell
Publishing Services Manager: Karen Eakin
Editorial Co-ordinator: Edie Franks
Copy Editor: Shirley Corriveau
Cover Design: Jack Steiner Graphic Design
Typesetting and Assembly: Q Composition Inc.
Printing and Binding: John Deyell Company

Printed in Canada

1 2 3 4 5   93 92 91 90 89

Whatever be the detail with which you cram
your students, the chance of their meeting in
after-life exactly that detail is almost
infinitesimal; and if they do meet it, they will
probably have forgotten what you taught them
about it. The really useful training yields a
comprehension of a few general principles with
a thorough grounding in the way they apply to
a variety of concrete details. In subsequent
practice the students will have forgotten your
particular details; but they will remember by an
unconscious common sense how to apply
principles to immediate circumstances.

Alfred North Whitehead
The Aims of Education and Other Essays

Preface

The most fundamental issue in designing an introductory accounting text is whether a procedural or conceptual approach should predominate. No text can be entirely one or the other; it is a question of achieving the optimal blend.

This text, in relation to other Canadian accounting texts, can be characterized as being highly conceptual. There are several reasons for this:

1. A majority of students taking the introductory financial accounting course are not majoring in accounting. This is likely to be the only accounting course they will take. Therefore, there is no point in burdening such students with extensive procedural detail.

2. Generally speaking, too little attention is paid on exposing students to the real-world usefulness and excitement of accounting and how it applies to them. If the first exposure to the discipline is an unpleasant one, students may decide against taking further accounting courses. Conceptually based courses are, in general, more interesting to students because they expose the students to those general, fundamental principles that they most certainly will use over and over again in many areas of their lives.

3. University courses should provide intellectual stimulation and focus on reasoning skills rather than memorization skills. Conceptual issues provide such stimulation.

4. An increasing number of students majoring in accounting have taken several years of bookkeeping/accounting in high school. This type of curriculum is highly procedural in orientation and it makes little sense to duplicate it in a university course.

5. Procedures can change as new standards are promulgated but the underlying concepts usually stay the same. Avoiding an undue stress on procedures will help students to be more flexible later on and to adapt to new methods as they arise.

6. Pedagogical theory often suggests a "top down" approach in teaching any material, which is consistent with introducing concepts and principles early.

7. The traditional approach to writing accounting texts reflects the historical roots of accounting—a collection of *ad hoc* procedures that, by whatever means, became generally accepted. Now that we have the rudiments of a conceptual framework and a theory of accounting, a deductive instead of an inductive approach to learning is more appropriate.

Of all the reasons that call for a conceptual approach, however, the most important stems from the calculus of accounting. Accounting is a highly dynamic discipline and the rate of change is increasing. Students well-grounded in concepts have less difficulty adapting to change. Indeed, such students are ideally suited to be the instruments of change.

In addition to containing a blend of concepts and procedures, this text adds a third dimension—the uses of accounting information. Decision usefulness is the central paradigm in accounting today and an understanding of the uses to which accounting information is put helps students as both future users and future preparers of financial statements. Specifically, concepts, methods, and uses are integrated as follows:

1. Concepts This text emphasizes the rationale for, and implications of, important accounting concepts. The ability to "conceptualize" material covered is an important part of the learning process. Without such conceptualization, students will have difficulty focusing on relevant issues in new and different situations. Accordingly, the important accounting concepts are identified early in each chapter. Following these are several numerical examples illustrating their application. Numerous short exercises are included at the end of each chapter to check the students' ability to apply the concepts to still different problem situations.

2. Methods Sufficient emphasis is placed on accounting procedures so that students can interpret, analyze, and evaluate published financial statements. However, procedures are not emphasized to such an extent that students bog down in detail. The determination of just how much accounting procedure is "enough" is a problem faced by all writers of accounting textbooks. Many feel, as do the authors of this text, that the most effective way to learn accounting concepts is to work numerous problems and exercises. However, when too much emphasis is placed on accounting procedures, there is a tendency for students to be lulled into the security of thinking they understand accounting concepts when they actually do not. The mixture of concepts and procedures in this book is one which has been experimented with extensively and has been found effective in classroom use.

Understanding the accounting implications of an event requires that students be able to construct the journal entry for that event. Throughout this book, journal entries are used in describing the nature of accounting events. Moreover, most chapters contain exercises and problems that require the analysis of transactions with debits and credits. Do not conclude, however, by a glance at this text, that it is primarily procedural. The principal objective is that students learn concepts; the procedures are required for learning the concepts.

3. Uses An attempt is made to bridge the gap between the preparation of financial statements and the uses to which the statements might be put. Extensive consideration is given to the effects of alternative accounting principles on the measurement of earnings and financial position and to the types of interpretations that should and should not be made. A complete set of financial statements and related notes appears in Appendix A at the back of the book. Discussion of these financial statements is appropriately integrated into each chapter. Numerous user-oriented cases appear at the end of most chapters.

Changes in This Edition

An extensive survey of third edition users indicated a strong preference to maintain the same basic structure for the fourth edition. Adopters of the fourth edition can be assured that all the successful features of the third edition have been retained.

Major changes in the fourth edition include:

1. Introduction of a new Chapter 14 entitled ''Statement of Changes in Financial Position: Revisited.'' Although an early introduction of this statement (Chapter 5) is desirable, students are unable to handle complex transactions at this point. Chapter 14 assimilates all the material in the book in terms of its impact on the statement of changes in financial position. For those instructors not wanting to cover this statement until the end of the course, Chapters 5 and 14 can be taught together as a unit.

2. Introduction of twenty-nine discussion modules spread evenly throughout the book. They serve two primary purposes. The first is to heighten student interest by introducing real-life examples, thought-provoking issues, or humorous anecdotes. The second purpose is to provide instructors with forums for classroom discussion to stimulate thinking in the students.

3. Addition of numerous new exercises and problems to provide even more choice for assignments. Several of these problems are adapted from CMA examinations.

4. Complete update of all material to reflect the most recent *CICA Handbook* pronouncements. All Handbook releases up to December 31, 1988 are incorporated.

5. Introduction of two Accounting Concepts Problems. The first is at the end of Chapter 4 and deals with a conceptual framework for accounting. The second is located at the end of Chapter 14 and deals with governmental accounting.

6. Inclusion of check figures for most problems (printed on the inside cover of the text) to give students more guidance during homework assignments.

7. Movement of the chapter on changing prices to an appendix because relatively few schools teach this topic at the introductory level. Interperiod tax allocation has been dropped from Chapter 11.

Organization

This book comprises four major parts. Part One, Overview of Financial Statements, contains Chapter 1; Part Two, Accounting Concepts and Methods, Chapters 2–6; Part Three, Measuring and Reporting Assets and Equities, Chapters 7–14; and Part

Four, Synthesis, Chapter 15. The four parts may be viewed as four tiers, or steps, for coverage of the material. Part One (Chapter 1) presents a general overview of the principal financial statements and the nature of accounting. Part Two (Chapters 2 through 6) discusses the basic accounting model used to generate the principal financial statements. Part Three (Chapters 7 through 14) considers the specific accounting principles or methods used in preparing the financial statements. Finally, Part Four (Chapter 15) serves as a synthesis for the entire book. This organization reflects the view that learning can take place most effectively when the student starts with a board picture, then breaks up that broad picture into smaller pieces until the desired depth is achieved, and finally synthesizes the various elements so that the relationship between the parts and the whole can be seen in perspective.

Chapter 1 presents a brief description of the principal activities of a business firm (investing, financing, and operating) and shows how the results of these activities are reported in the three principal financial statements: the balance sheet, the income statement, and the statement of changes in financial position.

Many students feel deluged with the multitude of new terms and concepts after reading Chapter 1. Most of these same students admit later, however, that the broad overview was useful in piecing material together as they later explored individual topics in greater depth.

Chapters 2 through 5 present the basic accounting model that generates the three principal financial statements. In each case, the discussion begins with a description of the important concepts underlying each statement. The accounting procedures employed to generate the statements are then described and illustrated. One of the unique features of the book is the integration in Chapter 3 of the accounting entries for transactions during a period with the related adjusting entries at the end of the period. When these two types of entries are discussed in separate chapters, students lose sight of the fact that both kinds of entries are required to measure net income and financial position.

Another unique aspect of the text is the early coverage, in Chapter 5, of the statement of changes in financial position. There are two purposes in placing it here. First, this placement elevates the statement to its rightful place among the three principal financial statements. Students can thereby integrate the concepts of profitability and cash flow more effectively and begin to understand that one does not necessarily accompany the other. When the funds statement is covered at the end of the course (in many cases, when time is running out), there is a tendency for the student to think it is less important. The second purpose for placing this chapter early in the book is that it serves to cement understanding of the basic accounting model in Chapters 2 through 4; preparing the statement of changes in financial position requires the student to work "backward" from the balance sheet and income statement to reconstruct the transactions that took place.

Chapter 6 introduces the topic of financial statement analysis. This topic is placed here to serve as a partial synthesis of the first five chapters. Students at this point ask how information in the statements might be used. This chapter presents an opportunity to answer some of these questions, even if at only an elementary level. Effective financial statement analysis requires an understanding of the specific accounting methods discussed in Part Three. Chapter 6 therefore serves as a springboard for what is to come.

Chapters 7 through 13 discuss the various "generally accepted accounting principles" employed in generating financial statements. Each chapter not only describes and illustrates the application of the various accounting methods but also considers their effects on the financial statements. This approach reflects the view that students should be able to interpret and analyze published financial statements and to understand the effect of alternative accounting methods on such assessments. Some of the more complicated topics have been placed in end-of-chapter appendices to provide flexibility in coverage. Some instructors may not wish to use this more advanced material.

Chapter 14 revisits the Statement of Changes in Financial Position for a more in-depth look. It draws upon material from most of the previous thirteen chapters.

The students who have used the previous edition of this book have found that Chapter 15, which synthesizes much of the material in the first fourteen chapters, is in many ways the most useful chapter in the book. Explicit consideration is given to the combined effects of alternative accounting methods on the financial statements and the significance of alternative accounting methods on financial statement analysis. The self-study problem and problems 20 and 21 at the end of Chapter 15 are major review problems for the whole book.

A comprehensive Glossary of financial accounting terms is included at the end of the book. This glossary serves as a useful reference tool for accounting and other business terms and provides additional descriptions of several topics considered only briefly in the text, such as *accounting changes* and *breakeven analysis*.

Related Materials Accompanying the Text

The following materials have been prepared for use with the text:

Instructor's Manual The instructor's manual, in addition to including responses to all questions and solutions to all exercises, problems and cases, presents suggested course outlines for courses of varying lengths, a list of chapter objectives, helpful teaching hints, detailed lecture and discussion outlines including the numbers of particularly germane problems, and sample examination questions and problems.

Study Guide A self-test study guide has been prepared which includes a listing of highlights from each chapter and is then followed by numerous short true/false, matching, and multiple-choice questions, with answers.

Test Bank Prepared by David Carter, this instructor's aid contains numerous examination-type questions.

Acknowledgements

I am, first and foremost, indebted to the authors of the American edition, Sidney Davidson, Clyde Stickney, and Roman Weil, for creating such a high-quality introductory text that emphasizes concepts rather than procedures. I am equally indebted to C.L. Mitchell, who has done such outstanding work on the first three Canadian editions.

The following individuals have reviewed portions of earlier editions and their efforts have contributed to the quality of the current edition: H. Babiak (University of Toronto), M. Bundy (University of Regina), P. Cunningham (Bishop's University), C. Duncan (St. Francis Xavier University), H. Elmslie (Lakehead University), B. Fleischer (Simon Fraser University), G.T. Gilbert (University of Toronto), C. Heywood (Wilfrid Laurier University), M. Hilton (University of Manitoba), J. Hughes (Memorial University), V.B. Irvine (University of Saskatchewan), B. Mallouk (University of Toronto), A.R. Marshall (McGill University), E. Peter (Memorial University), R. Rennie (University of Regina), A.W. Richardson (McMaster University), R.B. Schenk (Bishop's University), T. Var (Simon Fraser University) and Christopher Wright. Special thanks go to John McCutcheon (Wilfrid Laurier University) for preparing the Lecturer's Aid for the third edition. Parts of this volume have been incorporated into the instructor's manual.

I am grateful to Harry Elmslie (Lakehead University), Maureen Fizzell (University of Saskatchewan), John Heapy (McGill University), John Hughes (Memorial University), Duan Kennedy (University of Waterloo), Don Lockwood (University of British Columbia), John McCutcheon (Wilfrid Laurier University) and Peter Secord and Greg Walsh (Saint Mary's University) who acted as primary reviewers of the fourth edition. They contributed many valuable suggestions which have been utilized in the book. My colleagues at the University of Waterloo provided valuable advice. David Carter, in particular, gave thoughtful feedback on many of the changes in this edition. Also, he prepared the test bank for instructors.

I gratefully acknowledge the permission given by the Canadian Institute of Chartered Accountants to quote from their publications, *The CICA Handbook*, *Terminology for Accountants*, and *Financial Reporting in Canada*, and the permission given by the Society of Management Accountants of Canada to adapt some of their examination questions for this book.

David Collinge, publisher, Warren Laws, acquisitions editor, Rachel Campbell, editor, and Edie Franks, editorial co-ordinator of Holt, Rinehart, and Winston of Canada, Limited provided immense assistance in planning and preparing this edition.

The contributions of Karen Eakin, Shirley Corriveau, and Jack Steiner are also appreciated.

As any textbook author knows, the largest contribution of all comes from the patience and understanding of one's family for the long duration of the project. To Margaret and Cory – thank you.

> Brian G. Gaber
> University of Waterloo
> February, 1989

Publisher's Note to Instructors and Students

This text book is a key component of your course. If you are the instructor of this course, you undoubtedly considered a number of texts carefully before choosing this as the one that will work best for your students and you. The authors and publishers of this book spent considerable time and money to ensure its high quality, and we appreciate your recognition of this effort and accomplishment.

If you are a student, we are confident that this text will help you to meet the objectives of your course. You will also find it helpful after the course is finished, as a valuable addition to your personal library. So hold on to it.

As well, please don't forget that photocopying copyright work means the authors lose royalties that are rightfully theirs. This loss will discourage them from writing another edition of this text or other books, because doing so will simply not be worth their time and effort. If this happens, we all lose – students, instructors, authors, and publishers.

And since we want to hear what you think about this book, please be sure to send us the stamped reply card at the end of this text. This will help us to continue publishing high-quality books for your courses.

Table of Contents

Part Three	**Measuring and Reporting Assets and Equities Using Generally Accepted Accounting Principles**
	A Transitional Note: Generally Accepted Accounting Principles *324*
	Nature and Development of Generally Accepted Accounting Principles *324*

Chapter Seven	**Cash, Temporary Investments, and Receivables: The Liquid Assets** *327*
	Liquidity and Money-Like Assets *327*
	Cash *327*
	Cash Inclusions and Valuation *327*
	Cash Management *328*
	Controlling Cash *328*
	Controlling Cash Receipts and Disbursements *328*
	Undeposited Cash *330*
	Cash in Bank – Deposits *330*
	Cash in Bank – Issuance of Cheques *330*
	Control of Disbursements by Cheque *330*
	Petty Cash *331*
	The Bank Statement *331*
	Preparing the Bank Reconcilation *332*
	Adjusting Entries from the Bank Reconciliation *333*
	Summary of Accounting for Cash *335*
	Temporary Investments *335*
	Classification of Temporary Investments *335*

Part One   Overview of Financial Statements

Chapter 1 Overview of Financial Statements and Reporting Process

Accounting is a system for *measuring* the results of business activities and *communicating* those measurements to interested users. You are about to begin a study of (1) the concepts and procedures used by accountants to make these measurements and (2) the principal financial statements through which the measurements are communicated. Whether or not you become an accountant yourself, you will use accounting as a tool in making production, marketing, investment, or other business decisions. The goal of your study (and this book) is to help you gain sufficient understanding of accounting concepts and procedures so that you can use accounting data effectively.

Distinction Between Managerial and Financial Accounting

The field of accounting divides into two parts: managerial accounting and financial accounting.

Managerial accounting is concerned with the preparation of reports for use by persons within a firm. For example, a corporate treasurer might use a statement of projected cash receipts and disbursements in deciding whether short-term borrowing is necessary. A production manager might use a report on the productivity of various employees in deciding how a special order is to be routed through a factory. A sales manager might use a report on the cost of producing and selling different product lines in recommending the prices to be charged and the products to be emphasized by the sales staff. Users of information within a firm can specify the types of information they need for their decisions: managerial accounting reports are designed to satisfy these needs.

In contrast, *financial accounting* is concerned with the preparation of reports for use by persons outside a firm. For example, a bank may desire information on the cash-generating ability of a firm in deciding whether or not to grant a bank loan. A potential investor may desire information on a firm's profitability before deciding to purchase its common shares.

The format and content of financial accounting reports tend to be more standardized than those used in managerial accounting. The large number of uses and users of financial accounting reports creates the need for some degree of uniformity in reporting among firms.

The most common reports for external users are the financial statements included in annual reports to shareholders (owners) and potential investors. These financial statements are prepared to conform with *generally accepted accounting principles* (GAAP). Such "principles" have evolved over time or have been made "acceptable" by decree from an official rule-making body. The Accounting Standards

Committee (AcSC) of the Canadian Institute of Chartered Accountants (CICA) is the principal rule-making body in Canada.

This text discusses the principles that underlie the financial statements prepared by firms for external users. We begin by studying how a typical firm carries out its business activities. We then see how the results of these business activities are measured and reported in the principal financial statements. This chapter introduces material to be covered in greater depth in later chapters. The objective is to develop the "big picture" so that a perspective is provided for the concepts and procedures discussed later.

One Accounting Profession—or Three?

*T*here are three professional accounting organizations in Canada representing approximately 120,000 licenced accountants. A member of the Canadian Institute of Chartered Accountants (CICA) is a Chartered Accountant (CA). Members of The Society of Management Accountants of Canada (SMAC) are Certified Management Accountants (CMA). Members of the Certified General Accountants' Association of Canada are Certified General Accountants (CGA).

CMAs work principally in industry. CAs work in industry but are also licensed by ten provincial Acts to conduct independent audits of companies. The majority of CGAs are employed in industry, but in three provinces are also licensed to conduct audits. All three types of accountants are also found in government, the largest employer in Canada.

The three professions are marked by more similarities than differences, which is natural since any profession has many similar attributes. These include:
1. Mastery of an intellectual skill
2. Altruism (a desire to serve the public interest)
3. Self-regulation (including standards for admission, day-to-day conduct, and discipline)
4. Community sanction (which recognizes the group's professional status and grants it quasi-monopoly rights)
5. A code of ethical conduct more rigorous than that of the general population
6. Intellectual curiosity and a desire to expand the frontiers of known knowledge
7. Objectivity (a commitment to search for truth without the interference of bias)

Historically, medicine, theology, and law were deemed to be professions. In the twentieth century, other groups such as accountants, engineers, dentists, and architects have laid claim to professional status. In fact, a great many occupational classes aspire to professional status and have adopted the word "professional" in their title. However, community sanction and the right of self-regulation are granted to very few of these groups.

To be a professional accountant is a desirable goal. Accountants consistently rank in the top five occupational classes in Canada for average salary. Professions enjoy high social status and public respect, and the possession of a professional designation gives the holder considerable job mobility. The study program is long and the qualifying exams rigorous but the effort is well worth it.

Professional accountants in two Canadian provinces, British Columbia and Quebec, have recently put on ice plans for a proposed merger of the accounting bodies. In British Columbia the CAs and CMAs would have merged and in Quebec CAs, CMAs, and CGAs would have tied the knot.

Debate about the proposed mergers was just as emotional and vehement as the recent free trade debates in this country. Opposition to the union came principally from the CAs and appeared to be based on two themes. First, many CAs expressed the attitude "I worked so hard for my CA—why should I let others get the designation any easier." This view is predicated on the suspect logic that the hurdles to CAdom are considerably higher than for the other two designations. That may have been a correct assessment at one point in time, but the educational programs for CMAs and CGAs have undergone continued upgrading and are formidable in their own right. Now, with the recent move of CGAs to require university degrees, a major difference between educational programs will be removed.

The second, more serious concern of CAs (but never publically admitted) is fear of loss of monopoly rights (and revenues). In most of Canada's provinces, CAs are granted attestation rights by Act of Legislature that give them exclusive rights to conduct independent audits. A merger of the three accounting bodies would presumably open up cutthroat competition for slices of this lucrative audit pie.

This logic is also suspect. First, if auditors are providing quality service to clients, there is no particular reason for companies to switch auditors. Second, by necessity, the audits of large corporations are done normally by national, or multi-national, accounting firms. Few CGA firms are of this size. Third, CMAs operate in a specialized niche with no claim to providing attestation services. Finally, in the three provinces which allow CGAs attestation rights there have been no public outcries of lost business or hardship by CA firms.

Alberta may turn out to be the bellwether province on this issue. The provincial government recently passed legislation requiring harmonization of many aspects of accounting practice. This may turn out to be a *defacto* merger.

Despite the temporary setbacks in BC and Quebec, the three accounting bodies in Canada will eventually merge. History is often the best guide to the future. Note that on several occasions in Canadian history when there have been competing accounting bodies, merger was always the result.

More importantly, merger is in the public interest. The public has the right to demand a single standard of excellence from professional accountants. Do we have competing bodies of doctors, lawyers, or engineers? No—by definition each is a single profession, and accounting should be no different.

The CICA Long Range Strategic Planning Report holds the key to implementation. It proposes that the CA be a generalist designation (much like the GP in medicine) and then that there be separate specialist designations for tax, attestation, EDP, etc. All three current bodies could be granted the generalist designation and individuals would qualify for the individual specialist designations according to their needs and abilities. One accounting profession, one uniform standard of excellence, an idea whose time has come!

References:
"Will Canada's Accountants Ever Merge?" *The Financial Executive*, July/August 1988, pp. 8–9.
"Meeting the Challenge of Change." *Report of the CICA Long Range Strategic Planning Committee*, 1986.

Overview of Business Activities

Financial statements for external users attempt to present in a meaningful way the results of a firm's business activities. Understanding these financial statements requires an understanding of the business activities that they attempt to portray.

Example 1 Bill Marsh and Janet Nelson, while working toward degrees in engineering, developed a computerized mechanism for monitoring automobile engine performance. They received a patent on the device and, having recently graduated, want to set up their own firm to manufacture and sell it. The firm will be called Marnel Corporation.[1]

Some of the more important processes through which Marnel Corporation must go are described below.

Establishing Corporate Goals and Strategies

The *goals* of any firm are the targets, or end results, toward which the energies of the firm are directed. The *strategies* of the firm are the means for achieving these goals.

The detail in which goals and strategies are stated varies among firms. Some firms prefer to state goals and strategies in general terms only. For example, a firm might express its goal as ''be more profitable than our leading competitors.'' Its strategy might be to mechanize production so that it can manufacture quality products at a cost lower than its competitors.

Often firms might be more explicit. The goal might be to achieve a certain rate of profitability. The goals might also be broader than profitability alone and include concerns for employee welfare, environmental protection, and community involvement. Strategies might likewise be spelled out in detail, including step-by-step actions to accomplish the goals.

Marnel Corporation's goal is to develop a continuing stream of quality electronic products that can be manufactured and marketed profitably and thereby increase the value of the firm and the wealth of its owners. Its strategies include the following:

1. All electronic devices will be manufactured by Marnel Corporation, so as to ensure quality and provide some protection against other firms' attempts to imitate the devices.
2. The sales and servicing of the devices will be carried out by the firm's sales staff to provide close working relations with customers.
3. Investments will be made in research and development to ensure the ongoing creation of new products.

---

[1]Canadian companies are required by the Companies (Corporations) Acts of the provincial and federal governments to have attached to their name one of Limited, Ltd., Ltée, Incorporated, Inc., Corporation, Corp., depending on the jurisdiction of incorporation.

Obtaining Financing

Before Marnel Corporation can embark on its business activities, it must obtain the necessary funds. The principal sources of funds are owners and creditors.

Owners Owners provide funds to a firm and in return receive some evidence of their ownership. When a firm is organized as a corporation, ownership is evidenced by shares of common stock and the owners are called *shareholders*.[2] The firm need not repay the owners at a particular future date. Instead, the owners receive dividends if and when the firm decides to pay them. The owners also have a claim on all increases in the value of the firm resulting from future profitable operations. Usually shareholders are able to sell their shares to other persons at a bargained price.

Creditors Unlike owners, creditors provide funds but require that the funds be repaid, often with interest, at a specific date. The length of time that elapses until repayment varies. Long-term creditors may provide funds and not require repayment for 20 years or more. Such borrowings are usually evidenced by a *bond*. A bond is simply an agreement in which the borrowing company promises to pay the creditors interest on the amounts borrowed at specific dates in the future and then to repay the amount borrowed at the end of some stated period of years. Banks usually lend for periods between several months and several years. Bank borrowings are usually evidenced by a *note* in which the borrowing company promises to repay the amount borrowed plus interest at some future date. Suppliers of raw materials may not view themselves as sources of funds for a firm. Yet, when they supply raw materials but do not require payment for 30 days, they implicitly provide funds. Likewise, employees who are paid weekly or monthly and governmental units that are paid monthly or quarterly provide funds.

All firms must choose the proportion of funds to be obtained from owners, long-term creditors, and short-term creditors. Finance courses cover such financing decisions.

Making Investments

Once a firm has obtained funds, it usually invests them in various items (assets) needed to carry out its business activities, such as the following:

1. Land, buildings, and equipment — Such investments provide a firm with a capacity to manufacture and sell its products and usually take many years to provide all of the potential services for which they were acquired.
2. Patents, licences, and other contractual rights — Such investments provide a firm with the legal right to use certain property or processes in pursuing its business activities.
3. Common shares or bonds of other firms — A firm might invest in other firms (thereby becoming itself an owner or creditor). Such investments might be made for a few months with temporarily excess cash or for more long-term purposes.

---

[2]In other legal forms of business organizations, including sole proprietorships, partnerships, and co-operatives, the owners are not called shareholders. This text illustrates the corporate form of organization unless otherwise stated and the owners are called shareholders.

4. Inventories—The principal goal of many business firms is to sell their products to customers.[3] In order to satisfy the needs of customers as they arise, an inventory of products must be on hand. Funds are usually not invested in specific inventory items for very long, because the items will soon be sold to customers. Because a certain amount of inventory must always be on hand, however, firms must continually invest some amount of their funds in inventory items.
5. Accounts receivable from customers—When a firm sells its products to customers who are not required to pay immediately, the firm is providing financing to its customers. Carrying a certain amount of accounts receivable may be in the best interest of the firm if sales and profits are increased accordingly. In extending credit to customers, the firm forgoes collecting its cash right away. Funds to acquire other assets must be obtained elsewhere. Carrying accounts receivable, therefore, requires an investment of funds.
6. Cash—Most firms will leave a portion of their funds in the form of cash in chequing or savings accounts so that they can pay their bills currently, and to provide a cushion to handle unforeseen expenditures.

Managerial accounting courses cover the techniques for making proper investment decisions.

Carrying out Operations

A firm obtains financing and invests the funds in various resources in order to generate profit. The following comprises the operating activities of a firm:

1. Purchasing—The purchasing department of a *merchandising* firm acquires the amounts and types of products needed by its retail stores. The purchasing department of a *manufacturing* firm acquires the amounts and types of raw materials needed in production.
2. Production—The production department in a manufacturing firm combines raw materials, labour services, and other manufacturing inputs to produce the products, or outputs, of a firm.
3. Marketing—The marketing department oversees selling the product to customers.
4. Administration—The administrative activity of a firm supports purchasing, production, marketing, and other operating departments. Administration might include data processing, accounting, legal services, research and development, and other activities.

Managerial accounting, marketing, and production courses cover the appropriate basis for making operating decisions.

Summary of Business Activities

Figure 1.1 summarizes the four principal business activities discussed in this section and distinguishes between the short term and the long term. Although the time line dividing short- from long-term activities varies somewhat among firms, one year is generally the dividing line used, since one year is the normal interval between the preparation of full financial statements. Theoretically, the demarcation should

---

[3]Some firms, of course, sell services instead of products (e.g., an accounting firm).

be based on one year or one operating cycle, whichever is longer. An operating cycle is the normal length of time to turn cash into inventory, into receivables, and back into cash. For example, a distillery that ages its products might have an operating cycle of many years.

Figure 1.1   Summary of Business Activities

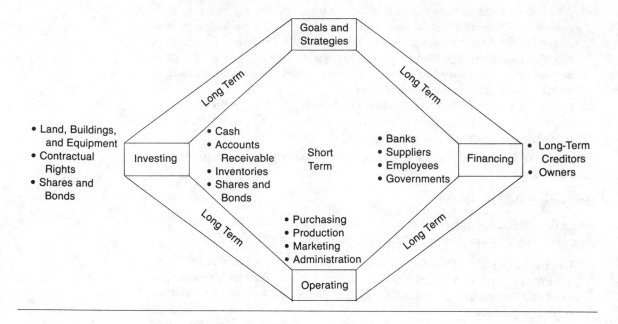

Principal Financial Statements

The annual report to shareholders typically includes a letter from the firm's president summarizing activities of the past year and assessing the firm's prospects for the coming year. Also frequently included are promotional materials, such as pictures of the firm's products and employees. The section of the annual report containing the financial statements comprises the following:[4]

1. Balance sheet
2. Income statement
3. Retained earnings statement
4. Statement of changes in financial position
5. Notes to the financial statements, including various supporting schedules and explanatory comments
6. Auditor's report

[4]An increasingly common addition to the financial statements is the *management report*, in which management acknowledges its primary responsibility for the content of the financial statements. Note also that the retained earnings statement is sometimes combined with the income statement instead of being shown as a separate schedule, and the auditor's report is included only for those companies requiring audited financial statements.

Balance Sheet

The balance sheet presents a snapshot of the financial position of the firm at an instant in time—the balance sheet date. This statement shows the accumulated wealth and the outstanding obligations of the enterprise. Each day the balance sheet would be different, reflecting further operating, financing, and investing activities. Exhibit 1.1 presents a comparative balance sheet for Marnel Corporation as of January 1, Year 1, and December 31, Year 1.

The balance sheet on January 1, Year 1, depicts Marnel Corporation on the day it was organized. Owners provided $500,000 of funds, long-term creditors provided $400,000, and suppliers provided $100,000. These funds were invested in inventories, land, building, equipment, and a patent; $70,000 was left in the firm's chequing account.

Exhibit 1.1
MARNEL CORPORATION
Comparative Balance Sheet

	December 31, Year 1	January 1, Year 1
Assets		
Current Assets:		
Cash	$ 190,000	$ 70,000
Accounts Receivable	180,000	—
Inventories	270,000	100,000
Total Current Assets	$ 640,000	$ 170,000
Property, Plant and Equipment:		
Land	$ 30,000	$ 30,000
Buildings (net of accumulated depreciation)	380,000	400,000
Equipment (net of accumulated depreciation)	230,000	250,000
Total property, plant and equipment	$ 640,000	$ 680,000
Patent (net of accumulated amortization)	120,000	150,000
Total Noncurrent Assets	$ 760,000	$ 830,000
Total Assets	$1,400,000	$1,000,000
Liabilities and Shareholders' Equity		
Current Liabilities:		
Accounts Payable	$ 130,000	$ 100,000
Salaries Payable	30,000	—
Income Taxes Payable	40,000	—
Total Current Liabilities	$ 200,000	$ 100,000
Noncurrent Liabilities:		
Bonds Payable (due Year 20)	450,000	400,000
Total Liabilities	$ 650,000	$ 500,000
Shareholders' Equity:		
Common Stock	$ 600,000	$ 500,000
Retained Earnings	150,000	—
Total Shareholders' Equity	$ 750,000	$ 500,000
Total Liabilities and Shareholders' Equity	$1,400,000	$1,000,000

The balance sheet on December 31, Year 1, presents the financial position of Marnel Corporation at the end of the first year. The amounts for most items in the balance sheet changed between the beginning and end of the year.

Note several aspects about the balance sheet.

Concepts of Assets, Liabilities, and Shareholders' Equity The balance sheet presents a listing of a firm's assets, liabilities, and shareholders' equity.

Assets are economic resources. An asset is an item that has the ability or potential to provide future benefits to a firm. For example, cash can be used to purchase inventory or equipment. Inventory can be sold to customers for an amount the firm hopes will be larger than was paid for it. Equipment can be used in transporting inventory to customers.

Liabilities are creditors' claims on the assets of a firm. Marnel Corporation has purchased inventories from its suppliers but has not paid for a portion of the purchases. As a result, these creditors have provided funds to the firm and have a claim on its assets. Labour services have been provided by employees for which payment has not been made as of December 31, Year 1. These employees likewise have provided funds to the firm and have a claim on its assets. Creditors' claims, or liabili-results from a firm's having received benefits (cash, inventories, labour services) previously, and typically have a specified amount and date at which they must be paid.

Shareholders' equity is the owners' claim on the assets of a firm in a corporate form of business. Unlike creditors, the owners have only a residual interest. That is, owners have a claim on all assets in excess of those required to meet creditors' claims. The shareholders' equity generally comprises two parts: contributed capital and retained earnings. *Contributed capital* reflects the funds invested by shareholders for an ownership interest. The owners initially contributed $500,000 for Marnel Corporation's common shares. They invested an additional $100,000 during Year 1 for more shares.

Retained earnings represent the earnings realized by a firm since its formation in excess of dividends distributed to shareholders. In other words, retained earnings are earnings reinvested by management for the benefit of shareholders. Management directs the use of a firm's assets so that over time more assets are received than are given up in obtaining them. This increase in assets, after any claims of creditors, belongs to the firm's owners. Most firms reinvest a large percentage of the assets generated by earnings for replacement of assets and growth rather than paying dividends.

Equality of Assets and Liabilities Plus Shareholders' Equity As the balance sheet for Marnel Corporation shows, there is an equality between (1) assets and (2) liabilities plus shareholders' equity. That is,

$$\text{Assets} = \text{Liabilities} + \text{Shareholders' Equity}$$

Assets reflect a firm's past investment decisions, and liabilities plus shareholders' equity reflect a firm's past financing decisions. Every dollar of funds obtained must be invested in something. Thus, we are viewing the same resources from two angles: a listing of the forms in which they are held (assets) and a listing of the parties (creditors and owners) who have provided financing and who, therefore, have a claim on those assets. Thus,

$$\text{Assets} = \text{Liabilities} + \text{Shareholders' Equity,}$$

or

$$\text{Investing} = \text{Financing.}$$

Balance Sheet Classification The balance sheet classifies assets and liabilities as being either current or noncurrent.

Current assets include cash and assets that are expected to be turned into cash, or sold, or consumed within approximately one year from the date of the balance sheet. Cash, temporary investments in securities, accounts receivable from customers, and inventories are the most common current assets. *Current liabilities* include liabilities that are expected to be paid within one year. Notes payable to banks, accounts payable to suppliers, salaries payable to employees, and taxes payable to governments are examples.

Noncurrent assets, typically held and used for several years, include land, buildings, equipment, patents, and long-term investments in securities. *Noncurrent liabilities* and *shareholders' equity* are a firm's longer-term sources of funds.

Valuation The dollar amount at which each asset and liability appears on the balance sheet is based on one of two valuation bases: (1) cash, or cash equivalent, valuation, or (2) acquisition, or historical, cost valuation.

Cash is stated at the amount of cash on hand or in the bank. Accounts receivable are shown at the amount of cash expected to be collected from customers. Liabilities are generally shown at the present value of the cash required to pay the liabilities. These assets and liabilities are sometimes referred to as *monetary items* because they are valued on a cash, or cash equivalent, basis.

The remaining assets are shown either at acquisition cost or at acquisition cost net of accumulated depreciation or amortization. For example, inventories and land are stated at the amount of cash or other resources that the firm originally sacrificed to acquire those assets. Buildings, equipment, and patents are likewise stated at acquisition cost, but this amount is adjusted downward to reflect the portion of the assets' services that has been used up since acquisition.

Common stock is reported at the amount invested by owners when the firm's common shares were first issued. Retained earnings is generally the sum of all prior years' earnings in excess of dividends.

Income Statement

The second principal financial statement is the income statement, which presents the results of the operating activities of a firm for a period of time. Exhibit 1.2 presents the income statement for Marnel Corporation for Year 1. This statement indicates the *net income* or *earnings* of a firm for a period of time. Net income is the difference between revenues and expenses. Note several aspects of the income statement.

Concepts of Net Income, Revenue, and Expense The terms *net income* and *earnings* are synonyms used interchangeably in corporate annual reports and throughout this text. Generating income from operating activities is the primary goal of most business firms. The income statement provides a measure of how successful a firm was in achieving this goal for a given time span. The income statement also reports the

Exhibit 1.2
MARNEL CORPORATION
Income Statement for Year 1

Sales of Electronic Devices		$2,250,000
Less: Cost of Goods Sold		1,400,000
Gross Profit		$ 850,000
Sale of Engineering Services		140,000
		$ 990,000
Less: Selling and Administrative Expenses		
Selling Expenses	$400,000	
Administrative Expenses	200,000	600,000
Operating Profit		$ 390,000
Less: Financial Expense (net):		
Interest Expenses	$ 50,000	
Less: Interest Revenue	10,000	40,000
Net Income before Income Tax		$ 350,000
Income Tax Expense		150,000
Net Income		$ 200,000

sources and amounts of a firm's revenues and the nature and amount of a firm's expenses that net to earnings for the period.

Revenues measure the inflows of assets (or reductions in liabilities) from selling goods and providing services to customers. During Year 1, Marnel Corporation sold electronic devices and provided engineering and financing services. From its customers, Marnel Corporation received either cash or promises to pay cash in the future, called Accounts Receivable from Customers. Both are assets. Thus, revenues were generated and assets increased.

Expenses measure the outflow of assets (or increases in liabilities) used up in generating revenues. *Cost of goods sold* (an expense) is a measure of the cost of inventories sold to customers. Selling expenses measure the cash payments made or the liabilities incurred to make future cash payments for marketing services received during the period. For each expense, either an asset decreases or a liability increases.

A firm strives to generate an excess of net asset inflows from revenues over net asset outflows from expenses required in generating the revenues. Net income indicates a firm's accomplishments (revenues) relative to the efforts required (expenses) in pursuing its operating activities. When expenses for a period exceed revenues, a firm incurs a *net loss*.

Classification of Income Statement The purpose of the income statement is to provide useful information about the flows of the firm so that persons outside the company can evaluate managerial performance and construct an estimate of future performance.

Expense flows are incurred to earn revenue. Some can be identified with particular revenue transactions, for example, the cost of goods sold, since the acquisition of the merchandise is a necessary condition to its sale. Other expense flows, such as advertising, can be identified only with particular classes of revenue, and others, such as general management expenses, only with the general operation of the business.

To distinguish the expenses and match them to the appropriate revenue, the income statement can be segregated into four steps. The first step matches the cost of goods sold with the revenue from the sale, the difference between the two representing the *gross profit*. The gross profit ratio, the ratio of gross profit to sales, will vary between industries and firms, but will alter significantly over time for one firm only if there have been dramatic changes in policy.

From the gross profit, the expenses of the operating functions, such as marketing, accounting, personnel, and general management, are deducted to derive the *operating profit* of the firm for the period. This is the second step. The operating profit is the result of the primary activities of the firm before considering the financing activities and the portion of the net income to be shared with government as income tax.

Some firms depend on the shareholders as a primary source of capital, whereas others borrow substantial sums from creditors for this purpose. The firms depending primarily on shareholders would incur no interest expense, in contrast with the latter group of firms. In order to enhance interfirm comparability and to evaluate the financial activity of a firm, the results of the financial function are deducted separately from the operating profit in the third step. The common result of the financial function is interest expense, but this expense may be offset by interest and dividends received from the investment in financial assets.

Corporations are individual legal entities and as such are subject to income tax. A full examination of corporate income tax requires a course wholly on that subject, but it will be discussed in Chapter 10. Briefly, the income tax payable by a firm is based on a fixed rate multiplied by the net income before income tax. After deducting income tax, the results of the recurring operations of the firm are presented as the *net income*. The net income represents the residual revenues attributable to the shareholders of the firm.

The *multiple-step* income statement described is ordinarily used for internal reporting; the format is altered for external reporting. This multiple-step form of income statement will be used throughout the text.

Retained Earnings Statement

The retained earnings statement links the balance sheet at the beginning with that at the end of the period and the income statement. Recall that retained earnings represent the sum of prior earnings of a firm in excess of dividends. The amount of net income helps explain the change in retained earnings between the beginning and end of the period. During Year 1, Marnel Corporation had net income of $200,000. Dividends declared and paid were $50,000. Exhibit 1.3 presents the retained earnings statement for Marnel Corporation for Year 1.

Exhibit 1.3
MARNEL CORPORATION
Retained Earnings Statement for Year 1

Retained Earnings, January 1, Year 1	$ 0
Add Net Income for Year 1	200,000
Subtract Dividends Declared and Paid during Year 1	(50,000)
Retained Earnings December 31, Year 1	$150,000

Summary of Balance Sheet and Income Statement

Recall that Figure 1.1 summarizes the principal business activities of a firm: financing, investing, and operating. Figure 1.2 now summarizes the relation between these business activities and the balance sheet and income statement.

Figure 1.2 Relationship Between Business Activities and Balance Sheet and Income Statement

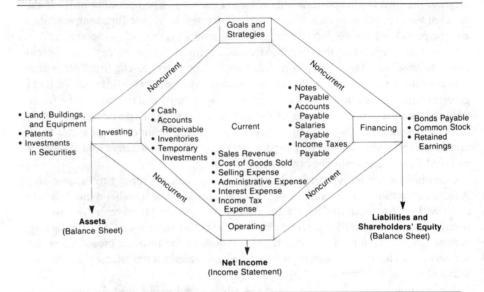

Statement of Changes in Financial Position

The fourth principal financial statement is the statement of changes in financial position. This statement reports the sources (inflows) and uses (outflows) of cash during a period of time. Exhibit 1.4 presents a statement of changes in financial position for

Exhibit 1.4
MARNEL CORPORATION
Statement of Changes in Financial Position for Year 1

Cash Provided By:	
Operations	$ 50,000[5]
New Financing: Issue of Bonds	50,000
Issue of Common Shares	100,000
Sale of Noncurrent Assets	—
Total Sources	$200,000
Cash Applied To:	
Dividends	$ 50,000
Reduction in Financing	—
Acquisition of Noncurrent Assets	30,000
Total Uses	$ 80,000
Net Increase in Cash for Year 1	$120,000

[5]Computation of this item, and proper formatting rules are discussed in Chapter 5.

Marnel Corporation for Year 1. Operations led to an increase in cash of $50,000. (Recall that not all revenues result in an immediate increase in cash and that not all expenses result in an immediate decrease in cash.) Also, cash was received when bonds and common shares were issued. Cash was used to pay dividends and to acquire equipment. Of what significance is a statement explaining or analyzing the change in cash during a period of time? This might be best understood with an example.

Example 2 Diversified Technologies Corporation began business four years ago. In its first four years of operations, net income was $100,000, $300,000, $800,000, and $1,500,000, respectively. The company retained all of its earnings for growth. Early in the fifth year, the company learned that despite the retention of all of its earnings, it was running out of cash. A careful study of the problem revealed that the company was expanding accounts receivable, inventories, buildings, and equipment so fast that funds were not being generated quickly enough by operations to keep pace with its growth.

This example illustrates a common phenomenon for business firms. Cash may not be generated in sufficient amounts or at the proper times to finance all ongoing or growing operations. If the firm is to continue operating successfully, it must generate more funds than it spends. In some cases the firm can borrow from creditors to replenish its cash, but future operations must generate funds to repay these loans.

Classification of Sources and Uses of Cash Exhibit 1.4 classifies the sources and uses of cash in parallel with the three principal business activities described earlier in the chapter. Figure 1.3 depicts these various sources and uses graphically.

Figure 1.3 Sources and Uses of Cash

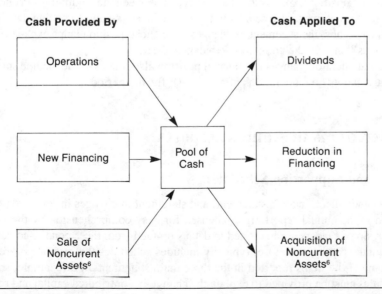

[6]These are called investing activities on the statement.

1. Sources: Operations — The excess of cash received from customers over the amount of cash paid to suppliers, employees, and others in carrying out a firm's operating activities is a primary source of funds for most firms. Although the cash received from customers could be included among the sources and the cash paid to suppliers, employees, and others included among uses, most firms net the sources from operations against the uses from operations.
2. Sources: New Financing — Firms often obtain additional financing by issuing bonds or common shares.
3. Sources: Sale of Noncurrent Assets — The sales of land, buildings, equipment, and other noncurrent assets generate cash.
4. Uses: Dividends — Most firms whose shares are widely held by the public regularly pay dividends. The payment of dividends might be viewed as a reduction in financing, because funds potentially invested by owners (through retained earnings) are now being distributed to them.
5. Uses: Reduction in Financing — Cash is used when a firm repays noncurrent liabilities or reacquires its common shares.
6. Uses: Acquisition of Noncurrent Assets — Firms that expect either to maintain current operating levels or to grow must continually acquire buildings, equipment, and other noncurrent assets.

Some people consider the statement of changes in financial position to be the most useful of the four statements. A major purpose of annual financial statements is to present a report on the activities of management during the past year to the investors who have entrusted their funds to management. The statement of changes best summarizes how this stewardship role was carried out and shows how these funds were deployed to produce the best possible return on investment for the owners.

Relationship to Balance Sheet and Income Statement The statement of changes in financial position explains the change in cash between the beginning and end of the period. The statement also sets forth the major investing and financing activities of the period. Thus, the statement of changes in financial position helps explain changes in various items on the comparative balance sheet.

The statement of changes in financial position also relates to the income statement in that it shows how operations affected cash for the period.

Other Items in Annual Reports

Notes and Supporting Schedules

The balance sheet, income statement, and statement of changes in financial position shown in the annual report are condensed for easy comprehension by the average reader. Some readers are interested in details omitted from these condensed versions. The annual report, therefore, typically includes schedules that provide more detail for some of the items reported in the three main statements. For example, separate schedules must be provided to explain the change in contributed capital and retained earnings, and may be provided to explain changes in other items in the balance sheet.

Every set of published financial statements also contains explanatory notes which are an integral part of the statements. As later chapters make clear, a firm must select the accounting methods followed in preparing its financial statements from a set of generally accepted methods. The notes indicate the actual accounting methods used by the firm, and also disclose additional information that elaborates on items presented in the three principal statements. To understand fully a firm's balance sheet, income statement, and statement of changes in financial position requires a careful reading of the notes. No such notes are presented for the financial statements of Marnel Corporation because they would not mean much at this stage. Do not conclude, however, that the notes are unimportant merely because they have been omitted from the statements presented in this chapter. See Appendix A, page 765 for examples of notes to the financial statements.

Auditor's Report

The annual financial statements present a "score card" on the activities of management and on the performance of the firm over the course of a year. Investment and lending decisions and the operation of capital markets are largely dependent on the signals generated by these financial statements. Yet we have the curious situation where management prepares its own "score card." Obviously, there is a natural tendency for management to want to present the financial position of the company in the most favourable light. In some cases, executive salaries are directly tied to the size of the earnings figure reported.

To add objectivity to this process, independent auditors, who are not employees of the corporation, are called in to make their own assessment of how fairly the financial statements portray the financial position and results of operation of the firm. Thus, the external audit adds credibility to the financial reporting process, and the auditor's report, contained in the annual report to the shareholders, is considered by readers as important as the financial statements themselves. The annual report to the shareholders contains the opinion of the independent auditor on the financial statements, supporting schedules, and notes.

The auditor's report generally follows a standard format, with some variations to meet specific circumstances. An auditor's report on the financial statements of Marnel Corporation might be as follows.

I have examined the comparative balance sheet of Marnel Corporation as at December 31, Year 1, and the statements of income, retained earnings and changes in financial position for the year then ended. My examination was made in accordance with generally accepted auditing standards, and accordingly included such tests and other procedures as I considered necessary in the circumstances.

In my opinion, these financial statements present fairly the financial position of Marnel Corporation at December 31, Year 1, and the results of its operations and the changes in financial position for the year then ended in accordance with generally accepted accounting principles applied on a basis consistent with that of the preceding year.

The report usually contains two paragraphs — a *scope paragraph* and an *opinion paragraph.* The scope paragraph indicates the financial presentations covered by the opinion and affirms that auditing standards and practices generally accepted by the accounting profession have been adhered to unless otherwise noted and described. Exceptions to the statement that the auditor's "examination was made in accordance with generally accepted auditing standards" are seldom seen in published annual reports. There are occasional references to the auditor's having relied on financial statements examined by other auditors, particularly for subsidiaries or for data from prior periods.

The opinion expressed by the auditor in the second paragraph is the heart of the auditor's report. The opinion may be *unreserved* or *reserved*. The great majority of opinions are unreserved; that is, there are no exceptions or reservations to the auditor's opinion that the statements "present fairly the financial position . . . in accordance with generally accepted accounting principles applied on a [consistent] basis."

Reservations to the opinion result when there is a departure from generally accepted accounting principles, or where there is a limitation in the scope of the auditor's examination. Examples of departures from generally accepted accounting principles would be a failure to report depreciation, an excessive provision for inventory obsolescence, or an inadequate explanation of a contingency. Examples of limitations to the scope of an auditor's examination would be when the auditor is unable to observe the inventory at the beginning of the year because his or her appointment was made during the year, when the accounting records are destroyed by fire, or when the auditor is not permitted to confirm the accounts receivable.

The auditor may be able to express a positive opinion on the financial statements taken as a whole, despite a reservation arising from the departure from generally accepted accounting principles or a limitation in the scope of this examination. In these cases, the auditor will insert a *reservation paragraph* between the scope and opinion paragraphs and qualify this opinion with an exception phrase. The reservation paragraph will explain the departure from generally accepted accounting principles and the impact of this departure on the financial statements, or alternatively provide full details of the limitation in and the reasons for the scope of the auditor's examinations.

If the departure from generally accepted accounting principles (GAAP) is so severe as to render the statements misleading, then an adverse opinion is given by the auditor. The opinion paragraph would conclude that the financial statements do not present fairly the financial position of the firm. Adverse opinions are rare in published reports.

Good-bye to the Ink-Stained Wretch

As a profession, accounting is still a parvenu. But new recruits are being lured by power, increasing prestige, and whopping salaries. The professions in North America are lined up in a kind of informal pecking order, certified by the twin laurels of success: money and so-cial standing. Doctors and lawyers generally occupy the uppermost ranks in the hierarchy, while teachers, architects, clerics, writers, scientists, and others fall in someplace behind. In this caste system, accountants have long been regarded as lowly unfortunates. Almost any accountant can provide a wealth of anecdotal evidence to prove the profession's reputation.

Accounting has never set the popular imagination to flights of rapturous veneration. The practitioners of other professions have all taken turns waltzing in the limelight, extolled in verse or song, held up as heroes. Yet one searches long and hard to find the accountant assigned *any* part in literature or theater, and when he is, it's usually as a bloodless drudge— Dicken's Uriah Heep. This nineteenth-century image seems to have endured, more or less intact, into the modern era. As recently as 1960, two social scientists, conducting a government-backed survey of attitudes among 1000 students at five unnamed but "highly selective" universities, found that in the students' eyes, "The accountant is the anti-hero of the occupational world. . . . The accountant is a conformist, with a minimum of social skills. . . . He is rated as passive, weak, soft, shallow, and cold." Even accounting's most distinguished scholars have been apologetic about their profession. For instance, Henry Rand Hatfield's famous treatise on accounting, first delivered as a speech in 1923, is entitled "An Historical Defense of Bookkeeping."

But things have been changing during the past two decades, and the profession is now in the midst of a full-fledged boom in terms of size, wealth, and even status. One business magazine, not long ago, quoted the chairman of a university accounting department as saying, "Suddenly students see accounting as glamorous, sexy. Many of our best students, who would have gone to law school a couple of years ago, are now going into public accounting." The reasons are no mystery: there are plenty of job openings in accounting and the salaries are increasingly attractive.

The causes of the profession's ascent are many and varied. But generally speaking, accounting is being assigned an expanded role in society as greater answerability is demanded of all institutions both public and private.

Accounting is control, and it is being used increasingly as an instrument of social control. Thus members of the accounting profession, it is said, should be society's tribunes, ensuring that the institutions to which power and authority have been granted are properly answerable to their constituents. It may be an exaggeration to suggest, as some have, that accountants constitute a "new elite" in America. Nonetheless, it is clear that the stereotypical image of the accountant as an ink-stained wretch wearing a green eyeshade and sitting on a three-legged stool is a relic of the past.

Because of its growth and ever broadening role, accounting is a many-faceted profession these days. Some accountants work for corporations, fashioning plans, budgets, and financial statements. Others, from the acounting firms, audit those numbers, while providing tax and management consulting services on the side. Accounting firms run the gamut from sole-practitioner outfits to the Big Eight concerns, employing thousands of workers and operating offices throughout the world. In addition, some accountants form a coterie of free-lance foreign-currency specialists clustered in the world's trading capitals—Hong Kong, Geneva, and other far-flung locales. Then, too, they are frequently becoming cops, as members of the state and local police, the RCMP or Revenue Canada, trying to ferret out white-collar crime. And while academia has generally been going through a period of contraction and austerity in recent years, accounting professors are in great demand.

The practice of accounting itself has become more and more complex, which tends to increase the level of specialization within the profession and adds to the demand for accountants. Fueling this trend has been the computer; it has spawned not only new techniques for gathering information, making decisions, and controlling operations, but also a vest new arena for technologically abetted crime. Tales of electronic thievery and fraud are by now well known, especially in the banking business. Crooks educated in the ways of computers have been able to tap into a bank's computer system, give the appropriate commands, and make off with millions, leaving scarcely a fingerprint in the Fortran. To cope with both the promise and the threat posed by computer technology, the large accounting firms have developed cadres of computer experts in recent years. One group, for instance, may counsel a corporate client on computerized management methods, while a separate team advises it on tightening security to lessen its vulnerability to computer crooks, either outsiders or employees.

It is sometimes said, and wisely suspected, that accounting is a craft by which the skilled practitioner can produce almost any result he desires. "Accounting is an art, and it contains a wide margin for personal judgment," Seidler observed. "Accountants can manipulate numbers, but only within certain limits. And in recent years, in the wake of the accounting fiascos of the sixties, things have been tightened up." To explain what accountants can and cannot do, within the boundaries of "generally accepted accounting principles," Seidler described a conversation he had in late 1979 with an acquaintance, the controller of a large oil company.

A few weeks before, most oil companies had reported their profits for the third quarter of 1979 and the increases were enormous, jumping more than 100 percent in some cases. Announcing such huge earnings was problematical for the industry, to put it mildly, at a time when the oil companies were being damned for profiteering at the expense of consumers. "You can be certain that the oil company accountants had been told to do everything they could to keep those profits down," said Seidler. So, seeing an opportunity for a little good-natured teasing, Seidler called his oil company friend and asked, "Hey, what happened? Why didn't you stuff that money into the black bag?" To that, the oil company executive replied, "Lee, it's full. Believe me, it's full."

The term "black bag," in this usage, does not mean illicit funds laundered through a Swiss bank account; it refers to the methods that can be employed legally to defer, or hide, profits. One such measure, for an oil company, might be setting aside a reserve to cover the eventual costs of scrapping offshore drilling platforms. To set up that sort of reserve fund is simply prudent business practice, even though such future costs are difficult to estimate and could vary greatly. One certainty, however, is that if possible, a company will establish the reserve in a good year, not in a rough one when it is straining for profits.

All companies similarly attempt to "manage" their year-to-year earnings, seeking a steadily, if gradually, ascending profit curve, which delights Bay Street investors, instead of an irregular pattern, which makes them skittish. As Seidler views it, the big oil industry profits in late 1979 were "a graphic example of how much accountants can't do, because they would have kept those earnings lower if they could have."

More generally, the problem, recognized by Seidler and others, is that as a profession, accounting is still in some respects a parvenu. While it has attained considerable size and wealth, the profession is struggling uneasily to fill the larger public role that society now demands of it. How ably and actively it moves into that broader domain will be of no little importance, particularly now that government regulation is in disrepute. The call for less regulation is a responsible tendency, it seems, only if there is some assurance that powerful private institutions can be held accountable without it. Providing that assurance is the mission of the accounting profession.

From "Good-Bye To The Ink-Stained Wretch" by Steve Lohr. Used with the special permission of *The Atlantic*, August 1980.

Objectives of Financial Reporting

Financial statements, such as those discussed in this chapter, provide information to investors, creditors, and others who commit funds to a firm. The Financial Accounting Standards Board, the official rule-making body in the private sector in the United States, has established a broad set of financial reporting objectives to guide the financial reporting process. Figure 1.4 summarizes these objectives, described briefly below, and their relation to the principal financial statements.

1. Financial reporting should provide information useful for making rational investment and credit decisions. This general-purpose objective states simply that financial reporting should be aimed primarily at investors and creditors and should strive to be useful to these individuals in their decisions.
2. Financial reporting should provide information to help investors and creditors assess the amount, timing, and uncertainty of cash flows. This objective flows from the first by defining ''useful'' information more fully. It states that investors and creditors are interested primarily in the cash they will receive from investing in a firm. Those cash flows are affected by the ability of the firm to generate cash flows.
3. Financial reporting should provide information about the economic resources of a firm and the claims on those resources. The balance sheet satisfies this objective.
4. Financial reporting should provide information about a firm's operating performance during a period. The income statement accomplishes this objective.
5. Financial reporting should provide information about how an enterprise obtains and uses cash. The statement of changes in financial position accomplishes this objective.
6. Financial reporting should provide information about how management has discharged its stewardship responsibility to owners. Stewardship refers to the prudent use of resources entrusted to a firm. No single statement helps in assessing stewardship. Rather, owners assess stewardship using information from all three financial statements and the notes.
7. Financial reporting should include explanations and interpretations to help users understand the financial information provided. Supporting schedules and notes to the financial statements satisfy this objective.

Summary

This chapter provided an overview of business activities and related them to the principal financial statements included in annual reports to shareholders. Perhaps more questions have been raised than answered. It is helpful, however, to have a broad overview of the various financial statements before examining the concepts and procedures that underlie each statement.

Chapters 2 through 5 discuss and illustrate the concepts and procedures underlying the balance sheet, income statement, and statement of changes in financial position. Chapter 6 considers techniques for analyzing and interpreting these financial statements. Chapters 7 through 14 explore more fully the principles of accounting for individual assets, liabilities, and shareholders' equities. Chapter 15 provides a synthesis of the book.

Figure 1.4 Summary of Reporting Process and Principal Financial Statements

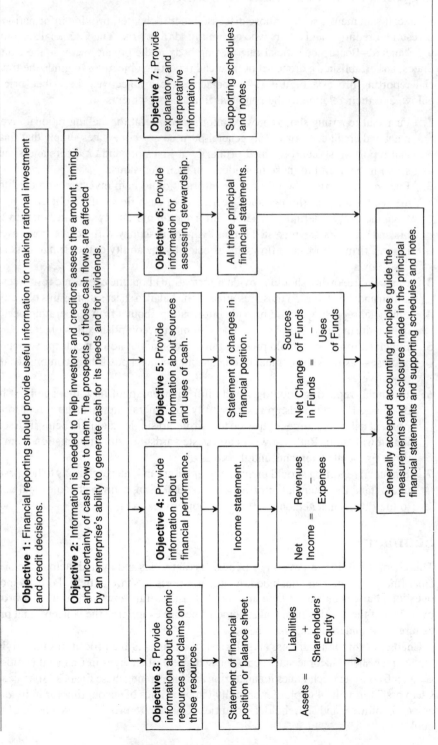

Now we turn to the study of financial accounting. One of the most effective means of comprehending the concepts and procedures in this book is the careful study of the numerical examples presented in each chapter and the diligent working of several problems, including the self-study problem(s), at the end of each chapter. Frequent reference should also be made to the Glossary of terms at the back of the book as well as to the financial statements and notes for General Products Limited presented in Appendix A.

Problem for Self-Study

The accounting records of Digital Electronics Corporation reveal the following:

	December 31	
	Year 2	Year 1
Balance Sheet Items:		
Accounts Payable to Suppliers	$295,000	$250,000
Accounts Receivable from Customers	320,000	240,000
Bonds Payable	120,000	100,000
Buildings (net of accumulated depreciation)	140,000	150,000
Cash	50,000	30,000
Common Stock	100,000	100,000
Equipment (net of accumulated depreciation)	220,000	140,000
Income Taxes Payable	70,000	40,000
Land	70,000	60,000
Merchandise Inventory	400,000	380,000
Retained Earnings	600,000	500,000
Salaries Payable	15,000	10,000
Income Statement Items for Year 2:		
Cost of Merchandise Sold	$ 620,000	
Depreciation Expense	40,000	
Income Tax Expense	100,000	
Insurance Expense	3,000	
Interest Expense	10,000	
Property Tax Expense	2,000	
Rental Revenue (rental of part of building)	30,000	
Salary Expense	135,000	
Sales Revenue	1,000,000	
Dividend Information for Year 2:		
Dividends Declared and Paid	$ 20,000	

a. Prepare a comparative balance sheet for Digital Electronics Corporation as of December 31, Year 1 and Year 2. Classify the balance sheet items into the following categories: current assets, noncurrent assets, current liabilities, noncurrent liabilities, and shareholders' equity.

b. Prepare a multistep income statement for Digital Electronics Corporation for Year 2.

c. Prepare a schedule explaining the changes in retained earnings during Year 2.

Suggested Solution

Exhibit 1.5 presents a comparative balance sheet, Exhibit 1.6 presents an income statement, and Exhibit 1.7 analyzes the change in retained earnings for Digital Electronics Corporation for Year 2.

Exhibit 1.5
DIGITAL ELECTRONICS CORPORATION
Comparative Balance Sheet
December 31, Year 1 and Year 2

	December 31 Year 2	December 31 Year 1
Assets		
Current Assets:		
Cash	$ 50,000	$ 30,000
Accounts Receivable from Customers	320,000	240,000
Merchandise Inventory	400,000	380,000
Total Current Assets	$ 770,000	$ 650,000
Noncurrent Assets:		
Land	$ 70,000	$ 60,000
Equipment (net of accumulated depreciation)	220,000	140,000
Buildings (net of accumulated depreciation)	140,000	150,000
Total Noncurrent Assets	$ 430,000	$ 350,000
Total Assets	$1,200,000	$1,000,000
Liabilities and Shareholders' Equity		
Current Liabilities:		
Accounts Payable to Suppliers	$ 295,000	$ 250,000
Salaries Payable	15,000	10,000
Income Taxes Payable	70,000	40,000
Total Current Liabilities	$ 380,000	$ 300,000
Noncurrent Liabilities:		
Bonds Payable	120,000	100,000
Total Liabilities	$ 500,000	$ 400,000
Shareholders' Equity:		
Common Stock	$ 100,000	$ 100,000
Retained Earnings	600,000	500,000
Total Shareholders' Equity	$ 700,000	$ 600,000
Total Liabilities and Shareholders' Equity	$1,200,000	$1,000,000

Exhibit 1.6
DIGITAL ELECTRONICS CORPORATION
Income Statement for Year 2

Sales	$1,000,000
Less: Cost of Merchandise Sold	620,000
Gross Profit	$ 380,000
Rental Revenue	30,000
	$ 410,000

Less: Selling and Administrative Expenses

Salaries	$135,000	
Property tax	2,000	
Insurance	3,000	
Depreciation	40,000	$ 180,000
Operating Profit		$ 230,000
Less: Interest Expense		10,000
Net Income before Income Tax		$ 220,000
Income Tax		100,000
Net Income		$ 120,000

Exhibit 1.7
DIGITAL ELECTRONICS CORPORATION
Retained Earnings Statement for Year 2

Retained Earnings, December 31, Year 1	$500,000
Plus Net Income	120,000
Less Dividends Declared and Paid	(20,000)
Retained Earnings, December 31, Year 2	$600,000

Questions, Exercises, Problems and Cases

Questions

1. Review the meaning of the following concepts or terms discussed in this chapter:

a. Managerial accounting
b. Financial accounting
c. Generally accepted accounting principles
d. Accounting Standards Committee
e. Operating profit
f. Goals and strategies
g. Financing activities
h. Investing activities
i. Operating activities
j. Balance sheet
k. Assets
l. Liabilities
m. Shareholders' equity

n. Contributed capital
o. Retained earnings
p. Cash equivalent value
q. Acquisition cost
r. Net income (earnings)
s. Net loss
t. Revenue
u. Expense
v. Dividends
w. Statement of changes in financial position
x. Unreserved, reserved and denial reports
y. Financial reporting objectives
z. Gross profit

2. Distinguish between financial accounting and managerial accounting. Suggest several ways in which the managers of a firm might use information presented in the three principal externally directed financial statements discussed in this chapter.

3. Suggest reasons why the format and content of financial accounting reports tend to be more standardized than is the case for managerial accounting reports.

4. What purpose is served by having a broad set of financial reporting objectives, such as those issued by the Financial Accounting Standards Board?

5. "Asset valuation and income measurement are closely related." Explain.

6. "Operating activities can be a source of financing." Explain.

7. Does the unreserved or "clean" opinion of a Chartered Accountant indicate that the financial statements are free of errors and misrepresentations? Explain.

Exercises

8. *Preparation of personal balance sheet.* Prepare a balance sheet of your personal assets, liabilities, and owner's equity. How does the presentation of owner's equity on your balance sheet differ from that in Exhibit 1.1?

9. *Account classification.* Various items are classified on the balance sheet or income statement in one of the following ways:

    CA — Current assets
    NA — Noncurrent assets
    CL — Current liabilities
    NL — Noncurrent liabilities
    CC — Contributed capital
    RE — Retained earnings
    NI — Income statement item (revenue or expense)
    X — Item would generally not appear on a balance sheet or income statement

Using the letters above, indicate the classification of each of the following items:

    a. Factory
    b. Interest revenue
    c. Common shares issued by a corporation
    d. Goodwill developed by a firm (see Glossary)
    e. Automobiles used by sales staff
    f. Cash on hand
    g. Unsettled damage suit against a firm
    h. Commissions earned by sales staff
    i. Supplies inventory
    j. Note payable, due in three months
    k. Increase in market value of land held
    l. Dividends
    m. Employee payroll taxes payable
    n. Note payable, due in six years

10. *Balance sheet relations.* Compute the missing balance sheet amounts in each of the four independent cases below:

	a	b	c	d
Noncurrent Assets	$400,000	$500,000	$340,000	?
Shareholders' Equity	?	250,000	290,000	$140,000
Total Assets	?	?	500,000	?
Current Liabilities	500,000	150,000	?*	?**
Current Assets	600,000	?	?*	?**
Noncurrent Liabilities	100,000	?	?	160,000
Total Liabilities and Shareholders' Equity	?	700,000	?	550,000

*Current assets − current liabilities = $70,000.
**Current assets − current liabilities = $80,000.

11. *Balance sheet relations.* Compute the missing balance sheet amounts in each of the four independent cases below:

	a	b	c	d
Noncurrent Assets	$700,000	$2,000,000	$340,000	?
Shareholders' Equity	?	1,550,000	380,000	$370,000
Total Assets	?	?	500,000	?
Current Liabilities	250,000	400,000	?*	?**
Current Assets	300,000	?	?*	?**
Noncurrent Liabilities	300,000	?	?	400,000
Total Liabilities and Shareholders' Equity	?	2,650,000	?	950,000

*Current assets − current liabilities = $40,000.
**Current assets − current liabilities = $70,000.

12. *Retained earnings relations.* Compute the missing amount affecting retained earnings for Year 2 in each of the independent cases below:

	a	b	c	d	e
Retained Earnings, Dec. 31, Year 1	$80,000	?	$458,000	$120,000	$240,000
Net Income	30,000	$260,000	260,000	?	(60,000)*
Dividends Declared and Paid	10,000	145,000	?	35,000	?
Retained Earnings Dec. 31, Year 2	?	766,000	598,000	110,000	180,000

*Net loss.

13. *Retained earnings relations.* Compute the missing amount affecting retained earnings for Year 2 in each of the independent cases below:

	a	b	c	d	e
Retained Earnings, Dec. 31, Year 1	$150,000	?	$320,000	$75,000	$ 40,000
Net Income (Loss)	50,000	$125,000	180,000	?	(30,000)
Dividends Declared and Paid	20,000	75,000	?	30,000	?
Retained Earnings Dec. 31, Year 2	?	500,000	470,000	90,000	10,000

14. *Relation of net income to balance sheet changes*. The comparative balance sheets of Sweet Limited as of December 31, Year 1, and December 31, Year 2, follow:

SWEET LIMITED
Comparative Balance Sheets
December 31, Year 1 and Year 2

| | December 31 | |
	Year 2	Year 1
Total Assets	$800,000	$500,000
Liabilities	$160,000	$100,000
Common Stock	290,000	250,000
Retained Earnings	350,000	150,000
Total Liabilities and Shareholders' Equity	$800,000	$500,000

Dividends declared and paid during Year 2 were $60,000.

a. Compute net income for the year ending December 31, Year 2, by analyzing the change in retained earnings.

b. Demonstrate that the following relation holds:

$$\frac{\text{Net}}{\text{Income}} = \frac{\text{Increase in}}{\text{Assets}} - \frac{\text{Increase in}}{\text{Liabilities}} - \frac{\text{Increase in}}{\substack{\text{Contributed} \\ \text{Capital}}} + \text{Dividends}.$$

15. *Income statement relations*. Compute the missing amounts affecting the net income for Year 1 in each of the independent cases below:

	a	b	c	d
Sales Revenue	$500	?	$390	$260
Cost of Goods Sold	250	$60	?	190
Selling and Administrative Expenses	120	30	70	?
Income Tax Expense	60	20	35	0
Net Income	?	15	35	(15)*

*Net loss.

16. *Statement of changes in financial position relations*. Compute the missing amounts affecting the change in cash for Year 1 in each of the independent cases below:

	a	b	c	d
Sources of Cash:				
Operations	$500	$250	$600	$(200)*
New Financing	200	100	?	300
Sale of Noncurrent Assets	50	20	0	100

*Net use of cash for operations.

	a	b	c	d
Use of Cash:				
Dividends	100	75	200	0
Reduction in Financing	80	0	50	50
Acquisition of Noncurrent Assets	550	?	800	120
Change in Cash	?	20	(50)**	?

**Decrease in cash.

17. *Relations between financial statements.* Compute the missing information in each of the independent cases below. The letters in parentheses refer to the following:

BS— Balance sheet
IS— Income statement
SCFP— Statement of changes in financial position

a. Accounts Receivable, Jan. 1, Year 2 (BS) .... $ 450
Sales on Account for Year 2 (IS) 1,700
Collections from Customers on Account During Year 2 (SCFP) 1,350
Accounts Receivable, Dec. 31, Year 2 (BS) .... ?
b. Salaries Payable, Jan. 1, Year 2 (BS) .... $ 120
Salary Expense for Year 2 (IS) .... ?
Payments to Salaried Employees During Year 2 (SCFP) 660
Salaries Payable, Dec. 31, Year 2 (BS) 90
c. Equipment (net of accumulated depreciation), Jan. 1, Year 2 (BS) .... $ 800
Depreciation Expense for Year 2 (IS) .... ?
Sales of Equipment During Year 2 (SCFP) 0
Acquisition of Equipment During Year 2 (SCFP) 250
Equipment (net of accumulated depreciation), Dec. 31, Year 2 (BS) 900
d. Retained Earnings, Jan. 1, Year 2 (BS) $1,250
Net Income for Year 2 (IS) 300
Dividends Declared and Paid During Year 2 (SCFP) .... ?
Retained Earnings, Dec. 31, Year 2 (BS) 1,430

18. *Balance sheet relations.* Compute the missing balance sheet amounts in each of the four independent cases that follow.

	a	b	c	d
Total Assets	$1,000,000	?	?	$270,000
Noncurrent Liabilities	350,000	$ 25,000	?	230,000
Noncurrent Assets	?	50,000	$600,000	?
Total Liabilities and Shareholders' Equity	?	300,000	?	?
Current Liabilities	250,000	?	40,000	60,000
Shareholders' Equity	?	75,000	110,000	?
Current Assets	350,000	?	50,000	30,000

Problems and Cases

19. *Preparation of balance sheet and income statement.* B. Stephens, L. Harris, and G. Winkle, recent graduates, set up a management consulting practice on December 31, Year 1, by issuing common shares for $750,000. The accounting records of S, H, & W Limited as of December 31, Year 2, reveal the following:

Balance Sheet Items:
Cash .... $ 50,000
Accounts Receivable from Clients 165,000
Supplies Inventory 5,000
Office Equipment (net of accumulated depreciation) 85,000
Office Building (net of accumulated depreciation) 500,000
Accounts Payable to Suppliers 10,000
Payroll Taxes Payable 5,000
Income Taxes Payable 20,000
Common Stock 750,000

Income Statement Items:

Revenue from Consulting Services	$300,000
Rental Revenue (from renting part of building)	30,000
Salaries Expense	215,000
Property Taxes and Insurance Expense	30,000
Supplies Expense	10,000
Depreciation Expense	25,000
Income Tax Expense	20,000

Dividend Information:

Dividends Declared and Paid	$ 10,000

a. Prepare an income statement for S, H, & W Limited, for the year ending December 31, Year 2. Refer to Exhibit 1.2 for help in designing the format of the statement.

b. Prepare a comparative balance sheet for S, H, & W Limited on December 31, Year 1, and December 31, Year 2. Refer to Exhibit 1.1 for help in designing the format of the statement.

c. Prepare an analysis of the change in retained earnings during Year 2.

20. *Preparation of balance sheet and income statement.* The accounting records of Laser Sales Corporation reveal the following:

	December 31 Year 2	December 31 Year 1
Balance Sheet Items:		
Accounts Payable	$1,513,000	$1,247,000
Accounts Receivable	820,000	740,000
Bank Loan Payable (due April 10, Year 3)	15,000	—
Bonds Payable (due Year 16)	100,000	80,000
Building (net of accumulated depreciation)	440,000	460,000
Cash	315,000	270,000
Common Stock	1,240,000	1,190,000
Equipment (net of accumulated depreciation)	1,023,000	825,000
Income Taxes Payable	30,000	25,000
Land	50,000	40,000
Merchandise Inventory	610,000	550,000
Note Receivable (due June 15, Year 3)	20,000	—
Note Receivable (due December 31, Year 10)	100,000	100,000
Retained Earnings	470,000	430,000
Salaries Payable	32,000	28,000
Supplies Inventory	22,000	15,000

Income Statement Items for Year 2:

Cost of Merchandise Sold	$2,611,000
Depreciation Expense	45,000
Income Tax Expense	55,000
Insurance Expense	8,000
Interest Expense	16,000
Interest Revenue	15,000
Payroll Tax Expense	80,000
Salary Expense	550,000
Sales Revenue	3,500,000
Supplies Expense	90,000

Dividend Information:

Dividends Declared and Paid During Year 2	$ 20,000

    a. Prepare a comparative balance sheet for Laser Sales Corporation as of December 31, Year 1 and Year 2. Classify the balance sheet items into the following categories: current assets, noncurrent assets, current liabilities, noncurrent liabilities, shareholders' equity.

    b. Prepare a multistep income statement for Laser Sales Corporation for Year 2.

    c. Prepare a schedule explaining, or accounting for, the change in retained earnings between the beginning and end of Year 2.

21. *Relations between principal financial statements.* The purpose of this problem is to illustrate the relations between the three principal financial statements. Exhibit 1.8 presents a comparative balance sheet for Articulation Inc. as of December 31, Year 1 and Year 2. Exhibit 1.9 presents an income statement and Exhibit 1.10 presents a statement of changes in financial position for Articulation Inc. for Year 2.

    Using amounts from these three financial statements, demonstrate that the following relations are correct:

    a. Retained earnings at the end of Year 1 plus net income for Year 2 minus dividends declared and paid for Year 2 equal retained earnings at the end of Year 2.

Exhibit 1.8
ARTICULATION INC.
Comparative Balance Sheets
December 31, Year 1 and Year 2

	December 31 Year 2	December 31 Year 1
Assets		
Current Assets:		
Cash	$180	$ 80
Accounts Receivable from Customers	340	300
Merchandise Inventory	160	150
Total Current Assets	$680	$530
Noncurrent Assets:		
Land	$ 55	$ 40
Buildings and Equipment (net of accumulated depreciation)	165	130
Total Noncurrent Assets	$220	$170
Total Assets	$900	$700

	December 31	
	Year 2	Year 1
Liabilities and Shareholders' Equity		
Current Liabilities:		
Accounts Payable	$350	$310
Income Taxes Payable	60	40
Total Current Liabilities	$410	$350
Noncurrent Liabilities:		
Bonds Payable	25	20
Total Liabilities	$435	$370
Shareholders' Equity:		
Common Stock	$245	$200
Retained Earnings	220	130
Total Shareholders' Equity	$465	$330
Total Liabilities and Shareholders' Equity	$900	$700

Exhibit 1.9
ARTICULATION INC.
Income Statement for Year 2

Sales Revenue		$1,000
Less: Cost of Goods Sold		600
Gross Profit		$ 400
Less: Operating Expenses		
Salaries	$100	
Depreciation	50	150
Operating Income		$ 250
Less: Interest Expense		$ 20
Net Income before Income Tax		$ 230
Less: Income Tax Expense		120
Net Income		$ 110

Exhibit 1.10
ARTICULATION INC.
Statement of Changes in Financial Position for Year 2

Sources of Cash:		
Operations:		
Revenues Increasing Cash	$960	
Expenses Decreasing Cash	790	
Total from Operations	$170	
Issue of Bonds	5	
Issue of Common Shares	45	
Total Sources		$220
Uses of Cash:		
Dividends Declared and Paid	$ 20	
Land Acquired	15	
Buildings and Equipment Acquired	85	
Total Uses		120
Net Change in Cash		$100

b. Change in total assets equals change in total liabilities plus change in common shares plus net income minus dividends.

c. Accounts receivable at the end of Year 1 plus sales (all on account) to customers less cash collections from customers (see statement of changes in financial position) equal accounts receivable at the end of Year 2.

d. Buildings and equipment at the end of Year 1 plus acquisitions of buildings and equipment minus dispositions of buildings and equipment minus depreciation for Year 2 equal buildings and equipment at the end of Year 2.

e. Bonds payable at the end of Year 1 plus new bonds issued during Year 2 minus outstanding bonds redeemed during Year 2 equal bonds payable at the end of Year 2.

f. Common stock at the end of Year 1 plus common shares issued during Year 2 minus outstanding common shares redeemed during year 2 equal common stock at the end of Year 2.

22. *Relations between financial statements. (Adapted from materials prepared by Professor Harvey Mann.)* Exhibit 1.11 presents a balance sheet on December 31, Year 1 (columns 1 and 2), an income statement for Year 2 (column 3), a statement of changes in financial position for Year 2 (column 4), and a balance sheet on December 31, Year 2 (columns 5 and 6) for Mann Co. Ltd.

Compute the amounts for each of the missing items labeled **a** through **j** in the exhibit.

23. *Interpretation of financial statements.* Refer to the financial statements and notes for General Products Limited presented in Appendix A at the back of the book. Respond to the following questions.

a. With respect to the consolidated balance sheet:

(1) Justify the inclusion of "inventories," and "property, plant, and equipment — net" as assets.

(2) Identify the valuation methods used in computing the amounts for the various assets shown on General Products Limited's balance sheet. (Note: You must refer to some of General Products Limited's notes to respond to this question.)

(3) What justification can you see for excluding General Products Limited's investment in a well-trained labour force or its good reputation with customers from its balance sheet?

(4) Liabilities and shareholders' equities represent sources of or claims on the assets of a firm. In what sense are "accounts payable," "taxes payable," and "retained earnings" sources of or claims on the assets of General Products Limited?

(5) The "net worth" of a firm has been described as the excess of a firm's assets over its liabilities. Assume that you have agreed to purchase all of the common shares of General Products Limited for its net worth as of December 31, 1988. Is $8.2 billion, the total shareholders' equity, a reasonable price to pay? Why or why not?

b. With respect to the consolidated income statement:

(6) Net income is defined as the excess of revenues over expenses. Using only

Exhibit 1.11
MANN CO. LTD.
Financial Statements for Year 2 (Problem 21)

	Balance Sheet December 31, Year 1		Income Statement for Year 2 (3)	Statement of Changes in Financial Position for Year 2 (4)	Balance Sheet December 31, Year 2	
	Assets (1)	Liabilities + Shareholders' Equity (2)			Assets (5)	Liabilities + Shareholders' Equity (6)
Accounts Receivable	$ 200		Sales $2,000	Collections from Customers $1,700	500 **a**	
Inventories	300		Cost of Goods Sold ...... 1200 **b**	Purchases of Merchandise ... 400 (1,300 400) 400	400	
Accounts Payable—Merchandise		$ 180		Change in Accounts Payable ... 440 40 440		$220
Salaries Payable		30	Salary Expense ...... (400)	Salaries Paid 50 (30) 50		40
Interest Payable		10 **d**	Interest Expense ...... (20)	Interest Paid 30 (20) 30		10
Income Taxes Payable		20	Income Tax Expense ...... (35)	Income Tax Paid ... −10 (10)		15
Other Current Liabilities		115	Other Expenses ...... 250 **e**	Other Expenses Paid ... −230 (220) (230)		145
				Cash from Operations .... (230)(465)		
Land, Building, and Equipment—Net	600		Depreciation Expense ...... (60)	Land, Building, and Equipment Acquired ... −430 (200) **g**	740	
Bonds Payable		200		Bonds Issued ... −230 200 (460)		400
Common Stock		300 **h**		Common Shares Issued ... 70 300 (160)		600
Retained Earnings		345	Net Income ...... $ 35	Dividend Paid ... 60 (10) (170)		370
Cash	100			Change in Cash ...... $ 60	160	
	$1,200	$1,200			$1,800	1,800

numerical amounts, rearrange the items in General Products Limited's income statement for 1988 into the following equation:

$$\text{Net Income} = \text{Revenues} - \text{Expenses}.$$

(7) Revenues are a measure of the inflows of assets (or reductions in liabilities) from selling goods and services to customers. Justify the inclusion of "sales" as revenues.

(8) Expenses are a measure of the outflows of assets (or increases in liabilities) used up in generating revenues. Justify the inclusion of "cost of goods sold," "depreciation," and "income taxes" as expenses.

(9) Net income has been described as a measure of the increase in wealth of a firm for a particular period of time. Do you agree?

c. With respect to the consolidated statement of changes in financial position:

(10) The factors causing a change in cash are depicted graphically in Figure 1.3 in the chapter. Classify each of the sources and uses of cash for General Products Limited for 1988 into one of these six categories.

d. Assume that you are a credit officer for a bank contemplating a loan of $500 million to General Products Limited as of February 1, 1989. The loan is to be repaid with interest on July 31, 1989. What information from General Products Limited's financial statements would you find useful in making this decision?

e. Assume that you are an independently wealthy investor contemplating the purchase of $500 million of General Products Limited's common shares. What information from General Products Limited's financial statements would you find useful in making this decision?

24. *Relation between net income and cash flows.* The ABC Co. Ltd. started the year in fine shape. The firm made widgets—just what the customer wanted. It made them for $.75 each and sold them for $1.00. The ABC Co. Ltd. kept an inventory equal to shipments of the past 30 days, paid its bills promptly, and collected cash from customers within 30 days after the sale. The sales manager predicted a steady increase of 500 widgets each month beginning in February. It looked like a great year, and it began that way:

January 1   Cash, $875; receivables, $1,000; inventory, $750.

January   In January, 1,000 widgets costing $750 were sold on account for $1,000. Receivables outstanding at the beginning of the month were collected. Production totaled 1,000 units at a total cost of $750. Net income for the month was $250. The books at the end of January showed:

February 1   Cash, $1,125; receivables, $1,000; inventory $750.

February   This month's sales jumped, as predicted, to 1,500 units. With a corresponding step-up in production to maintain the 30-day inventory, ABC Co. Ltd. made 2,000 units at a cost of $1,500. All receivables from January sales were collected. Net income so far, $625. Now the books looked like this:

March 1   Cash, $625; receivables, $1,500; inventory, $1,125.

March   March sales were even better: 2,000 units. Collections: On time. Production, to adhere to the inventory policy: 2,500 units. Operating results for the month, net income of $500. Net income to date: $1,125. The books:

April 1   Cash, $250; receivables, $2,000; inventory, $1,500.

April   In April, sales jumped another 500 units to 2,500, and the manager of ABC Co. Ltd. patted the sales manager on the back. Customers were paying right on time. Production was pushed to 3,000 units, and the month's business netted $625 for a net income to date of $1,750. The manager of ABC Co. Ltd. took off for Miami before the accountant's report was issued. Suddenly a phone call came from the treasurer: "Come home! We need money!"

May 1   Cash, $000; receivables, $2,500; inventory, $1,875.

a. Prepare an analysis that explains what happened to ABC Co. Ltd. (Hint: Compute the amount of cash receipts and cash disbursements for each month during the period January 1 to May 1.)
b. How can a firm show increasing net income but a decreasing amount of cash?
c. What insights are provided by the problem about the need for all three financial statements: balance sheet, income statement, and statement of changes in financial position?

25. *Preparation of balance sheet and income statement.* Keyes Manufacturing Corporation was organized on January 1, Year 1. The company issued common stock for $600,000 and long-term bonds for $400,000. The accounting records of Keyes Manufacturing Corporation as of December 31, Year 1, reveal the following:

Balance Sheet Items:

Cash	$ 50,000
Accounts Receivable from Customers	350,000
Inventories	300,000
Land	50,000
Buildings (net of depreciation)	400,000
Equipment (net of depreciation)	350,000
Accounts Payable to Suppliers	120,000
Salaries Payable to Workers	75,000
Bonds Payable	400,000
Common Stock	700,000

Income Statement Items:

Sales Revenue	$2,000,000
Cost of Goods Sold	1,200,000
Selling Expenses	200,000
Administrative Expenses	210,000
Interest Expense	40,000
Income Tax Expense	100,000

Dividend Information:	
Dividends Declared and Paid	$ 45,000

a. Prepare an income statement for Keyes Manufacturing Corporation for the year ending December 31, Year 1. Refer to Exhibit 1.2 for help in designing the format of the statement.

b. Prepare a comparative balance sheet for Keyes Manufacturing Corporation on January 1, Year 1, and December 31, Year 1. Refer to Exhibit 1.1 for help in designing the format of the statement.

c. Prepare an analysis of the change in retained earnings during Year 1.

Decision Problem 1-1

Sam Black has just completed a busy week organizing and supervising the annual April Fool's Day chicken, hot dog and beer barbecue sponsored by the students' society of his faculty as a combination public relations, fun, and fund-raising activity. The barbecue had been a success, and Sam had just returned from the bank where he had deposited the proceeds of $2,810 and proudly announced that the bank balance now stood at $2,858—which represented "the most successful result of any barbecue."

The following conversation took place between Sam Black and Herbert McAlister, the president of the students' society.

"Congratulations on the successful barbecue, Sam," said McAlister. "Would you please transfer the $2,858 to the society's bank account tomorrow, so I can pay for the advance booking of the graduating class dance?"

"I can't transfer all the money," said Black. "I still have two bills to pay — $347 for the chicken and $630 for the material needed to build the barbecue. The chicken was all sold, but the barbecue should last for another two years.

"And further," Black added, "ten of the 80 cases of beer that were delivered C.O.D. were not sold and are to be returned for a refund of $4.80 per case. And at the same time the 65 cases of empties will be picked up, and the deposit of $.60 a case will be returned.

"I managed to sell the 24 dozen buns left over for $.50 a dozen to Jill Rosen for a sorority party," continued Sam. "This was half the unit cost of the 120 dozen purchased, but at least they will be used. Jill didn't have the money with her and will pay me tomorrow."

Spurred on by Herbert's interest, Black said he had also purchased barbecue sauce, condiments, and charcoal for $78 cash. Although there was a little barbecue sauce left over, it was given to the student helpers. In addition, $370 had also been spent on promoting the event.

Intent on his explanation Sam was unaware that Bill Hahn, the society's treasurer, had sidled up and heard the story.

"From the sounds of it, last year's affair was more successful," announced Hahn. "Once you have paid your bills and repaid the $1,000 advance I gave you last week, you will have less than $900 left. This is $400 less than last year's 'Beer and Hot Dog' reported net income."

Sam was deflated by the last comment, as well as a little confused. Help Sam Black out of his confusion by preparing an income statement and a current balance sheet for the barbecue.

Decision Problem 1–2

Your friend, Alex Delvechio, has asked for your advice. He is considering purchasing a sporting goods store but knows nothing about accounting and doesn't know if this business looks like a good investment. He has obtained income statements showing net income averaging $40,000 a year. The most recent balance sheet shows assets of $180,000 and liabilities of $30,000. The current owner, Ted Dumas, is asking $200,000 for the business.

a. Alex cannot understand why he should pay more than the value of the net assets ($150,000), especially since this business is several years old and some of the assets may be worn out. What counsel can you provide him on this?

b. After examining the income statements you notice that there is no expense shown for salary by Dumas. When questioned on this, he replied that he got enough income from his other investments that it wasn't necessary to draw a salary. What impact will this information have on the advice you offer Alex? Alex has a full-time job at the university.

Part Two   **Accounting Concepts and Methods**

Chapter 2   Balance Sheet: Presenting the Investments and Financing of a Firm

Chapter 1 introduced the balance sheet, one of the three principal financial statements. Recall that the balance sheet presents a snapshot of the investments of a firm (assets) and financing of those investments (liabilities and owners' equity) as of a specific time. The balance sheet shows the following balance, or equality:

$$\text{Assets} = \text{Liabilities} + \text{Owners' Equity}$$

That is, a firm's resources are in balance with, or equal to, the claims on those resources by creditors and owners. In the balance sheet, we view resources from two angles: a listing of the specific forms in which they are held (for example, cash, inventory, equipment); and a listing of the persons or interests that provided the financing and therefore have a claim on them (for example, suppliers, employees, governments, shareholders). The introduction to the balance sheet in Chapter 1 left several important questions unanswered:

1. What limits are set in defining the business entity for which the balance sheet is prepared?
2. Which resources of a firm are recorded as assets?
3. What valuations are placed on these assets?
4. How are assets classified, or grouped, within the balance sheet?
5. Which claims against a firm's assets are recognized as liabilities?
6. What valuations are placed on these liabilities?
7. How are liabilities classified within the balance sheet?
8. What valuation is placed on the owners' equity in a firm, and how is the owners' equity disclosed?

In answering these questions, several accounting concepts underlying the balance sheet must be considered. This discussion not only provides a background for understanding the statement as it is currently prepared, but also permits an assessment of alternative methods of measuring financial position. After this introduction to important accounting concepts, the accounting procedures used in recording transactions and events for presentation in a balance sheet are described and illustrated.

Underlying Concepts and Conventions

Accounting Entity

Business activities are carried on through various units, or entities. The identification of the business entity is the starting point in designing an accounting system that will provide data for financial statements. Most problems of identifying the business entity are caused by differences between the definition of the entity used in accounting, or the *accounting entity*, and the definition of the entity prescribed by law, or the *legal entity*. In accounting we attempt to emphasize substance over form; that is, the focus is on the unit, or entity, engaged in business activity even though it may not be recognized as a separate legal entity.

Example 1 Joan Webster operates a hardware store in her neighborhood as a sole proprietorship. According to the laws for sole proprietorships in most provinces, Webster's business assets and personal assets are mingled. That is, suppliers of merchandise to the hardware store can obtain payment for their claims from some or all of her personal assets if business assets are insufficient. Even so, the accounting entity is the hardware store alone, because this is the organizational unit carrying on the business activity.

Example 2 Bill White and Roger Green own and manage an apartment complex, called the Leisure Living Apartments, as a partnership. Under the partnership laws of most provinces, their personal assets as well as the business assets are subject to the claims of creditors. Even so, the accounting entity is the apartment complex alone, because this is the organizational unit carrying on the business activity.

Example 3 The Wilson Corporation operates through its subsidiaries. Each subsidiary is organized as a separate legal corporation under the laws of the government where it is located. The accounting entity is a combination (or consolidation) of Wilson Corporation and all of its subsidiary corporations, because these legally separate units operate as a single business entity. For purposes of internal performance evaluation by management, or to report to a given creditor, however, Wilson Corporation might treat each subsidiary as a separate reporting entity. Thus, the scope of the accounting entity can be related to the purpose to be served by the financial statements.

The accounting entity for which a set of financial statements has been prepared can be determined from the heading of each statement. For the three examples above, the headings might read: Webster's Hardware Store, Leisure Living Apartments, and Wilson Corporation and Consolidated Subsidiaries.

Asset Recognition

Assets are resources that have the potential for providing a firm with future economic benefits. That benefit is the ability to generate future cash inflows or to reduce future cash outflows. The resources that are recognized as assets are those (1) for which the firm has acquired rights to their future use as a result of a past transaction or exchange and (2) for which the value of the future benefits can be measured, or quantified, with a reasonable degree of precision.

Example 4 Miller Corporation sold merchandise and received a note from the customer who agreed to pay $2,000 within four months. This note receivable is an asset of Miller Corporation, because a right has been established to receive a definite amount of cash in the future as a result of the previous sale of merchandise.

Example 5 Miller Corporation acquired manufacturing equipment costing $40,000 and agreed to pay the seller over three years. After the final payment, legal title to the equipment will be transferred to Miller Corporation. Even though Miller Corporation does not possess legal title, the equipment is Miller's asset because it has obtained the rights and responsibilities of ownership and can sustain those rights as long as the payments are made on schedule.

Example 6 Miller Corporation plans to acquire a fleet of new trucks next year to replace those wearing out. These new trucks are not now assets, because no exchange has taken place between Miller Corporation and a supplier and, therefore, no right to the future use of the trucks has been established.

Example 7 Miller Corporation has developed a good reputation with its employees, customers, and citizens of the community. This good reputation is expected to provide benefits to the firm in its future business activities. A good reputation, however, is generally *not* recognized as an asset. Although Miller Corporation has made various expenditures in the past to develop the reputation, the future benefits are considered to be too difficult to quantify with a sufficient degree of precision to warrant recognition as an asset.

Most of the difficulties in deciding which items to recognize as assets are related to unexecuted or partially executed contracts. In Example 6, suppose that Miller Corporation entered into a contract with a local truck dealer to acquire the trucks next year at a cash price of $60,000. Miller Corporation has acquired rights to future benefits, but the contract has not been executed. Unexecuted contracts of this nature are generally not recognized as assets in accounting. Miller Corporation will recognize an asset for the trucks when they are received next year.

To take the illustration one step further, assume that Miller Corporation advances the truck dealer $15,000 of the purchase price upon signing the contract. Miller Corporation has acquired rights to future benefits and has exchanged cash. Current accounting practice treats the $15,000 as an advance on the purchase of equipment and reports it as an asset under a title such as Advances to Suppliers. The trucks would not be shown as assets at this time, however, because Miller Corporation is not yet deemed to have received sufficient future rights to justify their inclusion in the balance sheet. Similar asset recognition questions arise when a firm leases buildings and equipment for its own use under long-term leases or manufactures custom-design products for particular customers. Later chapters discuss these issues more fully.

Some expenditures provide future benefits to the firm but are not recognized as assets because the benefit will be used up within the forthcoming year (for instance, supplies). It is more convenient to charge these expenditures immediately as expenses against operating revenues in the income statement. Other examples of items that theoretically qualify as assets but do not get recognized as such are expenditures such as advertising where it is too difficult to measure the future benefits, or expenditures of small dollar amounts where it requires too much effort to keep track of the items on the balance sheet (for instance, hand tools).

Asset Valuation Bases

An amount must be assigned to each asset in the balance sheet. Several methods of computing this amount might be used. Part III presents the application of these valuation bases to specific asset classes.

Acquisition or Historical Cost The acquisition, or historical cost, of an asset is the amount of cash payment (or cash-equivalent value of other forms of payment) made in acquiring the asset. This amount can generally be found by referring to contracts, invoices, and canceled cheques. Because a firm is not compelled to acquire a given asset, it must expect the future benefits from that asset to be at least as large as its acquisition cost. Historical cost then is a lower limit on the amount that a firm considered the future benefits of the asset to be worth at the time of acquisition.

Current Replacement Cost Each asset might be shown on the balance sheet at the current cost of replacing it. Current replacement cost is often referred to as an *entry value*, because it represents the amount required currently to acquire, or "enter" into, the rights to receive future benefits from the asset.

For assets purchased frequently, such as merchandise inventory, current replacement cost can often be determined by consulting suppliers' catalogs or price lists. The replacement cost of assets purchased less frequently, such as land, buildings, and equipment, is more difficult to ascertain. A major obstacle to implementing current replacement cost is the absence of well-organized secondhand markets for many used assets. Ascertaining current replacement cost in these cases requires finding the cost of a similar new asset and then adjusting that amount downward somehow for the services of the asset already used. There may be difficulties, however, in finding a similar asset. With technological improvements and other quality changes, equipment purchased currently will likely differ from equipment still being used but acquired ten years previously. Thus, there may be no similar equipment on the market for which replacement cost can be found. Alternatively, the current replacement cost of an asset capable of rendering equivalent services might be substituted when the replacement cost of the specific asset is not readily available. The approach, however, requires subjectivity in identifying assets with equivalent service potential.

Current Net Realizable Value Net realizable value is the net amount of cash (selling price less selling costs) that the firm would receive currently if it sold each asset separately. This amount is often referred to as an *exit value*, because it reflects the amount obtainable if the firm currently disposed of the asset, or "exited" ownership. In measuring net realizable value, one generally assumes that the asset is sold in an orderly fashion, rather than through a forced sale at some "distress" price.

Measuring net realizable value entails difficulties similar to those in measuring current replacement cost. There may be no well-organized secondhand market for used equipment, particularly when the equipment is specially designed for a single firm's needs. In this case, the current selling price of the asset (value in exchange) may be substantially less than the value of the future benefits to the firm from using the asset (value in use).

Present Value of Future Net Cash Flows Another possible valuation basis is the present value of future net cash flows. An asset is a resource that provides future benefits. This future benefit is the ability of an asset either to generate future net cash receipts or to reduce future cash expenditures. For example, accounts receivable from customers will lead directly to future cash receipts. Merchandise inventory can be sold for cash or promises to pay cash. Equipment can be used to manufacture products that can then be sold for cash. A building that is owned reduces future cash outflows for rental payments. Because these cash flows represent the future services, or benefits, of assets, they might be used in the valuation of assets.

Because cash can be invested to yield interest revenue over time, today's value of a stream of future cash flows, called the *present value*, is worth less than the sum of the cash amounts to be received or saved over time. The balance sheet is to be prepared as of a current date. If future cash flows are to be used to measure an asset's value, then the future net cash flows must be "discounted" to find their present value as of the date of the balance sheet. Chapters 10, 11, and Appendix B discuss the discounting methodology, but the following example presents the general approach.

Example 8 Miller Corporation sold merchandise to a reliable customer, General Models Co. Ltd., who promised to pay $10,000 one year from the date of sale. General Models Co. Ltd. signed a "promissory note" to that effect and gave the note to Miller Corporation. Miller Corporation judges that the current borrowing rate of General Models Co. Ltd. is ten percent per year. That is, a loan to General Models Co. Ltd. should yield a return to Miller Corporation of ten percent. Miller Corporation is to receive $10,000 one year from today. The $10,000 includes both the amount initially lent plus interest on that amount for one year. Today's value of the $10,000 to be received one year hence is not $10,000 but about $9,100. That is, $9,100 plus ten percent interest on $9,100 equals $10,000. Hence, the *present value* of $10,000 to be received one year from today is $9,100. (Miller Corporation is indifferent between receiving approximately $9,100 today and $10,000 one year from today.) The asset represented by General Models Co. Ltd.'s promissory note has a present value of $9,100. If the note was stated on the balance sheet at the present value of the future cash flows, it would be shown at approximately $9,100 on the date of sale.

Using discounted cash flows in the valuation of individual assets requires solving several problems. One is the difficulty caused by the uncertainty of the amounts of future cash flows. The amounts to be received can depend on whether or not competitors introduce new products, the rate of inflation, and many other factors. A second problem is allocating the cash receipts from selling a single item of merchandise inventory to all of the assets involved in its production and distribution (for example, equipment, buildings, sales staff's automobiles). A third problem is selecting the appropriate rate to be used in discounting the future cash flows back to the present. Is the interest rate at which the firm could borrow the appropriate one? Or is the rate at which the firm could invest excess cash the one that should be used? Or is the appropriate rate the firm's cost of capital (a concept introduced in managerial accounting and finance courses)? In the example above, the selected rate is General Models' borrowing rate.

Selecting the Appropriate Valuation Basis The valuation basis selected depends on the kind of financial report being prepared.

Example 9 Miller Corporation is preparing its income tax return for the current year. The Income Tax Act and Regulations specify that acquisition or adjusted acquisition cost valuation must be used in most instances.

Example 10 A fire recently destroyed the manufacturing plant, equipment, and inventory of Miller Corporation. The firm's fire insurance policy provides coverage in an amount equal to the cost of replacing the assets that were destroyed. Current replacement cost at the time of the fire is appropriate for supporting the insurance claim.

Example 11 Miller Corporation plans to dispose of one of its manufacturing divisions because it has been operating unprofitably. In deciding on the lowest price to accept for the division, the firm considers the net realizable value of each asset.

Example 12 Brown Corporation is considering the purchase of Miller Corporation. In deciding on the highest price to be paid, Brown Corporation would be interested in the present value of the future net cash flows to be realized from owning Miller Corporation.

Generally Accepted Accounting Asset Valuation Bases The asset valuation basis appropriate for financial statements issued to shareholders and other investors is perhaps less obvious. The financial statements currently prepared by publicly held firms are based on one of two valuation bases: one for monetary assets (cash and claims to cash) and one for non-monetary assets.

Monetary assets, such as cash and accounts receivable, are generally shown on the balance sheet at their present value — their current cash, or cash-equivalent, value. Cash is stated at the amount of cash on hand or in the bank. Accounts receivable from customers are stated at the amount of cash expected to be collected in the future. If the period of time until a receivable is to be collected spans more than one year, then the expected future cash receipt is discounted to a present value. Most accounts receivable, however, are collected within one to three months. The amount of future cash flows is approximately equal to the present value of these flows, and the discounting process is ignored.

Nonmonetary assets, such as merchandise inventory, land, buildings, and equipment, are stated at *acquisition cost*, in some cases adjusted downward for depreciation reflecting the services of the assets that have been consumed.

The acquisition cost of an asset may include more than its invoice price. Cost includes all expenditures made or obligations incurred in order to put the asset into usable condition. Transportation cost, costs of installation, handling charges and any other necessary and reasonable costs incurred in connection with the asset up to the time it is put into service should be considered as part of the total cost assigned to the asset. For example, the cost of an item of equipment might be calculated as follows:

Invoice Price of Equipment	$12,000
Less: 2 Percent Discount for Prompt Cash Payment	240
Net Invoice Price	$11,760
Transportation Cost	326
Installation Costs	735
Total Cost of Equipment	$12,821

The acquisition cost of this equipment to be recorded in the accounting records is $12,821.

Instead of disbursing cash or incurring a liability, other forms of consideration (for example, common shares, merchandise inventory, land) may be given in acquiring an asset. In these cases, acquisition cost is measured by the market value of the consideration given or the market value of the asset received, depending on which market value is more reliably measured.

Foundations for Acquisition Cost Accounting's use of acquisition-cost valuations for nonmonetary assets rests on three important concepts or conventions. First, a firm is assumed to be a *going concern*. That is, it is assumed that the firm will remain in operation long enough for all of its current plans to be carried out. Any increases in the market value of assets held will be realized in the normal course of business when the firm receives higher prices for its products. Current values of the individual assets are therefore assumed to be largely unimportant. Second, acquisition-cost valuations are considered to be more objective than those obtained from using the other valuation methods. *Objectivity* in accounting refers to the ability of several independent measurers to come to the same conclusion about the valuation of an asset. Obtaining consensus on what constitutes the acquisition cost of an asset is relatively easy. Differences among measurers can arise in ascertaining an asset's current replacement cost, current net realizable value, or present value of future cash flows. Objectivity is necessary if financial statements are to be subject to audits by independent accountants. Third, acquisition cost generally provides more conservative valuations of assets (and measures of earnings) relative to the other valuation methods. Many accountants feel that the possibility of misleading financial statement users will be minimized when assets are stated at lower rather than higher amounts. Thus, *conservatism* has evolved as a convention to justify acquisition-cost valuations.

The preceding description of generally accepted valuation bases does not justify them. The valuation basis — acquisition cost, current replacement cost, current net realizable value, or present value of future cash flows — most relevant to users is an empirical question for which convincing evidence has not yet been provided. As Appendix D discusses, many large, publicly held firms provide supplementary information on the current cost of their inventories, property, plant, and equipment. The required disclosure of such information is, to some extent, a response to the recognized deficiencies of historical cost valuations during periods of changing prices.

Asset Classification

The classification of assets within the balance sheet varies widely in published annual reports. The principal asset categories are described below.

Current Assets *Current assets* include "those assets ordinarily realizable within one year from the date of the balance sheet or within the normal operating cycle, where that is longer than a year."[1] The operating cycle refers to the period of time that elapses for a given firm during which cash is converted into salable goods and

---

[1] *CICA Handbook*, section 1510.

services, goods and services are sold to customers, and customers pay for their purchases with cash. Included in current assets are cash, marketable securities held for the short-term, accounts and notes receivable net of allowance for doubtful accounts, inventories of merchandise, raw materials, supplies, work in process, and finished goods and prepaid operating costs (for example, prepaid insurance, and prepaid rent). Prepaid costs, or prepayments, are current assets in that, if they were not paid in advance, then current assets would be required within the next operating cycle to acquire those services.

Investments A second section of the balance sheet, labeled "Investments," includes long-term investments in securities of other firms. For example, a firm might purchase common shares of a supplier to help assure continued availability of raw materials. Or common shares of a firm in another area of business activity might be acquired to permit the acquiring firm to diversify its operations. When one corporation (the parent) owns more than 50 percent of the voting shares in another corporation (the subsidiary), a single set of "consolidated" financial statements is usually prepared. That is, the specific assets, liabilities, revenues, and expenses of the subsidiary are merged, or consolidated, with those of the parent corporation. The securities shown in the Investments section of the balance sheet are therefore investments in firms whose assets and liabilities have *not* been consolidated with the parent or investor firm. Chapter 13 discusses consolidated financial statements.

The holders of a firm's long-term bonds may require that cash be set aside periodically so that sufficient funds will be available to retire the bonds at maturity. The funds are typically given to a trustee, such as a trust company, which invests the funds received. Funds set aside for this purpose are shown in a Sinking Fund account and classified under Investments on the balance sheet.

Property, Plant, and Equipment Property, plant, and equipment (sometimes called *plant assets* or *fixed assets*) designates the tangible, long-lived assets *used in a firm's operations* over a period of years and generally not acquired for resale. This category includes land, buildings, machinery, automobiles, furniture, fixtures, computers, and other equipment. The amount shown on the balance sheet for each of these items (except land) is acquisition cost less accumulated depreciation since the asset was acquired. The total cost of each category is usually presented, and the accumulated depreciation is shown separately as a deduction from the acquisition cost. Land is shown at acquisition cost.

Intangible Assets Intangible assets include such items as patents, trademarks, franchises, and goodwill. The expenditures made by the firm in developing intangible assets are usually not recognized as assets, because of the difficulty of ascertaining the existence and amount of future benefits. Only intangible assets purchased in market exchanges from other entities are recognized as assets.

Liability Recognition

A liability arises when a firm receives benefits or services and in exchange promises to pay the provider of those goods and services a reasonably definite amount at a reasonably definite future time. The payment is usually in cash but may be made in goods or services.

Example 13 Miller Corporation purchased merchandise inventory and agreed to pay the supplier $8,000 within 30 days. This obligation is a liability, because Miller Corporation has received the goods and must pay a definite amount at a reasonably definite future time.

Example 14 Miller Corporation borrowed $4 million by issuing long-term bonds. Annual interest payments of ten percent must be made on December 31 of each year, and the $4 million principal must be repaid in 20 years. This obligation is a liability because Miller Corporation has received the cash and must repay the debt in a definite amount at a definite future time. The interest payable on the bonds increases each day the bonds are outstanding but at the time of the original borrowing there is no liability. At the financial statement date, the number of days of unpaid interest will be calculated and set up as a liability on the balance sheet.

Example 15 Miller Corporation provides a three-year warranty on its products. The obligation to maintain the products under warranty plans creates a liability. The selling price for its products implicitly includes a charge for future warranty services. As customers pay the selling price, Miller Corporation receives a benefit (that is, the cash received). Past experience provides a basis for estimating the proportion of customers who will seek services under the warranty agreement and the expected cost of providing warranty services. Thus, the amount of obligation can be estimated with a reasonable degree of accuracy, and it is shown as a liability.

Example 16 Miller Corporation has signed an agreement with its employees' labour union, promising to increase wages six percent and to provide for medical and life insurance. This agreement does not immediately create a liability, because services have not yet been received from employees that would require any payments for wages and insurance. As labour services are received, a liability will arise.

The most troublesome questions of liability recognition relate to unexecuted contracts. The labour union agreement in Example 16 above is an unexecuted contract. Other examples include leases, pension agreements, purchase-order commitments, and employment contracts. Accounting does not currently recognize unexecuted contracts as liabilities, although the issue continues to be controversial.

Liability Valuation

Most liabilities are monetary, requiring payments of specific amounts of cash. Those due within one year or less are stated at the amount of cash expected to be paid to discharge the obligation. If the payment dates extend more than one year into the future (for example, as in the case of the bonds in Example 14 above), the liability is usually stated at the present value of the future cash outflows.

A liability that requires delivering goods or rendering services, rather than paying cash, is nonmonetary. For example, magazine publishers typically collect cash for subscriptions, promising delivery of magazines over many months. Cash is received currently, whereas the obligation under the subscription is discharged by delivering magazines in the future. Theaters and football teams receive cash for season tickets and promise to admit the ticket holder to future performances. Landlords receive cash in advance and promise to let the tenant use the property. Such nonmonetary obligations appear among liabilities. They are stated, however, at the amount of cash received rather than at the expected cost of publishing the magazines or of providing the theatrical or sporting entertainment. The title frequently used for liabilities of this type is Advances from Customers.

Liability Classification

Liabilities in the balance sheet are typically classified in one of the following categories.

Current Liabilities *Current liabilities* include "amounts payable within one year from the date of the balance sheet or within the normal operating cycle, where this is longer than a year (the normal operating cycle should correspond with that used for current assets)."[2] Included in this category are liabilities to merchandise suppliers, employees, and governmental units. Notes and bonds payable are also included to the extent that they will require the use of current assets within the next year.

Long-Term Debt Obligations having due dates or maturities more than one year after the balance sheet date are generally classified as *long-term debt*. Included are bonds, mortgages, and similar debts, as well as some obligations under long-term leases.

Other Long-Term Liabilities Obligations not properly considered as current liabilities or long-term debt are classified as *other long-term liabilities*. Included are such items as future income taxes and some pension obligations.

Owners' Equity Valuation and Disclosure

The owners' equity in a firm is a residual interest.[3] That is, the owners have a claim on all assets not required to meet the claims of creditors. The valuation of the assets and liabilities included in the balance sheet therefore determines the valuation of total owners' equity.

The remaining question concerns the manner of disclosing this total owners' equity. Accounting draws a distinction between contributed capital and income retained by a firm. The balance sheet for a corporation generally separates the amounts contributed directly by shareholders for an interest in the firm (that is, share capital) from the subsequent earnings realized by the firm in excess of dividends declared (that is, retained earnings).

In addition, where a company is authorized to issue *par value* shares, the amount received from shareholders is further divided into the par value of the shares issued and *contributed surplus*. The par or stated value of a share is a somewhat arbitrary amount assigned to comply with corporation laws of each jurisdiction[4] and will rarely

---

[2]*CICA Handbook*, section 1510.

[3]Although owners' equity is equal to assets minus liabilities, accounting provides an independent method for computing the amount. This method is presented in this and the next two chapters.

[4]The federal and each provincial government has the authority to incorporate companies.

equal the market price of the shares at the time they are issued. As a result, the distinction between par or stated value and contributed surplus contains little information, but is typically shown nonetheless. To overcome this anomaly, Companies Acts authorize a company to issue no-par-value shares. When no-par-value shares are issued, the full amount received from the shareholders is included in share capital. The Canada Business Corporations Act requires a company to issue only no-par-value shares. (Chapter 12 discusses these fine points of accounting for owners' equity.)

Example 17 Stephens Corporation was formed on January 1, Year 1. It issued 15,000 $10 par value common shares for $10 cash per share. During Year 1, Stephens Corporation had net income of $30,000 and paid dividends of $10,000 to shareholders. The shareholders' equity section of the balance sheet of Stephens Corporation on December 31, Year 1 is as follows:

Common Stock (par value of $10 per share, 15,000 shares issued and outstanding)	$150,000
Retained Earnings	20,000
Total Shareholders' Equity	$170,000

Example 18 Instead of issuing $10 par value common shares as in Example 17, assume that Stephens Corporation issued 15,000 common shares of $1 par value for $10 cash per share. (The market price of common shares depends on the economic value of the firm and not on the par value of the shares.) The shareholders' equity section of the balance sheet of Stephens Corporation on December 31, Year 1 is as follows:

Common Stock (par value of $1 per share, 15,000 shares issued and outstanding	$ 15,000
Contributed Surplus	135,000
Retained Earnings	20,000
Total Shareholders' Equity	$170,000

The balance sheets of firms that are organized as sole proprietorships or partnerships, rather than as corporations, do not distinguish between contributed capital and earnings retained in business.

Example 19 Joan Webster operates a hardware store as a sole proprietorship. She contributed $20,000 on January 1, Year 1 and used the cash to rent a building, acquire display equipment, and purchase merchandise inventory. During Year 1, she had net income of $15,000 and withdrew $10,000 cash for personal use. The owner's equity section of the balance sheet of Webster's Hardware Store on December 31, Year 1 is as follows:

Joan Webster, Capital	$25,000[a]
Total Owner's Equity	$25,000

[a]$20,000 + $15,000 − $10,000 = $25,000.

Example 20 Bill White and Roger Green own and manage an apartment complex as a partnership. Each partner contributed $50,000 cash to form the partnership on January 1, Year 1. During Year 1, net income from the apartment complex was $40,000, which the partners shared equally. Bill White withdrew $10,000 and Roger Green withdrew $5,000 from the partnership. The owners' equity section of the balance sheet on December 31, Year 1 for the apartment complex is as follows:

Bill White, Capital	$ 60,000[a]
Roger Green, Capital	65,000[b]
Total Owners' Equity	$125,000

[a]$50,000 + (.50 × $40,000) − $10,000 = $60,000.
[b]$50,000 + (.50 × $40,000) − $ 5,000 = $65,000.

Distinctly Canadian GAAP

*T*he differences between Canadian and U.S. GAAP are of concern to the senior financial officers who have to provide for reconciliations. According to Suresh Thadhani, the controller of Alcan, providing the two sets of figures is "a nuisance," and the reconciliation provides additional information to competitors who do not have to comply with the same standards of disclosure.

Ken Whiteside, senior vice president with TransCanada PipeLines, remarked that it's difficult enough to understand one bottom line. He feels that a higher corporate profit reported under Canadian GAAP, when compared with the U.S. number, raises questions about the quality of the numbers involved—which is preferable and which is right?

Why the differences?

Why are there so many differences between Canadian and U.S. GAAP? Some standard-setters on either side of the border may be tempted to say, "Ours are better." But in most instances a definitive case for either side would be difficult to argue. Certainly, there have been some marked differences in the economic and financial development of Canada and the U.S., but, again, these cannot be related directly to the differences in the two GAAPs.

Instead, it appears that standard-setting in the two countries is influenced by how each views the relative importance of the different components of the financial statements.

In any effort to set standards, there is always a trade-off between "getting it right" on the balance sheet or on the income statement. From the examples of differences cited, it becomes apparent that the Canadian leaning is towards deferral and amortization, in attempts to match revenue and expenses, to allow for cause and effect, or to recognize time and terms. The U.S. approach, on the other hand, seems to be directed more to the balance sheet, to arriving at valuations without distortions due to "matching."

One could argue that the Canadian GAAP looks at the income statement trends, while the FASB concentrates on the balance sheet snapshot. While the income statement under the U.S. GAAP, some would argue, may be subject to swings brought about by accounting standards, the U.S. GAAP balance sheet attempts to present a more meaningful report of a company's resources and obligations. The U.S. result flows from restricted definitions of assets and liabilities, combined with an income stream that has not been normalized. There is no question, however, that the effort "to get it right'' on the income statements results in what some would call, with great technical precision, ''funny'' items on the balance sheet. And the most misunderstood and criticized of those is, of course, deferred income taxes.

The regulatory climate

The regulatory surroundings of the two GAAPs is also quite different. The U.S. practice of push-down accounting, for example, is not a result of standard-setting by the FASB; it is an instance of RAP—regulated accounting principles—as the practice was dictated by the Securities and Exchange Commission. In Canada, governments and regulators have retained the power to issue RAP, but have delegated the responsibility for setting both accounting and auditing standards to the CICA. In the provincial securities acts and in the federal Canada Business Corporations Act and some provincial corporations legislation, the accounting standards for Canadian profit-oriented enterprises are defined as those set out in the *CICA Handbook*.

Another contributor to the gap in GAAPs is one of the philosophy of standard-setting. Both the U.S. and Canadian models place prime importance on the use of professional judgment, but Canadian standards, in effect, place much more reliance—some would say too much reliance—on the use of the judgment. Canadian standards are specifically designed so that they are not detailed rules. All accounting and auditing standards are contained in the *CICA Handbook*, a publication which runs to only a few hundred pages. It is not light or pleasant reading, but it is relatively straight-forward in setting out general standards. And the CICA seldom issues supplementary technical bulletins or lengthy rationales of *Handbook* material.

Of course, it can be said that this approach is necessary for the CICA, which has 45,000 members and far fewer resources than either the FASB or the AICPA. But it is an approach in line with the early development of standard-setting in England and Scotland, where so many of Canada's early chartered accountants came from. Relative to its size, the Canadian profession does devote considerable resources not only to developing Canadian standards but also to international harmonization of accounting standards and auditing practices.

At this time, however, Canada may have to make some changes in its standard-setting philosophy and practices. In Canada, as in the U.S., accountants are under a good deal of pressure from regulators and the business community. How they react and grow will help shape the financial environment in the future.

Reprinted with the special permission of *Financial Executive*, Sept./Oct., 1988 pp. 42–43, ''Why the Difference?''

Accounting Procedures for Preparing the Balance Sheet

Now that the concepts and conventions underlying the balance sheet have been discussed, the manner in which these concepts and conventions are applied in preparing the statement can be considered. The objective is to develop a sufficient understanding of the accounting process that generates the balance sheet so that the resulting statement can be interpreted and analyzed.

Dual Effects of Transactions on the Balance Sheet Equation

The equality between total assets and total liabilities plus shareholders' equity in the balance sheet equation is maintained by reporting the effects of *each* transaction in a way that maintains the equation. Any single transaction will have one of the following four effects or some combination of these effects:

1. It increases both an asset and a liability or shareholders' equity.
2. It decreases both an asset and a liability or shareholders' equity.
3. It increases one asset and decreases another asset.
4. It increases one liability or shareholders' equity and decreases another liability or shareholders' equity.

To illustrate the dual effects of various transactions on the balance sheet equation, consider the following selected transactions for Miller Corporation during January.

1. On January 1, 10,000 $10 par value common shares are issued for $100,000 cash.
2. Equipment costing $60,000 is purchased for cash on January 5.
3. Merchandise inventory costing $15,000 is purchased from a supplier on account on January 15.
4. The supplier in (3) is paid $8,000 of the amount due on January 21.
5. The supplier in (3) accepts 700 common shares at par value in settlement of the $7,000 amount owned.
6. A one-year fire insurance premium of $600 for coverage beginning February 1 is paid in cash on January 31.
7. Cash of $3,000 is received from a customer on January 31 for merchandise to be delivered during February.

Exhibit 2.1 illustrates the dual effects of these transactions on the balance sheet equation. Note that, after each transaction, assets equal liabilities plus shareholders' equity.

The dual effects reported for each transaction may be viewed as an outflow and an inflow. For example, common shares are issued to shareholders and cash is received from them. A cash expenditure is made and equipment is received. A promise to make a future cash payment is given to a supplier and merchandise inventory is received. Most transactions and events recorded in the accounting system result from exchanges. The accounting records reflect the inflows and outflows arising from these exchanges.

Purpose and Use of Accounts

A balance sheet could be prepared for Miller Corporation as of January 31, using information from the preceding analysis. Total assets are $110,000. To prepare a balance sheet, however, it would be necessary to retrace the effects of each transaction on total assets to ascertain what portion of the $110,000 represents cash, merchandise inventory, and equipment. Likewise, the effects of each transaction on total liabilities and shareholders' equity would have to be retraced to ascertain which liability and shareholders' equity amounts comprise the $110,000 total. Even with just a few transactions during the accounting period, this approach to preparing a balance sheet would be cumbersome. Considering the thousands of transactions during the accounting period for most firms, some more practical approach to accumulating amounts for the balance sheet is necessary. To accumulate the changes that take place in each balance sheet item, the accounting system uses a device known as an *account*.

Exhibit 2.1
Illustration of Dual Effects of Transactions on Balance Sheet Equation

Transaction	Assets	=	Liabilities	+	Share-holders' Equity
(1) On January 1, 10,000 $10 par value common shares are issued for $100,000 cash. (Increase in both an asset and shareholders' equity.)	+$100,000		$ 0	+	$100,000
Subtotal	$100,000	=	$ 0	+	$100,000
(2) Equipment costing $60,000 is purchased for cash on January 5. (Increase in one asset and decrease in another asset.)	− 60,000 + 60,000				
Subtotal	$100,000	=	$ 0	+	$100,000
(3) Merchandise inventory costing $15,000 is purchased from a supplier on account on January 15. (Increase in both an asset and a liability.)	+ 15,000		+ 15,000		
Subtotal	$115,000	=	$15,000	+	$100,000
(4) The supplier in (3) is paid $8,000 of the amount due on January 21. (Decrease in both an asset and a liability.)	− 8,000		− 8,000		
Subtotal	$107,000	=	$ 7,000	+	$100,000
(5) The supplier in (3) accepts 700 common shares at par value in settlement of $7,000 of the amount owed. (Increase in shareholders' equity and decrease in a liability.)			− 7,000	+	7,000
Subtotal	$107,000	=	$ 0	+	$107,000
(6) A one-year fire insurance premium of $600 for coverage beginning February 1 is paid in cash on January 31. (Increase in one asset and decrease in another asset.)	+ 600 − 600				
Subtotal	$107,000	=	$ 0	+	$107,000
(7) Cash of $3,000 is received from a customer on January 31 for merchandise to be delivered during February. (Increase in both an asset and a liability.)	+ 3,000		+ 3,000		
Total — January 31	$110,000	=	$ 3,000	+	$107,000

Requirement for an Account Because a balance sheet item that changes can only increase or decrease, all an account need do is to provide for accumulating the increases and decreases that have taken place during the period for a single balance sheet item. The balance carried forward from the previous statement is added to the total increases; the total decreases are deducted, and the result is the amount of the new balance for the current balance sheet. The collection of individual accounts is called a *general ledger*.

Form of an Account The account may take many possible forms, and several are commonly used in accounting practice.

Perhaps the most useful form of the account for textbooks, problems, and examinations is the *T-account*. This form of the account is not used in actual practice, except perhaps for memorandums or preliminary analyses. However, it satisfies the requirement of an account and is easy to use. As the name indicates, the T-account is shaped like the letter T and consists of a horizontal line bisected by a vertical line. The name or title of the account is written on the horizontal line. One side of the space formed by the vertical line is used to record increases in the item and the other side to record the decreases. Spaces for dates and other information can appear as well.

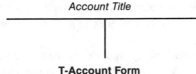

Account Title

T-Account Form

The form that the account takes in actual records depends on the type of accounting system being used. In manual systems the account may take the form of a single "ledger" sheet with columns for recording increases and decreases. In computer systems it may be a group of similarly coded items in a file. Whatever its form, an account contains the opening balance as well as the increases and decreases in the balance that result from the transactions of the period, and ordinarily the closing balance.

Placement of Increases and Decreases in the Account Given the two-sided account, we must choose which side will be used to record increases and which, decreases. By long-standing custom, the following rules are used:

1. Increases in assets are entered on the left side and decreases in assets on the right side.
2. Increases in liabilities are entered on the right side and decreases in liabilities on the left side.
3. Increases in owners' equity are entered on the right side and decreases in owners' equity on the left side.

This custom reflects the fact that a common format for a balance sheet shows assets on the left and liabilities and owners' equity on the right. Following this format, asset balances should appear on the left side of accounts; liability and shareholders' equity balances should appear on the right. But asset balances will appear on the left only if asset increases are recorded on the left side of the account. Similarly, right-hand liability and shareholders' equity balances can be produced only by recording liability and shareholders' equity increases on the right. When each transaction is properly analyzed into its dual effects on the accounting equation, and when the above three rules for recording the transaction are followed, then every transaction results in equal amounts in entries on the left- and right-hand sides of various accounts.

Debit and Credit Two terms may now be introduced, *debit* (Dr.) and *credit* (Cr.). These terms are convenient abbreviations: *debit* is an abbreviation for "record an entry on the left side of an account'' when used as a verb and is an abbreviation for ''an entry on the left side of an account'' when used as a noun or adjective. *Credit* is an abbreviation for ''record an entry on the right side of an account'' when used as a verb and is an abbreviation for ''an entry on the right side of an account'' when used as a noun or adjective. Often, however, the word *charge* is used instead of *debit*, both as a noun and as a verb. In terms of balance sheet categories, a debit or charge indicates (1) an increase in an asset, (2) a decrease in a liability, or (3) a decrease in a shareholders' equity item. A credit indicates (1) a decrease in an asset, (2) an increase in a liability, or (3) an increase in a shareholders' equity item.

In order to maintain the equality of the balance sheet equation, the amounts debited to various accounts for each transaction must equal the amounts credited to various accounts. Likewise, the sum of balances in accounts with debit balances at the end of each period must equal the sum of balances in accounts with credit balances.

Summary of Account Terminology and Procedure The conventional use of the account form and the terms debit and credit can be summarized graphically with the use of the T-account form, as follows:

Any Asset Account

Beginning Balance Increases + Dr.	Decreases – Cr.
Ending Balance	

Any Liability Account

Decreases – Dr.	Beginning Balance Increases + Cr.
	Ending Balance

Any Shareholders' Equity Account

Decreases – Dr.	Beginning Balance Increases + Cr.
	Ending Balance

Reflecting the Dual Effects of Transactions in the Accounts

The manner in which the dual effects of transactions change the accounts can now be illustrated. Three separate T-accounts are created: one for assets, one for liabilities, and one for shareholders' equity. The dual effects of the transactions of Miller Corporation for January, described earlier in the chapter, are entered in the T-accounts as shown in Exhibit 2.2.

The amount entered on the left side of, or debited to, the accounts for each transaction is equal to the amount entered on the right side of, or credited to, the accounts. Recording equal amounts of debits and credits for each transaction ensures that the balance sheet equation will always be in balance. At the end of January, the assets account has a debit balance of $110,000. The sum of the balances in the liabilities and shareholders' equity accounts is a credit balance of $110,000.

Exhibit 2.2
Summary T-Accounts Showing the
Transactions of Miller Corporation

	Assets		=	Liabilities		+	Shareholders' Equity	
	Increases (Dr.)	Decreases (Cr.)		Decreases (Dr.)	Increases (Cr.)		Decreases (Dr.)	Increases (Cr.)
(1) Issue of Common Shares for Cash	100,000							100,000
(2) Purchase of Equipment for Cash	60,000	60,000						
(3) Purchase of Merchandise on Account	15,000				15,000			
(4) Payment of Cash to Supplier in (3)		8,000		8,000				
(5) Issuance of Common Shares to Supplier in (3)				7,000				7,000
(6) Payment of Insurance Premium in Advance	600	600						
(7) Cash Received from Customer in Advance	3,000				3,000			
Balance	110,000				3,000			107,000

A balance sheet could be prepared for Miller Corporation from the information in the T-accounts. As was the case in the earlier illustration, however, it would be necessary to retrace the entries in the accounts during the period to ascertain which individual assets, liabilities, and shareholders' equity items make up the total assets of $110,000 and the total equities of $110,000.

So that the amount of each asset, liability, and shareholders' equity item can be computed directly, a separate account is used for each balance sheet item, rather than for the three broad categories alone. The recording procedure is the same, except that we must now consider which specific asset or equity account is debited and credited.

The transactions of Miller Corporation for January are recorded in Exhibit 2.3, using separate T-accounts for each balance sheet item. The number in parentheses refers to the seven transactions we have been considering for Miller Corporation.

Exhibit 2.3
Individual T-Accounts Showing
the Transactions of Miller Corporation

Cash (Asset)		Accounts Payable (Liability)	
Increases (Dr.)	Decreases (Cr.)	Decreases (Dr.)	Increases (Cr.)
(1) 100,000	60,000 (2)	(4) 8,000	15,000 (3)
(7) 3,000	8,000 (4)	(5) 7,000	
	600 (6)		
Balance 34,400			0 Balance

Merchandise Inventory (Asset)			**Advance from Customer (Liability)**	
Increases (Dr.)	Decreases (Cr.)		Decreases (Dr.)	Increases (Cr.)
(3) 15,000				3,000 (7)
Balance 15,000				3,000 Balance

Prepaid Insurance (Asset)			**Common Stock (Shareholders' Equity)**	
Increases (Dr.)	Decreases (Cr.)		Decreases (Dr.)	Increases (Cr.)
(6) 600				100,000 (1)
				7,000 (5)
Balance 600				107,000 Balance

Equipment (Asset)		
Increases (Dr.)	Decreases (Cr.)	
(2) 60,000		
Balance 60,000		

The balance sheet can be prepared using the amounts shown as balances in the T-accounts. The balance sheet of Miller Corporation after the seven transactions of January is shown in Exhibit 2.4.

Exhibit 2.4
MILLER CORPORATION
Balance Sheet, January 31

Assets
Current Assets:

Cash	$ 34,400
Merchandise Inventory	15,000
Prepaid Insurance	600
Total Current Assets	$ 50,000

Property, Plant, and Equipment

Equipment	60,000
Total Assets	$110,000

Liabilities and Shareholders' Equity
Current Liabilities:

Advance from Customer	$ 3,000

Shareholders' Equity:

Common Stock	107,000
Total Liabilities and Shareholders' Equity	$110,000

The Times They are a Changing

*N*ot too many years ago, the number of women in the accounting profession was roughly the same as the number of women playing defensive tackle in professional football. Not so today. Women make up roughly 14% of the accounting profession in this country which is twice the percentage of 5 years earlier. But when you consider that 30 to 40% of all accounting students today are female, you see that it is possible that the profession someday may be made up of a majority of female members.

Women are greatly attracted to all the professions today, which makes sense, since that's where the money and prestige is. However, a recent survey by Nelson, Andiappan, and Swartz has found that female members of the profession still lag behind male counterparts in salary.

Several successful female accountants interviewed gave the same advice to women looking to a career in accounting—the best possible education and hard work were seen as the prescription to success in the profession. Increasingly, excellence will find its own reward. Sounds like good advice for all of us.

Source: "The Bottom Line." June 1987, pp. 5, 6, 7.

An Overview of the Accounting Process

The double-entry recording framework is used in processing the results of various transactions and events through the accounts so that financial statements can be prepared periodically. The accounting system designed around this recording framework generally involves the following operations:

1. Entering the results of each transaction in the *general journal* in the form of a *journal entry*, a process called *journalizing*.
2. Posting the journal entries from the general journal to the accounts in the *general ledger*.
3. Preparing a *trial balance* of the accounts in the general ledger.
4. Making *adjusting* journal entries to accounts listed in the trial balance and posting them to the appropriate general ledger accounts.
5. Preparing financial statements from a trial balance after adjusting entries.

Figure 2.1 shows these operations. Each is described further and illustrated using the transactions of Miller Corporation during January.

Figure 2.1 Summary of the Accounting Process

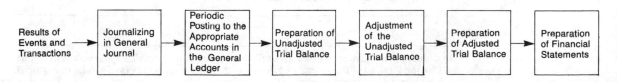

Journalizing

Each transaction is initially recorded in the general journal in the form of a *journal entry*. The standard journal entry format is as follows:

Date Account Debited .... Amount Debited
         Account Credited .... Amount Credited
         Explanation of transaction or event being journalized.

The *general journal* is merely a book or other device containing a listing of journal entries in chronological order. The general journal is often referred to as the "book of original entry," because transactions initially enter the accounting system through it.[5]

The journal entries for the seven transactions of Miller Corporation during January are presented below.

---

(1) Jan. 1   Cash $100,000
                 Common Stock $100,000
                 10,000 $10 par value common shares are issued for
                 cash.

(2) Jan. 5   Equipment .... $ 60,000
                 Cash .... $ 60,000
                 Equipment costing $60,000 is purchased for cash.

(3) Jan. 15 Merchandise Inventory .... $ 15,000
                 Accounts Payable .... $ 15,000
                 Merchandise inventory costing $15,000 is purchased
                 on account.

(4) Jan. 21 Accounts Payable .... $ 8,000
                 Cash .... $ 8,000
                 Liabilities of $8,000 are paid with cash.

(5) Jan. 21 Accounts Payable .... $ 7,000
                 Common Stock .... $ 7,000
                 700 $10 par value common shares are issued in
                 settlement of an account payable of $7,000.

(6) Jan. 31 Prepaid Insurance .... $ 600
                 Cash .... $ 600
                 One-year fire insurance premium of $600 is paid in
                 advance.

(7) Jan. 31 Cash .... $ 3,000
                 Advance from Customer .... $ 3,000
                 Advance of $3,000 is received from customer for
                 merchandise to be delivered in February.

---

[5]In addition to the general journal, most firms also maintain *specialized journals*. These journals are used instead of the general journal where there are large numbers of similar transactions. Appendix 3.1 discusses specialized journals more fully.

Journal entries are useful for indicating the effects of various transactions on a firm's financial statements and in preparing solutions to the problems at the end of each chapter. An accounting event will not be completely understood until it is analyzed into its required debits and credits and the proper journal entry prepared. Consequently, journal entries are used as tools of analysis throughout this text.

Posting

At periodic intervals (for example, weekly or monthly), the transactions journalized in the general journal are entered, or posted, to the individual accounts in the general ledger.[6] In manual systems, the *general ledger* is a book with a separate page for each account. In computerized systems, the general ledger takes the form of an access number in a computer's file. The T-account described earlier serves as a useful surrogate for a general ledger account. The journal entries from the general journal of Miller Corporation would be posted to the general ledger accounts in the manner shown previously in Exhibit 2.3.

As with journal entries, T-accounts are useful tools in preparing solutions to accounting problems and are used throughout this text.

Trial Balance Preparation

A *trial balance* is a listing of each of the accounts in the general ledger with its balance as of a particular date. The trial balance of Miller Corporation on January 31 appears in Exhibit 2.5.

When the sum of debit account balances equals the sum of credit account balances, it is likely that the double-entry recording procedure has been carried out accurately during the period. If the trial balance is out of balance, retracing the steps followed in processing the accounting data is necessary to locate the source of the error.

Exhibit 2.5
MILLER CORPORATION
Unadjusted Trial Balance, January 31

Account	Amounts in Accounts with Debit Balances	Amounts in Accounts with Credit Balances
Cash	$ 34,400	
Merchandise Inventory	15,000	
Prepaid Insurance	600	
Equipment	60,000	
Advance from Customer		$ 3,000
Common Stock		107,000
Totals	$110,000	$110,000

---

[6]There are also subsidiary ledgers, discussed in Appendix 3.1.

Trial Balance Adjustment and Correction

Any errors detected in the processing of accounting data must be corrected. More frequently, adjustment is necessary to account for unrecorded events that help to measure net income for the period and financial position at the end of the period. For example, at the end of February, the Prepaid Insurance account will be adjusted downward to reflect the coverage that expired during February. Chapters 3 and 4 discuss this type of adjustment more fully. Most corrections and adjustments are made by preparing a journal entry, entering it in the general journal, and then posting it to the general ledger accounts.

Financial Statement Preparation

The balance sheet and income statement can be prepared from the trial balance after adjustments and corrections. Because correcting or adjusting entries are not required for Miller Corporation, the balance sheet in Exhibit 2.4 is correct as presented. In subsequent chapters, the accounting procedures for preparing the income statement and the statement of changes in financial position are considered.

The results of various transactions and events are processed through the accounting system in a flow beginning with the journalizing operation and ending with the financial statements.

The audit of the financial statements by the independent auditor typically flows in the opposite direction. The auditor begins with the financial statements prepared by management and then traces various items back through the accounts to the source documents (for example, sales invoices, canceled cheques) that support the entries made in the general journal. Thus, it is possible to move back and forth among source documents, journal entries, general ledger postings, and the financial statements.

Balance Sheet Account Titles

The following list shows balance sheet account titles that are commonly used. The descriptions should help in your understanding the nature of various assets, liabilities, and shareholders' equities as well as in selecting appropriate terms for solving problems. Alternative account titles can be easily devised. The list does not show all the account titles used in this book or appearing in the financial statements of publicly held firms. The Glossary provides a more complete description of account titles.

Assets

Cash on hand Coins and currency, and such items as bank cheques and money orders. The latter items are merely claims against individuals or institutions, but by custom are called "cash."

Cash in Bank Strictly speaking, merely a claim against the bank for the amount deposited. Cash in bank consists of demand deposits, against which cheques can be drawn, and time deposits, usually savings accounts and certificates of deposit. In published statements, the two items of Cash on Hand and Cash in Bank usually are combined under the title *Cash*.

Temporary Investments Government bonds, or shares and bonds of corporations, that the firm plans to hold for a relatively short period of time. The word *temporary* implies that they can be bought and sold readily through a security exchange such as the Toronto Stock Exchange.

Accounts Receivable Amounts due from customers of a business from the sale of goods or services. The collection of cash occurs some time after the sale. These accounts are also known as "charge accounts" or "open accounts." The general term Accounts Receivable is used in financial statements to describe the figure representing the total amount receivable from all customers but, of course, the firm keeps a separate record for each customer.

Notes Receivable Amounts due from customers or from others to whom loans have been made or credit extended, when the claim has been put into writing in the form of a promissory note.

Interest Receivable Interest on assets such as promissory notes or bonds that has accrued, or come into existence, through the passing of time but that has not been collected as of the date of the balance sheet.

Merchandise Inventory Goods on hand that have been purchased for resale, such as canned goods on the shelves of a grocery store or suits on the racks of a clothing store.

Raw Materials Inventory Unused materials from which manufactured products are to be made.

Work-in-Process Inventory Partially completed manufactured products.

Finished Goods Inventory Completed but unsold manufactured products.

Supplies Inventory Lubricants, cleaning rags, abrasives, and other incidental materials used in manufacturing operations. Stationery, computer disks, pens, and other office supplies. Bags, twine, boxes, and other store supplies. Gasoline, oil, spare parts, and other delivery supplies.

Prepaid Insurance Insurance premiums paid for future coverage.

Prepaid Rent Rent paid in advance for future use of land, buildings, or equipment.

Advances to Suppliers The general name used to indicate payments made in advance for goods to be received at a later date. If no cash is paid by a firm when it places an order, then no asset is recognized.

Investment in Securities The cost of shares in other companies, where the firm's purpose is to hold the shares for relatively long periods of time.

Land Land occupied by buildings or used in operations.

Buildings Factory buildings, store buildings, garages, warehouses, and so forth.

Equipment Lathes, ovens, tools, boilers, computers, motors, bins, cranes, conveyors, automobiles, and so forth.

Furniture and Fixtures Desks, tables, chairs, counters, showcases, scales, and other such store and office equipment.

Accumulated Depreciation This account shows the cumulative amount of the cost of long-term assets (such as buildings and equipment) that has been allocated to the costs of production or to prior periods in measuring net income. The amount in this account is subtracted from the acquisition cost of the long-term asset to which it relates in ascertaining the *net book value* of the asset to be shown in the balance sheet. This account is an example of a *contra account*.

Leasehold The right to use property owned by someone else.

Deferred Charges Debt discount and expense, organization costs, deferred development costs, preproduction costs, and so forth.

Organization Costs Amounts paid for legal and incorporation fees, for printing the share certificates, for accounting, and any other costs incurred in organizing the business so it can begin to function.

Deferred Development and Preproduction Costs Expenditures made, additional to specific asset purchases, prior to the commencement of production or use of facilities.

Patents A right granted for up to 17 years by the federal government to exclude others from manufacturing, using, or selling a certain process or device. Under current generally accepted accounting principles, research and most development costs must be treated as an expense in the year incurred, rather than being recognized as an asset with future benefits.[7] As a result, a firm that develops a patent will not normally show it as an asset. On the other hand, a firm that purchases a patent from another firm or from an individual will recognize the patent as an asset. Chapter 9 discusses this inconsistent treatment of internally developed and externally purchased patents.

Goodwill An amount paid by one firm in acquiring another business enterprise that is greater than the sum of the then-current values assignable to individual, identifiable assets. A good reputation and other desirable attributes are generally not recognized as assets by the firm that creates or develops them. However, when one firm

---

[7]*CICA Handbook*, section 3450.

acquires another firm, these desirable attributes are indirectly recognized as assets, because they are a factor in the measurement of goodwill, and because they have to be paid for.

Liabilities

Bank Loans Amounts borrowed from a bank, frequently payable on demand.

Accounts Payable Amounts owed for goods or services acquired under an informal credit agreement. These accounts are usually payable within one or two months. The same items appear as Accounts Receivable on the creditors' books.

Notes Payable The face amount of promissory notes given in connection with loans from a bank or the purchase of goods or services. The same items appear as Notes Receivable on the creditors' books.

Payroll Taxes Payable Amounts withheld from wages and salaries of employees for payroll taxes that have not yet been remitted to tax authorities as well as the employer's share of such taxes.

Withheld Income Taxes Amounts withheld from wages and salaries of employees for income taxes that have not yet been remitted to the taxing authority. This is a tentative income tax on the earnings of employees, and the employer acts merely as a tax-collecting agent for the government.

Interest Payable Interest on obligations that has accrued or accumulated with the passage of time but that has not been paid as of the date of the balance sheet. The liability for interest is customarily shown separately from the face amount of the obligation.

Income Taxes Payable The estimated liability for income taxes, accumulated and unpaid, based on the taxable income of the business from the beginning of the taxable year to the date of the balance sheet. Because sole proprietorships and partnerships do not pay income taxes directly, this term will appear only on the books of a corporation or other taxable entity.

Advances from Customers The general name used to indicate payments received in advance for goods to be delivered or services to be furnished to customers in the future: a nonmonetary liability. If no cash is received when a customer places an order, then no liability is recorded.

Rent Received in Advance Another example of a nonmonetary liability. The business owns a building that it rents to a tenant. The tenant has prepaid the rental charge for several months in advance. The amount applicable to future months cannot be considered a component of income until the rent is earned, as service is rendered with the passage of time. Meanwhile the advance payment results in a liability payable in services (that is, in the use of the building). On the records of the tenant the same amount would appear as an asset, Prepaid Rent.

Mortgage Payable Long-term promissory notes that have been given greater protection by the pledge of specific pieces of property as security for their payment. If the loan or interest is not paid according to the agreement, the property can be sold for the benefit of the creditor.

Bonds Payable Amounts borrowed by the business for a relatively long period of time under a formal written contract or indenture. The loan is usually obtained from a number of lenders, each of whom receives one or more bond certificates as written evidence of his or her share of the loan.

Obligation under Capital Lease The present value of future commitments for cash payments to be made in return for the right to use property owned by someone else.

Future Income Taxes Certain income tax obligations are delayed beyond the current accounting period. These arise from timing differences in the deductibility of various expenses on the income statement versus the tax return, and also with respect to the period of inclusion of various revenue items.

Shareholders' Equity

Common Stock Amounts received for the par or stated value of a corporation's principal class of voting shares. Or, the total proceeds received for no-par-value shares.

Preferred Stock Amounts received for the par value of a class of a corporation's shares that has some preference relative to the common shares. Or, the total proceeds received for no-par-value preferred shares. This preference is usually with respect to dividends and to assets in the event the corporation is liquidated. Sometimes, preferred shares are convertible into common shares.

Contributed Surplus Amounts received from the issuance of common or preferred shares in excess of such shares' par or stated value. This account does not appear when a company is authorized to issue only no-par-value shares, except when property is donated to the company, or credit balances result from other capital transactions such as share redemptions, sale of treasury shares and capital reorganizations.

Retained Earnings An account reflecting the increase in net assets since the business was organized as a result of generating earnings in excess of dividend declarations. When dividends are declared, net assets are decreased, and retained earnings are reduced by an equal amount.

Treasury Shares This account shows the cost of shares originally issued but subsequently reacquired by the corporation. Treasury shares are not entitled to dividends and are not considered to be ''outstanding'' shares. The cost of treasury shares is shown on the balance sheet as a deduction from the total of the other shareholders' equity accounts. Chapter 12 discusses the accounting for treasury shares.

A balance sheet that includes many of the accounts described in this section is presented in Appendix A, Exhibit A.2, for General Products Limited (p. 761).

Analysis of Balance Sheet

The balance sheet reflects the effects of a firm's investment and financing decisions, and also reflects the results of operating decisions via the changes to the retained earnings account. In general, firms attempt to balance the term structure of their financing with the term structure of their investments. For example, firms such as retail stores, with large investments in current assets (receivables and inventories), tend to use significant short-term financing. Highly capital-intensive firms, such as electric utilities and steel manufacturers, tend to rely heavily on long-term debt and common shares.

Short-term financing refers to obligations payable within a year of the balance sheet date. A firm will want to be sure that it will have sufficient cash available within that time period to pay the obligations. Assets classified as ''current'' will be the assets most likely to generate the cash needed. Likewise, long-term financing is repaid, if at all, over a longer period. Because noncurrent assets tend to generate cash over a longer period of years, long-term financing for these assets is appropriate.

Refer to the balance sheet of General Products Limited in Exhibit A.2 in Appendix A (p. 761). At the end of 1988, current assets represent 53 percent of total assets, and current liabilities represent 41 percent of liabilities plus shareholders' equity. At the end of 1987, these percentages were 56 percent and 41 percent, respectively. To provide a cushion, the percentage for current assets tends to be higher than that for current liabilities.

A potential cause for concern occurs when the percentage of short-term financing begins to exceed the percentage of current assets. In this case, the firm is using short-term financing for noncurrent assets. A firm may face difficulties in obtaining sufficient cash from these noncurrent assets to meet required payments on short-term debt.

Summary

The balance sheet comprises three major classes of items — assets, liabilities, and shareholders' equity.

Resources are recognized as assets when a company has acquired rights to their future use as a result of a past transaction or exchange and when the value of the future benefits can be measured with a reasonable degree of precision. Monetary assets are, in general, stated at their current cash, or cash-equivalent, values. Nonmonetary assets are stated at acquisition cost, in most cases adjusted downward for the cost of services that have been consumed.

Liabilities represent obligations of a company to make payments of a reasonably definite amount at a reasonably definite future time for benefits already received. Shareholders' equity, the difference between total assets and total liabilities, is typically segregated for companies into contributed capital and retained earnings.

The equality of total assets and total liabilities plus shareholders' equity is maintained by recording the effects of each transaction in a dual manner in the accounts. The double-entry recording framework is summarized as follows:

Asset Accounts		=	Liability Accounts		+	Shareholders' Equity Accounts	
Increases (Debits)	Decreases (Credits)		Decreases (Debits)	Increases (Credits)		Decreases (Debits)	Increases (Credits)

The dual effects of each transaction are initially recorded in journal entry form in the general journal. These journal entries are then posted to the appropriate asset, liability, and shareholders' equity accounts in the general ledger. A trial balance of the ending balances in the general ledger accounts is prepared periodically as a check on the mathematical accuracy of the double-entry recording procedure. Any necessary adjustments of the account balances in the trial balance are then made in the general journal and posted to the accounts in the general ledger. The financial statements are prepared from the adjusted trial balance. Chapters 3 and 4 discuss the procedures for preparing the income statement. Chapter 5 discusses the statement of changes in financial position.

When analyzing a balance sheet, one looks for a reasonable balance between the term structure of assets and the term structure of liabilities plus shareholders' equity. The proportion of short- versus long-term financing should bear some relation to the proportion of current versus noncurrent assets.

Problem for Self-Study

The Electronics Appliance Corporation was organized on September 1. The following transactions occurred during the month of September.

(1) The firm issues 4,000 $10 par value common shares for $12 cash per share on September 1.
(2) The firm's lawyer is given 600 $10 par value common shares on September 2 in payment for legal services rendered in the organization of the corporation. The bill for the services is $7,200.
(3) A factory building is leased for the three years beginning October 1. Monthly rental payments are $5,000. Two months' rent is paid in advance on September 5.
(4) Raw materials are purchased on account for $6,100 on September 12.
(5) A cheque for $900 is received on September 15 from a customer as a deposit on a special order for equipment that Electronics plans to manufacture. The contract price is $4,800.
(6) Office equipment with a list price of $950 is acquired on September 20. After deducting a discount of $25 for prompt payment, a cheque is issued in full payment.
(7) The company hires three employees to begin work October 1. A cash advance of $200 is given to one of the employees on September 28.

(8) Factory equipment costing $27,500 is purchased on September 30. A cheque for $5,000 is issued, and a long-term mortgage liability is assumed for the balance.

(9) The labour costs of installing the new equipment in **(8)** are $450 and are paid in cash on September 30.

a. Prepare journal entries for each of the nine transactions.

b. Set up T-accounts and post each of the nine journal entries.

c. Prepare a balance sheet for Electronics Appliance Corporation as of September 30.

Suggested Solution

The journal entries for the nine transactions are as follows:

(1) Sept. 1	Cash	$48,000		
	Common Stock		$40,000	
	Contributed Surplus		8,000	
	Issuance of 4,000 $10 par value common shares for $12 cash per share.			
(2) Sept. 2	Organization Costs	$ 7,200		
	Common Stock		$ 6,000	
	Contributed Surplus		1,200	
	Issuance of 600 $10 par value common shares in settlement of $7,200 lawyer's bill connected with organization of the corporation.			
(3) Sept. 5	Prepaid Rent	$10,000		
	Cash		$10,000	
	Prepayment of rent for October and November on factory building.			
(4) Sept. 12	Raw Material Inventory	$ 6,100		
	Accounts Payable		$ 6,100	
	Raw materials costing $6,100 are purchased on account.			
(5) Sept. 15	Cash	$ 900		
	Advances from Customers		$ 900	
	An advance of $900 is received from a customer as a deposit on equipment to be manufactured in the future.			
(6) Sept. 20	Equipment	$ 925		
	Cash		$ 925	
	Equipment with a list price of $950 is acquired, after a discount, for $925.			
(7) Sept. 28	Advance to Employee	$ 200		
	Cash		$ 200	
	A cash advance of $200 is given to an employee beginning work on October 1.			
(8) Sept. 30	Equipment	$27,500		
	Cash		$ 5,000	
	Mortgage Payable		22,500	
	Acquisition of equipment for $5,000 cash and assumption of a $22,500 mortgage for the balance of the purchase price.			
(9) Sept. 30	Equipment	$ 450		
	Cash		$ 450	
	Installation cost on equipment acquired in (8) of $450 is paid in cash.			

Exhibit 2.6 presents T-accounts for Electronics Appliance Corporation and shows the posting of the nine entries to the accounts. The letters A, L, and SE are added after the account titles to indicate the balance sheet category of the accounts. Exhibit 2.7 presents a balance sheet as of September 30.

Exhibit 2.6
T-Accounts and Transactions during September
for Electronics Appliance Corporation

Cash (A)		Advances to Employees (A)		Raw Materials Inventory (A)		Prepaid Rent (A)	
(1) 48,000	10,000 (3)	(7) 200		(4) 6,100		(3) 10,000	
(5) 900	925 (6)						
	200 (7)						
	5,000 (8)						
	450 (9)						
32,325		200		6,100		10,000	

Equipment (A)		Organization Costs (A)		Accounts Payable (L)		Advances from Customers (L)	
(6) 925		(2) 7,200			6,100 (4)		900 (5)
(8) 27,500							
(9) 450							
28,875		7,200			6,100		900

Mortgage Payable (L)		Common Stock (SE)		Contributed Surplus (SE)	
	22,500 (8)		40,000 (1)		8,000 (1)
			6,000 (2)		1,200 (2)
	22,500		46,000		9,200

Exhibit 2.7
ELECTRONICS APPLIANCE CORPORATION
Balance Sheet, September 30

Assets

Current Assets:

Cash	$32,325	
Advances to Employees	200	
Raw Materials Inventory	6,100	
Prepaid Rent	10,000	
Total Current Assets		$48,625

Property, Plant, and Equipment:

Equipment		28,875

Intangibles:

Organization Costs		7,200
Total Assets		$84,700

Liabilities and Shareholders' Equity

Current Liabilities:

Accounts Payable	$6,100	
Advances from Customers	900	
Total Current Liabilities		$ 7,000

Long-Term Debt:

Mortgage Payable		22,500
Total Liabilities		29,500

Shareholders' Equity:

Common Shares, $10 Par Value	$46,000	
Contributed Surplus	9,200	
Total Shareholders' Equity		55,200
Total Liabilities and Shareholders' Equity		$84,700

Questions, Exercises, Problems and Cases

Questions

1. Review the meaning of the following concepts or terms discussed in this chapter.

   a. Accounting entity

   b. Legal entity

   c. Sole proprietorship

   d. Partnership

   e. Corporation

   f. Acquisition cost

   g. Current replacement cost

   h. Current net realizable value

   i. Present (discounted) value of future cash flows

   j. Monetary assets

   k. Nonmonetary assets

l. Going concern
m. Objectivity
n. Conservatism
o. Plant, or fixed, assets
p. Intangible assets
q. Par value
r. No par value
s. Debit

t. Charge
u. Credit
v. Journal entry
w. General journal
x. General ledger
y. T-account
z. Trial balance

2. How can you ascertain from a balance sheet whether the enterprise is a corporation, partnership, or sole proprietorship?

3. Conservatism is generally regarded as a convention in accounting. Indicate who might be hurt by conservatively stated accounting reports.

4. One of the criteria for the recognition of an asset or a liability is that there be a transaction, or exchange. What justification can you see for this requirement?

5. Accounting typically does not recognize either assets or liabilities for mutually unexecuted contracts. What justification can you see for this treatment?

6. Cash discounts taken on the purchase of merchandise or equipment are treated as a reduction in the amount recorded for the assets acquired. What justification can you see for this treatment?

7. A group of investors owns an office building, which is rented unfurnished to tenants. The building was purchased five years previously from a construction company and, at that time, was expected to have a useful life of 40 years. Indicate the procedures that might be followed in ascertaining the amount at which the building would be stated under each of the following valuation methods.
  a. Acquisition cost
  b. Current replacement cost
  c. Current net realizable value
  d. Present value of future cash flows

8. Some of the assets of one firm correspond to the liabilities of another firm. For example, an account receivable on the seller's balance sheet would be an account payable on the buyer's balance sheet. For each of the following items, indicate whether it is an asset or a liability and give the corresponding account title on the balance sheet of the other party to the transaction.
  a. Advances by Customers
  b. Bonds Payable
  c. Interest Receivable
  d. Prepaid Insurance
  e. Rental Fees Received in Advance

Exercises

9. *Asset recognition.* Indicate whether or not each of the following items would be recognized as an asset by a firm according to generally accepted accounting principles.

   a. A patent on a new invention purchased from its creator.
   b. A firm's chief scientist, who has twice won the Nobel prize.
   c. The right to use a building during the coming year. The rent for the period has already been paid.
   d. An automobile acquired with the issue of a note payable. Because the note has not been paid, legal title to the automobile has not yet passed to the firm.
   e. A degree in engineering from a reputable university, awarded to the firm's chief executive.
   f. A contract signed by a customer to purchase $1,000 worth of goods next year.
   g. A favorable reputation.

10. *Asset recognition and valuation.* Indicate whether or not each of the following immediately gives rise to an asset under generally accepted accounting principles. If an asset is recognized, state the account title and amount.
   a. A cheque for $300 has been sent to an insurance company for property insurance. The period of coverage begins next month (consider from the standpoint of the firm making the cash expenditure).
   b. A cheque for $3,000 is issued as a deposit on specially designed equipment. The equipment is to have a total purchase price of $20,000 and will be completed and delivered next year (consider from the standpoint of the firm making the cash expenditure).
   c. Common shares of Bell Canada Enterprises Inc. are acquired with temporarily excess cash for $12,000.
   d. Merchandise inventory with a list price of $800 is acquired, with payment made in time to secure a three percent discount for prompt payment. Cash discounts are treated as a reduction in the acquisition cost of the inventory.
   e. A well-known scientist has been hired to manage the firm's research and development activity. Employment begins next month. One-twelfth of the annual salary of $90,000 is payable at the end of each month worked.
   f. Bonds with a face value of $200,000 are purchased for $206,000. The bonds mature in 20 years. Interest is payable by the issuer at the rate of ten percent annually.
   g. An order for $700 worth of merchandise is received from a customer.
   h. Notice has been received from a manufacturer that raw materials billed at $2,000, with payment due in 30 days, have been shipped by freight. The buyer obtains title to the goods as soon as they are shipped by the seller.

11. *Asset recognition and valuation.* Indicate whether or not each of the following events immediately gives rise to the recognition of an asset under generally accepted accounting principles. If an asset is recognized, state the account title and amount.
   a. Raw materials with an invoice price of $4,800 are purchased on account from Greer Wholesalers.
   b. Defective raw material purchased in part **a** for $400 is returned to Greer Wholesalers and full credit is received.
   c. The bill of Greer Wholesalers (see parts **a** and **b**) is paid promptly. A discount of two percent offered by the seller for prompt payment is taken. Cash discount are treated as a reduction in the acquisition cost of the raw materials.
   d. A machine is purchased for $25,000 cash.

e. The cost of transporting the new machine in part **d** to the plant site is paid in cash, $450.

f. Material and labour costs incurred in installing the machine in part **d** total $300 and are paid in cash.

12. *Asset recognition and valuation.* Indicate whether or not each of the following events immediately gives rise to an asset under generally accepted accounting principles. If an asset is recognized, state the account title and amount.

a. An investment of $8,000 is made in a government bond. The bond will have a maturity value of $10,000 in three years. The firm intends to hold the bond to maturity.

b. A cheque for $900 is sent to a landlord for two months' rent in advance. (Consider from the standpoint of the firm issuing the cheque.)

c. A cheque for $1,000 is written to obtain an option to purchase a tract of land. The price of the land is $32,500. (Consider from the standpoint of the firm issuing the cheque.)

d. A firm signs a four-year employment agreement with its president for $500,000 per year. The contract period begins next month. (Consider from the standpoint of the firm.)

e. A patent has been purchased from its creator for $40,000.

f. A patent has been received on a new invention developed by a firm. Expenditures of $40,000 have been made to develop the patented invention.

g. Notice has been received from a supplier that materials billed at $4,000, with payment due in 30 days, have been shipped by freight. The seller retains title to the materials until received by the buyer.

13. *Asset recognition and valuation.* In each of the following transactions, give the title(s) and amount(s) of the asset(s) that would appear on the balance sheet.

a. A firm purchases an automobile with a list price of $8,000. The dealer allows a discount of $850 from the list price for payment in cash. Dealer preparation charges on the automobile amount to an extra $200. The dealer collects a four percent sales tax on the price paid for the automobile and preparation charges. In addition, the dealer collects a $75 fee to be remitted to the province for this year's licence plates and $300 for a one-year insurance policy provided by the dealer's insurance agency. The firm pays a body shop $75 for painting the firm's name on the automobile.

b. A firm acquires land that has been valued at $2 million by a real estate appraiser. The firm pays for the land by giving up shares in Imperial Oil Limited at a time when equivalent shares traded on the Toronto Stock Exchange have a market value of $2,100,000.

c. A firm acquires land that has been appraised at $2 million by a real estate appraiser. The firm pays for the land by giving up shares in Small Timers, Inc., whose shares are traded only on the Vancouver Stock Exchange. The last transaction in shares of Small Timers, Inc., occurred four days prior to this asset swap. Using the prices of the most recent trades, the shares of Small Timers, Inc., given in exchange for the building have a market value of $2,100,000.

14. *Liability recognition.* Indicate whether or not each of the following items is recognized as a liability according to generally accepted accounting principles.

    a. An obligation to provide magazines next year to subscribers who have paid one year's subscription fees in advance (consider from the standpoint of the magazine publisher).

    b. The reputation for poor quality control on products manufactured.

    c. An obligation to provide warranty services for three years after customers purchase the firm's products.

    d. The outstanding common shares of a corporation.

    e. Unpaid property taxes for the preceding year.

    f. The amount payable by a firm for a television advertisement that has appeared but for which payment is not due for 30 days.

    g. A tenant's obligation to maintain a rented warehouse in good repair.

    h. The firm's president has an incompetent son who is employed in the business.

15. *Liability recognition and valuation.* Indicate whether or not each of the following events immediately gives rise to the recognition of a liability under generally accepted accounting principles. If a liability is recognized, state the account title and amount.

    a. A company hires its president under a five-year contract beginning next month. The contract calls for $300,000 compensation per year.

    b. An insurance company receives $2,000 for six months' insurance coverage in advance (consider from the standpoint of the insurance company).

    c. A manufacturer agrees to produce a specially designed piece of equipment for $3 million. A down payment of $300,000 is received upon signing the contract, and the remainder is due when the equipment is completed (consider from the standpoint of the manufacturer).

    d. Additional common shares with a par value of $75,000 are issued for $80,000.

    e. Employees earned wages totaling $6,000 during the last pay period for which they have not been paid. The employer is also liable for payroll taxes of eight percent of the wages earned.

    f. A firm signs a contract agreeing to sell $6,000 of merchandise to a particular customer.

16. *Liability recognition and valuation.* Indicate whether or not each of the following events immediately gives rise to the recognition of a liability under generally accepted accounting principles. If a liability is recognized, indicate the account title and amount.

    a. A $600 cheque is received from a tenant for three months' rent in advance. (Consider from the standpoint of the lessor, or owner, of the building.)

    b. Utility services received during the past month of $240 have not been paid. (Consider from the standpoint of the firm using the utility services.)

    c. A $10,000 loan has been received from the bank, with the firm signing a note agreeing to repay the loan with interest at eight percent in six months.

    d. A firm has signed an agreement with its employees' labour union agreeing to increase the firm's contribution to the union pension fund by $20,000 per month, beginning next month. (Consider from the standpoint of the firm).

    e. Income taxes totaling $15,000 on last year's earnings have not been paid.

f. A firm has signed an employment contract with its controller for a three-year period beginning next month at a contract price of $200,000 per year. (Consider from the standpoint of the firm.)

17. *Liability recognition and valuation.* Indicate whether or not each of the following events immediately gives rise to a liability under generally accepted accounting principles. If a liability is recognized, state the account title and amount.

a. A landscaper agrees to improve land owned by a firm. The agreed price of the work is $2,500. (Consider from the standpoint of the firm owning the land.)

b. A cheque for $36 is received for a two-year, future subscription to a magazine. (Consider from the standpoint of the magazine publisher.)

c. A construction company agrees to build a bridge for $2 million. A down payment of $200,000 is received upon signing the contract, and the remainder is due when the bridge is completed.

d. Additional common shares with a par value of $60,000 are issued for $80,000.

e. A firm received a 60-day, ten percent loan of $10,000 from a local bank.

f. A firm signs a contract to purchase at least $6,000 worth of merchandise during the next year.

g. Refer to part **f.** An order for $1,500 of merchandise is placed with the supplier.

18. *Disclosure of owners' equity.* The assets of a business total $700,000, and liabilities total $550,000. Present the owners' equity section of the balance sheet under the following assumptions:

a. The business is a sole proprietorship owned by William Gleason.

b. The business is a partnership. William Gleason has a 35 percent interest. John Morgan has a 40 percent interest, and David Johnson has a 25 percent interest.

c. The business is a corporation. Outstanding common shares were originally issued for $80,000 of which $50,000 represented par value. The remainder of the owners' equity represents accumulated, undistributed earnings.

19. *Balance sheet classification.* Information may be classified with respect to a balance sheet in one of the following ways:

(1) Asset.
(2) Liability.
(3) Shareholders' equity.
(4) Item would not appear on the balance sheet as conventionally prepared.

Using these numbers, indicate the appropriate classification of each of the following items:

a. Salaries payable
b. Retained earnings
c. Notes receivable
d. Unfilled customer's orders (no deposits received)
e. Land
f. Interest payable
g. Work-in-process inventory
h. Mortgage payable

  i.   Organization costs
  j.   Advances by customers
  k.   Advances to employees
  l.   Patents
  m. Good credit standing
  n.   Common stock

20. *Balance sheet classification.* Information may be classified with respect to a balance sheet in one of the following ways:
  (1) Asset.
  (2) Liability.
  (3) Shareholders' equity.
  (4) Item would not appear on the balance sheet as conventionally prepared.

Using these numbers, indicate the appropriate classification of each of the following items:
  a. Preferred shares
  b. Furniture and fixtures
  c. Potential liability under lawsuit (case has not yet gone to trial)
  d. Prepaid rent
  e. Contributed surplus
  f. Cash on hand
  g. Goodwill
  h. Estimated liability under warranty contract
  i. Raw materials inventory
  j. Rental fees received in advance
  k. Bonds payable
  l. Unexpired insurance.

21. *Working backwards from journal entries.* Presented below are journal entries for a series of transactions. Describe the likely transaction that gave rise to each journal entry.

a. Equipment	$10,000	
Cash		$2,000
Note Payable		8,000
b. Cash	$6,000	
Acounts Receivable		$4,000
Advances from Customers		2,000
c. Accounts Payable	$2,500	
Merchandise Inventory		$2,500
d. Bonds Payable	$100,000	
Common Stock		$40,000
Contributed Surplus		60,000
e. Cash	$800	
Subscription Fees Received in Advance		$800
f. Prepaid Rent	$2,000	
Cash		$2,000

Problems and Cases

22. *Journal entries for various transactions.* Present journal entries for each of the following transactions of Mailor Corporation during April, its first month of operations.

(1) April 2: 250,000 $5 par value common shares are issued for $8 cash per share.

(2) April 3: A building costing $800,000 is acquired. A down payment of $200,000 is made in cash and a ten percent note maturing in three years is signed for the balance.

(3) April 8: A machine costing $15,000 is acquired for cash.

(4) April 15: Merchandise inventory costing $120,000 is acquired on account from various suppliers.

(5) April 18: A cheque for $400 is issued for insurance coverage for the period beginning May 1.

(6) April 20: A cheque for $800 is received from a customer for merchandise to be delivered on May 5.

(7) April 26: Invoices totaling $80,000 from the purchases on April 15 are paid, after deducting a two percent discount for prompt payment. Cash discounts are treated as a reduction in the acquisition cost of inventory.

(8) April 30: The remaining invoices from the purchases on April 15 are paid after the discount period has lapsed.

23. *Journal entries for various transactions.* Present journal entries for each of the following transactions of Area Corporation. You may omit dates and explanations for the journal entries.

(1) 20,000 $10 par value common shares are issued at par value for cash.

(2) Land and building costing $90,000 are acquired with the payment of $25,000 cash and the assumption of a 20-year, eight percent mortgage for the balance. The land is to be stated at $30,000 and the building at $60,000.

(3) A used lathe is purchased for $4,620 cash.

(4) Raw materials costing $3,600 are acquired on account.

(5) Defective raw materials purchased in **(4)** and costing $650 are returned to the supplier. The account has not yet been paid.

(6) The supplier in **(4)** is paid the amount due, less a two percent discount for prompt payment. Cash discounts are treated as a reduction in the acquisition cost of raw materials.

(7) A fire insurance policy providing $100,000 coverage beginning next month is obtained. The one year premium of $625 is paid in cash.

(8) A cheque for $2,000 is issued to Roger White to reimburse him for costs incurred in organizing and promoting the corporation.

(9) A cheque for $600 is issued for three months' rent in advance for office space.

(10) A patent on a machine process is purchased for $35,000 cash.

(11) Office equipment is purchased for $950. A down payment of $250 is made, with the balance payable in 30 days.

(12) $275 is paid to Express Transfer Company for delivering the equipment purchased in **(3)**.

24. *Journal entries for various transactions of a sole proprietorship.* Express the following transactions of Winkle Grocery Store, a sole proprietorship, in journal entry form. You may omit explanations for the journal entries.

(1) John Winkle contributes $50,000 cash to help set up the grocery store.
(2) A 60-day, eight percent note is signed in return for a $10,000 loan from the bank.
(3) A building is rented, with the annual rental of $6,000 paid in advance.
(4) Display equipment costing $16,000 is acquired. A cheque is issued.
(5) Merchandise inventory costing $35,000 is acquired. A cheque for $8,000 is issued, with the remainder payable in 30 days.
(6) A contract is signed with a nearby restaurant under which the restaurant agrees to purchase $6,000 of groceries each week. A cheque is received for the first two weeks' orders in advance.

25. *Journal entries for various transactions.* Express the following independent transactions in journal entry form. If an entry is not required, indicate the reason. You may omit explanations for the journal entries.
(1) Bonds of the Sommers Co. Ltd. with a face value of $60,000 and annual interest at the rate of eight percent are purchased for $58,500 cash.
(2) A cheque for $2,600 is received by a fire insurance company for premiums on policy coverage over the next two years.
(3) A corporation issues 20,000 $12 par value common shares in exchange for land, building, and equipment. The land is to be stated at $30,000, the building at $180,000, and the equipment at $75,000.
(4) A contract is signed by a manufacturing firm agreeing to purchase 100 dozen machine tool parts over the next two years at a price of $60 per dozen.
(5) 5,000 $1 par value preferred shares are issued to a lawyer for legal services rendered in organization of the corporation. The bill for the services is $9,500.
(6) A coupon book, redeemable in future movie viewings, is issued for $60 cash by a movie theatre.
(7) A firm has been notified that it is being sued for $30,000 damages by a customer who incurred losses as a result of purchasing defective merchandise.
(8) Merchandise inventory costing $2,000, purchased on account, is found to be defective and returned to the supplier for full credit.

26. *Effect of transactions on balance sheet equation.* Indicate the effects of the transactions below on the balance sheet equation using the following format:

Transaction Number	Assets	=	Liabilities	+	Shareholders' Equity
(1)	+$50,000		0		+$50,000
Subtotal	$50,000 =		0	+	$50,000

(1) 5,000 no par value common shares are issued for $50,000 cash.
(2) Equipment costing $12,000 is acquired. A down payment of $4,000 is made, with the remainder payable in six months with interest at nine percent.
(3) Raw materials costing $6,000 are acquired on account.
(4) Installation cost of $800 on the equipment in **(2)** is paid in cash.
(5) The property insurance premium of $420 for the year, beginning on the first day of next month, is paid.
(6) Raw materials acquired in **(3)** for $700 are found to be defective and returned to the supplier for full credit. The account had not yet been paid.
(7) Invoices from the purchases in **(3)** totaling $4,000 are paid after deducting a

one percent discount for prompt payment. Cash discounts are treated as a reduction in the acquisition cost of raw materials.

(8) 100 no par value common shares are issued to the firm's attorney for services in organizing the corporation. The attorney's bill was $1,000.

(9) Customers advanced the firm $250 for merchandise to be delivered next month.

27. *Effect of transactions on balance sheet equation.* Indicate the effects of the transactions below on the balance sheet equation using the following format:

Transaction Number	Assets	=	Liabilities	+	Shareholders' Equity
(1)	+$30,000		0		+$30,000
Subtotal	$30,000	=	0	+	$30,000

(1) 3,000 no par value common shares are issued for $30,000 cash.

(2) Merchandise costing $24,300 is purchased on account.

(3) Store equipment costing $4,800 is acquired. A cheque for $1,000 is issued and the balance is payable over three years under an installment contract.

(4) A cheque is issued for $900 covering two months' rent in advance.

(5) Refer to transaction **(3)**. Common shares with a market value of $3,800 are issued in full settlement of the installment contract.

(6) The merchandise supplier in transaction **(2)** is paid the amount due.

28. *T-account entries for various transactions.* Set up T-accounts for the following accounts. Indicate whether each account is an asset, liability, or shareholders' equity item, and enter the transactions described below:

Cash	Accounts Payable
Merchandise Inventory	Note Payable
Prepaid Insurance	Mortgage Payable
Building	Common Stock — Par Value
Equipment	Contributed Surplus

(1) 30,000 $5 par value shares are issued for $8 cash per share.

(2) A building costing $300,000 is acquired. A cash payment of $60,000 is made, and a long-term mortgage is assumed for the balance of the purchase price.

(3) Equipment costing $5,000 and merchandise inventory costing $7,000 are acquired on account.

(4) A three-year fire insurance policy is taken out and the $900 premium is paid in advance.

(5) A 90-day, six percent note is issued to the bank for a $10,000 loan.

(6) Payments of $8,000 are made to the suppliers in **(3)**.

29. *T-account entries and balance sheet preparation.* The Patterson Manufacturing Corporation is organized on January 1. During January, the following transactions occur:

(1) The corporation issues 15,000 no par value common shares for $210,000 in cash.

(2) The corporation issues 28,000 no par value common shares in exchange for land, building, and equipment. The land is to be stated at $80,000, the building at $220,000, and the equipment at $92,000.

(3) The corporation issues 2,000 no par value common shares to a lawyer in payment of legal services rendered in obtaining the corporate charter.

(4) Raw materials costing $75,000 are acquired on account from various suppliers.

(5) Manufacturing equipment with a list price of $6,000 is acquired. After deducting a $600 discount, the net amount is paid in cash. Cash discounts are treated as a reduction in the acquisition cost of equipment.

(6) Freight charges of $350 for delivery of the equipment in **(5)** are paid in cash.

(7) Raw materials costing $800 are found to be defective and returned to the supplier for full credit. The raw materials had been purchased on account [see **(4)**], and no payment had been made as of the time that the goods were returned.

(8) A contract is signed for the rental of a fleet of automobiles beginning February 1. The rental for February of $1,400 is paid in advance.

(9) Invoices for $60,000 of raw materials purchased in **(4)** are paid, after deducting a discount of three percent for prompt payment. Cash discounts are treated as a reduction in the acquisition cost of raw materials.

(10) Fire and liability insurance coverage is obtained from Northwest Insurance Company. The two-year policy, beginning February 1, carries a $400 premium, which has not yet been paid.

(11) A contract is signed with a customer for $20,000 of merchandise that Patterson plans to manufacture. The customer advanced $4,500 toward the contract price.

(12) A warehouse costing $60,000 is acquired. A down payment of $7,000 is made, and a long-term mortgage is assumed for the balance. No principal payments are to be made on the mortgage for two years.

(13) Raw materials inventory with an original list price of $1,500 is found to be defective and returned to the supplier. This inventory has already been paid for in **(9)**. The returned raw materials are the only items purchased from this particular supplier during January. A cash refund has not yet been received from the supplier.

(14) The firm purchased 6,000 $10 par value common shares of the General Cereal Corporation for $95,000. This investment is made as a short-term investment of excess cash. The shares of General Cereal Corporation are traded on the Toronto Stock Exchange.

The following assumptions will help you resolve certain accounting uncertainties: (i) Transactions **(2)** and **(3)** occurred on the same day as transaction **(1)**. (ii) The invoices paid in **(9)** are the only purchases for which discounts were made available to the purchaser. (iii) No depreciation is recorded for January.

    a. Enter these transactions in T-accounts. Indicate whether each account is an asset, liability, or shareholders' equity item. Cross-reference each entry to the appropriate transaction number.

    b. Prepare a balance sheet as of January 31.

30. *T-account entries and balance sheet preparation.* The Scott Products Co. Ltd. is organized on October 1. During October, the following transactions occur:

(1) The corporation issues 20,000 $5 par value common shares for $7 per share in cash.

(2) The corporation issues 200 $100 par value preferred shares at par value for cash.

(3) The corporation gives $40,000 in cash and 5,000 common shares in exchange for land and building. The land is to be stated at $5,000 and the building at $70,000.

(4) Equipment costing $26,000 is acquired. Cash of $3,000 is paid and an eight percent note, due in one year, is given for the balance.

(5) Transportation costs on the equipment in (4) of $800 are paid in cash.

(6) Installation costs on the equipment in (4) of $1,100 are paid in cash.

(7) Merchandise inventory costing $45,000 is acquired on account.

(8) License fees for the year beginning November 1 of $800 are paid in advance.

(9) Merchandise costing $1,300 from the acquisition in (7) are found to be defective and returned to the supplier for full credit. The account had not been paid.

(10) A patent is purchased from its creator for $15,000.

(11) The corporation signed an agreement to manufacture a specially designed machine for a customer for $60,000, to be delivered in January of next year. At the time of signing, the customer advanced $6,000 of the contract price.

(12) Invoices totaling $30,000 from the purchases in (7) are paid, after deducting a two percent discount for prompt payment. Cash discounts are treated as a reduction in the acquisition cost of inventory.

    a. Enter the transactions in T-accounts. Indicate whether each account is an asset, liability, or shareholders' equity item. Cross-reference each entry to the appropriate transaction number.

    b. Prepare a balance sheet for Scott Products Co. Ltd. as of October 31.

31. *T-account entries and balance sheet preparation*. The Sarwark Corporation is organized on January 1. During January, the following transactions occur:

(1) 10,000 no par value common shares are issued for $150,000.

(2) Bonds with a face and maturity value of $100,000 are issued at face value for cash.

(3) Land and building costing $200,000 is acquired. A cheque for $80,000 is issued, with the remainder payable over 20 years. The land is assigned $20,000 and the building is assigned $180,000 of the acquisition cost.

(4) Equipment costing $40,000 is acquired. After deducting a discount of two percent for immediate cash payment, the net amount due is paid.

(5) Merchandise costing $25,000 is acquired on account.

(6) Merchandise costing $2,000 is found to be defective and returned to the supplier. No cash payments have yet been made to this supplier.

(7) An insurance policy for a one-year period beginning February 1 is obtained. The premium for the one-year period of $1,200 is paid.

(8) A customer placed an order for $1,500 of merchandise to be delivered in February. The customer sent a cheque of $300 with the order.

(9) Merchandise suppliers in (5) are paid $18,000 of the amounts due. The remaining suppliers will be paid in February.

    a. Enter these transactions in T-accounts. Indicated whether each account is an asset, liability, or shareholders' equity item. Cross reference each entry to the appropriate transaction number.

    b. Prepare a balance sheet as of December 31.

32. *T-account entries and balance sheet preparation for a sole proprietorship*. The following transactions occur during March for Dryden's Book Store, a sole proprietorship, in preparation for its opening for business on April 1.

(1) H. R. Dryden contributes $6,000 in cash, 100 common shares of Western Cor-

poration, and an inventory of books to be sold. The shares of Western Corporation are quoted on the Vancouver Stock Exchange at $15 per share on the day they are contributed, and will be sold when additional cash is needed. The books are to be stated at $2,750.

(2) Two months' rent on a store building is paid in advance in cash. The bookstore will occupy the building on April 1. The monthly rental is $400.

(3) Store fixtures are purchased for $4,000, of which $800 is paid in cash. A note, to be paid in ten equal monthly installments beginning May 1, is signed for the balance.

(4) Books with an invoice price of $2,600 are purchased on account.

(5) A one-year insurance policy on the store's contents beginning April 1 is purchased. The premium of $160 is paid by cheque.

(6) A cheque for $320 is issued to the Darwin Equipment Co. Ltd. for a cash register and other operating equipment.

(7) Books costing $1,800 are ordered from a publisher. Delivery is scheduled for April 15.

(8) The books purchased in (4) are paid for by cheque. Payment is made in time to obtain a two percent cash discount for prompt payment. These are the only purchases for which discounts are available. Cash discounts are treated as a reduction in the acquisition cost of the books.

(9) An operating licence for the year beginning April 1 is obtained. A fee of $250 is paid by cheque.

   a. Enter these transactions in T-accounts. Indicate whether each account is an asset, liability, or owner's equity item. Cross-reference each entry to the appropriate transaction number.

   b. Prepare a balance sheet for this sole proprietorship as of March 31.

33. *T-account entries and balance sheet preparation for a partnership.* Priscilla Mullins and Miles Standish form a partnership to operate a laundry and cleaning business to be known as Pilgrim's One Day Laundry and Cleaners. The following transactions occur in late June, prior to the grand opening on July 1.

(1) Standish contributes $400 cash and cleaning equipment that is to be stated at $5,600.

(2) Mullins contributes $3,000 cash and a delivery truck to be stated at $2,500.

(3) The July rent for the business premises of $400 is paid in advance.

(4) Cleaning supplies are purchased on account from Wonder Chemical Ltd. for $2,500.

(5) Insurance coverage on the equipment and truck for a one-year period beginning July 1 is purchased for $425 cash.

(6) The firm borrows $2,000 from the First Canadian Bank. A 90-day, eight percent note is signed, with principal and interest payable at maturity.

(7) The Wonder Chemical Ltd. account is paid in full after deducting a two percent discount for prompt payment. Cash discounts are treated as a reduction in the acquisition cost of supplies.

(8) A cash register is purchased for $700. A down payment of $100 is made, and a note is signed for the remainder, payable in ten equal installments beginning August 1.

   a. Enter these transactions in T-accounts. Indicate whether each account is an asset, liability, or owners' equity item. Cross-reference each entry to the appropriate transaction number.

b. Prepare a balance sheet for the partnership as of June 30.

34. *Criticism of balance sheet formate and disclosure*. Comment on any unusual features of the balance sheet of the Western Sales Inc. shown in Exhibit 2.8.

Exhibit 2.8
WESTERN SALES INC.
Balance Sheet for the Year Ended December 31, Year 5

Assets

Current Assets:

Cash and Certificates of Deposit	$ 86,500	
Accounts Receivable — Net	193,600	
Merchandise Inventory	322,900	$ 603,000

Investments (substantially at cost):

Investment in Treasury Bills	$ 60,000	
Investment in Eastern Sales Corp.	196,500	256,500

Fixed Assets (at cost):

Land	$225,000	
Buildings and Equipment — Net	842,600	1,067,600

Intangibles and Deferred Charges:

Prepaid Insurance	$ 1,200	
Prepaid Rent	1,500	
Goodwill	2	2,702
Total Assets		$1,929,802

Liabilities and Shareholders' Equity

Current Liabilities:

Accounts Payable	$225,300	
Accrued Expenses	10,900	
Income Taxes Payable	89,200	$ 325,400

Long-Term Liabilities:

Bonds Payable	$500,000	
Pensions Payable	40,600	
Contingent Liability	100,000	640,600

Shareholders' Equity:

Common Stock — $10 par value, 50,000 shares issued and outstanding	$625,000	
Earned Surplus	338,802	963,802
Total Liabilities and Shareholders' Equity		$1,929,802

35. *Effect of recording errors on balance sheet equation*. Using the notation O/S (overstated), U/S (understated), or No (no effect), indicate the effects on assets, liabilities, and shareholders' equity of failing to record each of the following independent transactions or events. For example, a failure to record the issuance of common shares for $10,000 cash would be

Assets — U/S $10,000

Liabilities — No

Shareholders' equity — U/S $10,000

(1) Merchandise costing $6,000 is purchased on account.
(2) A machine costing $10,000 is acquired. A 25 percent down payment is made, with the remainder payable over five years.
(3) An order for $3,500 of merchandise is placed with a supplier.
(4) A cheque for $300 is received from a customer for merchandise to be delivered next month.
(5) A cheque for $800 was issued to cover rental of a warehouse for the next two months.
(6) Common shares with a market value of $1,500 were issued to lawyers for services rendered in setting up the firm.
(7) A note payable for $2,000, which had previously been correctly recorded on the books, was now paid in the amount of $2,000.
(8) A cheque for $1,000 is issued for an option to purchase a tract of land. The price of the land is $30,000. The option can be exercised within 90 days.

36. *Balance sheet analysis for General Products Limited.* Financial analysts typically use information from all three of the principal financial statements discussed in Chapter 1 (that is, balance sheet, income statement, and statement of changes in financial position) in making their analyses and interpretations. It is possible, however, to make some general observations about changes in the structure of a firm's assets and equities by studying comparative balance sheets only. These general observations are then examined further by studying the income statement and statement of changes in financial position.

Refer to the comparative balance sheet and related notes of General Products Limited in Appendix A on p. 761. Using this financial statement only, describe the most significant changes that occurred in the structure of General Products Limited's assets and equities between 1987 and 1988. (Hint: You may want to begin your analysis by expressing various balance sheet components as a percentage of other components. For example, current assets represent 53.4 percent of total assets on December 31, 1988.)

37. *Constructing a balance sheet from incomplete records.* Most of the financial records of the Rowland Novelty Company were removed by an employee who, apparently, took all the cash on hand from the store on October 31. From supplementary records, the following information is obtained:
(1) According to the bank, cash in bank was $5,730.
(2) Amounts payable to creditors were $4,720.
(3) Rowland's initial contribution to the business was $15,000, and the total interest in the business at the time of the theft was $17,500.
(4) Cost of merchandise on hand was $11,380.
(5) A one-year fire insurance policy was purchased on September 1 for $900.

(6) Furniture and fixtures are rented from the Anderson Office Supply Company for $200 per month. The rental for October has not been paid.

(7) A note for $1,200 was given by a customer. Interest due at October 31 was $45.

(8) Payments due for other customers amounted to $1,915.

(9) Rowland purchases a licence from the city for $300 on July 1. The licence allows retail operations for one year.

    a. Determine the probable cash shortage.

    b. Prepare a well-organized balance sheet presenting the financial position immediately preceding the theft.

38. *Constructing Statements from T-account analysis.* In early 1989, the president of Quebec City Candle Store contacted you for assistance. On January 4, 1989, the accountant of Quebec City Candle Store was hospitalized as a result of a traffic accident. You were hired as a consultant to prepare the financial statements for 1988. From the company records, you found the following account balances.

	January 1, 1987		December 31, 1987	
	Dr.	Cr.	Dr.	Cr.
Cash	$ 6,500		$ 3,000	
Accounts receivable	35,400		32,200	
Merchandise	10,500		45,800	
Supplies	1,500		1,200	
Prepaid insurance	1,800		1,400	
Land	22,500		22,500	
Buildings	45,000		45,000	
Accumulated depreciation—				
buildings		$ 6,000		$ 7,200
Equipment	12,000		15,000	
Accumulated depreciation—				
equipment		2,000		3,000
Accounts payable		14,200		37,500
Salaries payable		1,000		1,500
Capital stock		100,000		100,000
Retained earnings		12,000		16,900
TOTAL	$135,200	$135,200	$166,100	$166,100

Upon further investigation, you have found the following working papers prepared by the accountant:

1988 Purchases on account:	
Merchandise	270,000
Supplies	2,000
1988 Cash receipts:	
Sales of merchandise	75,000
Collections of customers' accounts	300,000
1988 Cash disbursements:	
Supplies	1,200
Delivery charges on outgoing merchandise	2,200
Insurance premium	800
Payments on account	285,000
Salesmen's salaries	18,900
Utility services	2,100
Purchase of equipment	3,000

You took inventory and found that merchandise on hand on December 31, 1988 was $65,000, and the inventory of supplies on December 31, 1988 was $900.

Further discussion with the sales manager revealed that 1988 sales on account were $310,000, and that unpaid salesmen's salaries accounted to $1,000.

Other information:

Depreciation for year on building		$1,200
Depreciation for year on equipment		1,500
Insurance expired during year		1,200
Earnings before extraordinary items	$110,200	$110,000
Less: Dividends—6% cumulative	30,000	
Subtotal	$ 80,200	$110,000
Extraordinary items	(2,900)	–
Earnings available to common shareholders, after extraordinary		
items	$ 77,300	$110,000
Weighted average	58,000	55,000
Earnings per share before extraordinary items	$1.38	$2.00
Earnings per share after extraordinary items	$1.33	$2.00

Adapted with permission from the Society of Management Accountants of Canada.

Decision Problem 2-1

Saul Levi, the owner-operator of a local hardware store, is planning to add a line of mechanized gardening equipment to his present stock. The cost of purchasing this new merchandise, the higher replacement costs of inventory, and the pressing demands for payment by his creditors have made him realize that he needs more cash. He approaches the manager of the local bank to arrange for a demand bank loan for $30,000, taking with him the following balance sheet he prepared for inclusion in his income tax return.

Saul Levi's Hardware Store
Balance Sheet
December 31, Year 7

Assets			Liabilities and Owner's Equity	
Cash on hand and in bank . .		$ 780	Accounts payable	$22,970
Accounts receivable		1,210	Notes payable	6,000
Inventory		12,000	Owner's equity	11,100
Land		10,000		
Building	$50,000			
Less Accumulated				
Depreciation	43,920	6,080		
Goodwill		10,000		
		$40,070		$40,070

Saul Levi has owned the building for 20 years and lives above the store. He did not originally operate the store, but decided to do so when the business of the tenant, Sam Brown, seriously declined because of Brown's failing health. Brown had fallen behind in his rent and had incurred substantial debts to his suppliers. In December Year 7, Levi agreed to take over the business assets and liabilities in consideration for $10,000, represented by the rental arrears of $4,000 and a noninterest-bearing note payable of $6,000, which falls due in December, Year 8.

The local bank manager, recognizing Levi's limited accounting background, asked a number of questions about the balance sheet, and discovered the following information:

(1) Included in the cash on hand was an I.O.U. from Saul's wife for $200, which Saul's assistant had put in the till when Mrs. Levi asked for $200 for household and personal expenses.

(2) In order to minimize his income tax, Levi had written off, as uncollectible, certain accounts receivable that were overdue. He estimated that he would collect 80 percent of the $2,500 overdue accounts.

(3) In addition, Saul had estimated conservatively the value of his inventory. He considered that, at today's prices, he would have to pay at least $18,000 to replace the inventory that would be sold at a regular price of $27,000 (150 percent above cost). In addition, he planned to sell the obsolete merchandise at a "clear out" rate for $6,000. He had ignored this inventory when preparing his balance sheet for the income tax department.

(4) Levi had made no additions to the counters, display cases, lighting fixtures, etc. since he began operating the business. No value had been placed on these items in the balance sheet when he took over the business since they were old, but still usable, and the proceeds of this sale would have been offset by the cost of repairing the store if they were removed. However, if replaced today, these items would cost $17,000. Saul estimated that the replacement fixtures would last twice as long as the present fixtures.

(5) The land and building were recorded at Saul's cost when purchased 20 years ago, although the segregation between the two was made on an arbitrary basis. He had recorded the depreciation on the building at the maximum permitted for income tax purposes. This resulted in accumulated depreciation considerably in excess of what he thought was necessary, since the building should last another 20 years without major repairs. Further, the city had assessed the land and building recently for real estate tax purposes at a current market value of $60,000, allocating $40,000 to the land and $20,000 to the building. Saul thought that the city assessment was fair, but that, if he sold the land and building at the assessed value, he would be required to pay a real estate commission of five percent.

(6) Levi had carried $10,000 of goodwill from the balance sheet of the previous owner, Brown.

The bank manager advised Saul Levi that, if a loan was granted, it would carry interest of 20 percent but, before he could make a final decision, he would need more realistic estimates of Saul's equity in the business.

a. Prepare a revised balance sheet of Saul Levi's Hardware Store at December 31, Year 7 to assist the bank manager when deciding on Levi's loan request.
b. Would the above balance sheet be different from that prepared in accordance with generally accepted accounting principles?
c. Do you think the bank manager would make a loan?

Chapter 3   Income Statement: Reporting the Results of Operating Activities

The second principal financial statement is the income statement. This statement provides a measure of the operating performance of a firm for some particular period of time. *Net income*, or *earnings*, is equal to revenues minus expenses.

Revenues measure the net assets (assets less liabilities) that flow into a firm when goods are sold or services are rendered. *Expenses* measure the net assets used up in the process of generating revenues. As measures of operating performance, revenues reflect the services rendered by the firm, and expenses indicate the efforts required.

This chapter considers the measurement principles and accounting procedures that underlie the income statement. We begin by considering the concept of an accounting period, the span of time over which operating performance is measured. Next, two common approaches to measuring operating performance, the cash basis and the accrual basis, are described and illustrated. Finally, the accounting procedures used in applying the accrual basis of accounting are illustrated for a merchandising firm. Chapter 4 explores more fully the application of the accrual basis of accounting for manufacturing, construction, and other types of businesses.

The Accounting Period Convention

The income statement reports operating performance over a specified period of time. Years ago, the length of this period varied substantially among firms. Income statements were prepared at the completion of some activity, such as after the round-trip voyage of a ship between England and its colonies or at the completion of a construction project.

The operating activities of most modern firms do not divide so easily into distinguishable projects. Instead, the income-generating activity is carried on continuously. For example, a plant is acquired and used in manufacturing products for a period of 40 years or more. Delivery equipment is purchased and used in transporting merchandise to customers for four, five, or more years. If the preparation of the income statement were postponed until all operating activities were completed, the report might be prepared only when the firm ceased to exist and, in any case, would be too late to help a reader appraise operating performance. An accounting period of uniform length facilitates timely comparisons and analyses among firms.

An accounting period of *one year* underlies the principal financial statements distributed to shareholders and potential investors. Most firms prepare their annual reports using the calendar year as the accounting period. A growing number of firms, however, use a *natural business year*. The use of a natural business year is an attempt to measure performance at a time when the cycle of earnings activities has been substantially concluded. The ending date of a natural business year varies from one firm to another. For example, the Hudson's Bay Company uses a natural business year ending on January 31, which comes after completion of the Christmas shopping season; Standard Broadcasting Corporation Limited uses a year ending August 31, just prior to the beginning of the new radio and television season; and Union Gas Limited uses a year ending March 31, coinciding with the end of winter, the major period of natural gas sales.

Reports of performance for periods shorter than a year are frequently prepared as indicators of progress during the year. These are known as "interim reports" or "reports for interim periods." Preparing interim reports does not remove the need to prepare an annual report.

Accounting Methods for Measuring Performance

Some operating activities both start and finish within a given accounting period. For example, merchandise might be purchased from a supplier, sold to a customer on account, and the account collected in cash, all within a particular accounting period. Few difficulties are encountered in measuring performance in these cases. The difference between the cash received from customers and the cash disbursed to acquire, sell, and deliver the merchandise represents earnings for this series of transactions.

Many operating activities, however, start in one accounting period and finish in another. Buildings and equipment are acquired in one period but used over a period of several years. Merchandise is sometimes purchased in one accounting period and sold during the next, with cash collected from customers during a third period. A significant problem in measuring performance for a specific accounting period is measuring the amount of revenues and expenses from operating activities that are in process at the beginning of the period or are incomplete at the end of the period. Two approaches to measuring operating performance are (1) the cash basis of accounting, and (2) the accrual basis of accounting.

Cash Basis of Accounting

Under the *cash basis of accounting*, revenues from selling goods and providing services are recognized in the period when cash is received from customers. Expenses are reported in the period in which payments are made for merchandise, salaries, insurance, taxes, and similar items. To illustrate the measurement of performance under the cash basis of accounting, consider the following example.

Donald and Joanne Allens open a hardware store on January 1, Year 1. They contribute $20,000 in cash and borrow $12,000 from a local bank. The loan is repayable on June 30, Year 1, with interest charged at the rate of 12 percent per year. A store building is rented on January 1, and two months' rent of $4,000 is paid in advance. The premium of $2,400 for property and liability insurance coverage for the year ending December 31, Year 1 is paid on January 1. During January, merchandise costing $40,000 is acquired, of which $26,000 is purchased for cash and $14,000 is purchased on account. Sales to customers during January total $50,000, of which $34,000 is sold for cash and $16,000 is sold on account. The acquisition cost of merchandise sold during January is $32,000, and various employees are paid $5,000 in salaries.

Exhibit 3.1
ALLENS' HARDWARE STORE
Performance Measurement on a Cash Basis
for the Month of January Year 1

Cash Receipts from Sales of Merchandise		$34,000
Less: Cash Payments for Merchandise and Services		
Merchandise	$26,000	
Salaries	5,000	
Rental	4,000	
Insurance	2,400	
Total Cash Payments		37,400
Excess of Cash Payments over Cash Receipts		($ 3,400)

Exhibit 3.1 presents a performance report for Allens' Hardware Store for the month of January Year 1 using the cash basis. Cash receipts from sales of merchandise of $34,000 represent the portion of the total sales of $50,000 made during January that was collected in cash. Although merchandise costing $40,000 was acquired during January, only $26,000 cash was disbursed to suppliers, and only this amount is subtracted in measuring performance under the cash basis. Cash payments during January for salaries, rent, and insurance are also subtracted in measuring performance, without regard to whether or not the services acquired were fully consumed by the end of the month. Cash payments made for merchandise and services exceeded cash receipts from customers during January by $3,400.[1]

As a basis for measuring performance for a particular accounting period (for example, January Year 1 for Allens' Hardware Store), the cash basis of accounting has two weaknesses. First, the cost of the efforts required in generating revenues is not adequately matched with those revenues. Performance of one period therefore gets mingled with the performance of preceding and succeeding periods. The store rental payment of $4,000 provides rental services for both January and February, but under the cash basis, the full amount is subtracted in measuring performance during January. Similarly, the annual insurance premium provides coverage for the full year, but under the cash basis of accounting none of this insurance cost will be subtracted in measuring performance during the months of February through December.

The longer the period over which future benefits are received, the more serious is this criticism of the cash basis of accounting. Consider, for example, the investments of a capital-intensive firm in buildings and equipment that might be used for 10, 20, or more years. The length of time between the purchase of these assets and the collection of cash for goods produced and sold can span many years.

A second criticism of the cash basis of accounting is that it postpones unnecessarily the time when revenue is recognized. In most cases, the sale (delivery) of goods or rendering of services is the critical event in generating revenue. Collecting cash is relatively routine, or at least highly predictable. In these cases, recognizing revenue at the time of cash collection may result in reporting the effects of operating activities

---

[1]Note that, under the cash method, financing transactions (cash received from owners and through borrowing) are not included in the performance report.

one or more periods after the critical revenue-generating activity has occurred. For example, sales to customers during January by Allens' Hardware Store totaled $50,000. Under the cash basis of accounting, $16,000 of this amount will not be recognized until the cash is collected during February or even later. If the credit worthiness of customers has been checked prior to making sales on account, the cash will probably be collected, and there is little reason to postpone recognition of the revenue.

The cash basis of accounting is used principally by lawyers, accountants, and other professional people. These professionals have relatively small investments in multi-period assets, such as buildings and equipment, and usually collect cash from their clients soon after services are rendered. Most such firms actually use a *modified cash basis of accounting*, under which the costs of buildings, equipment, and similar items are treated as assets when purchased. A portion of the acquisition cost is then recognized as an expense when services of these assets are consumed. Except for the treatment of these long-lived assets, revenues are recognized at the time cash is received, and expenses are reported when cash disbursements are made. When calculating taxable income, professional people using the modified cash basis must further modify their reporting system by extending the accrual concept to billings for services, to expenses, and possibly to work in process that has not been billed.

Most individuals use the cash basis of accounting for the purpose of computing personal income and personal income taxes. A business is *not* permitted to use the cash basis of accounting when calculating income subject to tax under the Income Tax Act, except for unincorporated farms and fishing operations whose owners elect to use the cash basis.

Accrual Basis of Accounting

The *accrual basis of accounting* typically recognizes revenue when goods are sold or services are rendered. It reports costs incurred as expenses in the period when the revenues that they helped produce are recognized. Thus, accrual accounting attempts to *match* expenses with associated revenues. Costs incurred that cannot be closely identified with specific revenue streams are treated as expenses of the period in which services of an asset are consumed and the future benefits of an asset disappear.

Exhibit 3.2
ALLENS' HARDWARE STORE
Income Statement for the Month of January
(Accrual Basis of Accounting)

Sales Revenue		$50,000
Less: Cost of Goods Sold		32,000
Gross Profit		$18,000
Less: Operating Expenses		
Salaries	$5,000	
Rent	2,000	
Insurance	200	7,200
Operating Profit		$10,800
Less: Interest Expense		120
Net Income		$10,680

Exhibit 3.2 presents an income statement for Allen's Hardware Store for January of Year 1 using the accrual basis of accounting. The entire $50,000 of sales during January is recognized as revenue, even though cash in that amount has not yet been received. Because the outstanding accounts receivable will probably be collected, the sale of the goods, rather than the collection of cash from customers, triggers the recognition of revenue. The merchandise sold during January cost $32,000. Recognizing this amount as an expense (cost of goods sold) matches the cost of the merchandise sold with revenue from sales. Of the advance rental payment of $4,000, only $2,000 applies to the cost of services consumed during January. The remaining rental of $2,000 applies to the month of February. Likewise, only $200 of the $2,400 insurance premium represents coverage used up during January. The remaining $2,200 of the insurance premium provides coverage for February through December and will be recognized as an expense during those months. The interest expense of $120 represents one month's interest on the $12,000 bank loan at an annual rate of 12 percent ($= \$12,000 \times .12 \times 1/12$). Although the interest will not be paid until the loan becomes due on June 30, Year 1, the firm benefited from having the funds available for its use during January; an appropriate portion of the total interest cost on the loan should therefore be recognized as an expense of January. The salaries, rental, insurance, and interest expenses, unlike the cost of merchandise sold, cannot be associated directly with revenues recognized during the period. These costs are therefore reported as expenses of January to the extent that services were consumed during the month.

Note that income tax expense is missing from Allens' Hardware Store's income statement. Since the accounting entity, Allens' Hardware Store, is not a limited company, it is not considered a taxable entity under the Income Tax Act and pays no income tax. For income tax purposes, the income from Allens' Hardware Store is assumed to flow directly and completely to Donald and Joanne Allens at the end of the fiscal year. The portion of the store's income allocated to Donald will be included as part of Donald's personal income subject to income tax and the remainder will be included as part of Joanne's personal income subject to income tax.

The accrual basis of accounting provides a better measure of operating performance for Allens' Hardware Store for the month of January than does the cash basis for two reasons:

1. Revenues more accurately reflect the results of sales activity during January.

2. Expenses are associated more closely with reported revenues.

Likewise, the accrual basis will provide a superior measure of performance for future periods, because activities of those periods will be charged with their share of the costs of rental, insurance, and other services to be consumed. Thus, the accrual basis focuses on *inflows of net assets* from operations (revenues) and the *use of net assets* in operations (expenses), regardless of whether those inflows and outflows currently produce or use cash.

Most business firms, particularly those involved in merchandising and manufacturing activities, use the accrual basis of accounting. The next section examines the measurement principles of accrual accounting.

Measurement Principles of Accrual Accounting

Reporting revenues and expenses under the accrual basis of accounting requires considering when revenues and expenses are recognized (timing questions) and how much is recognized or reported (measurement questions).

Timing of Revenue Recognition

The operating process for the acquisition and sale of merchandise might be depicted as shown in Figure 3.1. Revenue could conceivably be recognized at the time of purchase, sale, or cash collection, at some point(s) between these events, or even continuously. Answering the timing question requires a set of criteria for revenue recognition.

Figure 3.1 Earnings Process for the Acquisition and Sale of Merchandise

Criteria for Revenue Recognition The criteria currently required to be met before revenue is recognized under the accrual basis of accounting are as follows:

1. All, or a substantial portion, of the services to be provided have been performed.
2. Cash, a receivable, or some other asset susceptible to reasonably precise measurement has been received.

For the vast majority of firms involved in selling goods and services, revenue is recognized at the time of sale (delivery). The goods have been transferred to a buyer or the services have been performed. Future services, such as for warranties, are either insignificant, or if significant, can be estimated with reasonable precision. An exchange between an independent buyer and seller provides an objective measure of the amount of revenue. If the sale is made on account, past experience and an assessment of credit standings of customers provide a basis for predicting the amount of cash that will be collected. Thus, the criteria for revenue recognition are usually met at the time of sale.

Measurement of Revenue

The amount of revenue recognized is measured by the cash or cash equivalent value of other assets received from customers. As a starting point, this amount is the agreed-upon price between buyer and seller at the time of sale. Some adjustments to this amount may be necessary, however, if revenue is recognized in a period prior to the collection of cash.

Trade Discounts A trade discount is a reduction from the list price used to determine the final sales price to a customer. Trade discounts are used by manufacturers to establish different prices for different sets of customers. For example, a manufacturer may sell to wholesalers at 40 percent off the list price and to retailers at 30 percent off list price. Since trade discounts are a means of determining the final price, they are deducted from the list price in measuring the amount of revenue from a particular sale, and are not recorded separately in the accounts.

Impact of Sales Terms on Pricing

The concept of pricing is frequently confined to the identification of the price per unit charged to the customer on the sales invoice or as listed on the company's price sheet or in its catalogue. The terms and conditions of sale, often shown in fine print on the back of the invoice, are not always seen as having any direct bearing on price. In reality, they have a substantial impact on the actual price recovered, and in many instances serve to negate completely the effect of the pricing decision. Some of the sales terms are readily measurable as to the effect on price; others are not, being either hidden from view or misleading as to interpretation. In total they constitute an integral part of the pricing process, and the effects of each must be measured on a step-by-step basis to obtain the desired economic results.

One of the more obvious examples of pricing impact is the measurement of cash discounts allowed for early payment. Typical is the discount of "2% 10 days net 30." First, the discount is a direct reduction of 2% in the selling price, a reduction that will usually be taken by the customer, even beyond the 10-day period allowed. Second, the offer of a 2% reduction for payment 20 days early—in 10 days rather than 30—amounts to an annual interest rate of 36% per year, a payment for the use of money far in excess of the bank rate for funds even in times of double-digit inflation.

Taken together, these two points add up to the fact that cash discounts seldom work as intended, that in practice they routinely become nothing more than a price concession. Management is not deliberately offering 36% per annum for the use of money, but an alert customer will make the calculation properly and be quick to take advantage of it. Furthermore, the fact that many accounts take the discount well after the time allowed is evidence that customers regard it more as a price concession than a reward for early payment. Some companies attempt to charge back the unearned discount, a procedure that creates undesirable friction with their own customers, which the sales force would prefer to avoid.

Variations of the cash discount terms, such as "2% 10th prox," further complicate the picture by encouraging customers to bunch their orders around the first of the month to get the greatest leverage on the terms offered. This, obviously, can have the undesirable effect of creating peak work loads in order entry, shipping, and billing, with consequent dry periods toward month-end.

In short, cash discounts make little economic sense as payment for the use of funds and in practice become nothing more than a reduction of price. In recent years, the great majority of companies have found it to be an awkward vehicle for price adjustment and have abandoned it in favour of net terms.

Delayed Payments When the period between the sale of the goods or services and the time of cash collection extends over a year or more and there is no provision for explicit interest payments, the selling price probably includes an interest charge for the right to delay payment. Under the accrual basis of accounting, this interest element is recognized as interest revenue during the periods between sale and collection when the loan is outstanding. To recognize all potential revenue entirely in the period of sale would be to recognize too soon the return for services rendered over time in lending money. Thus, when cash collection is to be delayed beyond one year, the measure of revenue for the current period should be the selling price reduced to account for interest during future periods. Only the *present value* at the time of sale of the amount to be received should be recognized as revenue during the period of sale. For most accounts receivable, the period between sale and collection spans only two to three months. The interest element is likely to be relatively insignificant in these cases. As a result, in accounting practice no reduction for interest on delayed payments is made for receivables to be collected within one year or less. This procedure is a practical expedient rather than a strict following of the underlying accounting theory.

Timing of Expense Recognition

Assets provide future benefits to the firm. *Expenses* are a measurement of the assets consumed in generating revenue. Assets are *unexpired costs* and expenses are *expired costs* or "gone assets." Our attention focuses on *when* the asset expiration takes place. The critical question is "When have asset benefits expired — leaving the balance sheet — and becomes expenses — entering the income statement as reductions in shareholders' equity?" Thus:

Balance Sheet	**Income Statement**

Assets or Unexpired Costs ⟶ Expenses or Expired Costs (which reduce shareholders' equity on the balance sheet).

Expense Recognition Expenses are recognized as follows:

1. Asset expirations directly associated with particular types of revenue are expenses in the period in which the revenues are recognized. This treatment is called the *matching convention*, because cost expirations are matched with revenues.
2. Asset expirations not associated with revenues are expenses of the period in which services are consumed in operations.

Product Costs The cost of goods or merchandise sold is perhaps the easiest expense to associate with revenue. At the time of sale, the asset physically changes hands. Revenue is recognized, and the cost of the merchandise transferred is treated as an expense.

A *merchandising firm* purchases inventory and later sells it without changing its physical form. The inventory appears as an asset stated at acquisition cost on the balance sheet. Later, when the inventory is sold, the same amount of acquisition cost appears as an expense (cost of goods sold) on the income statement.

A *manufacturing firm*, on the other hand, incurs various costs in changing the physical form of the goods it produces. There are three types of cost: (1) direct material, (2) direct labour, and (3) manufacturing overhead (sometimes called indirect manufacturing costs). Direct material and direct labour costs are associated directly with particular products manufactured. Manufacturing overhead includes a mixture of costs that provide a firm with a capacity to produce. Examples of manufacturing overhead costs are expenditures for utilities, property taxes, and insurance on the factory, as well as depreciation on manufacturing plant and equipment. The services of each of these items are used up during the period while the firm is creating new assets—the inventory of goods being worked upon or held for sale. Benefits from direct material, direct labour, and manufacturing overhead are transferred to, or become part of, the asset represented by units of inventory. Because the inventory items are assets until sales are made to customers, the various direct material, direct labour, and manufacturing overhead costs incurred in producing the goods are included in the manufacturing inventory under the titles Work-in-Process Inventory and Finished Goods Inventory. Such costs, which are assets transformed from one form to another, are called *product costs*. Product costs are assets; they become expenses only when the goods in which they are embodied are sold. Chapter 4 discusses more fully the accounting for manufacturing costs.

Revenue-Related Expenses Revenue-related expenses are those expenses that occur after a sale has been made. Some of these expenses, such as sales commissions, are known with certainty at the time of sale. Others, such as *bad debts* and *cash discounts*, can only be estimated at the time of sale since the amount of the expense depends on the future action of the customer in paying the account by the discount date, or in failing to pay. These expenses should attach to the period when the revenue is recognized and not to a later period when the specific customer's account is found to be uncollectible, or when the customer has taken advantage of the discount for prompt payment. If the recognition of these items is postponed, reported income of the subsequent periods will be reduced by an earlier decision to extend credit and discount terms to the customer. Thus, the performance of the firm for both the period of sale and the subsequent period would be measured inaccurately.

A question arises whether bad debts and cash discounts should be considered as a reduction of revenue or as a business expense. Although theoretically it may be argued that these items are reductions in revenue, since revenue should be measured on a cash-equivalent basis, the general practice is to treat them as business expenses. The general practice will be followed in the illustrations in this chapter. Chapter 7 considers these problems further.

Selling Costs In most cases, the costs incurred in selling, or marketing, a firm's products relate to the units sold during the period. For example, salaries and commissions of the sales staff, sales literature used, and most advertising costs are incurred in generating revenue currently. Because these selling costs are associated with the revenues of the period, they are reported as expenses in the period when their services are used. It can be argued that some selling costs, such as advertising and other sales promotion, provide future-period benefits for a firm and should continue to be treated as assets. However, distinguishing the portion of the cost relating to the current period (to be recognized as an expense) from the portion relating to future periods (to be treated as an asset) can be extremely difficult. Accountants, therefore, treat selling and other marketing activity costs as expenses of the period when the services are used. These selling costs are treated as *period expenses* rather than as assets, even though they may enhance the future marketability of a firm's products.

Administrative Costs The costs incurred in administering the activities of the firm cannot be closely associated with units produced and sold and, like selling costs, are treated as period expenses. Examples include the president's salary, accounting and data-processing costs, and the costs of conducting various supportive activities, such as legal services and corporate planning.

Financial Costs Some firms limit the amount of funds provided by creditors and finance the majority of asset acquisition from funds received from the issue of shares, or from the retention of income that is not paid to the shareholders as cash dividends. Other firms minimize the shareholders' contribution to asset acquisition and borrow substantial amounts with a repayment obligation. The form of financing should not influence operating decisions, and financing activities are ordinarily separated from operating activities. To reflect this separation, the results of operating and financial activities may be separated in the income statement. The costs and revenues resulting from the financing activities arise from the passage of time and are treated as period expenses. Examples include interest paid on bank loans, notes payable, bonds payable, mortgages payable, and financial income from interest-bearing bank deposits, notes receivable, investment in bonds and shares of other companies, and investment in government bonds.

Measurement of Expenses

Expenses represent assets consumed during the period. The amount of an expense is therefore the cost of the expired asset. Thus, the basis for expense measurement is the same as for asset valuation. Because assets are primarily stated at acquisition cost on the balance sheet, expenses are measured by the acquisition cost of the assets that were either sold or used during the period.

Summary

The *amount* of income from operating activities is equal to the difference between the cash received from customers and the amount of cash paid to suppliers, employees, and other providers of goods and services. However, cash receipts from customers do not always occur in the same accounting period as the related cash expenditures to the providers of goods and services. To obtain a measure of operating performance in which outflows are matched more effectively with inflows, the accrual basis of accounting is used.

The accrual basis determines the *timing* of income recognition. Revenue is typically recognized at the time of sale under the accrual basis. Costs that can be associated directly with particular revenues become expenses in the period when revenues are recognized. The cost of acquiring or manufacturing inventory items is treated in this manner. Costs that cannot be closely associated with particular revenue streams become expenses of the period when goods or services are consumed in operations. Most selling and administrative costs are treated in this manner.

The accounting procedures for preparing the income statement are considered next.

Overview of Accounting Procedures

Relationship between Balance Sheet and Income Statement

Net income, or earnings, for a period measures the excess of revenues (net asset inflows) over expenses (net asset outflows) from selling goods and providing services. Dividends measure the net assets distributed to shareholders. The Retained Earnings account on the balance sheet measures the cumulative excess of earnings over dividends since the firm began operations. The following disaggregation of the balance sheet equation helps to show the relation of revenues, expenses, and dividends to the components of the balance sheet.

$$\text{Assets} = \text{Liabilities} + \text{Owners' Equity}$$

$$\text{Assets} = \text{Liabilities} + \text{Contributed Capital} + \text{Retained Earnings}$$

$$\text{Assets} = \text{Liabilities} + \text{Contributed Capital} + \begin{array}{c}\text{Retained Earnings}\\ \text{Beginning}\\ \text{of Period}\end{array} + \text{Net Income} - \text{Dividends}$$

$$\text{Assets} = \text{Liabilities} + \text{Contributed Capital} + \begin{array}{c}\text{Retained Earnings}\\ \text{Beginning}\\ \text{of Period}\end{array} + \text{Revenues} - \text{Expenses} - \text{Dividends}$$

Purpose and Use of Individual Revenue and Expense Accounts

Revenue and expense amounts could be recorded directly in the Retained Earnings account. For example, the sale of merchandise on account results in an increase in assets (accounts receivable) and retained earnings (sales revenue) and a decrease in assets (merchandise inventory) and retained earnings (cost of merchandise sold). Measuring the *amount* of net income would be relatively simple if revenues and expenses were recorded directly in the Retained Earnings account. Net income would be computed from the following equation:

$$\text{Net Income} = \frac{\text{Retained Earnings}}{\text{End of Period}} - \frac{\text{Retained Earnings}}{\text{Beginning of Period}} + \text{Dividends}$$

The income statement is not designed merely to report net income. As the equation above indicates, the amount of net income can be deduced from the change in the Retained Earnings account. Rather, the income statement is designed to report the sources and amounts of a firm's revenues and the nature and amounts of a firm's expenses that sum to income for the period. Knowledge of the components of a firm's net income is helpful both in appraising past performance and in forecasting future performance.

To help in preparing the income statement, individual revenue and expense accounts are maintained during the accounting period. These accounts begin the accounting period with a zero balance. During the period, revenues and expenses are recorded in the accounts as they arise. At the end of the period, the balance in each revenue and expense account represents the cumulative revenues and expenses *for the period.* These amounts are reported in the income statement, which shows the net income of the period.

Because revenues and expenses are basically components of retained earnings, the balance in each revenue and expense account is transferred at the end of the period to the Retained Earnings account. Each revenue and expense account will then have a zero balance after the transfer. Retained earnings will be increased by the amount of net income (or decreased by the net loss) for the period.

The end result of maintaining separate revenue and expense accounts during the period and transferring their balances to the Retained Earnings account at the end of the period is the same as if revenues and expenses were initially recorded directly in the Retained Earnings account. Using separate revenue and expense accounts facilitates preparation of the income statement, which shows specific types of revenues and expenses. Once this purpose has been served, the need for separate revenue and expense accounts *for a given accounting period* has ended. Having been reduced to a zero balance at the end of the accounting period, these accounts begin the following accounting period with a zero balance and are therefore ready for entry of the revenue and expense amounts of the following period.

The process of transferring the balances in revenue and expense accounts to retained earnings is referred to as the *closing process*, because each revenue and expense account is closed, or reduced to a zero balance. Revenue and expense accounts accumulate amounts for only a single accounting period, and are therefore *temporary accounts*. One the other hand, the balance sheet accounts reflect the cumulative changes in each account from the time the firm was first organized, and are not closed each period. The balances in these accounts at the end of one period are carried over as the beginning balances of the following period. Balance sheet accounts are *permanent accounts*.

Debit and Credit Procedures for Revenues, Expenses, and Dividends

Because revenues, expenses, and dividends are components of retained earnings, the recording procedures for these items are the same as for any other transaction affecting owner's equity accounts.

Shareholders' Equity

Decreases (Debit)	Increases (Credit)
	Issues of Share Capital
Expenses	Revenues
Dividends	

A transaction giving rise to revenue results in an increase in net assets (increase in assets or decrease in liabilities) and an increase in shareholders' equity. The usual journal entry to record a revenue transaction is therefore:

Asset (A) Increase or Liability (L) Decrease . . . .   Amount
    Revenue (SE) . . . .   Amount
Typical entry to recognize revenue.

A transaction giving rise to expense results in a decrease in net assets (decrease in assets or increase in liabilities) and a decrease in shareholders' equity. The usual journal entry to record an expense is therefore:

Expense (SE) . . . .   Amount
    Asset (A) Decrease or Liability (L) Increase . . . .   Amount
Typical entry to record expense.

Dividends result in a decrease in net assets and a decrease in shareholders' equity. As we discuss in Chapter 12, dividends may be paid either in cash or in other assets. Although the accounting procedures for dividends are similar regardless of the form of the distribution, we assume that cash is used unless information is provided to the contrary. The usual entry to record the declaration of a dividend by the board of directors of a corporation is:

Retained Earnings (SE) . . . .   Amount
    Dividends Payable (L) . . . .   Amount
Typical entry to record dividend declaration.

When the dividend is paid, the journal entry is:

Dividends Payable (L) . . . .   Amount
   Cash (A) . . . .   Amount
Typical entry to record dividend payment.

A conceptual error sometimes made is that of treating dividends as an expense on the income statement. *Dividends are not expenses*. They are not costs incurred in *generating* revenues. Rather, they represent *distributions* of assets arising from current and prior years' operations to the owners of the firm.[2]

Before illustrating the recording procedures for revenues and expenses, it may be helpful to review briefly the steps in the accounting process.

Review of the Accounting Process

The steps in the accounting process, discussed in Chapter 2, are summarized as follows:

Journalizing Each transaction or series of transactions during the period is recorded in journal entry form in the general journal (or in a special journal that supplements the general journal).

Posting At periodic intervals, the entries in the general journal are posted to the accounts in the general ledger.

Trial Balance At the end of the accounting period, the balance in each general ledger account is calculated and a trial balance is prepared. A trial balance is a listing of all accounts in the general ledger that have balances. If the recording process has been carried out properly, the total amount in accounts having debit balances must equal the total amount in accounts having credit balances.

Adjusting Entries During the period, some accounting events may be only partially recorded, not recorded at all, or recorded incorrectly. Before the financial statements can be prepared at the end of the period, the omissions must be accounted for and the errors corrected. The entries to do this are known as *adjusting* entries. These entries are made so that revenues and expenses are reported in appropriate accounts with correct amounts, and so that balance sheet accounts show correct amounts of assets and equities at the end of the period.

---

[2]An alternative method for recording dividends is to debit an account, Dividends Declared. At the end of the accounting period, the balance in the Dividends Declared account is closed to the Retained Earnings account, thereby reducing the balance of Retained Earnings. The end result is a debit to Retained Earnings and a credit to Dividends Payable for the amount of dividends declared during the period. Because the account, Dividends Declared, is closed in a manner similar to an expense account at the end of the accounting period, this method of recording the dividend sometimes leads to the erroneous treatment of dividends as expenses. In this book, declarations of dividends are debited directly to Retained Earnings.

Statement Preparation The balance sheet, income statement, statement of changes in financial position, and any desired supporting schedules (for example, an analysis of changes in the Cash, Buildings and Equipment, or Retained Earnings accounts) are then prepared.

Illustration of the Accounting Process for a Merchandising Firm

Stephen's Shoe Store, Inc., has been in business since Year 1. A trial balance taken from its general ledger accounts on January 1, Year 4, the first day of an accounting period, is shown in Exhibit 3.3. To facilitate understanding, in this illustration the asset accounts are designated (A), the liability accounts (L), and the shareholders' equity (including revenue and expense) accounts (SE). Trial balances do not usually contain such designations.

Exhibit 3.3
STEPHEN'S SHOE STORE, INC.
Trial Balance
January 1, Year 4

	Accounts with Debit Balances	Accounts with Credit Balances
Cash (A)	$ 30,000	
Accounts Receivable (A)	63,000	
Merchandise Inventory (A)	175,000	
Land (A)	100,000	
Building and Equipment (A)	525,000	
Accumulated Depreciation (XA)		$ 85,000
Accounts Payable (L)		115,000
Income Tax Payable (L)		20,000
Bonds Payable (L)		100,000
Common Stock (SE)		250,000
Contributed Surplus (SE)		200,000
Retained Earnings (SE)		123,000
Total	$893,000	$893,000

Note that the revenue and expense accounts do not appear in this trial balance; they have zero balances at the beginning of an accounting period. One of the accounts in the trial balance, Accumulated Depreciation, has not previously been considered. This account is presented on the balance sheet as a deduction from Building and Equipment. (See Exhibit 3.9 for balance sheet presentation of this account.) Because of this manner of disclosure, this account is referred to as a *contra account*. A contra account accumulates amounts that are subtracted from the amount in another account. The nature and use of these contra accounts are discussed later in this illustration. An asset contra account is designated (XA) in the trial balance (Exhibit 3.5).

Journalizing

The transactions of Stephen's Shoe Store during Year 4 and the appropriate journal entries at the time of the transactions follow.

1. The firm purchases merchandise on account costing $355,000.

Merchandise Inventory (A)	$355,000	
Accounts Payable (L)		$355,000

2. Sales during the year are $625,000, of which $225,000 are for cash and the remainder are on account.

Cash (A)	$225,000	
Accounts Receivable (A)	400,000	
Sales Revenue (SE)		$625,000

3. The cost of merchandise sold during Year 4 is $390,000.

Cost of Goods (SE).	$390,000	
Merchandise Inventory (A)		$390,000

4. The firm pays salaries in cash of $110,000 during the year.

Salaries Expense (SE)	$110,000	
Cash (A)		$110,000

5. The firm collects cash of $325,000 from customers who had purchased on account.

Cash (A)	$325,000	
Accounts Receivable (A)		$325,000

6. The firm pays $250,000 to merchandise suppliers for purchases which have been made on account.

Accounts Payable (L)	$250,000	
Cash (A)		$250,000

7. The firm makes payment of $20,000 to the government for Year 3 income taxes.

Income Tax Payable (L)	$20,000	
Cash (A)		$20,000

8. The firm pays a premium of $1,500 on January 1, Year 4, for a three-year property and liability insurance policy.

Prepaid Insurance (A)	$1,500	
Cash (A)		$1,500

The debit in this entry, made on January 1, Year 4, is to an asset account, because the insurance provides three years of coverage beginning on that date. The entry to reduce the Prepaid Insurance account and to record the insurance expense for Year 4 is one of the adjusting entries made at the end of the accounting period, and is illustrated later.

9. Warehouse space not needed in the company's operations is rented out for one year beginning December 1, Year 4. The annual rental of $600 is received at that time.

Cash (A)	$600	
Advances from Tenants (L)		$600

10. On December 31, Year 4, the firm pays annual interest at eight percent on the long-term bonds outstanding: $.08 \times \$100,000 = \$8,000$.

Interest Expense (SE)	$8,000	
Cash (A)		$8,000

11. A customer who had purchased merchandise on account for $10,000 has experienced financial difficulty and has been unable to pay for the goods on time. The customer now promises to pay $10,000 in 90 days with interest at nine percent per year. As evidence of that promise, the customer gives a promissory note. On November 1, Year 4, Stephen's Shoe Store accepts the 90-day note for $10,000 bearing interest at nine percent in settlement of the open account receivable.

Notes Receivable (A)	$10,000	
Accounts Receivable (A)		$10,000

12. The board of directors declared a cash dividend of $15,000 on December 28, Year 4. The dividend is to be paid on January 20, Year 5.

Retained Earnings (SE)	$15,000	
Dividends Payable (L)		$15,000

Exhibit 3.4
STEPHEN'S SHOE STORE, INC.
T-Accounts Showing Beginning Balances,
Transactions during Year 4, and Ending
Balance before Adjusting Entries

Cash (A)

Bal. 1/1	30,000		
(2)	225,000	110,000	(4)
(5)	325,000	250,000	(6)
		20,000	(7)
		1,500	(8)
(9)	600	8,000	(10)
Bal. 12/31	191,100		

Notes Receivable (A)

Bal. 1/1	0		
(11)	10,000		
Bal. 12/31	10,000		

Land (A)

Bal. 1/1	100,000		
Bal. 12/31	100,000		

Accounts Receivable (A)

Bal. 1/1	63,000		
(2)	400,000	325,000	(5)
		10,000	(11)
Bal. 12/31	128,000		

Merchandise Inventory (A)

Bal. 1/1	175,000		
(1)	355,000	390,000	(3)
Bal. 12/31	140,000		

Building and Equipment (A)

Bal. 1/1	525,000		
Bal. 12/31	525,000		

Prepaid Insurance (A)

Bal. 1/1	0		
		1,500	(8)
Bal. 12/31	1,500		

Accumulated Depreciation (XA)

		85,000	Bal. 1/1
		85,000	Bal. 12/31

Continued

Continued

Accounts Payable (L)

Debit	Credit
	115,000 Bal. 1/1
(6) 250,000	355,000 (1)
	220,000 Bal. 12/31

Income Tax Payable (L)

Debit	Credit
	20,000 Bal. 1/1
(7) 20,000	
	0 Bal. 12/31

Dividends Payable (L)

Debit	Credit
	0 Bal. 1/1
	15,000 (12)
	15,000 Bal. 12/31

Advances from Tenants (L)

Debit	Credit
	0 Bal. 1/1
	600 (9)
	600 Bal. 12/31

Bonds Payable (L)

Debit	Credit
	100,000 Bal. 1/1
	100,000 Bal. 12/31

Common Stock (SE)

Debit	Credit
	250,000 Bal. 1/1
	250,000 Bal. 12/31

Contributed Surplus (SE)

Debit	Credit
	200,000 Bal. 1/1
	200,000 Bal. 12/31

Retained Earnings (SE)

Debit	Credit
(12) 15,000	123,000 Bal. 1/1
	108,000 Bal. 12/31

Sales Revenue (SE)

Debit	Credit
	0 Bal. 1/1
	625,000 (2)
	625,000 Bal. 12/31

Cost of Goods Sold (SE)

Debit	Credit
Bal. 1/1 0	
(3) 390,000	
Bal. 12/31 390,000	

Salaries Expense (SE)

Debit	Credit
Bal. 1/1 0	
(4) 110,000	
Bal. 12/31 110,000	

Interest Expense (SE)

Debit	Credit
Bal. 1/1 0	
(10) 8,000	
Bal. 12/31 8,000	

Posting

The entries in the general journal are posted to the appropriate general ledger accounts. In this illustration, the posting operation takes place on December 31, Year 4. The T-accounts in Exhibit 3.4 show the opening balances from the trial balance in Exhibit 3.3 and the effects of transactions (1) through (12).

Trial Balance Preparation

The trial balance prepared at the end of the accounting period before adjusting and closing entries is called an *unadjusted trial balance*. The unadjusted trial balance of Stephen's Shoe Store as of December 31, Year 4 appears in Exhibit 3.5. The amounts in the unadjusted trial balance are taken directly from the ending balances in the T-accounts in Exhibit 3.4.

Exhibit 3.5
STEPHEN'S SHOE STORE, INC.
Unadjusted Trial Balance
December 31, Year 4

	Accounts with Debit Balances	Accounts with Credit Balances
Cash (A)	$ 191,100	
Accounts Receivable (A)	128,000	
Notes Receivable (A)	10,000	
Merchandise Inventory (A)	140,000	
Prepaid Insurance (A)	1,500	
Land (A)	100,000	
Building and Equipment (A)	525,000	
Accumulated Depreciation (XA)		$ 85,000
Accounts Payable (L)		220,000
Dividends Payable (L)		15,000
Advances from Tenants		600
Bonds Payable (L)		100,000
Common Stock (SE)		250,000
Contributed Surplus (SE)		200,000
Retained Earnings (SE)		108,000
Sales Revenue (SE)		625,000
Cost of Goods Sold (SE)	390,000	
Salaries Expense (SE)	110,000	
Interest Expense (SE)	8,000	
Totals	$1,603,600	$1,603,600

Adjusting Entries

The entries in the general journal made during the year result from transactions between the firm and outsiders (for example, suppliers, employees, customers, and governmental units). Other events continuously occur, however, for which no specific transaction signals the requirement for a journal entry, but which must be considered in measuring net income for the period and financial position at the end of the period. For example, building and equipment are used continuously in the process of generating revenue. Because the services of these assets are consumed during the period, a portion of their acquisition cost must be recorded as an expense. Similarly, insurance coverage expires continuously throughout the year. Because the services of the asset are gradually consumed, a portion of the asset, Prepaid Insurance, must be recorded as an expense.

Other kinds of events occur that affect the revenues and expenses of the period but for which a cash transaction with an outsider will not occur until a subsequent period. For example, salaries and wages are earned by administrative employees during the last several days of the current accounting period, but they will not be paid until the following accounting period. Such salaries and wages, although payable in the next period, are expenses of the current period when the labour services are consumed. Similarly, interest accrues on a firm's notes receivable or payable. Interest will be collected or paid in a subsequent period, but a portion of the interest should be recognized as revenue or expenses in the current period.

Adjusting entries are prepared at the end of the accounting period. These entries alter the balances in the general ledger accounts in order to recognize all revenues and expenses for the proper reporting of net income and financial position. The following sections illustrate several examples of adjusting entries for Stephen's Shoe Store.

Recognition of Accrued Revenues and Receivables   Revenue is earned as services are rendered. For example, rent is earned as a tenant uses the property. Interest, a "rent" for the use of money, is earned from a loan as time passes. Recording these amounts as they accrue day by day is usually not convenient, however. At the end of the accounting period, there may be some situations in which revenue has been earned but for which no entry has been made, either because cash has not been received or the time has not arrived for a formal invoice to be sent to the customer. A claim has come into existence that, although it may not be due immediately, should appear on the balance sheet as an asset and must be reflected in the revenues of the period. The purpose of the adjusting entry for interest eventually receivable by the lender is to recognize on the balance sheet the right to receive cash in an amount equal to the interest already earned and to recognize the same amount as revenue on the income statement for the period.

Stephen's Shoe Store received a 90-day note from a customer on November 1, Year 4. At year-end, the note already appears on the trial balance. Interest earned during November and December, however, does not appear in the unadjusted trial balance. The note earns interest at the rate of nine percent per year. By convention in business practice, interest rates stated on loans are almost always stated as annual interest rates. Also, by convention, a year equal to 12 months of 30 days each, or 360 days, is usually assumed to simplify the calculation of interest earned. Interest of $150 is earned by Stephen's Shoe Store, Inc., during November and December. This amount is equal to the $10,000 principal times the nine percent annual interest rate times the elapsed 60 days divided by 360 days ($150 = $10,000 × .09 × 60/360). The adjusting entry to recognize the asset, Interest Receivable, and the interest earned is:

365 int always per diem.

---

(13) Interest Receivable (A) $150

       Interest Revenue (SE) $150

Recognition of Accrued Expenses and Payables As various services are received, their cost should be reflected in the financial statements, whether or not payment has been made or an invoice received. Here, also, recording these amounts day by day is frequently not convenient. Some adjustment of expenses and liabilities will probably be necessary at the end of the accounting period.

Salaries and wages earned during the last several days of the accounting period, which will not be paid until the following accounting period, illustrate this type of adjustment. According to payroll records, employees of Stephen's Shoe Store earned salaries of $14,000 during the last several days of Year 4 that were not recorded at year-end. The adjusting entry is:

---

(14) Salaries Expense (SE) $14,000

       Salaries Payable (L) $14,000

Other examples of this type of adjusting entry include costs incurred for utilities, taxes, and interest.

Allocation of Prepaid Operating Costs Another type of adjustment arises because assets are required for use in the operations of the firm but are not completely used during the accounting period in which they are acquired. For example, Stephen's Shoe Store paid $1,500 on January 1, Year 4 for a three-year insurance policy. During Year 4, one-third of the coverage expired, so $500 of the premium should be removed from the asset account and reflected as insurance expense. The balance sheet on December 31, Year 4 should show $1,000 of prepaid insurance as an asset, because this portion of the premium is a future benefit—the asset of insurance coverage to be received over the next two years.

The nature of the adjusting entry to record an asset expiration as an expense depends on the recording of the original payment. If the payment resulted in a debit to an asset account, the adjusting entry must reduce the asset and increase the expense for the services used up during the accounting period. Stephen's Shoe Store had recorded in entry (8), as discussed on page 106, the payment of the insurance premium on January 1, Year 4 as follows:

| (8) Prepaid Insurance (A) . . . . | $1,500 | |
| Cash (A) . . . . | | $1,500 |

The adjusting entry is, therefore:

| (15) Insurance Expense (SE) . . . . | $500 | |
| Prepaid Insurance (A) . . . . | | $500 |

Insurance expense for Year 4 is $500, and prepaid insurance in the amount of $1,000 appears as an asset on the balance sheet on December 31, Year 4.

Alternative Procedure Instead of debiting an asset account at the time the premium is paid, some firms debit an expense account. For example, Stephen's Shoe Store might have recorded the original premium payment as follows:

| (8a) Insurance Expense (SE) . . . . | $1,500 | |
| Cash (A) . . . . | | $1,500 |

Because many operating costs become expenses in the period in which the expenditure is made (for example, monthly rent), this second procedure for recording expenditures during the year sometimes reduces the number of adjusting entries that must be made at year-end. In the situation with the insurance policy, however, not all of the $1,500 premium paid is an expense of Year 4. If the original journal entry had been (8a), the adjusting entry would then be:

| (15a) Prepaid Insurance (A) . . . . | $1,000 | |
| Insurance Expense (SE) . . . . | | $1,000 |

After the original entry in (8a) and the adjusting entry in (15a), insurance expense for Year 4 is reflected in the accounts at $500, and prepaid insurance at $1,000. The *end result* of these two approaches to recording the original payment of the premium is the same. The *adjusting entries*, however, are quite different. (See Problem 3 for Self-Study at the end of the chapter.)

Recognition of Depreciation When assets such as buildings, machinery, furniture, and trucks are purchased, their acquisition cost is debited to appropriate asset accounts. Although these assets may provide services for a number of years, their future benefits expire as time passes. The asset's cost is spread systematically over its estimated useful life. The charge made to the current operations for the portion of the cost of such assets consumed during the current period is called *depreciation*. Depreciation involves nothing new in principle; it is identical with the procedure for prepaid operating costs presented previously. For example, the cost of a building is a prepayment for a series of future services, and depreciation allocates the cost of the services to the periods in which services are received and used.

Various accounting methods are used in allocating the acquisition cost of long-lived assets to the periods of benefit. One widely used method is the *straight-line method*. Under this procedure, an equal portion of the acquisition cost less estimated salvage value is allocated to each period of the asset's estimated useful life. The depreciation charge for each period is computed as follows:

$$\frac{\text{Acquisition Cost} - \text{Estimated Salvage Value}}{\text{Estimated Useful Life in Periods}} = \frac{\text{Depreciation Charge for}}{\text{Each Period}}$$

Internal records indicate that the Building and Equipment account of Stephen's Shoe Store comprises a store building with an acquisition cost of $400,000 and a group of items of equipment with an acquisition cost of $125,000. At the time the building was acquired, it had an estimated 40-year useful life and a zero salvage value. Depreciation expense for each year of the building's life is calculated to be

$$\frac{\$400,000 - \$0}{40 \text{ years}} = \$10,000 \text{ per year.}$$

At the time the equipment was acquired, it had an estimated useful life of six years and an estimated salvage value of $5,000. Annual depreciation is, therefore.

$$\frac{\$125,000 - \$5,000}{6 \text{ years}} = \$20,000 \text{ per year.}$$

The adjusting entry to record depreciation of $30,000 (= $10,000 + $20,000) for Year 4 is:

(16) Depreciation Expense (SE)	$30,000	
Accumulated Depreciation (XA)		$30,000

The credit in entry (16) could have been made directly to the Building and Equipment account, because the credit records the portion of the asset's cost that has expired, or become an expense, during Year 4. The same end result is achieved by crediting the Accumulated Depreciation account, a contra-asset account, and then deducting the balance in this account from the acquisition cost of the assets in the Building and Equipment account on the balance sheet. Using the contra account enables the financial statements to show both the acquisition cost of the assets in use and the portion of that amount that has previously been recognized as an expense. Showing both acquisition cost and accumulated depreciation amounts separately provides a rough indication of the relative age of the firm's long-lived assets. (See Exercise 29 at the end of the chapter.)

Note that the Depreciation Expense account includes only depreciation for the current accounting period, while the Accumulated Depreciation account includes the cumulative depreciation charges on the present assets since acquisition.

Valuation of Liabilities When a firm receives cash from customers before it sells merchandise or renders services, it incurs a liability. For example, Stephen's Shoe Store received $600 on December 1, Year 4, as one year's rent on warehouse space. When the cash was received, the liability account, Advances from Tenants, was credited. One month's rent has been earned as of December 31, Year 4. The adjusting entry is

---

(17) Advances from Tenants (L) $50
         Rent Revenue (SE) $50
      To reduce liability from $600 to $550.

The remaining $550 of the cash collected for rent is yet to be earned and appears on the December 31, Year 4 balance sheet as a liability.

Income Tax Expense After the adjusting entries are recorded, a final entry for income tax expense is required for Stephen's Shoe Store, Inc. Corporate income tax payable for a period is based on the accounting net income before income tax of the period, adjusted for differences between accounting income and income for tax purposes. A rate specified by the Income Tax Act is applied to income for tax purposes.

For Year 4, there was no difference between accounting income before income tax and income for tax purposes. The rate of income tax was 40 percent and the income tax payable was $29,080 ($= .40 \times \$72,700$, from Exhibit 3.8).

---

(18) Income Tax Expense (SE) $29,080
         Income Tax Payable (L) $29,080

Trial Balance after Adjusting Entries The adjusting entries are posted or entered in the general ledger in the same manner as entries made during the year. A trial balance of the general ledger accounts after adjusting entries are made is called an *adjusted trial balance* and helps when preparing the financial statements. Exhibit 3.6 presents the trial balance data before and after adjusting entries for Stephen's Shoe Store. The exhibit indicates the effect of the adjustment process on the various accounts. The number in parentheses identifies the debit and credit components of each adjusting entry.

Preparing Income Statement The adjusted trial balance shows all revenue and expense accounts with their correct amounts for the period. The income statement can be prepared by listing all the revenue accounts, listing all the expense accounts, and showing the difference between the sum of the revenues and the sum of the expenses as net income. Revenue and expense accounts are temporary labels for portions of retained earnings. Once the adjusted trial balance has been prepared, the revenue and expense accounts have served their purpose for the current period and are closed.

Exhibit 3.6
STEPHEN'S SHOE STORE, INC.
Trial Balance before and after Adjusting Entries[a]
December 31, Year 4

Accounts	Unadjusted Trial Balance		Adjusting Entries		Adjusted Trial Balance	
	Debit	Credit	Debit	Credit	Debit	Credit
Cash (A)	$ 191,100				$ 191,100	
Accounts Receivable (A)	128,000				128,000	
Notes Receivable (A)	10,000				10,000	
Interest Receivable (A)			$ 150 (13)		150	
Merchandise Inventory (A)	140,000				140,000	
Prepaid Insurance (A)	1,500			$ 500 (15)	1,000	
Land (A)	100,000				100,000	
Building and Equipment (A)	525,000				525,000	
Accumulated Depreciation (XA)		$ 85,000		30,000 (16)		$ 115,000
Accounts Payable (L)		220,000				220,000
Salaries Payable (L)				14,000 (14)		14,000
Dividends Payable (L)		15,000				15,000
Income Tax Payable (L)				29,080 (18)		29,080
Advances from Tenants		600	50 (17)			550
Bonds Payable (L)		100,000				100,000
Common Stock (SE)		250,000				250,000
Contributed Surplus (SE)		200,000				200,000
Retained Earnings (SE)		108,000				108,000
Sales Revenue (SE)		625,000				625,000
Interest Revenue (SE)				150 (13)		150
Rent Revenue (SE)				50 (17)		50
Cost of Goods Sold (SE)	390,000				390,000	
Salaries Expense (SE)	110,000		14,000 (14)		124,000	
Interest Expense (SE)	8,000				8,000	
Insurance Expense (SE)			500 (15)		500	
Depreciation Expense (SE)			30,000 (16)		30,000	
Income Tax Expense (SE)			29,080 (18)		29,080	
Totals	$1,603,600	$1,603,600	$73,780	$73,780	$1,676,830	$1,676,830

[a]This convenient tabular form is often called a *work sheet*. Most work sheets are more elaborate than this one, but their purpose is the same—to display data in a form for easy computations and financial statement preparation. The typical work would not show just two final columns called Adjusted Trial Balance, but would show four columns: Income Statement Debit and Credit, and Balance Sheet Debit and Credit. The horizontal sum of the amounts in an income account is shown in the appropriate debit or credit income statement column of the work sheet. The horizontal sum of the amounts in a balance sheet account is shown in the appropriate debit or credit balance sheet column of the work sheet. See Appendix 3.2 for further explanation.

Closing of Temporary Accounts

The closing process transfers the balances in the temporary revenue and expense accounts to Retained Earnings. A temporary account with a debit balance is closed by crediting it with the amount equal to its balance at the end of the period and debiting Retained Earnings. A temporary account with a credit balance is closed by debiting the temporary account and crediting Retained Earnings. After closing entries, the balances in all temporary accounts are zero. The former debit (credit) balances in temporary accounts become debits (credits) in the Retained Earnings account.

Each temporary revenue and expense account could be closed by a separate entry. Some recording time is saved, however, by closing all revenue and expense accounts in a single entry as follows:

(19)	Sales Revenue (SE)	$625,000	
	Interest Revenue (SE)	150	
	Rent Revenue (SE)	50	
	Cost of Goods Sold (SE)		$390,000
	Salaries Expense (SE)		124,000
	Interest Expense (SE)		8,000
	Insurance Expense (SE)		500
	Depreciation Expense (SE)		30,000
	Income Tax Expense (SE)		29,080
	Retained Earnings (SE)		43,620

The amount credited to Retained Earnings is the difference between the amounts debited to revenue accounts and the amounts credited to expense accounts. This amount is the net income for the period.[3]

Alternative Closing Procedure An alternative closing procedure uses a temporary "Income Summary" account. Individual revenue and expense accounts are first closed to the Income Summary account. The income statement is prepared using information on the individual revenues and expenses in the Income Summary account. The balance in the Income Summary account, representing net income for the period, is then closed to Retained Earnings.

For example, the entry to close the Sales Revenue account under this alternative procedure is:

(19a)	Sales Revenue (SE)	$625,000	
	Income Summary (SE)		$625,000

---

[3]The amount credited to Retained Earnings in the closing entry is called a *plug* and is equal to the net income transferred. When making some journal entries in accounting, often all debits are known, as are all but one of the credits (or vice versa). Because double-entry recording procedure requires equal debits and credits, the unknown quantity can be found by subtracting the sum of the known credits from the sum of all debits (or vice versa). This process is known as *plugging*.

The entry to close the Cost of Goods Sold account is:

(19b)	Income Summary (SE)	$390,000	
	Cost of Goods Sold (SE)		$390,000

Similar closing entries are made for the other revenue and expense accounts. The Income Summary account will have a credit balance of $43,620 after all revenue and expense accounts have been closed. The balance in the Income Summary account is then transferred to Retained Earnings:

(19c)	Income Summary (SE)	$43,620	
	Retained Earnings (SE)		$43,620

The end result of both closing procedures is the same. Revenue and expense accounts, as well as the Income Summary account if one is used, have zero balances after closing entries, and the Retained Earnings account is increased by the net income for the period of $43,620. Exhibit 3.7 shows the Income Summary account for Stephen's Shoe Store after all revenue and expense accounts have been closed at the end of the period.

Exhibit 3.7
Illustration of Income Summary
Account for Stephen's Shoe Store, Inc.

Income Summary Account (SE)				Retained Earnings (SE)		
Cost of Goods Sold	$390,000	$625,000	Sales Revenue		$123,000	Beginning
Salaries Expense	124,000	150	Interest Revenue			Balance
Interest Expense	8,000	50	Rent Revenue	Dividends $15,000	43,620	Net Income
Insurance Expense	500	$625,200				
Depreciation Expense	30,000				$151,620	Ending
						Balance
Income Tax Expense	29,080					
To Close Income						
Summary Account	43,620					
	$625,200					

Financial Statement Preparation

if computerized systems are used, we would like to run I/S at will w/o closing to Income summary

The income statement, balance sheet, and any desired supporting schedules can be prepared from information in the adjusted trial balance. Exhibit 3.8 presents the income statement of Stephen's Shoe Store for Year 4. Exhibit 3.9 presents the comparative balance sheets for December 31, Year 3 and Year 4. Exhibit 3.10 presents an analysis of changes in retained earnings. Companies are required to prepare comparative income statements and statements of retained earnings as well as comparative balance sheets. To simplify the illustration, single year income and retained earnings statements are presented below.

Exhibit 3.8
STEPHEN'S SHOE STORE, INC.
Income Statement for the Year Ending
December 31, Year 4

Sales Revenue		$625,000
Less: Cost of Goods Sold		390,000
Gross Profit		$235,000
Less: Operating Expenses		
Salaries	$124,000	
Insurance	500	
Depreciation	30,000	154,500
Operating Profit		$ 80,500
Less: Financial Expenses		
Interest Expense	$ 8,000	
Less: Interest Earned	150	
Net Interest Expense	$ 7,850	
Less: Rent Earned	50	7,800
Net Income before Income Tax		$ 72,700
Less: Income Tax Expense		29,080
Net Income		$ 43,620

Exhibit 3.9
STEPHEN'S SHOE STORE, INC.
Comparative Balance Sheet
December 31, Year 3 and Year 4

ASSETS

		December 31, Year 4		December 31, Year 3
Current Assets:				
Cash		$191,100		$ 30,000
Accounts Receivable		128,000		63,000
Notes Receivable		10,000		—
Interest Receivable		150		—
Merchandise Inventory		140,000		175,000
Prepaid Insurance		1,000		—
Total Current Assets		$470,250		$268,000
Property, Plant, and Equipment:				
Land		$100,000		$100,000
Building and Equipment	$525,000		$525,000	
Less: Accumulated Depreciation	115,000		85,000	
Building and Equipment — net		410,000		440,000
Total Property, Plant, and Equipment		$510,000		$540,000
Total Assets		$980,250		$808,000

LIABILITIES AND SHAREHOLDERS' EQUITY	December 31, Year 4	December 31, Year 3
Current Liabilities:		
Accounts Payable	$220,000	$115,000
Salaries Payable	14,000	—
Dividends Payable	15,000	—
Income Tax Payable	29,080	20,000
Advances from Tenants	550	—
Total Current Liabilities	$278,630	$135,000
Long-Term Debt:		
Bonds Payable	100,000	100,000
Total Liabilities	$378,630	$235,000
Shareholders' Equity:		
Common Stock — at par value	$250,000	$250,000
Contributed Surplus	200,000	200,000
Retained Earnings	151,620	123,000
Total Shareholders' Equity	$601,620	$573,000
Total Liabilities and Shareholders' Equity	$980,250	$808,000

Exhibit 3.10
STEPHEN'S SHOE STORE, INC.
Statement of Retained Earnings for the Year Ending
December 31, Year 4

Retained Earnings, December 31, Year 3		$123,000
Net Income	$43,620	
Less: Dividends	15,000	
Increase in Retained Earnings		28,620
Retained Earnings, December 31, Year 4		$151,620

Summary

Measurements of net income *for the period* and of financial position *at the end of the period* are interrelated. Revenues result from selling goods or rendering services to customers and lead to increases in assets or decreases in liabilities. Expenses indicate that services have been used in generating revenue and result in decreases in assets or increases in liabilities. Because revenues represent increases in owners' equity, revenue transactions are recorded by crediting (increasing) an owners' equity account for the specific type of revenue and by debiting either an asset or liability account. Expenses represent decreases in owners' equity and are recorded by debiting (decreasing) an owners' equity account for the specific type of expense and crediting either an asset or a liability account. The revenue and expense accounts accumulate the revenues earned and expenses recognized during the period.

Computers in Accounting

*A*ccounting involves the collection, recording, and summarizing of financial data about an organization—data processing. Today, most organizations employ the technological assistance of computers in carrying out these activities, hence the term—*electronic data processing (EDP)*.

A computer performs the same functions as an individual in an accounting system. However, it can potentially perform them quicker, cheaper, and with less potential for error than an individual. In small companies computers are optional; in large companies they are a necessity.

The major difference between a DP and an EDP system is in storage media for the accounting data. In an EDP system, the journals and ledgers described in this chapter are stored on electromagnetic media (tape or disk). This has raised important new issues for the accountant to deal with, such as data integrity and data security.

A firm has the option of internally developing its own specialized programs for its accounting applications or purchasing ''canned software'' from commercial software houses. There are so many good packages available on the market today that most firms choose the latter option if they are using microcomputers.

These accounting software packages have the following general capabilities:

1. Transaction processing, journal and ledger maintenance, and financial statement preparation
2. Electronic spreadsheets
3. Database management systems

Programs that have the first capability are often referred to as general ledger packages. These packages include programs to handle the specialized journal functions we have discussed in this chapter, including receivables, payroll, payables, fixed assets, and inventory. The software will support the functions of journalizing and the updating of subsidiary ledgers, and control accounts. It can also include such functions as invoicing, preparing customer statements, and generating periodic reports. Most of the general ledger packages are quite user-friendly and relatively foolproof, so that accounting departments with little computer expertise can use them.

These systems can reduce clerical effort and errors, and some even have features that enhance internal control. A complete general ledger system can be acquired for under $5000.

Some of the systems available in Canada include ACCPAC. Accounting Plus, BPI, MBSI, New Views, Peachtree, Radio Shack, and Bedford. Every computer software store will carry one or more packages, and the sales staff can usually instruct purchasers on use.

Electronic spreadsheet software is used primarily for planning purposes in accounting. Such software is highly useful in ''what if?'' decisions. With one of these packages, the accountant can examine the effects of different sales prices, sales volumes, product costs, and so on. The computer algorithms will recast the income statement employing the new assumptions, so that the bottom-line impact of any accounting decision on income is immediately discernible.

Database management systems differ greatly in relative complexity and features. In general such a system can be used as the information management facility for the entire firm. Accounting, production, marketing, and human resources are all handled by the database system. The advantages of having one centralized information database increase with the size of the firm. Commercial packages include AB Master, RBase, dBase III Plus, Profile Plus, Watbase, and Info Star.

In general, an accountant no longer needs to know much about computers to enjoy the many advantages that computerized data processing can provide.

Some events will not be recorded as part of the regular day-to-day recording process during the period because no explicit transaction between the firm and some external party (such as a customer, creditor, or governmental unit) has taken place to signal the requirement for a journal entry. Such events require an adjusting entry at the end of the period so that periodic income and financial position can be properly reported on an accrual basis. After an adjusted trial balance has been prepared the balances in these temporary accounts are transferred, or closed, to the Retained Earnings account.

Appendix 3.1
Accounting Journal and Ledgers

This appendix describes and illustrates some of the more common types of journals and ledgers used in accounting systems.

Journals

The *journal* presents a chronological record of accounting events. *Journalizing* consists of analyzing the accounting events into the proper debits and credits and recording the results of the analysis in a journal. The journal contains accounting information classified by accounting event. Further, each accounting event is analyzed and recorded completely before the next one is entered. The journal is the first place in which a complete formal record of the accounting event is made. It is thus sometimes called *the book of original entry.* By recording all information relating to each accounting event in one place, the journal provides a chronological history, or running record, of the various events and transactions of the firm. The number of transactions, even in a small business, is so large that errors are bound to occur. It would be almost impossible to locate errors if a record such as the journal were not kept. Each journal entry can be checked independently for equal debits and credits, and postings in the ledger accounts can be traced back to the journal to determine the origin, authorization, and analysis of each transaction.

The journal may take three possible forms: (1) two-column journal, (2) multicolumn journal, or (3) specialized journal.

The Two-Column Journal Form The most common journal form is the two-column form presented in Exhibit 3.11. Essentials of the two-column form are a pair of columns to record the debits and credits and a place to indicate the names of the accounts affected by the transaction. As posting is done, there will be entered in the reference (Ref.) column the number, or page, of the account to which the amount has been posted, or perhaps a check mark to indicate that the posting has been done. A transaction involving the receipt of $150 from R. Wood as payment on an account receivable is shown in Exhibit 3.11 in the two-column journal.

The two-column journal form is the one commonly used for the general journal of a firm.

Exhibit 3.11
Two-Column Journal Form

Date		Accounts and Explanation	Ref.	Debit	Credit
9	1	Cash	✓	1 5 0 0 0	
		Accounts Receivable	✓		1 5 0 00
		Collection from R. Wood on Account			

Multicolumn Journal The process of posting, or transferring, figures from the journal to the general ledger accounts is laborious and monotonous. When the two-column journal form is used, each journal debit and credit must be copied into the general ledger individually. In practice this simple two-column form is usually replaced by a more elaborate journal or journals. One labor-saving device is to expand the journal into a multicolumn record. The *multicolumn* journal provides several debit and several credit columns to replace the two-column form. This subdivision permits separate columns to be reserved for the entering of debits or credits in accounts, such as Cash and Sales for a merchandising firm, that are used often. A simple multicolumn journal form is shown in Exhibit 3.12. The transaction involving the receipt of cash from R. Wood on account is entered in the multicolumn journal.

Exhibit 3.12
Multicolumn Journal

Date		Explanation	Cash		Merchandise Sales		Other Accounts			
			Debit	Credit	Debit	Credit	Debit	Credit	Ref.	Account Title
9	1	Collection from R. Wood on Account	150.00					150.00		Accounts Receivable

Designing a multicolumn journal requires selecting the accounts to be allocated special columns. Columns should be provided for the debits or credits, or both, of those accounts that are used most frequently. In practice it may not be easy to discover which will be used most often. If the business has been in operation for some time, the past transactions can be studied and a tabulation made of the number of entries to each side of each account. If there is no experience to use as a guide, an attempt is made to anticipate the types of transactions that will occur most frequently and a tentative set of column headings is selected. In any case, the column headings may have to be changed from time to time so that the multicolumn format may be used efficiently. When only one multicolumn journal is used, two columns must always be reserved to record the debits and credits to the accounts for which specialized columns are not provided. The multicolumn journal is composed of two segments:

(1) specialized columns for frequent items, and (2) an attached two-column journal form to provide for all other items.

The principal advantage of using specialized columns is the savings in posting time. The posting of a column total to the general ledger takes the place of the posting of each of the individual items that appear in the column. Specialized columns also facilitate the process of journalizing, because most bookkeepers find it easier to analyze transactions when the commonly used accounts are spread across a columnar sheet. Each entry also takes less vertical space and more entries can therefore be made on a journal page.

Specialized Journals The advantages of specialization can be extended further by replacing the multicolumn journal by a group of specialized journals. There is no standard set of journals suitable for all firms. However, in most concerns four specialized journals are likely to be used in addition to the general journal: cash receipts; cash disbursements; revenue recognition (particularly sales); and acquisition of goods and services (particularly purchases of merchandise and raw materials). The size of the firm and the nature of its operations will, of course, affect the number and types of specialized journals employed. A cash receipts journal and a cash disbursements journal are described briefly next.

Cash Receipts Journal A cash receipts journal provides a chronological listing of all transactions involving the receipt of cash. Exhibit 3.13 shows an example of a cash receipts journal. Each cash receipt is entered in the Cash Dr. column and the credit entry appears in either the Accounts Receivable Cr., Sales Cr., or Other Cr. column. At periodic intervals, such as weekly or monthly, the total amount in each column is posted to the appropriate general ledger accounts. For example, at the end of September, $995 would be debited to the Cash account in the general ledger. Likewise, $225 would be credited to the Accounts Receivable account in the general ledger.

Exhibit 3.13
Cash Receipts Journal

CASH RECEIPTS JOURNAL   Page 46

Date		Explanation	Cash Dr.	Accounts Receivable Cr.	Sales Cr.	Other Cr.	Account Title
9	1	Collection from R. Wood on account	150.00	150.00			
9	5	Sale of Merchandise to Customers	250.00		250.00		
9	12	Collection from J. Smith on Account	75.00	75.00			
9	19	Receipt of Dividend from Ford Motor Company	120.00			120.00	Dividend Revenue
9	25	Sales of Merchandise to Customers	400.00		400.00		
			995.00	225.00	650.00	120.00	

Cash Disbursements Journal A cash disbursements journal contains a sequential listing of all cash disbursements made. If all disbursements are made by cheque, a desirable procedure for control purposes, the cash disbursements journal will list each cheque written (credits to the Cash account) and the appropriate account debited. Exhibit 3.14 presents a typical cash disbursements journal. Each disbursement is entered in the Cash Cr. column. An entry is also made in either the Accounts Payable Dr., Selling and Administrative Expense Dr., or Other Dr. column. At periodic intervals, the total amount in the Cash Cr. column ($506) is posted to the credit side of the general ledger account for Cash. Similar entries are made on the debit sides of the other general ledger accounts.

Exhibit 3.14
Cash Disbursements Journal

CASH DISBURSEMENTS JOURNAL — Page 64

Date		Cheque Number	Payee	Cash Cr.	Accounts Payable Dr.	Selling and Adminis- trative Expense Dr.	Other Dr.	Account Title
9	4	246	G. Winkle	80.00		80.00		
9	7	247	Stephens Wholesale	163.00	163.00			
9	16	248	Harris Insurance	96.00			96.00	Prepaid Insurance
9	22	249	City of Norwich	62.00	62.00			
9	28	250	Burkett Supply	105.00		105.00		
				506.00	225.00	185.00	96.00	

Ledgers

A group of accounts arranged in orderly fashion is known as a *ledger*. The account is the unit of classification within the ledger for accumulating information. There are few essential requirements for the form of a ledger account. Space should be provided for the following data: account title; date of transaction; debit, credit and balance amounts; and a reference to trace the posting to its source in a journal. Space for other explanatory data may sometimes be useful. The standard ledger form presented in Exhibit 3.15 provides space for an explanation of each entry. An alternative T-account ledger form presents all debit entries on the left half of the page and credit entries on

Exhibit 3.15
Ledger Form

CASH

Date		Explanation	Ref.	Dr.	Cr.	Bal.
9	1	Balance		634.00		634.00
9	30	Cash Receipts Journal	46	995.00		1,629.00
9	30	Cash Disbursements Journal	64		506.00	1,123.00

the right half. The T-account form is frequently used for class presentation but seldom found in practice.

Note that the debit to the Cash account in the ledger is equal to the total cash receipts for September taken from the Cash Receipts Journal in Exhibit 3.13. Likewise, the credit to the Cash account is equal to the total cash disbursements for September listed in the Cash Disbursements Journal. The reference (Ref.) is to the appropriate page in these two specialized journals.

All firms maintain a general ledger. There is usually one ledger sheet for each balance sheet and income statement account. Some firms also maintain subsidiary ledgers. Subsidiary ledgers contain a listing of individual items that comprise the total in a general ledger account. A subsidiary accounts receivable ledger would contain a listing of the individual customers' accounts and amounts due. The sum of the amounts in the subsidiary ledger should equal the total in the general ledger account. The amounts shown in the two ledgers are reconciled periodically and any differences are investigated and corrected. When such a system of internal checks between the general ledger and subsidiary ledgers is used, the general ledger accounts are referred to as "controlling accounts." Exhibit 3.16 lists some common controlling accounts. Note that the subsidiary record is not always a group of ledger accounts in the standard ledger form. It may be a group of specially designed forms.

Exhibit 3.16
Examples of Controlling Accounts

General Ledger Controlling Account	Type of Subsidiary Record
Accounts Receivable	Individual customers' ledger accounts, or a file of uncollected sales invoices.
Accounts Payable	Individual ledger accounts, or a file of unpaid purchase invoices.
Common Stock	A record of the share certificates and number of shares held by each shareholder.
Notes Receivable	A file of uncollected notes receivable, or a "register" or book in which the notes are listed.
Raw Material Inventory	Separate record card for each item in inventory used in manufacturing.
Equipment	Separate record card for each item of equipment. This is often known as a plant ledger.
Land	Separate record cards showing description and cost of each parcel of land owned.

Micros in Accounting

*T*he computing and processing capabilities of a microcomputer approach those of the largest mainframe of only 20 years ago. Ever smaller, faster, cheaper, and easier to use, the microcomputer has enjoyed spectacular sales growth. Microcomputer sales in North America are now running over two million units per year. And the business market—as opposed to the home or hobbyist market—is now accounting for the lion's share of sales.

The small business is an obviously large market. Long closed out from the advantages of computer processing by prohibitive cost and the need for specially trained personnel, an increasing number of small businesses now find it feasible to use microcomputers to process their basic accounting transactions, to provide ready access to necessary operating data, and to handle correspondence.

But this use—essential as it is—is only the tip of the iceberg. Microcomputers expand the options available to businesses of all sizes. Using microcomputers, management can arrange data-processing facilities with much less concern for hardware costs. A micro might be used to automate activities that for reasons of cost or confidentiality are not suitable for processing on the company's mainframe. Typical business applications include the following:

(1) Forecasting, modelling, and financial statement consolidation are simplified by a microcomputer program known as an electronic spreadsheet. Once a model of relationships among a specific set of data has been established, an electronic spreadsheet program will automatically update all of the items affected by a change in one or more components. Some simple examples include the effect on the bottom line if sales double, if a division is sold, or if a union contract is settled at various possible levels.

(2) Data bases may be created for the use of individual executives or departments. Once a database file has been created in a common format, the information can be retrieved, summarized, sorted, rearranged, or used to prepare special purpose reports. The publications department might use a microcomputer to keep its mailing list current. Personnel data, meeting calendars, information on contracts with potential customers, tickler files, almost any type of data an individual or department needs to file and find for later use could become the subject of a microcomputer application. Applications that may not be cost-effective on the

company's mainframe computer might well be practicable on a micro.

(3) Graphics software available for microcomputers can reduce the time and cost associated with preparing illustrative charts for many types of presentations. The graphics capabilities of microcomputers are easily seen in the games run on home computers.

(4) Security portfolio analysis, trend analysis, and plotting are possible with specialized programs. Arrangements can be made to use the microcomputer as a terminal to access data bases of specialized information maintained by outsiders. Teleglobe and Informart are two of the major Canadian data bases. The Source and CompuServe are available in the United States. Prestel can be accessed in the United Kingdom, and so on.

Not so long ago corporate electronic data processing was highly centralized. The high cost of the computer carried with it the need to allocate service facilities principally to priority tasks. Relatively inexpensive machines with enough processing power were simply not available. That has changed—less expensive computers have put computer power into the hands of many individuals. The power of the computer is being dispersed throughout the business organization.

Microcomputers—ever smaller and less expensive machines—are accelerating this already widespread trend. Microcomputers will not replace the mainframe computer for large-scale applications, but microcomputers are becoming so inexpensive that it is quite reasonable to automate additional activities. Distributed data processing—the use of several different computers (and now including microcomputers) in different locations all connected by transmission facilities—is becoming more and more common.

From *Microcomputers: Their Use and Misuse in Your Business*, Price Waterhouse, 1983, pages 1–2.

Appendix 3.2
Preparation of a Work Sheet

To facilitate the preparation of the income statement and balance sheet at the end of an accounting period, a work sheet is often used. Exhibit 3.17 presents an example of a work sheet. This work sheet contains pairs of debit and credit columns for: — *ie AccPac.*

1. Unadjusted trial balance   *Horiz*
2. Adjusting entries
3. Adjusted trial balance

4. Income statement   *Vertical.*
5. Balance sheet

All of the required procedures at the end of an accounting period can be conveniently summarized in the work sheet, facilitating the preparation of the financial statements. A work sheet does not eliminate any of the usual end-of-period procedures. Adjusting and closing entries must still be made, entered in the general journal, and posted to the appropriate general ledger accounts. The work sheet is simply a mechanism for aggregating all of the data from these end-of-period procedures and organizing it in a useful form for preparing the financial statements.

Illustration of Work Sheet Preparation

The data presented in the chapter for Stephen's Shoe Store, Inc. are used to illustrate the preparation of a work sheet.

Unadjusted Trial Balance The first two columns contain the account balances taken from the general ledger at the end of the period before adjusting entries have been made. The debit and credit columns are summed to ensure that the trial balance is in balance.

Adjusting Entries The adjusting entries made at the end of the accounting period are entered in the next two columns. Note that the debits and credits for each entry are cross-referenced in the adjusting entries columns. The numbers used for cross-referencing in this case refer to the numbered journal entries in the chapter. Letters are often used as cross-references instead of numbers to avoid the possibility of confusing the amount of the adjusting entry with its cross-reference.

Adjusted Trial Balance The amounts in the adjusted trial balance columns are the sum or net amounts for each account in the first four columns. Adjusted trial balance columns are not essential in a work sheet, but they do facilitate the completion of the income statement and balance sheet columns.

Income Statement The amount in each income statement account in the adjusted trial balance is extended to the appropriate debit or credit column in the income statement section of the work sheet. A subtotal of the total debits (expenses) and the total credits (revenues) is then calculated. The difference between these two subtotals is net income or net loss for the period. For Stephen's Shoe Store, revenues exceed expenses by $43,620. This amount is entered in the debit column in the income statement section to equate the two income statement columns. The amount is also entered in the credit column in the balance sheet section. The placement of the net income amount in these two columns is analogous to the entry to close revenue and

Exhibit 3.17
STEPHEN'S SHOE STORE, INC.
Work Sheet
Year Ended December 31, Year 4

Accounts	Unadjusted Trial Balance Debit	Unadjusted Trial Balance Credit	Adjusting Entries Debit	Adjusting Entries Credit	Adjusted Trial Balance Debit	Adjusted Trial Balance Credit	Income Statement Debit	Income Statement Credit	Balance Sheet Debit	Balance Sheet Credit
Cash (A)	$ 191,100				$ 191,100				$ 191,100	
Accounts Receivable (A)	128,000				128,000				128,000	
Notes Receivable (A)	10,000				10,000				10,000	
Interest Receivable (A)			$ 150 (13)		150				150	
Merchandise Inventory (A)	140,000				140,000				140,000	
Prepaid Insurance (A)	1,500			$ 500 (15)	1,000				1,000	
Land (A)	100,000				100,000				100,000	
Building and Equipment (A)	525,000				525,000				525,000	
Accumulated Depreciation (XA)		$ 85,000		30,000 (16)		$ 115,000				$ 115,000
Accounts Payable (L)		220,000				220,000				220,000
Salaries Payable (L)				14,000 (14)		14,000				14,000
Dividends Payable (L)		15,000				15,000				15,000
Income Tax Payable (L)				29,080 (18)		29,080				29,080
Advances from Tenants (L)		600	50 (17)			550				550
Bonds Payable (L)		100,000				100,000				100,000
Common Stock (SE)		250,000				250,000				250,000
Contributed Surplus (SE)		200,000				200,000				200,000
Retained Earnings (SE)		108,000				108,000				108,000
Sales Revenue (SE)		625,000				625,000		$625,000		
Interest Revenue (SE)				150 (13)		150		150		
Rent Revenue (SE)				50 (17)		50		50		
Cost of Goods Sold (SE)	390,000				390,000		$390,000			
Salaries Expense (SE)	110,000		14,000 (14)		124,000		124,000			
Interest Expense (SE)	8,000				8,000		8,000			
Insurance Expense (SE)			500 (15)		500		500			
Depreciation Expense (SE)			30,000 (16)		30,000		30,000			
Income Tax Expense (SE)			29,080 (18)		29,080		29,080			
Subtotals							581,580		1,095,250	
Net income for the year							43,620			43,620
Totals	$1,603,600	$1,603,600	$73,780	$73,780	$1,676,830	$1,676,830	$625,200	$625,200	$1,095,250	$1,095,250

expense accounts to retained earnings. The credit in the balance sheet column is to
"net income for the year" instead of retained earnings. Retained earnings at the
end of the year must be calculated from the work sheet ($151,620 = $108,000 +
$43,620).

Balance Sheet The final step is to extend the amounts for each balance sheet account
from the adjusted trial balance to the appropriate debit and credit columns in the
balance sheet section of the work sheet. An equality between the debit and credit
columns serves as a check on the work sheet preparation procedures.

Alternative Work Sheet Formats

The particular columns used in a work sheet depend on a firm's accounting system
and the financial statements and schedules to be prepared. Two alternative work sheet
formats are discussed briefly below.

Combined Income and Retained Earnings Columns Some firms prepare a combined statement of income and retained earnings. The seventh and eighth columns in
the work sheet in Exhibit 3.17 can be altered to include information for both of these
statements. Exhibit 3.18 contains a partial work sheet to illustrate the procedure.
Dividends declared and paid during Year 4 were $15,000. For purposes of this
illustration, it is assumed that a Dividends Declared account was debited when the
dividend was declared instead of Retained Earnings. Thus, the balance in the Retained
Earnings account on the trial balance at the end of Year 4 is its balance as of January
1, Year 4.

Exhibit 3.18
STEPHEN'S SHOE STORE, INC.
Partial Work Sheet
Year Ended December 31, Year 4

Account	Income and Retained Earnings		Balance Sheet	
	Debit	Credit	Debit	Credit
Sales Revenue (OE)		$625,000		
Interest Revenue (OE)		150		
Rent Revenue (OE)		50		
Cost of Goods Sold (OE)	$390,000			
Salaries Expense (OE)	124,000			
Interest Expense (OE)	8,000			
Insurance Expense (OE)	500			
Depreciation Expense (OE)	30,000			
Income Tax Expense (OE)	29,080			
Subtotal	$581,580	$625,200		
Net Income for the Year	43,620			
Total	$625,200	$625,200		
Retained Earnings (beginning of year) .		123,000		
Net Income for the Year		43,620		
Dividends Declared	15,000			
Subtotal	$640,200	$791,820		
Retained Earnings (end of year)	151,620			$151,620
Total	$791,820	$791,820		

The revenues and expenses are extended from the adjusted trial balance columns to the income and retained earnings statement columns in Exhibit 3.18 precisely the same as was done in Exhibit 3.17. The difference between the subtotals of the two columns of $43,620 is net income for the year. This amount is again entered in the debit column to equate the two columns. Instead of being entered as a credit in the balance sheet columns, as was done in Exhibit 3.17, the amount is entered as a credit in the income and retained earnings columns. The retained earnings amount on the adjusted trial balance, assuming dividend declarations are debited to a Dividends Declared account, is the balance on January 1, Year 4, of $123,000. This amount is entered in the credit column. The dividends declared are entered in the debit column. A second subtotal is now taken. The difference between the column totals of $151,620 is the balance in the retained earnings at the end of the year. This amount is entered in the debit column of the income and retained earnings statement section to equate the two columns. It is also entered in the credit column in the balance sheet section. The principal difference between the work sheets in Exhibits 3.17 and 3.18 is that the ending balance in Retained Earnings is calculated explicitly in Exhibit 3.18, but must be calculated separately in Exhibit 3.17.

Merchandise Accounts in the Work Sheet The illustration in the text implicitly assumed that Stephen's Shoe Store used a perpetual inventory system. Purchases of inventory items were debited to the Merchandise Inventory account. At the time of sale, the cost of the merchandise sold was credited to the Merchandise Inventory account and debited to Cost of Goods Sold. The balance in the Merchandise Inventory account consequently is constantly updated and should show the inventory on hand at all times. Chapter 8 points out that many firms use a periodic inventory system. In a periodic system, purchases of merchandise inventory are usually debited to a Purchases account. Freight-in, returns, discounts, and allowances on items purchased are debited or credited as appropriate to separate accounts. Under a periodic system, the balance in the Merchandise Inventory account at any time *during* an accounting period is its balance as of the beginning of the period. No entry is made in the Merchandise Inventory account as items are either purchased or sold. At periodic intervals, usually quarterly or annually, inventory is counted to determine the amount of inventory still on hand. Any difference between the beginning inventory plus net purchases and the amount still on hand (ending inventory) is assumed to have been sold.

To illustrate the preparation of a work sheet when a periodic inventory system is in use, assume that the following data are obtained for Stephen's Shoe Store for Year 4:

Beginning Inventory, January 1, Year 4		$175,000
Plus: Purchases	$375,000	
Freight-in	10,000	
Less: Returns	(5,000)	
Discounts	(20,000)	
Allowances	(5,000)	
Net Purchases		$355,000
Less: Ending Inventory, December 31, Year 4		(140,000)
Cost of Goods Sold		$390,000

Exhibit 3.19 presents a partial work sheet for Stephen's Shoe Store assuming that a periodic inventory system is used. The amount in the Merchandise Inventory account in the adjusted trial balance at the beginning of the year is entered in the debit column in the income statement section of the work sheet. The amounts in the Purchases, Freight-in, Returns, Discounts, and Allowances accounts are likewise entered in their appropriate debit or credit columns. The amount in the ending inventory of $140,000, as determined by physical count, is entered in the credit column in the income statement section and the debit column in the balance sheet section. The total of the amounts in the debit column in the income statement section of $560,000 (= $175,000 + $375,000 + $10,000) exceeds the total of the amounts in the credit column of $170,000 (= $140,000 + $5,000 + $20,000 + $5,000) by $390,000. This is the Cost of Goods Sold for the period. The work sheet will not show a separate line for Cost of Goods Sold. Its amount is calculated implicitly when the income statement columns are summed.

Exhibit 3.19
STEPHEN'S SHOE STORE, INC.
Partial Work Sheet
Year Ended December 31, Year 4

Account	Adjusted Trial Balance		Income Statement		Balance Sheet	
	Debit	Credit	Debit	Credit	Debit	Credit
Merchandise Inventory ..	$175,000		$175,000	$140,000	$140,000	
Purchases	375,000		375,000			
Freight-in	10,000		10,000			
Returns		$ 5,000		5,000		
Discounts		20,000		20,000		
Allowances		5,000		5,000		

Problem 1 for Self-Study

Harris Equipment Corporation was organized on January 2, Year 2, with the issuance of 10,000 shares of $10 par value common stock for $15 cash per share. The company maintains a perpetual inventory system. The following transactions occurred during Year 2:

(1) January 2, Year 2: The firm acquired a building costing $80,000 and equipment costing $40,000. It paid cash in the amount of $60,000 and assumed a ten percent mortgage for the balance of the purchase price. Interest is payable on January 2 of each year, beginning one year after the purchase.

(2) January 2, Year 2: The firm bought a two-year fire insurance policy on the building and equipment. It paid the insurance premium of $1,200 for the two-year period in advance (debit an asset account).

(3) During Year 2: Merchandise acquired on account totaled $320,000. Payments to these suppliers during Year 2 totaled $270,000.

(4) During Year 2: Sales of merchandise totaled $510,000, of which $80,000 was for cash and $430,000 was on account. The cost of merchandise sold was $180,000. Collections from credit customers during Year 2 totaled $360,000.

(5) During Year 2: Salaries paid to employees totaled $80,000.

(6) During Year 2: Utility bills totaling $1,300 were paid.

(7) November 1, Year 2: A customer advanced $600 toward the purchase price of merchandise to be delivered during January, Year 3.

(8) November 1, Year 2: A customer gave a $1,000, nine percent, 90-day note to settle an open account receivable.

(9) December 1, Year 2: The firm rented out a portion of the building for a three-month period. It received the rent for the period of $900 in advance (credit a revenue account).

Give the journal entries to record these nine transactions *during Year 2*. (Adjusting entries at the end of Year 2 are analyzed in the next self-study problem.) Omit explanations for the journal entries.

Suggested Solution

(1) Jan. 2, Year 2	Building	$ 80,000	
	Equipment	40,000	
	Cash		$ 60,000
	Mortgage Payable		60,000
(2) Jan. 2, Year 2	Prepaid Insurance	1,200	
	Cash		1,200
(3) During Year 2	Merchandise Inventory	320,000	
	Accounts Payable		320,000
During Year 2	Accounts Payable	270,000	
	Cash		270,000
(4) During Year 2	Cash	80,000	
	Accounts Receivable	430,000	
	Sales Revenue		510,000
	Cost of Sales	180,000	
	Merchandise Inventory		180,000
During Year 2	Cash	360,000	
	Accounts Receivable		360,000
(5) During Year 2	Salary Expense	80,000	
	Cash		80,000
(6) During Year 2	Utilities Expense	1,300	
	Cash		1,300
(7) Nov. 1, Year 2	Cash	600	
	Advances from Customers		600
(8) Nov. 1, Year 2	Note Receivable	1,000	
	Accounts Receivable		1,000
(9) Dec. 1, Year 2	Cash	900	
	Rent Revenue		900

Problem 2 for Self-Study

Refer to the data for Harris Equipment Corporation in the preceding self-study problem. Give the adjusting entries on December 31, Year 2, to reflect the following items. You may omit explanations to the journal entries.

(10) The building acquired on January 2, Year 2, has a 20-year estimated life and zero salvage value. The equipment has a seven-year estimated life and $5,000 salvage value. The straight-line depreciation method is used.

(11) Interest expense on the mortgage liability for Year 2 is recognized.

(12) Salaries earned by employees during the last three days of December total $800 and will be paid on January 4, Year 3.

(13) Interest revenue is recognized on the note receivable [see transaction **(8)** in the preceding self-study problem].

(14) An adjusting entry is made to record the proper amount of rent revenue for Year 2 [see transaction **(9)** in the preceding self-study problem].

(15) Dividends of $25,000 are declared. The dividend will be paid on January 15, Year 3 (debit Retained Earnings).

(16) Income tax expense is recorded as 40 percent of accounting income before income tax.

Suggested Solution

(10) Depreciation Expense	4,000	
Accumulated Depreciation		4,000
($80,000 − $0)/20 = 4,000.		
Depreciation Expense — Equipment	5,000	
Accumulated Depreciation — Equipment		5,000
($40,000 − $5,000)/7 = $5,000.		
(11) Interest Expense	6,000	
Interest Payable		6,000
$60,000 × .10 = $6,000.		
(12) Salary Expense	800	
Salaries Payable		800
(13) Interest Receivable	15	
Interest Revenue		15
$1,000 × .09 × 60/360.		
(14) Rent Revenue	600	
Advances from Tenants		600
(15) Retained Earnings	25,000	
Dividends Payable		25,000
(16) Income Tax Expense	93,286	
Income Tax Payable		93,286
.4 × [($510,000 + $900 − $600 + $15) − ($80,000		
+ $800 + $1,300 + $9,000 + $180,000 + $6,000)] = $93,286.		

Problem 3 for Self-Study

To achieve efficient recording of day-to-day cash receipts and disbursements relating to operations, a firm may credit *all* cash receipts to revenue accounts and debit *all* cash disbursements to expense accounts. The efficiency stems from treating all receipts in the same way and from treating all disbursements in the same way. As a result, lower-paid clerks can be employed to make the routine and repetitive entries for receipts and disbursements. In the day-to-day recording of transactions, the clerk need not be concerned with whether a specific cash transaction reflects settlement of a past accrual, a revenue or expense correctly assigned to the current period, or a prepayment relating to a future period. Higher-paid accountants need be employed only at the end of the period to analyze the existing account balances and to construct the adjusting entries required to correct them. This process results in temporarily incorrect balances in some balance sheet and income statement accounts *during* the accounting period.

Construct the adjusting entry required for each of the following scenarios.

   a. On September 1, Year 2, a tenant paid $24,000 rent for the one-year period starting at that time. The tenant debited the entire amount to Rent Expense and credited Cash. The tenant made no adjusting entries for rent between September 1 and December 31. Construct the adjusting entry to be made on December 31, Year 2, to recognize the proper balances in the Prepaid Rent and Rent Expense accounts.

   b. The tenant's books for December 31, Year 2, after adjusting entries, show a balance in the Prepaid Rent account of $16,000. This amount represents rent for the period January 1 through August 31, Year 3. On September 1, Year 3, the tenant paid $30,000 for rent for the one-year period starting September 1, Year 3. The tenant debited this amount to Rent Expense and credited Cash, but made no adjusting entries for rent during Year 3. Construct the adjusting entry required on December 31, Year 3.

   c. The tenant's books for December 31, Year 3, after adjusting entries, show a balance in the Prepaid Rent account of $20,000. This amount represents rent for the period January 1 through August 31, Year 4. On September 1, Year 4, the tenant paid $18,000 for rent for the *six-month* period starting September 1, Year 4. The tenant debited this amount to Rent Expense and credited Cash, but made no adjusting entries during Year 4. Construct the adjusting entry required on December 31, Year 4.

   d. Whenever the firm makes payments for wages, it debits Wage Expense. At the start of April, the Wages Payable account had a balance of $5,000, representing wages earned but not paid during the last few days of March. During April, the firm paid $30,000 in wages, debiting the entire amount to Wage Expense. At the end of April, analysis of amounts earned since the last payday indicates that wages of $4,000 have been earned but not yet paid. Construct the required adjusting entry.

   e. A firm purchased an insurance policy providing one year's coverage from May 1, Year 1, and debited the entire amount to Insurance Expense. After the firm made adjusting entries, the balance sheet for December 31, Year 1, correctly showed Prepaid Insurance of $3,000. Construct the adjusting entry that must be made on January 31, Year 2, if the books are closed monthly and a balance sheet is to be prepared for January 31, Year 2.

   f. The record-keeping system for an apartment building instructs the bookkeeper always to credit rent revenue when a payment is received from tenants. At the beginning of Year 3, the liability account, Advances from Tenants, had a credit balance of $25,000 representing collections from tenants for rental services to be received during Year 3. During Year 3, collections from tenants of $250,000 were all debited to Cash and credited to Rent Revenue. No adjusting entries were made during Year 3. At the end of Year 3, analysis of the individual accounts indicates that of the amounts already collected, $30,000 represents collections for rental services to be provided to tenants during Year 4. Present the required adjusting entry.

g. When the firm acquired new equipment costing $10,000 on January 1, Year 1, the bookkeeper debited Depreciation Expense and credited Cash for $10,000, but made no further entries for this equipment during Year 1. The equipment has an expected service life of five years and an estimated salvage value of zero. Construct the adjusting entry required before a balance sheet for December 31, Year 1, can be prepared.

Suggested Solution

a. The Prepaid Rent account on the year-end balance sheet should represent eight months of prepayments. The rent per month is $2,000 (= $24,000/12), so the balance required in the Prepaid Rent account is $16,000 (= 8 × $2,000).

Prepaid Rent	$16,000	
Rent Expense		$16,000
To increase the balance in the Prepaid Rent account, reducing the amount in the Rent Expense account.		

b. The Prepaid Rent account on the balance sheet for the end of Year 3 should represent eight months of prepayments. The rent per month is $2,500 (= $30,000/12), so the required balance in the Prepaid Rent account is $20,000 (= 8 × $2,500). The balance in that account is already $16,000, so the adjusting entry must increase it by $4,000 (= $20,000 − 16,000).

Prepaid Rent	$4,000	
Rent Expense		$4,000
To increase the balance in the Prepaid Rent account, reducing the amount in the Rent Expense account.		

The Rent Expense account will have a balance at the end of Year 3 before closing entries of $26,000 (= $30,000 − $4,000). This amount comprises $16,000 (= $2,000 × 8) for rent from January through August and $10,000 (= $2,500 × 4) for rent from September through December.

c. The Prepaid Rent account on the balance sheet at the end of year 4 should represent two months of prepayments. The rent per month is $3,000 (= $18,000/6), so the required balance in the Prepaid Rent account is $6,000 (= 2 × $3,000). The balance in that account is $20,000, so the adjusting entry must reduce it by $14,000 (= $20,000 − $6,000).

Rent Expense..................................	$14,000	
Prepaid Rent		$14,000
To reduce the balance in the Prepaid Rent account, increasing the amount in the Rent Expense account.		

The Rent Expense account will have a balance at the end of Year 3 before closing entries of $32,000 (= $18,000 + $14,000). This amount comprises $20,000 (= $2,500 × 8) for rent from January through August and $12,000 (= $3,000 × 4) for rent from September through December.

d. The Wages Payable account should have a credit balance of $4,000 at the end of April, but it has a balance of $5,000 carried over from the end of March. The adjusting entry must reduce the balance by $1,000, which requires a debit to the Wages Payable account.

Wages Payable	$1,000	
Wage Expense		$1,000
To reduce the balance in the Wages Payable account, reducing the amount in the Wage Expense account.		

e. The Prepaid Insurance account balance of $3,000 represents four months of coverage. Thus, the cost of insurance is $750 (= $3,000/4) per month. The adjusting entry for a single month is

| Insurance Expense .... | $750 | |
| Prepaid Insurance .... | | $750 |

f. The Advances from Tenants account has a balance of $25,000 carried over from the start of the year. At the end of Year 3, it should have a balance of $30,000. Thus, the adjusting entry must increase the balance by $5,000, which requires a credit to the liability account.

Rent Revenue	$5,000	
Advances from Tenants		$5,000
To increase the balance in the Advances from Tenants account, reducing the amount in the Rent Revenue account.		

g. The Depreciation Expense for the year should be $2,000 (= $10,000/5). The balance in the Accumulated Depreciation account should also be $2,000 and, thus, the Depreciation Expense account must be reduced (credited) by $8,000 (= $10,000 − $2,000). The adjusting entry not only reduces recorded Depreciation Expense, but sets up the asset account and its accumulated depreciation contra account.

Equipment	$10,000	
Accumulated Depreciation		$2,000
Depreciation Expense		8,000
To reduce Depreciation Expense, setting up the asset and its contra account		

Questions, Exercises, Problems and Cases

Questions

1. Review the meaning of the following concepts or terms discussed in this chapter.

a. Revenue
b. Expense
c. Net income or net loss
d. Accounting period
e. Natural business year or fiscal period
f. Cash basis of accounting
g. Accrual basis of accounting
h. Unexpired costs
i. Expired costs
j. Matching convention

k. Product cost
l. Period expense
m. Expense versus dividend
n. Temporary and permanent accounts
o. General journal entries
p. Adjusting entries
q. Closing entries
r. Unadjusted trial balance
s. Adjusted trial balance
t. Contra account

2. What factors would a firm likely consider in its decision to use the calendar year versus a fiscal (natural business) year as its accounting period?

3. Which of the following types of businesses are likely to have a natural business year different from the calendar year?

a. A ski resort in British Columbia
b. A professional basketball team
c. A grocery store

4. Distinguish between a revenue and a cash receipt. Under what conditions will they be the same?

5. Distinguish between an expense and a cash expenditure. Under what conditions will they be the same?

6. "Cash flows determine the *amount* of revenue and expense but not the *timing* of their recognition." Explain.

7. "Accrual accounting focuses on the use, rather than the financing, of assets." Explain.

8. "Depreciation on equipment may be a product cost or a period expense depending on the type of equipment." Explain.

9. "Revenue and expense accounts are useful accounting devices, but they could be dispensed with." What is an alternative to using them?

10. Why are revenue and expense accounts closed at the end of each accounting period?

11. Before the books have been closed for an accounting period, what types of accounts will have nonzero balances? After the books have been closed, what types of accounts will have nonzero balances?

12. If each transaction occurring during an accounting period has been recorded properly, why is there a need for adjusting entries at the end of the period?

13. What is the purpose of using contra accounts? What is the alternative to using them?

Exercises

14. *Relation between cash flows and revenues and expenses.* Under the accrual basis of accounting, cash receipts and disbursements may precede, coincide with, or follow the period in which revenues and expenses are recognized. Give an example of each of the following:

    a. A cash receipt that precedes the period in which revenue is recognized.

    b. A cash receipt that coincides with the period in which revenue is recognized.

    c. A cash receipt that follows the period in which revenue is recognized.

    d. A cash disbursement that precedes the period in which expense is recognized.

    e. A cash disbursement that coincides with the period in which expense is recognized.

    f. A cash disbursement that follows the period in which expense is recognized.

15. *Revenue recognition.* Assume that the accrual basis of accounting is used and that revenue is recognized at the time the goods are sold or services are rendered. How much revenue is recognized during the month of May in each of the following transactions?

    a. Collection of cash from customers during May for merchandise sold and delivered in April, $8,200.

    b. Sales of merchandise during May for cash, $9,600.

    c. Sales of merchandise during May to customers to be collected in June, $2,400.

    d. A store building is rented to a toy shop for $800 a month, effective May 1. A cheque for $1,600 for two months' rent is received on May 1.

    e. Data in part (**d**) except that collection is received from the tenant in June.

16. *Revenue recognition.* Assume that the accrual basis of accounting is used and that revenue is recognized at the time goods are sold or services are rendered. Indicate the amount of revenue recognized in each of the months of April, May, and June relating to the following cash receipts during May.

    a. $4,600 collected from customers for merchandise sold and delivered in April.

    b. $8,900 collected from customers for merchandise sold and delivered in May.

    c. $1,800 collected from customers for merchandise to be delivered in June.

    d. $3,600 collected from subscribers for subscription fees to magazines for the one-year period beginning April 1.

    e. Same as part (**d**) except that the subscription period begins May 1.

    f. Same as part (**d**) except that the subscription period begins June 1.

17. *Revenue recognition.* Indicate the amount of revenue recognized, if any, from each of the following related events, assuming that the accrual basis of accounting is used.

    a. A firm receives purchase orders from regular customers for $8,400 of merchandise. A two percent discount is allowed, and generally taken, for prompt payment.

    b. The customers' orders are filled and shipped by way of the company's trucking division.

   c. The firm sends invoices totaling $8,400 to the customers.

   d. The merchandise is received by customers in the correct quantities and according to specifications.

   e. The firm receives cheques in the amount of $8,232 (= .98 × $8,400) from customers in payment of the merchandise.

   f. Upon reinspection, several days later, merchandise with a gross invoice price of $600 is found to be defective by customers and returned for appropriate credit.

18. *Revenue recognition.* Indicate which of the following transactions or events immediately gives rise to the recognition of revenue under the accrual basis of accounting.

   a. The receipt of an order from a customer for merchandise.

   b. The shipment of goods that have been paid for in advance.

   c. The issue of additional common shares.

   d. The completion of a batch of men's suits by a clothing factory.

   e. The sale of tickets by a major league baseball team for a game in two weeks.

   f. Same as part **(e)** except that sale was made by Ticketron, a ticket agent.

   g. The interest earned on a savings account between interest dates.

   h. A collection of cash from accounts receivable debtors.

   i. The rendering of accounting services to a customer on account.

19. *Expense recognition.* Give the amount of expense recognized, if any, from each of the following related events, assuming that the accrual basis of accounting is used.

   a. The purchasing department notifies the stockroom that the supply of 1 cm plywood has reached the minimum point and should be reordered.

   b. The firm sends a purchase order to Central Lumber Co. Ltd. for $10,000 of the material.

   c. The firm receives an acknowledgement of the order. It indicates that delivery will be made in 15 days but that the price has been raised to $10,200.

   d. The shipment of plywood arrives and is checked by the receiving department. The correct quantity has been delivered.

   e. The purchase invoice arrives. The amount of $10,200 is subject to a two percent discount if paid within ten days. Cash discounts are treated as a reduction in the acquisition cost of inventory.

   f. Upon reinspection, the firm finds plywood with a gross invoice price of $200 to be defective and returns it to the supplier.

   g. The balance of the amount due the Central Lumber Co. Ltd. is paid in time to obtain the discount.

   h. The firm sells the plywood to customers for $12,000.

20. *Expense recognition.* Assume that the accrual basis of accounting is used and that revenue is recognized at the time goods are sold or services are rendered. Indicate the amount of expense recognized during March, if any, from each of the following transactions or events.

   a. An insurance premium of $1,800 is paid on March 1 for one year's coverage beginning on that date.

   b. On April 3, a utilities bill totaling $460 for services during March is received.

    c. $700 worth of supplies was purchased on account during March. $500 of these purchases on account was paid in March and the remainder was paid in April. On March 1, supplies were on hand that cost $300. At March 31, supplies that cost $350 were still on hand.

    d. Data of (c), except that $200 of supplies was on hand at March 1.

    e. Property taxes of $4,800 on an office building for the year were paid in January.

    f. An advance of $250 on the April salary is paid to an employee on March 29.

21. *Expense recognition.* Assume that the accrual basis of accounting is used and that revenue is recognized at the time goods are sold or services are rendered. Indicate the amount of expense recognized in each of the months of April, May, and June relating to the following cash expenditures during May.

    a. $1,900 for advertising that appeared on television programs during April.

    b. $3,200 for sales commissions on sales made during May.

    c. $500 for rent on delivery equipment for the month of June.

    d. $600 for an insurance premium for coverage from May 1 until October 30.

    e. $800 as a deposit on equipment to be delivered during June.

    f. $1,200 for property taxes on an office building for the current calendar year.

22. *Income recognition.* Feltham Limited acquired used machine tools costing $75,000 from various sources. These machine tools were then sold to Mock Corporation. Delivery costs paid by Feltham Limited totaled $4,500. Mock Corporation had agreed to pay $100,000 cash for these tools. Finding itself short of cash, however, Mock Corporation offered some of its bonds to Feltham Limited. The bonds have a face value of $110,000 and mature in five years. The bonds promise eight percent interest per year. At the time the offer was made, the bonds could have been sold in public bond markets for $98,000.

Feltham Limited accepted the offer and held the bonds for three years. During the three years, it received interest payments of $8,800 per year, or $26,400 total. At the end of the third year, Feltham Limited sold the bonds for $95,000.

    a. What profit or loss did Feltham Limited recognize at the time of sale of machine tools to Mock Corporation?

    b. What profit or loss would Feltham Limited have recognized at the time of the sale of machine tools if it had sold the bonds for $98,000 immediately upon receiving them?

    c. What profit or loss would Feltham Limited have recognized at the time of the sale of machine tools if it had held the bonds to maturity, receiving $8,800 each year for another five years and $110,000 at the time the bonds matured?

23. *Identifying missing half of journal entries.* In the business world, many transactions are routine and repetitive. Because accounting records business transactions, many accounting entries are also routine and repetitive. Knowing one-half of an entry in the double-entry recording system often permits a reasoned guess about the other half. The items below give the account name for one-half of an entry. Indicate your best guess as to the nature of the transaction being recorded and the name of the account of the *routine* other half of the entry. Also indicate whether the other account is increased or decreased by the transaction.

    a. Debit: Cost of Goods Sold.

    b. Debit: Accounts Receivable.

   c. Credit: Accounts Receivable.
   d. Debit: Accounts Payable.
   e. Credit: Accounts Payable.
   f. Credit: Accumulated Depreciation.
   g. Debit: Retained Earnings.
   h. Credit: Prepaid Insurance.
   i. Debit: Property Taxes Payable.
   j. Debit: Merchandise Inventory.

24. *Asset versus expense recognition.* Give the journal entry that should be made upon the receipt of each of the following invoices by the South Appliance Company, assuming that no previous entry has been made.

(1) From Western Electric Supply Company, $385, for repair parts purchased.
(2) From Touch & Rose, chartered accountants, $800, for services in filing income tax returns.
(3) From the General Electric Company, $12,365, for refrigerators purchased.
(4) From the White Stationery Company, $250 for office supplies purchased.
(5) From the Showy Sign Company, $540, for a neon sign acquired.
(6) From Schutheis and Schutheis, attorneys, $1,000, for legal services in changing from the corporate to the partnership form of organization.
(7) From the Bell Telephone Company, $65, for telephone service for next month.
(8) From the Madison Avenue Garage, $43, for gasoline and oil used by the delivery truck.
(9) From the Municipal Electric Department, $105, for electricity used for lighting last month.

25. *Journal entries for notes receivable and notes payable.* The General Supply Co. Inc. received a $10,000, three-month, nine-percent promissory note, dated December 1, Year 6, from Widen Stores to apply on its open accounts receivable. The fiscal year end of both companies is December 31.
   a. Present journal entries for the General Supply Co. Inc. from December 1, Year 6, through collection at maturity. The books are closed quarterly. Include the closing entry for interest.
   b. Present journal entries for Widen Stores from December 1, Year 6, through payment at maturity. Include the closing entry for interest.

26. *Journal entries for notes payable.* Selected transactions of Burlson Limited are described below. Present dated journal entries for these transactions and adjusting entries at the end of each month from January 15, Year 2, through July 1, Year 2. Assume that only the notes indicated were outstanding during this period. The accounting period is one month.

(1) The company issued a $6,000, two-month, ten percent promissory note on January 15, Year 2, in lieu of payment on an account due that date to the Grey Wholesale Company.
(2) The note in (1) and interest were paid at maturity.
(3) The company issued a $2,000, three-month, nine percent promissory note to the Grey Wholesale Company on the date of purchase of merchandise, April 1, Year 2.

(4) The note in **(3)** and interest were paid at maturity.

27. *Journal entries for office supply inventories.* On January 1, Year 4, the Office Supplies Inventory account of the Harris Company had a balance of $4,200. During the ensuing quarter, supplies were acquired on account in the amount of $9,000. On March 31, Year 4, the inventory was taken and calculated to amount to $2,500.

Present journal entries to record the above acquisition and adjustments at the end of March in accordance with each of the following sets of instructions, which might be established in an accounting systems manual:

    a. An expense account is to be debited at the time supplies are acquired.

    b. An asset account is to be debited at the time supplies are acquired.

28. *Journal entries for rental receipts and payments.* The Regina Realty Co. Ltd. rents office space to Maddox Consultants at the rate of $600 per month. Collections have been made for rental through April 30, Year 3. The following transactions occurred on the dates indicated:

(1) May 1, Year 3: Collection, $600.
(2) June 1, Year 3: Collection, $1,200.
(3) August 1, Year 3: Collection, $1,800.

Present journal entries for the above transactions and for adjusting entries from May 1 to August 31, inclusive, as they relate to both companies, assuming that each company adjusts its books monthly.

29. *Using accumulated depreciation to estimate asset age.*

    a. Machine A costs $10,000, has accumulated depreciation of $4,000 as of year-end, and is being depreciated on a straight-line basis over ten years with an estimated salvage value of zero. How long ago was machine A acquired?

    b. Machine B has accumulated depreciation (straight-line basis) of $6,000 at year-end. The depreciation charge for the year is $2,000. The estimated salvage value of the machine at the end of its useful life is $1,000. How long ago was machine B acquired?

30. *Effect of recording errors on financial statements.* In recording transactions of Rogow Corporation during Year 7, the following errors were made:

(1) An expenditure of $2,000 to acquire a tract of land was debited to Administrative Expenses.

(2) Cash collections during Year 7 of $1,500 relating to sales made during Year 6 were credited to Sales Revenue of Year 7.

(3) An expenditure of $1,200 for insurance coverage from October 1, Year 7 to September 30, Year 8, was debited to Administrative Expenses on October 1, Year 7.

(4) Cash collections during Year 7 of $1,000 for goods to be delivered during Year 8 were credited to Sales Revenue of Year 7.

Indicate the cumulative effect (exclusive of income tax implications) of these errors on the following items in the financial statements prepared on December 31, Year 7.

    a. Current assets

    b. Property, plant, and equipment

    c. Current liabilities

   d. Sales revenue

   e. Administrative expenses

   f. Net income

   g. Retained earnings

31. *Effect of recording errors on financial statements.* In recording the adjusting entries of the Hammond Sales Company, Inc., at the end of Year 7, the following adjustments were omitted:

(1) Depreciation on the delivery truck of $3,000.

(2) Insurance expired on the delivery truck of $600.

(3) Interest accrued on notes payable of $150.

(4) Interest accrued on notes receivable of $330.

Indicate the cumulative effect (exclusive of income tax implications) of these omissions on the following items in the financial statements prepared on December 31, Year 7.

   a. Current assets

   b. Property, plant, and equipment

   c. Current liabilities

   d. Selling and administrative expenses

   e. Net income

   f. Retained earnings

32. *Effect of recording errors on financial statements.* Using the notation O/S (overstated), U/S (understated), and NO (no effect), indicate the effects on assets, liabilities, and shareholders' equity as of December 31, Year 5, of the following independent errors or omissions. Ignore income tax implications.

   a. An expenditure of $1,200 for insurance coverage for the one-year period beginning September 1, Year 5, was debited to Administrative Expenses.

   b. Sales commissions earned and paid during December Year 5 were debited to Interest Expense.

   c. Depreciation on delivery equipment for Year 5 of $1,500 was not recorded.

   d. A cheque for $900 was received from a customer during December Year 5 for merchandise to be delivered during January Year 6. Sales Revenue was credited when the cash was received.

   e. Interest accrued on Notes Payable of $400 as of December 31, Year 5, was not recorded.

   f. Interest accrued on Notes Receivable of $560 as of December 31, Year 5, was recorded as $650.

33. *Effect of recording errors on financial statements.* Using the notation O/S (overstated), U/S (understated), and NO (no effect), indicate the effects on assets, liabilities, and shareholders' equity as of December 31, Year 3, of the following independent errors or omissions. Ignore income tax implications.

   a. An expenditure of $600 made on December 1, Year 3, for six months' rent on an automobile was debited to Prepaid Rent. No adjusting entry was made on December 31, Year 3.

b. A microcomputer acquired on July 1, Year 3, for $6,000 was debited to Administrative Expenses. The microcomputer has an expected useful life of three years and zero estimated salvage value.

c. The company rented out excess office space for the six-month period beginning January 1, Year 3. A rental cheque for this period of $600 was received on December 26, *Year 2*, and correctly credited to Rental Fees Received in Advance. No further journal entries were made relating to this rental during Year 3.

d. Interest accrued on Notes Receivable of $500 as of December 31, Year 3, was not recorded.

e. A cheque for $250 was received from a customer on December 31, Year 3, in settlement of an account receivable. No journal entries have been made to record this cheque.

f. An expenditure of $740 for travel on December 31, Year 3, was recorded as $470.

34. *Allocation of Cost.* How should the cost of the following assets be allocated over their useful lives?

a. A building with an estimated useful life of 30 years.

b. A road leading to a timber tract. The road would normally last for 14 years before extensive reconstruction would be necessary, but it is expected that the timber will all be cut in 5 years.

c. Rent prepaid for 2 years on a warehouse in Regina.

d. A truck with an estimated service life of 90,000 miles.

e. Rent prepaid for a year on a shop used for boat repairs at a summer resort. The shop is open only from June 1 to September 1.

f. An ore deposit owned by a mining company.

35. *Reconstructing accounting records.* Most of the financial records of the Rowland Novelty Company were removed by an employee who apparently took all the cash on hand from the store on October 31. From supplementary records, the following information is obtained:

(1) According to the bank, cash in bank was $5,730.

(2) Amounts payable to creditors were $4,720.

(3) Rowland's initial contribution to the business was $15,000, and the total shareholders' equity at the time of the theft was $17,500.

(4) Cost of merchandise on hand was $11,380.

(5) A 1-year fire insurance policy was purchased on September 1 for $900.

(6) Furniture and fixtures are rented from the Anderson Office Supply Company for $200 per month. The rental for October has not been paid.

(7) A note for $1,200 was given by a customer. Interest due at October 31 was $45.

(8) Payments due from other customers amounted to $1,915.

(9) Rowland purchased a licence from the city for $300 on July 1. The licence allows retail operations for 1 year.

a. Determine the probable cash shortage.

b. Prepare a well-organized balance sheet presenting the financial position immediately preceding the theft.

36. *Miscellaneous transactions of adjusting entries.* Prepare journal entries for each of the following sets of data.

   a. The company rents out excess office space at a rate of $3,000 per month, payable in advance at the beginning of each calendar quarter of the year. The rental payment for the first quarter was received 2 months late on March 1. Assume that the books are closed monthly. Present the collection entry on March 1 and the adjusting entry made at the end of each month.

   b. On March 16, a $20,000, 2-month, 9-percent note was received by the company in full payment of an open account receivable. Assume that the books are closed monthly. Give all journal entries relating to the note, from March 16 until payment at maturity on May 15.

   c. The balance in the Prepaid Insurance account on January 1, Year 4, was $600. On March 1, Year 4, the company renewed its only insurance policy for another 3 years, beginning on that date, by payment of $14,400. Assume that the books are closed quarterly. Present journal entries for the renewal and adjusting entries for Year 4.

   d. The Repair Parts Inventory account showed a balance of $3,000 on January 1. During January, parts costing $8,000 were purchased and charged to Repair Expense. An inventory of repair parts at the end of January revealed that parts costing $3,800 were on hand. Present the adjusting entry required at the end of January.

   e. An office machine was acquired on July 1, Year 6, at a cost of $100,000. It was estimated to have a 10-year life and a $20,000 residual value. Assume that the books are closed annually. Present the adjusting entries on December 31, Year 6, and December 31, Year 7.

   f. Property taxes for the calendar year are assessed on January 1 but are paid on April 1. The company's property taxes for Year 8 of $24,000 were paid as required. Assume that the books are closed quarterly. Give the journal entries relating to property taxes for Year 8.

Problems and Cases

37. *Cash versus accrual basis of accounting.* J. Thompson opened a hardware store on January 1, Year 5. Thompson invested $10,000 and borrowed $8,000 from a local bank. The loan plus interest is repayable on June 30, Year 5, with interest at the rate of nine percent per year.

   Thompson rented a building on January 1, and paid two months' rent in advance in the amount of $2,000. Property and liability insurance coverage for the year ending December 31, Year 5, was paid on January 1 in the amount of $1,200.

   Thompson purchased $28,000 of merchandise inventory on account on January 2 and paid $10,000 of this amount on January 25. The cost of merchandise on hand on January 31 was $15,000.

   During January, cash sales to customers totaled $20,000 and sales on account totaled $9,000. Of the sales on account, $2,000 had been collected as of January 31.

   Other costs incurred and paid in cash during January were as follows: utilities, $400; salaries, $650; taxes, $350.

   a. Prepare an income statement for January, assuming that Thompson uses the accrual basis of accounting with revenue recognized at the time goods are sold (delivered).

   b. Prepare an income statement for January, assuming that Thompson uses the cash basis of accounting.

   c. Which basis of accounting do you feel provides a better indication of the operating performance of the hardware store during January? Why?

38. *Cash versus accrual basis of accounting.* Management Consultants, Inc., opened a consulting business on July 1, Year 2. Roy Bean and Sarah Bower each contributed $7,000 cash for the firm's common shares. The corporation borrowed $8,000 from a local bank on August 1, Year 2. The loan plus interest is repayable on July 31, Year 3, with interest at the rate of nine percent per year.

Office space was rented on August 1, with two months' rent paid in advance. The remaining monthly rental fees of $900 per month were made on the first of each month, beginning October 1. Office equipment with a four-year life was purchased for cash on August 1 for $4,800.

Consulting services rendered for clients between August 1 and December 31, Year 2, were billed at $15,000. Of this amount, $9,000 was collected by year-end.

Other costs incurred and paid in cash by the end of the year were as follows: utilities, $450; salary of secretary, $7,500; supplies, $450. Unpaid bills at year-end are as follows: utilities, $80; salary of secretary, $900; supplies, $70. All supplies acquired were used. Income tax is payable at the rate of 40 percent of accounting income before income tax calculated on an accrual basis.

   a. Prepare an income statement for the five months ended December 31, Year 2, assuming that the corporation uses the accrual basis of accounting, with revenue recognized at the time services are rendered.

   b. Prepare an income statement for the five months ended December 31, Year 2 assuming that the corporation uses the cash basis of accounting.

   c. Which basis of accounting do you feel provides a better indication of operating performance of the consulting firm for the period? Why?

39. *Cash versus accrual basis of accounting.* J. Hennessey opened a retail store on January 1, Year 8. Hennessey invested $20,000 and borrowed $10,000 from a local bank. The loan plus interest is repayable on December 31, Year 9, with interest at the rate of 12 percent per year. Hennessey rented a building on January 1 and paid a year's rent in advance in the amount of $8,000. Property and liability insurance coverage for the two-year period of $2,000 was paid on January 1, year 8.

Hennessey purchased $84,000 of merchandise on account during Year 8 and paid $76,000 of the amount by the end of Year 8. The cost of merchandise on hand on December 31, Year 8, was $12,000.

During Year 8, cash sales to customers were $30,000 and sales on account totaled $70,000. Of the sales on account, $62,000 was collected by December 31, Year 8.

Other costs incurred and paid in cash were salaries, $20,000; utilities, $1,500. Unpaid bills at year-end are as follows: salaries, $1,200; utilities, $120.

   a. Prepare an income statement for Year 8 assuming that the company uses the accrual basis of accounting, with revenue recognized at the time of sale.

b. Prepare an income statement for Year 8 assuming that the company uses the cash basis of accounting.

c. Which basis of accounting do you feel provides a better indication of operating performance for the retail store during Year 8? Why?

40. *Miscellaneous transactions and adjusting entries.* Present journal entries for each of the following separate sets of data:

   a. On January 15, Year 2, a $6,000, two-month, 12 percent note was received by the company. Present adjusting entries at the end of each month and the entry for collection at maturity.

   b. The company uses one Merchandise Inventory account to record the beginning inventory and purchases during the period. The balance in this account on December 31, Year 2, was $580,000. The inventory of merchandise on hand at that time was $60,000. Present the adjusting entry.

   c. The company rents out part of its building for office space at the rate of $900 a month, payable quarterly in advance on January 1, April 1, July 1, and October 1. The quarterly rental for the first quarter was received one month late on February 1, Year 2. Present collection and adjusting entries for the quarter. Assume that the books are adjusted monthly.

   d. The company leases branch office space at $3,000 a month. Payment is made by the company on the first of each six-month period. Payment of $18,000 was made on July 1, Year 2. Present payment and adjusting entries through August 31, Year 2. Assume that the books are adjusted monthly.

   e. The balance of the Prepaid Insurance account on October 1, Year 2, was $400. On December 1, Year 2, the company renewed its only insurance policy for another two years, beginning on that date, by payment of $3,000. Present journal entries for renewal and adjusting entries through December 31, Year 2. Assume that the books are adjusted quarterly at the end of March, June, September and December.

   f. The Office Supplies on Hand account had a balance of $400 on December 31, Year 2. Purchases of supplies in the amount of $580 were recorded in the Office Supplies Expense account during the month. The physical inventory of office supplies on December 31, Year 2, was $340. Present any necessary adjusting entry at December 31, Year 2.

   g. An office building was constructed at a cost of $560,000. It was estimated that it would have a useful life of 50 years from the date of occupancy, October 31, Year 2, and a residual value of $80,000. Present the adjusting entry for the depreciation of the building in Year 2. Assume that the books are closed annually at December 31.

41. *Miscellaneous transactions and adjusting entries.* Give the journal entry to record each of the transactions below as well as any necessary adjusting entries on December 31, Year 6, assuming that the accounting period is the calendar year and the books are closed on December 31.

   a. Harrison's Supply Company Ltd. received a 90-day note from a customer on December 1, Year 6. The note in the face amount of $3,000 replaced an open account receivable of the same amount. The note is due with interest at nine percent per year on March 1, Year 7.

b. Thompson's Wholesale Limited purchased a two-year insurance policy on September 1, Year 6, paying the two-year premium of $9,600 in advance.

c. William's Products Inc. acquired a machine on July 1, Year 6, for $20,000 cash. The machine is expected to have a $4,000 salvage value and a four-year life.

d. Greer Electronics Ltd. acquired an automobile on September 1, Year 5, for $5,000 cash. The automobile is expected to have $1,400 salvage value and a four-year life.

e. Devine Co. Ltd. rented out excess office space for the three-month period beginning December 15, Year 6. The first month's rent of $6,400 was received on this date.

f. Prentice Products Corporation began business on November 1, Year 6. It acquired office supplies costing $5,000 on account. Of this amount, $4,000 was paid by year-end. A physical inventory indicates that office supplies costing $2,400 were on hand on December 31, Year 6.

42. *Preparation of T-account entries and adjusted trial balance.* A corporation known as the Kirby Collection Agency Ltd. is organized by Betty Kirby and Charles Stevens on January 1, Year 3. The business of the firm is to collect overdue accounts receivable of various clients on a commission basis. The following transactions occurred during January:

(1) Kirby contributes office supplies worth $3,000 and cash of $12,000. She is issued share certificates for 500 shares with a par value of $30 a share.

(2) Stevens contributes $3,000 in cash and office equipment valued at $9,000. He is issued share certificates for 400 shares.

(3) The Kirby agency collects $400 on an account that was turned over to it by the Jiggly Market. The commission earned is 50 percent of the amount collected.

(4) The stenographer's salary during the month, $600, is paid.

(5) A bill is received from Lyband and Linn, chartered accountants, for $400 to cover the cost of installing a computer system.

(6) The amount due the Jiggly Market [see **(3)**] is paid.

(7) An office is leased for the year beginning February 1, Year 3, and the rent for two months is paid in advance. A cheque is drawn for $900.

(8) An automobile is purchased on January 30 for $4,500; $2,500 is paid by cheque and an installment contract, payable to the Scotch Automobile Sales Company, is signed for the balance.

a. Open T-accounts and record the transactions during January.

b. Prepare an adjusted, preclosing trial balance as of January 31, Year 3. Indicate, by ''R'' or ''E,'' accounts that are revenue or expense accounts.

43. *Preparation of T-account entries and adjusted trial balance.* Bill Wilson operates a restaurant that he has rented fully equipped from its owner. The trial balance of the restaurant on November 1, Year 6, the first day of an accounting period, is as follows:

Cash	$ 6,975	
Food on Hand	5,400	
Accounts Payable, Barry Meat Company		$ 2,050
Accounts Payable, Conell Wholesale Grocery		2,378
Bill Wilson, Capital		7,947
	$12,375	$12,375

A summary of the transactions for the month of November is as follows:

(1) Cash received for meals served, $26,550.
(2) November rent paid by cheque, $4,050.
(3) Food purchased on account from the Conell Wholesale Grocery, $7,650.
(4) Maintenance to equipment paid in cash, $450.
(5) Food purchased on account from the Barry Meat Company, $4,725.
(6) Payment to Barry Meat Company, $5,650.
(7) Payment to Conell Wholesale Grocery, $8,228.
(8) Salaries for the month totaling $6,273 are paid.
(9) Cost of food used, $11,925.

a. Open T-accounts for the accounts in the trial balance and enter the beginning balance. Record the transactions for the month of November in the T-accounts, opening additional T-accounts for individual revenues and expenses as needed.

b. Prepare an adjusted, preclosing trial balance to check the accuracy of your entries.

44. *Preparation of T-account entries, adjusted trial balance, income statement, and balance sheet.* The trial balance of Safety Cleaners and Dyers at February 28, Year 6, is shown below. The books have not been closed nor have adjusting entries been made since December 31, Year 5.

Cash	$ 3,400	
Accounts Receivable	15,200	
Supplies on Hand	4,800	
Prepaid Insurance	1,200	
Equipment	65,000	
Accumulated Depreciation		$ 9,680
Accounts Payable		7,900
P. O. Grey, Capital		60,000
Sales Revenue		46,060
Salaries and Wages Expense	26,600	
Cost of Outside Work	2,040	
Advertising Expense	400	
Repairs Expense	500	
Rent Expense	1,200	
Power, Gas, and Water Expense	880	
Supplies Used	—	
Depreciation Expense	—	
Miscellaneous Expense	2,420	
	$123,640	$123,640

A summary of the transactions for the month of March, Year 6 is as follows:

(1) Sales: For cash, $14,000; on account, $5,800.
(2) Collections on account, $10,000.
(3) Purchases of outside work (cleaning done by wholesale clearners), $800, on account.
(4) Purchases of supplies, on account, $2,800.
(5) Payments on account, $4,000.
(6) March rent paid, $600.
(7) Supplies used (for the quarter), $5,340.
(8) Depreciation (for the quarter), $2,420.
(9) March salaries and wages of $11,120 are paid.
(10) Bills received but not recorded or paid by the end of the month: advertising, $200; maintenance on equipment, $60; power, gas, and water, $380.
(11) Insurance expired (for the quarter), $400.

> **a.** Open T-accounts and enter the trial balance amounts.
> **b.** Record the transactions for the month of March in the T-accounts, opening additional T-accounts as needed. Cross-number the entries.
> **c.** Prepare an adjusted, preclosing trial balance at March 31, Year 6, an income statement for the three months ending March 31, Year 6, and a balance sheet as of March 31, Year 6.
> **d.** Enter closing entries in the T-accounts using an Income Summary account.

45. *Preparation of T-account entries, adjusted trial balance, income statement, and balance sheet.* The balance sheet accounts of Hanover Camera Repair Shop at June 30, Year 8, are as follows:

Cash	$1,920	
Repair Parts Inventory	600	
Office Supplies Inventory	80	
Equipment	2,200	
Accumulated Depreciation		$ 300
Accounts Payable		2,500
B. Greer, Capital		2,000
	$4,800	$4,800

A summary of the transactions during July is as follows:

(1) Performed repair services, for which $900 in cash was received immediately.
(2) Performed additional repair work, $200, and sent bills to customers for this amount.
(3) Paid creditors, $400.
(4) Took out insurance on equipment on July 1, and issued a cheque to cover one year's premium of $96.
(5) Paid $60 for a series of advertisements that appeared in the local newspaper during July.
(6) Issued a cheque for $130 for rent of shop space for July.
(7) Paid telephone bill for the month, $35.

(8) Collected $100 of the amount charged to customers in item **(2)**.

Adjusting entries required at the end of July relate to the following:

(9) The insurance expired during July is calculated at $8.

(10) Cost of repair parts used during the month, $180.

(11) Cost of office supplies used during July, $40.

(12) Depreciation of equipment for the month is $30.

    a. Open T-accounts and insert the July 1 balances. Record the transactions for the month in the T-accounts, opening additional T-accounts for individual revenue and expense accounts as needed.

    b. Prepare an adjusted, preclosing trial balance at July 31, Year 8.

    c. Prepare an income statement for the month of July and a balance sheet as of July 31, Year 8.

    d. Enter closing entries in the T-accounts using an Income Summary account.

46. *Preparation of T-account entries, adjusted trial balance, income statement, and balance sheet.* The trial balance of Jones Shoe Repair Shop at February 28, Year 2, is shown below. The books have not been closed since December 31, Year 1.

Cash	$ 6,060	
Accounts Receivable	15,200	
Supplies Inventory	4,800	
Prepaid Insurance	900	
Equipment	65,000	
Accumulated Depreciation		$ 11,460
Accounts Payable		6,120
W. R. Jones, Capital		62,360
Sales Revenue		46,060
Salaries and Wages Expense	26,600	
Cost of Outside Work	2,040	
Advertising Expense	900	
Rent Expense	1,200	
Power, Gas, and Water Expense	880	
Supplies used	—	
Depreciation Expense	—	
Miscellaneous Expense	2,420	
	$126,000	$126,000

A summary of the transactions during the month of March, Year 2 is as follows:

(1) Sales: for cash, $26,000; on account, $17,600.

(2) Collections on account, $22,000.

(3) Purchases of outside work (repair work done by another shoe repair shop for Jones), $1,600, on account.

(4) Purchases of supplies, on account, $2,800.

(5) Payments on account, $6,000.

(6) March rent paid, $1,200.

(7) March salaries and wages of $13,290 are paid.

Adjusting entries required at the end of March relate to the following:

(8) Supplies used (for the quarter), $4,960.
(9) Depreciation (for the quarter), $3,820.
(10) Bills received but not yet recorded or paid by the end of the month: advertising, $300; power, gas, and water, $620.
(11) Insurance expired (for the quarter), $300.

 a. Open T-accounts and enter the trial balance amounts.
 b. Record the transactions for the month of March in the T-accounts, opening additional T-accounts as needed. Cross-number the entries.
 c. Prepare an adjusted, preclosing trial balance at March 31, Year 2, an income statement for the three months ending March 31, Year 2, and a balance sheet, as of March 31, Year 2.
 d. Enter closing entries in the T-accounts using an Income Summary account.

47. *Preparation of journal entries, T-accounts, adjusted trial balance, income statement, and balance sheet.* The post-closing trial balance of Cunningham's Hardware Store Ltd. on September 30, Year 4, is as follows:

Cash	$ 88,400	
Accounts Receivable	54,500	
Merchandise Inventory	136,300	
Prepaid Insurance	800	
Equipment	420,000	
Accumulated Depreciation		$168,000
Accounts Payable		66,200
Note Payable		10,000
Salaries Payable		2,500
Capital Stock		300,000
Retained Earnings		153,300
Total	$700,000	$700,000

Transactions during October and additional information are as follows:

(1) Merchandise inventory purchased on account from various suppliers is $92,600.
(2) Sales, all on account, total $170,000; cost of merchandise sold, $73,000.
(3) Rent for the month of October of $23,500 is paid.
(4) Salaries paid to employees during October are $41,200.
(5) Accounts receivable of $68,300 are collected.
(6) Accounts payable of $77,900 are paid.
(7) Miscellaneous expenses of $6,400 are paid in cash.
(8) The premium on a one-year insurance policy was paid on June 1, Year 4.

Adjusting entries required at the end of October relate to the following:

(9) Equipment is depreciated over a ten-year life. Estimated salvage value of the equipment is considered to be negligible.
(10) Employee salaries earned during the last two days of October but not paid are $3,200. These are the only unpaid salaries at the end of October.

(11) The note payable is a 90-day, 12 percent note issued on September 30, Year 4.

(12) Merchandise inventory on hand on October 31, Year 4, totals $155,900.

(13) The company records income tax at the rate of 40 percent of accounting income before income tax.

> **a.** Prepare general journal entries to record the transactions during October.
>
> **b.** Set up T-accounts and enter the opening balances in the accounts on September 30, Year 4. Post the entries from part (**a**) in the T-accounts, creating additional accounts as required.
>
> **c.** Prepare an unadjusted trial balance as of October 31, Year 4.
>
> **d.** Prepare adjusting entries required at the end of October.
>
> **e.** Enter the trial balance from part (**c**) and the adjusting entries from part (**d**) in a work sheet and complete the work sheet.
>
> **f.** Prepare an income statement for the month of October.
>
> **g.** Prepare a balance sheet as of October 31, Year 4.

48. *Preparation of adjusting entries and work sheet.* The following unadjusted trial balance is taken from the books of the Kathleen Clothing Company Ltd. at July 31, Year 3.

Accounts Payable		$ 12,952
Accounts Receivable	$ 18,257	
Accumulated Depreciation		8,214
Advances by Customers		540
Capital Stock		40,000
Cash	9,000	
Equipment	2,640	
Depreciation Expense	—	—
Dividends Payable	—	—
Furniture and Fixtures	12,000	
Income Tax Expense	—	
Income Tax Payable		3,500
Insurance Expense	—	—
Leasehold	10,800	
Merchandise Cost of Goods Sold	—	—
Merchandise Inventory	49,500	
Miscellaneous Expense	188	
Prepaid Insurance	450	
Rent Expense	—	—
Retained Earnings		14,294
Salaries and Commissions Expense	2,020	
Salaries and Commissions Payable		500
Sales		25,000
Supplies Inventory	145	
	$105,000	$105,000

Additional data:

(1) Depreciation on equipment is to be calculated at ten percent of cost per year (assume zero salvage value).

(2) Depreciation on furniture and fixtures is to be calculated at 20 percent of cost per year (assume zero salvage value).

(3) The leasehold represents long-term rent paid in advance by Kathleen. The monthly rental charge is $600.

(4) One invoice of $420 for the purchase of merchandise from the Peoria Company on account was recorded during the month as $240. The account has not yet been paid.

(5) Commissions unpaid at July 31, Year 3, are $340. All salaries have been paid. The balance in the Salaries and Commissions Payable account represents the amount of commissions unpaid at July 1.

(6) Merchandise with a sales price of $350 was recently delivered to a customer, and charged to Accounts Receivable, although the customer had paid $350 in advance.

(7) The balance in the Prepaid Insurance account relates to a three-year policy that went into effect on January 1, Year 3.

(8) A dividend of $3,000 was declared on July 31, Year 3.

(9) The inventory of merchandise on July 31, Year 3, was $33,600.

(10) The company records income tax at the rate of 40 percent of accounting income before income tax.

Prepare a work sheet incorporating adjusting journal entries at July 31, Year 3. Use only the accounts listed in the trial balance.

49. *Preparation of closing entries.* The adjusted trial balance of Life Photographers, Inc., at June 30, Year 2, is presented in Exhibit 3.20.

    a. Present the journal entries to close the revenue and expense accounts directly to Retained Earnings as of June 30, Year 2.

    b. Set up in T-account form the revenue, expense, and retained earnings accounts. Insert the trial balance amounts and record the closing entries from part (**a**).

Exhibit 3.20
LIFE PHOTOGRAPHERS, INC.
Adjusted Trial Balance
June 30, Year 2

Accounts Payable		$ 3,641
Accounts Receivable	$ 3,900	
Accumulated Depreciation		1,995
Advertising Expense	1,500	
Cameras and Equipment	15,500	
Cash	2,994	
Common Stock		10,000
Depreciation Expense—Cameras and Equipment	180	
Depreciation Expense—Furniture and Fixtures	105	
Electricity Expense	300	
Equipment Repairs Expense	180	
Furniture and Fixtures	9,600	
Insurance Expense	330	
Photographic Supplies Expense	1,950	
Photographic Supplies on Hand	3,390	

Prepaid Insurance	270	
Rent Expense	1,425	
Retained Earnings		14,138
Revenue — Commercial Photography		18,090
Revenue — Printing Service		4,680
Salaries Expense	10,800	
Telephone Expense	120	
	$52,544	$52,544

50. *Working backwards to balance sheet at beginning of period.* (Problems 50 through 52 are adapted from problems by George H. Sorter.) The following data relate to the Prima Company Ltd.:

(1) Post-closing trial balance at December 31, Year 2.

Debits

Cash	$ 10,000
Temporary Investments	20,000
Accounts Receivable	25,000
Merchandise Inventory	30,000
Prepayments for Miscellaneous Services	3,000
Land, Buildings, and Equipment	40,000
Total Debits	$128,000

Credits

Accounts Payable (for merchandise)	$ 25,000
Interest Payable	300
Taxes Payable	4,000
Notes Payable (6 percent, long-term)	20,000
Accumulated Depreciation	16,000
Capital Stock	50,000
Retained Earnings	12,700
Total Credits	$128,000

(2) Income and retained earnings data for Year 2:

Sales		$200,000
Less: Cost of Goods Sold		130,000
Gross Profit		$ 70,000
Less: Operating Expenses:		
Depreciation Expense	$ 3,000	
Other	48,700	51,700
Operating Profit		$ 18,300
Less: Interest Expense		1,200
Net Income before Income Tax		$ 17,100
Income Tax		8,000
Net Income		$ 9,100
Less: Dividends		5,000
Increase in Retained Earnings		$ 4,100

(3) Summary of cash receipts and disbursements in Year 2:

Cash Receipts		
Cash Sales	$ 47,000	
Collection from Credit Customers	150,000	
Total Receipts		$197,000
Cash Disbursements		
Payment to Suppliers of Merchandise	$128,000	
Payment to Suppliers of Miscellaneous Services	49,000	
Payment of Taxes	7,500	
Payment of Interest	1,200	
Payment of Dividends	5,000	
Purchase of Temporary Investments	8,000	
Total Disbursements		198,700
Excess of Disbursements over Receipts		$ 1,700

(4) Purchases of merchandise during the period, all on account, were $127,000. All "Other Operating Expenses" were credited to Prepayments.

Prepare a balance sheet for January 1, Year 2. (*Hint:* Set up T-accounts for each of the accounts in the trial balance and enter the *ending* balances in the T-accounts. Starting with information from the income statement and statement of cash receipts and disbursements, reconstruct the transactions that took place during the year and enter the amounts in the appropriate T-accounts.)

51. *Working backwards to cash receipts and disbursements.* The Secunda Company Limited's trial balance at the beginning of Year 2 and the adjusted, preclosing trial balance at the end of Year 2 are presented below.

	12/31/Year 2	1/1/Year 2
Debits		
Cash	$ 9,000	$ 20,000
Accounts Receivable	51,000	36,000
Merchandise Inventory	60,000	45,000
Prepayments	1,000	2,000
Land, Buildings, and Equipment	40,000	40,000
Cost of Goods Sold	50,000	—
Interest Expense	3,000	—
Other Operating Expenses	29,000	—
Total Debits	$243,000	$143,000
Credits		
Accumulated Depreciation	$ 18,000	$ 16,000
Interest Payable	2,000	1,000
Accounts Payable	40,000	30,000
Mortgage Payable	17,000	20,000
Capital Stock	50,000	50,000

Retained Earnings	16,000	26,000
Sales	100,000	—
Total Credits	$243,000	$143,000

All goods and services acquired during the year were purchased on account. The Other Operating Expenses account includes depreciation charges and expirations of prepayments. Dividends declared during the year were debited to Retained Earnings.

Prepare a schedule showing all cash transactions for Year 2. (*Hint:* Set up T-accounts for each of the accounts listed in the trial balance and enter the amounts shown as of January 1, Year 2, and December 31, Year 2. Starting with the entries in revenue and expense accounts, reconstruct the transactions that took place during the year and enter the amounts in the appropriate T-accounts. The effect of earnings activities is not yet reflected in the Retained Earnings account because the trial balance is preclosing.)

52. *Working backwards to income statement.* Tertia Company Inc. presents the following incomplete post-closing trial balances, as well as a statement of cash receipts and disbursements:

	12/31/Year 2	1/1/Year 2
Debits		
Cash	$?	$?
Accounts and Notes Receivable	41,000	36,000
Merchandise Inventory	49,500	55,000
Interest Receivable	700	1,000
Prepaid Miscellaneous Services	5,200	4,000
Building, Machinery, and Equipment	47,000	47,000
Total Debits	$?	$?
Credits		
Accounts Payable (miscellaneous services)	$ 2,500	$ 2,000
Accounts Payable (merchandise)	41,000	34,000
Property Taxes Payable	1,500	1,000
Accumulated Depreciation	12,000	10,000
Mortgage Payable	30,000	35,000
Capital Stock	25,000	25,000
Retained Earnings	?	76,000
Total Credits	$211,200	$183,000

	Year 2
Cash Receipts	
1. Collection from Credit Customers	$144,000
2. Cash Sales	63,000
3. Collection of Interest	1,000
	$208,000

Less: Cash Disbursements

4. Payment to Suppliers of Merchandise	$114,000
5. Repayment on Mortgage	5,000
6. Payment of Interest	500
7. Prepayment to Suppliers of Miscellaneous Services	57,500
8. Payment of Property Taxes	1,200
9. Payment of Dividends	2,000
	$180,200
Increase in Cash Balance for Year	$ 27,800

Prepare a combined statement of income and retained earnings for Year 2. (*Hint:* Set up T-accounts for each of the balance sheet accounts listed in the trial balance and enter the amounts shown as of January 1, Year 2, and December 31, Year 2. Starting with the cash receipts and disbursements for the year, reconstruct the transactions that took place during the year and enter them in the appropriate T-accounts. The effect of earnings activities for the year is already reflected in the Retained Earnings account, because the trial balance shown is post-closing.)

53. *Analyses of General Products Limited.* Refer to the Consolidated Statements of Income and Retained Earnings for General Products Limited in Appendix A, p. 760. Prepare a common-size (see Glossary) income statement for each of the years 1986, 1987, and 1988 in which each income statement account is expressed as a percentage of sales revenue (that is, sales revenue equals 100 percent). What changes in the profitability of General Products Limited can be observed over this three-year period?

54. *Specialized journals and subsidiary ledgers.*

   a. What advantage is there to using multicolumn journals instead of two-column journals?
   b. What advantage is there to using specialized journals instead of multicolumn journals?
   c. What advantage is there to using subsidiary ledgers in conjunction with a general ledger?

55. *Specialized journals and subsidiary ledgers.* Indicate whether each of the following statements is true or false.

   a. Posting is the process of recording entries in a journal.
   b. A general journal is not needed when specialized journals are used.
   c. The balances in individual subsidiary ledger accounts are not included in the general ledger trial balance.
   d. Specialized journals are created to facilitate the recording of various types of frequent transactions.
   e. A controlling account represents a group of subsidiary ledger accounts that are kept in detail outside of the general ledger.
   f. A specialized journal must have an equal number of debit and credit columns.
   g. A journal must have at least one column for debits and at least another column for credits.
   h. The use of subsidiary ledgers facilitates the taking of a trial balance.

i. When a controlling account is credited, one of the subsidiary ledger accounts is debited.

j. There is usually more detail about an individual transaction in the general journal than in the general ledger.

56. *Accounting cycle with specialized journals.* The trial balance of the general ledger of the Renuit Shop, Inc., on July 1, Year 5, is as follows:

Cash	$ 700	
Supplies Inventory	425	
Tools	2,000	
Accumulated Depreciation		$ 800
Accounts Payable		625[a]
Common Shares		500
Retained Earnings		1,200
Repair Service Revenue		—
Cost of Repair Supplies Used	—	
Salary Expense	—	
Utilities Expense	—	
Depreciation Expense......................................	—	
Total	$3,125	$3,125

[a]Amount is payable to Handicraft Supply Company.

The transactions during July are as follows:

(1) Cash is received on July 3 for repair work done, $360.

(2) Supplies are purchased on account from Handicraft Supply Company on July 10, $185.

(3) Cash payments are made on July 31 as follows: salaries, $125; utilities, $13; Handicraft Supply Company on account, $725.

(4) Cash is received for repair work done on July 31, $310.

(5) Depreciation on tools for the month is $55.

(6) The cost of supplies used during the month is $255.

    a. Open T-accounts for the accounts listed in the trial balance on July 1, Year 5, and enter the opening balances.

    b. Construct a six-column journal with the following column headings: Cash, Debit and Credit; Revenue for Repair Services, Credit; Supplies, Debit; Other Accounts, Debit and Credit. Also include columns for Date, Explanation, and Other Account Titles.

    c. Enter transactions **(1)** through **(4)** in the six-column journal.

    d. Post amounts from the six-column journal to the appropriate T-accounts.

    e. Prepare an unadjusted trial balance.

    f. Prepare a two-column general journal. Enter the adjusting entries for items **(5)** and **(6)** on July 31, Year 5.

    g. Post the adjusting entries to the T-accounts.

    h. Prepare an adjusted trial balance.

    i. Enter the closing entries on July 31, Year 5 in the general journal and then post them to the general ledger accounts.

    j. Prepare a post-closing trial balance.

57. *Specialized journals.* The most common transactions of the Beal Antique Shop, Inc. are as follows:

Sales for cash and on account.
Payments for purchases of merchandise by cash and by cheque.
Collections of cash from customers.
Payments of operating expenses by cash and by cheque.
Deposits in the bank.

Subsidiary ledgers are used for customers' accounts and operating expense accounts. The following are the transactions for July 1–31:

July 1 Cash sales, $200.
4 Sale, on account, L. C. Jones, $80; cash sales, $60.
6 $500 of common shares are issued for cash.
11 Cash sales, $250.
15 Collection from a customer, A. C. Hines, $75.
17 Sale, on account, A. O. Brown, $85.
20 Store fixtures are purchased for $800 from the Office Supply Company. A cheque (No. 550) is issued, $200; the balance is covered by an installment contract.
23 Merchandise is purchased for $650 from the East Antique Company. Cheque (No. 551) is issued in full payment.
25 Cash sales, $200.
25 Collection from a customer, M. A. Cross, $90.
27 A note payable is issued to the bank, $1,000. The proceeds are added by the bank to the firm's account.
28 Sale, on account, W. I. Snow, $95; cash sales, $60.
29 A telephone bill is received from Bell Canada. Cheque (No. 552) is issued, $12.
30 Merchandise is acquired from the Specialty Furniture Company, $550. Cheque (No. 553) is issued in payment of the accompanying invoice.
31 The clerk is paid for the second half of the month. Cheque (No. 554) is issued for earnings of $300, less deductions of six percent for payroll taxes and $45 for income tax.

a. Prepare an 11-column journal with the following column headings: Cash (Dr. and Cr.); Accounts Receivable (Dr. and Cr.); Merchandise Inventory (Dr.); Selling and Administrative Expenses (Dr.); Sales (Cr.); Other Accounts (Dr. and Cr.). Also include columns for Date, Explanation, and Other Accounts Titles.
b. Enter each of the transactions during July in the 11-column journal.
c. Total columns.

58. *Specialized journals, posting, trial balance (if combined with Problem 59, a mini practice set).* E. S. Brady and R. E. Brady own and operate Brady Business Services, Inc., providing mimeographing and public stenographic services. At September 30, Year 3, the trial balance of the general ledger and the schedules of the subsidiary ledgers are as follows:

General Ledger

Cash	$ 5,500	
Accounts Receivable	9,500	
Supplies on Hand	3,300	
Prepaid Insurance	960	
Office Equipment	19,500	
Accumulated Depreciation		$ 7,200
Accounts Payable		4,900
Equipment Contract Payable		3,000
Share Capital		10,000
Retained Earnings		13,660
Total	$38,760	$38,760

Accounts Receivable

Baum & Co.	$ 1,220
Clark's Market	300
David Bros.	—
Forest Stores	1,800
H. B. Gross	590
Moll & Co.	750
Ohio Realty	—
Porter and Sons	290
A. B. Reck	1,450
Standard Service	3,100
Total	$ 9,500

Accounts Payable

Burton, Inc.	$ 250
City Supply Co.	2,360
Mears & Co.	450
P. A. Page, Ltd.	1,080
Snell Bros.	760
Total	$ 4,900

The following transactions took place during the month of October:

October 1 Received $450 in cash for secretarial work completed and delivered today.

 1 Completed and delivered mimeograph work for Moll & Company and invoiced them for $510.

 2 Issued cheque (No. 100) for $600 to K. M. Bear for rent for the month of October. (Cheques are issued in serial number order.)

 3 Received cheque for $1,800 from Forest Stores in payment of their account balance.

 6 Issued cheques (Nos. 101–104) in payment of September 30 balances to Burton, Inc., City Supply Company, P. A. Page, Ltd., and Snell Brothers.

 6 Acquired on account paper and other mimeograph supplies from City Supply Company, $1,050.

7   Cash receipts for the day were $330 for stenographic service and $1,250 for mimeograph work.

8   Received the following invoices: Mears & Company, $100, for repairs to office equipment; Burton, Inc., $480, for office supplies: P. A. Page, Ltd. $250 for mimeograph supplies.

10 Received cheques from the following customers for the September 30 balances: Baum & Company, Clark's Market, Moll & Company, Porter and Sons, and Standard Service.

10 Issued cheque (No. 105) for $150 for advertising invoice received from the *Daily Register*.

13 Issued cheque (No. 106) for $1,500 to Hall Office Equipment, Ltd. for monthly payment on the equipment purchase contract.

13 Completed and delivered the following mimeograph jobs and invoiced the customers: Ohio Realty, $460; Davis Brothers, $200; Standard Service, $930.

14 Receipts for the day for stenographic work, $620.

15 Issued cheque (No. 107) for $90 to Blott Typewriter Services for repairs on machines.

16 Received a cheque for $550 from S. V. Smith for mimeograph work completed and delivered today.

17 Receipts for the day: stenographic services, $100; mimeograph work, $850.

17 Issued cheques (Nos. 108–109) to Mears & Company and P. A. Page, Ltd., for invoices of October 8.

20 Issued cheque (No. 110) to City Supply Company for invoice of October 6.

20 Purchased the following operating supplies on account: City Supply Company, $1,500; Snell Brothers, $950.

20 Issued cheque (No. 111) to a customer, S. V. Smith, as an adjustment reducing the amount he had paid for mimeograph work, $50 (adjustment due to error in calculating the charge on October 16).

21 Received a cheque from H. B. Gross for $590 in payment of September 30 balance.

21 Other cash receipts for the day: stenographic services, $440; mimeograph work, $460.

23 Issued cheque (No. 112) for $450 to Mears & Company.

24 Billed the following customers for mimeograph work completed and delivered: Clark's Market, $210; Forest Stores, $445; Moll & Company, $1,070.

24 Issued a cheque (No. 113) for $500 to N. Stewart as a dividend.

28 Cash receipts for the day: stenographic services, $270; mimeograph work, $1,500.

29 Issued a credit memo to Moll & Company for $100 as an adjustment on invoice of October 24 (incorrect rate used).

30 Issued cheque (No. 114) to Southwestern Telephone Company for telephone bill for the month, $120.

31 Paid $50 out of cash on hand for machinery repair.

     31 Cash receipts for the day: mimeograph work, $435.

     31 Issued cheques (Nos. 115-116) for October salaries: E. S. Brady, $2,750; R. E. Brady, $2,500.

a. Open T-accounts for each of the general ledger accounts and insert the September 30 balances.

b. Record the October transactions in a 12-column journal. The amount-column headings in the journal are as follows: Cash, Dr. and Cr.; Accounts Receivable, Dr. and Cr.; Accounts Payable, Dr. and Cr.; Supplies on Hand, Dr.; Sales Revenue, Cr.; Other Accounts, Dr. and Cr. There should also be columns for Date, Explanation, and Other Accounts Titles.

c. Post the transactions during October from the journal to the general ledger T-accounts.

d. Prepare an unadjusted trial balance of the general ledger accounts as of October 31.

59. *Adjusting and closing journal entries and trial balance.* This problem is a continuation of Problem **58.** Additional information as of October 31, Year 3:

(1) Ending inventory of supplies amounts to $4,750.

(2) The insurance policy acquired on October 1, Year 2 runs for three years.

(3) Office equipment was acquired on September 30, Year 1, at a cost of $19,500. It was estimated that the salvage value of the equipment at the estimated retirement date, September 30, Year 6, would be $1,500.

(4) Income tax expense is estimated to be $600.

   a. Construct a two-column general journal. Prepare any adjusting entries required on October 31, Year 3 and enter them in the general journal.

   b. Post the adjusting entries to the general ledger T-accounts.

   c. Prepare an adjusted pre-closing trial balance.

   d. Prepare the closing entries for the revenue and expense accounts, enter them in the general journal, and post them to the general ledger T-accounts.

   e. Prepare a post-closing trial balance.

60. *Specialized Journals.* Referring to Problem **58**, prepare the following specialized journals:

(1) Cash receipts and disbursements journal with the following columns: Date; Cash on Hand, Dr. and Cr.; Accounts Receivable, Cr. (amount, name of customer); Sales Revenue, Cr.; Other Accounts, Dr. (amount, account title, explanation).

(2) Cheque register with the following columns: Date, Payee; Cheque Number; Cash in Bank, Cr.; Accounts Payable, Dr.; Other Accounts, Dr. (amount, account title, explanation).

(3) Revenue journal for use where credit is extended, with the following columns: Date; Name of customer; A single column for Accounts Receivable, Dr. and Sales Revenue, Cr.

(4) Invoice register with the following columns: Date: Name of Creditor; Accounts Payable, Cr.; Supplies on Hand, Dr.; Other Accounts, Dr. (amount, account title, explanation).

Record the transactions during October in the appropriate journal.

61. *Subsidiary ledgers.* Refer to Problem **58**. Prepare the subsidiary ledgers for Accounts Receivable and Accounts Payable as of October 31, Year 3, using the format shown in Problem **58**.

62. *Financial statement impact of cash vs. accrual assumption.* In 1988 the Glitter Corporation was a newly formed jewellery company. During its first year of operations, the company did not have a qualified accountant. The first year end closing, to say the least, was a bit chaotic.

The bookkeeper for the Glitter Corporation elected to use the cash method. The following were noted at year end:

(**1**) Depreciation for the office building was not entered.

(**2**) Interest on an outstanding note payable was not accrued.

(**3**) A down-payment for some jewellery to be delivered next year was recorded as sales.

(**4**) Although the contract was signed, the purchase of a shipment of gem stones was not recognized because the delivery date was one month after year end.

(**5**) Some credit sales were not booked as revenue for the year.

(**6**) The company bought a large quantity of rubies and sapphires and paid in advance. The gems being shipped are not expected to arrive until three months after the year end. By the end of the current year, due to a newly invented synthetic process for rubies, the ruby price had dropped by 20%. However, the sapphire price had increased by 10%, due to a shortage in the world markets. The purchase of these gems had not been recorded.

    a. Explain the difference between the cash and accrual bases of recording accounting transactions.

    b. What are the effects of items 1 to 6 (listed above) on assets, liabilities and owners' equity if accounting is done on an accrual basis? Show the direction of change and support your answer with corresponding journal entries. Use the following format:

Impact on Accounts
(Increase, Decrease or No Change)

Item	Assets	Liabilities	Owners' Equity	Journal Entry

Adapted with permission from the Society of Management Accountants of Canada.

63. *Working backwards from trial balance to journal entries.* Majestic Bodies Fitness Club Ltd. Offers free trial memberships to the general public to attract business. The customer must pay a deposit of $500, but if not satisfied after a month, he or she can withdraw and get a full refund. The following were taken from the trial balances of Majestic Bodies Fitness Club Ltd. during the month of December, 1988.

	Unadjusted Trial Balance	Adjusted Trial Balance
Club membership sales	$122,800 cr.	$141,300 cr.
Accumulated depreciation for fitness equipment	2,700 cr.	4,000 cr.
Interest revenue	1,280 cr.	1,540 cr.
Supplies expense	2,360 dr.	1,460 dr.

Unexpired liability insurance	0	2,800 dr.
Tanning booth revenue	3,200 cr.	4,900 cr.
Office salaries	6,500 dr.	7,980 dr.
Commissions payable	400 cr.	1,430 cr.

During the Christmas season, the club was selling gift certificates to promote its business. A gift certificate for 10 visits to the club's tanning facilities was selling for $50. A total of 20 certificates were sold.

During December 1988, 18 people used the gift certificates for a total of 40 visits.

  a. Reconstruct the journal entries that probably were prepared to adjust each of the trial balance accounts above.

  b. Journalize the sale of the gift certificates and the resulting revenue in December 1988.

Adapted with permission from the Society of Management Accountants of Canada.

Decision Problem 3-1

Your friend's mother, Mary Brooks, has opened Mary's Boutique Ltd. in a nearby shopping mall. She began her business on February 1, Year 1; she invested $20,000 in share capital and her husband, Tom, contributed another $20,000 as a loan to the firm, bearing interest at ten percent, of which none has been paid to date.

Mary Brooks has found the boutique exciting and appears to have succeeded as a businessperson — but how successful? She answers this question when preparing her income tax return; this in turn helps determine whether or not she should continue the business.

Brooks maintains a summary of selected transactions. This summary for the year ended January 31, Year 2 follows:

Cost of merchandise purchased on account	$34,600
Wages paid to assistant	9,200
Salary paid to M. Brooks	12,000
Rent paid	4,800
Business taxes and licences (11 months, Year 1)	330
Supplies purchased for cash	2,950
Miscellaneous expenses paid	6,340

During the year Mary's Boutique Ltd. sold merchandise for $57,600 — $8,900 for cash — and collected all credit sales except $5,300. However, Mary expected to collect only $4,100 from the accounts outstanding. Mary had recorded and summarized the cost of each item of merchandise sold and for the year the total was $24,800. The cost of the merchandise remaining was $8,700, leaving $1,100 of purchases unaccounted for. Brooks attributed this difference to theft or failure to record the cost of the item sold. At January 31, Year 2, Mary estimated the boutique had supplies on hand that cost about $250.

The bank had deducted interest and bank charges, totaling $1,400, from the boutique's account. The major portion of this deduction was for interest on the demand loan which, at January 31, Year 2, was $10,000. This demand loan was fully secured by a government bond Mary had purchased for the firm for $10,000 when she originally organized it and had excess cash on hand. The current market value of this bond was $10,200. The firm had received $600 interest on the bond during the year and $400 additional interest had been earned to January 31, Year 2. The bank balance at January 31, Year 2 was $7,480.

When Mary's Boutique Ltd. was formed, a friendly insurance agent had sold Mary Brooks a comprehensive policy for the business with a two-year premium of $480, which had been paid and included in the miscellaneous expenses.

The firm had paid the previous store occupant $20,000 for the existing furniture and fixtures, which are estimated to last for ten years.

Brooks has very good relations with her suppliers, to whom she owed $6,200 at January 31, Year 2.

Income tax is payable by Mary's Boutique Ltd. calculated at 20 percent of net income before income tax.

Prepare a set of financial statements for Mary's Boutique Ltd., to show the results of the first year of business. Do you think that Mary Brooks would have a successful career as a boutique operator?

Chapter 4 Income Statement: Extensions of the Accrual Concept

Chapter 3 points out that most business firms use an accrual, rather than a cash, basis of accounting. The two distinguishing features of the accrual basis are the following:

1. Revenue is recognized when all, or a substantial portion, of the services to be provided have been performed and cash, a receivable, or some other asset whose cash equivalent can be measured objectively has been received.
2. Expenses are recognized in the period when related revenues are recognized or, if not associated with a particular revenue stream, expenses are recognized in the period when goods or services are consumed in operations.

For most merchandising firms, revenue is recognized in the period when goods are sold. Expenses are then matched either directly with the revenue or with the period when goods or services are consumed. This chapter explores the application of the accrual concept to other types of businesses: firms involved in manufacturing, firms involved in long-term contract activities, and firms selling goods on an installment basis.

Accrual Basis for Manufacturers

A manufacturing firm incurs various costs in changing the physical form of the goods it produces. Figure 4.1 depicts the operating process for a typical manufacturing firm. A firm acquires productive facilities (plant and equipment) to provide capacity to manufacture goods. Raw materials for use in production are also acquired. Converting raw materials into a salable product requires labour and other manufacturing services (for example, utilities, insurance, taxes, and depreciation on production facilities) during the period of production. The finished product is held in inventory until sold. When the good is sold, either cash is collected or a receivable from the customer arises.

Figure 4.1
Earnings Process for Manufacturing Firm

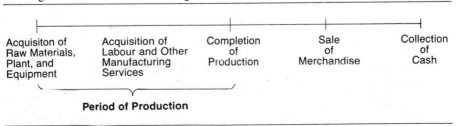

| Acquisiton of Raw Materials, Plant, and Equipment | Acquisition of Labour and Other Manufacturing Services | Completion of Production | Sale of Merchandise | Collection of Cash |

Period of Production

Most manufacturing firms recognize revenue at the time goods are sold. At this time, the production actvity has been completed, a customer has been identified and a selling price agreed upon, and an assessment of the customer's credit standing provides a reasonable basis for estimating the amount of cash that will be collected.

Accounting for Manufacturing Costs

As Chapter 3 points out, a merchandising firm acquires inventory items in finished form ready for sale. The acquisition cost of these items remains in the asset account, Merchandise Inventory, until the units are sold. At the time of sale, the cost of the items sold is transferred from the asset account, Merchandise Inventory, to the expense account, Cost of Goods Sold.

A manufacturing firm, on the other hand, incurs various costs in transforming raw materials into finished products. These manufacturing costs are generally classified into direct material (or raw material), direct labour, and manufacturing overhead. Manufacturing overhead includes a variety of indirect costs that provide a firm with productive capacity (depreciation, insurance, and taxes on manufacturing facilities, supervisory labour, and supplies for factory equipment). Until the units are sold and revenue is recognized, manufacturing costs are treated as product costs—assets—and accumulated in various inventory accounts.

A manufacturing firm, like a merchandising firm, also incurs various selling costs (commissions for the sales staff, depreciation, insurance and taxes on the sales staff's automobiles) and administrative costs (salary of president, depreciation on computer facilities). Selling and administrative costs are treated as period expenses by both merchandising and manufacturing firms. Figure 4.2 summarizes the nature and flow of various costs for a manufacturing firm.

Figure 4.2
Diagram of Cost Flows

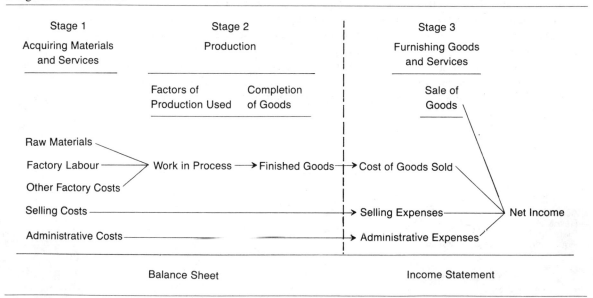

Separate inventory accounts are maintained by a manufacturing firm for product costs incurred at various stages of completion. The Raw Materials Inventory account includes the cost of raw materials purchased but not yet transferred to production. The balance in the Raw Materials Inventory account indicates the cost of raw materials on hand in the raw materials storeroom or warehouse. When raw materials are issued to producing departments, the cost of the materials is transferred from the Raw Materials Inventory account to the Work-in-Process Inventory account. The Work-in-Process Inventory account accumulates the costs incurred in producing units during the period. The Work-in-Process Inventory account is debited for the cost of raw materials transferred from the raw materials storeroom, the cost of direct labour services used, and the manufacturing overhead cost incurred. The Work-in-Process Inventory account is credited for the total manufacturing cost of units completed in the factory and transferred to the finished goods storeroom. The Finished Goods Inventory account includes the total manufacturing cost of units completed but not ye sold. The cost of units sold during the period is transferred from the Finished Goods Inventory account to the Cost-of-Goods-Sold account. Figure 4.3 show the flow of manufacturing cost through the various inventory and other accounts.

Illustration of the Accounting Process for a Manufacturing Firm

The accounting process for a manufacturing firm is illustrated with information about the operations of the Moon Manufacturing Co. Ltd. The company was formed on December 31, with the issuance of 10,000 no par value common shares for $30 per share. Transactions during January are described below, and the appropriate journal entries are provided:

1. A building costing $200,000 and equipment costing $50,000 are acquired for cash.

Building (A)	$200,000	
Equipment (A)	50,000	
Cash (A)		$250,000

2. Raw materials costing $25,000 are purchased on account.

Raw Materials Inventory (A)	$25,000	
Accounts Payable (L)		$25,000

3. Raw materials costing $20,000 are issued to producing departments.

Work-in-Process Inventory (A)	$20,000	
Raw Materials Inventory (A)		$20,000

4. The total payroll for January is $60,000. Of this amount, $40,000 is paid to factory workers, and $20,000 is paid to selling and administrative personnel.

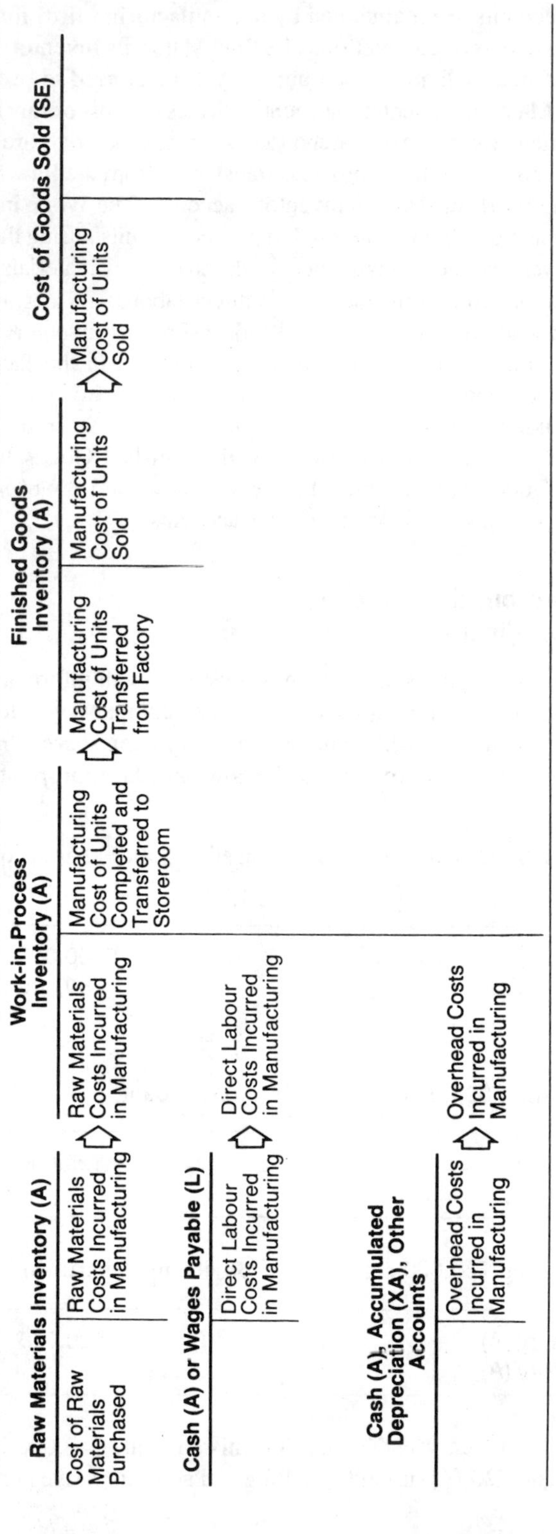

Figure 4.3
Flow of Manufacturing Costs through the Accounts

Raw Materials Inventory (A)

Cost of Raw Materials Purchased

Raw Materials Costs Incurred in Manufacturing

Cash (A) or Wages Payable (L)

Direct Labour Costs Incurred in Manufacturing

Cash (A), Accumulated Depreciation (XA), Other Accounts

Overhead Costs Incurred in Manufacturing

Work-in-Process Inventory (A)

Raw Materials Costs Incurred in Manufacturing

Direct Labour Costs Incurred in Manufacturing

Overhead Costs Incurred in Manufacturing

Manufacturing Cost of Units Completed and Transferred to Storeroom

Finished Goods Inventory (A)

Manufacturing Cost of Units Transferred from Factory

Manufacturing Cost of Units Sold

Cost of Goods Sold (SE)

Manufacturing Cost of Units Sold

Work-in-Process Inventory (A)	$40,000	
Salaries Expense (SE)	20,000	
Cash (A)		$60,000

Recall that nonmanufacturing costs are recorded as expenses of the period in which the services are consumed, because these costs rarely create assets with future benefits. Journal entry (4), as well as entries (5) and (6) below, illustrate the difference between the recording of a product cost and a period expense.

5. The expenditures for utilities during January are $1,200. Of this amount, $1,000 is attributable to manufacturing, and $200 to selling and administrative activities.

Work-in-Process Inventory (A)	$1,000	
Utilities Expense (SE)	200	
Cash (A)		$1,200

6. Depreciation on building and equipment during January is as follows: factory, $8,000; selling and administrative, $2,000.

Work-in-Process Inventory (A)	$8,000	
Depreciation Expense (SE)	2,000	
Accumulated Depreciation (XA)		$10,000

7. The manufacturing cost of units completed during January and transferred to the finished goods storeroom is $48,500.

Finished Goods Inventory (A)	$48,500	
Work-in-Process Inventory (A)		$48,500

8. Sales during January total $75,000, of which $25,000 is on account.

Cash (A)	$50,000	
Accounts Receivable (A)	25,000	
Sales Revenue (SE)		$75,000

9. The cost of the goods sold during January is $42,600.

Cost of Goods Sold (SE)	$42,600	
Finished Goods Inventory (A)		$42,600

10. The income tax for January is $2,000.

Income Tax Expense (SE)	$2,000	
Income Tax Payable (L)		$2,000

Exhibit 4.1 shows how the various manufacturing and other costs incurred flow through the accounts. Exhibit 4.2 presents an income statement for Moon Manufacturing Co. Ltd. for January.

Exhibit 4.1
MOON MANUFACTURING CO. LTD.
T-Accounts Showing Transactions during January

Raw Materials Inventory (At)				Work-in-Process Inventory (A)		
(2) 25,000	20,000 (3)			(3) 20,000	48,500 (7)	
				(4) 40,000		
				(5) 1,000		
				(6) 8,000		
Bal. 1/31 5,000				Bal. 1/31 20,500		

Finished Goods Inventory (A)			Cost of Goods Sold (SE)	
(7) 48,500	42,600 (9)		(9) 42,600	
Bal. 1/31 5,900			Bal. 1/31 42,600	

Cash (A)				Accounts Receivable (A)	
Bal. 1/1 300,000	250,000 (1)			(8) 25,000	
(8) 50,000	60,000 (4)				
	1,200 (5)				
Bal. 1/31 38,800				Bal. 1/31 25,000	

Building (A)			Equipment (A)	
(1) 200,000			(1) 50,000	
Bal. 1/31 200,000			Bal. 1/31 50,000	

Accumulated Depreciation (XA)			Salaries Expense (SE)	
	10,000 (6)		(4) 20,000	
	10,000 Bal. 1/31		Bal. 1/31 20,000	

Sales Revenue (SE)	
	75,000 (8)
	75,000 Bal. 1/31

Accounts Payable (L)	
	25,000 (2)
	25,000 Bal. 1/31

Utilities Expense (SE)	
(5) 200	
Bal. 1/31 200	

Depreciation Expense (SE)	
(6) 2,000	
Bal. 1/31 2,000	

Income Tax Expense (SE)	
(10) 2,000	
Bal. 1/31 2,000	

Income Tax Payable (L)	
	2,000 (10)
	2,000 Bal. 1/31

Exhibit 4.2
MOON MANUFACTURING CO. LTD.
Income Statement for the Month of January

Sales Revenue		$75,000
Less: Cost of Goods Sold		42,600
Gross Profit		$32,400
Less: Operating Expenses		
Salaries	$20,000	
Utilities	200	
Depreciation	2,000	22,200
Net Income before Income Tax		$10,200
Income Tax Expense		2,000
Net Income		$ 8,200

Summary of the Accounting for Manufacturing Operations

The accounting procedures for the selling and administrative costs of manufacturing firms resemble those for merchandising firms. These costs are treated as expenses of the period in which services are consumed. The accounting procedures for a manufacturing firm differ from those of a merchandising firm primarily in the treatment of inventories. A manufacturing firm incurs various costs in transforming raw materials into finished products. Until the units produced are sold, manufacturing costs are accumulated in inventory accounts — the Work-in-Process Inventory account or the Finished Goods Inventory account — depending on the stage of completion of each unit being produced. Product costs are therefore debited to inventory (asset) accounts until the time of sale.

Job Order Costing in Service Industries

Many firms in service industries use variations of job order costing systems for accumulating costs and developing billings to customers. Manufacturing firms typically accumulate costs by job or product while service firms accumulate costs by client (accounting and law firms) or by project (engineering and architectural firms).

For example, in a public accounting firm, revenues are based on services provided by professional staff. Each staff member keeps track of all time during the workweek according to classification codes such as the following:

001–900	Charge code for each client to be billed.
901	Unassigned (uncharge-able) time.
902	Training.
903	Client development and promotion.
904	Community service.
905	Service to the institute.

In addition, a suffix system might be used; for example:

A	Audit work.
B	Accounting services.
C	Tax services.
D	Management advisory services.
E	Other.

Some firms keep track of staff time to the nearest quarter hour.

In addition to the billable hours charged by professional staff, accounting firms have large administrative and support structures whose costs must also be recovered by fees billed to clients. These costs include secretarial support, library research staff, office space, computers, and even the managing partner's salary. Thus, an overhead charge is built into per diem billing rates of the professional staff. For instance, a staff assistant may be charged out at $30 an hour, although his or her hourly salary may be less than half that amount.

Accounting firms do not usually detail these overhead charges when invoicing clients, although breakdowns should be available to clients who request them. This is one area in which small accounting firms and sole practitioners have a distinct advantage over national and international accounting firms. Small firms have a much lower overhead structure and can pass on these savings through lower billing rates.

Control of costs is as important in an accounting firm as in any manufacturing firm. And because labour is a service firm's product, control of costs equals control of time. It is important, therefore, for accountants and other professionals to be "clock watchers."

Accrual Basis for Long-Term Contractors

The earnings process for a long-term contractor (for example, building construction, ship-building) differs from that of a manufacturing firm (depicted in Figure 4.1) in three important respects:

1. The period of construction (production) may span several accounting periods.
2. A customer is identified and a contract price agreed upon in advance (or at least in the early stages of construction).
3. Periodic payments of the contract price are often made by the buyer as work progresses.

The criteria for the recognition of revenue from long-term contracts are often satisfied during the period of construction. The existence of a contract indicates that a buyer has been identified and a price agreed upon. Either cash is collected in advance or an assessment of the customer's credit standing leads to a reasonable expectation that the contract price will be received in cash after construction is completed. Although future services required on these long-term construction contracts can be substantial at any given time, the costs to be incurred in providing these services can often be estimated with reasonable precision. In agreeing to a contract price, the firm must have some confidence in its estimates of the total costs to be incurred on the contract.

When the criteria for revenue recognition are met as construction progresses, revenue is usually recognized during the period of construction using the *percentage-of-completion method*. Under the percentage-of-completion method, a portion of the total contract price, based on the degree of completion of the work during the period, is recognized as revenue each period. This proportion is based either on engineers' or architects' estimates of the degree of completion or on the ratio of costs incurred to date to the total expected costs for the contract. The actual schedule of cash collections is *not* significant for the revenue recognition process when the percentage-of-completion method is used. Even if all of the contract price is collected at completion of construction, the percentage-of-completion method may still be used as long as reasonable estimates of the amount of cash to be collected and of the costs remaining to be incurred can be made as construction progresses.

As portions of the contract price are recognized as revenues, corresponding proportions of the total estimated costs of the contract are recognized as expenses. Thus, the percentage-of-completion method follows the accrual basis of accounting, because expenses are matched with related revenues.

To illustrate the percentage-of-completion method, assume that a firm agrees to construct a bridge for $5,000,000. Estimated costs are as follows: Year 1, $1,500,000; Year 2, $2,000,000; Year 3, $500,000. Thus, the expected profit from the contract is $1,000,000 (= $5,000,000 − $1,500,000 − $2,000,000 − $500,000).

Assuming that the degree of completion is based on the percentage of total costs incurred and that actual costs are incurred as anticipated, revenue and expense from the contract are as follows:

Year	Degree of Completion	Revenue	Expense	Profit
1	$1,500,000/$4,000,000 = 37.5%	$1,875,000	$1,500,000	$ 375,000
2	$2,000,000/$4,000,000 = 50.0%	2,500,000	2,000,000	500,000
3	$500,000/$4,000,000 = 12.5%	625,000	500,000	125,000
		$5,000,000	$4,000,000	$1,000,000

Some firms involved with construction contracts postpone the recognition of revenue until the construction project and the sale are completed. This method is the same as the completed sale basis, but is often referred to as the *completed contract method* of recognizing revenue. If the completed contract method were used in the example above, no revenue or expense from the contract would be recognized during Year 1 or Year 2. In Year 3, contract revenue of $5,000,000 and contract expenses of $4,000,000 would be recognized in measuring net income.

In some cases, the completed contract method is used because the contracts are of such short duration (such as a few months) that earnings reported with the percentage of completion method and the completed contract method are not significantly different. In these cases, the completed contract method is used because it is generally easier to implement. Firms use the completed contract method in situations when a specific buyer has not been obtained during the periods while construction is progressing, as is sometimes the case in constructing residential housing. In these cases, future selling efforts are required and substantial uncertainty may exist regarding the contract price ultimately to be established and the amount of cash to be received.

The primary reason for a contractor's not using the percentage-of-completion method when a contract exists is the uncertainty of total costs to be incurred in carrying out the project. If total costs cannot be reasonably estimated, the percentage of total costs incurred by a given date also cannot be estimated, and the percentage of services already rendered (revenue) cannot be determined.

Accrual Basis When Cash Collectibility Is Extremely Uncertain

Occasionally, estimating the amount of cash or cash equivalent value of other assets that will be received from customers is difficult. This may occur because the future financial condition of the buyer is highly uncertain or because the payments are spread over a very long period of time. Therefore, an objective measure of the present value of the cash to be received cannot be made at the time of the sale. Under these circumstances, revenue is recognized at the time of cash collection using either the installment method or the cost-recovery-first method described below. Unlike the cash method of accounting, however, there is an attempt to match expenses with revenues.

Installment Method

Under the installment method, revenue is recognized as parts of the selling price are collected in cash. At the same time, corresponding parts of the cost of the good or service sold are recognized as expenses. For example, assume that merchandise costing $60 is sold for $100. The buyer agrees to pay (ignoring interest) $20 per month for five months. Under the installment method, revenue of $20 is recognized each month as cash is received. Likewise, cost of goods sold is $12 (= $20/$100 × $60) each month. By the end of five months, total income of $40 [= 5 × ($20 − $12)] would be recognized.

The installment method is sometimes used by land development companies. These companies typically sell undeveloped land and promise to develop it over several future years. The buyer makes a nominal down payment and agrees to pay the remainder of the purchase price in installments over 10, 20, or more years. In these cases, future development of the land is a significant aspect of the earnings process. Also, substantial uncertainty often exists as to the ultimate collectibility of the installment notes, particularly those not due until several years in the future. The customer can always elect to stop making payments, merely losing the right to own the land.

Cost-Recovery-First Method

Under circumstances where there is great uncertainty about cash collection, the *cost-recovery-first method* of income recognition can also be used. Under this method, costs of generating revenues are matched dollar for dollar with cash receipts until all such costs are recovered. Revenues and total expenses are equal in each period until all costs are recovered. Only when cumulative cash receipts exceed total costs will profit (that is, revenue without any matching expenses) be shown in the income statement.

To illustrate the cost-recovery-first method, refer to the example above relating to the sale of merchandise for $100. During the first three months, revenue of $20 and expenses of $20 would be recognized. By the end of the third month, cumulative cash receipts of $60 would be exactly equal to the cost of the merchandise sold. During the fourth and fifth months, revenue of $20 per month would be recognized but without an offsetting expense. For the five months as a whole, total income of $40 would again be recognized, but in a different pattern than under the installment method.

Use of Installment and Cost-Recovery-First Methods

Generally accepted accounting principles permit the installment method and the cost-recovery-first method only when great uncertainty exists about cash collection. For most sales of goods and services, past experience and an assessment of customers' credit standings provide a sufficient basis for estimating the amount of cash to be received.

The installment method is allowable for income tax reporting under certain circumstances, even when cash collections are assured. Retailers and other firms selling on extended payment plans often use the installment method for income tax reporting (while recognizing revenue at the time of sale for financial reporting). The cost-recovery-first method is not permitted for income tax reporting.

Recognition of Revenue between Purchase and Sale

The period between the acquisition or production of inventory items and the sale of the items is referred to as a *holding period*. The current market prices of these assets could change during this holding period while the items are held in inventory. Such changes are described as *unrealized holding gains and losses*, because a transaction or exchange has not taken place.

Unrealized holding gains could be recognized as they occur. Accountants typically wait, however, until the asset is sold or exchanged in an arm's length transaction before recognizing any gain. At that time, an inflow of net assets subject to objective measurement takes place. Because the accountant assumes that the firm is a going concern, the unrealized gain will eventually be recognized as revenue in the ordinary course of business in a future period. The recognition of revenue and the valuation of assets are therefore closely associated. Nonmonetary assets are typically stated at acquisition cost until sold. At the time of sale, an inflow of net assets occurs (for example, cash, accounts receivable), and revenue reflecting the previously unreported unrealized gain is recognized. This treatment of unrealized holding gains has the effect of shifting income from periods when the asset is held and the market price increases to the later period of sale. The longer the holding period (as, for example, land held for several decades), the more is reported income likely to be shifted to later periods.

Current accounting practices do not treat all unrealized holding losses in the same way as unrealized holding gains. If the current market prices of inventory items or temporary investments decrease below acquisition cost during the holding period, the asset is usually written down with a credit to the asset account. The matching debit recognizes the unrealized loss in the period of price decline. This treatment of losses rests on the convention that earnings should be reported conservatively. Considering the estimates and predictions required in measuring revenues and expenses, some accountants prefer to provide a conservative measure of earnings so that statement users will not be misled into thinking the firm is doing better than it really is.

The inconsistent treatment of unrealized gains and unrealized losses does not seem warranted. The arguments used against recognizing unrealized gains apply equally well to unrealized losses. If gains cannot be measured objectively prior to sale, then how can losses be measured prior to sale? If losses can be measured objectively prior to sale, then why cannot gains? The accounting treatment of unrealized holding gains and losses is considered further in Chapters 7, 8, and 13.

Summary Illustration of Income Recognition Methods

Exhibit 4.3 illustrates various methods of income recognition discussed in Chapters 3 and 4. The illustration relates to a contract for the construction of a bridge for $12 million. The expected and actual pattern of cash receipts and disbursements under the contract is as follows:

Period	Expected and Actual Cash Receipts	Expected and Actual Cash Expenditures
1	$ 1,000,000	$1,600,000
2	1,000,000	4,000,000
3	2,000,000	4,000,000
4	4,000,000	—
5	4,000,000	—
Total	$12,000,000	$9,600,000

The bridge was completed in period 3. Exhibit 4.3 indicates the revenues, expenses, and income recognized each period under the contract using the cash basis of accounting, the percentage of completion method, the completed contract (completed sale) method, the installment method, and the cost-recovery-first method. Not all five methods of income recognition could be justified for financial reporting. They are presented merely for illustrative purposes. Note that the total revenues, expenses, and income recognized for the five years are the same for all methods. In historical cost accounting over long enough time periods, income is equal to cash inflows less cash outflows. The patterns of annual income differ significantly, however, depending on the accounting method.

Exhibit 4.3
Comprehensive Illustration of
Revenue and Expense Recognition
(All Dollar Amounts in Thousands)

Period	Cash Basis of Accounting[a]		
	Revenue	Expense	Income
1	$ 1,000	$1,600	$ (600)
2	1,000	4,000	(3,000)
3	2,000	4,000	(2,000)
4	4,000	—	4,000
5	4,000	—	4,000
Total	$12,000	$9,600	$2,400

Period	Percentage of Completion Method			Completed Contract Method		
	Revenue	Expense	Income	Revenue	Expense	Income
1	$ 2,000[d]	$1,600	$ 400	$ —	$ —	$ —
2	5,000[e]	4,000	1,000	—	—	—
3	5,000[e]	4,000	1,000	12,000	9,600	2,400
4	—	—	—	—	—	—
5	—	—	—	—	—	—
Total	$12,000	$9,600	$2,400	$12,000	$9,600	$2,400

Period	Installment Method[b]			Cost-Recovery-First Method[c]		
	Revenue	Expense	Income	Revenue	Expense	Income
1	$ 1,000	800[f]	$ 200	$ 1,000	$1,000	$ 0
2	1,000	800[f]	200	1,000	1,000	0
3	2,000	1,600[g]	400	2,000	2,000	0
4	4,000	3,200[h]	800	4,000	4,000	0
5	4,000	3,200[h]	800	4,000	1,600	2,400
Total	$12,000	$9,600	$2,400	$12,000	$9,600	$2,400

[a]The cash basis is not allowed for tax reporting, except for farming and fishing businesses.
[b]The installment method should be used for financial reporting only if extreme uncertainty exists as to the amount of cash to be collected from customers.
[c]The cost-recovery-first method is allowed for financial reporting only if extreme uncertainty exists as to the amount of cash to be collected from customers. It is not permitted for tax purposes.
[d]$1,600/$9,600 × $12,000.   [f]$1,000/$12,000 × $9,600.   [h]$4,000/$12,000 × $9,600.
[e]$4,000/$9,600 × $12,000.   [g]$2,000/$12,000 × $9,600.

Profits are ok, Says Society

*I*n "Can Ethics and Profits Live Under the Same Corporate Roof" (March/April), author Ralph Sorenson makes a valiant effort but is in trouble right from the title line.

"Ethics" and "profits" are not mutually exclusive words or concepts. It's a shame when we in the business community concede that fundamental argument right off the bat.

Corporations exist in our society to fulfill needs. Consider that the other alternative is to have some form of government organization fulfill those needs. Most would agree that there's no point in arguing which is more ethical.

Let's go on. Whether or not an individual corporation consciously realizes it, it has a raison d'etre, a reason for being. And every company's raison d'etre is different from that of the next company, but they all fit the same template: "Do something for somebody." (As an aside, the degree of success of corporations is closely aligned with how well the organization perceives and adheres to its raison d'etre.)

That's all very nice, but what about profits? While raisons d'etre come in all sizes and shapes, the corollary to them all is the same—the corporation must make a profit. Otherwise, how will you be able to fulfill your raison d'etre tomorrow?

Conceptually, profits are society's way of saying that they like and appreciate what you are doing for them and probably would like you to continue providing similar value tomorrow. Nothing unethical about that, is there?

John G. B. Howland
President
Coordinated Capital
Resources, Inc.
Glenview, Illinois

Reprinted with the special permission of *Financial Executive*. July/August 1988, p. 10.

Format and Classification Within the Income Statement

One of the major objectives in income statement presentation is to show the results of normal business operations as distinct from gains and losses resulting from highly infrequent or unusual transactions. Segregating these items makes it easier for financial statement users to predict future earnings performance of the company.

The income statement might contain some or all of the following additional sections or categories beyond those described previously, depending on the nature of the firm's income for the period:

1. Income before extraordinary items
2. Extraordinary gains and losses
3. Net income for the period
4. Earnings per share

The majority of income statements include only the Net Income and Earnings per Share sections. The other sections are added if necessary. The income statement for General Products Limited in Appendix A (p. 760) contains several of these classifications of income.

Income before Extraordinary Items Revenues, gains, expenses, and losses from continuing areas of business activity of a firm are presented in the first section of the income statement. A heading such as ''Net Income (or Net Earnings) for the Year'' is used if there are no other sections in the income statement. This segment of the income statement should show the following amounts separately, if material:[1]

1. Sales
2. Income from investments by major class
3. Income from operating and sales-type leases
4. Government assistance credited directly to income
5. Depreciation, depletion, and amortization of leasehold improvements
6. Amortization of deferred charges and intangible assets
7. Research and development costs
8. Interest expense by class of investment
9. Gains, losses, and provisions for losses resulting from normal business activities that are both abnormal in size and caused by rare or unusual circumstances
10. Income taxes

In addition, the income statement should include the amount of income from contingent and sub-lease rentals, the cost of goods sold, other major operating expenses, and rentals for the year under lease obligations.

The information presented above is frequently included in the footnotes to the financial statements rather than in the body of the statement.

Extraordinary Gains and Losses Extraordinary items are ''gains, losses and provisions for losses which, by their nature, are not typical of the normal business activities of the enterprise, are not expected to occur regularly over a period of years, and are not considered as recurring factors in any evaluation of the ordinary operations of the enterprise.''[2]

Examples of extraordinary items appearing in contemporary financial statements are:

1. Gains or losses from disposals of assets used in discontinued operations
2. Realization of taxable loss carry-forward
3. Sale or disposal of assets other than those of discontinued operations
4. Write-down of assets to their market value
5. Gains or losses on expropriation of property
6. Catastrophes and ''Acts of God'' such as earthquakes, floods, fires, etc.

Income taxes payable resulting from an extraordinary gain must be deducted from the gain and the ''aftertax'' total added to ''net income before extraordinary items'' to arrive at the ''net income for the period.'' The income tax recoverable from an extraordinary loss will be treated in a similar fashion.

This method is referred to as the ''net of tax'' treatment. Suppose Fisher Ltd. had pre-tax income from operations of $125,000 and, in addition, suffered an

---

[1] *CICA Handbook*, section 1520.
[2] *CICA Handbook*, section 3480.

extraordinary loss of $30,000 from a flood. Assuming a 40% income tax rate, the bottom section of the income statement would appear as follows:

Income before Taxes and Extraordinary Item		$125,000
Less: Income Taxes		50,000
Income before Extraordinary Item		$ 75,000
Extraordinary Item:		
Flood Loss (Note X)	$30,000	
Less: Tax Reduction from Flood Loss	12,000	18,000
Net Income		$ 57,000

The total income taxes payable of $38,000 [($125,000–$30,000) × 40%] is split on the statement as $50,000 on operating revenue, less a $12,000 reduction caused by claiming a flood loss. In this way, readers can readily see the tax impact of extraordinary gains and losses.

During the last decade extraordinary items have appeared in one-third of the income statements of companies included in the *Financial Reporting in Canada* sample.

Unusual or Nonrecurring Items These items do not meet the strict criteria for extraordinary items mentioned above but nevertheless are considered worthy of separate disclosure in the income statement because of their abnormal size or the circumstances creating them. Examples of such items include gains and losses from: (a) the writeoff or writedown of receivables and inventories (b) the exchange or translation of foreign currencies into Canadian dollars (c) the sale or abandonment of property, plant, or equipment used in the business (d) the effects of a strike, and (e) the adjustment of long-term contract accruals. The usefulness of the income statement is enhanced by reporting items such as these as a separate item in the statement.

Earnings per Share Probably the two most widely used numbers reported on financial statements are net income and earnings per share (EPS). These two statistics are important pieces of information in making investment decisions about a company. As the name suggests, EPS indicates the maximum current earnings that theoretically could be distributed to each shareholder after the prior claims of debt holders and preferred shareholders have been satisfied. Earnings per share data must be shown either on the face of the income statement or in a note to the financial statements cross-referenced to the income statement. With only a few exceptions, companies present this information on the face of the income statement.

Both basic and fully diluted earnings per share are to be presented in the income statement for income before extraordinary items (if relevant) and net income for the period.

The basic earnings per common share are conventionally calculated by dividing net income minus preferred share dividends by the weighted average number of outstanding common shares during the accounting period. For example, assume that a firm had a net income of $500,000 during the year 1986. Dividends declared and paid on outstanding preferred were $100,000. The average number of common shares outstanding during 1986 was one million shares. Earnings per common share would be $.40 [= ($500,000 − $100,000) ÷ 1,000,000].

Assume now this firm had 1,000,000 shares outstanding on January 1 but issued an additional 400,000 shares on September 1. The weighted average number of shares outstanding for the year ended December 31 would be calculated as follows:

Shares	Months Outstanding	Share Months
1,000,000	8	8,000,000
1,400,000	4	5,600,000
		13,600,000
		÷ 12
		= 1,133,333 shares

Where extraordinary items are presented in the income statement, earnings per share before extraordinary items will be shown in addition to the above. The difference between this figure and the basic earnings per common share will be the amount of extraordinary items divided by the average number of common shares outstanding.

If a firm has securities outstanding that can be converted into or exchanged for common shares, it may be required to present two sets of earnings per share amounts: *basic earnings per share* and *fully diluted earnings per share*. For example, some firms issue convertible bonds or convertible preferred shares, which can be exchanged directly for common shares. Also, many firms have employee stock option plans under which the company's common shares may be acquired by employees under special arrangements. If these convertible securities were to be converted or stock options were to be exercised and additional common shares were issued, the amount conventionally shown as earnings per share would probably decrease, or become *diluted*. When a firm has outstanding securities that, if exchanged for common shares, would decrease earnings per share, a dual presentation of basic and fully diluted earnings per share is required.

Problem 1 for Self-Study

The following data relate to the manufacturing activities of the Haskell Co. Ltd. during March:

	March 31	March 1
Raw Materials Inventory	$ 46,900	$42,400
Work-in-Process Inventory	63,200	75,800
Finished Goods Inventory	46,300	44,200
Factory Costs Incurred during the Month:		
Raw Materials Purchased	$ 60,700	
Labour Services Received	137,900	
Heat, Light, and Power	1,260	
Rent	4,100	

Expirations of Previous Factory Acquisitions and Prepayments:

Depreciation of Factory Equipment	$ 1,800
Prepaid Insurance Expired	1,440

Other Data Relating to the Month:

Sales	$400,000
Selling and Administrative Expenses	125,000
Estimated Income Tax Expense	25,000

   a. Calculate the cost of raw materials used during March.

   b. Calculate the cost of units completed during March and transferred to the finished goods storeroom.

   c. Calculate the cost of goods sold during March.

   d. Calculate net income for March.

Suggested Solution

The transactions and events relating to manufacturing activities are shown in the appropriate T-accounts in Exhibit 4.4.

Exhibit 4.4
T-Accounts and Transactions
for Haskell Co. Ltd.

Raw Materials Inventory			
Bal.	42,400		
(1)	60,700	56,200	(2)ⁱ
Bal.	46,900		

Work-in-Process Inventory			
Bal.	75,800		
(2)	56,200	215,300	(8)*
(3)	137,900		
(4)	1,260		
(5)	4,100		
(6)	1,800		
(7)	1,440		
Bal.	63,200		

Finished Goods Inventory			
Bal.	44,200		
(8)ⁱⁱ	215,300	213,200	(9)ⁱⁱⁱ
Bal.	46,300		

Cost of Goods Sold	
(9)	213,200

Cash or Various Liabilities		
	60,700	(1)
	137,900	(3)
	1,260	(4)
	4,100	(5)

Prepaid Insurance		
	1,440	(7)

Accumulated Depreciation		
	1,800	(6)

---

*Amount calculated by plugging.

   i. The cost of raw materials used is $56,200 (= $42,400 + $60,700 − $46,900).
  ii. The cost of units completed during March is $215,300.
 iii. The cost of units sold during March is $213,200 (= $44,200 + $215,300 − $46,300).
  iv. Net income is $36,800 (= $400,000 − $213,200 − $125,000 − $25,000).

Problem 2 for Self-Study

The Brennan Construction Co. Ltd. contracted on May 15, Year 2 to build a bridge for the city for $4,500,000. Brennan estimated the cost of constructing the bridge would be $3,600.000. Brennan incurred $1,200,000 in construction costs during Year 2, $2,000,000 during Year 3, and $400,000 during Year 4 in completing the bridge. The city paid $1,000,000 during Year 2, $1,500,000 during Year 3, and the remaining $2,000,000 of the contract price at the time the bridge was completed and approved in Year 4.

a. Calculate the net income (revenue less expenses before income tax) of Brennan on the contract during Year 2, Year 3, and Year 4, assuming that the percentage-of-completion method is used.

b. Repeat (**a**), assuming that the completed contract method is used.

c. Repeat (**a**), assuming that the installment method is used.

d. Repeat (**a**), assuming that the cost-recovery-first method is used.

Suggested Solution

a. Percentage-of-Completion Method:

Year	Incremental Percentage Complete	Revenue Recognized	Expenses Recognized	Net Income
2	12/36 (.333)	$1,500,000	$1,200,000	$300,000
3	20/36 (.556)	2,500,000	2,000,000	500,000
4	4/36 (.111)	500,000	400,000	100,000
Total	36/36 (1.000)	$4,500,000	$3,600,000	$900,000

b. Completed Contract Method:

Year	Revenue Recognized	Expenses Recognized	Net Income
2	$ 0	$ 0	$ 0
3	0	0	0
4	4,500,000	3,600,000	900,000
Total	$4,500,000	$3,600,000	$900,000

c. Installment Method:

Year	Cash Collected (=Revenue)	Fraction of Cash Collected	Expenses (=Fraction × Total Cost)	Net Income
2	$1,000,000	2/9	$ 800,000	$200,000
3	1,500,000	3/9	1,200,000	300,000
4	2,000,000	4/9	1,600,000	400,000
Total	$4,500,000	1.0	$3,600,000	$900,000

d. Cost-Recovery-First Method:

Year	Cash Collected (= Revenue)	Expenses Recognized	Net Income
2	$1,000,000	$1,000,000	$ 0
3	1,500,000	1,500,000	0
4	2,000,000	1,100,000	900,000
Total	$4,500,000	$3,600,000	$900,000

Problem 3 for Self-Study

The following information is available regarding the NEWCO Company:
   January 1, 1987—50,000 common shares issued
   December 1, 1987—1 for 10 stock dividend
   October 1, 1988—12,000 common shares issued for cash

	Years Ended December 31	
	1988	1987
Earnings before extraordinary item	$110,200	$110,000

Not included in the above earnings is:
In 1988, a major fire destroyed one of NEWCO's buildings, which is estimated to have a net loss of $2,900 (all figures are shown net of taxes).
a. What earnings per share figures would be required on the December 31, 1988 comparative income statement?
b. Assume that on January 1, 1988, the following shares, in addition to the common shares, were outstanding:
   5,000 6%, $100 par cumulative preferred shares,
   5,000 10%, $50 par noncumulative preferred shares.
   What earnings per share figures would be required on the December 31, 1988, comparative income statement if:
   (1) dividends were declared in 1988,
   (2) dividends were not declared in 1988?

Suggested Solution

a.

	1986	1985
	$	$
Earnings before extraordinary items	$110,200	$110,000
Extraordinary items	(2,900)	—
Earnings after extraordinary items	$107,300	$110,000
Outstanding common shares		
Weighted average		
50,000 + 5,000		55,000
55,000 + (12,000 × 3/12)	58,000	
Earnings per share		
Before extraordinary items	$ 1.90	$ 2.00
Net earnings per share	$ 1.85	$ 2.00

b.

	1986	1985
Earnings before extraordinary items	$110,200	$110,000
Less: Dividends—6% cumulative	30,000	
—10% non-cumulative	25,000	
Subtotal	$ 55,200	$110,000
Extraordinary items	(2,900)	—
Earnings available to common shareholders, after extraordinary items	$ 52,300	$110,000
Weighted average of Common	58,000	55,000
Earnings per share before extraordinary items	$ .95	$ 2.00
Earnings per share after extraordinary items	$ .90	$ 2.00

Adapted with permission from the Society of Management Accountants of Canada.

Questions, Exercises, Problems and Cases

Questions

1. Review the meaning of the following concepts or terms discussed in this chapter.

    a. Product cost
    b. Period expense
    c. Direct material
    d. Direct labour
    e. Manufacturing overhead
    f. "Flow of costs"
    g. Raw materials inventory
    h. Work-in-process inventory
    i. Finished goods inventory
    j. Percentage-of-completion method

    k. Completed sales, or completed contract, method
    l. Installment method
    m. Cost-recovery-first method
    n. Unrealized holding gain or loss
    o. Conservatism
    p. Extraordinary gains and losses
    q. Basic earnings per share
    r. Fully diluted earnings per share

2. "Depreciation on equipment may be a product cost or a period expense, depending on the type of equipment." Explain.

3. Compare and contrast the Merchandise Inventory account of a merchandising firm and the Finished Goods Inventory account of a manufacturing firm.

4. The percentage-of-completion method is often used by construction companies. Why isn't this method of income recognition used by a typical manufacturing firm?

5. Under both the installment method and the cost-recovery-first method, revenue is recognized when cash is received. Why, then, is the pattern of income (that is, revenues minus expenses) over time different under these two methods?

6. Compare and contrast the installment method and the cash basis of accounting.

7. "When the *total* amount of cash to be collected from a customer is highly uncertain, the cost-recovery-first method seems more appropriate than the installment method." Explain.

8. Economists typically define income as an increase in value, or wealth, while assets are held. Accountants typically recognize income when the criteria for revenue recognition are satisfied. Why does the accountants' approach to income recognition differ from that of the economists?

9. Why do income statements separate income relating to continuing operations from income relating to discontinued operations?

Exercises

 10. *Identifying product costs and period expenses.* Indicate whether each of the following types of wages and salaries is a (1) product cost or (2) period expense:

a.	Cutting-machine operators	**j.**	Nightwatch force at the factory
b.	Delivery labour	**k.**	General office clerks
c.	Factory janitors	**l.**	Operator of a lift truck in the shipping room
d.	Factory payroll clerks	**m.**	President of the firm
e.	Factory superintendent	**n.**	Sales manager
f.	General office secretaries	**o.**	Shipping room workers
g.	Guards at factory gate	**p.**	Sweepers who clean retail store
h.	Inspectors in factory	**q.**	Traveling salespersons
i.	Maintenance workers who service factory machinery		

11. *Identifying product costs and period expenses.* Indicate whether each of the following types of materials and supplies is a (1) product cost or (2) period expense:

a. Cleaning lubricants for factory machines
b. Paper for central office computer
c. Glue used in assembling products
d. Supplies used by factory janitor

    e. Gasoline used by salespersons
    f. Sales promotion pamphlets distributed
    g. Materials used in training production workers

12. *Identifying product costs, period expenses, and assets.* Indicate whether each of the following costs is a (1) period expense, (2) product cost, or (3) some balance sheet account other than those for product costs.
    a. Office supplies used
    b. Salary of factory supervisor
    c. Purchase of a fire insurance policy on the store building for the three-year period beginning next month
    d. Expiration of one month's protection of the insurance in (c)
    e. Property taxes for the current year on the factory building
    f. Wages of truck drivers who deliver finished goods to customers
    g. Wages of factory workers who install a new machine
    h. Wages of mechanics who repair and service factory machines
    i. Salary of the president of the company
    j. Depreciation of office equipment
    k. Factory supplies used

13. *Raw materials inventory transactions.* Compute the missing item in each of the independent cases below.

	a	b	c	d
Raw Materials Inventory, Jan. 1	$ 15,000	$ 76,900	$ 28,700	?
Purchases of Raw Materials	$297,000	$696,000	?	$76,700
Raw Materials Used	$290,000	?	$467,300	$71,700
Raw Materials Inventory, Dec. 31	?	$ 72,100	$ 37,900	$12,300

14. *Work-in-process inventory transactions.* Compute the missing item in each of the following independent cases.

	a	b	c	d
Work-in-Process Inventory, Jan. 1	$ 26,000	$ 55,600	$ 39,400	?
Raw Materials Used	$290,000	$700,800	$ 467,300	$ 71,700
Direct Labour Cost	$260,000	$675,800	?	$ 87,300
Manufacturing Overhead Costs	$180,000	$267,900	$ 136,900	$42,900
Cost of Units Completed	$724,000	?	$1,206,600	$193,400
Work-in-Process Inventory, Dec. 31	?	$ 72,300	$ 35,900	$ 41,700

15. *Finished goods inventory transactions.* Compute the missing item in each of the independent cases below.

	a	b	c	d
Finished Goods Inventory, Jan. 1	$ 71,000	$ 189,300	$ 110,300	?
Cost of Units Completed	$724,000	$1,627,800	?	$193,400
Costs of Units Sold	$701,000	?	$1,197,900	$187,200
Finished Goods Inventory, Dec. 31 ...	?	$ 179,600	$ 119,000	$ 22,100

16. *Income computation for a manufacturing firm.* The following data relate to a manufacturing firm for a period:

Sales	$250,000
Cost of Units Completed	240,000
Costs of Units Sold	210,000
Selling and Administrative Expenses	30,000

Compute net income before income tax for the period.

17. *Income computation for a manufacturing firm.* The following data relate to the United Manufacturing Corporation for the month of April.

	April 30	April 1
Raw Materials Inventory	$10,000	0
Work-in-Process Inventory	25,000	0
Finished Goods Inventory	22,000	0

Manufacturing cost (direct material used, direct labour, manufacturing overhead) incurred during April totaled $65,000. Sales revenue for April was $25,000 and selling and administrative expenses were $2,000.

Compute net income before income tax for April.

18. *Percentage-of-completion and completed contract methods of income recognition.* A construction company agreed to build a warehouse for $2,500,000. Expected and actual costs to construct the warehouse were as follows: Year 1, $600,000; Year 2, $1,000,000; Year 3, $400,000. The warehouse was completed in Year 3.

Compute revenue, expense, and net income before income tax for Year 1, Year 2, and Year 3 using the percentage-of-completion method and the completed contract method.

19. *Installment and cost-recovery-first methods of income recognition.* A real estate firm sold a tract of land costing $80,000 to a manufacturing firm for $100,000. The manufacturing firm agreed to pay $25,000 per year for four years (plus interest).

Compute revenue, expense, and net income for each of the four years using the installment method and the cost-recovery-first method. Ignore interest and income tax.

Problems and Cases

20. *Preparation of journal entries and income statement for a manufacturing firm.* Westside Products Inc. showed the following amounts in its inventory accounts on January 1.

Raw Materials Inventory	$15,000
Work-in-Process Inventory	65,000
Finished Goods Inventory	32,000

The following transactions occurred during January:

(1) Raw materials costing $28,500 were acquired on account.

(2) Raw materials costing $31,600 were issued to producing departments.

(3) Salaries and wages paid during January for services received during the month were as follows:

Factory Workers	$46,900
Sales Personnel	14,300
Administrative Officers	20,900

(4) Depreciation on buildings and equipment during January was as follows:

Manufacturing Facilities	$12,900
Selling Facilities	2,300
Administrative Facilities	1,800

(5) Other operating costs incurred and paid in cash were as follows:

Manufacturing	$15,600
Selling	4,900
Administrative	3,700

(6) The cost of goods manufactured and transferred to the finished goods storeroom totaled $85,100.

(7) Sales on account during January totaled $150,000.

(8) A physical inventory taken on January 31 revealed a finished goods inventory of $35,200.

    a. Present journal entries to record the transactions and events during January.

    b. Prepare an income statement for Westside Products Inc. for January (ignore income tax).

21. *Preparation of journal entries and an income statement for a manufacturing firm.* Southside Products Ltd. showed the following amounts in its inventory accounts on January 1.

Raw Materials Inventory	$40,000
Work-in-Process Inventory	96,000
Finished Goods Inventory	73,000

The following transactions occurred during January.

(1) Raw materials costing $122,700 were acquired on account.

(2) Raw materials costing $119,200 were issued to production.

(3) Salaries and wages paid during January for services received during the month were as follows:

Factory Workers	$87,600
Sales Personel	18,900
Administrative Personnel	27,400

(4) Depreciation on buildings and equipment during January was as follows:

Manufacturing Facilities	$14,700
Selling Facilities	2,400
Administrative Facilities	2,900

(5) Other operating costs incurred and paid in cash were as follows:

Manufacturing	$18,200
Selling	7,300
Administrative	4,400

(6) The cost of goods completed and transferred to the finished goods storeroom totaled $234,000.

(7) Sales on account during January totaled $325,000.

(8) A physical inventory taken on January 31 revealed a finished goods inventory of $68,000.

a. Present journal entries to record the transactions and events during January.

b. Prepare an income statement for Southside Products Ltd. for January. (Ignore income tax.)

22. *Flow of manufacturing costs through the accounts.* The following data relate to the manufacturing activities of Cornell Ltd. during June.

	June 30	June 1
Raw Materials Inventory	$ 43,600	$ 46,900
Factory Supplies Inventory	7,700	7,600
Work-in-Process Inventory	115,200	110,900
Finished Goods Inventory	71,400	76,700

Factory costs incurred during the month:

Raw Materials Purchased	$429,000
Supplies Purchased	22,300
Labour Services Received	362,100
Heat, Light, and Power	10,300
Insurance	4,200

Expirations of previous factory acquisitions and prepayments:

Depreciation on Factory Equipment	$36,900
Prepaid Rent Expired	3,600

a. Calculate the cost of raw materials and factory supplies used during June.
b. Calculate the cost of units completed during June and transferred to the finished goods storeroom.
c. Calculate the cost of goods sold during June.

23. *Flow of manufacturing costs through the accounts.* The following data relate to the activities of Myers Corporation during April.

	April 30	April 1
Raw Materials Inventory	$16, 400	$18,700
Work-in-Process Inventory	72,400	66,800
Finished Goods Inventory	29,800	32,900

Factory costs incurred during the month:

Raw Materials Purchased	$87,300
Labour Services Received	66,100
Heat, Light, and Power	2,700
Depreciation	15,600

Other data relating to the month:

Sales	$250,000
Selling and Administrative Expenses	38,100

a. Calculate the cost of raw materials used during April.
b. Calculate the cost of units completed during April and transferred to the finished goods storeroom.
c. Calculate net income before income tax for April.

24. *Preparing T-account entries, adjusted trial balance, income statement, and balance sheet for a manufacturing firm.* On July 1, the accounts of the Tampa Manufacturing Co. Ltd. contained the following balances:

Debit Balances		Credit Balances	
Cash	$ 110,000	Accumulated Depreciation . .	$ 30,000
Accounts Receivable	220,000	Accounts Payable	56,000
Raw Materials Inventory	80,000	Wages Payable	24,000
Work-in-Process Inventory . .	230,000	Capital Stock	1,000,000
Finished Goods Inventory . . .	170,000	Retained Earnings	200,000
Factory Supplies Inventory . .	20,000		
Manufacturing Equipment . . .	480,000		
Total	$1,310,000	Total	$1,310,000

Transactions for the month of July are listed below in summary form:

(1) Sales, all on account, were $310,000.

(2) Labour services furnished by employees during the period (but as yet unpaid) amounted to $80,000. All labour is employed in the factory.

(3) Factory supplies were purchased for $8,500; payment was made by cheque.

(4) Raw materials purchased on account, $100,000.

(5) Collections from customers, $335,000.

(6) Payment of $108,000 was made to raw materials suppliers.

(7) Payments to employees total $78,500.

(8) Rent of the factory building for the month, $8,000, was paid.

(9) Depreciation of manufacturing equipment for the month, $12,000.

(10) Other manufacturing costs incurred and paid, $40,000.

(11) All selling and administrative services are furnished by Clark and Company for $10,000 per month. Their bill was paid by cheque.

(12) Raw materials used during month, $115,000.

(13) Factory supplies used during month, $8,000.

(14) Cost of goods completed during month, $258,000.

(15) Goods costing $261,500 were shipped to customers during the month.

(16) Estimated income tax expense for July is $15,400.

    a. Open T-accounts and record the July 1 amounts. Record transactions **(1)** through **(15)** in the T-accounts, opening additional accounts as needed.

    b. Prepare an adjusted, preclosing trial balance as of July 31.

    c. Prepare a combined statement of income and retained earnings for July.

    d. Enter closing entries in the T-accounts using an Income Summary account.

    e. Prepare a balance sheet as of July 31.

25. *Preparing T-account entries and adjusted trial balance for a manufacturing firm.* Melton Plastics Limited was incorporated on September 16. By September 30, having rented a building for its manufacturing operations, the firm was ready to begin operations. The trial balance at that date was as follows:

Cash	$387,200	
Raw Materials Inventory	19,200	
Factory Equipment	136,000	
Accounts Payable		$ 22,400
Capital Stock		520,000
	$542,400	$542,400

The following data relate only to the manufacturing operations of the firm during October:

(1) Materials purchased on account, $161,600.
(2) Wages and salaries earned during the month, $148,000.
(3) Raw materials requisitioned and put into process during the month, $168,800.
(4) Equipment was acquired during the month at a cost of $112,000. A cheque for $40,000 was issued, and an equipment contract payable in eight equal monthly installments was signed for the remainder (ignore interest).
(5) Additional payments by cheque:

Raw Materials Suppliers	$140,000
Payrolls	112,420
Building Rent	6,000
Utilities	2,920
Insurance Premiums (for 1 year from October 1)	9,600
Miscellaneous Factory Costs	26,400
	$297,340

(6) Invoices received but unpaid at October 31:

City Water Department	$ 120
Hoster Machine Supply Co. Ltd. for additional equipment	2,400

(7) Depreciation on equipment for the month, $1,200.
(8) One month's insurance expiration is recorded.
(9) The cost of parts finished during October was $281,750.

 a. Open T-accounts and enter the amounts from the opening trial balance.
 b. Record the transactions during the month in the T-accounts, opening additional accounts as needed.
 c. Prepare an adjusted trial balance at October 31.

26. *Preparing T-account entries and financial statements for a manufacturing firm.* This problem is a continuation of Problem 25, Melton Plastics Limited. In addition to the manufacturing activities described in that problem, the following transactions relating to selling and administrative activities occurred during October.

(10) Sales, on account, $340,600.

(11) Collections from customers, $330,000.

(12) Salaries earned during the month: sales, $30,800; office, $31,200.

(13) Payments by cheque:

Sales Salaries	$27,630
Office Salaries	27,550
Advertising during October	7,200
Rent of Office and Office Equipment for October	2,200
Office Supplies	1,600
Miscellaneous Office Costs	1,400
Miscellaneous Selling Costs	2,800
Total	$70,380

(14) The inventory of office supplies on October 31 is $800.

(15) The inventory of finished goods on October 31 is $59,000.

   a. Employing the T-accounts of Problem 25 and additional accounts as needed, record the selling and administrative activities for the month in the T-accounts.

   b. Prepare a combined statement of income and retained earnings for the month (ignore income tax).

   c. Prepare a balance sheet as of October 31.

   d. Enter closing entries in the T-accounts, using an Income Summary account.

27. *Income recognition for shipbuilder.* Maine Shipbuilding Inc. agreed on June 15, Year 2, to construct an oil tanker for Global Petroleum Co. Ltd. The contract price of $80 million is to be paid as follows: at the time of signing, $8 million; December 31, Year 3, $32 million; at completion on June 30, Year 4, $40 million. Maine Shipbuilding Inc. incurred the following costs in constructing the tanker: Year 2: $21.6 million; Year 3: $36 million; Year 4: $14.4 million. These amounts conformed to original expectations.

   Calculate the amount of revenue, expense, and net income before income tax for Year 2, Year 3, and Year 4 under each of the following revenue recognition methods:

   a. Percentage-of-completion method

   b. Completed contract method

   c. Installment method

   d. Cost-recovery-first method

   e. Cash basis

   f. Which method do you feel provides the best measure of Maine Shipbuilding Inc.'s performance under the contract? Why?

28. *Income recognition for contractor.* The Humbolt Electric Co. Ltd. received a contract late in Year 1 to build a small electricity-generating unit. The contract price was $700,000, and it was estimated that total costs would be $600,000. Estimated and actual construction time was 15 months, and it was agreed that payments would be made by the purchaser as follows:

March 31, Year 2	$ 70,000
June 30, Year 2	105,000
September 30, Year 2	203,000
December 31, Year 2	161,000
March 31, Year 3	161,000
	$700,000

Estimated and actual costs of construction incurred by the Humbolt Electric Co. Ltd. were as follows:

January 1—March 31, Year 2	$120,000
April 1—June 30, Year 2	120,000
July 1—September 30, Year 2	180,000
October 1—December 31, Year 2	120,000
January 1—March 31, Year 3	60,000
	$600,000

The Humbolt Electric Co. Ltd. prepares financial statements quarterly at March 31, June 30, and so forth.

Calculate the amount of revenue, expense, and net income before income tax for each quarter under each of the following methods of revenue recognition:

  a. Percentage-of-completion method
  b. Completed contract method
  c. Installment method
  d. Cost-recovery-first method
  e. Which method do you feel provides the best measure of Humbolt's perform-ance under this contract? Why?
  f. Under what circumstances would the methods not selected in part (**e**) provide a better measure of performance?

29. *Point-of-sale versus installment method of income recognition.* The Freda Com-pany begins business on January 1, Year 8. Activities of the company for the first two years are summarized below.

	Year 9	Year 8
Sales, All on Account	$150,000	$100,000
Collections from Customers		
On Year 8 Sales	55,000	45,000
On Year 9 Sales	60,000	
Purchases of Merchandise	120,000	90,000
Inventory of Merchandise at 12/31	57,000	30,000
All Expenses Other than Merchandise, Paid in Cash	22,000	16,000

  a. Prepare income statements for Year 8 and Year 9, assuming that the com-pany uses the accrual basis of accounting and revenue is recognized at the time of sale (ignore income tax).

b. Prepare income statements for Year 8 and Year 9, assuming that the company uses the installment method of accounting (ignore income tax).

30. *Income recognition over two-year period.* The Webster Corporation produces a single product at a cost of $5 each, all of which is paid in cash when the unit is produced. The selling cost consists of a sales commission of $3 a unit and is paid in cash at the time of shipment. The selling price is $10 a unit; all sales are made on account. No uncollectible accounts are expected, and no costs are incurred at the time of collection.

During Year 2, the firm produced 200,000 units, shipped 150,000 units, and collected $1 million from customers. During Year 3, the firm produced 125,000 units, shipped 160,000 units, and collected $2 million from customers.

Calculate the amount of net income before income tax for Year 2 and Year 3:
   a. If revenue and expense are recognized at the time of production.
   b. If revenue and expense are recognized at the time of shipment.
   c. If revenue and expense are recognized at the time of cash collection.
   d. If revenue and expense are recognized on a cash basis.
   e. A firm experiencing growth in its sales volume will often produce more units during a particular period than it sells. In this way, inventories can be built up in anticipation of an even larger sales volume during the next period. Under these circumstances, will recognition of revenue and expense at the time of production, shipment, or cash collection generally result in the largest reported net income for the period? Explain.
   f. A firm experiencing decreases in its sales volume will often produce fewer units during a period than it sells in an effort to reduce the amount of inventory on hand for next period. Under these circumstances, will recognition of revenue and expense at the time of production, shipment, or cash collection generally result in the largest reported net income for a period? Explain.

31. *Classifying items in income statement.* The results of various transactions and events are usually classified within the income statement in one of the following two sections: (1) income before extraordinary items, and (2) extraordinary items. Using the appropriate number, identify the classification of each of the transactions or events below. State any assumptions you think necessary.
   a. Depreciation expense for the year on a company's automobile used by its president.
   b. Uninsured loss of a factory complex in Manitoba as a result of a flood.
   c. Gain from the sale of temporary investments.
   d. Loss from the sale of a delivery truck.
   e. Loss from the sale of a division that conducted all of the firm's research activities.
   f. Earnings during the year up to the time of sale of the division in (e).
   g. Loss in excess of insurance proceeds on an automobile destroyed during an accident.
   h. Loss of plant, equipment, and inventory held in a foreign country when confiscated by the government of that country.

32. *Classifying items in income statement.* Prepare a multi-step income statement for Nordic Enterprises, Inc. from the information shown in Exhibit 4.5 and comment on any unusual features of this statement.

Exhibit 4.5
NORDIC ENTERPRISES, INC.
Income Statement
December 31, Year 5

Revenues and Gains:		
Sales Revenue	$1,964,800	
Rental Revenue	366,900	
Interest Revenue	4,600	
Gain on Sale of Equipment	2,500	
Gain on Sale of Subsidiary	643,200	$2,982,000
Expenses and Losses:		
Cost of Goods Sold	$1,432,900	
Depreciation Expense	226,800	
Salaries Expense	296,900	
Interest Expense	6,600	
Loss of Plant Due to Fire	368,800	
Income Tax Expense	200,000	
Dividends Expense	100,000	2,632,000
Net Income		$ 350,000

33. *Revenue recognition for various types of businesses.* Discuss when revenue is likely to be recognized by firms in each of the following types of businesses:

    a. A shoe store
    b. A shipbuilding firm constructing an ice breaker under a government contract
    c. A real estate developer selling lots on long-term contracts with small down payments
    d. A barber shop
    e. An apple-growing farm
    f. A producer of television movies, where the rights to the movies for the first three years are sold to a television network and all rights thereafter revert to the producer
    g. A residential real estate developer who constructs only "speculative" houses and then later sells the houses to buyers
    h. A producer of fine whiskey that ages from 6 to 12 years before sale
    i. A credit union lending money for home mortgages
    j. A travel agency
    k. A printer who prints only custom-order stationery
    l. A seller of trading stamps to food stores redeemable by food store customers for various household products
    m. A wholesale food distributor
    n. A livestock rancher
    o. A shipping company that loads cargo in one accounting period, carries cargo

across the ocean in a second accounting period, and unloads the cargo in a third period. The shipping is all done under contract, and cash collection of shipping charges is relatively certain.

34. *Revenue recognition for franchise.* Pickin Chicken, Incorporated, and Country Delight, Incorporated, both sell franchises for their chicken restaurants. The franchisee receives the right to use the franchisor's products and to benefit from national training and advertising programs. The franchisee agrees to pay $50,000 for exclusive franchise rights in a particular city. Of this amount, $20,000 is paid upon signing the franchise agreement and the remainder is payable in five equal annual installments of $6,000 each.

   Pickin Chicken, Incorporated, recognizes francise revenue as franchise agreements are signed, whereas Country Delight, Incorporated, recognizes franchise revenue on an installment basis. In Year 2, both companies sold eight franchises. In Year 3, they both sold five franchises. In Year 4, neither company sold a franchise.

   a. Calculate the amount of revenue recognized by each company during Year 2, Year, 3, Year 4, Year 5, Year 6, Year 7, and Year 8.

   b. When do you feel that franchise revenue should be recognized? Why?

35. *Flow of manufacturing costs through the accounts.* The following data relate to the manufacturing activities of Quilt Manufacturing Company during July.

	July 1	July 31
Raw Materials Inventory	$ 56,300	$ 62,900
Factory Supplies Inventory	15,900	13,700
Work-in-Process Inventory	297,200	257,200
Finished Goods Inventory	83,700	86,200

Factory costs incurred during the month were as follows:

Raw Materials Purchased	$ 42,700
Supplies Purchased	9,200
Labour Services Received	187,600
Heat, Light, and Power	12,100
Insurance	6,000

Expirations of previous factory acquisitions and prepayments were as follows:

Depreciation on Factory Equipment	$15,000
Prepaid Rent Expired	2,000

   a. Calculate the cost of raw materials and factory supplies used during July.

   b. Calculate the cost of units completed during July and transferred to the finished goods storeroom.

   c. Calculate the cost of goods sold during July.

36. *Income recognition for contractor.* On March 15, year 1, Fuller Construction Company contracted to build a shopping centre at a contract price of $10 million. The schedule of expected and actual cash collections and contract costs is as follows:

Year	Cash Collections from Customers	Estimated and Actual Cost Incurred
1	$ 2,000,000	$1,200,000
2	3,000,000	3,200,000
3	4,000,000	1,600,000
4	1,000,000	2,000,000
	$10,000,000	$8,000,000

a. Calculate the amount of revenue, expense, and net income for each of the 4 years under the following revenue recognition methods:
1. Percentage-of-completion method.
2. Completed-contract method.
3. Installment method.
4. Cost-recovery-first method.

b. Which method do you believe provides the best measure of Fuller Construction Company's performance under the contract? Why?

37. *Revenue recognition policies.* The Omega Drilling Company of Black Squirrel, Alberta, specializes in oil well servicing and drilling for various oil companies. Orders are usually received one to three weeks before drilling begins. The drilling time for a well ranges from three days to one month, at the end of which time all services are performed and the invoice is sent to the customer. Collection records show that 80 percent of the customers pay within 45 days, the other 20 percent usually pay within 90 days. Lately, because of the economic downturn in the oil industry, Omega has experienced many collection defaults.

The problem of when to recognize revenue has been raised at a committee meeting at Omega Drilling Company. The following are the views of several key personnel of the company:

(1) Credit and collection manager: "Currently, with the decline in oil prices, we cannot be certain of revenue collection. Therefore, we shouldn't recognize any revenue until the entire transaction has been completed, i.e., after we have been paid."

(2) Office manager: "I think we should recognize the revenue as soon as we send the invoice to the customer. The invoice is proof that the customer owes us money."

(3) President: "I disagree. Revenue should be recognized as soon as the order is taken. We need to show the best financial picture at all times."

(4) Drilling manager: "You are all wrong. Revenue is earned throughout the entire drilling/service-billing-collection process. It should be recognized, therefore, as these stages progress. I would recommend that we recognize one third of it at the end of each of these three major and critical events."

As the only accountant within 300 miles, you are called in to resolve the company's problem.

a. For each of the above positions, indicate whether you agree or disagree and why.

b. What recommendation would you make in regard to revenue recognition for Omega Drilling Company? Give reasons.

Decision Problem 4-1

Your uncle, Bob Orsky, recently "made a killing" on the stock market and can realize his longstanding dream of becoming a gentleman farmer. He has been negotiating the purchase of Jessy Jones's farm and small dairy herd near Collingwood, since Jessy is planning to retire. Until his retirement in ten years' time, however, Orsky must hire a farm family to operate the farm for him; he has been advised that he should have no trouble finding a trustworthy farm family to operate the farm for him on payment of $18,000 per year.

Year 2 was a normal year for farms in the Collingwood area and Bob Orsky believes that the following statement of cash receipts and disbursements prepared by Jessy Jones is more or less typical of the results his farm manager could be expected to achieve.

Jessy Jones's Farm
Statement of Cash Receipts and Disbursements
For the Year Ended December 31, Year 2

Receipts:

Milk Deliveries		$60,000
Apple Deliveries		14,000
Sales of Calves (in excess of requirements)		2,500
Sale of Old, Tired Milking Cows		600
Proceeds of Expropriation of Land for Road Allowance		3,000
Total Cash Receipts		$80,100

Cash Disbursements:

Seed Grain	$ 900	
Cattle Food and Supplements	8,000	
Veterinary Fees	600	
Property Taxes	1,700	
Insurance on Building (3 years from January 1, Year 2)	4,500	
Gas and Oil	4,000	
Spray and Chemicals	900	
Mortgage Interest ($1,000) and Principal ($10,000)	11,000	
Purchase of Tractor	18,000	
Cost of Replacing 2 Milk Cows Hit by Lightning while in Pasture	2,000	51,600
Excess of Receipts over Disbursements		$28,500

Jessy is asking $350,000 for the farm, mortgage free, which corresponds closely to the money Uncle Bob has to invest. Bob considers that he should be able to earn at least 15 percent per annum, before income taxes, on average over the next ten years, in an investment with a similar risk.

The farm equipment is in good condition and today would cost $50,000 to replace new with an average life of ten years. The farm buildings are old but appear to have an unlimited life, as long as they are maintained at the same level that Jessy Jones has done.

Because of a fire in one of the local apple-packing plants, Jessy Jones has been required to defer the delivery of 60 percent of his apple crop until January or February Year 3, an unusual event. However, he anticipates no trouble selling them to the packing house for the same price as those delivered to date.

Would you advise Uncle Bob to buy Jessy Jones's farm or to wait until another farm comes on the market that would be a more profitable investment?

As mentioned in the Preface, a new feature in the fourth edition is two Accounting Concepts Problems. This one in Chapter 4 deals with a conceptual framework for accounting. The second is in Chapter 14 and concerns governmental accounting.

Review of Chapters 1, 2, 3, and 4—Accounting Concepts Problem 1

Exhibit 4.6 presents the new *CICA Handbook*, Section 1000 entitled "Financial Statement Concepts". With reference to this exhibit and to Chapters 1 through 4, answer the following questions:

a. What contribution will Section 1000 possibly make to accounting?

b. What are the primary objectives of financial statements?

c. Why does it help to understand the qualitative attributes of financial information?

d. Why does it help to define elements of financial statements?

e. To what does the term "recognition criteria" refer?

f. What is the measurement basis underlying financial statements in Canada?

g. What is GAAP and where does one find authoritative support to decide whether a proposed accounting treatment is within the framework of GAAP?

h. Does Section 1000 constitute a conceptual framework for accounting?

Exhibit 4.6
A. Handbook Section 1000

Financial Statement Concepts

PURPOSE AND SCOPE

.01   The purpose of this Section is to set out the concepts that underlie the development and use accounting principles in the general purpose financial statements of profit oriented enterprises. The conceptual material will provide a consistent source of reference to guide the future development accounting standards by the Committee.

.02   The material can also be used by preparers of financial statements and accounting practitioners in making judgments in applying generally accepted accounting principles and in establishing accounting policies in areas where there are no generally accepted accounting principles.

.03   The material does not define standards for any particular measurement or disclosure issue. Nothing in this Section overrides any specific Recommendation in other Sections of the Handbook. To the extent there may be inconsistencies between this Section and other Sections, it is intended that these will be resolved when those other Sections are reviewed by the Committee.

Financial statements

.04   Financial statements normally include a balance sheet, income statement, statement of retained earnings and statement of changes in financial position. Notes to financial statements and supporting schedules to which the financial statements are cross-referenced are an integral part of such statements.

.05   Financial statements are usually limited to information about economic transactions and events that are financial in nature and can be expressed in financial terms. Financial statements deal with measurements that may, by their nature, be imprecise and are generally based on representation of past rather than future transactions and events.

.06   In addition to the process of providing financial statements, financial reporting includes other types of reporting, such as information outside the financial statements in annual reports, prospectuses and other material distributed with financial statements. Financial reporting is accordingly broader in scope than the process of providing financial statements. While it is recognized that many financial statement concepts also apply to other types of financial reporting, this Section does not specifically set out concepts for other types of financial reporting.

.07 In the Canadian economic environment, the production of goods and the provision of services are, to a significant extent, carried out by investor-owned business enterprises in the private sector and to a lesser extent by government-owned business enterprises. Debt and equity markets act as an exchange mechanism for investment resources.

.08 Enterprise ownership is often segregated from management creating a need for external communication of economic information about the enterprise to investors. For the purposes of this Section, investors include present and potential debt and equity investors and their advisors. Creditors and others who do not have internal access to enterprise information also need external reports to obtain the information they require.

.09 It is not practicable to expect financial statements to satisfy the many and varied information needs of all external users of information about an enterprise. Consequently, the objective of financial statements focuses primarily on the information needs of investors and creditors. The Committee believes that financial statements prepared to satisfy these needs are often used by others who need external reporting of information about an enterprise.

.10 Investors and creditors are interested, for the purpose of making resource allocation decisions, in predicting the ability of the enterprise to generate cash flows in the future, to meet its obligations and to generate a return on investment.

.11 Investors also require information about how the management of an enterprise has discharged its stewardship responsibility to those that have provided resources to the enterprise.

Objective

.12 The objective of financial statements is to communicate information that is useful to investors and creditors in making resource allocation decisions and assessing management stewardship. Information provided in financial statements should fairly present: (1) an enterprise's economic resources, obligations and equity, (2) changes in the enterprise's economic resources, obligations and equity, and (3) the economic performance of the enterprise.

BENEFIT VERSUS COST CONSTRAINT

.13 The benefits expected to arise from providing information in financial statements should exceed the cost of doing so. This constraint applies to the development of accounting standards by the Committee and is a consideration in the preparation of financial statements in accordance with those standards. The Committee recognizes that the benefits and costs may fall to different parties and that the evaluation of benefits and costs is substantially a judgmental process.

MATERIALITY

.14 Investors and creditors are generally interested only in information that may affect their decision making. Materiality is the term used to describe the significance of information to decision makers. While materiality is a matter of judgment in the particular circumstances, as a general rule it should be judged in relation to the significance of an item in the making of decisions by an investor or creditor. If it is probable the item would change or influence a decision, it would be deemed to be material.

QUALITATIVE CHARACTERISTICS

.15 Qualitative characteristics define and describe the attributes of information provided in financial statements that make that information useful to investors and creditors. The four qualitative characteristics are understandability, relevance, reliability and comparability.

.16 a) Understandability

Given that the objective of financial statements is to communicate information that is useful to investors and creditors, an essential characteristic of the information provided in financial statements is that it is readily understandable by investors and creditors. For this purpose, investors and creditors are assumed to have a reasonable knowledge of business and economic activities and a willingness to study the information with reasonable diligence.

.17 b) Relevance

For the information provided in financial statements to be useful, it must be relevant to the decisions made by investors and creditors. Relevance is achieved through predictive and feedback value and timeliness.

i) *Predictive and feedback value*

Information that helps investors and creditors to predict future cash flows has predictive value. Although the information provided in financial statements will not normally be a prediction in itself, this does not preclude the information from being useful in making predictions. The predictive value of the income statement, for example, is enhanced if unusual, abnormal or infrequent items are separately disclosed. Information that confirms or corrects the earlier predictions of investors and creditors has feedback value. Information often has both predictive and feedback value.

ii) Timeliness

For information to be useful for decision making, it must be received by the decision maker before it loses its capacity to influence decisions. The usefulness of information for decision making declines as time elapses.

.18   c) Reliability

For the information provided in financial statements to be useful, it must be reliable. Reliability is achieved through representational faithfulness, verifiability and neutrality.

i) Representational faithfulness

Representational faithfulness is achieved when transactions and events affecting the enterprise are presented in financial statements in a manner that recognizes their economic substance.

ii) Verifiability

The financial statement representation of a transaction or event is verifiable if knowledgeable and independent observers would agree, with a reasonable degree of precision, that it corresponds to and adequately reflects the actual transaction or event.

iii) Neutrality

Information is neutral when it is free from bias that would lead investors and creditors towards making predetermined decisions. Bias in measurement occurs when a measure tends to overstate or understate the item being measured. In the selection of accounting principles, bias occurs when the selection is made with the interests of particular users or with particular economic or political objectives in mind.

Financial statements that do not include everything necessary for faithful representation of transactions and events affecting the enterprise would be incomplete and, therefore, potentially biased.

The neutrality of financial statements is affected in an acceptable manner by the use of conservatism in making judgments when conditions of uncertainty exist. When uncertainty exists, estimates of a conservative nature attempt to ensure net assets or net income are not overstated. However, conservatism does not encompass the deliberate understatement of net assets or net income.

.19   d) Comparability (including consistency)

Comparability is a characteristic of the relationship between two pieces of information rather than of a particular piece of information by itself. It enables investors and creditors to identify similarities in and differences between two sets of financial statements. Comparability is important when comparing the financial statements of two different enterprises and when comparing the financial statements of the same enterprise over two periods or at two different points in time.

.20   Comparability in financial statements of an enterprise is enhanced when the same accounting policies are used consistently from period to period. Consistency helps prevent misconceptions that might result from the application of different accounting policies in different periods. When a change in accounting policy is deemed to be appropriate, disclosure of the effects of the change is necessary to maintain comparability.

Qualitative characteristics trade-off

.21   The Committee recognizes that there is often a trade-off required in the degree to which qualitative characteristics can be achieved, particularly between relevance and reliability. For example, there is often a trade-off between the timeliness of producing financial statements and the reliability of the information reported in the statements. Generally, the objective is to achieve an appropriate balance among the characteristics. The relative importance of the characteristics in different cases is a matter of judgment.

FUNDAMENTAL CONCEPTS

The following fundamental concepts normally underlie the preparation of financial statements:

a) Accrual

Revenues and expenses are recognized in the period in which they are considered to have been earned or incurred, respectively, whether or not they have been settled by the receipt or payment of cash or its equivalent. The accrual concept encompasses deferrals that occur when the recognition of a cash receipt or payment occurs prior to the criteria for recognition of revenue or expense being satisfied (see paragraph 1000.24).

b) Matching

Revenues and expenses that are linked to each other in a cause and effect relationship are included in income in the same accounting period.

c) Going concern

Financial statements are prepared on the assumption that the enterprise will continue in operation for the foreseeable future. Assets, therefore, are normally accounted for on the basis of continued use as opposed to liquidation. The going concern concept is not applied when the enterprise is not expected to continue in operation for the foreseeable future.

d) Substance over form

Transactions and events are accounted for and presented in a manner that conveys their economic substance rather than their legal or other form.

e) Historical cost

Transactions and events are initially recognized and subsequently included in the financial statements at the value ascribed to them when they took place.

f) Nominal dollar financial capital

Capital is measured in financial terms and no adjustment is made for the effect of a change in the general purchasing power of the currency during the period. The concept of capital used in financial statements is important because income exists only after the capital of an enterprise has been maintained. Thus, income is the increase in the amount of capital at the end of the period over the beginning of the period, after excluding the effects of capital contributions and withdrawals.

ELEMENTS OF FINANCIAL STATEMENTS

.22 Elements of financial statements are the basic categories of items portrayed in financial statements. There are two types of elements: those that describe the economic resources, obligations and equity of an enterprise at a point in time (balance sheet elements), and those that describe changes in economic resources, obligations and equity (income statement elements). A statement of changes in financial position consists primarily of changes in balance sheet elements. Notes to financial statements, while an integral part of financial statements, are not considered to be an element.

.23 The elements defined herein are the most common categories of items portrayed in financial statements. The existence of other items is not precluded. In practice, a balance sheet may include, as a category of assets or liabilities, deferred charges or credits that arise from a delay in income statement recognition. Criteria for the recognition of items in financial statements are discussed in paragraph 1000.24.

.24 Net income is the residual amount after expenses and losses are deducted from revenues and gains. Net income is important because it is frequently used as a measure of economic performance.

a) Assets

.25 Assets are resources controlled by an enterprise as a result of past transactions or events from which future economic benefits may be obtained.

.26 Assets have two essential characteristics:
   i) they embody a future benefit that involves a capacity, singly or in combination with other assets, to contribute directly or indirectly to future net cash flows; and
   ii) the transaction or event giving rise to the enterprise's right to, or control of, the benefit has already occurred.

.27 It is not essential for the future benefit to be legally enforceable for the resource to be an asset provided that the enterprise can control the use of the future benefit through other means.

b) Liabilities

.28 Liabilities are obligations of an enterprise arising from past transactions or events, the settlement of which may result in the transfer of assets, provision of services or other yielding of economic benefits in the future.

.29 Liabilities have two essential characteristics:
   i) they embody a duty or responsibility to others that entails settlement by future transfer or use of assets at a specified or determinable date, on occurrence of a specified event, or on demand; and
   ii) the transaction or event obligating the enterprise has already occurred.

.30 Liabilities do not have to be legally enforceable provided that they otherwise meet the definition of liabilities; they can be based on equitable or constructive obligations. An equitable obligation is a duty based on ethical or moral considerations. A constructive obligation is one that can be inferred from the facts in a particular situation as opposed to a contractually based obligation.

.31 c) Equity

Equity is the ownership interest in the assets of an enterprise after deducting its liabilities. It may include, for example, various types of share capital, contributed surplus and retained earnings. Capital contributions and withdrawals are equity transactions that do not give rise to revenues, expenses, gains or losses.

.32 d) Revenues

Revenues are increases in economic resources, either by way of inflows of assets or reductions of liabilities, arising in the course of the ordinary activities of an enterprise, normally from the sale of goods, the rendering of services and the use by others of enterprise resources yielding interest, royalties and dividends.

.33   e) Expenses

Expenses are decreases in economic resources, either by way of outflows of assets or incurrences of liabilities, arising in the course of the ordinary activities of an enterprise.

.34   f) Gains

Gains are increases in equity from peripheral or incidental transactions and events affecting an enterprise and from all other transactions, events and circumstances affecting the enterprise except those that result from revenues or capital contributions.

.35   g) Losses

Losses are decreases in equity from peripheral or incidental transactions and events affecting an enterprise and from all other transactions, events and circumstances affecting the enterprise except those that result from expenses or withdrawals of capital.

RECOGNITION CRITERIA

.36   Recognition is the process of including an item in the financial statements of an enterprise. Recognition consists of a narrative description of the item in a statement (e.g., "inventory" or "sales") and the addition of the amount involved into statement totals. Similar items may be grouped together in the financial statements for the purpose of disclosure.

.37   Recognition means inclusion of an item within one or more individual statements and does not mean disclosure in the notes to the financial statements. Notes either provide further details about items recognized in the financial statements, or provide information about items that do not meet the criteria for recognition and thus are not recognized in the financial statements.

.38   The recognition criteria below provide general guidance on when an item is recognized in the financial statements. Whether any particular item is recognized or not will require the application of judgment in considering whether the specific circumstances meet the recognition criteria.

.39   The recognition criteria are as follows:
a) the item has an appropriate basis of measurement and a reasonable estimate can be made of the amount involved; and
b) for items involving obtaining or giving up future economic benefits, it is probable that such benefits will be obtained or given up.

.40   It is possible that an item will meet the definition of an element but still not be recognized in the financial statements because it is not probable that future economic benefits will be obtained or given up or because a reasonable estimate cannot be made of the amount involved.

Measurement

.44   Measurement is the process of determining the amount at which an item is recognized in the financial statements. There are a number of bases on which the amount can be measured. One of the fundamental concepts of financial statements is that they are prepared using the historical cost basis of measurement (see paragraph 1000.17).

.45   Other bases of measurement are also used but only in certain limited circumstances. The main ones are:

a) Replacement cost—the amount that would be needed currently to acquire an equivalent asset. This may be used, for example, when inventories are valued at the lower of historical cost and replacement cost.

b) Realizable value—the amount that would be received by selling the asset in the ordinary course of business. This may be used, for example, to value temporary and portfolio investments. Realizable value encompasses market value, which is a way of estimating realizable value when a market for the asset exists.

c) Present value—the discounted amount of future cash flows expected to be received from an asset or required to settle a liability. This is used, for example, to estimate the cost of pension benefits.

GENERALLY ACCEPTED ACCOUNTING PRINCIPLES

.48   Generally accepted accounting principles is the term used to describe the basis on which financial statements are normally prepared. There are special circumstances where a different basis of accounting may be appropriate, for example, in financial statements prepared in accordance with regulatory legislation or contractual requirements.

Generally accepted accounting principles encompass the Recommendations of this Handbook and those other accounting principles that have gained general acceptance. An accounting principle not covered by the Recommendations of the Handbook is considered to have gained general acceptance when it is actually being used in similar circumstances by a significant number of enterprises in Canada.

.49 Where there is no generally accepted accounting principle for a transaction or event, accounting principles will be developed, using judgment, through the application of the concepts contained in this Section and by referring to other sources including the following:

- the Handbook;
- practice in analogous situations;
- Accounting guidelines published by the CICA Accounting Standards Steering Committee;
- International Accounting Standards published by the International Accounting Standards Committee;
- standards published by bodies authorized to establish financial accounting standards in other jurisdictions;
- CICA research studies; and
- other sources of accounting literature such as text books and journals.

Review of this material may also help determine whether an accounting principle is generally accepted.

.50 In those rare circumstances where following a Handbook Recommendation would result in misleading financial statements, generally accepted accounting principles encompass appropriate alternative principles.

Chapter 5   Flow of Funds and the Statement of Changes in Financial Position

Chapter 1 pointed out that three major financial statements are useful to those interested in understanding the financial activities of a business. Chapter 2 discussed the balance sheet, a snapshot of the *investments* and *financing* of a firm at a moment in time. Chapters 3 and 4 considered the income statement, a report on the revenues and expenses related to *operations* for a period of time. This chapter discusses a third major statement, the statement of changes in financial position. The statement of changes in financial position reports the flows of cash into and out of a business during a period of time. This statement is also sometimes referred to as the ''funds statement.'' This comes from the historical name of the statement, ''The Statement of Sources and Applications of Funds.'' The term funds was used because firms could define funds as cash or working capital (working capital = current assets − current liabilities).

In 1985, the CICA decided that the definition of funds should be cash only. This change was attributable largely to the fact that in an increasing number of business failures, analysis of the firm's working capital position failed to point out its solvency problems.

The accounting profession has concluded that the primary objective of financial statements is to assist users in predicting future cash flows. A cash basis statement of changes in financial position reflects the financial community's growing preoccupation with cash flow analysis and cash management.

Rationale for the Statement of Changes in Financial Position

Recall from Chapter 1 the relation between the principal activities of a business and the two financial statements already discussed, the balance sheet and the income statement. These relations are shown in Figure 5.1.

Figure 5.1

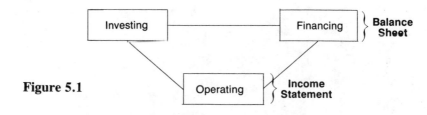

Investing, financing, and operating might be thought of as three interconnected cog-wheels, each turning on its own, yet connected in important ways with the other activities (Figure 5.2).

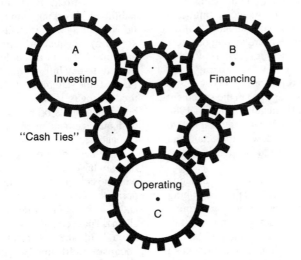

Figure 5.2

Cash ties these three activities together and keeps them running smoothly. If cash cannot be generated in sufficient amounts and at the right times, then a firm faces financial difficulty and even bankruptcy.

Example Solinger Electric Corporation was formed during January, Year 1, to operate a retail electrical supply business. It obtained financing from creditors and owners and invested the funds in buildings and equipment. The firm operated profitably since opening, with net income increasing from $3,000 in Year 1 to $20,000 in Year 4. The firm has had increasing difficulty, however, paying its monthly bills as they become due. Management is puzzled as to how net income could be increasing while, at the same time, the firm continually finds itself strapped for cash.

Relationship between Income Flows and Cash Flows

Revenues and expenses reported in the income statement for a period differ in amount from cash receipts and disbursements for the period. The differences arise for two principal reasons.

1. The accrual basis of accounting is used in measuring net income. Thus, the recognition of revenues does not necessarily coincide with receipts of cash from customers. Likewise, the recognition of expenses does not necessarily coincide with disbursements of cash to suppliers, employees, and other creditors. As Chapter 3 pointed out, the accrual basis of accounting focuses on the use of assets in generating earnings and not on their associated cash receipts and disbursements.

Cash Flow—a Concept for the Nineties

*I*f there is such a thing as being fashionable or trendy in accounting, it is trendy these days to talk about cash flow. Terms frequently heard among business analysts today include "cash flow statements," "cash flow per share," and "cash flow projections." The CICA's definition of funds used in the statement of changes in financial position in 1986 was changed from working capital to cash. Why is cash flow so important and what led to the sudden interest in this concept?

Historically, cash was the bad guy of the balance sheet. Near the beginning of this century, the accounting profession embraced matching and accrual-based accounting as central pillars in accounting. Matching is the attempt to get revenues and all costs associated with generating those revenues into the same income statement. Accrual-based accounting is recognizing expenses as soon as they are incurred and revenues as soon as they are earned, rather than waiting for the cash flow to trigger a recording entry.

Both of these concepts are the antithesis of cash basis accounting, in which all recording activity in the accounts is triggered by a cash flow in or out of the firm. Your chequebook is a perfect illustration of cash basis accounting. Accounting pundits, however, saw cash basis statements as a distortion of true income measurement. More importantly, cash basis statements allowed management to manipulate reported profits. All management had to do was alter the timing of a disbursement or a cash receipt to radically alter the bottom line on the income statement. We call deliberate efforts by management to change net income by employing accounting tactics *income smoothing* (which has also had a bad name in accounting lore).

Consequently, cash took a back seat to another concept—working capital—which is current assets minus current liabilities. Working capital was supposed to be a better indicator of a firm's solvency because it represented the amount of current assets left over after the day-to-day bills were paid. Thus, in the past, the statement of changes measured changes in working capital, and business schools offered courses not in cash management but in working capital management.

The beginning of the end for working capital came in the mid seventies, with the collapse of two major U.S. corporations—Penn Central (a railway) and W. T. Grant (a department store chain). These collapses sent shock waves throughout the financial community because traditional working capital analysis had failed to foretell their collapse. Subsequent business failures have brought the financial community to the realization that working capital tells very little about a company's solvency. Two of the principal components of working capital, receivables and inventories, do not always convert as readily into cash as we would like to believe. History is full of examples of bankrupt firms with warehouses filled with inventory. Cash pays bills, working capital does not. It's as simple as that.

The accounting profession recognized the pre-eminence of cash in the blue-ribbon American Institute of Certified Public Accountants' study "The Objectives of Financial Statements," which concluded that the primary objective of financial statements is to assist users in predicting future cash flows. The culmination of cash's ascendancy came in 1986 when the profession changed the statement of changes from a working capital basis to a cash basis. With the growing preoccupation with measuring corporate solvency, cash management will continue to play a larger role in financial statement presentation.

2. The firm receives cash from sources that are not related directly to operations, such as issuing shares or bonds. Similarly, the firm makes cash disbursements for such things as dividends and the acquisition of equipment that are not related directly to operations during the current period.

To illustrate the differences between income flows and cash flows, refer to the data for Solinger Electric Corporation for Year 4 in Exhibit 5.1. Sales revenue reported in the income statement totaled $125,000. However, only $90,000 was collected in cash from customers. The remaining amount of sales was not collected by the end of the year and is reflected in the increase in the Accounts Receivable account on the balance sheet.[1] Likewise, the cost of goods sold shown on the income statement totaled $60,000. Only $50,000 cash was disbursed to suppliers during the year. Similar differences between income flows and cash flows can be seen for salaries and for other expenses. Note that there is no specific cash flow associated with depreciation expense

Exhibit 5.1
SOLINGER ELECTRIC CORPORATION
Income Statement and Statement of
Cash Receipts and Disbursements for the Year 4

	Income Statement[a]	Statement of Cash Receipts and Disbursements	
Sales Revenue	$125,000	$ 90,000	... Collections from Customers
Less: Expenses			Less: Disbursements
Cost of Goods Sold ..	$ 60,000	$ 50,000	... To Merchandise Suppliers
Salaries	20,000	19,000	... To Employees
Depreciation	10,000	0	... —
Other	15,000	13,000	... To Other Suppliers
Total Expenses	$105,000	$ 82,000	... Total Disbursements to Suppliers and Employees
Net Income	$ 20,000	$ 8,000	... Net Cash Inflow from Operations
		100,000	... Receipts from Issuing Long-Term Bonds
		$108,000	... Total Receipts from Operations and Bond Issue
		$ 10,000	... Disbursements for Dividends
		125,000	... Disbursements for Equipment
		$135,000	... Total Disbursements for Dividends and Equipment
		$ 27,000	... Net Decrease in Cash

[a]To facilitate comparison, a single-step income statement is used in this illustration.

[1]This example has been simplified for purpose of illustration. In a realistic situation, some of the receipts would have been from collection of receivables existing at the start of the year. Similarly, some of the payments would have been for liabilities existing at the start of the year. To further simplify, we have included income tax with "other expenses."

during Year 4. Cash was used in some earlier periods for the acquisition of buildings and equipment, but the amount of cash spent earlier was not reported then as an expense in accrual accounting. Rather, it was reflected in the balance sheet as an increase in the asset account for buildings and equipment and shown in the statement of changes in financial position as a use of funds. Now, as the buildings and equipment are being used, the cost of the assets' services used is reported as expense of the period even though there is now no outflow of cash. Although the operating activities generated $20,000 in net income, these activities led to an increase in cash of only $8,000 during Year 4.

The Solinger Electric Corporation engaged in other activities affecting cash during Year 4, as is reported in the lower portion of Exhibit 5.1. Cash in the amount of $100,000 was received from the issue of bonds, $10,000 was disbursed for dividends, and $125,000 was disbursed for the acquisition of new equipment. The result of all of the firm's activities is a decrease in cash of $27,000.

The experience of Solinger Electric Corporation is not unusual. Many firms, particularly those growing rapidly, discover that their cash position is deteriorating despite an excellent earnings record. The statement of changes in financial position explains how the financing, investing, and operating activities of a firm affect cash for a period.

Objective of the Statement of Changes in Financial Position

The statement of changes in financial position reports the major sources and uses of cash flowing through a firm during a period of time. Figure 5.3 shows the major sources and uses, which are described following.

Figure 5.3
Sources and Uses of Cash

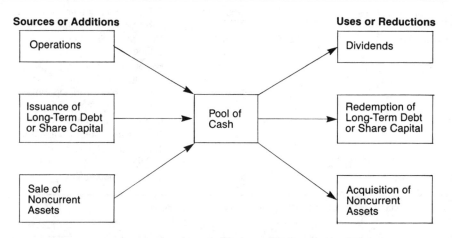

1. *Sources — Operations* The net amount of cash generated from selling goods and providing services is one of the most important sources of funds for a financially healthy company. When assessed over several years, cash provided by opera-

tions indicates the extent to which the operating or earnings activities have generated more than is used up. The excess from operations can then be used for dividends, acquisition of buildings and equipment, or repayment of long-term debt as necessary.

2. *Sources — Issuance of Long-Term Debt or Share Capital*   In the long run, a firm must generate most of its cash from operating activities. Potential shareholders are not willing to invest in unprofitable firms. Neither are banks willing to lend large amounts of cash to firms that do not generate profits. A potentially profitable firm finds that it can raise cash by issuing shares to owners or by borrowing. The amount of cash that can be generated by issuing shares or by borrowing is limited, however, by the marketplace's assessment of the firm's prospects.

3. *Sources — Sales of Noncurrent Assets*   The sale of buildings, equipment, and other noncurrent assets increases cash. These sales generally are not a major source of financing for an ongoing firm. The amounts received from the sales are not likely to be sufficient to replace the assets sold.

4. *Uses — Dividends*   Dividends are generally a recurring use of cash. Most publicly held firms are reluctant to omit the payment of dividends, even during a year of poor earnings performance. Because dividends use cash that might otherwise be retained and used elsewhere, they generally increase the need for other forms of financing.

5. *Uses — Redemption of Long-Term Debt or Share Capital*   In most instances, publicly held firms redeem or pay long-term debt at maturity with the proceeds of another debt issue. Thus, these redemptions often have little effect on the *net* change in cash. Some firms also occasionally reacquire, or redeem, their own share capital for various reasons (discussed in Chapter 12).

6. *Uses — Acquisition of Noncurrent Assets*   The acquisition of noncurrent assets, such as buildings and equipment, usually represents the most important continuing use of cash. Such assets must be replaced as they wear out, and additional noncurrent assets must be acquired if a firm is to grow.

Firms sometimes issue long-term debt or shares directly to the seller in acquiring buildings, equipment, or other noncurrent assets. These transactions technically do not affect cash. However, the transaction is reported in the statement of changes in financial position as though two transactions took place: the issuance of long-term debt or shares for cash and the immediate use of that cash in the acquisition of noncurrent assets. This is called the *dual transactions assumption*. Such a transaction would normally be disclosed in the statement of changes in financial position as both a source and use of cash of equal amounts, with a note referring to the link between the two items.

Uses of Information in the Statement of Changes in Financial Position

The statement of changes in financial position provides information that may be used in:

1. Assessing changes in a firm's liquidity, and
2. Assessing changes in the structure of a firm's assets and equities.

Note:

Liquidity Perhaps the most important factor not reported on either the balance sheet or income statement is how the operations of a period affected the liquidity of a firm. It is easy to conclude that increased earnings mean increased cash or other liquid assets. Such a conclusion may not be valid. The successful firm may acquire a new plant, so that it has less cash after a good year than before. On the other hand, increased liquidity can accompany reduced earnings. Consider, for example, a firm that is gradually reducing the scope of its operations. Such a firm is likely to report reduced net income or even losses over time. But because it is not replacing plant and equipment, it is likely to be accumulating cash or other liquid assets.

Very important to investors who wish to protect themselves

Structure of Assets and Equities In addition to providing information about changes in a firm's liquidity during a period, the statement of changes in financial position indicates the major transactions causing changes in the structure of a firm's assets (investments) and its liabilities and shareholders' equity (financing). For example, acquisitions and sales of specific types of assets (buildings, equipment, patents) are reported. Likewise, issues and redemptions of long-term debt and share capital are disclosed. These transactions are difficult to observe by looking at the income statement or the balance sheet or both. For example, the change in the account, Buildings and Equipment—Net of Accumulated Depreciation, could be attributable to depreciation charges, to acquisition of new buildings and equipment, to disposition of old buildings and equipment, or to a combination of these. The income statement and comparative balance sheets do not provide sufficient information about these three items individually for the reader to disaggregate the net change in the account during the period. A statement of changes in financial position is required to report this information.

Cash Defined

Define Cash. Cash - demands on cash.

The *CICA Handbook* defines cash as **cash plus cash equivalents net of short-term bank borrowings.**[2] This broader measure gives a more accurate representation of short-term liquidity. To avoid confusion, the phrase **cash position** will be used in this text whenever the CICA definition is employed.

Although the choice of the phrase *cash position* is arbitrary, there is a degree of logical support for its use. The accounting profession has embraced the term *statement of financial position*, which is gradually supplanting the historical phrase *balance sheet*. One of the major functions of this statement is to allow readers to assess the liquidity of the firm. *Cash position* is liquidity under distress conditions. A number of leading Canadian corporations now use the term *cash position*.

---

[2]Judgment is necessary in deciding what items to include in this algorithm. For instance, if a certificate of deposit was a one-year GIC, non-cashable before maturity, then it would not be a cash equivalent. Similarly if a bank note payable was a 12-month note and not a demand note then it would not be a factor in assessing short-run liquidity.

Corporate cash: why its meaning differs between treasurers and controllers

Richard P. Kramer
Assistant Treasurer
PLM Companies Inc.

*E*veryone knows what cash is. You reach in your pocket, pull out some bills, and that's cash—it's simple. As for money, that's another matter; the monetary aggregates used by economists (M-1, M-2, etc.) are confusing at best. The meaning of cash, as well, is not simple in the corporate world of cash managers (treasurers) and accountants (controllers).

Determining how much cash a corporation has is another task that's not easy. Dictionary definitions of cash are not particularly helpful because they do not take into account the dynamics of either modern cash management or current accounting practices. Also, all corporations do not use the same accounting treatment for cash. The problem of measuring corporate cash is further compounded by the fact that corporate treasurers and controllers use different definitions of cash. These different definitions and different accounting treatments can cause misunderstandings and problems within the corporation, as well as for users of published financial statements.

Different definitions

Two key objectives of modern corporate cash management are maximization of the return on liquid assets and minimization of the cost of financing the assets used by corporations. The minimization of idle cash balances is basic to the achievement of these objectives. Corporations should either invest all available cash to produce investment income or use cash to reduce debt and the cost of borrowing. One way that corporate cash management groups minimize idle cash is to wait until outstanding checks issued by the corporation are presented for payment at the corporation's banks before depositing money into the bank accounts to cover them.

From a cash management point of view, the objective is to have a bank balance of zero at the end of each day. Banks provide "controlled disbursing" programs to assist corporations in achieving their zero-balance objectives. Many treasurers are so successful at eliminating bank account balances that they are able to consistently maintain a negative account balance (for cash) on the corporation's accounting books.

The negative accounting balance for corporate cash results from the fact that the accepted accounting procedure is to reduce the cash account when checks are issued. When the value of outstanding but uncleared checks exceeds the amount of cash in the corporate bank accounts, the corporation's accounting records show a deficit cash balance. This result is especially likely when a corporation uses a controlled disbursing program to keep bank account balances at zero.

Public corporations almost always maintain accounting records and financial statements on an accrual basis, in accordance with "generally accepted accounting principles." One of the basic objectives of accrual accounting is to record and report revenues and expenses in the same period in which they are incurred. Standard accounting practice calls for the reduction of the cash account balance and a debit to accounts payable—or some other liability or expense account—when a check is prepared and mailed to the payee. On the other hand, treasury cash management practices recognize a reduction in cash balances only when a bank debits a corporate bank account. The bank's daily reports of cash balances are based upon cash disbursements and do not reflect any outstanding checks that have not been presented for payment. The difference between the treasurer's cash records and the balance in the controller's cash account is simply the timing difference—the number of days it takes for the check to be delivered, deposited, and cleared through the banking system to the company's bank account. In cash management parlance, the dollar amount of outstanding checks is known as "disbursement float."

Deposit float, the mirror image of disbursement float, refers to the receipt of checks rather than the issuance of checks. Generally accepted accounting principles dictate that the accounting cash balance be increased as checks are deposited in the bank. However, the treasurer's cash management staff does not record an increase in cash until the banks have credited the corporate bank accounts with cleared funds.

The preceding sounds basic to anyone familiar with modern corporate cash management practices and accrual accounting. The point is that "cash" takes on different meanings as one moves from the realm of cash management into the world of accounting. If nothing else were involved, these two corporate departments could use different definitions of cash without being concerned about what is being done elsewhere. Unfortunately, neither group can take a myopic view of what cash is. The following section describes a few of the problems that arise from the use of different definitions of cash by treasurers and controllers.

The problem with definitions

One of the most important problems associated with the difference in definitions of cash is the economic cost incurred by corporations that are reluctant to publish financial statements showing "bank overdrafts" (outstanding checks in excess of bank balances) on their balance sheet. It is very common for senior corporate executives to establish, as a cash target, the amount of cash they want to show on published financial statements. Unfortunately for these executives, the cash figure cannot be buried in financial statements; U.S. accounting rules require that "cash" be shown on corporate balance sheets as a separate line item.

Under certain conditions, cash can be combined with short-term investments, but it may not be combined with other current asset items in published financial statements. Also, the accounting profession insists that the dollar figure reported as cash should be the amount available for the payment of debts—and should not include bank account balances against which checks are outstanding.

It is not entirely clear why most corporate executives believe that a positive cash figure is so desirable. A few large corporations report bank overdrafts without any apparent ill effects. In fact, those familiar with modern cash management practices know that a large positive cash figure on a corporate balance sheet may be a symptom of either poor cash management or window dressing. One reason that has been advanced to justify cash window dressing is that both investors and lending institutions view with disfavor those companies that show either a zero cash balance or bank overdrafts in published financials. However, informal discussions with both investment professionals and bankers suggest that they do not downgrade corporations that report a zero cash figure or book overdrafts. Investment professionals do look at financial ratios, such as the current ratio and quick ratio that include cash, but they do not focus on cash as an important item. If a company's financial ratios are of an investment grade, then investment professionals are not concerned about bank overdrafts on the balance sheet.

Similarly, commercial banks take many objective and subjective factors into account as a part of their loan approval process. In their eyes, the presence of bank overdrafts in financial statements is not sufficient to affect the lending decision. However, a zero cash or overdraft position may be the symptom of fundamental liquidity or profit problems that would cause a bank to reject a loan request.

There is a very real economic cost associated with cash window dressing in published financial statements. In corporations that wish to show a particular balance in the cash amount at the end of financial reporting periods, the treasurer's staff must do two things: First, they must estimate how large a cash deposit will be required to offset the disbursement float on the last day of the reporting period. Second, they must obtain the cash and put it in the bank for at least one day (longer if weekends or holidays follow the end of the accounting period). This idle cash has an economic cost. That is, investments must be foregone or interest must be paid on borrowed funds.

In some cases, the cost can be significant. For example, the cost of $100 million for two days four times per year at 10 percent per year is approximately $219,000. This figure does not include the cost of information systems and staff time.

Some solutions

Corporations deal with the problem of the economic cost of cash window dressing in different ways. A few companies generate improved reported cash balances by changing their accounting treatment rather than by actually increasing the bank balances. These companies have been successful in persuading their accountants and auditors to add disbursement float back to the cash account at the end of the financial reporting period. This adjustment on the asset side of the balance sheet must be accompanied by an offsetting adjustment to liabilities. In some cases, the liability item is descriptive (e.g., "Outstanding Checks in Excess of Bank Balances"), but other companies include the addition to liabilities in a nondescriptive account such as "Accounts Payable."

Making payments with drafts is another way to deal with the problem of

the difference between cash and accrual accounting. A draft is a written order (by the company as drawer) instructing a bank (the drawee) to pay a third party (the payee). Legally, a draft is not the same as a check; however, in appearance, a draft is almost indistinguishable from a check. The difference is that a draft is drawn against a bank rather than against a company's bank account. The company need not pay a draft until it is approved by the corporation, honored by the bank, and charged against the corporation's bank account. Consequently, accrual accounting practices do not require a reduction in the cash account balance until the company is charged by the bank. The disadvantage of drafts (vs. checks) is that the companies issuing them are responsible for verifying signatures and approving the bank's payments to the payees. The verification of signatures on tens of thousands or millions of drafts can be a labor-intensive and expensive activity. However, companies can separately authorize their banks to verify the signatures on drafts. Because signature verification is a normal bank service, this contractual shifting of responsibility for signature verification results in a per-item cost equal to the cost of checks.

How then can the differing objectives and accounting treatments for cash be accommodated with a minimum of effort and cost?

☐ Continue the current cash management and accounting practices.
☐ Discontinue window dressing for published financial statements.
☐ Use drafts rather than checks to pay obligations.
☐ Adjust the accounting practice to add back issued but uncleared checks to the accounting book balance at the end of financial reporting periods.

Reprinted with permission of *Financial Executive*. Jan./Feb. 1988, pp. 53–55.

Statement Format

Since the CICA introduced the new recommendations for the statement of changes in financial position in 1986, there has been a proliferation of formats for the statement. For instance, *Financial Reporting in Canada* (1987 ed.) shows fourteen different variations. In our opinion, many of these variations are punitive to readers since sources and applications of cash are mixed together and the statements employ extensive use of bracketed figures.

We believe the format shown in Figure 5.4 is easy to understand and conceptually elegant:

Figure 5.4

The Every Firm Statement of Changes in Financial Position
For the year ended —

Cash Provided by	
Operations[a]	$
Financing Activities	$
Investing Activities	$
Cash Applied to	
Financing Activities	$
Investing Activities	$
Dividends	$
Increase (Decrease) in Cash Position[b]	$
Cash Position Beginning of Year	$
Cash Position End of Year	$

[a]Schedule of reconciliation of net income to cashflow provided here
[b]Cash position is defined as cash plus cash equivalents net of short-term bank borrowings

Analysis of the Effects of Transactions on Cash

Algebraic Formulation

The effects of various transactions on cash might be seen by reexamining the accounting equation. In doing so, the following notation is used:

C — cash

NCA — noncash assets

L — liabilities

SE — shareholders' equity

Δ — the change in an item, whether positive (an increase) or negative (a decrease) from the beginning of a period to the end of the period.

The accounting equation states that:

$$\text{Assets} = \text{Liabilities} + \text{Shareholders' Equity}$$
$$\text{C} + \text{NCA} = \text{L} + \text{SE}$$

Furthermore, this equation must be true for balance sheets constructed at both the start of the period and the end of the period. If the start-of-the-period and end-of-the-period balance sheets maintain the accounting equation, then the following equation must also be valid:

$$\Delta C + \Delta NCA = \Delta L + \Delta SE$$

Rearranging terms in this equation, we obtain the equation for changes in cash:

$$\Delta C = \Delta L + \Delta SE - \Delta NCA$$

The left-hand side of the above equation represents the change in cash. The right-hand side of the equation, reflecting changes in all noncash accounts, must also be equal in amount to the net change in cash. The equation states that increases (decreases) in cash (left-hand side) are equal to, or caused by, the increases in liabilities plus the increases (decreases) in shareholders' equity less the increases (decreases) in non-cash assets (right-hand side). Next, we illustrate how the changes in the accounts on the right-hand side bring about the change in cash on the left-hand side.

Illustration of Transactions Analysis

We can analyze some typical transactions to demonstrate how the equation is maintained and how cash is affected.

Assume that the following events occur during Year 4 for the Solinger Electric Corporation, considered earlier in Exhibit 5.1.

1. Merchandise costing $70,000 is acquired on account.
2. Merchandise costing $60,000 is sold to customers on account for $125,000.
3. Salaries of $19,000 are paid in cash.
4. Other expenses of $13,000 are paid in cash.
5. Cash collections of customers' accounts total $90,000.
6. Cash payments to suppliers of merchandise total $50,000.
7. Salaries earned but not paid as of December 31, Year 4 are accrued, $1,000.
8. Other expenses not paid as of December 31, Year 4 are accrued, $2,000.
9. Depreciation for Year 4 is recorded, $10,000.
10. Long-term debt is issued for cash, $100,000.
11. Dividends of $10,000 are declared and paid.
12. Equipment costing $125,000 is acquired for cash.

The effects of these transactions on cash are analyzed in Exhibit 5.2. Cash decreased by $27,000 during Year 4. Both sides of the equation show this net change. The net change in cash during a period (left-hand side of the equation at the top of Exhibit 5.2) can therefore be explained, or analyzed, by focusing on the changes in noncash accounts (right-hand side of the equation). For Solinger Electric Corporation, the net decrease in cash of $27,000 is explained as follows:

Increases in Cash:	
From Operations	$ 8,000
From Issuing Long-Term Debt	100,000
Total Increases	$108,000
Decreases in Cash:	
For Dividends	$ 10,000
For Acquisition of Equipment	125,000
Total Decreases	$135,000
Net Decrease in Cash	$ 27,000

Note that the recording of depreciation for the period does not affect cash. A noncash asset is decreased and shareholders' equity is decreased. Cash is not affected. (Cash was reduced in the period when the noncurrent asset was purchased.)

The information necessary to prepare the statement of changes in financial position could be developed using the transactions analysis approach illustrated in Exhibit 5.2. This approach quickly becomes cumbersome, however, as the number of transactions increases. The next section describes an alternative procedure for preparing the statement of changes in financial position that uses the T-account discussed in previous chapters.

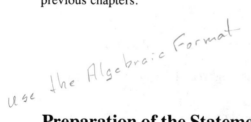

Preparation of the Statement of Changes in Financial Position

As with the balance sheet and income statement, knowing how to prepare a statement of changes in financial position is not essential in order to use it effectively. Nevertheless, learning how to construct this statement facilitates understanding its rationale and content. This section presents a step-by-step procedure for preparing the statement of changes in financial position. This procedure is then illustrated using the transactions of Solinger Electric Corporation for Year 4.

Unlike the balance sheet and income statement, the statement of changes in financial position is not generated as a regular output of a firm's record-keeping system. The statement of changes in financial position is usually prepared with a work sheet or other analysis after the balance sheet and income statement have been prepared.

Exhibit 5.2
Analysis of the Effects of Solinger Electric Corporation's Transactions
During Year 4 on Cash and Noncash Accounts

Transactions	Changes in Cash ΔC	=	ΔL	+	Changes in Noncash Accounts ΔSE	−	ΔNCA
(1) Merchandise costing $70,000 is acquired on account, increasing a noncash asset and a noncash liability ..	$ 0	=	$ 70,000	+	0	−	(+$ 70,000)
(2) Merchandise costing $60,000 is sold to customers on account for $125,000, increasing a noncash asset, accounts receivable, by $125,000, decreasing the noncash asset, inventory, by $60,000, and increasing shareholders' equity by $65,000 (= $125,000 − $60,000)...	0	=		+	$65,000	−	(+$125,000) / (−$ 60,000)
(3) Salaries of $19,000 are paid in cash, decreasing cash and shareholders' equity	(−$ 19,000)	=	0	+	(−$19,000)	−	0
(4) Other expenses of $13,000 are paid in cash, decreasing cash and shareholders' equity	(−$ 13,000)	=	0	+	(−$13,000)	−	0
(5) Cash collections of customers' accounts total $90,000, increasing cash and decreasing the noncash asset, accounts receivable	$ 90,000	=	0	+	0	−	(−$ 90,000)
(6) Payments to suppliers of merchandise total $50,000, decreasing cash and a liability	(−$ 50,000)	=	(−$ 50,000)	+	0	−	0
(7) Salaries of $1,000 earned but not paid as of December 31, Year 4, are accrued, increasing a liability and decreasing shareholders' equity	0	=	$ 1,000	+	(−$ 1,000)	−	0
(8) Other expenses of $2,000 not paid as of December 31, Year 4, are accrued, increasing a liability and decreasing shareholders' equity	0	=	$ 2,000	+	(−$ 2,000)	−	0
(9) Depreciation for Year 4 of $10,000 is recorded, decreasing shareholders' equity and noncash assets	0	=	0	+	(−$10,000)	−	(−$ 10,000)
Total from operations	$ 8,000	=	$ 23,000	+	$20,000	−	$ 35,000
(10) Long-term debt is issued for $100,000, increasing cash and a liability	$100,000	=	$100,000	+	0	−	0
(11) Dividends of $10,000 are declared and paid, decreasing cash and shareholders' equity	(−$ 10,000)	=	0	+	(−$10,000)	−	0
(12) Equipment costing $125,000 is acquired for cash, decreasing cash and increasing noncash assets	(−$125,000)	=	0	+	0	−	(+$125,000)
Net change in cash and noncash accounts	−$27,000	=	$123,000	+	$10,000	−	$160,000

Effect on Cash

The Procedure and an Illustration

Step 1 Obtain balance sheets for the beginning and end of the period covered by the statement of changes in financial position. Exhibit 5.3 presents the comparative balance sheets of Solinger Electric Corporation for December 31, Year 3 and Year 4.

Exhibit 5.3
SOLINGER ELECTRIC CORPORATION
Comparative Balance Sheets for
December 31, Year 3 and Year 4

Assets	December 31,	
Current Assets:	**Year 4**	**Year 3**
Cash	$ 3,000	$ 30,000
Accounts Receivable	55,000	20,000
Merchandise Inventory	50,000	40,000
Total Current Assets	$108,000	$ 90,000
Noncurrent Assets:		
Buildings and Equipment (Cost)	$225,000	$100,000
Accumulated Depreciation	(40,000)	(30,000)
Total Noncurrent Assets	$185,000	$ 70,000
Total Assets	$293,000	$160,000

Equities		
Current Liabilities:		
Accounts Payable — Merchandise Suppliers	$ 50,000	$ 30,000
Accounts Payable — Other Suppliers	12,000	10,000
Salaries Payable	6,000	5,000
Total Current Liabilities	$ 68,000	$ 45,000
Noncurrent Liabilties:		
Bonds Payable	$100,000	$ 0
Shareholders' Equity:		
Common Stock	$100,000	$100,000
Retained Earnings	25,000	15,000
Total Owners' Equity	$125,000	$115,000
Total Equities	$293,000	$160,000

Step 2 Prepare a T-account *work sheet*. An example of such a T-account work sheet is shown in Exhibit 5.4. At the top of the work sheet is a master T-account titled Cash. Note that this T-account has sections labeled Operations, Financing, Investing, and Dividends. Transactions affecting cash during the period are classified under one of these headings to aid in the preparation of the statement of changes in financial position. This procedure is explained later in this section. The beginning and ending amounts of cash are then entered in the master T-account. The beginning and ending amounts of cash for Solinger Electric Corporation are $30,000 and $3,000 respectively. The check marks indicate that the figures are balances. The number at the top of the T-account is the opening balance; the one at the bottom is the closing

balance. Note that the T-account, Cash, is another means of expressing the left-hand side of the equation for changes in cash in Exhibit 5.2.

After the T-account for Cash has been prepared (as at the top of Exhibit 5.4), the work sheet is completed by preparing T-accounts for *each* noncash asset and liability and shareholders' equity account. Enter the beginning and ending balances in each account for the period as given in Exhibit 5.3. The lower portion of Exhibit 5.4 shows the T-accounts for each noncash account. Note that the sum of the changes in these individual T-accounts is another means of expressing the right-hand side of the equation for changes in cash in Exhibit 5.2.

Exhibit 5.4
T-Account Work Sheet for Solinger Electric Corporation

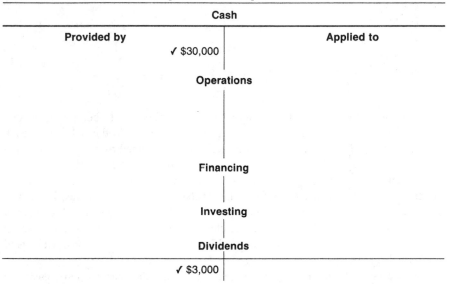

Salaries Payable	Bonds Payable	Common Stock
5,000 ✓	0 ✓	100,000 ✓
6,000 ✓	100,000 ✓	100,000 ✓

Retained Earnings
15,000 ✓
25,000 ✓

Step 3 Explain the change in the master cash account between the beginning and end of the period by explaining, or accounting for, the change in the balance of each noncash account during the period. This step is accomplished by *reconstructing the entries originally recorded in the accounts during the period*. The reconstructed entries are written in the appropriate T-accounts on the work sheet. These reconstructed entries are called *analytical entries*. Once the net change in each of the noncash accounts has been accounted for, sufficient information will have been generated to account for the net change in cash. That is, if the changes in the right-hand side of the cash equation have been explained, the causes of the changes in cash itself on the left-hand side will also have been explained.

The process of reconstructing the transactions during the year is usually easiest if information supplementary to the balance sheet is accounted for first. Assume the following information concerning the Solinger Electric Corporation for Year 4:

1. Net income is $20,000.
2. Depreciation expense is $10,000.
3. Dividends declared and paid total $10,000.

The analytical entry to record the information concerning net income is:

(1) Cash (Operations — Net Income)	$20,000	
Retained Earnings		$20,000

To understand this entry, review the process of recording revenues and expenses and the closing entries for those temporary accounts from Chapter 3. All of the journal entries that together record the process of earning $20,000 net income are equivalent to the following single journal entry:

Net Assets (= All Assets − All Liabilities)	$20,000	
Retained Earnings		$20,000
Summary entry equivalent to recording earnings of $20,000		

The summary journal entry debits Net Assets. The initial assumption at this stage of preparing the statement of changes in financial position is that all of the net assets generated by the earnings process were cash. Thus, in the analytic entry (1) above, the debit results in showing a provisional increase in cash from operations in an amount equal to net income for the period.

Not all of the items recognized as expenses and deducted in calculating net income, however, decrease cash (refer to Exhibit 5.1). The portion of the expenses that does not affect cash is added to the provisional increase in cash to calculate the net amount of cash from operations. One expense not using cash is depreciation, illustrated in analytical entry (2).

follow through to 232-33

(2) Cash (Sources: Operations — Depreciation Expense		
Addback)	$10,000	
Accumulated Depreciation		$10,000

Because depreciation expense was deducted in calculating net income but did not reduce cash, the amount of depreciation expense must be added back to net income in calculating the amount of cash provided by operations. A more complete explanation is provided on pages 232–233.

The supplementary information concerning dividends of $10,000 declared and paid is recorded in the analytical entry that follows:

(3) Retained Earnings	$10,000	
Cash (Uses: Dividends)		$10,000
Dividends reduce retained earnings and cash.		

Dividends create a classification problem within the operating/investing/financing format. *Financial Reporting in Canada* (1987 ed.) showed that 58% of companies surveyed treat dividends as a financing activity, 8% as an operating activity, and 34% as a separate category altogether. Since the logic supporting their inclusion as operating or financing activities is weak, we support the classification of dividends as a separate item on the statement of changes in financial position.

Once the supplementary information has been reflected in the T-accounts, it is necessary to make inferences about the reasons for the remaining changes in the noncash accounts on the balance sheet. (If the statement of changes in financial position were being prepared for an actual firm, such inferences might not be necessary, because sufficient information regarding the change in each account is likely to be available from the firm's accounting records.) The changes in noncash accounts are explained in the order of their appearance.

The Accounts Receivable account shows an increase of $35,000. The analytical entry to record this assumed information in the work sheet is:

(4) Accounts Receivable	$35,000	
Cash (Uses: Operations — Subtractions)		$35,000

The operations of the period generated sales. Not all of these sales resulted in an increase in cash. Some of the sales resulted in an increase in Accounts Receivable. Because we start the statement of changes in financial position with net income, in deriving the amount of cash from operations we must *subtract that portion of revenues not producing cash* (that is, the excess of sales on account over cash collections from customers).

The next noncash account showing a change is that for Merchandise Inventory. That account shows an increase during the year of $10,000. As the operations of the firm have expanded, so has the amount carried in inventory. The analytical entry of the work sheet to explain the change in Merchandise Inventory is:

(5) Merchandise Inventory	$10,000	
Cash (Uses: Operations — Subtractions)		$10,000

Solinger Electric Corporation found it necessary to increase the amount of inventory carried to make possible increased future sales. An increase in inventory is ordinarily an operating use of cash. Because we start the statement of changes in financial position with net income, in deriving cash from operations we must subtract from net income the incremental investment in inventories during the year (that is, the excess of purchases over the cost of goods sold).

The next noncash account showing a change is that for Buildings and Equipment (Cost). The Buildings and Equipment (Cost) account shows a net increase of $125,000 (= $225,000 − $100,000). Because we have no other information, we must assume or deduce that buildings and equipment costing $125,000 were acquired during the year. The analytical entry is:

(6) Buildings and Equipment (Cost)	$125,000	
Cash (Uses: Investing — Acquisitions of Buildings and Equipment)		$125,000

Acquisition of buildings and equipment is a nonoperating use of cash.

The next noncash account showing a change is that for Accounts Payable — Merchandise Suppliers. As the amounts carried in inventory have increased, so have the amounts owed to suppliers of inventory. The analytical entry to explain the increase in the amount of Accounts Payable — Merchandise Suppliers is:

(7) Cash (Sources: Operations — Additions)	$20,000	
Accounts Payable — Merchandise Suppliers		$20,000

explain the inverse of accounts receivable.

Ordinarily, acquiring inventory requires cash. Suppliers who allow a firm to pay later for goods (and services) received now are effectively supplying the firm with cash. Thus an increase in the amount of accounts payable for inventory results from a transaction where inventory increased but cash did not decrease, which is equivalent to saying that an increase in payables provides cash, even if only temporarily. The increase in cash resulting from increased payables for inventory is an operating source of funds.

The next noncash account showing a change is Accounts Payable — Other Suppliers. As the scope of operations has increased, so has the amount owed to others. The analytical entry to explain the increase in the amount of Accounts Payable — Other Suppliers is:

(8) Cash (Sources: Operations — Additions)	$2,000	
Accounts Payable — Other Suppliers		$2,000

ditto

The reasoning behind this entry is the same as for entry (7). Creditors who permit a firm to owe them effectively provide cash. The same reasoning applies to an increased amount of Salaries Payable, the next noncash account showing a change. The analytic entry to record the increase in Salaries Payable is:

(9) Cash (Sources: Operations — Additions)	$1,000	
Salaries Payable		$1,000

ditto

Employees who do not demand immediate payment for salaries earned have provided their employer with cash, at least temporarily.

The final noncash account showing a change not yet explained is Bonds Payable. It shows a net increase of $100,000 for the year. Because no other information is given, it must be assumed that long-term bonds were issued during the year. The analytic entry is:

(10) Cash (Sources: Financing — Long-Term Bond		
Issue)	$100,000	
Bonds Payable		$100,000

ditto

Exhibit 5.5 presents the completed T-account work sheet for Solinger Electric Corporation for Year 4. All changes in the noncash T-accounts have been explained with the ten entries. If the work is correct, the causes of the change in the Cash account will have been presented in the entries in the master Cash account.

Exhibit 5.5
T-Account Work Sheet for
Solinger Electric Corporation

Cash

Provided by			Applied to
	✓ 30,000		

Operations

Net Income	(1)	20,000	35,000	(4)	Increased Accounts Receivable
Depreciation Expense	(2)	10,000	10,000	(5)	Increased Merchandise Inventory
Increased Accounts Payable to Merchandise Suppliers	(7)	20,000			
Increased Accounts Payable to Other Suppliers	(8)	2,000			
Increased Salaries Payable	(9)	1,000			

Financing

Long-Term Bonds Issued	(10)	100,000		

Investing

		125,000	(6)	Acquisition of Buildings and Equipment

Dividends

		10,000	(3)

	✓ 3,000	

Accounts Receivable			Merchandise Inventory			Buildings and Equipment (Cost)	
✓ 20,000			✓ 40,000			✓ 100,000	
(4) 35,000			(5) 10,000			(6) 125,000	
✓ 55,000			✓ 50,000			✓ 225,000	

Accumulated Depreciation			Accounts Payable Merchandise Suppliers			Accounts Payable Other Suppliers	
	30,000 ✓			30,000 ✓			10,000 ✓
	10,000 (2)			20,000 (7)			2,000 (8)
	40,000 ✓			50,000 ✓			12,000 ✓

Salaries Payable			Bonds Payable			Retained Earnings	
	5,000 ✓			0			15,000 ✓
	1,000 (9)			100,000 (10)	(3) 10,000		20,000 (1)
	6,000 ✓			100,000 ✓			25,000 ✓

Step 4 The final step is the preparation of a formal statement of changes in financial ~~List~~ position. Exhibit 5.6 presents the statement for Solinger Electric Corporation. The statement is prepared directly from the information provided in the master T-account for Cash in the completed work sheet.

Exhibit 5.6
Solinger Electric Corporation
Statement of Changes in Financial Position
For the year ended December 31, 19X4

Cash Provided By

Operations (Note 1)	$ 8,000
Investing Activities	—
Financing Activities	
Sale of bonds	100,000
	$108,000

Cash Applied To

Investing Activities	
Acquisition of plant assets	125,000
Financing Activities	—
Dividends	10,000
	$135,000
Net Decrease in Cash Position[a]	(27,000)
Cash Position Beginning of Year	30,000
Cash Position End of Year	3,000

Note 1—Cash Provided by Operations

Net Income	$ 20,000
Add (deduct) non-cash items	
Depreciation expense	10,000
Working Capital Accounts	
Cash provided by net increases in accounts payable and salaries payable	23,000
Cash applied to net increases in accounts receivable and inventory	(45,000)
Cash Provided by Operations	$ 8,000

[a]Cash position is defined as cash plus cash equivalents net of short-term bank borrowings.

The first item disclosed in the statement is the amount of cash generated by operations. In deriving cash from operations, published annual reports typically start with net income. Expenses not using cash are then added to net income, and revenues not providing cash are subtracted to obtain cash from operations. If the reconciliation of net income to cash provided by operations is placed in a separate schedule below the main statement, a much "cleaner" looking statement results. Exhibit 5.6 illustrates this format. Because depreciation expense is added to net income to calculate cash provided by operations, some readers of financial statements incorrectly conclude that depreciation expense is a source of cash. As Exhibit 5.2 illustrated, the recording of depreciation expense does not affect cash. A noncash asset is decreased and a shareholders' equity account is decreased. Cash is not affected. Cash from operations results from selling goods and services to customers. If no sales are made, then there will be no cash provided by operations regardless of how large the depreciation charge may be.

A definition of the components of cash position should always be provided somewhere on the face of the statement.

Depreciation Is Not a Source of Funds To demonstrate that depreciation is not a source of funds, refer to the income statement of Solinger Electric Corporation (Exhibit 5.1) and the cash flow from the operations section of the statement of changes in financial position (Exhibit 5.6). Exhibit 5.7 reproduces them in condensed form. Suppose that depreciation for Year 4 had been $25,000 rather than $10,000. Then the condensed income statement and cash flow from operations would appear as in Exhibit 5.8. Note that the total cash flow from operations remains $8,000, which is the difference between receipts from revenues and all expenses that did use cash. The only effects on cash of transactions involving long-term assets are that: (1) cash is typically used when a long-term asset is acquired, and (2) cash is provided when the asset is sold.

Exhibit 5.7
SOLINGER ELECTRIC CORPORATION
Year 4
Depreciation $10,000

Income Statement		Cash Flow from Operations	
Revenues	$125,000	Net Income	$20,000
Expenses Except Depreciation	(95,000)	Additions:	
	$ 30,000	Depreciation	10,000
Depreciation Expense	(10,000)	Other	23,000
		Subtractions	(45,000)
		Cash Flow Provided by	
Net Income	$ 20,000	Operations	$ 8,000

Exhibit 5.8
SOLINGER ELECTRIC CORPORATION
Year 4
Depreciation $25,000

Income Statement		Cash Flow from Operations	
Revenues	$125,000	Net Income	$ 5,000
Expenses Except Depreciation	(95,000)	Additions:	
	$ 30,000	Depreciation	25,000
		Other	23,000
Depreciation Expense	(25,000)	Subtractions:	(45,000)
		Cash Flow Provided by	
Net Income	$ 5,000	Operations	$ 8,000

An alternative procedure for deriving cash flow from operations is to list all revenue items that provide cash and then to subtract all expense items that use cash. The right-hand column of Exhibit 5.1 illustrates this approach. This alternative presentation is appealing because depreciation expense does not appear as an element in the calculation of cash flow provided by operations. The latter presentation, although acceptable, is rarely used in published financial statements. If this approach was followed for Solinger, cash flow from operations would be computed as follows:

Collections from customers		
Opening balance Accounts Receivable	$ 20,000	
+ Sales	125,000	
− Receivables at end of period	(55,000)	
		$90,000
Payments to Suppliers and Creditors		
(from data on p. 221, $19,000 + $13,000 + $50,000)		($82,000)
Cash flow from operations		$ 8,000

Extension of the Illustration

The illustration for Solinger Electric Corporation considered so far in this chapter is simpler than the typical published statement of changes in financial position in at least four respects:

1. There were only a few balance sheet accounts whose changes are to be explained.
2. Several types of more complex transactions that affect the sources of cash from operations were not involved.
3. Each transaction involved only one debit and one credit.
4. Each explanation of a noncash account change involved only one analytic entry on the work sheet, except for the Retained Earnings account.

Notes

Most of the complications that arise in interpreting published statements of changes in financial position relate to accounting events that are not discussed until later chapters. As these transactions are discussed, their effects on the statement of changes in financial position will be illustrated. One complication caused by a supplementary disclosure can be illustrated at this time, however. Suppose that the firm sold some of its buildings and equipment during the year. For now, and until we address the issue again in Chapter 9, assume that the firm disposes of existing buildings and equipment at their book value; the cash proceeds from disposition are equal to acquisition cost less accumulated depreciation of the assets. With this assumption, there will be no gain or loss on disposition.

Reconsider the Solinger Electric Corporation example with the following new information. Solinger Electric Corporation sold some equipment during Year 4. This equipment cost $10,000 and was sold for $3,000 at a time when accumulated depreciation on the equipment sold was $7,000. The actual entry made during the year to record the sale of the equipment was as follows:

Cash	$3,000	
Accumulated Depreciation	7,000	
Buildings and Equipment (Cost)		$10,000
Journal entry for sale of equipment.		

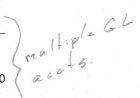

multiple GL accts.

Follow this"

Assume that the comparative balance sheets as shown in Exhibit 5.3 are correct and thus that the net decrease in cash for Year 4 is still $27,000. The entries in the T-accounts must be altered to reflect this new information. The following entry in the T-account work sheets is required to recognize the effect of the sale of equipment:

(1a) Cash (Sources — Sale of Equipment)	$3,000	
Accumulated Depreciation	$7,000	
Buildings and Equipment (Cost)		$10,000

The debit to Cash (Sources: Sale of Equipment) shows the proceeds of the sale.

As a result of entry (1a), the T-accounts for Buildings and Equipment (Cost) and Accumulated Depreciation would appear as follows:

Buildings and Equipment (Cost)		Accumulated Depreciation	
✓ 100,000			30,000 ✓
	10,000 (1a)	(1a) 7,000	
✓ 225,000			40,000 ✓

When the time comes to explain the change in the account, Buildings and Equipment (Cost), the T-account indicates that there is an increase of $125,000 and a credit entry (1a) of $10,000 to recognize the sale of equipment. The net increase in the Buildings and Equipment (Cost) account can be accounted for, given the decrease already entered, only by assuming that new buildings and equipment have been acquired during the period for $135,000.

The reconstructed entry to complete the explanation of the change in this account would be as follows:

(6a) Buildings and Equipment (Cost)	$135,000	
Cash (Uses: Acquisition of Buildings and		
Equipment)		$135,000

Likewise, when the change in the T-account for Accumulated Depreciation is explained, there is a net credit change of $10,000 and a debit entry (1a) of $7,000 to recognize the sale. Thus, the depreciation charge for Year 4 must have been $17,000. The reconstructed entry to complete the explanation of the change in the Accumulated Depreciation account would be as follows:

(2a) Cash (Source — Depreciation Expense		
Addback)	$17,000	
Accumulated Depreciation		$17,000

Exhibit 5.9 presents a revised T-account work for Solinger Electric Corporation incorporating the new information on the sale of equipment.

Exhibit 5.9
Revised T-Account Work Sheet for
Solinger Electric Corporation

Cash		
Provided by		**Applied to**

✓ 30,000

Operations

Net Income	(1) 20,000	35,000 (4) Increased Accounts Receivable
Depreciation Expense	(2a) 17,000	10,000 (5) Increased Merchandise Inventory
Increased Accounts Payable to Merchandise Suppliers	(7) 20,000	
Increased Accounts Payable to Other Suppliers	(8) 2,000	
Increased Salaries Payable	(9) 1,000	

Financing

| Long-Term Bonds Issued | (10) 100,000 | |

Investing

| Sale of Equipment | (1a) 3,000 | 135,000 (6a) Acquisition of Buildings and Equipment |

Dividends

| | | 10,000 (3) Dividends Declared and Paid |

✓ 3,000

Accounts Receivable		Merchandise Inventory		Buildings and Equipment (Cost)	
✓ 20,000		✓ 40,000		✓ 100,000	
(4) 35,000		(5) 10,000		(6a) 135,000	10,000 (1a)
✓ 55,000		✓ 50,000		✓ 225,000	

Accumulated Depreciation		Accounts Payable Merchandise Suppliers		Accounts Payable Other Suppliers	
	30,000 ✓		30,000 ✓		10,000 ✓
(1a) 7,000	17,000 (2a)		20,000 (7)		2,000 (8)
	40,000 ✓		50,000 ✓		12,000 ✓

Salaries Payable		Bonds Payable		Retained Earnings	
	5,000 ✓		0 ✓		15,000 ✓
	1,000 (9)		100,000 (10)	(3) 10,000	20,000 (1)
	6,000 ✓		100,000 ✓		25,000 ✓

Analysis of Statement of Changes in Financial Position

The principal questions that the statement of changes in financial position is designed to answer include the following:

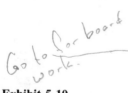

1. What is the relation between the various sources of cash (operations, new financing, sale of noncurrent assets)?
2. What is the relation between the various uses of cash (dividends, reduction in financing, acquisition of noncurrent assets)?
3. What is the relation between the total sources and the total uses of cash?

   In analyzing the statement of changes in financial position, it is often useful to express each source as a percentage of total sources and each use as a percentage of total uses. Such an analysis appears in Exhibit 5.10 for General Products Limited, whose financial statements appear in Appendix A. Because the percentages for any particular year can be significantly affected by a large debt or common stock issue in that year, it is often useful to combine the data for several years as is done in the far-right column of Exhibit 5.10.

   Note the following regarding General Products Limited.

1. Approximately 84 percent of the funds needed over the three-year period were generated from operations. Such a percentage is characteristic of a financially healthy firm.
2. Approximately 60 percent of the funds used were for the acquisition of plant, equipment, and other noncurrent assets. Such percentages are likewise typical of a manufacturing firm experiencing significant growth.
3. More funds were obtained from operations than were paid out as dividends. Thus, the firm is not liquidating itself, or shrinking. Instead, the excess cash generated from operations is being used for replacement and growth of assets.

   General Products Limited is a sound, financially healthy company. For a contrast, refer to Problem 27 at the end of the chapter, which involves analysis of the statement of changes in financial position for a financially troubled company.

Exhibit 5.10
GENERAL PRODUCTS LIMITED
Statement of Changes in Financial Position
(amounts in millions)

	1988		1987		1986		Combined	
Cash Provided by								
Operations	$1,963	83.0%	$2,322	88.6%	$1,742	79.0%	$6,027	83.8%
Financing Activities	258	10.9	198	7.5	289	13.1	745	10.4
Investing Activities	143	6.0	102	3.9	173	7.8	418	5.8
Total Sources	$2,364	100.0%	$2,622	100.0%	$2,204	100.0%	$7,190	100.0%
Cash Applied to								
Dividends	$ 670	22.6%	$ 624	24.9%	$ 570	25.8%	$1,864	24.6%
Reduction in Financing	214	7.2	253	13.6	582	26.4	1,049	13.8
Investing Activities	2,077	70.1	1,543	61.5	1,055	47.8	4,675	61.6
Total Uses	$2,961	100.0%	$2,420	100.0%	$2,207	100.0%	$7,588	100.0%

Summary

Generally accepted accounting principles require that a statement of changes in financial position be presented whenever a firm presents an income statement and a balance sheet.[3] The statement of changes in financial position reports on flows of cash into and out of a business during a period.

The statement of changes in financial position helps explain the major reasons for a change in a firm's liquidity. In particular, it shows the relation between net income and cash generated by operations. The statement also reports the reasons for significant shifts in the structure of a firm's assets (changes in receivables, inventories, plant and equipment) and in the structure of a firm's liabilities and shareholders' equity (changes in accounts payable, bonds payable, common stock, retained earnings). These types of information are difficult to observe from a balance sheet or income statement alone.

The statement of changes in financial position is basically derived from an analysis of changes in balance sheet accounts during the accounting period. If the double-entry recording process has been applied properly, the net change in cash (or other definition of funds) should equal the net change in all noncash accounts. By reconstructing the entries made in noncash accounts and explaining their net change during the period, the net change in cash is also explained.

The statement of changes in financial position usually begins with net income for the period. Adjustments are then made for revenues not providing cash and expenses not using cash. The result is cash generated by operations. Other sources (new financing, sale of noncurrent assets) are then shown. From the total sources are subtracted the uses of cash (dividends, reductions in financing, acquisition of noncurrent assets) to derive the net change in cash for the period.

When analyzing a statement of changes in financial position, the focus is on the relations between the various sources, among the various uses, and between the total sources and total uses. A financially healthy firm typically obtains a majority of its funds from operations and invests a large percentage in plant and equipment.

Chapter 5 constitutes an introduction to the statement of changes in financial position. In subsequent chapters as we introduce more types of transactions, reference will be made to the impact on this statement. Chapter 14 will synthesize these references and work through a comprehensive illustration.

Problem 1 for Self-Study

Exhibit 5.11 presents a comparative balance sheet for Robbie Corporation as of December 31, Year 1 and Year 2. During Year 2, no plant and equipment was sold and no dividends were declared or paid.

Prepare a T-account work sheet for the preparation of a statement of changes in financial position.

---

[3]Technically, the *CICA Handbook* strongly recommends but does not require a statement of changes in financial position. Some incorporating acts such as the Canada Business Corporations Act do require such a statement. *Financial Reporting in Canada* showed that for a survey of 300 public companies in Canada in 1986, 299 presented the statement of changes.

Exhibit 5.11
ROBBIE CORPORATION
Comparative Balance Sheet
December 31, Year 1 and Year 2
(amounts in 000's)
(Problem 1 for Self-Study)

	December 31, Year 2	December 31, Year 1		December 31, Year 2	December 31, Year 1
Assets			**Liabilities and Shareholders' Equity**		
Current Assets:			**Current Liabilities:**		
Cash	$ 25	$10	Accounts Payable	$ 40	$30
Accounts Receivable	20	15	Total Current Liabilities	$ 40	$30
Merchandise Inventories	25	20	**Long-Term Debt:**		
Total Current Assets	$ 70	$45	Bonds Payable	$ 15	$10
			Total Liabilities	$ 55	$40
Property, Plant, and Equipment ...	$ 60	$50	**Shareholders' Equity:**		
			Common Stock	$ 20	$10
Less: Accumulated Depreciation ...	(30)	(25)	Retained Earnings	25	20
Total Property, Plant, and Equipment	$ 30	$25	Total Shareholders' Equity	$ 45	$30
Total Assets	$100	$70	Total Liabilities and Shareholders' Equity	$100	$70

Suggested Solution

Exhibit 5.12 presents a completed T-account work sheet for Robbie Corporation.

Exhibit 5.12
T-Account Work Sheet for Robbie Corporation
Funds Defined as Cash
(amounts in 000's)

Cash			
Provided by		**Applied to**	
	✓ 10		
Operations			
Depreciation Expense	(4) 5	5 (1)	Increased Accounts Receivable
Increase Accounts Payable to Merchandise Suppliers	(5) 10	5 (2)	Increased Merchandise Inventories
Net Income	(8) 5		
Financing			
Long Term Bonds Issued	(6) 5		
Shares Issued	(7) 10		

Investing

		Property Plant and
10	(3)	Equipment Purchased

✓   25

Accounts Receivable	**Merchandise Inventories**	**Property, Plant and Equipment**
✓ 15	✓ 20	✓ 50
(1) 5	(2) 5	(3) 10
✓ 20	✓ 25	✓ 60

Accumulated Depreciation	**Accounts Payable**	**Bonds Payable**
25 ✓	30 ✓	10 ✓
5 (4)	10 (5)	5 (6)
30 ✓	40 ✓	15 ✓

Common Stock	**Retained Earnings**
10 ✓	20 ✓
10 (7)	5 (8)
20 ✓	25 ✓

Problem 2[4] for Self-Study

Exhibit 5.13 presents comparative balance sheets for Gordon Corporation as of December 31, Year 1 and Year 2. The following information pertains to Gordon Corporation for Year 2.

1. Net income was $200,000.
2. Dividends declared and paid were $120,000.
3. Depreciation expense totaled $80,000.
4. Buildings and equipment originally costing $50,000 and with accumulated depreciation of $40,000 were sold for $10,000.

   a. Prepare a T-account work sheet for the preparation of a statement of changes in financial position, defining funds as cash.

   b. Prepare a T-account work sheet for the preparation of a statement of changes in financial position, defining funds as working capital.

   c. Convert working capital provided by operations to cash flow provided by operations.

---

[4]Although working capital is no longer used as a definition of funds in Canada, this exercise is useful in helping students understand the relationship between cash and working capital.

Exhibit 5.13
GORDON CORPORATION
Comparative Balance Sheets
December 31, Year 1 and Year 2
(amounts in 000's)

	December 31	
	Year 2	Year 1
Assets		
Current Assets:		
Cash	$ 40	$ 70
Accounts Receivable	420	320
Merchandise Inventories	470	360
Prepayments	70	50
Total Current Assets	$1,000	$ 800
Property, Plant, and Equipment:		
Land	$ 250	$ 200
Building and Equipment (net of accumulated depreciation of $800 and $840)	1,150	1,000
Total Property, Plant, and Equipment	$1,400	$1,200
Total Assets	$2,400	$2,000
Liabilities and Shareholders' Equity		
Current Liabilities:		
Accounts Payable	$ 440	$ 320
Income Taxes Payable	80	60
Other Current Liabilities	360	170
Total Current Liabilities	$ 880	$ 550
Noncurrent Liabilities:		
Bonds Payable	$ 200	$ 250
Total Liabilities	1,080	800
Shareholders' Equity:		
Common Stock	$ 540	$ 500
Retained Earnings	780	700
Total Shareholders' Equity	$1,320	1,200
Total Liabilities and Shareholders' Equity	$2,400	$2,000

Suggested Solution

Exhibit 5.14 shows the analytical entries posted to Exhibits 5.15 and 5.16. Note that the changes to current assets and current liabilities posted to Exhibit 5.15 as analytical entries 5, 6, 7, 10, 11, and 12 are not posted to Exhibit 5.16, in which funds are defined as working capital.[5] Exhibit 5.15 presents a completed T-account work sheet for Gordon Corporation with funds defined as cash. Exhibit 5.16 presents a completed T-account work sheet with funds defined as working capital. Exhibit 5.17

---

[5]Prior to 1986 this was the prevalent definition of funds in Canada.

shows the conversion of working capital provided by operations to cash flow provided by operations.

Exhibit 5.14
Analytical Entries for Gordon Corporation
for Exhibits 5.15 and 5.16
(amounts in 000's)

Entry Exhibit 5.15	Exhibit 5.16	T-Account	Amount Dr.	Cr	Comment
(1)	(1)	Cash (Operations)	$200		Net income.
		Retained Earnings		$200	
(2)	(2)	Retained Earnings	120		Dividends.
		Cash (Other)		120	
(3)	(3)	Cash (Operations)	80		Depreciation expense.
		Bldgs. and Equip. — Net		80	
(4)	(4)	Bldgs. and Equip. — Net	40		Sale of buildings and
		Cash (Other)	10		equipment.
		Bldgs. and Equip. — Net		50	
(5)	—	Accounts Receivable	100		Accounts receivable
		Cash (Operations)		100	increase.
(6)	—	Merchandise Inventories	110		Merchandise inventories
		Cash (Operations)		110	increase.
(7)	—	Prepayments	20		Prepayments increase.
		Cash (Operations)		20	
(8)	(5)	Land	50		Purchase of land.
		Cash (Other)		50	
(9)	(6)	Bldgs. and Equip. — Net	240		Purchase of buildings and
		Cash (Other)		240	equipment.
(10)	—	Cash (Operations)	120		Accounts payable
		Accounts Payable		120	increase.
(11)	—	Cash (Operations)	20		Income tax payable
		Income Tax Payable		20	increase.
(12)	—	Cash (Operations)	190		Other current liabilities
		Other Current Liabilities		190	increase.
(13)	(7)	Bonds Payable	50		Noncurrent bonds payable
		Cash (Other)		50	decrease.
(14)	(8)	Cash (Other)	40		Share issue.
		Common Stock		40	

Exhibit 5.15
T-Account Work Sheet for Gordon Corporation
Funds Defined as Cash
(amounts in 000's)

	Cash	
Provided by		**Applied to**
	✓ 70	
	Operations	
Net Income (1) 200	100	(5) Accounts Receivable Increase
Depreciation Expense (3) 80	110	(6) Inventories Increase
Accounts Payable Increase (10) 120	20	(7) Prepayments Increase
Income Tax Payable Increase (11) 20		
Other Current Liabilities Increase (12) 190		

Financing

Share Issue	(14) 40		
		50	(13) Bonds Payable Decrease

Investing

Bldgs. and Equip. Sale	(4) 10	50	(8) Land Purchase
		240	(9) Bldgs. and Equip. Purchase

Dividends

	120 (2)

✓ 40	

Accounts Receivable

✓	320
(5)	100
✓	420

Merchandise Inventories

✓	360
(6)	110
✓	470

Prepayments

✓	50
(7)	20
✓	70

Land

✓	200
(8)	50
✓	250

Buildings and Equipment — Net

✓	1,000		
(4)	40	80	(3)
(9)	240	50	(4)
✓	1,150		

Accounts Payable

320	✓
120	(10)
440	✓

Income Taxes Payable

60	✓
20	(11)
80	✓

Other Current Liabilities

170	✓
190	(12)
360	✓

Bonds Payable

	250	✓
(13) 50		
	200	✓

Common Shares

500	✓
40	(14)
540	✓

Retained Earnings

	700	✓
(2) 120	200	(1)
	780	✓

Exhibit 5.16
T-Account Work Sheet for Gordon Corporation
Funds Defined as Working Capital
(amounts in 000's)

Working Capital

Sources		Uses
	✓ 250	

Operations

Net Income	(1) 200	
Depreciation Expense	(3) 80	

Financing

Share Issue	(8) 40	50 (5)	Bonds Payable Decrease

Investing

Bldgs. and Equip. Sale	(4) 10	240 (6)	Bldgs. and Equip. Purchase
		50 (7)	Land Purchase

Dividends

	120 (2)
✓ 120	

Land		Buildings and Equipment — Net		Bonds Payable	
✓ 200		✓ 1,000			250 ✓
(5) 50		(4) 40	80 (3)	(7) 50	
		(6) 240	50 (4)		
✓ 250		✓ 1,150			200 ✓

Common Stock		Retained Earnings	
	500 ✓		700 ✓
	40 (8)	(2) 120	200 (1)
	540 ✓		780 ✓

Exhibit 5.17
Gordon Corporation Conversion
of Working Capital Provided by
Operations to Cash Flow Provided by Operations
(amounts in 000's)

Working Capital Provided by Operations	$280
Plus:	
Increase in Accounts Payable	120
Increase in Income Taxes Payable	20
Increase in Other Current Liabilities	190
Less:	
Increase in Accounts Receivable	(100)
Increase in Merchandise Inventories	(110)
Increase in Prepayments	(20)
Cash Provided by Operations	$380

Questions, Exercises, Problems and Cases

Questions

1. Review the meaning of the following concepts or terms discussed in this chapter.
   a. Relation between income flows and cash flows
   b. Cash provided by operations
   c. Liquidity
   d. Dual transactions assumption
   e. T-account work sheet
   f. Depreciation is not a source of funds
   g. Alternative definitions of funds

2. "The reporting objective of the income statement under the accrual basis of accounting and the reporting objective of the statement of changes in financial position could be more easily accomplished by issuing a single income statement using the cash basis of accounting." Evaluate this proposal.

3. The text indicates that the statement of changes in financial position provides information about changes in the structure of a firm's assets and equities. Of what value is information about the structure of a firm's assets and equities?

4. The text states that the statement of changes in financial position can be used for assessing changes in both (1) liquidity and (2) the structure of assets, liabilities, and shareholders' equity. The acquisition of equipment by assuming a noncurrent liability is a transaction that must be disclosed (using the dual transactions assumption) even though it does not involve cash. This disclosure is made primarily for the second rather than the first use of the statement of changes in financial position listed above. Explain.

5. One writer stated, "Depreciation expense is the chief source of cash for growth in industries." A reader criticized this statement by replying: "The fact remains that if the companies listed had elected, in any year, to charge off $10 million more depreciation than they did charge off, they would not thereby have added one dime to the total of their cash available for plant expansion or for increasing inventories or receivables. Therefore, to speak of depreciation expense as a source of cash has no significance in a discussion of fundamentals."

Comment on these statements, ignoring income tax effects.

6. A firm generated net income for the current year, but cash flow relating to operations was negative. How can this happen?

7. A firm operated at a net loss for the current year, but cash flow relating to operations was positive. How can this happen?

8. The acquisition of equipment by assuming a mortgage is a transaction that must be disclosed either in the statement of changes in financial position or in a supplemental schedule. Of what value is information about the disclosure of this type of transaction?

Exercises

9. *Effect of various transactions on cash.* Prepare a work sheet with the following headings.

Effect of Transaction or Event on:

Transaction or Event	Cash	Other Current Assets	Noncurrent Assets	Current Liabilities	Noncurrent Liabilities	Shareholders' Equity

   a. For each of the transactions or events listed below, indicate the effect on the balance sheet categories shown in the work sheet.

(1) Purchase of merchandise on account, $5,000.

(2) Payment of $4,000 of amount due for purchases in (1).

(3) Sale of merchandise to customers on credit. Selling price is $7,000; cost of goods sold is $3,500.

(4) Collection of $5,500 of amount due from customers from sales in (3).

(5) Depreciation expense for the period is $600.

(6) Employees earn salaries of $1,200 [also see transaction (7)].

(7) Employees are paid $1,100 of amount due in (6).

(8) Insurance premium of $200 is paid for coverage to begin next period.

(9) Income taxes for the period are accrued, $900 [also see transaction (10)].

(10) Income taxes of $600 are paid.

(11) Bonds payable are issued, $200.

(12) Equipment costing $1,500, and on which $1,000 of depreciation had been taken, is sold for $500.

(13) Equipment costing $300 is acquired for cash.

(14) Equipment costing $200 is acquired and a noncurrent liability of $200 is assumed for the purchase price.

(15) Dividends of $700 are declared and paid.

   b. Indicate whether each of the transactions or events affecting cash relates to an operating, financing, or investing activity.

10. *Calculating cash provided by operations.* The following items were found in the financial statements of Maher Company Ltd. for Year 2:

Sales	$90,000
Depreciation Expense	45,000
Income Taxes	10,000
Other Expenses	20,000
Common Shares Issued During Year	17,500

The changes in current asset and current liability accounts were as follows:

Accounts Receivable	$45,000 Increase
Merchandise Inventories	30,000 Increase
Prepayments	5,000 Decrease
Accounts Payable	15,000 Increase
Income Taxes Payable	7,500 Decrease

Compute the amount of cash provided by operations.

11. *Calculating cash provided by operations.* Compute the amount of cash provided by operations in each of the independent cases below.

	a	b	c	d
Net Income (Loss)	$100	$50	$70	$(40)
Depreciation Expense	15	10	12	18
Increase (Decrease) in:				
Accounts Receivable	20	15	(10)	12
Merchandise Inventories	25	(10)	15	15
Prepayments	10	(3)	4	(6)
Accounts Payable	15	10	(20)	14
Income Taxes Payable	18	(8)	14	(16)
Other Current Liabilities	12	(9)	(7)	11

12. *Working backwards from changes in buildings and equipment account.* The comparative balance sheet of the Kanodia Co. Ltd. showed a balance in the Buildings and Equipment account at December 31, Year 5, of $24,600,000; at December 31, Year 4, the balance was $24,000,000. The Accumulated Depreciation account showed a balance of $8,600,000 at December 31, Year 5, and $7,600,000 at December 31, Year 4. The statement of changes in financial position reports that expenditures for buildings and equipment for the year totaled $1,300,000. The income statement indicates a depreciation charge of $1,200,000 for the year. Buildings and equipment were sold during the year at their book value.

Calculate the acquisition cost and accumulated depreciation of the buildings and equipment retired during the year and the proceeds from their disposition.

13. *Preparing statement of changes in financial position; working backwards from changes in plant asset accounts.* The balance in the Property, Plant, and Equipment (Cost) account was $200 on January 1 and $260 on December 31. The balance in the Accumulated Depreciation account was $120 on January 1 and $140 on December 31. During the year, equipment costing $25 and with accumulated depreciation of $15 was sold for $10. No dividends were paid during the year, nor were there any changes in the Bonds Payable or the Common Stock accounts. Cash provided by operations totaled $80, and the net change in cash for the year was an increase of $5.

Prepare a statement of changes in financial position for the year.

14. *Preparing statement of changes in financial position using changes in balance sheet accounts.* The accounting records of Kropp Corporation reveal the following for the current year.

Account	Amount	Change
Cash	$120	Increase
Accounts Receivable	15	Increase
Merchandise Inventories	20	Decrease
Property, Plant, and Equipment	50[a]	Increase
Accumulated Depreciation	10	Increase
Accounts Payable	25	Increase
Bonds Payable	20	Increase
Common Stock	30	Increase
Retained Earnings	80[b]	Increase

[a]There were no dispositions of property, plant, and equipment during the year.
[b]Net income was $130; dividends were $50.

Prepare a statement of changes in financial position, explaining the change in cash for the year.

15. *Preparing statement of changes in financial position using changes in balance sheet accounts.* The accounting records of Baker Corporation reveal the following for the current year.

Account	Amount	Change
Cash	$75	Decrease
Accounts Receivable	40	Increase
Merchandise Inventories	30	Increase
Property, Plant, and Equipment	60[a]	Increase
Accumulated Depreciation	20[a]	Increase
Accounts Payable	25	Decrease
Bonds Payable	35[b]	Decrease
Common Stock	45	Increase
Retained Earnings	50[c]	Increase

[a]Equipment costing $15 and with accumulated depreciation of $12 was sold for $3 during the year.
[b]Bonds with a face value and book value of $50 were retired during the year at no gain or loss.
[c]Dividends declared and paid totaled $20 during the year.

Prepare a statement of changes in financial position, explaining the change in cash for the year.

16. *Reformulating statement of changes in financial position.* Guerrero Corporation has prepared the statement of changes in financial position appearing in Exhibit 5.18. Recast this statement into a properly formulated statement of changes in financial position as shown in Figure 5.4.

Exhibit 5.18
GUERRERO CORPORATION
Statement of Changes in Financial Position
for the Current Year

Sources of Cash	
Proceeds from Issue of Bonds	$ 20,000
Proceeds from Issue of Common Stock	30,000
Proceeds from Sale of Equipment	4,000
Net Income	40,000
Depreciation Expense	10,000
Increase in Accounts Payable	15,000
Total Sources	$119,000
Uses of Cash	
Acquisition of Equipment[a]	$ 60,000
Payment of Dividends	12,000
Repayment of Bonds Payable	8,000
Increase in Accounts Receivable	16,000
Increase in Merchandise Inventory	11,000
Total Uses	$107,000
Net Change in Cash	$ 12,000

[a]In addition, equipment costing $25,000 was acquired and a noncurrent liability assumed for the purchase price.

✓ **17.** *Effect of various transactions on statement of changes in financial position.* Exhibit 5.19 shows a *simplified* statement of changes in financial position for a period. Eleven of the lines in the statement are numbered. Other lines are various subtotals and grand totals; these are to be ignored in the remainder of the problem. Assume that the accounting cycle is complete for the period and that all of the financial statements have been prepared. Then it is discovered that a transaction has been overlooked. That transaction is recorded in the accounts and all of the financial statements are corrected. For each of the following transactions, indicate which of the numbered lines of the statement of changes in financial position are affected. Define funds as cash. If net income, line (1), is affected, be sure to indicate whether it decreases or increases. Ignore income tax effects.

   a. Depreciation expense on office computer

   b. Purchase of machinery for cash

   c. Declaration of a cash dividend on common shares; the dividend was paid by the end of the fiscal year.

   d. Issue of common shares for cash

   e. Proceeds of sale of common share investment, a noncurrent asset, for cash. The investment was sold for book value.

   f. Amortization of patent, treated as an expense

   g. Amortization of patent, charged to production activities. The items being produced have not yet been completed.

   h. Acquisition of a factory site by issue of share capital

   i. Purchase of inventory on account

   j. Uninsured fire loss of merchandise inventory

   k. Collection of an account receivable

   l. Issue of bonds for cash

   m. Proceeds from sale of equipment. The equipment was sold for its book value.

Exhibit 5.19
Simplified Statement of
Changes in Financial Position

Cash Provided By	
From Operations:	
Net Income	(1)
Addback for Expenses and Losses Not Using Working Capital	(2)
Additions for Decreases in Current Asset Accounts Other than Cash and for Increase in Current Liability Accounts	(3)
Subtractions for Revenues and Gains Not Producing Working Capital from Operations	(4)
Subtractions for Increases in Current Asset Accounts Other than Cash and for Decreases in Current Liability Accounts	(5)
Total Cash Provided by Operations [= (1) + (2) + (3) − (4) − (5)]	$
Financing Activities	
Increases in Debt or Capital Stock	(6)
Investing Activities	
Proceeds from Dispositions of Noncurrent Assets	(7)
Total "Other" Sources of Cash [= (6) + (7)]	$
Total Sources of Cash	$

Cash Applied to

Dividends	(8)
Financing Activities	
Reduction in Debt or Capital Stock	(9)
Investing Activities	
Acquisition of Noncurrent Assets	(10)
Total Uses of Cash [= (8) + (0) + (10)]	$
Change in Cash for the Period	(11)

Problems and Cases

18. *Preparing statement of changes in financial position.* Exhibit 5.20 presents a comparative balance sheet for Bragg Corporation as of the beginning and end of the current year. During the year, there were no dispositions of property, plant, and equipment, and no dividends were declared or paid.

Prepare a statement of changes in financial position for Bragg Corporation for the current year, supporting the statement with a T-account work sheet.

Exhibit 5.20
BRAGG CORPORATION
Comparative Balance Sheet

	December 31	January 1
Assets		
Current Assets:		
Cash	$ 10,000	$ 6,000
Accounts Receivable	82,000	72,000
Merchandise Inventories	110,000	95,000
Total Current Assets	$202,000	$173,000
Property, Plant, and Equipment	$425,000	$350,000
Less: Accumulated Depreciation	(135,000)	(123,000)
Total Property, Plant, and Equipment	$290,000	$227,000
Total Assets	$492,000	$400,000
Liabilities and Shareholders' Equity		
Current Liabilities:		
Accounts Payable	$121,000	$ 95,000
Income Taxes Payable	15,000	10,000
Total Current Liabilities	$136,000	$105,000
Long-Term Debt:		
Bonds Payable	75,000	50,000
Total Liabilities	$211,000	$155,000
Shareholders' Equity:		
Common Stock	$106,000	$105,000
Retained Earnings	175,000	140,000
Total Shareholders' Equity	$281,000	$245,000
Total Liabilities and Shareholders' Equity	$492,000	$400,000

19. *Preparing statement of changes in financial position.* Condensed financial statement data for the Harris Company for the current year appear in Exhibits 5.21 and 5.22. During the current year, equipment costing $10,000 and with $8,000 of accumulated depreciation was sold for $2,000.

Exhibit 5.21
HARRIS CO. LTD.
Comparative Balance Sheets

	December 31	January 1
Assets		
Cash	$ 24,000	$ 20,000
Accounts Receivable	58,000	52,000
Inventory	81,000	79,000
Land	15,000	15,000
Buildings and Equipment (Cost)	$415,000	$400,000
Less: Accumulated Depreciation	(252,000)	(240,000)
Total Assets	$341,000	$326,000
Liabilities and Shareholders' Equity		
Accounts Payable for Inventory	$ 65,000	$ 62,000
Interest Payable	4,000	6,000
Mortgage Payable	55,000	60,000
Common Stock	130,000	120,000
Retained Earnings	87,000	78,000
Total Liabilities and Shareholders' Equity	$341,000	$326,000

Exhibit 5.22
HARRIS CO. LTD.
Statement of Income and Retained Earnings
For the Current Year

Sales		$200,000
Less: Cost of Goods Sold		100,000
Gross Profit		$100,000
Less: Operating Expenses		
Wages and Salaries	$30,000	
Depreciation	20,000	50,000
Net Income before Income Tax		$ 50,000
Income Tax Expense		11,000
Net Income		$ 39,000
Dividends on Common Shares		30,000
Addition to Retained Earnings for Year		$ 9,000
Retained Earnings, January 1		78,000
Retained Earnings, December 31		$ 87,000

Prepare a statement of changes in financial position for the year, supporting the statement with a T-account work sheet. Define funds as cash.

20. *Preparing statement of changes in financial position.* Financial statement data for the Perkerson Supply Co. Inc. for the current year appear in Exhibit 5.23.

Additional information:

(1) Net income for the year was $324,000; dividends declared and paid were $70,000.
(2) Depreciation expense for the year was $305,000 on buildings and machinery.
(3) Machinery originally costing $125,000 and with accumulated depreciation of $110,000 was sold for $15,000.

Exhibit 5.23
PERKERSON SUPPLY CO. INC.
Comparative Balance Sheets

	December 31	January 1
Assets		
Current Assets:		
Cash	$ 162,000	$ 179,000
Accounts Receivable	526,000	473,000
Inventory	604,000	502,000
Total Current Assets	$1,292,000	$1,154,000
Noncurrent Assets:		
Land	$ 315,000	$ 297,000
Buildings and Machinery	4,773,000	4,339,000
Less: Accumulated Depreciation	(2,182,000)	(1,987,000)
Total Noncurrent Assets	$2,906,000	$2,649,000
Total Assets	$4,198,000	$3,803,000
Liabilities and Shareholders' Equity		
Current Liabilities:		
Accounts Payable	$ 279,000	$ 206,000
Income Taxes Payable	145,000	137,000
Other Short-Term Payables	363,000	294,000
Total Current Liabilities	$ 787,000	$ 637,000
Noncurrent Liabilities:		
Bonds Payable	967,000	992,000
Total Liabilities	$1,754,000	$1,629,000
Shareholders' Equity:		
Common Stock	$ 852,000	$ 836,000
Retained Earnings	1,592,000	1,338,000
Total Shareholders' Equity	$2,444,000	$2,174,000
Total Liabilities and Shareholders' Equity	$4,198,000	$3,803,000

Prepare a statement of changes in financial position for the Perkerson Supply Co. Inc. for the year with funds defined as cash. Support the statement with a T-account work sheet.

21. (This problem should not be attempted until Problem **(20)** has been worked.) Refer to problem **(20)** concerning the Perkerson Supply Co. Inc. Convert cash provided by operations to working capital provided by operations.

22. Refer to Problem **(20)** concerning the Perkerson Supply Co. Inc. Work the problem using a definition of funds as working capital.

23. *Preparing income statement and statement of changes in financial position.* Condensed financial statement data for Victoria Ltd. for the year appear in Exhibit 5.24.

Expenditures on new plant and equipment for the year amounted to $121,000. Old plant and equipment that had cost $94,000 were sold during the year. It was sold for cash at book value.

Exhibit 5.24
VICTORIA LTD.
Post-closing Trial Balance
Comparative Data

	December 31	January 1
Debits:		
Cash	$ 55,000	$ 62,000
Accounts Receivable	163,000	135,000
Inventory	262,000	247,000
Plant and Equipment (cost)	1,389,000	1,362,000
Total Debits	$1,869,000	$1,806,000
Credits:		
Accounts Payable	$ 75,000	$ 72,000
Accumulated Depreciation	573,000	508,000
Long-Term Debt	215,000	200,000
Capital Stock	509,000	509,000
Retained Earnings	497,000	517,000
Total Credits	$1,869,000	$1,806,000
Income Statement Data		
Sales	$1,338,000	
Cost of Goods Sold (excluding depreciation)	932,000	
Selling and Administrative Expenses	313,000	
Depreciation Expense (manufacturing)	93,000	
Interest Expense	20,000	

a. Prepare an income statement (including a reconciliation of retained earnings) for the year.

b. Prepare a statement of changes in financial position for Victoria Ltd. for the year, defining funds as cash. Support the statement of changes in financial position with a T-account work sheet.

24. *Preparing statement of changes in financial position.* Exhibit 5.25 presents a comparative balance sheet for Psilos Corporation as of the beginning and end of the current year. Additional information related to the year is as follows:

Net Income	$40,000
Dividends Declared and Paid	50,000
Property, Plant, and Equipment Acquired:	
For Cash	40,000
By Assuming Long-Term Debt	15,000
Proceeds from Sale of Property, Plant, and Equipment Sold at Book Value	5,000

Prepare a statement of changes in financial position for Psilos Corporation for the current year, supporting the statement with a T-account work sheet.

Exhibit 5.25
PSILOS CORPORATION
Comparative Balance Sheet

	December 31	January 1
Assets		
Current Assets:		
Cash	$ 16,000	$ 28,000
Accounts Receivable	109,000	125,000
Merchandise Inventories	163,000	147,000
Total Current Assets	$288,000	$300,000
Property, Plant, and Equipment	$240,000	$210,000
Less: Accumulated Depreciation		
Total Property, Plant, and Equipment		
Total Assets	$443,000	$423,000
Liabilities and Shareholders' Equity		
Current Liabilities:		
Accounts Payable	$175,000	$177,000
Income Taxes Payable	30,000	23,000
Total Current Liabilities	$205,000	$200,000
Long-Term Debt:		
Bonds Payable	75,000	50,000
Total Liabilities	$280,000	$250,000
Shareholders' Equity:		
Common Stock	$ 10,000	$ 10,000
Retained Earnings	153,000	163,000
Total Shareholders' Equity	$163,000	$173,000
Total Liabilities and Shareholders' Equity	$443,000	$423,000

Do in
class

25. *Preparing statement of changes in financial position over two-year period.* Condensed financial statement data of the Alberta Co. Ltd. for the years ending December 31, Year 1, Year 2, and Year 3, are presented in Exhibits 5.26 and 5.27.

Exhibit 5.26
ALBERTA CO. LTD.
Post-closing Trial Balance
Comparative Data

	12/31/Year 3	12/31/Year 2	12/31/Year 1
Debits:			
Cash	$ 97,000	$ 87,000	$ 55,000
Accounts Receivable	105,000	120,000	110,000
Merchandise Inventories	140,000	115,000	125,000
Total Current Assets	$ 342,000	$ 322,000	$ 290,000
Property, Plant, and Equipment	1,875,000	1,679,000	1,616,000
Total Debits	$2,217,000	$2,001,000	$1,906,000
Credits:			
Accounts Payable	$ 83,000	$ 80,000	$ 81,000
Accumulated Depreciation	745,000	720,000	697,000
Bonds Payable	135,000	90,000	106,000
Common Stock	514,000	423,000	377,000
Retained Earnings	740,000	688,000	645,000
Total Credits	$2,217,000	$2,001,000	$1,906,000

Exhibit 5.27
ALBERTA CO. LTD.
Income and Retained Earnings
Statement Data

	Year 3	Year 2
Sales	$970,000	$910,000
Interest and Other Revenue	7,000	5,000
Cost of Goods Sold (excluding depreciation)	413,000	370,000
Selling and Administrative Expenses	301,000	320,000
Depreciation	98,000	87,000
Income Taxes	66,000	55,000
Dividends Declared	47,000	40,000

a. Prepare a statement of changes in financial position for Year 2. Support the statement with a T-account work sheet. The original cost of the property, plant, and equipment sold during Year 2 was $108,000. These assets were sold for cash at their net book value.

b. Prepare a T-account work sheet and a statement of changes in financial position for Year 3. Property, plant, and equipment were sold during the year at book value. Expenditures on new property, plant, and equipment amounted to $318,000 during Year 3.

26. *Working backwards through statement of changes in financial position.* The Quinta Co. Ltd. presents the post-closing trial balance shown in Exhibit 5.28 and statement of changes in financial position shown in Exhibit 5.29 for Year 5.

Investment, equipment, and land were sold for cash at their net book value. The accumulated depreciation of the equipment sold was $20,000.

Prepare a balance sheet for the beginning of the year, January 1, Year 5.

Exhibit 5.28
QUINTA CO. LTD.
Post-closing Trial Balance
December 31, Year 5

Debit Balances:

Cash	$ 25,000
Accounts Receivable	220,000
Merchandise Inventories	320,000
Land	40,000
Buildings and Equipment	500,000
Investments (noncurrent)	100,000
Total Debits	$1,205,000

Credit Balances:

Accumulated Depreciation	$ 200,000
Accounts Payable	280,000
Other Current Liabilities	85,000
Bonds Payable	100,000
Common Stock	200,000
Retained Earnings	340,000
Total Credits	$1,205,000

Exhibit 5.29
QUINTA CO. LTD.
Statement of Changes in Financial Position
For Year Ended December 31, 19X5

Cash Provided By
   Operations

Net Income	$200,000
Additions:	
Depreciation Expense	60,000
Increase in Accounts Payable	25,000

Subtractions:		
Increase in Accounts Receivable		(30,000)
Increase in Merchandise Inventories		(40,000)
Decrease in Other Current Liabilities		(45,000)
Total Sources from Operations		$170,000
Financing Activities		
Common Share Issue	$60,000	
Bond Issue	40,000	
Investing Activities		
Sale of Investments	$40,000	
Sale of Buildings and Equipment	15,000	
Sale of Land	10,000	
Total Sources of Cash		$335,000
Cash Applied to		
Dividends		$200,000
Investing Activities		
Acquisition of Buildings and Equipment		130,000
Total Uses of Cash		$330,000
Increase in Cash During the Year		$ 5,000

27. *Interpretative case using statement of changes in financial position (adapted from a problem by Leonard Morrissey).* RV Suppliers, Incorporated, founded in January, Year 1, manufactures "Kaps." A "Kap" is a relatively low-cost camping unit attached to a pickup truck. Most units consist of an extruded aluminum frame and a fiberglass skin.

After a loss in its initial year, the company was barely profitable in Year 2 and Year 3. More substantial profits were realized in Years 4 and 5, as indicated in the financial statements shown in Exhibits 5.30 and 5.31.

Exhibit 5.30
RV SUPPLIERS, INCORPORATED
Income Statements
(amounts in 000's)

	Year 6	Year 5	Year 4
Net Sales	$247.4	$424.0	$266.4
Cost of Goods Sold	210.6	314.6	191.4
Gross Profit	$ 36.8	$109.4	$ 75.0
Operating Expenses[a]	55.2	58.4	35.5
Income (loss) Before Income Taxes	$(18.4)	$ 51.0	$ 39.5
Income Taxes	(5.0)	16.4	12.3
Net Income (loss)	$(13.4)	$ 34.6	$ 27.2

[a]Includes depreciation expense of $1.7 in Year 4, $4.8 in Year 5, and $7.6 in Year 6.

Exhibit 5.31
RV SUPPLIERS, INCORPORATED
Balance Sheet
(amounts in 000's)
(Problem 27)

	Dec. 31 Year 6	Dec. 31 Year 5	Dec. 31 Year 4
Assets			
Current Assets:			
Cash	$ 5.2	$ 12.0	$ 14.0
Accounts Receivable	24.2	55.6	28.8
Inventories	81.0	85.6	54.0
Income Tax Recoverable	5.0	0	0
Prepayments	5.6	7.4	4.8
Total Current Assets	$121.0	$160.6	$101.6
Property, Plant, Equipment—Net (Note 1) ...	72.2	73.4	30.2
Total Assets	$193.2	$234.0	$131.8
Liabilities and Shareholders' Equity			
Current Liabilities:			
Bank Notes Payable	$ 70.0	$ 52.0	$ 10.0
Accounts Payable	17.4	53.4	31.6
Income Taxes Payable	0	7.0	5.8
Other Current Liabilities	4.4	6.8	4.2
Total Current Liabilities	$ 91.8	$119.2	$ 51.6
Shareholders' Equity:			
Capital Stock	$ 44.6	$ 44.6	$ 44.6
Retained Earnings	56.8	70.2	35.6
Total Shareholders' Equity	$101.4	$114.8	$ 80.2
Total Liabilities and Shareholders' Equity ...	$193.2	$234.0	$131.8

Note 1	Year 6	Year 5	Year 4
Acquisitions	$ 11.8	$ 48.4	$ 13.4
Depreciation Expense	(7.6)	(4.8)	(1.7)
Book Value and Sales Proceeds from Retirements ...	(5.4)	(.4)	(.4)
Net Change in Property, Plant, and Equipment ...	$ (1.2)	$ 43.2	$ 11.3

However, in Year 6, ended just last month, the company suffered a loss of $13,400. Sales dropped from $424,000 in Year 5 to $247,400 in Year 6. The outlook for Year 7 is not encouraging. Potential buyers continue to shun pickup trucks in preference to more energy-efficient small foreign and domestic automobiles.

How did the company finance its rapid growth during the year ended December 31, Year 5? What were the sources and uses of cash during the year? Similarly, how did the company manage its financial affairs during the abrupt contraction in business during the year just ended last month?

Decision Problem 5-1

Bill Wanda had been a successful public accountant before his death four years ago. On his death, his wife, Kit, was left with a portfolio of securities along with the proceeds of a life insurance policy and a mortgage-free house to look after herself and her three young children. In the past, the investment portfolio had paid sufficient interest and dividends to provide Kit's major source of income. During the last year, Kit's cash needs had increased as a result of growing children and rising price levels. At the same time, the dividends from one of her major shareholdings, Price Sisters Ltd., had declined. She had read in the president's report of the company that the dividends had been reduced in order to fund the company's expansion program, since the profit potential was large—as evidenced by the increased profits reported in Year 4. Kit interpreted this statement to mean that the company's net income was increasing, but, she said, "The income is meaningless to me since I can't buy food with it."

The comparative balance sheets and income statements of Price Sisters Ltd. for Year 4, included in the company's Annual Report, was presented in Exhibits 5.32 and 5.33.

Exhibit 5.32
PRICE SISTERS LTD.
Comparative Balance Sheets
As at December 31
(amounts in 000's)

	Year 4		Year 3	
Assets				
Current Assets:				
Cash		21		22
Accounts Receivable		533		410
Inventory		540		427
		$1,094		$ 859
Plant and Equipment	$2,624		$1,980	
Less: Accumulated Depreciation	1,397	1,227	1,217	763
Autos and Trucks	$ 203		$ 132	
Less: Accumulated Depreciation	69	134	48	84
		$2,455		$1,706
Liabilities and Shareholders' Equity				
Current Liabilities:				
Bank Loan		$ 391		$ 100
Accounts Payable		332		251
		$ 723		$ 351
Bonds Payable		740		540
Shareholders' Equity:				
Share Capital	$ 500		$ 500	
Retained Earnings	492	992	315	815
		$2,455		$1,706

Exhibit 5.33
PRICE SISTERS LTD.
Condensed Comparative Income Statement
Years Ended December 31
(amounts in 000's)

	Year 4	Year 3
Sales	$3,604	$2,772
Less: Cost of Sales[a]	2,172	1,675
Gross Profit	$1,432	$1,097
Expenses[a]	1,015	841
Net Income before Income Tax	$ 417	$ 256
Income Tax	200	133
Net Income	$ 217	$ 123
Deduct Dividends	40	80
Addition to Retained Earnings	$ 177	$ 43

[a]Including depreciation of $221,000 (plant and equipment $180,000; autos and trucks $41,000) for each year.

During Year 4, ten autos and trucks (one-third of the fleet) with an original cost of $33,000 were replaced for a cost of $52,000, after deducting the trade-in allowance (equal to their net book value) of $13,000. In addition, the fleet was expanded to 36 vehicles with the purchase of six additional vehicles for $39,000.

Explain to Kit Wanda why the dividends have been cut in half at the same time that the net income has increased by three-quarters over that reported in the previous year. Is Price Sisters Ltd. in a better financial position at December 31, Year 4 than it was at December 31, Year 3? If not, why not?

Integrative Problem 5-1

H. R. Franck was admitted to the Law Society of Nova Scotia on November 15, Year 4 and immediately set up her own practice in Halifax. Since she was uncertain about the amount of business she would have, she arranged with a recently qualified Chartered Accountant, C. M. Lindsay, to share office space and secretarial and reception facilities. Franck and Lindsay agreed that they would pay for the secretarial services used by both at the rate of $10 per hour and the remainder of the office costs would be shared equally. Each of them deposited $40,000 in a joint account to pay for the costs of furniture and equipment, joint supplies used by the secretary, and monthly expenses. At the end of each month Lindsay prepared a statement of joint operating expenses and each of them reimbursed the joint account for her portion.

Franck and Lindsay were responsible for furnishing their own offices and purchasing their own letterhead stationery.

An analysis of Franck's bank statements from the opening of her practice on December 1, Year 4 to November 30, Year 5 follows:

Deposits:

ℝ Collection of Fees Billed	$ 22,600
Receipt of Trust Funds from Clients	30,100
Loan from Parents	40,000
Demand Loan from Bank	20,000
Deposit of Personal Funds	6,000
Total Deposits	$118,700

Withdrawals:

E Share of Office Expenses to October 31, Year 5	$ 19,800
E Purchase of Letterhead	900
Transfer to Joint Account	40,000
E % Purchase of Office Equipment	6,500
E Personal Withdrawals	10,800
Law Society Fees, Year 5	360
Payment of Trust Funds on Behalf of Clients	26,400
Bank Interest	1,600
Bank Charges	200
Payments on Demand Loan	4,000
Total Withdrawals	$110,560

The bank statement for December Year 5 includes the following items that may relate to the year ended November 30, Year 5.

Payment of trust funds held for clients	$ 600
Payment of joint expenses for November Year 5	3,100
Payment of letterhead purchased on October 15, Year 5 (cheque dated November 25)	300

Approximately one-third of the letterhead stationery purchased during the year was on hand on November 30. The fees billed but not collected at November 30 were $8,200 and included one for $700 that had been billed in December Year 4 — which Franck does not expect to collect since her client was found guilty and is currently serving a five-year sentence.

Franck's parents loaned her $40,000 interest free, but Franck felt a moral obligation to repay the loan in a couple of years with interest at ten percent compounded annually.

Franck estimates that the billings accumulated for the cases she had worked on but has neither completed nor billed by November 30 amount to $1,400.

Franck has been living comfortably for the past year and, with a bank balance of about $8,000, considers she has begun a successful practice.

To eliminate the need for two sets of records, Franck has decided to claim the maximum capital cost allowance of 20 percent for her furniture when calculating taxable income, and to record depreciation in an equal amount.

Prepare a complete set of financial statements for Franck including a statement of changes in financial position to demonstrate the degree of financial success she has achieved as a lawyer to November 30, Year 5.

Chapter 6   Introduction to Financial Statement Analysis

Chapters 1 through 5 have considered the three principal financial statements needed to understand the financial activities of a business: the balance sheet, the income statement, and the statement of changes in financial position. For each financial statement, we have examined its purpose, its underlying concepts, the procedures for preparing it, and some of the uses that can be made of information contained in the statement.

Chapters 7 through 13 explore the generally accepted accounting principles used in preparing these financial statements. Before embarking on a study of generally accepted accounting principles, it will be useful to pause and introduce some of the possible techniques for analyzing financial statements. Such analysis can be done only at an elementary level at this point; effective financial statement interpretation and analysis require a fuller understanding of the impact of accounting principles on the reported amounts. Introducing the tools and techniques of financial statement analysis at this time, however, provides an opportunity to synthesize the material in the preceding five chapters.

Objectives of Financial Statement Analysis

The first question likely to be raised in analyzing a set of financial statements is "What do I look for?" The response to this question requires an understanding of investment decisions.

To illustrate, assume that you recently inherited $25,000 and must decide what to do with the bequest. You have narrowed the investment decision to purchasing either a certificate of deposit at a local bank or common shares of Horrigan Corporation, currently selling for $40 per share. Your decision will be based on the *return* anticipated from each investment and the *risk* associated with that return.

The bank is currently paying interest at the rate of ten percent annually on certificates of deposit. Because it is unlikely that the bank will go out of business, you are virtually certain of earning ten percent each year.

The return from investing in the common shares of Horrigan Corporation has two components. First, the firm paid a cash dividend in their most recent year of $.625 per share, and it is anticipated that this dividend will continue in the future. Second, the market price of the shares is likely to change between the date the shares are purchased and the date in the future when they are sold. The difference between the eventual selling price per share and the $40 purchase price, often called a *capital gain*, is a second component of the return from buying the shares.

The return from the common share investment is more risky than the interest on the certificate of deposit. Future dividends and market price changes are likely to be associated, at least partially, with the profitability of the firm. Future income might be less than is currently anticipated if competitors introduce new products that erode Horrigan Corporation's share of its sales market. Future income might be greater than currently anticipated if Horrigan Corporation makes important discoveries or introduces successful new products.

The market price of Horrigan Corporation's shares will probably also be affected by economy-wide factors such as inflation and changes in international tensions. Also, specific industry factors, such as raw materials shortages or government anti-trust actions, may influence the market price of the shares. Because most individuals prefer less risk to more risk, you will probably demand a higher expected return from the purchase of Horrigan Corporation's shares than if you invest the inheritance in a certificate of deposit.

Theoretical and empirical research has shown that the expected return from investing in a firm is, in part, related to its expected profitability.[1] A firm's past operating, or earnings, performance is analyzed as a basis for forecasting its future profitability.

Investment decisions also require that the risk associated with the expected return be assessed.[2] A firm may find itself with a shortage of cash and be unable to repay a short-term loan coming due. Or the amount of long-term debt in the capital structure may be so large that the firm has difficulty meeting the required interest and principal payments. The financial statements provide information for assessing how these and other elements of risk affect expected return.

Most financial statement analysis, therefore, is directed at some aspect of a firm's *profitability* or its *risk*.

Usefulness of Ratios

The various items in financial statements may be difficult to interpret in the form in which they are presented. For example, the profitability of a firm may be difficult to assess by looking at the amount of net income alone. It is helpful to compare earnings with the assets or capital required to generate those earnings. This relation, and other important ones between various items in the financial statements, can be expressed in the form of ratios. Some ratios compare items within the income statement; some use only balance sheet data; others relate items from more than one of the three principal financial statements. Ratios are useful tools of financial statement analysis because they conveniently summarize data in a form that is more easily understood, interpreted, and compared.

Ratios are, by themselves, difficult to interpret. For example, does a rate of return on common shares of 8.6 percent reflect a good performance? Once calculated, the ratios must be compared with some standard. Several possible standards might be used:

1. The planned ratio for the period being analyzed.
2. The corresponding ratio during the preceding period for the same firm.
3. The corresponding ratio for a similar firm in the same industry.
4. The average ratio for other firms in the same industry.

Difficulties encountered in using each of these bases for comparison are discussed later.

[1]Ray Ball and Phillip Brown, ''An Empirical Evaluation of Accounting Income Numbers,'' *Journal of Accounting Research*, Autumn 1968, pp. 159–178.
[2]Modern finance makes a distinction between systematic (market) risk and nonsystematic (firm-specific) risk. The discussion in this chapter does not differentiate between these two dimensions of risk.

Good-looking Balance Sheets can be Assets for Companies

*L*enders judge businesses by their financial statements. So common sense dictates that they look as good as possible. Year-end is "the one time of the year they take a picture of your company," says Steven N. Delit, of the New York CPA firm of Delit Friedman & Co., "and you want it to look its best."

There are a number of perfectly legitimate things a business can do to put the best face on its balance sheet. Some can be done near the end of the year, but it is better to operate a company with financial results in mind all the time.

Business owners need "an element of perspicacity" about producing a good balance sheet each year, says James McNeil Stancil, a professor of finance at the University of Southern California. As an example, he cites a company that borrows regularly against its receivables from a finance company, as many companies do.

The business normally takes cash it collects on its receivables and promptly pays off the finance company. One day its bank balance is impressive, the next it is anemic. If it has a skimpy bank balance the last day of the year, Mr. Stancil says, its balance sheet will look bad. It wouldn't matter that the company "has $5 million of assets," he says. "Someone will look at the cash account and say, 'My God! You are broke!'"

That can be avoided by having the finance company agree to slower repayment for a week or more near year-end, so the business can accumulate late cash for its balance sheet.

Ratio analysis is a common way lenders analyze balance sheets. Most familiar is the current ratio, computed by dividing current assets—cash accounts receivable, inventory—by current liabilities, or debt due within a year.

A company can strengthen this ratio by paying off current debt. If a business has, say, $40,000 cash (its only current asset) and $20,000 of current liabilities, its current ratio is 2:1. If $10,000 of the cash is used to reduce debt, however, the ratio improves significantly to 3:1.

A financial statement can be enhanced by borrowing long term to payoff short-term debt. "If you can get debt out of short term into long term, it cleans up the balance sheet," says Edward H. Pendergast, chairman of Kennedy & Lehan CPAs Inc., North Quincy, Mass. But this isn't mere window dressing, he says. "The company is much stronger because it is more liquid. Current demands on the business have been reduced considerably."

Bankers look carefully at the equity a small business has in relationship to debt. "There's nothing like equity," says the executive vice president of a $7 billion bank. "It's your cushion in the event something comes up that could damage the company." In the past, nothing less than a one-to-one debt equity ratio would satisfy most banks. Nowadays, debt one and a half times greater than equity is usually acceptable. And some banks won't balk if it exceeds this, says David F. Nasman, president of Bellingham National Bank, Tacoma, Wash.

High debt-equity ratios could be acceptable, Mr. Nasman says, for a young company "that is strong and operating and growing well." But, he says, a bank would view with alarm "a company in business for 25 years whose debt-equity ratio starts to slide." The difference, he says, is that the young profitable company probably can "increase the equity along the way."

Profits left in the business become retained earnings and increase equity. However, small-business owners usually try to minimize profits for income tax purposes, and often do this by paying themselves year-end bonuses. One way to satisfy tax considerations and bolster the financial statement is for the owner to take the bonus, providing the company a tax deduction, and then loan the money back to the company.

"If you indicate that the company doesn't have to pay the owner back for a year," says Herbert C. Speiser, a partner at Touche Ross & Co., CPAs, "a banker will consider it equity."

Such a solution isn't always possible, however. "Sometimes tax planning goes against the financial statement, says Irwin Math, a partner in the CPA firm of Laventhol & Horwath. "Sometimes I tell a client to pay taxes and strengthen your statement." In some small companies this means valuing year-end inventory as high as possible to maximize profits, and thus incur higher taxes.

Manufacturers should try to reduce raw materials inventory by turning it into finished goods, Mr. Math says. Large year-end raw-materials inventory suggests "you have a problem of not being able to sell your product," he says. A bulge in finished-goods inventory looks

better because "finished goods are what you can convert to cash quickly."

However, when the business is having a terrible year, says John J. O'Leary, partner in the accounting firm of Alexander Grant & Co., "you can't pull a rabbit out of the hat in the last quarter." Don't wait for year-end to tell the bank the business is in trouble, he says. "It rubs bankers the wrong way."

Henry R. Pearson, a Dallas CPA, says he doesn't window dress statements for clients. "We dress down; we are very conservative." The way to impress lenders is to repay them on time, he says. "If you're not paying your debts," he says, "no matter what you say to your banker he isn't going to be happy."

Sanford L. Jacobs, "Good-Looking Balance Sheets Can Be Assets for Companies." *Wall Street Journal*, September 23, 1985, p. 31. Reprinted by permission of *Wall Street Journal*, © Dow Jones & Company, Inc., 1985. All rights reserved.

The sections that follow describe several ratios useful for assessing profitability and various dimensions of risk. To demonstrate the calculation of various ratios, we use data for Horrigan Corporation for years 2 through 4 as shown in Exhibit 6.1 (comparative balance sheets), Exhibit 6.2 (comparative income statements), and Exhibit 6.3 (comparative statements of changes in financial position). Our analysis for Horrigan Corporation is based on a study of the changes in its various ratios over the three-year period. Such an analysis is referred to as *time-series analysis*. Comparison of a given firm's ratios with those of other firms for the same period is referred to as *cross-section analysis*. Cross-section analysis requires an understanding of the accounting principles used by different firms and is considered in Chapter 15.

Exhibit 6.1
HORRIGAN CORPORATION
Comparative Balance Sheets
(amounts in millions)

	December 31			
	Year 4	Year 3	Year 2	Year 1
Assets				
Cash	$ 12	$ 8	$ 14	$ 10
Accounts Receivable (net)	76	46	36	26
Inventories	83	46	30	14
Total Current Assets	$171	$100	$ 80	$ 50

Land	$ 60	$ 60	$ 30	$ 20
Building	190	150	150	150
Equipment	313	276	192	70
Less: Accumulated Depreciation	(84)	(66)	(52)	(40)
Total Noncurrent Assets	$479	$420	$320	$200
Total Assets	$650	$520	$400	$250

Liabilities and Shareholders' Equity

Accounts Payable	$ 50	$ 35	$ 30	$ 25
Salaries Payable	20	15	13	10
Income Taxes Payable	20	10	7	5
Total Current Liabilities	$ 90	$ 60	$ 50	$ 40
Bonds Payable	150	100	50	50
Total Liabilities	$240	$160	$100	$ 90
Common Stock ($10 par value)	$160	$160	$150	$100
Contributed Surplus	120	120	100	20
Retained Earnings	130	80	50	40
Total Shareholders' Equity	$410	$360	$300	$160
Total Liabilities and Shareholders' Equity	$650	$520	$400	$250

Exhibit 6.2
HORRIGAN CORPORATION
Comparative Income Statements
(amounts in millions)

	Years Ended December 31		
	Year 4	Year 3	Year 2
Sales Revenue	$475	$310	$210
Less: Cost of Goods Sold	280	179	119
Gross profit	$195	$131	$ 91
Less: Operating Expenses			
Selling	$ 46	$ 38	$ 36
Administrative	15	13	12
Depreciation	18	14	12
Total Operating Expenses	$ 79	$ 65	$ 60
Operating Profit	$116	$ 66	$ 31
Less: Interest	16	10	5
Net Income before Income Tax	$100	$ 56	$ 26
Income Tax Expense	40	22	10
Net Income	$ 60	$ 34	$ 16

Exhibit 6.3
HORRIGAN CORPORATION
Comparative Statements of
Changes in Financial Position
(amounts in millions)

	For the Year Ended December 31		
	Year 4	Year 3	Year 2
Sources of Cash			
Operations:			
Net Income	$ 60	$ 34	$ 16
Additions:			
Depreciation Expense	18	14	12
Increase in Accounts Payable	15	5	5
Increase in Salaries Payable	5	2	3
Increase in Income Taxes Payable	10	3	2
Subtractions:			
Increase in Accounts Receivable	(30)	(10)	(10)
Increase in Inventories	(37)	(16)	(16)
Cash Provided by Operations	$ 41	$ 32	$ 12
Issuance of Bonds	50	50	—
Issuance of Common Shares	—	30	130
Total Sources	$ 91	$112	$142
Uses of Cash			
Dividends	$ 10	$ 4	$ 6
Purchase of Land	—	30	10
Purchase of Building	40	—	—
Purchase of Equipment	37	84	122
Total Uses	$ 87	$118	$138
Increase (Decrease) in Cash	$ 4	$ (6)	$ 4

Analysis of Profitability

The operating activities of a firm are carried out in order to generate net income. Three measures of profitability discussed in this section are:

1. Rate of return on assets
2. Rate of return on common shareholders' equity
3. Earnings per common share

Rate of Return on Assets

The rate of return on assets is a measure of a firm's performance in using assets to generate earnings independent of the financing of those assets. In terms of the three principal business activities (investing, financing, and operating) discussed in previous chapters, the rate of return on assets relates the results of *operating* performance to the *investments* that a firm has made without regard to how the acquisition of those investments was *financed*.

The rate of return on assets is calculated as follows:

$$\frac{\text{Net Income Plus Interest Expense}}{\text{Net of Income Tax Savings}}$$
$$\frac{}{\text{Average Total Assets}}$$

Because the rate of return on assets measures a firm's performance in using assets independent of the financing of those assets, the earnings figure used in calculating the rate of return on assets is income before deducting any payments or distributions to the providers of capital. Because interest is a payment to a provider of capital, interest expense should not be deducted in measuring the return on total assets. To derive income before interest charges, it is usually easier to start with net income and add to that figure. The amount added to net income is not, however, the interest expense shown on the income statement. Because interest expense is deductible in calculating taxable income, interest expense does not reduce *aftertax* net income by the full amount of interest expense. The amount added back to net income is interest expense reduced by income tax savings.

For example, interest expense for Horrigan Corporation for Year 4, as shown in Exhibit 6.2, is $16 million. The income tax rate is assumed to be 40 percent of pretax income. The income taxes saved, because interest is deductible in computing taxable income, is $6.4 million ($= .40 \times \$16$ million). The amount of interest expense net of income tax savings that is added back to net income is therefore $9.6 million ($= \$16$ million $- \$6.4$ million). There is no need to add back dividends paid to shareholders, because they are not deducted as an expense in calculating net income.

Because the earnings rate *during the year* is being computed, the measure of investment should reflect the average amount of assets in use during the year. A crude, but usually satisfactory, figure for average total assets is one-half the sum of total assets at the beginning and at the end of the year.

The calculation of rate of return on assets for Horrigan Corporation for Year 4 is:[3]

$$\frac{\begin{array}{c}\text{Net Income Plus}\\\text{Interest Expense}\\\text{Net of Income Tax}\\\text{Savings}\end{array}}{\text{Average Total Assets}} = \frac{\$60 + (\$16 - \$6.4)}{\frac{1}{2}(\$520 + \$650)} = 11.9\%$$

Thus, for each dollar of assets used, the management of Horrigan Corporation was able to earn $.119 during Year 4 before payments to the suppliers of capital. The rate of return on assets was 5.8 percent in Year 2 and 8.7 percent in Year 3. Thus, the rate of return has increased steadily during this three-year period.

---

[3]Throughout the remainder of this chapter, we omit reference to the fact that the amounts for Horrigan Corporation are in millions of dollars.

One might question the rationale for a measure of return that is independent of the means of financing. After all, the assets must be financed and the cost of that financing must be covered if the firm is to be profitable.

The rate of return on assets is of particular concern to lenders, or creditors, of a firm. These creditors have a senior claim on earnings and assets relative to common shareholders. Creditors receive their return in the form of interest. This return typically comes from earnings generated from assets before any other suppliers of capital receive a return (for example, dividends). When extending credit or providing debt capital to a firm, creditors would want to be sure that the return generated by the firm on that capital (assets) exceeded its cost.

The rate of return on assets is also useful to common shareholders in assessing financial leverage, a topic discussed later in this chapter.

Disaggregating the Rate of Return on Assets

One means of studying changes in the rate of return on assets is to disaggregate the ratio into two other ratios as follows:

$$
\begin{array}{ccc}
\text{Rate of} & \text{Profit Margin Ratio} & \text{Total Assets} \\
\text{Return} = & \text{(before interest expense} & \times \quad \text{Turnover} \\
\text{on Assets} & \text{and related income tax effects)} & \text{Ratio}
\end{array}
$$

or

$$
\frac{\substack{\text{Net Income Plus} \\ \text{Interest Expense} \\ \text{Net of Income} \\ \text{Tax Savings}}}{\substack{\text{Average Total} \\ \text{Assets}}} = \frac{\substack{\text{Net Income Plus} \\ \text{Interest Expense} \\ \text{Net of Income} \\ \text{Tax Savings}}}{\text{Revenues}} \times \frac{\text{Revenues}}{\substack{\text{Average Total} \\ \text{Assets}}}
$$

The profit margin ratio is a measure of a firm's ability to control the level of costs, or expenses, relative to revenues generated. By holding down costs, a firm will be able to increase the profits from a given amount of revenue and thereby improve its profit margin ratio. The total assets turnover ratio is a measure of a firm's ability to generate revenues from a particular level of investment in assets, or to put it another way, the total assets turnover measures a firm's ability to control the level of investment in assets for a particular level of resources.

Exhibit 6.4 shows the disaggregation of the rate of return on assets for Horrigan Corporation for Year 2, Year 3, and Year 4 into profit margin and total assets turnover ratios. Much of the improvement in the rate of return on assets between Year 2 and Year 3 results from an increase in the profit margin ratio from 9.1 percent to 12.9 percent. The total assets turnover ratio remained relatively stable between these two years. On the other hand, most of the improvement in the rate of return on assets between Year 3 and Year 4 can be attributed to the increased total assets turnover. The firm was able to generate $.81 of sales from each dollar invested in assets during Year 4 as compared to $.67 of sales per dollar of assets in Year 3. The increased total

assets turnover, coupled with an improvement in the profit margin ratio, permitted Horrigan Corporation to increase its rate of return on assets during Year 4. We must analyze the changes in the profit margin ratio and total assets turnover ratio in greater depth to pinpoint the causes of the changes in Horrigan Corporation's profitability over this three-year period. We return to this analysis shortly.

Exhibit 6.4
Disaggregation of Rate of Return
on Assets for
Horrigan Corporation
for Year 2, Year 3, and Year 4

$$\frac{\text{Net Income Plus Interest Expense Net of Income Tax Savings}}{\text{Average Total Assets}} = \frac{\text{Net Income Plus Interest Expense Net of Income Tax Savings}}{\text{Revenues}} \times \frac{\text{Revenues}}{\text{Average Total Assets}}$$

Year 2: $\dfrac{\$16 + (\$5 - \$2)}{\frac{1}{2}(\$250 + \$400)} = \dfrac{\$16 + (\$5 - \$2)}{\$210} \times \dfrac{\$210}{\frac{1}{2}(\$250 + \$400)}$

$\qquad\qquad 5.8\% \quad = \quad 9.1\% \quad \times \quad 65\%$

Year 3: $\dfrac{\$34 + (\$10 - \$4)}{\frac{1}{2}(\$400 + \$520)} = \dfrac{\$34 + (\$10 - \$4)}{\$310} \times \dfrac{\$310}{\frac{1}{2}(\$400 + \$520)}$

$\qquad\qquad 8.7\% \quad = \quad 12.9\% \quad \times \quad 67\%$

Year 4: $\dfrac{\$60 + (\$16 - \$6.4)}{\frac{1}{2}(\$520 + \$650)} = \dfrac{\$60 + (\$16 - \$6.4)}{\$475} \times \dfrac{\$475}{\frac{1}{2}(\$520 + \$650)}$

$\qquad\qquad 11.9\% \quad = \quad 14.7\% \quad \times \quad 81\%$

Improving the rate of return on assets can be accomplished by increasing the profit margin ratio, the rate of asset turnover, or both. Some firms, however, may have little flexibility in altering one of these components. For example, a firm committed under a three-year labour union contract may have little control over wage rates paid. Or a firm operating under market- or government-imposed price controls may not be able to increase the prices of its products. In these cases, the opportunities for improving the profit margin ratio may be limited. In order to increase the rate of return on assets, the level of investment in assets such as inventory, plant, and equipment must be reduced or, to put it another way, revenues per dollar of assets must be increased.

Analyzing Changes in the Profit Margin Ratio

Profit, or net income, is measured by subtracting various expenses from revenues. To identify the reasons for a change in the profit margin ratio, changes in a firm's expenses relative to revenues must be examined. One approach is to express individual expenses and net income as a percentage of revenues producing a common-size statement. Such an analysis is presented in Exhibit 6.5 for Horrigan Corporation. Note that we have altered somewhat the conventional income statement format in this analysis by subtracting interest expense (net of its related income tax effects) as the last expense item. The percentages on the line, Income before Interest and Related Income Tax Effect, correspond (except for rounding) to the profit margin ratios (before interest and related tax effects) shown in Exhibit 6.4.

The analysis in Exhibit 6.5 indicates that the improvement in the profit margin ratio over the three years for Horrigan Corporation can be attributed primarily to decreases in selling, administrative, and depreciation expenses as a percentage of sales. The reasons for these decreasing percentages should be explored further with management. Does the decrease in selling expenses as a percentage of sales reflect a reduction in the rate of advertising expenditures that could hurt future sales? Does the decrease in depreciation expense as a percentage of sales reflect a failure to expand plant and equipment as sales have increased? On the other hand, do these decreasing percentages merely reflect the realization of economies of scale as fixed selling, administrative, and depreciation expenses are being spread over a larger number of units?[4]

Exhibit 6.5
Net Income and Expenses as a
Percentage of Sales for
Horrigan Corporation for
Year 2, Year 3, and Year 4

	Years Ended December 31		
	Year 4	Year 3	Year 2
Sales	100.0%	100.0%	100.0%
Less: Cost of Goods Sold	58.9	57.7	56.7
Gross Profit	41.1%	42.3%	43.3%
Less: Operating Expenses			
Selling	9.7%	12.3%	17.1%
Administrative	3.2	4.2	5.7
Depreciation	3.8	4.5	5.7
Total Operating Expenses	16.7%	21.0%	28.5%
Operating Profit	24.4%	21.3%	14.8%
Income Taxes at 40 percent	9.7	8.4	5.7
Income before Interest and Related Income Tax Effect	14.7%	12.9%	9.1%
Interest Expense Net of Income Tax Effect	2.1	1.9	1.5
Net Income	12.6%	11.0%	7.6%

[4]This phenomenon is called *operating leverage* and is discussed more fully in managerial accounting textbooks.

The amount or trend in a particular ratio cannot, by itself, be the basis for investing or not investing in a firm. Ratios merely indicate areas where additional analysis is required. For example, the increasing percentage of cost of goods sold to sales should be explored further. It may reflect a successful, planned pricing policy of reducing gross profit (selling price less cost of goods sold) in order to increase the volume of sales. On the other hand, the replacement cost of inventory items may be increasing without corresponding increases being made in selling prices. Or, the firm may be accumulating excess inventories that are physically deteriorating or becoming obsolete.

Analyzing Changes in the Total Assets Turnover Ratio

The total assets turnover ratio depends on the turnover ratios for its individual asset components. Three turnover ratios are commonly calculated: accounts receivable turnover, inventory turnover, and fixed asset turnover.

Accounts Receivable Turnover The rate at which accounts receivable turn over gives an indication of their nearness to being converted into cash. The accounts receivable turnover is calculated by dividing net sales on account by average accounts receivable. For Horrigan Corporation, the accounts receivable turnover for Year 4, assuming all sales are on account (that is, none are for immediate cash), is calculated as follows:

$$\frac{\text{Net Sales on Account}}{\text{Average Accounts Receivable}} = \frac{\$475}{\frac{1}{2}(\$46 + \$76)} = 7.8 \text{ times per year}$$

The concept of accounts receivable turnover is often expressed in terms of the average number of days receivables are outstanding before cash is collected. The calculation divides the accounts receivable turnover ratio into 365 days. The average number of days that accounts receivable are outstanding for Horrigan Corporation for Year 4 is 46 days ($= 365$ days/7.8 times per year). Thus, on average, accounts receivable are collected approximately one and one-half months after the date of sale. The interpretation of this average collection period depends on the terms of sale. If the terms of sale are "net 30 days," the accounts receivable turnover indicates that collections are not being made in accordance with the stated terms. Such a ratio would warrant a review of the credit and collection activity for an explanation and for possible corrective action. If the firm offers terms of "net 45 days," then the results indicate that accounts receivable are being handled better.

Inventory Turnover The inventory turnover ratio is considered to be a significant indicator of the efficiency of operations for many businesses. It is calculated by dividing cost of goods sold by the average inventory during the period. The inventory turnover of Horrigan Corporation for Year 4 is calculated as follows:

$$\frac{\text{Cost of Goods Sold}}{\text{Average Inventory}} = \frac{\$280}{\frac{1}{2}(\$46 + \$83)} = 4.3 \text{ times per year}$$

Thus, inventory is typically on hand an average of 84 days (= 365 days/4.3 times per year) before it is sold.

The interpretation of the inventory turnover figure involves two opposing considerations. Management would like to sell as many goods as possible with a minimum of capital tied up in inventories. An increase in the rate of inventory turnover between periods would seem to indicate more profitable use of the investment in inventory. On the other hand, management does not want to have so little inventory on hand that shortages result and customers are turned away. An increase in the rate of inventory turnover in this case may mean a loss of customers and thereby offset any advantage gained by decreased investment in inventory. Some trade-offs are therefore required in deciding the optimum level of inventory for each firm, and thus the desirable rate of inventory turnover.

The inventory turnover ratio is sometimes calculated by dividing sales, rather than cost of goods sold, by the average inventory. As long as there is a relatively constant relationship between selling prices and cost of goods sold, changes in the *trend* of the inventory turnover can usually be identified with either measure. It is inappropriate to use sales in the numerator if the inventory turnover ratio is to be used to calculate the average number of days inventory is on hand until sale.

Plant Asset Turnover The plant asset turnover ratio is a measure of the relationship between sales and the investment in plant assets such as property, plant, and equipment. It is calculated by dividing revenues by average plant assets during the year. The plant assets turnover ratio for Horrigan Corporation for Year 4 is:

$$\frac{\text{Sales}}{\text{Average Plant Assets}} = \frac{\$475}{\frac{1}{2}(\$420 + \$479)} = 1.1 \text{ times per year}$$

Thus, for each dollar invested in plant assets during Year 4, $1.10 was generated in revenues.

Changes in the plant asset turnover ratio must be interpreted carefully. Investments in plant assets (for example, production facilities) are often made several periods before the time when sales are generated from products manufactured in the plant. Thus, a low or decreasing rate of plant asset turnover may be indicative of an expanding firm preparing for future growth. On the other hand, a firm may cut back its capital expenditures if the near-term outlook for its products is poor. Such action could lead to an increase in the plant asset turnover ratio.

We noted earlier that the total assets turnover for Horrigan Corporation was relatively steady between Year 2 and Year 3 but increased dramatically in Year 4. Exhibit 6.6 presents the four turnover ratios we have discussed for Horrigan Corporation over this three-year period. The accounts receivable turnover ratio increased steadily over the three years, indicating either more careful screening of credit applications or more effective collection efforts. The inventory turnover ratio decreased during the three years. Coupling this result with the increasing percentage of cost of goods sold to sales shown in Exhibit 6.5 indicates that there may be excessive investments in inventories that are physically deteriorating or becoming obsolete.

Note

Exhibit 6.6
Asset Turnover Ratios for
Horrigan Corporation for
Year 2, Year 3, and Year 4

	Year 4	Year 3	Year 2
Total Assets Turnover	.81	.67	.65
Accounts Receivable Turnover	7.6	7.8	.68
Inventory Turnover	4.3	4.7	5.4
Plant Asset Turnover	1.1	.8	.8

Most of the increase in the total assets turnover between Year 3 and Year 4 can be attributed to an increase in the plant assets turnover. We note in the statement of changes in financial position for Horrigan Corporation in Exhibit 6.3 that total capital expenditures on land, building, and equipment have decreased over the three-year period, possibly accounting for the increase in the plant assets turnover. The reasons for this decrease should be investigated.

Summary of the Analysis of the Rate of Return on Assets This section began by stating that the rate of return on assets is a useful measure for assessing a firm's performance in using assets to generate earnings. The rate of return on assets was then disaggregated into profit margin and total assets turnover components. The profit margin ratio was, in turn, disaggregated by relating various expenses and net income to sales. The total assets turnover was further analyzed by calculating turnover ratios for accounts receivable, inventory, and plant assets.

The analysis revealed the following:

1. The rate of return on assets increased steadily over the three-year period from Year 2 to Year 4.
2. The improved rate of return on assets can be attributed to an increasing profit margin over all three years and an improved total asset turnover during Year 4.
3. The improved profit margin is in large measure attributable to a decrease in the percentage of selling expenses to sales. The reason for this decrease should be explored further to ascertain whether advertising and selling efforts are being curtailed currently in a way that might adversely affect future sales.
4. The changes in the total assets turnover reflect the effects of increasing accounts receivable and plant asset turnover and a decreasing inventory turnover. The increasing plant asset turnover might be attributable to a reduction in the level of investment in new property, plant, and equipment that could hurt future productive capacity and should be explored further. The decreasing rate of inventory turnover coupled with the increasing percentage of cost of goods sold to sales may be indicative of inventory control problems (build-up of obsolete inventory) and should likewise be explored further.

Rate of Return on Common Share Equity

A second measure of profitability is the *rate of return on common shareholders' equity*. The rate of return on common shareholders' equity measures a firm's performance in using assets to generate earnings but, unlike the rate of return on assets, explicitly considers the financing of those assets. Thus, this measure of profitability incorporates the results of operating, investing, and financing decisions. This measure of profitability is of primary interest to investors in a firm's common shares. The rate of return on common shareholders' equity is calculated as follows:

$$\frac{\text{Net Income} - \text{Dividends on Preferred Shares}}{\text{Average Common Shareholders' Equity}}$$

To calculate the amount of earnings assignable to common shareholders' equity, the earnings allocable to any preferred share equity — usually the dividends on preferred shares declared during the period — must be deducted from net income. The capital invested during the period by common shareholders can be calculated by averaging the aggregate par value of common shares, contributed surplus on common shares, and retained earnings (or by deducting the equity of preferred shareholders from total shareholders' equity) at the beginning and end of the period.

The rate of return on common share equity of Horrigan Corporation for Year 4 is calculated as:

$$\frac{\text{Net Income} - \text{Dividends on Preferred Shares}}{\text{Average Common Shareholders' Equity}} = \frac{\$60 - \$0}{\frac{1}{2}(\$360 + \$410)} = 15.6\%$$

The rate of return on common shareholders' equity was 7.0 percent in Year 2 and 10.3 percent in Year 3. Thus, like the rate of return on assets, the rate of return on common shareholders' equity increased dramatically over the three years.

Relationship Between Return on Assets and Return on Common Shareholders' Equity

Figure 6.1 graphs the two measures of rate of return discussed thus far for Horrigan Corporation for Year 2, Year 3, and Year 4. In each year, the rate of return on common shareholders' equity exceeded the rate of return on assets. What accounts for this relation?

Recall that the rate of return on assets measures the profitability of a firm *before* any payments to the suppliers of capital. This return on assets must then be allocated among the various providers of capital. Creditors are allocated an amount equal to any contractual interest to which they have a claim. Preferred shareholders, if any, are allocated an amount equal to the stated dividend rate on the preferred shares. *Any remaining return* belongs to the common shareholders. That is, common sharehold-

Figure 6.1 Rates of Return for Horrigan Corporation

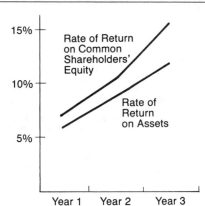

ers have a residual claim on all earnings after creditors and preferred shareholders have received amounts contractually owed them. Thus,

$$
\begin{array}{c}
\text{Rate of Return} \\
\text{on Assets}
\end{array}
\rightarrow
\begin{array}{c}
\text{Return to} \\
\text{Creditors} \\
\text{(interest)}
\end{array}
+
\begin{array}{c}
\text{Return to} \\
\text{Preferred} \\
\text{Shareholders} \\
\text{(dividends)}
\end{array}
+
\begin{array}{c}
\text{Return to} \\
\text{Common} \\
\text{Shareholders} \\
\text{(residual)}
\end{array}
$$

We can now see how the rate of return on common shareholders' equity can be larger than the rate of return on assets. The rate of return on assets must exceed the aftertax cost of debt capital (Horrigan Corporation has no preferred stock outstanding). For Year 4, the rate of return on assets was 11.9 percent and the aftertax cost of debt was 4.8 percent [= (1 − .4)($16)/.5($160 + $240); see Exhibits 6.1 and 6.2]. This excess return belongs to the common shareholders.

thus the concept of leveraging

The common shareholders earned a higher return only because the shareholders undertook more risk in their investment. They were placed in a riskier position because the firm incurred debt obligations with fixed payment dates. The phenomenon of common shareholders trading extra risk for a potentially higher return is called financial leverage and is described next.

Financial Leverage: Trading on the Equity

Financing with debt and preferred shares to increase the potential return to the residual common shareholders' equity is referred to as *financial leverage* or *trading on the equity*. So long as a higher rate of return can be earned on assets than is paid for the capital used to acquire those assets, then the rate of return to common shareholders can be increased. Exhibit 6.7 explores this phenomenon. Leveraged Limited and No-Debt Limited both have $100,000 of assets. Leveraged Limited borrows $40,000 at

Exhibit 6.7
Effects of Leverage on Rate of
Return of Shareholders' Equity
(Income Tax Rate Is 40 Percent of
Pretax Income)

	Long-Term Equities		Income after Taxes but before Interest Charges[a]	Aftertax Interest Charges[b]	Net Income	Rate of Return on Total Assets[c] (Percent)	Rate of Return on Common Share-holders' Equity
	Long-Term Borrowing at 10 Percent per Year	Share-holders' Equity					
Good Earnings Year							
Leveraged Limited	$40,000	$ 60,000	$10,000	$2,400	$ 7,600	10.0%	12.7%
No-Debt Limited	—	100,000	10,000	—	10,000	10.0	10.0
Neutral Earnings Year							
Leveraged Limited	40,000	60,000	6,000	2,400	3,600	6.0	6.0
No-Debt Limited	—	100,000	6,000	—	6,000	6.0	6.0
Bad Earnings Year							
Leveraged Limited	40,000	60,000	4,000	2,400	1,600	4.0	2.7
No-Debt Limited	—	100,000	4,000	—	4,000	4.0	4.0

[a]But not including any income tax savings caused by interest charges. Income before taxes and interest for *good* year is $16,667; for *neutral* year is $10,000; for *bad* year is $6,667.
[b]$40,000 (borrowed) × .10 (interest rate) × [1 − .40 (income tax rate)]. The numbers shown in the preceding column for aftertax income do not include the effects of interest charges on taxes.
[c]In each year, the rate of return on assets is the same for both companies as the rate of return on common shareholders' equity for No-Debt Limited: 10%, 6%, and 4%, respectively.

a ten percent annual rate. No-Debt Limited raises all its capital from common share-holders. Both companies pay income taxes at the rate of 40 percent.

Consider first a "good" earnings year. Both companies earn $10,000 before interest charges (but after taxes except for tax effects of interest charges).[5] This represents a rate of return on assets for both companies of ten percent:

$$\frac{\$10,000}{\$100,000} = 10\%$$

Leveraged Limited's net income is $7,600:

$$\$10,000 - (1 - .40 \text{ tax rate}) \times (.10 \text{ interest rate} \times \$40,000 \text{ borrowed}) = \$7,600$$

The net income represents a rate of return on common shareholders' equity of 12.7 percent:

$$\frac{\$7,600}{\$60,000} = 12.7\%$$

[5] That is, income before taxes and before interest charges is $16,667; $10,000 = (1 − .40) × $16,667.

Net income of No-Debt Limited is $10,000, representing a rate of return on shareholders' equity of ten percent. Leverage increased the rate of return to shareholders of Leveraged Limited, because the capital contributed by the long-term debtors earned ten percent but required an aftertax interest payment of only six percent [= (1 − .40 tax rate) × (.10 interest rate)]. This additional four percent return on each dollar of assets increases the return to the common shareholders.

Although leverage increased the return to the common share equity during the "good" earnings year, the increase would be larger if a larger proportion of the assets were financed with long-term borrowing and the firm were made more risky. For example, assume that the assets of $100,000 were financed with $50,000 of long-term borrowing and $50,000 of shareholders' equity. Net income of Leveraged Limited in this case would be:

$$\$10,000 - (1 - .40 \text{ tax rate}) \times (.10 \times \$50,000 \text{ borrowed}) = \$7,000$$

$$10,000 - (.6 \times .1 \times 50,000)$$

The rate of return on common share equity would be:

$$\frac{\$7,000}{\$50,000} = 14\%$$

This rate compares with a rate of return on common share equity of 12.7 percent when long-term debt was only 40 percent of the total capital provided.

Financial leverage increases the rate of return on common share equity when the rate of return on assets is higher than the aftertax cost of debt. The greater the proportion of debt in the capital structure, however, the greater the risk borne by the common shareholders. Debt cannot, of course, be increased without limit. As more debt is added to the capital structure, the risk of default or insolvency becomes greater. Lenders, including investors in a firm's bonds, will require a higher and higher return (interest rate) to compensate for this additional risk. A point will be reached when the aftertax cost of debt will exceed the rate of return that can be earned on assets. At this point, leverage can no longer increase the potential rate of return to common share equity. For most large manufacturing firms, liabilities represent between 30 percent and 60 percent of total capital.

The leverage ratio is a measure of the financial leverage practised by the firm on behalf of the common shareholders during a year. The leverage ratio is calculated by dividing the total assets by the common shareholders' equity averaged over the year. The leverage ratio for No-Debt Limited is 1 (= $100,000/$100,000) and for Leveraged Limited is 1.7 (= $100,000/$60,000).

Exhibit 6.7 also demonstrates the effect of leverage in a "neutral" earnings year and in a "bad" earnings year. In the "neutral" earnings year, the rate of return to common shareholders is neither increased nor decreased by leverage, because the return on assets is 6 percent and the aftertax cost of long-term debt is 6 percent. In the "bad" earnings year, the return on assets of 4 percent is less than the aftertax cost of debt of 6 percent. The return on common share equity therefore drops — to only 2.7 percent — below the rate of return on assets. Clearly, financial leverage can work in two ways. It can enhance owners' rate of return in good years, but owners run the risk that bad earnings years will be even worse than they would be without the borrowing.

Disaggregating the Rate of Return on Common Shareholders' Equity

The rate of return on common shareholders' equity can be disaggregated into several components in a manner similar to the disaggregation of the rate of return on assets. The rate of return on common shareholders' equity might be disaggregated as follows:

$$
\begin{array}{c}
\text{Rate of Return} \\
\text{on Common} \\
\text{Shareholders'} \\
\text{Equity}
\end{array}
=
\begin{array}{c}
\text{Profit Margin Ratio} \\
\text{(after interest} \\
\text{expense and} \\
\text{preferred dividends)}
\end{array}
\times
\begin{array}{c}
\text{Total} \\
\text{Assets} \\
\text{Turnover} \\
\text{Ratio}
\end{array}
\times
\begin{array}{c}
\text{Leverage} \\
\text{Ratio}
\end{array}
$$

The profit margin percentage indicates the portion of the revenue dollar left over for the common shareholders after all operating costs have been covered and all claims of creditors and preferred shareholders have been subtracted. The total assets turnover, as discussed earlier, indicates the revenues generated from each dollar of assets. The leverage ratio indicates the extent to which capital (= total assets) has been provided by common shareholders. The larger is the leverage ratio, the smaller is the portion of capital provided by common shareholders and the larger the proportion provided by creditors and preferred shareholders. Thus, the larger the leverage ratio, the greater will be the extent of financial leverage.

The disaggegation of the rate of return on common shareholders' equity ratio for Horrigan Corporation for Year 4 is as follows:

$$
\frac{\$60}{\frac{1}{2}(\$360 + \$410)} = \frac{\$60}{\$475} \times \frac{\$475}{\frac{1}{2}(\$520 + \$650)} \times \frac{\frac{1}{2}(\$520 + \$650)}{\frac{1}{2}(\$360 + \$410)}
$$

$$
15.6 \text{ percent} = 12.6 \text{ percent} \times \quad .81 \quad \times \quad 1.5
$$

Exhibit 6.8 shows the disaggregation of the rate of return on common shareholders' equity for Horrigan Corporation for Year 2, Year 3, and Year 4. Most of the increase in the rate of return on common shareholders' equity can be attributed to an increasing profit margin over the three-year period plus an increase in total assets turnover in Year 4. The leverage ratio remained reasonably stable over this period.

Exhibit 6.8
Disaggregation of Rate of Return
on Common Shareholders' Equity for Horrigan Corporation

Year	Rate of Return on Common Shareholders' Equity	=	Profit Margin	×	Total Assets Turnover	×	Leverage Ratio
Year 2	7.0%	=	7.6%	×	.65	×	1.4
Year 3.	10.3%	=	11.0%	×	.67	×	1.4
Year 4	15.6%	=	12.6%	×	.81	×	1.5

Earnings per Common Share

Earnings per share for Horrigan Corporation for Year 4 is calculated as follows:

$$\dfrac{\begin{array}{c}\text{Net} \quad \text{Preferred Share} \\ \text{Income} \ - \ \text{Dividend}\end{array}}{\begin{array}{c}\text{Weighted Average} \\ \text{Number of Common Shares} \\ \text{Outstanding} \\ \text{During the Period}\end{array}} = \dfrac{\$60 - \$0}{16 \text{ shares}^6} = \$3.75 \text{ per share}$$

Earnings per share were \$1.28 (= \$16/12.5) for Year 2 and \$2.19 (= \$34/15.5) for Year 3.

If a firm has securities outstanding that can be converted into or exchanged for common shares, it may be required to present two earnings per share amounts: *basic earnings per share* and *fully diluted earnings per share*. For example, some firms issue convertible bonds or convertible preferred shares that can be exchanged directly for common shares. Also, many firms have employee stock option plans under which the company's common shares may be acquired by employees under special arrangements. If these convertible securities were converted or stock options were exercised and additional common shares were issued, the amount conventionally shown as earnings per share would probably decrease, or become *diluted*. When a firm has outstanding securities that, if exchanged for common shares, would decrease earnings per share by a material amount, a dual presentation of basic and fully diluted earnings per share is required.[7]

Interpreting Earnings per Share Earnings per share has been criticized as a measure of profitability because it does not consider the amount of assets or capital required to generate that level of earnings. Two firms with the same earnings and earnings per share will not be equally profitable if one of the firms requires twice the amount of assets or capital to generate that earnings than does the other firm.

Earnings per share amounts are also difficult to interpret when comparing firms. For example, assume that two firms have identical earnings, common shareholders' equity, and rates of return on common shareholders' equity. One firm may have a lower earnings per share simply because it has a larger number of shares outstanding (owing perhaps to the use of a lower par value for its shares or from different earnings retention policies; see Problem 21 at the end of this chapter).

Price-Earnings Ratio

Earnings per share amounts are often compared with the market price of the shares. This is usually expressed as a *price-earnings ratio* (= market price per share/earnings per share). For example, the common shares of Horrigan Corporation are selling for \$40 per share at the end of Year 4. The price-earnings ratio, also called the P/E ratio,

---

[6] Exhibit 6.1 indicates that the par value of a common share is \$10 and that the common stock account has a balance of \$160 million throughout 1982. The shares outstanding were therefore 16 million.

[7] *CICA Handbook*, section 3500.

is 10.67 to one (= $40/$3.75). This ratio is often presented in tables of stock market prices and in financial periodicals. The relationship is sometimes expressed by saying that ''the shares are selling at 10.7 times earnings.''

The relation between earnings and market price per share might be expressed as a rate (= earnings per share/market price per share). This calculation, 9.4 percent (= $3.75/$40) for Horrigan Corporation, is less common than the price-earnings ratio.

inverse

Summary of Profitability Analysis

Three broad measures for assessing a firm's profitability have been discussed in this chapter. Because the rate of return on assets and rate of return on common shareholders' equity relate earnings to some measure of the capital required to generate those earnings, most of our attention has been focused on the two profitability measures.

Exhibit 6.9 summarizes the analysis discussed. On the most general level, the concern is with overall measures of profitability and the effectiveness of financial leverage. On the next level, the overall measures of profitability are disaggregated into profit margin, asset turnover, and leverage components. On the third level, the profit margin and asset turnover ratios are further disaggregated to gain additional insights into reasons for changes in profitability. The depth of analysis required in any particular case depends on the differences or changes in profitability observed.

Exhibit 6.9 Profitability Ratios

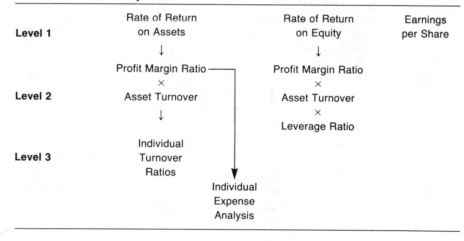

Profitability

Analysis of Risk

The second parameter in investment decisions after profitability is risk. There are various factors that affect the risk of business firms:

1. Economy-wide factors, such as increased inflation or interest rates, unemployment, or recessions.
2. Industry-wide factors, such as increased competition, lack of availability of raw materials, changes in technology, or increased government antimonopoly actions.

Securities Analysis—Art or Science?

*T*he prediction of corporate economic performance by financial statement analysis is one of the most heavily researched of all human endeavours. A whole industry of financial analysts has been spawned by investors' unquenchable thirst for predictive information. Most investment brokers and securities analysts use the techniques illustrated in this chapter. There are, however, some additional methods in use—some uncontroversial and some controversial. These include the statisticians, the bullionists, the hemliners, and the tippers.

Interviewing of corporate financial executives is a standard tool in the financial analyst's kit. Theoretically, an individual investor could call on a company and ask for information. In reality, this task is left to financial analysts. An American department store chain, J.C. Penny, reported that in one year it granted 1,500 one-hour interviews to analysts. Consequently, some large firms hire someone full-time just to talk to these analysts.

One of the oldest forms of corporate predictive tools, charting, is based on the premise that if you chart economic activity long enough, cycles are discernable. These sawtooth diagrams, often seen in movies and cartoons, are examples of charting. Chartists eventually go looney because they discover cycles within cycles within cycles, all depending on how long a time horizon has been taken.

Statisticians have refined charting using a rigorous method called time series analysis, which is, simply stated, regression over time. Despite a period of academic popularity, the latest view is that the behaviour of most securities can be depicted as a random walk (i.e., its future behaviour is unpredictable).

Bullionists believe that stock market performance and the price of gold bullion are inversely related. When the economy is deteriorating (along with the companies responsible for the economy), people flee paper investments and put their funds into gold and diamonds.

Hemlining has reappeared several times in the twentieth century. A hemliner believes that stock market prices move in the same direction as ladies' hemlines. It is unknown how many people use this technique.

The tipper is the most popular of all techniques. Most investments today are based on "hot tips." Few investors have not suffered the pangs of remorse after failing to act on one of these tips and then seeing the company's stock price take off like a rocket. Strangely enough, those tips we do act on usually blow up on the launching pad. Where do tips come from? Some come from the people who do financial statement analysis. But most come from something called *insider information*. Somebody knows somebody who knows somebody inside the company who has access to important information not yet known to the public. For instance, when a gold mining company strikes a motherlode, there is an interval of time before this information is made public, and if the company's shares are purchased before this release, a killing can be made because the share prices will surely jump later on. One problem with acting on insider information is that it is illegal.

In summary, there are numerous techniques available for predicting stock performance. However, if someone attempts to sell you or give you advice based on any of these approaches, ask yourself one question before you accept that advice: if the method works, why isn't this person fabulously wealthy?

3. Firm-specific factors, such as labour strikes, loss of facilities due to fire or other casualty, or poor health of key managerial personnel.

The ultimate risk is that a firm will be forced into bankruptcy and creditors and investors will lose the capital they provided to the firm.

When assessing risk, the focus is generally on the relative *liquidity* of a firm. Cash and near-cash assets provide a firm with the resources needed to adapt to these various dimensions of risk as potential losses arise. That is, liquid resources provide a firm with *financial flexibility*. Cash is also the connecting link that permits the operating, investing, and financing activities of a firm to continue operating smoothly and effectively.

When assessing liquidity, time is of critical importance. Consider the following three questions:

1. Does a firm have sufficient cash to repay a loan due tomorrow?
2. Will the firm have sufficient cash to repay a note due in six months?
3. Will the firm have sufficient cash to repay bonds due in five years?

In answering the first question, the analysis would probably focus on the amount of cash on hand and in the bank relative to obligations coming due tomorrow. In answering the second question, consideration would be given to the amount of cash expected to be generated from operations during the next six months, as well as to any new borrowing, relative to obligations coming due during that period. In answering the third question, the focus would shift to the longer-run cash-generating ability of a firm relative to the amount of long-term debt that would become due.

Measures of Short-Term Liquidity Risk

This section discusses four measures for assessing short-term liquidity risk: (1) current ratio, (2) quick ratio, (3) operating cash flow to current liabilities ratio, and (4) working capital turnover ratio.

Current Ratio

The *current ratio* is calculated by dividing current assets by current liabilities. It is commonly expressed as a ratio such as "2 to 1" or "2:1," meaning that current assets are twice as large as current liabilities. The current ratio of Horrigan Corporation on December 31, Year 1, Year 2, Year 3, and Year 4 is:

$$\frac{\text{Current Assets}}{\text{Current Liabilities}} = \frac{\text{Current}}{\text{Ratio}}$$

$$\text{December 31, Year 1:} \frac{\$\ 50}{\$\ 40} = 1.25 \text{ to } 1.0$$

$$\text{December 31, Year 2:} \frac{\$\ 80}{\$\ 50} = 1.60 \text{ to } 1.0$$

$$\text{December 31, Year 3:} \frac{\$100}{\$\ 60} = 1.67 \text{ to } 1.0$$

$$\text{December 31, Year 4:} \frac{\$171}{\$\ 90} = 1.90 \text{ to } 1.0$$

This ratio is presumed to indicate the ability of the firm to meet its current obligations, and is therefore of particular significance to short-term creditors. Although an excess of current assets over current liabilities is generally considered desirable from the creditor's viewpoint, changes in the trend of the ratio may be difficult to interpret. For example, when the current ratio is larger than 1 to 1, an increase of equal amount in both current assets and current liabilities results in a decline in the ratio, whereas equal decreases result in an increased current ratio. *Note*

In a recession period, business is contracting, current liabilities are paid, and, even though the current assets may be at a low point, the ratio may go to high levels. In a boom period, just the reverse effect might occur. In other words, a very high current ratio may accompany unsatisfactory business conditions, whereas a falling ratio may accompany profitable operations.

Furthermore, the current ratio and the quick ratio below are susceptible to "window dressing"; that is, management can take deliberate steps to produce a financial statement that presents a better current ratio at the balance sheet date than the average or normal current ratio. For example, toward the close of a fiscal year normal purchases on account may be delayed. Or loans to officers, classified as noncurrent assets, may be collected and the proceeds used to reduce current liabilities. These actions may be taken so that the current ratio will appear as favourable as possible in the annual financial statements at the balance sheet date. *Accts action ∴ CICA Rules*

Although the current ratio is probably the most common liquidity ratio presented in statement analysis, there are limitations in its use as discussed above. Its trends are difficult to interpret and, if overemphasized, it can easily lead to undesirable business practices as well as misinterpretation of financial condition.

Quick Ratio

A variation of the current ratio, usually known as the *quick ratio* or *acid-test ratio*, is computed by including in the numerator of the fraction only those current assets that could be converted quickly into cash. The numerator customarily includes cash, temporary investments, and receivables, but it would be better to make a study of the facts in each case before deciding whether or not to include receivables and to exclude inventories. In some businesses, the inventory of merchandise might be converted into cash more quickly than the receivables of other businesses.

Assuming that the accounts receivable of Horrigan Corporation are included but that inventory is excluded, the quick ratio on December 31, Year 1, Year 2, Year 3 and Year 4 is:

$$\frac{\text{Cash, Accounts Receivable}}{\text{Current Liabilities}} = \frac{\text{Quick}}{\text{Ratio}}$$

$$\text{December 31, Year 1:} \frac{\$36}{\$40} = .90 \text{ to } 1.0$$

$$\text{December 31, Year 2:} \frac{\$50}{\$50} = 1.0 \text{ to } 1.0$$

$$\text{December 31, Year 3:} \frac{\$54}{\$60} = .90 \text{ to } 1.0$$

$$\text{December 31, Year 4: } \frac{\$88}{\$90} = \quad .98 \text{ to } 1.0$$

Therefore

Whereas the current ratio increased steadily over the period, the quick ratio remained relatively constant. The increase in the current ratio results primarily from a build-up of inventories.

Operating Cash Flow to Current Liabilities

✓

Both the current ratio and quick ratio can be criticized in that they are calculated using amounts at a specific point in time. If financial statement amounts at that particular time are unusually large or small, the resulting ratios will not reflect more normal conditions.

What is operating cash flow

To overcome these deficiencies, the operating cash flow to current liabilities ratio can be calculated. The numerator of this ratio is cash provided by operations for the year. The denominator is average current liabilities for the year. The operating cash flow to current liabilities ratios for Horrigan Corporation for Year 2, Year 3, and Year 4 are as follows:

	$\dfrac{\text{Cash Provided by Operations}}{\text{Average Current Liabilities}}$ =	Operating Cash Flow to Current Liabilities
Year 2..............	$\dfrac{\$12}{\frac{1}{2}(\$40 + \$50)}$ =	26.7 percent
Year 3..............	$\dfrac{\$32}{\frac{1}{2}(\$50 + \$60)}$ =	58.2 percent
Year 4..............	$\dfrac{\$41}{\frac{1}{2}(\$60 + \$90)}$ =	54.7 percent

A ratio of 40 percent or more[8] is common for a healthy firm. Thus, the liquidity of Horrigan Corporation improved dramatically between Year 2 and Year 3. The decrease between Year 3 and Year 4 is due primarily to a build-up in current liabilities (which, in turn, is probably related to the build-up in inventories noted above).

Working Capital Turnover Ratio

Net WC is used from chapt. 5

The *operating cycle* of a firm is a sequence of activities in which:

1. Inventory is purchased on account from suppliers
2. Inventory is sold on account to customers
3. Customers pay amounts due
4. Suppliers are paid amounts due

This cycle occurs continually for most business firms. The longer the cycle, the longer is the time that funds are tied up in receivables and inventories. The interest cost on

---

[8]Cornelius Casey and Norman Bartczak, "Operating Cash Flow Data and Financial Distress: Some Empirical Evidence," *Journal of Accounting Research*, Spring 1985, pp. 384–401.

funds required to carry receivables and inventory reduces net income and hurts profitability. Funds tied up in receivables and inventory also have negative effects on the short-run liquidity of a firm. The more quickly inventory and receivables are turned into cash, the more liquid is a firm.

The working capital turnover ratio is a measure of the length of the operating cycle. It is calculated by dividing sales by the average working capital for the year. Working capital is equal to current assets minus current liabilities. The working capital turnover ratio for Horrigan Corporation is as follows:

	$\dfrac{\text{Sales}}{\text{Average Working Capital}}$	$=$	Working Capital Turnover Ratio
Year 2..........................	$\dfrac{\$210}{\frac{1}{2}(\$10 + \$30)}$	$=$	10.5 times
Year 3..........................	$\dfrac{\$310}{\frac{1}{2}(\$30 + \$40)}$	$=$	8.9 times
Year 4..........................	$\dfrac{\$475}{\frac{1}{2}(\$40 + \$81)}$	$=$	7.9 times

The turnover rate has decreased over the three-year period, primarily because inventories net of current liabilities increased faster than sales.

The working capital turnover ratio is often converted to the number of days required for one revolution of the operating cycle by dividing the turnover ratio into 365 days. Thus, working capital turned over on average every 34.8 days (= 365/10.5) during Year 2. The corresponding amounts for Year 3 and Year 4 were 41.0 days and 46.2 days, respectively.

The working capital turnover ratio varies significantly across firms depending on the nature of their businesses. The working capital turnover for grocery stores is approximately 12 times per year, whereas for a construction company the turnover is sometimes less than one. When using the working capital turnover ratio to evaluate short-term liquidity, the analyst must be aware of the type of business in which the firm is involved.

Summary of Short-Term Liquidity Analysis

The current and quick ratios give snapshot measures of liquidity at particular points in time. These ratios for Horrigan Corporation are at reasonably adequate levels at the end of each year, although they indicate a build-up of inventories in Year 4.

The cash flow from operations to current liabilities and the working capital turnover ratios provide measures of short-term liquidity for a period of time. Both ratios indicate a significant improvement in liquidity between Year 2 and Year 3, due primarily to increased cash flow from operations. Both ratios decreased during Year 4 owing to the build-up of inventory. However, the levels of the ratios during Year 4 do not yet indicate serious short-term liquidity problems for Horrigan Corporation. Given the growth rate in sales during the past two years (approximately 50 percent per year), a build-up of inventories may be justified.

Measures of Long-Term Liquidity Risk

Measures of long-term liquidity risk are used in evaluating the firm's ability to meet interest and principal payments on long-term debt and similar obligations as they become due. If the payments cannot be made on time, the firm becomes *insolvent* and may have to be reorganized or liquidated.

Perhaps the best indicator for assessing long-term liquidity risk is a firm's ability to generate profits over a period of years. If a firm is profitable, it will either generate sufficient capital from operations or be able to obtain needed capital from creditors and shareholders. The measures of profitability discussed previously are therefore applicable for this purpose as well. Three other commonly used measures of long-term liquidity are debt ratios, the cash flow from operations to total liabilities ratio, and the number of times that interest charges are earned.

Debt Ratios

There are several variations of the debt ratio, but the one most commonly encountered in financial analysis is the *long-term debt ratio*. It reports the portion of the firm's long-term capital that is furnished by debt holders. To calculate this ratio, divide total long-term debt by the sum of total long-term debt and total shareholders' equity.

Another form of the debt ratio is the *debt-equity ratio*. To calculate the debt-equity ratio, divide total liabilities (current and noncurrent) by total equities (liabilities plus shareholders' equity = total assets).

Exhibit 6.10 shows the two forms of the debt ratio for Horrigan Corporation on December 31, Year 1, Year 2, Year 3, and Year 4. In general, the higher these ratios, the higher the likelihood that the firm may be unable to meet fixed interest and principal payments in the future. The decision for most firms is how much financial leverage with its attendant risk they can afford to assume. Funds obtained from issuing bonds or borrowing from a bank have a relatively low interest cost but require fixed, periodic payments that increase the likelihood of bankruptcy.

Exhibit 6.10
HORRIGAN CORPORATION
Debt Ratios

$\dfrac{\text{Total Long-Term Debt}}{\substack{\text{Total Long-Term Debt} \\ \text{Plus Shareholders'} \\ \text{Equity}}} = $ Long-Term Debt Ratio		$\dfrac{\text{Total Liabilities}}{\substack{\text{Total Liabilities Plus} \\ \text{Shareholders'} \\ \text{Equity}}} = $ Debt-Equity Ratio	
Dec. 31, Year 1: $\dfrac{\$50}{\$210} =$	24%	Dec. 31, Year 1: $\dfrac{\$90}{\$250} =$	36%
Dec. 31, Year 2: $\dfrac{\$50}{\$350} =$	14%	Dec. 31, Year 2: $\dfrac{\$100}{\$400} =$	25%
Dec. 31, Year 3: $\dfrac{\$100}{\$460} =$	22%	Dec. 31, Year 3: $\dfrac{\$160}{\$520} =$	31%
Dec. 31, Year 4: $\dfrac{\$150}{\$560} =$	27%	Dec. 31, Year 4: $\dfrac{\$240}{\$650} =$	37%

In assessing the debt ratios, analysts customarily vary the standard in direct relation to the stability of the firm's earnings and cash flow from operations. The more stable the earnings, and cash flow, the higher the debt ratio that is considered acceptable or safe. The debt ratios of public utilities are customarily high, frequently on the order of 60 to 70 percent. The stability of public utility earnings and cash flow, makes these ratios acceptable to many investors who would be dissatisfied with such high leverage for firms with less stable earnings and cash flows. The debt ratios of Horrigan Corporation are about average for an industrial firm.

Because several variations of the debt ratio appear in corporate annual reports, care in comparing debt ratios among firms is necessary.

Cash Flow from Operations to Total Liabilities Ratio

The debt ratios give no recognition to the varying liquidity of assets for covering various levels of debt. The cash flow from operations to total liabilities ratio overcomes this deficiency. This cash flow ratio is similar to the one used in assessing short-term liquidity risk, but here all liabilities (both current and noncurrent) are included in the denominator. The cash flow from operations to debt ratio for Horrigan Corporation is:

Note importance of calculation.

	$\dfrac{\text{Cash Flow from Operations}}{\text{Average Total Liabilities}}$ =	Cash Flow from Operations to Debt Ratio
Year 2...................	$\dfrac{\$12}{\frac{1}{2}(\$90 + \$100)}$ =	12.6 percent
Year 3...................	$\dfrac{\$32}{\frac{1}{2}(\$100 + \$160)}$ =	24.6 percent
Year 4...................	$\dfrac{\$41}{\frac{1}{2}(\$160 + \$240)}$ =	20.5 percent

A ratio of 20 percent or more is normal for a financially healthy company. Thus, the long-term liquidity risk decreased significantly between Year 2 and Year 3 but increased again in Year 4. The level of the ratio in Year 4, though, is still adequate.

Interest Coverage: Times Interest Charges Earned

Another measure of long-term solvency is the *number of times that interest charges are earned*, or covered. This ratio is calculated by dividing net income before interest and income tax expenses by interest expense. For Horrigan Corporation, the times interest earned ratios for Year 2, Year 3, and Year 4 are:

$$\frac{\text{Net Income before Interest and Income Taxes}}{\text{Interest Expense}} = \frac{\text{Times Interest}}{\text{Charges Earned}}$$

$$\text{Year 2:} \quad \frac{\$16 + \$5 + \$10}{\$5} = 6.2 \text{ times}$$

$$\text{Year 3:} \quad \frac{\$34 + \$10 + \$22}{\$10} = 6.6 \text{ times}$$

$$\text{Year 4:} \quad \frac{\$60 + \$16 + \$40}{\$16} = 7.3 \text{ times}$$

Thus, whereas the bonds payable increased sharply during the three-year period, the growth in net income before interest and income taxes was sufficient to provide increasing coverage of the fixed interest charges.

The purpose of this ratio is to indicate the relative protection of bondholders and to assess the probability that the firm will be forced into bankruptcy by a failure to meet required interest payments. If periodic repayments of principal on long-term liabilities are also required, the repayments might also be included in the denominator of the ratio. The ratio would then be described as the *number of times that fixed charges were earned*, or covered.

The times interest or fixed charges earned ratios can be criticized as measures for assessing long-term liquidity risk, because the ratios use earnings rather than cash flows in the numerator. Interest and other fixed payment obligations are paid with cash, and not with earnings. When the value of the ratio is relatively low (for example, two to three times), some measure of cash flows, such as cash flows from operations, may be preferable in the numerator.

Summary of Long-Term Liquidity Analysis

The focus of long-term liquidity analysis is on the amount of debt, particularly long-term debt, in the capital structure and the adequacy of earnings and cash flows for debt service—making interest and principal payments as they become due. Although both short- and long-term debt of Horrigan Corporation have increased over the three-year period, increases in sales, earnings, and cash flows from operations all appear to be increasing sufficiently to cover the current levels of debt.

Limitations of Ratio Analysis

For convenient reference, Exhibit 6.11 summarizes the calculation of the ratios discussed in this chapter. The analytical computations discussed in this chapter have a number of limitations that should be kept in mind by anyone preparing or using them. Several of the more important limitations are the following:

1. The ratios are based on financial statement data and are therefore subject to the same criticisms as the financial statements (for example, use of acquisition cost rather than current replacement cost or net realizable value; the latitude permitted firms in selecting from among various generally accepted accounting policies).
2. Changes in many ratios are highly associated with each other. For example, the changes in the current ratio and quick ratio between two different times are often in the same direction and approximately proportional. It is therefore not necessary to compute all the ratios to assess a particular factor.
3. When comparing the size of a ratio between periods for the same firm, one must

recognize conditions that have changed between the periods being compared (for example, different product lines or geographical markets served, changes in economic conditions, changes in prices).

4. When comparing ratios of a particular firm with those of similar firms, one must recognize differences between the firms (for example, use of different methods of accounting, differences in the method of operations, type of financing, and so on).

Exhibit 6.11
Summary of Financial
Statement Ratios

Ratio	Numerator	Denominator
Profitability Ratios		
Rate of Return on Assets . . .	Net Income + Interest Expense (net of tax effects)[a]	Average Total Assets During the Period
Profit Margin Ratio (before interest effects) . .	Net Income + Interest Expense (net of tax effects)[a]	Revenues
Various Expense Ratios	Various Expenses	Revenues
Total Assets Turnover Ratio	Revenues	Average Total Assets During the Period
Accounts Receivable Turnover Ratio	Net Sales on Accounts	Average Accounts Receivable During the Period
Inventory Turnover Ratio . . .	Cost of Goods Sold	Average Inventory During the Period
Plant Asset Turnover Ratio	Revenues	Average Plant Assets During the Period
Rate of Return on Common Shareholders' Equity	Net Income — Preferred Stock Dividends	Average Common Shareholders' Equity During the Period
Profit Margin Ratio (after interest expense and preferred dividends)	Net Income — Preferred Stock Dividends	Average Common Shareholders' Equity During the Period
Leverage Ratio	Average Total Assets During the Period	Average Common Shareholders' Equity During the Period
Earnings per Share of Stock[b]	Net Income — Preferred Stock Dividends	Weighted-Average Number of Common Shares Outstanding During the Period
Short-Term Liquidity Ratios		
Current Ratio	Current Assets	Current Liabilities
Quick or Acid Test Ratio	Highly Liquid Assets (ordinarily, cash, temporary investments, and receivables)[c]	Current Liabilities

Cash Flow from Operations to Current Liabilities Ratio	Cash Provided by Operations	Average Current Liabilities During the Period
Working Capital Turnover Ratio	Revenues	Average Working Capital During the Period
Long-Term Liquidity Ratios		
Long-Term Debt Ratio	Total Long-Term Debt	Total Long-Term Debt Plus Shareholders' Equity
Debt-Equity Ratio	Total Liabilities	Total Equities (liabilities plus shareholders' equity)
Cash Flow from Operations to Total Liabilities Ratio	Cash Provided by Operations	Average Total Liabilities During the Period
Times Interest Charges Earned	Net Income Before Interest and Income Taxes	Interest Expense

[a]If a consolidated subsidiary is not owned entirely by the parent corporation, the minority interest share of earnings must also be added back to net income. See the description in Chapter 13.
[b]This calculation can be more complicated when there are convertible securities, options, or warrants outstanding.
[c]Receivables could conceivably be excluded for some firms and inventories included for others. Such refinements are seldom employed in practice.

Results of financial statement analyses cannot be used by themselves as direct indications of good or poor management. Such analyses merely indicate areas that might be investigated further. For example, a decrease in the turnover of raw materials inventory, ordinarily considered to be an undesirable trend, may reflect the accumulation of scarce materials that will keep the plant operating at full capacity during shortages when competitors have been forced to restrict operations or to close down. Ratios derived from financial statements must be combined with an investigation of other facts before valid conclusions can be drawn.

Summary

This chapter began by raising the question, ''Should you invest your inheritance in a certificate of deposit or in the common shares of Horrigan Corporation?'' Analysis of Horrigan Corporation's financial statements indicates that it has been a growing, profitable company with few indications of either short-term liquidity or long-term liquidity problems. At least three additional inputs are necessary before making the investment decision. First, consideration must be given to other sources of information besides the financial statements to determine if information relevant for projecting rates of return or for assessing risk needs to be considered. Second, you must decide your attitude toward, or willingness to assume, risk. Third, you must decide if you think the stock market price of the shares makes them an attractive purchase.[9]

[9]Other important factors cannot be discussed here, but are in finance texts. Perhaps the most important question of all is how a particular investment fits in with the investor's entire portfolio. Modern research suggests that the suitability of a potential investment depends more on the attributes of the other components of an investment portfolio and the risk attitude of the investor than it does on the attributes of the potential investment itself.

It is at this stage in the investment decision that the analysis becomes particularly subjective.

Problem 1 for Self-Study

Exhibit 6.12 presents a comparative balance sheet for Cox Co. Ltd. as of December 31, Year 1 and Year 2, and Exhibit 6.13 presents an income statement for Year 2. Using information from these financial statements, compute the following ratios. (The income tax rate is 40 percent. Cash provided by operations totals $3,300.)

Exhibit 6.12
COX CO. LTD.
Comparative Balance Sheet
December 31, Year 1 and Year 2

	December 31	
	Year 2	Year 1
Assets		
Current Assets:		
Cash	$ 750	$ 600
Accounts Receivable	4,300	3,600
Merchandise Inventories	7,900	5,600
Prepayments	380	300
Total Current Assets	$13,330	$10,100
Property, Plant, and Equipment:		
Land	$ 600	$ 500
Buildings and Equipment (net)	10,070	9,400
Total Property, Plant, and Equipment	$10,670	$ 9,900
Total Assets	$24,000	$20,000
Liabilities and Shareholders' Equity		
Current Liabilities:		
Notes Payable	$ 4,000	$ 2,000
Accounts Payable	3,300	3,500
Other Current Liabilities	1,900	1,500
Total Current Liabilities	$ 9,200	$ 7,000
Noncurrent Liabilities:		
Bonds Payable	2,800	4,000
Total Liabilities	$12,000	$11,000
Shareholders' Equity:		
Preferred Stock	$ 1,000	$ 1,000
Common Stock	4,300	3,500
Retained Earnings	6,700	4,500
Total Shareholders' Equity	$12,000	$ 9,000
Total Liabilities and Shareholders' Equity	$24,000	$20,000

Exhibit 6.13
COX CO. LTD.
Income and Retained Earnings Statement
For Year 2

Sales		$30,000
Less: Cost of Sales		18,000
Gross Profit		$12,000
Less: Operating Expenses		
Selling	$4,500	
Administrative	1,800	6,300
Operating Profit		$ 5,700
Less: Interest Expense		700
Net Income before Income Tax		$ 5,000
Income Tax		2,000
Net Income		$ 3,000
Less: Dividends		
Preferred	$ 100	
Common	700	800
Increase in Retained Earnings for Year 2		$ 2,200
Retained Earnings, December 31, Year 1		4,500
Retained Earnings, December 31, Year 2		$ 6,700

a. Rate of return on assets
b. Profit margin ratio (before interest and related tax effects)
c. Cost of goods sold to sales percentage
d. Selling expense to sales percentage
e. Total assets turnover
f. Accounts receivable turnover
g. Inventory turnover
h. Plant asset turnover
i. Rate of return on common shareholders' equity
j. Profit margin (after interest)
k. Leverage ratio
l. Current ratio (both dates)
m. Quick ratio (both dates)
n. Cash flow from operations to current liabilities
o. Working capital turnover
p. Long-term debt ratio (both dates)
q. Debt-equity ratio (both dates)
r. Cash flow from operations to total liabilities
s. Time interest charges earned

Suggested Solution

a. Rate of return on assets $= \dfrac{\$3,000 + (1 - .40)(\$700)}{.5(\$20,000 + \$24,000)} = 15.5\%$

b. Profit margin ratio $= \dfrac{\$3,000 + (1 - .40)(\$700)}{\$30,000} = 11.4\%$

c. Cost of goods sold to sales percentage $= \dfrac{\$18,000}{\$30,000} = 60.0\%$

d. Selling expense to sales percentage $= \dfrac{\$4,500}{\$30,000} = 15.0\%$

e. Total assets turnover $= \dfrac{\$30,000}{.5(\$20,000 + \$24,000)} = 1.4$ times per year

f. Accounts receivable turnover $= \dfrac{\$30,000}{.5(\$3,600 + \$4,300)} = 7.6$ times per year

g. Inventory turnover $= \dfrac{\$18,000}{.5(\$5,600 + \$7,900)} = 2.7$ times per year

h. Plant asset turnover $= \dfrac{\$30,000}{.5(\$9,900 + \$10,670)} = 2.9$ times per year

i. Rate of return on common shareholders' equity $= \dfrac{\$3,000 - \$100}{.5(\$8,000 + \$11,000)} = 30.5\%$

j. Profit margin (after interest) $= \dfrac{\$3,000 - \$100}{\$30,000} = 9.7\%$

k. Leverage ratio $= \dfrac{.5(\$20,000 + \$24,000)}{.5(\$8,000 + \$11,000)} = 2.3$

l. Current ratio

December 31, Year 1: $\dfrac{\$10,100}{\$7,000} = 1.4{:}1$

December 31, Year 2: $\dfrac{\$13,330}{\$9,200} = 1.4{:}1$

m. Quick ratio

December 31, Year 1: $\dfrac{\$4,200}{\$7,000} = .6{:}1$

December 31, Year 2: $\dfrac{\$5,050}{\$9,200} = .5{:}1$

n. Cash flow from operations to current liabilities $= \dfrac{\$3,300}{.5(\$7,000 + \$9,200)} = 40.7\%$

o. Working capital turnover $= \dfrac{\$30,000}{.5(\$3,100 + \$4,130)} = 8.3$ times per year

p. Long-term debt ratio

December 31, Year 1: $\dfrac{\$4,000}{\$13,000} = 30.8\%$

$$\text{December 31, Year 2: } \frac{\$2,800}{\$14,800} = 18.9\%$$

q. Debt-equity ratio

$$\text{December 31, Year 1: } \frac{\$11,000}{\$20,000} = 55.0\%$$

$$\text{December 31, Year 2: } \frac{\$12,000}{\$24,000} = 50.0\%$$

r. Cash flow from operations to total liabilities $= \dfrac{\$3,300}{.5(\$11,000 + \$12,000)} = 28.7\%$

s. Times interest charges earned $= \dfrac{\$3,000 + \$2,000 + \$700}{\$700} = 8.1 \text{ times}$

Problem 2 for Self-Study

Exhibit 6.14 presents a ratio analysis for Abbott Corporation for Year 1 to Year 3.
a. What is the likely explanation for the decreasing rate of return on assets?
b. What is the likely explanation for the increasing rate of return on common share-holders' equity?
c. What is the likely explanation for the behaviour of the current and quick ratios?
d. What is the likely explanation for the decreases in the two cash flow from operations to liabilities ratios?

Exhibit 6.14
Ratio Analysis for Abbott Corporation

	Year 3	Year 2	Year 1
Rate of Return on Assets	9.2%	9.6%	10.0%
Profit Margin (before interest and related tax effects)	6.1%	6.1%	6.0%
Total Assets Turnover	1.5	1.6	1.7
Cost of Goods Sold/Revenues	62.6%	62.3%	62.5%
Selling Expenses/Revenues	10.4%	10.2%	10.3%
Interest Expense/Revenues	2.5%	2.0%	1.5%
Accounts Receivable Turnover	4.2	4.3	4.3
Inventory Turnover	3.6	3.4	3.2
Plant Asset Turnover	.6	.7	.8
Rate of Return on Common Shareholders' Equity	14.5%	14.2%	14.0%
Profit Margin (after interest)	4.6%	4.9%	5.1%
Leverage Ratio	2.1	1.8	1.6
Current Ratio	1.2	1.3	1.4
Quick Ratio	1.0	.9	1.0
Cash Flow from Operations to Current Liabilities	36.4%	37.3%	38.2%
Working Capital Turnover	5.2	5.0	4.8
Long-term Debt Ratio	43.3%	33.8%	37.5%
Debt-Equity Ratio	52.4%	44.4%	37.5%
Cash Flow from Operations to Total Liabilities	11.1%	13.4%	16.3%
Times Interest Charges Earned	4.1	5.1	6.7

Suggested Solution

a. Given that the profit margin (before interest expense and related tax effects) is stable over the three years, the decreasing rate of return on assets is attributable to a decreasing total assets turnover. The decreasing total assets turnover is caused primarily by a decreasing plant asset turnover (the accounts receivable turnover is stable while the inventory turnover increased). Explanations for a decreasing plant asset turnover include (1) acceleration of capital expenditures in anticipation of higher sales in the future, and (2) decreasing use of plant capacity so that depreciation expense must be covered by fewer units sold.

b. Given that the rate of return on assets is decreasing, the increasing rate of return on common shareholders' equity must be due to increased financial leverage. The increased financial leverage is evident from the leverage ratio, as well as the percentage of interest expense to sales and the difference between the profit margin measures before and after interest expense.

c. Because the primary difference between the current and quick ratios relates to inventories, the decreasing current ratio coupled with a stable quick ratio must be caused by more efficient inventory management. This explanation is supported by the increasing inventory turnover.

d. Given the stability of the profit margin (before interest expense and related tax effects) and the accounts receivable turnover and given the increased inventory turnover, we must look to the impact of interest expense on operating cash flows for the explanation. The increasing debt load has decreased the profit margin (after interest) and drained greater and greater amounts of cash for interest payments. These drains on operating cash flows coupled with increasing amounts of debt, particularly long-term debt, have driven the cash flow ratios down.

Questions, Exercises, Problems and Cases

Questions

1. Review the meaning of the following concepts or terms discussed in this chapter:

    a. Return and risk
    b. Profitability
    c. Short-term liquidity risk
    d. Long-term liquidity risk
    e. Time-series analysis
    f. Cross-section analysis
    g. Rate of return on assets
    h. Profit margin and expense ratios
    i. Total assets turnover ratio
    j. Accounts receivable turnover ratio
    k. Inventory turnover ratio
    l. Plant asset turnover ratio
    m. Rate of return on common shareholders' equity
    n. Financial leverage
    o. Leverage ratio

    p. Earnings per share

    q. Basic and fully diluted earnings per share

    r. Current ratio

    s. Quick ratio

    t. Cash flow from operations to current liabilities ratio

    u. Working capital turnover ratio

    v. Long-term debt ratio

    w. Debt-equity ratio

    x. Cash flow from operations to total liabilities ratio

    y. Times interest charges earned

2. Describe several factors that might limit the comparability of a firm's financial statement ratios over several periods.

3. Describe several factors that might limit the comparability of one firm's financial statement ratios with those of another firm in the same industry.

4. "I can understand why interest expense is added back to net income in the numerator of the rate of return on assets, but I don't see why an adjustment is made for income taxes." Provide an explanation.

5. One company president stated: "The operations of our company are such that we must turn inventory over once every four weeks." Another company president in a similar industry stated: "The operations of our company are such that we can live comfortably with a turnover of four times each year." Explain what these two company presidents probably had in mind.

6. It has been suggested that for any given firm at a particular time there is an optimal inventory turnover ratio. Explain.

7. Under what circumstances will the rate of return on common shareholders' equity be greater than the rate of return on assets? Under what circumstances will it be less?

8. A company president recently stated: "The operations of our company are such that we can effectively use only a small amount of financial leverage." Explain.

9. Define financial leverage. As long as a firm's rate of return on assets exceeds its aftertax cost of borrowing, why doesn't the firm increase borrowing to as close to 100 percent of financing as possible?

10. Illustrate with amounts how a decrease in working capital can accompany an increase in the current ratio.

Exercises

11. *Calculation and disaggregation of rate of return on assets.* The following data are taken from the most recent annual reports of Manitoba Ltd. and Ontario Inc.

    a. Calculate the rate of return on assets for each company.

    b. Disaggregate the rate of return in part (**a**) into profit margin and total assets turnover components.

    c. Comment on the relative profitability of the two companies.

	Manitoba Ltd.	Ontario Inc.
Revenues	$2,000,000	$2,400,000
Expenses Other than Interest and Income Taxes	1,700,000	2,150,000
Interest Expense	100,000	50,000
Income Tax Expense at 40 percent	80,000	80,000
Net Income	120,000	120,000
Average Total Assets During the Year	1,500,000	1,000,000

12. *Profitability analysis for two types of retailers.* The following information is taken from the annual reports of two companies, one of which is a retailer of quality men's clothes and the other of which is a discount household goods store. Neither company had any interest-bearing debt during the year. Identify which of these companies is likely to be the clothing retailer and which is likely to be the discount store. Explain.

	Company A	Company B
Sales	$3,000,000	$3,000,000
Net Income	60,000	300,000
Average Total Assets	600,000	3,000,000

13. *Analysis of accounts receivable for two companies.* The following information relates to the activities of Quebec Corporation and N.B. Corporation for the current year.

	Quebec Corp.	N.B. Corp.
Sales on Account	$4,050,000	$2,560,000
Accounts Receivable, January 1	960,000	500,000
Accounts Receivable, December 31	840,000	780,000

    a. Compute the accounts receivable turnover of each company.
    b. Compute the average number of days that accounts receivable are outstanding for each company.
    c. Which company is managing its accounts receivable more efficiently?

14. *Analysis of inventories over four years.* The following information relates to the activities of Carlson Corporation.

	Year 4	Year 3	Year 2	Year 1
Sales	$8,000	$5,000	$2,500	$1,000
Cost of Goods Sold	5,120	3,150	1,550	600
Average Inventory	2,050	1,170	550	200

    a. Compute the inventory turnover for each year.
    b. Compute the average number of days that inventories are held for each year.
    c. How well has Carlson Corporation been managing its inventories?

15. *Analysis of plant assets over four years.* The following information relates to Steele Limited.

	Year 4	Year 3	Year 2	Year 1
Sales	$3,000	$1,500	$800	$500
Average Plant Assets	2,630	1,290	670	400
Expenditures on Plant Assets	2,700	1,200	500	250

    a. Compute the plant asset turnover for each year.
    b. How well has Steele Limited been managing its investment in plant assets?

16. *Calculation and disaggregation of rate of return on common shareholders' equity.* The following data are taken from the financial statements of Alta Corporation.

	Year 4	Year 3	Year 2	Year 1
Revenues	$2,750	$2,500	$2,250	$2,000
Net Income	220	200	180	160
Average Total Assets	809	694	592	500
Average Common Shareholders' Equity	1,517	1,333	1,160	1,000

    a. Calculate the rate of return on common shareholders' equity.
    b. Disaggregate the rate of return on common shareholders' equity into profit margin, total assets turnover, and leverage components.
    c. How has the profitability of Alta Corporation changed over the four years?

17. *Profitability analysis for three companies.* The data below show five items from the financial statements for three companies for a recent year in millions of dollars.

	Company A	Company B	Company C
For Year			
Revenues	$3,438	$ 632	$3,137
Income Before Interest and Related Taxes[a]	96	303	107
Net Income to Common Shareholders[b]	77	215	27
Average During Year			
Total Assets	1,041	3,058	1,774
Common Shareholders' Equity	615	946	509

[a]Net Income + Interest Charges × (1 − Tax Rate).
[b]Net Income − Preferred Stock Dividends.

    a. Compute the profit margin (after interest) ratio for each company. Which company seems to be the most successful according to this ratio?
    b. How many dollars of sales on average does each of the companies make for each dollar's worth of average assets held during the year?
    c. Compute the rate of return on assets for each company. Which company seems to be the most successful according to this ratio?
    d. Compute the rate of return on common shareholders' equity for each company. Which company seems to be the most successful according to this ratio?

e. The three companies are Trans Alta Utilities Corporation, Canada Safeway Limited, and Simpsons-Sears Limited. (Dollar amounts shown are actually in thousands.) Which of the companies corresponds to A, B, and C? What clues did you use in reaching your conclusion?

18. *Relation of profitability to financial leverage.*

a. Compute the ratio of return on common shareholders' equity in each of the following independent cases.

Case	Total Assets	Interest-Bearing Debt	Common Share-holders' Equity	Rate of Return on Assets	Aftertax Cost of Interest-Bearing Debt
A	$200	$100	$100	6%	6%
B	$200	$100	$100	8%	6%
C	$200	$120	$ 80	8%	6%
D	$200	$100	$100	4%	6%
E	$200	$ 50	$100	6%	6%
F	$200	$ 50	$100	5%	6%

b. In which cases is leverage working to the advantage of the common shareholders?

19. *Analysis of financial leverage.* The Borrowing Co. Ltd. has total assets of $100,000 during the year. It has borrowed $20,000 at a ten percent annual rate and pays income taxes at a rate of 40 percent of pretax income. Shareholders' equity is $80,000.

a. What must net income be for the rate of return on shareholders' equity to equal the rate of return on assets?
b. What is the rate of return on common shareholders' equity for the net income determined in part (a)?
c. What must income before interest and income taxes be to achieve this net income?
d. Repeat parts (a), (b), and (c), assuming borrowing of $80,000 and common shareholders' equity of $20,000.
e. Compare the results from the two different debt-equity relations. What generalizations can be made?

20. *Ratio analysis of profitability and risk.* Refer to the data below for the Adelsman Co. Inc.

	Year 3	Year 2	Year 1
Rate of Return on Common Shareholders' Equity	11%	10%	8%
Earnings per Share	$4.40	$4.00	$3.00
Net Income/Total Interest Expense[a]	4	5	10
Debt-Equity Ratio (liabilities/all equities)	60%	50%	20%

[a]Note that this computation does not represent "times interest earned" as defined in the chapter.

The income tax rate was 40 percent in each year and 100,000 common shares were outstanding throughout the period.

  a. Did the company's profitability increase over the three-year period? How can you tell? (*Hint:* Compute the rate of return on assets.)
  b. Did risk increase? How can you tell?
  c. Are shareholders better off in Year 3 than in Year 1?

21. *Interpreting changes in earnings per share.* A Inc. and B Ltd. both start Year 1 with $1 million of shareholders' equity and 100,000 common shares outstanding. During Year 1, both companies earn net income of $100,000, a rate of return of ten percent on common shareholders' equity. A Inc. declares and pays $100,000 of dividends to common shareholders at the end of Year 1, whereas B Ltd. retains all its earnings, declaring no dividends. During Year 2, both companies earn net income equal to ten percent of shareholders' equity at the beginning of Year 2.

  a. Compute earnings per share for A Inc. and for B Ltd. for Year 1 and for Year 2.
  b. Compute the rate of growth in earnings per share for A Inc. and B Ltd., comparing earnings per share in Year 2 with earnings per share in Year 1.
  c. Using the rate of growth in earnings per share as the criterion, which company's management appears to be doing a better job for its shareholders? Comment on this result.

22. *Working backwards from profitability ratios to financial statement data.* The revenues of Lev Limited were $1,000 for the year. A financial analyst computed the following ratios for Lev Limited, using the year-end balances for balance sheet amounts. The Lev Limited has no preferred shares outstanding.

Debt-Equity Ratio (all liabilities/all equities)	73⅓ percent
Income Tax Expense as a Percentage of Pretax Income	40 percent
Net Income as a Percentage of Revenue	12 percent
Rate of Return on Common Shareholders' Equity	10 percent
Rate of Return on Assets	6 percent

From this information, compute each of the following items.

  a. Interest expense
  b. Income tax expense
  c. Total expenses
  d. Net income
  e. Total assets
  f. Total liabilities

23. *Effect of financing strategy on earnings per share (CMA adapted).* The Virgil Co. Ltd. is planning to invest $10 million in an expansion program that is expected to increase income before interest and taxes by $2.5 million. Currently, Virgil Co. Ltd. has total equities of $40 million, 25 percent of which is debt and 75 percent of which is shareholders' equity, represented by one million shares. The expansion can be financed with the issuance of 200,000 new shares at $50 each or by issuing long-term debt at an annual interest rate of ten percent. The following is an excerpt from the most recent income statement.

Earnings Before Interest and Taxes	$10,500,000
Less: Interest Charges	500,000
Earnings Before Income Taxes	$10,000,000
Income Taxes (at 40 percent)	4,000,000
Net Income	$ 6,000,000

Assume that Virgil Co. Ltd. maintains its current earnings on its present assets, achieves the planned earnings from the new program, and that the tax rate remains at 40 percent.

a. What will be earnings per share if the expansion is financed with debt?
b. What will be earnings per share if the expansion is financed by issuing new shares?
c. At what level of earnings before interest and taxes will earnings per share be the same, whichever of the two financing programs is used?
d. At what level of earnings before interest and taxes will the rate of return on shareholders' equity be the same, whichever of the two financing plans is used?

24. *Relation between book and market rates of return.* Net income attributable to common shareholders' equity of Quebec Corporation during the current year was $250,000. Earnings per share were $.50 during the period. The average common shareholders' equity during the year was $2,500,000. The market price at year-end was $6.00.

a. Calculate the rate of return on common shareholders' equity for the year.
b. Calculate the rate of return currently being earned on the market price of the shares (the ratio of earnings per common share to market price per common share).
c. Why is there a difference between the rates of return calculated in parts (a) and (b)?

25. *Calculation and interpretation of short-term liquidity ratios.* The following data are taken from the financial statements of Maloney Corporation.

For the Year	Year 4	Year 3	Year 2	
Revenues	$281	$270	$245	
Cash Flow from Operations	137	105	79	

On December 31	Year 4	Year 3	Year 2	Year 1
Quick Assets	$350	$330	$225	$200
Current Assets	455	420	375	320
Current Liabilities	350	300	250	200

a. Compute the current and quick ratios as of December 31 of each of the Years 1 through 4.

b. Compute the cash flow from operations to current liabilities ratio and the working capital turnover ratio for each of the Years 2 through 4.

c. How has the short-term liquidity risk of Maloney Corporation changed over the three-year period?

26. *Calculating changes in current ratio and working capital.* Merchandise inventory costing $30,000 is purchased on account. Indicate the effect (increase, decrease, no effect) of this transaction on (1) working capital and (2) the current ratio, assuming that current assets and current liabilities immediately prior to the transaction were as follows:

a. Current assets, $120,000; current liabilities, $120,000.

b. Current assets, $120,000; current liabilities, $150,000.

c. Current assets, $120,000; current liabilities, $80,000.

27. *Relation of profitability to short-term liquidity.* Following is a schedule of the current assets and current liabilities of the Lewis Company, Ltd.

	December 31	
	Year 2	**Year 1**
Current Assets:		
Cash	$ 355,890	$ 212,790
Accounts Receivable	389,210	646,010
Inventories	799,100	1,118,200
Prepayments	21,600	30,000
Total Current Assets	$1,565,800	$2,007,000
Current Liabilities:		
Accounts Payable	$ 152,760	$ 217,240
Accrued Payroll, Taxes, etc.	126,340	318,760
Notes Payable	69,500	330,000
Total Current Liabilities	$ 348,600	$ 866,000

During Year 2, the Lewis Company Ltd. operated at a loss of $100,000. Depreciation expense during Year 2 was $30,000.

a. Calculate the current ratio for each date.

b. Calculate the amount of cash provided by operations for Year 2.

c. Explain how the improved current ratio is possible under the Year 2 operating conditions.

28. *Calculation and interpretation of long-term liquidity ratios.* The following data are taken from the financial statements of Saskatchewan Corporation.

For the Year	Year 4	Year 3	Year 2
Net Income Before Interest and Income Taxes	$360	$325	$200
Cash Flow from Operations	184	155	115
Interest Expense	60	50	40

On December 31	Year 4	Year 3	Year 2	Year 1
Current Liabilities	$ 362	$ 304	$ 250	200
Total Liabilities	1,018	822	650	500
Total Assets	1,818	1,522	1,250	1,000

   a. Compute the long-term debt ratio and the debt-equity ratio at the end of each
      of the Years 1 through 4.
   b. Compute the cash flow from operations to total liabilities ratio and the times
      interest charges earned ratio for each of the Years 2 through 4.
   c. How has the long-term liquidity risk of Sask. Corporation changed over this
      three-year period?

29. *Effect of various transactions on financial statement ratios.* Indicate the immediate effects (increase, decrease, no effect) of each of the independent transactions
below on (1) rate of return on common shareholders' equity, (2) current ratio, and
(3) debt-equity ratio. State any necessary assumptions.
   a. Merchandise inventory costing $205,000 is purchased on account.
   b. Merchandise inventory costing $120,000 is sold on account for $150,000.
   c. Collections from customers on accounts receivable total $100,000.
   d. Payments to suppliers on accounts payable total $160,000.
   e. A machine costing $40,000, on which $30,000 of depreciation had been taken,
      is sold for $10,000.
   f. Dividends of $80,000 are declared. The dividends will be paid during the
      next accounting period.
   g. Common shares are issued for $75,000.
   h. A machine costing $60,000 is acquired. Cash of $10,000 is given and a note
      for $50,000 payable five years from now is signed for the balance of the
      purchase price.

30. *Effect of various transactions on financial statement ratios.* Indicate the effects
(increase, decrease, no effect) of the independent transactions below on (1) earnings
per share, (2) working capital, and (3) quick ratio, where accounts receivable are
included but merchandise inventory is *excluded* from "quick assets." State any necessary assumptions.
   a. Merchandise inventory costing $240,000 is sold on account for $300,000.
   b. Dividends of $160,000 are declared. The dividends will be paid during the
      next accounting period.
   c. Merchandise inventory costing $410,000 is purchased on account.
   d. A machine costing $80,000, on which $60,000 depreciation had been taken,
      is sold for $20,000.
   e. Merchandise inventory purchased for cash in the amount of $7,000 is returned
      to the supplier because it is defective. A cash reimbursement is received.
   f. 10,000 no par value common shares were issued on the last day of the account-
      ing period for $15 per share. The proceeds were used to acquire the assets of
      another firm composed of the following: accounts receivable, $30,000; mer-
      chandise inventory, $60,000; plant and equipment, $100,000. The acquiring
      firm also agreed to assume current liabilities of $40,000 of the acquired
      company.

31. *Profitability analysis for three companies.* The following data show five items from the financial statements of three companies for a recent year.

	Company A	Company B	Company C
For Year			
Revenues	$28,947,200	$13,639,900	$9,716,900
Income before Interest and Related Taxes[a]	4,295,800	824,600	156,400
Net Income to Common Shareholders[b]	2,915,800	522,600	148,600
Average during Year			
Total Assets	77,107,200	10,885,000	1,532,400
Common Shareholders' Equity	29,769,200	5,118,800	743,830

[a]Net Income + Interest Expense × (1 − Tax Rate).
[b]Net Income − Preferred Stock Dividends.

a. Compute the profit margin ratio (after interest) for each company. Which company seems to be the most successful according to this ratio?
b. On average, how many dollars of sales does each of the companies earn for each dollar's worth of assets held during the year?
c. Compute the rate of return on assets for each company. Which company seems to be the most successful according to this ratio?
d. Compute the rate of return on common shareholders' equity for each company. Which company seems to be the most successful according to this ratio?
e. The three companies are American Telephone & Telegraph, Safeway Stores, and Sears, Roebuck and Company. (Dollar amounts shown are actually in thousands.) Which of the companies corresponds to A, B, and C? What clues did you use in reaching your conclusion?

Problems and Cases

32. *Calculation of profitability and risk ratios.* The following data are taken from the financial statements of the Press Co. Inc.:

	December	January
Current Assets	$210,000	$180,000
Noncurrent Assets	275,000	255,000
Current Liabilities	78,000	85,000
Long-Term Liabilities	75,000	30,000
Common Stock (10,000 shares)	300,000	300,000
Retained Earnings	32,000	20,000

	Operations
Net Income	$72,000
Interest Expense	3,000
Income Taxes (40 percent rate)	48,000
Cash Provided by Operations	30,970
Dividends Declared	60,000

Calculate the following ratios:

    a. Rate of return on assets.
    b. Rate of return on common shareholders' equity.
    c. Earnings per common share.
    d. Current ratio (both months).
    e. Cash flow from operations to current liabilities.
    f. Debt-equity ratio (both months).
    g. Cash flow from operations to total liabilities.
    h. Times interest charges earned.

33. *Calculation of profitability and risk ratios.* The comparative balance sheets, income statement, and statement of changes in financial position of Solo Corporation for the current year are shown in Exhibits 6.15, 6.16, and 6.17.

    a. Calculate the ratios listed in Exhibit 6.11 in the chapter for Solo Corporation for the current year. You may omit expense ratios. Balance sheet ratios are to be computed at the end of the year.
    b. Was Solo Corporation successfully leveraged during the current year?
    c. Assume that the bonds were issued on November 1. At what annual interest rate were the bonds apparently issued?
    d. If Solo Corporation earns the same rate of return on assets next year as it realized this year, and issues no more debt, will the firm be successfully leveraged next year?

Exhibit 6.15
SOLO CORPORATION
Comparative Balance Sheets
(Problem 33)

	December 31	January 1
Assets		
Current Assets:		
Cash	$ 3,000	$ 30,000
Accounts Receivable	55,000	20,000
Merchandise Inventory	50,000	40,000
Total Current Assets	$108,000	$ 90,000

Noncurrent Assets:

Buildings and Equipment (cost)	$225,000	$100,000
Accumulated Depreciation	(40,000)	(30,000)
Total Noncurrent Assets	$185,000	$ 70,000
Total Assets	$293,000	$160,000

Liabilities and Shareholders' Equity
Current Liabilities:

Accounts Payable — Merchandise Suppliers	$ 50,000	$ 30,000
Accounts Payable — Other Suppliers	12,000	10,000
Salaries Payable	6,000	5,000
Total Current Liabilities	$ 68,000	$ 45,000

Noncurrent Liabilities:

Bonds Payable	100,000	0
Total Liabilities	$168,000	$ 45,000

Shareholders' Equity:

Common Stock ($10 par value)	$100,000	$100,000
Retained Earnings	25,000	15,000
Total Shareholders' Equity	$125,000	$115,000
Total Liabilities plus Shareholders' Equity	$293,000	$160,000

Exhibit 6.16
SOLO CORPORATION
Income Statement for the Current Year
(Problem 33)

Sales		$125,000
Less: Cost of Goods Sold		60,000
Gross Profit		$ 65,000
Less: Operating Expenses		
Salaries	$19,667	
Depreciation	10,000	29,667
Operating Profit		$ 35,333
Less: Interest Expense		2,000
Net Income before Income Tax		$ 33,333
Income Tax Expense		13,333
Net Income		$ 20,000

Exhibit 6.17
SOLO CORPORATION
Statement of Changes in Financial Position
for the Current Year
(Problem 33)

Sources of Cash

Net Income	$20,000
Additions:	
Depreciation Expense	10,000

Increase in Accounts Payable:	
Merchandise Suppliers	20,000
Other Suppliers	2,000
Increase in Salaries Payable	1,000
Subtractions:	
Increase in Accounts Receivable	(35,000)
Increase in Merchandise Inventory	(10,000)
Cash Provided by Operations	$ 8,000
Proceeds from Long-Term Bonds Issued	100,000
Total Sources of Cash	$108,000
Uses of Cash	
Dividends	$ 10,000
Acquisition of Buildings and Equipment	125,000
Total Uses of Cash	$135,000
Net Decrease in Cash during the Year	
(Sources minus Uses)	$ 27,000

34. *Calculation of profitability and risk ratios.* Comparative balance sheets, income statement, and statement of changes in financial position of Nykerk Electronics Corporation for the current year are presented in Exhibits 6.18, 6.19, and 6.20, respectively.

    a. Calculate the ratios listed in Exhibit 6.11 in the chapter for Nykerk Electronics Corporation for the current year. You may omit expense ratios. Balance sheet ratios are to be computed at the end of the year.

    b. Was Nykerk Electronics Corporation successfully leveraged during the year?

Exhibit 6.18
NYKERK ELECTRONICS CORPORATION
Comparative Balance Sheets
(Problem 34)

	(In 000's of dollars)	
	December 31	January 1
Assets		
Current Assets:		
Cash	$ 1,600	$ 1,400
Accounts Receivable (net)	2,600	2,500
Inventories	7,300	6,900
Total Current Assets	$11,500	$10,800
Noncurrent Assets:		
Plant and Equipment	$ 5,200	$ 4,500
Less: Accumulated Depreciation	1,300	1,000
Net Plant and Equipment	$ 3,900	$ 3,500
Land	1,200	1,200
Total Noncurrent Assets	$ 5,100	$ 4,700
Total Assets	$16,600	$15,500

Liabilities and Shareholders' Equity
Current Liabilities:

Accounts Payable	$ 1,600	$ 1,700
Accrued Payables	800	900
Income Taxes Payable	300	200
Notes Payable	1,900	1,200
Total Current Liabilities	$ 4,600	$ 4,000

Long-Term Liabilities:

Bonds Payable (8 percent)	$ 2,000	$ 2,100
Mortgage Payable	200	200
Total Long-Term Liabilities	$ 2,200	$ 2,300
Total Liabilities	$ 6,800	$ 6,300

Shareholders' Equity:

Preferred Stock (6 percent, $100 par)	$ 2,000	$ 2,000
Common Stock ($1 par)	3,000	3,000
Total Contributed Capital	$ 5,000	$ 5,000
Retained Earnings	4,800	4,200
Total Shareholders' Equity	$ 9,800	$ 9,200
Total Liabilities and Shareholders' Equity	$16,600	$15,500

Exhibit 6.19
NYKERK ELECTRONICS CORPORATION
Statement of Income and Retained Earnings
for the Current Year
(Problem 34)

	(in 000's of dollars)
Sales	$26,500
Less: Sales Allowance, Returns, and Discounts	600
Net Sales	$25,900
Less: Cost of Goods Sold	20,500
Gross Profit	$ 5,400

Less: Operating Expenses		
Selling Expenses	$2,120	
Administrative Expenses	1,000	
Depreciation	300	3,420
Operating Profit		$ 1,980

Financial Income:		
Interest Income	$ 200	
Less: Interest Expense	180	20
Net Income before Income Tax		$ 2,000

Income Tax Expense	800
Net Income	$ 1,200
Retained Earnings, January 1	4,200
	$ 5,400

Less: Dividends Paid		
On Preferred Shares	$ 120	
On Common Shares	480	600
Retained Earnings, December 31		$ 4,800

Exhibit 6.20
NYKERK ELECTRONICS CORPORATION
Statement of Changes in Financial Position
for the Current Year
(Problem 34)

	(in 000's of dollars)
Cash Provided by	
Operations:	
Net Income	$1,200
Additions:	
Depreciation Expense	300
Increase in Income Taxes Payable	100
Subtractions:	
Increase in Accounts Receivable	(100)
Increase in Inventories	(400)
Decrease in Accounts Payable	(100)
Decrease in Accrued Payables	(100)
Cash Provided by Operations	$ 900
New Financing by Bank Note	700
Total Sources of Cash	$1,600
Cash Applied to	
Dividend on Preferred Shares	$ 120
Dividend on Common Shares	480
Purchase of Plant and Equipment	700
Redemption of Bonds Payable	100
Total Uses of Cash	$1,400
Increase in Cash for the Year	$ 200

35. *Calculation of profitability and risk ratios.* Refer to the financial statements for General Products Limited in Appendix A on p. 760.

   a. Calculate the rate of return on assets for 1988. Assume an income tax rate of 46 percent in computing the tax effect of interest expense. In computing income before distributions to providers of capital, add to net income the $21 million shown as the minority interest in earnings of consolidated affiliates. Chapter 13 explains minority interest.

b. Disaggregate the rate of return on assets for 1988 into profit margin (before interest) and asset turnover components. Note that "Other Income" should be included in revenues.

c. Calculate the accounts receivable turnover, inventory turnover, and plant asset turnover ratios for 1988. The numerator of the accounts receivable and plant asset turnover should include sales revenue but exclude "Other Income."

d. Calculate the rate of return on common shareholders' equity for 1988.

e. Disaggregate the rate of return on common shareholders' equity for 1988 into profit margin (after interest), asset turnover, and leverage components.

f. Calculate the current and quick ratios as of December 31, 1987 and 1988, and the cash flow to current liabilities and working capital turnover ratios for 1988. Include "Other Income" in the numerator of the working capital turnover ratio.

g. Calculate the long-term debt and debt equity ratios as of December 31, 1987 and 1988, and the cash flow from operations to total liabilities and times interest charges earned ratios for 1988. Include "Other (noncurrent) Liabilities" in long-term debt. Include "Minority Interest in Equity of Consolidated Affiliates" in the denominator of the long-term debt ratio. Include "Minority Interest in Earnings of Consolidated Affiliates" in the numerator of the times interest charges earned ratio.

36. *Analysis of profitability and risk for two companies.* Exhibits 6.21 and 6.22 present the income statements and balance sheets of Toronto Corporation and Regina Corporation.

Cash flow provided by operations was $600,000 for Toronto Corporation and $550,000 for Regina Corporation.

Exhibit 6.21
Income Statements for the Current Year
(Problem 36)

	Toronto Corp.	Regina Corp.
Sales	$4,300,000	$3,000,000
Less: Cost of Goods Sold	2,800,000	1,400,000
Gross Profit	$1,500,000	$1,600,000
Less: Selling and Administrative Expenses	330,000	580,000
Operating Profit	$1,170,000	$1,020,000
Interest Expense	100,000	200,000
Net Income before Income Tax	$1,070,000	$ 820,000
Income Tax Expense	428,000	328,000
Net Income	$ 642,000	$ 492,000

Exhibit 6.22
Balance Sheets December 31
(Problem 36)

	Toronto Corp.	Regina Corp.
Assets		
Cash	$ 100,000	$ 50,000
Accounts Receivable (net)	700,000	400,000
Merchandise Inventory	1,200,000	750,000
Plant and Equipment (net)	4,000,000	4,800,000
Total Assets	$6,000,000	$6,000,000
Liabilities and Shareholders' Equity		
Accounts Payable	$ 572,000	$ 172,000
Income Taxes Payable	428,000	328,000
Long-Term Bonds Payable (10 percent)	1,000,000	2,000,000
Common Stock	2,000,000	2,000,000
Retained Earnings	2,000,000	1,500,000
Total Liabilities and Shareholders' Equity	$6,000,000	$6,000,000

Assume that the balances in asset and equity accounts at year-end approximate the average balances during the period. The income tax rate is 40 percent. On the basis of this information, which company is:

   a. More profitable?
   b. Less risky in terms of short-term liquidity?
   c. Less risky in terms of long-term liquidity?

Use financial ratios, as appropriate, in your analysis.

37. *Detective analysis: identify company.* In this problem, you become a financial analyst/detective. The condensed financial statements in Exhibit 6.23 are constructed on a percentage basis. In all cases, total sales revenues are shown as 100.00%. All other numbers were divided by sales revenue for the year. The 13 companies (all corporations except for the accounting firm) shown here represent the following industries:

   a. Advertising and public opinion survey firm
   b. Beer brewery
   c. Department store chain (that carries its own receivables)
   d. Distiller of hard liquor
   e. Drug manufacturer
   f. Finance company (lends money to consumers)
   g. Grocery store chain
   h. Insurance company
   i. Manufacturer of tobacco products, mainly cigarettes
   j. Public accounting (CA) partnership
   k. Soft drink bottler
   l. Steel manufacturer
   m. Utility company.

Exhibit 6.23
Data for Ratio Detective Exercise
(Problem 37)

	Company Numbers						
	(1)	(2)	(3)	(4)	(5)	(6)	(7)
Balance Sheet at End of Year							
Current Receivables	0.31%	29.11%	6.81%	25.25%	3.45%	38.78%	17.64%
Inventories	7.80	0.00	3.14	0.00	6.45	14.94	20.57
Net Plant and Equipment*	8.50	9.63	11.13	19.88	49.87	15.59	37.60
All Other Assets	2.16	7.02	25.59	32.93	24.05	15.54	30.07
Total Assets	18.77%	45.76%	46.67%	78.06%	83.82%	84.85%	105.88%
*Cost of Plant and Equipment (gross)	14.64%	14.80%	19.57%	29.03%	79.03%	24.80%	59.73%
Current Liabilities	6.08%	9.82%	6.41%	17.49%	14.83%	35.28%	27.68%
Long-Term Liabilities	2.12	7.96	0.00	0.00	0.00	8.33	1.33
Owners' Equity	10.58	27.98	40.25	60.57	69.00	41.24	76.86
Total Equities	18.78%	45.76%	46.66%	78.06%	83.83%	84.85%	105.87%
Income Statement for Year							
Revenues	100.00%	100.00%	100.00%	100.00%	100.00%	100.00%	100.00%
Cost of Goods Sold (excluding depreciation) or Operating Expenses[a]	78.97	53.77	48.21	59.07	68.62	60.88	33.29
Depreciation	1.04	1.39	1.72	2.07	4.07	1.09	3.02
Interest Expense	0.16	0.52	0.00	0.08	0.02	1.35	0.73
Advertising Expense	3.72	0.00	11.43	0.06	4.39	2.93	2.28
Research and Development Expense	0.00	1.00	0.00	0.00	0.15	0.00	9.06
Income Taxes	1.28	0.53	9.59	6.52	7.87	3.78	8.55
All Other Items (net)	13.34	18.88	‡8.58	24.52	6.40	24.39	27.66
Total Expenses	98.51%	76.09%	89.53%	92.32%	91.52%	94.42%	84.59%
Net Income	1.50%	23.92%	10.47%	7.68%	8.49%	5.59%	15.41%

	Company Numbers					
	(8)	(9)	(10)	(11)	(12)	(13)
Balance Sheet at End of Year						
Current Receivables	12.94%	9.16%	25.18%	27.07%	13.10%	653.94%
Inventories	15.47	56.89	79.53	0.00	1.62	0.00
Net Plant and Equipment*	70.29	28.36	19.22	2.64	251.62	2.88
All Other Assets	18.37	26.42	24.72	223.91	23.68	200.37
Total Assets	117.07%	120.83%	148.65%	253.62%	290.02%	857.19%
*Cost of Plant and Equipment (gross)	167.16%	42.40%	35.08%	4.45%	320.90%	3.81%
Current Liabilities	19.37%	33.01%	20.42%	161.37%	28.01%	377.56%
Long-Term Liabilities	20.62	34.07	36.09	10.62	115.50	280.79
Owners' Equity	77.09	53.74	92.13	81.63	146.51	198.83
Total Equities	117.08%	120.82%	148.64%	253.62%	290.02%	857.18%

	Company Numbers					
	(8)	(9)	(10)	(11)	(12)	(13)
Income Statement for Year						
Revenues	100.00%	100.00%	100.00%	100.00%	100.00%	100.00%
Cost of Goods Sold (excluding depreciation) or Operating Expenses[a]	81.92	57.35	42.92	82.61	45.23	47.69
Depreciation	5.81	1.90	1.97	0.05	14.55	0.00
Interest Expense	1.23	2.69	3.11	1.07	7.15	24.33
Advertising Expense	0.00	6.93	13.04	0.00	0.00	0.00
Research and Development Expense	0.76	0.00	0.00	0.00	0.71	0.00
Income Taxes	2.15	7.47	10.63	3.92	8.73	12.89
All Other Items (net)	3.81	14.82	17.99	2.97	11.51	−5.57
Total Expenses	95.68%	91.16%	89.66%	90.62%	87.88%	79.34%
Net Income	4.32%	8.84%	10.34%	9.38%	12.11%	20.65%

[a]Represents operating expenses for the following companies: Advertising/public opinion survey firm, insurance company, finance company, and the public accounting partnership.

Use whatever clues you can to match the companies in Exhibit 6.23 with the industries listed above. You may find it useful to refer to average industry ratios compiled by Dun & Bradstreet. Copies of this document can be found in most libraries.

38. *Interpretation of ratio analysis.* Exhibit 6.24 presents a ratio analysis for Sarwark Limited.

   a. What is the likely explanation for the stable rate of return on assets coupled with the decreasing rate of return on common shareholders' equity?
   b. What is the likely reason for the increasing plant asset turnover?

Exhibit 6.24
Ratio Analysis for Sarwark Limited
(Problem 38)

	Year 3	Year 2	Year 1
Rate of Return on Assets	9.9%	10.2%	10.1%
Profit Margin (before interest and related tax effects)	9.6%	10.0%	11.9%
Total Assets Turnover	1.03	1.02	0.85
Cost of Goods Sold/Revenues	73.8%	73.9%	72.4%
Selling and Administrative/Revenues	10.5%	10.4%	10.5%
Interest Expense/Revenues	4.0%	3.5%	2.1%
Income Tax Expense/Revenues	3.8%	4.1%	4.2%
Accounts Receivable Turnover	4.6	4.7	4.6
Inventory Turnover	3.7	3.6	3.7
Plant Asset Turnover	1.7	1.5	1.2
Rate of Return on Common Shareholders' Equity	14.7%	15.2%	15.5%

	Year 3	Year 2	Year 1
Current Ratio	1.2:1	1.4:1	1.6:1
Quick Ratio	.5:1	.7:1	.9:1
Total Liabilities/Total Liabilities and Shareholders' Equity	60.0%	48.0%	42.0%
Long-Term Liabilities/Total Liabilities and Shareholders' Equity	25.0%	26.0%	25.0%
Revenues as Percentage of Year 1 Revenues	130%	115%	100%
Assets as Percentage of Year 1 Assets	125%	113%	100%
Capital Expenditures as Percentage of Year 1 Capital Expenditures	120%	112%	100%

39. *Interpretation of ratio analysis.* Exhibit 6.25 presents a ratio analysis for Widdicombe Corporation for Year 1 through Year 3.

   a. What is the likely explanation for the increasing rate of return on assets coupled with the decreasing rate of return on shareholders' equity?
   b. How effectively has the firm been managing its inventories?
   c. What is the likely explanation for the increasing total assets turnover?

Exhibit 6.25
Ratio Analysis for Widdicombe Corporation
(Problem 39)

	Year 3	Year 2	Year 1
Rate of Return on Assets	12%	11%	10%
Profit Margin (before interest and related taxes)	14%	16%	18%
Total Asset Turnover	.86	.69	.56
Cost of Goods Sold/Revenues	65%	63%	62%
Selling and Administrative/Revenues	10%	10%	8%
Interest Expense/Revenues	8%	12%	16%
Income Tax Expense/Revenues	7%	5%	4%
Accounts Receivable Turnover	2.4	2.5	2.6
Inventory Turnover	2.5	2.8	3.2
Fixed Asset Turnover	.7	.5	.3
Rate of Return on Common Shareholders' Equity	14%	16%	18%
Profit Margin (after interest)	10%	10%	10%
Asset Turnover	.86	.69	.56
Leverage Ratio	1.6	2.3	3.2
Revenues as Percentage of Year 1 Revenues	99%	102%	100%
Assets as Percentage of Year 1 Assets	105%	104%	100%
Net Income as Percentage of Year 1 Net Income	99%	102%	100%
Capital Expenditures as Percentage of Year 1 Capital Expenditures	85%	90%	100%

40. *Case analysis of bankruptcy.* On October 2, 1975, W.T. Grant Company filed for bankruptcy. At that time, it reported assets of $1.02 billion and liabilities of $1.03 billion. The company had operated at a profit for most years prior to 1974, but it reported an operating loss of $177 million for its fiscal year January 31, 1974, to January 31, 1975.

The accompanying Exhibits 6.26 through 6.29 contain:

1. Balance sheets, income statements, and statements of cash flows for W.T. Grant Company for the 1971 through 1975 fiscal periods.
2. Additional financial information about W.T. Grant Company, the retail industry, and the economy for the same period.

Prepare an analysis that explains the major causes of Grant's collapse. Assume an income tax rate of 48 percent.

Exhibit 6.26
W.T. GRANT COMPANY
Comparative Balance Sheet
(Problem 40)

	January 31				
	1971	1972	1973	1974	1975
Assets					
Cash and Marketable Securities	$ 34,009	$ 49,851	$ 30,943	$ 45,951	$ 79,642
Accounts Receivable	419,731	477,324	542,751	598,799	431,201
Inventories	260,492	298,676	399,533	450,637	407,357
Other Current Assets	5,246	5,378	6,649	7,299	6,581
Total Current Assets	$719,478	$831,229	$ 979,876	$1,102,686	$ 924,781
Investments	23,936	32,367	35,581	45,451	49,764
Property, Plant, and Equipment					
(net)	61,832	77,173	91,420	100,984	101,932
Other Assets	2,382	3,901	3,821	3,862	5,790
Total Assets	$807,628	$944,670	$1,110,698	$1,252,983	$1,082,267
Equities					
Short-Term Debt	$246,420	$237,741	$ 390,034	$ 453,097	600,695
Accounts Payable	118,091	124,990	112,896	103,910	147,211
Current Deferred Taxes	94,489	112,846	130,137	133,057	2,000
Total Current Liabilities	$459,000	$475,577	$ 633,067	$ 690,064	$ 749,906
Long-Term Debt	32,301	128,432	126,672	220,336	216,341
Noncurrent Deferred Taxes	8,518	9,664	11,926	14,649	—
Other Long-Term Liabilities	5,773	5,252	4,694	4,195	2,183
Total Liabilities	$505,592	$618,925	$ 776,359	$ 929,244	$ 968,430
Preferred Stock	$ 9,600	$ 9,053	$ 8,600	$ 7,465	$ 7,465
Common Stock	18,180	18,529	18,588	18,599	18,599
Additional Paid-in Capital	78,116	85,195	86,146	85,910	83,914
Retained Earnings	230,435	244,508	261,154	248,461	37,674
Total	$336,331	$357,285	374,488	$ 360,435	$ 147,652
Less Cost of Treasury Stock	(34,295)	(31,540)	(40,149)	(36,696)	(33,815)
Total Shareholders' Equity	$302,036	$325,745	$ 334,339	$ 323,739	$ 113,837
Total Equities	$807,628	$944,670	$1,110,698	$1,252,983	$1,082,267

Exhibit 6.27
W.T. GRANT COMPANY
Statement of Income and Retained Earnings

	Years Ended January 31				
	1971	1972	1973	1974	1975
Sales	$1,254,131	$1,374,811	$1,644,747	$1,849,802	$1,761,952
Concessions	4,986	3,439	3,753	3,971	4,238
Equity in Earnings	2,777	2,383	5,116	4,651	3,086
Other Income	2,874	3,102	1,188	3,063	3,376
Total Revenues	$1,264,768	$1,383,735	$1,654,804	$1,861,487	$1,772,652
Cost of Goods Sold	$ 843,192	$ 931,237	$1,125,261	$1,282,945	$1,303,267
Selling, General, and					
Administration	329,768	373,816	444,377	518,280	540,953
Interest	18,874	16,452	21,127	51,047	199,238
Taxes: Current	21,140	13,487	9,588	(6,021)	(19,439)
Deferred	11,660	13,013	16,162	6,807	(98,027)
Other Expenses	557	518	502	—	24,000
Total Expenses	$1,225,191	$1,348,523	$1,617,017	$1,853,058	$1,949,992
Net Income	$ 39,577	$ 35,212	$ 37,787	$ 8,429	$ (177,340)
Dividends	(20,821)	(21,139)	(21,141)	(21,122)	(4,457)
Other	—	—	—	—	(28,990)
Change in Retained Earnings	$ 18,756	$ 14,073	$ 16,646	$ (12,693)	$ (210,787)
Retained Earnings—					
Beg. of Period	211,679	230,435	244,508	261,154	248,461
Retained Earnings—					
End of Period	$ 230,435	$ 244,508	$ 261,154	$ 248,461	$ 37,674

Exhibit 6.28
W.T. GRANT COMPANY
Statement of Changes in Financial Position

	Years Ended January 31				
	1971	1972	1973	1974	1975
Cash Provided by					
New Financing:					
Short-Term Bank Borrowing	$ 64,288	—	$152,293	$ 63,063	$147,898
Issue of Long-Term Debt	—	$100,000	—	100,000	—
Sale of Common Stock:					
to Employees	5,218	7,715	3,492	2,584	886
On Open Market	—	2,229	174	260	—
Other Sources (net)	—	—	2,307	—	—
Total Sources of Cash	$ 69,506	$109,944	$158,266	$165,907	$148,784
Cash Applied to					
Net Income	$ 39,577	$ 35,212	$ 37,787	$ 8,429	$(177,340)
Additions:					
Depreciation and Other	9,619	10,577	12,004	13,579	14,587
Decrease in Accounts Receivable	—	—	—	—	121,351
Decrease in Inventories	—	—	—	—	43,280
Increase in Accounts Payable	13,947	6,900	—	—	42,028
Increase in Deferred Taxes	14,046	18,357	17,291	2,920	—

Subtractions:					
Equity in Earnings and Other	(2,470)	(1,758)	(1,699)	(1,344)	(16,993)
Increase in Accounts Receivable	(51,464)	(57,593)	(65,427)	(56,047)	—
Increase in Inventories	(38,365)	(38,184)	(100,857)	(51,104)	—
Increase in Prepayments	(209)	(428)	(1,271)	(651)	(11,032)
Decrease in Accounts Payable	—	—	(12,093)	(8,987)	—
Decrease in Deferred Taxes	—	—	—	—	(101,078)
Cash Used by Operations	$ 15,319	$ 26,917	$114,265	$ 93,205	$ 85,197
Reduction in Financing:					
Repayment of Short-Term Borrowing					
(net)	—	$ 8,680	—	—	—
Retirement of Long-Term Debt	$ 1,538	5,143	$ 1,760	$ 6,336	$ 3,995
Reacquisition of Preferred Stock	948	308	252	618	—
Reacquisition of Common Stock	13,224	—	11,466	133	—
Dividends	20,821	21,138	21,141	21,122	4,457
Total for Reductions in Financing	$ 36,531	$ 35,269	$ 34,619	$ 28,209	$ 8,452
Investments in Noncurrent Assets:					
Property, Plant, and Equipment	$ 16,141	$ 25,918	$ 26,250	$ 23,143	$ 15,535
Investments in Securities	436	5,951	2,040	5,700	5,182
Total for Investments	$ 16,577	$ 31,869	$ 28,290	$ 28,843	$ 20,717
Other Uses (net)	$ 47	$ 47	—	$ 642	$ 727
Total Uses of Cash	$ 68,474	$ 94,102	$177,174	$150,899	$115,093
Increase (decrease) in Cash	$ 11,032	$ 15,842	$(18,908)	$ 15,008	$ 33,691

Exhibit 6.29
Additional Information

	Fiscal Years Ending January 31				
	1971	1972	1973	1974	1975
W.T. Grant Company					
Range of Stock Price, Dollar per Share[a]	$41\frac{7}{8}$–$70\frac{5}{8}$	$34\frac{3}{4}$–$48\frac{3}{4}$	$9\frac{7}{8}$–$44\frac{3}{8}$	$9\frac{5}{8}$–41	$1\frac{1}{2}$–12
Earnings per Share in Dollars	$2.64	$2.25	$2.49	$0.76	$(12.74)
Dividends per Share in Dollars	$1.50	$1.50	$1.50	$1.50	$ 0.30
Number of Stores	1,116	1,168	1,208	1,189	1,152
Total Store Area, Thousands of Square Feet	38,157	44,718	50,619	53,719	54,770
	1970	1971	1972	1973	1974
Retail Industry[b]					
Total Chain Store Industry Sales in Millions					
of Dollars	$6,969	$6,972	$7,498	$8,212	$8,714
	1970	1971	1972	1973	1974
Aggregate Economy[c]					
Gross National Product in Billions of Dollars	$1,075.3	$1,107.5	$1,171.1	$1,233.4	$1,210
Bank short-Term lending Rate	8.48%	6.32%	5.82%	8.30%	11.28%

[a]Source: *Standard and Poor's Stock Reports.*
[b]Source: *Standard Industry Surveys.*
[c]Source: *Survey of Current Business.*

Decision Problem 6-1

In February Year 6, the president of Alba Ltd. is preparing for a meeting of the finance committee of the board of directors to discuss the financial plans of the company for the coming year. He wants to continue to expand the company's activities, but will need more funds provided for the purpose from outside the company. He has asked you to play the role of representative of the financial community to evaluate the attached financial statements of the company for the four preceding years. He would like you, in turn, to represent the views of a bank credit officer considering an expansion of the loan to the company, an investment manager of an insurance company considering a purchase of the company's bonds, and a stock broker advising his clients who are present or potential shareholders of the company.

ALBA LTD.
Comparative Balance Sheets
December 31, Year 2 to Year 5

| | (thousands of dollars) | | | |
	Year 5	Year 4	Year 3	Year 2
Assets				
Current Assets:				
Cash	$ 48	$ 29	$ 21	$ 212
Accounts Receivable	882	709	601	541
Inventories	2,903	1,183	789	578
Total Current Assets	$3,833	$1,921	$1,411	$1,331
Plant and Equipment:	$4,917	$3,884	$2,853	$2,491
Less: Accumulated Depreciation	1,915	1,643	1,472	1,499
Net Plant & Equipment	$3,002	$2,241	$1,381	$ 992
Total	$6,835	$4,162	$2,792	$2,323
Liabilities and Shareholders' Equity				
Current Liabilities:				
Bank Loan	$1,609	$ 518	$ 386	$ 238
Trade Accounts Payable	974	471	272	184
Other Liabilities	146	79	39	17
Total Current Liabilities	$2,729	$1,068	$ 697	$ 439
Long-Term Debt	2,542	1,558	702	526
Total Liabilities	$5,271	$2,626	$1,399	$ 965
Shareholders' Equity:				
Common Share Capital	$1,000	$1,000	$1,000	$1,000
Retained Earnings	564	536	393	358
Total Shareholders' Equity	$1,564	$1,536	$1,393	$1,358
Total	$6,835	$4,162	$2,792	$2,323

ALBA LTD.
Comparative Income Statements
For the Years Ended December 31, Year 2 to Year 5

	(thousands of dollars)			
	Year 5	Year 4	Year 3	Year 2
Sales	$9,658	$7,853	$6,647	$5,942
Less: Cost of Sales	5,796	4,709	3,991	3,560
Gross Profit	$3,862	$3,144	$2,656	$2,382
Expenses	3,329	2,621	2,158	1,918
	$ 533	$ 523	$ 498	$ 464
Interest	479	248	104	83
Net Income before Income Tax	$ 54	$ 275	$ 394	$ 381
Income Tax (48 percent)	26	132	189	183
Net Income	$ 28	$ 143	$ 205	$ 198
Deduct Dividends Paid	—	—	170	160
Increase in Retained Earnings	$ 28	$ 143	$ 35	$ 38

Prepare calculations and notes that you would take to the meeting with the president.

Do you think that any of the above members of the financial community would be willing to provide funds to the company? If not, what do you recommend the company should do during the next few years?

Decision Problem 6-2

Western Printers Ltd. had operated a commercial printing business in Vancouver since it was founded by Mr. P. R. Robson several years ago. Robson suffered a heart attack in July, Year 3 and retired from active interest in the business, delegating complete responsibility to Phil Grange, who had joined the company in Year 1. A month ago, Robson died, and willed the majority interest in the company to his son, Barry, currently completing his final year studying philosophy at university. Barry Robson approached you to advise him whether Grange has been performing in a competent fashion and should be retained or replaced.

Barry Robson has with him condensed financial statements of the company for the past few years and, for the same period, comparative data for the printing industry. A review of these statements leads you to the conclusion that the financial statements for Year 5 and Year 6 attached are representative of the financial statements of both the company and the industry for the past few years.

    a. From the information available, advise Barry Robson whether he should retain Phil Grange as manager of the company, look for a replacement, or make some modification of these alternatives.

    b. List the four most important additional bits of financial information that you consider necessary to confirm these impressions.

Condensed Balance Sheet
For Years Ended December 31, Year 5 and Year 6

	Western Printers Ltd. $000s		Total Industry $000,000s	
	Year 6	Year 5	Year 6	Year 5
Assets				
Current Assets:				
Cash	$ 30	$ 24	$ 7	$ 11
Temporary Investments (at market value)	11	9	9	9
Accounts Receivable	34	30	36	40
Inventory	26	20	29	24
	$101	$ 83	$ 81	$ 84
Land	$ 3	$ 3	$ 4	$ 5
Buildings	$111	$109	$136	$122
Less: Accumulated Depreciation	(64)	(56)	(74)	(66)
	$ 47	$ 53	$ 62	$ 56
Total	$151	$139	$147	$145
Liabilities and Shareholders' Equity				
Current Liabilities:				
Bank Loan	$ 18	$ 18	$ 9	$ 11
Accounts Payable	7	7	18	16
Due to Finance Companies	18	14	1	3
Taxes Payable	4	4	5	5
	$ 47	$ 43	$ 33	$ 35
Mortgages	—	—	12	14
	$ 47	$ 43	$ 45	$ 49
Shareholders' Equity:				
Share Capital	$ 30	$ 30	$ 32	$ 32
Retained Earnings	74	66	70	64
	$104	$ 96	$102	$ 96
	$151	$139	$147	$145

Condensed Income Statement
For Year Ended December 31, Year 6

	Western Printers Ltd. $000s	Total Industry $000,000s
Sales	$212.2	$237.5
Cost of Sales	141.1	160.6
Gross Profit	$ 71.1	$ 76.9
Selling and Administrative Expenses	53.3	61.1
Operating Income	$ 17.8	$ 15.8
Interest Paid	$ 3.1	$ 1.5
Less: Interest and Dividends Received	0.3	0.6
Net Interest Expense	$ 2.8	$ 0.9
Net Income before Income Tax	$ 15.0	$ 14.9
Income Tax	4.4	4.4
Net Income	$ 10.6	$ 10.5
Dividends	2.7	4.4
Addition to Retained Earnings	$ 7.9	$ 6.1

Part Three   Measuring and Reporting Assets and Equities Using Generally Accepted Accounting Principles

A Transitional Note: Generally Accepted Accounting Principles

By now, most of the basic concepts and procedures of financial accounting have been introduced. The purpose of accounting, its theoretical framework, and some of its procedures have been discussed. Tools for analyzing financial statements have been presented. From this point onward, generally accepted accounting principles (GAAP) will be considered in approximate balance sheet order: liquid assets in Chapter 7, inventories in Chapter 8, noncurrent assets in Chapter 9, liabilities and owners' equity in Chapters 10, 11, and 12. Chapter 13, somewhat out of "balance sheet order," focuses on accounting for certain long-term investments in securities of other companies. Before examining GAAP for liquid assets, it will be helpful to explore the nature and development of accounting principles.

Nature and Development of Generally Accepted Accounting Principles

Generally accepted accounting principles, or GAAP, are the accounting methods and procedures used by firms in preparing their financial statements. The primary source of statements of GAAP is the CICA Handbook prepared following due process by the Accounting Standards Committee of the Canadian Institute of Chartered Accountants. Where the Handbook makes no reference to an item, additional sources may be the Companies Acts, Securities Commissions statements, common Canadian practice, and standards of other countries. This section considers the nature of these principles and the process through which they are developed.

Nature of Accounting Principles To understand the nature of principles in accounting, contrast them with principles in fields such as physics and mathematics. In physics and other natural sciences, a principle (or theory) is evaluated by asking how well the predictions of the principle correspond with physically observed phenomena. Mathematicians evaluate a principle (or theorem) by comparing its internal consistency with the structure of definitions and underlying axioms. In accounting, principles stand or fall on their general acceptability to preparers and users of accounting reports. Unlike those in the physical sciences, principles in accounting do not exist naturally, merely awaiting discovery. Unlike mathematics, accounting has no structure of definitions and concepts that can be used unambiguously to develop accounting principles. For example, one generally accepted accounting principle requires land to be stated at its acquisition cost as long as it is held by a firm. Changes in the market value of the land are not reflected in the financial statements until the land is sold. This accounting principle cannot be "proven" to be correct. It has simply been judged to be the generally acceptable method of accounting for land. Accounting principles might more aptly be called "accounting conventions."

Development of Accounting Principles Accounting principles result from an essentially political process. Various persons or groups have power, or authority, in the decision process that yields generally accepted accounting principles. The next few paragraphs describe the most important participants in this process.

The Companies Acts The fundamental and superior authorities for establishing and monitoring companies are the legislatures of the provincial and the federal governments. This authority is given expression through the Companies Acts (or Corporations Acts) that have been passed in each of the provinces and by the federal government. Attempts continue to be made to achieve uniformity in this legislation, with limited success. Since no uniform Companies Act exists, and all laws are subject to change, references to law will be limited to the Canada Business Corporations Act enacted by the federal government. Under this Act, the authority for establishing generally accepted accounting principles has been delegated to the Canadian Institute of Chartered Accountants (CICA), with a few minor exceptions.

The Securities Commissions A second group concerned with generally accepted accounting principles is the provincial securities commissions. They have authority specified by legislation to regulate accounting practices for companies under their jurisdiction, generally limited to those companies whose securities are traded in the relevant province. There is considerable uniformity in the major practices of the provincial securities commissions. As with the Canada Business Corporations Act, the primary responsibility for establishing generally accepted accounting principles has been delegated by these securities commissions to the CICA.

The Canadian Institute of Chartered Accountants The CICA is the primary accounting body responsible for establishing generally accepted accounting principles. The CICA has delegated the authority to the Accounting Standards Committee (AcSC), whose origin dates from 1946. The operation of the AcSC is financed by the CICA but operates independently. The majority of the Committee members are chartered accountants, but members from related associations are included to represent providers and users of financial statements.

The due process procedure used by the Committee for setting accounting standards is complex and is summarized below:

1. An issue is identified and placed on the AcSC's agenda.
2. The research staff collects and summarizes material related to the problem, including statements issued by standard-setting bodies in other countries.
3. Where major initiatives are undertaken, a Research Study by a consultant may be commissioned.
4. On completion of the Research Study, the project is allocated, where necessary, to a regional section of the AcSC.
5. A regional section of the AcSC with staff support, prepares a proposal for consideration of the AcSC.
6. The AcSC may return the proposal to the regional section for modification or may modify the proposal and prepare an Exposure Draft.
7. The Exposure Draft is circulated widely with a request for comment by a specified date.
8. The comments are analyzed by the AcSC staff and considered by the AcSC.
9. The AcSC may modify the Exposure Draft.
10. Where the modifications are significant a Re-Exposure Draft may be issued and the Exposure Draft Review Process repeated.

11. Where the modifications are not significant, the AcSC will vote on the amended Exposure Draft and on approval of at least two-thirds of the members will authorize additions or revisions of the *CICA Handbook*.

12. The Handbook revisions and additions are prepared by the staff and issued to the members of the CICA in Handbook Revisions Releases with the effective date stated.

Accounting Practices of Other Nations Canada traditionally has been influenced by the customs, laws, and culture of the United Kingdom and the United States. This influence is particularly significant in economic affairs since traditionally capital and skills have been drawn from these two countries. Today many Canadian companies are owned by American and British companies and the shares of several Canadian companies are listed for trading on American stock exchanges. Consequently, Canadian accounting practice has drawn extensively from the United Kingdom and United States experiences. This has occurred not only for the traditional reasons, but also because those companies whose shares are owned by foreign companies, or are traded in American stock exchanges, are subject to the laws of those jurisdictions, including the generally accepted accounting principles. Significant lack of congruence between Canadian and American generally accepted accounting principles creates questions in Canada and costly conversion processes when conforming to American practices. Consequently, when determining generally accepted accounting principles in Canada, the members of the CICA committees must be aware of the comparable generally accepted accounting principles in other countries, and particularly those of the United States.

Canadian accounting institutes have been active members in the International Accounting Standards Committee, whose objective is to formulate and publish accounting and auditing standards, and to promote their world-wide acceptance and observance. Although the standards issued by the committee have no legal force in Canada, the AcSC supports the objective of international harmonization of accounting standards. When the International Accounting Standards Committee issues a standard, it is compared with present Canadian practice and, where a significant difference exists, serious consideration is given to incorporating this standard in the *CICA Handbook*.

Future Development of Accounting Principles Unless governments unexpectedly decide to exert their legal authority, we see little reason for the future development of accounting principles to differ materially from that in the past. The process will continue to be a political one, with opposing viewpoints attempting to exert influence on the decision process. Positions taken or opinions rendered by participants in this process must be not only carefully developed but also effectively marketed if the positions are to become generally acceptable to the persons who prepare and use financial statements. To provide guidance to the standard-setting process, the AcSC should strive to relate its pronouncements on particular topics to general-purpose financial reporting objectives.

Chapter 7   Cash, Temporary Investments, and Receivables: The Liquid Assets

Liquidity and Money-Like Assets

Chapters 5 and 6 point out that liquidity is essential for business operations. An insolvent company, one that cannot pay its bills and meet its commitments as they mature, will not survive no matter how large its shareholders' equity. Most bankrupt companies show positive shareholders' equity on their balance sheets at the time of bankruptcy. Bankruptcy is usually caused by an inability to meet debts as they become due. One of the largest bankruptcies in Canada of recent times occurred in 1965 when the Atlantic Acceptance Corporation Limited was placed in bankruptcy. At December 31, 1964 the Atlantic Acceptance Corporation Limited had almost $133 million of assets, financed by $117 million of debts and $16 million of shareholders' equity. Nevertheless, the company became insolvent because it could not meet "only" a $5 million cheque.

Money-like assets are an important determinant of a firm's liquidity. Cash, temporary investments, accounts receivable, and notes receivable are the principal liquid assets of a business. These assets are generally stated at their current cash, or cash-equivalent, values on the balance sheet. This chapter explores various inclusion and valuation questions related to each of these liquid assets. The objective of the chapter is to present the methods of accounting and reporting for money-like assets so that assessments can be made of a firm's liquidity at a moment in time and changes in that liquidity over time.

Cash

Cash is the most liquid asset. It is also the most vulnerable because of its susceptibility to theft or embezzlement. This section considers cash inclusions and valuation as well as cash management and control.

Cash Inclusions and Valuation

To be counted as cash on the balance sheet, an item should be freely available for use as a medium of exchange. Coins, currency, travellers' cheques, and undeposited cheques qualify. Most cash is cash in the bank in the form of demand deposits and savings accounts. Although banks can restrict the immediate withdrawal of funds from savings accounts and term deposits, these items are usually sufficiently available for use as a medium of exchange to be included in cash. Cash includes foreign currency unless a firm's ability to use the currency is severely restricted. For example, foreign currency held by a division located in a country that forbids the outflow of funds would not be included. Also, funds set aside or restricted for a particular purpose would not be included. For example, firms are often required to establish "sinking funds" to retire outstanding debt. The cash in a sinking fund appears as Investments, rather than in Cash, on the balance sheet.

Once an item meets the criteria to be included in cash, there are few valuation problems. Cash is normally stated at its face amount. Foreign currency must be translated to its Canadian dollar-equivalent amount using the exchange rate in effect on the date of the balance sheet.

Cash Management

The management of cash involves two distinct goals. First, a firm establishes a system of internal controls to ensure that cash is safeguarded from theft or embezzlement. Typical internal control procedures include the separation of duties of individuals handling cash receipt and disbursement, depositing cash receipts immediately, disbursing cash only by authorized cheques, and preparing bank account reconciliations regularly.

Second, management wants to regulate cash balances so that neither too much nor too little cash is available at any time. Cash on hand or in chequing accounts generally does not earn interest. In fact, during inflationary periods, idle cash loses purchasing power and thus decreases in real value. A firm does not want to maintain excessive cash balances. On the other hand, a firm does not want to be short of cash and unable to meet its obligations as they become due or unable to take advantage of cash discounts.

A weekly or monthly budget of cash receipts and disbursements aids cash management. Such a budget indicates both the amounts and times when excess cash will be available for investment or when additional borrowing will become necessary.

Controlling Cash

Of all assets, cash is the most vulnerable—the most difficult to safeguard from theft. This section discusses the usual procedures of accounting for and controlling cash. For internal control purposes, most firms maintain two cash accounts, Cash on Hand and Cash in Bank.

Controlling Cash Receipts and Disbursements

The system for controlling cash receipts should be designed to ensure that all money collected for the firm benefits the firm. In most businesses, collections are received primarily through the mail in the form of bank cheques or in currency for cash sales. The need to control the collections of currency and coins is obvious. All collections for cash sales should be recorded promptly, either in a cash register or some other device that both records the receipts and locks in the amount of the collection. Other kinds of collections are more susceptible to mishandling because they occur less often. These include receipts from the sale of assets not normally intended to be sold, receipts from dividends and interest on investments, collections on notes receivable, proceeds of bank loans, and proceeds of share or bond issues.

In-house Thieves

*F*ew people, from corporate executives on down, realize how big employee theft is. The fact is, it's a crime that amounts to 1% of the Gross National Product, and just about every employee this side of sainthood will commit it some time during his or her working life. Moreover, employee theft accounts for 80% of all crime against corporations.

Security experts divide internal crime into three categories—the theft of things such as raw materials, finished products, cash, and tools; the theft of information; and fraud.

The theft of raw materials occurs primarily in the manufacturing and construction businesses. For a manufacturing firm, it most often occurs in the shipping and receiving or warehouse end of the operation, where controls are notoriously lax. With hundreds of shipments going in and out of a docking area each day, keeping an eye on materials is taxing, and the opportunity for theft astounding.

At construction sites, there are often hundreds of workers performing a wide variety of tasks and trucks coming and going with materials. It is relatively easy for an employee to slip off the job to nab some lumber, plasterboard, or insulating material and stash it in a pickup truck, or to arrange for a commercial truck to pick up material and haul it away.

The illegal siphoning off of crude and refined oil plagues the oil industry. The measurement of how much oil goes into a tank is relatively imprecise, so employees are able, undetected, either to siphon oil from a storage tank or to pump only part of the oil in a tanker truck into a tank.

When it comes to the outright theft of money, banks are where the big action is. In one such instance, an employee in a bank's operations department fiddled with customer accounts entered in the bank computers and embezzled about $21 million in a two-year period before he was caught.

Theft of information, though less prevalent than the theft of objects or services, can be disastrous. The energy industry is a frequent target of such thefts. Seismic surveys and exploration data, which cost millions of dollars to collect, have been pilfered from major oil companies and sold to small independent drillers or to foreign concerns.

Fraudulent schemes are the most costly form of employee theft. "The creation of dummy or shell companies is on the upswing, and it is not especially difficult to arrange," says Errol M. Cook, a security expert. He tells of one executive who formed an "offshore" insurance company. This executive had the authority to place insurance, so he bought a policy from the dummy company and pocketed the premiums. Cook notes that "where phony insurance companies are used, the type of insurance placed is usually where claims would not be occurring—officers' and directors' liability and bonding insurance, for example."

Employees in a payroll department can easily rip off a company. At one hospital, a worker added the names of two friends to the payroll and managed to funnel $40,000 their way before she was caught.

The most distressing thing about employee theft, security experts say, is that companies make it so easy. They leave valuable items unlocked or do not check to see that supplies actually exist. "It is just astounding the number of . . . corporations . . . that have woefully inadequate security systems. I should know, because many of them are my clients," says August Bequai, a lawyer, author, and consultant in the area of corporate security.

From Lynn Adkins. "The High Cost of Employee Theft." Reprinted with the special permission of Dun's *Business Month* (formerly *Dun's Review*), October 1982, pages 66–73, Dun & Bradstreet Publications Corporation.

One way to provide effective control of cash receipts would be to maintain duplicate sets of records, each under separate supervision. But doing so would be expensive. The business need not undertake this expensive control device, however, if it (1) designs its cash-handling techniques so that the monthly statement received from its bank effectively serves as a duplicate record and (2) separates the functions of cash handling and record keeping. To use the bank statement as an effective cash-controlling device requires prompt depositing of all receipts and making all disbursements by cheque.

Undeposited Cash

If a firm follows the desirable practice of depositing all receipts intact each day, disbursements will usually be made only from chequing accounts. Any balance in the Cash on hand account will represent cash received since the last deposit. A daily record of cash on hand is desirable. Cash registers facilitate the accumulation of such cash data. There are many types, but the usual cash register is a combination of a cash drawer and a multiple-register adding machine. The transactions are entered by hand. Then they are recorded and accumulated by the register so that at the end of the day the totals are available for each of several divisions of the day's activities — the total cash sales (sometimes classified according to products or departments), total collections on account, and total sales of each salesperson.

Cash in Bank — Deposits

A deposit slip provides the information for preparing the journal entry to record the deposit of cash funds in the chequing account. The deposit slip should be prepared in duplicate; the bank keeps the original and the firm keeps the duplicate. The duplicate is often initialed by the bank teller and used as a receipt for the deposit of the funds. The total on the deposit slip is entered in a journal as a debit to Cash in Bank and a credit to Cash on Hand.

Cash in Bank — Issuance of Cheques

The information for the entry to record cheques drawn in payment of bills comes from the document authorizing the payment. The customary entry will be a debit to Accounts Payable and a credit to Cash in Bank.

Control of Disbursements by Cheque

All cash payments except for those of very small amounts should be made by cheque. The firm can thereby restrict the authority for payments to a few employees. Firms often provide further control by requiring that all cheques be signed by two employees. Another control device is the use of a Cash Disbursements Journal or Cheque Register in which all cheques issued are recorded. Using such a journal provides control because a single person, who is not allowed to authorize payments or to sign cheques, is responsible for recording all payments.

In any case, control over disbusements should ensure that:

1. Payments are made only by authorized persons.
2. Adequate records support each payment. Such records attest that disbursement was for goods and services procured by proper authority and actually received by the business. The records attest that payment is made in accordance with the purchase contract.
3. The transaction is entered properly in the formal account records.
4. Authorization of payment is separate from making payment, and record keeping is separate from both.

Petty Cash

It is inefficient for small payments to be made by cheque. Small payments may be made by cash and yet come within the cheque control system by the use of an *imprest petty cash fund* operated as follows:

1. Establishment of the fund: A cheque is prepared for a round amount that will provide for small cash payments for a reasonable time, and cashed by the petty cashier responsible for the cash payments. The establishment of the fund is recorded by debiting Petty Cash and crediting Cash.
2. Payments from fund: When payments are made by the petty cashier receipts or other memos are saved to show that the money was spent.
3. Replenishment of fund: When the cash in the fund is almost exhausted by payments, the receipts and memos are batched and totaled and reimbursement requested. A cheque will be made payable to the petty cashier for the total of the batched receipts and memos accompanying the request for replenishment. The cheque will be reported as a normal expenditure, with a debit to expenses and a credit to Cash. When the cheque is cashed by the petty cashier the cash in the fund will equal the amount on hand when the fund was established.

Note that:

1. The only entry made in the petty cash account is to establish the fund or to change the total amount.
2. The petty cashier should have cash, receipts and memos on hand equal to the amount of the fund.
3. The payments made by the petty cashier will not be recorded in the accounting records until the replenishment cheque is prepared.

The Bank Statement

At the end of each month (or other regular interval), the bank sends a statement together with the canceled cheques that have been paid and deducted from the depositor's account, and memorandums of any other additions or deductions that have been made by the bank. When the bank statement is received, it should be compared promptly with the record of deposits, cheques drawn, and other bank items on the records of the firm.

The balance shown on the bank statement will rarely correspond to the balance of the Cash in Bank account. The two basic causes of the difference are time lag and errors. In the normal course of business activities, some items will have been recorded by either the bank or the firm without having reached the recording point on the other set of records, hence a *time lag* difference. Causes of such differences include: cheques outstanding (that is, cheques recorded by the drawing firm but not yet received by the bank on which they were drawn), deposits made just before the bank statement date that do not appear on the bank statement, and transactions (such as service charges and collections of notes or drafts) that have not been recorded on the firm's books. The other basic difference is caused by errors in record keeping by either the firm or the bank. The process of comparing the bank statement with the books is known as *reconciling* the bank account, and the schedule that is prepared to demonstrate the results of the comparing is called a *bank reconciliation*. Exhibit 7.1 shows a typical reconciliation.

Exhibit 7.1
LIPSCOMB CORPORATION
Bank Reconciliation
National Bank
April 1

Balance shown on bank statement, April 1		$3,941.43
Deposits of March 30 and 31, not yet recorded by bank		753.25
Cheque of F. Lipscomb deducted by bank in error		102.00
		$4,796.68
Outstanding cheques:		
#2443	$ 79.67	
#2459	242.53	
#2471	131.26	
#2472	32.44	
#2473	243.55	
Less: Total outstanding cheques		(729.45)
Adjusted bank balance[a]		$4,067.23
Balance shown on books, April 1		$3,588,23
Items unrecorded on books:		
Collection of note of J. B. Ball:		
Face amount of note	$500.00	
Less collection charge	(15.00)	485.00
Less: Bank service charge for March		(24.00)
Adjusted book balance before correction of errors		$4,049.23
Cheque #2467 for $268.81 was entered in the cheque register as		
$286.81. It was issued in March to pay a bill for office equipment . .		18.00
Adjusted book balance[a]		$4,067.23

[a]This is the amount that would be shown in the Cash in Bank account if a balance sheet were prepared as of April 1.

Preparing the Bank Reconciliation

The bank reconciliation explains the difference between the book balance of Cash in Bank and the bank's statement of the firm's cash on deposit. It indicates the required adjustments of the firm's accounts. If the bank statement is used as a control device, the bank reconciliation is the final step in the monthly procedure for controlling cash receipts and disbursements. The bank reconciliation provides a convenient summary of the adjusting entries that must be made by the firm to account for previous errors in recording cash-related transactions or for cash transactions that have not yet been recorded.

Preparing the bank reconciliation typically involves the following steps:

1. Enter at the top of the reconciliation the balance as shown on the bank statement.
2. Enter next any deposits that have not been recorded on the bank statement. Such items usually occur because the bank has prepared the statement before the deposits for the last day or two have been recorded. If there are any time or date breaks in the list of deposits for the period, the bank should be notified promptly.
3. Enter any other adjustments of the bank's balance, such as errors in recording canceled cheques or deposits, or the return of cheques belonging to some other customer of the bank. Errors on bank statements are infrequent.
4. Obtain a total.
5. List the outstanding cheques. A list should be prepared, beginning with the cheques still outstanding from the previous period and continuing with the cheques outstanding that were drawn during the current period.
6. Deduct the sum of the outstanding cheques from the total obtained in step (4). The balance is the adjusted bank balance — the balance that would be shown on the bank statement if all deposits had been entered, all cheques written had been returned, and no errors had been made; it is the final figure for this first section of the statement.

These steps will frequently conclude the reconciliation because this balance should correspond to the balance of the Cash in Bank account as of the bank statement date when there are no unrecorded transactions or errors. If these two amounts are not equal at this point, the following steps must be taken and shown in a second section of the reconciliation.

7. Enter the Cash in Bank account balance as shown on the books as of the bank statement date.
8. Add or deduct any errors or omissions that have been disclosed in the process of reviewing the items returned by the bank. These will include such items as errors in recording deposits or cheques, unnumbered cheques that have not been entered in the cheque register, and service charges and collection fees deducted by the bank.
9. The net result is the adjusted book balance, and it must correspond to the adjusted bank balance derived in the first section. If it does not, the search must be continued for other items that have been overlooked.

Adjusting Entries from Bank Reconciliation

The bank reconciliation shows two distinct kinds of differences:

1. Differences between the balance shown on the bank statement and the adjusted bank balance.
2. Differences between the account balance on the firm's books and the adjusted bank balance.

The Paperless Society

*B*illions of paper cheques are written each year by businesses and individuals. The costs of processing this large volume of cheques have motivated financial institutions to develop systems for transferring funds among parties electronically, without the need for paper cheques. The exchange of cash through such a system is called **electronic funds transfer (EFT)**.

A typical example of EFT is the payment of a payroll. An employer firm obtains authorizations from its employees to deposit their payroll cheques directly to their chequing accounts. The firm then sends to the bank a magnetic tape coded with the appropriate payroll data. The bank's computer processes the magnetic tape, deducts the total payroll amount from the firm's chequing account, and adds each employee's payroll amount to his or her chequing account.

Banks are attempting to introduce EFT into retailing in situations where customers typically pay for goods with a cheque at the time of purchase. At the check-out counter, the customer uses a plastic card to activate a computer terminal connected with the bank. These cards are referred to as **debit cards**. Funds to pay for the groceries are immediately transferred from the customer's chequing account to the store's account at the bank. This procedure not only eliminates the cost of processing the paper cheques for the bank, but also eliminates the risk of bad cheques for the grocery store. So far, Canadian consumers have been more resistant than American consumers to the use of debit cards.

The use of EFT will increase with the development of expanded computer networks capable of handling electronic funds transfers. The specific controls over cash transactions handled through EFT, of course, may vary from the internal control procedures under a paper cheque system. However, adequate controls are no less important in an electronic funds transfer system.

Some people foresee these debit cards entirely replacing cheques in the future. This is part of the movement to what has been called the ''paperless society.'' An advanced version of this card is now being tested by the banks. It incorporates a keyboard on the card and an internal memory. With each use, the individual can see the current balance, a history of past transactions, and so on.

The major factor standing in the way of the paperless society is consumer fear of outside control over their cash balances. For example, there is currently a controversy over the limit of bank responsibility if an automated teller banking machine shortchanges a user. The banks claim this is impossible, but there have been newspaper reports of Canadians complaining to the banks about such errors. It appears that the banks will have to conduct a massive promotional campaign to assure people that internal control over EFT is adequate before we see the paperless society in this country.

Only the second type of difference requires entries on the firm's books. Any deposits not credited by the bank will presumably have been recorded by the time the reconciliation is prepared and, in any event, represent funds that the depositor may assume are in the bank and available for use.

Entries must be made for all of the differences between the firm's account balance on the books and the adjusted book balance, because they represent errors or omissions. The reconciliation illustrated in Exhibit 7.1 requires adjustments for bank service charges, for the collection of a note, and for the cheque whose amount was incorrectly recorded. (The bank must, of course, correct any error on its books when the mistake is called to its attention.) The entries would be:

Bank Service Charge Expense	$ 24	
Cash in Bank		$ 24
Service charges for month of March.		
Cash in Bank	$485	
Collection Expense	15	
Notes Receivable, J. B. Ball		$500
Note collected by bank.		
Cash in Bank	$ 18	
Accounts Payable		$ 18
To correct entry of cheque #2467.		

Summary of Accounting for Cash

Cash is an enterprise's most vulnerable resource. An internal control system is essential to the proper management of cash. One way to provide control is to maintain duplicate and independent records of cash flows, but the monthly bank statement can serve as the duplicate record. Using the bank statement as an effective control device requires depositing receipts daily and making all disbursements by cheque or through petty cash funds. By this means the bank reconciliation serves as a control device, because the bank record will reflect the cash inflows and outflows of the enterprise.

Temporary Investments

A business may find itself with more cash than it needs for current and near-term business purposes. Rather than allow cash to remain unproductive, the business may invest some of its currently excess cash in income-yielding securities, such as Canadian government bonds and treasury bills or shares or bonds of other companies. Such liquid assets appear under the caption of *Temporary investments* in the Current Asset section of the balance sheet.

    A business may also acquire securities intending to hold them for a longer period. Such securities are treated as long-term investments. Thus, the classification of a security as a current or noncurrent asset is a function of management's intentions. This section considers the classification and valuation of securities held temporarily. Securities intended to be held for a longer period are considered in Chapter 13.

Classification of Temporary Investments

Securities are classified as Temporary investments among current assets as long as they can be readily converted into cash *and* management intends to do so when it needs cash. Securities that do not meet both of these criteria are included under Portfolio Investments on the balance sheet.

Example 1 Morrissey Manufacturing Corporation invested $150,000 of temporarily excess funds in Canada Treasury Bills. The bills mature in three months. This investment appears among temporary investments, because the bills can be sold at any time and, even if not sold, the cash will be collected within three months.

Example 2 Suppose that Morrissey Manufacturing Corporation had acquired 20-year bonds of Greer Electronics Limited instead of the Canada Treasury Bills. Its intent in acquiring the bonds was the same as before: the investment of temporarily excess cash. These bonds would similarly be classified as temporary investments, because they can be traded in an established marketplace.

Example 3 West Corporation acquired ten percent of the outstanding shares of Haskell Corporation on the open market for $10 million. West Corporation plans to hold these shares as a long-term investment. Even though the shares of Haskell Corporation are readily marketable, they would not be classified as temporary investments, because West Corporation does not intend to turn the securities into cash within a reasonably short period. These securities appear as Portfolio Investments on the balance sheet.

In published financial statements, all securities properly classified as the current asset Temporary Investments appear together on a single line on the balance sheet. However, when temporary investments include holdings of securities issued by affiliated companies, these should be set out separately, distinguishing those of subsidiaries.

Valuation of Temporary Investments

Temporary investments are initially recorded at acquisition cost. Acquisition cost includes the purchase price plus any commissions, taxes, and other costs incurred. For example, if temporary investments are acquired for $10,000 plus $300 for commissions and taxes, the entry is:

Temporary Investments	$10,300	
Cash		$10,300

Dividends on temporary investments become revenue when declared. Interest revenue is recognized when earned.[1] Assuming that a dividend of $250 was declared and $300 of interest was earned on temporary investments and these amounts were immediately received in cash, the entry is:

Cash	$550	
Dividend Revenue		$250
Interest Revenue		300

There is nothing unusual about the valuation of temporary investments at date of acquisition or the recording of dividends and interest. The valuation of temporary investments after acquisition, however, departs from strict historical cost accounting.

---

[1]This reflects application of the accrual concept. For convenience, many firms wait until receipt of the interest or dividend cheque. As long as the impact on revenues is not materially different, such treatment is acceptable.

Lower of Cost and Market

The *CICA Handbook* requires that "when the market value of temporary investments has declined below the carrying value, they should be carried at market value." This statement is a specific way of saying that marketable securities should be valued at the *lower of cost and market*. Under the lower of cost and market method, decreases in the market value of securities are recognized as holding losses each period as the decreases occur, even though a market transaction has not taken place.

The lower of cost and market may be interpreted in a number of ways. The two alternatives acceptable under generally accepted accounting principles are the lower of individual cost and market, and the lower of aggregate cost and market.

Lower of Individual Cost and Market   The lower of cost and market rule is based on the concept of conservatism that requires a company to "provide for all losses but anticipate no profits." Once a loss has been provided for by reducing the carrying value of a security to market value, which is lower than cost, the reduced carrying value will never be increased. When the security is sold, the gain on the sale will be calculated on the carrying value of the individual security.

Example 4   Wolfson Limited acquired temporary investments during Year 3 as shown in Exhibit 7.2.[2] The entry to record the acquisition of shares of A Ltd., B Ltd., and C Ltd. during Year 3 is:

Temporary Investments (A Ltd.)	$50,000	
Temporary Investments (B Ltd.)	30,000	
Temporary Investments (C Ltd.)	20,000	
Cash		$100,000

Exhibit 7.2
Data for Illustration of Accounting for Temporary Investments of Wolfson Limited

			Market Value			
Security	Date Acquired	Acquisition Cost	Dec. 31, Year 6	Dec. 31, Year 5	Dec. 31, Year 4	Dec. 31, Year 3
A Ltd.	4/1/Year 3	$ 50,000	$43,000	$52,000	$54,000	$53,000
B Ltd.	6/1/Year 3	30,000	—	—[a]	22,000	27,000
C Ltd.	8/1/Year 3	20,000	—[b]	24,000	23,000	16,000
Total		$100,000	$43,000	$76,000	$99,000	$96,000

[a]Holdings of B Ltd. sold during Year 5 for $32,000.
[b]Holdings of C Ltd. sold during Year 6 for $17,000.

Unrealized Holding Loss   At the end of Year 3, the market value of the shares of A Ltd. increased from the date of purchase, but the market value of the shares of B Ltd.

---

[2]In reality, a firm holding these securities for four years would likely classify them as portfolio investments, a noncurrent asset. For purposes of illustration, we have shown the accounting for a portfolio of temporary investments over several years.

and C Ltd. declined. Following the rule of conservatism that a company should anticipate no profits but provide for all losses, a write-down of $7,000 is required to recognize the unrealized holding loss on the investment in shares of B Ltd. and C Ltd. The entry to record the write-down is:

Holding Loss on Temporary Investments[a] $7,000
    Temporary Investment (B Ltd.) $3,000
    Temporary Investment (C Ltd.)   4,000
To record reduction in carrying value of investments to market value.

---

[a] An alternative way of recording this is to create a *valuation allowance*, instead of writing down the asset directly. Valuation allowances are used commonly with receivables. The benefit of the allowance method is that it preserves more information (the original carrying value of the asset).

The holding loss appears in the income statement for Year 3 as a reduction of financial income.[3] The Temporary Investments are presented in the December 31, Year 3 balance sheet, valued at the lower of cost and market of $93,000 ($= $50,000 + $27,000 + $16,000$). The market value of $96,000 will be noted.

    During Year 4 the market value of B Ltd. shares declined and the market value of A Ltd. and C Ltd. shares increased. To recognize the unrealized holding loss of $5,000 ($= $27,000 - $22,000$) on the shares of B Ltd. a write-down of $5,000 is required. The entry is:

Holding Loss on Temporary Investments $5,000
    Temporary Investment (B Ltd.) $5,000

The increase in the market value of the shares of A Ltd. and C Ltd. will not be recorded. At the end of Year 4, the temporary investments have an original cost of $100,000 ($= $50,000 + $30,000 + $20,000$) and a carrying value (lower of individual cost and market) of $88,000 ($= $50,000 + $22,000 + $16,000$). The cost has been decreased by a reduction of financial income of $7,000 in Year 3 and $5,000 in Year 4. The Temporary Investments would be shown on the December 31, Year 4 balance sheet at the carrying value of $88,000 with the market value of $99,000 noted.

Realized Gain through Sale During Year 5 the shares of B Ltd. are sold for $32,000, the market value of A Ltd. shares declined but remain above cost, and the market value of C Ltd. shares increased. When an individual temporary investment is sold, the realized gain or loss is the difference between the selling price and the carrying value. Because the current buying and selling price will be the same, the "operating profit," as defined in Chapter 3, is zero. All gains or losses are therefore holding gains and losses. The entry to record the sale is:

---

[3] For income tax purposes, losses (or gains) are reported only when realized, generally by sale.

Cash	$32,000	
Temporary Investments (B Ltd.)		$22,000
Holding Gain on Temporary Investments		10,000

The gain on sale is a combination of the unrealized holding losses provided for in Year 3 and Year 4 of $8,000 (= $3,000 + $5,000) and the realized holding gain above cost of $2,000 (= $32,000 − $30,000). The gain on the sale of temporary investments would be included in financial income for Year 5.

At December 31, Year 5, the carrying value of the temporary investments is $66,000, consisting of the cost of A Ltd. shares of $50,000 and the lowest market value of C Ltd. shares of $16,000 at December 31, Year 3. Note that the market value of A Ltd. shares has consistently exceeded cost. The carrying value of each investment is the lower of cost and market, where market is defined as the lowest year-end price since the shares were purchased.

During Year 6 the market values of the shares of A Ltd. declined by $9,000 (= $52,000 − $43,000) and the shares of C Ltd. were sold for $17,000. The shares in C Ltd. had a carrying value of $16,000, which represents the cost of $20,000, less the unrealized holding loss during Year 3 of $4,000. The entry to record the sale of C Ltd. shares is:

Cash	$17,000	
Temporary Investments (C Ltd.)		$16,000
Holding Gain on Temporary Investments		1,000

The decline in market value of the shares of A Ltd. during Year 6 exceeds the net unrealized holding gains since acquisition at December 31, Year 5 of $2,000 (= $52,000 − $50,000) and the market value is below cost. To recognize the net unrealized holding loss of $7,000 (= $50,000 − $43,000) on the shares of A Ltd., a write-down is required. The entry is:

Holding Loss on Temporary Investments	$7,000	
Temporary Investments (A Ltd.)		$7,000

The Temporary Investments are shown on the December 31, Year 6 balance sheet at $43,000, the market value of the shares in A Ltd. Income from temporary investments is reduced by $6,000 (= $7,000 − $1,000) as a result of the unrealized loss from holding A Ltd. and the realized gain from the sale of shares of C Ltd.

Lower of Aggregate Cost and Market The lower of aggregate cost and market is also based on the concept of conservatism. The lower of cost and market rule is applied to the total portfolio of temporary investments rather than to each security within the portfolio. The lower of aggregate cost and market is implemented either by adjusting the carrying value of each individual security to market value when aggregate market value is less than cost, or by establishing a contra account to the total portfolio of temporary investments, usually called Allowance for Decline in Temporary Investments. Using a separate contra account enables the simultaneous identification of both the acquisition cost and the amount of decline, if any, in the market value of the portfolio of temporary investments. Separate identification of the cost of individual investments is required because, when a security is sold, the difference between the sale price and cost must be determined to record the gain or loss realized on sale. Realized gains and losses are computed from original cost. Realized losses are charged to the contra account. Realized gains are recorded in the income statement as financial income and are offset by any unrealized holding loss added to the contra account. The entries to record the lower aggregate cost and market value using a contra account, based on the data provided in Exhibit 7.2, are presented below.

Example 5 Wolfson Limited acquired temporary investments during Year 3 as shown in Exhibit 7.2. The entry to record the acquisition of the shares of A Ltd., B Ltd., and C Ltd. during Year 3 is:

Temporary Investments	$100,000	
Cash		$100,000

Unrealized Holding Loss At the end of Year 3, the aggregate cost of the portfolio of temporary investments of $100,000 is $4,000 above the aggregate market value of $96,000. Applying the lower-of-cost-and-market rule a provision of $4,000 is required. The entry is:

Holding Loss on Temporary Investments	$4,000	
Allowance for Decline in Temporary Investments		$4,000

To record the creation of an allowance account to reduce the carrying value of temporary investments to the lower of the aggregate cost or market.

The loss account appears in the Year 3 income statement as a reduction of financial income, and the Temporary Investments are included in current assets at $96,000 (= $100,000 − $4,000).

Unrealized Holding Gain During Year 4 the market value of the temporary investments increased, so that at December 31 the aggregate market value exceeds the carrying value by $3,000 [= $99,000 − ($100,000 − $4,000)]. Regardless of the absence of the need for the $4,000 balance in the contra account, the balance in the account remains unchanged, since Allowances for Unrealized Losses cannot be reduced except through sale. No entry is recorded in Year 4 and the Temporary Investments are included in current assets of $96,000, unchanged from December 31, Year 3.

Realized Holding Gain through Sale During Year 5 a gain was realized on the sale of B Ltd. shares. The entry to record the sale of B Ltd. shares for $32,000 is:

Cash	$32,000	
Temporary Investments		$30,000
Holding Gain on Temporary Investments		2,000

The cost of temporary investments at December 31, Year 5 is $70,000 (= $50,000 + $20,000). The market value is $76,000 and the Allowance for Decline in Temporary Investments is $4,000. Since the market value exceeds cost, the Allowance for Decline in Temporary Investments is unnecessary. However, the balance in this account is reduced only for realized losses or on the ultimate disposal of all temporary investments. Consequently no entry is made.

The gain on sale appears in the Year 5 income statement as an addition to financial income. The Temporary Investments are included in current assets at their carrying value of $66,000 (= $50,000 + $20,000 − $4,000) with the market value of $76,000 noted.

Realized Holding Loss through Sale During Year 6 the market value of the shares of A Ltd. declined to $43,000 and the company sold the C Ltd. shares for $17,000.

The balance in the Allowance for Decline in Temporary Investments absorbs the loss on sale of C Ltd. shares. The entry to record the sale is:

Cash	$17,000	
Allowance for Decline in Temporary Investments	3,000	
Temporary Investments		$20,000

The balance in the allowance account is now $1,000 (= $4,000 − $3,000), which is insufficient to reduce the investment in shares of A Ltd. (the remaining temporary investment) to its market vlaue. To provide for this deficiency, the allowance account is increased to $7,000 (= $50,000 − $43,000). The entry to record this increase is:

Holding Loss on Temporary Investments	$6,000	
Allowance for Decline in Temporary Investments		$6,000

The loss account appears in the Year 6 income statement as a reduction in financial income and the Temporary Investments are included in current assets at $43,000 (= $50,000 − $7,000).

Evaluation of Alternatives Exhibit 7.3 summarizes the financial statement effect of the two alternative methods of determining and recognizing the holding gains and losses on temporary investments and consequent balance sheet valuations. The lower of individual cost and market method represents the more conservative alternative since unrealized gains on some securities cannot offset unrealized losses on others.

A review of Exhibit 7.3 illustrates this statement. For each of Year 3 and Year 4, the lower of individual cost and market method reports the largest holding loss and the lowest balance sheet values, since the unrealized gain of A Ltd. shares cannot offset the unrealized losses in the other investments. In Year 5 both lower of cost and market alternatives report the same balance sheet values and the cumulative reductions in financial income over the three years. In Year 6 the balance sheet values reported under each alternative are the same, as the market value of the remaining security is below cost for the first time since it was purchased.

Exhibit 7.3
Items in Income Statement and
Balance Sheet of Wolfson Limited Illustrating Transactions in
Marketable Securities as Temporary Investments — Current Assets
Under Two Alternatives

	Year 6	Year 5	Year 4	Year 3	Total
Alternative 1: Individual Cost or Market					
Excerpts from Income Statement for Year					
Dividends Earned (Assumed)	$ 6,000	$ 8,000	$10,000	$10,000	$34,000
Holding Gain (Loss) on Temporary Investments	(6,000)	10,000	(5,000)	(7,000)	(8,000)
Financial Income from Temporary Investments	$ —	$18,000	$ 5,000	$ 3,000	$26,000
Balance Sheet Item at Year-End					
Temporary Investments at Lower-of-Cost-and-Market	$43,000	$66,000	$88,000	$93,000	
(Market Value)	$43,000	$76,000	$99,000	$96,000	
Alternative 2: Aggregate Cost or Market					
Excerpts from Income Statement for Year					
Dividends Earned (Assumed)	$ 6,000	$ 8,000	$10,000	$10,000	$34,000
Holding Gain (Loss) on Temporary Investments	(6,000)	2,000	—	(4,000)	(8,000)
Financial Income from Temporary Investments	$ —	$10,000	$10,000	$ 6,000	$26,000
Balance Sheet Item at Year-End					
Temporary Investments at Lower-of-Cost-and-Market	$43,000	$66,000	$96,000	$96,000	
(Market Value)	$43,000	$76,000	$99,000	$96,000	

Accounts Receivable

The third liquid asset this chapter considers is accounts receivable. Trade accounts receivable typically arise when goods or services are sold on account. The entry is:

Accounts Receivable	$250	
Sales Revenue		$250

Receivables sometimes also arise from transactions other than sales. For example, advances might be made to officers or employees, deposits might be made to guarantee performance or cover potential damages, or claims may be made against insurance companies, governmental bodies, common carriers, or others. These receivables are classified as either current assets or investments, depending on the expected collection date. This section focuses on trade accounts receivable, considering both their valuation and their management.

Accounts Receivable Valuation

Individual accounts receivable are initially recorded at the amount owed by each customer. The recording is made in a subsidiary ledger either as a manual accounting system, discussed in Chapter 3, or in a separately coded section of a computer memory bank. The sum of the amounts in individual customers' accounts appears in the master, or "control," account for Accounts Receivable. The Accounts Receivable account records the total of the amounts in individual customers' accounts.

The amount in the master account for Accounts Receivable is reduced for estimated uncollectible (doubtful) accounts, sales discounts, and sales returns and allowances. The reporting objective is to state accounts receivable at the amount expected to be collected in cash. The difference between the amounts owed by customers and the amounts expected to be collected in cash must be charged against revenue. The charge against revenue for expected uncollectible amounts, sales discounts, and sales returns and allowances is preferably made in the period when the sales occur. In this way, revenue and net income for a period will reflect the amounts expected to be collected for services rendered during the period.

Receivables Management

When a firm extends credit to customers, the possibility arises that one or more of them will not pay the money they owe. Usually this occurs because the customer has liquidity problems—an inability to pay. In some cases the customer is just unwilling to pay—because of a disagreement over the quality of goods and services received or because of dishonesty. Regardless of the reason, the firm must try to estimate at each balance sheet date the percentage of its receivables that will eventually turn out to be uncollectible. This is another example of the principle of conservatism—anticipate all losses, which result in current assets being carried at net realizable value.

Firms have some control over the amount of bad-debt losses they will experience by:
1. the credit policy established
2. the collection policy established

The credit policy is a formal decision rule as to which customers the firm will grant credit. A very liberal credit policy will boost sales but may boost bad debts also. A very stringent credit policy will have the reverse impact. Many firms will have a credit officer to judge whether potential customers should be granted credit. The objective for every firm is to find the ideal credit policy; that which maximizes net cash flow from sales.

An aggressive collection policy can also reduce bad debts. Customers should be contacted as soon as the account is overdue. For balances long overdue, the use of a collection agency may be advisable.

These policies fall under the heading of receivables management. In general, firms that actively manage their receivables suffer fewer losses than firms that do not.

Firms use two methods of accounting for doubtful accounts, (1) the direct charge-off method and (2) the allowance method.

Direct Charge-off Method

The direct charge-off method recognizes losses from doubtful accounts in the period in which a specific customer's account is determined to be uncollectible. The method is sometimes called the "direct write-off method." For example, if it is decided that the account receivable of John Mahoney for $200 has become uncollectible, the following entry would be made:

Bad Debts Expense	$200	
Accounts Receivable		$200
To record loss from an uncollectible customer's account.		

The direct charge-off method has three important shortcomings. First, the loss from doubtful accounts is usually not recognized in the period in which the sale occurs and revenue is recognized. Too much income is recognized in the period of sale and too little in the period of write-off. Second, the amount of losses from doubtful accounts recognized in any period is susceptible to intentional misrepresentation, because it is difficult to decide when a particular account becomes uncollectible. Third, the amount of accounts receivable on the balance sheet does not reflect the amount of cash expected to be collected. The direct charge-off method is not appropriate when such losses are significant in amount, occur frequently, and are reasonably predictable. However, a firm that has not had any bad debts for several years would be able to justify using this method.

Allowance Method

When amounts of uncollectibles can be estimated with reasonable precision, accounting requires an alternative procedure, the allowance method. The allowance method involves:

1. Estimating the amount of doubtful accounts that will occur over time in connection with the sales of each period.
2. Making an adjusting entry increasing the reported expense of the period for the estimated uncollectible amount.
3. Making a corresponding adjustment to the amount of accounts receivable so that the balance sheet figure reports the amount expected to be collected.

The entry involves a debit to Bad Debts Expense and a credit to Allowance for Doubtful

Accounts, which is an account contra to the total of Accounts Receivable. The credit must be made to a contra account rather than to Accounts Receivable because no specific, individual account is being written off at the time of entry.[4] Because the Allowance for Doubtful Accounts is a contra to Accounts Receivable, its balance at the end of the period will be deducted from Accounts Receivable. Since it is assumed that an adequate allowance for doubtful accounts has been made in the absence of a contrary statement, it is not considered necessary to refer to such allowance. The Bad Debts Expense is normally shown as a Selling, or Administration, Expense.[5]

To illustrate the allowance method, assume that two percent of the credit sales made during the present period are estimated never to be collected. If sales on account are $90,000, then the entry to increase expense and reduce the amount of Accounts Receivable to the amount expected to be collected would be:

Bad Debts Expense $1,800
   Allowance for Doubtful Accounts $1,800
To record estimate of uncollectible accounts arising from current
period's sales (.02 × $90,000).

When a particular customer's account is judged uncollectible, it is written off against the Allowance for Doubtful Accounts. If, for example, it is decided that a balance of $200 due from John Mahoney will not be collected, the entry to charge off the account is:

Allowance for Doubtful Accounts $200
   Accounts Receivable $200
To write off John Mahoney's account.

The entry to write off specific accounts may be made during the period, as information about specific customers' accounts is obtained, or at the end of the period as an adjusting entry.

---

[4]Recall that Accounts Receivable is a master, or "control," account showing the total of all amounts receivable from specific customers. There is a separate account for each customer in a subsidiary ledger; the Accounts Receivable account merely records their total.

---

[5]Views differ as to the type of account—expense or revenue contra—debited when providing for doubtful accounts. Many firms debit Bad Debts Expense and include its amount among total expenses on the income statement. Their rationale is that a certain amount of bad debts is a necessary "cost" of generating revenues. Advocates of using a revenue contra account point out that its use permits net sales to be shown at the amount of cash expected to be collected. When the provision is debited to an expense account and included among total expenses on the income statement, net sales will overstate the amount of cash expected to be received. More important, though, advocates of using a revenue contra account point out that uncollectible accounts cannot be an expense. Accounts that, at the time of recording, were not expected to be collected were never assets to begin with. Although the arguments for using a revenue contra account may be persuasive, Bad Debts Expense is the account debited in this book because that account is more widely used in practice. In either case, income remains the same.

Under the allowance method, the expense for the period of sale is increased by the amount of uncollectibles that is estimated to arise from that period's sales. Some time later, when the attempts at collection are finally abandoned, the specific account is written off. Net assets are not affected by writing off the specific account. The reduction in net assets took place earlier, when the Allowance for Doubtful Accounts was credited in the entry recognizing the estimated amount of eventual uncollectibles.

Estimating Uncollectibles

Accountants use two basic methods for calculating the amount of the adjustment for doubtful accounts: the *percentage of sales method* and the *aging of accounts receivable method*.

Percentage of Sales Method The easiest method in most cases is to multiply the total sales on account during the period by an appropriate percentage, because it seems reasonable to assume that doubtful account amounts will vary directly with the volume of credit business. (The example on page 344 used the percentage of sales method.) The percentage to be used is estimated by studying the experience of the business or by inquiring into the experience of similar enterprises. The rates found in use will generally be within the range of one-quarter percent to two percent of credit sales.

To illustrate, assume that sales on account total $1,500,000, and experience indicates that the appropriate percentage of doubtful accounts is two percent. The entry is:

Bad Debts Expense $30,000
    Allowance for Doubtful Accounts $30,000
To provide for estimate of uncollectibles computed as a
percentage of sales.

If cash sales occur in a relatively constant proportion of credit sales, the estimated uncollectibles percentage, proportionately reduced, can be applied to the total sales for the period. The total amount of all sales may be more readily available than that for sales on account.

Aging of Accounts Receivable Method A more time-consuming but more accurate method of calculating the amount of the adjustment, often called *aging the accounts*, involves classifying each customer's account as to the length of time for which the account has been uncollected. Common intervals used for classifying individual accounts receivable are:

1. Not yet due
2. Past due 30 days or less
3. Past due 31 to 60 days
4. Past due 61 to 180 days
5. Past due more than 180 days

The accountant presumes that the balance in the Allowance for Doubtful Accounts should be large enough to cover substantially all accounts receivable past due for more than 180 days and smaller portions of the more recent accounts. The actual portions are estimated from past experience.

As an example of the adjustment to be made, assume that the present balance in the Accounts Receivable account is $850,000 and the balance in the Allowance for Doubtful Accounts before the adjusting entry for the period is $36,000. An aging of the accounts receivable balance ($850,000), shown in Exhibit 7.4, results in an estimate that $68,000 of the accounts will probably become uncollectable. The adjustment requires that the Allowance for Doubtful Accounts balance be $68,000, an increase of $32,000. The adjusting entry at the end of the period is:

Bad Debts Expense	$32,000	
Allowance for Doubtful Accounts		$32,000
To increase Allowance account to $68,000 computed by an		
aging analysis; $68,000 − $36,000 = $32,000.		

Exhibit 7.4
Illustration of Aging Accounts Receivable

Classification of Accounts	Amount	Estimated Uncollectible Percentage	Estimated Uncollectible Amounts
Not yet due	$680,000	0.5%	$ 3,400
1–30 days past due	60,000	6.0	3,600
31–60 days past due	30,000	25.0	7,500
61–180 days past due	50,000	50.0	25,000
Over 180 days past due	30,000	95.0	28,500
	$850,000		$68,000

Even when the percentage of sales method is used, aging the accounts should be done periodically as an occasional check on the accuracy of the percentage being used. If the aging analysis shows that the balance in the Allowance for Doubtful Accounts is apparently too large or too small, the percentage of sales to be charged to Bad Debts Expense can be lowered or raised so that the apparent error will work itself out through future adjustments.

When the percentage of sales method is used, the periodic provision for doubtful accounts (for example, $30,000) is merely added to the amounts provided in previous periods in the account, Allowance for Doubtful Accounts. When the aging method is used, the balance in the account, Allowance for Doubtful Accounts, is adjusted (for example, by $32,000) to reflect the desired ending balance. If the percentage used under the percentage of sales method reasonably reflects collection experience, the *balance* in the allowance account should be approximately the same at the end of each period under these two methods of estimating doubtful accounts.

Exhibit 7.5 illustrates the operation of the allowance method for uncollectibles over two periods. In the first period the percentage method is used. In the second period the aging method is used. Normally, a firm would use the same method in all periods.

Exhibit 7.5
Review of the Allowance Method
of Accounting for Doubtful Accounts

Transactions in the First Period:
(1) Sales are $1,000,000.
(2) Cash of $937,000 is collected from customers in payment of their accounts.
(3) At the end of the first period, it is estimated that uncollectibles will be two percent of sales; .02 × $1,000,000 = $20,000.
(4) Specific accounts totaling $7,000 are written off as uncollectible.
(5) The bad debts expense and other temporary accounts are closed.

Transactions in the Second Period:
(6) Sales are $1,200,000.
(7) Specific accounts totaling $22,000 are written off during the period as information on their uncollectibility becomes known. The debit balance of $9,000 will remain in the Allowance account until the adjusting entry is made at the end of the period; see (9).
(8) Cash of $1,100,000 is collected from customers in payment of their accounts.
(9) An aging of the accounts receivable shows that the amount in the Allowance account should be $16,000. The amount of the adjustment is $25,000. It is computed as the difference between the desired $16,000 credit balance and the current $9,000 debit balance in the Allowance account.
(10) The bad debts expense and other temporary accounts are closed.

Cash		Accounts Receivable		Allowance for Doubtful Accounts	
		(1) 1,000,000			20,000 (3)
(2) 937,000			937,000 (2)		
			7,000 (4)	(4) 7,000	
Bal. ?		Bal. 56,000			13,000 Bal.
		(6) 1,200,000			
			22,000 (7)	(7) 22,000	
(8) 1,100,000			1,100,000 (8)		
					25,000 (9)
Bal. ?		Bal. 134,000			16,000 Bal.

Bad Debts Expense		Sales Revenue	
(3) 20,000			1,000,000 (1)
	Closed (5)	(5) Closed	
(9) 25,000			1,200,000 (6)
	Closed (10)	(10) Closed	

Cash Discounts

Often the seller of merchandise offers a reduction from its invoice price for prompt payment. Such reductions are called *cash discounts*.[6] There is nothing incongruous in the proposition that goods may have two prices: a cash price or a higher price if goods are sold on credit. The seller offers a cash discount not only as an interest allowance on funds paid before the bill is due—the implied interest rate is unreasonably large—but also an incentive for prompt payment so that additional book-keeping and collection costs can be avoided.

The goods are sold for a certain price if prompt payment is made, and a penalty is added in the form of a higher price if the payment is delayed. The bills rendered by some public utilities illustrate this approach. The amount of cash discount made available to customers, then, should be considered as one of the adjustments in the measurement of net sales revenue.

The need to prepare operating statements for relatively short periods leads to alternative possibilities for recording cash discounts and computing the amount of cash discounts reported for a period. The issue is whether the amount of cash discount should be deducted from sales revenue in the period when the sales revenue is recognized or in the period of cash collection. In computing the amount of cash discounts recognized for a period, the major alternatives are the following:

1. To recognize discounts when taken by the customer, without regard to the period of sale (called the *gross price method*).
2. To estimate the total amount of discounts that will be taken on the sales made during the period (called the *allowance method*).
3. To record sales amounts reduced by all discounts made available to customers and to recognize additional revenue when a discount lapses (called the *net price method*).

Intermediate accounting texts discuss these methods.

Trade Discounts

A common business practice is to allow customers who buy in large quantity a lower unit purchase cost. For instance Alpha Company might quote a list price of $500 for their machine but if 100 are purchased, 20% reduction in list price is granted and if more are purchased a further 5% reduction is allowed. If Beta Company ordered 140 machines, the invoice price would be:

On the first 100 units

List ($500 × 100)	$50,000
Less 20%	10,000
	$40,000

---

[6]See Glossary at the back of the book for the definition of a *discount* and a summary of the various contexts where this word is used in accounting.

On the next 40 units

List ($500 × 40)	$20,000
Less 25%	5,000
	$15,000
Invoice gross cost	$55,000
Unit cost	$ 393

Both the sale and the purchase would be recorded at $55,000 so the trade discount is not reflected in the accounts. Any cash discount allowed would be calculated on the $55,000.

The advantage of trade discounts, besides stimulating volume sales, is that a sales catalogue can be published once, showing list prices. The firm can use the same catalogue for all customers and allow trade discounts as it sees fit.

Sales Returns

When a customer returns merchandise, the sale has been canceled, and an entry that reverses the sale would be appropriate. In analyzing sales activities, however, management may be interested in the amount of goods returned. If so, a sales contra account is used to accumulate the amount of returns for a particular period.

A cash refund, such as might be made in a retail store when a customer returns merchandise that had been purchased for cash, would be entered as:

Sales Returns	$23	
Cash on hand		$23

Return of goods by a customer who buys "on account" would usually involve the preparation of a credit memorandum, which is the reverse of a sales invoice. The credit memorandum lists the goods that have been returned and indicates the amount that is to be allowed the customer. The entry to record the issuance of the credit would normally be a debit to the sales returns account and a credit to the Accounts Receivable account.

Misleading sales and income amounts can result if goods are returned in a period after the one of sale. If there is no adjustment in the period of sale for estimated returns, the sales and income amounts for the period of sale are overstated, because they reflect transactions that are later canceled. Further, sales and revenue amounts are correspondingly understated in the period when the goods are returned. An allowance method for estimated returns similar to that for estimated uncollectible accounts could be used. Because the amounts of sales returns for most businesses are usually relatively small, however, an allowance method is not often used.

Sales Allowances

A *sales allowance* is a reduction in price granted to a customer, usually after the goods have been delivered and found to be unsatisfactory or damaged. Again, as for sales returns, the effect is a reduction in the sales revenue, but it may be desirable to accumulate the amount of such adjustments as a separate item. An account, Sales Allowances, may be used for this purpose, or a combined account title, Sales Returns and Allowances, may be used. The record-keeping problems are similar to those caused by sales returns.

Presentation of Sales Adjustments in the Income Statement

In discussing the complications that accompany accounts receivable, several adjustments to sales that are accumulated in revenue contra accounts have been introduced. All these adjustments — for cash discounts, for returns, and for allowances — are illustrated in the Alexis Co. Ltd.'s income statement, Exhibit 7.6.

Exhibit 7.6
Income Statement Illustration of Sales and
Sales Adjustments, Alexis Co. Ltd.
Partial Income Statement
for the Year Ended June 30, Year 6

Revenues:		
Sales — Gross		$515,200
Less: Sales Adjustments		
Cash Discounts Taken[a]	$33,900	
Allowances	11,000	
Returns	8,600	
Total Sales Adjustments		53,500
Net Sales		$461,700

[a]The gross price method is used. If the net price method were used, discounts taken would not be shown and there would be an *addition* to revenue for the amount of sales discounts that lapsed.

Turning Receivables into Cash

A firm may find itself temporarily short of cash and unable to borrow from its usual sources. In such instances, accounts receivable can be used to obtain funds. A firm may *assign* its accounts receivable to a bank or finance company to obtain a loan. The borrowing company physically maintains control of the accounts receivable, collects amounts remitted by customers, and then forwards the proceeds to the lending institution. Alternatively, the firm may *pledge* its accounts receivable to the lending agency. If the borrowing firm is unable to make loan repayments when due, the lending agency has the power to sell the accounts receivable in order to obtain payment. Finally, the accounts receivable may be *factored* to a bank or finance company to obtain cash. In this case, the accounts receivable are, in effect, sold to the lending institution, which physically controls the receivables and collects payments from customers. If accounts receivable have been assigned or pledged, a footnote to the financial statements should indicate this fact. The collection of such accounts receivable will not increase the liquid resources available to the firm to pay general trade creditors. Accounts receivable that have been factored will not appear on the balance sheet, because they have been sold.

Notes Receivable

The last liquid asset considered in this chapter is notes receivable. Many business transactions involve written promises to pay sums of money at a future date. These written promises are called promissory notes. The holder of a promissory note has a liquid asset, notes receivable. A promissory note is a written contract in which one person, known as the *maker*, promises to pay to another person, known as the *payee*, a definite sum of money. The money may be payable either on demand or at a definite future date. A note may or may not provide for the payment of interest in addition to the principal amount.

Promissory notes are used most commonly in connection with obtaining loans at banks or other institutions, the purchase of various kinds of property, and as a temporary settlement of an open or charge account balance when payment cannot be made within the usual credit period. A note may be *secured* by a mortgage on real estate (land and buildings) or personal property (machinery and merchandise), or by the deposit of specific collateral (share certificates, bonds, and so forth). If the secured note is not collected at maturity, the lender can take possession of the real estate, personal property, or other collateral, sell it, and apply the proceeds to the repayment of the note. Any proceeds in excess of the amount due under the note are then paid to the borrower. Alternatively, the note may be *unsecured*, in which case it has about the same legal position as an account receivable.

Calculation of Interest Revenue

Interest is the price paid for the use of borrowed funds. From the lender's point of view, it is revenue. The interest price is usually expressed as a percentage rate of the principal, with the rate being stated on an annual basis. Thus, a two-month, 12-percent note would have interest equal to two percent of the principal; a four-month, 15-percent note would have interest equal to five percent of principal, and so on. Because interest is a payment for the use of borrowed funds for a period of time, it accrues with the passage of time. Although interest accrues every day (indeed, every time the clock ticks), firms usually record interest only at the time of payment or at the end of an accounting period.

Most short-term notes receivable from customers are based on *simple interest* calculations.[7] The general formula for the calculation of simple interest is:

$$\text{Interest} = \text{Base (Principal or Face)} \times \text{Interest Rate} \times \text{Elapsed Time}$$

---

[7]Most long-term notes involve *compound interest*, which is discussed in Appendix B.

The calculation of simple interest for a year or for any multiple or fraction of a year is an elementary arithmetic computation. For example, the interest at the rate of 12 percent a year on $20,000 is $200 for one month, $400 for two months, $1,200 for six months and so on. The calculation for shorter periods, although still not an involved mathematical problem, is complicated by the odd number of days in a year and the variations in the number of days in a month. Simple interest at the rate of 12 percent a year on $20,000 for 90 days would be $20,000 × .12 × 90/365, or $592, if an exact computation were made. For many purposes, especially the calculation of accrued interest, a satisfactory approximation of the correct interest can be obtained by assuming that the year has 360 days and that each month is one-twelfth of a year. Thus, 30 days is the equivalent of one month, and 60 days is the equivalent of two months, or one-sixth of a year. Under this method, the interest at 12 percent on $20,000 for 90 days would be the same as the interest for three months, or one-quarter of a year, or $600. Keep in mind that nearly all quotations of simple interest rates state the rate per year, unless some other period is specifically mentioned. In the formula for simple interest, Principal × Rate × Elapsed Time, "time" should be expressed in terms of years, or portions of a year, because the rate is the rate per year.

For the sake of uniformity and simplicity, we shall use the following rules in connection with the calculation of interest throughout the text and problems:

1. When the maturity terms are given in months, consider one month to be one-twelfth of a year; three months to be one-fourth of a year; six months to be half a year, and so on, regardless of the actual number of days in the period. This is equivalent to regarding any one-month period as being 30 days in a 360-day year.
2. When the maturity terms are given in days, use the 360-day year. Consider 30 days to be one-twelfth of a year, 60 days to be one-sixth of a year, 17 days to be 17/360 of a year, and so on. Calculate maturity dates and elapsed time by using the actual number of days.

Accounting for Interest-Bearing Notes Receivable

The notes to be discussed in this section, so-called interest-bearing notes, are those that indicate a face, or principal, amount together with explicit interest at a stated fair market rate for the time period stated in the note.[8] For example, the basic elements of such a note might read: "Two months after date (June 30), the Suren Co. Ltd. promises to pay to the order of the Mullen Co. Inc. $3,000 with interest from date at the rate of 12 percent per annum." At the maturity date, August 31, the maturity value would be the face amount of $3,000 plus interest of $60 calculated in accordance with the preceding discussion ($60 = $3,000 × .12 × 2/12), or a total of $3,060.

Among the transactions related to a note receivable discussed in this section are the following: receipt of note, interest recognition at an interim date, transfer prior to maturity, and collection at maturity date.

---

[8]Both non-interest-bearing notes, where the face amount is the same as the maturity value, and notes where the stated rate differs from the fair market rate, involve compound interest calculations; Chapters 10 and 11 discuss them.

Receipt of Notes and Collection at Maturity Promissory notes usually are received from customers in connection with sales or with the settlement of an open account receivable. The customer is usually the maker, but the customer may transfer a note that has been received from another. It is common practice to allow the customer full credit for the face value and accrued interest, if any, although a different value might be agreed upon in some instances.

If, on June 30, the Mullen Co. Inc. were to receive a 60-day, 12-percent note for $3,000, dated June 30, from the Suren Co. Ltd., to apply on its account, the entry would be:

June 30 Notes Receivable	$3,000	
Accounts Receivable—Suren Co. Ltd.		$3,000

Assuming that the accounting period of the Mullen Co. Inc. is the calendar year, the entry upon collection at maturity would be:

Aug. 31 Cash	$3,060	
Notes Receivable		$3,000
Interest Revenue		60

Assuming instead that the accounting period of the Mullen Co. Inc. is one month, the interest adjustment at the interim date, July 31, would be:

July 31 Interest Receivable	$30	
Interest Revenue		$30
($3,000 × .12 × 30/360 = $30.)		

The entry upon collection at maturity would then be:

Aug. 31 Cash	$3,060	
Notes Receivable		$3,000
Interest Receivable		30
Interest Revenue		30

At the maturity date, the note may be collected, as illustrated above, renewed, partially collected with renewal of the balance, or dishonored by the maker. These other possibilities involve more advanced accounting procedures and are not discussed in this book.

Transfer of Notes Receivable To obtain cash, a note may be transferred to another party *without recourse*. This procedure is equivalent to a sale of the note, because the transferor has no further liability even if the maker fails to pay at maturity.

If Mullen Co. Inc. transferred without recourse the two-month, 12-percent, $3,000 note to Lane Trust Company for $3,030 one month after the date of the note, the entry would be:

July 31 Cash	$3,030	
Notes Receivable		$3,000
Interest Revenue		30
To record transfer of note without recourse.		

Most businesses that "purchase" notes are, however, unwilling to acquire them without recourse. Such firms do not want to be responsible for investigating the credit-worthiness of the maker or for any collection efforts required for dishonored notes. Consequently, most notes that are transferred are done so *with recourse*.

A transfer with recourse places a potential or "contingent" obligation on the transferor if the maker fails to pay at maturity. Such a transfer is not a completed transaction because of the possibility that the endorser will have to pay the note in case the maker defaults at maturity.

Chapter 10 discusses contingent obligations, such as those for notes transferred with recourse or for the potential loss arising from an unsettled damage suit. Contingent obligations do not appear in the accounts, but are merely disclosed in notes to the balance sheet.

If Mullen Co. Inc. transferred with recourse the 60-day, 12-percent $3,000 note to Lane Trust Company one month after the date of the note, the entry would be the same as if the note was transferred without recourse. If Mullen Co. Inc. prepared financial statements before Lane Trust Company collected from the maker, however, the notes to Mullen's balance sheet would contain a statement such as the following:

Contingencies. The firm is contingently liable for a note transferred and accrued interest thereon to the Lane Trust Company. The face value of the transferred note is $3,000.

Illustration of Balance Sheet Presentation

The balance sheet accounts discussed in this chapter include Cash, Term Deposits, Temporary Investments, Notes Receivable, and Accounts Receivable. Exhibit 7.7 illustrates the presentation of these items in the balance sheet, which includes all of the current assets for the Alexis Co. Ltd. as of June 30, Year 6.

Exhibit 7.7
Detailed Illustration of Current Assets on the Balance Sheet
Alexis Co. Ltd. Balance Sheet (Excerpts)
June 30, Year 6 and Year 5

	June 30, Year 6		June 30, Year 5	
Current Assets:				
Cash in Change and Petty Cash Funds		$ 1,000		$ 800
Cash in Bank		14,500		12,500
Term Deposits		8,000		7,500
Temporary Investments at Acquisition Cost	$30,000		$25,000	
Less: Allowance for Excess of Cost of Temporary Investments over Market Value (On June 30, Year 5, market value of $31,000 exceeds cost)	(3,000)		—	
Temporary Investments at Lower of Cost and Market		27,000		25,000
Notes Receivable (See Note A)		12,000		10,000
Interest and Dividends Receivable		500		400
Accounts Receivable		54,500		53,700
Merchandise Inventory[a]		72,000		67,000
Prepayments		4,800		4,300
Total Current Assets		$194,300		$181,200

Note A. The amount shown for Notes Receivable does not include notes with a face amount of $2,000 that have been discounted with recourse at the First National Bank. The company is contingently liable for these notes, should the makers not honor them at maturity. The estimated amount of our liability is zero.

[a]Additional required disclosures for this item omitted here. See Chapter 8.

Effect of Transactions Involving Liquid Assets on the Statement of Changes in Financial Position

Temporary Investments

Recall from Chapter 5, page 216, that the CICA definition of cash for the statement of changes in financial position includes cash equivalents. These are synonymous with temporary investments by definition.

A write-down of the portfolio of temporary investments in applying the lower of cost or market method results in a loss that does not use cash. The funds statement shows an addition to net income for the loss in computing cash provided by operations.

Accounts Receivable

Unlike purchases and sales of temporary investments, transactions changing accounts receivable clearly involve operations. Because the change in accounts receivable is added to or subtracted from net income to derive cash provided by operations, no special entry need be made in preparing the funds statement.

Summary

This chapter has examined the accounting for cash and other liquid, or cash-like, assets. Among the questions addressed were the following:

1. What items are included in each of the liquid asset accounts?
2. At what amount are they stated?

Problem 1 for Self-Study

Refer to the data in Exhibit 7.2 showing transactions in temporary investments for Wolfson Limited over four years. Assume that in addition to those transactions, Wolfson Limited purchased 1,000 shares of D Ltd. on October 1, Year 1, for $40 per share, $40,000 in total. Shares of D Ltd. had a market value of $45 per share at the end of Year 1, $36 per share at the end of Year 2, $30 per share at the end of Year 3, and $50 per share at the end of Year 4.

a. For each of the four years, determine the amount reported as Temporary Investments in the December 31 balance sheet, and the amount reported as Holding Gain or Loss on Temporary Investments in the income statement, where Wolfson Limited uses each of the following bases to value Temporary Investments: lower of individual cost and market; or lower of aggregate cost and market.

b. Assume that during Year 5 Wolfson Limited sold the D Ltd. shares for $32,000 in place of selling the B Ltd. shares. At December 31, Year 5, the market value of the B Ltd. shares was $30,000. Compare the holding gain (loss) as originally reported and the amount reported under this alternative, under each of the bases of valuing temporary investments listed in (a) above.

Suggested Solution

a. See Exhibit 7.8.

Exhibit 7.8
Self-Study Problem 1
(Suggested Solution to Part **a**)

	Year 6	Year 5	Year 4	Year 3
Lower of Individual Cost and Market				
Balance Sheet Value at Dec. 31				
A Ltd.	$43,000^m	$ 50,000^c	$ 50,000^c	$ 50,000^c
B Ltd.	—	—	22,000^m	27,000^m
C Ltd.	—	16,000^{cv}	16,000^{cv}	16,000^m
D Ltd.	30,000^{cv}	30,000^m	36,000^m	40,000^c
Total	$73,000	$ 96,000	$124,000	$133,000
Holding Gain (Loss) during Year				
A Ltd.	$(7,000)	$ —	$ —	$ —
B Ltd.	—	10,000	(5,000)	(3,000)
C Ltd.	1,000	—	—	(4,000)
D Ltd.	—	(6,000)	(4,000)	—
Total	$(6,000)	$ 4,000	$ (9,000)	$ (7,000)
Lower of Aggregate Cost and Market				
Balance Sheet Value at Dec. 31				
Cost—A Ltd.	$50,000	$ 50,000	$ 50,000	$ 50,000
B Ltd.	—	—	30,000	30,000
C Ltd.	—	20,000	20,000	20,000
D Ltd.	40,000	40,000	40,000	40,000
Total	$90,000	$110,000	$140,000	$140,000
Less: Allowance for Decline	2,000	5,000	5,000	—
Carrying Value	$88,000^{cv}	$105,000^{cv}	$135,000^m	$140,000^c
Holding Gain (Loss) during Year				
On Sales	$(3,000)	$ 2,000	$ —	$ —
Other	3,000	—	(5,000)	—
Total	$ —	$ 2,000	$ (5,000)	$ —

^{c} = cost; ^{m} = market value; ^{cv} = carrying value.

b. See Exhibit 7.9.

Exhibit 7.9
Self-study Problem 1
(Suggested Solution to Part **b**)

Holding Gain (Loss) Reported
Year Ended December 1, Year 5

	Gain (Loss)	
	Original	Revised
Lower of Individual Cost or Market		
Investment A Ltd.	$ —	$ —
Investment B Ltd.	10,000	—
Investment C Ltd.	—	—
Investment D Ltd.	(6,000)	(4,000)
Total	$ 4,000	$ (4,000)

	B Ltd.	D Ltd.
Lower of Aggregate Cost or Market		
Gain (Loss on Sale of Shares):		
Sale Price	$32,000	$32,000
Less: Original Cost	30,000	40,000
Gain (Loss)	$ 2,000	$ (8,000)
Charged to Allowance for Decline	—	5,000
Holding Gain (Loss) Reported	$ 2,000	$ (3,000)

Problem 2 for Self-Study

Refer to the data in Exhibit 7.5 showing sales and collection activities for two periods. At the end of the third period, the *unadjusted* trial balance included the following accounts and amounts: Accounts Receivable — $75,000 debit; Allowance for Doubtful Accounts — $8,000 debit; Bad Debts Expense — zero (adjusting entries have not yet been made); Sales Revenue — $1,300,000. No further specific accounts receivable need be written off for the period.

a. Reconstruct the transactions of the third period, assuming all sales were made on account.

b. What were the total cash collections for the third period from customers who paid their accounts?

c. Reconstruct the transactions of the third period, assuming that only $1 million of the $1.3 million total sales were made on account.

d. What were the total cash collections for the third period, including collections both from customers who paid cash and from customers who paid their accounts?

e. Does one need to know the actual split of sales between cash sales and sales on account to know the total amount of cash collected from customers, that is, the sum of cash sales and collections on account? Why or why not?

f. Assume that two percent of all sales for the third period is estimated to be uncollectible. What is the adjusting entry to be made at the end of the third period for estimated uncollectibles? What net balance of Accounts Receivable will appear on the balance sheet at the end of the third period?

g. Independent of the answer to (**f**), assume that an aging of accounts receivable indicates that the amount in the Allowance for Doubtful Accounts appropriate for the status of outstanding accounts at the end of the third period is $20,000. What is the adjusting entry to be made at the end of the third period for estimated uncollectibles?

Suggested Solution

a. Sales were $1,300,000, debited to Accounts Receivable. Specific accounts receivable of $24,000 (= $16,000 credit at start of period plus $8,000 debit by the end of period) were written off with debits to the Allowance for Doubtful Accounts and credits to Accounts Receivable. Thus, the balance in accounts receivable before cash collections was $1,410,000 (= $134,000 + $1,300,000 − $24,000). Because the ending balance is actually $75,000, the cash collections from customers who bought on account are $1,335,000 (= $1,410,000 − $75,000).

b. $1,335,000, as derived above.

c. Sales were $1,300,000, debited $300,000 to Cash and $1,000,000 to Accounts Receivable. Specific accounts receivable of $24,000 were written off with debits to the Allowance for Doubtful Accounts and credits to Accounts Receivable. The amount is derived as in (**a**). The write-off of specific accounts left a balance of $1,110,000 (= $134,000 + $1,000,000 − $24,000), but the actual ending balance was $75,000, so $1,035,000 (= $1,110,000 − $75,000) of accounts must have been collected in cash.

d. $1,335,000 = $300,000 cash sales plus $1,035,000 from collections on account.

e. No. Once cash from a sale on account has been collected, the overall effect of the sale on the financial statements is identical with a cash sale. Thus, cash sales and collected credit sales have the same effects on the financial statements.

---

f. Bad Debts Expense $26,000

   Allowance for Doubtful Accounts $26,000

   Amount is equal to .02 × $1,300,000. Ending balance in the
   allowance account is $18,000 (= $26,000 credit less $8,000
   debit).

The net Accounts Receivable balance at the end of the third period is $57,000 (= $75,000 − $18,000).

---

g. Bad Debts Expense $28,000

   Allowance for Doubtful Accounts $28,000

   A $28,000 credit is required to establish a $20,000 credit
   balance in an account with a tentative $8,000 debit balance.

Questions, Exercises, Problems and Cases

Questions

1. Review the meaning of the following concepts or terms discussed in this chapter.

a. Generally accepted accounting principles	**m.** Lower of individual cost and market
b. AcSC	**n.** Lower of aggregate cost and market
c. Canada Business Corporations Act	**o.** Market value
d. Liquidity	**p.** Bad Debts Expense
e. Insolvent	**q.** Aging of accounts receivable
f. Cash	**r.** Sales Discounts
g. Demand deposits	**s.** Sales Returns and Allowances
h. Term deposit	**t.** Simple interest
i. Foreign currency	**u.** Recourse
j. Allowance for doubtful accounts	**v.** Factoring
k. Temporary investments	**w.** Contingent obligation
l. Investments (noncurrent)	

2. What purpose is served by having a broad set of financial reporting objectives, such as those issued by the FASB?

3. Generally accepted accounting principles are the methods of accounting used by publicly held firms in preparing their financial statements. A principle in physics, such as the law of gravity, serves as a basis for developing theories and explaining the relations among physical objects. In what ways are generally accepted accounting principles similar to and different from principles of physics?

4. What are the strengths and weaknesses of the standard-setting process followed by the Accounting Standards Committee of the CICA?

5. Distinguish between a Research Study, an Exposure Draft of a Proposed Handbook Revision, and a Handbook Revision Release.

6. What evidence of cash control have you observed in a cafeteria? A department store? A theatre? A gasoline station?

7. The Tastee Delight ice cream stores prominently advertise on signs in the stores that the customer's purchase is free if the clerk does not present a receipt. Oakland's Original hot dog stand says that the customer's purchase is free if the cash register receipt contains a red star. What control purposes do such policies serve?

8. Current assets are defined as those assets that are expected to be turned into cash, or sold, or consumed within the next operating cycle. Cash is not always classified as a current asset, however. Explain.

9. Does application of the lower of cost and market valuation method to the portfolio of temporary investments or to each temporary investment individually result in the most conservative asset values and net income amounts?

10. Which of the two methods for treating uncollectible accounts (direct write-off or allowance) implies recognizing income reductions earlier rather than later? Why?

11. a. An old adage in tennis holds that if your first serves are always good, then you are not hitting them hard enough. An analogous statement in business might be that if you have no uncollectible accounts, then you probably are not selling enough on credit. Comment on the validity of this statement.
   b. When are more uncollectible accounts better than fewer uncollectible accounts?
   c. When is a higher percentage of uncollectible accounts better than a lower one?

12. The customary method of accounting for sales results in adequate reporting for the returned sales when the goods are returned in the same period in which they are sold. If the goods are returned in a period subsequent to that of the sale, distortion of the reported income results. Explain how sales returns may produce each of the described effects.

13. Under what circumstances will the Allowance for Doubtful Accounts have a debit balance during the accounting period? The balance sheet figure for the Allowance for Doubtful Accounts at the end of the period should never show a debit balance. Why?

14. What is the effect on the financial statements of discounting, or transferring, a note with recourse versus without recourse?

Exercises

15. *Inclusions in Cash account.* Indicate if each of the following items should be included in "cash" on the balance sheet. If not, indicate how the item should be reported.

   a. Cash that has been collected from customers and is awaiting deposit in the firm's chequing account.
   b. Cash left in cash registers each day, which serves as a change fund.
   c. Cash set aside in a special savings account to accumulate funds to replace equipment as it wears out. The firm is not legally obligated to use the funds for this purpose.
   d. Cash set aside in a special savings account to accumulate funds to retire debt as it becomes due. The firm is legally obligated to use the funds for this purpose.
   e. A postdated cheque received from a customer. The cheque is dated 60 days after the date of the balance sheet.
   f. A money order received from a customer.
   g. Postage stamps.
   h. Cash held for small miscellaneous expenditures, such as freight charges and executive lunches.

16. *Inclusions in Cash account.* You are asked to compute the amount that should be shown as Cash on the balance sheet as of December 31 for Zeff Transportation Limited from the following information.

a. Coins, currency, and cheques received from customers on December 31, but not yet deposited, $6,500.

b. Cash held for making small miscellaneous cash expenditures. The fund normally has a balance of $100, but expenditures of $22 were made on December 31.

c. The firm's postage meter was "filled" on December 31 and contains $500 of postage.

d. The books indicate that the balance in the firm's chequing account on December 31 is $45,800. When the bank statement is received on the next January 10, it is learned that one customer's cheque for $800, which was deposited on December 28, was returned for insufficient funds. In addition, during December the bank collected $2,200 for a note receivable from one of Zeff's customers and added the amount to Zeff's bank account. The note had a face value of $2,000 and interest of $200.

e. Term deposit for a face value of $10,000. The deposit was acquired on July 1 of this year and matures on June 30 of next year. Simple interest of 12 percent per year accumulates on the note and is payable at maturity with the principal.

f. British sterling currency, £10,000. The exchange rate on December 31 is $1.60 per pound sterling.

17. *Bank reconciliation.*

   a. Arrange the following data related to Antle Inc. in bank reconciliation form.

Adjusted Bank Balance	$6,713
Adjusted Book Balance	6,713
Balance per Bank Statement, October 31	7,873
Balance per Books, October 31	6,028
Error in Deposit of October 28; $457 Deposit Entered on Books as $547	90
Outstanding Cheques	1,305
Payroll Account Cheque Deducted from This Account in Error	145
Proceeds on Note of W. Y. Smith, Taken by the Bank for Collection, Less Collection Fee of $25	775

   b. Present journal entries on the books of Antle Inc. to record the adjustments indicated in the bank reconciliation schedule.

18. *Bank reconciliation.*

   a. Prepare a bank reconciliation schedule at July 31 for the Home Appliance Co. Ltd. from the following information:

Balance per Bank Statement, July 29	$1,240
Balance per Ledger, July 31	714
Deposit of July 30 Not Recorded by Bank	280
Debit Memo — Service Charges	8
Credit Memo — Collection of Note by Bank	300

An analysis of canceled cheques returned with the bank statement reveals the following: Cheque #901 for purchase of supplies on account was correctly drawn for $58 but was recorded as $85. The manager wrote a cheque for traveling expenses of $95 while out of town. The cheque was not recorded. The following cheques are outstanding:

#650	$120
#721	162
#728	300
	$582

    b. Journalize the adjusting entries required by the information revealed in the bank reconciliation.

19. *Bank reconciliation.* On May 31, the books of the Griffin Co. Ltd. show a debit balance in the Cash in Bank account of $4,720. The bank statement at that date shows a balance of $6,000. The deposit of May 31 of $250 is not included in the bank statement. Notice of collections made by the bank on mortgages of the company in the amount of $350, including interest of $250, and of bank service charges of $20 have not previously been received. Outstanding cheques at May 31 total $1,200.

    a. Prepare a bank reconciliation for the Griffin Co. Ltd. at May 31.
    b. Journalize the entries required upon preparation of the bank reconciliation.

20. *Classify temporary investments.* Indicate the classification of each of the securities below in the balance sheet of Bower Corporation on December 31.

    a. Treasury Bills, acquired on October 15. The bills mature next April 15.
    b. Shares of Brazil Coffee Corporation, a major supplier of raw materials for Bower Corporation's products.
    c. Shares of Overland Transportation Limited. The shares were originally acquired as a temporary investment of excess cash. Overland Transportation Limited has been so profitable that Bower Corporation plans to increase its ownership percentage, eventually obtaining 51 percent of the outstanding shares.
    d. Ontario Hydro bonds that mature in three years. The bonds were acquired with a cash advance from a customer on a contract for the manufacture of machinery and will be sold, as needed, to pay costs of manufacturing. The manufacturing process will take three years.

21. *Journal entries for holdings of temporary investments.* The following list gives all events for Germont Inc.'s actions with respect to its current asset portfolio of temporary investments during the period August, Year 1, through January, Year 2.

    8/21   Germont Inc. purchases 1,000 shares of Grenvil Co. Ltd. for $15 per share. In addition, it pays $150 in brokerage commissions to its stockbroker.

    9/1   The stockbroker calls Germont Inc. to report that Grenvil Co. Ltd. shares closed on the preceding day at $18 per share.

9/30   Grenvil Co. Ltd. declares a dividend of $.25 per share.

10/25   Germont Inc. receives a dividend cheque for $250.

12/31   The stockbroker calls Germont Inc. to report that Grenvil Co. Ltd. shares closed the year at $11 per share. The books are closed for the year.

1/31   Germont Inc. sells 600 shares of Grenvil Co. Ltd. for $13 per share, the closing price for the day. Brokerage commissions, deducted from the proceeds, are $100.

1/31   Germont Inc. prepares an up-to-date balance sheet as part of an application for a loan.

Prepare dated journal entries as required by the events described above.

22. *Journal entries for portfolio of temporary investments.* The aggregate cost and aggregate market value of the portfolio of temporary investments, current assets, of Elson Corporation at various dates appear below:

Date	Aggregate Cost	Aggregate Market Value
December 31, Year 1	$150,000	$140,000
December 31, Year 2	160,000	144,000
December 31, Year 3	170,000	185,000
December 31, Year 4	180,000	160,000

No temporary investments were sold during these years. Give the journal entry required at the end of each year, assuming that the accounting period is the calendar year.

23. *Journal entries for the allowance method.* The trial balance of the Walker Co. Ltd. at the end of its first year of operations included $20,000 of outstanding customers' accounts. An analysis reveals that 80 percent of the total credit sales of the year had been collected and that no accounts had been charged off as uncollectible.

The credit manager estimated that two percent of the total credit sales would be uncollectible. On the next January 31, the account of H. J. Williams, who had owed a balance of $300 for six months, was judged uncollectible and was written off.

On July 1, the amount owed by H. J. Williams, previously written off, was collected in full.

Present dated journal entries to record the following:

  a. Adjustment for estimated uncollectible accounts on December 31.

  b. Write-off of the H. J. Williams account on January 31.

  c. Collection of the H. J. Williams account on July 1. Assume that it is felt that there is evidence that the account should never have been written off as uncollectible, and that total uncollectibles are likely not to be different from the original estimates.

24. *Reconstructing events when allowance method is used.* The balance sheets of Wilton Corporation on December 31, Year 1 and Year 2, showed gross accounts receivable of $8,300,000 and $9,700,000, respectively. You are advised that the balances in the Allowance for Doubtful Accounts account at the beginning and end of Year 2, after closing entries, were credits of $750,000 and $930,000, respectively. The income statement for Year 2 shows that the bad debts expense was $300,000, which was one percent of sales. All sales are made on account. There were no recoveries during Year 2 of accounts written off in previous years.

Give all the journal entries made during Year 2 that have an effect on Accounts Receivable and Allowance for Doubtful Accounts.

25. *Aging accounts receivable.* Love Limited's accounts receivable show the following balances by ages:

Age of Accounts	Balance Receivable
0–30 Days	$300,000
31–60 Days	75,000
61–120 Days	30,000
More than 120 Days	15,000

The credit balance in the Allowance for Doubtful Accounts is now $6,000.

Love Limited's credit manager suggests that the following percentages be used to compute the estimates of amounts that will eventually prove uncollectible: 0–30 days, .5 of 1 percent; 31–60 days, 1 percent; 61–120 days, 10 percent; more than 120 days, 60 percent.

Prepare a journal entry that will carry out the credit manager's suggestion.

26. *Aging accounts receivable.* Rozay Corporation's accounts receivable show the following balances:

Age of Accounts	Balance Receivable
0-30 Days	$500,000
31–60 Days	175,000
61–120 Days	80,000
More than 120 Days	40,000

An adjusting entry based on the percentage of sales method has already been made for the period. The credit balance in the Allowance for Uncollectible Accounts is now $30,000. The Bad Debt Expense account has a balance of $35,000.

Analysis of recent collection experience suggests that the following percentages be used to compute the estimates of amounts that will eventually prove uncollectible: 0–30 days, .5 of 1 percent; 31–60 days, 1 percent, 61–120 days, 10 percent; more than 120 days, 40 percent.

Prepare the indicated adjusting entry.

27. *Simple interest computations.* Calculate simple interest on a base of $6,000 for the following intervals and rates, using a 360-day year.

    a. 60 days at 12 percent
    b. 90 days at 9 percent

c. 60 days at 16 percent

d. 15 days at 16 percent

e. 5 months, 15 days at 12 percent

28. *Journal entries for notes.* On May 10, the Dukes Co. Ltd. receives a note from one of its customers, Salk Builders, Inc., to apply on its account. The six-month, 12 percent note for $6,000, issued on May 10, is valued at its face amount, $6,000.

On July 25, the Dukes Co. Ltd. endorses the note and transfers it with recourse to Beaver Ltd. to settle an account payable. The note is valued at its face amount plus accrued interest.

On November 12, the Dukes Co. Ltd. is notified that the note was paid at maturity.

    a. Present dated entries on the books of the Dukes Co. Ltd., assuming that it closes its books quarterly on March 31, June 30, and so on.

    b. Present dated entries on the books of Beaver Ltd., assuming that it closes its books quarterly on March 31, June 30, and so on.

29. *Effect of compensating balances on effective interest rate.* Davidoff Corporation borrowed $1 million from the local bank on July 1. The bank charged Davidoff Corporation interest at its prime lending rate of 13.5 percent. The principal and interest on the loan are repayable on the following June 30. Davidoff Corporation must maintain a $100,000 compensating balance in an interest-free chequing account at the bank during the term of the loan.

    a. What is the effective annual interest rate that Davidoff Corporation is paying on this loan?

    b. What message to Davidoff Corporation is implicit in the bank's requirement that a compensating balance be maintained?

30. *Journal entries for the allowance method.* The trial balance of the Biddle Company at the end of its first year of operations included $25,000 of outstanding customers' accounts. An analysis revealed that 90 percent of the total credit sales of the year had been collected and that no accounts had been charged off as uncollectible.

The auditor estimated that 1 percent of the total credits sales would be uncollectible. On the next January 31, the account of Robert Jesse, who had owed a balance of $500 for 6 months, was judged uncollectible and was written off.

On August 1, the amount owed by Robert Jesse, previously written off, was collected in full.

Present dated journal entries to record the following:

    a. Adjustment for estimated uncollectible accounts for December 31.

    b. Write-off of the Robert Jesse account on January 31.

    c. Collection of the Robert Jesse account on August 1. Assume that it is believed there is evidence that the account should never have been written off as uncollectible and that total uncollectibles are likely not to be different from the original estimates.

Problems and Cases

31. *Bank reconciliation and journal entries.* The bank reconciliation of the Clovis Company at March 31 was as follows:

Balance per Bank Statement, March 31	$3,965
Unrecorded Deposit	475
Outstanding Cheques	820
Adjusted Bank and Book Balance, March 31	3,620

The bank statement, returned cheques, and other documents received from the bank at the end of April provide the following information:

Balance, April 29	$ 3,800
Deposit of March 31	475
Deposits of April 1–29 Including a Credit Memo for a Collection of a Note, $860	16,160
Canceled Cheques Issued Prior to April 1	600
Canceled Cheques Issued During April	16,200

The Cash in Bank account of the Clovis Company for the month of April shows deposits of $16,140 and cheques drawn of $17,015. The credit memo has not as yet been recorded on the books of the company; it represents the collection of a note with $800 face value on which $40 of the $60 total interest had already been accrued as of March 31.

    a. Prepare a bank reconciliation for the Clovis Company at April 30.

    b. Present in journal entry form any adjustment of the company's books resulting from the information generated by the bank reconciliation.

32. *Journal entries and financial statement presentation of temporary investments.* The information below summarizes data about the temporary investments of Albion Corporation.

					Market Value	
Security	Date Acquired	Acquisition Cost	Date Sold	Selling Price	Dec. 31, Year 1	Dec. 31, Year 2
A	1/5/Year 1	$40,000	11/5/Year 2	$50,000	$30,000	—
B	6/12/Year 1	85,000	—	—	90,000	$82,000
C	2/22/Year 2	48,000	—	—	—	46,000
D	3/25/Year 2	25,000	12/5/Year 2	18,000	—	—
E	4/25/Year 2	36,000	—	—	—	50,000

    a. Give all journal entries relating to these temporary investments during Year 1 and Year 2, assuming that the calendar year is the accounting period, when the company values temporary investments at: the lower of individual cost and market; or the lower of aggregate cost and market.

    b. Indicate the manner in which temporary investments would be presented in the balance sheet and related notes on December 31, Year 1, under each alternative listed in (**a**).

    c. Indicate the manner in which temporary investments would be presented in the balance sheet and related notes on December 31, Year 2, under each alternative listed in (**a**).

33. *Financial statement presentation of temporary investments.* Exhibit 7.10 gives data on holdings of temporary investments of Sprouse Limited for Year 1 and Year 2. There were no sales of securities during Year 1. During Year 2 Sprouse Limited purchased new shares in Security F. During Year 2 the following sales of securities took place:

	Net Proceeds of Sale	Cost	Realized Gain (Loss)
Security A	$125,000	$100,000	$ 25,000
Security B	65,000	100,000	(35,000)
	$190,000	$200,000	$(10,000)

Exhibit 7.10
Data on Temporary Investments for Sprouse Limited

	Year 2		Year 1	
	Cost	Market	Cost	Market
In Current Assets:				
Security A	$100,000	$100,000	$200,000	$250,000
B	200,000	150,000	300,000	250,000
C	200,000	175,000	200,000	150,000
D	150,000	100,000	150,000	200,000
E	50,000	100,000	50,000	75,000
F	200,000	225,000	—	—
Total of Portfolio	$900,000	$850,000	$900,000	$925,000

The company wishes to determine the impact on the financial statements of valuing temporary investments at: the lower of individual cost and market; or the lower of aggregate cost and market. Ignore income taxes.

    a. Prepare in parallel columns for year-end 2 and 1 the data that appear in the December 31, Year 2 balance sheet for each alternative valuation.

    b. Determine the holding gains and losses that would be included in calculating net income for Year 1 and Year 2 for each alternative valuation.

34. *Effects of applying lower of cost and market to entire portfolios, rather than security by security.* Information relating to the temporary investments of TSS Limited is shown below:

					Market Value	
Security	Date Acquired	Acquisition Cost	Date Sold	Selling Price	Dec. 31, Year 2	Dec. 31, Year 1
H	4/26/1	$18,000	2/9/2	$15,000	—	$16,000
I	5/25/1	25,000	8/10/2	26,000	—	24,000
J	11/24/1	12,000	—	—	$15,000	14,000
K	2/26/2	34,000	—	—	33,400	—
L	12/17/2	8,000	—	—	8,800	—

    a. Compute the net holding gain or loss reported in the Year 1 and Year 2 income statements where the company values temporary investments at: the lower of individual cost and market; the lower of aggregate cost and market; and market value.

    b. Which alternative results in the most conservative asset values and measure of income?

35. *Allowance method; working "backwards."* The sales, all on account, of the Needles Inc. in Year 1, its first year of operations, were $600,000. Collections totaled $500,000. On December 31, Year 1, it was estimated that 1.5 percent of all sales would probably be uncollectible. On that date, specific accounts in the amount of $3,000 were written off.

The company's *unadjusted* trial balance (but after all nonadjusting entries were made) on December 31, Year 2, included the following accounts and balances:

Accounts Receivable (Dr.)	$60,000	
Allowance for Doubtful Accounts (Dr.)	4,000	
Bad Debt Expense	—	
Sales (Cr.)		$700,000

In Year 2, Needles Inc. switched to the aging method for estimating uncollectibles. It estimated that the Year 2 ending balance of accounts receivable contained $12,000 of probable uncollectibles. You may assume, although it is not necessary to do so (why?), that all sales in Year 2 were made on account.

Present journal entries for the following:

    a. Transactions and adjustments of Year 1 related to sales and customers' accounts.

    b. Transactions of Year 2 resulting in the above trial balance amounts.

    c. Adjustment for estimated uncollectibles for Year 2.

36. *Reconstructing events when allowance method is used.* The amounts in certain accounts on January 1, and before adjusting entries on December 31, appear below:

	December 31	January 1
Accounts Receivable	$ 500,000 Dr.	$400,000 Dr.
Allowance for Doubtful Accounts	20,000 Dr.	30,000 Cr.
Bad Debt Expense	0	0
Sales	2,000,000 Cr.	0

During the year, 90 percent of sales were on account and three percent of credit sales are judged to be uncollectible. During the year one account for $1,500 was collected, although it had been written off as uncollectible during the preceding year. When the written-off account was reinstated, the credit was to the Allowance account.

    a. Give the journal entries made during the year that explain the changes in the four accounts as listed above.

    b. Give any adjusting entries required on December 31.

37. *Estimating percentage of uncollectibles.* The data in the following schedule pertain to the first eight years of the Glidden Limited's credit sales and experiences with uncollectible accounts.

Year	Credit Sales	Related Uncollectible Accounts	Year	Credit Sales	Related Uncollectible Accounts
1	$200,000	$5,100	5	$500,000	$6,000
2	300,000	6,450	6	550,000	5,400
3	400,000	7,450	7	560,000	5,750
4	450,000	8,000	8	580,000	5,950

Glidden Limited has not previously used an Allowance for Doubtful Accounts but has merely charged accounts written off directly to Bad Debts Expense.

What percentage of credit sales for a year would you recommend that Glidden Limited charge to Bad Debts Expense if the allowance method were to be adopted at the end of Year 8?

38. *Decision to extend credit to a new class of cusotmers.* The Feldman Company has a gross margin on credit sales of 30 percent. That is, cost of goods sold on account is 70 percent of sales on account. Uncollectible accounts amount to two percent of credit sales. If credit is extended to a new class of customers, credit sales will increase by $10,000, eight percent of the new credit sales will be uncollectible, and all other costs, including interest to finance extra inventories, will increase by $1,000.

   a. Would Feldman Company be better or worse off if it extended credit to the new class of customer and by how much?

   b. How would your answer to part **(a)** differ if $3,000 of the $10,000 increase in credit sales had been made anyway as sales for cash? (Assume that the uncollectible amount on new credit sales is $800.)

39. *Decision to extend credit; working backwards to uncollectible rate.* The Hanrahan Company has credit sales of $100,000, a gross margin on those sales of 25 percent, with three percent of the credit sales uncollectible. If credit is extended to a new class of customers, sales will increase by $40,000, other expenses will increase by $2,500, and uncollectibles will be five percent of *all* credit sales. Verify that Hanrahan Company will be $3,500 better off if it extends credit to the new customers. What percentage of the new credit sales are uncollectible?

40. *Journal entries for notes.* On November 1, Year 1, Atlas Corp. receives a note from one of its customers to apply on its open account receivable. The nine-month, 18 percent note for $8,000, issued November 1, Year 1, is valued at its face amount.

On January 31, Year 2, Atlas Corp. endorses the note and transfers it with recourse to First Canadian Bank in return for a cash payment of $8,100. The company's chequing account at this bank is increased for the proceeds, $8,100.

On August 1, Year 2, Atlas Corp. is notified by the bank that the note was collected from the customer at maturity.

Atlas Corp. closes its books annually on December 31.

Present dated journal entries on the books of Atlas Corp. relating to this note.

41. *Reconstructing events from journal entries.* Give the likely transaction or event that would result in making each of the independent journal entries below:

a. Notes Receivable	$300	
Accounts Receivable		$300
b. Temporary Investments	$10,000	
Cash		$10,000
c. Bad Debts Expense	$2,300	
Allowance for Doubtful Accounts		$2,300
d. Holding Loss on Valuation of Temporary Investments	$4,000	
Allowance for Excess of Cost of Temporary Investments		
over Market Value		$4,000
e. Cash	$295	
Notes Receivable		$285
Interest Revenue		10
f. Cash	$1,200	
Loss on Sale of Temporary Investments	200	
Temporary Investments		$1,400
g. Allowance for Doubtful Accounts	$450	
Accounts Receivable		$450
h. Bad Debts Expense	$495	
Accounts Receivable		$495
i. Accounts Receivable	$285	
Allowance for Doubtful Accounts		$285

42. *Funds statement effects.* Refer to the Simplified Statement of Changes in Financial Position Statement for a Period in Exhibit 5.19 on page 248. Eleven of the lines in the statement are numbered. Ignore the unnumbered lines in responding to the questions below.

Assume that the accounting cycle is complete for the period and that all of the financial statements have been prepared. Then it is discovered that a transaction has been overlooked. That transaction is recorded in the accounts, and all of the financial statements are corrected. Define *funds* as *cash*.

For each of the following transactions or events, indicate which of the numbered lines of the funds statement is affected and by how much. Ignore income tax effects.

    a. Estimated uncollectibles equal to one percent of the year's sales of $1 million are recognized. An entry is made increasing the Allowance for Doubtful Accounts.

    b. The specific account receivable of Eli Worman in the amount of $2,000 is written off by a firm using the allowance method.

    c. The specific account receivable of Eli Worman in the amount of $3,000 is written off by a firm using the direct write-off method.

    d. A firm owns temporary investments. Dividends of $30,000 are declared on the shares owned. The payment will be received next period.

    e. The portfolio of temporary investments acquired this period has a market value of $60,000 less than their net amount shown on the balance sheet at the end of the current accounting period. An entry is made changing the allowance account contra to the current asset, temporary investments.

    f. The market value of the same portfolio of temporary investments referred to in part (**e**) has increased $40,000 by the end of the next period.

43. *Prepare funds statement; adapted from a problem by Stan Baiman.* Exhibit 7.11 shows comparative balance sheets and an income statement of Trimolet Limited for Year 2.

    Prepare the Year 2 statement of changes in financial position with funds defined as cash.

Exhibit 7.11
TRIMOLET LIMITED
Comparative Balance Sheets and Income Statement

	December 31	
Balance Sheets	**Year 2**	**Year 1**
Cash	$130,000	$ 50,000
Accounts Receivable	110,000	100,000
Less: Allowance for Doubtful Accounts	(25,000)	(20,000)
Inventory	90,000	100,000
Prepaid Rent	250,000	220,000
Total Assets	$555,000	$450,000
Accounts Payable	$ 40,000	$ 20,000
Capital Stock	135,000	200,000
Retained Earnings	380,000	230,000
Total Equities	$555,000	$450,000
Year 2 Income Statement		
Gross Sales		$500,000
Less: Sales Discounts		5,000
Net Sales		$495,000
Cost of Goods Sold		200,000
Gross Profit		$295,000
Less:		
Bad Debts Expense	$15,000	
Rent Expense	30,000	45,000
Net Income Before Income Tax		$250,000
Income Tax Expense		100,000
Net Income		$150,000

Note: During Year 2, $6,000 in specific accounts receivables were defaulted upon and written off as uncollectible.

44. *Management of investment portfolios to affect income and financial statement ratios.* The chief financial officer (CFO) of Easton Limited is nervous about the state of the company's financial affairs, as reflected in its tentative post-closing trial balance at the end of the current year, which appears in Exhibit 7.12. The CFO worries that the current ratio is too low.

    Several years ago, the company borrowed $6 million in the form of a long-term bond issue, maturing 15 years from now, carrying an interest rate of 7.5 percent per year. Interest rates have increased substantially since then, and comparable borrowings would now cost the firm more than ten percent per year. The CFO worries about terms of the bond agreement that require the firm to maintain a ratio of current assets to current liabilities of at least 1.20 to 1.00. If the current ratio falls below that amount, then the bond issue becomes due immediately, rather than maturing at its original maturity date, which is still 15 years in the future. The CFO knows it will be costly to borrow new funds to replace the old.

Over the past several years Easton Limited has acquired various holdings of temporary investments, some as current assets and some as noncurrent assets. Data on these holdings appear in Exhibit 7.12. The decline in value of C Corp. and D. Co. Ltd. occurred during the current year and is considered temporary. The holdings of any one company were acquired in a single transaction. The CFO wonders what, if anything, can be done with the holdings of temporary investments to keep the call provision of the bond issue from being triggered.

The chief executive officer (CEO) of Easton Limited has discussed these problems with the CFO and raises another issue. The CEO's compensation package contains a bonus clause. As things now stand, the CEO will not receive a bonus because income for the year is $1.5 million short of the minimum for a bonus to be earned. Neither the CFO nor the CEO want the firm to incur any extra income tax payments, as will become payable at a rate of 40 percent on any gains realized on sale of securities. Both the CEO and the CFO seek your advice.

a. Is the bond issue in danger of being declared due for current payment? Why or why not?

b. What actions, if any, can management of Easton Limited undertake to protect the outstanding bond issue from coming due at the end of the current year without having to pay additional income taxes? Provide journal entries that record the actions you suggest. What is the effect on income? On shareholder's equity?

c. What actions, if any, can management undertake to boost reported income sufficiently so that the CEO will receive a bonus? Provide journal entries that record the actions you suggest. How will these actions affect the current ratio?

Exhibit 7.12
EASTON LIMITED
Tentative Post-Closing Trial Balance at Current Year-End
(dollar amounts in thousands)
(Problem 44)

	Dr.	Cr.
Allowance for Excess of Cost of Temporary Investments over Market Value (current asset contra)		$ 2,500
Current Liabilities		5,500
Portfolio Investments (noncurrent assets)	$ 3,000	
Temporary Investments (current assets), at Cost	3,500	
Noncurrent Liabilities		6,000
Other Current Assets	5,000	
Other Noncurrent Assets, Net	12,000	
Owner's Equity Accounts		9,500
Totals	$23,500	$23,500

Holdings of Equity Securities

	Cost	Year-End Market-Value
Current Assets:		
A Ltd.	$ 2,000	$ 600
B Inc.	1,500	400
Total	$ 3,500	$ 1,000
Noncurrent Assets:		
C Corp.	$ 1,000	$ 5,000
D Co. Ltd.	2,000	1,600
Total	$ 3,000	$ 6,600

45. *Preparing an income statement.* Selected balance sheet accounts for Richman Enterprises as at December 31 are as follows:

	1988	1987
Accounts receivable	$ 13,400	$ 11,500
Inventory	27,000	15,000
Accounts payable for merchandise	(14,000)	(9,000)
Accrued liabilities for operating expenses	(12,000)	(16,000)
Owner's equity (E. Richman)	(122,000)	(110,000)

An analysis of the cash account as at December 31, 1988, revealed the following:

(1) $160,000 had been paid to merchandise suppliers during the year;
(2) $42,000 had been paid for operating expenses;
(3) $24,000 had been withdrawn from the business by E. Richman in the form of dividends;
(4) $237,000 had been collected from customers.

Depreciation on buildings and equipment is $10,000 per year. A reasonable estimate of bad debts is 4% of sales and is recorded in the Allowance for Doubtful Accounts Receivable account. Write-offs of uncollectible accounts during 1988 were $7,975. Assume that all sales, purchases, and operating expenses are made on account.

a. Prepare in good form an income statement for 1988 from the information given above. Ignore taxes and show all calculations.

Adapted with permission from the Society of Management Accountants of Canada.

46. *Temporary investments.* The following schedule shows the Sackman Corporation's portfolio of temporary investments at December 31, of each year:

	1988		1987	
	Cost	Market	Cost	Market
Security A	$150,000	$100,000	$150,000	$135,000
B	100,000	75,000	200,000	180,000
C	50,000	80,000	50,000	60,000
D	70,000	60,000	70,000	75,000
	$370,000	$315,000	$470,000	$450,000

The initial portfolio was acquired during 1987. During 1988, one half of the investment in Security B was sold for $130,000.

The management of Sackman would like to determine the impact on income of valuing temporary investments at the lower of individual cost and market, or the lower of portfolio (i.e., aggregate) cost and market.

    a. Determine the effect on income of the temporary investments for 1987 and 1988 using:
     (i) the lower of individual cost and market.
    (ii) the lower of portfolio (aggregate) cost and market.
    Show all supporting calculations.
    b. Determine the unrealized holding gains included in income under each valuation alternative in 1987.
    c. Prepare a journal entry to record the sale of Security B, assuming the portfolio (i.e., aggregate) method was used in 1987.
    d. One investor was heard to say, ''The only section of the balance sheet that I feel confident in is the current asset section. Cash, temporary investments and accounts receivable are each specified in dollar amounts, so the reporting can't vary in any way.'' Comment on the validity of the investor's confidence with specific reference to each of these accounts.

Adapted with permission from the Society of Management Accountants of Canada.

Decision Problem 7-1

Mark Wong is a recent graduate of a well known west coast business school. After graduation he set up a marketing consulting firm ''Mark Wong Western.'' On July 1, Year 1, he began the business with $12,000 in cash received from a legacy. He leased an automobile, furniture, and office equipment in order to preserve his capital. To provide for the eventual purchase of his own office building, he had limited his withdrawals from the business to $800 per month during the first year.

Having completed 12 months of frenetic activity and becoming cramped for space, Wong is considering moving to larger quarters, possibly purchased. To assist him in the purchase of office facilities he considers it necessary to produce financial statements for a potential lender showing the first year results of his business in a favorable light. He has also been advised that he will have to prepare financial statements for income tax purposes and, in order to maximize his cash, wants to minimize his income tax payments.

Mark Wong has heard of the ''triple-entry bookkeeping system'' — one entry for the tax department, one entry for the creditors, and one for the owner. He would like to know the results of this system applied to the first year of his business and comes to you.

You find that Wong's financial data had been thrown out inadvertently with his market survey records. However, he advises you that the business has no debts and has the following assets:

1. Cash on hand in change fund $200.
2. Undeposited cheque in an amount of $700 for a small market survey completed but not yet billed.
3. Balance per bank statement, $5,340. Wong believes that he issued two cheques at the end of June totaling $873, which have not been deducted from the bank statement.
4. During the year, as his bank balance increased, he invested the excess in bonds and shares, the certificates for which he has stored in an envelope in a filing cabinet. On opening the envelope, you find a $10,000, 12 percent bond of Manning Oil Ltd. with an interest coupon attached for $600 representing six months' interest to March 31, Year 2. Attached is a note stating that the bonds had been purchased on September 30, Year 1 at par value. You call Wong's broker and she advises you that the bond could be sold at June 30, Year 2 for $9,600 plus accrued interest.

   Also in the envelope is a certificate for 200 shares of Nalgoma Mines Ltd. and a broker's note attached indicating that the shares were purchased for $25 each plus brokerage of $200. The market value of the shares at June 30 amounted to $6,700.

   Out of the bottom of the envelope flutters a note receivable by the company for $1,000 signed by Bill Wood dated December 31, Year 1. The note bore interest at eight percent per annum payable at the due date, December 31, Year 2. You find that the note was received in return for a loan to Mark Wong's brother-in-law, who had planned to borrow from the finance company at 20 percent interest.

Wong maintains a copy of each invoice billed in a separate file, notes the money (if any) received, and extracts the invoice when paid in full. The file at present includes invoices totaling $5,720, of which $150 has been received in payment. Mark examines the bills and advises you that he expects to collect 90 percent of the amounts outstanding, although he could make a case that $2,500 would not be collected since it is two months' overdue.

Mark Wong had no other assets except his B.Comm., good looks, and confidence.

a. Prepare statements of the business's net worth at June 30, Year 2 that could be prepared for a banker (an optimistic view), for the tax department (a pessimistic view), and for Mark Wong's private information (a realistic view). Finally, prepare a net worth statement in conformity with generally accepted accounting principles.

b. Calculate the income earned by the business according to each of the above statements.

Chapter 8 Inventories: The Source of Operating Profits

This chapter introduces the choices that a firm must make in accounting for inventories and shows the impact of these decisions on reported expenses and net income for the period. The choices made in accounting for inventories can make two companies that are basically alike appear to be quite different.

Inventory Terminology

The term *inventory* means a stock of goods or other items owned by a firm and held for sale, or for processing before being sold, as part of a firm's ordinary business operations. Tools, for example, are inventory in the hands of a tool manufacturer or hardware store, but not in the hands of a carpenter. Marketable securities are inventory in the hands of a securities broker or dealer, but not in the hands of a manufacturer who is holding them as a temporary investment.

Goods held for sale by a retail or wholesale business are called *merchandise inventory*; goods held for sale by a manufacturing concern are called *finished goods inventory*. The inventories of manufacturing firms also include *raw materials* (materials being stored that will become part of goods to be produced) and *work in process* (partially completed products in the factory). The balance sheet may also include inventories of supplies to be consumed in administrative, selling, and manufacturing operations.

To "inventory" a stock of goods means to prepare a list of the items on hand at some specified date, to assign a unit cost to each item, and to calculate the total cost of the goods.

Significance of Accounting for Inventories

Financial accounting attempts to measure periodic income. Accounting for inventories affects income measurement by assigning costs to various accounting periods as expenses. The total cost of goods available for sale during a period must be allocated between the current period's usage (cost of goods sold, an expense) and the amounts carried forward to future periods (end-of-period inventory, an asset now, but later an expense).

Inventory Equation

The inventory equation aids understanding of accounting for inventory. In the following equation, all quantities are measured in physical units.

$$\underbrace{\begin{array}{c}\text{Beginning}\\\text{Inventory}\end{array} + \text{Additions}} - \text{Withdrawals} = \begin{array}{c}\text{Ending}\\\text{Inventory}\end{array}$$

Goods Available for
Use or Sale

If we begin a period with 2,000 kilograms of sugar (beginning inventory) and if we purchase (add) 4,500 kilograms during the period, then there are 6,500 (= 2,000 + 4,500) kilograms available for use. If we use (withdraw) 5,300 kilograms during the period, then there should be 1,200 kilograms of sugar left at the end of the period (ending inventory). The inventory equation can also be rewritten as:

$$\underbrace{\begin{array}{c}\text{Beginning}\\\text{Inventory}\end{array} + \text{Additions}} - \begin{array}{c}\text{Ending}\\\text{Inventory}\end{array} = \text{Withdrawals}$$

Goods Available for
Use or Sale

If we begin the period with 2,000 kilograms of sugar, if we purchase 4,500 kilograms of sugar, and if we observe 1,200 kilograms on hand at the end of the period, then we know that 5,300 (= 2,000 + 4,500 − 1,200) kilograms of sugar were used, or otherwise withdrawn from inventory, during the period. The sum of Beginning Inventory plus Additions is usually called "Goods Available for Use or Sale." In this example, there are 6,500 kilograms of sugar available for use or sale.

If accounting were concerned merely with tracing physical quantities, there would be few conceptual problems in accounting for inventories. But, of course, accounting reports are stated in dollar amounts, not physical quantities. When prices remain constant, inventory accounting problems are minor, because all items carry the same per-unit cost. Any variation in values of inventories results only from changes in quantities. The major problems in inventory accounting arise because the unit acquisition costs of inventory items fluctuate over time.

To illustrate, suppose that an appliance store had a beginning inventory of one television set, "TV set 1," which cost $250. Suppose, further, that two TV sets are purchased during the period, TV set 2 for $290 and TV set 3 for $300, and that one TV set is sold for $550. The three TV sets are exactly alike in all physical respects; only their costs differ. Assume that there is no way to know which TV set was sold.

The inventory equation can be written as follows, with all quantities measured in dollars of cost:

$$\underbrace{\begin{array}{c}\text{Beginning}\\\text{Inventory}\end{array} + \begin{array}{c}\text{Net}\\\text{Purchases}\end{array}} - \begin{array}{c}\text{Ending}\\\text{Inventory}\end{array} = \begin{array}{c}\text{Cost of}\\\text{Goods Sold}\end{array}$$
$$\underbrace{\$250 \quad + \quad \$590} - \quad ? \quad = \quad ?$$

Cost of Goods
Available for Sale
$840

Since financial statements are prepared with amounts measured in dollar terms, then some assumption must be made about which TV set was sold. There are at least four assumptions that can be made in applying the inventory equation to determine the Cost of Goods Sold expense for the income statement and the ending inventory for the balance sheet. Exhibit 8.1 shows these assumptions. As the inventory equation and the TV set example both show, the higher the Cost of Goods Sold, the lower must be the Ending Inventory. Which particular pair of numbers appears — one in the income statement and one in the balance sheet — reflects the *cost-flow assumption*, a major accounting issue discussed below.

Exhibit 8.1
Assumptions for Inventory Illustrations

Assumed Item Sold	Cost of Goods Available for Sale (beginning inventory = plus purchases)[a]	Cost of Goods Sold (for income) statement)	Ending Inventory + (for balance sheet)
TV Set 1	$840	$250	$590
TV Set 2	840	290	550
TV Set 3	840	300	540
"Average" TV Set	840	280[b]	560[b]

[a]Cost of goods available for sale = cost of (TV Set 1 + TV Set 2 + TV Set 3) = ($250 + $290 + $300) = $840.
[b]Average cost of a TV set = $840/3 = $280.

Problems of Inventory Accounting

The remainder of this chapter discusses four problems of inventory accounting:

1. The costs to be included in acquisition cost.
2. The valuation basis to be used for items in inventory.
3. The frequency of carrying out inventory computations, periodically or perpetually.
4. The cost flow assumption used to trace the movement of costs into and out of inventory, which may not parallel the physical movement of goods.

Problem 1:
Costs Included in Inventory at
Acquisition

Components of Inventory Cost

The amount on a balance sheet for inventory includes all costs incurred to acquire goods and prepare them for sale. For a merchandising firm, such costs should include purchasing, transportation, receiving, unpacking, inspecting, and shelving costs, as well as any bookkeeping and office costs for recording purchases.[1] Example 8 on page 44 (in Chapter 2), showing the computation of the cost of some equipment, applies to inventory as well.

---

[1]Because the amounts involved are often relatively small, and because it is difficult to assign a definite dollar amount for many of these costs to specific purchases, practice tends to restrict the actual additions to a few significant items that can easily be identified with particular goods, such as transportation costs. The costs of operating a purchasing department, the salaries and expenses of buyers, the costs of the receiving and warehousing departments, and the costs of handling and shelving are usually treated as expenses of the period in which they are incurred, even though they must be incurred to make merchandise ready for sale.

For a manufacturing firm, inventory costs include direct materials, direct labour, and manufacturing overhead. In a manufacturing firm, *all* production costs are debited to Work-in-Process Inventory. The process of recording *all* manufacturing costs in Work-in-Process Inventory is straightforward. The later allocation of costs in Work-in-Process Inventory to individual items transferred to the Finished Goods Inventory is not conceptually difficult, but requires special techniques of cost accounting, beyond the scope of this book. See the Glossary at ''flow of costs.'' The procedure followed is called *absorption* (or *full*) *costing*.[2]

The Purchase Transaction

The purchase transaction includes receiving goods, inspecting them, and recording the purchase. Legally, purchases should be recorded in the formal accounting records when title to the goods passes. The timing of title passage is often a technical question, whose answer depends on many circumstances of the transaction. For convenience, the accountant usually recognizes purchases only after the invoice and the goods are received and inspected. Adjustments may be made at the end of the accounting period to reflect the legal formalities for goods in transit that belong to the purchaser or for goods on hand that still belong to the seller.

Merchandise Purchases Adjustments

The invoice price of goods purchased seldom measures the total acquisition cost. Additional costs are incurred in transporting and handling the goods; deductions may be required for cash discounts, goods returned, and other adjustments of the invoice price. All of these adjustments could be debited or credited to the Merchandise Inventory account. Freqently, however, a number of contra and adjunct accounts are used for these adjustments so that a more complete analysis of the cost of purchases is available. Purchase Discounts, Freight-in, Purchase Returns, and Purchase Allowances accounts are used to provide the needed detail. The accounting for purchase adjustments closely parallels the accounting for sales adjustments discussed in Chapter 7.

The largest adjustment to the invoice price of merchandise is likely to be that for purchase discounts. Sellers often offer a discount from the invoice price for prompt

---

[2]An alternative procedure, known as *variable costing* (or, sometimes, *direct costing*), may be superior for internal management purposes.

In the variable costing procedure, product costs are classified into variable manufacturing costs (those that tend to vary with output) and fixed manufacturing costs (those that tend to be relatively unaffected in the short run by the number of units produced). Nonvariable (fixed) manufacturing costs are treated in the same way as selling and administrative costs; that is, they are treated as expenses assigned to the period of incurrence rather than as costs assignable to the product produced. Nonvariable manufacturing costs are charged in their entirety against revenues in calculating net income for the period.

When absorption costing is used, unit costs of product manufactured tend to vary inversely with the total number of units produced because a given amount of fixed costs is allocated to all the units produced. The larger is the number of units produced, the smaller is the per-unit cost.

Managerial accounting courses discuss the criticism of absorption costing and suggested benefits of variable costing for internal management uses. Variable costing is seldom used in external reporting.

Effective Purchasing: A Direct Route to New Profits

As a financial executive, you are not responsible to increase sales. But your eye is definitely on profitability. And you have in your company a resource that can fatten the bottom line just as surely as a big sales boost—and much more quickly and directly.

The resource is your purchasing department. Consider: Typically, for every $20 million of sales, about $1 million ends up as profit. If you can save $1 million internally, the effect on profit is as good as a $20-million sales increase. And purchasing, more than any other function, has the potential for savings that can reach into the millions—if it is used right.

That is a big "if." For while the best-managed, most successful companies have long recognized purchasing's direct impact on profit, too many others overlook the goldmine at their feet. This oversight has always been wasteful and costly. In today's competitive world economy, it can threaten a company's survival.

Also, many successful companies who are doing a good job on purchasing for the bill-of-materials frequently overlook the secondary goldmine of MRO (maintenance, repair, and operating costs) and advertising and marketing materials, where, though less dollars are spent than for bill-of-materials, frequently millions of dollars are spent. It is not unusual on this classification of materials to save as much as 25 percent. Also, MRO and advertising savings are easier to accomplish because they do not affect the product.

Why, then, do many companies fail to tap the profit potential of effective purchasing? There are many reasons, but perhaps the biggest is simply the burden of purchasing's traditional role. The purchasing department has long been considered a support or service function,

existing to serve the objectives of manufacturing. Its main imperative was to assure supplies to keep production lines running. A second objective, imposed in some companies, would be to assure supplies, while at the same time reduce inventory investment. Purchasing was a tactical way to achieve the objectives of other functions. There was no recognition that purchasing could be used in a genuinely strategic way.

Inevitably, this idea of purchasing affected the way the function was conducted. It was treated largely as a clerical, rather than professional, function. It did not attract the highest-caliber people. But if it did, they soon were promoted to "faster-track" jobs in manufacturing or marketing. It was not equipped by management with the most advanced computers. Typically, for lack of both decision support and a clearly defined mission, purchasing spent 80 percent of its time on activities that affected only 20 percent of the dollars it spent—and vice versa.

In a few instances, exceptional individuals in purchasing were promoted to the level of division president. This is a double-edged sword, because in order to attract exceptional people in purchasing, there must be a clear career path to top management. However, if exceptional people are "pirated" without the career path, there will not be talented layers of management in this critical function. At Travenol Laboratories, a career path was established several years ago and, to date, two directors of purchasing are now operating unit presidents. The result of this career path is an exceptional purchasing department that helps to support a high-quality, low-cost product line.

The traditional positioning of the purchasing function as a drain on profitability continues to exist. Today, this is completely out of touch with industrial reality. A new Industrial Revolution has transformed dominant industries from manufacturing to assembly. This has made effective purchasing—not production—the key to competitiveness and profitability. Companies that fail to recognize the transformation are clinging to outdated thinking, and often with disastrous financial results.

What are the trends driving this transformation? First, complexity. Most industrial products contain so many different kinds of parts, and require so many different technologies, that almost no company can any longer make most of its components cost-effectively. By choosing to buy components rather than make them, a company positions itself to benefit from the specialized capabilities and the economies of scale that outside supplies can provide.

A second trend transforming industry from manufacturing to assembly is the emergence of a truly worldwide industrial economy, including third world countries that manufacture technological products. The steady rise of new industrial nations means that American buyers have a continually expanding choice of outside suppliers—many characterized by extremely low wage costs.

The final transforming influence is competition. In the past, many companies could rely on marketing strategies emphasizing *either* quality *or* price. These days an either/or strategy is inadequate. The Japanesee example has taught us that it is possible—and crucial—to compete in quality and price together. American companies are under demand from their customers to do so. To survive, they have no choice but to make the same demand of their suppliers.

I.B.M. is a perfect example. The company manufactures very little. They design, subcontract, assemble, and support their products. The net result is a very high-quality, reasonably priced product. And I.B.M. has shown that this

strategy can work. They are virtually competing with the entire nation of Japan—and winning.

An Ongoing Analysis

The most effective purchasing departments have long made use of make-or-buy analyses. Whether the analysis favored making a component in-house or buying it outside depended on the individual company, its markets, its suppliers, and a great many other highly special factors. These days, for American companies, such analyses more and more tend to favor buying. We often find that as much as 50 percent of components made in-house could be purchased from outside suppliers with greater cost-effectiveness.

An effective purchasing department must be engaged in continuing make-or-buy analyses. It should treat the company's internal manufacturing operation as if it were a vendor—gathering comprehensive cost data by each stage of the production process, and comparing costs against those of outside suppliers, in the U.S. and elsewhere, to uncover opportunities for cost-effective purchases.

In the past, an ongoing make-or-buy analysis was too burdensome for most purchasing departments. Today, thanks to personal computers and a new generation of software, such analysis is only one of many easily accessible tools for effective purchasing.

Computers enable purchasing to handle vastly greater amounts of information than ever before. With the right software, targeted specifically for purchasing's objectives, a company has the power to make continuing make-or-buy analyses, as well as other strategic and tactical purchasing decisions. Here are some of these applications.

Parts Coding

Many companies don't know, in effect, what they purchase. That is, they don't have easily accessible information on the great variety of parts and components they buy for different divisions or different end uses. The result, even in the best cases, is costly duplication of purchases. Still worse, different purchases of the same or similar items may be made at a whole range of prices at different locations within the same organization, rather than at the best available price. And the company misses out on the savings possible through ganged or cluster production for longer runs.

A newly available computer-based parts coding system can solve these problems. the system gives the user a 10-character field for coding parts by family, group, and subgroup—plus a 15-character field for easy sequential part numbering. And this coding system can be expanded if larger fields are required.

With such a system, each purchased part can be given its own exclusive identification. Once the ID's are in the data base, it becomes a powerful management tool. One can review the demand and purchase history for individual parts. Families of items can be scanned to determine their budget impact, and cost-saving buying strategies can be developed based on volume discounts and long-term contracts.

ABC Analysis

As mentioned earlier, purchasing has sometimes been prone to devoting too much time and effort to activities that account for only small proportions of dollars spent. ABC Analysis is the best cure for this problem. This process divides all purchased items into three classes. In a typical case, if you multiply the quantity of an item purchased each year by the unit cost, and arrange the totals in descending order, you find that:

☐ 10 percent of the items account for 75–80 percent of the dollars spent. This is the A group.

☐ Another 15 percent of items account for another 15 percent of dollars spent. This is the B group.

☐ The other 75 percent of items purchased accounts for only 10-15 percent of dollars spent. This is the C group.

ABC Analysis is a detailed application

of Pareto's Law, which says that in any situation a small proportion of causes produces a large share of results. Because the three classes of purchased items have such a widely different impact on spending, they deserve different management priorities. Group A should be geared to rapid inventory turnover and regular individual attention in light of current conditions of demand, supply, and technology, which can have cost-reducing potential. Group B can be controlled more loosely with preset reorder points and reorder quantities. Group C should be managed to prevent stockouts with adequate buffer stocks (achievable with a low level of inventory investment), and to minimize management and clerical effort.

By tailoring purchasing and inventory policy to the cost impact of specific groups of purchased items, most companies can immediately allocate management time for cost reductions while reducing inventory investment. In addition, ABC Analysis can serve as a guide to setting management priorities and can identify opportunities for savings available through value analysis.

Value Analysis

The relationship of function, design, and cost is the focus of value analysis. It aims to reduce costs through changes in design, in materials, in manufacturing processes, or in suppliers. Value analysis requires detailed knowledge of how a purchased item is produced, and how much each stage of the production process adds to the cost. With the right computer software, this information can be at a buyer's fingertips. The user can ask "What if . . . ?" about potential changes in materials or production processes, or elimination of certain frills. Conversely, the user can model the additional cost—if any—of adding a desirable feature to the product. The right software can provide buyers with a decision support system that organizes the detailed knowledge required by value analysis to locate savings opportunities. The buyer can then reap the savings in

any number of ways: by having the production process changed, substituting a standard part for a special part, or switching from a brand name specifi-	cation to a generic of equivalent performance. Reprinted with permission of *Financial Executive*, Feb. 1986, pp. 37–39.

payment. For example, the terms of sale "2/10, net/30" mean that a two percent discount from invoice price is offered if payment is made within ten days and, otherwise, the full invoice price is due within 30 days.[3] Purchase discounts become a reduction in the purchase price. Two methods for recording purchases and the later treatment at time of payment (depending on whether the discount is actually taken) are the *gross price method* and the *net price method*. Problem 27 at the end of the chapter describes and illustrates these methods of record keeping.

Problem 2: Bases of Inventory Valuation

The basis for valuing inventory — the rule for assigning a cost to a physical unit — affects both periodic net income and the amount at which inventories appear on the balance sheet. At least five valuation bases are used for one purpose or another: acquisition cost, current cost measured by replacement cost, current cost measured by net realizable value, lower of (acquisition) cost and market, and standard cost. Some of the following discussion reviews fundamentals considered in Chapter 2. Generally accepted accounting principles require the use of the lower of cost market basis for most purposes.

Acquisition Cost Basis

The acquisition cost basis values units in inventory at their historical cost until sold. In accounting, the terms *acquisition cost* and *historical cost* mean the same thing.

Using acquisition costs implies using the *realization convention:* gains (or losses) caused by increases (or decreases) in the market value of assets do not appear in income until the particular assets are sold. When the acquisition cost basis is used, only sales transactions affect income. Any changes in the value of inventory items occurring between the time of acquisition and the time of sale are not recognized. The figure shown on the balance sheet for inventory becomes out of date to the extent that prices have changed since the items were acquired. The longer the time since acquisition, the more likely the current value of the inventory will differ from its acquisition cost.

The determination of acquisition cost depends on the components included in acquiring the unit of inventory and the cost-flow assumption adopted. The former is discussed on page 380, and the latter in the section beginning on page 391.

---

[3]Problem 29 at the end of Appendix B demonstrates that the interest rate implied in these terms of sales is about *45 percent per year*. That is, a purchaser who does not take such a discount is borrowing money at an interest rate of about 45 percent per year. Most purchasers find it advantageous to take such discounts and to borrow elsewhere at lower rates.

Current Cost Basis

A current cost basis values units in inventory at a current market price. Two current cost bases discussed below are (1) current entry value, often called *replacement cost*, and (2) current exit value, often called *net realizable value*. When inventories are stated at current cost, gains and losses from changes in prices are recognized during the holding period that elapses between acquisition (or production) and the time of sale.

Whereas acquisition cost for inventory shows objective, verifiable information that may be out of date, current cost shows up-to-date information, which can be more useful, but the amount shown may be more difficult to measure and to audit.

Replacement Cost (Entry Value) The replacement cost of an item at a given time is the amount a firm would have to pay to acquire the item at that time. In computing replacement cost, one assumes a fair market (or arm's length) transaction between a willing buyer and a willing seller. One also assumes that the inventory is bought in the customary fashion in the customary quantities. Replacement cost does not imply the forced purchase of inventory by a frantic buyer from a hoarding seller (which probably implies a premium price) or purchases of abnormally large quantities (which often can be bought at a lower than normal price) or purchases of abnormally small quantities (which usually cost more per unit to acquire).

Net Realizable Value (Exit Value) The amount that a firm could realize as a willing seller (not a "distressed seller") in an arm's length transaction with a willing buyer in the ordinary course of business is *net realizable value*. The measurement of net realizable value can present problems for items of inventory not yet ready for sale (for example, partially complete inventory in a manufacturing firm). Additional manufacturing costs will have to be incurred before the item can be sold. Also, a sales commission and other selling costs, such as packaging and freight costs, will probably be incurred. In these cases, net realizable value is the estimated final selling price of the inventory less the estimated costs necessary to make the item ready for sale and to sell it. Consider as examples, agricultural products and precious metals on hand at the close of an accounting period. These are often stated at net realizable value. It may be easier to estimate a market price less selling costs than to measure the historical cost of a bushel of apples harvested from an orchard.

Lower of Cost and Market Basis

The lower of cost and market valuation basis is the lesser of the two amounts; acquisition cost or "market value," the latter generally measured as net realizable value. The *CICA Handbook* discourages the use of "market value" in describing inventory value because of its lack of precision. To replace "market value" the Handbook recommends that a more descriptive term be used such as "replacement cost," "net realizable value," or "net realizable value less normal profit margin."[4]

A decline of $5,000 in the market value of inventory is recognized with the following entry:

---

[4]*CICA Handbook*, section 3030.

Loss from Decline in Value of Inventory	$5,000
Inventory	$5,000

The entry directly credits the Inventory account, not a contra account as may be done for temporary investments (explained in Chapter 7), because subsequent recoveries in market value are not recorded as gains. Under some approaches to inventory accounting, the above entry is not recorded explicitly; instead, the loss appears as a higher cost of goods sold. Consider, for example, the calculation in Exhibit 8.2 of cost of goods sold when beginning inventory is $19,000, purchases are $100,000, and ending inventory has a cost of $25,000 but has a replacement cost of $20,000.

Exhibit 8.2
Calculating Cost of Goods Sold Illustrating
Different Bases of Inventory Valuation

	Cost Basis	Lower of Cost and Market Basis
Beginning Inventory	$ 19,000	$ 19,000
Purchases	100,000	100,000
Goods Available for Sale	$119,000	$119,000
Less: Ending Inventory	(25,000)	(20,000)
Cost of Goods Sold	$ 94,000	$ 99,000

Note that cost of goods sold is $5,000 larger under the lower of cost and market basis than under the acquisition cost basis. The loss of $5,000 is not reported separately, but income will be $5,000 smaller than when the acquisition cost basis is used. If the amount of the write-down to market is so large that the reader of the statements will be misled without separate disclosure of the decline in replacement cost, then the write-down can be shown as an adjustment to cost of goods sold or as a loss, separately reported as part of operating activities.

The lower of cost and market basis for inventory valuation is called a "conservative" policy because (1) losses from decreases in market value are recognized before goods are sold, but gains from increases in market value are not recorded before a sale takes place; and (2) inventory figures on the balance sheet are never greater, but may be less, than acquisition cost. That is, *holding losses* are reported currently, whereas *holding gains* are not reported until the goods are sold.

Over long enough time spans, however, income equals cash-in less cash-out. For any one unit, there is only one total gain or loss figure — the difference between its selling price and its acquisition cost; the valuation rule merely determines how this gain or loss is spread over the accounting periods between acquisition and final disposition. When the lower of cost and market basis is used, the net income of the present period may be "conservatively" lower than if the acquisition cost basis were used, but the net income of a later period, when the unit is sold, will be higher.

Standard Costs

Standard cost is a predetermined estimate of what items of *manufactured* inventory *should* cost. Studies of past and estimated future cost data provide the basis for standard costs. Manufacturing firms frequently use standard cost systems for internal performance measurement and control. Managerial and cost accounting texts discuss these uses. Standard cost is also used occasionally as the valuation basis for preparing financial statements. Units in inventory may be valued at standard cost, especially in the preparation of monthly or quarterly statements.

Generally Accepted Accounting Basis for Inventory Valuation

Accounting uses a historical cost basis for most assets. Because the "market value" of some inventory items can be significantly less than acquisition cost, either because of price changes for this kind of inventory generally or because of physical deterioration of the particular items in an inventory, generally accepted accounting practice favours the use of lower of cost or market for inventory.[5] This is the same as saying that "market values" must be used in some cases. Computing market value requires either replacement cost or net realizable value amounts. Thus, generally accepted accounting principles for inventory valuation and measurement of cost of goods sold may require a combination of three valuation bases: acquisition cost, replacement cost, and net realizable value. In a period of rising prices, replacement cost and net realizable value are likely to be higher than acquisition cost, so valuation at cost and the lower of cost and market usually give the same valuation.

The *CICA Handbook* recommends supplementary disclosure by large firms of the current cost of beginning inventory, ending inventory, and cost of goods sold in notes to the financial statements even though the financial statements are based on lower of cost and market values.[6]

Problem 3: Timing of Computations

Two principal approaches to calculating the physical quantity and dollar amount of an inventory are the *periodic* inventory system and the *perpetual* inventory system. The periodic inventory system is less expensive to use than the perpetual inventory system because it involves fewer accounting computations, but the perpetual inventory system provides useful information not provided by the periodic inventory system.

Periodic Inventory System

In a periodic inventory system, the ending inventory figure for each item on hand results from making a physical count of units on hand at the end of an accounting period and multiplying the quantity on hand by the cost per unit. The cost of the total ending inventory is calculated by summing the ending inventory figure for each item. Then the inventory equation calculates the withdrawals that represent the cost-of-goods-sold expense. The following form of the inventory equation computes the cost of goods sold under a periodic system:

---

[5]The *CICA Handbook* makes no recommendation on inventory valuations. However, 81 percent of the survey companies included in the 1987 edition of *Financial Reporting in Canada* valued all, or part of, their inventory at the lower of cost and market.
[6]*CICA Handbook*, section 4510.

$$\underbrace{\begin{array}{c}\text{Beginning}\\\text{Inventory}\\\text{(known)}\end{array} + \begin{array}{c}\text{Purchases}\\\text{(known)}\end{array}}_{\begin{array}{c}\text{Goods Available}\\\text{for Use or Sale}\end{array}} - \begin{array}{c}\text{Ending}\\\text{Inventory}\\\text{(counted}\\\text{and costed)}\end{array} = \begin{array}{c}\text{Cost of}\\\text{Goods Sold}\\\text{(solved for)}\end{array}$$

When a periodic system is used, no entry is made for withdrawals (cost of goods sold) until the inventory on hand at the end of the accounting period is counted and costed.

To illustrate the periodic system, assume that sales during the year amounted to $165,000. The entries made to record sales during the year would have the combined effect of the following entry:

Cash and Accounts Receivable	$165,000	
Sales		$165,000
To record cash and credit sales for the year.		

At the end of the year, a physical count is taken, inventory costs are assigned, and the cost of the withdrawals is computed from the inventory equation. Exhibit 8.2 derives cost of goods sold for the lower of cost and market basis embedded in a periodic inventory system. We assume that all purchases have been debited to the Merchandise Inventory account. The cost-of-goods-sold expense is recognized in a single entry:

Cost of Goods Sold	$99,000	
Merchandise Inventory		$99,000
Cost of goods sold recognized under a periodic inventory system.		

A periodic inventory system generates no separate information to aid in controlling the amount of inventory shrinkage (the general name for losses from such causes as breakage, theft, evaporation, and waste). All goods not in the physical ending inventory count are assumed to have been either sold or used. Any losses from shrinkage appear in the cost of goods sold amount. Furthermore, physically counting the inventory at the end of the accounting period can seriously interfere with normal business operations for several days. Some firms using the periodic inventory system even close down and engage a large staff in physically counting the items on hand. Preparing income statements more frequently than once a year is expensive when the inventory figures result only from physically counting inventories.[7]

---

[7]The gross margin method and retail inventory methods provide for approximating ending inventory costs when counts cannot easily be taken. These methods are outlined on page 399 and 400.

Perpetual Inventory System

In a *perpetual (continuous)* inventory system, cost of goods sold is calculated and recorded whenever an item is taken from inventory. A perpetual inventory system requires a constant tracing of costs as items move into and out of inventory. Such entries as the following may be made from day to day:

Accounts Receivable	$800	
Sales		$800
Cost of Goods Sold	$475	
Finished Goods Inventory		$475

To record the cost of goods withdrawn from inventory and sold for $800.

After postings for a period have been completed, the balance in the Merchandise Inventory account is the cost of the goods that should be on hand. Statements can be prepared without carrying out a physical count of inventory. In a perpetual inventory system, the following form of the inventory equation computes goods expected to remain in the ending inventory after each acquisition or withdrawal:

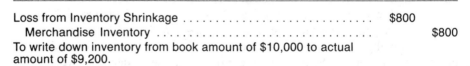

$$\underbrace{\begin{matrix} \text{Beginning} \\ \text{Inventory} \\ \text{(known)} \end{matrix} + \begin{matrix} \text{Purchases} \\ \text{(known)} \end{matrix}}_{\substack{\text{Goods Available} \\ \text{for Use or Sale}}} - \begin{matrix} \text{Withdrawals} \\ \text{(recorded)} \end{matrix} = \begin{matrix} \text{Ending} \\ \text{Inventory} \\ \text{(solved for)} \end{matrix}$$

Using a perpetual inventory system does not eliminate the need to take a physical inventory in which the items of inventory on hand are counted and costed. A physical count and assigning of costs to remaining items provides a check on the perpetual inventory and enables the measurement of any loss from shrinkage. The loss is the difference between the amounts in the Inventory account and the cost of the goods actually on hand. To illustrate, assume a book balance for inventory of $10,000 and an amount based on a physical count of $9,200. The entry to record the shrinkage is:

Loss from Inventory Shrinkage	$800	
Merchandise Inventory		$800

To write down inventory from book amount of $10,000 to actual amount of $9,200.

The credit reduces the book amount of inventory from its recorded amount, $10,000, to the correct amount, $9,200. The debit is to a Loss account or, if immaterial, to Cost of Goods Sold. In either case, it reduces net income for the current period.

Some businesses using a perpetual approach make a complete physical check at the end of the accounting period, in the same way as when a periodic inventory is used. A more effective procedure is available. Rather than taking the inventory of all items at one time, the count may be staggered throughout the period. For example, a college bookstore may check actual physical amounts of textbooks and inventory account amounts at the end of the school year, whereas the comparison for beach wear might be done in November. All items should be counted at least once during every year, but not all items need be counted at the same time. The count of a particular item should be scheduled for a time when the stock on hand is near its low point for the year.

Choosing Between Periodic and Perpetual Inventory Systems

A perpetual inventory system helps maintain up-to-date information on quantities actually on hand. It is justified when being ''out of stock'' may lead to costly consequences, such as customer dissatisfaction or the need to shut down production lines. In such cases, a perpetual inventory system might keep track of the physical quantities of inventory but not the dollar amounts. Controlling losses is easier under a perpetual system because inventory records always indicate the goods that should remain. A periodic inventory system usually costs less than a perpetual inventory system, but it provides no data on shrinkages.

As with other choices that have to be made in business, costs should be compared with benefits. A periodic inventory system is likely to be cost-effective when being out of stock will not be extremely costly, when there is a large volume of items with a small value per unit, or when items are hard to steal or pilfer. Perpetual inventory systems are cost-effective when there is a small volume of high-value items or when running out of stock is costly.

As the cost of record keeping with computers declines, the cost of perpetual inventories declines. Their use, therefore, increases over time.

Problem 4: Cost Flow Assumptions

Specific Identification and the Need for a Cost Flow Assumption

Individual units sold can sometimes be physically matched with a specific purchase. If so, then no special problems arise in ascertaining the acquisition cost of the units withdrawn from inventory and the cost of the units still on hand. For example, cost can be marked on the unit or on its container, or the unit can be traced back to its purchase invoice or cost record. The inventory and cost of goods sold of an automobile dealer or of a dealer in diamonds or fur coats might be computed using specific identification of costs.

In most cases, however, new items are mixed with old units on shelves, in bins, or in other ways, and physical identification is impractical. Accounting traces cost flows, not flows of goods. Moreover, to assume that cost flows differ from physical flows of goods may be desirable (for reasons to be discussed in this section).

Flow of Historical Costs

The inventory *costing* problem arises because of *two* unknowns in the inventory equation:

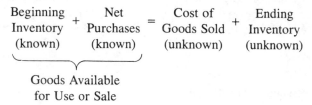

$$\underbrace{\begin{array}{ccc} \text{Beginning} \\ \text{Inventory} \\ \text{(known)} \end{array} + \begin{array}{ccc} \text{Net} \\ \text{Purchases} \\ \text{(known)} \end{array}}_{\begin{array}{c} \text{Goods Available} \\ \text{for Use or Sale} \end{array}} = \begin{array}{ccc} \text{Cost of} \\ \text{Goods Sold} \\ \text{(unknown)} \end{array} + \begin{array}{ccc} \text{Ending} \\ \text{Inventory} \\ \text{(unknown)} \end{array}$$

We know the costs of the beginning inventory and net purchases but not the amounts for cost of goods sold and for ending inventory. The question is whether to compute amounts for the units in ending inventory using the most recent costs, the oldest costs, the average cost, or some other choice. Of course, the question could have been put in terms of computing amounts for the cost of goods sold, for once we place an amount on one unknown quantity, the inventory equation automatically determines the amount of the other. The sum of the two unknowns, Cost of Goods Sold and Ending Inventory, must equal the cost of goods available for sale (= beginning inventory plus net purchases). The higher the cost assigned to one unknown, the lower must be the cost assigned to the other.

When prices are changing, no historical cost-based accounting method for costing ending inventory and cost of goods sold allows the accountant to show recent costs on both the income statement and the balance sheet. For example, in a period of rising prices, if recent, higher acquisition prices are used in measuring cost of goods sold for the income statement, then older, lower acquisition prices must be used in costing the ending inventory for the balance sheet. As long as cost of goods sold and ending inventory are based on acquisition costs, financial statements can present current amounts in the income statement or the balance sheet, but not in both. Of course, combinations of current and out-of-date information can appear in both statements.

If more than one purchase is made of the same item at different prices and specific identification is not feasible, then some assumption must be made about the flow of costs. Using a cost flow assumption, the accountant computes the acquisition cost applicable to the units remaining in the inventory. One of three cost flow assumptions is typically used for this purpose. These cost flow assumptions are:

1. First-in, first-out (FIFO)
2. Last-in, first-out (LIFO) and
3. Weighted average.

The following demonstrations of each of these methods use the TV set example introduced earlier and repeated at the top of Exhibit 8.3. The example of the three TV sets illustrates most of the important points about the cost flow assumption required in accounting for inventories and cost of goods sold. The first problem for self-study at the end of this chapter illustrates the techniques more realistically, but contains no new concepts.

Exhibit 8.3
Comparison of Cost Flow Assumptions
Historical Cost Basis

Assumed Data

Beginning Inventory: TV Set 1 Cost		$250
Purchases:	TV Set 2 Cost	290
	TV Set 3 Cost	300
Cost of Goods Available for Sale		$840
Sales: One TV set—Sales Price		$550

Financial Statements	Cost Flow Assumption		
	FIFO (1)	Weighted Average (2)	LIFO (3)
Sales	$550	$550	$550
Cost of Goods Sold	250[a]	280[b]	300[c]
Gross Profit on Sales	$300	$270	$250
Ending Inventory	$590[d]	$560[e]	$540[f]

[a]TV set 1 costs $250.
[b]Average TV set costs $280 (= $840/3).
[c]TV set 3 costs $300.
[d]TV sets 2 and 3 cost $290 + $300 = $590.
[e]Two average TV sets cost 2 × $280 = $560.
[f]TV sets 1 and 2 cost $250 + $290 = $540.

First-In, First-Out

The first-in, first-out cost flow assumption (FIFO) assigns the cost of the earliest units acquired to the withdrawals and the cost of the most recent acquisitions to the ending inventory. This cost flow assumes that the oldest materials and goods are used first. This cost flow assumption conforms to good business practice in managing physical flows, especially in the case of items that deteriorate or become obsolete. Column (1) of Exhibit 8.3 illustrates FIFO. TV set 1 is assumed to be sold, whereas TV sets 2 and 3 are assumed to remain in inventory. The designation FIFO refers to the cost flow of units sold. A parallel description for ending inventory is last-in, still-here, or LISH.

Last-In, First-Out

The last-in, first-out cost flow assumption, abbreviated LIFO, assigns the cost of the latest units acquired to the withdrawals and the cost of the oldest units to the ending inventory. Some theorists argue that LIFO matches current costs to current revenues and therefore that LIFO better measures income. Column (3) of Exhibit 8.3 illustrates LIFO. The $300 cost of TV set 3 is assumed to leave, whereas the costs of TV sets 1 and 2 are assumed to remain in inventory. The designation of LIFO refers to the cost flow for units sold. A parallel description for ending inventory is first-in, still-here, or FISH.

In a period of consistently rising prices, LIFO results in a higher cost of goods sold and a lower reported periodic income than either FIFO or weighted-average cost flow assumptions. LIFO usually does not reflect physical flows but is used because it produces a cost-of-goods-sold figure based on more up-to-date prices. In a period of rising prices, LIFO's higher (than FIFO's) cost-of-goods-sold figure reduces reported income.

Revenue Canada consistently has refused to permit companies to use the LIFO method of inventory valuation when determining taxable income. Primarily as a result of the tax department's position, this method is used rarely in Canada. Canadian practice varies dramatically from that used in the United States, where the LIFO method of inventory valuation is accepted for income tax purposes so long as it is used in financial reports to owners.

Weighted Average

Under the weighted-average cost flow assumption, the average of the costs of all goods available for sale (or use) during the accounting period, including the cost applicable to the beginning inventory, must be calculated.[8] The weighted-average cost is applied to the units sold and those on hand at the end of the month. Column (2) in Exhibit 8.3 illustrates the weighted-average cost flow assumption. The weighted-average cost of TV sets available for sale during the period is $280 [$= \frac{1}{3} \times$ ($250 + $290 + $300)]. Cost of Goods Sold is thus $280 and ending inventory is $560 ($= 2 \times 280).

Comparison of Cost Flow Assumptions

FIFO results in balance sheet figures that are closest to current cost, because the latest purchases dominate the ending inventory amounts. Remember LISH — last-in, still-here. The cost-of-goods-sold expense tends to be out of date, however, because FIFO assumes that the earlier prices of the beginning inventory and the earliest purchases are charged to expense. When prices rise, FIFO usually leads to the highest reported net income of the three methods, and to the smallest when prices are falling.

Because LIFO ending inventory can contain cost of items acquired many years previously, LIFO produces balance sheet figures usually much lower than current costs. LIFO's cost-of-goods-sold figure closely approximates current costs. Exhibit 8.4 summarizes the differences between FIFO and LIFO. Of the cost flow assumptions, LIFO usually implies the smallest net income when prices are rising (highest cost of goods sold), and the largest when prices are falling (lowest cost of goods sold). Also, LIFO results in the least fluctuation in reported income in businesses where selling prices tend to change as current prices of inventory items change.

---

[8]This description is technically correct only when a periodic inventory system is used. The first problem for self-study at the end of this chapter explores the procedures for applying the weighted-average method in a perpetual inventory system.

Exhibit 8.4
Age of Information About Inventory Items

Cost Flow Assumption	Income Statement	Balance Sheet	Inventory-on-Hand Assumption
FIFO	Old Prices	Current Prices	LISH
LIFO	Current Prices	Very[a] Old Prices	FISH

[a]The oldest prices on the FIFO income statement are just over one year old in nearly all cases and the *average* price on the FIFO income statement (for a year) is slightly more than $\frac{1}{2}$ year old. The larger the rate of inventory turnover, the closer the average age on the income statement is to $\frac{1}{2}$ year. LIFO balance sheet items are generally much older than the FIFO income statement items.

The weighted-average cost flow assumption falls between the other two in its effect on both the balance sheet and the income statement. It is, however, much more like FIFO than like LIFO in its effects on the balance sheet. When inventory turns over rapidly, the weighted-average inventory costs reflect present prices almost as much as FIFO.

Identifying Operating Profit and Holding Gains

The reported net income under FIFO is generally larger than under LIFO during periods of rising prices. This higher reported net income is caused by including a larger *realized holding gain* in reported net income under FIFO than under LIFO. This section illustrates the significance of holding gains in the calculation of net income under FIFO and LIFO.

The conventionally reported gross profit (sales minus cost of goods sold) consists of:

1. An operating profit, and
2. A realized holding gain (or loss).

(Unrealized holding gains and losses do not appear in income, but can be computed from information in notes to the financial statements when current costs of inventory are disclosed.)

The difference between the selling price of an item and its replacement cost at the time of sale is called an *operating profit*. This operating profit gives some indication of the relative advantage that a particular firm has in the market for its goods, such as a reputation for quality or service. The difference between the current replacement cost of an item and its acquisition cost is called a *holding gain* (or *loss*). The holding gain (or loss) reflects the change in cost of an item during the period while the inventory item is held. Holding gains indicate increasing prices and the skill (or luck) of the purchasing department in timing acquisitions.

To demonstrate the calculation of the operating profit and holding gain, consider the TV set example discussed in this chapter. The acquisition cost of the three items available for sale during the period is $840. Assume that one TV set is sold for $550. The replacement cost of the TV set at the time it was sold is $320. The current replacement cost at the end of the period for each item in ending inventory is $350. The top portion of Exhibit 8.5 illustrates the separation of the conventionally reported gross profit into the operating profit and the realized holding gain.

The operating profit is the difference between the $550 selling price and the $320 replacement cost at the time of sale. The operating profit of $230 is the same under both the FIFO and LIFO cost flow assumptions. The *realized holding gain* is the difference between cost of goods sold based on replacement cost and cost of goods sold based on acquisition cost. The realized holding gain under FIFO is larger than under LIFO, because the earlier purchases at lower costs are charged to cost of goods sold under FIFO. The larger realized holding gain under FIFO explains why net income under FIFO is typically larger than under LIFO during periods of rising prices. In conventional financial statements, the realized holding gain does *not* appear separately, as in Exhibit 8.5. Sometimes the realized holding gain on inventory is called *inventory profit*.

Exhibit 8.5
Reporting of Operating Profits
and Holding Gains for TV Sets
Using the Periodic Inventory Method

	Cost Flow Assumption			
	FIFO		LIFO	
Sales Revenue	$550		$550	
Less: Replacement Cost of Goods Sold	320		320	
Operating Profit on Sales		$230		$230
Realized Holding Gain on TV Sets:				
Replacement Cost (at time of sale) of Goods Sold	$320		$320	
Less: Acquisition Cost of Goods Sold				
(FIFO—TV set 1; LIFO—TV set 3)	250		300	
Realized Holding Gain on TV Sets (inventory profit)		70		20
Conventionally Reported Gross Profit[a]		$300		$250
Unrealized Holding Gain:				
Replacement Cost of Ending Inventory (2 × $350)	$700		$700	
Less: Acquisition Cost of Ending Inventory				
(FIFO—TV sets 2 and 3; LIFO—TV sets 1 and 2)	590		540	
Unrealized Holding Gain on TV Sets		110		160
Economic Profit on Sales and Holding Inventory of				
TV Sets (not reported in financial statements)		$410		$410

[a]Note that Exhibit 8.3 stops here.

The calculation of an unrealized holding gain on units in ending inventory also appears in Exhibit 8.5. The *unrealized holding gain* is the difference between the current replacement cost of the ending inventory and its acquisition cost.[9] This unrealized holding gain on ending inventory is not reported in the income statement as presently prepared. The unrealized holding gain under LIFO is larger than under

---

[9]The unrealized holding gain for a *given year* on items on hand both at the beginning and at the end of the year is the difference between year-end current cost and beginning-of-year current cost. The examples in this chapter do not illustrate this complication; all items on hand at the end of the year are purchased during the year. See the Glossary at *inventory profit* for an illustration of the computation of holding gains for the year where there is a beginning inventory that includes unrealized holding gains from preceding periods.

FIFO, because earlier purchases with lower costs remain in ending inventory under LIFO. The sum of the operating profit plus all holding gains (both realized and unrealized), called "Economic Profit" in Exhibit 8.5, is the same under FIFO and LIFO. Most of the holding gain under FIFO, that is, the realized portion, is recognized in computing net income each period, whereas most of the holding gain under LIFO, that is, the unrealized portion, is not currently recognized in the income statement. Instead, under LIFO the unrealized holding gain remains unreported, so long as the older acquisition costs are shown on the balance sheet as ending inventory.

The total increase in wealth for a period includes both realized and unrealized holding gains. That total increase, $410 in the example, is independent of the cost flow assumption, but does not appear in financial statements under currently accepted accounting principles.

The *CICA Handbook* recommends supplementary disclosure in notes of the realized and unrealized holding gains on inventory (and plant) under certain conditions.

Current Cost Basis Removes the Need for a Cost Flow Assumption

The preceding sections illustrate the difficulty in constructing useful financial statements in historical cost accounting for inventory in times of changing prices. If a FIFO cost flow assumption is used, then the income statement reports out-of-date cost of goods sold. If a LIFO cost flow assumption is used, then the balance sheet reports out-of-date ending inventory. (See Exhibit 8.4.)

A current cost basis for inventory allows up-to-date information to be shown on both statements, eliminating the need for a cost flow assumption. But using a current cost basis eliminates the realization convention from accounting, incurs additional costs, and requires the accountant to make estimates of current costs. Some accountants find the resulting loss of objectivity and verifiability, and additional costs of collecting the information, to outweigh the potential benefits from using current cost data. Other accountants think that the benefits of current data outweigh the costs of having less auditable numbers.

Exhibit 8.6 illustrates the TV set example when both cost of goods sold and ending inventory are valued at replacement cost.

The first income figure, $230, is labeled *Operating Profit*. This figure shows selling price less replacement cost of goods sold at the time of sale. This number may have significance for companies operating in unregulated environments. The significance can perhaps be understood by considering the following assertion. If the retailer of the TV sets pays out more than $230 in other expenses, taxes, and dividends, then there will be insufficient funds retained in the firm for it to replace inventory and to allow it to continue in business carrying out the same physical operations next period as it did this period. On the date of sale, a new TV set costs $320; the historical cost of the TV set sold, whether $250 or $230 or some amount in between, does not help the retailer to understand the costs required to maintain its productive assets intact, given the *current* economic conditions.

The second income item shown in Exhibit 8.6 is called *Holding Gains*. Holding

Exhibit 8.6
Using Replacement Cost Data to Analyze Components of Income

Assumed Data

Beginning Inventory: TV Set 1 Cost		$250
Purchases:	TV Set 2 Cost	290
	TV Set 3 Cost	300
Historical Cost of Goods Available for Sale		$840
Sales: One TV Set for		$550
Replacement Cost of TV Sets on:		
Date of Sale		$320
At End of Period		$350

Income Statement

Sales	$550
Replacement Cost of Goods Sold	320
Operating Profit	$230
Holding Gains for Year[a] (see calculation below)	180
Economic Income	$410

Calculation of Holding Gains for Year

Replacement Cost at Time of Sale[a]	$ 320
Replacement Cost of Ending Inventory (2 × $350)	700
Total Replacement Cost	$1,020
Historical Cost of Goods Available for Sale	840
Total Holding Gains for Year	$ 180
Ending Inventory (two TV sets, $350 current cost each)	$ 700

[a]To give some recognition to the realization convention, the total holding gain might be divided into realized and unrealized portions. To do so requires knowing the acquisition cost of the TV set sold, and that requires a cost flow assumption. As Exhibit 8.5 indicates, if a LIFO assumption is made, then the realized holding gain is $20 and the realized income of $250 could be between the operating profit of $230 and the economic income of $410.

gains of $180 occurred during the period on the TV sets held in inventory. At the time of sale, the replacement cost of TV sets had increased to $320. Thus, the holding gain on three TV sets, on the date of sale of one of them, was $120 [= 3 × $320 − ($250 + $290 + $300)]. By the end of the accounting period there was another $60 [= 2 × ($350 − $320)] holding gain on the two TV sets still held in inventory as the replacement cost increased to $350 from $320.

The $410 income figure shown after the inclusion of holding gains may also be significant. It represents the increase in wealth of the firm without regard to the realization convention. Some economists define income as the change in wealth during the period. They judge realization through arm's length transactions to be unimportant. Economic income, including all holding gains, is $410 in the example.

In recent years, generally accepted accounting principles recommend that major corporations disclose the current cost of goods sold computed at the time of sale and the current cost of ending inventory as supplementary information. Such information makes possible measuring operating profit and holding gains. Appendix D discusses current costs more fully.

You Can Trust Your Accountant

*T*oday, business is generally seen as a cutthroat environment with little room for ethics and integrity. Even the professions, always considered a bastion of trustworthiness, are coming under attack.

Lord Benson[a] attributes this to some problems of the professions own making, but also to media sensationalism of these problems and a middle class dislike for the bourgeoisie elitist concept with which professions historically were associated.

However, accountants have been able to maintain a better than average image in the eyes of the public.

A Harris poll conducted in the United States found "that even though people tend to have little faith in the integrity and honesty of most business dealings,

accountants are still seen as the moral and ethical pillars of the business community."

Professional accountants were ranked first in terms of ethics and morality, followed by university professors, bankers, and doctors. Newspaper and magazine editors and newscasters were also viewed in positive terms. Politicians and even members of the clergy were rated negatively.

Three out of four people polled believed that the accounting profession is performing better now than ever. They also credited accountants with high marks for honesty, competence, reliability, and objectivity. Take a bow, accountants!

[a]"The Professions and the Community," *Journal of Accountancy*, April 1983.
Source: *Bottom Line*, January 1987, p. 36.

Estimating Inventory Values when the Periodic Method Is Used

To count every item in inventory is generally expensive. Firms try to do it as seldom as possible, consistent with requirements of generally accepted accounting principles and proper inventory control. When the periodic inventory method is used and financial statements are to be prepared, say at the end of a month or quarter, reasonably good estimates of Ending Inventory and Cost of Goods Sold amounts can often be obtained with the various *gross profit methods* and *retail methods*. The details of these methods are covered in intermediate accounting books, but we can introduce the general idea.

The foundation of these estimating methods is the fact that most businesses mark up the cost of similar kinds of merchandise by a relatively constant percentage in obtaining selling prices. For example, nearly every college bookstore sets the selling price of a textbook 25 percent more than its cost to the bookstore. Put another way, the manager of the bookstore would say that the gross profit (= retail selling price less cost) is 20 percent of selling price.[10] To take another example, men's clothing in

---

[10]This is one of the most confusing areas in business terminology. If you buy a share of stock for $8 and sell it for $10, both you and your stock broker would call that a 25 percent (= $2/$8) *gain*. You would compute the gain percentage with the denominator being original cost. A retailer, however, speaks of the *markup* on an item selling for $10 that cost $8 as being 20 percent (= $2/$10). The retailer uses selling price, not cost, as the denominator. It is common practice and the effective participant in the business world will have to understand these differences in terms.

a department store is likely to carry a selling price twice the cost to the store. The selling price of most types of retail items stands in a relatively constant percentage to their costs. This fact is used in estimating Ending Inventory and Cost of Goods Sold.

We find it easier to illustrate the procedure than to define it. The method is illustrated in Exhibit 8.7 and is often called the *gross profit method*. The gross profit percentage is defined by

$$\text{Gross Profit Percentage} = \frac{\text{Selling Price} - \text{Acquisition Cost}}{\text{Selling Price}}$$

Assume that the data shown at the top of Exhibit 8.7 are available from the records for a month. (The kinds of information assumed available would typically be available in nearly all businesses.) In this business firm, all goods carry a gross profit percentage of 25 percent. That is, if the selling price of an item is $100, it cost $75; $25/$100 = 25 gross profit percentage.

The cost of goods sold and inventory at the end of January are computed as shown at the bottom of Exhibit 8.7. This method results in the precisely correct figures for

Exhibit 8.7
Illustration of Gross Profit Method
(Gross Profit Percentage is 25
Percent of Selling Price)

Assumed Data

Cost of Inventory, January 1	$150,000
Invoice Cost of Purchases during January	220,000
Transportation-in on Purchases during January	2,000
Invoice Cost of Purchases Made during January but Returned to Seller during January (purchase returns)	7,000
Sales Made during January	310,000
Selling Price of Goods Sold during January but Returned by Customers (sales returns)	10,000

Application of Gross Profit Method to Assumed Data

Cost of Inventory, January 1		$150,000
Net Purchases:		
Purchases	$220,000	
Plus Transportation-in	2,000	
Less: Purchase Returns	(7,000)	215,000
Total Cost of Goods Available for Sale		$365,000
Estimated Cost of Goods Sold:		
Sales	$310,000	
Less: Sales Returns by Customers	(10,000)	
Net Sales	$300,000	
Less: Estimated Gross Profit (= .25 × 300,000)	(75,000)	
Estimated Cost of Goods Sold		225,000
Estimated Cost of Ending Inventory, January 31		$140,000

the cost of goods sold and ending inventory if each item has a gross profit percentage of exactly 25 percent. The method results in approximations if the individual items have different gross profit percentages whose average is 25 percent.

There are many variants of this method. In the retail method, the gross profit percentage is itself estimated from data on costs and selling prices of goods. The variants of the retail method result from various assumptions about the fate (whether sold or not by the end of the period) of goods that have been marked down from their original retail price or that have been marked up still further from their original retail price.

Effects of Transactions Involving Inventory on the Statement of Changes in Financial Position

Inventory is a current asset and, hence, part of working capital. Thus all transactions involving inventory affect the operations section of the statement of changes in financial position. None of the transactions involving inventory discussed in this chapter requires special adjustments in deriving cash provided by operations, because insofar as they do not change cash they do change other working capital accounts.

Consider, for example, the adjusting entry to recognize cost of goods sold in a perpetual inventory system:

Cost of Goods Sold	$12,000	
Inventory		$12,000

Although this entry recognizes an expense that does not use cash, it does reduce the net balance in the Inventory account. Reductions in Inventory, like other reductions in current assets, appear in the operating section of the statement of changes in financial position as a use of cash. Refer to Exhibit 5.19 on page 248. The expense reduces income and cash from operations; the reduction in Inventory increases cash from operations. The total leaves cash from operations unchanged, which is correct because cash did not change.

Or, consider the entry recognizing the acquisition of inventory:

Inventory	$140,000	
Accounts Payable		$140,000

The current asset for Inventory increases, absorbing cash from operations, but the current liability for Accounts Payable also increases, providing cash from operations. The net effect is that cash provided by operations does not change. Later, when the payable is paid, the entry is:

Accounts Payable	$140,000	
Cash		$140,000

The current liability Accounts Payable declines, absorbing cash from operations.

Summary

Inventory measurements affect both the cost-of-goods-sold expense on the income statement for the period and the amount shown for the asset, inventory, on the balance sheet at the end of the period. The sum of the two must be equal to the beginning inventory plus the cost of purchases, at least in accounting based on acquisition costs and market transactions. The allocation between expense and asset depends primarily on the valuation basis and the cost flow assumption used.

Additional inventory problems include dealing with the inclusions (absorption and variable costing) and timing inventory computations (periodic and perpetual approaches).

Common business terminology often inhibits clear thinking about the four problems because the term "inventory method" is so often used. For example, the terms "absorption costing method," "acquisition cost method," "perpetual method," and "LIFO method" are often used, but these are not alternatives to one another. An inventory method results from a combination of choices, one from each of the following:

1. Inclusion: absorption or variable costing.
2. Basis: historical cost, lower of cost and market, current cost, or standard cost, among others.
3. Frequency of computations: periodic or perpetual.
4. Cost flow assumption: FIFO, LIFO, or weighted average.

Be prepared for the ambiguous use of the term "inventory method," realizing that one of several distinctions may be at issue:

Problem 1 for Self-Study

Exhibit 8.8 presents data on beginning amounts of, additions to, and withdrawals from the inventory of item X during June. Beginning inventory is assumed to be 100 units, costing $10 each, in all cases.[11]

    a. Compute cost of goods sold and ending inventory using a FIFO cost flow assumption. Note that periodic and perpetual approaches give the same results.

---

[11]To simplify the problem, beginning inventory is shown as having the same opening valuation of $1,000 under all cost flow assumptions. If costs had varied in the past, then the opening unit costs would differ across cost flow assumption.

b. Compute cost of goods sold and ending inventory using a LIFO cost flow assumption with a periodic inventory.

c. Compute cost of goods sold and ending inventory using a LIFO cost flow assumption with a perpetual inventory.

d. Compute cost of goods sold and ending inventory using a weighted-average cost flow assumption in a periodic inventory.

e. Compute cost of goods sold and ending inventory using a weighted-average cost flow assumption in a perpetual inventory.

Exhibit 8.8
Data for Illustration
of Inventory Calculations

Item X	Units	Unit Cost	Total Cost
Beginning Inventory, June 1	100	$10.00	$1,000
Purchases, June 7	400	11.00	4,400
Purchases, June 12	100	12.50	1,250
Total Goods Available for Sale at Cost	600		$6,650
Withdrawals, June 5	25		?
Withdrawals, June 10	10		?
Withdrawals, June 15	200		?
Withdrawals, June 25	260		?
Total Withdrawals During June	495		?
Ending Inventory, June 30	105		?
Replacement Cost per Unit, June 30		$13.60	

Suggested Solution

a. See Exhibit 8.9   **d.** See Exhibit 8.12
b. See Exhibit 8.10   **e.** See Exhibit 8.13
c. See Exhibit 8.11

Exhibit 8.9
Ending Inventory and Cost of Goods Sold Computation
Using a Periodic Inventory and a FIFO Cost Flow Assumption

Item X

Ending Inventory Computation

100 units @ $12.50 (from June 12 purchase)	$1,250
5 units @ $11.00 (from June 7 purchase)	55
Ending Inventory, June 30	$1,305

Cost of Goods Sold Computation

Cost of Goods Available for Sale	$6,650
Less: Ending Inventory	1,305
Cost of Goods Sold	$5,345

Exhibit 8.10
Ending Inventory and Cost of Goods Sold Computation
Using a Periodic Inventory and a LIFO Cost Flow Assumption

Item X

Ending Inventory Computation

100 units @ $10.00 (from beginning inventory)	$1,000
5 units @ $11.00 (from first purchase, June 7)	55
Ending Inventory at Cost	$1,055

Cost of Goods Sold Computation

Cost of Goods Available for Sale	$6,650
Less: Ending Inventory	1,055
Cost of Goods Sold	$5,595

Exhibit 8.11
Ending Inventory and
Cost of Goods Sold Computation
Using a Perpetual Inventory
and a LIFO Cost Flow Assumption

Item X
Cost of Goods Sold Computation

Date	Received			Issued			Balance		
	Units	Cost	Amount	Units	Cost	Amount	Units	Cost	Amount
6/1							100	$10.00	$1,000
6/5				25	$10.00	$ 250	75	10.00	750
6/7	400	$11.00	$4,400				{ 75	10.00	750
							{ 400	11.00	4,400
6/10				10	11.00	110	{ 75	10.00	750
							{ 390	11.00	4,290
6/12	100	12.50	1,250				{ 75	10.00	750
							{ 390	11.00	4,290
							{ 100	12.50	1,250
6/15				100	12.50	1,250	{ 75	10.00	750
				100	11.00	1,100	{ 290	11.00	3,190
6/25				260	11.00	2,860	{ 75	10.00	750
							{ 30	11.00	330
Cost of Goods Sold						$5,570			

Ending Inventory Computation

75 units @ $10.00	$ 750
30 units @ $11.00	330
Ending Inventory	$1,080

Alternative Cost of Goods Sold Computation

Cost of Goods Available for Sale	$6,650
Less: Ending Inventory	1,080
Cost of Goods Sold	$5,570

Exhibit 8.12
Ending Inventory and Cost of Goods Sold Computation
Using Periodic Inventory and a
Weighted-Average Cost Flow Assumption

Ending Inventory Computation

6/1	100 units @ $10.00	$1,000
6/7	400 units @ $11.00	4,400
6/12	100 units @ $12.50	1,250
	600 units @ $11.08 (= $6,650/600)	$6,650
Ending inventory (105 units @ $11.08)		$1,163

Cost of Goods Sold Computation

Cost of Goods Available for Sale	$6,650
Less: Ending Inventory	1,163
Cost of Goods Sold	$5,487[a]

[a]Because of rounding error, this number is *not* 495 (= 600 − 105) units × $11.08 = $5,485. In general, the weighted-average unit price should be applied either to ending inventory or to cost of goods sold. After being applied to one, the other is found from the inventory equation.

Exhibit 8.13
Ending Inventory and Cost of Goods Sold Computation
Using a Perpetual Inventory and a
Moving-Average Cost Flow Assumption

Item X
Ending Inventory and Cost of Goods Sold Computation

	Received			Issued			Balance		
Date	Units	Cost	Amount	Units	Cost	Amount	Units	Total Cost	Unit Cost[a]
6/1							100	$1,000	$10.00
6/5				25	$10.00	$ 250	75	750	10.00
6/7	400	$11.00	$4,400				475	5,150	10.84
6/10				10	10.84	108	465	5,042	10.84
6/12	100	12.50	1,250				565	6,292	11.14
6/15				200	11.14	2,228	365	4,064	11.13[b]
6/25				260	11.13	2,894	105	1,170	11.14
Cost of Goods Sold						$5,480			

Alternative Cost-of-Goods-Sold Computation

Cost of Goods Available for Sale	$6,650
Less: Ending Inventory	1,170
Cost of Goods Sold	$5,480

[a]Unit cost = total cost/units.
[b]Note how the rounding effects change the unit cost even though no new units were acquired.

Problem 2 for Self-Study

Refer to the data for Item X in Exhibits 8.9 and 8.10, showing cost of goods sold and ending inventory in a periodic inventory, using FIFO and LIFO cost flow assumptions, respectively. Assume that the 495 units withdrawn from inventory were sold for $15 each, $7,425 in total. Construct a schedule that both separates operating profit from holding gains and separates *realized* holding gains from *unrealized* holding gains. Show the results for FIFO and LIFO in parallel columns. The total of operating profit and realized holding gain should be equal to the gross profit reported in historical cost income statements. The total of operating profit and all holding gains should be the same for LIFO as for FIFO. Assume that the replacement cost of item X remained unchanged until a purchase was made.

Suggested Solution

See Exhibit 8.14.

Exhibit 8.14
Reporting of Operating Profits
and Holding Gains for Item X

	Cost Flow Assumption			
	FIFO		LIFO	
Periodic Inventory Method				
Sales Revenue from Item X (495 × $15.00)	$7,425		$7,425	
Less: Replacement Cost of Goods Sold [(25 × $10.00) + (10 × $11.00) + (460 × $12.50)]	6,110		6,110	
Operating Profit on Sales of Item X		$1,315		$1,315
Realized Holding Gain on Item X:				
Replacement Cost of Goods Sold	$6,110		$6,110	
Less: Acquisition Cost of Goods Sold (FIFO—Exhibit 8.9; LIFO—Exhibit 8.10)	5,345		5,595	
Realized Holding Gain on Item X		765		515
Conventionally Reported Gross Profit		$2,080		$1,830
Unrealized Holding Gain on Item X:				
Replacement Cost of Ending Inventory (105 × $13.60; see Exhibit 8.8)	$1,428		$1,428	
Less: Acquisition Cost of Ending Inventory (FIFO—Exhibit 8.9; LIFO—Exhibit 8.10)	1,305		1,055	
Unrealized Holding Gain on Item X		123		373
Economic Income on Sales and Holding Inventory of Item X		$2,203		$2,203

Problem 3 for Self-Study

Canadian Steel Ltd. uses a LIFO cost flow assumption for inventories. Its year-end financial statements show the following amounts.

Balance Sheet Inventories:	
Beginning of Year	$1,500,000
End of Year	$1,700,000
Income Statement Amounts:	
Cost of Goods Sold	$8,000,000
Income Before Taxes	800,000
The Excess of FIFO Cost over Reported LIFO Cost of Inventory is:	
Beginning of Year	$1,650,000
End of Year	$1,850,000

a. Compute the inventory turnover ratio from the published financial statements based on LIFO cost flow.

b. Compute the difference in income before taxes between LIFO and FIFO.

c. Compute the inventory turnover ratio computed from the financial statements as they would appear using FIFO cost flow.

Suggested Solution

a. $$\text{Inventory Turnover} = \frac{\text{Cost of Goods Sold}}{\text{Average Inventory During Year}}$$

$$= \frac{\$8,000,000}{.5(\$1,500,000 + \$1,700,000)}$$

$$= 5 \text{ times per year}$$

b. Pretax income would be larger by the amount that cost of goods sold would be smaller. Cost of goods sold would be smaller by $200,000 = $1,850,000 − $1,650,000.

c. $$\frac{\text{Inventory}}{\text{Turnover}} = \frac{\text{Cost of Goods Sold}}{\text{Average Inventory During Year}}$$

$$= \frac{\$8,000,000 - \$200,000}{.5[(\$1,500,000 + \$1,650,000) + (\$1,700,000 + \$1,850,000)]}$$

$$= \frac{\$7,800,000}{\$3,350,000}$$

$$= 2.33 \text{ times per year}$$

Questions, Exercises, Problems and Cases

Questions

1. Review the meaning of the following concepts or terms discussed in this chapter.

a. Inventory (as both a noun and a verb)	**b.** Inventory equation
	c. Purchases

d.	Purchase returns	**o.**	Variable (direct) costing
e.	Purchase discounts	**p.**	Cost flow assumption
f.	Shrinkages	**q.**	FIFO
g.	Periodic inventory	**r.**	LIFO
h.	Perpetual inventory	**s.**	Weighted average
i.	Acquisition cost basis	**t.**	Inventory measured by gross
j.	Replacement cost		profit method
k.	Net realizable value	**u.**	Current cost basis
l.	Lower of cost and market basis	**v.**	Realized holding gain
m.	Standard cost	**w.**	Unrealized holding gain
n.	Absorption (full) costing	**x.**	Inventory profit

2. Under what circumstances would the perpetual and periodic inventory systems both yield the same inventory amount if the weighted-average flow assumption were used?

3. During a period of rising prices, will the FIFO or LIFO cost flow assumption result in the higher ending inventory amount? The lower inventory amount? Assume no changes in physical quantities during the period.

4. Refer to the preceding question. Which cost flow assumption will result in the higher ending inventory amount during a period of declining prices? The lower inventory amount? Ignore the lower of cost and market method.

5. a. During a period of rising prices, will a FIFO or LIFO cost flow assumption result in the higher cost of goods sold? The lower cost of goods sold? Assume no changes in physical quantities during the period.
   b. Which cost flow assumption, LIFO or FIFO, will result in the higher cost of goods sold during a period of declining prices? The lower cost of goods sold? Ignore the lower of cost and market method.

6. "Cost flow assumptions for inventory are required only because specific identification of items sold is costly. Specific identification is theoretically superior to any cost flow assumption and eliminates the possibility for income manipulation available with some cost flow assumptions." Comment.

7. Assume that a steel manufacturer and a retailing firm have identical sales and income and that the costs of their purchased inputs of goods and services increase at the same rate. The steel company has inventory turnover of about four times per year, whereas the retailer has inventory turnover of about ten times per year.
   Which of the two firms is more likely to increase income through switching from FIFO to LIFO? Explain.

8. "LIFO provides a more meaningful income statement than FIFO, even though it provides a less meaningful balance sheet." Does it ever? Does it always?

9. Assume that the cost basis for inventory is changed from historical cost to current cost, that current costs exceed historical costs at the end of the year of change, and that all year-end inventory is sold during the following year. Ignore income tax effects.

What will be the impact of the change on net income for the year of change? On income for the following year? On total income over the two years?

10. Would you expect to find a periodic or perpetual inventory system used in each of the following situations?
- **a.** The greeting card department of a retail store.
- **b.** The fur coat department of a retail store.
- **c.** Supplies storeroom for an automated production line.
- **d.** Automobile dealership.
- **e.** Wholesale dealer in bulk salad oil.
- **f.** Grocery store.
- **g.** College bookstore.
- **h.** Diamond ring department of a jewelry store.
- **i.** Ballpoint pen department of a jewelry store.

11. A noted accountant once claimed that firms which use a LIFO cost flow assumption will find that historical cost of goods sold is *greater than* replacement cost of goods sold computed as of the time of sale. Under what circumstances is this assertion likely to be true? (*Hint:* Compare the effects of periodic and perpetual approaches on LIFO cost of goods sold.) Do you agree that the assertion is likely to be true?

Exercises

12. *Journal entries for periodic and perpetual inventories.* Goods that cost $1,500 are sold for $2,000 cash. Present the normal journal entries at the time of the sale:
- **a.** When a periodic inventory is used.
- **b.** When a perpetual inventory is used.

13. *Computations involving different cost flow assumptions.* The inventory at September 1 and the purchases during September of Hanna Ltd.'s raw material were as follows:

9/1 Inventory	1,000 kg	$ 4,500
9/5 Purchased	3,000 kg	13,500
9/14 Purchased	3,500 kg	17,500
9/27 Purchased	3,000 kg	16,500
9/29 Purchased	1,000 kg	8,000

The inventory at September 30 is 1,800 kilograms.

Assume a periodic inventory system. Compute the cost of the inventory on September 30 under each of the following cost flow assumptions:
- **a.** FIFO
- **b.** Weighted average
- **c.** LIFO

14. *Compute acquisition cost of inventory and record sales transaction using perpetual inventory.* Ducru Ltd. ordered from an overseas suppliers 10,000 shirts that had a list price of $12 each, requesting the normal trade discount. The invoice arrived showing a discount of 40 percent from list price. Ducru Ltd. paid its customs broker

$750 for taxes and paid a trucking company $250 to deliver the goods. Later, it sold 1,000 shirts for $12 each on account. Ducru Ltd. uses a perpetual inventory.

Prepare journal entries to record the sales transaction.

15. *Over long enough time spans, income is cash-in less cash-out; cost flow assumptions.* Gazin Inc. was in business for four years. Exhibit 8.15 shows its purchases and sales during that four-year period. Ignore income taxes.

Exhibit 8.15
GAZIN INC.
Purchases and Sales
(Exercise 15)

	Purchases		Sales	
	Units	Unit Cost	Units	Unit Price
Year 1	12,000	$10	9,000	$15
Year 2	11,000	11	10,000	17
Year 3	10,000	12	11,000	19
Year 4	9,000	13	12,000	21
Totals	42,000		42,000	

a. Compute income for each of the four years assuming FIFO cost flow.
b. Compute income for each of the four years assuming LIFO cost flow.
c. Compare total income over the four-year period. Does the cost flow assumption matter?

16. *Over long enough time spans, income is cash-in less cash-out; cost basis for inventory.* The Sales Co. Ltd. began business on January 1, Year 1. Information concerning merchandise inventories, purchases, and sales for the first three years of operations follows:

	Year 3	Year 2	Year 1
Sales	$450,000	$330,000	$300,000
Purchases	350,000	260,000	280,000
Inventories, Dec. 31:			
At cost	95,000	95,000	80,000
At market	100,000	80,000	75,000

a. Compute the gross profit on sales (sales minus cost of goods sold) for each year, using the lower of cost and market basis in valuing inventories.
b. Compute the gross profit on sales (sales minus cost of goods sold) for each year, using the acquisition cost basis in valuing inventories.
c. Indicate your conclusion whether the lower of cost and market basis of valuing inventories is "conservative."

17. *When goods available for sale exceed sales, income can be manipulated, even when specific identification is used.* Langoa Limited has 300 identical TV sets available for sale during December, when it expects to sell 200 sets for $500 each. These TV sets were acquired as follows: 100 in June for $200 each, 100 in August for $300 each, and 100 in November for $250 each. Assume that sales for December are 200 units at $500 each.

   a. Compute gross profit for December assuming FIFO.

   b. Compute gross profit for December assuming specific identification of sales and sets sold to minimize reported income for tax purposes.

   c. Compute gross profit for December assuming specific identification of sales and sets sold to maximize reported income, so as to increase the store manager's profit-sharing bonus for the year.

18. *Computations involving cost flow assumptions and periodic or perpetual approaches.* The following information concerning Arpesfeld Limited's inventory of merchandise is available:

Nov. 2	Inventory	4,000 kg @ $5
9	Sold	3,000 kg
16	Purchased	7,000 kg @ $6
23	Sold	3,000 kg
30	Sold	3,000 kg

Compute the cost of goods sold and the cost of ending inventory on November 30 for each of the following combinations of inventory systems and cost flow assumptions.

   a. Periodic FIFO

   b. Perpetual FIFO

   c. Periodic weighted average

   d. Perpetual weighted average

   e. Periodic LIFO

   f. Perpetual LIFO

19. *Computing cost of goods sold under various treatments of cost flows with periodic and perpetual systems.* The Central Supply Co. Ltd. has in its inventory on May 1 three units of item K, all purchased on the same date at a price of $60 per unit. Information relative to item K is as follows:

Date		Explanation	Units	Unit Cost	Tag Number
May 1		Inventory	3	$60	K–515,516,517
3		Purchase	2	65	K–518,519
12		Sale	3		K–515,518,519
19		Purchase	2	76	K–520,521
25		Sale	1		K–516

Compute the cost of units sold in accordance with the following:

   a. Specific identification of units sold.

   b. FIFO cost flow assumption and periodic inventory system.

   c. FIFO cost flow assumption and perpetual inventory system.

   d. LIFO cost flow assumption and periodic inventory system.

   e. LIFO cost flow assumption and perpetual inventory system.

   f. Weighted-average cost flow assumption and perpetual inventory system.

   g. Weighted-average cost flow assumption and periodic inventory system.

20. *LIFO provides opportunity for income manipulation.* Lagrange Ltd. began the year with 20,000 units of product on hand that cost $10 each. During the year, it produced another 30,000 units at a cost of $18 each. Sales for the year were expected to total 50,000 units. During November, the company had to make a decision about production for the remainder of the year. No additional units need be produced this year beyond the 30,000 units already produced. Up to 60,000 additional units could be produced; the cost would be $22 per unit regardless of the quantity produced. The company uses a periodic LIFO inventory. Assume that sales are 50,000 units for the year at an average price of $25 per unit.

    a. What production for the remainder of the year gives the largest cost of goods sold for the year? What is that cost of goods sold?

    b. What production for the remainder of the year gives the smallest cost of goods sold for the year? What is that cost of goods sold?

    c. Compare the gross margins implied by the two production plans devised in the preceding parts.

21. *Calculations combining cost basis and cost flow assumptions.* The Sanlex Co. Ltd. started the year with no inventories on hand. It manufactured two batches of inventory, 100 units each, which were identical except that the variable costs of producing the first batch were $120 and the variable costs of producing the second batch were $200 because of rising prices. By the end of the year, Sanlex Co. Ltd. had sold 75 units from the first batch for $300 and none of the second batch. The ending inventory had a market value of $305. Total fixed manufacturing costs for the year were $160. Under the absorption costing procedure, $100 of fixed manufacturing costs allocated to units produced remained in inventory at the close of the year. Selling and administrative expenses for the year were $40.

  Prepare a statement of pretax income for the Sanlex Co. Ltd. for the year under each of the following sets of assumptions.

    a. FIFO, acquisition cost basis

    b. LIFO, acquisition cost basis

    c. FIFO, lower of cost and market basis

22. *Effects on funds statement.* Indicate the effect on Cash Provided by Operations of the following independent transactions. Include the effects of income taxes, assuming a rate of 40 percent of pretax income, that the accounting methods used on the tax return are the same as on the financial statements, and that taxes have been paid in cash.

    a. A firm using the lower of cost and market basis for inventories writes ending inventory down by $100,000.

    b. A firm has been using FIFO. It switches to weighted average cost at the end of the current year and finds that the cost of goods sold is $200,000 larger than it would have been under FIFO.

23. *Separating operating profit from holding gains.* On January 1, the merchandise inventory of Revsine Appliance Store consisted of 1,000 units acquired for $450 each. During the year, 2,500 additional units were acquired at an average price of $600 each while 2,300 units were sold for $900 each. The replacement cost of these units at the time they were sold averaged $600 during the year. The replacement costs of units on December 31 was $750 per unit.

a. Calculate cost of goods sold under both FIFO and LIFO cost flow assumptions.
b. Prepare partial statements of income showing gross profit on sales as revenues less cost of goods sold with both FIFO and LIFO cost flow assumptions.
c. Prepare partial income statements separating the gross profit on sales into operating profits and realized holding gains under both FIFO and LIFO.
d. Append to the bottom of the statements prepared in part (**c**) a statement showing the amount of unrealized holding gains and the total of realized income plus unrealized holding gains.
e. If you did the above steps correctly, the totals in part (**d**) are the same for both FIFO and LIFO. Is this equality a coincidence? Why or why not?

24. *Effect of inventory errors (adapted from a problem by S. Zeff).* Pollack Company reported net income of $106,000 in Year 1 and $88,000 in Year 2. Early in Year 3, Pollack Company discovered that it had *overstated* its Year 1 ending inventory by $6,000 and had *understated* its Year 2 inventory by $10,000.

What should have been the company's reported net incomes for Year 1 and Year 2? Ignore income taxes.

Problems and Cases

25. *Effect of inventory errors.* On December 30, Year 1, merchandise amounting to $1,000 was received by the Warren Co. Ltd. and was counted in its December 31 listing of all inventory items on hand. The invoice was not received until January 4, Year 2, at which time the acquisition was recorded as a Year 2 acquisition. The acquisition should have been recorded for Year 1. Assume that the error was not ever discovered by the firm. Warren Co. Ltd. uses a periodic inventory system. Indicate the effect (overstatement, understatement, none) on each of the following amounts. Ignore income taxes.
a. Inventory, 12/31/Year 1
b. Inventory, 12/31/Year 2
c. Cost of goods sold, Year 1
d. Cost of goods sold, Year 2
e. Net income, Year 1
f. Net income, Year 2
g. Accounts payable, 12/31/Year 1
h. Accounts payable, 12/31/Year 2
i. Retained earnings, 12/31/Year 2

26. *Analysis of adjunct and contra accounts used for purchases and sales.* The accounts listed below might appear in the records of a retail store. Their use is never required, but accounts such as these often provide details about purchase activity useful to management. From the name of the account and your understanding of the accounting for purchase and sales, indicate:
a. Whether the account is a permanent account (to appear as such on the balance sheet) or a temporary account (to be closed at the end of the accounting period).
b. The normal balance, debit or credit, in the account. If the account is a temporary one, give the normal balance prior to closing.

   c. If the account is a temporary one, the kind of account it is closed to—balance sheet asset, balance sheet liability, balance sheet owners' equity through a revenue account, or balance sheet owners' equity through an expense (or revenue contra) account.

   (1) Merchandise Purchases
   (2) Merchandise Purchase Allowances
   (3) Merchandise Purchase Returns
   (4) Purchase Returns
   (5) Sales Tax on Purchases
   (6) Freight-in on Purchases
   (7) Sales Allowances
   (8) Allowance for Sales Discounts
   (9) Provincial Sales Taxes Payable on Sales

(The next three items should not be attempted until Problem 27 has been read.)

   (10) Purchase Discounts
   (11) Purchase Discounts Taken
   (12) Purchase Discounts Lost

27. *Gross and net price methods for treating purchase discounts.* The chapter mentions two alternatives for treating discounts on merchandise purchases often used in practice: (1) the gross price method, which recognizes the amount of discounts taken on payments made during the period, without regard to the period of purchase, and (2) the net price method, which deducts all discounts made available from the gross purchase invoice prices at the time of purchases. This problem explains the two methods.

Alternative 1: Gross Price Method The gross price method of accounting for purchases records invoices at the gross price and accumulates the amount of discounts taken on payments made. Suppose that goods with a gross invoice price of $1,000 are purchased, 2/10, net/30. (That is, a two percent discount from invoice price is offered if payment is made within ten days and the full invoice price is due, in any case, within 30 days.) The entries to record the purchase and the payment (1) under the assumption that the payment is made in time to take the discount, and (2) under the assumption that the payment is too late to take advantage of the discount, are as follows:

Gross Price Method	(1) Discount Taken		(2) Discount Not Taken	
Purchases (or Inventory)	$1,000		$1,000	
Accounts Payable		$1,000		$1,000
To record purchase.				
Accounts Payable	$1,000		$1,000	
Cash		$ 980		$1,000
Purchase Discounts (or Inventory)		20		—
To record payment.				

The balance in the Purchase Discounts account is deducted from the balance in the Purchases account in calculating net purchases for a period. Such a deduction approximates the results achieved by treating purchase discounts as a reduction in purchase price at the time of purchase. It is only an approximation because the total adjustment includes discounts taken on payments made this period, without regard to the period of purchase.

An accurate adjustment would require eliminating the discounts taken related to purchases of previous periods while including the amount of discounts available at the end of the accounting period that are expected to be taken during the following period. This refinement in the treatment of purchase discounts is seldom employed in practice.

Alternative 2: Net Price Method In recording purchases, the purchase discount is deducted from the gross purchase price immediately upon receipt of the invoice, and the net invoice price is used in the entries. The example used previously of a $1,000 invoice price for goods subject to a two percent cash discount would be recorded as follows under the net price method:

Net Price Method	(1) Discount Taken		(2) Discount Not Taken	
Purchases (or Inventory)	$980		$980	
Accounts Payable		$980		$980
To record purchase.				
Accounts Payable	$980		$980	
Purchase Discounts Lost	—		20	
Cash		$980		$1,000
To record payment.				

The balance in the Purchase Discounts Lost account could be added to the cost of the merchandise purchased and, therefore, viewed as an additional component of goods available for sale. Most accountants believe, however, that discounts lost should be shown as a general operating expense rather than as an addition to the cost of purchases, because lost discounts may indicate an inefficient office force or inadequate financing. In this text, we treat purchase discounts lost as an expense unless an explicit contrary statement is made.

a. Attempt to decide which of these two alternatives is preferable and why. You might find working part (b), below, helpful in making your decision.

b. Prepare a journal form with two pairs of columns, one headed Net Price Method and the other headed Gross Price Method. Using this journal form, show summary entries for the following events in the history of Evans and Foster Ltd., furniture manufacturers.

   (1) During the first year of operations, materials with a gross invoice price of $60,000 are purchased. All invoices are subject to a two percent cash discount if paid within ten days.

   (2) Payments to creditors during the year amount to $53,000, settling $54,000 of accounts payable at gross prices.

    (3) Of the $6,000, gross, in unpaid accounts at the end of the year, the discount time has expired on one invoice amounting to $400. It is expected that all other discounts will be taken. This expectation is reflected in the year-end adjustment.

    (4) During the first few days of the next period, all invoices are paid in accordance with expectations.

28. *Gross and net price methods for recording purchase discounts.* (This problem should not be attempted until Problem 27 has been read.) The following are selected transactions of the Skousen Appliance Store:

(1) A shipment of refrigerators is received from the Standard Electric Corp., $15,000. Terms 2/30, n/60.

(2) Part of the shipment of **(1)** is returned. The gross invoice price of the returned goods is $1,200, and a credit memorandum for this amount is received from the Standard Electric Corp.

(3) The invoice of the Standard Electric Corp. is paid in time to take the discount.

    a. Give entries on the books of the Skousen Appliance Store, assuming that the net price method is used.

    b. Give entries on the books of the Skousen Appliance Store, assuming that the gross price method is used.

29. *Fundamentals of the gross margin method for approximating inventory amounts.* The merchandise inventory of Parks Store was destroyed by fire on July 4. The accounting records were saved and provided the following information:

Cost of Merchandise Inventory on Hand, January 1	$ 45,000
Purchases of Merchandise, January 1 to July 4	125,000
Sales, January 1 to July 4	180,000

The average retail markup over cost of the goods sold during the year before the fire was 50 percent of the acquisition cost. That is, selling price equals 150 percent of cost.

    a. Estimate the cost of the goods on hand at the time of the fire.

    b. Give the journal entry to record the loss, assuming that it was uninsured.

    c. Give the journal entry to record the loss, assuming that all goods were fully insured for their acquisition cost.

30. *Fundamentals of the retail inventory method for approximating inventory amounts.* Refer to the data in the preceding problem. Assume that the store owner does not know the average retail markup over cost for the destroyed goods. The accounting records show that the total sales revenue during the four years preceding the fire amounted to $1,000,000 and the total cost of goods sold over the same period was $650,000.

    a. Assume that the ratio of sales prices to cost of goods sold for the last four years reflects this year's operations as well. Estimate the cost of the goods destroyed in the fire.

b. Assume the same facts as above, except that the $1,000,000 represents the original selling price of the goods sold during the last four years. Certain goods were marked down before sale so that the actual sales revenue was only $975,000. Assuming that the same percentage of goods was marked down by the same price percentage during the first six months of this year as in the previous four years, estimate the cost of the goods destroyed by the fire.

31. *Detailed comparison of various choices for inventory accounting.* The Harrison Corporation was organized and began retailing operations on January 1, Year 1. Purchases of merchandise inventory during Year 1 and Year 2 were as follows:

	Quantity Purchased	Unit Price	Acquisition Cost
1/10/Year 1	1,000	$10	$10,000
6/30/Year 1	400	15	6,000
10/20/Year 1	200	16	3,200
Total Year 1	1,600		$19,200

	Quantity Purchased	Unit Price	Acquisition Cost
2/18/Year 2	300	$18	$ 5,400
7/15/Year 2	100	20	2,000
12/15/Year 2	500	22	11,000
Total Year 2	900		$18,400

The number of units sold during Year 1 and Year 2 was 900 units and 1,100 units, respectively. Harrison Corporation uses a periodic inventory system.

    a. Calculate the cost of goods sold during Year 1 under the FIFO cost flow assumption.

    b. Calculate the cost of goods sold during Year 1 under the LIFO cost flow assumption.

    c. Calculate the cost of goods sold during Year 1 under the weighted-average cost flow assumption.

    d. Calculate the cost of goods sold during Year 2 under the FIFO cost flow assumption.

    e. Calculate the cost of goods sold during Year 2 under the LIFO cost flow assumption.

    f. Calculate the cost of goods sold during Year 2 under the weighted-average cost flow assumption.

    g. For the two years taken as a whole, will FIFO or weighted-average result in reporting the larger net income? What is the difference in net income for the two-year period under FIFO as compared to weighted-average? Assume an income tax rate of 40 percent for both years.

    h. Which method, weighted-average or FIFO, should Harrison Corporation probably prefer and why?

32. *Continuation of preceding problem introducing current cost concepts.* (This problem should not be attempted until Problem 31 has been done.) Assume the same data for the Harrison Corporation as given in the previous problem. In addition, assume the following:

Selling Price per Unit:	
Year 1	$25
Year 2	30
Average Current Replacement Cost:	
Year 1	$15
Year 2	20
Current Replacement Cost:	
December 31, Year 1	$17
December 31, Year 2	22

    a. Prepare an analysis for Year 1 that identifies operating margins, realized holding gains and losses, and unrealized holding gains and losses for the FIFO, LIFO, and weighted-average cost flow assumptions.

    b. Repeat part **(a)** for Year 2.

    c. Demonstrate that over the two-year period, the income plus holding gains before taxes of Harrison Corporation are independent of the cost flow assumption.

33. *Impact on financial statements of the choice between a FIFO and a LIFO flow assumption.* Take 12 pieces of paper and mark each one with a number between 1 and 12 inclusive. Sort the pieces of paper into a pile with the numbers in consecutive order facing up, so that number 1 is on top and number 12 is on bottom. These 12 pieces of paper are to represent 12 identical units of merchandise purchased over three periods at prices increasing from $1 to $12. Assume that four of the units are purchased each period for three periods, that three units are sold each period, and that a periodic inventory system is used.

    a. Compute the cost of goods sold and ending inventory amounts for each of the three periods under a FIFO flow assumption.

    b. Compute the cost of goods sold and ending inventory amounts for each of the three periods under a LIFO flow assumption.

    c. Re-sort the 12 pieces of paper into decreasing order to represent declining prices for successive purchases. Compute the cost of goods sold and ending inventory amounts for each of the three periods under a FIFO flow assumption.

    d. Repeat part **(c)** using a LIFO flow assumption.

    e. Convince yourself that the following are all true statements.

        (1) In periods of rising prices and increasing physical inventories, FIFO implies higher reported income than does LIFO.

        (2) In periods of declining prices and increasing physical inventories, LIFO implies higher reported income than does FIFO.

        (3) Under FIFO, current prices are reported on the balance sheet and old prices are reported on the income statement.

        (4) Under LIFO, current prices are reported on the income statement and very old prices are reported on the balance sheet.

        (5) In periods of rising prices and increasing physical inventories, the difference between FIFO and LIFO balance sheet amounts for inventory at the end of each period after the first one is larger than the differences between FIFO and LIFO reported net income for each period after the first one.

f. Assume that in period 4, only one unit (number 13) is purchased for $13, but three are sold. What additional "truth" can you deduce from comparing LIFO and FIFO cost of goods sold when physical quantities are declining and prices are rising?

g. The LIFO portion of Figure 8.1 represents a periodic inventory. In this part of the question, assume that in each period the first item is acquired before any sales occur. Then one item is sold; then the two items are purchased; then one more item is sold; then the last purchase is made and the last sale occurs. (If P represents purchase and S represents sale, the events of each period are PSPPSPS.) Draw a figure similar to those in Figure 8.1 to represent a LIFO cost flow assumption coupled with a perpetual inventory system. Convince yourself that in times of rising prices the LIFO cost of goods sold figure with a periodic inventory exceeds LIFO cost of goods sold computed with a perpetual inventory.

Figure 8.1 To Aid in Understanding Problem 33

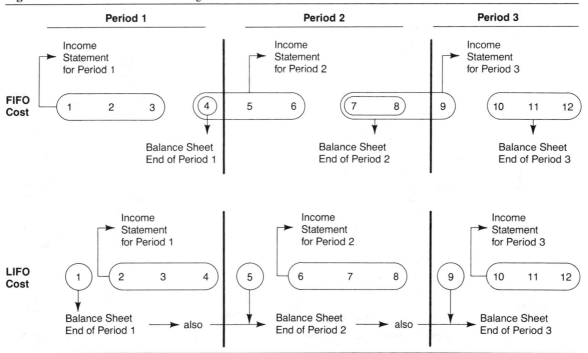

34. *Exploring the relation between replacement cost of goods sold and historical LIFO cost of goods sold.* The points to grasp in this problem are as follows:

(1) LIFO cost of goods sold is generally larger in a periodic inventory than in a perpetual inventory.

(2) LIFO cost of goods sold for most companies is insignificantly different from replacement cost of goods sold using replacement costs as of the time of sale.

(3) Historical LIFO cost of goods sold in a periodic inventory is likely to be larger (although not significantly) than the replacement cost of goods sold using replacement cost at the time of sale.

The data in Exhibit 8.16 are hypothetical. They are constructed from ratios of an actual retailing firm selling grocery products. Sales revenue for the year is $2,820,000. All expenses (including income taxes) other than cost of goods sold are $144,000 for the year. Exhibit 8.16 shows cost of goods available for sale. The costs of the grocery items for this company increase during the year at a steady rate of about one percent per month. The company starts the year with an inventory equal to $1\frac{1}{2}$ months' sales. These items were acquired at the end of December of Year 1 for $300,000. At the end of each month during Year 2, the firm is assumed to acquire inventory in physical quantities equal to the next month's sales requirements. We assume that all sales occur at mid-month during each month and that all purchases occur at the end of a month to be sold during the next month. (These artificial assumptions capture the reality of a firm acquiring inventory on average $\frac{1}{2}$ month before it is sold and an inventory turnover rate of about eight times per year.) Identical physical quantities are purchased and sold each month.

Exhibit 8.16
Data for Problem 34

	Replacement Cost of Goods Measured at	
	Sales Dates (mid-month)	Purchases Dates (end of month)
December Year 1	—	$ 300,000
January Year 2	$ 201,000	202,000
February Year 2	203,000	204,000
March Year 2	205,000	206,000
April Year 2	207,000	208,000
May Year 2	209,000	210,000
June Year 2	211,000	212,000
July Year 2	213,000	214,000
August Year 2	215,000	216,000
September Year 2	217,000	218,000
October Year 2	219,000	220,000
November Year 2.	221,000	222,000
December Year 2	223,000	224,000
Replacement Cost of Goods Sold at Times of Sale	$2,544,000	
Cost of Goods Available for Sale		$2,856,000

Exhibit 8.16 shows the actual cost of the items purchased at the end of each month and the replacement cost of those items if they had been acquired at mid-month.

At the end of the year, ending physical inventory is equal in amount to $1\frac{1}{2}$ months' sales, which is the same as the physical quantity on hand at the start of the year.

a. Compute LIFO historical cost of goods sold and net income for Year 2 using a periodic inventory system.

b. Compute LIFO historical cost of goods sold and net income for Year 2 using a perpetual inventory system.

c. Compute net income for Year 2 using replacement cost of goods sold at the time of sale.

d. What is the percentage difference between the largest and smallest cost of goods sold figures computed in the preceding three parts?

e. What is the percentage error in using LIFO costs of goods sold to approximate replacement cost of goods sold? (Compute percentage errors for both LIFO periodic and LIFO perpetual calculations.)

35. *Comparing LIFO and FIFO with declines in inventory quantities.* The LIFO Company and the FIFO Company both manufacture paper and cardboard products. Prices of timber, paper pulp, and finished paper products have generally increased by about five percent per year through the *start of this year*. Inventory data for the beginning and end of the year are shown below:

	Inventory Amounts	
	December 31	January 1
LIFO Company Inventory (last-in, first-out; historical cost)	$15,870,000	$19,695,000
FIFO Company Inventory (first-in, first-out; lower of cost and market)	38,250,000	46,284,000

Income statements for the two companies for the year ending December 31 are as follows:

	LIFO Company	FIFO Company
Sales	$57,000,000	$129,000,000
Less: Cost of Goods Sold	44,580,000	108,000,000
Gross Profit	$12,420,000	$ 21,000,000
Less: Operating Expenses		
Depreciation	$ 5,400,000	$ 12,000,000
Other	2,220,000	5,400,000
Total	$ 7,620,000	$ 17,400,000
Net Income before Income Tax	4,800,000	3,600,000
Income Tax (40 percent[a])	1,920,000	1,440,000
Net Income	$ 2,880,000	$ 2,160,000

[a]Assume the companies calculate income tax expense as a percentage of net income before income tax.

a. Assuming that the prices for timber, paper pulp, and finished paper had remained unchanged during the year, how would the two companies' respective inventory choices affect the interpretation of their financial statements for the year?

    b. How would the answer to part **(a)** differ if prices at the end of the year had been higher than at the beginning of the year?

36. *Reconstructing underlying events from ending inventory amounts (adapted from CPA examination).* The Burch Corporation began a merchandising business on January 1, Year 1. It acquired merchandise costing $100,000 in Year 1, $125,000 in Year 2, and $135,000 in Year 3. Exhibit 8.17 shows information about Burch Corporation's inventory as it would appear on the balance sheet under different inventory methods.

Exhibit 8.17
BURCH CORPORATION
Inventory Valuations for Balance Sheet
Under Various Assumptions

December 31	LIFO Cost	FIFO Cost	Lower of LIFO Cost and Market	Lower of FIFO Cost and Market
Year 1	$40,200	$40,000	$37,000	$37,000
Year 2	36,400	36,000	34,000	34,000
Year 3	41,800	44,000	41,800	44,000

In answering each of the following questions, indicate how the answer is deduced. You may assume that in any one year, prices moved only up or down, but not both.
    a. Did prices go up or down in Year 1?
    b. Did prices go up or down in Year 3?
    c. Which inventory method would show the highest income for Year 1?
    d. Which inventory method would show the highest income for Year 2?
    e. Which inventory method would show the highest income for Year 3?
    f. Which inventory method would show the lowest income for all three years combined?
    g. For Year 3, how much higher or lower would income be on the FIFO cost basis than it would be on the lower-of-FIFO-cost-and-market basis?

37. *Reconstructing accounting policies from financial statement data.* Data for Company A and Company B in Exhibit 8.18 are taken from the annual reports of two actual companies for a recent year. One of these companies uses a LIFO cost flow assumption for 100 percent of its inventories, and the other uses LIFO for about 45 percent of its inventories. Answer the following questions, making explicit the reasoning used in each case.
    a. From the cost of goods sold data alone, which of the companies appears to be the 100 percent LIFO company? The 45 percent LIFO company?
    b. From the ending inventory data alone, which of the companies appears to be the 100 percent LIFO company? The 45 percent LIFO company?
    c. From your answers to parts **(a)** and **(b)**, draw a conclusion as to which of the companies appears to be which.
    d. Note that Company A earned net income equal to 2.1 percent of sales whereas

Exhibit 8.18
Data for Analysis of LIFO and FIFO
Effects on Financial Statements

	Dollar Amounts in Millions	
	Company A	Company B
Sales Revenue	$5,151	$5,042
Cost of Goods Sold:ᵃ		
Historical Cost Basis	3,638	3,720
Replacement Cost Basis	3,675	3,720
Net Income	108	383
Ending Inventory:		
Historical Cost Basis	1,026	1,245
Replacement Cost Basis	1,056	2,169
Ratio of Net Income to Revenue	2.1 percent	7.6 percent

ᵃExcludes depreciation charges.

Company B earned net income equal to 7.6 percent of sales. Can you conclude that Company A is less profitable than Company B? Why or why not?

e. Which of the two companies is more likely to be involved in retailing, and which is more likely to be involved in manufacturing? Explain.

38. *Cost flow assumptions and financial statement ratios.* The financial statements of the General Products Limited (GP) are included in Appendix A starting on page 760. Refer to the data for 1988.

a. GP uses a FIFO cost flow assumption. There is sufficient information given in the notes for you to construct hypothetical financial statements assuming that GP used a current cost basis for inventories, without any cost flow assumption. For each of these treatments — FIFO, current cost — compute each of the following ratios (ignoring income tax effects):

(1) Current ratio
(2) Inventory turnover ratio
(3) Rate of return on shareholders' equity.

(Make current cost adjustments only for effects on inventory, ignoring effects for property, plant, and equipment. When assuming a current value basis for inventory, be sure to increase owners' equity by the same amount that you increase ending inventory. When you hypothetically debit ending inventory to increase it, you must also credit owners' equity.)

b. What inferences can you draw about the comparison of financial statements using historical cost accounting for inventories with those based on current values measured by replacement cost?

39. *Analysis of statement of changes in financial position; change definition of funds to exclude inventories.* For many years, General Motors Corporation (GM) defined funds as working capital (= current assets − current liabilities) in its statement of changes in financial position. Exhibit 8.19 presents condensed excerpts of GM's funds statements for several recent years with funds defined as working capital. During this five-year period GM changed the definition of funds to cash and temporary investments. Today, companies present the funds statement with funds defined as cash or cash plus temporary investments net of short-term borrowings. One implication of the difference is that changes in inventories become sources or uses of funds, rather than mere alterations of the components of funds.

Derive funds provided by operations for GM, defining funds as cash plus temporary investments. Treat changes in working capital accounts other than cash and temporary investments as *operating* sources and uses of funds. Analyze the apparent differences in changes in liquidity by comparing your statements to those in Exhibit 8.19. Try to form an opinion as to which funds statement you as an analyst would prefer to use.

Exhibit 8.19
GENERAL MOTORS CORPORATION
Excerpts from Statement of Changes in Financial Position
with Working Capital Definition of Funds
(dollars amounts in millions)
(Problem 39)

	Year 5	Year 4	Year 3	Year 2	Year 1
Total Working Capital Provided by Current Operations	$5,589.0	$4,807.6	$3,726.7	$5,758.8	$6,479.7
Increase (Decrease) in Working Capital Items by Element:					
Cash and Temporary Investments	$1,805.5	($2,394.5)	$ 728.8	($1,068.4)	$ 814.8
Accounts and Notes Receivable	(778.8)	(125.1)	(1,262.0)	(608.3)	957.6
Inventories	(1,038.5)	(72.3)	(844.1)	499.6	401.0
Prepaid Expenses and Deferred Income Taxes	341.1	820.6	243.1	(259.9)	(131.1)
Accounts Payable	99.0	268.0	(586.4)	307.0	893.3
Loans Payable	543.3	51.3	(752.4)	466.2	57.3
Accrued Liabilities	(474.3)	498.7	(1,065.9)	(590.0)	(773.1)
Increase (Decrease) in Working Capital Items	$ 497.3	($ 953.3)	($3,538.9)	($1,253.8)	$2,219.8

40. *Decision making and cost basis for inventories.* Imagine that you take frequent business trips. You have discovered a major airline's Bonus Travel tickets, which enable the holder to fly round trip anywhere that the airline flies. These tickets are bought and sold by special ticket brokers, and their price fluctuates almost daily in the market place. The schedule shown here presents data on tickets purchased and used.

Ticket Number	When Bought	Price Paid	When Used
1	May	$400	May
2	May	400	?
3	May	425	June
4	June	450	July
5	June	475	August
6	June	500	September
7	July	440	?
8	August	550	?

In October, you decide to take a good friend with you on a weekend vacation to New York and to use two of the tickets you have for the trip. At the time you take the October vacation, you have three tickets in your desk drawer: numbers 2, 7, and 8. During the week of the trip you have the option to purchase new tickets for $600 each, and your broker offers to buy tickets from you or anyone else for $480 each.

Your friend wants to reimburse you for the "cost" of the travel but has not made clear what is meant by *cost*. Your friend does not intend to audit the cost you quote. What is the "cost" of your friend's travel under each of the following sets of facts?

a. For the trip you use ticket numbers 2 and 8, putting the friend's name on ticket 2 and yours on ticket 8.

b. For the trip you use ticket numbers 2 and 8, putting the friend's name on ticket 8 and yours on ticket 2.

c. Just before you depart, your broker, in tribute to your being such a good customer, offers you one ticket for the bargain price of $480 and offers to sell you other tickets for $600. You purchase the ticket, but not until after the vacation weekend. For the trip you use ticket numbers 2 and 8, putting the friend's name on ticket 2 and yours on ticket 8.

d. Same facts as c, except that you do purchase the bargain-priced ticket and use it during the vacation, putting your friend's name on it.

e. Indicate how your answers to parts a through d change (if they do) when you assume that your traveling companion is a business associate, not your friend, and the trip is a business trip, not a vacation.

f. Should the cost you impose on your friend or your business associate depend on which particular ticket happens to be used in travel?

41. *Detailed comparison of various choices for inventory accounting.* the Freeman Corporation was organized and began retailing operations on January 1, Year 1. Purchases of merchandise inventory during Year 1 and Year 2 were as follows:

	Quantity Purchased	Unit Price	Acquisition Cost
1/10/Year 1	600	$10	$ 6,000
6/30/Year 1	200	12	2,400
10/20/Year 1	400	15	6,000
Total Year 1	1,200		$14,400

	Quantity Purchased	Unit Price	Acquisition Cost
2/18/Year 2	500	$18	$ 9,000
7/15/Year 2	500	20	10,000
12/15/Year 2	800	24	19,200
Total Year 2	1,800		$38,200

The number of units sold during Year 1 and Year 2 was 1,000 units and 1,500 units, respectively. Freeman Corporation uses a periodic inventory system.

a. Calculate the cost of goods sold during Year 1 under the FIFO cost flow assumption.

   b. Calculate the cost of goods sold during Year 1 under the LIFO cost flow assumption.

   c. Calculate the cost of goods sold during Year 1 under the weighted-average cost flow assumption.

   d. Calculate the cost of goods sold during Year 2 under the FIFO cost flow assumption.

   e. Calculate the cost of goods sold during Year 2 under the LIFO cost flow assumption.

   f. Calculate the cost of goods sold during Year 2 under the weighted-average cost flow assumption.

42. *Computation of mark-up ratios and holding gains/losses.* The following data pertain to the first two years of operations of the Macheral Company:

	1988	1987
Sales	$462,500	$331,250
Purchases	300,000	230,000
Ending Inventory:		
at cost	75,000	22,500
at market	82,500	28,125

   a. Compute Macheral Company's gross profit for 1987 and 1988, assuming inventory is valued at cost.

   b. Express gross profit for 1988 as a percentage of sales. What is the average markup on cost?

   c. Distinguish between the terms gross profit and operating profit.

   d. In 1987, a supplier representative indicated to Macheral's management that there would be a significant price increase in its product line. Acting on this tip, Macheral made all its 1987 purchases within a one week period, before any sales had occurred. Subsequently, the market value of these goods increased over the initial cost by the same percentage as reflected in Macheral's 1987 ending inventory (i.e., market vs. cost). Compute any holding gains or losses included in the 1987 income.

Adapted with the permission of the Society of Management Accountants of Canada.

Decision Problem 8-1

Barbara Distributors Ltd. imports and distributes a variety of products produced in the Pacific Rim countries. At the present time the company imports about 30 lines of merchandise with about 20 varieties in each line.

   The sales staff is motivated to sell the products, but must have some flexibility in setting prices to meet the competition. To provide a guide and control in setting prices and to ensure that each line makes an adequate contribution, the buyers are required to set a retail price on each item of merchandise they purchase. The salespeople are required to advise the sales manager when these prices are changed. The accounting staff makes a notation of the original retail price on all purchase invoices showing the percent markup expected. A copy of each purchase invoice with this information is given to the main buyer and to the sales manager. At the same time a memo record of the initial retail price is made for each invoice and summarized monthly.

Unfortunately, on November 17, one of the shipments from Taiwan was piled too close to the heat register and caught fire. The fire spread quickly and by the time it was put out the company's entire merchandise inventory was either destroyed or smoke and water damaged.

The insurance company sent an adjustor to determine the insurance claim that should be paid under the company's insurance policy. The policy provides that the insurance company will reimburse the insured by an amount equal to the "cost" of the inventory "less salvage value." With considerable difficulty the adjustor has taken a physical inventory of the merchandise, referred to the current invoice prices and arrived at a "cost" of $293,000, which he is willing to recommend that the insurance company pay for the inventory, which would then be sold by the insurance company.

As a check on the adequacy of the adjustor's recommendation, the accountant judged that accounting information might be useful. He had the books entered up to the date of the fire and extracted the following information from them for the period from January 1, the start of the current fiscal year, to November 17.

Cost of Material Purchased (Sales Price $1,234,100)	$668,400
Freight on Merchandise Purchased	$ 68,200
Custom Duty and Brokerage	$ 80,400

The operating costs of the various functions for the year to date were as follows:

Buying Office	$ 52,300
Warehousing	$ 48,000
Marketing	$119,600
Accounting	$ 41,900
General Administration	$63,600

The accountant estimated that 30 percent of the warehouse cost was incurred to receive, unpack, and store incoming shipments and the remainder incurred on outgoing shipments. The benefits from the accounting and administrative functions were received by the buying, warehousing, and marketing functions in proportion to the direct operating costs incurred by these three functions.

The sales for the year to date were $1,073,400 and the sales returns $52,800.

The balance sheet at December 31 last showed that the inventory, valued at the lower of cost and market, was $244,900. At that date the retail value of the inventory was $428,700.

Should the company accept the insurance claim proposed by the insurance adjustor? If the claim is not accepted, what alternative claim would you propose? What uncertainties exist about the adjustor's estimate and that of the alternative you propose?

Chapter 9   Plant, Equipment, and Intangible Assets: The Source of Operating Capacity

Assets are future benefits, short-lived or long-lived. A business acquires a short-lived asset, such as insurance coverage, in one period and uses up its benefits within a year. A long-lived asset is different: to reap its benefits, the owner uses it for several years. In these cases, the accountant allocates the cost of the asset over the several accounting periods of benefit. This general process is called *amortization*. Amortization of *plant assets*, which include the fixtures, machinery, equipment, and physical structures of a business, is called *depreciation*.

In addition to its plant assets, a company such as Petro Canada Limited owns natural resources, called *wasting assets*. Oil wells, coal mines, uranium deposits, and other natural resources are eventually used up. Amortization of the cost of these wasting assets is called *depletion*.

Businesses may also acquire *intangible assets* and, although there are many examples of them, some of the best-known ones are everyday words such as *Coca-Cola*, *Kleenex*, and *Kodak*, all famous trademarks. A firm may purchase a McDonald's or Kentucky Fried Chicken franchise. Other intangible assets are goodwill, copyrights, and patents. Although such intangibles may have indefinite economic lives, the accountant generally amortizes their costs to the periods of benefit. There is no specific term for the amortization of intangibles; the general term *amortization* is used to describe the process of writing off the cost of all intangibles.

Most of this chapter deals with depreciation because plant assets[1] are the most common long-lived assets and depreciation problems are typical of almost all other amortization problems.

The problems of plant asset valuation and depreciation measurement can be conveniently separated into the consideration of four separate kinds of events:

1. Recording the acquisition of the asset
2. Recording its use over time
3. Recording adjustments for changes in capacity or efficiency and for repairs or improvements
4. Recording its retirement or other disposal

Acquisition of Plant Assets

The cost of a plant asset includes all charges necessary to prepare it for rendering services, and it is often recorded in a series of transactions. Thus, the cost of a piece

---

[1] The terms *plant assets* and *fixed assets* are often used interchangeably. They refer to long-lived assets used in the operations of trading, service, and manufacturing enterprises, and include land, buildings, machinery, and equipment. The ordinary use of the terms *plant assets* and *fixed assets* often does not adequately encompass the class of long-lived assets that includes all land, buildings, machinery, and equipment. *Plant assets* is sometimes used too narrowly to mean only items in a factory or plant. *Fixed assets* is sometimes used too narrowly to mean only items such as land and buildings that are immovable.

of equipment will be the sum of the entries to recognize the invoice price (less any discounts), transportation costs, installation charges, and any other costs incurred before the equipment is ready for use. See the example on page 45.

Computing the acquisition cost of an asset acquired in a trade-in transaction presents special problems. A trade-in transaction involves both the retirement of an old asset and the acquisition of a new one. Although its problems might be discussed with acquisitions, this chapter discusses trade-in transactions in the section on retirements. Computing the acquisition cost of a self-constructed asset presents other problems, discussed next.

Self-Constructed Assets

When a firm constructs its own buildings or equipment, many entries to record the labor, material, and overhead costs will normally be required before the total cost is recorded. One of these costs may be interest paid during construction. The amount may be significant during periods of double-digit interest rates and for projects with long construction periods. The *CICA Handbook* makes no recommendation on capitalization of interest during construction and, as a consequence, there is no standard Canadian practice. Most public utilities, such as electric and gas, pipeline, telephone and cablevision, and land development companies, capitalize interest during construction. A few companies in other industries also follow this practice. The amount of interest that is capitalized is usually based on the entity's actual borrowings and interest payments. It is intended to be the interest cost incurred during the assets' acquisition periods that in principle could have been avoided if the assets had not been acquired.

If there is a specific new borrowing in connection with the asset being constructed, the interest rate on that borrowing should be used. If the expenditures on plant exceed such specific new borrowings, the interest rate to be applied to such excess is the weighted average of rates applicable to other borrowings of the enterprise. If there are no specific new borrowings, then the average interest rate on old borrowings is used to compute the total amount to be capitalized. The total amount of interest included cannot exceed total interest costs for the period. The capitalization of interest into plant during construction reduces otherwise reportable interest expense and increases income during periods of construction. In later periods, the plant will have higher depreciation charges, reducing income.

Example Assume the following long-term debt structure:

Construction Loan at 15 Percent on Building under Construction	$1,000,000
Other Borrowings at 12 Percent Average Rate	3,600,000
Total Long-Term Debt	$4,600,000

The account Building under Construction has an average balance during the year of $3,000,000. The amount of interest to be capitalized is based on all of the new construction-related borrowings, $1,000,000, and enough of the older borrowings, $2,000,000, to bring the total to $3,000,000. The interest capitalized is computed as:

$1,000,000 × .15	$150,000
2,000,000 × .12	240,000
$3,000,000	$390,000

The entries to record interest and then to capitalize the required amounts might be:

Interest Expense	$582,000	
Interest Payable		$582,000

To record all interest as expense: $582,000 =
(.15 × $1,000,000) + (.12 × $3,600,000) =
$150,000 + $432,000.

Building under Construction	$390,000	
Interest Expense		$390,000

To record interest capitalized as part of the cost of the building,
reducing interest expense.

The preceding two entries might be combined as one:

Interest Expense	$192,000	
Building under Construction	390,000	
Interest Payable		$582,000

To record interest payable, part charged to expense and part
charged to the cost of the building.

Both total interest for the year, $582,000, and the amount capitalized, $390,000, should be disclosed in notes. The income statement will report interest expense, $192,000, in the example. The amount shown in future years for depreciation of the plant will be larger than otherwise because of interest capitalization in earlier years. Over the life of the asset, from construction through retirement, total income is unaffected by capitalizing interest, because the increased income in the construction period is later exactly offset with larger depreciation charges. Over long enough time spans, total expense must equal total cash expenditure.

Depreciation — Fundamental Concepts

Purpose of Depreciation

Most plant assets can be kept intact and in usable operating condition for more than a year, but, except for land, eventually they must be retired from service. Depreciation systematically allocates the cost of these assets to the periods of their use.

Allocation of Cost The cost of a depreciating asset is the price paid for a series of future services. The asset account is like a prepayment, similar to prepaid rent or insurance — a payment in advance for services to be received. As the asset is used in each accounting period, a portion of the investment in the assets is treated as the cost of the service received and is recognized as an expense of the period or as part of the cost of goods produced during the period.

Depreciation is a process of cost allocation, not one of valuation. This chapter discusses the problems of *allocating* the cost of assets to the periods of benefit. A depreciation problem will exist whenever (1) funds are invested in services to be rendered by a plant asset, and (2) at some date in the future, the asset must be retired from service with a residual value less than its original cost.

No uniquely correct amount for the periodic charge for depreciation can be computed. The cost of the plant asset is a *joint cost* of the several benefited periods. That is, each of the periods of the asset's use benefits from its services. There is usually no single correct way to allocate a joint cost. The depreciation process assigns periodic charges that reflect systematic calculations.

Return of Capital A business attempts to earn both a return *of* capital and a return *on* capital. Before there can be a return *on* capital (as measured by accounting profits), all costs must be recovered. The purpose of amortization is to charge against revenues the cost of noncurrent assets. To understand the role of amortization in this process, reconsider the installment method and the cost-recovery-first method of recognizing revenue, introduced in Chapter 4. In the cost-recovery-first method, there is no accounting income until all costs are recovered. The accounting under cost recovery first charges to expense an amount equal to cash collections so that there is no accounting income until all anticipated costs have been debited to expense. In contrast, under the installment method, costs are allocated over the time of cash collections so that each dollar collected represents identical proportions of cost recovery and profits. In accounting for noncurrent assets, one might, in principle, debit expense and credit plant assets so that there is no profit until the costs of plant assets have been written off. The early periods of a noncurrent asset's life could have no income but the later periods would show no expense for plant and, consequently, larger net income. Instead, accounting estimates the life of the noncurrent asset and writes off its cost over its life, in principle allowing each period to show both cost recovery and income. The amortization process provides for the gradual return of the investment in a noncurrent asset. In historical cost accounting, the process is designed to provide a return of the cost of the asset, no more and no less.[2] But the return of costs is designed to occur over the asset's life, not all in the early periods of its life.

Depreciation Is Not a Decline in Value

In ordinary conversation, "depreciation" frequently means a decline in value. Over the entire service life of a plant asset, there is a decline in value of the asset from

---

[2]As inflation has become a major economic problem, accountants increasingly recognize that basing depreciation charges on acquisition costs will not, in most cases, charge amounts to expense that are sufficient to maintain the productive capacity of the business. Basing depreciation on acquisition costs will enable a business to recover its initial cash investment but not necessarily enough to replace the physical productive capacity purchased with the cash.

Section 4510 of the *CICA Handbook* requires major corporations to disclose as supplemental information depreciation charges based on current costs. The formal financial statements continue to report acquisition cost measured in nominal dollars. Appendix D describes the calculation and reporting of depreciation to reflect the effect of changing prices.

acquisition until it is retired from service. The charge made to the operations of each accounting period does not result from declines in value during that period but, rather, from the process of ensuring a return of capital invested. If, in a given period, an asset increases in value, there will still be depreciation during that period. There have been two partially offsetting processes: (1) a holding gain on the asset, which usually is not recognized in historical cost-based accounting, and (2) depreciation of the asset's historical cost to achieve a return of investment.

The Causes of Depreciation

The causes of depreciation are the causes of decline in an asset's service potential and of its ultimate retirement. Unless the asset must eventually be retired from its planned use, there is no depreciation. When the services provided by land do not diminish over time, land is not depreciated; all costs are recovered when the land is sold. Many factors lead to the retirement of assets from service, but the causes of decline in service potential can be classified as either *physical* or *functional*. The physical factors include such things as ordinary wear and tear from use, chemical action such as rust or electrolysis, and the effects of wind and rain. The most important functional (nonphysical) cause is *obsolescence*. Inventions, for example, may result in new processes that reduce the unit cost of production to the point where continued operation of old equipment is not economical, even though it may be relatively unimpaired physically. Retail stores often replace display cases and storefronts long before they are worn out in order to make the appearance of the store more attractive. Changed economic conditions may also become functional causes of depreciation, such as when an old airport becomes inadequate and must be abandoned, and a new, larger one is built to meet the requirements of heavier traffic, or when an increase in the cost of gasoline causes a reduction in demand for automobile products, which results in a reduced scale of operations in automobile manufacturing.

Identifying the specific causes of depreciation is not essential for measuring it. Almost any physical asset will eventually have to be retired from service, and in some cases the retirement will become necessary at a time when physical deterioration is negligible. Understanding the specific causes can, nevertheless, help in estimating an asset's useful life.

Depreciation Accounting Problems

The three principal accounting problems in allocating the cost of an asset over time are:

1. Measuring the depreciable basis of the asset
2. Estimating its useful service life
3. Deciding on the pattern of expiration of asset cost over the useful service life

Depreciable Basis of Plant Assets — Cost Less Salvage Value

Depreciation charges in historical cost accounting are based on the acquisition cost of the asset less the estimated residual value — the amount to be received when the asset is retired from service. The amounts invested in an asset that will be recovered when the asset is retired need not be recovered through depreciation charges. Recall that land is not depreciated because its utility will not be impaired and it is likely that its cost will be recovered at the time of sale. Similarly, the amount estimated to be recovered from a depreciating plant asset at its retirement need not be depreciated; that portion of the initial investment is recovered at retirement.

Estimating Salvage Value Depreciation charges are based on the difference between acquisition cost and the asset's estimated salvage value or net residual value. The terms *salvage value* and *net residual value* refer to estimated proceeds on disposition of an asset less all removal and selling costs. Salvage value must be an estimate at any time before the asset is retired. Hence, before retirement, the terms *salvage value* and *estimated salvage value* are synonymous.

For buildings, common practice assumes a zero salvage value. This treatment rests on the assumption that the cost to be incurred in tearing down the building, or disposing of other assets kept for their physical lives, will approximate the sales value of the scrap materials recovered. For other assets, however, the salvage value may be substantial and should be taken into account in making the periodic depreciation charge. For example, a car rental firm will replace its automobiles at a time when other owners can use the cars for several years more. The rental firm will be able to recover a substantial part of acquisition cost (and return of part of the capital invested) from the sale of used cars. Past experience usually forms the best basis for estimating salvage value. (Salvage value can be negative. Consider, for example, the cost of dismantling a nuclear electricity-generating plant.)

Estimates of salvage value are necessarily subjective and in the past were the source of conflict between companies and income tax assessors. A major revision of the income tax treatment of depreciation, explained in detail below, eliminated this conflict by using a declining-balance method that ignores the residual value. Companies are not required to record the income tax depreciation in their accounts, and the majority do not follow this method of depreciation. In calculating depreciation in problems in this text, the entire salvage value is to be taken into account unless explicit contrary instructions are given.

Unit of Account Whenever feasible, depreciation should be computed for individual items such as a single building, machine, or automobile. Where similar items are in use and each one has a relatively small cost, individual calculations may be impractical and the depreciation charge is usually calculated for the group as a whole. Furniture and fixtures, tools, and telephone poles are examples of assets that are usually depreciated in groups. Group depreciation techniques are treated in more advanced financial accounting courses. The basic principles of depreciating individual items discussed here apply, however, to group depreciation situations.

Estimating Service Life

The depreciation calculation requires an estimate of the economic service life of the asset. In making the estimate, both the physical and the functional causes of depreciation must be considered. Experience with similar assets, corrected for differences in the planned intensity of use or alterations in maintenance policy, is usually the best guide for this estimate.

Despite abundant data from experience, estimating service lives for financial reporting is the most difficult task in the entire depreciation calculation. Allowing for obsolescence is particularly difficult because most obsolescence results from forces outside the firm. Estimates will probably prove to be incorrect. For this reason, estimates of useful service life of assets are reconsidered every few years.

Pattern of Expiration of Costs

Once the cost is measured and both salvage value and service life are estimated, the total of depreciation charges for the whole life of the asset has been determined. If salvage value is assumed to be zero, then the entire cost will be depreciated. The problem remains of selecting the pattern for allocating those charges to the specific years of the life. Depreciation based on the passage of time follows one of five basic patterns. They are labeled E, A, S, D, and N in Figures 9.1 and 9.2.

The next section discusses the patterns in more detail. A represents *accelerated* depreciation; S, *straight-line* depreciation; D, *decelerated* depreciation. (Understanding the terms "accelerated" and "decelerated" is easier if you compare the depreciation charges in the early years to straight-line depreciation. See Figure 9.2.) Pattern D is seldom used in financial reporting, but is useful for certain managerial accounting problems. Pattern E represents immediate expensing of the item. All costs are charged to the period when the cost is incurred. The section on intangibles discusses this pattern. Pattern N represents the situation, such as for land, where there are no periodic amortization charges. The asset is shown on the books at acquisition cost until sold or otherwise retired.

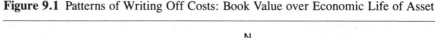

Figure 9.1 Patterns of Writing Off Costs: Book Value over Economic Life of Asset

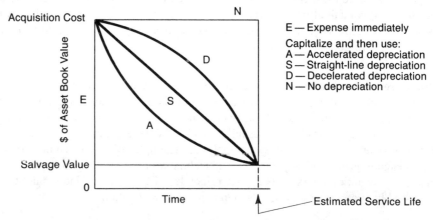

Figure 9.2 Patterns of Annual Depreciation Charge over Economic Life of Asset

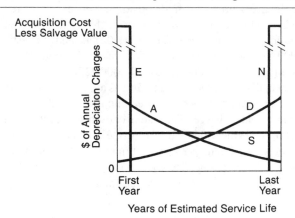

Depreciation Methods

All depreciation methods systematically allocate the cost of the asset minus its estimated salvage value to the periods in which it is used. The methods discussed here are as follows:

1. Straight-line (time) method (pattern S)
2. Production or use (straight-line use) method
3. Declining-balance method (pattern A)
4. Compound interest methods (pattern D)

When a depreciable asset is acquired or retired during an accounting period, depreciation should be calculated only for that portion of the period during which the asset is used. However, to simplify the calculation, many companies record a full year's depreciation in the year of acquisition and no depreciation on a depreciable asset in the year of disposal. In these cases the companies in fact assume that all acquisitions and disposals are made at the beginning of the year.

Straight-Line (Time) Method

The allocation method that is used most commonly for financial reporting is the *straight-line* method. Eighty-five percent of the sample companies included in the CICA's 1987 edition of *Financial Reporting in Canada* used this method of depreciation for some or all of their assets. Under the straight-line method, the cost of the asset, less any estimated salvage value, is divided by the number of years of its expected life in order to arrive at the annual depreciation:

$$\text{Annual Depreciation} = \frac{\text{Cost Less Estimated Salvage Value}}{\text{Estimated Life in Years}}$$

For example, if a machine costs $12,000, has an estimated salvage value of $1,000, and has an expected useful life of five years, the annual depreciation will be $2,200

[= ($12,000 − $1,000)/5]. Occasionally, instead of a positive salvage value, the cost of removal exceeds the gross proceeds on disposition. This excess of removal costs over gross proceeds should be added to the cost of the asset in making the calculation. Thus, if a building is constructed for $37,000,000, and it is estimated that it will cost $5,000,000 to remove it at the end of 25 years, the annual depreciation would be $1,680,000 [= ($37,000,000 + $5,000,000)/25].

A common practice, especially when the salvage value is assumed to be zero, is to apply an appropriate percentage, known as the depreciation rate, to the *acquisition cost* in order to calculate the annual charge. The rate is chosen so that it will charge the entire acquisition cost off over the estimated life. A rate of ten percent will write off the cost of an asset in ten years, a rate of 25 percent in four years, and so on. The machine referred to in the preceding paragraph would be depreciated annually at the rate of 20 percent of acquisition cost less salvage value for five years.

Units of Production Method

Many assets are not used uniformly over time. Manufacturing plants often have seasonal variations in operation so that certain machines may be used 24 hours a day at one time and eight hours or less a day at another time of year. Trucks are not likely to receive the same amount of use in each year of their lives. The straight-line (time) method of depreciation may result in depreciation patterns unrelated to patterns of use.

When the rate of use varies over periods and when the total use of an asset over its life can be estimated, a depreciation charge based on actual use during the period may be used. It is commonly assumed that an equal benefit is received from each unit of use resulting in the adoption of the straight-line use method where the same cost is allocated to each unit of use. For example, depreciation of a truck for a period could be based on the ratio of kilometres driven during the period to total kilometres expected to be driven over the truck's life. The depreciation cost per unit (kilometre) of use is:

$$\text{Depreciation Cost per Unit} = \frac{\text{Cost Less Estimated Salvage Value}}{\text{Estimated Number of Units}}$$

Assume that a truck costs $24,000, has an estimated salvage value of $1,200 and is expected to be driven 100,000 kilometres before it is retired from service. The depreciation per kilometre is $.228 [= ($24,000 − $1,200)/100,000]. If the truck is operated 2,000 kilometres in a given month, the depreciation charge for the month is 2,000 × $.228 = $456.

One-fifth of the sample companies included in the CICA's 1987 edition of *Financial Reporting in Canada* used the units of production method of depreciation.

Accelerated Depreciation (Declining-Balance Method)

The earning power of some plant assets declines as the assets grow older. Cutting tools lose some of their precision; printing presses are shut down more frequently for repairs; rentals in an old office building are lower than those from a new one. Some assets provide more and better services in the early years of their lives while requiring increasing amounts of maintenance as they grow older. Where this is the case, methods that recognize larger depreciation charges in early years and progressively smaller depreciation charges later may be justified. Such methods are referred to as *accelerated depreciation* methods because the depreciation charges in the early years of the asset's life are larger than in later years. Accelerated depreciation leads to a pattern such as A in Figures 9.1 and 9.2.

For convenience, the depreciation charges for a year, however they are determined, are allocated on a straight-line basis to periods *within* the year.

The *declining-balance*, or diminishing balance, method is one accelerated depreciation method. In this method, the depreciation charge is calculated by multiplying the *net book value* of the asset (cost less accumulated depreciation) at the start of each period by a fixed rate. The estimated salvage value is not subtracted from the cost in making the depreciation calculation, but the asset should not be written down below its estimated salvage value. Because the net book value declines from period to period, the result is a declining periodic charge for depreciation throughout the life of the asset.[3] The rate most commonly used is the maximum one permitted for income tax purposes. If a machine costing $5,000 is purchased on January 1, Year 1 and depreciated on a declining-balance basis with a rate of 40 percent, the depreciation charges would be calculated as shown in Exhibit 9.1.

Exhibit 9.1
Declining-Balance Depreciation Asset with 5-Year Life

Year	Acquisition Cost (1)	Accumulated Depreciation as of Jan. 1 (2)	Net Book Value as of Jan. 1 = (1) − (2) (3)	Depreciation Rate (4)	Depreciation Charge for the Year = (3) × (4) (5)
1	$5,000	$ 0	$5,000	.40	$2,000
2	5,000	2,000	3,000	.40	1,200
3	5,000	3,200	1,800	.40	720
4	5,000	3,920	1,080	.40	432
5	5,000	4,352	648	.40	259
6	5,000	4,611	389	—	—

The undepreciated cost as of December 31, Year 5, as shown in Exhibit 9.1, is $389 (= $648 − $259). This amount is unlikely to equal the salvage value at that time.

---

[3]Under the declining-balance method, as strictly applied, the fixed depreciation rate used is one that will charge the cost less salvage value of the asset over its service life. The formula for computing the rate is:

$$\text{Depreciation Rate} = 1 - \sqrt[n]{\frac{s}{c}} = 1 - \left(\frac{s}{c}\right)^{1/n}$$

In this formula n = estimated periods of service life, s = estimated salvage value, and c = cost.

Estimates of salvage value have a profound effect on the rate. Unless a positive salvage value is assumed, the rate is 100 percent — that is, all depreciation is charged in the first period. For an asset costing $10,000, with an estimated life of five years, the depreciation is 40 percent per period if salvage value is $778, but it is 60 percent if salvage value is $102.

The effect of small changes in salvage value on the rate and the seeming mathematical complexity of the formula have resulted in widespread use of approximations or rules of thumb instead of the formula.

The problem may be anticipated and solved by adjusting the depreciation charge in one or more of the later years.

With a few exceptions, the declining-balance method applied on a group basis is used when determining the maximum depreciation (called *capital cost allowance*) that may be claimed as an expense when deriving taxable income. Further details of capital cost allowance are provided below.

Twenty-six percent of the sample companies included in the CICA's 1987 edition of *Financial Reporting in Canada* used the declining-balance method of depreciation for financial reporting purposes, for some or all of their assets.

Decelerated Depreciation (Compound Interest Methods)

Compound interest methods are seldom used in financial accounting except for real estate development operations, but they are theoretically sound for many management decisions. For plant assets producing equal annual net inflows of cash, compound interest depreciation leads to a pattern like D in Figures 9.1 and 9.2. This text does not illustrate compound interest methods, but see Problem 41 at the end of this chapter.

Capital Cost Allowance

Under the Income Tax Act a company is not permitted to deduct depreciation when deriving taxable income. In place of depreciation a company may claim a capital cost allowance as specified in the Act and Regulations.

When framing the capital cost allowance (CCA) provisions the government hoped to achieve three objectives. The first objective was to permit a company to deduct from taxable income, over the life of the company, the cost of utilizing depreciable assets. The cost to be allowed was defined as the initial acquisition cost less the proceeds of the ultimate disposal. A corollary of this objective was that the differences between the disposal price and the net book value of depreciable assets on the disposal date were considered to be corrections of the CCA claimed over the life of the assets rather than capital gains or losses, except to the extent that the disposal price exceeded the original cost to the company.

The second objective was to permit the company to select the pattern of allocating the cost of the asset to each year, subject only to a liberal maximum annual allowance. This annual allowance was in most cases double the normal straight-line rate of depreciation.

Thirdly, the method that was adopted should be simple for the company to compute and for the income tax department to administer in order to reduce the cost to the company and the government of administering the regulations.

These objectives were attained by framing legislation that has the following features:

1. No allowance for depreciation would be permitted as a deduction from revenue to compute taxable income, except as permitted by the capital cost allowance regulations.
2. All depreciable assets are grouped into about 35 classes, roughly based on the term of life of the asset from the date it was originally constructed until it was

scrapped. For each class a maximum rate of depreciation (called capital cost allowance) is permitted, varying from one percent to 100 percent and applied to the class as a whole.

3. The treatment of individual assets is ignored, except when an asset is sold for more than its cost to the company. In this case, the excess of the proceeds of the disposal of the asset over the cost is considered as a capital gain, and only half of the excess is considered taxable income.

4. In computing the maximum capital cost allowance permitted to be deducted when computing taxable income, the undepreciated capital cost of a class is utilized as the base to which the stated rates apply. The undepreciated capital cost of a class consists of the acquisition cost of the assets in the class less the sum of the accumulated capital cost allowances claimed and the proceeds of the sales of assets of the class, reduced by any portion of the proceeds considered to be a capital gain.

5. It is assumed that all depreciable assets are purchased in the middle of the fiscal period. Consequently, only 50 percent of the CCA may be claimed in the year of acquisition. When a fiscal period is less than 12 months, a proportion of the annual amount may be claimed. With these exceptions, the balances in each class at the end of each fiscal year are used as the base for computing the maximum capital cost allowance for that year, with the full rates adopted.

The maximum capital cost allowance permitted to be claimed in any one year is computed as follows:

1. Determine the undepreciated cost at the beginning of the year for each class of asset owned by the company. This balance is available from the income tax return submitted in the previous year.

2. Add to the opening balance of the undepreciated cost of each class of assets the cost of assets purchased in that class during the year.

3. Deduct from this total for each class the proceeds of the sales of assets in the class during the year, except to the extent that a portion of the proceeds (the excess of the sale proceeds over the cost) is considered to be a capital gain. The balance of the undepreciated cost on completion of steps 1, 2, and 3 becomes the class base for capital cost allowances for that year.

4. Multiply the base for each class of asset by the rate stated in the regulations. The resultant product is the maximum capital cost allowance permitted under the Act. Illustrations of the rates applicable to particular classes follow:

Brick, stone, concrete buildings .... Class 3   5%
Frame, stucco on frame, galvanized buildings .... Class 6   10%
Furniture and machinery not otherwise specified .... Class 8   20%
Automobiles and trucks .... Class 10   30%

5. Deduct one half of the capital cost allowance claimed on the cost of the assets acquired during the year less the proceeds of disposals.

6. A special situation arises when all of the assets in a class are disposed of, or when the proceeds of the sale of assets in a class exceed the undepreciated cost of the class at the beginning of the fiscal year plus the cost of additions made during the year.

   When all of the assets in a class are disposed of and the proceeds of the disposal (reduced by any capital gain) are less than the undepreciated cost of the class at the end of the year, the undepreciated cost, reduced by the proceeds of the disposal, may be deducted from taxable income in that year. On the other hand, when the proceeds of disposal (reduced by any capital gains), whether or not all of the assets of the class are disposed of, exceed the undepreciated cost of the class at the end of the year, the excess must be included in the taxable income of the year of disposal, subject to certain exceptions. For example, where an asset disposal is involuntary, resulting from a fire, theft or expropriation, special provisions apply.

A company is not required to claim any capital cost allowance in a year, but if not claimed, the capital cost allowance cannot be carried forward except as part of the undepreciated cost.

Exhibit 9.2
CCA LIMITED
Analysis of Capital Cost Allowance
Fiscal Year-End December 31

	Class 6 10%	Class 8 20%	Class 10 30%
Jan. 1, Year 1 Purchased frame building	$100,000		
Jan. 15, Year 1 Purchased manufacturing equipment		$300,000	
Feb. 13, Year 1 Purchased: 1 fork lift truck			$ 4,000
3 delivery trucks @ $5,000.			15,000
1 automobile			3,000
Undepreciated capital cost, Dec. 31, Year 1	$100,000	$300,000	$22,000
Capital cost claimed for the year[a]	—	—	—
Undepreciated capital cost, Jan. 1, Year 2 and Dec. 31, Year 2 (there were no transactions during Year 2)	$100,000	$300,000	$22,000
Capital cost claimed for Year 2[b]	10,000	60,000	6,600
Undepreciated capital cost, Jan. 1, Year 3	$ 90,000	$240,000	$15,400
Oct. 20, Year 3 Sold building for $110,000[c]	(100,000)		
Oct. 20, Year 3 Sold machinery for $320,000[c]		(300,000)	
Dec. 20, Year 3 Sold fork lift truck for $5,000[c]			(4,000)
Dec. 20, Year 3 Sold automobile for $1,000			(1,000)
Dec. 20, Year 3 Sold 1 truck for $4,000			(4,000)
Dec. 31, Year 3 Purchased a new factory building (frame)	150,000		
Undepreciated capital cost, Dec. 31, Year 3	$140,000	$(60,000)	$ 6,400
Capital cost claimed for Year 3[d]	5,000		
The $60,000 must be taken into current income		60,000	
Undepreciated capital cost, Jan. 1, Year 4	$135,000	—	$ 6,400
Jan. 5, Year 4 Purchased machinery		$400,000	
June 30, Year 4 Sold 2 trucks for $3,000 each			6,000
Undepreciated capital cost, Dec. 31, Year 4	$135,000	$400,000	$ 400
Maximum capital cost allowance claimed for Year 4	13,500	40,000[f]	400[e]
Undepreciated capital cost, Jan. 1, Year 5	$121,500	$360,000	—

[a]Because the company suffered a loss during the first year, no capital cost allowance was claimed.
[b]Maximum capital cost allowance claimed.
[c]Sale proceeds in excess of the original cost of the asset are considered to be capital gains and are exempt from taxation.
[d]The company achieved a small taxable income before capital cost allowance, so only enough capital cost allowance to produce a taxable income of zero was claimed.
[e]The entire balance may be claimed because there are no assets remaining in class 10.
[f]Only 50 percent of the normal CCA may be claimed in the year the machinery was purchased.

An illustration of the capital cost allowances claimed by CCA Limited, incorporated on January 1, Year 1, is presented in Exhibit 9.2.

The maximum capital cost allowance permitted to be deducted in deriving taxable income for assets falling in nine classes is computed using the straight-line method. These asset classes were established for assets whose useful lives to the taxpayer were determined by legal contract or depletion of a nonrenewable resource, and assets for which accelerated rates of capital cost allowances were granted to encourage companies to acquire and use the specific type of asset. Examples of these classes and the basis of computing their capital cost allowance follow:

Class 13 Leasehold improvements — over the life of the lease plus one renewal period (minimum five years, maximum 40 years).

Class 14 Patents, franchises, licenses, etc. — over the life of the asset.

Class 15 Woods assets — depreciated on the basis of a rate applied to the cords or board feet of timber cut during the year.

Class 24 Water pollution control equipment — 50 percent.

Class 29 Certain machinery and equipment acquired after May 8, 1972 for use in Canada primarily in the manufacture or processing of goods — 50 percent (maximum in first year only).

Over the years, various accelerated rates have been introduced to spur the economy or to give recognition to unusual conditions (e.g., double depreciation for manufacturers of defense materials in wartime). At other times, the deduction of capital cost allowance has been deferred or restricted.

Factors To Consider in Choosing the Depreciation Method

Depreciation affects both income reported in the financial statements and taxable income on tax returns. The firm need not choose the same depreciation method for both financial and tax reporting purposes. If it chooses different methods for the two purposes, the difference between depreciation in the financial statements and CCA on the tax return leads to a problem in accounting for income taxes, discussed in intermediate texts.

Financial Reporting Financial reporting for long-lived assets seeks an income statement that realistically measures the expiration of their benefits and provides a "reasonable" pattern of cost recovery. No one knows, however, just what portion of the service potential of a long-lived asset expires in any one period. The cost of the plant asset is a joint cost of the several periods of use, and no uniquely correct way of allocating joint costs exists. All that can be said is that financial statements should report depreciation charges based on reasonable estimates of asset expirations. Chapter 15 discusses more fully the firm's selection from alternative accounting principles, including the choice of depreciation methods.

Tax Reporting It seems clear that in selecting the amount of capital cost allowance claimed for tax reporting, the goal of the firm should be to maximize the present value of the reductions in tax payments from claiming capital cost allowance. Earlier deductions are worth more than later ones, because a dollar saved today is worth more than a dollar saved tomorrow. A firm will generally choose an amount that meets the general goal of paying the least amount of tax, as late as possible, within the law. This goal is sometimes called the *least and latest rule*.

Accounting for Periodic Depreciation

The debit made in the entry to record periodic depreciation is usually either to an expense account or to a product cost account. In a manufacturing concern, the depreciation of factory buildings and equipment is a product cost, a part of the cost of work-in-process and finished product. Depreciation on sales equipment is a selling expense. Depreciation on office equipment is a general or administrative expense. The matching credit for periodic depreciation could, in principle, be made directly to the asset account affected, such as buildings or equipment. Although such an entry is sometimes made, usually the credit is to a contra asset account. This leaves the acquisition cost of the asset undisturbed and permits easy computation of the total amount written off through depreciation. The effect, however, is precisely the same as a direct credit to the asset account. Accumulated Depreciation is the title of the contra asset account credited.

The entry to record periodic depreciation of office facilities, a period expense, is:

Depreciation Expense	$1,500	
Accumulated Depreciation		$1,500

The entry to record periodic depreciation of manufacturing facilities, a product cost, is:

Work-in-Process Inventory	$4,500	
Accumulated Depreciation		$4,500

The Depreciation Expense account is closed at the end of the accounting period as a part of the regular closing-entry procedure. The Work-in-Process Inventory account is an asset. Product costs, such as depreciation on manufacturing facilities, accumulate in the Work-in-Process account until the goods being produced are completed and transferred to Finished Goods Inventory. The Accumulated Depreciation account remains open at the end of the period and appears on the balance sheet as a deduction from the asset account to which it refers. The balance in the Accumulated Depreciation account represents the total charges prior to the balance sheet date for the depreciation on assets currently in use. The difference between the balance of the asset account and the balance of its accumulated depreciation account is called the *net book value* of the asset.

In preparing a statement of changes in financial position, the periodic depreciation charge is an addback in the "operations" section. It represents an expense that does not use funds but instead uses a noncurrent asset.

Changes in Periodic Depreciation

The original depreciation schedule for a particular asset may require changing. Estimates of useful life (and of salvage value as well) may be judged incorrect in the light of new information, which may become apparent at any time during its life. The accuracy of the estimates improves as retirement approaches. If the change in estimate has a material impact, corrective action must be taken. The generally accepted procedure is to make no adjustment for the past estimate error, but to spread the remaining undepreciated balance less the revised estimate of salvage value over the new estimate of remaining service life of the asset.

To illustrate the accounting for changes in periodic depreciation, assume the following facts. An office machine was purchased on January 1, Year 1, for $9,200. It was estimated that the machine would be operated for 15 years with a salvage value of $200. The depreciation charge recorded for each of the years from Year 1 through Year 5 under the straight-line method would have been $600 [= ($9,200 − $200)/15]. On December 31, Year 6, before the books are closed for the year, it is decided that a total useful life of ten years is more likely, but the salvage estimate of $200 is still reasonable.

The accepted procedure for recognizing this substantial decrease in service life is to revise the future depreciation so that the correct total will be accumulated in the Accumulated Depreciation account at the end of the revised service life. No adjustments of amounts previously recorded may be made. In our example, the total amount of acquisition cost yet to be depreciated before the Year 6 adjustments is $6,000 [= ($9,200 − $200) − (5 × $600)]. The new estimate of the *remaining* life is five years (the year just ended plus the next four), so the new annual depreciation charge is $1,200 (= $6,000/5). The only change in the accounting procedure is to substitute the new amount of $1,200 for the former annual depreciation of $600. The depreciation entry on December 31, Year 6, and each year thereafter would be

Depreciation Expense	$1,200	
Accumulated Depreciation		$1,200
To record depreciation for Year 6 based on revised estimates.		

Figure 9.3 illustrates the revised depreciation path.

Figure 9.3
Illustration of Revised Depreciation Schedule. Asset's service life estimate is decreased from 15 to 10 years at the start of Year 6. The straight-line method is used. Asset cost is $9,200 and has estimated salvage value of $200.

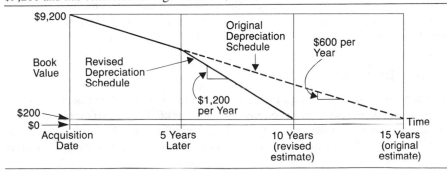

Repairs and Improvements

Depreciation is not the only cost of using a plant asset. Repair and maintenance costs during the life of the asset will be incurred. The repair policy adopted by the business will often affect the depreciation rate. If, for example, machinery, trucks, and other plant assets are checked and repaired frequently, such assets will have a longer useful life, and therefore a lower depreciation rate than otherwise. The more commonly used estimates of service life and depreciation rates assume that normal repairs will be made during the life of an asset.

Repairs must be distinguished from improvements (sometimes called *betterments*). *Repairs* do not extend estimated service life materially or otherwise increase productive capacity. They restore future benefits to originally estimated levels. *Improvements* involve making an asset substantially better, improving its productive capacity. Repairs maintain or restore service potential; improvements and betterments extend service beyond that originally anticipated.

Whether a particular expenditure is a repair, treated as a period expense, or is an improvement, treated as an asset, can be difficult to decide. The line between maintaining service and improving or extending it is not distinct. Some expenditures may both restore and extend service potential. Consider, for example, an aircraft engine repair during which improved alloy materials are installed where inferior alloy parts had been used before. There is frequent disagreement between Revenue Canada and taxpayers, as well as among accountants, over this question in specific situations.

Unit of Account Sometimes Distinguishes Repair from Improvement

Some assets are actually composites of assets. Consider, for example, a truck, which might simplistically be thought of as a chassis, an engine, and a set of tires.

Although some major parts of a composite asset may have shorter lives than the asset as a whole, accounting for them with separate asset accounts is frequently impractical. Thus, the cost of a replacement set of tires is usually charged to repairs expense, although the tires could be treated as a separate asset. In some cases, composite assets are disaggregated for the purposes of depreciation. Exhibit 9.3 illustrates the effects on the timing and amounts of depreciation and repair expense of treating a truck either as a single asset or as a group of assets. At the time the truck is acquired, replacing the tires every second year and the engine after three years was anticipated. The repair to the windows in Year 5 was not. The truck has a six-year life and zero estimated salvage value. When the truck is depreciated as a single asset, replacement of tires or the engine is a repair. When separate accounts are used, replacing the tires is an improvement, the acquisition of a new asset.

Retirement of Assets

When an asset is retired from service, the cost of the asset and the related amount of accumulated depreciation must be removed from the books. As part of this entry, the amount received from the sale or trade-in and any difference between that amount and book value must be recorded. The difference between the proceeds received on

Exhibit 9.3
Unit of Account Influences Depreciation and Maintenance Charges
Truck: Cost $48,000; 6-Year Life
Engine: Cost $9,000; 3-Year Life
Tires: Cost $1,200; 2-Year Life
Windows: Repair Cost $800 in Year 5
(straight-line depreciation)

| | Depreciation of | | | | |
	Chassis	Engine	Tires	Maintenance	Total Expense
Separate Asset Accounts					
Year 1	$ 6,300[a]	$ 3,000[b]	$ 600[c]	—	$ 9,900
Year 2	6,300	3,000	600	—	9,900
Year 3	6,300	3,000	600[c]	—	9,900
Year 4	6,300	3,000[b]	600	—	9,900
Year 5	6,300	3,000	600[c]	$ 800[c]	10,700
Year 6	6,300	3,000	600	—	9,900
	$37,800	$18,000	$3,600	$ 800	$60,200
Single Asset Account	**Truck**				
Year 1	$ 8,000[e]	—	—	—	$ 8,000
Year 2	8,000	—	—	$ 1,200[f]	9,200
Year 3	8,000	—	—	9,000[g]	17,000
Year 4	8,000	—	—	1,200[f]	9,200
Year 5	8,000	—	—	800[d]	8,800
Year 6	8,000	—	—	—	8,000
	$48,000			$12,200	$60,200

[a]Chassis ($48,000 − $9,000 − $1,200)/6.
[b]Engine: $9,000/3.
[c]Tires: $1,200/2.
[d]Window repair.
[e]$48,000/6.
[f]Tires.
[g]Engine.

retirement and book value is a gain (if positive) or a loss (if negative). Before making the entry to write off the asset and its accumulated depreciation, an entry should be made to bring the depreciation up to date; that is, the depreciation that has occurred between the start of the current accounting period and the date of disposition is recorded. Because of the inherent uncertainties and the insignificant amount, this entry is frequently ignored in practice.

To illustrate the retirement of an asset, assume that sales equipment which cost $5,000, was expected to last four years, and had an estimated salvage value of $200, is depreciated on a straight-line basis at $1,200 [= ($5,000 − $200)/4] per year. Depreciation has been recorded for two years, and the equipment is sold at mid-year in the third year. The depreciation from the start of the accounting period to the date of sale of $600 [= $\frac{1}{2}$ × ($5,000 − $200)/4] is recorded:

Depreciation Expense	$600	
Accumulated Depreciation		$600
To record depreciation charges up to the date of sale.		

The book value of the asset is now its cost less two and one-half years of straight-line depreciation of $1,200 per year or $2,000 (= $5,000 − $3,000). The entry to record the retirement of the assets depends on the amount of the selling price.

1. Suppose that the equipment were sold for $2,000 cash. The entry to record the sale would be:

Cash	$2,000	
Accumulated Depreciation	3,000	
Equipment		$5,000

2. Suppose that the equipment were sold for $2,300. The entry to record the sale would be:

Cash	$2,300	
Accumulated Depreciation	3,000	
Equipment		$5,000
Gain on Retirement of Equipment		300

3. Suppose that the equipment were sold for $1,500. The entry to record the sale would be:

Cash	$1,500	
Accumulated Depreciation	3,000	
Loss on Retirement of Equipment	500	
Equipment		$5,000

Retirement Entries in the Statement of Changes in Financial Position

The cash received from the disposition of a plant asset is a nonoperating source of funds. It appears on the funds statement as a source, "Proceeds from Disposition of Noncurrent Assets." The loss on retirement of equipment reduces net income but does not use cash. Thus, in deriving cash from operations, the amount of the loss is an addback to net income. Its presentation is similar to that for depreciation expense.

If there is a gain on retirement of equipment, the entire proceeds from disposition of the asset as a nonoperating source of funds and thus requires treating the gain on retirement as a subtraction in computing cash from operations. The subtraction would be classified under the general heading of revenues not producing cash from operations, because all cash produced is shown under the heading of proceeds from disposition of noncurrent assets.

Trade-in Transactions

Instead of being sold when it is retired from service, the asset may be traded in on a new unit, a common practice for automobiles. The trade-in transaction can best be viewed as a sale of the old asset followed by a purchase of the new asset. The accounting for trade-in transactions determines simultaneously the gain or loss on disposal of the old asset and the acquisition cost recorded for the new asset. The procedures depend on the data available about the market value of the asset traded in and the cash equivalent cost of the new asset.

Using Market Value of Old Asset If the fair market value of the old asset traded in can be found, that amount plus the cash given up generally determines the valuation of the new asset. Assume that used equipment originally costing $5,000 with $3,000 of accumulated depreciation has a fair market value of $1,300 and is traded in on a new piece of equipment, along with an additional $5,500 of cash. The new equipment had a list price of $7,300. The entries could be:

Accumulated Depreciation	$3,000	
Trade-in Allowance	1,300	
Loss on Disposition of Equipment	700	
Equipment		$5,000
To record disposition of old equipment; plug for loss.		
Equipment	$6,800	
Trade-in Allowance		$1,300
Cash		5,500
To record acquisition of new equipment; plug for cost of new equipment. The Trade-in Allowance account is not required but is used to split the transaction into two components: the sale of the old asset and purchase of the new.		

Note that the *list* price of the new equipment does not affect the entries shown above. Valuation of the used asset in established secondhand markets almost always offers more reliable information than quoted list prices.

Using Market Value of New Asset If, however, a reliable valuation of the used asset is not available, then the lowest available cash price for the new asset (which is sometimes the list price) will determine the valuation of the new asset as well as the gain or loss on disposition of the old asset. If the list price of the new equipment in the preceding example were $7,000 and there were no other reliable information available, the entries would be:

Equipment	$7,000	
Cash		$5,500
Trade-in Allowance		1,500
To record acquisition at list price; plug for trade-in allowance.		
Accumulated Depreciation	$3,000	
Trade-in Allowance	1,500	
Loss on Disposition of Equipment	500	
Equipment		$5,000
To record disposition of old equipment. Loss is determined by list price of new equipment.		

The recording of the two methods has been illustrated with a two-step approach. The two entries could be combined into one, removing the need for a Trade-in Allowance account. The same analysis and same type of entries would be made if there were a gain on disposition.

The capital cost allowance regulations under the Income Tax Act ignore the gain or a sale on disposal of an individual asset. They require a company to deduct the lesser of the disposal proceeds and the capital cost from the undepreciated capital cost of the assets in the class, hence reducing the undepreciated capital cost of the class. This reduction in the undepreciated capital cost subsequently diminishes the capital cost allowance that may be claimed as a deduction from income in the current and future years. Any gain or loss recorded by a company on disposal of plant assets is eliminated in computing taxable income.

The Investment Tax Credit

In order to stimulate investment in machinery and equipment, the federal government has passed tax laws that permit the purchaser of machinery and equipment to claim a credit against income taxes otherwise payable. The credit reduces the purchaser's income tax liability and the capital cost of the asset is reduced by the amount of the investment tax credit claimed in a year. The rate of the credit and the property eligible for the credit have varied through the years as the federal government has amended the tax laws. The examples in this section assume a ten percent tax credit on all equipment purchases.

If a firm buys $900,000 of equipment with an estimated service life of eight years this year, it will receive a $90,000 (= .10 × $900,000) investment tax credit. If its income tax liability shown on the tax return before the investment tax credit is $600,000, the following entry would be made:

Income Tax Expense	$600,000	
Income Tax Payable		$600,000
To record income taxes before the investment tax credit.		

The investment credit will reduce income taxes payable by $90,000 in the year the credit is earned, independent of the financial accounting treatment of the credit. There are two generally accepted methods of recording the investment tax credit for financial reporting—the flow-through method and the deferral method.[4] Two major options, the deferred-credit method and the cost-reduction method are included in the deferral method.

Under the flow-through method, the entire investment credit realized during the year by all asset acquisitions is recorded as a reduction in income tax expense of the year. (It all "flows through" to income this year.) The entry would be:

---

[4]Problem 32 at the end of this chapter explores the theoretical possibilities one might consider in choosing the methods in practice.

Income Tax Payable	$90,000	
Income Tax Expense		$90,000
To record the investment tax credit (= .10 × $900,000) for the year.		

The deferral method spreads the benefit from the investment tax credit over the years of the service life of the equipment acquired. The entire investment tax credit reduces the amount of income taxes payable in the year of acquisition, even though the reported reductions in income tax expense are spread over the years of service life. In the example, the entry in the year of acquisition, using the deferred-credit method, would be:

Income Tax Payable	$90,000	
Income Tax Expense		$11,250
Deferred Investment Tax Credit		78,750
Part ($\frac{1}{8}$ × $90,000) of investment tax credit reduces the income tax expense in first year. The remaining portion will reduce expense in later years. The entire effect on taxes payable occurs in the first year.		

The Deferred Investment Tax Credit account appears on the balance sheet either as an asset contra account or among the noncurrent liabilities. At the end of each of the seven following years, the following entry would be made:

Deferred Investment Tax Credit	$11,250	
Income Tax Expense		$11,250
To amortize the deferred investment tax credit. Recorded income tax expense is reduced by $11,250 in each year 2 through 8. Income tax payable is reduced by $90,000 in Year 1.		

The cost reduction method considers the reduction in income taxes payable to be a government grant reducing the cost of the equipment purchased. As in the deferred credit method, the cost-reduction method spreads the benefits from reduced income taxes payable over the years of service of the new equipment, but records this benefit by reducing the amount of the depreciation expense. In the example the entry in the year of acquisition using the cost-reduction method, would be:

Income Tax Payable	$90,000	
Machinery and Equipment		$90,000
To record the investment tax credit (= .10 × $900,000)		

The depreciation on the new machinery and equipment will be based on the reduced cost of $810,000 (= $900,000 − $90,000). At the end of each of the eight years of the asset, the following entry would be made:

Depreciation	$10,125	
Accumulated Depreciation		$10,125

To record depreciation on new machinery and equipment
equal to $\frac{1}{8}$ of the net cost of $810,000.

Effects over Time

Income tax expense is reduced by the full amount of the investment tax credit under both methods, but over different time periods.

If the deferral approach is used, income tax expense is reduced not only by a part of this year's investment tax credit but also portions of the investment tax credit relating to earlier years that are still being amortized. For a firm in equilibrium (and assuming no recent change in the tax law with regard to the investment tax credit), income tax expense and net income will be the same under the flow-through and deferral approaches. For a growing firm, the flow-through method produces higher reported net income in all years during the growth period.

If the deferral method is used, income tax expense for a growing firm will be greater than taxes paid or taxes currently payable. This excess represents an expense that does not use funds. It is added to net income in the operating section of the statement of changes in financial position to derive funds provided by operations.

Until 1984 the *CICA Handbook* made no reference to the accounting treatment of the investment tax credit. During the preceding decade the flow-through method became the alternative favoured by Canadian companies[5]. In 1984 the *CICA Handbook* recognized the investment tax issue and, contrary to existing practice, recommended that the cost-reduction approach be used for fiscal years beginning on or after January 1, 1985.[6]

Wasting Assets and Depletion

The costs of finding natural resources and preparing to extract them from the earth should be capitalized and amortized. Whether all costs of exploration or the costs of only the successful explorations are capitalized into the asset accounts remains an open accounting question. Generally accepted accounting principles allow two treatments. Under *full costing*, the costs of all explorations (both successful and unsuccessful) are capitalized so long as the expected benefits from the successful explorations will more than cover the cost of all explorations. Under *successful efforts costing*, only the cost of the successful efforts is capitalized; the costs of unsuccessful exploration efforts become expenses of the period when the fact becomes apparent that the efforts will not result in productive sites.

[5]In 1986, eighty-seven percent of the *Financial Reporting in Canada* sample who reported investment tax credits followed the cost-reduction method.
[6]*CICA Handbook*, section 3805.

Amortization of wasting assets, or natural resources, is called *depletion*. The depletion method most often used is the *units-of-production* method. For example, if $4.5 million in costs are incurred to discover an oil well that contains an estimated 1.5 million barrels of oil, then the costs of $4.5 million would be amortized (depleted) at the rate of $3 (= $4,500,000/1,500,000) for each barrel of oil removed from the well. The major accounting problem of extractive industries stems from uncertainty about the eventual total of units that will result from exploratory efforts.

Intangible Assets and Amortization

Assets can provide future benefits without having physical form. Such assets are called *intangibles*. Examples are research costs, advertising costs, patents, trade secrets, know-how, trademarks, and copyrights. The first problem with intangibles is to decide:

1. Whether expenditures made to acquire or develop intangibles have future benefits and can be quantified with a sufficient degree of precision so that they should be "capitalized" (set up as assets) and amortized over time; or
2. Whether they have no future benefits and thus are expenses of the period in which the costs are incurred.

If the latter, the immediate expensing of the asset's cost appears as pattern E in Figures 9.1 and 9.2.

The second problem to solve is how to amortize the costs if they have been capitalized. Deciding the period of amortization (the estimated service life) is a difficult question. Amortization of capitalized intangibles is usually recorded using the straight-line method, but other methods can be used if they seem appropriate. This section discusses some common intangibles and the issues involved in deciding whether to expense or to capitalize their costs. The *CICA Handbook* gives no recommendation to solve this problem, except for goodwill arising from a business combination. In this case the *Handbook* recommends that a company amortize goodwill on a straight-line basis over its estimated life, not exceeding 40 years.[7] Exhibit A.4 in Appendix A (p. 763) and Note 12 of the financial statements for General Products Limited (p. 770) illustrate the typical disclosure for amortization of intangibles.

Name That Brand

*T*hese days a good name is hard to find. The R.J. Reynolds Tobacco division of R.J. Reynolds Industries thought the perfect brand name for a new cigarette aimed at fashion-conscious, young women smokers would be Ritz, as in puttin' on the . . . Not so

fast, said the Ritz Hotel in Paris, haunt of several generations of American romantics. The hotel, which, as it happens, markets a brand of cigarettes called Ritz Paris, brought a trademark infringement suit against Reynolds.

Was RJR intentionally infringing the

---

[7]*CICA Handbook*, section 1580.

Paris hotel's trademark? That's for the courts to decide; the suit is pending in a New York federal court. But name overlap can happen innocently these days. In the last four years alone more than 150,000 trademarks were registered with the U.S. Patent & Trademark Office. That's double the number of names registered in the preceding four years. It makes picking a name a big problem.

But be of good cheer. Some smart businessess are willing to relieve you of the problem. For a price. "The days when clients asked their advertising agencies to crank out a few names or held a company contest are over," declaims Frank Delano, chairman of the New York firm of Delano Goldman & Young, Inc. Its business is making up names. "We can clear a name in North America in about four hours and foreign countries in about five days."

What's in a name? Plenty, says Larry goldman, Delano's partner. Apple Computer's name was a good choice, he explains, because it separated the company from thousands of others using the word computer as part of their trademark. Goldman claims he told Apple that Lisa was a poor name choice for its later product. "Too feminine," says Goldman.

Where do companies get their names? Some let their computers spew out thousands of letter combinations. Other sources include foreign words, trees, flowers, even words that don't mean anything but do imply desirable qualities—such as Ford's Merkur, which sounds, as it is intended to, German and vaguely high tech. The challenge in these cases is to match the name with the image of the product.

For big jobs, like naming cars or motorcycles, Delano Goldman & Young might charge $100,000 or more. A smaller job might cost $20,000. Clearly, the name business is profitable. Delano says that last year his company generated $1.2 million in revenues, with pre-

tax earnings of 22%, and he expects to do $2 million in 1985.

Delano Goldman is not without competition. NameLab, Inc., in San Francisco, works from morphemes—the core semantic unit within a word. For example, "tra" in transport, used by NameLab in the name Softra for a California software distributor. There are approximately 6,200 morphemes in the English language, the root of most of the 150,000-word stock of the language. Ira Bachrach, NameLab's president, says he has programmed each morpheme into his computer through the use of a notational system. The end result: coinages like Compaq (morpheme: pak, meaning a small object).

"Most of the morphemes are Indo-European, the root of most of the major Western languages. By choosing the right morphemes," says Bachrach, "you can create names that have an impact worldwide." One example: Acura, the name of Honda's new luxury car. Bachrach thinks the word conveys precision—as in accurate—which was Honda's intention. Acura also meets the technical demands of a coined word, Bachrach explains. Because it ends with the suffix *a*, it is read as a noun and, therefore, a name. The word also starts and ends with the same letter, making it more memorable, and contains three clearly voiced syllables in only five letters.

Suzanne Leff, vice president of Interbrand, Inc., a New York company in the name business, points to Lozol, a drug for treating high blood pressure, manufactured by USV Laboratories, a unit of Revlon. "The name is a palindrome—it is spelled the same backwards and forwards—which is an advantage because such words tend to have pleasant sounds and are well balanced," says Leff.

Needless to say, the name was created by Leff's company.

From *Forbes*, April 8, 1985, pages 128 and 130. "Name That Brand," by Jeffrey A. Trachtenberg.

Research and Development

One common intangible is the benefit provided by expenditures on research and development (R&D). Such costs are incurred for various reasons. Perhaps the firm seeks to develop a technological or marketing advance in order to have an edge on competition. Or it might wish to explore possible applications of existing technology to design a new product or improve an old one. Other research may be undertaken in response to a government contract, in preparing for bids on potential contracts, or in pursuit of "discoveries," with no specific product in mind. Whatever the reason, practically all research costs will yield their benefits, if any, in future periods. Herein lies the accounting issue: should research and development costs be charged to expense immediately as they are incurred, or should they be capitalized and amortized over future periods?

Generally accepted accounting principles[8] distinguish between the accounting treatment of research costs and development costs. Research costs result from a planned investigation undertaken with the hope of gaining new scientific or technical knowledge and understanding. Such investigation may or may not be directed toward a specific practical aim or application. Development costs result from a translation of research findings or other knowledge into a plan or design for new or substantially improved materials, devices, products, processes, systems, or services prior to the commencement of commercial production or use. In both cases costs include all direct costs of a research or development project and in addition a fair share of overhead costs.

Generally accepted accounting principles require immediate expensing of research costs. This requirement is based on arguments that the future benefits from most research efforts are too uncertain to warrant capitalization and that writing them off as soon as possible is more conservative. Nevertheless, others consider that there must be future benefits in many cases or else efforts would not be pursued. Theoretically, research costs should be matched with the benefits produced by the research expenditures through the capitalization procedure with amortization over the benefited periods.

Development expenditures are incurred after the research phase has been completed, with a consequent reduction in the uncertainty of future benefits. In recognition of this fact, generally accepted accounting principles recommend that development costs be capitalized where they meet stringent criteria to assure reasonable future expense recovery. Under these circumstances the development costs would be amortized over future years commencing with the commercial production or use of the product or process and charged as an expense in a systematic and rational basis. The deferred development cost of each project would be reviewed at the end of each accounting period to ensure that the cost will still be recovered at that time. Any cost that is not expected to be recovered should be written off as an expense of the period. Where development costs fail to meet the criteria they would be expensed as incurred.

Note 2 of the financial statements of General Products Limited in the Appendix (p. 765) illustrates the required disclosures. Note that all development expenditures

---

[8]*CICA Handbook*, section 3450.

are expensed as incurred. Where a company defers development costs, it must additionally disclose in the financial statements the unamortized balance of the development costs, the amount of development costs deferred during the year, and the amortization of development costs charged to expense during the year. It is also encouraged to present a general description of the general nature of the projects whose costs have been deferred.

Advertising

Advertising expenditures are designed to increase sales currently and in the future, but there is a lag between the incurrence of these costs and their impact. The impact of advertising probably extends into subsequent periods.

Common practice immediately expenses all advertising and sales promotion costs, regardless of the timing of their impact (see pattern E in Figures 9.1 and 9.2). Those supporting this practice argue that: (1) it is more conservative to do so; (2) it is almost impossible to quantify the future effects and timing of benefits derived from these costs; and (3) when these costs remain stable from year to year, income is not affected by the capitalization policy after the first few years. Nevertheless, some accountants support the capitalization treatment because doing so will better report assets and match costs with resulting benefits.

Patents

A patent is a right obtained from the federal government to exclude others from the benefits from an invention. The legal life of patent protection may be as long as 17 years, although the economic life of the patent may be considerably less. The accounting for patent costs depends on whether the patent was purchased from another party or developed internally. If the former, the purchase price is capitalized. If the latter, the total cost of product development and patent application is treated as a research and development cost and may be expensed or capitalized. Patent costs are usually amortized over the shorter of: (1) the remaining legal life, or (2) its estimated economic life. If for some reason the patent becomes worthless, the remaining capitalized cost is recognized immediately as an expense of that period.

Goodwill

Goodwill is an intangible asset that will be mentioned here only briefly. More details follow in Chapter 13. Goodwill arises from the purchase of one company or operating unit by another company and is measured as the difference between the amount paid for the acquired company as a whole and the sum of the current value of its individual assets less its liabilities. Thus, goodwill will appear in the financial statements of the company making the acquisition. Under present practice, goodwill acquired after March 1974 must be amortized over a time period not longer than 40 years[9]. Most companies use a considerably shorter amortization period. Goodwill is generally not recognized by a company that develops it, even though large expenditures for advertising and other publicity may be made annually. All such expenditures are charged to expense as incurred. Notes 1 and 12 of General Products Limited financial statements (pp. 765 and 770) illustrate the typical disclosure for amortization of intangibles.

---

[9]*CICA Handbook*, section 1580.

Should Human Resources Be Reflected on the Balance Sheet?

*T*he annual report for a large firm begins with the statement: "People are our most important asset." But an analysis of the firm's financial statements reveals no human assets. The reason is simple: Everyone agrees that people are important to an organization, but no one knows how to place a monetary value on their importance.

An executive's job is to allocate and administer scarce resources to achieve a goal—that is, maximize owner wealth. But if investments in assets are distorted, decisions of managers, investors, and appraisers may not be the optimum ones. Recognition of this has stimulated interest in the valuation of intangible assets, especially human assets.

Humans fall into a large and complex category of assets known as intangibles. Included among such assets are patents, copyrights, trademarks, and a variety of intangible assets commonly listed under the term "goodwill," such as a favorable business name or location, or a group of knowledgeable or skilled employees. While important to the success and value of a firm, many of these intangible assets do not appear on a firm's balance sheet because there is usually no objective cost basis at which to value them. In addition, tax laws discourage the allocation of costs to goodwill because goodwill, unlike equipment and other tangible assets, cannot be depreciated. Consequently, buyers tend to minimize the amount of the purchase costs allocated to goodwill in financial statements.

For many years, accountants have attempted to build human value into financial statements. Although their efforts have not been completely successful, they have generated many ideas that may be helpful to financial executives.

It wasn't until the 1960s that a theory of human resource accounting was developed. Since then, many have applied their knowledge and skills to the valuation of human resources.

Accountants generally desire to provide information to improve the decision-making ability of managers. Thus, early accounting literature defined *human resource valuation* as the process of identifying, measuring, and communicating information about human resources to assist management decision-making within an organization. Within a few years, the definition was modified to read "identifying and measuring data about human resources and communicating this information to interested parties." Interested parties are divided into two basic groups: investors and managers.

Research demonstrates that investors change their decisions concerning investments when human resource information about a firm is disclosed. Such a reaction would not be unusual if humans were normally considered an asset of the firm. Their inclusion as assets, however, has raised several questions. The most prominent is, obviously, what is an asset?

From the accountants' point of view, things of value should be recognized, valued, and placed on a firm's balance sheet as an asset. Valuing humans, however, creates a tremendous problem because they do not conform to the traditional definition of an asset. the classical definition of something owned by a firm cannot be applied to humans. This is true even in professional sports. A firm may own a player's contract but not the player.

When defined in terms of characteristics, assets should have utility, scarcity, and exchangeability. Arthur Andersen & Co. applied this definition to human resources and conclude that humans lack exchangeability and thus are not assets. The firm advised, however, that if obtaining and training human assets required large expenditures, these should be reported in special statements rather than in the traditional financial statements.

When analyzed from a broader, more philosophical point of view, humans can be classified as assets. The word "asset" can have many different meanings. When applied in a particular chain of reasoning, it has a known and constant meaning that is not bound by tradition, but based upon use. If assets are considered tangibles or intangibles that possess certain properties, and if accounting statements are to provide a realistic reflection of the usefulness or value of these properties, humans can be assets. If one property is that an asset should be subject to control by the firm, that control need not be absolute. For instance, goodwill is currently considered an asset, but it is subject to many forces outside the firm.

Thus, assets are something that possess utility or value. They are acquired not for their own sake, but for what they can contribute to a firm's cash flow. This definition avoids controversies over ownership, control, and exchangeability. Once it is accepted, the real challenge is measuring the value of all assets.

Human resource accounting advocates argue that a firm's value is understated when finance statements fail to recognize the value of human assets. Some accountants still reject the concept of considering humans an asset, but the more basic objection is that human valuation is too subjective or difficult to measure. Attempts to measure human value have generally been split between two theories: historical cost theory and replacement cost theory. Among accountants, the historical cost theory seems to be favored because it is similar to conventional accounting practices. Because historical costs are not as useful in making decisions about the present or future, many have reason to prefer replacement cost theory.

Historical cost valuation records objective and verifiable input values. When cost theory is applied to human resource valuation, two questions arise: Which costs are relevant, and which of these costs are to be expensed or capitalized. One approach has been to classify human resource costs as either training or educational. Training costs relate to a current job, whereas educational costs relate to the preparation for advancement. Training costs are expensed, and educational costs are capitalized.

A second approach includes all recruiting, testing, training, and development costs. Whether to expense or capitalize a particular cost is determined by how long the firm is expected to benefit from the cost. A formula has been developed to calculate whether it is reasonable to assume that the benefit would exceed 12 months. If so, the cost is capitalized. This method was actually implemented by the R.G. Barry Corporation. (See Bertha Proffitt, "Human Resource Accounting in Practice at R.G. Barry Corporation," *The Woman CPA*, October 1974. Historical cost models have also been used by the Atlanta Braves, Flying Tigers Corporation, Upjohn Company, and Touche Ross & Co.)

The benefit of using the historical cost method is that it incorporates the value of human resources in financial statements. Consequently, attention is focused on both the costs and the benefits associated with recruiting, training, and educating human resources.

The replacement cost method of human resource valuation is based upon established economic theory. People, like any other resource, have value because they are capable of providing future utility or service. Consequently, the current value of an individual to an organization can be defined as the present value of the future services he or she is expected to provide the firm.

An individual's value to a firm can be calculated by determining a "conditional value" and the probability that the individual will remain with the firm. The conditional value is the present worth of the services an individual could perform if he remains with the firm throughout his productive working life.

With the exception of cash or claims

on cash, the values assigned to balance sheet assets recorded at historical costs do not represent realistic measures. The classic example is fixed investments. Their initial value is based upon cost, but all future financial statement values are determined by a variety of depreciation techniques, life expectancies, salvage values, etc. Accountants record an input cost and then allocate cost to a series of future income flows. While these allocations are frequently less than perfect, they are of some value to management, investors, appraisers, etc.

Why should human resources be treated any differently? Input costs are indeed associated with the acquisition of human assets. Thus, these costs should be recognized. At issue is not whether the costs are measured perfectly or allocated exactly but whether human resources receive the value they deserve. This objective can only be accomplished if human resources are recorded and integrated with information about other assets.

Human resource valuation is of concern to people in many professions: the plant manager with high employee turnover, the financial analyst making investment recommendations, the investor deciding between alternative investment opportunities, and the business appraiser. There are no simple or exact solutions on how to appropriately report and use human resource valuations.

While recognizing that human resource valuation data are useful to managers, analysts, investors, and appraisers, accountants have spent much of their efforts debating whether humans are assets, and if they are, what about them can be measured. The accuracy of such measurements has been overly debated to the detriment of financial statement users who need human resource information to make informed investment and business decisions. If accuracy were the main issue, a strong case could be made for deleting from financial statements depreciation and inventory valuations, which are based on arbitrary historical cost assumptions.

The true value of a business is generated by an integrated valuation system that cannot be derived by merely summarizing and adding the individual valuation elements of the system. While each valuation element, including the human resource element, is important and deserves consideration, the value of a business may be greater than or less than the sum total of the individual valuation elements. Consequently, accountants should continue their efforts to place human resource valuations in financial statements. To accomplish this goal, they may need to place less emphasis upon historical cost data and more emphasis on the present value of future benefits.

Reprinted with permission of *Financial Executive* Feb. 1986 pp. 37–39.

Summary

Three major classes of long-lived operating assets are plant assets, wasting assets (non-renewable natural resources), and intangibles. The major accounting problems for each class are the same: (1) calculating the cost of the asset to be capitalized as an asset, (2) estimating the total period of benefit or the amount of expected benefits, and (3) assigning the cost to the benefited periods or units produced in a systematic and reasonable fashion so that investment in the asset is recovered through charges to income.

This chapter emphasizes depreciable plant assets and their depreciation. The cost figure to be charged off is reduced by any salvage value. The period (or number of units) of benefit is determined by judgment based on experience. The pattern of depreciation charges over the asset's life is usually based on some conventional method — the most common methods in practice are straight-line, declining-balance, and unit-of-production. The Income Tax Act does not permit a company to deduct depreciation when computing taxable income but replaces it with a maximum capital cost allowance that may be claimed, using the declining-balance basis for most asset classes.

If the asset is retired before the end of the estimated service life for an amount different from its book value, a gain or loss will be recognized. Under the capital cost allowance regulations, the gain or loss will not be recognized in the year of disposal but will be deferred to the future.

Intangibles such as trademarks, copyrights, patents, and computer programs are among the most valuable resources owned by some firms. The accounting treatment of *purchased* intangibles is the same as for tangible assets. For most intangibles developed by a firm, accounting requires the immediate expensing of the development costs. This accounting drastically alters the look of some financial statements. The firms most likely to be affected are service, rather than manufacturing, companies.

Problem 1 for Self-Study

Purdy Inc. acquires two used trucks from Foster Inc. Although the trucks are not identical, they both cost $15,000. Purdy Inc. knew when it negotiated the purchase price that the first truck required extensive engine repair, expected to cost about $4,000. The repair was made the week after acquisition and actually cost $4,200. Purdy Inc. thought the second truck was in normal operating condition when it negotiated the purchase price but discovered on using the truck that certain bearings needed replacing. The cost of this repair, made the week after acquisition, was $4,200.

- **a.** What costs should be recorded in the accounts for the two trucks?
- **b.** If the amounts recorded above are different, then distinguish between the two "repairs."

Suggested Solution

- **a.** First truck recorded at $19,200. Second truck recorded at $15,000, with $4,200 debited to expense or loss.
- **b.** At the time the first truck was acquired, Purdy Inc. knew it would have to make the "repair." The purchase price was presumably reduced because of the known cost to be incurred. At the time of acquisition, the cost was anticipated to be required in order to produce the expected service potential of the asset. The fact that the cost is $4,200, rather than "about $4,000," seems not to violate the Purdy Inc.'s expectations at the time it acquired the truck. If the repair had cost significantly more than $4,000, say $7,000, then the excess would be loss or expense.

The second truck was assumed to be operable when the purchase price was agreed. The cost of the repair is incurred to bring about the level of service potential already thought to have been acquired. There are no more future benefits after the repair than had been anticipated at the time of acquisition. Therefore, the $4,200 is expense or loss.

Problem 2 for Self-Study

Jensen Limited purchased land with a building standing on it as the site for a new plant it planned to construct. The company received bids from several independent contractors for demolition of the old building and construction of the new one. It rejected all bids and undertook demolition and construction using company labour, facilities, and equipment.

All transactions relating to these properties were debited or credited to a single account, Real Estate. Various items in the Real Estate account are described below. The Real Estate account is to be closed. All amounts in it should be taken out and reclassified into one of the following accounts:

(1) Land account
(2) Buildings account
(3) Revenue, gain, or expense contra account
(4) Expense, loss, or revenue contra account
(5) Some other account

You may reclassify amounts of the following transactions into two or more of the above. If you use **(5)**, some other account, indicate the nature of the account.

- **a.** Cost of land, including old building.
- **b.** Legal fees paid to bring about purchase of land and to transfer its title.
- **c.** Invoice cost of materials and supplies used in construction.
- **d.** Direct labour and materials cost incurred in demolition of old building.
- **e.** Direct costs of excavating raw land to prepare it for the foundation of the new building.
- **f.** Discounts earned for prompt payment of item **c**.
- **g.** Interest for year on notes issued to finance construction.
- **h.** Amounts equivalent to interest on Jensen Limited's own funds used in construction that would have been invested in temporary investments if an independent contractor had been used. The amount was debited to Real Estate and credited to Interest Revenue so that the cost of the real estate would be comparable to its cost if it had been built by an independent contractor.
- **i.** Depreciation for period of construction on trucks that were used both in construction and regular company operations.
- **j.** Proceeds of sale of materials salvaged from old buildings were debited to Cash and credited to Real Estate.
- **k.** Cost of building permits.

   l. Salaries of certain corporate engineering executives can be allocated between Salary Expense and Real Estate. The portion debited to Real Estate represents an estimate of the portion of the time spent during the year on planning and construction activities for the new building.

   m. Payments for property taxes on plant site owed by its former owner but assumed by Jensen Limited.

   n. Payments for property taxes on plant site for construction period.

   o. Insurance premiums to cover workers engaged in demolition and construction activities. The insurance policy contains various deductible clauses, requiring the company to pay the first $5,000 of damages from any accident.

   p. Cost of injury claims for $2,000 paid by the company because the amount was less than the deductible amount in the policy.

   q. Costs of new machinery to be installed in building.

   r. Installation costs for the machinery above.

   s. Profit on construction of new building (computed as the difference between lowest independent contractor's bid and the actual construction cost) was debited to Real Estate and credited to Construction Revenue.

Suggested Solution

(Note that three items are included in more than one account)

(1) a, b, d, j, l, m, o.
(2) c, e, f, g, i, k, l, n, o, p.
(3) — .
(4) h, i, s.
(5) i, q, r.

Comments and Explanations

   f. The reduction in cost of materials and supplies will reduce the cost of the buildings. The actual accounting entries depend on the method used to record the potential discount. These issues are not discussed in this book, but see Problem 27 at the end of Chapter 8.

   h. Although one capitalizes explicit interest, one may not capitalize opportunity-cost interest or interest imputed on one's own funds used. The adjusting entry credits Real Estate and debits Interest Revenue or its contra. In any case, the debit reduces income, removing the revenue that had been recognized by the company.

   i. Computation of the amounts to be allocated requires an estimate. Once the amounts are estimated, they are debited to Building or to Depreciation Expense and Work-in-Process Inventory, as appropriate for the regular company operations.

   j. Credit to Land account, reducing its cost.

   l. Allocate to Land and Building based on estimate of how time was spent.

Given the description, most of these costs are probably for the building. If all of the salaries had been debited to Real Estate, then some must be reclassified as Salary Expense.

m. Part of the cost of the land.

n. Capitalized as part of the Building account for the same reasons that interest during construction is capitalized. Some accountants would treat this item as expense.

p. Most accountants would treat this as an expense or loss for the period. Others would treat it as part of the cost of the building for the same reason that the explicit insurance cost is capitalized. If, however, the company was irrational in acquiring insurance policies with deductible clauses, then this item is expense or loss. Accounting usually assumes that most managements make rational decisions most of the time.

q. Debit to Machinery and Equipment account, an asset account separate from Building.

r. Treat the same as preceding item; installation costs are part of the cost of the asset. See Chapter 2.

s. The effect of recognizing revenue is reversed. The Real Estate account is credited and Construction Revenue or its contra is debited.

Problem 3 for Self-Study

Central Electric Co. Ltd. constructed a nuclear generating power plant at a cost of $200 million. The plant is expected to last 50 years before being retired from service. The company estimates that at the time the plant is retired from service, $20 million in "decommissioning costs" (costs to dismantle the plant and dispose of the radioactive materials) will be incurred. Straight-line depreciation is computed and charged once per year, at year-end.

During the eleventh year of operation, new regulations governing nuclear waste disposal are enacted. The estimated decommissioning costs increase from $20 million to $24 million.

During the thirty-first year of operation, the life of the plant is revised. It will last 60 years in total, not 50 years.

At the end of the thirty-fifth year, the plant is sold to another utility company for $80 million.

a. What is the depreciation charge for the first year?

b. What is the depreciation charge for the eleventh year?

c. What is the depreciation charge for the thirty-first year?

d. Record the journal entry for the sale of the plant at the end of the thirty-fifth year.

Suggested Solution

(Dollar amounts in millions.)

a. $4.4 per year = ($200 + $20)/50 years.

  b. $4.5 per year = ($200 + $20 + $4 − $4.4 per year × 10 years)/40 years remaining life.

$$= (\$224 - \$44)/40.$$
$$= \$180/40.$$

  c. $3.0 per year = ($180 − $4.5 × 20 years)/30 years remaining life.

$$= (\$180 - \$90)/30.$$
$$= \$90/30.$$

  d. Accumulated depreciation at time of sale

$$= (\$4.4 \times 10) + (\$4.5 \times 20) + (\$3.0 \times 5) = \$149.0.$$

December 31 of Year 35

Cash	80.0	
Accumulated Depreciation on Power Plant	149.0	
Power Plant		200.0
Gain on Disposal of Plant		29.0

Problem 4 for Self-Study

Widdicomb Corp. is considering changing from the flow-through method to the deferral method of accounting for the investment tax credit. It expects to acquire assets subject to increasing dollar amounts of investment tax credits each year for the foreseeable future.

Part 1:   Indicate the effect on each of the following items in the financial statements two years hence if the deferral, rather than flow-through, method is used, starting now and continuing for the indefinite future.

    a. Recorded Cost of Assets Acquired   **e.** Depreciation Expense
    b. Income Taxes Payable   **f.** Net Income for year
    c. Income Tax Expense   **g.** Retained Earnings
    d. Deferred Investment Credits on   **h.** Total Equities
        balance sheet

Part 2:   Indicate the effect on the financial items (**a**) to (**h**) in the financial statements two years hence if the cost-reduction deferral option rather than the deferred-credit deferral option was used.

Suggested Solution

Part 1:   Larger under the deferral method than under the flow-through method: (**c**), (**d**).
Smaller under the deferral method than under the flow-through method: (**f**), (**g**).
The same under both methods: (**a**), (**b**), (**e**), (**h**).

Part 2:   Larger under the cost-reduction option than under the deferred-credit option: (**c**) (**d**).

Smaller under the cost-reduction option than under the deferred-credit option: (**a**), (**e**).

The same under both methods: (**b**), (**f**), (**g**), (**h**).

Questions, Exercises, Problems and Cases

Questions

1. Review the meaning of the following concepts or terms discussed in this chapter.

   a. Amortization
   b. Plant assets and depreciation
   c. Interest during construction
   d. Wasting assets and depletion
   e. Intangibles
   f. Capitalize
   g. Improvements
   h. Repairs
   i. Maintenance
   j. Joint cost
   k. Value
   l. Residual or salvage value
   m. Service or depreciable life
   n. Asset depreciation range

   o. Units of production method
   p. Declining-balance methods
   q. Capital cost allowance
   r. Book Value
   s. Treatment of changes in estimates of useful lines and residual values of long-lived assets
   t. Trade-in transaction
   u. Research and development
   v. Goodwill
   w. Investment tax credit
   x. Flow-through method
   y. Deferral method

2. **a.** ''Accounting for depreciating assets would be greatly simplified if accounting periods were only long enough or the life of the assets short enough.'' What is the point of the quotation?

   b. ''The major purpose of depreciation accounting is to provide funds for the replacement of assets as they wear out.'' Do you agree? Explain.

3. ''Showing both acquisition cost and accumulated depreciation amounts separately provides a rough indication of the relative age of the firm's long-lived assets.''

   a. Assume that the Poyfer Co. Ltd. acquired an asset with a depreciable cost of $100,000 several years ago. Accumulated depreciation as of December 31, recorded on a straight-line basis, is $60,000. The depreciation charge for the year is $10,000. What is the asset's depreciable life? How old is the asset?

   b. Assume straight-line depreciation. Devise a formula that, given the depreciation charge for the year and the asset's accumulated depreciation, can be used to determine the age of the asset.

4. **a.** What is the effect of capitalizing interest on reported net income summed over all the periods of the life of a given self-constructed asset, from building through use, until eventual retirement? Contrast with a policy of expensing interest as incurred.

   b. Consider a company engaging in increasing dollar amounts of self-construction activity each period over periods when interest rates do not decline. What is the effect on reported income each year of capitalizing interest in contrast to expensing interest as incurred?

Exercises

5. *Classification of expenditures as asset or expense.* For each of the following expenditures or acquisitions, indicate the type of account debited. Classify the accounts as asset other than product cost, product cost (Work-in-Process Inventory), or expense. If the account debited is an asset account, then specify whether it is current or noncurrent.

    a. $150 for repairs of office machines
    b. $1,500 for emergency repairs to an office machine
    c. $250 for maintenance of delivery trucks
    d. $5,000 for a machine acquired in return for a three-year note
    e. $4,200 for research staff salaries
    f. $3,100 for newspaper ads
    g. $6,400 for wages of factory workers engaged in production
    h. $3,500 for wages of factory workers engaged in installing equipment
    i. $2,500 for salaries of office work force
    j. $1,000 for legal fees in acquiring an ore deposit
    k. $1,200 for a one-year insurance policy beginning next month
    l. $1,800 for Treasury Bills, to be sold to pay the next installment due on income taxes
    m. $4,000 for royalty payment on a patent used in manufacturing
    n. $10,000 for purchase of a trademark
    o. $100 filing fee for copyright registration application

6. *Journal entries for trade-in transactions and depreciation.* On April 30, Year 6, the Tico Wholesale Co. Ltd. acquired a new machine with a fair market value of $14,000. The seller agreed to accept the company's old machine, $7,000 in cash, and a 12 percent, one-year note for $4,000 in payment.

The old machine was purchased on January 1, Year 1, for $10,000. It was estimated that the old machine would be useful for eight years, after which it would have a salvage value of $400. It is estimated that the new machine will have a service life of ten years and a salvage value of $800.

Assuming that the Tico Co. Ltd. uses the straight-line method of depreciation and closes its books annually on December 31, give the entries that were made in Year 6.

7. *Computations and journal entries for retirement of plant.* On July 1, Year 2, a building and land were purchased for $96,000 by The Hub, a retail clothing store. Of this amount, $40,000 was allocated to the land and the remainder to the building. The building is depreciated on a straight-line basis.

On July 1, Year 24 (no additions or retirements having been recorded in the meanwhile), the net book value of the building was $25,200. On March 31, Year 25, the building and site were sold for $60,000. The fair market value of the land was $50,000 on this date.

The firm closes its books annually at June 30. Give the entries required on March 31, Year 25. (*Hint:* First compute what the annual depreciation charges must be, based on the facts given.)

8. *Journal entries for plant acquisition, depreciation, and retirement.* Journalize the following transactions:

a. A piece of office equipment is purchased for $850 cash.

b. Depreciation for one year of $170 is recorded.

c. The equipment is sold for $400. At the time of the sale, the Accumulated Depreciation shows a balance of $340. Depreciation of $170 for the year of the sale has not yet been recorded.

9. *Journal entries for revising estimate of life.* Give the journal entries for the following selected transactions of the Eagle Manufacturing Co. Inc. The company uses the straight-line method of calculating depreciation and closes its books annually on December 31.

a. A machine is purchased on November 1, Year 9, for $30,000. It is estimated that it will be used for ten years and that it will have a salvage value of $600 at the end of that time. Give the journal entry for the depreciation at December 31, Year 9.

b. Record the depreciation for the year ending December 31, Year 10.

c. In August Year 15, it is decided that the machine will probably be used for a total of 12 years and that its salvage value will be $400. Record the depreciation for the year ending December 31, Year 19.

d. The machine is sold for $1,000 on March 31, Year 20. Record the entries of that date, assuming that depreciation is recorded as indicated in part (**c**).

10. *Straight-line depreciation, working backwards.* On March 1, one of the buildings owned by the Metropolitan Storage Co. Ltd. was destroyed by fire. The cost of the building was $100,000. The balance in the Accumulated Depreciation account at January 1 was $38,125. A service life of 40 years with a zero salvage value had been estimated for the building. The company uses the straight-line method. The building was not insured.

a. Give the journal entries made at March 1.

b. If there have been no alterations in the service life estimate, how many years previously was the building acquired?

11. *Journal entries to correct accounting errors.* Give correcting entries for the following situations. In each case, the firm uses the straight-line method of depreciation and closes its books annually on December 31. Recognize all gains and losses currently.

a. A cash register was purchased for $300 on January 1, Year 1. It was depreciated at a rate of ten percent of original cost per year. On June 30, Year 6, it was sold for $200 and a new cash register was acquired for $500. The bookkeeper made the following entry to record the transaction:

Store Equipment	$300	
Cash in Bank		$300

b. A used truck was acquired for $4,000. Its cost, when new, was $6,000, and the bookkeeper made the following entry to record the purchase:

Truck	$6,000	
Accumulated Depreciation		$2,000
Cash		4,000

c. A testing mechanism was purchased on April 1, Year 4, for $600. It was depreciated at a ten percent annual rate. On June 30, Year 6, it was stolen. The loss was not insured, and the bookkeeper made the following entry:

Theft Loss	$600	
Testing Mechanism		$600

12. *Journal entries for acquisition of asset with a note and subsequent recognition of depreciation and interest.* The Grogan Manufacturing Company Ltd. started business on January 1, Year 3. At that time it acquired machine A for $20,000, payment being made by cheque.

Because of an expansion in the volume of business, machine B, costing $25,000, was acquired on September 30, Year 4. A cheque for $15,000 was issued, with the balance to be paid in annual installments of $2,000 plus interest at the rate of 12 percent on the unpaid balance. The first installment is due on September 30, Year 5.

On June 30, Year 5, machine A was sold for $13,000 and a larger model, machine C, was acquired for $30,000.

All installments are paid on time.

All machines have an estimated life of ten years with an estimated salvage value equal to ten percent of acquisition cost. The company closes its books on December 31. The straight-line method is used.

Prepare dated journal entries to record all transactions through December 31, Year 5, including year-end adjustments but excluding closing entries.

13. *Cost of self-constructed assets.* The Dickhaut Manufacturing Co. Ltd. purchased a plot of land for $90,000 as a plant site. There was a small office building on the plot, conservatively appraised at $20,000, which the company will continue to use with some modification and renovation. The company had plans drawn for a factory and received bids for its construction. It rejected all bids and decided to construct the plant itself. Below are listed additional items that management feels should be included in plant asset accounts:

(1) Materials and Supplies	$200,000
(2) Excavation	12,000
(3) Labour on Construction	140,000
(4) Cost of Remodeling Old Building into Office Building	13,000
(5) Interest on Money Borrowed by Dickhaut[a]	6,000
(6) Interest on Dickhaut's Own Money Used	9,000
(7) Cash Discounts on Materials Purchased	7,000
(8) Supervision by Management	10,000
(9) Workers' Compensation Insurance Premiums	8,000
(10) Payment of Claims for Injuries Not Covered by Insurance	3,000
(11) Clerical and Other Expenses of Construction	8,000
(12) Paving of Streets and Sidewalks	5,000
(13) Architect's Plans and Specifications	4,000
(14) Legal Costs of Conveying Land	2,000
(15) Legal Costs of Injury Claim	1,000
(16) Income Credited to Retained Earnings Account, Being the Difference Between the Foregoing Cost and the Lowest Contractor's Bid	11,000

[a]This interest is the entire amount of interest paid during the construction period.

Show in detail the items to be included in the following accounts: Land, Factory Building, Office Building, and Site Improvements. Explain why you excluded any items that you did not include in the four accounts.

14. *Calculations for various depreciation methods.* Calculate the depreciation charge for the first and second years of the asset's life in each of the following cases.

Asset	Cost	Estimated Salvage Value	Life (years)	Depreciation Method
a. Blast Furnace	$800,000	$25,000	20	Declining-Balance[a]
b. Hotel	500,000	50,000	45	Straight-Line
c. Tractor	18,000	1,500	10	Declining-Balance[a]
d. Delivery Truck	22,000	5,200	6	Straight-Line

[a]The declining-balance rate is double the straight-line rate.

15. *Calculations for various depreciation methods.* On January 1, Year 5, the Central Production Company Ltd. acquired a new turret lathe for $36,000. It was estimated to have a useful life of four years and no salvage value. The company closes its books annually on December 31. Indicate the amount of the depreciation charge for each of the four years under:
   a. The straight-line method
   b. The declining-balance method at twice the straight-line rate

16. *Amount of interest capitalized during construction.* Chan Ltd. builds some of its own chemical processing plants. At the start of the year the Construction-in-Process account had a balance of $1 million. Construction activity occurred uniformly throughout the year. At the end of the year the balance was $5 million. The borrowings of the company during the year were as follows:

New Construction Loans at 20 Percent per Year	$ 2,000,000
Old Bond Issues Maturing at Various Times, Averaging 10 Percent Rate	8,000,000
Total Interest-Bearing Debt	$10,000,000

   a. Compute the amount of interest to be capitalized into the Construction-in-Process account for the year.
   b. Present journal entries for interest for the year.

17. *Calculations for various depreciation methods.* A machine is acquired for $8,900. It is expected to last eight years and to be operated for 25,000 hours during that time. It is estimated that its salvage value will be $1,700 at the end of that time. Calculate the depreciation charge for each of the first three years using:
   a. The straight-line (time) method.
   b. The declining-balance method using a 25 percent rate.
   c. The units-of-production method. Operating times are as follows: first year, 3,500 hours; second year, 2,000 hours; third year, 5,000 hours.

18. *Revision of estimated service life changes depreciation schedule.* The Slowpoke Shipping Co. Ltd. buys a new car for $10,000 on January 1, Year 4. It is estimated that it will last six years and have a salvage value of $1,000. Early in Year 6, it is discovered that the car will last only an additional two years, or four years in total. The company closes its books on December 31. Present a table showing the depreciation charges for each year from Year 4 to Year 7 and give the adjusting entry made in Year 6. Follow the instructions for each of the depreciation methods listed below:

    a. The straight-line method.

    b. The declining-balance method with depreciation at twice the straight-line rate. The remaining undepreciated cost less salvage value is to be written off in the last year.

19. *Retirement of plant assets.* The Lindahl Manufacturing Co. Ltd. acquires a new machine for $7,200 on July 1, Year 1. It is estimated that it will have a salvage value of $900. The company closes its books annually on June 30.

    a. Compute the depreciation charges for each year of the asset's life assuming the straight-line method.

    b. If the machine were sold for $700 on October 30, Year 6, give the journal entries that would be made on that date.

20. *Trade-in transactions.* The Twombly Co. Ltd. purchased a new panel truck in May Year 3. The truck cost $18,600. It was estimated that the truck would be driven for 200,000 kilometers before being traded in and that its salvage value at that time would be $2,600.

    Odometer readings are as follows:

December 31, Year 3	24,000
December 31, Year 4	100,000
December 31, Year 5	164,000
June 16, Year 6	196,000

On June 16, Year 6, the truck was traded in for a new one with a list price of $22,000. The old truck had a fair market of $2,600, but the dealer allowed $3,000 on it toward the list price of the new one. The balance of the purchase price was paid by cheque.

    a. Compute the depreciation charges for each year through Year 5, using a ''production'' or ''use'' method.

    b. Record the entries for June 16, Year 6, assuming that the list price of the new truck is unreliable, whereas the fair market value of the old is reliable.

    c. Record the entries for June 16, Year 6, assuming that there were no reliable estimates for the fair market value of the old truck.

21. *Funds statement; loss on disposal of plant.* Refer to the data in Problem 19 at the end of Chapter 5 on page 250 for the Harris Co. Ltd. Assume that the proceeds of sale of the equipment amount to $400 rather than $2,000. As a result, net income declines from $39,000 to $37,400, and dividends are reduced from $30,000 to $28,400. All other items remain unchanged. Prepare a statement of changes in financial position for Year 5, using a cash definition of funds.

22. *Funds statement: gain on disposal of plant.* Refer to the data in problem 19 at the end of Chapter 5 on page 250 for the Harris Co. Ltd. Assume that the proceeds of sale of the equipment amount to $3,000 rather than $2,000. As a result, net income increases from $39,000 to $40,000, and dividends are increased from $30,000 to $31,000. All other items remain unchanged. Prepare a statement of changes in financial position for Year 5, using a cash definition of funds.

23. *Journal entries for investment tax credit.* The Libby Co. Inc. has income tax expense, before any investment tax credits, of $50,000 each year. At the start of the first year, it acquires an asset with a depreciable life of four years. Assume that the asset qualifies for an investment credit of $4,000.

    a. Record income taxes and the entries related to the investment tax credit for the four years of the asset's life using the flow-through method.

    b. Record entries related to income taxes and the investment tax credit for the four years of the asset's life using the deferral method.

24. *Whether a single asset account or separate asset accounts are used affects classification of expenditures as repairs or improvements.* Lafleur Inc. purchased a delivery truck for $20,000 at the start of Year 1. The truck is expected to last for four years, but the engine is expected to be replaced at the end of Year 2 at a cost of $6,000. Lafleur Inc. must choose between depreciating the truck as a single unit or as two separate assets — the engine and the rest of the truck. The company uses straight-line depreciation for financial reporting.

    a. Compute total expense for each of the four years of the truck's life, depreciating the entire cost of $20,000 in a single asset account.

    b. Compute total expense for each year of the truck's life, depreciating the engine and the rest of the truck in separate asset accounts.

25. *Working backwards to derive proceeds of disposition of plant.* Balance sheets of Rasmussen Company at the beginning and end of the year contained the following data:

	End of Year	Beginning of Year
Property, Plant, and Equipment (at cost)	$350,000	$300,000
Accumulated Depreciation	165,000	170,000
Net Book Value	$185,000	$130,000

During the year, machinery and equipment was sold at a gain of $2,000. New machinery and equipment was purchased at a cost of $80,000. Depreciation charges on machinery and equipment for the year amounted to $20,000.

    Calculate the proceeds received from the sale of the machinery and equipment.

Problems and Cases

26. *Allocation of cost in "basket" purchases.* In each of the following situations, compute the amounts of gain or loss to be shown on the income statement for the year, as well as the amount of asset to be shown on the balance sheet as of the end of the year. Show the journal entry or entries required, and provide reasons for your decisions.

a. A company wishes to acquire a five-acre site for a new warehouse. The land it wants is part of a ten-acre site that the owner insists be purchased as a whole for $18,000. The company purchases the land, spends $2,000 in legal fees for rights to divide the site into five-acre plots, and immediately offers half of the land for resale. The two best offers are

(1) $12,000 for the east half, and
(2) $13,000 for the west half.

The company sells the east half.

b. The same data as in part (**a**), except the two best offers are

(1) $5,000 for the east half, and
(2) $12,000 for the west half.

The company sells the west half.

27. *Composite depreciation versus individual-item depreciation.* The Alexander Company Inc. acquired three used machine tools for a total price of $49,000. Costs to transport the machine tools from the seller to Alexander Company's factory were $1,000. The machine tools were renovated, installed, and put to use in manufacturing the firm's products. The costs of renovation and installation were as follows:

	Machine Tool A	Machine Tool B	Machine Tool C
Renovation Costs	$1,700	$800	$950
Installation Costs	300	550	250

The machine tools have the following estimated lives: tool A — four years; tool B — ten years; tool C — six years.

a. Assume that each machine tool is capitalized in a separate asset account and that the remaining life of each machine tool is used as the basis for allocating the joint costs of acquisition. Compute the depreciable cost of each of the three machine tools.

b. Present journal entries to record depreciation charges for years 1, 5, and 8, given the assumption in part (**a**). Use the straight-line method.

c. Assume that the three machine tools are treated as one composite asset in the accounts. If management decides to depreciate the entire cost of the composite asset on a declining balance basis with a rate of 20 percent, what is the depreciation charge for each year?

28. *Funds statement effect.* Refer to the Simplified Statements of Changes in Financial Position for a Period in Exhibit 5.19 on page 248. Eleven of the lines in the statement are numbered. Ignore the unnumbered lines in responding to the questions below.

Assume that the accounting cycle is complete for the period and that all of the financial statements have been prepared. Then it is discovered that a transaction has been overlooked. That transaction is recorded in the accounts and all of the financial statements are corrected. Define *funds* as *cash*. For each of the following transactions, indicate which of the numbered lines of the funds statement is affected and by how much. Ignore income tax effects.

    a. A machine that cost $10,000 and that has $7,000 of accumulated depreciation is sold for $4,000 cash.

    b. A machine that cost $10,000 and that has $7,000 of accumulated depreciation is sold for $2,000 cash.

    c. A machine that cost $10,000 and that has $7,000 of accumulated depreciation is traded in on a new machine. The new machine has a cash price of $12,000. A trade-in allowance for the old machine of $4,000 is given, so that $8,000 cash is paid.

    d. A fire destroys a warehouse. The loss is uninsured. The warehouse cost $80,000 and at the time of the fire had accumulated depreciation of $30,000.

    e. Refer to the facts of part **(d)**. Inventory costing $70,000 was also destroyed. The loss was uninsured. Record effects of only these new facts.

29. *Effects of investment tax credit on funds statement.* Refer to the instructions in the preceding question. Follow the instructions for the transactions or events below relating to the investment tax credit. During the year, qualifying assets with a ten-year depreciable life are acquired, and investment tax credits of $10,000 are realized.

    a. The flow-through method of accounting is used. Record the effects for the year the assets are acquired.

    b. The flow-through method of accounting is used. Record the effects for the year after the assets are acquired.

    c. The deferral method is used. Record the effects for the year the assets are acquired.

    d. The deferral method is used. Record the effects for the year after the assets are acquired.

30. *Preparing funds statements (adapted from a problem by Stan Baiman).* Exhibit 9.4 shows comparative balance sheets, an income statement of Ormes Limited for Year 2, and supplementary notes.

    Prepare the Year 2 statement of changes in financial position with funds defined as *cash*.

Exhibit 9.4
ORMES LIMITED
Comparative Balance Sheets and Income Statement
(Problem 30)

	December 31	
	Year 2	Year 1
Balance Sheet		
Cash	$130,000	$ 30,000
Accounts Receivable	95,000	80,000
Inventory	80,000	100,000
Plant and Equipment	750,000	700,000
Accumulated Depreciation	(500,000)	(380,000)
Total Assets	$555,000	$530,000

Accounts Payable	$ 30,000	$ 20,000
Capital Stock	145,000	200,000
Retained Earnings	380,000	310,000
Total Equities	$555,000	$530,000

Year 2 Income Statement

Net Sales		$795,000
Less: Cost of Goods Sold		315,000
Gross Profit		$480,000
Less: Depreciation Expense	$140,000	
Other Expenses	200,000	340,000
		140,000
Plus: Gain on Sale of Equipment		110,000
Income before Income Tax		$250,000
Income Tax Expense		100,000
Net Income		$150,000

Notes: (1) During Year 2, Ormes acquired property, plant, and equipment at a cost of $200,000.
   (2) All depreciation charges are expensed.
   (3) Dividends declared have been paid in cash.

31. *Investment tax credits for a firm growing to equilibrium.* Refer to the data in Exercise 23 for the Libby Co. Inc. Assume that each year the Babiak Equilibrium Co. Ltd. acquires an asset with a depreciable life of four years. Each year the asset acquired qualifies for an investment tax credit of $4,000, and income tax expense before any investment tax credits is $50,000.

   a. Record entries related to income taxes and the investment tax credit for each of the first five years using the flow-through method.
   b. Record entries related to income taxes and the investment tax credit for each of the first five years using the deferral method.
   c. Assuming that Babiak Equilibrium Co. Ltd.'s income taxes, asset acquisitions, and investment tax credits continue in the following years as in the first four years, describe the effects on the financial statements of the two methods of accounting for the investment tax credit.
   d. Assume the same data as in part **(c)**, but that the new asset's cost increases by ten percent each year and that the amount of the investment tax credit earned increases by ten percent each year. Describe the effects on the financial statements of the two methods of accounting for the investment tax credit.

32. *Choosing between the deferral and flow-through methods for the investment credit.* Three companies have each recently made investments in equipment designed to save fuel. The equipment purchased by each company costs $200,000 and has a ten-year service life. In all three cases, the company was entitled to $10,000 investment tax credit when it purchased the asset during the current year. The income taxes otherwise payable of all three companies were reduced by $10,000 during the current year. In all three companies, management had made careful studies of the costs and benefits of acquiring the new equipment.

   Management of Company A decided that the equipment purchased would provide operating cost savings with a present value of $250,000. The company is delighted to acquire the asset.

Management of Company B decided that the equipment it purchased would provide operating cost savings with a present value of $190,000. The equipment was worth acquiring only because of the investment tax credit.

Management of Company C decided that the equipment it purchased provided operating cost savings with a present value of $196,000. The equipment was acquired only because the investment tax credit made the investment worthwhile.

a. Discuss the considerations the management of each of these companies might give to accounting for the investment tax credit.

d. What can you conclude from this problem about the method of accounting for the investment tax credit that reflects managerial decisions?

33. *Capitalizing versus expensing advertising costs: effects on financial statements and rate of return.* The Consumer Products Co. Ltd. has $300,000 of total assets. The Consumer Products Co. Ltd. has been earning $45,000 per year and generating $45,000 per year of cash flow from operations. Each year the Consumer Products Co. Ltd. distributes its earnings by paying cash of $45,000 to owners. Management of the Consumer Products Co. Ltd. believes that a new advertising campaign now will lead to increased sales over the next four years. The anticipated net cash flows of the project are as follows:

Beginning of Year	Net Cash Inflow (outflow)
1	($24,000)
2, 3, and 4	10,000 each year

Assume that the advertising campaign is undertaken, that cash flows are as planned, and that the Consumer Products Co. Ltd. makes payments to owners of $45,000 at the end of the first year and $47,000 at the end of each of the next three years. Assume that there are no interest expenses in any year. Ignore any income tax effects.

a. Compute net income and the rate of return on assets of the Consumer Products Co. Ltd. for each of the four years, assuming that advertising expenditures are expensed as they occur. Use the year-end balance of total assets in the denominator of the rate-of-return calculation.

b. Compute net income and the rate of return on assets of the Consumer Products Co. Ltd. for each year of the project, assuming that advertising costs are capitalized and then amortized on a straight-line basis over the last three years. Use the year-end balance of total assets in the denominator of the rate of return on assets.

c. How well has the management of the Consumer Products Co. Ltd. carried out its responsibility to its owners? On what basis do you make this judgment? Which method of accounting seems to reflect performance more adequately?

34. *Accounting for intangibles.* In Year 1, Epstein Inc. acquired the assets of Falk Limited. The assets of Falk Limited included various intangibles. Discuss the accounting for the acquisition in Year 1, and in later years, for each of the following items.

a. Registration of the trademark Thyrom® for thyristors expires in three years. Epstein Inc. thought that the trademark had a fair market value of $100,000. It expects to continue making and selling Thyrom thyristors indefinitely.

b. The design patent covering the ornamentation of the containers for displaying Thyrom expires in five years. Epstein Inc. thought that the design patent had a fair market value of $30,000 and expects to continue making the containers indefinitely.

c. An unpatented trade secret on a special material used in manufacturing thyristors was viewed as having a fair market value of $200,000.

d. Refer to the trade secret in part (**c**). Suppose that in Year 2 a competitor discovers the trade secret, but does not disclose the secret to other competitors. How should the accounting policies be changed?

e. During Year 1, Epstein Inc. produced a sales promotion film, *Using Thyristors for Fun and Profit*, at a cost of $45,000. The film is licensed to purchasers of thyristors for use in training their employees and customers. The film is copyrighted.

35. *Expensing versus capitalizing advertising costs for firm advertising every year.* Equilibrium Ltd. plans to spend $60,000 at the beginning of each of the next several years advertising the company's brand names and trademarks. As a result of the advertising expenditure for a given year, aftertax income (not counting advertising expense) is expected to increase by $24,000 a year for three years, including the year of the expenditure itself. Equilibrium Ltd. has other aftertax income of $20,000 per year. The controller of Equilibrium Ltd. wonders what will be the effect on the financial statements of following one of two accounting policies with respect to advertising expenditures:

(1) Expensing the advertising costs in the year of expenditures.

(2) Capitalizing the advertising costs and amortizing them over three years, including the year of the expenditure itself.

Assume that the Company does spend $60,000 at the beginning of each of four years and that the planned increase in income occurs. Ignore income tax effects.

a. Prepare a four year condensed summary of net income, assuming that policy **(1)** is followed and advertising costs are expensed as incurred.

b. Prepare a four year condensed summary of net income, assuming that policy **(2)** is followed and advertising costs are capitalized and amortized over three years. Compute also the amount of Deferred Advertising Costs (asset) to be shown on the balance sheet at the end of each of the four years.

c. In what sense is policy **(1)** a conservative policy?

d. What will be the effect on net income and on the balance sheet if Equilibrium Ltd. continues to spend $60,000 each year and the effects on aftertax income continue as in the first four years?

36. *Improvements versus repairs or maintenance.* The balance sheet of Woolf's Department Store Ltd. shows a building with an original cost of $800,000 and accumulated depreciation of $660,000. The building is being depreciated on a straight-line basis over 40 years. The remaining depreciable life of the building is seven years. On January 2 of the current year, an expenditure of $28,000 was made on the street-level display windows of the store. Indicate the accounting for the current year if the expenditure of $28,000 was made under each of the following circumstances. Each of these cases is to be considered independently of the others, except where noted. Ignore income tax effects.

    a. Management decided that improved display windows would make the store's merchandise seem more attractive. The windows are a worthwhile investment.

    b. A violent hailstorm on New Year's Day destroyed the display windows previously installed. There was no insurance coverage for this sort of destruction. The new windows installed are physically identical to the old windows. The old windows had a book value of $28,000 at the time of the storm.

    c. Vandals destroyed the display windows on New Year's Day. There was no insurance coverage for this sort of destruction. The new windows installed are physically identical to the old windows. The old windows had a book value of $28,000 at the time of destruction.

    d. The old displays contained windows constructed of nonshatterproof glass. Management had previously considered replacing its old nonshatterproof windows with new ones but had decided that there was *zero* benefit to the firm in doing so. New shatterproof windows are installed because a new law was passed requiring that all stores must have shatterproof windows on the street level. The alternative to installing the new windows was to shut down the store. In responding to this part, assume *zero* benefits result from the new windows. Part **(e)** below considers the more realistic case of some benefits.

    e. Management had previously considered replacing its old, nonshatterproof windows with new ones, but decided that the new windows would produce future benefits of only $7,000 and so were not a worthwhile investment. However, a new law [see part **(d)**] now requires them to do so (or else shut down), and the new windows are installed.

37. *Capitalizing versus expensing: if capitalized, what amortization period?* In each of the following situations, compute the amounts of revenue, gain, expense, and loss to be shown on the income statement for the year and the amount of asset to be shown on the balance sheet as of the end of the year. Show the journal entry or entries required, and provide reasons for your decisions. Straight-line amortization is used. The reporting period is the calendar year. The situations are independent of each other, except where noted.

    a. Because of a new fire code, a department store must install an additional fire escape on its building. Management had previously considered installing the additional fire escape. It had rejected the idea because it had already installed a modern sprinkler system, which was even more cost-effective, instead. The new code gives management no alternative except to close the store. The fire escape is acquired for $28,000 cash on January 1. The building is expected to be demolished seven years from the date the fire escape was installed.

    b. Many years ago, a firm acquired shares of stock in Seagram Co. Ltd. for $100,000. On December 31, the firm acquired a building with an appraised value of $1 million. The company paid for the building by giving up its shares in Seagram Co. Ltd. at a time when equivalent shares traded on the Toronto Stock Exchange for $1,050,000.

    c. Same data as part **(b)**, except that the shares represent ownership in Small Timers, Inc., whose shares are traded on a regional stock exchange. The last transactions in shares of Small Timers, Inc., occurred on December 27. Using the prices of the most recent trades, the shares of Small Timers, Inc., given in exchange for the building have a market value of $1,050,000.

d. A company decides that it can save $3,500 a year for ten years by switching from small panel trucks to larger delivery vans. To do so requires remodelling costs of $18,000 for various garages. The first fleet of delivery vans will last for five years, and the garages will last for twenty years. The garages are remodeled on January 1.

e. A company drills for oil. It sinks ten holes during the year at a cost of $1 million each. Nine of the holes are dry, but the tenth is a gusher. By the end of the year, the oil known to be recoverable from the gusher has a net realizable value of $40 million, and another oil company has offered to buy the well for $40 million. No oil was extracted during the year.

f. A company manufactures aircraft. During the current year, all sales were to the government under defense contracts. The company spent $400,000 on institutional advertising to keep its name before the business community. It expects to resume sales of small jet planes to corporate buyers in twenty years.

g. A company runs a large laboratory that has, over the years, found market-able ideas and products worth tens of millions of dollars. On average, the successful products have a life of ten years. Expenditures for the laboratory this year were $1,500,000.

h. A textile manufacturer gives $250,000 to the Textile Engineering Depart-ment of a local university for basic research in fibers. The results of the research, if any, will belong to the general public.

i. On January 1, an automobile company incurs costs of $6 million for special-ized machine tools necessary to produce a new model automobile. Such tools last for six years, on average, but the new model automobile is expected to be produced for only three years.

j. On January 1, an airline purchased a fleet of airbuses for $100 million cash. The airbuses have an expected useful life of ten years and no salvage value. At the same time the airline purchased spare parts for use with those airbuses for $20 million cash. The spare parts have no use, now or in the future, other than replacing broken or worn-out airbus parts. During the first year of operation, no spare parts were used.

k. Refer to the data in the preceding part. In the second year of operation, $1 million of spare parts were used.

38. *Effect on net income of changes in estimates for depreciable assets.* A major airline has $3 billion of assets, including airplanes costing $2.5 billion with net book value of $1.6 billion. It earns income before income tax equal to approximately six percent of total assets. Airplanes have been depreciated for financial reporting pur-poses on a straight-line basis over ten-year lives to a salvage value equal to ten per-cent of original cost. The airline has announced a change in depreciation policy; it will use 14-year lives and salvage values equal to 12 percent of original cost. Assume that the airplanes are all four years old.

What will be the approximate impact on net income of the change in depreciation policy? Compute both dollar and percentage effects.

39. Prepare the Year 2 capital cost allowance schedule for the Dumpty Co. Ltd. from the following information about events occurring in Year 2, using the CCA rates in the chapter.
   (1) The undepreciated capital cost as at December 31, Year 1 for Class 6 was $6,700; Class 8, $62,750; and Class 10, $43,800.
   (2) Proceeds from the sale of a truck were $6,000. This amount was less than the original capital cost.
   (3) Proceeds from the sale of a specialized machine were $12,000, which was $1,000 more than the capital cost.
   (4) Purchases during the year: Class 8, $16,000; Class 10, $8,000; and special water pollution equipment, $8,400.
   (5) A lease for five years with a five-year renewal option was signed and $16,000 was paid for improvements to the premises.
   (6) A patent with five years' life left was purchased for $7,500.
   (7) The last asset included in Class 6, a galvanized building, was sold for $12,700, which was less than its original capital cost.
   (8) The company claimed the maximum capital cost allowance for the year ended December 31, Year 2.

40. *Analysis of financial statement disclosure of effects of depreciation policy.* A recent annual report of Caterpillar Tractor Company contained the following statement of depreciation policy:

> Depreciation is computed principally using accelerated methods for both income tax and financial reporting purposes. These methods result in a larger allocation of the cost of buildings, machinery, and equipment to operations in the early years of the lives of assets than does the straight-line method.

Then Caterpillar discloses the amounts for "Buildings, Machinery, and Equipment — Net" as they would appear if the straight-line method had always been used. Exhibit 9.5 shows these amounts and other data from the financial statements for three recent years.

Exhibit 9.5
Excerpts from Annual Report of Caterpillar Tractor Company
(dollar amounts in millions)
(Problem 40)

	Year 3	Year 2	Year 1
Buildings, Machinery, and Equipment — Net:			
As Reported	$3,339	$3,300	$2,928
If Straight-Line Depreciation Were Used	4,020	3,894	3,431
Depreciation Expense Reported	505	448	370

   a. What amounts would be reported for depreciation expense for Years 2 and 3 if the straight-line method had always been used?
   b. Now assume a 40 percent tax rate, that straight-line depreciation had been used always for both income tax and financial reporting purposes, and that Buildings, Machinery, and Equipment — Net on the balance sheet amounted to $4,020 at the end of Year 3. What other items on the balance sheet for the end of Year 3 would probably change and by how much?

41. *Straight-line depreciation is probably too ''conservative''; it usually writes off an asset's cost faster than future benefits disappear.* (This problem requires material from Appendix B.) Assets are acquired for their future benefits — the future cash flows they produce, either cash inflows or savings of cash outflows. As the near-term cash flows are received, the future benefits decline, but the future cash flows come closer to being received, *increasing* the value of the future benefits. The present value of future cash flows may, in total, increase or decrease during any one year. This problem explores changes in the present value of future cash flows with the passage of time and illustrates the phenomenon that for many business projects the present value of future benefits (that is, future cash flows) declines at a rate much slower than implied by straight-line depreciation.

Pasteur Limited plans to acquire an asset that will have a ten-year life and promises to generate cash flows of $10,000 per year at the end of each of the ten years of its life. Given the risk of the project that uses the asset, Pasteur Limited judges that a 12 percent rate is appropriate for discounting its future cash flows. Using a 12 percent discount rate, the present value of $1 received at the end of each of the next ten years is $5.65022 (see Table 4 on page 817, ten-period row, 12 percent column). Because the project is expected to generate $10,000 per year, the present value of the cash flows is $56,502 (= $10,000 × 5.65022). Assume that Pasteur Limited purchases the asset for exactly $56,502 at the beginning of Year 1. Exhibit 9.6 shows for each

Exhibit 9.6
Pattern of Expiration of Future Benefits Measured as the
Net Present Value of Future Cash Flows
(Problem 41)

Asset Cost $56,502 and Has Ten-Year Life
Asset Yields $10,000 per Year of Cash Inflow
Discount Rate = 12 Percent per Year

Beginning of Year (1)	Years Remaining (2)	Present Value of Remaining Cash Flows (3)	Percentage of Present Value of Cash Flows Remaining (4)	Percentage of Loss in Value During Preceding Year (5)	Straight-line Depreciation for Preceding Year (6)
1	10	$56,502	100%		
2	9	53,282	94	6%	10%
3	8	49,676	88	6	10
4	7	45,638	81	7	10
5	6	41,114	73	8	10
6	5	36,048	64	9	10
7	4	30,373	54	10	10
8	3	24,018	43	11	10
9	2	16,901	30	13	10
10	1	8,929	16	14	10
11	0	0	0	16	10
Total ...				$100%	$100%

Column (3) from Table 4 (at back of book), 12 percent column, row corresponding to number in column (2) here multiplied by $10,000.
Column (4) = number in column (3)/$56,502.
Column (5) = column (4) preceding year − column (4) this year.

year the present value of the cash flows remaining at the beginning of each year of the asset's life. The numbers in column (3) are $10,000 multiplied by the number appearing in Table 4, 12 percent column, for the number of periods remaining in the asset's life. Column (4) shows the percentage of the asset's present value of the cash flows remaining, and column (5) shows the percentage loss in present value of cash flows during the preceding year.

Column (6) shows the percentage write-off in cost each year using straight-line depreciation — ten percent per year. Note that the decline in present value of cash flows is less than straight-line in the first five years, but greater in the last four years.

   a. Construct an exhibit similar to Exhibit 9.6 for an asset with a five-year life promising $10,000 of cash flows at the end of each year. Use a discount rate of 15 percent per year. The asset cost is $33,522. Compare the resulting decline in present value with straight-line depreciation.

   b. Now consider another asset with a five-year life with risk appropriate for a 15 percent discount rate. This asset also has net present value of cash flows of $33,522, but the expected cash flows are $11,733 at the end of the first year, $10,767 at the end of the second year, $9,722 at the end of the third year, $8,716 at the end of the fourth year, and $7,710 at the end of the fifth year. Construct an exhibit similar to Exhibit 9.6 for this asset. You should find that the present value of future cash flows disappears at the rate of 20 percent per year of $33,522, the initial present value.

   c. Using the results of your work above, comment on the nature of conservatism of straight-line depreciation.

42. *Analysis of financial statements to compute the change in property and plant assets required to sustain sales growth (developed from a suggestion by Katherine Schipper).* Exhibit 9.7 shows data from several recent years for the General Electric Company (GE). Assume that analysis of GE's markets indicates that GE can sustain sales growth of ten percent per year for the next several years. The corporate treasurer must plan ways to raise the new funds that will be required to finance the expansion of assets needed to support such increased sales. Assume that GE's financial policy calls for financing of new property and plant with long-term financing, owners' equity (including earnings and retentions), and long-term borrowings, whereas financing for current assets, such as receivables and inventory, can be generated with current liabilities, such as increases in payables and short-term bank borrowings.

   Past relations appear in Exhibit 9.7; note the computation of the fixed asset turnover ratio and the total asset turnover ratio. These ratios show the average amount of sales per dollar of investment in plant and equipment and the average amount of sales per dollar of investment in total assets. The total asset turnover ratio averages 1.42, indicating that $1.42 of sales requires about $1.00 of total assets. Putting it another way, about $.70 (= $1/1.42) of assets is required for each dollar of sales. The average fixed asset turnover ratio of 4.94 indicates that about $1 of net property and plant is required for $4.94 of sales, or that $1 of sales requires about $.20 (= $1/4.94) of property and plant. From these data, management has tentatively concluded that to increase sales by $1 will require about $.70 of new assets, of which about $.20 will be invested in new property and plant, with the remaining $.50 invested in current

Exhibit 9.7
GENERAL ELECTRIC COMPANY
Data on Sales, Plant/Equipment, and Total Assets
(dollar amounts in millions)

			Plant and Equipment			Total Assets			
Year (1)	Sales (2)	Dollar Change from Preceding Year (3)	Balance Sheet Total Net of Accumulated Depreciation December 31 (4)	Dollar Change from Preceding Year (5)	New Acquisitions for Year (6)	Balance Sheet Total December 31 (7)	Dollar Change from Preceding Year (8)	Turnover Ratios Fixed Assets (9)	Turnover Ratios Total Assets (10)
12 ..	$27,240	$2,281	$6,844	$1,064	$2,025	$20,942	$2,431	4.32	1.38
11 ..	24,959	2,498	5,780	1,167	1,948	18,511	1,867	4.80	1.42
10 ..	22,461	2,807	4,613	590	1,262	16,644	1,608	5.20	1.42
9 ..	19,654	2,135	4,023	439	1,055	15,036	1,339	5.17	1.37
8 ..	17,519	1,822	3,584	228	823	13,697	1,647	5.05	1.36
7 ..	15,697	1,592	3,356	175	740	12,050	1,309	4.80	1.38
6 ..	14,105	187	3,181	565	588	10,741	1,372	4.87	1.40
5 ..	13,918	1,973	2,616	255	813	9,369	1,045	5.59	1.57
4 ..	11,945	1,471	2,361	224	735	8,324	922	5.31	1.52
3 ..	10,474	917	2,137	111	501	7,402	514	5.03	1.47
2 ..	9,557	723	2,026	277	711	6,888	689	5.06	1.46
1 ..	8,834		1,749		685	6,199			
Weighted average								4.94	1.42

Columns (2), (4), (6), (7): taken from annual reports
Columns (3), (5), (8): amount for a given year computed by subtracting amount for preceding year from amount for given year, using data in preceding column.

$$\text{Column (9)} = \frac{\text{Column (2)}}{.5 \times [\text{Column (4)} + \text{Column (4), Preceding Year}]}$$

$$\text{Column (10)} = \frac{\text{Column (2)}}{.5 \times [\text{Column (7)} + \text{Column (7), Preceding Year}]}$$

assets such as receivables and inventories. Thus, to increase sales by ten percent, or $2.7 billion, will require about $1.9 (= .70 × $2.7) billion of new funds, with about $540 million (= .20 × $2.7 billion) required from long-term sources.

Can you sharpen and improve this analysis? Consider the *incremental* sales achieved by past incremental investments in both property/plant and total assets. Consider that turnover ratios deal with average relations, whereas the questions at issue require analysis of incremental relations — how much additional investment is required for additional sales.

43. *Analysis of effects of capitalization of interest and other funds into construction work in progress.* Regulated public utilities capitalize into their plant assets under construction not only explicit interest costs, but also an amount for the cost of funds provided by owners. These amounts are often called AFUDC—allowance for funds used during construction; see the Glossary for an explanation of the term and an indication of why this is done.

Exhibit 9.8 reproduces excerpts from the recent financial statements of Trans Alta Utilities Corporation, a regulated producer of electricity. The balance sheet amount for Construction Work in Progress includes amounts for interest and owners' equity capitalized as AFUDC. The income statement shows credits to income each year for the amounts of AFUDC.

    a. Compute the rate of return on common shareholders' equity, using the average of beginning- and end-of-year balances.

    b. Compute the net income to common shareholders before AFUDC and the implied rates of return on common shareholders' equity, as in the preceding part.

    c. Estimate the average construction period for Trans Alta Utilities Corporation's plant by dividing the average balance of Construction Work in Progress by the Construction Expenditures for the year.

Exhibit 9.8
TRANS ALTA UTILITIES CORPORATION
Financial Statement Excerpts

(dollars in thousands)	Year 4	Year 3	Year 2	Year 1
Property Under Construction	$ 671	$ 881	$ 479	$ 211
Utility Plant (net)	2,212	1,602	1,457	1,379
Other Assets (net)	413	337	434	349
Total Assets	$3,296	$2,820	$2,370	$1,939
Liabilities and Deferred Credits	$1,586	$1,352	$1,107	$ 891
Preferred Stock Equity	622	664	476	442
Common Stock Equity:				
Contributed Capital	666	454	477	352
Retained Earnings	422	350	310	254
	$3,296	$2,820	$2,370	$1,939

Income Statement for Year

	Year 4	Year 3	Year 2	Year 1
Operating Income	$ 234	$ 190	$ 164	$ 132
Total Interest Expense and Preferred Share Dividend Requirements[a]	(204)	(164)	(118)	(88)
Amounts Capitalized into Property Under Construction	97	85	35	21
Other (net)	22	23	25	9
Net Income to Common Shares	$ 149	$ 134	$ 106	$ 74

Statement of Changes in Financial Position

	Year 4	Year 3	Year 2	Year 1
Construction Expenditures[b]	$ 492	$ 622	$ 407	$ 271
Interest Rate Used for Capitalization	12.91%	13.08%	11.74$	10.66%

[a]Before capitalization into plant
[b]Including amounts capitalized into property under construction

Income tax advantage of capital cost allowances.

44. Griffin Co. Limited purchased for $10,000 an asset which has a useful life of ten years, no salvage value, and is included in Class 8 for income tax purposes. What is the first-year tax advantage (computed to the nearest dollar) of the income tax method over the straight-line method, assuming a constant tax rate of 50 percent? What is the tax advantage over the life of the asset ignoring present value and assuming the asset is one of several in Class 8?

45. *Effects of recording errors on financial statements*. O'Keefe Company manufactures small machine tools. Its inventory turnover (= cost of goods sold ÷ average inventory during year) is about 3. The company uses a FIFO cost flow assumption. During the current year, inventory increased. The firm depreciates its plant assets over 7 years, using the straight-line method. Below are described several transactions and the incorrect way these events were recorded. Indicate the effect of the mistake (overstatement, understatement, no effect) on each of the following items:
(1)   Plant Assets (net of depreciation), end of current year.
(2)   Selling, General, and Administrative Expenses for the current year.
(3)   Cost of Goods Sold for the current year.
(4)   Total Assets, end of next year.
(5)   Net Income for next year.
(6)   Owners' Equity, end of next year.
For example, if the effect of recording is that net income is too low, the right response is *understatement*.

    a. During the current year, expenditures for testing a new factory machine were debited to Work-in-Process Inventory.

    b. During the current year, the company completed self-construction of a warehouse for finished goods, but it failed to charge any general supervisory overhead costs of construction to the plant account. All costs were expensed.

    c. The local electric utility installed new time-of-day metering devices to enable peak-load pricing of electricity. The O'Keefe Company paid the utility a $5,000 deposit, which will be returned in 3 years if the meters have not been negligently damaged by the company. O'Keefe Company debited this payment to Work-in-Process Inventory.

    d. Maintenance cost of office machines was debited to Accumulated Depreciation on Plant Assets.

    e. Maintenance of factory machines was debited to Accumulated Depreciation on Plant Assets.

    f. In the current year, O'Keefe acquired new land to be used for a warehouse. It incorrectly debited the cost of independent appraisals of the property to general expenses rather than to a plant account.

    g. O'Keefe Company carried out a significant rearrangement of its factory plant layout during the current year and properly accounted for all costs that were recorded. A bill from Stephens Moving Company will not arrive until the next year. When it is paid, the amount will be debited to a general expense account.

46. *Trade-ins (adapted from a problem by S. Zeff)*. Werner Company traded in a machine for an essentially identical machine. The journal entry, which correctly reflects the application of proper accounting practice, was as follows:

Machine	33,400	
Accumulated Depreciation	12,700	
Loss on Disposition	3,700	
Machine		29,800
Cash		20,000

  a. What is the fair market value of the old machine?

  b. Suppose that all the facts of the trade-in were the same except that the amount of cash given was $15,000 instead of $20,000, changing the $3,700 loss to a $1,300 gain. Give the journal entry that should be made.

47. *Comparing depreciation methods.* The Hobson Company has been in business since July, 1986, providing a gravel hauling service. Six trucks were purchased on July 1, 1986, at a cost of $35,000 each. These trucks were expected to have a useful life of eight years and a ten percent salvage value. They have been depreciated on a straight-line basis.

On April 1, 1987, one of the drivers experienced a brake failure and overturned his truck. At this time the truck was written off. The driver sued the company for negligence, charging that the company had not maintained the trucks properly. The suit was successful, and the Hobson Company was ordered on November 16, 1988, to pay $100,000 in damages.

On January 20, 1989, when the accountant was preparing the financial statements, he recommended that the production method would provide a better matching of truck depreciation expense to revenue. At the date of purchase, each truck was estimated to have a useful economic life of 80,000 kilometers. Hauling contracts had been somewhat erratic; total kilometers for all trucks in 1986, 1987 and 1988 were 12,000, 55,000 and 40,000 respectively.

Income was reported to be $96,000 and $136,000 in 1986 and 1987 respectively. In 1988, income before depreciation was $154,000.

  a. Prepare a journal entry to record the write-off of the truck on April 1, 1987.

  b. What would be the difference in income for each of the three years if depreciation had been calculated on the production method rather than on the straight-line method? Show all supporting calculations.

  c. What would be a valid rationale for the production method in this case? Be specific.

  d. What is the required accounting treatment for the $100,000 in damages that Hobson Company was ordered to pay in 1988?

Adapted, with permission, from the Society of Management Accountants of Canada.

48. *Limitations of GAAP.* Mr. Goldwin runs an antiques store in Kingston, Ontario. His store has established a reputation that the antiques in stock will always appreciate in value. When Mr. Goldwin applied for a bank loan, the bank manager assessed the store as having $500,000 worth of goodwill and inventory appreciation, although it is not recorded in the books. Mr. Goldwin discussed the bank manager's statements with his accountant and asked to have the goodwill recorded. His accountant replied, "Conventional accounting principles result in many assets being carried at values that do not reflect their true economic value to the firm. In addition, many of the firm's assets are not recorded at all."

a. Explain the accountant's statement including a discussion of why accounting principles have not been altered to correct this situation. Include in your explanation a recommendation, with reference to generally accepted accounting principles, as to whether the goodwill should be recorded.

Adapted, with permission, from the Society of Management Accountants of Canada.

Decision Problem 9-1

Acme Trucking Ltd. recently expanded its operations into Alberta by purchasing 60 percent of the shares of Alberta Transport Ltd. from the estate of the company's founder. The remaining shares are held by members of the founder's family who do not wish to sell their shares at this time.

Shortly after gaining control through the share purchase, in order to permit the expansion of the Alberta operations, Alberta Transport, on Acme's direction and financing, sold its existing warehouse and purchased for $400,000 a replacement frame warehouse with greater storage capacity. For the coming year Alberta expected to use only 60 percent of the warehouse, but over the next ten years the steady increase in business was expected to result in full capacity use. Because of the ample supply of warehouse space in Alberta, there did not appear to be an alternate use for the excess capacity during this time. The warehouse had been constructed on leased land with 40 years to expire on lease. At the expiration of the lease, the salvage value of the warehouse was expected to be $20,000 in excess of the costs of demolition.

In the past, Alberta Transport had recorded depreciation on frame buildings equal to the maximum capital cost allowance of ten percent. Bill Buck, the president of Acme, had questioned this policy and has asked you to consider the continuation of the policy or some other alternative (or alternatives) that would present a fair set of financial statements that could be used:

(1) To evaluate the performance of Jack Doe, the new manager of Alberta Transport.
(2) To report on the results of the company's operations to the minority shareholders and
(3) To minimize the payments of corporate income tax.

Before finalizing a policy proposal on depreciation you have collected the following information that may be relevant to the policy:

(1) Jack Doe will be evaluated on the return on investment (R.O.I.) achieved on net operating assets (less current liabilities).
(2) The minority shareholdings were expected to be purchased by Acme over the next two years. Consequently, it was considered to be in Acme's interest to minimize the reported income since this policy might encourage the founder's family to sell its shares at a lower price.

(3) Sixty percent of Alberta Transport's reported income is to be included in the financial statements of Acme. Since Bill Buck has a ten-year contract with a profit-sharing clause, he was interested in increasing the income of Acme during this period.

(4) It was in the interest of all parties to minimize the payments for corporate income tax.

Prepare a statement of depreciation policy that would be suitable for the new warehouse of Alberta Transport, indicating in full the reasons for the policy recommended.

Chapter 10   Liabilities: Introduction

This chapter and the next two examine the accounting concepts and procedures for the right-hand side of the balance sheet, which shows the sources of a firm's financing. The funds used to acquire assets come from two sources: owners and nonowners. Chapter 12 discusses owners' equity. This chapter and Chapter 11 discuss obligations incurred by a business that result from raising funds from nonowners. Banks and creditors providing debt on a long-term basis understand their role as providers of funds. Suppliers and employees, who do not require immediate cash payment for goods provided or services rendered, usually do not think of themselves as contributing to a firm's funds, but they do. Likewise, customers who advance cash to a firm prior to delivery of a good or service provide funds to the firm. The obligations of a business to these non-owning contributors of funds are *liabilities*.

Basic Concepts of Liabilities

In accounting, an obligation is generally recognized as a liability of an entity if it has three essential characteristics:[1]

1. The obligation involves a probable future sacrifice of resources — a future transfer of cash, goods, or services or the forgoing of a future cash receipt — at a specified or determinable date. The cash equivalent value of resources to be sacrificed must be measurable with reasonable precision.
2. The entity has little or no discretion to avoid the transfer.
3. The transaction or event giving rise to the entity's obligation has already occurred.

A thorough understanding of liabilities requires knowledge of compound interest and present value computations. In these computations, payments made at different times are made comparable by taking into account the interest that cash can earn over time. Appendix B at the back of the book introduces the computations.

Example 1 Miller Corporation's employees have earned wages and salaries that will not be paid until the next payday, two weeks after the end of the current accounting period. Miller Corporation's suppliers are owed substantial amounts for goods sold to Miller Corporation, but these debts are not due for ten to thirty days after the end of the period. Miller Corporation owes the federal government for taxes, but the payments are not due until the 15th of next month. Each of these items meets the three criteria to be a liability. Thus, they are shown as liabilities under titles such as Wages Payable, Salaries Payable, Accounts Payable, and Taxes Payable.

---

[1] Financial Accounting Standards Board, *Statement of Financial Accounting Concepts No. 3*, "Elements of Financial Statements of Business Enterprises," 1980, par. 29.

Example 2 When Miller Corporation sells television sets, it gives a warranty to repair or replace any faulty parts within one year after sale. This obligation meets the three criteria of a liability. Because some television sets will surely need repair, the future sacrifice of resources is probable. The obligation to make repairs is Miller Corporation's. The transaction giving rise to the obligation, the sale of the television set, has already occurred.

The amount is not known with certainty, but Miller Corporation has had sufficient experience with its own television sets to be able to estimate with reasonable precision what the expected costs of repairs or replacements will be. The repairs or replacements will occur within a time span, one year, known with reasonable precision. Miller Corporation will thus show Estimated Liability for Warranty Payments on its balance sheet.

Example 3 Miller Corporation signs a binding contract to supply certain goods to a customer within the next six months. In this case, there is an obligation, definite time, and definite amount (of goods, if not cash), but there has been no past or current transaction. Chapter 2 pointed out that accounting does not recognize assets or liabilities for executory contracts—the mere exchange of promises where there is no mutual performance. Without some mutual performance, there is no current or past benefit. Thus no liability is shown in this case.

Example 4 Facts are the same as in Example 3, except that the customer has made a $10,000 cash deposit on signing the order. Here, there has been more than an exchange of promises. The customer has paid cash and Miller Corporation has accepted it. It will show a liability called Advances from Customers in the amount of $10,000. The remainder of the order is still executory and is not recognized in accounting. Such arrangements are called "partially executory contracts."

Example 5 Miller Corporation has signed a three-year, noncancelable lease with the IBM Corporation to make payments of $3,000 per month for use of a computer system with a three-year life. Definite amounts are due at definite times, and a transaction has occurred—a computer system has been received. Therefore, Miller Corporation will show a liability called Obligation under Capital Leases on its balance sheet.

Example 6 Miller Corporation is defendant in a lawsuit alleging damages of $10 million. The lawsuit was filed by customers who claim to have been injured by misleading advertising about Miller Corporation's television sets. Lawyers retained by the corporation think that there is an adequate defense to the charges. Because there is no obligation to make a payment at a reasonably definite time, there is no liability. The notes to the financial statements will disclose the existence of the lawsuit, but no liability will be shown on the balance sheet.

Example 7 Miller Corporation has signed a contract promising to employ its president for the next five years and to pay the president a salary of $250,000 per year. The salary is to be increased in future years at the same rate as the Consumer Price Index, published by the government, increases. Miller Corporation has an obligation to make payments (although the president may quit at any time without penalty). The payments are of reasonably certain amounts and are to be made at definite times. At the time the contract is signed, no mutual performance has occurred. The contract is purely executory. Because a transaction is deemed not to have taken place, no liability appears on the balance sheet. A liability will, of course, arise as the president performs services over time.

Example 8 Miller Corporation has signed a contract with Horizon Oil Pipe Line Limited to ship at least 10,000 barrels of crude oil per month for the next three years. Miller Corporation must pay for the shipping services, whether or not it actually ships oil. An arrangement such as this, called a *throughput contract*, is not recorded as a liability because the event giving rise to the obligation is viewed as being actual shipment, which has not yet occurred. Such an obligation is merely disclosed in notes. Similarly, long-term obligations for so-called take-or-pay contracts, where the "purchaser" is obliged to pay for certain quantities of goods, whether or not the purchaser actually takes delivery of them, is not a formal liability, but must be disclosed. Both throughput and take-or-pay contracts are viewed as executory.

Valuation

In *historical*-cost accounting, liabilities appear on the balance sheet as the present value of payments to be made in the future. The interest rate used in computing the present-value amount throughout the life of a liability is the interest rate that the specific borrower was required to pay at the time the liability was initially incurred. That is, the *historical* interest rate is used.

As Chapter 2 mentions, most current liabilities appear at the amount payable because the difference between the amount ultimately payable and its present value is immaterial.

Classification

Liabilities are generally classified on the balance sheet as *current* or *noncurrent*. The criterion generally used for dividing current from noncurrent liabilities is the length of time that will elapse before payment must be made. The dividing line between the two is one year, or the length of the operating cycle if more than one year.

Contingencies — Potential Obligations

One of the criteria used by the accountant to recognize a liability is that there be a probable future sacrifice of resources. The world of business and law is full of uncertainties. At any given time a firm may find itself potentially liable for events that have occurred in the past. Contingencies of this nature are not recognized as accounting liabilities. They are potential future obligations rather than current obligations. The potential obligations arise from events that occurred in the past but whose outcome is not now known. Whether an item becomes a liability, and how large a liability it will become, depends on a future event, such as the outcome of a lawsuit.

Suppose that the company is sued for damages in a formal court proceeding for an accident involving a customer who was visiting the company. The suit is not scheduled for trial until after the close of the accounting period. If the company's lawyers and auditors agree that the outcome is likely to be favorable for the company or that, if unfavorable, the amount of the damage settlement will not be large, then no liability will be recognized on the balance sheet. The notes to the financial statements must disclose, however, significant contingencies.

The *CICA Handbook* recommends that an estimated loss from a contingency should be recognized in the accounts only if both of the following conditions are met:[2]

(a) Information available prior to the issuance of the financial statements indicates that the chance is high that a future event will confirm that an asset had been impaired or that a liability had been incurred.

(b) The amount of the loss can be reasonably estimated.

An example is that of a toy manufacturer who has sold products for which a safety hazard has been discovered. The toy manufacturer thinks it likely that liabilities have been incurred. Test (b) would be met if experience or other information enabled the manufacturer to make a reasonable estimate of the loss. The journal entry would be:

Loss on Damage Claim	$50,000	
Estimated Liability for Damages		$50,000
To recognize estimated liability for expected damage		
arising from safety hazard of toys sold.		

The debit in the above entry is to a loss account (presented among other expenses on the income statement), and the credit is to an estimated liability which should be treated as a current liability, similar to the Estimated Warranty Liability account, on the balance sheet. In practice, an account with the title "Estimated Liability for Damages" would seldom, if ever, appear in published financial statements, because it would be perceived as an admission of guilt. Such an admission is likely to affect adversely the outcome of the lawsuit. The liability account would be combined with others for financial statement presentation.

The term *contingent liability* is used only when the item is not recognized in the accounts but rather in the footnotes. (A note receivable sold *with* recourse, described in Chapter 7, gives rise to another example of a contingent liability.) Footnote disclosure is required when the existence of a contingent liability is likely (the chance is high), but the amount cannot be reasonably estimated; or when there exists an exposure to loss in excess of the amount accrued; or when the occurrence of the confirming future event is not determinable.

The 1982 annual report of VS Services Ltd. illustrates the disclosure of contingent liabilities as follows:

---

[2]*CICA Handbook*, section 3290.

Commitments and Contingencies (*in part*)

An action was commenced against the Company in 1972 by Canada Square Corporation Limited claiming damages for alleged breach of contract in the amount of $3,000,000. A court decision, upheld on appeal, that there was an enforceable agreement has been rendered in favour of the plaintiff. The issue of the amount of damages has not been considered. Provision for loss is not presently determinable. Any loss would be treated as a prior period adjustment.

If a contingency arises that may result in a gain to a company and whether or not the above conditions for recognition are met, the *CICA Handbook* recommendations prohibit the accrual of the gain.

Current Liabilities

Current liabilities are those due within one year, or the current operating cycle if more than one year. They include accounts payable to creditors, payroll accruals, short-term notes payable, taxes payable, and a few others. Current liabilities are continually discharged and replaced with new ones in the course of business operations.

These obligations may not be paid for several weeks or months after the current balance sheet date. Their present value is therefore less than the amount that will be paid. Nevertheless, these items are shown at the full amount to be paid, because the difference is usually so small that separate accounting for the difference and subsequent interest expense is judged not worth the trouble.

Accounts Payable to Creditors

Companies seldom pay for goods and services when received. Payment is usually deferred until a bill is received from the supplier. Even then, the bill might not be paid immediately, but instead, accumulated with other bills until a specified time of the month when all bills are paid. Because explicit interest is not paid on these accounts, management tries to obtain as much capital as possible from its creditors by delaying payment as long as possible. Failure to pay creditors according to schedule can, however, lead to poor credit ratings and to restrictions on future credit.

Wages, Salaries, and Other Payroll Items

When employees earn wages, they owe part of their earnings to governments for income and other taxes. Employees may also owe other amounts for union dues and insurance plans. The amounts, although wage expense of the employer, are not paid directly to employees, but are paid on their behalf to the governments, unions, and insurance companies.

In addition, the employer must pay various payroll taxes and may have agreed to pay for other fringe benefits because wages were earned. Employers owe Unemployment Insurance and Canada Pension Plan (CPP) contributions, whose rates vary over time; the amounts used in this book are approximately correct.

Employers in most provinces are required to provide paid vacations or vacation pay to employees. The employer must accrue the costs of the earned but unused vacations (including the payroll taxes and fringe benefits on them) at the time the employees earn them, not the later time when employees take vacations and are paid. In this way, the accountant will charge each quarter of the year with a portion of the cost of vacations, rather than allocating all to the summer when most employees take the majority of their vacation days.

Example 9 Assume that employees earn $100,000, that the employees' withholding rates for income taxes average 24 percent and that employees owe eight percent of their wages for Unemployment Insurance and CPP. In addition, employees, in aggregate, owe $500 for union dues to be withheld by the employer and $3,000 for health insurance plans.

The employer must make Unemployment Insurance and CPP payments of $9,400 and $4,500 to provide life and health insurance coverage. Employees have earned vacation pay estimated to be $4,000; estimated employer payroll taxes and fringe benefits are 18 percent of the gross amount.

The journal entries below record these wages. If some of the wages were earned by production workers, some of the debits would be to Work-in-Process Inventory, rather than to Wage and Salaries Expense. Although three journal entries are used (one for payments to employees, one for employer payroll taxes, and one for the accrual for estimated vacation pay), in practice these might be prepared as 11 separate entries or even as a single entry.

Wages and Salaries Expense	$100,000	
Withholding Taxes Payable		$24,000
Payroll Taxes Payable		8,000
Withheld Dues Payable to Union		500
Insurance Premiums Payable		3,000
Wages and Salaries Payable		64,500
Record wage expense.		
Wages and Salaries Expense	$13,900	
Payroll Taxes Payable		$ 9,400
Insurance Premiums Payable		4,500
Employer's expense for amounts not payable directly to employees.		
Wages and Salaries Expense	$ 4,720	
Estimated Vacation Wages and Fringes Payable		$ 4,720
Estimate of vacation pay and fringes thereon earned during the current period: .18 × $4,000 = $720.		

On payday, the employer pays $64,500 to employees, discharging the direct liability to them. The employer writes cheques at various times to the federal government, the union, and the insurance companies. The insurance might be paid in advance with the debit being made to Prepaid Insurance; if so, the credits when wages are recorded will be to the Prepaid Insurance account. The amounts paid to employees taking vacation are debited to the liability account, Estimated Vacation Wages and Fringes Payable, not to an expense account.

Short-Term Notes and Interest Payable

Businesses obtain interim financing for less than a year from banks or other creditors in return for a short-term note called a *note payable*. Chapter 7 discusses such notes from the point of view of the lender, or note holder. The treatment of these notes by the borrower is the mirror image of the treatment by the lender. Where the lender records an asset, the borrower records a liability. When the lender records interest receivable and revenue, the borrower records interest payable and expense.

Income Taxes Payable

Businesses organized as corporations must pay income taxes based on their taxable income from business activities. In contrast, business entities organized as partnerships or sole proprietorships do not pay income taxes. Instead, the income of the business entity is taxed to the individual partners or sole proprietor. Each partner or sole proprietor adds his or her share of business income to income from all other (nonbusiness) sources in preparing an individual income tax return.

The details of the income tax on corporations are subject to change. The rates and schedules of payments mentioned below should not be taken as an indication of the exact procedure in force at any particular time, but rather as an indication of the type of accounting procedures that are involved. Throughout the remainder of the text, an income tax rate of 40 percent is used in almost all illustrations for ease of calculation.

Companies must pay income taxes on a monthly basis throughout the year. The monthly installment is based on the lesser of the amount paid in the prior year or the company's estimate of the taxes to be paid during the current year. The final payment for a year is made two or three months after the fiscal year-end. This is frequently described as "pay-as-you-go" taxation.

Example 10 The fiscal year of Bongo Ltd. begins on January 1 and ends on December 31. The Year 6 income tax payable by Bongo Ltd. was $60,000 and the company estimates the Year 7 income tax payable will be $45,000. The company is required to make 12 monthly payments of $3,750 ($= \frac{1}{12} \times \$45,000$) commencing in January, Year 7, as Year 7 income tax installments. A final payment, equal to the taxes payable according to the income tax return (say $47,000) less the 12 installments, is due on March 31, Year 8.

The journal entries made for Bongo Ltd. to record Year 6 income tax related transactions follow:

Year 7			
Monthly Entry	Income Tax Payable — Year 7	$ 3,750	
	Cash		$ 3,750
	To record the instalment payments on Year 7 income tax ($^1/_{12} \times \$45,000$).		
December	Income Tax Expense	$47,000	
	Income Tax Payable — Year 7		$47,000
	To record Year 7 income tax payable		
Year 8			
March 31	Income Tax Payable — Year 7	$ 2,000	
	Cash		$ 2,000
	To record the final payment due on Year 7 income tax [$47,000 − (12 × $3,750)]		

Deferred Performance Liabilities

Another current liability arises when customers make advance payments for goods or services to be delivered in the future. This liability, unlike the preceding ones, is discharged by delivering goods or services rather than by paying cash. This liability represents "unearned" and, therefore, unrecognized, revenue; that is, cash is received before the goods or services are furnished to the customer.

An example of this type of liability is the advance sale of theatre tickets, say, for $200. Upon the sale, the following entry is made:

Cash	$200	
Advances from Customers		$200
To record sale of tickets for future performances.		

These deferred performance obligations qualify as liabilities. The account credited is called Advances from Customers or Liability for Advance Sales. After the theatre performance, or after the tickets have expired, revenue is recognized and the liability is removed by recording the following entry:

Advances from Customers	$200	
Performance Revenue		$200
Service has been rendered and revenue is recognized.		

Deferred performance liabilities also arise in connection with the sale of magazine subscriptions, transportation tickets, and service contracts.

Product Warranties

Most firms today must guarantee the quality of their products in order to sell the product. It would be unthinkable to buy a car, or a television without such a guarantee of product performance. This guarantee is called a *product warranty* and can run from 30 days to the lifetime of the consumer.

Accounting for warranties would be trivial if entries were made only as claims were submitted. The matching principle, however, attempts to place the estimated cost of warranty service on sales in the same income statement as the associated revenue. A firm must thus estimate two quantities: the percentage of units sold that will come back for service in the warranty period, and the average cost of honouring each warranty claim.

Assume that Eckel Ltd. sells cellular phones for $2,000 each and offers a one-year warranty against defects. Past experience indicates that 4% of the units will prove defective and the average repair cost for each is $70. This past year, 40,000 phones were sold and 500 of these have already been returned for service. The accrued liability for product warranties at the end of the year would be calculated as follows:

Number of units sold	40,000
Rate of defective units	×.04
Total units expected to fail	1,600
Less units already failed	500
Number of units sold this year expected to still fail in warranty period ...	1,100
Average repair cost per unit	$70
Estimated liability for product warranties at year end	$77,000

The journal entry at year end would be

Product Warranty Expense	$77,000	
Estimated Liability for Product Warranty		$77,000

As each unit subsequently is brought in for repair the liability would be debited and the credit would go to Cash, Supplies, Labour, etc.

The bad guys vs. the good guys

Nelson Luscombe, CA

At the XIII World Congress of Accountants in Tokyo last October (covered in this issue), Akio Morita, co-founder and chairman of the giant Sony Corporation, opened his keynote address with an anecdote about his most memorable "tangle" with the accounting profession.

Sony, then in its infancy, was struggling to establish itself in a war-ravaged country, and Morita and his co-founder, Masaru Ibuka, decided the ideal product to make its reputation with was a machine that could record sound on a long piece of magnetic tape.

"We were set on developing and manufacturing Japan's first tape-recorder," Morita explained, "although at the time we didn't even know what material the tape should be made of. We were confident, however, that if we succeeded, our prospects would be promising.

"We took our idea to our chief (in fact, our only) financial officer. He listened carefully to our plan and then proceeded to show us that, based on our financial situation at the time, and the development cost we had projected, it would be disastrous if we were to commit ourselves to such an expensive high-risk venture.

"It looked as though our first step toward the development of Japan's first tape recorder would have to be the development of our chief financial officer. So Mr. Ibuka and I invited this gentlemen out one evening for what we called a 'discussion'—to a cozy little restaurant next to our office. At that time, the only way to obtain 'alcoholic instruments of persuasion' was on the black market, but on this occasion, we considered it an R&D cost.

"Well, it was a good discussion, and by the end of the evening we'd managed to convince our CFO that the tape-recorder wasn't really such a dangerous idea after all. That was my first indication that numbers sometimes look different at different times."

That incident may be 40 years old, but it illustrates a characteristic of accountants criticized even today. Morita wasn't really referring to any tendency on the part of accountants to succumb to alcoholic persuasion. I expect we can hold our own in that regard. He was referring to the tendency of many of us to focus on costs and short-term benefits when long-term vision is called for.

"In my experience with accountants," said Morita, "when they are told of an idea for a new product, they immediately do a cost analysis. Their cost estimates, in most cases, are very high, and they are reluctant to give their support." Still, he allowed, accountants have their place.

"The tension between the product developer, who is burning with an idea, and the financial officer whose job is to keep the company from shoving all the chips into the middle of the table at one time, is a very common occurrence in business: the engineer versus the accountant; the spenders versus the savers; the good guys versus the bad guys. I am not saying which is which. The truth is, we really need each other. And if an organization is working the way it should, we complement each other."

But good management goes far beyond number crunching, says Morita. It's about taking risks—even when the numbers might speak against it.

"There is no accounting system in the world that could have justified the decision we made to commit ourselves to an extremely expensive digital-recording developmental program, for example. What numbers we did see at the time indicated we were crazy to go on with it, but we didn't seek justification.

"I think sometimes management worries too much about justification through numbers. Instead, I tell my people that good managers develop a sense of intuition, hunch or sixth sense when it comes to decision making. In order to make a rational decision, you have to know all of the facts and figures and the environment surrounding the facts. But it is impossible for a person to know everything. So in order to run the busines, I tell them, 'Take risks based on the numbers, but also have faith in your sixth sense. Don't let the facts and the figures, the elements of justification, turn you away from a new idea.' "

It's a good message for accountants everywhere to ponder as we open the page on a new year.

Reprinted with permission of CA Magazine, January 1988.

Sales Taxes

A major revenue source for provinces in Canada is the imposition of a *sales tax* on the sale of goods and services. Although the tax is imposed on the consumer, the provinces force retailers to act as collection agents for the government and periodically remit these taxes back to the government. Assume that a particular product selling for $1000 is subject to a 6% sales tax. The sale is recorded as follows:

Cash (or Accounts Receivable)	$1,060	
Sales		1,000
Retail Sales Tax Payable		60

When remittance is made to the government, the liability is debited and cash credited. Governments may allow the retailer to retain a small portion of the tax collected as partial compensation for the expense incurred in collecting it.

Long-Term Liabilities

The principal long-term liabilities are mortgages, notes, bonds, and leases. The significant differences between long-term and short-term, or current, liabilities are that: (1) interest on long-term liabilities is ordinarily paid at regular intervals during the life of a long-term obligation, whereas interest on short-term debt is usually paid in a lump sum at maturity; (2a) the principal of long-term obligations is often paid back in installments, or (2b) special funds are accumulated by the borrower for retiring long-term liabilities.

Accounting for all long-term liabilities generally follows the same procedures. Those procedures are outlined next and illustrated throughout the rest of this chapter and the next.

Procedures for Recording Long-Term Liabilities

Long-term liabilities are initially recorded at the present value of all promised payments to be made using the market interest rate at the time the liability is incurred. This market interest rate is also used to compute the amount of interest expense throughout the life of the liability. A portion (perhaps all) of each cash payment represents interest expense. Any excess of cash payment over interest expense is used to reduce the liability itself (often called the *principal*). If a given payment is not sufficient to discharge the entire interest expense that has accrued since the last payment date, then the liability principal increases by the excess of interest expense over cash payment.

Retirement of long-term liabilities can occur in several ways, but the process is the same. The net amount shown on the books for the obligation is debited, the asset given up in return (usually cash) is credited, and any difference is recognized as a gain or loss on retirement of the debt.

Mortgages and Interest-Bearing Notes

In most Canadian provinces a mortgage is considered a lien on property, which may be registered with a government agency as security for a loan made by the "mortgagee" to the borrower. The lien may be removed when the mortgage is paid in full. The mortgaged property is collateral for the loan.[3] The customary terminology designates the lender as the "mortgagee" and the borrower as the "mortgagor."[4]

As long as the mortgagor meets the obligations under the mortgage agreement, the mortgagee does not have the ordinary rights of an owner to possess and use the property. If the mortgagor defaults on either the principal or interest payments, the mortgagee can usually arrange to have the property sold for his or her benefit through a process called *foreclosure*. The mortgagee has first rights to the proceeds from the foreclosure sale for satisfying any unpaid claim. If there is an excess, it is paid to the

---

[3]Accountants are generally careful to use the word *collateral*, rather than *security*, in this context. Whether the loan is "secured" is a matter of legal judgment; moreover, accountants do not wish to imply that the value of the collateral will be sufficient to satisfy the debt, as "secured" might imply.

[4]When you borrow money to finance your home purchase, you give the bank a mortgage, not vice versa.

mortgagor. If the proceeds are insufficient to pay the remaining loan, the lender becomes an unsecured creditor of the borrower for the unpaid balance.

A note is similar to a mortgage except that no property is typically pledged as collateral.

Accounting for Mortgages and Interest-Bearing Notes

Some of the more common problems in accounting for mortgages are presented in the following illustration.

On October 1, Year 1, the Western Co. Ltd. borrows $125,000 for five years from the Home Insurance Company to obtain funds for additional working capital. As collateral, Western Co. Ltd., gives Home Insurance Company a mortgage on several parcels of land that it owns and that are on its books at a cost of $50,000. Interest is charged on the unpaid balance of the loan principal at an interest rate of 12 percent per year compounded semiannually. Payments are due on April 1 and October 1 of each year. Western agrees to make ten payments over the five years of the mortgage so that when the last payment is made on October 1, Year 6, the loan and all interest will have been paid. The first nine payments are to be $17,000 each. The tenth payment is to be just large enough to discharge the balance of the loan. The Western Co. Ltd. closes its books annually on December 31. (The derivation of the semiannual payment of $17,000 is shown in Example 11 in Appendix B, page 800.)

The entries from the time the mortgage is issued through December 31, Year 2, are as follows:

10/1/Year 1	Cash	$125,000	
	Mortgage Payable		$125,000
	Loan obtained from Home Insurance Company for 5 years at 12 percent compounded semiannually.		

As Example 11 in Appendix B shows, $125,000 is approximately equal to the present value of 10 semiannual cash payments of $17,000, each discounted at 12 percent compounded semiannually.

12/31/Year 1	Interest Expense	$3,750	
	Interest Payable		$3,750
	Adjusting entry: Interest expense on mortgage from 10/1/Year 1 to 12/31/Year 1		

Interest expense on the loan for the first six months is $7,500 ($= .06 \times \$125,000$). To simplify the calculations, accounting typically assumes that the interest accrues evenly over the six-month period. Thus, interest expense for October, November, and December is half of the $7,500, or $3,750.

4/1/Year 2	Interest Expense	$3,750	
	Interest Payable	3,750	
	Mortgage Payable	9,500	
	Cash		$17,000

Cash payment made requires an entry. Interest expense on mortgage from 1/1/Year 2 to 4/1/Year 2, payment of 6 months' interest, and reduction of loan by the difference, $17,000 − $7,500 = $9,500.

After the cash payment on April 1, Year 2, the unpaid principal of the loan is $115,500 (= $125,000 − $9,500). Interest expense during the second six-month period is based on this unpaid principal amount.

10/1/Year 2	Interest Expense	$ 6,930	
	Mortgage Payable	10,070	
	Cash		$17,000

Cash payment made requires an entry. Interest expense for the period 4/1/Year 2 to 10/1/Year 2 is $6,930 [= .12 × ($125,000 − $9,500) × $\frac{1}{2}$]. The loan is reduced by the difference, $17,000 − $6,930 = $10,070.

12/31/Year 2	Interest Expense	$3,163	
	Interest Payable		$3,163

Adjusting entry: Interest expense from 10/1/Year 2 to 12/31/Year 2 = [.12 × ($125,000 − $9,500 − $10,070) × $\frac{3}{12}$].

Amortization Schedule

Exhibit 10.1 presents an "amortization schedule" for this mortgage. For each period it shows the balance at the beginning of the period, the interest for the period, the payment for the period, the reduction in principal for the period, and the balance at the end of the period. (The last payment, $16,782 in this case, often differs slightly from the others because of the cumulative effect of rounding errors.) *All* long-term liabilities have analogous amortization schedules, which aid in understanding the timing of payments to discharge the liability. Amortization schedules for various long-term liabilities appear throughout this chapter and the next.

Exhibit 10.1
Amortization Schedule for $125,000 Mortgage (or Note),
Repaid in 10 Semiannual Installments of $17,000,
Interest Rate of 12 Percent, Compounded Semiannually

6-Month Period (1)	Loan Balance Start of Period (2)	Interest Expense for Period (3)	Payment (4)	Portion of Payment Reducing Principal (5)	Loan Balance End of Period (6)
0					$125,000
1	$125,000	$7,500	$17,000	$ 9,500	115,500
2	115,500	6,930	17,000	10,070	105,430
3	105,430	6,326	17,000	10,674	94,756
4	94,756	5,685	17,000	11,315	83,441
5	83,441	5,006	17,000	11,994	71,448
6	71,448	4,287	17,000	12,713	58,734
7	58,734	3,524	17,000	13,476	45,259
8	45,259	2,715	17,000	14,285	30,974
9	30,974	1,858	17,000	15,142	15,832
10	15,832	950	16,782	15,832	0

Note: In preparing this table, calculations were rounded to the nearest cent. Then, for presentation, results are rounded
   to the nearest dollar.
Column (2) = Column (6) from Previous Period.
Column (3) = .06 × Column (2).
Column (4)   Given, except row 10, where it is the amount such that Column (4) = Column (2) + Column (3).
Column (5) = Column (4) − Column (3).
Column (6) = Column (2) − Column (5).

Bonds

Whenever funds can be borrowed from one lender, the firm usually issues mortgages
or notes. When larger amounts are needed, the firm may have to borrow from the
general investing public with a bond issue. Bonds are used primarily by corporations
and governmental units. The distinctive features of a bond issue are as follows:

1. A *bond indenture*, or agreement, is drawn up that shows in detail the terms of the
   loan and the rights and duties of the borrower and other parties to the contract.
   Bond indentures typically limit the borrower's right to declare dividends and to
   make other distributions to owners in order to provide better protection to
   bondholders.
2. *Bond certificates* are used. Engraved certificates are prepared, each one representing a portion of the total loan. The usual minimum denomination in business
   practice is $1,000, although smaller denominations are occasionally used. Some
   government bonds are issued in denominations as small as $50.
3. If property is pledged as collateral for the loan (as in a mortgage bond), then a
   trustee is named to represent the bondholders and is usually a trust company.
4. An agent is appointed, usually a trust company, to act as *registrar* and *disbursing
   agent*. The borrower deposits interest and principal payments with the disbursing agent, who distributes the funds to the bondholders.

5. Most bonds are *coupon bonds*. Coupons attached to the bond certificate represent promises to make interest payments throughout the life of the bond. When a coupon comes due, the bondholder cuts it off and deposits it with a bank. The bank sends the coupon through the bank clearing system to the disbursing agent for payment, which is deposited in the bondholder's account at the bank.

6. Bonds are frequently *registered as to principal*, which means that the holder's name appears on the bond certificate and on the records of the registrar. Sometimes both the principal and interest of bonds are registered, in which case the interest payments are mailed directly to the bondholder and coupons are not used. Registered bonds are easily replaced if lost, but the transfer from one holder to another is cumbersome. Unregistered bonds may be transferred merely by delivery, whereas registered bonds have to be assigned formally from one holder to another.

7. The entire bond issue is usually issued by the borrower to an investment banking firm, or to a group of investment bankers known as a *syndicate*, which takes over the responsibility of reselling the bonds to the investing public. Members of the syndicate usually bear the risks and rewards of interest-rate fluctuations during the period while the bonds are being sold to the public.

Types of Bonds

Mortgage bonds carry a mortgage on real estate as collateral for the repayment of the loan. *Collateral trust bonds* are usually secured by shares and bonds of other corporations. The most common type of corporate bond, except in the railroad and public utility industries, is the *debenture bond*. This type carries no special collateral; instead, it is issued on the general credit of the business. To give added protection to the bondholders, provisions are usually included in the bond indenture that limit the dividends that can be declared or the amount of subsequent long-term debt that can be incurred. *Convertible bonds* are debentures that the holder can exchange, possibly after some specific period of time has elapsed, for a specific number of shares. A detailed discussion of accounting for convertible bonds is presented in Chapter 12.

Almost all bonds provide for the payment of interest at regular intervals, usually semiannually. The amount of interest is typically expressed as a percentage of the principal. For example, a 12-percent, ten-year, semiannual coupon bond with face amount of $1,000 promises to pay $60 every six months. Here, we assume, the first payment occurs six months after the issue date. A total of 20 payments are made. At the time of the final $60 coupon payment, the $1,000 principal is also due. The coupon rate is 12 percent in this case. The principal amount of a bond is its face, or par, value. The terms *face value* and *par value* are synonymous in this context. In general, the par value multiplied by the coupon rate equals the amount of cash paid per *year*, whether in quarterly, semiannual, or annual installments. By far the majority of corporate bonds provide for semiannual coupon payments. A bond can be issued and subsequently traded in the marketplace for amounts below par, at par, or above par.

Proceeds of a Bond Issue

The amount received by the borrower will usually differ from the par value of the bonds issued. The difference arises because the coupon rate printed on the bond certificates differs from the interest rate the market requires given the risk of the borrower, the general level of interest rates in the economy, and other factors. Whatever the market rate, at time of issue or at any time thereafter, the annual cash payments for a bond remain the product of the face value multiplied by the coupon rate. If the coupon rate is less than the rate the market requires the firm to pay, then the bonds will sell for less than par. The difference between par and selling price is called the *discount* on the bond. The issuer will pay the full amount at maturity. The difference between the face amount and the initial issue proceeds is part of the interest the market requires the borrower to pay. Even though the payment occurs at maturity, the accounting procedures are designed to record that interest systematically over the life of the bond. If the coupon rate is larger than the rate the market requires, then the bonds will sell above par. The difference between selling price and par is called the *premium* on the bond.

The presence of a discount or premium in and of itself indicates nothing about the credit standing of the borrower. A firm with a credit standing that would enable it to borrow funds at 11 percent might issue ten-percent bonds that would sell at a discount, whereas another firm with a lower credit standing, that would require it to pay 11.5 percent on loans, might issue bonds at 14 percent that would sell at a premium.

Issued at Par The Macaulay Corporation issues $100,000 face value of 12-percent semiannual coupon debenture bonds. The bonds are dated July 1, Year 1. The principal amount is repayable on July 1, Year 6 or five years later. Interest payments (coupons) are due on July 1 and January 1 of each year. The coupon payments promised at each interest payment date total $6,000. Figure 10.1 presents a time line for the two sets of cash flows associated with this bond. Assuming that the issue was taken by Penman & Co. Inc., investment banker, on July 1, Year 1, at a rate to yield 12 percent compounded semiannually, the calculation of the proceeds to Macaulay would be as follows. (Appendix B at the back of the book explains the present value calculations.)

Figure 10.1
Time Line for 5-Year Semiannual Coupon Bonds, 12-Percent
Annual Coupons. $100,000 Par Value Issued at Par.

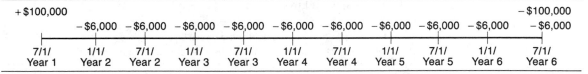

The issue price would be stated as 100.0 (that is, 100 percent of par), which implies that the market interest rate was 12 percent compounded semiannually, the same as the coupon rate.

(a) Present value of $100,000 to be paid at the end of 5 years . . . . $ 55,839
   (Appendix C, Table C.2, page 815, shows the present value of $1 to be
   received in 10 periods at 6 percent per period to be $.55839;
   $100,000 × .55839 = $55,839.)

(b) Present value of $6,000 to be paid each 6 months for 5 years   44,161
   (Appendix C, Table C.4, page 817, shows the present value of an ordinary
   annuity of $1 per period for 10 periods discounted at 6 percent to be
   $7.36009; $6,000 × 7.36009 = $44.161.)

Total Proceeds $100,000

Issued at Less than Par Assume that these same bonds were issued at a price to
yield 14 percent compounded semiannually. The promised cash flows after July 1,
Year 1, associated with these bonds (payments of periodic interest plus repayment of
principal) are identical to those in the time line shown in Figure 10.1. These future
cash flows would be discounted to their present value, however, using a 14 percent
discount rate compounded semiannually. The calculation of the issue proceeds (that
is, initial market price) would be as follows. (Why it is that ''12-percent'' bonds
can be issued to yield 14 percent is discussed below on pages 504 and 505.)

(a) Present value of $100,000 to be paid at the end of 5 years $50,835
   (Present value of $1 to be received in 10 periods at 7 percent per period is
   $0.50835; $100,000 × 0.50835 = $50,835.)

(b) Present value of $6,000 to be paid each 6 months for 5 years   42,141
   (Present value of an ordinary annuity of $1 per period for 10 periods, discounted
   at 7 percent per period = $7,02358; $6,000 × 7.02358 = $42,141.)

   Total Proceeds $92,976

If the issue price were stated on a conventional pricing basis in the market at 92.98
(92.98 percent of par), the issuing price would be $92,980. This amount implies a
market yield of slightly less than 14 percent compounded semiannually.

Issued at More than Par Assume that the bonds were issued at a price to yield ten
percent compounded semiannually. The cash flows, after July 1, Year 1, would again be
identical to those shown in Figure 10.1. They would be discounted at ten percent
compounded semiannually to calculate their present value. The calculation of the
proceeds would be as follows:

(a) Present value of $100,000 to be paid at the end of 5 years . . . . $ 61,391
   (Present value of $1 to be received in 10 periods at 5 percent per period is
   $0.61391; $100,000 × 0.61391 = $61,391.)

(b) Present value of $6,000 to be paid each 6 months for 5 years   46,330
   (Present value of an ordinary annuity of $1 per period for 10 periods,
   discounted at 5 percent per period = $7.72173;
   $6,000 × 7.72173 = $46,330.)

Total Proceeds $107,721

If the issue price were stated on a conventional pricing basis in the market at 107.72 (107.72 percent of par), the issuing price would be $107.720.[5] The price would imply a market yield of slightly more than ten percent compounded semiannually.

Bond Tables

These tedious calculations need not be made every time a bond issue is analyzed. *Bond tables* show the results of calculations like those just described. Examples of such tables are included in Tables C.5 and C.6 on pages 818 and 819. Table C.5 shows the price for ten-percent, semiannual coupon bonds as a percent of par for various market interest rates (yields) and years to maturity. Table 6 shows market rates and implied prices for 12-percent, semiannual coupon bonds. (Some modern electronic calculators make the calculations represented by these tables in a few seconds.)

The percentages of par shown in these tables represent the present value of the bond indicated. Because the factors are expressed as a percent of par, they have to be multiplied by ten to find the price of a $1,000 bond. If you have never used bond tables before now, turn to Table C.6 and find in the fifth-year row the three different prices for the three different market yields used in the preceding examples. Notice further that a bond will sell at par if, and only if, it has a market yield equal to its coupon rate.

These tables are useful whether a bond is being issued by a corporation or resold later by an investor. The approach to computing the market price will be the same in either case, although the years to maturity will be less than the original term of the bond when it is resold. The following generalizations can be made regarding bond prices:

1. When the market interest rate equals the coupon rate, the market price will equal par.
2. When the market interest rate is greater than the coupon rate, the market price will be less than par.
3. When the market interest rate is less than the coupon rate, the market price will be greater than par.

Accounting for Bonds Issued at Par

The following illustration covers the more common problems associated with bonds issued at par.

---

[5]In many contexts, bond prices are quoted in dollars plus thirty-seconds of a dollar. A bond selling for about 107.721 percent of par would be quoted at $107\frac{23}{32}$, which would be written as 107.23. In order to read published bond prices, you must know whether the information after the "decimal" point refers to fractions expressed in one-hundredths or in thirty-seconds. (If you are reading published bond prices and see any number larger than 31 after the decimal point, then you can be sure that one-hundredths are being used. If you see many prices, but none of the numbers shown after the point is larger than 31, then you can be reasonably sure that thirty-seconds are being used.)

We use the data presented in the previous sections for the Macaulay Corporation, where the bonds were issued at par and we assume that the books are closed semi-annually on June 30 and December 31. The entry at the time of issue would be:

7/1/Year 1	Cash	$100,000	
	Debenture Bonds Payable		$100,000
	$100,000 of 12-percent, 5-year bonds issued at par.		

The entries for interest would be made at the end of the accounting period and on the interest payment dates. Entries through January 1, Year 2 would be:

12/31/Year 1	Interest Expense	$6,000	
	Interest Payable		$6,000
	To accrue 6 months' interest.		
1/1/Year 2	Interest Payable	$6,000	
	Cash		$6,000
	To record payment of 6 months' interest.		

Bond Issued between Interest Payment Dates The actual date that a bond is issued seldom coincides with one of the payment dates. Assuming these same bonds were actually brought to market on September 1, rather than July 1, and were issued at par, the purchaser of the bond would be expected to pay Macaulay Corporation for two months' interest in advance. After all, on the first coupon Macaulay Corporation promises a full $60, for six months' interest, but would have had the use of the borrowed funds for only four months. The purchasers of the bonds would pay $100,000 plus two months' interest of $1,000 (= .12 × $100,000 × $\frac{2}{12}$) and would get the $2,000 back when the first coupons are redeemed. The journal entries made by Macaulay Corporation, the issuer, would be:

9/1/Year 1	Cash	$102,000	
	Bonds Payable		$100,000
	Interest Payable		2,000
	To record issue of bonds at par between interest payment dates. The purchasers pay an amount equal to interest for the first 2 months but will get it back when the first coupons are redeemed.		

Accounting for Bonds Issued at Less than Par

The following illustrates the more common problems associated with bonds issued for less than par.

Assume the data presented for the Macaulay Corporation, where 12-percent, $100,000-par value, five-year bonds were issued to yield approximately 14 percent compounded semiannually. The issue price was shown previously to be $92,976. The journal entry at the time of issue would be:

7/1/Year 1	Cash	$92,976	
	Discount on Debenture Bonds Payable[6]	7,024	
	Debenture Bonds Payable		$100,000
	$100,000 of 12-percent, 5-year bonds issued at 92.476.		

The issuance of these bonds for $92,976, instead of the $100,000 par value, indicates that 12 percent is not a sufficiently high rate of interest for the bonds to induce purchasers to pay the full par value in the open market. If purchasers of these bonds paid the full $100,000 par value, they would earn only 12 percent compounded semiannually, the coupon rate. Purchasers desiring a rate of return of 14 percent will postpone their purchases until the market price drops to $92,976. At this price, purchasers of the bonds will earn the 14 percent return they require. The return will be composed of ten $6,000 coupon payments over the next five years plus $7,024 (= $100,000 − $92,976) as part of the payment at maturity.

For Macaulay Corporation, the total interest expense over the life of the bonds is equal to $67,024 (periodic interest payments totaling $60,000 plus $7,024 paid at maturity). Two methods of allocating the total interest expense of $67,024 to the periods of the loan are the effective-interest method and the straight-line method.

Interest Expense under the Effective-Interest Method

Under the effective interest method, interest *expense* each period is equal to the market interest rate at the time that bonds were initially issued (14 percent compounded semiannually in this example) multiplied by the *net book value* of the liability[7] at the

---

[6]Bond discount may be considered a contra liability account, reducing the liability below its face (redemption) value, or as a deferred charge classified as a noncurrent asset. The advocates of the contra liability view consider that the liability should be shown at the present value of the bond face value discounted at the bond yield rate at the date of issue. This objective is accomplished by deducting the bond discount from the face value on the balance sheet. The advocates of the deferred charge view consider that bond discount represents a prepayment of interest by the company at the issue date in lieu of larger regular interest payments over the life of the bond. Further, they declare that the liability to repay is the face value and may become due at any time if the company fails to meet its interest payments and other commitments. Consequently, the liability is shown at its face value and the discount as a noncurrent asset at amortized value. *CICA Handbook* Sections 1520 and 3070 imply that the deferred charge alternative be adopted. To be consistent, unamortized bond premium would be considered as a deferred credit.

[7]The net book value is par value of bonds payable less bond discount, or plus bond premium.

The Credit Card Mentality

*O*ur nation thrives on credit. Most sales today are on credit. Chapter 7 deals with sales on account and the need to establish valuation allowances. fortunately, this problem is disappearing for most companies that sell at the retail level. Instead of setting up accounts in the store for customers and worrying about collectibility, we just say "will that be cash or charge?" (that is, "will it be cash or Visa, Mastercard, or American Express?"). For a fixed monthly fee these credit card companies take the worry out of sales—collectibility is their problem.

Today, civilization as we know it could not exist without the credit card. The colour of your card is even a symbol of your social status. "Some people need an American Express Gold Card and its $10,000 limit of pure power. Others need that platinum card with its $100,000 spending limit to feel really powerful."

A new credit card is out that puts all others to shame. A plastic card has been issued to members of the United States Congress which members insert into a computer terminal to vote on bills. As Congressman DioGuardi says:

"I've got a card that puts those two to shame. My Congressional voting card. This is the most expensive credit card in the world. The card has no limit . . . Last year our national debt reached 2 trillion dollars—the established limit. And what did we do? We decided to raise the limit. You see, we've got a credit card mentality in this country."

Adapted from The Financial Executive Sept./Oct. 1988 "Why doesn't the government understand accounting?" Diogardi, pp. 27–31.

---

beginning of the interest period. For example, interest expense for the period from July 1, Year 1 to December 31, Year 1, the first six-month period, is $6,508 [= .07 × ($100,000 − $7,024)]. The bond indenture provides that only $6,000 (= .06 × $100,000) need be paid on January 2, Year 2. This amount is equal to the coupon rate times the par value of the bonds. The difference between the interest expense of $6,508 and the interest currently payable of $6,000 is deducted from bond discount. The journal entry made on December 31, Year 1 to recognize interest for the last six months of Year 1 is:

12/31/Year 1	Interest Expense	$6,508	
	Interest Payable		$6,000
	Discount on Debenture Bonds Payable		508
	To recognize interest expense for 6 months.		

The Interest Payable account would be shown as a current liability on the balance sheet at the end of Year 1. Discount on Debenture Bonds Payable of $6,516 (= $7,024 − $508) would be reported as a noncurrent asset.

On January 2, Year 2, the first periodic cash payment is made.

1/2/Year 2	Interest Payable	$6,000	
	Cash		$6,000
	To record payment of interest for 6 months.		

Interest expense for the second six months, from January 1, Year 2 through June 30, Year 2, is $6,544 (= .07 × $93,484). Interest expense for the second six months of $6,544 is larger than the $6,508 for the first six months because the recorded net book value of the liability at the beginning of the second six months is larger. The journal entry on July 1, Year 2 to record interest expense is:

7/1/Year 2	Interest Expense	$6,544	
	Interest Payable		$6,000
	Discount on Debenture Bonds Payable		544
	To recognize interest expense for 6 months.		

An amortization schedule for these bonds over their five-year life is shown in Exhibit 10.2.

Exhibit 10.2
Effective-Interest Amortization Schedule for $100,000 of 12-Percent, 5-Year Bonds Issued for 92.976 Percent of Par To Yield 14 Percent, Interest Payable Semiannually

Semiannual Journal Entry
Dr. Interest Expense .... Amount in Column (3)
   Cr. Cash .... Amount in Column (4)
   Cr. Discount on Debenture Bonds Payable .. Amount in Column (5)

Period (6-month intervals) (1)	Net Liability at Start of Period (2)	Effective Interest: 7 Percent per Period (3)	Coupon Rate: 6 Percent of Par (4)	Bond Discount		Net Liability at End of Period (7)
				Amort- ization (5)	At End of Period (6)	
0					$7,024	$ 92,976
1	$92,976	$ 6,508	$ 6,000	$ 508	6,516	93,484
2	93,484	6,544	6,000	544	5,972	94,028
3	94,028	6,582	6,000	582	5,390	94,610
4	94,610	6,623	6,000	623	4,767	95,233
5	95,233	6,666	6,000	666	4,101	95,899
6	95,899	6,713	6,000	713	3,388	96,612
7	96,612	6,763	6,000	763	2,625	97,375
8	97,375	6,816	6,000	816	1,809	98,191
9	98,191	6,873	6,000	873	936	99,064
10	99,064	6,936	6,000	936	0	100,000
Total		$67,024	$60,000	$7,024		

Note: In preparing this table, calculations were rounded to the nearest cent. Then, for presentation, results were rounded
to the nearest dollar.
Column (2) = Column (7) from Previous Period.
Column (3) = .07 × Column (2).
Column (4)   Given.
Column (5) = Column (3) − Column (4).
Column (6) = Column (6) from Previous Period − Column (5) of This Period.
Column (7) = Column (2) + Column (5).

The effective interest method of recognizing interest expense on a bond has the following financial statement effects.

1. On the income statement, interest expense will be a constant percentage of the recorded net liability at the beginning of each interest period. This percentage will be equal to the market interest rate for these bonds when they were initially issued. When bonds are issued for less than par value, the *dollar amount* of interest expense will increase each period as the recorded net principal amount increases.

2. On the balance sheet at the end of each period, the net balance of the bonds less the unamortized discount will be the present value of the *remaining* cash outflows discounted at the market rate of interest when the bonds were initially issued. For example, on July 1, Year 2, the present value of the remaining cash payments is as follows:

Present Value of July 1, Year 2, Interest Payment	$ 6,000
Present Value of 8 remaining semiannual interest payments discounted at 14 percent, compounded semiannually (Table C.4, page 817, shows the present value of an ordinary annuity of $1 per period for 8 periods discounted at 7 percent to be $5.97130; $6,000 × 5.97130 = $35,827)	35,827
Present value of $100,000 to be paid at the end of 4 years (Table C.2, page 815, shows the present value of $1 to be paid at the end of 8 periods discounted at 7 percent to be $.58201; $100,000 × .58201 = $58,201)	58,201
Total Present Value	$100,028
Less: Amount Shown as Current Liability	6,000
Equals Par Value of Bonds Less Bond Discount	$ 94,028

The amount $94,028 appears in column (7) of Exhibit 10.2 for the net liability at the end of the second six-month period.

Interest Expense under the Straight-Line Method

The second method for recording interest expense over the life of the bond issue is the straight-line method. Under this method, total interest expense (periodic coupon payments plus any amount paid at the time of maturity) is spread evenly over the life of the bonds. In the example of Macaulay Corporation, total interest expense is $67,024 [= ($6,000 × 10) + ($100,000 − $92,976)]. Interest expense each six months will therefore be $6,702.40 (= $67,024/10). The journal entry to record interest expense at the end of each six months is:

Interest Expense	$6,702.40	
Interest Payable		$6,000.00
Discount on Debenture Bonds Payable		702.40
To recognize interest expense for 6 months.		

The straight-line method of computing interest expense is computationally easier than the effective-interest method. It has two theoretical weaknesses, however.

1. When bonds are issued for less than par value, interest expense will be a decreasing percentage of the net bond liability (par value less unamortized discount) at the beginning of each period. That is, interest expense (numerator) will be constant

but the net bond liability (denominator) will increase as the maturity date approaches. In contrast, the effective-interest method provides an amount for interest expense that is a constant percentage of the beginning-of-the-period net liability.

2. The balance sheet values of the bonds less the bond discount that are presented each period will not equal the present value of the remaining cash flows relating to the bond discounted at the historical-interest rate.

Preferred Method of Amortizing Bond Discount

In practice, many (even most) companies use the straight-line method of amortizing bond discount. Most of the accountants working in these companies were trained in the era preceding inexpensive calculating devices. They act as though the calculations required by the effective-interest method are too tedious to be done regularly. The effective-interest method may appear more difficult but it is based on the same concepts and procedures used for mortgages, explained earlier in the chapter, and for leases, to be explained later. We prefer the effective-interest method, but the difference between the two methods is not usually material.

Interest on Bonds Issued for Less than Par and the Statement of Changes in Financial Position

Recognizing interest expense on bonds issued for less than par requires special treatment in computing cash provided by operations in the statement of changes in financial position. Interest expense reported for the first six months is $6,508: $6,000 in coupon payments and $508 in decreased deferred charge. Notice that only $6,000 of cash was used for the expense. There was an increase in Interest Payable of $6,000 followed by discharge of that current liability with cash payment. The remainder of the interest expense, $508, is a decrease in the deferred charge, Discount on Debenture Bonds Payable. Consequently, there must be an *addback* to net income in computing "funds provided by operations" in the statement of changes in financial position. The amount of the addback is the amount of the expense that did not use cash, $508.

Accounting for Bonds Issued for More than Par

The following discussion illustrates the more common problems associated with bonds issued for more than par.

Assume the data presented for the Macaulay Corporation, in which 12-percent, $100,000-par value, five-year bonds were issued to yield approximately ten percent compounded semiannually. The issue price derived previously is $107,721. The journal entry at the time of issue is:

7/1/Year 1	Cash	$107,721	
	Debenture Bonds Payable		$100,000
	Premium on Debentures Bonds		
	Payable		7,721
	$100,000 of 12-percent, 5-year bonds issued at 107.721.		

The firm borrows $107,721. The issuance of these bonds for $107,721, instead of the $100,000 par value, indicates that 12 percent is a higher rate of interest for the bonds than the purchasers demand. If purchasers of these bonds paid the $100,000 par value, they would earn 12 percent compounded semiannually, the coupon rate. Purchasers requiring a rate of return of only ten percent will bid up the market price to $107,721. At this price, purchasers of the bonds will earn only the ten-percent demanded return. The return comprises ten $6,000 coupon payments over the next five years reduced by $7,721 (= $107,721 − $100,000) lent but not repaid at maturity.

For Macaulay Corporation, the total interest expense over the life of the bonds is equal to $52,279 (periodic interest payments totaling $60,000 less $7,721 not repaid at maturity.) Two methods of allocating the total interest expense of $52,279 to the periods of the loan are the effective-interest method and the straight-line method.

Interest Expense under the Effective-Interest Method

Under the effective-interest method, interest *expense* each period is equal to the market interest rate at the time the bonds were initially issued (ten percent compounded semiannually in this example) multiplied by the net recorded liability at the beginning of the interest period. For example, interest expense for the period from July 1, Year 1 to December 31, Year 1, the first six-month period, is $5,386 [= .05 × ($100,000 + $7,721)]. The bond indenture provides that $6,000 (= .06 × $100,000) be paid on January 1, Year 2. This amount is equal to the coupon rate times the par value of the bonds. The difference between the payment of $6,000 and the interest expense of $5,386 reduces the amount to be paid at maturity. The journal entry made on December 31, Year 1, to recognize interest for the last six months of Year 1 is:

12/31/Year 1	Interest Expense	$5,386	
	Premium on Debenture Bonds Payable . . .	614	
	Interest Payable		$6,000
	To recognize interest expense for 6 months.		

The Interest Payable account would be shown as a current liability on the balance sheet at the end of Year 1. Debenture Bonds Payable of $100,000 and Premium on Debenture Bonds Payable of $7,107 (= $7,721 − $614) appear as noncurrent liabilities.

On January 1, Year 2, the first periodic cash payment is made.

1/01/Year 2	Interest Payable	$6,000	
	Cash		$6,000
	To record payment of interest for 6 months.		

Interest expense for the second six months, from January 1, Year 2 through June 30, Year 2 is $5,355 (= .05 × $107,107). Interest expense for the second six months of $5,355 is smaller than the $5,386 for the first six months because the unpaid balance of the net liability at the beginning of the second six months is smaller. The journal entry on June 30, Year 2 to record interest expense is:

7/01/Year 2	Interest Expense	$5,355	
	Premium on Debenture Bonds Payable . . .	645	
	Interest Payable		$6,000
	To recognize interest expense for 6 months.		

An amortization schedule for these bonds over their five-year life appears in Exhibit 10.3.

The effective-interest method of recognizing interest expense on a bond has the following financial statement effects.

Exhibit 10.3
Effective-Interest Amortization Schedule for $100,000 of 12-Percent,
5-Year Bonds Issued for 107.721 Percent of Par To Yield 10 Percent,
Interest Payable Semiannually

Semiannual Journal Entry
Dr. Interest Expense . . . . Amount in Column (3)
Dr. Premium on Debenture Bonds Payable . . . . Amount in Column (5)
  Cr. Cash . . . . Amount in Column (4)

Period (6-month intervals) (1)	Net Liability at Start of Period (2)	Effective Interest: 5 Percent per Period (3)	Coupon Rate: 6 Percent of Par (4)	Bond Premium Amort- ization (5)	At End of Period (6)	Net Liability at End of Period (7)
0					$7,721	$107,721
1	$107,721	$ 5,386	$ 6,000	$ 614	7,107	107,107
2	107,107	5,355	6,000	645	6,462	106,462
3	106,462	5,323	6,000	677	5,785	105,785
4	105,785	5,289	6,000	711	5,074	105,074
5	105,074	5,254	6,000	746	4,328	104,328
6	104,328	5,216	6,000	784	3,544	103,544
7	103,544	5,177	6,000	823	2,721	102,721
8	102,721	5,136	6,000	864	1,857	101,857
9	101,857	5,093	6,000	907	950	100,950
10	100,950	5,050	6,000	950	0	100,000
Total		$52,279	$60,000	$7,721		

Column (2) = Column (7) from Previous Period.
Column (3) = .05 × Column (2).
Column (4)   Given.
Column (5) = Column (4) − Column (3).
Column (6) = Column (6) from Previous Period − Column (5) of This Period.
Column (7) = Column (2) − Column (5).

1. On the income statement interest expense will be a constant percentage of the recorded net liability at the beginning of each interest period. This percentage will be equal to the market interest rate when the bonds were initially issued. When bonds are issued for more than par value, the *dollar amount* of interest

expense will decrease each period as the unpaid principal amount decreases to the maturity value.

2. On the balance sheet at the end of each period, the balance of the bonds plus the unamortized premium will be stated at the present value of the *remaining* cash flow discounted at the market rate of interest when the bonds were initially issued. For example, on June 30, Year 2, the present value of the remaining cash payments is as follows:

Present Value of July 1, Year 2, Interest Payment	$ 6,000
Present Value of 8 remaining semiannual interest payments discounted at 10 percent, compounded semiannually (Table C.4, page 817, shows the present value of an ordinary annuity of $1 per period for 8 periods discounted at 5 percent to be $6.46321; $6,000 × 6.46321 = $38,779)	38,779
Present value of $100,000 to be paid at the end of 4 years (Table C.2, page 815, shows the present value of $1 to be paid at the end of 8 periods discounted at 5 percent to be $.67684; $100,000 × .67684 = $67,684)	67,684
Total Present Value	$112,463
Less: Amount Shown as Current Liability	6,000
Equals Amount Shown for Debenture Bonds Payable Plus Bond Premium	$106,463

The amount $106,462, different because of rounding effects, appears in column (7) of Exhibit 10.3 for the liability at the end of the second six-month period.

Premium on Bonds Payable Account

Accounting has traditionally shown Bonds Payable at par value with a liability adjunct account, Premium on Bonds Payable, carrying the amount to add to par value to show book value. If the Premium on Bonds Payable account were used, the balance sheet on June 30, Year 2, after two semiannual interest periods would show:

Bonds Payable—Par Value	$100,000
Plus: Premium on Bonds Payable	6,462
Bonds Payable—Net Book Value	$106,462

Interest Expense under the Straight-Line Method

Under the straight-line method, total interest expense (periodic coupon payments reduced by the excess of initial issue proceeds over amounts paid at maturity) is spread evenly over the life of the bonds. In the example for Macaulay Corporation, total interest expense is $52,279 [= ($6,000 × 10) − ($107,721 − $100,000)]. Interest expense each six months will therefore be $5,227.90 (= $52,279/10). The journal entry to record interest expense at the end of each six months is:

Interest Expense	$5,227.90	
Premium on Debenture Bonds Payable	772.10	
Interest Payable.		$6,000.00
To recognize interest expense for 6 months.		

The straight-line method of computing interest expense is computationally easier than the effective-interest method. It has two theoretical weaknesses, however.

1. When bonds are issued for more than par value, interest expense will be an increasing percentage of the net bond liability at the beginning of each period. That is, interest expense (numerator) will be constant but the net bond liability (denominator) will decrease as the maturity date approaches. In contrast, the effective-interest method provides an amount for interest expense that is a constant percentage of the beginning-of-the-period net liability.
2. The net amount at which the bonds are stated on the balance sheet each period will not equal the present value of the remaining cash flows relating to the bond discounted at the historical-interest rate.

Effects on Statement of Changes in Financial Position

Interest expense on bonds originally issued above par is less than the periodic amounts of cash disbursed. The excess of cash disbursed (or current liability for Interest Payable recorded) over interest expense is a repayment of a portion of the bond liability to the lenders. This payment can be interpreted in either of two ways.

1. It is an operating use of cash. Because the amount of cash disbursed exceeds interest expense, there must be a subtraction in the statement of changes in financial position in deriving "cash provided by operations." The amount subtracted is the excess of cash disbursed over interest expense.
2. It is a nonoperating use of cash and appears as a (partial) retirement of debt in the section showing uses of cash for financing.

The problems and examples in this book use the first interpretation, although the second is supportable.

Bond Retirement

Many bonds remain outstanding until the stated maturity date. Refer to Exhibit 10.2, the Macaulay example, where the 12 percent coupon bonds were issued to yield 14 percent. The company pays the final coupon, $6,000, and the face amount, $100,000, on the stated maturity date. The entries are:

7/1/Year 6	Interest Expense	$6,936	
	Cash		$6,000
	Debenture Bonds Payable		936
	See row 10 of Exhibit 10.2.		
	Debenture Bonds Payable	$100,000	
	Cash		$100,000
	Retirement at maturity of bonds.		

Retirement before Maturity A firm sometimes purchases its own bonds on the open market before maturity. Because market interest rates constantly change, the purchase price will seldom equal the recorded book value of the bonds. Assume that Macaulay Corporation originally issued its bonds at par to yield 12 percent compounded semiannually. Assume that three years later, on July 1, Year 4, interest rates in the marketplace have increased so that the market then requires a 15 percent interest rate to be paid by Macaulay Corporation. Refer to Table C.6 on page 819, 2-year row, 15 percent column, which shows that 12 percent bonds with two years until maturity will sell in the marketplace for 94.9760 percent of par if the current interest rate is 15 percent compounded semiannually.

The marketplace is not constrained by the principles of historical cost accounting. Even though Macaulay Corporation shows the Debenture Bonds Payable on the balance sheet at $100,000, the marketplace puts a price of only $94,976 on the entire bond issue. From the point of view of the marketplace, these bonds are the same as two-year bonds issued on July 1, Year 4 at an effective yield of 15 percent and, so, carry a discount of $5,024 (= $100,000 − $94,976).

If, on July 1, Year 4 Macaulay Corporation purchases $10,000 of par value of its own bonds, it would have to pay only $9,498 (= .94976 × $10,000) for those bonds. The journal entries it would make at the time of purchase are:

7/1/Year 4	Interest Payable	$6,000	
	Cash		$6,000
	To record payment of coupons, as usual.		
	Debenture Bonds Payable	$10,000	
	Cash		$9,498
	Gain on Retirement of Bonds		502
	To record purchase of bonds for less than the current amount shown in the accounting records.		

The adjustment to give equal debits and credits in the second journal entry is recorded as a gain. The gain arises because the firm is able to retire a liability recorded at one amount, $10,000, for a smaller cash payment, $9,498. This gain actually occurred as interest rates increased between Year 1 and Year 4. In historical cost accounting, the gain is reported only when realized — in the period of bond retirement. This phenomenon is analogous to a firm's purchasing temporary investments, holding those investments as prices increase, selling the investments in a subsequent year, and reporting all the gain in the year of sale. It is caused by the historical cost accounting convention of recording amounts at historical cost and not recording increases in wealth until those increases are realized in arm's length transactions with outsiders.

During the 1970s, interest rates jumped upward from their levels in the 1960s. Many companies had issued bonds at prices near par with coupon rates of only three or four percent per year in the 1960s. When interest rates in the 1970s jumped to 12 or 15 percent per year, these bonds sold in the marketplace for substantial discounts from par value. Many companies repurchased their own bonds, recording substantial gains in the process.

Since there is no alternative in historical cost accounting to showing a gain (or loss) on bond retirement (the debits must equal the credits), and since the gain (or loss) does not meet the criteria of an extraordinary item, generally accepted accounting principles[8] require that all gains or losses on bond retirements be recorded as unusual items in arriving at the net income before extraordinary items. This unusual item must be recorded separately only if it is abnormal in size. This ruling enables companies to manage their reported income before extraordinary items by repurchasing bonds.

Special Provisions for Bond Retirement

Serial Bonds The bond indenture may require the issuing firm to make a special provision for retiring the bond issue. There are two major types of retirement provisions. One provides that certain portions of the principal amount will come due on a succession of maturity dates; the bonds of such issues are known as *serial bonds*. (The bonds considered so far in this chapter are not serial bonds.)

Sinking-Fund Bonds The other major type of retirement provision in bond indentures requires the firm to accumulate a fund of cash or other assets that will be used to pay the bonds when the maturity date arrives or to reacquire and retire portions of bond issue. Funds of this type are commonly known as *sinking funds*, although *bond-retirement funds* would be a more descriptive term. The trustee of the bond issue usually holds the sinking fund. It appears on the balance sheet as a noncurrent asset in the "Investments" section.

Re-funded Bonds Some bond indentures make no provision for installment repayment or for accumulating sinking funds for the payment of the bonds when they come due. Such bonds are usually well protected with property held by the trustees as collateral or by the high credit standing of the issuer. Under these circumstances, the entire bond liability may be paid at maturity out of cash in the bank at that time. Quite commonly, however, this procedure is not followed. Instead, the bond issue is *re-funded* — a new set of bonds is issued to obtain the funds to retire the old ones when they come due.

Callable Bonds A common provision gives the issuing company the right to retire portions of the bond issue before maturity if it so desires, but does not require it do so. To facilitate such reacquisition and retirement of the bonds, the bond indenture can provide that the bonds shall be *callable*. That is, the issuing company has the right to reacquire its bonds at prices specified in the bond indenture. When the bonds are called for redemption the trustee will notify the holder to present all remaining coupons and the bond principal for payments equal to the call price plus accrued interest.

The *call price* is usually set a few percentage points above the par value and declines as the maturity date approaches. Because the call provision may be exercised by the issuing company at a time when the market rate of interest is less than the coupon rate, callable bonds usually are sold in the marketplace for something less than otherwise similar, but noncallable, bonds.

Assume, for example, that a firm had issued 12 percent semiannual coupon bonds at par, but the market interest rates and the firm's credit standing at a later date would

---

[8]*CICA Handbook*, section 3480.

currently allow it to borrow at ten percent. If $100,000 par value bonds issued at par are called at 105, the entry, in addition to the one to record the accrued interest expense, would be:

Debenture Bonds Payable	$100,000	
Loss on Retirement of Bonds	5,000	
Cash		$105,000
Bonds called and retired.		

This loss recognized on bond retirement, like the analogous gain, is generally classified as an unusual item in the income statement.

When bonds are retired, the book value of the bonds at the time of retirement must be removed from the accounting records. Suppose that $100,000 par value bonds were issued for more than par value several years ago and that the book value of the bonds is now $103,500. If $10,000-par value bonds are called at 105, the entry to record the retirement would be:

Bonds Payable	$10,000	
Premium on Bonds Payable	350	
Loss on Retirement of Bonds	150	
Cash		$10,500
Partial retirement of bonds originally issued for more than par value.		

The market rate of interest a firm must pay depends on two factors: the general level of interest rates and its own creditworthiness. If the market rate of interest has risen since bonds were issued (or the firm's credit rating has declined), the bonds will sell in the market at less than issue price. A firm that wanted to retire such bonds would not *call* them, because the call price is typically greater than the face value. Instead the firm would probably purchase its bonds in the open market and realize a gain on the retirement of bonds.

Unifying Principles of Accounting for Long-Term Liabilities

Long-term liabilities are obligations to pay fixed amounts at definite future times more than one year in the future. The obligations appear on the balance sheet at the present value of the future payments. The present value computations use the historical rate of interest — the market interest rate on the date the obligation was incurred.

The method of accounting for all long-term liabilities and related expenses are conceptually and procedurally identical — the effective-interest method. The liability is initially recorded at the cash equivalent value received, which will equal the present value of the future contractual payments using the interest rate relevant for the borrower on the date the loan begins. At any subsequent interest accrual or interest payment date, Interest Expense is computed by multiplying the book value of the net liability by the historical interest rate. The amount of interest expense increases liabilities. The amount of any cash payment made reduces the liabilities. The difference between interest expense and the cash payment decreases the discount of premium on bonds payable.

Amoritization schedules, such as those in Exhibits 10.1, 10.2, 10.3, 10.4, and in Chapter 11, illustrate this unchanging procedure for a variety of long-term liabilities.

Summary

A liability is an obligation by an entity involving a probable future sacrifice of resources. The amount of the obligation and the timing of its payment can be estimated with reasonable certainty. The transaction causing the obligation to arise has already occurred.

Accounting for long-term liabilities is accomplished by recording these obligations at their present value at the date the obligation is incurred (which equals the cash equivalent value received at the time of the borrowing) and then showing the change in that present value as the maturity date of the obligation approaches. In historical cost accounting, the interest rate used throughout the life of the liability is the firm's borrowing rate at the time the liability was originally incurred. Retirement of long-term liabilities can be brought about in a variety of ways, but in each case, the process is the same. The net obligation is offset against what is given in return, usually cash, with gain or loss on retirement recognized as appropriate.

Problem 1 for Self-Study

On June 30, Year 0 Avner Incorporated issues a three-year, $100,000 note bearing interest at the rate of 15 percent per year. That is, Avner Incorporated promises to pay $15,000 on June 30, Year 1, $15,000 on June 30, Year 2, and $115,000 on June 30, Year 3. The market rate of interest on the date the note is issued is ten percent.
a. Compute the proceeds Avner Incorporated receives for its note.
b. Prepare an amortization schedule similar to Exhibit 10.1 for the life of the note.
c. Prepare journal entries that would be made on three dates: the date of issue, six months after the date of issue (assuming the books were closed then), and one year after the date of issue, assuming an interest payment is made then.

Suggested Solution

a. Present value of 3 payments of $15,000, discounted at 10 percent; see Table
    C.4, page 817, 3-period row, 10-percent column: $15,000 × 2.48685 . . . . $ 37,303

    Present value of 1 payment of $100,000 discounted at 10 percent for 3
    periods; see Table C.2, page 815, 3-period row, 10-percent column:
    $100,000 × .75131   75,131

    Net Proceeds from Issue of Note $112,434

b. See Exhibit 10.4.

Exhibit 10.4
Amortization Schedule for Note with Face Value of $100,000
Issued for $112,434, Bearing Interest at the Rate of 15 Percent
of Face Value per Year, Issued To Yield 10 Percent
(Problem 1 for Self-Study)

June 30 Year (1)	Loan Balance Start of Period (2)	Interest Expense for Period (3)	Payment (4)	Note Premium Amort- ization (5)	Note Premium At end of Period (6)	Net Loan Balance End of Period (7)
0					$12,434	$112,434
1	$112,434	$11,243	$ 15,000	$ 3,757	8,677	108,677
2	108,677	10,868	15,000	4,132	4,545	104,545
3	104,545	10,455	115,000	4,545	0	0

Column (2) = Column (7) from Previous Period.
Column (3) = .10 × Column (2).
Column (4)   Given.
Column (5) = Column (4) − Column (3) except Year 3.
Column (6) = Column (6) from Previous Period − Column (5) of This Period.
Column (7) = Column (2) − Column (5) − $100,000 in Year 3.

c. 6/30/Year 0: Cash $112,434
    Note Payable $100,000
    Premium on Note Payable   12,434
    Proceeds of issue of note.
    12/31/Year 0: Interest Expense .... $ 5,622
    Interest Payable .... $ 5,622
    See Exhibit 10.4; accrual of 6 months' interest =
    $11,243/2.
    6/30/Year 1: Interest Expense .... $ 5,621
    Interest Payable   5,622
    Premium on Note Payable   3,757
    Cash .... $ 15,000
    Interest expense for the remainder of the first year and
    cash payment made. Excess of cash payment over in-
    terest expense reduces note premium.

Problem 2 for Self-Study

Generally accepted accounting principles require that long-term monetary net liabilities
be stated at the present value of the future cash flows discounted at the market rate of
interest appropriate to the monetary items at the time they were initially recorded.
Obligations under warranties are excluded from this rule and warranties are stated at
the estimated cost of providing warranty goods and services in the future.

Assume that the estimated future costs of a three-year warranty plan on products
sold during Year 1 are as follows:

Year	Expected Cost
2	$ 500,000
3	600,000
4	900,000
Total	$2,000,000

Actual costs coincided with expectations both as to timing and amount.

a. Prepare the journal entries for each of the Years 1 through 4 for this warranty plan following current generally accepted accounting principles.

b. Now, assume that generally accepted accounting principles allow these liabilities to be shown at their present value. Prepare the journal entries for each of the Years 1 through 4 for this warranty plan assuming that the warranty liability is stated at the present value of the future costs discounted at ten percent. To simplify the calculations, assume that all warranty costs are incurred on December 31 of each year.

c. What theoretical arguments can be offered for the valuation basis in (**b**)?

Suggested Solution

a. Year 1   Warranty Expense $2,000,000

            Estimated Warranty Liability $2,000,000

     Year 2   Estimated Warranty Liability .... $ 500,000

            Cash and Other Accounts .... $ 500,000

     Year 3   Estimated Warranty Liability .... $ 600,000

            Cash and Other Accounts .... $ 600,000

     Year 4   Estimated Warranty Liability .... $ 900,000

            Cash and Other Accounts .... $ 900,000

b. The present value of the future costs amounts on December 31, Year 1, discounted at ten percent, is:

Year 2	$500,000 × .90909	$ 454,545
Year 3	$600,000 × .82645	495,870
Year 4	$900,000 × .75131	676,179
	Total	$1,626,594

     Year 1   Warranty Expense $1,626,594

            Estimated Warranty Liability $1,626,594

     Year 2   Interest Expense .... $ 162,659

            Estimated Warranty Liability .... $ 162,659

            .10 × $1,626,594 = $162,659.

Year 2	Estimated Warranty Liability	$ 500,000		
	Cash and Other Accounts		$ 500,000	
Year 3	Interest Expense	$ 128,925		
	Estimated Warranty Liability		$ 128,925	
	.10 × ($1,626,594 + $162,659 − $500,000) = $128,925.			
Year 3	Estimated Warranty Liability	$ 600,000		
	Cash and Other Accounts		$ 600,000	
Year 4	Interest Expense	$ 81,818		
	Estimated Warranty Liability		$ 81,818	
	.10 × ($1,626,594 + $162,659 − $500,000 + $128,925 − $600,000) = .10 × $818,178 = $81,818.			
Year 4	Estimated Warranty Liability	$ 899,996		
	Interest Expense	4		
	Cash and Other Accounts		$ 900,000	
	There is a rounding error of $4 in the Estimated Warranty Liability account at the end of Year 4. Interest expense for Year 4 is, therefore, increased by $4.			

c. The goods and services provided under the warranty plan must first be acquired for cash. Thus, even though customers will receive goods and services, the firm must expend cash at some point. To be consistent with monetary liabilities, these amounts should be discounted to their present value.

Questions, Exercises, Problems and Cases

Questions

1. Review the meaning of the following concepts or terms discussed in this chapter.
   a. Liability
   b. Executory contract
   c. CPP
   d. Call price
   e. Contingent liability and estimated liability
   f. Mortgage, mortgagee, mortgagor
   g. Collateral
   h. Bond indenture
   i. Coupon bond
   j. Debenture bond
   k. Convertible bond
   l. Yield or effective rate of bond
   m. Bond tables
   n. Amortization of bonds using the straight-line and effective interest methods.
   o. Sinking fund
   p. Serial bonds
   q. Bond refunding

2. For each of the following items, indicate whether the item meets all of the criteria of a liability. If so, how is it valued?
   a. Interest accrued but not paid on a note
   b. Advances from customers for goods and services to be delivered later
   c. Firm orders from customers for goods and services to be delivered later

d. Mortgages payable

e. Bonds payable

f. Product warranties

g. Fifteen-year cancelable lease on an office building

h. Damages the company must pay if a pending lawsuit is lost

i. Cost of restoring strip-mining sites after mining operations are completed

j. Contractual promises to purchase natural gas for each of the next ten years

3. Describe the similarities and differences between the allowance method for uncollectibles (see Chapter 7) and the allowance method for estimated warranty costs.

4. Generally accepted accounting principles specifically require the accrual of earned but unpaid wages and fringe benefits thereon. Generally accepted accounting principles specifically require the accrual of earned but unused vacation pay under most circumstances. Generally accepted accounting principles do not mention fringe benefits attached to vacation pay. Explain why the text might say that accrual of these items is required even though there is no specific pronouncement that mentions such a requirement.

5. A noted accountant once remarked that the optimal number of faulty TV sets for the General Electric Co. Ltd. to sell is "not zero," even if GE promises to repair all faulty GE sets that break down, for whatever reason, within two years of purchase. Why could the optimal number be "not zero"?

6. A private school has a reporting year ending June 30. It hires teachers for the ten-month period, September of one year through June of the following year. It contracts to pay teachers in 12 monthly installments over the period September of one year through August of the next year. For the current academic year, the total contractual salaries to be paid to teachers is $360,000. How should this amount be accounted for in the financial statements issued June 30, at the end of the academic year?

7. While shopping in a store on July 5, Year 1, a customer slipped on the floor and sustained back injuries. On January 15, Year 2, the customer sued the store for $1 million. The case came to trial on April 30, Year 2. The jury's verdit was rendered on June 15, Year 2, with the store found guilty of gross negligence. A damage reward of $400,000 was granted to the customer. The store, on June 25, Year 2 appealed the decision to a higher court on the grounds that certain evidence had not been admitted by the lower court. The higher court ruled on November 1, Year 2 that the evidence should have been admitted. The lower court reheard the case beginning on March 21, Year 3. Another jury, on April 20, Year 3, again found the store guilty of gross negligence and awarded $500,000. On May 15, Year 3, the store paid the $500,000 judgment. When should a loss from these events be recognized by the supermarket? Explain your reasoning.

8. What factors determine the amount of money a firm actually receives when it offers a bond issue to the market?

9. A call premium is the difference between the call price of a bond and its par value. What is the purpose of such a premium?

10. The Discount on Bonds Payable account has a debit balance and, as such, could be treated as deferred charge or as a liability contra. Present the reasons supporting each alternative.

11. If a company borrows $1,000,000 by issuing, at par, 20-year, ten-percent bonds with semiannual coupons, the total interest expense over the life of the issue is $2,000,000 (= 20 × .10 × $1,000,000). If a company undertakes a 20-year mortgage or note with an implicit borrowing rate of ten percent, the annual payments are $1,000,000/8.51356 = $117,460. (See Table C.4, page 817, 20-period row, 10 percent column.) The total mortgage payments are $2,349,200 (= 20 × $117,460), and the total interest expense over the life of the note or mortgage is $1,349,200 (= $2,349,200 − $1,000,000).

Why are the amounts of interest expense different for these two means of borrowing for the same length of time at identical interest rates?

12. The following questions compare the effective interest method and the straight-line method of accounting for interest expense on bonds.

    a. Which method gives higher interest expense in the first year for a bond issued at less than par value?

    b. Which method gives higher interest expense in the first year for a bond issued at more than par value?

    c. Which method gives higher interest expense in the last year for a bond issued at less than par value?

    d. Which method gives higher interest expense in the last year for a bond issued at more than par value?

    e. Which method involves the larger adjustment to net income in deriving funds provided by operations in the first year for a bond issued at more than par value?

    f. Which method involves the larger adjustment to net income in deriving funds provided by operations in the first year for a bond issued at less than par value?

    g. What are the relative advantages and disadvantages of the straight-line method versus the effective interest method of accounting for interest expense on a bond?

13. Are high-quality, long-term bonds always sound investments? A friend has $20,000 to invest to pay for a child's education expenses. The funds will be needed in four years. The friend believes that the ten percent semiannual coupon bonds of the Canadian government maturing in the year 2010 would be as safe and sound an investment as any available. What advice can you give?

14. Critics of historical cost accounting for long-term debt argue that the procedures give management unreasonable opportunity to "manage" income with the timing of bond retirements. What phenomenon do these critics have in mind?

15. What purposes do restrictions placed on borrowing firms by bond indentures serve?

Exercises

16. *Journal entries for payroll.* During the current period, office employees earned wages of $200,000. $38,000 of this amount must be withheld from payments for income taxes, and eight percent must be deducted for Social Insurance taxes. The employer must pay 11 percent of gross wages for Social Insurance taxes. The employer has promised to contribute four percent of gross wages to a profit-sharing fund, whose proceeds are used to pay workers when they retire. Employees earned vacation pay estimated to be $9,000; estimated fringes are 20 percent of that amount.

    a. Prepare journal entries for these wage-related items.

    b. What is total wage and salary expense?

17. *Journal entries for payroll.* Prepare journal entries for the following wages, fringes, and accruals of Bages Limited. Factory employees earned $90,000 and office employees earned $60,000. The company must pay $27,000 to the government for withheld income taxes and eight percent to the government for withheld Social Insurance taxes. The employer also owes 11 percent for Social Insurance taxes. The employer pays all costs of insurance plans; it owes $5,000 for health and life insurance premiums. The employer awards paid vacations to employees who have been working for a year or more. During the current period, employees earning 90 percent of the gross wages are expected to earn paid vacations, which is estimated to be four percent of their gross wages. Payroll taxes and fringe benefits are estimated to be 20 percent of vacation pay.

18. *Journal entries for estimated warranty liabilities and subsequent expenditures.* A new product introduced by Junn Corp. carries a two-year warranty against defects. The estimated warranty costs as a percentage of dollar sales are three percent in the year of sale and five percent in the next year. Sales (all on account) and actual warranty expenditures (all paid in cash) for the first two years of the product's life were as follows:

	Sales	Actual Warranty Expenditures
Year 1	$400,000	$10,000
Year 2	500,000	35,000

    a. Prepare journal entries for the events of Year 1 and Year 2. Closing entries are not required.

    b. What is the balance in the Estimated Warranty Liability account at the end of Year 2?

19. *Using bond tables.* The Gonedes Co. Ltd. issues 12 percent semiannual coupon bonds maturing in ten years. The face amount of the bonds is $1 million. The net cash proceeds to Gonedes Co. Ltd. from the bond issue amounts to $944,907.

    What interest rate will be used in applying the effective interest method over the life of this bond issue?

20. *Using bond tables.* Refer to Table C.6 on page 819 for 12 percent semiannual coupon bonds issued to yield 13 percent per year compounded semiannually. All of the questions below refer to $1 million face value of such bonds.

    a. What are the initial issue proceeds for bonds issued to mature in 30 years?

      b. What is the book value of those bonds after five years?

      c. What is the book value of the bonds when they have 20 years until maturity?

      d. What are the initial issue proceeds of bonds issued to mature in 20 years? (Compare to your answer above.)

      e. Write an equation for interest expense for the last six months before maturity.

      f. If the market rate of interest on the bonds is 14 percent, what is the market value of the bonds when they have 20 years to maturity?

      g. When the bonds have 10 years until maturity, they trade in the market for 112.46 percent of par. What is the effective market rate at that time?

21. *Using bond tables; computing interest expense.* Refer to Table C.5, page 818, for ten percent semiannual coupon bonds. On January 1, Year 1, Souverain Limited issued $1 million of face-value, ten-percent semiannual coupon bonds maturing in 20 years (on December 31, Year 20) at a price to yield 14 percent per year, compounded semiannually. Use the effective interest method of computing interest expense.

      a. What were the proceeds of the original issue?

      b. What was the interest expense for the first half of Year 1?

      c. What was the interest expense for the second half of Year 1?

      d. What was the book value of the bonds on January 1, Year 6 (when the bonds have 15 years until maturity)?

      e. What was the interest for the first half of Year 6?

22. *Funds statement effects; gain or loss on bond retirement.* Refer to the data in the preceding exercise for Souverain Limited.

      a. By what amount did cash used for debt service differ from interest expense, and how does this amount affect the fund statement's derivation of cash provided by continuing operations for Year 1?

      b. On January 1, Year 11 (when bonds have ten years to maturity), $100,000 face value of bonds are purchased in the open market and retired. The market rate of interest at the time of purchase is 12 percent compounded semiannually. What gain or loss will Souverain Limited report?

23. *Journal entry for short-term note payable.* On December 1, the O'Brien Co. Ltd. obtained a 90-day loan for $15,000 from the Twin City Bank at an annual interest rate of 12 percent. On the maturity date the note was renewed for another 30 days, with a cheque being issued to the bank for the accrued interest. The O'Brien Co. Ltd. closes its books annually at December 31.

      a. Present entries on the books of the O'Brien Co. Ltd. to record the issue of the note, the year-end adjustment, the renewal of the note, and the payment of cash at maturity of the renewed note.

      b. Present entries at maturity date of the original note for the following variations in the settlement of the note of the O'Brien Co. Ltd.

         (1) The original note is paid at maturity.

         (2) The note is renewed for 30 days; the new note bears interest at 15 percent per annum. Interest on the old note was not paid at maturity.

24. *Partial amortization schedule for note.* The Holmes Sales Co. Inc. sells a building lot to N. Wolfe on September 1 for $27,000. The down payment is $3,000, and minimum payments of $265 a month are to be made on the contract. Interest at the rate of 12 percent per annum on the unpaid balance is deducted from each payment, and the balance is applied to reduce the principal. Payments are made as follows: October 1, $265; November 1, $265; December 1, $600; January 2, $265.

Prepare a partial amortization schedule showing payments, interest and principal, and remaining liability at each of these dates. Round amounts to the nearest dollar.

25. *Partial amortization schedule for mortgage.* Lynne Michals secures a mortgage loan of $112,000 from the Canada Trust Co. Ltd. The terms of the mortgage require monthly payments of $1,660. The interest rate to be applied to the unpaid balance is nine percent per year.

Prepare a partial amortization schedule showing payments, interest and principal, and remaining liability for the first four months of the loan. Round amounts to the nearest dollar.

26. *Journal entries for effective interest and straight-line methods of computing bond interest.* On October 1, Year 1, Howell Stores, Inc. issues 20-year, first mortgage bonds with a face value of $1,000,000. The proceeds of the issue are $1,060,000. The bonds bear interest at the rate of ten percent per year, payable semiannually at April 1 and October 1. Howell Stores, Inc., closes its books annually at December 31. Round amounts to the nearest dollar.

    a. Present dated journal entries related to the bonds from October 1, Year 1, through October 1, Year 2, inclusive. Assume that Howell Stores, Inc., uses the straight-line method to recognize interest expense.

    b. Repeat instructions for part (**a**) but assume that the company uses the effective interest method. The effective interest rate to be used is 9.3 percent, compounded semiannually.

27. *Amortization schedule for bonds.* Hanouille Inc. issues ten-percent semiannual coupon bonds maturing five years from the date of issue. Interest of five percent of the face value of $100,000 is payable January 1 and July 1. The bonds are issued to yield 12 percent, compounded semiannually.

    a. What are the initial issue proceeds received by Hanouille Inc.?

    b. Construct an amortization schedule for this bond issue, similar to Exhibit 10.2.

    c. By how much does interest expense for the first year (note *year*, not first six-month period) of the bond's life under the effective interest method differ from that under the straight-line method?

    d. Assume that at the end of the third year of the bond's life, $10,000 face value of bonds are called and retired for 103 percent of par. Give the journal entry to record the retirement.

28. *Accounting for bond issue and subsequent interest including journal entries.* The Central Power Company Ltd. issued $2 million bonds in two series, A and B. Each series had face amount of $1 million and was issued at prices to yield 11 percent. Issue A contained semiannual ten percent coupons. Issue B contained 12 percent semiannual coupons. Issues A and B both mature 30 years from issue date.

    Answer the following questions for issue A. Round amounts to the nearest dollar.

    a. What is the issuing price of the bonds?

    b. Make the journal entry for the date of bond issue.

    c. Using the effective interest method, show the journal entries made on the first semiannual interest payment date.

    d. Repeat part (**c**) for the second and third payment dates.

    e. Show the semiannual entry if straight-line method is used.

29. *Accounting for bond issue and subsequent interest including journal entries.* Refer to the data in Exercise **28**. Work the problem for issue B.

30. *Liability for sales tax.* The new bookkeeper for Courtis Company forgot to set up a special account for the 5% provincial sales tax and included the tax in sales. Eighty percent of the company's sales are subject to sales tax; the remainder are sales to tax exempt wholesalers. The sales account has a balance of $834,288 at the end of the period. Make the appropriate entry to remit the sales tax and correctly state revenues. What is the correct amount of sales?

31. *Liability for product warranties.* Kennedy Corp., sells a product with a one-year warranty. At December 31, 19X1 after closing adjustments, the liability account has a balance of $60,000 reflecting 800 units sold this past year still expected to come in for warranty service. The expected failure rate for this product is 3% and the average warranty cost per item serviced equals 5% of selling price. Thirteen hundred items sold in 19X1 were returned for service before years end. What was the amount of 19X1 sales?

32. *Using present value tables for bond computations.* Refer to Tables 2 and 4, which appear after Appendix A. Assume that $100,000 par value, 8-percent semi-annual coupon bonds maturing in 10 years are issued to yield 10 percent per year, compounded semiannually.

    a. Compute the book value of the bonds 2 years after issue.

    b. Compute the market value of the bonds 2 years after issue if the bonds then have a market yield of 6 percent, compounded semiannually.

Problems and Cases

33. *Allowance method for warranties; reconstructing transactions.* Colantoni Co. Inc. sells appliances, all for cash. All acquisitions of appliances during a year are debited to the Merchandise Inventory account. The company provides warranties on all its products, guaranteeing to make repairs within one year of the date of sale as required for any of its appliances that break down. The company has many years of experience with its products and warranties.

    The schedule shown in Exhibit 10.5 contains trial balances for the Colantoni Co. Inc. at the ends of Year 1 and Year 2. The trial balances for the end of Year 1 are the Adjusted Preclosing Trial Balance (after all adjusting entries have been properly made) and the final Post-Closing Trial Balance. The trial balance shown for the end of Year 2 is taken before any adjusting entries of any kind, although entries have been made to the Estimated Liability for Warranty Repairs account during Year 2, as repairs have been made. Colantoni Co. Inc. closes its books once each year.

    At the end of Year 2, the management of Colantoni Co. Inc. analyzes the appliances sold within the preceding 12 months. All appliances in the hands of customers that are still covered by warranty are classified as follows: those sold on or before

June 30 (more than six months old), those sold after June 30, but on or before November 30 (more than one month, but less than six months old), and those sold on or after December 1. One-half of one percent of the appliances sold more than six months ago are estimated to require repair, five percent of the appliances sold one to six months before the end of the year are estimated to require repair, and eight percent of the appliances sold within the last month are assumed to require repair. From this analysis, management estimated that $5,000 of repairs still would have to be made in Year 3 on the appliances sold in Year 2. Ending inventory on December 31, Year 2, is $120,000.

Exhibit 10.5
COLANTONI CO. INC.
(Problem 33)

Trial Balances — End of Year 1	Adjusted Preclosing		Post-Closing	
	Dr.	Cr.	Dr.	Cr.
Estimated Liability for Warranty Repairs . . .		$ 6,000		$ 6,000
Merchandise Inventory	$ 100,000		$100,000	
Sales		800,000		
Warranty Expense	18,000			
All Other Accounts	882,000	194,000	110,000	204,000
Totals	$1,000,000	$1,000,000	$210,000	$210,000

Trial Balance — End of Year 2	Unadjusted Trial Balance	
	Dr.	Cr.
Estimated Liability for Warranty Repairs	$ 15,000	
Merchandise Inventory	820,000	
Sales		$1,000,000
Warranty Expense	—	—
All Other Accounts	265,000	100,000
Totals	$1,100,000	$1,100,000

    a. What were the total acquisitions of merchandise inventory during Year 2?
    b. What is the cost of goods sold for Year 2?
    c. What was the dollar amount of repairs made during Year 2?
    d. What is the Warranty Expense for Year 2?
    e. Give journal entries for repairs made during Year 2, for the warranty expense for Year 2, and for cost of goods sold for Year 2.

34. *Nonmonetary liabilities; reconstructing transactions.* The Myrtle Lunch sells coupon books that patrons may use later to purchase meals. Each coupon book sells for $17 and has a face value of $20. That is, each book can be used to purchase meals with menu prices of $20. On July 1, redeemable unused coupons with face value of $1,500 were outstanding. During July, 250 coupon books were sold; during August, 100; during September, 100. Cash receipts exclusive of coupons were $1,200 in July, $1,300 in August, and $1,250 in September. Coupons with a face value of $2,700 were redeemed by patrons during the three months.

a. If the Myrtle Lunch had a net income of $500 for the quarter ending September 30, how large were expenses?

b. What effect, if any, do the July, August, and September coupon sales and redemptions have on the right-hand side of the September 30 balance sheet?

35. *Nonmonetary liabilities; journal entries.* The Lambert Co. Ltd. sells service contracts to repair copiers at $300 per year. When the contract is signed, the $300 fee is collected and the Service Contract Fees Received in Advance account is credited. Revenues on contracts are recognized on a quarterly basis during the year in which the coverage is in effect. On January 1, 1,000 service contracts were outstanding. Of these, 500 expired at the end of the first quarter, 300 at the end of the second quarter, 150 at the end of the third quarter, and 50 at the end of the fourth quarter. Sales and service during the year came to these amounts (assume that all sales occurred at the beginning of the quarter):

	Sales of Contracts	Service Expenses
First Quarter	$120,000 (400 contracts)	$50,000
Second Quarter	240,000 (800 contracts)	60,000
Third Quarter	90,000 (300 contracts)	45,000
Fourth Quarter	60,000 (200 contracts)	55,000

a. Prepare journal entries for the first three quarters of the year for the Lambert Co. Ltd. Assume that quarterly reports are prepared on March 31, June 30, and September 30.

b. What is the balance in the Service Contract Fees Received in Advance account on December 31?

36. *Journal entries for purchase with existing mortgage; subsequent interest entries.* On June 1, the Loebbecke Co. Inc. purchases a warehouse from F. S. Brandon for $600,000, of which $100,000 is assigned to the land and $500,000 to the building. There is a mortgage on the property payable to the London Life Insurance Co. Ltd., which, together with the accrued interest, will be assumed by the purchaser. It bears interest at the rate of 12 percent per year. The balance due on the mortgage is $240,000. The principal of the mortgage will be paid on April 1 and October 1 of each year in installments of $20,000 each. The principal payments of $20,000 are in addition to the interest of six percent per six-month period on the outstanding balance. A ten-year second mortgage for $150,000 is issued to F. S. Brandon; it bears interest at the rate of 15 percent per year, payable on June 1 and December 1. A cheque is drawn to complete the purchase.

The Loebbecke Co. Inc. closes its books once a year on December 31. Prepare journal entries for June 1, October 1, and December 1.

37. *Accounting for investment in bonds.* On April 1, Year 1, the Oliver Co. Ltd. acquired $1,000,000 par value of bonds of Bret Corp. for $1,398,000. Costs of acquisition amounted to an additional $2,000. The bonds bear interest at 15 percent per year payable on March 31 and September 30 and mature on March 31, Year 10. Use the straight-line method to recognize interest revenue.

a. Present journal entries on the books of the Oliver Co. Ltd. from April 1, Year 1, through March 31, Year 2, inclusive. Assume that the books are closed annually on December 31.

b. Present the journal entry (or entries) for the sale of the bonds on August 1, Year 4, at 103.5 plus accrued interest.

38. *Operations of a syndicate and risk of interest rate fluctuations.* During October 1979, MBI arranged with a syndicate of investment bankers to borrow $1 billion. MBI and the syndicate reached agreement on MBI's borrowing rate and the amounts the syndicate would pay to MBI on a Friday. Over the weekend, the Bank of Canada took actions that drastically increased interest rates. The members of the syndicate were responsible for any difference between the amount they had obligated themselves to pay to MBI and the amount for which they could sell the bonds during the following week.

a. Did the syndicate gain or lose by the change in interest rates over the weekend?

b. What sorts of actions might members of the syndicate take to insulate themselves from involuntary speculation in interest rates over the weekend?

39. *Preparing funds statement (adapted from a problem by Stan Baiman).* Exhibit 10.6 shows comparative balance sheets, an income statement for Year 2, and supplementary notes of Branaire Limited.

Prepare the Year 2 statement of changes in financial position with funds defined as cash.

Exhibit 10.6
BRANAIRE LIMITED
Comparative Balance Sheets and Income Statement
(Problem 39)

	December 31	
	Year 2	Year 1
Balance Sheets		
Cash	$130,000	$ 30,000
Accounts Receivable	95,000	80,000
Inventory	150,000	140,000
Plant and Equipment	855,000	800,000
Accumulated Depreciation	(500,000)	(380,000)
Total Assets	$730,000	$670,000
Accounts Payable	$ 25,000	$ 20,000
Bonds Payable	110,000	100,000
Premium on Bonds Payable	44,000	40,000
Capital Stock	206,000	200,000
Retained Earnings	345,000	310,000
Total Equities	$730,000	$670,000

Year 2 Income Statement

Net Sales		$895,000
Less: Cost of Goods Sold		415,000
Gross Profit		$480,000
Less: Depreciation Expense	$140,000	
Other Expenses	200,000	340,000
		$140,000
Gain on Sale of Equipment		110,000
Net Income Before Income Tax		$250,000
Income Tax Expense		100,000
Income Before Extraordinary Items		$150,000
Extraordinary Loss on Bond Retirement		4,000
Net Income		$146,000

Notes:

(1) During Year 2, Branaire sold property, plant, and equipment that had originally cost $200,000.

(2) All depreciation charges are expensed.

(3) Dividends declared have been paid in cash.

(4) New bonds due in 15 years were issued for $10,000 more than face value.

(5) Bonds with face value of $20,000 and unamortized premium of $6,000 were retired at a loss (which has no income tax effects).

40. *Funds statement effects.* Refer to the Simplified Statement of Changes in Financial Position for a Period in Exhibit 5.19 on page 248. Eleven of the lines in the statement are numbered. Ignore the unnumbered lines in responding to the questions below.

Assume that the accounting cycle is complete for the period and that all of the financial statements have been prepared. Then it is discovered that a transaction has been overlooked. That transaction is recorded in the accounts and all of the financial statements are corrected. Define *funds* as *cash*. For each of the following transactions, indicate which of the numbered lines of the funds statement is affected and by how much. Ignore income tax effects.

    a. Bonds are issued for $100,000 cash.

    b. Bonds with a fair market value of $100,000 are issued for a building.

    c. Bonds with a book value of $100,000 are retired for $90,000 cash.

    d. Bonds with a book value of $100,000 are called for $105,000 cash and retired.

    e. Interest expense for half a year on bonds is recorded using the effective interest method. The bonds have a face value of $100,000 and a current book value of $90,000. The coupon rate is ten percent, paid semiannually, and the bonds were originally issued to yield 12 percent, compounded semiannually.

    f. Interest expense for half a year on bonds is recorded using the effective interest method. The bonds have a face value of $100,000 and a book value of $105,000. The coupon rate is 12 percent paid semiannually, and the bonds were originally issued to yield ten percent, compounded semiannually.

41. *Managing income and the debt-equity ratio through bond retirement.* Meyney Limited issued $40 million of 5 percent semiannual coupon bonds many years ago at par. The bonds now have 20 years until scheduled maturity. Because market interest rates have risen to 12 percent, the market value of the bonds has dropped to 63 percent of par. Meyney Limited has $5 million of current liabilities and $35 million of owners' equity in addition to the $40 million of long-term debt in its financial structure. The debt-equity ratio is 56 percent [= ($40 + $5)/($5 + $40 + $35)]. (Owners' equity includes an estimate of the current year's income.) The president of Meyney Limited is concerned about boosting reported income for the year, which is about $8 million for the year in the absence of any other actions. Also, the debt-equity ratio appears to be larger than that of other firms in the industry. The president wonders what would be the impact on net income and the debt-equity ratio of issuing at par new 12 percent semiannual coupon bonds to mature in 20 years and using the proceeds to retire the outstanding bond issue. Assume that such action is taken and that any gain on bond retirement is a non-taxable capital gain.

  a. Prepare the journal entries for the issue of new bonds in amount required to raise funds to retire the old bonds and retirement of the old bonds.
  b. What is the effect on income for the year? Give both dollar and percentage amounts.
  c. What is debt-equity ratio after the transaction?

42. *Financial institutions holding bonds of issuers in financial difficulties may find the book value and the market of the bonds to be quite different; should this change be recognized in accounting; troubled debt restructuring.* On January 1, Year 1, First National Bank (FNB) acquired $10 million of face value bonds issued on that date by the Occidental Oceanic Power Systems (OOPS). The bonds carry 12 percent, semiannual coupons and were to mature 20 years from the issue date. The bonds were issued by OOPS, and purchased by FNB, at par.

  By Year 6, OOPS was in severe financial difficulty and threatened to default on the bonds. After much negotiation with FNB (and other creditors), it agreed to repay the bond issue, but only on less burdensome terms. OOPS agreed to pay five percent per year, semiannually, for 25 years and to repay the principal on January 1, Year 31 or 25 years after the negotiation. FNB will receive $250,000 each six months starting with July 1, Year 6, and $10 million on January 1, Year 31. By January 1, Year 6, OOPS was being charged 20 percent per year, compounded semiannually, for its new long-term borrowings.

  a. What is the value of the bonds that FNB holds? That is, what is the present value of the newly promised cash payments when discounted at OOPS' current borrowing rate?
  b. Consider two accounting treatments for this negotiation.
    (1) Write down the bonds to the value computed in the preceding part and base future interest revenue computations on that new book value and the new historical interest rate of 20 percent per year, compounded semiannually. (What loss would FNB recognize?)
    (2) Make no entry to record the negotiation and record interest revenue as the amount of cash, $250,000, received semiannually.

    Over the new life of the bond issue, how will total income vary as a function of the method chosen?
  c. Which of these two methods would you recommend and why?

Decision Problem 10-1

Your Aunt Maud recently received an inheritance and is considering the purchase of $50,000 to $100,000 in shares of Feltham Inc. or Mattesich Ltd. She has given you condensed financial statements of these two companies for the current period, presented in Exhibit 10.7.

Having been advised in advance of Aunt Maud's interest, you made inquiries about the operations of the two companies and find that the operations of the two companies are similar and, except for their size, there appears to be no apparent difference between them except their financing activities. The financial statements appear to reflect the operating similarities. The companies own similar productive assets of the same age.

You determine that one difference between the two companies is their bond financing. On January 1, Year 2, both companies issued bonds with interest payable annually on December 31. Feltham Inc. issued at par $800,000, seven percent bonds maturing on December 31, Year 11, and Mattesich Ltd. issued at 110.59, $400,000, eight percent bonds maturing on December 31, Year 21. On December 31, Year 11, Feltham Inc. redeemed the seven percent issue primarily from the proceeds of an issue at 90.33 of $800,000, 14-percent bonds maturing on December 31, Year 21, yielding a return of 16 percent.

Both companies follow the policy of amortizing the bond premium or discount by the effective-interest method.

The shares of Feltham Inc. are currently trading at $15.00 per share and the shares of Mattesich Ltd. at $7.40 per share.

Which company's shares would you advise Aunt Maud to purchase?

Explain how you arrived at your recommendation.

Exhibit 10.7
Feltham Inc. and Mattesich Ltd.
Condensed Financial Statements

<table>
<tr><td colspan="5" align="center">Balance Sheets
December 31, Year 11
(thousands of dollars)</td></tr>
<tr><td></td><td>Feltham Inc.</td><td>Mattesich Ltd.</td><td></td><td>Feltham Inc.</td><td>Mattesich Ltd.</td></tr>
<tr><td>Current Assets . . . .</td><td>$ 542</td><td>$ 268</td><td>Current Liabilities . . . . .</td><td>$ 268</td><td>$ 133</td></tr>
<tr><td>Plant and Equipment . .</td><td>2,051</td><td>1,027</td><td>Bonds Payable . . . .</td><td>800</td><td>400</td></tr>
<tr><td>Bond Discount . . . .</td><td>77</td><td>—</td><td>Bond Premium . . . .</td><td>—</td><td>28</td></tr>
<tr><td></td><td></td><td></td><td>Shareholder's Equity . .</td><td>1,602</td><td>734</td></tr>
<tr><td></td><td>$2,670</td><td>$1,295</td><td></td><td>$2,670</td><td>$1,295</td></tr>
</table>

Income Statement
Year Ended December 31, Year 11
(dollars in thousands except per share amounts)

	Feltham Inc.	Mattesich Ltd.
Sales	$2,398	$1,204
Less: Cost of Sales	1,439	722
Gross Profit	$ 959	$ 482
Selling and Administrative Expenses	501	253
Operating Profit	$ 458	$ 229
Bond Interest	56	30
Net Income before Income Tax	$ 402	$ 199
Income Tax	161	80
Net Income	$ 241	119
Earnings per Share	$2.41	$1.19

Liabilities: Interest Imputation, Leases, Off-Balance-Sheet Financing, and Pensions

The preceding chapter discussed the concept of an accounting liability and described the accounting for current liabilities, long-term bonds, and long-term notes. This chapter examines more controversial issues in liability recognition, valuation, and accounting. The chapter treats the accounting for long-term notes payable where the historical interest rate must be imputed, the accounting for leases and pensions, and off-balance-sheet financing.

Contracts and Long-Term Notes: Interest Imputation

Real estate is often purchased on a *land contract*. Equipment is frequently acquired on the installment plan, and the liability is called an *equipment contract*. Such contracts usually require periodic payments. Sometimes the contract provides for an explicit interest rate. Many contracts, however, do not state an explicit interest rate. Instead, so-called *carrying charges* are added to the purchase price and the total is divided over a certain number of months without any specific charge being indicated for interest. The "principal" or "face amount" in this case actually includes *implicit* interest.

Long-term liabilities carrying no explicit interest should be stated at the present value of the future cash payments.[1] The interest rate used in discounting is the rate appropriate to the particular borrower given the amount and terms of the borrowing arrangement. It is called the *imputed interest rate*. The difference between the present value and the face value of the liability represents interest to be recognized over the period of the loan. The next two sections discuss two acceptable ways to compute the present value of the liability and the amount of imputed interest.

Base Interest Rate on Market Value of Asset

The first approach uses the market value of the assets acquired as a basis for computing the present value of the liability. For example, assume that a piece of equipment

---

[1]The CICA has applied the concept of present value in a limited way because of the uncertainties of estimating future cash flows and selecting a discount rate. The concept is applied in the *CICA Handbook* recommendation on capitalizing capital leases and pensions considered later in this chapter and reporting the effects of changing prices considered in Appendix D. On the other hand, the application of the concept to future income tax assets and liabilities is explicitly rejected. It appears that the *CICA Handbook* would recommend the use of present value as a general practice only where the future cash flows and the discount rate can be reasonably and objectively estimated. At the time of writing, the *CICA Handbook* does not include a recommendation on the use of present value for discounting long-term liabilities, except when determining the fair value of noncurrent assets or obligations in business combinations. In this limited case, discounting may be considered an aid in valuation.

can be bought for $10,520 cash. The equipment is purchased in return for a single-payment note with face amount of $16,000 payable in three years. The implied interest rate is about 15 percent per year. (That is, $1.15^3 \times 10,520$ is approximately equal to $16,000.) The journal entry using this approach would be:

Equipment	$10,520	
Note Payable		$10,520

To record purchase of equipment using the known cash price. The amount for the note is inferred from the known cash price of the equipment.

At the end of each accounting period that intervenes between the acquisition of the equipment and repayment of the note, journal entries would be made for depreciation of the equipment. These are not shown. Journal entries must also be made to recognize interest expense. Assume that the note was issued at the beginning of a year. The entries for the three years would be:

(1) Interest Expense	$ 1,578	
Note Payable		$ 1,578

Entry made 1 year after issuance of note. Interest is .15 × $10,520. The amount is not paid in cash but is added to the principal amount of the liability.

(2) Interest Expense	$ 1,815	
Note Payable		$ 1,815

Entry made 1 year after entry above, 2 years after issuance of note. Interest is .15 × ($10,520 + $1,578).

(3) Interest Expense	$ 2,087	
Note Payable		$ 2,087

Entry is made one year after entry above, 3 years after issuance of note. Interest is .15 × ($10,520 + $1,578 + $1,815). Balance in note payable now $16,000 (= $10,520 + $1,578 + $1,815 + $2,087).

(4) Note Payable	$16,000	
Cash		$16,000

To repay note at maturity.

Of the $16,000 paid at maturity, $5,480 represents interest accumulated on the note since its issue.

Use of Market Interest Rate to Establish Market Value of Asset and Present Value of Note

If the firm purchased used equipment with the same three-year note, it might be unable to establish a reliable estimate of the current market value of the asset acquired. The firm would then use the interest rate it would have to pay for a similar loan in the open market to find the present value of the note. This is the second acceptable method for quantifying the amount of the liability and computing the imputed interest. Suppose that the market rate for notes such as the one above is 12 percent compounded annually, rather than 15 percent. The present value at 12 percent per year of the $16,000 note due in three years is $11,388 (= $16,000 × .71178; see Table C.2 on page 815, three-period row, 12 percent column). The entry to record the purchase of used equipment and payment with the note would be:

Equipment	$11,388	
Note Payable		$11,388

To record purchase of equipment. Cost of equipment is inferred from known interest rate.

Entries would be made at the end of each period to recognize interest expense and to increase the principal amount of the liability. After the third period, the principal amount of the liability would be $16,000. See Exercise 14 at the end of this chapter.

Funds Statement Effects of Interest Imputation

The process just described for imputing interest on long-term notes results in the recognition of interest expense even though no cash is disbursed (at least until the last period when the note is discharged). In deriving cash provided by operations, there must be an addback to net income in the amount of expense that is credited to the long-term liability account, rather than to a cash account.

Total Expense is Independent of Interest Rate

In the first case, the equipment is recorded at $10,520 and there is $5,480 of imputed interest. In the second case, the equipment is recorded at $11,388 and there is $4,612 of imputed interest. The total expense over the combined lives of the note and the equipment — interest plus depreciation — is the same, $16,000, no matter which interest rate is used. Over long enough time periods, total expense equals the total cash expenditure; accrual accounting changes only the timing of the expense recognition.

Long-Term Notes Held as Receivables

A note that is the long-term liability of the borrower is a long-term asset of the lender who will show the asset in the Long-Term Note Receivable account at its present value. The rate at which the lender discounts the note should in theory be the same as that used by the borrower, but in practice the two rates sometimes differ. The lender's accounting mirrors the borrower's; the lender has interest revenue where the borrower has interest expense.

Leases

Many firms acquire rights to use assets through long-term noncancelable leases. A company might, for example, agree to lease an office for five years, or an entire building for 40 years, promising to pay a fixed periodic fee for the duration of the lease. Promising to make an irrevocable series of lease payments commits the firm just as surely as a bond indenture or mortgage, and the accounting is similar in many cases.

This section examines two methods of accounting for long-term, noncancelable leases: the operating lease method and the capital lease method. The accounting for leases is based on the concept that the party that carries substantially all the risks and benefits should reflect the asset in its financial statements.

To illustrate these two methods, suppose that Myers Inc. wants to acquire a computer that has a three-year life and costs $45,000. Assume that Myers Inc. can borrow money for three years at 15 percent per year. The computer manufacturer is willing to sell the equipment for $45,000 or to lease it for three years. Myers Inc. is responsible for maintenance and repair of the computer whether leased or purchased.

Assume that the lease is signed on January 1, Year 1, and that payments on the lease are due on December 31, Year 1, Year 2, and Year 3. In practice, lease payments are usually made in advance, but the computations in the example are simpler if we assume payments at the end of the year. Compound-interest computations show that each lease payment must be $19,709. (The present value of $1 paid at the end of this year and each of the next two years is $2.28323 when the interest rate is 15 percent per year. See Table C.4, page 817. Because the lease payments must have present value of $45,000, each payment must be $45,000/2.28323 = $19,709.)

Operating Lease Method

In an *operating lease*, the owner, or lessor, transfers the rights to use the property to the lessee for specified periods of time. At the end of the lease period, the property is returned to the lessor. For example car rental companies lease cars by the day or week on an operating basis. If the Myers Inc. lease is cancelable and Myers Inc. can stop making payments and return the computer at any time, then the lease is considered an *operating lease*. No entry would be made on January 1, Year 1, when the lease is signed, and the following entry would be made on December 31, Year 1, Year 2, and Year 3:

Rent Expense	$19,709	
Cash		$19,709
To recognize annual expense of leasing computer.		

Capital-Lease Method

If this lease is noncancelable, then the arrangement is a form of borrowing to purchase the computer. It would be accounted for as a *capital lease*.[2] This treatment recognizes the signing of the lease as the simultaneous acquisition of a long-term asset, called a *leasehold*, and the incurring of a long-term liability for lease payments. At

---

[2]*CICA Handbook*, section 3065.

the time the lease is signed, both the leasehold and the liability are recorded on the books at the present value of the liability, $45,000 in the example, which is also the fair value of the leased property.

The entry made at the time Myers Inc. signed its three-year noncancelable lease would be:

Computer Leasehold — (Asset) $45,000
    Obligation under Capital Lease — (Liability) $45,000
To recognize acquisition of asset and the related liability.

At the end of the year, two separate entries must be made. The leasehold is a long-term asset and, like most long-term assets, it must be amortized over its useful life. The first entry made at the end of each year recognizes the amortization of the lease-hold asset. Assuming that Myers Inc. uses straight-line amortization of its leasehold, the entries made at the end of Year 1, Year 2, and Year 3 would be:

Amortization Expense (on Computer Leasehold) $15,000
    Asset — Computer Leasehold $15,000

(An alternative treatment credits a contra-asset account, Accumulated Amortization of Computer Leasehold.)

The second entry made at the end of each year recognizes the lease payment, which is part payment of interest on the liability and part reduction in the liability itself. The entries made at the end of each of the three years would be:

December 31, Year 1
Interest Expense .... $ 6,750
Liability — Obligation under Capital Lease 12,959
    Cash $19,709
To recognize lease payment, interest on liability for year (.15 $\times$ $45,000 = $6,750) and reduction in the liability. The present value of the liability after this entry is $32,041 = $45,000 − $12,959.

December 31, Year 2
Interest Expense .... $ 4,806
Liability — Obligation under Capital Lease 14,903
    Cash $19,709
To recognize lease payment, interest on liability for year (.15 $\times$ $32,041 = $4,806) and the reduction in the liability. The present value of the liability after this entry is $17,138 = $32,041 − $14,903.

December 31, Year 3
Interest Expense .... $ 2,571
Liability — Obligation under Capital Lease 17,138
    Cash $19,709
To recognize lease payment, interest on liability for year (.15 $\times$ $17,138 = $2,571) and the reduction in the liability. The present value of the liability after this entry is zero (= $17,138 − $17,138).

Exhibit 11.1 shows the amortization schedule for this lease. Note that its form is exactly the same as in the mortgage amortization schedule shown in Exhibit 10.2. The underlying principle uses the effective interest method of computing interest each period.

Exhibit 11.1
Amortization Schedule for $45,000 Lease Liability,
Repaid in Three Annual Installments of $19,709 Each,
Interest Rate 15 Percent, Compounded Annually

Annual Journal Entry

Dr. Interest Expense . . . .   Amount in Column (3)
Dr. Liability — Obligation under Capital Lease . .   Amount in Column (5)
   Cr. Cash . . . .   Amount in Column (4)

Year (1)	Lease Liability Start of Year (2)	Interest Expense for Year (3)	Payment (4)	Portion of Payment Reducing Lease Liability (5)	Lease Liability End of Year (6)
0					$45,000
1	$45,000	$6,750	$19,709	$12,959	32,041
2	32,041	4,806	19,709	14,903	17,138
3	17,138	2,571	19,709	17,138	0

Column (2) = Column (6), Previous Period.
Column (3) = .15 × Column (2).
Column (4)   Given.
Column (5) = Column (4) − Column (3).
Column (6) = Column (2) − Column (5).

Accounting Method Determines Timing, but Not Amount, of Total Expense

Notice that, in the capital lease method, the total expense over the three years is $59,127, consisting of $45,000 (= $15,000 + $15,000 + $15,000) for amortization expense and $14,127 (= $6,750 + $4,806 + $2,571) for interest expense.

Exhibit 11.2
Comparison of Expense
Recognized under Operating- and
Capital-Lease Methods

Year	Expense Recognized Each Year under	
	Operating-Lease Method	Capital Lease Method
1982	$19,709	$21,750 (= $15,000 + $ 6,750)
1983	19,709	19,806 (= 15,000 + 4,806)
1984	19,709	17,571 (= 15,000 + 2,571)
Total	$59,127[a]	$59,127 (= $45,000[b]+ $14,127[c])

[a]Rent expense.
[b]Amortization expense.
[c]Interest expense.

This is exactly the same as the total expense recognized under the operating lease method described above ($19,709 × 3 = $59,127). The capital lease method recognizes expense sooner than does the operating lease method, as summarized in Exhibit 11.2. But, over long enough time periods, expense is equal to the cash expenditure. One difference between the operating lease method and the capital method is the *timing* of the expense recognition. The other difference is that the capital lease method recognizes both the asset (leasehold) and the liability on the balance sheet.

Choosing the Accounting Method

When a journal entry debits an asset account and credits a liability account, the debt-equity ratio increases, making the company appear more risky. Thus, given a choice, most managements prefer not to show an asset and a related liability on the balance sheet. These managements prefer an operating lease to either an installment purchase or capital lease, where both the asset and liability appear on the balance sheet. Many managements would also prefer to recognize expenses later rather than sooner for financial reporting. These preferences have led managements to structure asset acquisitions so that the financing takes the form of an operating lease.

The *CICA Handbook* has established relatively stringent requirements for accounting for long-term noncancelable leases. A lease must be accounted for as a capital lease if it meets any one of three conditions.[3]

The most critical of these conditions compares the contractual lease payments discounted at an ''appropriate'' market interest rate with 90 percent of the fair value of the asset at the time the lease is signed. (The interest rate must be appropriate, given the creditworthiness of the lessee.) When the present value of lease payments exceeds 90 percent of the fair value, then the capital-lease method must be used. Other criteria are that the capital-lease method must be used if the lease period is 75 percent or more of the asset's expected remaining economic life, or that the lessee will likely obtain ownership at the end of the lease term. The major risks and rewards of ownership have been transferred from the lessor to the lessee. Thus, in economic substance, the lessee has acquired an asset and agreed to pay for it under a long-term contract, to be recognized as a liability.

Effects on Lessor

The lessor uses the same criteria for classifying a lease as a capital lease or an operating lease as does the lessee. However, the term ''capital lease'' is replaced by ''sales-type lease'' or ''direct financing lease.'' A lessee who is a manufacturer or dealer usually enters into a sales-type lease whereas a financing intermediary usually enters into a direct financing lease. At the time that a sales-type lease is signed, the lessor recognizes revenue in an amount equal to the present value of all future lease payments and recognizes expense (analogous to cost of goods sold) in an amount equal to the book value of the leased asset. The difference between the revenue and expense is the lessor's gain or loss on the ''sale'' of the asset. The lease receivable is recorded

---

[3]*CICA Handbook*, section 3065.

as any other long term receivable at the present value of the future cash flows. Interest revenue is then recognized over the collection period of the payments. When a direct financing lease is signed only interest revenue is recognized. Lessors tend to prefer sales-type lease accounting because it enables the recognition of a gain on the "sale" of the asset on the date the lease is signed. Under the operating lease method, all lease revenue is recognized gradually over time as lease payments are received.

Off-Balance-Sheet Financing[4]

Firms generally obtain debt financing either directly from banks and other financial institutions or by issuing bonds to investors. These arrangements result in a debit to cash and a credit to a liability account, and increase the debt-equity ratio. Under some other financing arrangements, the resulting obligations do not have to be recorded on the balance sheet as liabilities.

Keeping Debt off the Balance Sheet

To be an accounting liability, an obligation must be incurred for a past or current benefit received—the event or transaction giving rise to the obligation must already have happened. If the obligation arises from an executory contract, in which both parties have exchanged only promises but there has been no event in which economic risk is transferred, accounting typically does not recognize a liability. This criterion for recognizing a long-term liability focuses on the transfer of risks and rewards of ownership, not just on the undertaking of commitments to make fixed payments.

Example (Land Option) Miller Corporation desires to acquire land costing $25 million, on which it will build a shopping center. It could borrow the $25 million from its bank, paying interest at 12 percent, and buy the land outright from the seller. If so, both an asset and a liability will appear on the balance sheet. Instead, it borrows $5 million and purchases for $5 million from the seller an option to buy the land from the seller at any time within the next six years for a price of $20 million. The option costs Miller Corporation $5 million immediately and provides for continuing "option" payments of $2.4 million per year, which is just equal to Miller Corporation's borrowing rate multiplied by the remaining purchase price of the land: $2.4 million = .12 × $20 million. Although Miller Corporation need not continue payments and can let the option lapse at any time, it also has an obligation to begin developing on the site immediately. Because Miller Corporation has invested a substantial sum in the option, will invest more, and will begin immediately developing the land, Miller Corporation is almost certain to exercise its option before it expires. The seller of

---

[4]This section was developed from materials by Richard Dieter, David L. Landsittel, John E. Stewart, and Arthur R. Wyatt, all of Arthur Andersen & Co. See Landsittel and Stewart, "Off-Balance Sheet Financing; Commitments and Contingencies," in *Handbook of Modern Accounting*, 3rd ed., edited by S. Davidson and R. L. Weil, McGraw-Hill Book Company (New York: 1983), Chap. 26.

the land can take the option contract to the bank and borrow $20 million, paying interest at Miller Corporation's borrowing rate, 12 percent per year. The continuing option payments from Miller Corporation will be sufficient to enable the seller to make its payments to the bank. Generally accepted accounting principles view Miller Corporation as having acquired an option for $5 million, rather than having acquired land costing $25 million in return for $5 million cash and a liability of $20 million. As a result, Miller Corporation keeps $20 million of ''debt'' off the balance sheet until it borrows more funds to exercise the option.

The techniques for off-balance-sheet financing generally exploit the requirement that to be a liability in accounting, there must have been mutual performance. That is, benefits must have been received in the past obligating the firm to make payments in the future. When the mutual performance will occur in the future (as in executory contracts), accounting typically does not recognize a liability. In the example above, the buyer is viewed as not yet having performed beyond having purchased an option, even though the terms of the option make its eventual exercise by Miller Corporation a virtual certainty.

Why Remove Debt from the Balance Sheet?

When debt is left off the balance sheet, ratios (such as the debt-equity ratio) that have proved useful to analysts for many years will appear more favorable to the borrower. One motive may be to prevent an adverse debt-equity ratio from developing later. The entity may foresee reaching the danger point in its debt-equity relations based on historical standards. Future credit ratings might be lowered and future borrowing costs might increase.

Accounting's Response

The accounting profession has begun to recognize that certain off-balance-sheet financing arrangements have the economic substance of notes or bonds and should be recognized as accounting liabilities. The AcSC has dealt with the transactions on a case-by-case basis, without having promulgated principles to deal with all such transactions. For leases (discussed earlier in this chapter) the accounting profession attempted for more than ten years to develop a set of criteria that specify clearly which lease obligations must be recognized as liabilities. Some accountants think that there will never be a satisfactory solution until accounting requires the recording of a liability whenever there is an obligation to pay a reasonably definite amount at a reasonably definite time, independent of the executory nature of the contract.

Pensions

Under a pension plan, an employer promises to make payments to employees after retirement. Private pension plan systems have grown so rapidly in number and size over the last several decades that the major asset of many individuals is the present value of their pension benefits and a significant obligation of many firms results from their pension promises. The basic operations of a pension plan are simple, but the concepts can be lost in a variety of details. In a pension plan:

1. The employer sets up a pension plan, specifying the eligibility of employees, the types of promises to employees, the method of funding, and the pension plan administrator.
2. The employer computes a pension expense each period according to some formula. The employer debits Pension Expense for that amount and credits Pension Liability. This process is called "expensing pension obligations."
3. The employer transfers cash to the plan administrator each period according to some formula. The employer debits Pension Liability and credits Cash. This process is called "funding pension liabilities." The amounts funded in this step are usually, but *not* necessarily, the same as the amounts expensed in step (2).

The preceding steps constitute the employer's accounting for pensions. The employer is sometimes called the "plan sponsor." The following steps are carried out by the pension plan administrator.

1. The administrator receives cash each period from the plan sponsor. In the accounting records of the administrator, Cash is debited and Liability for Payments to Employees is credited.
2. Funds received are invested to generate income. The income is not part of the employer's (sponsor's) income for the period, but is reported by the administrator in separate financial statements of the pension plan.
3. The administrator makes payments to those entitled to receive them. The administrator debits Liability for Payments to Employees and credits Cash.

Section 3460 of the *CICA Handbook* governs the *employer's* accounting and reporting for the pension plan. There is no specific reference in the *Handbook* to the administrator's accounting and reporting for the pension plan.

Introduction to Pension Plans

There are almost as many different kinds of pension plans as there are employers who have them. The basic variables of a pension plan are the following:

1. Its requirement for contributions by employers and employees
2. Vesting provisions
3. Funding provisions
4. The kinds of promises made by the employer
5. Treatment of "accrued actuarial obligation," if any

Each of these variables is explained and discussed.

Contributions Under a *noncontributory* plan, the employee makes no explicit contribution of funds to the pension plan; only the employer contributes. Under a *contributory* plan both the employee and the employer contribute, but they do not necessarily contribute equal amounts. Employees retain a claim to their explicit contributions under virtually all plans. The employee's rights to the employer's contributions are determined by the *vesting* provisions. The rest of this section considers noncontributory plans or, if the plan is contributory, only the employer's contributions.

Vesting Provisions An employee's rights under a pension plan may be fully vested or partially vested. When the rights are *fully vested*, the pension benefits purchased with the employer's contributions cannot be taken away from the employee. If the rights are not vested, the employee will lose rights to the employer's contributions if he or she leaves the company. Under *partially vested* plans, rights vest gradually. For example, an employee in the fifth year of work might have no vested rights, but by the time he or she has been employed for 15 years, all rights will be vested. The nature of vesting provisions will influence the present value of the expected pension liabilities generated during an accounting period. If employees leave their jobs, then their rights, and therefore the employer's liabilities, are less if the benefits are only partially vested than when the benefits are fully vested.

Funding Provisions A pension plan may be *fully funded* or *partially funded*. Under a fully funded plan, the employer sets aside cash, or pays cash to an outside trustee, such as an insurance company, equal to the present value of all expected pension liabilities. Partially funded plans have cash available in an amount less than the present value of all pension obligations.

Employer Promises

Employers make essentially two different kinds of pension promises to employees:

1. A few employers make promises about the amounts to be contributed to the pension plan without specifying the benefits to be received by retired employees. Such plans are referred to as *defined-contribution* plans.[5] Employer inputs, or contributions to the plan, are defined. The amounts eventually received by employees depend on the investment performance of the pension fund.
2. Most employers make promises about the amount each employee will receive during retirement based on wages earned and number of years of employment. The plan does not specify the amounts the employer will contribute to the plan. Such plans are called *defined-benefit* plans.[6] Payments to employees are defined. The employer must make contributions to the plan so that those amounts plus their earnings are large enough to make the promised payments.

Defined-Contribution Plans In a defined-contribution plan, the employer promises to contribute an amount determined by formula to each employee's pension account. An employer, for example, promises to contribute between six and 12 percent of income before the contribution (the exact amount depending on some other factors) to the pension plan each year. An employee's share in the company's pension fund depends on his or her annual compensation. Another employer might

---

[5]Also called *money-purchase* or *cost-based* plans.
[6]Also called *unit-benefit* or *benefit-based* plans.

agree to contribute an amount equal to five percent of an employee's salary to a pension fund. Subject to reasonable investment risks, the funds are managed to produce as large a series of payments as is possible during the employee's retirement. No specific promises are made to employees about the amount of the eventual pension. Inputs are defined; total outputs depend on investment performance. In a defined-contribution plan, the investment and actuarial risks are carried by the employees.

The accounting for defined-contribution plans is straightforward. If the employer contributes $75,000 to a trustee to be managed for employees' retirement benefits, the journal entry is:

Pension Expense	$75,000	
Cash		$75,000

Other than periodically overseeing the activities of the plan administrator to ensure that investment policies are being carried out prudently, the employer's obligation under the pension plan is largely completed once the cash is paid to the plan administrator. Neither the assets of the pension plan nor the amounts expected to be paid to retired employees appear in the employer's financial statements. The income from pension fund investments each period is not included in the net income of the employer, but in separate financial statements of the plan.

Defined-Benefit Plans In a defined-benefit plan, the employer promises the employee a series of payments at retirement based on a formula. The typical formula takes into account the employee's length of service and some measure of average earnings. For example, the employer might promise to pay during retirement an annual pension equal to a stated percentage of the average annual salary earned during the five highest-paid working years for all employees. The percentage might increase by two percent points for each year of service, so that an employee with 40 years of service would get a pension equal to 80 percent of his or her average salary during the five highest-paid working years. The defined-benefit formula is

$$\begin{matrix} \text{Pension Benefit} \\ \text{per Year during} \\ \text{Retirement} \end{matrix} = .02n \times \begin{matrix} \text{Average Salary for} \\ \text{the 5 Highest-Paid} \\ \text{Years of} \\ \text{Employment} \end{matrix}$$

where n is the number of years of the employee's employment. Payments are defined by formula; the exact amount to be paid later to employees is not known currently and therefore must be estimated. This amount depends on factors such as mortality, inflation, and future wages. In a defined-benefit plan the investment and actuarial risks are carried by the employer.

The employer must set aside funds to fulfill its pension obligations to employees and report expenses for these amounts. The amount depends on, among other factors, the rate of return to be earned on pension fund investments. Because defined-benefit pension plans are based on numerous estimates, accounting for such plans must cope with misestimates as they become apparent.

Comparison of Types of Promises Most corporate pension plans are defined-benefit plans. Some employees prefer a defined-benefit plan because it reduces the employee's risk in planning for retirement. Employers tend to prefer defined-contribution plans because of the reduced uncertainty of pension expenses and contributions. The plan used in any given firm is likely to be the result of labour-management negotiations.

Accounting for Defined-Benefit Plans

The overriding principle that determines the accounting for defined-benefit pension plans is that the pension expense recognized in a period is a function of trying to match the total cost of the pension plan with the years in which employees provide service to the organization. The computation of the expense is *not*, however, tied to actual funding payments made to the pension plan.

An actuary for the pension plan estimates the number of eligible service years accumulated by employees to date. The projected benefits the company will incur as a result of this service are calculated by an algorithm called by the defined-benefit formula, such as the one shown on the previous page. The present value of benefits payable and attributable to services rendered to date is the principal component of the expense recognized for the current period. We will call this component the *normal cost*.

Adjustments to the Current Expense In addition to the normal cost, other components that affect the calculation of the current period expense include:
1. The amortization of adjustments arising from amendments to the plan or to assumptions underlying the plan, such as when past service costs are recognized.
2. The amortization of experience gains or losses on the plan.
3. Amortization of the difference between the value of the pension fund assets and the present value of the accrued pension benefits, calculated at the time when the recommendation of the *CICA Handbook* are first applied.[7]

Past Service Costs

The recognition of an obligation for past service costs by an employer is going to increase its costs of providing pension benefits to its employees. How should these additional costs be recognized for accounting purposes? A liability for these costs is not recognized in the accounting records. Instead, the total additional cost of this past service obligation is amortized over the remaining service life of the employees entitled to past service benefits as an increment to the normal pension expense shown each year.

For example, if it was determined that the company had an additional obligation of $900,000 and the remaining service life of employees was 15 years, then the pension expense for each of the next 15 years would increase by $60,000 ($900,000 ÷ 15).

---

[7]The current rules on accounting for pensions were implemented in December, 1986. Previous to this, most companies recognized an expense equal to the funding requirement for the year.

Other Pension Plan Adjustments When estimating the liability for future pensions a company must make assumptions about such things as investment returns, employee turnover, salary and wage changes, and mortality rates. Periodically these assumptions are compared with the experience. The difference between an assumption and the experience may be a result of a short-term fluctuation or evidence of a long-run trend. Short-term fluctuations will be considered experience gains or losses and may be automatically corrected in the future. Long-term trends are not self-correcting and will require changes to the original assumptions. Both experience gains or losses and changes in pension liabilities resulting from changes in assumptions will require an adjustment to pension expense. GAAP require that these adjustments should be normally amortized over the expected average remaining service life of the employee group covered by the pension plan.[8]

Summary of Corporate Pension Accounting by Employer

Total corporate pension expense for a period under a defined-benefit plan is made up of the sum of the charge for current service benefits earned during the period plus the charge for the gradual recognition of past service costs, gains and losses, and amounts arising from changes in assumptions.

Generally accepted accounting principles require certain minimum disclosures for pension plans by the employer. The notes to the balance sheet must disclose[9] the present value of accrued pension benefits attributable to services rendered to date and the market value of the pension fund assets.

In addition, it may be desirable to disclose the current period expense and accrual, the basis of valuing pension assets, assumptions used in determining the expense and accrual, the method and period used to amortize adjustments to the plan, a general description of the plan, and the date of the most recent actuarial valuation.

Generally Accepted Accounting Principles by the *Plan* for Defined-Benefit Pensions

The pension plan receives the cash paid by the employer/sponsor and invests it until paid to retired employees. The plan administrator keeps his or her own accounting records and reports to the company, pensioners, and employees. Note 2 in Appendix A (page 765) illustrates the required disclosures for General Products Limited.

The plan administrator ordinarily reports the plan assets, usually investments of various sorts, at fair market value. The fluctuations in market value each year are part of the earnings or losses of the pension plan.

---

[8]*CICA Handbook*, section 3460.

[9]*CICA Handbook*, section 3460.

Problem 1 for Self-Study

The Chang Company purchased a truck from Guttman's Auto Agency. The truck had a list price of $25,000, but discounts of ten to 15 percent from list price are common in purchases of this sort. Chang Company paid for the truck by giving a noninterest-bearing note due two years from the date of purchase. The note had a face value of $28,730. The rate of interest that Chang Company paid to borrow on secured two-year loans ranged from ten to 15 percent during the period when the purchase occurred.

a. Record the acquisition of the truck on Chang Company's books assuming that the fair market value of the truck was computed using a ten-percent discount from list price.

b. What imputed interest rate will be used throughout the loan for computing interest expense if the acquisition is recorded as in part (a)?

c. Record the acquisition of the truck on Chang Company's books, assuming that the estimated interest rate Chang Company must pay to borrow is deemed reliable and is 12 percent per year.

d. Record the acquisition of the truck on Chang Company's books, assuming that the interest rate Chang Company must pay to borrow is one percent per month.

e. Prepare journal entries to record the loan and to record interest over two years, assuming that the truck is recorded at $23,744 and the interest rate implicit in the loan is ten percent per year.

f. Throughout, this book has stressed that over long enough time periods, total expense is equal to cash outflow. In what sense is the total expense for this transaction the same, independent of the interest rate (and, therefore, the interest expense)?

Suggested Solution

(See Appendix B, page 793, for present value computation)

a. Truck $22,500
        Note Payable $22,500
        .90 × $25,000 = $22,500

b. $28,730/$22,500 = 1.27689. The truck has fair market value of $22,500 (= .90 × $25,000); $(1 + r)^2 = 1.27689$ implies that $r = \sqrt{1.27689} - 1$ = .13 or 13 percent per year. That is, $22,500 grows to $28,730 in two years when the interest rate is 13 percent per period.

c. Truck $22,903
        Note Payable $22,903
        $(1.12)^{-2}$ = .79719; .7919 × $28,730 = $22,903.

d. $(1.01)^{-24}$ = .78757. (See Table C.2, page 815, 24-column row, one-percent column.) .78757 × $28,730 = $22,627.

Truck	$22,627	
Note Payable		$22,627

e. Truck	$23,744	
Note Payable		$23,744
Year 1		
Interest Expense (= .10 × $23,744)	$ 2,374	
Note Payable		$ 2,374
Year 2		
Interest Expense [= .10 × ($23,744 + $2,374)] ..	$ 2,612	
Note Payable		$ 2,612

f. Total expense equals interest expense on note *and* depreciation on truck. Interest expense is $28,730 less the amount at which the truck is recorded. Depreciation expense is equal to the amount at which the truck is recorded less estimated salvage value. Thus, over the life of the truck, or two years, whichever is longer, the total expense equals $28,730 less salvage value of the truck.

Problem 2 for Self-Study

Landlord Co. Ltd., as lessor, entered into a long-term lease agreement with Tenant Limited, as lessee. The present value of the lease payments and the fair value of the property exceeded the lessor's cost of manufacturing the asset. Both companies accounted for the lease as an operating lease, whereas both companies should have accounted for it as a capital lease. What effect — understated, overstated, or none — does this error have on each of the following items in the financial statements of each of the companies for the first year of the lease?

a. Current assets   **d.** Expense
b. Liabilities   **e.** Net income
c. Revenue   **f.** Retained earnings

Suggested Solution

	Tenant Limited	Landlord Co. Ltd.
a. Current Assets	None	Understated[a]
b. Liabilities	Understated	None
c. Revenue	None	Understated[b]
d. Expense	Understated	Understated[b]
e. Net Income	Overstated	Understated[b]
f. Retained Earnings	Overstated	Understated[b]

[a]Lease receivables are part current and part noncurrent.
[b]In a capital lease, the lessor treats the signing of the lease as an installment sale. The lessor has sales revenue, cost of goods sold, and a new asset, the long-term receivable.

Problem 3 for Self Study

Rachel Limited adopted a defined benefit pension plan at the beginning of 19X1. An actuarial valuation at this date showed the following:

Accrued benefits	$8,000,000
Market value of pension fund assets	9,000,000
Expected coverage remaining service life of employees	25 years
Rate of return expected on invested fund assets	7%
Expected salary increase rate	8%
Funding requirement for 19X1	$250,000
Increase in accrued benefits attributable to 19X1 service rendered	160,000
Estimated benefit payments for 19X1	50,000

a. Calculate 19X1 pension expense.

b. What amount will be shown on Rachel's balance sheet?

c. Give the journal entries made in 19X1. (Assume all assumptions are realized so no experience gain or loss occurs.)

Suggested Solution

a. Components of the 19X1 expense

Costs related to current services rendered	$160,000
Amortization of experience gains/losses	nil
Amortization of adjustments arising from plan amendments or changes in assumptions	nil
Amortization of the net pension asset (surplus) arising on implementation of the current pension plan $\left(\dfrac{\$9,000,000 - \$8,000,000}{25 \text{ years}}\right)$	(40,000)

Interest on the accrued pension benefits

Opening balance	$8,000,000	
Accrual for current year service	160,000	
Benefit payments this year[a]	(25,000)	
	$8,135,000	
@8%		650,800

Interest on the pension fund assets

Opening balance	$9,000,000	
Funding contributions[a]	125,000	
Benefit payments this year[a]	(25,000)	
@7%		(637,000)
Net expense		**$ 133,800**

[a]The $50,000 in benefit payments are assumed to occur evenly throughout the year. For interest calculations, the mid-year point is chosen ($50,000 ÷ 2 = $25,000). The same assumption is used for funding contributions.

b. The balance sheet would show a liability of $33,800:

$133,800 .... expense
100,000 .... funding requirement
$ 33,800[b]

[b]If the expense is less than the funding requirement, the difference is shown as a deferred charge (*CICA handbook* 3460.57).

c. The compound journal entry for 19X1 is:

Pension Expense	$133,800	
Cash		100,000
Liability for pension benefits		33,800

Questions, Exercises, Problems and Cases

Questions

1. Review the meaning of the following concepts or terms discussed in this chapter.

a. Interest-bearing note	**g.** Off-balance-sheet financing
b. Noninterest-bearing note	**h.** Pension plan
c. Implicit interest	**i.** Defined-benefit plan
d. Imputed interest rate	**j.** Defined-contribution plan
e. Capital lease	**k.** Current service costs
f. Operating lease	**l.** Past service obligation

2. In what sense is the historical cost accounting for noncurrent liabilities subsequent to the date of issuance based on historical costs?

3. Brealey Limited negotiated a five-year loan for $1 million with its bank. The terms of the loan require that the interest rate can be changed as the bank chooses, but that the company can repay the loan at any time. Interest is to be paid quarterly. How should Brealey Limited classify this note on its balance sheet?

4. Demonstrate that the amortization schedule in Exhibit 11.1 conforms to the "unifying principles of accounting for long-term liabilities" described on pages 516 and 517 of Chapter 10.

5. Why is the question, "Who enjoys the potential rewards and bears the risks of an asset?" important for lease accounting?

6. In what ways is the economic substance of a capital lease by a lessee similar to, and different from, that of an installment purchase?

7. Distinguish between the lessee's accounting for a capital lease and for an installment purchase.

8. In what sense is the total expense from a lease independent of the method of accounting for it by the lessee?

9. Why do many managements find off-balance-sheet financing attractive?

10. What are the economic and accounting differences between a defined-benefit pension plan and a defined-contribution plan?

11. Why does the amendment ("sweetening") of a defined-benefit plan ordinarily increase the past service obligation, whereas a change with the same cost in a defined-contribution plan does not?

12. The Hicks Co. Ltd. is adopting a defined-benefit pension plan. Who, the employee or the Hicks Co. Ltd., is more likely to bear the risks and rewards of fluctuating market returns on funds invested to pay the pension?

Exercises

13. *Nature of liabilities.*
  a. For each of the following items, indicate whether the item meets all of the criteria of the accountant's usual definition of a liability.
  b. If the item is recognized as a liability, how is the amount of the liability computed?
  (1) Fifteen-year cancelable lease on an office building.
  (2) Twenty-year noncancelable lease on a factory building.
  (3) Anticipated future cost of restoring strip-mining sites after mining operations are completed.
  (4) Obligation to pay pensions under defined-benefit formula for labour services during current year.
  (5) Obligation to pay pensions under defined-benefit formula with retroactive credit given to employees for labour services provided before the plan was adopted.

14. *Journal entries for equipment contract with imputed interest.* Refer to the example on page 535 of the chapter where equipment is acquired in exchange for a single-payment note for $16,000 due in three years. The issuer of the note pays 12 percent interest for borrowings of this sort. The present value of the note on the date of issue is $11,388. Assume the note is issued on January 1, Year 1, and that the firm closes its books annually.

Provide adjusting entries for the end of Years 1, 2, and 3 and an entry for the payment of the note at maturity.

15. *Funds statement effects of leases.* Refer to the Simplified Statement of Changes in Financial Position for a Period in Exhibit 5.19 on page 248. Eleven of the lines in the statement are numbered. Ignore the unnumbered lines in responding to the questions below.

Assume that the accounting cycle is complete for the period and that all of the financial statements have been prepared. Then it is discovered that a transaction has been overlooked. That transaction is recorded in the accounts and all of the financial statements are corrected. Define *funds* as *cash*. For each of the following transactions, indicate which of the numbered lines of the funds statement is affected and by how much. Ignore income tax effects except where taxes are explicitly mentioned.

For the following questions, assume that an asset with an economic life of ten years, costing $100,000, is leased for $19,925 per year, paid at the end of each year.

    a. The lessor, using the operating lease method, records depreciation for the year.

    b. The lessor, using the operating lease method, records receipt of a cash payment for the year. Revenue has not previously been recognized.

    c. The lessee, using the operating lease method, records payment of cash for the year. Expense has not previously been recognized.

    d. The lessor, using the capital lease method, records receipt of cash at the end of the first year and uses an interest rate of 15 percent per year. $15,000 is interest and $4,925 is receipt of principal. No entries have previously been made recognizing revenues.

    e. The lessee, using the capital lease method, records payment of cash for the first year and uses an interest rate of 15 percent per year. $15,000 is interest and $4,925 is payment of principal.

16. *Pension disclosures.* The CICA Handbook (Section 3460.61) recommends rather than requires several pension related disclosures such as: the pension expense for the period, the amount of the deferred charge or accrual, the basis of valuing fund assets, the salary and interest rate assumptions, the method and amortization period for all adjustments, a general description of the plan, the date of the most recent actuarial valuation, and any matters which might affect comparability.

Go to the library and photocopy the pension footnote(s) from the annual report of any Canadian public corporation. Prepare for class discussion a critique of how its disclosure compares with these guidelines.

17. *Funds statement effects of pensions.* Refer to the instructions in Exercise 15. For each of the following transactions, indicate which of the numbered lines of the funds statement is affected and by how much. Ignore income tax effects.

    a. A pension plan is adopted with credit given for past service; an obligation of $100,000 arises.

    b. A past service obligation is expensed and funded in the amount of $100,000.

    c. Current Service costs of $40,000 are recognized and funded.

18. *Amortization schedule for note where explicit interest differs from market rate of interest.* On January 1, Year 1, the beginning of the fiscal year, Garstka Limited acquires a computer from Berney's Computer Store. The cash price (fair market value) of the computer is $50,568. Garstka Limited gives a three-year, interest-bearing note with maturity value of $60,000. The note requires annual interest payments on December 31 of nine percent of face value, $5,400 per year. The interest rate implicit in the note is 16 percent per year.

    a. Prepare an amortization schedule for the note.

    b. Prepare journal entries for Garstka Limited over the life of the note.

19. *Operating lease accounting (adapted from CPA Examination).* The Jackson Co. Ltd. manufactured a piece of equipment at a cost of $7 million, which is held for resale from January 1 to June 30 at a price of $8 million. On July 1, Jackson leased the equipment to the Crystal Co. Ltd. The lease is appropriately recorded as an operating lease for accounting purposes. The lease is for a three-year period. Equal monthly payments under the lease are $115,000 and are due on the first of the month. The first payment was made on July 1. The equipment is being depreciated on a straight-line basis over an eight-year period with no residual value expected.

    a. What expense should Crystal record as a result of the above facts for the current year ended December 31? Show supporting computations in good form.

    b. What income or loss before income taxes should Jackson record as a result of the above facts for the year ended December 31? Show supporting computations in good form.

20. *Understanding pension disclosures in financial statements.* From the notes to financial statements of Imperial Oil Ltd. determine the following:

    a. the type of plan

    b. the expense for pension costs shown in the 1986 income statement

    c. how much the company actually pays into the pension plan each year

    d. the adequacy of the pension fund in relation to Imperial Oil's obligations to its employees for its *regular* pension plans

    e. Are the pension numbers reported by Imperial Oil for 1986 and 1985 comparable? Are any caveats to readers in order?

IMPERIAL OIL LTD.
In Summary of Accounting Policies

Retirement plans

The company's pension plans cover almost all employees. Pension-benefit obligations are determined annually by independent actuaries using the projected-unit-credit method. Valuation of assets is based on market values at December 31 of each year. The amounts contributed by the company to the plans are established according to accepted actuarial procedures. Prior to 1986, the amount funded was also the pension expense for the year. In 1986, the Canadian Institute of Chartered Accountants published new standards for accounting for pension plans. As a result, starting in 1986 the amount expensed is determined on the accrual basis, which reflects the service of employees for the year rather than the amount contributed by the company to the plans.

Note to Financial Statements

16. *Employee retirement plans*

The pension plans cover almost all company employees and generally are based on length of service and on average earnings during the final three years of employment. The plans are funded by the company based on actuarial valuation, the most recent being December 31, 1985. As well, the amounts include the company's share of the pension plans for the Syncrude joint venture.

Funded status at December 31	1984	1985	1986
	(millions of dollars)		
Market value of assets	1057	1296	1319
Accumulated benefit obligation (1)	842	898	1067
Assets excess	215	398	252
Unearned benefit obligation (1)	308	328	222
(Unfunded liability) Surplus	(93)	70	30

The benefit obligation for 1986 is affected by the 1986 early-retirement program and an updating of the actuarial assumptions.

The surplus/unfunded liability is credited/charged to expense over the average remaining service life of employees, which is currently 17 years.

In addition, actuarially determined obligations to surviving spouses (which are paid directly by the company) amount to $150 million at December 31, 1986.

Annual pension expense

In accordance with new accounting standards, the pension expense for 1986 is calculated on the accrual basis rather than the funding basis used in prior years. (See summary of significant accounting policies.)

	1984	1985	1986
	(millions of dollars)		
Current service cost	—	—	33
Interest cost	—	—	5
Plan amendment amortization	—	—	1
Expense for 1984 and 1985 based on funding method	32	34	—
Pension expense before 1986 early-retirement program	32	34	39
Expense of 1986 early-retirement program (2)	—	—	109
Total pension expense	32	34	148

Assumptions

The measurement of the retirement obligation and expense involves making assumptions about economic and other factors over an extended future period. In order to aid in understanding the information provided above, the following provides the most significant assumptions and their impact:

	1984	1985	1986
Rate of return on the plan's assets (percent)	7.0	7.0	8.5
Salary escalation rate (percent)	5.0	5.0	6.0

	(millions of dollars)
Impact of a one percent increase in rate of return on	
total benefit obligation (1)	(160)
annual expense	(9)
Impact of a one percent increase in salary escalation on	
total benefit obligation (1)	22
annual expense	1

(1) The total benefit obligation is the amount the pension fund needs to have invested at the assumed rate of return (currently 8.5 percent) in order to be able to pay pensions for service rendered to date. This obligation has two parts. The accumulated benefit obligation is based on current salaries and the unearned benefit obligation is the estimated additional amount due to salary escalation by the time of retirement. (2) This amount is part of the work-force reduction program included in unusual items (note 10).

21. *Computation of pension expense.* The actuaries of Campbell Corporation have provided the following information on its pension plan as of 12/31/19X0:

	12/31/19X0[a]
Average service life remaining of employees covered by the plan	20 years
Expected salary rate increase	6%
Rate of return expected on fund assets.....................................	7%
Funding requirement for 19X1	$800,000
Increase in accrued benefits attributable to 19X1 service rendered	$200,000
Estimate of benefits to be paid out in 19X1	$100,000
Market value of fund assets at 12/31/19X0	$6,000,000
Accrued benefits at 12/31/19X0	$7,000,000

[a]It adopted a defined benefit plan at this date.

Compute the 19X1 pension expense and the amount to be shown on the balance sheet at 12/31/19X1.

Problems and Cases

22. *Comparing expense for operating lease with capital lease.* Maher Co. Ltd. has calculated that the annual payment in arrears to amortize a $1 million loan over 25 years at 15 percent interest is $154,700.

    a. What is rent expense for the first year of an operating lease when the rent payment is $154,700?

    b. What is lease expense for the first year of a 25-year capital lease for use of an asset costing $1 million requiring annual payments in arrears of $154,700? Use straight-line amortization of leasehold.

    c. How much larger in percentage terms is the lessee's expense in the first year under the capital lease than under the operating lease?

23. *Criteria for classifying leases as operating or capital.* Assume that Rich's Department Stores Inc. is about to sign four separate leases for stores in four separate shopping centres. Each of the stores would cost $20 million if purchased outright and has an economic life of 20 years. Assume that the company currently must pay interest at the rate of 15 percent per year on long-term borrowing when sound collateral backs the loan. The lease payments are to be made at the end of each year in all four cases.

Based on the information given here, decide whether each of the four leases requires accounting as operating leases or as capital leases. Give your reasoning.

	Lease Term	Annual Lease Payment
a. Cumberland Mall	16 Years	$2,500,000
b. Normandale Centre	16 Years	2,600,000
c. Eastbrook Haven	12 Years	3,300,000
d. Peachtree Parkview	12 Years	3,400,000

24. *Comparison of borrow/buy with operating and capital leases.* The Carom Co. Ltd. plans to acquire, as of January 1, Year 1, a computerized cash register system that costs $100,000 and has a five-year life and no salvage value. The company is considering two plans for acquiring the system.

(1) Outright purchase. To finance the purchase, $100,000 of par value, ten percent semiannual coupon bonds will be issued January 1, Year 1, at par.

(2) Lease. The lease requires five annual payments to be made on December 31, Year 1, Year 2, Year 3, Year 4, and Year 5. The least payments are such that they have a present value of $100,000 on January 1, Year 1, when discounted at ten percent per year.

Straight-line amortization methods will be used for all depreciation and amortization computations for assets.

    a. Verify that the amount of the required lease payment is $26,380 by constructing an amortization schedule for the five payments. Note that there will be a $2 rounding error in the fifth year. Nevertheless, you may treat each payment as being $26,380 in the rest of the problem.

    b. What balance sheet amounts will be affected if plan **(1)** is selected? If plan **(2)** is selected, the lease is cancelable, and the operating lease treatment is used? If plan **(2)** is selected, the lease is noncancelable, and the capital lease treatment is used?

    c. What will be the total depreciation and interest expenses for the five years under plan **(1)**?

    d. What will be the total expenses for the five years under plan **(2)** if the lease is accounted for as an operating lease? As a capital lease?

    e. Why are the answers in part **(d)** the same? Why are the answers in part **(c)** different from those in part **(d)**?

    f. What will be the total expenses for Year 1, under plan **(1)**? Under plan **(2)** accounted for as an operating lease? Under plan **(2)** accounted for as a capital lease?

    g. Repeat part **(f)** for the fifth year, Year 5.

25. *Analysis of risks and rewards of lease contracts.* Pacific Eastern Air Lines (PEA) leased three Boeing 707 aircraft in Year 1 from Sally Leasing Limited (Sally). The aircraft had a purchase price of $6.64 million each. The leases covered 13-year terms, were noncancelable, contained no purchase options, and required monthly payments of $71,115. The rental cost per month of $71,115 was several hundred dollars less than PEA would have had to pay for conventional financing at the then-prevalent interest rate.

    a. What, if anything, did PEA give up in return for its savings of several hundred dollars per month for 13 years? What, if anything, did Sally get for giving up several hundred dollars per month for 13 years?

    b. Who bore the risks and rewards of ownership in these leases?

    c. Verify that the interest rate implicit in the least contract is about three-fourths of one percent per month.

    d. Assume that Section 3065 of the *CICA Handbook* had been in effect when these leases were signed. To ascertain how the leases would be accounted for, what further information would you need?

26. *Possible accounting treatments for past service obligations.* When a company adopts a defined-benefit pension plan giving credit to current employees for past service, an obligation, perhaps in large amounts, arises. This amount is currently disclosed in notes and is only gradually recognized in the balance sheet.

    Assume that the amount is immediately credited to a liability when it comes into existence. What accounts might be debited? Give justifications for debiting an asset account or an expense account, or directly debiting Retained Earnings.

27. *Preparing funds statement (adapted from a problem by Stan Baiman).* Exhibit 11.3 shows comparative balance sheets and income statement of Hermitage Limited for Year 2, and supplementary notes.

Exhibit 11.3
HERMITAGE LIMITED
Comparative Balance Sheets and Income Statement

Balance Sheets	December 31	
	Year 2	Year 1
Cash	$130,000	$ 30,000
Accounts Receivable (net)	95,000	80,000
Inventory	150,000	140,000
Plant and Equipment	875,000	800,000
Accumulated Depreciation	(520,000)	(380,000)
Total Assets	$730,000	$670,000
Accounts Payable	$ 25,000	$ 20,000
Taxes Payable	76,000	60,000
Deferred Investment Tax Credits	13,000	10,000
Future Income Taxes	64,000	40,000
Capital Stock	210,000	200,000
Retained Earnings	342,000	340,000
Total Equities	$730,000	$670,000

Year 2 Income Statement

Net Sales		$605,000
Less: Cost of Goods Sold		200,000
Gross Profit		$405,000
Less: Depreciation	$140,000	
Other Expenses	15,000	155,000
Net Income Before Income Tax		$250,000
Income Tax		
Current	$76,000	
Deferred	24,000	100,000
Net Income		$150,000

Notes:
(1) All depreciation charges are expensed.
(2) Dividends declared have been paid in cash.
(3) During Year 2, Hermitage acquired property, plant, and equipment to be depreciated over ten years for financial reporting. The items are eligible for an investment tax credit of $7,500; income taxes for Year 2 are already decreased by this amount.
(4) Hermitage uses the deferral method for the investment tax credit and deferred 90 percent of the investment tax credit earned during Year 2. Current income tax expense was reduced by $4,500 because of the investment tax credit.

a. How much of the $7,500 investment tax credit earned during Year 2 was deferred? Why does the Deferred Investment Tax Credits account increase by only $3,000, an amount smaller than this?

b. Prepare the Year 2 statement of changes in financial position with funds defined as cash.

28. *Analysis of attempts to achieve off-balance-sheet financing* [*adapted from "Off-Balance-Sheet Financing," Case 4.1 in* Accounting and Auditing Case Studies (*The Trueblood Professors' Seminar*), *The Touche Ross Foundation and The American Accounting Association, 1983, pp. 21–22*]. Container Limited has developed a process for manufacturing plastic bottles at a cost lower than any competitor's. Gigantic Drugs, Inc., has offered to purchase enough of the bottles so that Container will have to build a new plant just to fill Gigantic's orders. The new plant will be built next to Gigantic's plant, with a conveyor belt to carry the bottles into Gigantic's plant. Container will operate the plant. The problem is that Container does not have, and is unable to raise, sufficient funds to finance construction of the new plant. Gigantic is willing to provide its financial backing to raise the necessary funds but has insufficient cash to finance the project. Moreover, it is unwilling to borrow the funds if doing so increases the recorded debt on its balance sheet because of potential default on some of its own debt covenants and some other new plans it has to raise funds by borrowing. The financial executives of Container and Gigantic have devised two plans to finance the plant while attempting to satisfy Gigantic's requirements. Under both plans, Container will create a subsidiary, Borrower Inc. to borrow all the funds required from a bank to build the plant.

Plan 1. Borrower will lease the plant to Gigantic for 40 years with lease payments matched in size and timing to Borrower's debt service payments to the bank. Gigantic is sufficiently solvent and profitable that its promised lease payments and the plant itself will induce a bank to provide 100 percent financing at Gigantic's borrowing rate. Borrower would contract with Container to manage the new plant.

Plan 2. Gigantic will sign a contract to purchase bottles from the new plant. It will buy all the bottles produced by the plan when it operates at normal capacity. Contractual payments will cover all variable manufacturing costs, debt service on the bank loan, and the payments to Container to manage the new plant. If Gigantic does not wish to purchase the entire output of the plant and if Borrower is unable to sell the bottles to other bottle users, then Gigantic will agree to make a cash payment to Borrower for the difference so that Borrower can meet all its cash obligations. Any cash that Borrower can generate from selling bottles to other bottle users for amounts larger than variable manufacturing costs will reduce the payments Gigantic makes to Borrower.

Discuss these two plans from two perspectives.

    a. Consider the auditor who must decide whether each arrangement requires recognition on the balance sheet or whether footnote disclosure is enough.

    b. Consider an investment banker who is planning to bid on the new bond issue Gigantic will use to raise funds for a different purpose. The banker must take into account, among other things, Gigantic's entire financial structure.

29. *Analysis of take-or-pay contract including capitalization of future payments and possible losses.* Natural gas pipelines sign take-or-pay contracts with producers of natural gas. Under these contracts the pipelines agree to purchase the natural gas in fixed (or computable) quantities at fixed (or computable) prices or to pay for the gas even if they do not take delivery. By the mid-1980s, there was a large quantity of natural gas contracted for relative to the amounts that could be sold by the pipelines. *A Business Week* article on the subject said:

> Most of the unfavorable contracts were hastily signed after the cold winters of 1977 and 1978, when the gas shortage assumed crisis proportions. The pipeline industry faced the prospect of . . . lawsuits over its inability to supply contracted-for fuel. . . . Aggressively bidding for new supplies, the pipelines bought their way out of the problem — and into an even greater mess. They now find themselves stuck with massive numbers of "take-or-pay" agreements. . . . The fear of another icy, gasless winter, some say, drove pipeline executives to close one bad deal after another. Tenneco . . . had 4 billion cu. ft. per day of gas available for delivery and sales of just over 2 billion cu. ft. per day . . . [The] costs [of natural gas had] soared to $3.48 per thousand cu. ft. . . . and price escalators in many contracts threaten to keep costs rising, especially after [price] controls expire. . . .

The financial statements of Tenneco showed total assets of $17.4 billion, current liabilities of $6.9 billion, long-term debt of $5.0 billion, and owners' equity of $5.5 billion. Notes to the statements indicate that some of Tenneco's take-or-pay contracts extend 25 years into the future.

    a. Compute the long-term debt ratio [= long-term debt/(long-term debt + owners' equity)] from the financial statement data.

    b. Compute the present value of the obligation to take 4 billion cubic feet of gas per day for ten years. Assume a price of $3.50 per thousand cubic feet, a year of 300 business days, and a discount rate of 15 percent per year. Payments occur at year-end.

    c. Assume that these contractual payments are capitalized on the balance sheet and that an asset is recorded in the same amount. Compute the long-term debt ratio.

    d. Now assume that Tenneco will be able to sell only 60 percent of the contracted-for gas. The other 40 percent will be paid for, but because it is not taken, there is no offsetting asset for this amount, only a loss. Assume that the loss is tax deductible and an income tax rate of 46 percent. Recompute owners' equity and the long-term debt ratio for the financial statements excerpted above.

30. *Attempts to achieve off-balance-sheet financing (adapted from materials by Richard Dieter, David L. Landsittel, John E. Stewart, and Arthur R. Wyatt).* Brion Limited wishes to raise $50 million cash but, for various reasons, does not wish to do so in a way that results in a newly recorded liability. It is sufficiently solvent and profitable that its bank is willing to lend up to $50 million at the prime interest rate. Brion Limited's financial executives have devised six different plans, described below.

Transfer of Receivables with Recourse Brion Limited will transfer to Credit Corp. its long-term accounts receivable, which call for payments over the next two years. Credit Corp. will pay an amount equal to the present value of the receivables less an allowance for uncollectibles and a discount because it is paying now, but will collect cash later. Brion Limited must repurchase from Credit Corp. at face value any receivables that become uncollectible in excess of the allowance. In addition, Brion Limited may repurchase any of the receivables not yet due at face value less a discount specified by formula and based on the prime rate at the time of transfer. (This option permits Brion Limited to benefit if an unexpected drop in interest rates occurs after the transfer.) The accounting issue is whether the transfer is a sale (where Brion Limited debits Cash, credits Accounts Receivable, and debits expense or loss on transfer) or whether the transfer is merely a loan collateralized by the receivables (where Brion Limited debits Cash and credits Notes Payable at the time of transfer).

Product Financing Arrangement Brion Limited will transfer inventory to Credit Corp., who will store the inventory in a public warehouse. Credit Corp. may use the inventory as collateral for its own borrowings, whose proceeds will be used to pay Brion Limited. Brion Limited will pay storage costs and will repurchase all the inventory within the next four years at contractually fixed prices plus interest accrued for the time elapsed between the transfer and later repurchase. The accounting issue is whether the inventory is sold to Credit Corp., with later repurchases treated as new acquisitions for Brion's inventory, or whether the transaction is merely a loan, with the inventory remaining on Brion's balance sheet.

Throughput Contract Brion Limited requires a branch line of a railroad to be built from the main rail line to carry raw material directly to its own plant. It could, of course, borrow the funds and build the branch line itself. Instead, it signs an agreement with the railroad to ship specified amounts of material each month for ten years. Even if it does not ship the specified amounts of material, it will pay the agreed shipping costs. The railroad will take the contract to its bank and, using it as collateral, borrow the funds to build the branch line. The accounting issue is whether Brion Limited would debit an asset for future rail services and credit a liability for payments to the railroad. The alternative is to make no accounting entry except when Brion makes payments to the railroad.

Construction Partnership Brion Limited and Mission Inc. will jointly undertake to build a plant to manufacture chemicals both need in their own production processes. Each will contribute $5 million to the project, called Chemical. Chemical will borrow another $40 million from a bank, with Brion, only, guaranteeing the debt. Brion and Mission are each to contribute equally to future operating expenses and debt service payments of Chemical, but, in return for its guaranteeing the debt, Brion will have an option to purchase Mission's interest for $20 million four years hence. The accounting issue is whether Brion Limited would recognize a liability for the funds borrowed by Chemical; because of the debt guarantee, debt service payments will ultimately be the responsibility of Brion Limited. Alternatively, the debt guarantee is a commitment merely to be disclosed in notes to Brion Limited's financial statements.

Research and Development Partnership Brion Limited will contribute a laboratory and preliminary finding about a potentially profitable gene-splicing discovery to a partnership, called Venture. Venture will raise funds by selling the remaining interest in the partnership to outside investors for $2 million and borrowing $48 million from a bank, with Brion Limited guaranteeing the debt. Although Venture will operate under the management of Brion Limited, it will be free to sell the results of its further discoveries and development efforts to anyone, including Brion Limited. Brion Limited is not obligated to purchase any of Venture's output. The accounting issue is whether the liability would be recognized by Brion Limited. (Would it make any difference if Brion Limited has either the *option* to purchase or an *obligation* to purchase the results of Venture's work?)

Hotel Financing Brion Limited owns and operates a profitable hotel. Brion could use the hotel as collateral for a conventional mortgage loan. Instead, it considers selling the hotel to a partnership for $50 million cash. The partnership will sell ownership interests to outside investors for $5 million and borrow $45 million from a bank on a conventional mortgage loan, using the hotel as collateral. Brion Limited guarantees the debt. The accounting issue is whether Brion Limited would record the liability for the guaranteed debt of the partnership.

Consider each of these proposed arrangements from the viewpoint of the auditor (who must decide whether the transaction will result in a liability to be recorded or whether footnote disclosure will suffice) and from the viewpoint of an investment banker (who must assess the financing structure of Brion Limited in order to make a competitive bid on a proposed new underwriting of Brion Limited common shares).

Decision Problem 11-1

Shifty Moving Ltd. is considering the acquisition of a warehouse to provide storage for its moving customers. R.U. Shifty, the president and sole shareholder, has designed a suitable frame building which he can have constructed for $100,000 on land leased for 40 years. He is considering alternative methods of financing the construction.

Shifty Moving Ltd. is subject to a 40 percent marginal rate of income tax.

R.U. Shifty has approached an insurance company that is prepared to lend Shifty Moving $100,000 in exchange for a first mortgage for the same amount bearing interest at 12 percent, with payments of principal and interest of $12,130 per year in arrears. The mortgage would be paid in full in 40 years.

As an alternative, Shifty is considering financing the warehouse from a trust fund established for his children by his father. He and his two unmarried sisters are the trustees of the fund. His sisters follow his advice, since Shifty pays them an annual gift of $1,600 a month as a balm to his conscience for paying them only 20 percent of the real value of the shares in Shifty Moving Ltd. when these were willed to the three of them by their father.

Shifty has considered that the trust fund can purchase the building and lease it to the company for $12,130 per year in arrears on a 40-year lease. Shifty Moving Ltd. would pay all taxes and maintenance costs and the building would have no value in 40 years time.

Shifty has heard that, if he considers the lease a "Capital Lease," he will be required to record the asset and liability on his books and present them in his financial statements in a similar fashion to the presentation made if he chose the mortgage issue alternative. On the other hand, if he considers the lease to be an "Operating Lease," he need not show the asset and liability in his financial statements.

Because of his indirect control of the trust fund, Shifty judges that the lease could be written so that it might be considered either as a "Capital Lease" or as an "Operating Lease." In both cases the annual payment, in arrears, would be $12,130 over a period of 40 years.

Evaluate the alternative methods of financing the construction (mortgage purchase, capital lease, operating lease).

Chapter 12 Owners' Equity

The economic resources of a firm come from two major sources. Nonowners provide funds to a firm; the sources of these funds are shown on the balance sheet as *liabilities*, discussed in chapters 10 and 11. Owners provide funds; the sources of these funds are shown on the balance sheet as *owners' equity*.

The accounting equation states that:

$$\text{Assets} = \text{Claims to Assets}$$
or
$$\text{Assets} = \text{Liabilities} + \text{Owners' Equity}$$

This chapter discusses **corporate** owners' equity. There are three major advantages to incorporation:

1. The corporate form provides the owner (shareholder) with limited liability. That is, should the corporation become insolvent, creditors' claims are limited to the assets of the corporate entity. The corporation's creditors cannot claim the assets of the individual owners. On the other hand, creditors of partnerships and sole proprietorships have a claim on both the owners' personal and the business assets to settle such firms' debts.[1]
2. The corporate form allows the raising of funds by the issuing of shares. The general public can acquire the shares in varying amounts. Individual investments can range from a few dollars to hundreds of millions of dollars.
3. The corporate form makes transfer of ownership interests relatively easy, because individual shares can be sold by current owners to others without interfering with the ongoing operations of the business. Changes in ownership do not affect the continuity of the management and of operations.

There are also disadvantages to incorporation. The major disadvantage is double taxation—corporations must pay income tax on earnings whether distributed to shareholders or not. Remaining earnings, distributed as dividends, are taxed again in the shareholders' hands. Another disadvantage is that corporations are generally subject to more government regulation and supervision than unincorporated businesses.

This chapter discusses the accounting for capital contributed by owners; the accounting for income earned by the firm, which may be retained or distributed to owners; and other changes in owners' equity accounts.

Incorporating Acts

A corporation is an artificial legal "person" created with the approval of government. As such, it can sue, be sued, enter into contracts, and pay income taxes as

---

[1]Note that with small firms the directors/owners are often required to guarantee the firm's liabilities.

would an individual. A firm may choose to be incorporated federally under the jurisdiction of the Canada Business Corporations Act (CBCA) or provincially under one of the provincial corporations Acts. Variations exist in the rules among these Acts, especially with respect to the accounting and disclosure of capital transactions. The most significant of these involve whether par value shares and treasury shares are allowed. Throughout the chapter we will differentiate between CBCA and non-CBCA requirements.

Public Versus Private Corporations

Two fundamentally different types of corporations exist in Canada: *public* and *private*. Although the terms were created under the predecessor Canada Corporations Act and have been discontinued in the CBCA, they are still widely used.

A public company offers its shares to the general public and is usually listed on one of the five Canadian stock exchanges. Most of the largest companies in Canada are public, although there are some exceptions, such as the T. Eaton Company. A private company is *closely held*. This means that its shares are owned by a small number of people and that they are not marketed to the general public or sold on public stock exchanges.

From an accounting perspective, the key distinction between these two types of companies is that private companies are not legally required to have an annual audit unless a shareholder requests one and are not required to file annual financial statements with the Director of Companies or with the provincial securities commission. In order to qualify for this exemption, the CBCA imposes a size test. The corporation must have gross revenues less than ten million dollars and total assets under five million dollars.

Two implications arise from these exemptions. First, small closely held companies can escape much of the costly bureaurcratic red tape that large corporations face. Second, because most Canadian companies are small, closely held companies, the public has no access to their financial statements.

Capital Contributions

The corporation is a legal entity separate from its owners. Individuals or other entities make capital contributions under a contract between themselves and the corporation. Because those who contribute funds receive and hold share certificates, they are known as "shareholders."[2] The rights and obligations of a shareholder are governed by:

1. The corporation laws of the jurisdiction in which incorporation takes place.
2. The articles of incorporation or *charter*. This is a contract between the firm and a provincial or the federal government under whose laws the business is incor-

---

[2]The terminology in the USA is stockholder (and stock instead of shares). Many Canadian companies now say "Capital Stock" instead of "Share Capital."

porated. The enterprise is granted the privilege of operating as a corporation for certain stated purposes and of obtaining its capital through the issue of shares.

3. The bylaws of the corporation. The board of directors adopt bylaws, which are the rules and regulations governing the internal affairs of the corporation.
4. The share contract. Each type of share capital has its own provisions as to such matters as voting, sharing in earnings, distribution of earnings, and sharing in assets in case of dissolution.

Some closely held corporations have a small number of shareholders and operate much like a partnership. The few people involved agree to the amount of capital to be contributed, elect each other to be members of the board of directors and officials to the firm, and agree on policies regarding dividends and salaries. They may restrict the transfer of shares to outsiders, and may even become liable for debts of the corporation by endorsing its notes and bonds.

In the case of large, widely owned corporations, the effect of the corporation's being a separate legal entity is more pronounced. Officials and directors may own few or no shares in the corporation. Actual control is likely to be in the hands of a few individuals or a group who own or control enough shares to elect a majority of the board of directors. Most "minority" shareholders think of their share holdings merely as passive investments, and they participate little, if at all, in the conduct of the affairs of the corporation. The shareholders assume no obligation for the debts of the business. Shares change hands at the will of the shareholders, and the record of who owns shares is usually kept by a trust company.

Classes of Shares

Corporations are often authorized to issue more than one class of shares, each representing ownership in the business. Most shares issued are either *common* or *preferred*. Occasionally, there may be several classes of common or preferred shares, each with different rights and privileges. All corporations must have at least one class of shares. They are usually called "common shares," but they may be designated by another name, such as Class A shares. Preferred shares may, but need not be, issued by a corporation.

Common shares have the claim to earnings of the corporation after commitments to preferred shareholders have been satisfied. Frequently, common shares are the only voting shares of the company. In the event of corporate dissolution, all of the proceeds of asset disposition, after settling the claims of creditors and required distributions to preferred shareholders, are distributable to the common shareholders.

Preferred shares have special privileges. Although these privileges vary considerably from issue to issue, a preferred share usually entitles its holder to dividends at a certain rate, which must be paid before dividends can be paid to common shareholders. Sometimes, though these dividends may be postponed or omitted.

Dividend Preference

The amount is specified in dollars per share. However, the amount is owed to the shareholders only if declared.

Preferred dividends are usually *cumulative*—that is, regular dividends to preferred shareholders omitted in past years must be paid in addition to the current year's dividend before any distribution is made to common shareholders. For example, a dividend may not be declared in an unprofitable year. If a $6 preferred stock dividend is one year in arrears and a dividend is declared in the current year, preferred shareholders would receive $12 per share before common shareholders received anything. If a preferred share is noncumulative, omitted dividends do not carry forward. Because investors normally consider the cumulative feature unattractive, noncumulative preferred shares are rarely issued.

Dividends in arrears (that is, omitted in past years) on cumulative preferred shares are not an accounting liability and do not appear in the liability section of the balance sheet. They do not become an obligation of the corporation until the board of directors formally declares such dividends. Any arrearages are typically disclosed to investors in a footnote to the balance sheet.

Ordinarily, preferred shareholders receive a fixed amount and do not participate further in distributions made by the corporation. In rare circumstances, however, the corporation may decide to make the preferred share a *participating share*.

This feature is illustrated in the footnote taken from an annual report of a Canadian Company, shown here as Exhibit 12–1. Let us assume the following dividend distribution by this company:

(a) $1,000,000, (b) $2,500,000, and (c) $10,000,000

(a)	Class A	Class B
Outstanding shares	18,384,157	10,182,538
Dividend declared $1,000,000		
Payable to Class A	$ 1,000,000	
(5.43¢ per share)		
Payable to Class B		—

(b)	Class A	Class B
Outstanding shares	18,384,157	10,182,538
Dividend declared $2,500,000		
Payable to Class A (10¢/share)	$ 1,838,416	
Payable to Class B (6.5¢/share)		$ 661,584

(c)	Class A	Class B
Outstanding shares	18,384,157	10,182,538
Dividend declared $10,000,000		
Payable to Class A (10¢/share)	$ 1,838,416	
Payable to Class B (10¢/share)		$ 1,018,254
Remainder allocated equally		
(25¢/share [rounded])*	4,597,105	2,546,225

*$7,143,330/(18,384,157 + 10,182,538) = 25.01 cents

Exhibit 12.1
Example of Note Disclosure for Capital Stock

	1989	1988
Capital stock (note 10)	63,168	61,135

Note to financial statements

10. Capital Stock

Authorized

The Corporation is authorized to issue:

(a) an unlimited number of Class "A" non-voting shares without nominal or par value (the "Class 'A' shares");

(b) an unlimited number of Class "B" common shares without nominal or par value (the "Class 'B' shares"); and

(c) an unlimited number of preference shares without nominal or par value, which shall rank in priority to the Class "A" and Class "B" shares and may be issued from time to time in series with the designation, right, privileges, restrictions and conditions attaching to each series as and in the manner set out in its Articles.

The holders of the Class "A" shares are entitled, voting separately as a class on the basis of one vote per share, to elect annually three members of the Board of Directors of the Corporation. Subject to applicable law, the holders of the Class "A" shares do not otherwise have a right to vote at meetings of shareholders but are entitled to notice of and to attend all shareholders' meetings except class meetings of the holders of another class of shares. The holders of the Class "B" shares are entitled to one vote per share at all meetings of shareholders.

In each fiscal year, the holders of the Class "A" shares are entitled to receive non-cumulative dividends aggregating $0.10 per share before any dividends may be paid on the Class "B" shares. No further dividends can be paid to the holders of the Class "A" shares until dividends aggregating $0.10 per share have been declared or paid on the Class "B" shares, and thereafter the Class "A" shares and the Class "B" shares participate equally as to all dividends declared. The former rate of $0.20 per share was adjusted to reflect the 2:1 stock split on July 18, 1988.

In the event of the liquidation, dissolution or winding-up of the Corporation, the holders of the Class "A" shares and the holders of the Class "B" shares would be entitled to share equally, share for share, in all distributions of the assets of the Corporation.

Issued and outstanding

At March 31, the following shares were issued and outstanding:

	1989		1988	
	Shares	**Amount**	**Shares**	**Amount**
Class "A"	18,384,157	$ 53,952	18,265,054	$ 51,919
Class "B"	10,182,538	9,216	10,182,538	9,216
	28,566,695	$ 63,168	28,447,592	$ 61,135

Many preferred shares issued by corporations in recent years have been *redeemable*. Redeemable preferred shares can be reacquired by the corporation at a specified price, which may vary according to a preset time schedule. Redeemability is commonly thought to be for the benefit of the corporation. If financing becomes available at a lower cost than the rate fixed for the preferred shares, a corporation may wish to reduce the relatively fixed commitment of preferred dividends (as compared to common). It can do so by exercising its option to redeem the preferred shares. This option is valuable to the corporation but makes the shares less attractive to potential owners. Other things being equal, nonredeemable shares will be issued for a higher price than will redeemable shares. Thus, the degree to which the corporation benefits by making shares redeemable is not clear-cut.

Preferred shares with a conversion feature also have become increasingly popular. *Convertible preferred shares* may be converted by their owner into a specified amount of common shares at specified times. The conversion privilege may appear advantageous to both the individual shareholder and the corporation. The preferred shareholder enjoys the security of a relatively assured dividend as long as the shares are held. The shareholder also has the opportunity to realize capital appreciation by converting the shares into common shares if the market price of the common shares rises sufficiently. Because of this feature, the change in the market price of convertible preferred shares will often parallel changes in the market price of the common shares.

The firm may also benefit from the conversion option. By including it in the issue, the company is usually able to specify a lower dividend rate on the preferred than otherwise would have been required to issue the shares for a given price.

In recent years a number of firms have issued *term preferred* shares. The holder of these shares is allowed to trade them with the firm for cash or bonds at specified dates and prices or conversion ratios. Although term preferred shares have many of the attributes of bonds, a *CICA Guideline* recommends that companies clarify them as shareholders' equity. However, the *Guideline* requires that the unique characteristics of term preferred shares be clearly disclosed in the financial statements

On the balance sheet, generally accepted accounting principles[3] require each class of share to be shown separately disclosing the authorized and issued shares. Full details of each class of share authorized must be presented. The issued share capital will disclose the number of shares outstanding, the amount attributable to capital from the shares issued and where the shares are not fully paid the details of the amounts outstanding. The company will also disclose, if relevant, details of shares issued or redeemed during the year, commitments to issue or resell shares and the amount of preferred dividends in arrears. Customarily, preferred shares are listed before common shares in the balance sheet.

Par and No-Par Value Shares

Par value and no-par value are legal terms. *Par value* is a dollar value given to each share as specified by the articles of incorporation of a company. It does not necessarily mean that the share will sell at this price. The Canada Business Cor-

---

[3]*CICA Handbook*, section 3240.

porations Act requires the use of *no-par value* shares, wherein the entire proceeds from the sale of the shares is the amount shown in the Common Share account. Companies incorporated in some provinces may issue par value shares, and the term is still used in the United States. This section briefly describes its use.

For companies in jurisdictions where the incorporating act permits it, the corporate charter may stipulate a par value for each share of any class. This value can be set at any amount: it rarely has any relationship to the market value of the share.

A *premium* is the amount in excess of par value received when a corporation issues shares. The excess of par value over the amount received may be called *discount*. In some jurisdictions, people purchasing shares for less than par value may have a liability for the discount should creditor claims remain unsatisfied after the company's liquidation. Shares are rarely sold at a discount—in certain areas this practice is even forbidden.

To record differences between amounts received for shares and par value, the accountant uses appropriately descriptive accounts. When an amount greater than par value is received, we may use the account Premium on Stock. The account Discount on Stock can be used when a discount is involved.

To illustrate, let us assume that in its first year of operations, a corporation had the following transactions:

(1) Sold 1,000 shares of $100 par value, preferred stock at $107 per share.
(2) Sold 1,000 shares of $100 par value, preferred stock at $98 per share.
The two journal entries would be:

Cash	107,000	
Preferred Shares		100,000
Premium on Preferred Shares[a]		7,000
Cash	98,000	
Discount on Preferred Shares		2,000
Preferred Shares		100,000

[a] Part of Contributed Surplus.

Thus, no matter what the selling price of a share, under a par value system, only the par value is recorded in the share account itself.

Issuances of Shares for Cash

In issuing its shares, a corporation may use the services of an investment broker, often called an underwriter, who is a specialist in marketing securities to investors. The broker may underwrite an issue of shares—that is, the broker buys the shares from the corporation and resells them to investors. The corporation does not risk being unable to sell its shares. The underwriter bears this risk in return for the profits generated by selling the shares to investors at a price higher than that paid to the corporation. An investment broker who is unwilling to underwrite an issue of shares may handle them on a *best efforts* basis. In this case, the broker agrees to sell as many shares as possible at a set price, but the corporation bears the risk of unsold shares.

Costs of Issuing Shares

In order to issue and market its shares, a company may incur legal fees, accounting fees, underwriting commissions, and mailing, registration, and advertising costs. It is common practice to treat these costs as a reduction of the net proceeds received for the share issuance. Theoretically, a company will benefit many years from these expenditures and should set them up as an intangible asset called *organization costs*. This asset would be amortized systematically over 40 years or less.

Share Subscriptions

Sometimes a corporation sells shares directly to investors rather than through an investment broker. The corporation may obtain signatures of prospective purchasers on *subscription contracts* prior to issuing shares. Frequently, such contracts provide for installment payments. When subscriptions are obtained, the corporation debits a receivable account, Share Subscriptions Receivable. Instead of crediting the regular Common Shares account, the firm credits a temporary paid-in capital account called Common Shares Subscribed. The use of a temporary account signifies that the shares have not yet been paid for or issued. The CBCA does not allow the issue of shares until they are fully paid for. Until the shares are paid for, the account is shown separately in the shareholders' equity section of the balance sheet. Share Subscriptions Receivable appears with the current assets. After all payments have been received and the shares are issued, the corporation debits the temporary account, Common Shares Subscribed, and credits the regular account, Common Shares.

To illustrate the journal entries for share subscription transactions, let us assume that 500 shares were sold on subscription for $120 a share, paid in installments of $40 and $80. The entries would be:

To record receipt of subscriptions		
Share Subscriptions Receivable—Common	60,000	
Common Shares Subscribed		60,000
Received subscriptions for 500 shares at $120 per share.		
To record collection of first installment		
Cash	20,000	
Share Subscriptions Receivable—Common		20,000
Collected first installment of $40 per share.		
To record collection of final installment and issuance of shares		
Cash	40,000	
Share Subscriptions Receivable—Common		40,000
Collected final installment of $80 per share.		
Common Shares Subscribed	60,000	
Common Shares		60,000
To record issuance of 500 shares.		

Issuances of Shares for Assets Other Than Cash

When shares are issued for property other than cash or for services, the accountant must carefully determine the amount recorded. Property or services acquired should be recorded at their current fair value or at the fair value of the shares issued, whichever is more clearly determinable. If the shares are actively traded on a securities exchange, the market price of the shares issued may indicate an appropraite value. For example, if the current market price is $140 per share and 500 shares are issued for a parcel of land, this land may be valued, in the absence of other price indicators, at $70,000. An effort should be made, however, to determine a fair value for the property. Certainly, all aspects of the transaction should be carefully scrutinized to ascertain that the number of shares issued was objectively determined. Obviously, if no market value for the shares is available, we would seek an independently determined value for the property or services received.

Assuming its market value is the best indicator of the property's fair value, the entry to record the transaction would be

Land	70,000	
Common Shares		70,000
To record issuance of 500 shares for land valued at $70,000.		

Treasury Stock

Treasury stock refers to shares that a corporation purchased on the open market. A company might do this to attempt to influence the market price of the shares, to buy out a particular shareholder, or to have shares on hand to satisfy employee stock options.

The CBCA allows a corporation to acquire its own shares as long as the solvency of the corporation is not impaired. However, the Act requires immediate cancellation of these shares, which means that a Canadian corporation cannot have treasury shares for resale; therefore, the accounting issues that arise in the United States, where such a practice is common, do not apply here. In jurisdictions that allow treasury stock, the most prevalent accounting practice is to debit an account called Treasury Stock for the cost of the reacquired shares and to show this debit balance account as a deduction from Shareholders' Equity.

Provincial Corporations Acts

Some of the provincial corporations acts do allow the use of treasury stock. For companies incorporated under these acts, the *CICA Handbook* requires the following accounting treatment for treasury shares.

The acquired shares are set up at cost, debiting Treasury Stock and crediting Cash. Treasury Stock is deducted from total shareholders' equity in the balance sheet. Suppose a corporation had outstanding 2,000 shares of no par value common stock originally issued at $100 per share, and then repurchased 100 shares at $120 per share. The entry for the repurchase would be

Treasury Stock	12,000	
Cash		12,000
To record purchase of 100 shares		
of treasury stock at $120 per share.		

The corporation may accept any price for the reissue of treasury stock. Treasury stock transactions are not part of a firm's normal operating activities, and any additional capital obtained from reissuing such shares at more than cost is not regarded as earnings and is not added to retained earnings. The corporation should regard any additional amounts paid by subsequent purchasers as excess capital. Therefore, increases in capital from the reissue of purchased treasury shares should be credited to an account called Contributed Surplus: Treasury Stock. Decreases on reissue of treasury stock at less than cost offset previously recorded credits to Contributed Surplus: Treasury Stock, or, if that is not possible, Retained Earnings.

Let us assume that 50 shares of the treasury stock reacquired are resold by the corporation at $130 per share. The entry to record the reissue would be

Cash	6,500	
Treasury Stock		6,000
Contributed Surplus: Treasury Stock		500
To record sale of 50 shares of		
treasury stock at $130 per share.		

Observe that Treasury Stock is credited at the cost price of $120 per share, a basis consistent with the original debit to the account. The excess over cost is credited to Contributed Surplus: Treasury Stock. If a balance sheet is prepared after this transaction, the shareholders' equity section would appear as shown below (assuming retained earnings of $40,000):

Shareholders' Equity

Common Shares, No Par Value, authorized and issued 2,000 shares;	
50 shares in treasury, 1,950 shares outstanding	$200,000
Contributed Surplus: Treasury Stock	500
Retained Earnings	40,000
	$240,500
Less: Treasury Stock (50 shares) at Cost	6,000
Total Shareholders' Equity	$234,500

Note that the $200,000 stated value of all issued stock is shown, although 50 shares are no longer outstanding. The total cost of the 50 shares, however, is later deducted from total shareholders' equity.

In the above owners' equity situation, the corporation apparently has $40,000 retained earnings unfettered by any legal restrictions; the entire amount can be distributed as dividends if the corporation's cash position permits. In some jurisdictions, however, the corporation must restrict (reduce) the retained earnings available for declaration of dividends by the cost of any treasury stock held. Then, in our illustration, only $34,000 in retained earnings would be available for dividends, and the reason would be disclosed in the shareholders' equity section.

Contributed Surplus

The previous section introduced an account called Contributed Surplus: Treasury Stock. Under the Canada Business Corporations Act, any capital contributed other than through the issue of shares should be shown as Contributed Surplus. Shareholders' Equity may, therefore, show three subheadings: Capital Stock, Contributed Surplus, and Retained Earnings. Other examples of transactions creating contributed surplus include redemption of shares and certain dividend transactions.

Donated Capital

Sometimes corporations receive donations of assets from shareholders or from governmental units. How should these donations be reflected in the accounts?

A donation from a shareholder is really an additional investment by the shareholder and as a result would represent Donated Capital (sometimes referred to as Contributed Surplus), a shareholders' equity account.

For donations from outsiders, under generally accepted accounting principles these donations are not part of capital but are, in fact, an income item. The donation or government assistance either relates to one period or is treated as deferred revenue (or deferred government assistance), which is amortized to income.

Reacquisition of Shares by Redemption

The CBCA treats redemption of callable preferred shares and acquisition of common shares in the open market in the same way: solvency must be maintained by the corporation and the reacquired shares must be cancelled.

Assume the Arctic Corporation had the following equity accounts:

Preferred Shares	
2,000,000 no-par shares redeemable at $1.50	$1,000,000
Common Shares	
500,000 no-par shares	$4,000,000
Retained Earnings	$5,000,000

The CBCA states that when a corporation redeems its own shares, the stated capital account maintained *for the class or series of shares acquired* would be reduced on a *proportionate* basis.

The amount to be deducted from the stated capital would be calculated as

$$\left(\frac{\text{stated capital before acquisition}}{\text{number of shares before acquisition}} \right) \times \text{number of shares acquired}$$

Assume 100,000 preferred shares are redeemed at the call price of $1.50. Using this formula we calculate

$$\left(\frac{\$1,000,000}{\$2,000,000} \right) \times 100,000 = \$50,000$$

The remainder of the $150,000 would be charged against Retained Earnings. If a Contributed Surplus account existed it would be drawn down first. The entry on this redemption would be

Preferred Shares	50,000	
Retained Earnings	100,000	
Cash		150,000

It is important to remember that any type of capital transaction, such as the redemption or issue of shares, affects only capital accounts and is never a determinant of current net income.

Should a Firm Raise New Funds by Issuing Shares or Bonds?

A major consideration in the issue of common or preferred shares is that dividends are not deductible in calculating taxable income. Bond interest is, however, deductible. Thus, the aftertax accounting cost of borrowing may be less than the aftertax accounting cost of issuing shares, even though the interest rate on the bonds is higher than the dividend rate. Exhibit 12.2 illustrates this phenomenon. The accounting figures, however, do not reflect the economic costs of risk. When bonds are issued, both preferred and common shares become more risky, because bond-holders have a claim on future cash flows senior to the claim of shareholders. When preferred shares are issued, common shares become more risky. When shares become more risky, all else being equal, the rate of return on those shares required by the market increases. (For a given dollar amount of return from an investment in a share, this means that the price of the share must fall.) Even though a project financed with a bond issue may result in a larger earnings-per-share increase than one financed by a common stock issue, one cannot conclude that raising new funds by borrowing is better than raising new funds with share issues. As Chapter 6 pointed out, leverage (the raising of funds by borrowing) is a two-edged sword. Corporate finance texts discuss whether there is an optimal way to raise new funds.

Exhibit 12.2
Accounting Benefit of Raising New Funds by
Borrowing Rather than by Issuing Common Shares (financial leverage)

Current operations — expected to continue
Income Tax Rate: 40 Percent
Net Income: $216,000
Shares Outstanding: 90,000
Market Price per Share: $20.00
Earnings per Share: $2.40 (= $216,000/90,000 shares)

Assumptions About New Project
Requires New Funds of $1,000,000
Generates Income Before Financing Charges and Taxes of $200,000 per Year

Assumptions About New Financing Options
Issue $1,000,000 of Bonds at Par with Annual Coupon Rate of 12.5 Percent
or Issue 50,000 New Common Shares at $20 Each

Pro Forma Income Statements After New Financing

	Issue Bonds	Issue Shares
Income from New Project Before Interest and Taxes	$200,000	$200,000
Less: Interest Expense (= .125 × $1,000,000)	(125,000)	—
Less: Additional Income Taxes at 40 Percent	(30,000)	(80,000)
Additional Income	$ 45,000	$120,000
Current Income	216,000	216,000
Revised Income	$261,000	$336,000
Shares Outstanding	90,000	140,000
Earnings per Share	$2.90	$2.40
Rate of Return on Market Value of Share of $20	14.5%	12.0%

If the new project undertaken by the firm illustrated in Exhibit 12.2 has the same risk characteristics as the other, older projects of the firm, it is likely that the market value after either form of financing will remain at about $20 per share. If so, the return required by the market of the bond-financed firm increases from 12.0 percent to 14.5 percent. Although projected earnings per share increase, so does risk.

When Two Plus Two Equals Three

As anyone who's ever had reason to regret falling for a sales pitch knows only too well, form may promise substance but doesn't always deliver. What you see isn't always what you get.

As I write this, this morning's *Toronto Star* headline blares: "RCMP probing alleged fraud of $22 million at failed banks" and, underneath it, reporter Diane Francis unravels a tale of loans by the now-defunct Canadian Commercial and Northland banks to Insurance Premium Finance, an Alberta corporation. Those loans were made on the basis of insurance policies that — according to an affidavit filed by CCB's receiver, Coopers & Lybrand—never existed or, perhaps more correctly, existed but in counterfeit or forged form only.

The story reminded me of something Mike Mackenzie had said when I interviewed him a week earlier, just after the government announced his appointment as Canada's new Inspector General of Banks and soon-to-be first Superintendent of Financial Institutions

. . . It was related to the form over substance idea, but had an added dimension.

Called the "real world versus the symbolic world" concept, Mike first heard of it from an old professor of his at the Harvard Business School. In essence, it is that the real world is made up of a series of activities like, say, catching fish, which are then processed, sold, cooked and put on the table. Real economic wealth, as the argument goes, can come only from activities that provide jobs to create products. Those products, in turn, require manufacturing facilities and the funds to build them, thus stimulating investment and contributing to a vibrant economy.

The symbolic world, by contrast, is the world overlying this economic structure: an elaborate superstructure comprising activities engaged in by bankers, brokers, investment dealers, insurance companies, lawyers and, yes dare we say it?—even chartered accountants. This is the world that produces not fish on the table but symbols such as "earnings per share" and "return on investment."

''Both worlds are necessary,'' Mike's professor told him. ''But if the symbolic world departs too much from the real world, there could be trouble ahead.''

The student, now occupying a super-regulatory role over the financial institutions of this country, echoes his mentor's concerns: ''I'm not saying that banks and insurance companies don't offer real products to real people, because they do,'' Mike admits. ''But I have this uneasy feeling that so much of our brainpower and so much of our investment has gone into this 'overhead' world rather than into the true, economic world. I suspect if you could measure the amount of credit, money movement velocity and financial products, and assign a number to the amount of those available, and another to the real economic world, you'd find that the former world is getting bigger in relation to the underlying real world.''

Bank of Montreal Chairman Bill Mulholland said as much recently in connection with the rash of corporate takeovers in this country. In his ''Chairman's Letter to Shareholders,'' in the bank's latest annual report, he writes: ''Corporate takeovers are not bad *per se* or even necessarily unconstructive. Sometimes two plus two does equal five, but equally it can sometimes equal only three. . . .

''Corporate takeover activity should not only serve a basic economic purpose—that is, provide net value added—but it must be seen to do so.''

Those engaged in this activity argue, sometimes correctly, he says, that they serve a legitimate economic and social purpose by identifying areas of opportunity and, by their actions, force a more efficient use of capital. ''Even when true, this is a tough argument to sell,'' he says. ''Try selling it to the employees of a business that is dismembered or a business that is dismembered or a plant that is shut down to help finance the acquisitor's purchase or to turn a quick profit.''

Mulholland is even more graphic in a *Maclean's* interview with Peter Newman. ''Who has put up a new factory, brought in a new mine, put up a new pulp mill in the past five or 10 years?'' he asks. ''I can count them on my fingers. It's sick. the world's monetary system is flooded with liquidity, but it ain't being productively employed the way it used to be. People are finding it's cheaper making money with money than to make better goods or new products, or bring in new resources. . . . This wave of takeovers without productive investment is wrong, just *wrong*.

As a citizen, taxpayer and bank depositor in this country, I'm heartened to hear such concerns expressed by individuals of the stature and influence of Mike Mackenzie and Bill Mulholland. And as a CA, I'm particularly pleased I can call one of them a professional colleague.

Reprinted with permission of *CA Magazine*.

Retained Earnings

After a new business has established itself and is profitable, it usually generates additional owners' equity from undistributed earnings. These undistributed earnings represent the accumulated periodic net income that remains after dividends have been declared. Retained earnings increase shareholders' equity and provide capital for expansion or for replacing assets at higher costs.

Net Income and Cash Position

One misconception about net income is that it represents a fund of cash available for distribution or expansion. Earnings from operations usually involve cash at some stage: goods are sold to customers, the cash is collected, more goods are acquired, bills are paid, more sales are made, and so on. Assets generated by earnings do not, however, remain in the form of cash.[4] Only under most unrealistic conditions, with net plant and equipment, inventories, receivables, and liabilities remaining at constant amounts, would earnings correspond to the increase in cash. The statement of changes in financial position shows how the funds provided by operations and other sources are used during a period.

A well-managed firm keeps its cash at a reasonable minimum. If cash starts to accumulate, the firm may pay some obligations, increase its inventory, buy more equipment, or declare dividends. Thus, there is no way of knowing how retaining earnings affects the individual asset and liability accounts. The only certain statement is that an increase in retained earnings results in increased *net assets* (that is, an increase in the excess of all assets over all liabilities).

Cash Dividends

The shareholders of a corporation do not directly control distributions of corporate assets generated by net income. Corporation bylaws almost always delegate the authority to declare dividends to the board of directors. When a dividend is declared, the entry is:

Retained Earnings	$150,000	
Dividends Payable		$150,000

To record declaration of dividends. (Sometimes an account called Dividends or Dividends Declared is debited. The Dividends account is a temporary account and is closed to Retained Earnings at the end of the period.)

Once the board of directors declares a dividend, the dividend becomes a legal liability of the corporation. Dividends Payable is shown as a current liability on the balance sheet if the dividends have not been paid at the end of the accounting period. When the dividends are paid, the entry is:

---

[4]For many businesses, increased net income is frequently associated with decreased cash, whereas contraction of net income may be accompanied by an increase in cash. In the first stages of a business decline, cash may start to build up from the liquidation of inventories and receivables that have not been replaced, as well as from postponing replacement or expansion of plant. When conditions improve, inventories and receivables are expanded, new plant acquired, and a cash shortage may develop.

Dividends Payable	$150,000	
Cash		$150,000
To record payment of dividends.		

A distribution of a corporation's assets other than cash to its shareholders is called a *dividend in kind* or a *property dividend.* Such dividends are accounted for just like cash dividends, except that when the dividend is paid, the asset given up, rather than cash, is credited. The amount debited to Retained Earnings is the fair market value of the assets distributed. Any gain or loss is part of income for the period.

Stock Dividends

The retention of earnings may lead to a substantial increase in shareholders' equity, which represents a relatively permanent commitment by shareholders to the business. The commitment is relatively permanent because the net assets generated have been invested in operating assets such as inventories and plant. To indicate such a permanent commitment of reinvested earnings, the board of directors may declare a *stock dividend.* The accounting involves a debit to Retained Earnings and a credit to the capital accounts. When a stock dividend is issued, shareholders receive additional shares in proportion to their existing holdings. If a five-percent stock dividend is issued, each shareholder receives one additional share for every 20 shares held before the dividend.

The usual accounting practice is that the valuation of the newly issued shares be based on the market value of the shares issued. For example, the directors of a corporation may decide to issue a stock dividend of 10,000 additional shares with a par value of $10 per share at a time when the market price of a share is $38. The entry would be:

Retained Earnings	$380,000	
Common Stock — Par		$100,000
Contributed Surplus		280,000
Declaration and issue of a stock dividend — recorded using market price of shares to quantify the amounts: $38 × 10,000 shares = $380,000.		

The stock dividend relabels a portion of the retained earnings that had been legally available for dividend declarations as a more permanent form of owners' equity. A stock dividend formalizes the fact that some of the funds represented by past earnings have been used for plant expansion, to replace assets at increased prices, or to retire bonds. Such funds are therefore unavailable for cash dividends.

Stock dividends have little economic substance for shareholders: the same ownership is spread over more pieces of paper. If the distributed shares are of the same type as those held before, each shareholders' proportionate interest in the capital of the corporation and proportionate voting power have not changed. Although the book value per common share (total common shareholders' equity divided by number of common shares outstanding) decreases a proportionally larger number of shares will be held, so the total book value of each shareholder's interest will remain unchanged. The market value per share should decline, but, all else being equal, the total market value of an individual's shares will not change. To describe such a distribution of shares as a "dividend"—meaning a distribution of earnings—is potentially misleading. It is, nevertheless, generally accepted terminology.

Dividend Policy

The directors, in considering whether or not to declare cash dividends, must conclude both (1) that the declaration of a dividend is legal and (2) that it is financially expedient.

Statutory Limits on Dividends

Corporation law limits directors' freedom to declare dividends. These limitations are designed to protect creditors, whose interest might be jeopardized because neither shareholders nor directors are liable for debts of the corporation.

Generally, the laws provide that dividends may not be declared and paid if a company is currently or potentially insolvent, or if the dividend is paid out of capital. The Canada Business Corporations Act prohibits a company from declaring a dividend if there are reasonable grounds for believing that the company is, or would after the payment be, unable to pay its liabilities as they become due (the test of solvency), or, if the realizable value of the company's assets would thereby be less than the aggregate of its liabilities and capital of all classes (the test of capital).

For most companies, these statutory limits have little influence on the accounting for shareholders' equity and dividends. A balance sheet does not spell out all the legal details of amounts available for dividends, but it ought to disclose information necessary for the user to apply the legal rules of the jurisdiction in which the business is incorporated. For example, statutes can provide that "treasury shares may be acquired only with retained earnings." That is, dividends cannot exceed the amount of Retained Earnings reduced by the cost of treasury shares. If treasury shares are acquired under these circumstances, then the amount of this limit on dividends should appear as a footnote to the balance sheet.

The statutory requirements for declaring dividends can be met by building up a balance in retained earnings. Such a balance does not mean that a fund of cash is available for the dividends. Managing cash is a specialized problem of corporate finance; cash for dividends must be anticipated just as well as cash for the purchase of equipment, the retirement of debts, and so on. Borrowing from the bank to pay the regular dividend is not unsound if the corporation's financial condition justifies the resulting increase in liabilities.

Contractual Limits on Dividends

Contracts with bondholders, other lenders, and preferred shareholders often limit dividend payments and thereby compel the retention of earnings. A bond contract might provide that the retirement of the debt be made "out of earnings." Such a provision involves curtailing dividends so that the necessary debt service payments, plus any dividends, will not exceed the amount of net income for the period. Such a provision forces the shareholders to increase their investment in the business by limiting the amount of dividends that might otherwise be made available to them. Financial statement notes must disclose significant limitations on dividend declarations. For example, a recent balance sheet of the Great Lakes Forest Products Ltd. contains the following footnote:

---

4. Dividend Restriction

Certain of the indentures relating to the company's long-term debt contain convenants limiting dividends. The most restrictive of these requires that, after any dividend is declared, working capital (which for these purposes is before the deduction of the current portion of long-term debt) must be over $10 million and shareholders' equity must be over $50 million.

Dividends and Corporate Financial Policy

Dividends are seldom declared up to the maximum legal limit. The directors may allow the retained earnings to increase as a matter of corporate financial policy for several reasons:

1. Earnings are not reflected in a corresponding increase of available cash.
2. Restricting dividends in prosperous years may permit continued dividend payments in poor years.
3. Funds may be needed for expansion of working capital or plant and equipment.
4. Reducing the amount of borrowings, rather than paying dividends, may seem prudent.

The statement of changes in financial position helps the reader understand how funds provided by earnings and other sources have been used.

Stabilization of Dividends Many corporate shareholders want to receive a predictable cash return. To accommodate such shareholders and to create a general impression of stability, directors commonly attempt to declare a regular dividend. They try to maintain the regular dividend through good years and bad. When earnings and financial policy permit, they may declare "extra" dividends.

Financial Policy Some shareholders prefer a policy that restricts dividends in order to finance expansion. When dividends are declared, such shareholders will use the funds received to acquire an equivalent amount of the new shares issued to finance the expansion. These shareholders will be saved transaction costs if earnings are retained. If the corporation pays dividends, the shareholders may pay income taxes on the receipts before they can be reinvested. If the funds are reinvested directly by the corporation, there may be a deferral of, and possibly a permanent avoidance of, personal income taxes.

Other shareholders may want a steady flow of cash but do not wish to sell a portion of their shares to raise cash. Such shareholders will resent being forced to reinvest in the corporation when expansion is financed through the curtailing of dividends. They may change their investment to corporations that declare regular dividends.

How to finance expansion is a problem of managerial finance, not accounting. Research in finance suggests that, within wide limits, what a firm does makes little difference so long as it tends to follow the same policy over time. Shareholders who want earnings reinvested can invest in shares of firms that finance expansion with earnings, whereas others who want a steady flow of cash can invest in shares of firms that regularly pay dividends.

Other Changes in Owners' Equity Accounts

Stock Splits

Stock splits (or, more technically, *split ups*) are like stock dividends. Additional shares are issued to shareholders in proportion to existing holdings. No additional assets are brought into the firm. In a stock split, the par value of all the shares in the issued class is reduced. A corporation may, for example, have 1,000 shares of $10 par value outstanding, and, by a stock split, exchange those shares for 2,000 shares of $5 par value (a two-for-one split), or 4,000 shares of $2.50 par value (a four-for-one split), or any number of shares of no par value. If the shares outstanding have no par value, then the shareholders keep the existing certificates and receive additional ones.

A stock split generally does not require a journal entry. The amount of retained earnings is not reduced. The amount shown in the share capital account represents a larger number of shares. Of course, the additional number of shares held by each shareholder must be recorded in the subsidiary share capital records. Sometimes stock splits are accounted for as stock dividends — with a transfer from Retained Earnings to the Contributed Capital account. If so, the amounts are based on the market value of the shares on the date of the split. There is no easy way to distinguish stock splits from stock dividends. Usually, small percentage distributions are treated as stock dividends and larger ones as stock splits.

A stock split (or a stock dividend) usually reduces the market value per share, all other factors remaining constant, in inverse proportion to the split (or dividend). Thus a two-for-one split could be expected to result in a 50 percent reduction in the market price per share. Stock splits have, therefore, usually been used to keep the market prices per share from rising to a price level unacceptable to management. For example, the board of directors might think that a market price of $30 to $40 is an effective trading range for its shares. (This is a purely subjective estimate, and it is almost never supported by convincing evidence.) If the share prices have risen to $60 in the market, then the board of directors may declare a two-for-one split. The only certain result of stock splits and dividends is increased record-keeping costs. Stock splits and stock dividends are used primarily by corporations whose shares are currently, or soon to be, traded on a stock exchange.

Stock Options

Stock options are often a part of employee compensation plans. Under such plans, employees are granted an option to purchase shares in their company. Stock options present two kinds of accounting problems: (1) recording the granting of the option and (2) recording its exercise or lapse.

Granting the Option The generally accepted accounting treatment for options usually results in no entry being made at the time the options are granted. The *exercise price of an option* is the price the option holder will have to pay to acquire a share. If the exercise price is equal to the market price of the share on the date the option is granted, then the granting of the option is not viewed as resulting in compensation to the employee or expense to the employer and no entry is made. If the exercise price is less than the market price of the share on the date of the grant, then compensation expense may have to be recognized under some circumstances.

Exercise or Lapse When the option is exercised, the conventional entry treats the transaction simply as an issue of shares at the option price.

Cash	$35,000	
Common Shares		$35,000
To record issue of 1,000 no par value shares upon exercise of options and receipt of $35,000 cash.		

If the option lapses or expires without being exercised, no entry is required.

Disclosure of Options Generally accepted accounting principles require that the terms of options granted, outstanding, and exercised during a period be disclosed in text or notes accompanying the financial statements.[5] For example, Note 19 to the financial statements of General Products Limited in Appendix A, pages 772 and 773, discloses data on stock options.

Share Rights and Warrants

Opportunities to buy shares may be granted through *share rights* and *share warrants*.

Share Rights Share rights are similar to stock options, but there are some differences. Stock options are granted to employees, are nontransferable, and are a form of compensation. In contrast, share rights are granted to current shareholders and can usually be traded in public markets. They are generally exercisable for only a limited period but occasionally are good indefinitely. Share rights are ordinarily associated with attempts to raise new capital for a firm from current shareholders.

---

[5]*CICA Handbook*, section 3240.

Share rights entitle the owner to purchase shares at a specified price. Journal entries are not necessary when share rights are granted to current shareholders. When the rights are exercised, the entry is like the one to record the issue of new shares at the price paid.

Share Warrants Share warrants are issued to the general investing public for cash or used as a "bonus" with other security issues. They are exercisable for a limited period in most cases. Assume that a corporation issues warrants for $15,000 cash. The entry would be:

Cash	$15,000	
Common Share Warrants		$15,000

To record issue of warrants to the public. The Common Share Warrants account would normally be included with Contributed Surplus for balance sheet presentation.

When the options to purchase contained in these warrants are exercised and 10,000 common shares of no par value arc issued in exchange for the warrants plus $200,000, the entry would be:

Cash	$200,000	
Common Share Warrants	15,000	
Common Stock—No Par Value		$215,000

To record the issue of 10,000 shares for $200,000 cash and the redemption of warrants. (The amount originally received for the warrants is transferred to Common Stock.)

If the warrants expire without having been exercised, the entry would be:

Common Share Warrants	$15,000	
Contributed Surplus		$15,000

To record expiration of common share warrants and the transfer to permanent contributed capital

---

Convertible Bonds

Convertible bonds are, typically, semiannual coupon bonds like the ones discussed in Chapter 10—with one added feature. The holder of the bond can *convert* the bond into shares. The bond indenture specifies the number of shares to be received when the bond is converted, the dates when conversion can occur, and other details. Convertible bonds are usually callable.

Investors often find convertible bonds attractive. The owner is promised a regular interest payment. In addition, should the company business be so successful that its share prices rise on the stock market, then the holder of the bond can convert the investment from debt into equity. The creditor has become an owner and can share in the good fortune of the company. Of course, an investor does not get something for nothing. Because of the potential participation in the earnings of the company once the bonds are converted into common shares, an investor in the bonds must accept a lower interest rate than would be received if the bonds were not convertible into shares. From the company's point of view, convertible bonds allow borrowing at lower rates of interest than is required on ordinary debt, but the company must promise to give up an equity interest if the bonds are converted. The purchaser of the convertible bond is paying something for the option to acquire common shares later. Thus, a portion of the proceeds from the issue of convertible bonds actually represents a form of capital contribution, even though it is not so recorded.

Issue of Convertible Bonds Suppose, for example, that the Johnson Co. Ltd.'s credit rating would allow it to issue $100,000 of ordinary ten-year, 14-percent semiannual coupons bonds at par. The firm prefers to issue convertible bonds with a lower coupon rate. Assume that Johnson Co. Ltd. issues at par $100,000 of ten-year, ten-percent semiannual coupon bonds, but each $1,000 bond is convertible into 50 Johnson Co. Ltd. $5 par value common shares. (The entire issue is convertible into 5,000 shares.) The following entry is required:

Cash	$100,000	
Convertible Bonds Payable		$100,000
Issue of convertible bonds at par.		

This entry effectively treats convertible bonds just like ordinary, nonconvertible bonds and records the value of the conversion feature at zero. (Generally accepted accounting principles do recognize the potential issue of common shares implied by the conversion feature in the calculations of earnings per share figures.)

Recognizing the Value of the Conversion Feature Is Not Permitted Table C.5, page 818 (for ten-percent coupon bonds), indicates that ten-percent, ten-year semi-annual (nonconvertible) coupon bonds sell for about 79 percent of par when the market rate of interest is 14 percent. Thus, if the ten-percent convertible bonds can be issued at par, then the conversion feature must be worth about 21 ($= 100 - 79$) percent of par. Then 21 percent of the proceeds from the bond issue is actually a capital contribution by the bond buyers for the right to acquire common shares later. The logical entry to record the issue of these ten percent convertible bonds at par would be:

Cash	$100,000	
Discount on Bonds Payable	21,000	
Convertible Bonds Payable		$100,000
Contributed Surplus		21,000
Issue of 10 percent semiannual coupon convertible bonds at a time when ordinary 10 percent bonds could be issued for 79 percent of par.		

Notice that the calculation of the amounts for this entry requires that we know what the proceeds would be of an issue of nonconvertible bonds that are otherwise similar to the convertible bonds. Because auditors are often unable to ascertain this information in a reasonably objective manner, this alternative is seldom followed in Canada and is prohibited under generally accepted accounting principles in the United States. The entry is simply a debit to Cash and a credit to Convertible Bonds Payable for $100,000.

Conversion of Bonds Assume that the common shares of the Johnson Co. Ltd. increase in the market to $30 a share so that one $1,000 bond, which is convertible into 50 shares, can be converted into shares with a market value of $1,500. If the entire convertible issue were converted into common shares at this time, then 5,000 shares of $5 par value would be issued on conversion.

The usual entry to record the conversion of bonds into shares ignores current market prices in the interest of simplicity and merely shows the swap of shares for bonds at their book value.

Convertible Bonds Payable	100,000	
Common Stock — $5 Par Value		25,000
Contributed Surplus		75,000

To record conversion of 100 convertible bonds with a book value of $100,000 into 5,000 shares of $5 par value.

An alternative treatment recognizes that market prices provide information useful in quantifying the market value of the shares issued. Under the alternative treatment, when the market price of a share is $30 and the fair market value of the 5,000 shares issued on conversion is $150,000, the journal entry would be:

Convertible Bonds Payable	$100,000	
Loss on Conversion of Bonds	50,000	
Common Stock — $5 Par Value		$ 25,000
Contributed Surplus		125,000

To record conversion of 100 convertible bonds into 5,000 shares of $5 par value at a time when the market price of a share is $30.

The alternative entry results in the same total owners' equity: smaller retained earnings (because the Loss on Conversion of Bonds will reduce current net income and thus Retained Earnings), but larger contributed capital. It is the equivalent of the following two entries:

Cash	$150,000	
Common Stock — $5 Par Value		$ 25,000
Contributed Surplus		125,000

To record issue of 5,000 shares of $5 par value at $30 per share.

Convertible Bonds Payable $100,000
Loss on Retirement of Bonds   50,000
  Cash $150,000
Retirement by purchase for $150,000 of 100 convertible bonds
carried on the books at $100,000.

Potential Dilution of Earnings per Share

Chapter 6, page 279, explained that earnings per common share is conventionally calculated by dividing net income attributable to the common shareholders by the weighted-average number of common shares outstanding during the period. When a firm has outstanding securities that, if exchanged for common shares, would decrease earnings per share as conventionally calculated, then the earnings per share calculations become somewhat more complicated. Stock options, share rights, warrants, and convertible bonds all have the potential of reducing earnings per share and must be taken into account in calculating earnings per share. These complications are discussed in intermediate accounting books, but are introduced in Problem 38 at the end of this chapter.

A Telephone Number Says It All

*A*ndrew Agnew, a certified financial analyst addressing a Society of Management Accountants symposium has pleaded for professional accountants to take the lead in promoting fuller disclosure in corporate financial reports.

"Individually, there are numerous companies which have excellent disclosure . . . The immediate problem . . . is to bring the laggards up to a desirable minimum of disclosure."

Canadian companies are weak in disclosing revenues and profits by product line, their corporate goals and strategies, and their sensitivity to external forces.

He noted that some companies can also be criticized for the way they valued their assets, covered up the details of their involvement in joint ventures, and provided a lack of information about the different segments of their businesses.

Agnew noted that some companies even fail to list their telephone number in the annual report. "To me, this reflects management's state of mind towards shareholders—let's keep them in the dark."

Source: *The Bottom Line*. July 1986, p. 3.

Reporting Income and Retained Earnings Adjustments

The Income Statement Reconsidered

What is the purpose of the income statement? It is *not* just to show net income for the period. The reader of the financial statements can generally ascertain net income by subtracting the beginning balance of Retained Earnings from its ending balance and adding dividends. The purpose of the income statement is to show the *causes* of income.[6] Then, a company's performance can be compared with other companies or with itself over time, and more informed projections can be made about the future.

To help the reader understand the causes of income, generally accepted accounting principles require the separate reporting of (1) Income before Extraordinary Items and (2) Net Income for the Year. In addition the company must report gains and losses resulting from normal business activities which are both abnormal in size and caused by rare or unusual circumstances. What is included as an unusual or extraordinary item is a matter of judgment.[7]

With this information the reader is able to select or calculate the measure of income that is relevant to the decision.

Direct Adjustments to Retained Earnings

Nearly all items that cause the total of retained earnings to change during a period result from transactions reported in the income statement for that period. The major exception to this general rule is the declaration of dividends. Dividend declarations are distributions that reduce the balance in the Retained Earnings account but do not affect reported income. There are four other exceptions to the general rule that changes in retained earnings arise from transactions reported in the income statement. These are *losses from treasury share transactions*, *corrections of prior-period errors, retroactive changes in accounting policy*, and *other prior period adjustments* that meet restrictive criteria.

Corrections of prior period errors are rare and would include mistakes in computation or errors made in a prior year because of lack of information normally available to management. Examples of retained earnings adjustments resulting from changes in accounting policies are changes in lease capitalization, foreign currency translation, basis of consolidation, depreciation method, accounting for exploration and development expenses, and interest capitalization. Changes in accounting policies are the most common adjustment to retained earnings. Approximately 25 percent of the companies included in the CICA's 1987 *Financial Reporting in Canada* disclosed a change in accounting policy in an average year during the 1984 to 1986 period.

Except for corrections of prior-period errors and changes in accounting policies, prior-period adjustments (which should be rare) should have four characteristics. They should be specifically identified with and directly related to the business activities of particular prior periods; they should depend primarily on decisions or determinations by persons other than management or owners; they should not be attributable to economic events occurring subsequent to the date of the financial statements for such prior periods; and they could not be reasonably estimated prior to such decisions or determinations. Examples of prior-period adjustments that may meet these

---

[6]Parallel statements can be made about the funds statement. The purpose of the statement of changes in financial position is *not* to report the change in cash for the period. That can be deduced by subtracting the balance in the Cash account at the start of the period from that at the end of the period. The purpose is to report the *causes* of the change in the Cash account.

[7]Section 3480 of the *CICA Handbook*, summarized on page 180, provides guidance when making this judgment.

criteria would be settlements of claims resulting from litigation and settlements of prior-period income taxes. Prior-period adjustments *should not* include normal adjustments arising from modification of estimates commonly used in accounting, such as adjustments arising from changes in the estimated useful life of fixed assets. They would also not include, regardless of size, bad debt losses, inventory losses, amounts written off deferred development costs, or income tax reductions realized from the carry-forward of a loss.

Exhibit 12.3 shows the presentation of prior-period adjustments in the financial statements when a company has been required to pay additional income taxes for prior years.

Exhibit 12.3
Prior-Period Adjustment Ltd.
Statement of Retained Earnings
for the Year Ended December 31, Year 5
(amounts in 000's)

	Year 5	Year 4
Retained earnings, beginning of year		
As previously reported	$60,100	$54,100
Adjustments of prior years' income taxes (Note x)	7,500	5,100
As restated	$52,600	$49,000
Net income for the year	5,300	5,600
	$57,900	$54,600
Dividends	2,000	2,000
Retained earnings, end of year	$55,900	$52,600

Note x: As a result of income tax reassessments applicable to the years 1 to 4, the balance of retained earnings at December 31, Year 4 previously reported as $60,100,000 has been restated to show a retroactive charge of $7,500,000 representing the cumulative amount by which income taxes as at December 31, Year 4 had been increased. Of the $7,500,000, $2,400,000 is applicable to Year 4 and has been charged to income for that year. The remaining $5,100,000 is applicable to years prior to January 1, Year 4 and has been charged to retained earnings at that date, previously reported as $54,100,000.

When presenting the Year 5 comparative financial statements the company would amend the Year 4 income statement, presented last year, by increasing income tax expense by $2,400,000 and decreasing net income by the same amount from the $8 million balance originally reported.

Disclosure of Changes in Owners' Equity

The changes in all owners' equity accounts must be explained in the annual reports to shareholders.[8] As previous chapters have pointed out, the reconciliation of retained

---

[8] *CICA Handbook*, section 3240.

earnings may appear in the balance sheet, in a statement of income and retained earnings, or in a separate statement. The financial statements of General Products Limited in Appendix A show the reconciliation of retained earnings at the bottom of the combined statement of income and retained earnings (Exhibit A.1) and the causes of all other changes in owners' equity accounts in a separate schedule in Note 17, page 772.

Journal Entries for Changes in Owners' Equity

To review the accounting for owners' equity, Exhibit 12.4 reconstructs the journal entries for 1987 and 1988 that resulted in the changes in owners' equity disclosed for General Products Limited in Exhibits A.1 and Note 17 (pages 760 and 772).

Exhibit 12.4
Journal Entries Illustrating Transactions Involving Owner's Equity for General Products Limited, 1987–1988

	Millions of Dollars			
Entry and Explanation	1987		1988	
(1) Income Summary	$1,409		$1,514	
Retained Earnings		$1,409		$1,514
Net income for the year, recorded assuming that an Income Summary account is used. This entry, in effect, closes all temporary revenue and expense accounts, with the credit balance being reported as income for the year.				
(2) Retained Earnings	$ 624		$ 670	
Dividends Payable—Common Shares		$ 624		$ 670
Cash dividends declared on common shares.				
(3) Treasury Shares, at Cost	$ 156		$ 145	
Cash		$ 156		$ 145
Acquisitions of treasury shares in market transactions with outsiders.				
(4) Cash	$ 146		$ 139	
Contributed Surplus ("Loss")	2		—	
Treasury Shares, at Cost		$ 148		$ 136
Contributed Surplus ("Gain")		—		3
Issue of shares to employees under share plan and savings and share ownership, incentive compensation and stock option plans. The shares issued in 1987 had market value on date of reissue of $2 million less than their cost. The "loss" is debited to the Contributed Surplus account. The shares issued in 1988 had market value on date of reissue of $3 million more than their cost. The "gain" is credited to the Contributed Surplus account.				

Changes in Owners' Equity Reported in the Statement of Changes in Financial Position

The transactions affecting owners' equity generally affect funds and are reported in the statement of changes in financial position. Exhibit A.3 in Appendix A, page 762, presents the statement of changes in financial position for General Products Limited. The effects of net income can be seen in the statement of changes in financial position. The "Cash Provided by" section also shows the amounts for "Newly Issued Common Shares" and "Disposition of Treasury Shares" for the various compensation and savings plans. The section "Cash Applied to" shows lines for Dividend Declarations and Purchase of Treasury Shares.

Summary

Accounting for owners' equity in a corporation is based on the premise that there should be a separate account for each source of capital contributed by owners. The sources of capital from shareholders include:

1. Receipts from issues of no par value shares.
2. Receipts from issues of shares at par value.
3. Receipts in excess of par value of share issues.
4. Earnings retentions.
5. Capital transactions and prior period adjustments.

The detail of most changes in retained earnings are reported via the income statement. Dividend declarations are the major exception.

Problem 1 for Self-Study

Exhibit 12.5 shows the owners' equity accounts for Lorla Corporation at the ends of Year 1 and Year 2. During Year 2, Lorla Corporation issued new shares for $40 a share and reacquired 60 shares for the treasury at $42 per share. Still later in the year, it sold some of the treasury shares. Revenues for Year 2 were $90,100 and net income was $10,100.

Exhibit 12.5
Lorla Corporation Owners' Equity Accounts

	December 31	
	Year 2	Year 1
Common Stock ($5-par value)	$ 5,500	$ 5,000
Contributed Surplus	33,620	30,000
Retained Earnings	66,500	59,100
	$105,620	$94,100
Less: Cost of Treasury Shares	(840)	—
Total Owners' Equity	$104,780	$94,100

Reconstruct all of the transactions involving owners' equity accounts for Year 2 and show the journal entries for those transactions.

Suggested Solution

Cash	$4,000	
Common Sotck ($5 par value)		$ 500
Contributed Surplus		3,500

Because the Common Stock account went up by $500 and the par value is $5 per share, 100 shares (= $500/$5 per share) must have been issued. The issue price was $40 per share; hence the cash raised was $4,000 (= $40 × 100 shares).

Treasury Shares	$2,520	
Cash		$2,520

Acquisition of 60 shares for the treasury at $42 per share; 60 × $42 = $2,520.

Cash	$1,800	
Treasury Shares		$1,680
Contributed Surplus		120

Because the year-end balance in the treasury shares account is $840, 20 shares (= $840/$42 per share) must remain in the treasury. Thus, 40 (= 60 − 20) shares were resold. Because the year-end Contributed Surplus account is $120 [= $33,620 − ($30,000 + $3,500)] larger than is explained by the issue of new shares, a "gain" of $120 must have been realized on the resale of the shares from the treasury. Because 40 shares were resold, the total "gain" was $120, and the "gain" per share must have been $3 (= $120/40 shares). Thus, the total resale price per share must have been $45 (= $42 + $3). Cash raised must have been $1,800 = $45 per share × 40 shares.

Revenue Accounts	$90,100	
Expense Accounts		$80,000
Retained Earnings		10,100

Closing entries for revenue and expense accounts, given that revenues were $90,100 and net income was $10,100 for the year.

Retained Earnings	$2,700	
Dividends Payable		$2,700

The Retained Earnings account increased by only $7,400 for the year. Dividends must have been $10,100 − $7,400 = $2,700.

Problem 2 for Self-Study

Patell Limited owns 100,000 shares of Alcan Aluminium Limited, which it has held as an investment. The shares had cost $2 million, $20 each, and now have a fair market value of $50 each. Patell Limited declares a dividend in kind, distributing the shares of Alcan Aluminium Limited to its shareholders.

a. Prepare the journal entry to record the declaration. Under generally accepted accounting principles, dividends in kind are recorded at the market value, not the cost, of the assets distributed.

b. Prepare a journal entry that would record the dividend using the cost of the shares. This treatment is not generally acceptable.

c. Compare the effects on net income, retained earnings, and total owners' equity of the two treatments.

Suggested Solution

a. Retained Earnings	$5,000,000	
Investments		$2,000,000
Gain on Disposition of Investments		3,000,000

To record the declaration of a dividend in kind recorded at market value. The excess of the market value over cost is recognized.

b. Retained Earnings	$2,000,000	
Investments		$2,000,000

To record the declaration of a dividend in kind measured at cost.

c. Net income is larger when the dividend is recorded at fair market value. In both cases, Retained Earnings and total owners' equity decline by $2 million. The difference is that in the former treatment, income is increased by $3 million, the holding gain on the shares, which offsets the larger debit to Retained Earnings for the larger amount of dividend recognized.

Questions, Exercises, Problems and Cases

Questions

1. Review the meaning of the following concepts or terms discussed in this chapter.

a.	Corporation	**k.**	Treasury shares
b.	Corporate charter	**l.**	Earnings are not cash
c.	Corporate bylaws	**m.**	Convertible bond
d.	Share capital, common shares, preferred shares	**n.**	Stock dividend
		o.	Stock split
e.	Cumulative preferred shares	**p.**	Stock option
f.	Redeemable preferred shares	**q.**	Share right
g.	Convertible preferred shares	**r.**	Share warrant
h.	Term preferred shares	**s.**	Correction of error
i.	Par value	**t.**	Prior period adjustment
j.	Contributed surplus		

2. Under what circumstances would you expect par value shares to be issued at a price in excess of par? What is the entry to record such an issue?

3. A construction corporation is attempting to borrow money on a note secured by some of its property. A bank agrees to accept the note, provided that the president of the corporation will personally endorse it. What is the point of this requirement?

4. "Par value of preferred shares is frequently a significant figure, but par value of common shares possesses little significance." Why may par value of preferred shares be significant?

5. Why is the amount in the Retained Earnings account for a profitable, growing company that has been in business for several decades unlikely to be of much value for predicting future dividend declarations?

6. What are treasury shares? How are they reported on the balance sheet?

7. A certain corporation retained almost all of its earnings, only rarely paying a cash dividend. When some of the shareholders objected, the reply of the president was "Why do you want cash dividends? You would just have to go to the trouble of reinvesting them. Where can you possibly find a better investment than our own company?" Comment.

8. Compare the position of a shareholder who receives a cash dividend with that of one who receives a stock dividend.

9. At the annual shareholders' meeting, the president of the Santa Cris Corporation made the following statement. "The net income for the year, after taxes, was $1,096,000. The directors have decided that the corporation can afford to distribute only $500,000 as a cash dividend." Are the two sentences of this statement compatible?

10. The text says, "Convertible bonds are usually callable." The call feature is included so that the issuer can force conversion of the bonds. Explain.

11. Are accumulated, but unpaid, dividends to preferred shareholders, which must be paid before dividends can be declared on common shares, liabilities? Explain.

12. What are prior period adjustments? Why do some accountants think that GAAP should only rarely allow them?

13. Interest on bonds is deductible for tax purposes. Dividends on preferred share issues are not. Assume that a company can raise $100 million either by assuming bonds promising 12 percent annual interest or by issuing preferred shares, convertible into common shares promising 12 percent annual dividends. The firm expects to continue to have income (in excess of all interest payments) taxable at the rate of 40 percent per year.
   a. Which of the two financing methods will show a larger income available for common shares?
   b. Why does this book suggest that, in spite of the answer above, one financing method is not necessarily preferred to the other?

Exercises

14. *Effects of transactions involving owners' equity.* Indicate whether each of the following statements is true or false and justify your response. Ignore the effects of income taxes.
   a. Cash dividends reduce the book value per share.
   b. A stock dividend does not affect the Retained Earnings account.
   c. Stock dividends reduce the book value per share.
   d. The declaration of a cash dividend does not reduce the amount of the shareholders' equity.

e. The distribution of a stock dividend tends to reduce the market value per share.

f. A stock split generally does not affect the Retained Earnings account.

g. A stock dividend declaration is usually accompanied by a reduction in par value per share.

15. *Effects of transactions on Retained Earnings and owners' equity.* Indicate the effect of each of the following transactions on (1) the balance in the Retained Earnings and (2) the total shareholders' equity.

a. Bonds are issued at a discount.

b. A cheque is written to the Receiver General of Canada for additional income taxes levied on past years' income (no previous entry).

c. A stock split is voted by the directors. The par value per share is reduced from $20 to $5, and each shareholder is given four new shares in exchange for each old share.

d. The manager is voted a bonus of $35,000 by the directors.

e. Notes payable in the face amount of $50,000 are paid by cheque.

f. A dividend in preferred shares is issued to common shareholders (no previous entry).

g. Securities held as a long-term investment are sold at book value.

h. A building site is received as a donation by the company from the local chamber of commerce.

i. A building is sold for less than its book value.

16. *Journal entries for transactions involving owners' equity.* Present the journal entries for each of the following transactions. These transactions do not relate to the same set of records.

a. The no par value shares of a corporation are selling on the market at $100 a share. In order to bring the market value down to a ''more popular'' figure, the board of directors votes to issue four shares to shareholders in exchange for each share already held by them. The shares are issued.

b. The treasurer of the corporation reports that cash on hand exceeds normal requirements by $300,000. Pending a decision by the board of directors on the final disposition of the funds, temporary investments in marketable securities in the amount of $299,600 are purchased.

c. The net income for the year is $150,000. The directors vote to issue 1,000 shares of 10 percent, $100 par value preferred shares as a stock dividend on the 2,500 no par value common shares outstanding. The preferred's market price is $102 a share. The common's market price is $50 a share.

d. After the books are closed and the financial statements are issued, it is discovered that an arithmetic error was made in calculating depreciation on office equipment for the preceding period. The depreciation expense was $8,000 too large.

17. *Analyzing changes in owners' equity accounts.* The comparative balance sheet of the Forty-Misty Co. Inc. shows the following data:

	Dec. 31, Year 2	Dec. 31, Year 1
Common Stock	$1,320,000	$1,200,000
Retained Earnings	400,000	460,000
Total Shareholders' Equity	$1,720,000	$1,660,000

During Year 2, common shareholders received $60,000 in cash dividends and $120,000 in stock dividends. A refund on Year 0 taxes of $30,000 was received on March 1, Year 2, and was credited directly to Retained Earnings. A loss on retirement of plant assets of $5,600 occurred during the year and was debited directly to Retained Earnings.

   a. What net income is reported for Year 2, after the accounting was done as described?

   b. What net income should actually be reported for Year 2? Show your calculations.

18. *Analyzing changes in owners' equity accounts.* The comparative balance sheet of the Royal Corporation shows the following information:

	Dec. 31, Year 2	Dec. 31, Year 1
Preferred Stock (6 percent)	$ 600,000	$ 750,000
Common Stock	1,550,000	1,400,000
Retained Earnings	372,000	324,000
Total Shareholders' Equity	$2,522,000	$2,474,000

During Year 2, stock dividends of $150,000 were issued to common shareholders. In addition, common shareholders received $70,000 in cash dividends; the preferred shareholders received $36,000 in cash dividends. On July 1, Year 2, preferred shares with a par value of $150,000 were redeemed at 104; that is, $156,000 was paid to retire the shares. The call premium was debited to the Retained Earnings account.
   What net income is reported to shareholders for Year 2?

19. *Journal entries for transactions involving owners' equity.* Give journal entries for the following transactions.

   a. Outstanding shares are acquired by the issuing corporation for its treasury at a cost of $100,000.

   b. Dividends are declared on preferred shares, $220,000.

   c. A dividend is paid to common shareholders consisting of preferred shares in the same corporation with a par value of $200,000.

   d. A dividend is paid to common shareholders consisting of no-par-value common shares in the same corporation. The amount assigned to these shares is $600,000.

   e. The building is mortgaged for $100,000, and this amount is distributed to the common shareholders as a cash dividend.

20. *Journal entries for transactions involving owners' equity and other accounts.* Give journal entries, if required, for the following transactions, which are unrelated unless otherwise specified.

a. The regular quarterly dividend is declared on the ten percent, $100-par-value preferred shares. There are 10,000 shares authorized, 8,000 shares issued, of which 1,600 shares have been reacquired and are held in the treasury.

b. The dividend on the preferred shares [see part (a)] is paid.

c. A stock dividend of $250,000 of no par value common shares is issued to common shareholders.

d. A building replacement fund of $125,000 is created. The fund is to be used to purchase a new building when the present one becomes inadequate.

e. Bonds with $500,000 par value are retired at par out of the sinking fund created for that purpose.

f. The no par value common shares of the corporation are selling on the market at $300 a share. In order to bring the market value down to a more popular price and thereby broaden the distribution of its shareholdings, the board of directors votes to issue four extra shares to shareholders for each share already held by them. The shares are issued.

21. *Journal entries for transactions involving owners' equity.* Journalize the following transactions.

a. A cash dividend of $2 a share is declared on the outstanding preferred shares. There are 5,000 shares authorized, 3,000 shares issued, and 100 shares reacquired and held in the treasury.

b. A cash dividend of $1 a share is declared on the no par common shares, of which there are 10,000 shares authorized, 7,000 shares issued, and 1,000 shares reacquired and held in the treasury.

c. The dividend on the preferred shares is paid.

d. The dividend on the common shares is paid.

22. *Restrictions on dividend declarations.* Daley Limited has total retained earnings of $100 million and has acquired treasury shares at a cost of $25 million. Its loan agreements limit dividend declarations that would reduce retained earnings below $60 million. The corporation laws of the province of Daley Limited's incorporation do not allow dividend declarations if the amount of retained earnings is less than the cost of treasury shares held.

What is the maximum amount of dividends that Daley Limited can declare?

23. *Stock splits and stock splits accounted for as stock dividends.* The Horngren Co. Ltd. has 5 million common shares outstanding with a par value of $5 per share and retained earnings of $600 million. The common shares have a market price of $80 each. The board of directors wishes to increase the number of shares in circulation to 10 million either by declaring a two-for-one stock split or by declaring a 100 percent stock dividend to be accounted for as a stock split.

a. Give journal entries for each of these treatments.

b. Explain the relative advantages and disadvantages of each.

24. *Transactions to incorporate and run a business.* The following events relate to shareholders' equity transactions of the Richardson Copper Co. Ltd. during the first year of its existence. Present journal entries for each of the transactions.

a. January 2. Articles of incorporation are filed with the provincial registrar of companies. The authorized share capital consists of 5,000 $100 par value preferred shares, which offers an eight-percent annual dividend, and 50,000 no par value common shares. The original incorporators are issued 100 common shares at $20 per share; cash is collected for the shares.

b. January 6. 1,600 common shares are issued for cash at $20 per share.

c. January 8. 3,000 preferred shares are issued at par.

d. January 9. Certificates for the preferred shares are issued.

e. January 12. The tangible assets and goodwill of Richardson Copper Works, a partnership, are acquired in exchange for 600 preferred shares and 10,000 common shares. The tangible assets acquired are valued as follows: inventories, $40,000; land, $45,000; buildings, $80,000; and equipment, $95,000.

f. July 3. The semiannual dividend on the preferred shares outstanding is declared, payable July 25, to shareholders of record on July 12.

g. July 5. Operations for the first six months have been profitable, and the decision is made to expand. The company issues 20,000 common shares for cash at $33 per share.

h. July 25. The preferred share dividend declared July 3 is paid.

i. October 2. The directors declare a dividend of $1 per share on the common shares payable October 25, to shareholders of record on October 12.

j. October 25. The dividend on common shares declared on October 2 is paid.

25. *Transactions to incorporate and run a business.* The following data are selected from the records of capital stock and retained earnings of the Wheellock Inc. Present journal entries for these transactions.

a. July 5, Year 1. Articles of incorporation are filed with the director of the Canada Business Corporations Act. The authorized share capital consists of 1,000 Class B preferred shares with a preferred dividend of $6 per share and 10,000 Class A common shares.

b. July 8, Year 1. The company issues 3,000 common shares for cash at $60 per share.

c. July 9, Year 1. The company issues 6,000 common shares for the assets of the partnership of Wheellock and Wheellock. Their assets are valued as follows: accounts receivable, $30,000; inventories, $60,000; land, $80,000; buildings, $90,000; and equipment, $100,000.

d. July 13, Year 1. 750 preferred shares are issued for $75,000.

e. December 31, Year 1. The balance in the Income Summary account, after closing all expense and revenue accounts, is $300,000. That account is to be closed to the Retained Earnings account.

f. January 4, Year 2. The regular semiannual dividend on the preferred shares and a dividend of $2 per share on the common shares are declared. The dividends are payable on February 1.

g. February 1, Year 2. The dividends declared on January 4 are paid.

h. July 2, Year 2. The regular semiannual dividend on the preferred shares is declared. The dividend is payable on August 1.

i. August 1, Year 2. The dividend declared on July 2 is paid.

26. *Accounting for convertible bonds.* On January 2, Year 1, the Ogopogo Corporation issues $1 million of 20-year, $1,000 par value, ten percent semiannual coupon bonds at par. Each $1,000 bond is convertible into 40 no par value common shares. The Ogopogo Corporation's credit rating is such that it would have to issue 15-percent semiannual coupon bonds if the bonds were not convertible and if they were to be issued at par. On January 2, Year 5, the bond issue is converted into common shares. A common share has a market price of $45 a share on January 2, Year 5.

Present the journal entries made on January 2, Year 1 and Year 5, under generally accepted accounting principles, to record the issue and conversion of the issue.

27. *Granting stock options to executives involves an element of compensation.* Assume that accounting were to require recognition of compensation expense on the date that stock options were granted to an employee. A precise measure of the amount of the compensation expense would not be possible, but various approximations could be made. How might the accountant put a dollar amount on the compensation expense granted through stock options? You may assume that the exercise price is the market price on the date the option is granted.

Problems and Cases

28. *Reconstructing transactions involving owners' equity.* The Chelex Co. Ltd. began business on January 1. Its balance sheet on December 31 contains the shareholders' equity section shown in Exhibit 12.6.

Exhibit 12.6
CHELEX CO. LTD.
Shareholders' Equity as of December 31

Share Capital ($10 par value)	$ 50,000
Contributed Surplus	78,000
Retained Earnings	10,000
Less: 300 Shares Held in Treasury	(6,000)
Total Shareholders' Equity	$132,000

During the year, Chelex Co. Ltd. engaged in the following share capital transactions:

(1) Issued shares for $25 each.
(2) Acquired a block of 500 shares for the treasury in a single transaction.
(3) Reissued some of the treasury shares.

Assuming that these were all of the share capital transactions during the year, answer the following questions:

    a. How many shares were issued for $25?
    b. What was the price at which the treasury shares were acquired?
    c. How many shares were reissued from the block of treasury shares?
    d. What was the price at which the treasury shares were reissued?
    e. What journal entries must have been made during the year?

29. *Reconstructing transactions involving owners' equity.* The Worman Co. Inc. began business on January 1. Its balance sheet on December 31 contains the shareholders' equity section shown in Exhibit 12.7.

Exhibit 12.7
WORMAN CO. INC.
Shareholders' Equity as of December 31

Share capital ($5 par value)	$ 50,000
Contributed Surplus	254,800
Retained Earnings	25,000
Less: 600 Shares Held in Treasury	(16,800)
Total Shareholders' Equity	$313,000

During the year, Worman Co. Inc. engaged in the following share capital transactions:

(1) Issued shares for $30 each.
(2) Acquired a block of 1,000 shares for the treasury in a single transaction.
(3) Reissued some of the treasury shares.

Assuming that these were the only share capital transactions during the year, answer the following questions:

a. How many shares were issued for $30 each?
b. What was the price at which the treasury shares were acquired?
c. How many shares were reissued from the block of treasury shares?
d. What was the price at which the treasury shares were reissued?
e. What journal entries must have been made during the year?

30. *Funds statement effects.* Refer to the Simplified Statement of Changes in Financial Position for a Period in Exhibit 5.19 on page 248. Eleven of the lines in the statement are numbered. Ignore the unnumbered lines in responding to the questions below.

Assume that the accounting cycle is complete for the period and that all of the financial statements have been prepared. Then it is discovered that a transaction has been overlooked. The transaction is recorded in the accounts and all of the financial statements are corrected. Define *funds* as *cash*. For each of the following transactions, indicate which of the numbered lines of the funds statement is affected and by how much. Ignore income tax effects.

a. Common shares are issued for $200,000.
b. Common shares originally issued for $50,000 are repurchased for $75,000 and retired.
c. Convertible bonds with a book value of $100,000 and a market value of $240,000 are converted into common shares with a par value of $10,000 and a market value of $240,000.
d. Treasury shares acquired for $20,000 are reissued for $15,000.
e. A stock dividend is declared. The par value of the shares issued is $1,000 and their market value is $300,000.
f. A cash dividend of $70,000 is declared.
g. A previously declared cash dividend of $70,000 is paid.
h. Share rights are exercised. The shares have a par value of $1,000 and market value of $35,000 on the date of exercise. The exercise price is $20,000, and $20,000 cash is received.

31. *Dilutive effects of stock options.* Refer to the schedule reproduced in Exhibit 12.8, which shows employee stock option data for the International Products Co. Ltd. (IP). At December 31, Year 3, there were 2.7 million options outstanding to purchase shares at an average of $54 per share. Total shareholders' equity at December 31, Year 3, was about $2.5 billion.

a. If IP were to issue 2.7 million shares in a public offering at the market price per share on December 31, Year 3, what would be the proceeds of the issue?

b. If IP were to issue 2.7 million shares to employees who exercised all outstanding stock options, what would be the proceeds of the issue?

Exhibit 12.8
INTERNATIONAL PRODUCTS CO. LTD.
Disclosure of Employee Stock Options

Stock Options	Shares Subject to Option	Average per Share Option Price	Average per Share Market Price
Balance at December 31, Year 1	2,388,931	$45	$72
Options Granted	475,286	77	77
Options Exercised	(297,244)	42	76
Options Terminated	(90,062)	45	—
Balance at December 31, Year 2	2,476,911	50	83
Options Granted	554,965	75	75
Options Exercised	(273,569)	42	74
Options Terminated	(58,307)	52	—
Balance at December 31, Year 3	2,700,000	54	77

c. Are IP's shareholders better off under **(a)** or under **(b)**?

d. The text accompanying the stock option data in the IP annual report reads, in part, as follows:

Option price under these plans is the full market value of International Products common shares on date of grant. Therefore, participants in the plans do not benefit unless the share's market price rises, thus benefiting all share owners.

IP seems to be saying that shareholders are not harmed by these options, whereas your answers to parts **(a)** and **(b)** show shareholders are worse off when options are exercised than when shares are issued to the public. Attempt to reconcile IP's statement with your own analysis in parts **(a)** and **(b)**.

32. *Reporting nonrecurring gains in the income statement.* In 1982 Dominion Textile Inc. undertook a comprehensive review of the corporation's business units. As a result of this review the directors decided to discontinue a number of lines of business and to redeploy the corporation's resources to a narrower range of products.

Accordingly the corporation deducted $11,500,000 from income for 1982, made up as follows:

Write-down of fixed assets	$ 9,600,000
Provision for anticipated cash costs	10,300,000
	19,900,000

Less: Reduction in income taxes		
Deferred	$4,100,000	
Current	4,300,000	8,400,000
		$11,500,000

Before considering the above the corporation reported a loss of $2,900,000 for 1982.

  a. Give the journal entry made by Dominion Textiles Inc. to record the above event.

  b. How do you think the above event should be reported in the financial statements?

33. *Dividend policy and dividend reinvestment plans.* Many companies have "automatic dividend reinvestment plans." Shareholders notify the company that they wish to reinvest all cash dividends in common shares. The company arranges to have common shares purchased at current market value for the accounts of the shareholders.

General Products Limited, whose financial statements appear in Appendix A, has such an automatic dividend reinvestment plan. At the end of 1988 it declared and paid a dividend of $2 per share. Holders of 10 percent of the shares have elected the automatic dividend reinvestment option. The market price of a share on the date of reinvestment is $60. General Products Limited instructs a stockbroker to purchase the required shares on the Toronto Stock Exchange.

  a. Give the journal entries, if any, that General Products Limited makes for the dividend declaration and for the automatic reinvestment of dividends.

  b. A shareholder complained that if the company would refrain from paying dividends, only to have them reinvested, it would save paperwork and the shareholders would save income taxes. Comment.

34. *Dilution of earnings per share.* In May of Year 1, the A-Tat Co. Ltd. issued 100,000 no par value convertible preferred shares for $50 a share. The shares promised a dividend of $6. All shares were issued for cash. These shares were convertible into common shares at a rate of 5 common shares for each preferred share. The preferred shares are *not* regarded as equivalent to common shares in the calculation of earnings per share.

The company's earnings increased sharply during the next four years, and during January of Year 5, all preferred shares were converted into common shares. One million common shares were outstanding before conversion of the shares. If the conversion had not taken place, the net income to common for Year 5 would have been $3,000,000. Other data are as follows:

	Jan. Year 5	May Year 1
Market Prices:		
A-Tat Common Shares	$ 20	$10
A-Tat $6 Preferred Shares	100	50
Book Value per A-Tat Common Share (before conversion of preferred)	18	14

  a. Prepare journal entries to record the issuance and conversion of the preferred shares.

b. Compute earnings per common share before conversion of the shares. What was the effect of the conversion on book values and on earnings per common share?

c. Did the conversion of the preferred shares into common shares lead to a dilution of the common shareholders' equity? Explain your reasoning.

35. *Accounting for detachable warrants.* After several years of rapid expansion, the Alcher Co. Ltd. approached the Bank of Nova Montreal for a $1 million, five-year loan. The bank was willing to lend the money at an interest rate of 12 percent per year. Alcher Co. Ltd. then approached an individual investor who was willing to provide the same funds for only eight percent per year, provided that the Alcher Co. Ltd. gave the investor an option to purchase 20,000 no par value common shares of Alcher Co. Ltd. for $20 per share at any time within five years of the initial date of the loan.

Alcher weighed both opportunities and decided to borrow from the investor. At the time of the loan, the common shares had a market price of $15 per share. Five years after the initial date of the loan, the investor exercised the option and purchased 20,000 shares for $20 each. At that time, the market price of the common shares was $45 each.

a. Did the use of the "detachable warrants" (the technical name for the option granted to the investor) reduce the Alcher Co. Ltd.'s cost of borrowing?

b. How should the loan and annual interest payments of $80,000 be recorded in the books of the Alcher Co. Ltd. to reflect the economic reality of the transaction?

c. How might the exercise of the warrants (and the purchase of the 20,000 shares) be recorded?

d. Did exercise of the option dilute the owners' equity of the other shareholders on the date the option was exercised?

e. What disclosures during the life of the loan do you think appropriate? Why?

36. *Comprehensive review of accounting for owners' equity.* The shareholders' equity section of the balance sheet of the Reis Corporation at December 31 is shown below.

Shareholders' Equity

Common Stock — $10 Par Value, 500,000 Shares Authorized and 100,000 Shares Outstanding	$1,000,000
Contributed Surplus	500,000
Retained Earnings	3,000,000
Total Shareholders' Equity	$4,500,000

a. Calculate the total book value and the book value per common share as of December 31.

b. For each of the following transactions or events, give the appropriate journal entry and determine the total book value and the book value per common share of the Reis Corporation after the transaction. The transaction and events are independent of each other, except where noted.

(1) A ten percent stock dividend is declared when the market price of Reis Corporation's common shares is $60 per share.

    (2) A two-for-one stock split is declared, and the par value of a common share is reduced from $10 to $5. The new shares are issued immediately.

    (3) Ten thousand common shares of Reis Corporation are purchased on the open market for $50 per share and held as treasury shares.

    (4) Ten thousand common shares of Reis Corporation are purchased on the open market for $30 per share and held as treasury shares.

    (5) The shares acquired in **(3)** are sold for $70 per share.

    (6) The shares acquired in **(3)** are sold for $40 per share.

    (7) The shares acquired in **(3)** are sold for $30 per share.

    (8) Options to acquire 10,000 shares of Reis Corporation are exercised by officers for $15 per share.

    (9) Same as **(8)**, except that the exercise price is $50 per share.

    (10) Convertible bonds with a book value of $300,000 and a market value of $340,000 are exchanged for 10,000 common shares having a market value of $34 per share. No gain or loss is recognized on the conversion of bonds.

    (11) Same as **(10)**, except that gain or loss is recognized on the conversion of bonds into shares. Ignore income tax effects.

  c. Using the results from part **(b)**, summarize the transactions and events that result in a reduction in:

    (1) Total book value.

    (2) Book value per share.

37. *Reconstructing events affecting owners' equity.* Exhibit 12.9 reproduces the statement of changes in owners' equity accounts for Granof Inc. for Year 2.

  a. Identify the most likely events or transaction for each of the events numbered **(1)** to **(6)** in the exhibit.

  b. Prepare journal entries for each of these events or transactions.

Exhibit 12.9
GRANOF INC.
Statement of Changes in Owners' Equity Accounts for Year 2

	Common Shares					
	Market Value per Share[a]	Number of Shares	Par Value	Contributed Surplus	Retained Earnings	Total Owners' Equity
Balances, Dec. 31, Year 1	$100	2,000,000	$12,000,000	$48,000,000	$40,000,000	$100,000,000
Events Causing Changes						
Event **(1)**	$105	4,000,000	—	—	—	—
Event **(2)**	$ 40	600,000	1,200,000	22,800,000	(24,000,000)	—
Event **(3)**	$ 45	100,000	200,000	4,300,000	—	4,500,000
Event **(4)**	$ 48	50,000	100,000	1,400,000	—	1,500,000
Event **(5)**	$ 50	—	—	—	45,000,000	45,000,000
Event **(6)**	$ 53	—	—	—	(6,750,000)	(6,750,000)
Balances, Dec. 31, Year 2		6,750,000	$13,500,000	$76,500,000	$54,250,000	$144,250,000

[a]Before event.

38. *Case introducing earnings per share calculations for a complex capital structure.* The Layton Ball Corporation has a relatively complicated capital structure. In addition to common shares, it has issued stock options, warrants, and convertible bonds. Exhibit 12.10 summarizes some pertinent information about these items. Net income for the year is $9,500, and the income tax rate used in computing income tax expense is 40 percent of pretax income.

Exhibit 12.10
LAYTON BALL CORPORATION
Information on Capital Structure
for Earnings per Share Calculation
(Problem 38)

Assume the following data about the capital structure and earnings for the Layton Ball Corporation for the year:

Number of Common Shares Outstanding Throughout the Year	2,500 shares
Market Price per Common Share Throughout the Year	$25
Options Outstanding During the Year:	
Number of Shares Issuable on Exercise of Options	1,000 shares
Exercise Price per Share	$15
Warrants Outstanding During the Year:	
Number of Shares Issuable on Exercise of Warrants	2,000 shares
Exercise Price per Share	$30
Convertible Bonds Outstanding:	
Number (issued 15 years ago)	100 bonds
Proceeds per Bond at Time of Issue (= par value)	$1,000
Shares of Common Issuable on Conversion (per bond)	10 shares
Coupon Rate (per year)	$4\frac{1}{6}$ percent

a. First, ignore all items of capital except for the common shares. Calculate earnings per common share.

b. In past years, employees have been issued options to purchase shares. Exhibit 12.10 indicates that the price of the common shares throughout the year was $25, but that the stock options could be exercised at any time for $15 each. The holder of an option is allowed to surrender it along with $15 cash and receive one share in return. Thus, the number of shares would be increased, which would decrease the earnings per share figure. The company would, however, have more cash. Assume that the holders of options were to tender their options, along with $15 each, to purchase shares, and that the company would use the cash to purchase shares for the treasury at a price of $25 each. Compute a new earnings per share figure. (Treasury shares are *not* counted in the denominator of the earnings per share calculation.)

c. Exhibit 12.10 indicates that there are also warrants outstanding in the hands of the public. Anyone who owns such a warrant is allowed to turn in that warrant along with $30 cash and to purchase one share. If the warrants are exercised, then there would be more shares outstanding, which would reduce earnings per share. The company would, however, have more cash, which it could use to purchase shares for the treasury, reducing the number of shares outstanding. Assume that all holders of warrants were to exercise them. Assume that the company were to use the cash to purchase outstanding shares for the treasury. Compute a new earnings per share figure. (Ignore the information about options and the calculations in part (b) at this point.) Note that a rational warrant holder would *not* exercise his or her warrants for $30 when a share can be purchased for $25.

   d. There are convertible bonds outstanding. A holder of a convertible bond is entitled to trade in that bond for ten shares. If a bond is converted, the number of shares would increase, which would tend to reduce earnings per share. On the other hand, the company would not have to pay interest and thus would have no interest expense on the bond, because it would no longer be outstanding. This would tend to increase income and earnings per share. Assume that all holders of convertible bonds were to convert their bonds into shares. Compute a new net income figure (do not forget income tax effects on income of the interest saved) and a new earnings per share figure. (Ignore the information about options and warrants and the calculations in parts (b) and (c) at this point.)

   e. Now consider all the above calculations. Which sets of assumptions from parts (b), (c), and (d) would lead to the lowest possible earnings per share when they are all made simultaneously? Compute a new earnings per share under the most restrictive set of assumptions about reductions in earnings per share.

   f. Accountants publish several earnings per share figures for companies with complicated capital structures and complicated events during the year. The *Financial Post*, however, publishes only one figure in its weekly columns (where it reports the price-earnings ratio—the price of a share divided by its earnings per share). Which of the figures computed above for earnings per share do you think should be reported by the *Financial Post* as *the* earnings per share figure? Why?

39. *Stated value.* Brenda's Edit Shoppes, Inc., has the following equity account balances:

Preferred Shares, 40,000 no-par shares issued and outstanding	$ 60,000
Common Shares, 50,000 no-par shares issued and outstanding	100,000
Retained Earnings	40,000

The company reacquires 10,000 of its common shares on the open market at $2.50 per share and retires them. What is the *stated capital* of common shares after this transaction?

40. *Shareholders' equity—transactions, balance sheet presentation, and book value per share.* The shareholders' equity section of the Western Economic Fund Corporation, a crown corporation, at January 1 of the current year appears below:

Preferred Shares, $1.50 Dividend Per Share, No Par Value, 10,000 shares authorized;	
5,200 shares issued and outstanding	$208,000

Common Shares, No Par Value, 200,000 shares authorized;
   60,000 shares issued and outstanding   600,000
Retained Earnings   325,000

During the current year, the following transactions occurred:

Jan.   10   Issued 11,000 common shares for $13 cash per share.

       23   Issued 6,000 common shares at $14 per share.

Mar.   2   The federal government, the majority shareholder, donated $44,200 to Western.

July   15   Issued 1,200 preferred shares to acquire special equipment with a fair market value of $54,000.

Sept.   15   Received subscriptions to 10,000 common shares at $21 per share. One-third of the subscription price was received in cash.

Nov.   15   Received the balance due on the September 15 share subscriptions in cash, and issued the share certificates.

Dec.   31   Closed the net income of $95,800 from the Income Summary account to Retained Earnings.

a. Set up T accounts for the shareholders' equity accounts at the beginning of the year and enter January 1 balances.

b. Prepare general journal entries to record the foregoing transactions, and post to T accounts (set up any additional T accounts needed). Determine the ending balances for the shareholders' equity accounts.

c. Prepare the December 31 shareholders' equity section of the balance sheet.

41. *Shareholders' equity—transaction descriptions from account data.* The T accounts below contain keyed entries representing six transactions involving the shareholders' equity of Lawson, Inc.

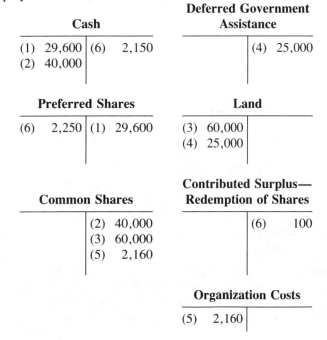

a. Using this information, give detailed descriptions for each of the six transactions.

42. *Dividends, share redemptions, and earnings per share.* The Cracker Corporation had the following shareholders' equity at January 1, 1988:

Common shares, no par value, 100,000 shares outstanding	$1,200,000
$12 Preferred, no par value, 20,000 shares outstanding, cumulative and	
redeemable at 104	2,000,000
Retained Earnings	1,875,000
	$5,075,000

Although earnings were satisfactory in the past, no cash dividends had been declared in the last two years, i.e., in 1986 and 1987. In 1988, however, Cracker Corporation was confident that it would be able to afford to distribute $1,000,000 in cash dividends. After distribution of the dividends, it planned to redeem 5,000 of the preferred shares. This could be accomplished either through a purchase in the market or by "calling" these shares for redemption.

a. Calculate the amount of the dividend that would be paid to the preferred shareholders and to the common shareholders if dividends of $1,000,000 were declared in 1988.
b. Calculate the effect on assets of calling the preferred stock for redemption.
c. Preferred shares are more like debt security than an equity security. Explain what is meant by this statement.
d. Dividends are said to be a distribution of earnings. Cracker Corporation has a large Retained Earnings balance. How could they not have been able to afford to pay dividends in 1986 and 1987?
e. Ignoring the redemption of preferred shares, if earnings for 1988 were $635,000, calculate the earnings per share for 1988.

Adapted, with permission, from the Society of Management Accountants of Canada.

Decision Problem 12-1

In early January Year 3, B. R. Baine (B. R.), the president of Fanco Ltd., a diversified public company, faced the problem of determining the means of financing a major project recently approved by the board of directors. This project requires an investment of $1,000,000 and is expected to produce an operating income before financing costs and income taxes of $200,000 a year, with the principal returned at the end of the fifth year. Fanco Ltd. is subject to an income tax rate of 40 percent.

The corporate treasurer has advised B. R. that the following alternative sources of financing are available:

(1) Issue rights to common shareholders to purchase common shares at $20 per share.
(2) Arrange a five-year bank loan with 14 percent interest payable annually in arrears.
(3) Issue five-year convertible bonds with ten percent interest payable annually. Each $100 bond would be convertible into 4.5 common shares.

(4) Issue cumulative, redeemable, convertible $1.75 preferred shares. The preferred shares are redeemable in five years at their issue price and convertible into common shares on the basis of one common share for each preferred share. The preferred shares would be issued at $25 per share.

B. R. Baine owns no Fanco Ltd. common shares, but is paid an annual bonus of 10,000 times the reported earnings per common share before bonus. The earnings per share for this purpose is calculated by dividing net income less preferred dividends by the common shares outstanding at the fiscal year-end. In Year 2, Fanco Ltd. reported income of $420,000 and earnings per share of $2.10.

After careful consideration, B. R. estimated that it was likely that 20 percent of the bonds or preferred shares would be converted at the end of the first year and a further 40 percent at the end of each of the third and fifth years.

Determine the form of financing that B. R. should select to maximize his bonus, in the first, third and fifth years of the project.

Integrative Problem 12-1

Part I

Smith, Jones, and Able had been equal partners in a chain of photographic shops in Hamilton for a number of years. Able was approaching 65 and wished to retire from the business and spend his golden years in Florida. He proposed that he retire from the partnership by changing from a partner to a creditor of the partnership, with his capital to be repaid at the rate of $40,000 per year, plus ten percent interest on the outstanding balance. At the same time, Jones and Smith thought they should convert the form of business to that of a limited company to provide more permanence and the flexibility to admit new employees as owners through the purchase of shares.

Jones and Smith considered that the book value of the assets and liabilities of the partnership were an inadequate measure of the value of the business, but did provide a list of the assets. To overcome the "historical cost" handicap of the book values, they had each asset and liability individually appraised at current market value and agreed upon by all partners. The following balance sheet presents the book values and agreed appraised values.

Since the business will remain essentially unchanged when Able retires, the partners decided to maintain the present accounting system. The new company, Smith, Jones, and Able Ltd., is to issue 5,000 shares of no par value (for a consideration of $30 each) to each of Smith and Jones as partial consideration for their interest in the partnership.

Prepare the journal entries necessary to record the revaluation of assets, the retirement of Able, and the conversion to a limited company.

Part II

Five years later, when the retained earnings of the company amounted to $240,300 and the share capital, $500,000, Smith decided to retire. Rather than have the present shareholders — now increased by the addition of the six store managers — purchase the shares, it was decided to have the company purchase them for $46 a share. The shares would be held for subsequent reissue or cancellation.

a. Prepare the journal entry to record the purchase by the company of the shares of Smith.

b. Prepare the shareholders' equity segment of the balance sheet prepared immediately following the share purchase.

Smith Jones & Able
Balance Sheet
October 31, Year 5

Assets

		Book Value	Appraised Value
Current Assets:			
Cash on Hand and in Bank		$ 12,500	$ 12,500
Temporary Investments		8,000	12,600
Accounts Receivable		17,600	17,200
Inventory		96,900	99,200
Prepaid Expenses		700	700
Total Current Assets		$135,700	$142,200
Land, Buildings, and Equipment:			
Land		$ 72,000	$169,500
Buildings	$ 68,200		272,000
Furniture and Fixtures	57,500		42,600
Automobiles	14,900		6,700
	$140,600		
Less: Accumulated Depreciation	61,700	78,900	
Total Plant and Equipment		$150,900	$490,800
Goodwill		2,500	46,300
Total Assets		$289,100	$679,300

Liabilities and Partners' Equity

		Book Value	Appraised Value
Current Liabilities:			
Accounts Payable		$ 6,400	$ 6,400
Accruals		700	700
		$ 7,100	$ 7,100
Mortgage Payable		106,400	98,200
Total Liabilities		$113,500	$105,300
Partners' Equity:			
Smith		30,100	
Jones		41,300	
Able		104,200	
		$175,600	574,000
		$289,100	$679,300

Chapter 13 Long-Term Investments in Corporate Securities

For a variety of reasons, corporations often acquire the shares or bonds of other corporations. For example, a corporation may temporarily hold excess cash that is not needed for operations. Rather than permit the cash to remain idle in its bank account, the corporation may invest in the common shares of another corporation. Relatively short-term investments of excess cash in corporate securities are usually classified as Temporary Investments and are shown in the Current Assets section of the balance sheet. Chapter 7 discusses the accounting for short-term investments.

A corporation may acquire another corporation's shares for some long-term purpose.[1] For example, a firm may acquire shares of a major raw materials supplier to help assure continued availability of raw materials. Or, a firm may wish to diversify its operations by acquiring a controlling interest in an established firm in some new area of business. Long-term investments in corporate securities are typically classified on the asset side of the balance sheet in a separate section called "Investments."

Types of Long-Term Investments

The accounting for long-term investments depends on the extent one company is able to exercise *significant influence* over the other. Significant influence over the operating and financial decisions of another company is indicated by such things as representation on the board of directors, participation in policy-making processes, material intercompany transactions, interchange of technical personnel, or provision of technical information. The extent of share ownership is one of the determinants of significant influence. Refer to Figure 13.1. Three types of long-term investments can be identified:

1. Portfolio Investments — Shares of another corporation are viewed as a good long-term investment and are acquired for the dividends and capital gains (increases in the market price of the shares) anticipated from owning the shares. The percentage owned of the other corporation's shares is not so large that the acquiring company can control or exert significant influence over the other company. Generally accepted accounting principles view investments of less than 20 percent of the voting shares of another company as portfolio investments, unless significant influence is clearly demonstrated.[2]

2. Minority Investments — Shares of another corporation are acquired so that the acquiring corporation can exert significant influence over the other company's activities. Because the shares of most publicly held corporations are widely dis-

---

[1]Industrial firms seldom acquire bonds of other corporations as long-term investments. Consequently, this chapter focuses on long-term investments in capital stock.
[2]*CICA Handbook*, section 3050.

persed among numerous individuals, many of whom do not vote their shares, it is possible to exert significant influence over another corporation with ownership of less than a majority of the voting shares. Generally accepted accounting principles view investments of between 20 percent and 50 percent of the voting shares of another company as minority investments. However, ownership of 20 percent or more of the voting shares is insufficient by itself to confirm the ability to exercise significant influence.

3. Majority Investments — Shares of another corporation are acquired so that the acquiring corporation can control the other company. This control is typically at both the broad policy-making level and at the day-to-day operational level. Ownership of more than 50 percent of the voting shares of another company implies an ability to control, unless there is evidence to the contrary.

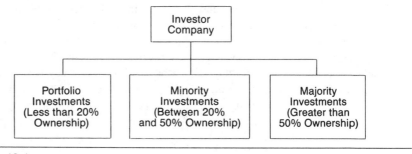

Figure 13.1
Types of Intercorporate Investments in Securities

The section that follows discusses the accounting for these three types of investments. Throughout the chapter, the acquiring corporation is designated P, for *purchaser* or for *parent*, depending on the context, and the acquired corporation is designated S, for *seller* or for *subsidiary*. Unless stated otherwise, company S issues only common shares.

Portfolio Investments

If a firm does not own a sufficient percentage of the voting shares of another corporation to control or significantly influence it (assumed to be 20 percent or more), the management of the investment involves two activities: (1) awaiting the receipt of dividends and (2) deciding when the investment should be sold for a capital gain or loss. Portfolio investments must be accounted for by using the *cost method* in accordance with generally accepted accounting principles.[3]

The following illustration presents typical transactions in portfolio investments.

Suppose that P acquires 1,000 shares of S (10 percent of the issued shares) for $40,000. The entry to record the acquisition would be:

---

[3]*Ibid.*

| Investment in S . . . . | $40,000 | |
| Cash . . . . | | $40,000 |

If, while P holds these shares, S pays a dividend of $2 per share, P would make the following entry:

| Cash . . . . | $2,000 | |
| Dividend Revenue . . . . | | $2,000 |

If P sells all of its shares of S, P will debit Cash for the proceeds, credit the Investment in S account to reduce the balance in that account to zero, and credit Gain on Sale of Shares (or debit Loss on Sale of Shares) to complete the entry. If P sells its 1,000 shares of S for $40,500, and they are still recorded at a cost of $40,000, the entry would be:

Cash	$40,500	
Investment in S		$40,000
Gain on Sale of Investment		500

To summarize, when company P accounts for its investment in company S using the cost method:

1. Company P reports as income each period its share of the dividends declared by company S.
2. Company P reports on the balance sheet the cost of the shares in company S.
3. Company P recognizes gains on the income statement from holding the shares of company S at the time the shares are sold.

Under the cost method, the carrying value of the investment is not affected by changes in the market value of the investment.[4] Since the investment is expected to be held for a long time, there is no point in recognizing market fluctuations that are likely to reverse themselves eventually.

However, if a decline in market value below the carrying value is deemed to be a permanent decline, then the investment should be written down. If there is subsequent rise in the market value, the carrying value would not be readjusted.

Minority Investments

Judgment is required in ascertaining when significant influence can be exercised over another company when less than a majority of the voting shares is owned. As a rule of thumb, generally accepted accounting principles presume that one company can significantly influence another company when 20 percent or more of the voting shares of the other company is owned. Significant influence may be present when less than 20

---

[4]Recall from Chapter 7 that investments classified as temporary should be carried at the lower of cost and market.

percent is owned, but in these cases management must demonstrate clearly to the independent accountants that it exists.

Minority investments, those where ownership is between 20 percent and 50 percent, must be accounted for using the *equity method*. Under the equity method, the firm owning shares in another firm recognizes as revenue (expense) each period its share of the net income (loss) of the other firm. Dividends received from S are not recognized as income but as a return of capital.

Equity Method: Rationale

The rationale for the equity method when significant influence is present can be best understood by considering the financial statement effects of using the cost method in these circumstances. Under the cost method, P recognizes income or loss on the income statement only when it receives a dividend, when there is a permanent decline in value, or when it sells all or part of the investment. Suppose, as often happens, that S follows a policy of financing its own growing operations through retention of earnings and consistently declares dividends significantly less than its net income. The market price of S's shares will probably increase to reflect the retention of assets generated by earnings. Under the cost method, P will continue to show the investment at acquisition cost and P's only reported income from the investment will be the modest dividends received. P, because of its ownership percentage, can influence the dividend policy of S and thereby the amount of income recognized under the cost method. Under these conditions, the cost method may not reasonably reflect the earnings of S generated under P's influence. The equity method is designed to provide a better measure of a firm's earnings and of its investment when, because of its ownership interest, significant influence can be exerted over the operations of another firm.

Equity Method: Procedures

Under the equity method, the initial purchase of an investment is recorded at acquisition cost, the same as under the cost method. Company P treats as revenue, each period, its proportionate share of the periodic earnings, not the dividends, of company S. Dividends declared by S are then treated by P as a reduction in its Investment in S.

Suppose that P acquires 30 percent of the outstanding shares of S for $600,000. The entry to record the acquisition would be:

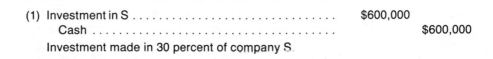

(1) Investment in S $600,000
        Cash $600,000
        Investment made in 30 percent of company S.

Between the time of the acquisition and the end of P's next accounting period, S reports income of $180,000. P, using the equity method, would record:

(2) Investment in S		$54,000	
Revenue from Investments[5]			$54,000
To record 30 percent of income earned by company S, accounted for using the equity method.			

If S pays a dividend of $70,000, P would be entitled to receive $21,000 and would record:

(3) Cash		$21,000	
Investment in S			$21,000
To record dividends received from company S, accounted for using the equity method, and the resulting reduction in the investment account.			

Notice that the credit is to the Investment in S account. P records income earned by S as an *increase* in investment. The dividend becomes a return of capital or a *decrease* in investment.[6] P's Investment in S account now has a balance of $633,000 as follows:

Investment in S

(1)	600,000	21,000	(3)
(2)	54,000		
Bal.	633,000		

If P now sells one-quarter of its shares for $165,000, P's entry to record the sale would be:

Cash		$165,000	
Investment in S			$158,250
Gain on Sale of Investment in S			6,750
($\frac{1}{4}$ × $633,000 = $158,250.)			

The equity method as described above is simple enough to use. To make financial reports that use the equity method more realistic, generally accepted accounting princi-

---

[5] In practice, this account is frequently called "Equity in Earnings of Unconsolidated Affiliates."
[6] Students often have difficulty understanding journal entry (3), particularly the credit by the investor when a dividend is declared by the investee company. The transaction and entries are analogous to an individual's ordinary savings account at a local bank. Assume that you put $600 in a savings account, that later interest of 9 percent (or $54) is added by the bank to the account, and that still later you withdraw $21, from the savings account. Journal entries (1)–(3) in the text could be recorded for these three events, with slight changes in the account titles: Investment in S changes to Savings Account, Revenue from Investments changes to Interest Revenue. The cash withdrawal reduces the amount invested in the savings account. Similarly, the declaration of a cash dividend by an investee company accounted for with the equity method reduces the investor's investment in the company.

ples require some modification of the entries under certain circumstances, described next.

When the equity method is used, the amount of income recorded by P should be equal to the amount that would be recognized if S's operations had been consolidated with P's. These modifications will be discussed and illustrated later in the chapter, but for present purposes we note two of them here.

Where either P or S sells goods to the other during the year and the goods have not been resold to other customers by the end of the year, the income from the sales is considered unrealized. The cost of the products recorded by the purchaser will usually exceed the cost to the seller by the amount of the income from the transaction recorded by the seller. In these circumstances the unrealized income attributed to P will be excluded from P's income from Investment in S, and the value of the unsold goods reduced. Further elaboration of this concept will be discussed and illustrated later in the chapter.

An additional complication in using the equity method arises when the acquisition cost of P's shares exceeds P's proportionate share of the carrying value of the net assets (= assets minus liabilities), or shareholders' equity, of S at the date of acquisition. For example, assume that P acquires 25 percent of the shares of S for $400,000, when the total shareholders' equity of S is $1 million, and the carrying value of the net assets of S equals their fair value. The excess of P's cost over carrying value acquired is $150,000 (= $400,000 − .25 × $1,000,000) and is called *goodwill*. Goodwill must be amortized over a period not greater than 40 years.[7] Accounting for goodwill, including its amortization, is discussed later in this chapter.

On the balance sheet, an investment accounted for on the equity method is shown separately in the Investments section. The amount shown will generally be equal to the acquisition cost of the shares plus P's share of S's undistributed earnings since the date the shares were acquired. On the income statement, P shows its share of S's income as a revenue each period. (The financial statements of the investee, S, are not affected by the accounting method used by the investor, P.)

Equity Method and the Statement of Changes in Financial Position

When company P uses the cost method to account for its investment in company S, all dividend revenues recognized in computing net income also produce cash. No adjustment to net income is therefore required in calculating Cash Provided by Operations.

Accounting for investments using the equity method, however, requires an adjustment to net income to compute Cash Capital Provided by Operations. Suppose that company P prepares its financial statements at the end of a year during which transactions (1)–(3), above, occurred. P's revenue from its investment in S is $54,000. P's income increased $54,000 because of its investment. However, P's cash increased by only $21,000 [transaction (3)] as a result of S's dividend declarations. Consequently, there must be a *subtraction* from net income of $33,000

---

[7]*CICA Handbook*, section 1580.

(= $54,000 − $21,000) in computing Cash Provided by Operations to show that cash did not increase by as much as the amount of revenue recognized under the equity method.

In preparing P's statement of changes in financial position using the T-account method, the following change in a noncurrent asset account would have to be explained:

Investment in S	
Bal. 0	
Bal. 633,000	

The entries to explain this debit change of $633,000 would be:

Investment in S	$600,000	
Cash (Use—Acquisition of Investment)		$600,000
To recognize use of cash for an investment in a noncurrent asset.		
Investment in S	$ 33,000	
Cash (Subtraction — Undistributed Income Under Equity Method)		$33,000
To recognize that cash was not increased by the full amount of revenue recognized under the equity method.		

Keep in mind that these two entries are not formally made in the accounting records, but are made only in the work sheet used for preparing the statement of changes in financial position.

Equity Method Illustrated

The equity method can be illustrated using information for General Products Limited found in Appendix A. The balance sheet (Exhibit A.2, page 761) indicates that investments were $1,691 million on December 31, 1985 and $1,820 million on December 31, 1986. Note 11 to the financial statements indicates that the investment in General Products Credit Corporation, a wholly owned, unconsolidated finance affiliate is, included in investments on the balance sheet. Because General Products Limited owns all of General Products Credit Corporation's outstanding common shares, but chooses not to consolidate it, the equity method of accounting is used.

The change in the Investment in General Products Credit Corporation account during 1988 is as follows (amounts in millions):

Investment in General Products Credit Corporation, December 31, 1987 (Note 11)	$817
Plus: Equity In Earnings of General Products Credit Corporation for 1988 (Note 3) ..	115
Additional Investments (change in Share Capital account of General Products Credit Corporation Note (11)	92
Less: Dividends Received (Note 11)..	(93)
Investment in General Products Credit Corporation, December 31, 1988 (Note 11)	$931

Income generated from this investment totaled $115 million during 1988. However, only $93 million was received in cash. Thus, the statement of changes in financial position must show a subtraction of $22 (= $115 − $93) million for income that did not produce cash. Also included among other uses of cash will be $92 million for additional investments in the credit subsidiary.

Majority Investments

When one firm, P, owns more than 50 percent of the voting shares of another company, S, P can control the activities of S. The majority investor in this case is called the *parent* and the majority-owned company is called the *subsidiary*. Generally accepted accounting principles require majority-owned investments to be combined, or *consolidated*, with those of the parent, except under certain conditions. Where these conditions are present, consolidated financial statements are not prepared. Instead, the investment is reported using the equity method.

Reasons for Legally Separate Corporations

There are many reasons why a business firm prefers to operate as a group of legally separate corporations, rather than as a single legal entity. From the standpoint of the parent company, the more important reasons for maintaining legally separate subsidiary companies include the following:

1. To reduce the financial risk. Separate corporations may be used for mining raw materials, transporting them to a manufacturing plant, producing the product, and selling the finished product to the public. If any one part of the total process proves to be unprofitable or inefficient, losses from insolvency will fall only on the owners and creditors of the one subsidiary corporation.
2. To meet more effectively the requirements of corporation laws and tax legislation. If an organization does business in a number of countries or provinces, it is often faced with overlapping and inconsistent taxation, regulations, and requirements. Organizing separate corporations to conduct the operations in the various local areas may be more economical.
3. To expand or diversify with a minimum of capital investment. A firm may absorb another company by acquiring a controlling interest in its voting shares. The result may be accomplished with a substantially smaller capital investment, as well as with less difficulty, inconvenience, and risk, than if a new plant had been constructed or the firm had geared up for a new line of business.

Purpose of Consolidated Statements

For a variety of reasons, then, a single *economic entity* may exist in the form of a parent and several legally separate subsidiaries. (MacMillan Bloedel Limited, for example, consists of about 75 legally separate companies.) A consolidation of the financial statements of the parent and each of its subsidiaries presents the results of operations, financial position, and changes in financial position of an affiliated group of companies under the control of a parent, essentially as if the group of companies were a single entity. The parent and each subsidiary are legally separate entities, but they operate as one centrally controlled *economic* entity. Consolidated financial statements generally provide more useful information to the shareholders of the parent corporation than would separate financial statements of the parent as investor and each subsidiary as an operating company.

Consolidated financial statements also generally provide more useful information than does use of the equity method. The parent, because of its voting interest, can effectively control the use of all of the subsidiary's assets. Consolidation of the individual assets and equities of both the parent and the subsidiary provides a more realistic picture of the operations and financial position of the single economic entity.

The Canada Business Corporations Act and the Corporation Acts of most of the provinces permit companies to replace the separate statements of the parent corporation by consolidated financial statements.

To GAAP or not to GAAP . . . that is the question.

*T*he Ontario Securities Commission expects to make a decision in two weeks on whether Crownx Inc. and Trilon Financial Corp., both of Toronto, should be allowed to consolidate the results of their life insurance subsidiaries with their other businesses.

"The principles . . . are so important we would like to go through a percolation period," said OSC chairman Peter Dey.

The OSC's financial analyst, Syl Gorecki, takes the purist view that it would be improper to consolidate the results of a life insurance company, which follows statutory rules of accounting, with the results of the parent company following generally accepted accounting principles (GAAP). At their simplest, accounting rules try to avoid the mixing of apples and oranges.

However, both Crownx and Trilon believe that the disclosed-basis-of-accounting section of the Canadian Institute of Chartered Accountants handbook gives them a free hand to consolidate their life insurance businesses in order to present a more realistic financial picture. They argue that the results should be shown as "a single economic group."

Two OSC panels, one convened to hear Trilon's case and the other for Crownx, must first decide whether consolidating the life insurance companies is in accordance with GAAP. If the OSC panels rule in favor of their staff that consolidation is not in accordance with GAAP, the commissioners must then decide whether or not to grant the companies an exemption from the need to follow GAAP principles.

Traditionally, life insurance companies are accounted for on a modified equity basis of accounting. The consolidated balance sheet discloses the ownership in the life insurance company as an investment, while the income statement shows on one line the parent's share in the profit of the insurance company. The reported profit is not adjusted to GAAP. The life insurance company figures are shown separately.

The OSC staff argues that if Trilon and Crownx want to consolidate their life insurance companies, the two financial conglomerates must adjust the insurance companies results to meet generally accepted accounting principles.

The two financial conglomerates take the position that they should be allowed to consolidate the life insurance companies using accounts prepared to meet statutory requirements. They are both relying on the professional judgments of their auditors that such accounting practices are appropriate.

"This whole thing can drive you crazy," said an exasperated Stephen Paddon, Crownx's lawyer, as the arguments got bogged down in accounting deriqueur.

"(Mr. Paddon) does the handbook an injustice," said OSC lawyer Harry Malcolmson. "One might think that the handbook is an ogre."

It is the OSC's position that the handbook clearly and purposely prohibits consolidating life insurance companies and the OSC should not change that standard. "Professional judgment is not to be a licence to depart from the recommendations made in the handbook," said Mr. Malcolmson.

In the past the OSC has been loathe to permit departures from GAAP principles or to become an arbiter in accounting squabbles. "We want to minimize the circumstances where professional judgments are exercised," said Mr. Dey at one point.

The dilemma the OSC faces is a result of a lag in the development of accounting standards. For eight years, a joint task force of chartered accountants and actuaries tried to work on GAAP rules for life insurance companies that would permit consolidation. The group disbanded in September, 1982, after filing a final report, which has yet to be acted upon. The recommendations could require changes both to the accounting handbook and in legislation.

A CICA panel set up to advise the OSC has recommended "urgent action" by CICA standard-setting committees to deal with the accounting problems faced by owners of life insurance companies.

Consolidation Policy

Consolidated financial statements are generally prepared when all of the following four criteria are met:

1. The parent owns more than 50 percent of the voting shares of the subsidiary.
2. There are no important restrictions on the ability of the parent to exercise effective control of the subsidiary.
3. The asset and equity structure of the subsidiary is not significantly different from that of the parent.
4. There are no legal restrictions prohibiting the consolidation of certain subsidiaries.

Ownership of more than 50 percent of the subsidiary's voting shares implies an ability to exert control over the activities of the subsidiary. For example, the parent can control the subsidiary's corporate policies and dividend declarations. There may be situations, however, where control of the subsidiary's activities cannot be carried out effectively, despite the ownership of a majority of the voting shares. For example, the subsidiary may be located in a foreign country that has severely restricted the withdrawal of funds from that country. Or the subsidiary may be in bankruptcy and under the control of a court-appointed group of trustees. In these cases, the financial statements of the subsidiary probably will not be consolidated with those of the parent. When the parent owns more than 50 percent of the shares and can exercise effective control, but consolidated statements are not prepared, then the equity method would normally be used.

If the asset and equity structure of the subsidiary is significantly different from that of the parent, the subsidiary's financial statements are frequently not consolidated with those of the parent and the equity method is used. For example, a consolidated statement might not be prepared if the parent is a manufacturing concern with heavy investments in property, plant, and equipment, whereas the subsidiary is a finance or insurance company with large holdings of cash, receivables, and temporary investments. The presentation of consolidated financial statements of corporations with significantly different asset and equity structures is sometimes thought to submerge potentially important information about the individual corporations. This is particularly true when the assets of the subsidiary are not, by law, fully available for use by the parent, such as when the subsidiary or parent is in a regulated industry, such as a public utility, a bank, or an insurance company.

Where the consolidated group of companies spans several industries, markets, or geographical areas, the consolidation of the subsidiaries results in a loss of useful information. To correct for this loss, segmented reporting should be implemented. Refer to Appendix A, pages 773–775, for an example of segment reporting by General Products Limited.

Example 1 Canadian Pacific Limited has organized its enterprises into two distinct groups. The company, directly and through its transportation subsidiaries, carries on the transportation enterprises, whereas Canadian Pacific Enterprises Limited, in which Canadian Pacific Limited holds 70 percent of the voting shares, is the vehicle through which all other operations are carried on. Canadian Pacific Limited controls subsidiaries with assets of $18 billion, including controlled assets of Canadian Pacific Enterprises Limited of about $12 billion. Canadian Pacific Limited controls subsidiaries operating in eight different industries. In evaluating the operations and financial position of Canadian Pacific Limited (and Canadian Pacific Enterprises Limited), it is more useful to consider all of the assets under its control, not just those of the parent, whose major assets are investments. Consolidated statements are easier to comprehend than separate statements for each of its operating subsidiaries.

Example 2 General Motors Limited and Canadian General Electric Company Limited, among others, have wholly owned finance subsidiaries. These subsidiaries make many of their loans to customers who wish to purchase the products of the parent company. The financial statements of these subsidiaries are not consolidated with those of the parent company. The assets of these subsidiaries are largely receivables. It is argued that statement readers may be misled as to the relative liquidity of these firms if consolidated statements were prepared and the assets of the parent, largely noncurrent manufacturing plant and equipment, were combined with the more liquid assets of the finance subsidiary.

Example 3 The Anglo-Canadian Telephone Company owns a controlling interest in two major Canadian telephone companies and one telephone company in the Dominican Republic. The assets and liabilities and revenues and expenses of the Canadian telephone companies are consolidated. However, during 1977 management decided to place the earnings of the Dominican subsidiary (Compania Dominicana de Telefonos, C. por A.) on a cost basis, reasoning as follows in the company's 1983 annual report:

The Company does not consolidate a wholly-owned subsidiary, Compania Dominicana de Telefonos, C. por A. ("Dominicana"), operating in the Dominican Republic, because of severe restrictions which limit the Company's ability to control distribution of earnings from this investment. The Company has not recorded earnings of this subsidiary since 1977, except as dividends were remitted, and elected beginning in 1981 to reduce the book value of its investment by the amount of any cash dividends received. The Company further elected during 1983 to write off this investment due to the uncertainty involved in its ultimate realization. This item was treated as an extraordinary item in the accompanying financial statements.

A summary of the financial information for Dominicana, translated to Canadian dollars, is as follows:

	1983	1982
	(Thousands of dollars)	
Telecommunications property, less accumulated depreciation	$144,652	$128,374
Total assets	206,000	186,695
Long-term debt	37,645	49,988
Net book value	131,158	106,469
Net earnings before unrealized gain or loss on translation from pesos to Canadian dollars	42,047	23,990

Disclosure of Consolidation Policy The summary of significant accounting policies in financial statements includes a statement about the consolidation policy of the parent. If a significant majority-owned subsidiary is not consolidated, then its financial statements are often included in the notes to the financial statements. For example, Exhibit A.4 for General Products Limited (page 763) indicates that all significant majority-owned subsidiaries are consolidated, with the exception of its finance company. For this subsidiary, the equity method is required and used. The financial statements of the finance company are themselves presented in Note 11 page 769.

Understanding Consolidated Statements

The remainder of this section discusses the following five concepts essential for understanding published consolidated statements:

1. Substitution
2. External relationship
3. Consolidated entity cost
4. Indivisibility
5. Acquisition cost (Goodwill)

You may need to apply these concepts to prepare consolidated financial statements showing the results of several companies as if they were a single entity.

Each concept will be defined, explained, and illustrated through to its application to the consolidated balance sheet. The impact of these concepts will be explained briefly as they apply to the consolidated income statement and the consolidated statement of changes in financial position.

Concept of Substitution The concept of substitution is applied so that the subsidiary's detailed financial data are substituted for the aggregated totals appearing in the parent's single-company financial statements. This substitution is accomplished in the balance sheet by eliminating (1) the balance in the "Investment in S" account appearing on P's balance sheet and (2) the balance in the shareholders' equity section appearing on S's balance sheet, and then by combining the remaining balances reported on S's balance sheet with the corresponding balances in P's single-company balance sheet. This substitution is accomplished in the income statement by eliminating the "Income from S" from P's income statement and combining the revenues and expenses of S with the corresponding revenues and expenses of P.[8] Where the parent uses the equity basis of accounting for the investment in S, a complete substitution occurs but, where the investment in S is recorded on a cost basis, the balance must be converted to the equity basis to achieve a complete substitution.

The concept of substitution is applied whenever consolidated financial statements are prepared.

For example, the parent company's balance sheet shows an asset, Investment in S. The balance sheet of S shows its individual assets and liabilities balanced by the shareholders' equity. In the simple case where S has no liabilities, the assets of S are substituted for the Investment in S and combined with the corresponding assets of P.

When the only asset of S is Cash, the Investment in S (a noncurrent asset) would be replaced by Cash (a current asset), increasing the liquidity of P. If in another case the only asset of S was land, there would be no change in the liquidity of P. The additional detail provided through the application of the concept of substitution is of significant value to the reader of the financial statements.

When S's balance sheet includes liabilities the amount of the assets would be increased over the previous case by the amount of the liability. For example, where S acquired additional land in return for issuing a demand note, the application of this concept would result in a reduction in the liquidity of P, since the total current liability is increased but not the current assets.

To understand the eliminations from the right-hand side of the balance-sheet, recall that the right-hand side shows the sources of the firm's financing. The subsidiary is financed by creditors (liabilities) and by owners (shareholders' equity). Assume that the parent owns 100 percent of the subsidiary's voting shares. Then the assets on the consolidated balance sheet of the single economic entity are financed by the creditors of both companies and by the parent's shareholders. That is, the equities of the consolidated entity are the liabilities of both companies and the shareholders' equity is that of the parent alone. If the shareholders' equity accounts of the subsidiary were added to those of the parent, then the financing from the parent's shareholders would be counted twice (once on the parent's books and once on the subsidiary's books). Hence, when the parent's investment account is eliminated from the sum of the two companies' assets, the accounting equation is maintained by eliminating the shareholders' equity accounts of the subsidiary.

The substitution and combination process explained above and the consolidation eliminations referred to below are made on a consolidation work sheet and are not recorded on the books of any of the legal entities being consolidated. The consoli-

---

[8]In some cases, discussed below, additional balances are created or revised valuations occur.

dated financial statements are then prepared directly from the work sheet. There are no separate books for the consolidated entity.

Concept of External Relationship This concept means that the consolidated financial statements show only the results of transactions between the consolidated group of companies and other parties. Account balances resulting from transactions between companies in the consolidated group are eliminated when consolidated statements are prepared. This elimination to balance sheet accounts is accomplished by eliminating all asset balances appearing on one entity's balance sheet that represent claims due from another entity, and eliminating the corresponding payables from the other entity's balance sheet. The elimination in the income statement is accomplished by eliminating the billed price of intercompany sales of goods and services from revenue reported by the entity providing the goods and services, and from the corresponding cost or expense reported by the receiving entity. This process prevents double counting of receivables and payables and of revenues and expenses that would otherwise occur.

For example, a parent may lend funds to its subsidiary. If the separate balance sheets were merely added together, those funds would be counted twice: once as a note receivable on the parent's books and again as cash or other asset on the subsidiary's books. Consolidated balance sheets eliminate intercompany transactions that would not be reported for a single, integrated enterprise. Thus, the note receivable of the parent and the note payable of the subsidiary are eliminated in preparing the consolidated balance sheet. These adjustments are referred to as *intercompany eliminations*.

Concept of Consolidated Entity Cost The fundamental accounting realization convention generally requires a company to defer the recognition of increase in value and recognition of gains until the assets are sold to an independent person in an arm's length transaction. Legally each affiliated company is an independent person; assets transferred between them will generally be sold at market price, usually in excess of cost. As a result, realized gains will be reported by the seller and the purchaser will record the asset at the market value at the date of purchase. Often, however, the asset purchased from an affiliate at market price remains on hand at the balance sheet date. At that time it may be valued at more than the cost to the affiliated company which first purchased the asset. The historical cost concept applied to the economic entity requires that the assets owned by members of the consolidated group must be valued at the cost when first acquired by the group. Any unrealized gain must be eliminated.

The elimination of the unrealized gain from the balance sheet is accomplished by eliminating the unrealized gain from the asset to which it is attached and from the retained earnings of the entity that made the sale and recorded the gain. The reduction in the retained earnings of the entity that made the sale results from the elimination from the income statement of this entity of the sales and cost of sales of the merchandise remaining unsold.

For example, P imported a quantity of cameras from Japan for a laid down cost of $100 each for sale to retailers for $120 each. A subsidiary, S, which operates a retail camera store, purchased five cameras for $600 (= 5 × $120). These cameras were unsold at the fiscal year-end. S would properly record these cameras in its inventory at $600, since this represents the cost to S. From a consolidated viewpoint, however, the $600 cost includes $100 of gain recognized by P. The cost of the cameras to the consolidated group remains $500. The application of the concept of consolidated entity cost results in a reduction in the consolidated value of the cameras to $500 and the elimination of the $100 unrealized gain from P's consolidated retained earnings and income. As a result, the cost of the assets included in the consolidated balance sheet is defined as cost when first purchased by a member of the affiliate group plus any costs incurred to modify the product subsequent to purchase.

Concept of Indivisibility In many cases, the parent will not own 100 percent of the voting shares of a consolidated subsidiary. The owners of the remaining voting shares are called *external minority shareholders*, or the *minority interest*.[9] These shareholders continue to have a proportionate interest in the net assets (or total assets minus total liabilities) of the subsidiary as shown on the subsidiary's separate corporate records. They also have a proportionate interest in the earnings of the subsidiary.

An issue in the generally accepted accounting principles for consolidated statements is whether the statements should show only the parent's share of the assets and liabilities of the subsidiary (proportionate consolidation), or whether they should show all of the subsidiary's assets and liabilities along with the minority interests in them (full consolidation).

The law clearly establishes that the ownership of shares in a company does not entitle a shareholder to a proportional claim to individual company assets. Further, the parent, with its controlling voting interest, can effectively direct the use of all the assets and liabilities, not merely an amount equal to the parent's percentage of ownership.

The concept of indivisibility rejects the proportionate consolidation alternative and requires that the individual assets and liabilities of a company may not be prorated between the majority and minority shareholders, and that the consolidated financial statements include all of the assets and liabilities of the subsidiary. The consolidated balance sheet and income statement in these instances, however, must disclose the interest of the minority shareholders in the subsidiary that has been consolidated.

The amount of the minority interest shown on the balance sheet is generally the result of multiplying the common shareholders' equity of the subsidiary — reduced by unrealized gains on goods sold by the subsidiary — by the minority's percentage of ownership. For example, if the common shareholders' equity (or assets minus liabilities) of a consolidated subsidiary totals $500,000 and the minority owns 20 percent of the common shares, then the minority interest shown on the consolidated balance sheet is $100,000 (= .20 × $500,000).

The minority interest is typically presented among the equities on the consolidated balance sheet between the liabilities and shareholders' equity. See, for example, the General Products Limited consolidated balance sheet in Exhibit A.2 on page 761. Note that "Minority Interest" is shown among the liabilities but is not clearly labeled as one. This presentation is typical of many published financial statements. The right-

[9]Do not confuse this minority interest in a consolidated subsidiary with a firm's own minority investments, discussed earlier. The minority *interest* belongs to others outside the parent and its economic entity. The parent's minority *investments* are those for which the parent owns less than 50 percent of the shares.

hand side of the balance sheet contains only liabilities and owners' equity items, so that the minority interest should appear as one or the other. Because the minority interest has no maturity date it does not meet the criteria to be a liability discussed in Chapter 10. It might be classified as an indeterminate-term liability, much the same as future income taxes.

The amount of the minority interest in the subsidiary's income shown on the consolidated income statement is generally the result of multiplying the *subsidiary's* net income by the minority's percentage of ownership. The consolidated income is allocated to show the portions applicable to the parent company and the portion of the subsidiary's income applicable to the minority interest. Refer again to General Products Limited's consolidated income statement shown in Exhibit A.1, page 760. Notice the deduction of $21 million for the "Minority Interest in Income of Consolidated Subsidiaries" before the consolidated net income figure for 1988. The consolidated net income includes only that portion of the net income of subsidiary companies allocable to the shareholders of General Products Limited. Typically, the minority interest in the subsidiary's income is shown as a deduction in calculating consolidated net income.

Concept of Acquisition Cost (Goodwill) When a company gains a majority interest in another established company through the purchase of shares, the cost of the shares purchased by the parent will ordinarily differ from their book value calculated from the balance sheet of the subsidiary.

Two issues in the generally accepted accounting principles for consolidated statements arise under these circumstances: the presentation of the difference between the cost and book value of the shares purchased, and the valuation of the assets and liabilities when presented on the consolidated financial statements.

The purchase of majority share interest in a going concern is analogous to purchasing a share of the assets less liabilities of the firm, since in both cases the purchaser acquires control over the resources. When the assets of a going concern are purchased and the liabilities assumed, the value of the individual assets and liabilities (usually their fair market value) would ordinarily be specified in the sales contract. The sum of the contract values of the individual assets, less the liabilities assumed, would ordinarily differ from the total contracted price, the difference being attributed to goodwill. In this case, providing that the contract value for the individual assets and liabilities did not materially differ from the current market prices, the contract values would be considered as cost for accounting purposes, and the goodwill reported as an asset and amortized by a charge to income over a period not exceeding 40 years.

The above accounting treatment for the purchase of assets of a going concern is used as a precedent for resolving the accounting issues that arise when majority control of a going concern is acquired through the purchase of shares. The concept of acquisition cost requires that, where a majority interest in a subsidiary is acquired through share purchase, the parent's interest in identifiable assets acquired and liabilities assumed would be based on their fair value at the date of acquisition. An exception is made when the fair value of the acquired interest in the net assets exceeds the total cost of acquiring the shares. In this case, the fair value should be adjusted to equal the total cost of acquisition.

The excess of the acquisition cost over the fair value of the acquired interest in the net assets is recorded as goodwill in the consolidated balance sheet. This goodwill is amortized over its estimated life, not exceeding 40 years. For example, a parent company purchases for $400,000 all the shares of a company which owns an apartment complex and has assets which consist of the apartment land and buildings with a book value of $100,000, and has no liabilities. Two factors could be identified for causing the difference of $300,000 (= $400,000 − $100,000) between the cost and book value of the shares. The book value of the land and buildings is based on historical cost and fails to consider changes in construction costs and increases in land values. An estimate of $350,000 for the depreciated replacement cost of the land and buildings could be considered the fair value of the assets. The remainder of the purchase price ($50,000) is attributed to the goodwill of the business. On the consolidated balance sheet at the date the shares are purchased, the land and buildings of the subsidiary would be valued at acquisition cost to the parent of $350,000 and goodwill on consolidation recorded at $50,000. The depreciation on the building in the consolidated income statement would subsequently be based on the portion of the acquisition cost allocated to the building.

Where P uses the equity method for recording the investment in S, the goodwill will be amortized by an entry on P's books reducing the balances in the accounts, Investment in S and Income from S, by the amounts of the annual amortization.

Setting GAAP

M ost of the generally accepted accounting principles you encounter in this text are presented to you without discussion of the alternatives they supplant. In some cases accounting principles have been chosen because they are perceived as generally accepted. In other cases they are established by fiat— a handbook pronouncement by the CICA.

Mergers and acquisitions are a good example of an economic event in which several plausible accounting alternatives are possible. One of the choices the Accounting Standards Committee has had to make involves the problem of what values to use for the assets of the subsidiary when bringing them forward to the consolidated balance sheet.

When less than 100 percent of the shares of S are purchased and consolidated statements are prepared by P, a problem arises in recording the value of the assets of S on the consolidated balance sheet. At least three alternative solutions could be considered. The assets of S could be included in the consoli-

dated balance sheet at their value on S's books; at their fair value at the date P purchased S's shares (the date of acquisition); or at S's book value plus P's proportion of the difference between fair market value and book value at the date of acquisition.

If S's assets were included in the consolidated balance sheet at S's book value, the concept of acquisition cost would be disregarded on the consolidated balance sheet. Consequently, this alternative has been rejected.

If S's assets (including goodwill) were included in the consolidated balance sheet at the fair market value at the date of acquisition, a portion of the excess would be allocated to the minority interest. Since the minority interest represents the minority shareholders' equity in S *as recorded on S's books* and, since S does not record the unrealized gain in conformity with the cost principle, the alternative has also been rejected.

If S's assets were included in the consolidated balance sheet at S's book value plus P's share of the difference between book value and fair market value at date of acquisition, the resulting consolidated balance sheet would conform to the concept of acquisition cost and the amount of the minority interest would be based on the book value of S's books. This method is required to be adopted under Canadian generally accepted accounting principles.[10]

To illustrate these alternatives, assume that in the previous example the parent company purchased only 80 percent of the shares of S for $320,000.

Under the first alternative, the consolidated balance sheet would include S's land and buildings at the book value of $100,000, minority interest of $20,000 (= .20 × $100,000), and goodwill of $240,000 [= $320,000 − (.80 × $100,000). This alternative ignores the fact that the fair market value of S's land and buildings at the date of acquisition was $350,000 and consequently overstates goodwill.

Under the second alternative, the consolidated balance sheet would include S's land and buildings at their fair market value at date of acquisition of $350,000, goodwill of $50,000, (= $400,000 − $350,000), and minority interest of $80,000 (= .20 × $400,000). This alternative recognizes the unrealized increase in value of S's land and buildings and the goodwill implied in

the purchase price of S's shares. However, these amounts are not recorded on S's balance sheet and do not represent the minority's share in the shareholders' equity of S of $20,000 (= .20 × $100,000).

Under the third alternative, the land and buildings would be valued on the consolidated balance sheet at historical cost plus P's share in the unrealized gain at the date of acquistion of $300,000 [= $100,000 + .80 × ($350,000 − $100,000)], the goodwill of $40,000 [= .80 × ($400,000 − $350,000)], and minority interest of $20,000 (= .20 × $100,000). Another way to calculate the consolidated balance sheet value of the land and buildings is to combine P's share in the market value at the date of acquisition and the minority interest's share of S's book value (.80 × $350,000 + .20 × $100,000 = $300,000).

The amounts, appearing on the consolidated balance sheet for land and buildings, goodwill, and minority interest under each of the alternatives are shown below. Note that the net balance under each alternative equals the cost of P's investment in S's shares of $320,000.

It should be noted that the subsidiary would record no change in the valuation of the land and buildings but would continue to report them in its financial statements as depreciated historical cost of $100,000.

	Alternative 1	Alternative 2	Alternative 3
Land and Buildings	$100,000	$350,000	$300,000
Goodwill	240,000	50,000	40,000
Total	$340,000	$400,000	$340,000
Less: Minority Interest	20,000	80,000	20,000
Cost of S's Shares	$320,000	$320,000	$320,000

[10]*CICA Handbook*, section 1600.

Consolidated Income and Retained Earnings The amount of consolidated net income for a period is the same as the amount that would be reported if the parent company used the equity method of accounting for the intercorporate investment. That is, consolidated net income is equal to:

$$\begin{matrix} \text{Parent Company's} \\ \text{Net Income} \end{matrix} + \begin{matrix} \text{Parent's Share of Sub-} \\ \text{sidiary's Net Income} \end{matrix} - \begin{matrix} \text{Unrealized Profit (or Plus Loss)} \\ \text{on Intercompany Transactions} \end{matrix}$$

The principal difference between the consolidated income statement and the income statement where the subsidiary is accounted for under the equity method relates to the components of income presented. When a consolidated income statement is prepared, the individual revenues and expenses of the subsidiary (less intercompany adjustments) are combined with those of the parent. When the equity method is used for an unconsolidated subsidiary, the parent's share of the subsidiary's net income minus gain (or plus loss) on intercompany transactions is shown on a single line of the income statement with a title such as "Equity in Earnings (Loss) of Unconsolidated Subsidiary." (See Note 3 of the General Products Limited statement, page 766.)

The amount shown on the consolidated balance sheet for retained earnings is likewise the amount that would be reported if the parent company used the equity method of accounting for the intercorporate investment. That is, consolidated retained earnings is equal to:

$$\begin{matrix} \text{Parent's} \\ \text{Retained} \\ \text{Earnings} \end{matrix} + \begin{matrix} \text{Parent's Share of the Change} \\ \text{in Subsidiary's Retained} \\ \text{Earnings since Acquisition} \end{matrix} - \begin{matrix} \text{Unrealized Profit (or Plus} \\ \text{Loss) on Intercompany} \\ \text{Transactions} \end{matrix}$$

Consolidation and Equity Method Compared

The only difference between the consolidation and the equity method is financial statement presentation. Under the equity method there is one-line disclosure of the investment on the balance sheet and one-line disclosure of the investee earnings[11] on the income statement. Under the consolidation method, the underlying balance sheet accounts are substituted for the one line. "Investment in S" and the underlying revenue and expense accounts are substituted for the one line on the income statement, "Equity in earnings of S." In fact, for 364 days of the year the parent accounts for subsidiaries using the equity method. Only when year-end consolidated financial statements are to be prepared is it necessary to deviate from the one-line presentation used for investments under the equity method. Since we have previously said that income reported from the investment must be identical under both equity and consolidation methods, it follows that all the intercompany eliminations are identical also. Exhibit 13.1 summarizes use of the equity method.

Statement of Changes in Financial Position The consolidated statement of changes in financial position is constructed from the consolidated balance sheet, income statement, and supplementary information in the same way as explained in Chapter 5 for a single company. Three items may appear in the consolidated statement, however, that do not usually appear on single-company funds statements.

---

[11] Assuming the investee has no extraordinary items in its income statement.

Exhibit 13.1

Components of the investment account during the year for long-term intercorporate investments using the equity method

(a) Acquisition cost of investment	**(c)** Cash dividends received
(b) Proportionate share of investee earnings recognized for the period	**(d)** Amortization of goodwill (excess of purchase price over proportionate share of fair value of net assets acquired)
	(e) Additional depreciation on the fair value increment attributed to undervalued plant assets
	(f) Elimination of unrealized profit on intercompany sales still held in inventory

Underlying Entries	**Circumstances**
(a) Investment in S 　　Cash	Each time additional shares in S acquired.
(b) Investment in S 　　Revenue from Investments	Made annually on receipt on financial statements from S. If S has a loss, then P will record a loss, not revenue.
(c) Cash 　　Investment in S	As dividends received
(d) Goodwill amortization expense 　　Investment in S	Each financial statement date
(e) Depreciation expense 　　Investment in S	Each financial statement date
(f) Sales Revenue (P) 　　Inventory (S) 　　Sales Revenue (S) 　　Inventory (P)	Each financial statement date

The first item in consolidated funds statements that does not appear in single-company statements is the addback to net income for the minority interest in earnings. As we pointed out in the discussion of minority interest above, General Products Limited shows a deduction of $21 million for the minority's share of earnings before the final net income figure in Exhibit A.1. This deduction did not require the use of any cash. Consequently, there must be an addback to derive "Cash Provided by Operations" in the consolidated statement of changes in financial position. General Products Limited shows the addback of $21 million in its statement of changes in financial position, Exhibit A.3, page 762, as "Minority Interest in Earnings of Consolidated Subsidiaries."

Second, the amortization of goodwill may appear in consolidated income statements. Just like other amortization charges, amortization of goodwill causes a reduction in reported net income without using any cash. Therefore, there must be an addback to net income in the amount of that amortization in order to derive the amount of cash provided by operations. Often, however, as in the case of the consolidated statement of changes in financial position of General Products Limited shown in Exhibit A.3, the amount of this amortization is so small that it does not warrant separate disclosure and is included with "Other" items.

Third, where a parent purchases a majority interest in a going concern for cash, the resulting reduction in the consolidated working capital will be presented as a use of funds in the consolidated statement of changes of financial position. The amount of cash reported as used will be the cost of the shares less the cash of the subsidiary at the date of acquisition. Where the shares are not purchased for cash then the consolidated cash will be increased by the amount of the subsidiary's cash at the date of purchase. For example, if the parent purchases 100 percent of the shares of the subsidiary for $600,000 cash when the subsidiary had cash of $200,000, then the consolidated cash used as a result of this acquisition would be $400,000 (= $600,000 − $200,000). When the parent company purchases less than 100 percent of the shares of a subsidiary, the cash used is further reduced. In this case all of the subsidiary's cash is added to the consolidated cash, but the cash required for the purchase is reduced since less than 100 percent of the shares were purchased. If in the previous case the parent purchased 60 percent of the shares of the subsidiary for $360,000 (.60 × $600,000), the cash used to achieve control is $160,000 (= $360,000 − $200,000). In certain cases the consolidated cash may increase as a result of a cash purchase of shares. If the parent purchased, for $600,000 cash, 60 percent of the shares of a highly liquid going concern with total cash of $900,000, then the acquisition would result in an increase of consolidated cash of $300,000 (= $900,000 − $600,000). Where the share purchase was partially consummated through the issue of long-term debt or preferred shares, the cash would be further increased.

Limitations of Consolidated Statements

The consolidated statements do not replace those of individual corporations; rather, they supplement those statements and aid in their interpretation. Creditors must rely on the resources of one corporation and may be misled if forced to rely entirely on a consolidated statement that combines the data of a company in good financial condition with those of one verging on insolvency.

Preparing Consolidated Financial Statements

This section illustrates the preparation of consolidated financial statements for P Ltd. and S Ltd. Knowing how to construct consolidated financial statements is not essential for learning how to interpret and to analyze them. Nevertheless, it helps.

Data for the Illustration

The illustration covers a five-year period during which time transactions occur that demonstrate the application of each of the five concepts presented above. For the sake of simplicity the illustration is limited to the preparation of the consolidated balance sheet.

Work sheets are used to prepare consolidated financial statements. The data include the post-closing trial balances of each company included in the consolidation, and supplementary information. The work sheet illustrated below differs from that adopted in Chapter 3 in the following ways:

1. There is a separate self-balancing work sheet for each financial statement.
2. There is a separate column for each company included in the consolidation. The post-closing trial balances of each single company will be inserted in these columns.
3. The assets are separated from the equities in the balance sheet work sheet.
4. The two Adjustment columns are replaced by one Elimination column.
5. Only one column is required for the consolidated statement.

Keep in mind that the Elimination entries are recorded only on the work sheet used to prepare the consolidated statements — not in the accounting records of the company. There is no "consolidated" set of books.

Year 1 — The Concept of Substitution

To illustrate the process of substitution and to demonstrate the use of consolidated working papers, the following facts are assumed:

1. P Ltd. starts a subsidiary company, S Ltd., on December 15, Year 1 and pays $60,000 for the shares of the subsidiary. The subsidiary purchases land to construct a building for $20,000 cash, and purchases inventory for $28,000, paying $18,000 on account.
2. The balance sheet of S Ltd. at December 31, Year 1, the fiscal year-end of both the parent and subsidiary, after the above transactions have been recorded, is shown in Exhibit 13.2.

Exhibit 13.2
S Ltd.
Balance Sheet
December 31, Year 1

Assets		Equities	
Cash	$22,000	Accounts Payable	$10,000
Inventory	28,000	**Shareholders' Equity:**	
Land	20,000	Share Capital	60,000
Total Assets	$70,000	Total Equities	$70,000

3. The balance sheet of the parent company at December 31, Year 1 is shown in Exhibit 13.3.

Exhibit 13.3
P Ltd.
Balance Sheet
December 31, Year 1

Assets		Equities		
Cash	$ 26,000	Accounts Payable		$ 29,000
Accounts Receivable	37,000	**Shareholders' Equity:**		
Inventory	64,000	Share Capital	$100,000	
Investment in S Ltd.	60,000	Retained Earnings	58,000	158,000
Total Assets	$187,000	Total Equities		$187,000

The parent company wishes to prepare a consolidated balance sheet that presents the state of affairs as though the two companies were one economic entity.

The parent's investment account equals the parent's ownership of the subsidiary's share capital. Before adding together the single-company balance sheet items to determine consolidated totals, the parent's Investment in S Ltd. must be eliminated so that the subsidiary's assets and the parent's investment in those assets are not both shown on the consolidated balance sheet.

The shareholders' equity of the consolidated entity is provided by the shareholders of the parent. If the shareholders' equity of the parent and of the subsidiary were merely added together, then equities would be counted twice. When the investment account is eliminated to avoid double counting of assets, the subsidiary's shareholders' equity accounts corresponding to the parent's investment are eliminated to avoid double counting of these equities.

To eliminate the parent's investment account and the subsidiary's shareholders' equity accounts, offset the subsidiary's Share Capital against the Investment in S account. The entry in Exhibit 13.4 to eliminate P Ltd.'s investment in S Ltd. is:

(A) Share Capital (S Ltd.)	$60,000	
Investment in S		$60,000
To eliminate the investment in S Ltd. account and the Share Capital account of S Ltd.		

Exhibit 13.4
P Ltd.
Consolidated Balance Sheet Work Sheet
December 31, Year 1

	Balance Sheets P Ltd.	S Ltd.	Intercompany Eliminations	Consolidated Balance Sheet
Assets				
Cash	$ 26,000	$22,000		$ 48,000
Accounts Receivable	37,000	—		37,000
Inventory	64,000	28,000		92,000
Investment in S Ltd.	60,000	—	A $(60,000)	—
Land	—	20,000		20,000
Total Assets	$187,000	$70,000	$(60,000)	$197,000
Equities				
Accounts Payable	$ 29,000	$10,000		$ 39,000
Share Capital:				
P Ltd.	100,000	—		100,000
S Ltd.	—	60,000	A $(60,000)	—
Retained Earnings				
P Ltd.	58,000	—		58,000
Total Equities	$187,000	$70,000	$(60,000)	$197,000

Intercompany Eliminations:
A — Parent's Investment in S Ltd. and the subsidiary's Share Capital.

This entry is entered in the consolidated balance sheet work sheet, Exhibit 13.4. Remember that this entry is not made in the books of either company. The consolidated balance sheet follows in Exhibit 13.5.

Exhibit 13.5
P Ltd.
Consolidated Balance Sheet
December 31, Year 1

Assets		**Equities**		
Cash	$ 48,000	Accounts Payable		$ 39,000
Accounts Receivable	37,000	**Shareholders' Equity:**		
Inventory	92,000	Share Capital	$100,000	
Land	20,000	Retained Earnings	58,000	158,000
Total Assets	$197,000	Total Equities		$197,000

A comparison of the parent company's balance sheet unconsolidated with the consolidated balance sheet shows that the only difference between the two is that the "Investment in S Ltd. . . . $60,000" has been eliminated and the balances of the underlying assets and liabilities have been substituted and aggregated with similar items on the parent company's balance sheet.

Year 2 — The Concept of External Relationship

To illustrate the concept of external relationship, the following facts are assumed during Year 2 for P Ltd. and S Ltd:

1. S Ltd. carried on an active business, reported an income of $18,000 for the year and paid a dividend to P Ltd., its sole shareholder, of $12,000. P Ltd. was not so successful and earned only $10,000 from its operations (before recognition of Income from Investment in S Ltd.). Because funds were required for expansion, P Ltd. paid no dividends.
2. At December 31, Year 2, P Ltd. advanced $50,000 to S Ltd. in return for a note.
3. At December 31, Year 2, P Ltd. owed S Ltd. $6,000 on current account.

A parent may sell goods on account or buy goods on account from a subsidiary and treat the resulting obligation as an account receivable or an account payable. The subsidiary will treat the obligation as an account payable or an account receivable. A parent often makes loans to subsidiaries that appear as Note Receivable, Investment in Bonds, or Advances to Subsidiary on the parent's books. The subsidiary would show Note Payable, Bonds Payable, or Advances from Parent on its books. A single company would not show Accounts Receivable and Accounts Payable for departments within the company. The balances resulting from these transactions must be eliminated from the consolidated balance sheet so that the resulting statement will appear as that of a single company.

In Exhibit 13.6, P Ltd.'s Note Receivable consists of $50,000 due from S Ltd., and S Ltd.'s Accounts Receivable include $6,000 due from P Ltd. The entries to record the elimination of the intercompany receivable and payables in Exhibit 13.6 is:

(A) Note Payable to P Ltd.	$50,000	
Note Receivable from S Ltd.		$50,000
(B) Due to S Ltd.	$ 6,000	
Due from P Ltd.		$ 6,000
To eliminate intercompany payables and receivables.		

Entry (C) is similar to entry (A) in Year 1 and described at the bottom of the work sheet. The balance sheet data for P Ltd. and S Ltd. extracted from their individual post-closing trial balances are shown in the consolidated balance sheet work sheet presented in Exhibit 13.6. The consolidated balance sheet follows in Exhibit 13.7.

Exhibit 13.6
P. Ltd.
Consolidated Balance Sheet Work Sheet
December 31, Year 2

	Balance Sheets P Ltd.	S Ltd.	Intercompany Eliminations		Consolidated Balance Sheet
Assets					
Cash	$ 2,000	$ 3,000			$ 5,000
Accounts Receivable	52,000	27,000			79,000
Due from P Ltd.		6,000	B $	(6,000)	—
Inventory	76,000	51,000			127,000
Land	—	20,000			20,000
Building^a	—	72,000			72,000
Investment in S Ltd.	66,000^b		C	(66,000)	—
Note Receivable from S Ltd.	50,000		A	(50,000)	—
Total Assets	$246,000	$179,000		$(122,000)	$303,000
Equities					
Bank Loan	$ 30,000	$ 40,000			$ 70,000
Accounts Payable	24,000	23,000			47,000
Due to S Ltd.	6,000		B $	(6,000)	—
Note Payable to P Ltd.		50,000	A	(50,000)	—
Share Capital:					
P Ltd.	100,000	—			100,000
S Ltd.	—	60,000	C	(60,000)	—
Retained Earnings:					
P Ltd.	86,000^c	—			86,000
S Ltd.	—	6,000^d	C	(6,000)	—
Total Equities	$246,000	$179,000		$(122,000)	$303,000

Intercompany Eliminations:
A — Intercompany notes.
B — Intercompany current accounts.
C — Parent's Investment in S Ltd. and the subsidiary's Share Capital and Retained Earnings.

^{a}Net of accumulated depreciation.
^{b}$60,000 + $18,000 − $12,000 = $66,000.
^{c}$58,000 + $10,000 + $18,000 = $86,000.
^{d}$18,000 − $12,000 = $6,000.

Exhibit 13.7
P Ltd.
Consolidated Balance Sheet
December 31, Year 2

Assets		Equities		
Cash	$ 5,000	Bank Loan		$ 70,000
Accounts Receivable	79,000	Accounts Payable		47,000
Inventory	127,000	Current Liabilities		117,000
Current Assets	211,000	**Shareholders' Equity:**		
Land	20,000	Share Capital	$100,000	
Building (net)	72,000	Retained Earnings	86,000	186,000
Total Assets	$303,000	Total Equities		$303,000

Note that all intercompany balances are excluded from the consolidated balance sheet and that the parent's Shareholders' Equity remains unchanged, since the parent used the equity basis of accounting for investment in the subsidiary.

Year 3 — The Concept of Consolidated Entity Cost

To illustrate the process of implementing the concept of consolidated entity cost, the following events are assumed to occur to P Ltd. and S Ltd. in Year 3:

1. During the year, P Ltd. incurred a loss of $2,000 from its own operations. S Ltd. reported earnings of $7,000 from its normal operations plus $17,000 gain on the sale of land to P Ltd., as detailed below. Since the $17,000 gain on the sale of the land has not been realized through sale outside the affiliated group, it was excluded from S Ltd.'s income recorded by P Ltd. Neither company paid dividends during the year.

2. To facilitate the financing of the consolidated group, it was decided that S Ltd. would sell to P Ltd. the land it purchased in Year 1. The sale was recorded at the current market price of $37,000 and the land was leased by the parent to the subsidiary for an annual rental of $3,600 per year. The proceeds from the sale of land helped the subsidiary repay the $50,000 Note Payable to the parent.

3. At December 31, Year 3, the subsidiary owed the parent $25,000 on current account.

A common feature of affiliated company activities is the sale of assets from one company to another. As single companies, the sale is usually transacted at the normal market price, which frequently exceeds cost. If the subsidiary had been organized as a department of the parent rather than as a separate legal entity, it is likely that the assets would have been transferred at cost, since the realization convention requires the deferral of revenue and profit until the sale is completed to a person outside the company. As single companies, however, the profit from the sale will be recognized by the vendor and cost to the purchaser will be the contracted price.

Since one purpose of consolidated statements is to report the results of the economic entity as if it was one legal entity, the cost of the assets transferred, if held by the purchaser at the balance sheet date, must be adjusted to the cost when acquired by the consolidated group. In this way the asset value appearing on the consolidated balance sheet will appear as if the group was a single company.

In Exhibit 13.8, land is recorded on the single-company post-closing trial balance of P Ltd. at the $37,000 cost to P Ltd. However, since the sale is made between the subsidiary and the parent, the increase in market value cannot be recognized and the land must be reduced to the cost of $20,000 when purchased by S Ltd. The entry to record the elimination of the unrealized profit in Exhibit 13.8 is:

(B)	Retained Earnings S Ltd.	$17,000	
	Land		$17,000

To eliminate the unrealized profit from the sale of land (= $37,000 − $20,000).

Entry A is similar to Entry B in Year 2, and Entry C is similar to Entry C in Year 2.

Exhibit 13.8
P. Ltd.
Consolidated Balance Sheet Work Sheet
December 31, Year 3

	Balance Sheets P Ltd.	S Ltd.	Intercompany Eliminations	Consolidated Balance Sheet
Assets				
Cash	$ 4,000	$ 3,000		$ 7,000
Accounts Receivable	51,000	32,000		83,000
Due from S Ltd.	25,000		A $ (25,000)	—
Inventory	84,000	44,000		128,000
Land	37,000	—	B (17,000)	20,000
Building[a]	—	69,000		69,000
Investment in S Ltd.	73,000[b]		C (73,000)	—
Total Assets	$274,000	$148,000	$(115,000)	$307,000
Equities				
Bank Loan	$ 30,000	—		$ 30,000
Accounts Payable	53,000	$ 33,000		86,000
Due to P Ltd.		25,000	A $ (25,000)	—
Share Capital:				
P Ltd.	100,000	—		100,000
S Ltd.	—	60,000	C (60,000)	—
Retained Earnings:				
P Ltd.	91,000[c]	—	B (17,000)	91,000
S Ltd.	—	30,000[d]	C (13,000)	—
Total Equities	$274,000	$148,000	$(115,000)	$307,000

Intercompany Eliminations:
A — Intercompany current accounts.
B — Reduction in value of land to subsidiary's cost.
C — Parent's Investment in S Ltd. and the subsidiary's Share Capital and Retained Earnings.

[a]Net of accumulated depreciation.
[b]$66,000 + $7,000 = $73,000.
[c]$86,000 − $2,000 + $7,000 = $91,000.
[d]$6,000 + $7,000 + $17,000 = $30,000.

The consolidated balance sheet work sheet of P Ltd. and S Ltd. at December 31, Year 3 is presented in Exhibit 13.8, and the consolidated balance sheet in Exhibit 13.9.

Exhibit 13.9
P Ltd.
Consolidated Balance Sheet
December 31, Year 3

Assets		**Equities**		
Cash	$ 7,000	Bank Loan		$ 30,000
Accounts Receivable . .	83,000	Accounts Payable		86,000
Inventory	128,000	Current Liabilities . . .		116,000
Current Assets	218,000	**Shareholders' Equity:**		
Land	20,000	Share Capital	$100,000	
Building (net)	69,000	Retained Earnings	91,000	191,000
Total Assets	$307,000	Total Equities		$307,000

Year 4 — The Concept of Indivisibility

To illustrate the concept of indivisibility, the following events are assumed to occur to P Ltd. and S Ltd. in Year 4:

1. On January 1, P Ltd. sold for $40,000 the land it had purchased from S Ltd. in Year 3.
2. On January 1, P Ltd. sold 20 percent of the shares of S Ltd. to the senior executives of S Ltd. for $18,000.
3. During the year P Ltd. earned income from its normal operations of $5,000 plus $3,000 (= $40,000 − $37,000) from the sale of land. S Ltd. reported income of $15,000.
4. During the year, P Ltd. paid a dividend of $14,000 and S Ltd. a dividend of $10,000.

Since P Ltd. sold 20 percent of the shares of S Ltd. at January 1, Year 4, minority shareholders of S Ltd. have been created. These minority shareholders have a 20 percent interest in the net assets and income of S Ltd.

The concept of indivisibility requires that the entire assets, liabilities, revenues, and expenses of the consolidated group be combined, since they represent the items under the control of the parent company's shareholders.

The amount of the minority shareholders' interest in the net assets and net income will be their proportional interest in the company in which they hold shares. In Exhibit 13.10, the minority interest in the net assets of S Ltd. at December 31, Year 4 is $19,000 [= .20 × ($60,000 + $35,000)] and their interest in the net income is $3,000 (= .20 × $15,000). The minority interest in the net assets is presented in the balance sheet between Liabilities and Shareholders' Equity and the minority interest in the net income is presented as a deduction in determining consolidated income. In place of an entry to record the minority share of the net assets, it is customary to create an additional column in the consolidated work sheet where the minority share is recorded and totaled.

Entry (A) is similar to entry (A) in Year 3 and entry (B) is similar to entry (C) in Year 3.

The consolidated work sheet at December 31, Year 4 is presented in Exhibit 13.10, and the consolidated balance sheet in Exhibit 13.11.

Exhibit 13.10
P. Ltd.
Consolidated Balance Sheet Work Sheet
December 31, Year 4

	Balance Sheets P Ltd.	S Ltd.	Intercompany Eliminations	Minority Interest	Consolidated Balance Sheet
Assets					
Cash	$ 47,000	$ 4,000			$ 51,000
Accounts Receivable ...	43,000	37,000			80,000
Due from S Ltd.	28,000		A $ (28,000)		—
Inventory	77,000	57,000			134,000
Building[a]	—	66,000			66,000
Investment in S Ltd.	76,000[b]		B (76,000)		—
Total Assets	$271,000	$164,000	$(104,000)		$331,000
Equities					
Accounts Payable	$ 57,000	$ 41,000			$ 98,000
Due to P Ltd.		28,000	A $ (28,000)		—
Share Capital:					
P Ltd.	100,000	—			100,000
S Ltd.	—	60,000	B (48,000)	$12,000	—
Retained Earnings:					
P Ltd.	114,000[c]				114,000
S Ltd.		35,000[d]	B (28,000)	7,000	—
Minority Interest				$19,000	19,000
Total Equities	$271,000	$164,000	$(104,000)		$331,000

Intercompany Eliminations:

A — Intercompany current accounts.

B — Parent's Investment in S Ltd. and the parent's share of the subsidiary's Share Capital and Retained Earnings.

[a] Net of accumulated depreciation.
[b] $73,000 + $17,000 − $18,000 + (.80 × $15,000) − (.80 × $10,000) = $76,000.
[c] $91,000 + $5,000 + $3,000 + $17,000 + (.80 × $15,000) − $14,000 = $114,000.
[d] $30,000 + $15,000 − $10,000 = $35,000.

Exhibit 13.11
P Ltd.
Consolidated Balance Sheet
December 31, Year 4

Assets		Equities		
Cash	$ 51,000	Accounts Payable		$ 98,000
Accounts Receivable . .	80,000	Minority Interest		19,000
Inventory	134,000	**Shareholders' Equity:**		
Current Assets	265,000	Share Capital	$100,000	
Building (net)	66,000	Retained Earnings	114,000	214,000
Total Assets	$331,000	Total Equities		$331,000

Year 5—The Concept of Acquisition Cost (Goodwill)

To illustrate the concept of acquisition cost (goodwill), the following events are assumed to occur to P Ltd., S Ltd., and SS Ltd. in Year 5:

1. Effective January 1, P Ltd. sold its remaining shares in S Ltd. for $90,000. During the year, the parent recorded operating income of $15,000 and paid dividends to its shareholders of $6,000.
2. Using in part the proceeds from the sale of the shares in S Ltd., P Ltd. purchased 60 percent of the shares in SS Ltd., one of its major suppliers, for $135,000 at December 31. The balance sheet of SS Ltd. at the date of acquisition, showing both the book value and the fair value of the indentifiable assets is presented in Exhibit 13.12.

Exhibit 13.12
SS Ltd.
Balance Sheet
December 31, Year 5

	Book Value	Fair Value	Increase (Decrease)
Assets			
Cash	$ 17,000	$ 17,000	—
Accounts Receivable	77,000	76,000	$ (1,000)
Inventory	69,000	79,000	10,000
Land	7,000	21,000	14,000
Buildings and Machinery (net)	52,000	67,000	15,000
Total Assets	$222,000	$260,000	$38,000
Equities			
Accounts Payable	$ 59,000	$ 59,000	
Shareholders' Equity:			
Share Capital	100,000		
Retained Earnings	63,000		
Total Equities	$222,000		

The book value of the 60 percent of the shares of SS Ltd. purchased by P Ltd. was $97,800 [= .60 × ($100,000 + $63,000)], whereas the cost of the shares purchased was $135,000. The difference (purchase discrepancy) of $37,200 can be attributed to two factors. The balance sheet values of the net assets may differ from their fair value, and other attributes of the company may not be recorded on the balance sheet.

To determine the amount attributed to each of the above two factors, P Ltd. undertook a detailed examination of the net assets and found that the fair value was $38,000 greater than the book value. P Ltd.'s share of this difference was $22,800 (= .60 × $38,000). The remainder of the difference between the cost of the shares to P Ltd. and 60 percent of the book value of the net asset, of $14,400 (= $37,200 − $22,800) is assumed to be attributed to ''off the balance sheet'' factors and is called Goodwill.

To record the parent's share of the net assets at fair value, at the date of the share purchase, the following entry is recorded in the consolidated balance sheet work sheet:

(A) Inventory		$6,000	
Land		8,400	
Buildings and Machinery		9,000	
Accounts Receivable			$ 600
Investment in SS Ltd.			22,800

The purchase discrepancy attributed to Goodwill appears at the time that the following substitution entry is recorded:

(B) Share Capital (SS Ltd.)		$60,000[1]	
Retained Earnings (SS Ltd.)		37,800[2]	
Goodwill		14,400[3]	
Investment in SS Ltd.			$112,200

1 60 percent × $100,000 = $60,000,
2 60 percent × $63,000 = $37,800.
3 $135,000 − $22,800 − $60,000 − $37,800 = $14,400.

The consolidated balance sheet work sheet at December 31, Year 5, following the acquisition of SS Ltd. is presented in Exhibit 13.13 and the consolidated balance sheet in Exhibit 13.14.

Exhibit 13.13
P. Ltd.
Consolidated Balance Sheet Work Sheet
December 31, Year 5

	Balance Sheets P Ltd.	SS Ltd.	Intercompany Eliminations and Adjustments		Minority Interest	Consolidated Balance Sheet
Assets						
Cash	$ 25,000	$ 17,000				$ 42,000
Accounts Receivable . . .	52,000	77,000	A $	(600)		128,400
Inventory	85,000	69,000	A	6,000		160,000
Land	—	7,000	A	8,400		15,400
Building & Machinery[a] . .	—	52,000	A	9,000		61,000
Investments in S Ltd.	135,000[b]		B	(112,200)		—
			A	(22,800)		—
Goodwill			B	14,400		14,400
Total Assets	$297,000	$222,000	$	(97,800)		$421,200
Equities						
Accounts Payable	$ 60,000	$ 59,000				$119,000
Share Capital:						
P Ltd.	100,000					100,000
SS Ltd.		100,000	B	(60,000)	$40,000	
Retained Earnings:						
P Ltd.	137,000[c]					137,000
SS Ltd.		63,000	B	(37,800)	25,200	
Minority Interest					$65,200	65,200
Total Equities	$297,000	$222,000	$	(97,800)		$421,200

Intercompany Eliminations:
A — To include the parent's interest in the difference between the book value and fair value of identifiable assets at the date of acquisition.

B — Parent's Investment in SS Ltd., the parent's share of the subsidiary's Share Capital and Retained Earnings, and a difference attributable to Goodwill.

[a]Net of accumulated depreciation.
[b]Cost of shares at balance sheet date.
[c]$114,000 + $15,000 + ($90,000 − $76,000) − $6,000 = $137,000.

Exhibit 13.14
P. Ltd.
Consolidated Balance Sheet
December 31, Year 5

Assets		Equities		
Cash	$ 42,000	Accounts Payable		$119,000
Accounts Receivable . .	128,400	Minority Interest		65,200
Inventory	160,000			
Current Assets	330,400			
Land	15,400	**Shareholders' Equity:**		
Building and Machinery (net)	61,000	Share Capital	$100,000	
Goodwill	14,400	Retained Earnings	137,000	237,000
Total Assets	$421,200	Total Equities		$421,200

The 40 percent minority interest of SS Ltd. is presented under the equities between the Accounts Payable and the Shareholders' Equity. It consists of 40 percent of the $163,000 book value of the subsidiary's shareholders' equity.

The consolidated assets are valued at book value to the company plus the parent's share in the difference between book value and fair value of subsidiary's assets.

The following schedule of the Inventory value in the consolidated balance sheet illustrates this calculation.

Book Value of Inventory:		
P Ltd.		$ 85,000
SS Ltd.		69,000
Total		$154,000
Excess of Fair Value of Inventory of SS Ltd. over Book Value:		
Fair Value	$79,000	
Book Value	69,000	
Excess	$10,000	
Parent's Interest (60% of $10,000)		$ 6,000
Inventory on Consolidated Balance Sheet		$160,000

The Goodwill presented in the consolidated balance sheet represents the cost of purchasing 60 percent of the shares of SS Ltd. for $135,000 less 60 percent of the fair value of the net assets at the date of purchase [= $135,000 − .60 × ($260,000 − $59,000)]. In the formal consolidated balance sheet the Goodwill may be described as "Goodwill on purchase of shares of subsidiary SS Ltd."

Summary

Businesses acquire shares in other businesses for a variety of reasons and in a variety of ways. The acquisition of shares of another company as a long-term investment is generally recorded as follows:

Investment in S	$X
Cash or Other Consideration Given	$X

The investment account is recorded at the amount of cash given or the market value of other consideration exchanged.

The accounting for the investment subsequent to acquisition depends on the ability of one company, the investor, to exercise significant influence over another. The investor's ownership of 20 percent or more of the voting shares of another company is a major indicator of significant influence. The increase of the investor's ownership of the voting shares to 50 percent indicates that the investor (now called the *parent*) controls the other company, which is now called the *subsidiary*. The cost method is used where the investor does not exercise significant influence (generally less than 20 percent ownership). The equity method is used when the investor exercises significant influence but does not control the other company (generally less than 50 percent ownership). Consolidated statements are generally prepared when the parent owns more than 50 percent of the voting shares of the subsidiary. Exhibit 13.15 summarizes the accounting for investments subsequent to the acquisition.

Exhibit 13.15
Effects of Various Methods of Accounting for Long-Term Investments in Corporate Securities

Method of Accounting	Balance Sheet	Income Statement	Statement of Changes in Financial Position
Cost method. Parent unable to exercise significant influence (generally when ownership is less than 20 percent).	Investment account shown at acquisition cost as a noncurrent asset. Unrealized losses that are other than a temporary decline reduce the value of the investment and are charged against income.	Dividends declared by investee shown as revenue of investor. Unrealized losses are reported in the income statement when they are other than a temporary decline in value. Gains and losses (from original cost reduced as noted above) are reported in the income statement as realized in arm's length transactions with outsiders.	Dividends declared by investee included in cash provided by operations of investor.
Equity method (generally when parent is able to exercise significant influence but owns not more than 50 percent of the shares).	Investment account shown at cost plus share of investee's net income less share of investee's dividends since aquisition.	Equity in investee's net income shown as revenue in period that investee earns income.	Equity in investee's undistributed earnings is subtracted from net income to derive cash provided by operations of investor. Cash from operations is thus increased only by the amount of dividend declarations.
Consolidation (generally when ownership percentage is greater than 50 percent)	Investment account is eliminated and replaced with individual assets and liabilities of subsidiary. Minority interest in subsidiary's net assets shown among equities.	Individual revenues and expenses of subsidiary are combined with those of parent. Minority interest in subsidiary's net income shown as a subtraction.	Individual sources and uses of cash of subsidiary are combined with those of parent. Minority interest in net income is added to net income to obtain cash provided by operations.

Under the cost method, income is recognized only when dividends become receivable by the investor or when the securities are sold.

Consolidated statements and the equity method both have the same effect on net income. The parent shows as income its proportional share of the acquired firm's periodic income after acquisition. Income statement amounts of revenues and expenses will be larger under the consolidation method, however, because the revenues and expenses of the acquired company are combined with those of the parent. Balance sheet components will be larger under the consolidation method than under the equity method, because the individual assets and liabilities of the acquired company will be substituted for the investment balance on the parent company's books.

Problem for Self-Study

Reynolds Corporation acquired common shares of R Ltd., S Inc., and T Corp. on January 2 as long-term investments. These are the only long-term investments in securities of Reynolds Corporation. Data relating to the acquisitions are shown below.

Company	Percentage Acquired	Book Value and Market Value of Total Net Assets on January 2	Acquisition Cost	Net Income for Year	Dividends Declared for Year
R Ltd.	10%	$5,000,000	$ 540,000	$1,000,000	$400,000
S Inc.	30	5,000,000	1,700,000	1,000,000	400,000
T Corp.	100	5,000,000	5,000,000	1,000,000	400,000

Any goodwill arising from the acquisitions is amortized over ten years.
a. Give the journal entries made to acquire the shares of R Ltd. and to account for the investment during the year, using the cost method.
b. Give the journal entries made to acquire the shares of S Inc. and to account for the investment during the year, using the equity method.
c. Give the journal entries made to acquire the shares of T Corp. and to account for the investment during the year, using the equity method.
d. Give the consolidation balance sheet work sheet entry to eliminate the Investment in Shares of T Corp. account at the end of the year, assuming that the equity method is used and that the work sheet is based on post-closing trial balance amounts. T Corp. had $2,000,000 in its Common Share Capital account throughout the year and a zero balance in Contributed Surplus.
e. Assume that the shares of T Corp. had been acquired for $5,500,000, instead of $5,000,000. Give the journal entries made during the year to acquire the shares of T Corp. and to account for the investment, using the equity method. Any excess of cost over book value is considered goodwill and is amortized over ten years.
f. Refer to (e) above. Give the consolidation work sheet entry to eliminate the Investment in Shares of T Corp. account, assuming the work sheet is based on post-closing trial balance data.
g. Assume that Reynolds Corporation had paid $4,000,000 for 80 percent of the

shares of T Corp. on January 2. Give the journal entries made during the year to acquire the shares of T Corp. and to account for the investment, using the equity method.

h. Refer to **(g)**, above. Give the consolidation balance sheet work sheet entries to eliminate the Investment in Shares of T Corp. account, assuming the work sheet is based on post-closing trial balance data. A separate column is used on the work sheet to accumulate the minority interest.

Suggested Solution

a.	Investment in Shares of R Ltd.	$540,000	
	Cash		$540,000
	To record acquisition of shares of R Ltd.		
	Cash and Dividends Receivable	$ 40,000	
	Dividends Revenue		$ 40,000
	To record dividends received or receivable.		

b.	Investment in Shares of S Inc.	$1,700,000	
	Cash		$1,700,000
	To record acquisition of shares of S Inc.		
	Investment in Shares of S Inc.	$ 300,000	
	Equity in Earnings of S Inc.		$ 300,000
	To accrue share of S Inc.'s earnings; $300,000 = .30 × $1,000,000		
	Cash or Dividends Receivable	$ 120,000	
	Investment in Shares of S Inc.		$ 120,000
	To record dividends received or receivable; $120,000 = .30 × $400,000		
	Equity in Earnings of S Inc.	$ 20,000	
	Investment in Shares of S Inc.		$ 20,000
	To record amortization of goodwill implicit in purchase price; $20,000 = ($1,700,000 − $1,500,000) ÷ 10		

c.	Investment in Shares of T Corp.	$5,000,000	
	Cash		$5,000,000
	To record acquisition of shares of T Corp.		
	Investment in Shares of T Corp.	$1,000,000	
	Equity in Earnings of T Corp.		$1,000,000
	To accrue earnings of T Corp.; $1,000,000 = 100% × $1,000,000.		
	Cash or Dividends Receivable	$ 400,000	
	Investment in Shares of T Corp.		$ 400,000
	To record dividends received or receivable.		

d. Common Stock T Corp. $2,000,000
Retained Earnings T Corp. (December 31) 3,600,000
   Investment in Shares of T Corp. $5,600,000
To eliminate investment account on consolidation
work sheet.

---

e. Investment in Shares of T Corp. $5,500,000
   Cash $5,500,000
To record acquisition of shares of T Corp.

Investment in Shares of T Corp. $1,000,000
   Equity in Earnings of T Corp. $1,000,000
To accrue earnings of T Corp.

Cash or Dividends Receivable .... $ 400,000
   Investment in Shares of T Corp. .... $ 400,000
To record dividends received or receivable.

Equity in earnings of T Corp. .... $ 50,000
   Investment in Shares of T Corp. .... $ 50,000
To record amortization of goodwill implicit in purchase
price; $50,000 = ($5,500,000 − $5,000,000) ÷ 10.

---

f. Common Stock T Corp. $2,000,000
Retained Earnings T Corp. 3,600,000
Goodwill 450,000
   Investment in Shares of T Corp. $6,050,000
To eliminate investment account on consolidation
work sheet; $6,050,000 = $5,500,000 + $1,000,000
− $400,000 − $50,000.

---

g. Investment in Shares of T Corp. $4,000,000
   Cash $4,000,000
To record acquisition of shares of T Corp.

Investment in Shares of T Corp. .... $ 800,000
   Equity in Earnings of T Corp. .... $ 800,000
To accrue share of T Corp.'s earnings;
$800,000 = .80 × $1,000,000.

Cash or Dividends Receivable .... $ 320,000
   Investment in Shares of T Corp. .... $ 320,000
To record dividends received or receivable;
$320,000 = .80 × $400,000.

---

h. Common Stock T Corp. $1,600,000
Retained Earnings T Corp. 2,880,000
   Investment in Shares of T Corp. $4,480,000
To eliminate investment account on consolidation
work sheet; $4,480,000 = $4,000,000 +
$800,000 − $320,000.

Questions, Exercises, Problems and Cases

Questions

1. Review the meaning of the following concepts or terms discussed in this chapter.
    a. Marketable securities classified as Temporary Investments or as Portfolio Investments
    b. Portfolio investments
    c. Minority investments
    d. Majority investments
    e. Cost method for portfolio investments
    f. Significant influence by an investor over an investee
    g. Equity method
    h. Parent
    i. Subsidiary
    j. Consolidated financial statements
    k. Consolidation policy
    l. Economic entity versus legal entity
    m. Adjustments and eliminations in a consolidation work sheet
    n. Intercompany transactions
    o. Minority interest in a consolidated subsidiary
    p. Goodwill

2. Unrealized holding losses from price declines of temporary investments classified as current assets are recognized as they arise in calculating net income. Similar unrealized holding losses from portfolio investments accounted for using the cost method are not recognized as they arise in calculating net income unless the decline is considered to be permanent. What is the rationale for this difference in accounting treatment?

3. Compare and contrast each of the following pairs of accounts.
    a. Dividend Revenue, and Equity in Earnings of Unconsolidated Affiliates
    b. Equity in Earnings of Unconsolidated Affiliate, and Minority Interest in Earnings of Consolidated Subsidiary
    c. Minority Interest in Earnings of Consolidated Subsidiary, and Minority Interest in Net Assets of Consolidated Subsidiary.

4. "Dividends received or receivable from another company may be either an item of revenue in calculating net income or a return of capital, depending on the method of accounting used." Explain.

5. Why is the equity method sometimes called a *one-line consolidation*? Consider both the balance sheet and the income statement in your response.

6. Distinguish between minority investments in other companies and the minority interest in a consolidated subsidiary.

7. "Net income will be the same regardless of whether an investment in a subsidiary is accounted for using the equity method and not consolidated or whether the subsid-

iary is consolidated. Total assets will be different, however, depending on whether or not the subsidiary is consolidated.'' Explain.

Exercises

8. *Amount of income recognized under various methods of accounting for investments.* On January 1, Buyer Limited acquired common shares of X Inc. At the time of acquisition, the book value and fair market value of X Inc.'s net assets were $200,000. During the year, X Inc. earned $50,000 and declared dividends of $40,000. How much income would Buyer Limited report for the year from its investment under the assumption that Buyer Limited:

    a. Paid $30,000 for 15 percent of the common shares and uses the cost method for its investment in X Inc.?

    b. Paid $40,000 for 15 percent of the common shares and uses the cost method for its investment in X Inc.?

    c. Paid $60,000 for 30 percent of the common shares and uses the equity method to account for its investment in X Inc.?

    d. Paid $80,000 for 30 percent of the common shares and uses the equity method to account for its investment in X Inc.? Give the maximum income that Buyer Limited can report from the investment.

9. *Consolidation work sheet: inter-company balances.* Listed below are balances of the pre-closing trial balances for Billy Ltd. and Tommy Ltd. at December 31, Year 1. On January 1, Year 1 Billy Ltd. purchased all the outstanding shares of Tommy Ltd. for $125,000. Included in Tommy Ltd.'s December 31st payables is $100,000 due Billy Ltd.

	Billy Ltd.	Tommy Ltd.
Assets		
Cash	$ 15,000	$ 10,000
Accounts Receivable	355,000	130,000
Inventories	100,000	60,000
Net Fixed Assets	140,000	80,000
Investment in Tommy Ltd.	145,000	
Equities		
Accounts Payable	150,000	135,000
Common Stock	125,000	100,000
Retained Earnings	440,000	25,000
Dividends	15,000	5,000
Revenues		
Sales	220,000	100,000
Equity in T's Income	25,000	
Expenses		
Cost of Goods Sold	150,000	50,000
Other Expenses	20,000	10,000
Income Tax	20,000	15,000

Required: Prepare consolidated financial statements.

10. *Journal entries to account for investments on an equity basis.* Johnson Corporation made three long-term intercorporate investments on January 2. Data relating to these investments for the year are as follows:

Company	Percentage Acquired	Book Value and Market Value of Net Assets on January 2	Acquisition Cost	Net Income for the Year	Dividends Declared During the Year
X	20%	$2,000,000	$ 400,000	$200,000	$ 80,000
Y	25	3,000,000	800,000	300,000	120,000
Z........	30	4,000,000	1,300,000	400,000	160,000

Give the journal entries to record the acquisition of these investments and to apply the equity method during the year. Goodwill is amortized over 20 years.

11. *Journal entries under various methods of accounting for investments.* Maddox Corporation made three long-term intercorporate investments on January 2. Data relating to these investments are as follows:

Company	Percentage Acquired	Book Value and Market Value of Net Assets on January 2	Acquisition Cost	Net Income for the Year	Dividends Declared During the Year
A Ltd.	10%	$1,800,000	$ 200,000	$100,000	$40,000
B Ltd.	25	1,800,000	500,000	100,000	40,000
C Inc.	60	1,800,000	1,400,000	100,000	40,000

Assume that these were the only three intercorporate investments of Maddox Corporation. Goodwill is amortized over 40 years.

    a. Give the journal entries on Maddox Corporation's books to record these acquisitions of common shares and to account for the intercorporate investments under generally accepted accounting principles. The investment in C Inc. is not consolidated. Be sure to include any required year-end adjusting entries.

    b. Assume that the financial statements of C Inc. are consolidated with those of Maddox Corporation, that the investment in C Inc. is accounted for using the equity method, and that the consolidation work sheet is based on post-closing trial balance data. Give the work sheet entry to eliminate the Investment in Shares of C Inc. account on December 31. The Common Stock account of C Inc. has a balance of $1,000,000, and Contributed Surplus has a zero balance.

12. *Consolidated policy and principal consolidation concepts.* The CAR Corporation manufactures computers in Canada. It owns 75 percent of the voting shares of Charles of U.S.A., 80 percent of the voting shares of Alexandre de France (in France), and 90 percent of the voting shares of R Credit Corporation (a finance company). The CAR Corporation prepares consolidated financial statements consolidating Charles of U.S.A., using the equity method for R Credit Corporation, and using the cost method for its investment in Alexandre de France. Data from the annual reports of these companies are given below.

	Percentage Owned	Net Income	Dividends	Accounting Method
CAR Corporation Consolidated	—	$1,000,000	$ 70,000	—
Charles of U.S.A.	75%	100,000	40,000	Consolidated
Alexandre de France	80	80,000	50,000	Cost
R Credit Corporation	90	120,000	100,000	Equity

    a. Which, if any, of the companies is incorrectly accounted for by CAR according to generally accepted accounting principles?

Assuming the accounting for the three subsidiaries shown above to be correct, answer the following questions.

    b. How much of the net income reported by CAR Corporation Consolidated is attributable to the operations of the three subsidiaries?

    c. What is the amount of the minority interest now shown on the income statement, and how does it affect net income of CAR Corporation Consolidated?

    d. If all three subsidiaries had been consolidated, what would have been the net income of CAR Corporation Consolidated?

    e. If all three subsidiaries had been consolidated, what would be the minority interest shown on the income statement?

13. *Equity method and consolidation elimination entries.* The Hart Co. Ltd. acquired control of Keller Inc. on January 2, by purchasing 80 percent of its outstanding shares for $700,000. The entire excess of cost over book value acquired is attributable to goodwill, which is amortized over 40 years. The shareholders' equity account of Keller Inc. appeared as follows on January 2 and December 31 of the current year.

	Dec. 31	Jan. 2
Common Shares	$600,000	$600,000
Retained Earnings	420,000	200,000

Keller Inc. had earnings of $250,000 and declared dividends of $30,000 during the year. The accounts receivable of the Hart Co. Ltd. at December 31 include $4,500, which is due it from Keller Inc. Hart Co. Ltd. accounts for its investment in Keller Inc. on its single-company books using the equity method.

    a. Give the journal entries to record the acquisition of the shares of Keller Inc. and to apply the equity method during the year on the books of Hart Co. Ltd.

    b. Give the required elimination entries for a consolidation work sheet at the end of the year assuming that the work sheet is based on post-closing trial balance data.

14. *Equity method and consolidation elimination entries.* The Roe Co. Ltd. purchased 80 percent of the common shares of Danver Limited on January 2 at book value, $480,000. The total common stock of Danver Limited at this date was $450,000, and the retained earnings balance was $150,000. During the year, net income of the Danver Limited was $90,000; dividends declared were $36,000. The Roe Co. Ltd. uses the equity method to account for the investment.

    a. Give the journal entries made by Roe Co. Ltd. during the year to account for its investment in Danver Limited.

    b. Give the elimination entry for the investment account, assuming that the consolidation work sheet is based on post-closing trial balance data.

15. *Equity method and consolidation work sheet entries.* The Little Corp. is a subsidiary of the Butler Co. Inc. and is accounted for using the equity method on the single-company books of the Butler Co. Inc.

    a. Present journal entries for the following selected transactions. Record the set of entries on the books of the Little Corp. separately from the set of entries on the books of the Butler Co. Inc.

        (1) On January 2, the Butler Co. Inc. acquired on the market, for cash, 80 percent of all the common shares of the Little Corp. The outlay was $325,000. The total share capital outstanding was $300,000; the retained earnings balance was $80,000. The excess of cost over book value acquired is all attributed to goodwill and is amortized over ten years.

        (2) The Little Corp. purchased materials from the Butler Co. Inc. on account at the latter's cost, $23,000.

        (3) The Little Corp. obtained an advance of $9,000 from the Butler Co. Inc. The funds were deposited in the bank.

        (4) The Little Corp. paid $19,000 on the purchases in **(2)**.

        (5) The Little Corp. repaid $7,500 of the loan received from the Butler Co. Inc. in **(3)**.

        (6) The Little Corp. declared and paid a dividend of $24,000 during the year.

        (7) The net income of the Little Corp. for the year was $40,000.

    b. Prepare the adjustment and elimination entries that would be necessary in the preparation of the December 31 consolidated balance sheet, recognizing the effects of only the above transactions. Assume that the work sheet is based on pre-closing financial statement data.

16. *Intercompany inventory transactions between consolidated entities.* P Ltd. owns 70 percent of a consolidated subsidiary, S Ltd. During the year, P Ltd.'s sales to S Ltd. amounted to $50,000. The cost of those sales was $35,000. The following data are taken from the two companies' income statements:

	P Ltd.	S Ltd.
Sales	$120,000	$250,000
Cost of Goods Sold	70,000	150,000

    a. Compute consolidated sales and consolidated cost of goods sold for the year, assuming that S Ltd. sold all the goods purchased from P Ltd.

    b. Compare the consolidated sales, cost of goods sold, and gross profit on sales to the sum of the sales, cost of goods sold, and gross profit of the separate companies.

17. *Working backwards to consolidation relationships.* A parent company owns shares in one other company. It has owned them since the other company was formed. The parent company has retained earnings from its own operations independent of intercorporate investments of $100,000. The consolidated balance sheet shows no goodwill and retained earnings of $160,000. Consider each of the following questions independently of the others.

a. If the parent owns 80 percent of its consolidated subsidiary, what are the retained earnings of the subsidiary?

b. If the subsidiary has retained earnings of $96,000, what fraction of the subsidiary does the parent own?

c. If the subsidiary had not been consolidated but instead had been accounted for by the equity method, how much revenue in excess of dividends received would the parent have recognized over the life of the investment?

18. *Working backwards from consolidated income statements.* Sealco Enterprises Inc. published the consolidated income statement for the year that is shown in Exhibit 13.16. The unconsolidated affiliate retained 20 percent of its earnings of $100,000 during the year, having paid out the rest as dividends. The consolidated subsidiary earned $200,000 during the year and declared no dividends.

Exhibit 13.16
SEALCO ENTERPRISES INC.
Consolidated Income Statement

Sales		$1,000,000
Less: Cost of Goods Sold		765,000
Gross Profit		$ 235,000
Less: Administrative Expenses	$100,000	
Amortization of Goodwill	5,000	105,000
Operating Income		$ 130,000
Equity in Earnings of Unconsolidated Affiliate		40,000
Net Income before the Undernoted		$ 170,000
Less: Income Tax Expense Currently Payable	$ 42,000	
Deferred	10,000	52,000
		$ 118,000
Less: Minority Interest in Earnings of Consolidated Subsidiary		30,000
Net Income		$ 88,000

a. What percentage of the unconsolidated affiliate does Sealco Enterprises Inc. own?

b. What dividends did Sealco Enterprises Inc. receive from the unconsolidated affiliate during the year?

c. What percentage of the consolidated subsidiary does Sealco Enterprises Inc. own?

19. *Working backwards from the statement of changes in financial position.* Lesala Corporation purchased most of the common shares of its subsidiary in Year 1. The subsidiary earned $1 million in Year 3 but declared no dividends. Exhibit 13.17 is an excerpt from Lesala Corporation's financial statements issued for Year 3.

Exhibit 13.17
LESALA CORPORATION
Consolidated Statement of
Changes in Financial Position
for the Year 3

Sources of Cash:

Consolidated Net Income		$3,000,000
Additions:		
Depreciation of Plant	$150,000	
Amortization of Goodwill Arising from Acquisition of Consolidated Subsidiary	10,000	
Minority Interest in Earnings of Consolidated Subsidiary	200,000	
Increases in Current Liabilities	75,000	
Subtractions:		
Increases in Current Assets Other than Cash	(90,000)	345,000
Cash Provided by Operations		$3,345,000

a. What percentage of the consolidated subsidiary does Lesala Corporation own?

b. Goodwill arising from the acquisition of the consolidated subsidiary is being amortized, using the straight-line method, to show the minimum charges allowed by generally accepted accounting principles. What was the excess of the subsidiary's market value as a going concern over the market value of the actual assets shown on its books as of the date of acquisition? Assume that the acquisition occurred on January 1, Year 1.

20. *Effect of transactions on the statement of changes in financial position.* Refer to the Simplified Statement of Changes in Financial Position for a Period in Exhibit 5.19 on page 248. Eleven of the lines in the statement are numbered. Ignore the unnumbered lines in responding to the questions below.

Assume that the accounting cycle is complete for the period and that all of the financial statements have been prepared. Then it is discovered that a transaction has been overlooked. The transaction is recorded in the accounts, and all of the financial statements are corrected. Define *funds* as *cash*. For each of the following transactions or events, indicate which of the numbered lines of the statement of changes in financial position is affected and by how much. Ignore income tax effects.

a. A 100 percent-owned affiliate accounted for on the equity method earns $10,000 and pays dividends of $4,000.

b. A 100 percent-owned affiliate accounted for on the equity method reports a loss for the year of $5,000.

c. Minority interest in income of a consolidated subsidiary is recognized in the amount of $20,000.

d. Minority interest in the losses of a consolidated subsidiary is recognized in the amount of $8,000.

e. A 100 percent-owned consolidated subsidiary sold merchandise to the parent company for $10,000. The subsidiary's cost of the goods sold was $6,000.

The parent sold the merchandise for $12,000. An elimination of the intercompany transactions is made.

f. A security in Portfolio Investments accounted for with the cost method is written down from $10,000 to $8,000.

g. A dividend of $7,000 is received on shares held as a *portfolio investment* and accounted for with the cost method.

h. The market value of securities accounted for as *current assets* (Temporary Investments) is $5,000 less than the net amount shown for the same portfolio on the balance sheet at the end of the previous accounting period. The amount in the allowance contra to Temporary Investments is changed to reflect this decline in market value.

21. *Effect of errors on financial statements.* Using the notation O/S (overstated), U/S (understated), or No (no effect), indicate the effects on assets, liabilities, and shareholders' equity of each of the independent errors below. Ignore income tax effects.

a. In applying the cost method to portfolio investments, dividends received were incorrectly credited to the Investment account.

b. In applying the equity method, P correctly accrued its share of S's net income for the year. However, when a dividend was received, Dividend Revenue was credited.

c. P acquired 30 percent of S on January 1 of the current year for an amount in excess of the market value of S's net assets. P correctly accounted for its share of S's net income and dividends for the year but neglected to amortize any of the excess purchase price.

d. During the current year, P sold inventory items to S, its wholly owned subsidiary, at a profit. These inventory items were sold by S and P has paid for them before the end of the year. No elimination entry was made for this intercompany sale on the consolidation work sheet. Indicate the effect of this error on consolidated assets, liabilities, and net income.

e. Refer to part (**d**). Assume that one-fourth of these goods were not sold by S during the year and therefore remain in ending inventory.

f. Refer to part (**d**). Assume that S owes P $10,000 for intercompany purchases at year-end. No elimination entry is made for this intercompany debt. Indicate the effect on consolidated assets, liabilities, and net income.

g. P owns 90 percent of S. The minority interest in consolidated subsidiaries is treated as part of shareholders' equity. In preparing a consolidated work sheet, no entry was made to accrue the minority interest's share of S's net income or of S's net assets.

Problems and Cases

22. *Consolidation work sheet for wholly owned subsidiary purchased at book value.* The trial balances of High Ltd. and Low Inc. on December 31, Year 6 are shown in Exhibit 13.18.

High Ltd. acquired all of the common shares of Low Inc. on January 1, Year 6, for $80,000. The receivables of High Ltd. and the liabilities of Low Inc. contain $5,000 of advances from High Ltd. to Low Inc.

Exhibit 13.18
HIGH LTD. and LOW INC.
Pre-Closing Trial Balances
(Problems 22 and 23)

	High Ltd.	Low Inc.
Debits:		
Cash	$ 50,000	$ 5,000
Account Receivable	80,000	15,000
Investment in Shares of Low Inc. (at equity)	90,000	—
Other Assets	360,000	100,000
Cost of Goods Sold	160,000	60,000
Selling and Administrative Expenses	50,000	20,000
Income Tax Expense	40,000	10,000
Totals	$830,000	$210,000
Credits:		
Accounts Payable	$ 70,000	$ 30,000
Bonds Payable	100,000	—
Common Shares	150,000	50,000
Retained Earnings	200,000	30,000
Sales Revenue	300,000	100,000
Equity in Earnings of Low Inc.	10,000	—
Totals	$830,000	$210,000

Prepare a consolidation balance sheet work sheet for High Ltd. and Low Inc. on December 31, Year 6. The elimination column should contain entries to:

(1) Eliminate the investment account.
(2) Eliminate intercompany receivables and payables.

23. *Consolidation work sheet entries for less than wholly owned subsidiary purchased for more than book value.* Refer to the data for High Ltd. and Low Inc. in Problem 22. Give the consolidation balance sheet work sheet elimination entries under each of the following independent situations:

a. High Ltd. paid $100,000, instead of $80,000, for all of the common shares of Low Inc. on January 1, Year 6. The market values of Low Inc.'s recorded assets and liabilities equaled their book values. Goodwill is amortized over ten years.

b. High Ltd. paid $64,000 for 80 percent of the common shares of Low Inc. on January 1, Year 6. The Investment in Shares of Low Inc. account showed a balance of $72,000 on December 31, Year 6.

24. *Consolidation work sheet for less than wholly owned subsidiary purchased for book value.* The pre-closing trial balances of L Corp. and M Inc. on December 31, Year 2 are shown in Exhibit 13.19. L Corp. acquired 90 percent of the common shares of M Inc. on January 2, Year 1, for $270,000. On this date, the shareholders' equity accounts of M Inc. were as follows:

Common Stock	$100,000
Retained Earnings	200,000
Total	$300,000

During Year 2, L Corp. sold merchandise costing $30,000, on account, to M Inc. for $40,000. Of the amount, $10,000 remains unpaid at year-end. M Inc. sold all of the merchandise during Year 2.

Exhibit 13.19
L CORP. and M INC.
Pre-Closing Trial Balances
(Problem 24)

	L Corp.	M Inc.
Debits:		
Receivables	$ 60,000	$130,000
Investment in Shares of M Inc.	319,500	—
Other Assets	761,500	285,000
Cost of Goods Sold	550,000	150,000
Other Expenses	120,000	10,000
Dividends Declared	30,000	15,000
Totals	$1,841,000	$590,000
Credits:		
Accounts Payable	$ 80,000	$ 20,000
Other Liabilities	90,000	40,000
Common Shares	400,000	100,000
Retained Earnings	435,000	230,000
Sales Revenue	800,000	200,000
Equity in Earnings of M Inc.	36,000	—
Totals	$1,841,000	$590,000

    a. Prepare a consolidated balance sheet work sheet for L Corp. and M Inc. for Year 2. The elimination column should contain entries to:

        (1) Eliminate the investment account.

        (2) Eliminate intercompany receivables and payables.

    b. Prepare a consolidated balance sheet as of December 31, Year 2.

25. *Consolidation work sheet for less than wholly owned subsidiary purchased for more than book value.* The condensed balance sheets of Ely Corp. and Sims Ltd. at December 31 are shown in Exhibit 13.20.

    The receivables of the Ely Corp. and the liabilities of Sims Ltd. contain an advance from the Ely Corp. to Sims Ltd. of $5,500. The Ely Corp. acquired 85 percent of the share capital of Sims Ltd. on the market at January 2 of this year for $80,000. At that date, the balance in the Retained Earnings account of Sims Ltd. was $30,000. Amortize goodwill, if any, over 40 years.

Prepare a consolidated balance sheet work sheet for Ely Corp. and Sims Ltd. The elimination column should contain entries to:

(1) Eliminate the Investment in the Sims Ltd. account.

(2) Eliminate intercompany obligations.

Exhibit 13.20
ELY CORP. and SIMS LTD.
Balance Sheet Data
(Problem 25)

	Ely Corp.	Sims Ltd.
Assets		
Cash	$ 60,000	$ 5,000
Receivables	120,000	15,000
Investment in Sims Ltd. shares (at equity)	88,200	—
Other Assets	540,000	100,000
	$808,200	$120,000
Liabilities and Shareholders' Equity		
Current Liabilities	$250,000	$ 30,000
Common Shares	400,000	50,000
Retained Earnings	158,200	40,000
	$808,200	$120,000

26. *Consolidation work sheet subsequent to year of acquisition.* The condensed balance sheets of R Ltd. and S Ltd. on December 31, Year 2 are shown in Exhibit 13.21. Additional information:

R Ltd. owns 90 percent of the share capital of S Ltd. The shares of S Ltd. were acquired on January 1, Year 1, when S Ltd.'s retained earnings amounted to $20,000.

R Ltd. holds a note issued by S Ltd. in the amount of $8,200.

Excess of cost over book value acquired is all attributable to goodwill, to be amortized over 40 years. The company has recorded Year 2 goodwill amortization.

Prepare a work sheet for a consolidated balance sheet.

Exhibit 13.21
R LTD. and S LTD.
Balance Sheet Data
(Problem 26)

	R Ltd.	S Ltd.
Assets		
Cash	$ 18,000	$ 13,000
Accounts and Notes Receivable	90,000	25,000
Inventories	220,000	125,000
Investment in Shares of S Ltd. (at equity)	312,450	—
Plant Assets	300,000	212,000
Total Assets	$940,450	$375,000

Liabilities and Shareholders' Equity

Accounts and Notes Payable	$ 55,000	$ 17,000
Dividends Payable	—	12,500
Other Liabilities	143,000	11,000
Common Shares	600,000	250,000
Contributed Surplus	—	50,000
Retained Earnings	$142,450	$ 34,500
Total Liabilites and Shareholders' Equity	$940,450	$375,000

27. *Total consolidated assets, unrealized inventory profit.* The assets included in the balance sheets of Parent Co. Ltd. and Subsidiary Co. Ltd. at December 31, Year 1 are shown in Exhibit 13.22

Exhibit 13.22
PARENT CO. LTD. and SUBSIDIARY CO. LTD.
Balance Sheet Assets

	Parent Co. Ltd.	Subsidiary Co. Ltd.
Assets		
Current Assets		
Cash	$ 40,000	$ 30,000
Accounts Receivable — Customers	88,200	59,000
Advances to Subsidiary Co. Ltd.	8,000	
Inventory	150,000	100,000
Prepaid Expenses	1,800	1,000
Total Current Assets	$288,000	$190,000
Property, Plant, and Equipment:		
Land	$100,000	$ 50,000
Buildings	300,000	200,000
Accumulated Depreciation	(140,000)	(60,000)
Equipment	150,000	120,000
Accumulated Depreciation	(68,000)	(40,000)
Total	$342,000	$270,000
Investment in Subsidiary Co. Ltd.[a]	300,000	
Total Assets	$930,000	$460,000

( ) Deduction.
[a]Recorded on the equity basis.

Parent Co. Ltd. owns 80 percent of the common shares of Subsidiary Co. Ltd., which it purchased when Subsidiary Co. Ltd. was formed.

All of the inventory of Subsidiary Co. Ltd. was purchased from Parent Co. Ltd. The inventory cost Parent Co. Ltd. $85,000.

The chief accountant of Parent Co. Ltd. must prepare a consolidated balance sheet. Determine the total that will be shown for the asset side of the consolidated balance sheet.

28. *Consolidated balance sheet, unrealized inventory profit.* The condensed balance sheets of Saginaw Co. Limited and Valley Co. Ltd. at December 31, Year 2 are shown in Exhibit 13.23.

Exhibit 13.23
SAGINAW CO. LIMITED and VALLEY CO. LTD
Balance Sheets

	Saginaw Co. Limited	Valley Co. Ltd.
Assets		
Current Assets	$ 90,000	$ 50,000
Investment in Valley Co. Ltd.	110,000	
Property, Plant, and Equipment — Net of		
Accumulated Depreciation	200,000	110,000
Total Assets	$400,000	$160,000
Equities		
Current Liabilities	$ 60,000	$ 30,000
Long-Term Liabilities	40,000	20,000
Shareholders' Equity:		
Share Capital	200,000	100,000
Retained Earnings	100,000	10,000
Total Equities	$400,000	$160,000

Saginaw Co. Limited organized Valley Co. Ltd. one year ago and holds all of the outstanding share capital of the subsidiary.

   a. Prepare the December 31, Year 2 consolidation balance sheet. A consolidation work sheet is not required.

   b. Assume that the following data relate to the next year, which ends December 31, Year 3.

	Saginaw Co. Limited	Valley Co. Ltd.
Net Income (single-company operations)*	$25,000	$10,000
Dividends paid	10,000	5,000
*Excluding any income from Valley Co. Ltd.		

Compute the consolidated retained earnings as of December 31, Year 3.

   c. In addition to the information provided in (**b**), assume that Saginaw Co. Limited made intercompany sales to Valley Co. Ltd. of $5,000, on which there was $500 of intercompany profit, and that the goods are included in the December 31, Year 3 inventory of Valley Co. Ltd. Compute the consolidated retained earnings as of December 31, Year 3.

29. *Minority interest.* The condensed balance sheets of Alpha Co. Limited and Gamma Limited at December 31, Year 9 are shown in Exhibit 13.24.

On December 31, Year 1, Alpha Co. Limited acquired 90 percent of the share capital of Gamma Limited at a cost of $117,000. On this date the balances of the retained earnings accounts of the two companies were:

Alpha Co. Limited	$48,900
Gamma Limited	30,000

Exhibit 13.24
ALPHA CO. LIMITED and GAMMA LTD.
Condensed Balance Sheets

	Alpha Co. Limited	Gamma Limited
Assets		
Current Assets	$ 34,730	$ 10,100
Investment in Gamma Limited	102,870	
Property, Plant, and Equipment — net	134,500	122,400
Total Assets	$272,100	$132,500
Equities		
Current Liabilities	$ 46,800	$ 18,200
Share Capital	150,000	100,000
Retained Earnings	75,300	14,300
Total Equities	$272,100	$132,500

    a. Compute the amount of minority interest that would be included in the December 31, Year 9 consolidated balance sheet.

    b. Prepare the Shareholders' Equity section of the December 31, Year 9 consolidated balance sheet.

30. *Consolidation work sheet and balance sheet, minority interest, purchase discrepancy, unrealized inventory profit.* The June 30, Year 8 balance sheets of Vapor Co. Ltd. and Trail Co. Limited are shown in Exhibit 13.25. Vapor Co. Ltd. accounts for its investment in Trail Co. Limited on the equity basis. Vapor Co. Ltd. acquired its 80 percent interest in Trail Co. Limited for $37,000 on July 1, Year 1 on which date the balance of retained earnings of Trail Co. Limited was $1,500. On this date there was evidence that the land owned by Trail Co. Limited was worth $5,000 more than its book value. Vapor Co. Ltd. had amortized $1,100 of goodwill on acquisition to June 30, Year 8.

On June 30, Year 8, the inventory of Trail Co. Limited included merchandise purchased from Vapor Co. Ltd. for $6,400, which was $1,500 above cost to Vapor Co. Ltd.

    a. Prepare the consolidated balance sheet work sheet as of June 30, Year 8.

    b. Prepare the consolidated balance sheet as of June 30, Year 8.

Exhibit 13.25
VAPOR CO. LTD. and TRAIL CO. LIMITED
Balance Sheets

	Vapor Co. Ltd.	Trail Co. Limited
Assets		
Cash	$ 18,400	$ 6,800
Accounts Receivable	46,100	10,200
Advance to Trail Co. Limited	25,000	
Inventory	83,500	18,500
Prepaid Expenses	6,400	2,600
Investment in Trail Co. Limited	40,000	
Land	15,000	6,400
Buildings, net of Accumulated Depreciation	108,600	20,100
Furniture and Equipment, net of Accumulated Depreciation	138,900	12,300
Total Assets	$481,900	$76,900
Equities		
Accounts Payable	$ 18,900	$14,200
Income Tax Payable	62,400	4,200
Advance from Vapor Co. Ltd.		25,000
Share Capital	300,000	25,000
Retained Earnings	100,600	8,500
Total Equities	$481,900	$76,900

31. *Consolidated balance sheets, investment on a cost basis, purchase discrepancy, unrealized inventory profit.* The condensed balance sheets of Par Ltd. and Sub Ltd. at December 31, Year 7, are shown in Exhibit 13.26. Par Ltd. records the Investment in Sub Ltd. on a cost basis and follows the practice of amortizing any goodwill arising from consolidation on a straight-line basis over a 20-year period.

Prepare a condensed consolidated balance sheet for each of the following separate cases.

a. The parent purchased all of the shares of the subsidiary for $120,000 when the retained earnings of the subsidiary amounted to $20,000.

b. The parent purchased 80 percent of the subsidiary's shares for $120,000 when the retained earnings of the subsidiary amounted to $50,000.

c. On December 31, Year 2, the parent purchased 70 percent of the subsidiary's shares for $120,000 when the retained earnings of the subsidiary amounted to $50,000. At the date of acquisition the fair value of the land was $10,000 above the book value. Intercompany profit in the inventory of the subsidiary was as follows:

December 31, Year 6	$2,000
December 31, Year 7	3,000

Exhibit 13.26
PAR LTD. and SUB LTD.
Condensed Balance Sheets
(Problem 31)

	Par Ltd.	Sub Ltd.
Assets		
Current Assets	$ 40,000	$ 30,000
Investment in Sub Ltd.	120,000	—
Property, Plant, and Equipment	220,000	150,000
Total Assets	$380,000	$180,000
Equities		
Current Liabilities	$ 30,000	$ 20,000
Share Capital	240,000	100,000
Retained Earnings	110,000	60,000
Total Equities	$380,000	$180,000

32. *Determine specific consolidated financial statement numbers, purchase discrepancy, minority interest, unrealized inventory profit.* The condensed balance sheets of P Ltd. and S Ltd. at December 31, Year 7, are shown in Exhibit 13.27.

Exhibit 13.27
P LTD. and S LTD.
Condensed Balance Sheets
(Amounts in 000's)

	P Ltd.	S Ltd.
Assets		
Current Assets	$212	$140
Investment in S Ltd.	158	—
Other Assets	420	180
Total	$790	$320
Equities		
Current Liabilities	$100	$170
Long-Term Debt	200	—
Share Capital	200	100
Retained Earnings	290	50
Total	$790	$320

In addition the following information is provided.

(1) P Ltd. acquired 80 percent of the shares of S Ltd. on December 31, Year 6, for $160,000. At that date the balance of shareholders' equity of S Ltd. was $142,500. Neither company issued shares during the year.

(2) On May 15, Year 7, P Ltd. sold merchandise to S Ltd. for a price of $60,000. The merchandise had cost P Ltd. $50,000 when purchased on December 20, Year 6. S Ltd. had resold half of the merchandise by December 31, Year 7.

(3) On November 30, Year 7, P Ltd. had advanced S Ltd. $40,000 on a 90-day note. The note was still outstanding at December 31, Year 7.

(4) At December 31, Year 6, the fair value of the land owned by S Ltd. exceeded the book value by $20,000. This was the sole difference between fair value and book value of S Ltd.'s assets at that date. No land was sold during Year 7.

(5) P Ltd. followed the policy of amortizing goodwill over ten years on a straight-line basis by reducing the book value of the investment in S Ltd.

(6) S Ltd. declared and paid no dividends during Year 7.

   a. Calculate the following balances appearing on the consolidated balance sheet at December 31, Year 7. (Show details of your calculation.)
   - **(i)** Current liabilities
   - **(ii)** Other assets (excluding goodwill on consolidation)
   - **(iii)** Consolidated retained earnings
   - **(iv)** Minority interest
   - **(v)** Goodwill on consolidation
   - **(vi)** Current assets

   b. Determine the income of S Ltd. for the year ended December 31, Year 7.

   c. Determine the amount and describe the location of references to minority interest in the Statements of Consolidated Income, Consolidated Balance Sheet, and Consolidated Retained Earnings for the year ended December 31, Year 7.

33. *Effect of accounting methods for investments on financial statements.* General Manufacturing (G.M) Limited manufactures heavy-duty industrial equipment and consumer durable goods. To enable its customers to make convenient credit ar-

Exhibit 13.28
GENERAL MANUFACTURING LIMITED and
CONSOLIDATED AFFILIATES
(Problems 33, 34, 35)

	(In millions of $) December 31		
Balance Sheet	**Year 3**	**Year 2**	**Year 1**
Investment in G.M. Credit Corporation	$ 260.0	$ 231.9	$ 190.0
Other Assets	7,141.8	6,655.9	6,008.5
Total Assets	$ 7,401.8	$6,887.8	$6,198.5
Total Liabilities	$ 4,317.2	$4,086.0	$3,644.9
Shareholders' Equity	3,084.6	2,801.8	2,553.6
Total Equities	$ 7,401.8	$6,887.8	$6,198.5

	For the Years		
Income Statement	**Year 3**	**Year 2**	**Year 1**
Sales	$10,387.6	$9,546.4	$8,813.6
Equity in Net Earnings of Credit Corporation	41.1	30.9	19.9
Total Revenues	$10,428.7	$9,577.3	$8,833.5
Expenses	(9,898.7)	(9,105.5)	(8,505.0)
Net Income	$ 530.0	$ 471.8	$ 328.5

rangements, G.M. Limited organized General Manufacturing Credit Corporation several years ago. G.M. Credit Corporation is 100-percent owned by G.M. Limited. G.M. Limited accounts for its investment in G.M. Credit Corporation using the equity method. G.M. owns shares of many other companies, and consolidates several of them in its financial statements. Refer to the comparative balance sheets and income statements for the two companies in Exhibits 13.28 and 13.29.

Exhibit 13.29
GENERAL MANUFACTURING CREDIT CORPORATION
(Problems 33, 34, 35)

Balance Sheet	(In millions of $) December 31		
	Year 3	Year 2	Year 1
Total Assets	$2,789.5	$2,358.7	$2,157.0
Total Liabilities	$2,529.5	$2,126.8	$1,967.0
Share Capital	$ 110.0	$ 90.0	$ 55.0
Retained Earnings	150.0	141.9	135.0
Shareholders' Equity	$ 260.0	$ 231.9	$ 190.0
Total Equities	$2,789.5	$2,358.7	$2,157.0

Statement of Income and Retained Earnings	For the Years		
	Year 3	Year 2	Year 1
Revenues	$ 319.8	$ 280.0	$ 247.5
Less: Expenses	278.7	249.1	227.6
Net Income	$ 41.1	$ 30.9	$ 19.9
Less: Dividends	33.0	24.0	15.0
Earnings Retained for Year	$ 8.1	$ 6.9	$ 4.9
Retained Earnings at January 1	141.9	135.0	130.1
Retained Earnings at December 31	$ 150.0	$ 141.9	$ 135.0

a. Given that G.M. Limited accounted for its investment in G.M. Credit Corporation by the equity method, identify, for Year 3, the components of G.M. Limited's income that are attributable to the Credit Corporation's dividends and earnings.

b. Assume that G.M. Limited had accounted for its investment in the Credit Corporation using the cost method, and market value has exceeded acquisition cost at all times since acquisition.

(i) Show the components of G.M. Limited's income from the Credit Corporation, and compute how much larger or smaller G.M. Limited's income would have been for Year 3 than was reported.

(ii) Identify any G.M. Limited balance sheet accounts that would have different balances, and calulate the differences from what is shown in the actual statements and what would be shown had the alternative treatment been used.

c. Assume that G.M. Limited had accounted for its investment in the Credit Corporation by consolidating it. Perform the same computations as required in **(i)** and **(ii)** of **(b)**, above, for Year 3. Notice that when a 100-percent-owned subsidiary — accounted for with the equity method — is consolidated, the effect on balance sheet totals and subtotals can be summarized as follows:

(1) Total owners' equity on the parent's books remain unchanged.

(2) Total liabilities on the parent's books increases by the amount of the subsidiary's total liabilities (assuming there are no intercompany receivables and payables).

(3) Total assets on the parent's books increases net by an amount equal to the subsidiary's liabilities. (All of the subsidiary's assets are put onto the parent's books, but the parent's investment in the subsidiary, an amount equal to the subsidiary's owners' equity, is removed. The net effect is to increase assets by the amount of the subsidiary's total assets − subsidiary's owners' equity = subsidiary's liabilities.)

d. Compute the following ratios for G.M. from the annual report as published for Year 3. (Refer to Exhibit 6.11 if you have forgotten how to compute these ratios.)

(1) Rate of return on assets. (Insufficient information is given to allow an addback to the numerator for interest payments net of tax effects; ignore that adjustment to net income that is ordinarily required. Use the year-end balance of total assets for the year's average.)

(2) Debt-equity ratio.

e. For Year 3, compute the two ratios required in part **(d)**, assuming that G.M. had consolidated the Credit Corporation, rather than accounting for it with the equity method. Use the information derived in part **(c)**.

f. Compare the results in parts **(d)** and **(e)**. What conclusions can you draw from this exercise about comparing financial ratios for companies that consolidate their subsidiaries with those of companies that do not?

34. Repeat Problem **(33)** for Year 2.

35. Repeat Problem **(33)** for Year 1.

36. *Impact of consolidation policy on debt ratios.* This problem illustrates the impact that consolidation policy can have on financial statements and financial statement analysis. Sears, Roebuck & Co. and J. C. Penney Company are large retailers who have similar operations. Both companies have organized financing subsidiaries. Each subsidiary borrows funds in credit markets and lends the funds to customers who purchase goods or services from the retailers. Each subsidiary is 100 percent owned by its parent company. Sears consolidates its financing subsidiary (Sears, Roebuck Acceptance Corp.) in published financial statements. Penney's uses the equity method for its financing subsidiary (J. C. Penney Financial Corporation) and shows the separate financial statements of the financing subsidiary in notes to the published financial statements.

In this problem we focus on the debt ratio, because the effects are easy to illustrate. Other ratios could be used as well. Throughout this text, the debt-equity ratio has been defined as

$$\text{Debt-Equity Ratio} = \frac{\text{Total Liabilities}}{\text{Total Equities}}$$

Many financial analysts prefer to use a form of the debt ratio such as

$$\text{Debt Ratio} = \frac{\text{Total } \textit{Long-Term} \text{ Debt}}{\text{Total Shareholders' Equity}}$$

Such analysts feel that this version of the debt ratio focuses more attention on the risk of companies being analyzed. (The notion is that the percentage of current liabilities to total equities is, to a large degree, determined by the nature of the business and that so long as current assets are as large as current liabilities, the percentage of current liabilities in total equities is not important.)

The accompanying Exhibit 13.30 shows pertinent data from recent financial statements for both Sears and Penney's. Both versions of the debt ratio mentioned above are presented. The data for Sears are taken directly from the financial statements. For Penney's, the exhibit shows data from the published balance sheet in column (1), data from the statements of the financing subsidiary in column (2), and presents a column for Penney's hypothetical financial statements, assuming consolidation of the financing subsidiary. Column (3) represents the accounting for Penney's that is analogous to Sears' accounting.

Exhibit 13.30
Effect of Consolidation Policy
(all dollar amounts in millions)

	J. C. Penney Company			Sears, Roebuck & Co.
	Financial Statements as Issued (1)	Financing Subsidiary Statements as Shown in Notes (2)	Hypothetical Financial Statements if Subsidiary Were Consolidated (3)	Financial Statements as Issued (4)
Total Assets	$3,483.8	$1,458.1	?	$12,711.5
Total Liabilities	1,567.2	1,078.9	?	6,774.6
Long-Term Debt	355.5	517.0	?	1,563.5
Shareholders' Equity	1,916.6	379.2	?	5,936.9
Debt-Equity Ratio (Total Liabilities/ Total Equities)	45.0%	72.3%	58.0%	53.3%
Long-Term Debt/ Shareholders' Equity . .	18.5%	136.3%	45.5%	26.3%

a. Complete column (3) for Penney's. (The ratios shown are correct; you can check your work from them.) You may find the summary in part (c) of Problem (33) to be useful.
b. As measured by the debt ratios (and ignoring other factors — scc Problem

(19) in Chapter 15), which company appears to be the more risky? Which company do you think is more risky and why?

c. Assume that the managements of Penney's and Sears are both considering additional long-term financing to raise funds. Managements of both companies are concerned about how the marketplace will react to new debt financing on the one hand or new common share issues on the other. How are financial analysts who are concerned with risk (as measured in part by debt ratios) likely to react to these two companies? How are managements of the two companies likely to react in making their financing decisions if they anticipate the reaction of financial analysts?

37. *Preparation of statement of changes in financial position (adapted from problem by Stan Baiman)*. Exhibit 13.31 presents a comparative balance sheet for Cherry Corporation for Year 6.

Exhibit 13.31
CHERRY CORPORATION
Comparative Balance Sheets
December 31

	Year 6	Year 5
Assets		
Current Assets		
Cash	$ 450,000	$ 287,000
Accounts Receivable	645,000	550,000
Inventories	460,000	298,000
Total Current Assets	$1,555,000	$1,135,000
Investments:		
Common Shares of Roy Inc. (3 percent)	$ 0	$ 39,000
Common Shares of Zuber Ltd. (90 percent)	246,300	0
Plant Assets	455,000	381,000
Less: Accumulated Depreciation	(193,000)	(144,000)
Patents (net)	26,000	19,000
Unamortized Bond Discount	49,000	47,000
Total Assets	$2,138,300	$1,477,000
Liabilities and Shareholders' Equity		
Current Liabilities:		
Dividends Payable	$ 181,000	$ 0
Accounts Payable	170,000	70,000
Accrued Liabilities	24,800	41,800
Total Current Liabilities	$ 375,800	$ 111,800
Long-Term Bonds Payable	223,000	180,000
Total Liabilities	$ 598,800	$ 291,800
Preferred Stock at par ($3)	$ 63,500	$ 53,000
Common Stock—No Par Value	774,500	712,100
Retained Earnings	701,500	420,100
Total Shareholders' Equity	$1,539,500	$1,185,200
Total Liabilities and Shareholders' Equity	$2,138,300	$1,477,000

Additional Information:

(1) For the year ended December 31, Year 6, Cherry reported net income of $496,000.

(2) On January 3, Year 6, Cherry acquired 90 percent of the outstanding common stock of Zuber Ltd. To consummate this transaction, Cherry paid $72,000 cash and issued 3,500 of its preferred and 2,400 of its common shares. The market price of Cherry's preferred shares on January 3, Year 6, was $3 a share and the market price of its common shares was $12 a share. The market value of the cash and shares given up by Cherry was equal to its share of Zuber's net book value.

   Zuber Ltd. is considered to be an unrelated business and not compatible with Cherry's operations. Therefore Zuber is not consolidated with Cherry. Rather the investment in Zuber is accounted for on Cherry's financial statement using the equity method. For the year ended December 31, Year 6, Zuber Ltd. reported $160,000 of net income and declared and paid cash dividends of $10,000.

(3) Cherry's investment in the common stock of Roy Inc. was made in Year 2 and represented a three percent interest. On January 1, Year 6, Cherry sold this investment for $46,000. In addition, Cherry acquired new plant assets at a cost of $81,000. Plant assets with a cost of $22,000 and accumulated depreciation of $17,600 were sold for $3,200. The remaining increase in plant assets resulted from major repairs that were accounted for properly as capital expenditures.

(4) Amortization of patents for Year 6 was $3,000. A new patent was acquired for cash.

(5) On January 2, Year 6 (before the purchase of Zuber), Cherry declared and issued a four percent stock dividend on its common shares, where were recorded at the market price on that date of $33,600. On December 31, Year 6, cash dividends of $145,000, on the common shares and $36,000 on the preferred shares were declared.

(6) During Year 6, bonds with a face value of $20,000 and unamortized bond discount of $3,000 were repurchased for $17,000. During Year 6, bond discount of $4,000 was amortized against interest expense. During Year 6, new bonds were issued at a discount.

   a. Prepare a T-account work sheet for a statement of changes in financial position, defining funds as cash.

   b. Prepare a statement of changes in financial position for Cherry Corporation for Year 6.

38. *Pooling-of-interests method.* When one corporation acquires all, or substantially all, of another corporation's common shares in a single transaction, the transaction is referred to as a *corporate acquisition*. Two methods of accounting for corporate acquisitions are permitted under generally accepted accounting principles, depending on the manner in which the acquisition is structured.

Purchase Method The purchase method is a direct extension of acquisition-cost accounting. The Investment in Subsidiary account on the parent's books is recorded initially at the amount of cash or market value of other consideration given in the exchange. When the consolidation work sheet is prepared, any difference between the amount in the investment account on the date of acquisition and the book value of the net assets acquired is allocated to individual assets and liabilities, based on their market values. Thus, under the purchase method, the assets and liabilities of the acquired company are reported in the consolidated balance sheet based on their market value at the date of acquisition. The consolidated income statement will show expenses (depreciation and amortization) based on these market values. The principles of the purchase method have implicitly been used throughout this chapter.

Pooling-of-Interests Method   The pooling-of-interests method accounts for a corporate acquisition as the uniting of ownership interests of two companies by exchange of equity (common shares) securities. The exchange of equity interests is viewed as a change in *form*, not in *substance*. That is, the shareholders of the predecessor companies become shareholders in the new combined enterprise. Each of the predecessor companies continues carrying out its operations as before. Because there is no change in the substance of either the ownership interest or the nature of the activities of the enterprises involved, no new basis of accountability arises. That is, the book values of the assets and liabilities of the predecessor companies are carried over to the new combined, or consolidated, enterprise. Unlike the purchase method, assets and liabilities do not reflect market values at the date of acquisition on the consolidated balance sheet.

In Canada the CICA requires that the purchase method be used except in those rare circumstances where it is not possible to identify one of the parties as the acquirer.

This problem demonstrates the impact of the purchase method versus the pooling-of-interests method on the consolidated balance sheet and income statement.

P Ltd. and S Inc. decide to combine operations. Management estimates that the combination will save $50,000 a year in expenses of running the combined businesses. Columns (1) and (2) in Exhibit 13.32 show abbreviated single-company financial statements for P Ltd. and S Inc. before combination. S Inc. has 20,000 shares outstanding that sell for $84 per share in the market. The market value of S Inc. as a going concern is, then, $1,680,000. As shown in Column (3), S's shareholders have $1,230,000 of equity not recorded on the books. Of this $1,230,000, $400,000 is attributable to undervalued noncurrent assets, and $830,000 is attributable to goodwill. P Ltd. has 100,000 shares outstanding, which have a $5-par value and sell for $42 each in the market. Ignore income taxes throughout this problem.

    a. Assume that P Ltd. purchases S Inc. to combine their operations. P Ltd. issues (sells) 40,000 additional shares on the market for $42 each, or $1,680,000 in total, and uses the proceeds to purchase all shares of S Inc. for $84 each. (Each share of S Inc. is, in effect, "sold" for two shares of P Ltd.) P Ltd. has acquired 100 percent of the shares of S Inc. and now owns S Inc. P Ltd.'s acquisition of S Inc. would be accounted for as a purchase. P Ltd. decides to amortize the revalued asset costs over five years and to amortize the goodwill over 40 years. Complete column (4) to show the effects of purchase accounting.

    b. Assume that P Ltd. issued the 40,000 shares directly to the owners of S Inc. in return for their shares. The merger is treated as a pooling of interests. Complete column (5) to show the effects of pooling accounting.

c. Suggest reasons why managers of business firms involved in corporate acquisition might prefer the pooling-of-interests method.

Exhibit 13.32
Consolidated Statements
Comparing Purchase and
Pooling-of-Interest Methods
(Problem 38)

	Historical Cost		S Inc. Shown at Current Values (3)	P Ltd. & S Inc. Consolidated at Date of Acquisition	
	P Ltd. (1)	S Inc. (2)		Purchase (4)	Pooling of Interests (5)
Balance Sheets					
Assets:					
Current Assets	$1,500,000	$450,000	$ 450,000	$1,950,000	$1,950,000
Long-Term Assets Less Accumulated Depreciation	1,700,000	450,000	850,000	?	?
Goodwill	—	—	830,000	?	—
Total Assets	$3,200,000	$900,000	$2,130,000	$5,330,000	$4,100,000
Equities:					
Liabilities	$1,300,000	$450,000	$ 450,000	$1,750,000	$1,750,000
Share Capital ($5 par)	500,000	100,000	100,000	?	?
Contributed Surplus	200,000	150,000	150,000	?	?
Retained Earnings	1,200,000	200,000	200,000	?	?
Unrecorded Equity at Current Valuation	—	—	1,230,000	—	—
Total Liabilites and Shareholders' Equity . . .	$3,200,000	$900,000	$2,130,000	$5,330,000	$4,100,000

Income Statements					
(Ignoring Income Taxes)	**Actual**			**Projected**	
Precombination Income from Combination	$ 300,000	$160,000		$ 460,000	$ 460,000
Cost Savings (Projected)	—	—		50,000	50,000
Extra Depreciation Expense	—	—		?	—
Amortization of Goodwill	—	—		?	—
Net Income	$ 300,000	$160,000		$ 409,250	$ 510,000
Number of Common Shares Outstanding . . .	100,000	20,000		?	?
Earnings per Share	$3.00	$8.00		?	?
Rate of Return on Assets (Using Balances at Merger Date)				?	?
Rate of Return on Owners' Equity (Using Balances at Merger Date)				?	?

Assumptions: (1) S Inc. has 20,000 shares outstanding that sell for $84 each in the market.
          (2) P Ltd.'s shares sell for $42 each in the market. P Ltd. issues 40,000 shares for the purpose of acquiring
              S Inc.

39. *Determine specific balances on statements for six conditions.* The condensed,
single-company Balance Sheets and Statements of Retained Earnings of P Ltd. and S
Ltd. at December 31, Year 1, and Year 2 follow:

P Ltd. & S Ltd.
Condensed Comparative Balance Sheets
at December 31

	P Ltd.		S Ltd.	
	Year 2	Year 1	Year 2	Year 1
Current assets	$200,000	$160,000	$ 60,000	$ 40,000
Plant & Equipment	210,000	240,000	60,000	70,000
Investments (Note A)	220,000	200,000	—	—
Total Assets	$630,000	$600,000	$120,000	$110,000
Current Liabilities	$ 80,000	$ 70,000	$ 15,000	$ 10,000
Share Capital	200,000	200,000	60,000	60,000
Retained Earnings	350,000	330,000	45,000	40,000
Total Equities	$630,000	$600,000	$120,000	$110,000

(Note A) including investment in S Ltd. at amounts indicated below.

P Ltd. & S Ltd.
Statement of Retained Earnings
Years Ended December 31

	P Ltd.		S Ltd.	
	Year 2	Year 1	Year 2	Year 1
Opening Balance	$330,000	$300,000	$ 40,000	$ 30,000
Plus: Net Income	80,000	90,000	25,000	30,000
Less: Dividends	(60,000)	(60,000)	(20,000)	(20,000)
Closing Balance	$350,000	$330,000	$ 45,000	$ 40,000

When preparing P Ltd.'s financial statements, presented above, the bookkeeper incorrectly recorded the investment in S Ltd. on a cost basis—hence dividends received from S Ltd. are recorded as income of P Ltd.

It is the company's policy to amortize goodwill, if any, on the purchase of S Ltd. shares on a straight-line basis over ten years.

Alternatives (A-F) below represent unrelated events that occurred during Year 2.

Alternative A
P Ltd. purchased 100% of the shares of S Ltd. on January 1, Year 2 for $100,000.

Alternative B
P Ltd. purchased 10% of the shares of S Ltd. on January 1, Year 2 for $13,000. At December 31, Year 2, P Ltd. owed S Ltd. $12,000 on current account for merchandise purchased from S Ltd. which remained unsold at December 31. These goods cost S Ltd. $9,000.

Alternative C
P Ltd. purchased 80% of the shares of S Ltd. on January 1, Year 2 for $80,000. At December 31, Year 2, P Ltd. owed S Ltd. $13,000.

Alternative D
P Ltd. purchased 60% of the shares of S Ltd. on January 1, Year 2 for $63,000.

Alternative E

P Ltd. purchased 30% of the shares of S Ltd. on January 1, Year 2 for $36,000. At December 31, Year 2, S Ltd. owed P Ltd. $30,000 on current accounts for merchandise purchased from P Ltd. which remained unsold at December 31. These goods cost P Ltd. $16,000.

Alternative F

P Ltd. purchased 70% of the shares of S Ltd. on January 1, Year 2 for $84,000. At that date it was determined that the land owned by S Ltd. had a fair value of $25,000 in comparison with a book value of $10,000. At December 20, Year 2, P Ltd. sold S Ltd. on account a machine, with a book value of $40,000, for $60,000. The account had not been paid on December 31, Year 2.

For each of these events, A to F, calculate the amounts that would be reported in the Year 2 financial statements of P Ltd. (prepared in accordance with generally accepted accounting principles) for each of the following captions:

1. Investment in S Ltd.
2. Net Income
3. Minority Interest
4. Goodwill on Consolidation
5. Income from S Ltd. Investment
6. Total Assets

If the caption does not appear in the financial statements of P Ltd., insert ''N/A'' beside the caption.

40. *Determining specific balances on investor's statements.* On January 1, Year 1, P Ltd. purchased shares of X Ltd., Y Ltd., and Z Ltd. These were the only purchases made by P Ltd. in shares of other companies. None of these shares were sold in the next three years. The following information has been extracted from the consolidated balance sheet of P Ltd.:

	December 31	
	Year 3	Year 2
Investment in X Ltd.	$120,000	$120,000
Investment in Z Ltd.	18,000	16,000
Land (owned by Y Ltd.)	89,000	89,000
Minority interest in Y Ltd.	15,000	13,000
Goodwill on consolidation of Y Ltd.	14,000	16,000

In addition, the following information was made available from the footnotes to the financial statements, or direct enquiry:

1. P Ltd. follows the policy of amortizing goodwill on consolidation on a straight line basis over ten years.
2. P Ltd. purchased 90 percent of the shares of Y Ltd. on January 1, Year 1.
3. During Year 3 the following dividends were paid:

By X Ltd.	$200,000
By Y Ltd.	12,000
By Z Ltd.	7,500

4. The land presented above was owned by Y Ltd. on January 1, Year 1. At the date the fair value was $10,000 more than the book value.
5. During Year 3 the following incomes were reported by the companies:

P Ltd.	$107,000
X Ltd.	240,000
Y Ltd.	not available
Z Ltd.	not available

6. Income from long-term share investments reported in P Ltd.'s financial statements (prepared in conformity with GAAP) follow:

X Ltd.	$18,000
Y Ltd.	not available
Z Ltd.	5,000

7. The shares of Z Ltd. were purchased at their book value.
    Required: Calculate the following (show details of your calculations):
    1. The balance of shareholders' equity of Y Ltd. at December 31, Year 3.
    2. The percentage of shares of X Ltd. purchased by P Ltd.
    3. The income reported in the financial statements of Y Ltd. for the year ended December 31, Year 3.
    4. The cost of the land owned by Y Ltd. referred to above.
    5. The percentage of shares of Z Ltd. purchased by P Ltd.
    6. The total excess of the cost of shares in Y Ltd. over the book value of these shares on January 1, Year 1.

Decision Problem 13-1

"You mean that the company can *increase* its working capital by purchasing shares in Equity Corp.? That's creative accounting!!"

The above remark was made by C. Bartello, the president of Conglo Inc., who was concerned that the working capital of the company would fall below the amount specified in the company's bank loan agreements.

The controller of Conglo Inc. had suggested that, rather than sell the common shares in Equity Corp. for less than their book value, the company purchase an additional six percent of the shares for $400,000. This purchase would increase Conglo's common share investment in Equity Corp. from 45 percent to 51 percent. The Investment in Equity Corp. account has a current balance of $3,600,000.

The condensed balance sheet of Equity Corp. at a current date is presented in Exhibit 13.33.

The controller further recommended that, in order to increase the income of Conglo Inc., a portion of the increased working capital be used to purchase an additional four percent of the shares of Cost Ltd. for about $800,000. This purchase would increase the investment in the common shares of Cost Ltd. from 17 percent to 21 percent and would enable Conglo Inc. to exercise significant influence over Cost Ltd. The income of Cost Ltd. for the current year was $4,000,000 and was expected to increase by ten percent each year as a consequence of the company policy of reinvesting about half of each year's income for expansion.

Exhibit 13.33
EQUITY CORP.
Condensed Balance Sheet
at a Current Date
(thousands of dollars)

Current Assets	$ 5,000	Current Liabilites	$ 2,000
Plant and Equipment (net)	12,000	Noncurrent Liabilities	7,000
		Shareholders' Equity	8,000
Total	$17,000	Total	$17,000

Was the result of the controller's suggestion valid? Did it conform to generally accepted accounting principles?

Chapter 14   Statement of Changes in Financial Position: Revisited

Chapter 5 introduced the statement of changes in financial position, discussing its rationale and illustrating a T-account approach for preparing the statement. Subsequent chapters have described briefly the impact of various transactions on the statement of changes in financial position. This chapter synthesizes these chapter-by-chapter discussions by providing a comprehensive example of a statement of changes in financial position.

Before beginning to read this Chapter, it is suggested that you review Chapter 5 as well as the sections on pages 356, 401, 446, 509, 513, 590 and 616.

Review of T-Account Procedure for Preparing Statement of Changes in Financial Position

The statement of changes in financial position is typically prepared after the balance sheet and income statement. The procedure described and illustrated in Chapter 5 is summarized as follows:

Step 1 Obtain a balance sheet for the beginning and end of the period for which the statement of changes in financial position is to be prepared.

Step 2 Prepare a T-account work sheet. At the top of the work sheet is a master T-account for cash position.[1] The T-account has sections labeled Operations, Investing, Financing, and Dividends. The beginning and ending balances of cash position are entered in the master T-account. The T-account work sheet is completed by preparing a T-account for each balance sheet account other than cash position and entering the beginning and ending balances.

Step 3 Explain the change in the cash position account between the beginning and end of the period by explaining, or accounting for, the changes in the other balance sheet accounts. This step is accomplished by reconstructing the entries originally made in the accounts during the period and entering them in appropriate T-accounts on the work sheet. Once the changes in these other balance sheet accounts have been explained, the change in cash position will have been explained.

Step 4 Prepare a statement of changes in financial position using information in the T-account work sheet.

---

[1] In Chapter 5 the T-account was entitled Cash. This was acceptable because none of the examples involved cash equivalents or short-term bank borrowings. However, these additional components of cash position (see page 215) are introduced in this chapter so the T-account should be properly labeled Cash Position.

Comprehensive Illustration of Statement of Changes in Financial Position

Data for Courtis Corporation for Year 2 is used in this comprehensive illustration of the statement of changes in financial position. Exhibit 14.1 presents a comparative balance sheet as of December 31, Year 1 and Year 2; Exhibit 14.2 presents an income statement for Year 2; Exhibit 14.3 presents the T-accounts; and Exhibit 14.4 presents the completed statement of changes in financial position. In the sections that follow, each of the line items in Exhibit 14.4 is discussed.

Cash Position

From Exhibit 14.1, cash position can be computed:

	Cash Position Beginning of Year 2	Cash Position End of Year 2
Cash	$ 1,150	$ 1,050
Certificates of Deposit	1,800	980
Temporary Investments	—	—
Short-term bank indebtedness	(2,000)	(2,750)
	$ 950	($720)

These numbers become the starting and ending balances in the master T-account for cash position and on the statement of changes in financial position.

Exhibit 14.1
COURTIS CORPORATION
Consolidated Balance Sheet

	December 31	
	Year 1	Year 2
Assets		
Current Assets:		
Cash	$ 1,150	$ 1,050
Certificate of Deposit	1,800	980
Accounts Receivable (net)	3,400	4,300
Inventory	1,500	2,350
Prepayments	800	600
Total Current Assets	$ 8,650	$ 9,280
Investments:		
Investment in Company A (15%)	$ 1,200	$ 1,200
Investment in Company B (40%)	2,100	2,420
Total Investments	$ 3,300	$ 3,620
Property, Plant, and Equipment:		
Land	$ 1,000	$ 1,000
Buildings	8,600	8,900
Equipment	10,840	11,540
Less Accumulated Depreciation	(6,420)	(6,490)
Total Property, Plant, and Equipment	$14,200	$14,950

	December 31	
	Year 1	Year 2
Intangible Assets:		
Patent	$ 2,550	$ 2,550
Less Accumulated Amortization	(600)	(750)
Total Intangible Assets	$ 1,950	$ 1,800
Total Assets	$28,100	$29,650
Liabilities and Shareholders' Equity		
Current Liabilities:		
Bank Notes Payable	$ 2,000	$ 2,750
Accounts Payable	2,250	3,000
Warranties Payable	1,200	1,000
Advances from Customers	600	900
Total Current Liabilities	$ 6,050	$ 7,650
Noncurrent Liabilities:		
Bonds Payable	$ 2,820	$ 1,370
Capitalized Lease Obligation	1,800	2,100
Future Income Taxes	550	650
Total Noncurrent Liabilities	$ 5,170	$ 4,120
Minority Interest in Consolidated Subsidiary	$ 200	$ 230
Shareholders' Equity:		
Preferred Shares	$ 1,000	$ 1,200
Common Shares	2,000	2,100
Contributed Surplus	4,000	4,200
Retained Earnings	9,930	10,530
Total	$16,930	$18,030
Less Cost of Treasury Shares	(250)	(380)
Total Shareholders' Equity	$16,680	$17,650
Total Liabilities and Shareholders' Equity	$28,100	$29,650

Exhibit 14.2
COURTIS CORPORATION
Consolidated Income Statement for Year 2

Revenues:	
Sales	$10,500
Interest and Dividends	320
Equity in Earnings of Affiliate	480
Gain on Sale of Equipment	50
Total Revenues	$11,350

Expenses:

Cost of Goods Sold	$ 6,000
Selling and Administration	3,550
Interest	450
Income Taxes	300
Total Expenses	$10,300
Net Income before Minority Interest	$ 1,050
Less Minority Interest in Earnings	(50)
Net Income	$ 1,000

Exhibit 14.3 presents a T-account work sheet for Courtis Corporation for Year 2.

Exhibit 14.3
COURTIS CORPORATION
T-Account Work Sheet

Cash Position

✔ 950

Operations

Net Income	(10)	1,000	50	(15)	Bond Premium Amortization
Depreciation Expense Addback	(11)	700	30	(1)	Gain on Sale of Equipment
Amortization Expense Addback	(12)	150	320	(16)	Equity in Undistributed Earnings
Minority Interest in Consolidated Subsidiary	(13)	50	900	(20)	Increase in Accounts Receivable
Future Income Taxes	(14)	100	850	(21)	Increase in Inventories
Decrease in Prepayment	(19)	200	200	(22)	Decrease in Warranties Payable
Increase in Accounts Payable	(17)	750			
Increase in Advances from Customers	(18)	300			

Investing

Sale of Equipment	(1)	180	1,300	(6)	Acquisition of Equipment
			300	(3)	Acquisition of Building through Capital Lease

Financing

Capital Lease Obligation Incurred in Acquisition of Building	(3)	300	300	(5)	Conversion of Long-Term Bonds into Common Shares
Long-Term Bonds Issued	(2)	400	1,500	(7)	Retirement of Long-Term Debt
Preferred Shares Issued	(4)	200	130	(8)	Acquisition of Common Shares
Common Shares Issued on Conversion of Bonds	(5)	300			

Dividends   420 (9)

✔ 720

Accounts Receivable	
✔ 3,400	
(20) 900	
✔ 4,300	

Inventories	
✔ 1,500	
(21) 850	
✔ 2,350	

Prepayments	
✔ 800	
	200 (19)
✔ 600	

Investment in Company A	
✔ 1,200	
✔ 1,200	

Investment in Company B	
✔ 2,100	
(16) 320	
✔ 2,420	

Land	
✔ 1,000	
✔ 1,000	

Buildings	
✔ 8,600	
(3) 300	
✔ 8,900	

Equipment	
✔ 10,840	
(6) 1,300	600 (1)
✔ 11,540	

Accumulated Depreciation	
	6,240 ✔
(1) 450	700 (11)
	6,490 ✔

Patent	
✔ 2,550	
✔ 2,550	

Accumulated Amortization	
	600 ✔
	150 (12)
	750 ✔

Accounts Payable	
	2,250 ✔
	750 (17)
	3,000 ✔

Warranties Payable	
	1,200 ✔
(22) 200	
	1,000 ✔

Advances from Customers	
	600 ✔
	300 (18)
	900 ✔

Bonds Payable	
	2,820 ✔
(15) 50	400 (2)
(5) 300	
(7) 1,500	
	1,370 ✔

Capitalized Lease Obligation	
	1,800 ✔
	300 (3)
	2,100 ✔

Future Income Taxes	
	550 ✔
	100 (14)
	650 ✔

Minority Interest in Consolidated Subsidiary	
	200 ✔
(9) 20	50 (13)
	230 ✔

Preferred Shares	
	1,000 ✔
	200 (4)
	1,200 ✔

Common Shares	
	2,000 ✔
	100 (5)
	2,100 ✔

Contributed Surplus	
	4,000 ✔
	200 (5)
	4,200 ✔

Retained Earnings	
	9,930 ✔
(9) 400	1,000 (10)
	10,530 ✔

Treasury Stock	
✔ 250	
(8) 130	
✔ 380	

Exhibit 14.4
COURTIS CORPORATION
Consolidated Statement of Changes in Financial Position for Year 2

Cash Provided by:

Operations		$ 900
Investing Activities		
(1) Sale of equipment		180
Financing Activities		
(2) Long-term bonds issued	$ 400	
(3) Capital lease obligation incurred	300	
(4) Preferred shares issued	200	
(5) Common shares issued	300	
		1,200
		$ 2,280

Cash Applied To:

Investing Activities		
(6) Acquisition of equipment	$(1,300)	
(3) Acquisition of building through capital lease	(300)	
		(1,600)
Financing Activities		
(7) Retirement of long-term debt	$(1,500)	
(5) Conversion of long-term bonds and common shares	(300)	
(8) Treasury shares acquired	(130)	
		(1,930)
(9) Dividends		(420)
		$(3,950)
Increase (Decrease) in Cash Position		$(1,670)
Cash Position at Beginning of Year		950
Cash Position at End of Year		$ (720)

Cash Provided by Operations	
(10) Net Income	$ 1,000
Add (deduct) items not affecting cash flow	
(11) Depreciation	700
(12) Amortization of patent	150
(13) Minority interest in consolidated earnings	50
(14) Future income taxes	100
(15) Amortization of bond premium	(50)
(1) Gain on sale of equipment	(30)
(16) Equity in undistributed earnings of affiliate	(320)
	1,600

Working Capital Accounts	
Cash provided by net increases in Accounts Payable (17), and Advances on Contracts (18)	1,050
Cash provided by net decrease in prepayments (19)	200
Cash applied to net increase in Receivables (20) and Inventory (21)	(1,750)
Cash applied to net decrease in Warranties Payable (22)	(200)
Cash Provided by Operations	$ 900

Item 1: Gain on Sale of Equipment   The accounting records indicate that a machine originally costing $600 and on which accumulated depreciation of $450 had been taken was sold for $180 during Year 2. The journal entry made to record this sale was as follows:

(1) Cash	180	
Accumulated Depreciation	450	
Equipment		600
Gain on Sale of Equipment		30

The cash proceeds of $180 are shown as an increase in cash from an investing activity. The $30 gain on the sale is included in net income. To avoid overstating the amount of cash derived from this sale, the $30 gain must be subtracted from net income in computing cash from operations.

(1) Cash (Investing—Sale of Equipment)	180	
Accumulated Depreciation	450	
Equipment		600
Cash (Operations—Gain on Sale of Equipment		
Subtraction)		30

Note that all cash proceeds are classified as investing activities and none as operating activities. Most firms acquire and sell plant assets with the objective of providing a capacity to carry out operations rather than as a means of generating operating income.

   If plant assets are sold at a loss instead of a gain, the loss must be added back to net income in deriving cash flow from operations. The typical work sheet entry would be as follows:

Cash (Investing—Sale of Equipment)	X	
Accumulated Depreciation	X	
Cash (Operations—Loss on Sale of Equipment Addback) ..	X	
Equipment		X

Item 2: Long-Term Bonds Issued   Long-term bonds totaling $400 were issued during Year 2.

(2) Cash (Financing—Long-Term Bonds Issued)	400	
Bonds Payable		400

Item 3: Acquisition of Building through Capital Lease   A long-term lease was signed during Year 2 for a building. This lease was classified as a capital lease and recorded in the accounts as follows:

(3) Building	300	
Capitalized Lease Obligations		300

Note that this entry does not affect cash. It does affect the investing and financing activities of Courtis Corporation and can be shown either in the statement of changes in financial position or in a supplementary schedule. Courtis Corporation indicates the transaction in its statement of changes in financial position with the following work sheet entry:

(3) Cash (Investing—Acquisition of Building through Capital Lease)	300	
Cash (Financing—Capital Lease Obligation Incurred in Acquisition of Building)		300

Should companies be made to air their forecasts?

Jack McArthur

Stop talking about yesterday. How do you see tomorrow?

Investors, stock market analysts and securities regulators constantly urge this upon the often reluctant bosses of companies with shares available for trading.

One such advocate is Stanley Beck, chairman of the Ontario Securities Commission. He says the commission is thinking of introducing a sweeping requirement that companies tell investors, in some detail, of trends and events that may affect how they'll do in the future.

He and many others say that the now-extensive discussion of the past and the present doesn't really represent good corporate disclosure.

The key to investor decisions—to buy, ignore, sell or continue to own a stock—hinges less on history than on the future and what the company plans for it. That will determine whether or not the company will prosper and whether or not the investors make money on their investments.

So, it's natural that there's a pressure for such information, especially because it's sure to exist. Any company will have its own formal or informal analysis of the trends and a program for coping with them.

The normal corporate impulse, though, is to be secretive. Forecasts are dicey. It's easy to be wrong and no one likes to risk the embarrassment of being wrong in public.

Another thing: corporate judgments of the future are subject to constant alteration, especially in times as uncertain

as these. That would put a heavy burden on the company to keep updating its disclosures. And, when an earlier analysis is wrong, and a company changes its view, some investors are bound to be angry, even suspicious of motives. They made decisions on the basis of one forecast and now they're left out on a limb! The results differ from the forecasts and the company has changed its tune.

Shareholders may ask antagonistic questions at the next annual meeting. Analysts may make pointed comments.

Obviously, this is not an easy matter for companies, no matter how eager they are to build a good reputation for good disclosure. Still, they have little choice but to do more future thinking for the public. The pressure is too great to resist.

That's clear from the comments of the judges in the latest *Financial Post* contest for the best corporate annual reports, held last November. One judge had cited as a "common omission" any "clear statement or discussion of corporate goals and strategies"—a future-oriented topic. Another wanted "more specific information about objectives and plans." Said another, "all too often companies still say little of substance about the future or they bury comments about the outlook."

In a general sense, it's true that much of business is in a constant state of being dragged kicking and screaming into the information age. With honourable exceptions, companies with shares in the public's hands are slow to venture on to new frontiers in providing clear, comprehensive details on themselves.

It has always taken pressure from regulators to achieve much progress. Disclosure does, after all, take money and time. It sometimes edges into the area of telling competitors more than is comfortable.

While voluntary efforts to play fair with investors are reasonably widespread among larger corporations—many small resource companies are simply disgusting—it has long been clear that most executives have to be pushed.

Indeed, voluntarism can be a problem. It's better that all should be forced to meet certain standards, otherwise the secretive, bad guy may win an advantage. But it's wrong to hang shareholders or prospective shareholders out to dry. They deserve a generous flow of material useful for making good choices.

If that bothers a company—and it can be hurtful or embarrassing at times—it should leave the arena. It shouldn't expect to enjoy the benefits of having public shareholders and escape any drawbacks.

As to the future, let's consider a certain irony concerning Canada Trustco. The big trust company was the winner of the grand prize for best-in show of *The Financial Post's* contest.

Canada Trustco, despite its own objections, was recently taken over by Genstar. That makes the trust firm's marvelous disclosure policies less meaningful for investors. Now that Genstar has snapped up almost all of Canada Trustco's shares, it has only about 1,200 shareholders compared with the earlier 6,700.

The latest (as of this writing) monthly report to Canada Trustco shareholders, signed by chairman Arthur Mingay and president Mervyn Lahn, says of the future:

"The emerging Canada Trust" (assuming its merger with the large Canada Permanent, also controlled by Genstar) "will be both bigger and better—a unique and significant competitor . . . ideally positioned . . ."

Well, maybe. But these same executives would have had a different attitude a few months earlier. Then they were bitterly resisting any thought that Canada Trustco should be taken over, merged with some other company or controlled by a single owner. They thought that was bad for Canada and the company.

You can see that opinions about the future do indeed change radically in a short time.

Reprinted with permission of *The Bottom Line*, January 1986.

Item 4: Preferred Shares Issued   Preferred shares totaling $200 were issued during the year.

(4) Cash (Financing—Preferred Share Issued)	200	
Preferred Shares		200

Item 5: Conversion of Debt to Common Shares   The conversion of debt to common share is a transaction that does not directly affect cash but represents a financing transaction. It is disclosed as a source and as an application in offsetting amounts. An analysis of the balance sheet for Courtis Corporation shows that Contributed Surplus increased by $200. It can be inferred that the conversion of bonds into common shares resulted in the following entry:

Bonds Payable	300	
Common Shares		100
Contributed Surplus		200

| (5) Cash (Financing—Conversion of Long-Term Bonds into Common Shares) .... | 300 | |
| Cash (Financing—Issue of Common Shares in Bond Conversion) .... | | 300 |

Item 6: Acquisition of Equipment   Equipment costing $1,300 was acquired during Year 2. The analytic entry for this investing activity is as follows:

| (6) Equipment .... | 1,300 | |
| Cash (Investing—Acquisition of Equipment) .... | | 1,300 |

Item 7: Retirement of Long-Term Debt   Courtis Corporation retired $1,500 of long-term debt at maturity and would make the following work sheet entry:

| (7) Bonds Payable .... | 1,500 | |
| Cash (Financing—Retirement of Long-Term Debt) ... | | 1,500 |

If the debt had been retired prior to maturity, it is likely that a gain or loss would have been recognized. The gain or loss would have been eliminated from net income in computing cash flow from operations, and the full amount of cash used to retire the debt would have been classified as a financing activity.

Item 8: Acquisition of Common Shares   Common shares costing $130 were acquired during Year 2.

| (8) Treasury Shares .... | 130 | |
| Cash (Financing—Acquisition of Common Shares) ... | | 130 |

Item 9: Dividends   Courtis Corporation declared and paid $400 of dividends to its shareholders during Year 2. In addition, a consolidated subsidiary paid $20 of dividends to minority shareholders (see discussion of Line 13). The analytic entry is as follows:

(9) Retained Earnings	400	
Minority Interest in Consolidated Subsidiary	20	
Cash (Dividends)		420

Item 10: Net Income   The income statement indicates that net income for the period was $1,000. The work sheet entry presumes that cash is provisionally increased by the amount of net income.

| (10) Cash (Operations—Net Income) .... | 1,000 | |
| Retained Earnings .... | | 1,000 |

Item 11: Depreciation Expense Addback   Internal records indicate that depreciation of $500 was included in cost of goods sold and depreciation of $200 was included in selling and administrative expenses. None of this $700 of depreciation required an operating cash outflow during Year 2. Thus it must be added back to net income in deriving cash flow from operations.

(11) Cash (Operations—Depreciation Expense Addback) ...	700	
Accumulated Depreciation		700

Item 12: Amortization of Patent   The treatment of patent amortization is identical to that of depreciation. Company records indicate that patent amortization of $150 was recorded during Year 2 and was included in cost of goods sold. The work sheet entry is as follows:

(12) Cash (Operations—Amortization Expense Addback)	150	
Accumulated Amortization		150

Item 13: Minority Interest in Consolidated Earnings   The financial statement in Exhibits 14.1, 14.2, and 14.4 are consolidated statements for Courtis Corporation and its majority-owned subsidiaries. Courtis does not own all of the shares of some of its consolidated subsidiaries. The minority shareholders in these subsidiaries have a claim on the earnings of their respective subsidiaries. The income statement in Exhibit 14.3 indicates that the minority interest in earnings of $50 has been subtracted in computing consolidated net income. This amount does not use cash and must be added back to net income to compute cash flow from operations. The analytic entry on the work sheet is as follows:

(13) Cash (Operations—Minority Interest)	50	
Minority Interest in Consolidated subsidiary		50

The balance sheet in Exhibit 14.2 indicates that the account titled Minority Interest in Consolidated Subsidiary increased during Year 2 by $30 (= $230 − $200). Because the account increased by $50 for the minority interest in earnings, dividends of $20 must have been paid to these shareholders during the year. The work sheet entry for these dividends is discussed in conjunction with the consideration of dividends (Item 9).

Item 14: Future Income Taxes   Notes to the financial statements of Courtis Corporation indicate that income tax expense of $300 is composed of $200 of currently payable taxes and $100 of future income taxes. The $100 of future income taxes reduced net income but did not require a cash outflow during Year 2. This amount must, therefore, be added back to net income.

(14) Cash (Operations—Future Tax Addback)	100	
Future Income Taxes		100

Item 15: Amortization of Bond Premium   Included in Bonds Payable on the balance sheet is one series of bonds that were initially issued at a premium (that is,

the coupon rate exceeded the required market rate of interest). The bond premium must be amortized over the life of the bonds as a reduction in interest expense. The entry made in the accounting records for this bond during the period was as follows:

(15) Interest Expense	300	
Bonds Payable	50	
Cash		350

Cash of $350 was expended even though only $300 of interest expense had been subtracted in computing net income. An additional $50 must be subtracted from net income to derive cash flow from operations.

(15) Bonds Payable	50	
Cash (Operations—Bond Premium Amortization		50
Subtraction)		

Note that cash used for interest expense is classified as an operating, not a financing, activity because it is viewed as a cost of carrying out operations.

Item 16: Equity in Undistributed Earnings of Affiliate   The balance sheet indicates that Courtis Corporation owns 40 percent of the common stock of Company B. During Year 2, Company B earned $1,200 and paid $400 of dividends. Courtis Corporation made the following entries on its books during the year.

(16) Investment in Company B	480	
Equity in Earnings of Affiliate		480
Cash	160	
Investment in Company B		160
.40 × $400 = $160.		

Net income of Courtis Corporation in Exhibit 14.4 includes $480 of equity income. Only $160 of cash was received. Thus a subtraction of $320 (= $480 − $160) must be made from net income in deriving cash from operations.

(16) Investment in Company B	320	
Cash (Operations—Equity in Undistributed Earnings		
Subtraction)		320

The investment in Company A shown in the balance sheet in Exhibit 14.2 is accounted for using cost method. During Year 2, dividends of $100 were received and included in Interest and Dividends on the income statement. Because these dividends provided cash, no adjustment is made to net income in computing cash flow from operations.

Item 17: Increase in Accounts Payable   An increase in accounts payable indicates that more costs were incurred on account and cash payments delayed than the amount paid during Year 2 for previous purchases on account. This increase in accounts payable, a credit change in an operating current liability account, implicitly increases cash from operations.

| (17) Cash (Operations—Increase in Accounts Payable) . . . . . | 750 | |
| Accounts Payable . . . . | | 750 |

Item 18: Increase in Advances from Customers   The $300 increase in customer advances means that $300 more cash was received during Year 2 than was recognized as revenue. The excess must be added to net income in deriving cash flow from operations.

| (18) Cash (Operations—Increase in Advances on Contracts) | 300 | |
| Advances from Customers . . . . | | 300 |

Item 19: Decrease in Prepayments   Because prepayments decreased by $200 during Year 2, less cash was expended during Year 2 for new prepayments than was amortized from prepayments of earlier years. Thus $200 must be added to net income for this credit change in an operating current asset account.

| (19) Cash (Operations—Decrease in Prepayments) . . . . | 200 | |
| Prepayments . . . . | | 200 |

Item 20: Increase in Accounts Receivable   The increase in accounts receivable indicates that less cash was collected from customers than the amount shown for sales on account. Thus the increase in accounts receivable, a debit change in an operating current asset account, must be subtracted from net income.

| (20) Accounts Receivable . . . . | 900 | |
| Cash (Operations—Increase in Accounts Receivable) | | 900 |

Note that this entry automatically incorporates the effect of any change in the Allowance for Uncollectible Accounts. Separate work sheet entries could be made for the change in gross accounts receivable and allowance for uncollectible accounts.

Item 21: Increase in Inventories   The increase in inventories indicates that more merchandise was purchased than was sold during Year 2. Thus more cash was used than the amount shown for cost of goods sold.[2] A subtraction from net income is required for this debit change in an operating current asset account.

| (21) Inventories . . . . | 850 | |
| Cash (Operations—Increase in Inventories) . . . . | | 850 |

Item 22: Decrease in Warranties Payable   Recall that Warranties Payable is increased for the estimated cost of future warranty services on products sold during the period and is decreased by the actual cost of warranty services performed. During Year 2, $200 more in costs was incurred and paid in cash than was included in

---

[2]To correctly compute the cash flow effect, the change in accounts payable must also be considered. See Item 17.

expenses on the income statement. This decrease in Warranties Payable, a debit change in an operating current liability account, must be subtracted from net income.

(22) Warranties Payable	200	
Cash (Operations—Decrease in Warranties Payable)		200

Cash flow from operations is $900 for Year 2.

Cash management in Canada: How the system works

*T*he basic principles and objectives of cash management within the United States and Canada are very similar. But despite the similarities, differences in the payment and banking systems in each country have resulted in very different methods being used to meet these objectives. American cash managers who are unfamiliar with these differences often request their Canadian subsidiaries to use specific cash management techniques and services which may be effective in the U.S. but are inappropriate or unnecessary in Canada. Opportunities are often missed because American cash managers are unaware that Canada's nationwide banking and payment systems provide cash management benefits that are unavailable in most other countries, including the U.S.

The U.S. has nearly 15,000 banks (of which the top six hold 20 percent of American bank assets), and more than 10,000 thrift institutions.

In the U.S., banks have been restricted geographically and operationally by federal law from setting up an interstate branch network. While there has been a recent emergence of limited interstate branching, it is governed by various restrictive regulations that will hinder the move toward nationwide branching.

In Canada, the chartered banks include nine Schedule A banks and 55 Schedule B banks. All operate within the mandate set out in the federal Bank Act, which allows a nationwide system of branch banking.

The six largest Schedule A banks have a long history of growth and sta-

bility. Their extensive on-line systems and advanced automated services have linked their national branch networks coast to coast and have permitted centralization of the financial operations of major corporations. Collectively, these six banks own 97 percent of Canada's 7,000 bank branches, which are located almost everywhere in the country and in many parts of the world.

Most of the Schedule B banks are foreign-bank subsidiaries, which concentrate on specialized lending to specific target markets. Only a few offer a full range of services or comprehensive service delivery networks. Even fewer provide cash management capabilities in Canada.

The remaining members of the Canadian banking system include approximately 70 trust companies and 3,000 credit unions ("near banks").

Although the Canadian payment system has looser geographic restrictions than does the American system, Canadian banks do have legislative restrictions on their activities. Traditionally, the Canadian financial system has been based on the concept of four separate "pillars"—banking, insurance, trusts, and securities—with rigidly defined functions. For example, the Bank Act restrains banks from offering data processing services for nonbank activities, engaging in fiduciary activities, underwriting or handling private placement of corporate securities, and providing investment advice.

This traditional separation of core functions is being revised and does not apply to Canadian bank development outside Canada, where Canadian banks operate trust, securities, and investment or merchant banking subsidiaries in conjunction with their primary functions of commercial and consumer lending.

Check-clearing system

Check clearing in the U.S. is not centralized. Most checks are cleared through the Federal Reserve and, in addition, there are local clearing houses, automated clearing houses (some under the control of the Federal Reserve and some under private control), and "direct-send" arrangements between numerous combinations of correspondent banks. Consequently, when a check is deposited, the funds are held and availability may not be given to the depositor until the check has been withdrawn from the payor's account.

When multiple local banks or out-of-town checks are involved, availability may not be given for two or three days. Because so many banks and near banks operate in the U.S., the "bank float" problem will not soon disappear.

In contrast, the Canadian check and electronic clearing system is controlled by the Canadian Payments Association, whose membership comprises the chartered banks and several other financial institutions. The current 119 members clear their own items and act as clearing agents for other banks or near banks. Although funds transfers may originate with any of the financial institutions, most corporate transactions move through Canada's "Big Six" Schedule A banks and their branches.

The strong nationwide branch system and a long history of financial stability and interaction among the relatively few Canadian banks have fostered a high level of trust among them. This allows same-day settlement and availability for all Canadian dollar items deposited, regardless of the banks involved or where in Canada the bank accounts are located.

The efficiency of the Canadian payment system, which settles checks overnight through the Bank of Canada, has precluded the need for payment techniques such as remote or controlled disbursement.

Multibank balance reporting

In the U.S., the larger number of banks and the state branching restrictions have imposed a need for multiple banking relationships, delayed credit for deposits, and caused a need for precise float measurement.

A large corporation may deal with several hundred unaffiliated banks every day. Even a small retail chain with five outlets in one city might have to deal with five or six banks. When it became economically unsound for large corporations to leave surplus funds in non-interest-bearing accounts at all their banks to make payments and to compensate the banks, the need became more critical to monitor these balances daily.

Multibank balance reporting services meet this need to assist American cash managers to determine the consolidated cash positions of their organizations. Once these are confirmed, the funds are mobilized in order to meet corporate financial objectives.

There is less need for multibank balance reporting in Canada because of the national branch networks—even the smallest communities are served by a major bank, and often by more than one. Since the 1970s, Canadian banks have provided their customers with numerous reporting options through on-line multibranch balance reporting. Consequently, the banking needs of a very large Canadian corporation can be fulfilled by dealing with one or two banks.

Intrabank funds concentration

In the U.S., deferred availability makes it difficult to accurately determine total funds for use. Complex interbank routines are required even for intracompany movement of collected funds. Typically, an organization's concentration bank must issue and send depository transfer checks (DTCs) to each remote bank to draw down funds. Even electronic DTCs do not provide same-day availability.

Electronic items are cleared separately from checks by means of a network of automated clearing houses. To expedite the settlement of high-value payments, wire transfer systems have been developed. These include Fed-Wire, BankWire, CHIPS, and systems operated by local clearing house associations.

In Canada, electronic items are exchanged at the check clearing points. Intra-bank funds concentration (and disbursement) is simple, quick, and inexpensive because of nationwide branch and on-line computer networks.

The Canadian system allows bank clients to consolidate or disburse their funds electronically. Regardless of geographic distance, deposits made at a local branch can receive same day value through automatic transfers to a concentration branch (or funds can be disbursed from the concentration account to the field account). This reduces the number of banks (or branches) with which the cash manager must do business and allows easy centralization or disbursement of funds to meet the company's needs.

Although specific features and options differ from bank to bank, Canada's centralized banking system can provide a daily snapshot of the net position of an entire organization and gives full value for the total cash pool. This can reduce a company's overall borrowing requirements because cash-generating subsidiaries can fund those that need cash. The corporation has all the benefits of a central operation, tighter control over bank accounts and funds at the local level, and the maximum use of its funds, without taking away local autonomy in the management of payables and receivables.

Some banks offer enhancements to this service. For example, an automated interest allocation reporting system exists that identifies the suppliers and users of funds within a firm. This information allows company treasurers to act, in effect, as internal bankers for their organizations. It also helps in charging back

the interest expense to the subsidiaries that are users of cash and in crediting interest income to those that are contributors of cash. Sophisticated services of this sort can usually be delivered through the head office's bank branch or through an in-office microcomputer.

Computerized delivery systems

The major Canadian banks can provide in-office delivery of bank products through interactive terminal facilities. The systems are similar in their general features, but differ greatly in their specific capabilities. In general, they provide information on balances, transactions, and rates; reports or raw data for various banking services; the ability to input and receive information for payroll preparation or security transactions; and the ability to initiate various types of funds transfers.

On most Canadian in-office delivery systems, the ''start-of-day consolidated balance'' is a statement of the organization's net position. Generally, it reflects all activity and all check clearings of the previous business day.

Multibank reporting on a Canadian in-office delivery system, as with American systems, is subject to the reliability of the banks reporting into the system. Multibank information may, therfore, be less accurate or timely than multi-branch information.

Intrabank services delivered through interactive terminal facilities are accurate and easy to use. This is because many activities—such as offsetting, netting, zero balancing, and money movement—are automatic. Moreover, in the Canadian payment system, features such as availability reports and target balancing are not needed.

Most Canadian in-office delivery systems can be accessed worldwide. This means a multinational corporation can monitor its Canadian banking network from anywhere in the world.

Disbursement services

Canadian banks offer a direct deposit service—similar to an ACH credit—that electronically credits payee accounts on specified value dates. This service is particularly useful when combined with the payroll systems available through the major Canadian banks. The Canadian subsidiary of a multinational corporation can provide the payroll service supplier with payment information on magnetic tape or transmit the information directly to the data centers. The payments are prepared and can be distributed throughout the banking system to any branch of any financial institution in Canada. In addition to payrolls, this service is also valuable for pensions, stock dividends, annuities, insurance payments, and almost all recurring payments.

In Canada, there is currently no formal method for corporate-to-corporate electronic payments that is similar to the Corporate Trade Payment program offered by the National Automated Clearing House Association. However, a number of different programs for inter-institutional payments are evolving and standards are being developed. The smaller number of financial institutions in Canada makes domestic interbank funds concentration comparatively easier.

The efficiency of the Canadian payment system in the area of disbursement services has afforded less room for creativity; Canadian banks emphasize precise regulation, information, and automation, as opposed to float maximization.

In both countries, the type of collection services required by a company is determined by its customer base and the payment system in which it operates.

In the U.S., the ban on interstate branching has made the lock box service a necessity for corporations that collect payments in more than one state. Corporations with nationwide lock boxes must use a lock box network or cope with the problem of transferring funds through wire transfers or DTCs (both paper and electronic varieties) to their major concentration bank. Availability of funds and mail times are the key to lock box decisions.

In Canada, less emphasis is placed on lock box services. The branch banking system allows the major banks to offer concentration services to enable a company's local offices to collect payments and deposit them at the nearest branch of the company's bank from which the funds are transferred automatically. That allows them same-day value at the concentration branch.

Results from a number of Canadian studies show that mail times are generally longer and more variable than those in the U.S. The use of lock boxes in Canada is justified on the basis of mail time savings and reduced internal processing. Canadian banks can do computerized lock box location analyses to determine if the savings are worthwhile.

Lengthy mail delays place a premium on intercepting large value northbound and southbound payments in both countries before they cross the border. An American company with Canadian revenues but no sales office in Canada may find it useful to have at least one lock box location in Canada for collecting its Canadian dollar receipts. Depending on the location of the American collection bank, a five- to ten-day cash flow saving could result from the use of a lock box in Canada.

Canadian banks can be paid for financial services with fees or compensating balances. An account analysis in Canada is usually conducted annually and is based on an actual sample from an agreed-upon typical operating period. The amount and type of compensation is agreed upon for the year.

Bank compensation in Canada takes service fees, balances, and Bank of Canada reserve requirements into account. Most banks provide ''unbundled'' pricing for each of their operating services. This pricing takes the form of a monthly fee and/or a per item charge, as is the case for transaction-based services.

The majority of the differences between Canada and U.S. cash management products are based on the distinctive banking systems that exist in the two countries. The primary Canadian cash management goal is not float management but rather a combination of up-to-date information, improved efficiency, and considerable flexibility in reporting formats and bank/business arrangements.

The major Canadian banks offer many sophisticated cash management services that take advantage of the country's national banking structure. American cash managers who seek to structure the cash management procedures of their

Canadian subsidiaries should be knowledgeable about the Canadian banking and payment systems and should seek professional advice on available products and services to capitalize on these systems.

Reprinted with permission of *Financial Executive.* Sept./Oct. 1987.

Problems and Cases

1. *Effect on Statement of Changes in Financial Position.* Refer to Exhibit 5.19, where a simplified statement of changes in financial position is presented. For each of the transactions that follow, indicate the number(s) of the line(s) in Exhibit 5.19 that would be affected. If net income is affected, be sure to indicate if it increases or decreases. Ignore income tax effects. (See page 248.)

   a. Long-term bonds are retired, using funds in a bond sinking fund.
   b. A cash dividend is received from an unconsolidated subsidiary accounted for using the equity method.
   c. Accounts are written off as uncollectible when the allowance method is used.
   d. Marketable securities are purchased for cash.
   e. Land is sold for an amount greater than its acquisition cost.
   f. A firm's annual cash contribution to a bond sinking fund is made.
   g. A fully amortized patent is written off.
   h. Land is given in settlement of annual legal fees of the corporate lawyer.
   i. Preferred stock is converted into common stock.
   j. Inventory items are written down to reflect a lower-of-cost-or-market valuation.
   k. The Future Income Tax (Credit) account is increased for the year.
   l. The Premium on Bonds Payable account is amortized for the year.
   m. A majority interest in the common stock of a supplier is acquired by issuing long-term convertible bonds.
   n. The liability account Rental Fees Received in Advance is reduced when the rental services are provided.
   o. A 10-percent stock dividend is declared and issued.
   p. Long-term debt maturing within the next year is reclassified as a current liability.
   q. Provision is made for estimated uncollectible accounts when the allowance method is used.
   r. Income is recognized using the percentage-of-completion method for long-term contracts.
   s. Land is donated to a firm by a local government as an inducement to locate manufacturing facilities in the area.
   t. Long-term investments in securities are written down to reflect a permanent decline in value.
   u. Research and development costs are paid during the period.

   v. Depreciation is recorded on selling and administrative facilities.
   w. Depreciation is recorded on manufacturing facilities.
   x. Treasury stock is sold for an amount less than its repurchase price.
   y. A 3-month loan is obtained from a local bank.

Work through the following problems:

2. 7.42 on p. 370	**8.** 9.28 on p. 468	**14.** 11.17 on p. 553
3. 7.43 on p. 371	**9.** 9.29 on p. 471	**15.** 11.27 on p. 558
4. 8.22 on p. 410	**10.** 9.30 on p. 471	**16.** 12.30 on p. 600
5. 8.39 on p. 421	**11.** 10.22 on p. 524	**17.** 13.20 on p. 654
6. 9.21 on p. 466	**12.** 10.39 on p. 529	**18.** 13.37 on p. 668
7. 9.22 on p. 466	**13.** 10.40 on p. 530	

19. *Preparation of statement of changes in financial position (adapted from CPA examination).* The management of Taylor Corporation, concerned over a decrease in cash, has provided you with the comparative analysis of changes in account balances between December 31, Year 4, and December 31, Year 5, shown in Exhibit 14.5.
   During Year 5, the following transactions occurred:

(1) New machinery was purchased for $386,000. In addition, certain obsolete machinery, having a book value of $61,000, was sold for $48,000. No other entries were recorded in Machinery and Equipment or related accounts other than provisions for depreciation.

(2) Taylor paid $2,000 of legal costs in a successful defense of a new patent, which was correctly debited to the Patents account. Amortization of patents amounting to $4,200 was recorded.

(3) Preferred shares, par value $100, were purchased at 110 and subsequently canceled. The premium paid was charged to retained earnings.

(4) On December 10, Year 5, the board of directors declared a cash dividend of $.20 per share payable to holders of common shares on January 10, Year 6.

Exhibit 14.5
TAYLOR CORPORATION
Changes in Account Balances between December 31, Year 4 and
December 31, Year 5

	December 31	
	Year 5	**Year 4**
Debit Balances		
Cash	$ 145,000	$ 186,000
Accounts Receivable	255,000	273,000
Inventories	483,000	538,000
Securities Held for Plant Expansion Purposes	150,000	—
Machinery and Equipment	927,000	647,000
Leasehold Improvements	87,000	87,000
Patents	27,800	30,000
Totals	$2,074,800	$1,761,000

Credit Balances

Allowance for Uncollectible Accounts	$ 16,000	$ 17,000
Accumulated Depreciation of Machinery and Equipment ..	416,000	372,000
Allowance for Amortization of Leasehold Improvements ..	58,000	49,000
Accounts Payable	232,800	105,000
Cash Dividends Payable	40,000	—
Current Portion of 6-Percent Serial Bonds Payable	50,000	50,000
6-Percent Serial Bonds Payable	250,000	300,000
Preferred Shares	90,000	100,000
Common Shares	500,000	500,000
Retained Earnings	422,000	268,000
Totals	$2,074,800	$1,761,000

(5) A comparative analysis of retained earnings as of December 31, Year 5 and Year 4, is presented as follows:

	December 31	
	Year 5	Year 4
Balance, January 1	$268,000	$131,000
Net Income	195,000	172,000
	$463,000	$303,000
Dividends Declared	(40,000)	(35,000)
Premium on Preferred Stock Repurchased	(1,000)	—
Balance, December 31	$422,000	$268,000

(6) Accounts totaling $3,000 were written off as uncollectible during Year 5.
   a. Prepare a T-account work sheet for the preparation of a statement of changes in financial position.
   b. Prepare a formal statement of changes in financial position for Taylor Corporation for the year ending December 31, Year 5.

20. *Preparation of statement of changes in financial position (adapted from CPA examination).* Feltham Company has prepared its financial statements for the year ended December 31, Year 6, and for the 3 months ended March 31, year 7. You have been asked to prepare a statement of changes in financial position for the 3 months ended March 31, year 7. The company's balance sheet data at December 31, Year 6, and March 31, year 7, are shown in Exhibit 14.6, and its income statement data for the 3 months ended March 31, Year 7, are shown in Exhibit 14.7. You have previously satisfied yourself as to the correctness of the amounts presented.

   Your discussion with the company's controller and a review of the financial records have revealed the following information:
   (1) On January 8, Year 7, the company sold marketable securities for cash. These securities had been held for more than 6 months. No marketable securities were purchased during Year 7.

Exhibit 14.6
FELTHAM COMPANY
Balance Sheet

	Dec. 31 Year 6	Mar. 31, year 7
Cash	$ 25,300	$ 87,400
Marketable Securities	16,500	7,300
Accounts Receivable (net)	24,320	49,320
Inventory	31,090	48,590
Total Current Assets	$ 97,210	$192,610
Land	40,000	18,700
Building	250,000	250,000
Equipment	—	81,500
Accumulated Depreciation	(15,000)	(16,250)
Investment in 30-Percent-Owned Company	61,220	66,980
Other Assets	15,100	15,100
Total Assets	$448,530	$608,640
Accounts payable	$ 21,220	$ 17,330
Dividend Payable	—	8,000
Income Taxes Payable	—	34,616
Total Current Liabilities	$ 21,220	$ 59,946
Other Liabilities	186,000	186,000
Bonds Payable	50,000	115,000
Discount on Bonds Payable	(2,300)	(2,150)
Future Income Taxes	510	846
Preferred Shares	30,000	—
Common Shares	80,000	110,000
Dividends Declared	—	(8,000)
Retained Earnings	83,100	146,998
Total Equities	$448,530	$608,640

Exhibit 14.7
FELTHAM COMPANY
Income Statement Data for the 3 Months Ended March 31, Year 7

Sales	$242,807
Gain on Sale of Marketable Securities	2,400
Equity in Earnings of 30-Percent-Owned Company	5,880
Gain on Condemnation of Land	10,700
Total Revenues	$261,787
Cost of Sales	$138,407
General and Administration Expenses	22,130
Depreciation	1,250
Interest Expense	1,150
Income Taxes	34,952
Total Expenses	$197,889
Net Income	$ 63,898

(2) The company's preferred shares are convertible into common shares at a rate of one share of preferred for two shares of common. The preferred shares and common shares have par values of $2 and $1, respectively.

(3) On January 17, Year 7, three acres of land were condemned. An award of $32,000 in cash was received on March 22, year 7. Purchase of additional land as a replacement is not contemplated by the company.

(4) On March 25, year 7, the company purchased equipment for cash.

(5) On March 29, Year 7, bonds payable were issued by the company at par for cash.

(6) The investment in the 30-percent-owned company included an amount attributable to goodwill of $3,220 at December 31, Year 6. Goodwill is being amortized at an annual rate of $480.

   a. Prepare a T-account work sheet for the preparation of statement of changes in financial position, defining funds as cash and cash equivalents.

   b. Prepare a formal statement of changes in financial position for Feltham Company for the 3 months ending March 31, year 7.

21. *Preparation of statement of changes in financial position (adapted from CPA examination).* Exhibit 14.8 presents a comparative statement of financial position for McDonald Corporation as of December 31, Year 1 and Year 2. Exhibit 14.9 presents an income statement for Year 2. The following additional information has been obtained.

(1) On February 2, Year 2, McDonald issued a 10-percent stock dividend to shareholders of record on January 15, Year 2. The market price per share of the common stock on February 2, Year 2, was $15.

(2) On March 1, Year 2, McDonald issued 3,800 common shares for land. The common shares and land had current market values of approximately $40,000 on March 1, Year 2.

(3) On April 15, Year 2, McDonald repurchased long-term bonds with a face and book value of $50,000. The gain of $22,000 was reported as an extraordinary item on the income statement.

Exhibit 14.8
MCDONALD CORPORATION
Statement of Financial Position

	December 31	
	Year 2	**Year 1**
Assets		
Current Assets:		
Cash	$ 100,000	$ 90,000
Accounts Receivable (net of allowance for doubtful accounts of $10,000 and $8,000 respectively)	210,000	140,000
Inventories	260,000	220,000
Total Current Assets	$ 570,000	$ 450,000
Land	325,000	200,000
Plant and Equipment	580,000	633,000
Less Accumulated Depreciation	(90,000)	(100,000)
Patents	30,000	33,000
Total Assets	$1,415,000	$1,216,000

Liabilities and Shareholders' Equity

Liabilities:

Current Liabilities:

Accounts Payable	$ 260,000	$ 200,000
Accrued Liabilities	200,000	210,000
Total Current Liabilities	$ 460,000	$ 410,000
Future Income Taxes	140,000	100,000
Long-Term Bonds (due December 15, Year 13)	130,000	180,000
Total Liabilities	$ 730,000	$ 690,000

Shareholders' Equity:

Common Shares, Par Value $5, Authorized 100,000 Shares, Issued and Outstanding 50,000 and 42,000 Shares, Respectively	$ 250,000	$ 210,000
Contributed Surplus	233,000	170,000
Retained Earnings	202,000	146,000
Total Shareholders' Equity	$ 685,000	$ 526,000
Total Liabilities and Shareholders' Equity	$1,415,000	$1,216,000

(4) On June 30, Year 2, McDonald sold equipment costing $53,000, with a book value of $23,000, for $19,000 cash.

(5) On September 30, Year 2, McDonald declared and paid a $.04 per share cash dividend to shareholders of record on August 1, Year 2.

(6) On October 10, Year 2, McDonald purchased land for $85,000 cash.

(7) Future income taxes represent timing differences relating to the use of different depreciation methods for income tax and financial statement reporting.

    a. Prepare a T-account work sheet for the preparation of statement of changes in financial position.

    b. Prepare a formal statement of changes in financial position for McDonald Corporation for the year ended December 31, Year 2.

Exhibit 14.9
MCDONALD CORPORATION
Income Statement for the Year Ended December 31, Year 2

Sales	$1,000,000
Expenses:	
Cost of Goods Sold	$ 560,000
Salary and Wages	190,000
Depreciation	20,000
Amortization	3,000
Loss on Sale of Equipment	4,000
Interest	16,000
Miscellaneous	8,000
Total Expenses	$ 801,000
Income before Income Taxes and Extraordinary Item	$ 199,000
Income Taxes	
Current	$ 50,000
Future	40,000
Provision for Income Taxes	$ 90,000
Income before Extraordinary Item	$ 109,000

Extraordinary Item—Gain on Repurchase of Long-Term Bonds (net of $10,000 income tax)	12,000
Net Income	$ 121,000
Earnings per Share:	
Income before Extraordinary Item	$2.21
Extraordinary Item	.24
Net Income	$2.45

22. *Preparation of statement of changes in financial position (adapted from CPA examination).* The comparative balance sheets for the Crandall Corporation are shown in Exhibit 14.10.

The following additional information relates to Year 5 activities:

(1) The Retained Earnings account was analyzed as follows:

Retained Earnings, December 31, Year 4		$758,200
Add Net Income after Extraordinary Items (loss of $3,000)		236,580
Subtotal		$994,780
Deduct:		
Cash Dividends	$130,000	
Loss on Reissue of Treasury Shares	3,000	
Stock Dividend	100,200	233,200
Retained Earnings, December 31, Year 5		$761,580

(2) On January 2, Year 5, marketable securities costing $110,000 were sold for $127,000. The proceeds from this sale, the funds in the bond sinking fund, and the amount received from the issuance of the 8-percent debentures were used to retire the 6-percent mortgage bonds. Any gain or loss on the retirement is taxed currently at 40 percent.

(3) The treasury shares were reissued on February 28, Year 5. All "losses" on the reissue of treasury shares are charged to retained earnings.

(4) The stock dividend was declared on October 31, Year 5, when the market price of Crandall Corporation's shares was $12 per share.

(5) On April 30, Year 5, a fire destroyed a warehouse that cost $100,000 and on which depreciation of $65,000 had accumulated. The loss was not insured.

(6) Plant and equipment transactions consisted of the sale of a building at its book value of $4,000 and the purchase of machinery for $28,000.

(7) Accounts receivable written off as uncollectible were $16,300 in Year 4 and $18,500 in Year 5. Expired insurance was $4,100 recorded in Year 4 and $3,900 in Year 5.

(8) The subsidiary, which is 80-percent owned, reported a loss of $22,400 for Year 5.

  a. Prepare a T-account work sheet for Crandall Corporation for Year 5, defining funds as cash and cash equivalents.

  b. Prepare a formal statement of changes in financial position for the year ending December 31, Year 5.

Exhibit 14.10
CRANDALL CORPORATION
Comparative Balance Sheets
December 31, Year 5 and Year 4

	Year 5	Year 4
Assets		
Cash	$ 141,100	$ 165,300
Marketable Securities (at cost)	122,800	129,200
Accounts Receivable (net)	312,200	371,200
Inventories	255,200	124,100
Prepayments	23,400	22,000
Bond Sinking Fund	—	63,000
Investment in Subsidiary (at equity)	134,800	152,000
Plant and Equipment (net)	1,443,700	1,534,600
Total Assets	$2,433,280	$2,561,400
Equities		
Accounts Payable	$ 238,100	$ 213,300
Notes Payable—Current	—	145,000
Accrued Payables	16,500	18,000
Income Taxes Payable	97,500	31,000
Future Income Taxes (noncurrent)	127,900	128,400
6-Percent Mortgage Bonds Payable (due Year 17)	—	300,000
Premium on Mortgage Bonds	—	10,000
8-Percent Debentures Payable (due Year 25)	125,000	—
Common Shares, $10 Par Value	1,033,500	950,000
Contributed Surplus	67,700	51,000
Retained Earnings	761,580	758,200
Treasury Shares—at Cost of $3 per Share	(34,500)	(43,500)
Total Equities	$2,433,280	$2,561,400

Accounting Concepts Problem 2

With respect to Exhibit 14.11 answer the following questions:
a. When politicians speak of reducing the deficit, which definition are they using?
b. Which of the definitions is most relevant to the average Canadian taxpayer?
c. What fundamental deficiency in GAAP does Exhibit 14.11 illustrate?

Exhibit 14.11
Confusing Terminology—or a Deficit by any other Name will give you a Different Number

It has become obvious that, whatever else, government deficits have become a cause for public anxiety. Such anxiety undermines public confidence in political and economic institutions and would undoubtedly affect performance in the long run.

Current information about government deficits may be inadequate—but it is certainly voluminous. In fact, a problem for anyone wanting to use governments' financial data is not finding it, it's sorting out the wheat from the chaff.

There are, broadly speaking, three ways to measure the federal deficit:

(1) The budgetary deficit. This most commonly used definition, derived from the Public Accounts, is a figure that indicates the amount that budgetary expenditures in the Main Estimates (the estimates of what the government will spend in the year) currently exceed the budgetary revenue. It is called "budgetary" because it excludes so-called "nonbudgetary" outflows such as loans, investments, and advances for specified purposes such as for unemployment insurance or for a Crown corporation. (The Main Estimates include both budgetary and nonbudgetary items, but other amounts are added in the Budget to make up the number that is called the financing requirment.)

(2) The National Accounts deficit. Because the Public Accounts of Canada do not jibe with the numbers or methods used by the provinces or used by other countries, Statistics Canada takes the government figures and "translates" them into a more comparable form to use in calculating gross national product—the National Accounts. The Public Accounts contains one version of this, called the extended National Accounts presentation, which is placed ahead of the official audited financial statements of Canada, thereby further confusing the reader as to which one is the "right" one.

(3) The financing requirement. That is the actual amount of money the federal government will need to raise over the annual period to meet its obligations on a cash basis.

Most people use the budgetary deficit figure when discussing The Deficit. That figure is not, however, a completely reliable indicator of a government's financial performance.

And that's an accounting problem.

There are two principal documents the public and the media use to judge a government's financial condition and deficit, and accordingly its managements ability. The future-oriented document is the budget setting out spending intentions; these plans can be compared to the audited financial statements issued after the fiscal year is over.

Unfortunately, the figures in the documents do not tell the whole story. The budgets and financial statements of individual Canadian governments are characterized by uncertain principles, widely diverse practices, and summary information that is often incomplete.

In the cases of our federal and provincial governments, accounting statements are neither consistent nor comparable. In part, these varying practices are due to the way government accounting has developed. It used to be that, as a means of legislative control, all revenues went into one *consolidated revenue fund* and were then appropriated for various government expenditures. As long as the consolidated fund was comprehensive, budgets and financial reports covered all transactions. As government operations became more widespread and complex, various funds, agencies and authorities were set up. Some government revenues continued to go into the consolidated fund; others went into funds, trusts, or Crown corporations.

Under such circumstances, the figure reported as a government's deficit does not necessarily cover all operations, and the figure need not reflect all the government's outstanding obligations or assets. Large expenditures, such as those for unemployment insurance, can be omitted from the calculation of the deficit, for example, by financing such programs through special funds.

In the past, some governments were always able to report a balanced budget on a current basis by reclassifying expenditures financed from borrowings. Governments no longer use such means to create balanced budgets. Also, the reported deficits of a single government are sometimes arrived at differently in successive years. It is difficult to assess, for instance, the growth over time of the federal deficit, when deficit-producing activities such as the Post Office become separate entities, to be reported separately.

Poor financial information, or badly organized good information, is useless for decision-making, and this is now a major concern being addressed by governments and the CICA. Although governments issue annual audited financial statements, these are difficult to interpret. Considerable attention is directed to the size and growth of a reported government deficit. However, as pointed out by the federal Auditor General, that figure may be misleading. The federal deficit in 1983, for example, was reported as $24.7 billion. But the Auditor General gave the government's financial statements a qualified audit opinion, noting:

> The increase in the national debt is important to all Canadians. Parliamentarians have the need—and all Canadians the right—to know the actual deficit, the actual debt as precisely as can be stated. My opinion on the financial statements of Canada illustrates that those amounts would differ by many billions of dollars from what is presented in those statements if the government were to prepare the statements with the primary aim of providing the clearest possible picture of its financial position to the people of Canada.

According to Mr. Dye, the reported 1982–83 federal deficit of $24.7 billion was understated by $5.3 billion.

If the gap between what is reported in the accounts and actual economic reality continues to increase, it will become more and more difficult to form judgements on the impact of the deficit and the national debt on the economy.

Adapted from "Government Deficits: How Far Down is the Bottom Line?" The Canadian Institute of Chartered Accountants, December 1985. Reprinted by permission.

Part Four   Synthesis

Chapter 15   Significance and Implications of Alternative Accounting Policies

The shareholders' auditor expresses an unreserved opinion on a firm's financial statements by stating that the statements were prepared in accordance with "generally accepted accounting principles." Accounting policies are the specific principles and the methods used in their application that are selected by a company as being most appropriate in the circumstances.[1] Previous chapters have described and illustrated most of the important accounting policies currently employed in preparing financial statements. This chapter focuses on the following questions:

1. What criteria should a firm employ in selecting its accounting policies from among those that are considered "generally acceptable"?
2. What are the effects of using alternative accounting policies on the principal financial statements?
3. What are the effects of using alternative accounting policies on investors' decisions to invest their capital resources?

One who understands the significance and implications of alternative generally accepted accounting policies is a more effective reader and interpreter of published financial statements. Throughout this chapter, we use the terms *accounting policies*, *methods*, and *procedures* interchangeably.

Summary of Generally Accepted Accounting Policies

This section lists the major currently acceptable accounting policies, most of which have been discussed in previous chapters. These accounting policies might be classified into two broad groups based on the flexibility permitted to firms in selecting alternative methods of accounting for a specific item. In some instances, the firm has wide flexibility in choosing among alternative methods, such as in the selection of depreciation methods. In other instances, the specific conditions associated with a transaction or event dictate the method of accounting that must be used. For example, the method of accounting for investments in the common shares of other firms depends on the presence of significant influence of which the percentage of share ownership is partial evidence. Although a list of major currently acceptable accounting policies is given below, remember that a particular firm does not have wide flexibility in selecting its accounting methods in all instances.

---

[1]*CICA Handbook*, section 1505.

Revenue Recognition A firm may recognize revenue at the time goods are sold or services are rendered, as is typically done under the accrual basis of accounting, at the time cash is collected (installment method or cost-recovery-first method), or as production progresses (percentage-of-completion method for long-term contracts).

Doubtful Accounts The amount that a firm recognizes as bad debts expense under the allowance method depends partly on the method used to make the estimate. A firm may estimate the expense as a percent of sales or by estimating the amount of the allowance for doubtful accounts. Several alternative methods are available when applying the second alternative.

Inventories A firm may cost inventories on one of several bases: acquisition cost, lower of acquisition cost or market, standard cost, and, in the case of some byproducts and precious minerals, net realizable value. When the cost of the specific goods sold cannot be ascertained, the firm must make a cost-flow assumption. The cost-flow assumption may be FIFO, LIFO, or weighted average, although LIFO may not be used when determining taxable income.

Investments in Securities A firm accounts for investments in the common shares of other firms using either the cost method or the equity method, or else prepares consolidated statements. The method used depends primarily on the degree of influence exercised by one firm over another. The percentage ownership of the voting shares is *prima facie* evidence of influence.

Machinery, Equipment, and Other Depreciable Assets These plant assets may be depreciated using the straight-line, declining-balance, compound-interest, or units-of-production method. Estimates of service lives of similar assets may differ among firms. The depreciation recorded in the financial statements is disregarded when determining taxable income, but is replaced by a company's capital cost allowance claimed, ordinarily the maximum allowed in the Income Tax Act.

Intangible Resources Development Cost The costs incurred in creating intangible resources, such as preproduction costs or store opening expenses, can be treated as an expense in the year the costs are incurred, or capitalized and amortized over some period of years. Thus, advertising and some development costs may be either capitalized when incurred and subsequently amortized, or expensed when incurred. Research costs, however, must be recognized as an expense in the year in which the costs are incurred.

Leases A firm may set up as an asset and subsequently amortize as a capital lease the rights to the use of property acquired under lease or give no recognition to the lease except at the time that lease payments are due each period (operating-lease method). Likewise, the lessor can set up the rights to receive future lease payments as a receivable at the inception of the lease (capital-lease method), or give no recognition to the lease except to the extent that lease payments become due each period (operating-lease method). Whether the capital or operating lease method is used depends on such factors as the life of the lease relative to the life of the leased asset and the present value of the lease payments relative to the market value of the leased property. The facts of each lease agreement determine the method to be used. Both the lessor and the lessee will generally use the same method for any lease.

Interest Revenue and Expense on Long-Term Investments and Debt A firm recognizes interest revenue and expense on long-term investments and debt using the effective-interest method, although the straight-line method can be used.

The preceding list of alternative acceptable accounting policies is not exhaustive. Also, remember that a firm does not always have a choice of methods. The factors that a firm might consider in selecting its accounting policies are discussed next.

The Firm's Selection of Alternative Accounting Policies

The methods of accounting used for income tax and financial reporting purposes generally do not have to be the same. Because the firm might pursue different objectives for financial and tax reporting, the selection of accounting policies for the two types of reports is discussed separately.

Financial Reporting Purposes

Accurate Presentation One of the criteria for assessing the usefulness of accounting information is *accuracy in presentation* of the underlying events and transactions. This criterion might be used by the firm as a basis for selecting its methods of accounting. For example, assets have been defined as resources having future service potential and expenses as a measurement of the services consumed during the period. In applying the accuracy criterion, the firm would select the inventory cost-flow assumption and depreciation method that most accurately measured the pattern of services consumed during the period and the amount of services still available at the end of the period. As a basis for selecting accounting methods, this approach has at least one serious limitation. The accountant can seldom directly observe the services consumed and the service potential remaining. Without this information, the accountant cannot ascertain which accounting policies lead to the most accurate presentation of the underlying events. This criterion can serve only as a normative criterion toward which the development and selection of accounting policies should be directed.

Conservatism In choosing among alternative, generally acceptable, methods, the firm might select the set that provides the most conservative measure of net income. Considering the uncertainties involved in measuring benefits received as revenues and services consumed as expenses, some have suggested that a conservative measure of earnings should be provided, thereby reducing the possibility of unwarranted optimism by users of financial statements. As a criterion for selecting accounting policies, *conservatism* implies that methods should be chosen that minimize cumulative reported earnings. That is, expenses should be recognized as quickly as possible, and the recognition of revenue should be postponed as long as possible. This reporting objective would lead to selecting the declining-balance depreciation method, selecting the LIFO cost-flow assumption if periods of rising prices are anticipated, and expensing of intangible development costs in the year incurred.

The rationale for conservatism as a reporting objective has been challenged. Over the whole life of the firm, income is equal to cash receipts minus cash expenditures. Thus, to the extent that net income of earlier periods is smaller, earnings of later periods must be larger. The "later" periods when income must be larger may, however, be many periods later, sometimes even the last period of the firm's existence. Also, some statement users may be misled by earnings reports based on conservative reporting policies. Consider, for example, investors who sell shares because they consider that the firm is not operating in a sufficiently profitable manner with the resources available, when earnings reported in a less conservative manner would not have induced the sale. Or, consider the potential investors who do not purchase securities because they are misled by the published "conservative" statement of earnings.

Profit Maximization A reporting objective having an effect opposite to conservatism might be employed in selecting among alternative generally accepted accounting policies. Somewhat loosely termed *reported profit maximization*,[2] this criterion suggests the selection of accounting methods that maximize cumulative reported earnings. That is, revenue should be recognized as quickly as possible, and the recognition of expense should be postponed as long as possible. For example, the straight-line method of depreciation would be used and, when periods of rising prices were anticipated, the FIFO cost-flow assumption would be selected. The use of profit maximization as a reporting objective is an extension of the notion that the firm is in business to generate profits and the firm should present as favorable a report on performance as possible within currently acceptable accounting methods. Profit maximization is subject to a similar, but mirror-image, criticism as the use of conservatism as a reporting objective. Reporting income earlier under the profit maximization criterion must mean that smaller income will be reported in some later period.

Income Smoothing A final reporting objective that might be used in selecting accounting policies is referred to as *income smoothing*. This criterion suggests the selection of accounting methods that result in the smoothest earnings trend over time. As discussed later in this chapter, empirical research has shown that changes in stock prices are related to changes in earnings. Advocates of income smoothing suggest that if a company can minimize fluctuations in earnings, then the perceived risk of investing in its shares will be reduced and, all else equal, its share price will be higher. Note that this reporting criterion suggests that net income, not revenues and expenses individually, is to be smoothed. As a result, the firm must consider the total pattern of its operations before selecting the appropriate accounting methods. For example, the straight-line method of depreciation may provide the smoothest amount of depreciation expense on a machine over its life. If, however, the productivity of the machine

---

[2]The concept of profit maximization as a reporting objective is not the same as the profit-maximization dictum of microeconomics.

declines with age so that revenues decrease in later years, net income using the straight-line method may not provide the smoothest net income stream. In this case, perhaps the declining-balance method should be used.

Summary The principal message of this section is that accurate presentation, although perhaps a desirable reporting objective, is not operational for selecting accounting policies. As a result, firms may select from among the methods included in the set of generally acceptable accounting policies using whatever reporting criteria they choose.

Where does this flexibility permitted in selecting accounting policies leave the user of financial statements? The *CICA Handbook*[3] requires firms to disclose the accounting policies used in preparing financial statements, either in a separate statement or as a note to the principal statements. An example of such disclosure for General Products Limited is presented at the beginning of Exhibit A.4 in Appendix A, page 763. The effect of alternative accounting policies on investment decisions is discussed later in the chapter.

Income Tax Reporting Purposes

In selecting accounting procedures for income tax purposes, the corporation's objective should be to select those methods that minimize the present value of the stream of income tax payments. The operational rule, sometimes called the *least and latest rule*, is to pay the least amount of taxes as late as possible within the law. The least and latest rule generally translates into a policy of recognizing expenses as quickly as possible and postponing the recognition of revenue as long as possible. This policy might be altered somewhat if income tax rates are expected to change, if the firm had losses in earlier years, or if the firm is a sole proprietorship or partnership where earnings of the firm are subject to graduated income tax rates of the owners.

The desire to recognize expenses as quickly as possible suggests claiming the maximum capital cost allowance and immediate expensing of research and development, advertising, and similar costs. Using the installment basis of recognizing revenue is generally desirable for income tax purposes where permitted by the Income Tax Act and Regulations, because it results in postponing the recognition of revenue and the resulting income tax payments until cash is collected.

What investors want in an annual report

What influences investor decisions, and how do annual reports fit into that decision-making process? Such questions prompted the Financial Executives Research Foundation to commission a study on the subject in 1986. The initial results were reported at the FEI conference on Current Financial Reporting Issues by Errol Alexander,

director, corporate financial services, of SRI International, which conducted the study.

The findings revealed the decision-making process to be a complex one, and corporate executives were found to have some misperceptions. For example, that individual investors want less information. "There is a grain of truth

---

[3]*CICA Handbook*, section 1505.

in that there is a lot of information that investors do not know what to make of,'' said Alexander. However, when you talk to them, he added, they show that they do want ''more information, but they want it to be more usable, more palatable, more in tune with the way they think.'' He also said they did not want ''to be denied information they think is available to others.'' Survey respondents particularly did not want ''different versions of the annual report for different audiences.''

When asked to indicate additional information they would like to see in annual reports, investors cited company reputation, company outlook, potential risk, and industry outlook. Business segment information was not rated important by individual investors, Alexander said. In talking to CEOs and CFOs of 26 companies, he also reported, ''these people were all very comfortable with the credibility level of their annual report. [However,] both professional and individual investors say very much otherwise.''

But why, then, do these same investors say that annual reports ''are the most frequently used source of information?'' The answer, Alexander said, is because they are so available. But while they are used, he reported, they are not influential in the decision-making process. ''No one relies heavily on information in the annual report unless he can confirm it through other means,'' he explained. For example, in talking to professional investors, he said, ''rarely did one say 'annual report' without saying '10 K' in the same or next sentence.''

Asked to characterize the readers of annual reports, Alexander described individual investors as ''scanners'' and professionals as ''selective.'' Both types of investors, he said, ranked financial statements the highest in importance, in contrast to corporate executives, who believe the letter to shareholders is the most important part of the annual report and the most read. Investors did not agree. ''They want to know what's really going on,'' Alexander said, and they see innate biases ''that push the chairman's letter way down on the list of what's important.''

It is important to investors, Alexander said, to know the company's plans for the future. In addition, professional investors want to know the company's view of its competitive standing, even though they will confirm this information from other sources as well. They would also like to see projections and forecasts in annual reports, even though they will generate their own from other sources. On the other hand, individual investors, the study reports, would like to see more key financial ratios, along with a short explanation.

Alexander cited a seeming conflict: individual investors said that annual reports could be improved by being shorter and less redundant, but they also said they desired more information in clearer detail. The answer, he said, was that these investors want more information of the right kind, which can be in keeping with shorter, less redundant information. However, he said that the most frequently cited area for improvement ''was frank reporting of poor company performance.''

Further details can be found in the FERF study, now available, Alexander said. He concluded by saying that management needed to set a primary objective for its annual report—that it be a stewardship document or a document to influence investors, for example. Then a primary target audience should be selected, and the report written to accommodate the characteristics and information needs of that primary audience. Finally, put one person in charge of the entire report—the letter, the narrative, and the financials. That person, he said, should have a working understanding of public relations and marketing as well as the financial side of the business.

Reprinted with permission of *Financial Executive*, March/April, 1987.

An Illustration of the Effects of Alternative Accounting Policies on a Set of Financial Statements

This section illustrates the effects of using different accounting policies on a set of financial statements. The illustration has been constructed so that the accounting policies used create significant differences in the financial statements. Therefore, inferences should not be drawn about the usual magnitude of the effects of alternative methods from this example.

The Scenario

On January 1, two corporations are formed to purchase two similar merchandising businesses. The two firms are alike in all respects except for their methods of accounting. Conservative Limited chooses the accounting policies that will minimize its reported net income. High Flyer Inc. chooses the accounting policies that will maximize its reported net income. The following events occur during the year.

1. Both corporations issue 2 million no-par-value shares on January 1 for $23 million cash.
2. On January 1 both firms acquire the equipment of their predecessors for $18 million cash. The equipment has a fair value of $14 million and an estimated life of ten years with no salvage value creating goodwill valued at $4 million.
3. Both firms make the following purchases of merchandise inventory:

Date	Units Purchased	Unit Price	Cost of Purchases
January 1	170,000	$60	$10,200,000
May 1	190,000	$63	11,970,000
September 1	200,000	$66	13,200,000
Total	560,000		$35,370,000

4. During the year, both firms sell 420,000 units at an average price of $100 each. All sales are made for cash.
5. During the year, both firms have selling, general, and administrative expenses, excluding depreciation and amortization of goodwill, of $7.1 million.
6. The income tax rate is assumed to be 46 percent.

Accounting Policies Used

The methods of accounting used by each firm in preparing its financial statements are described below.

Inventory Cost-Flow Assumption Conservative Limited makes a LIFO cost-flow assumption, whereas High Flyer Inc. makes a FIFO assumption. Both firms use the

FIFO method when deriving taxable income, since LIFO is not permitted for income tax purposes. Because the beginning inventory is zero, the cost of goods available for sale by each firm is equal to the purchases during the year of $35,370,000. Both firms have 140,000 units in ending inventory. Conservative Limited therefore reports a cost of goods sold of $26,970,000 [= $35,370,000 − (140,000 × $60)], whereas High Flyer Inc. reports a cost of goods sold of $26,130,000 [= $35,370,000 − (140,000 × $66)].

Depreciation Conservative Limited decides to claim the maximum capital cost allowance, using a rate of 20 percent, for income tax purposes and to record depreciation on its books in an equal amount. High Flyer Inc. decides to use the straight-line method in reporting income to shareholders but to claim the maximum capital cost allowance in its tax return. Conservative Limited therefore reports depreciation expense of $2.8 million (= .2 × $14,000,000), whereas High Flyer Inc. reports depreciation expense of $1.4 million (= $\frac{1}{10}$ × $14,000,000) to shareholders and $2.8 million on its tax return.

Amortization of Goodwill Conservative Limited decides to amortize goodwill on a straight-line basis over five years. High Flyer Inc. decides to amortize goodwill over the maximum period allowed of 40 years on a straight-line basis. A taxpayer may claim 50 percent of goodwill purchased as an expense for tax purposes at a straight-line rate of ten percent. Each company claims the maximum deduction. Conservative Limited therefore reports goodwill amortization of $800,000 (= $4,000,000/5), High Flyer Inc. reports goodwill amortization of $100,000 (= $4,000,000/40) and both companies claim the maximum income tax deduction of $200,000 (= 10% × .5 × $4,000,000).

Comparative Income Statements

Exhibit 15.1 presents comparative income statements for Conservative Limited and High Flyer Inc. for the year ending December 31. Conservative Limited reports a larger deduction for cost of sales and amortization of goodwill in its financial statements than it is allowed to deduct from its income tax return. The difference in cost of sales and one-half the difference in amortization of goodwill is viewed as a timing difference. The taxes currently payable exceed the deduction from income and a future income tax debit is recorded. High Flyer Inc. reports larger deductions from revenues on the income tax return than it reports to shareholders. The difference for depreciation on equipment is viewed as a timing difference. A portion of the income tax expense shown on the income statement of High Flyer Inc. is not payable currently, and therefore a future tax liability will appear on the balance sheet. In this illustration, net income and earnings per share of High Flyer Inc. are almost double the amounts shown for Conservative Limited.

Comparative Balance Sheets

Exhibit 15.2 presents comparative balance sheets for Conservative Limited and High Flyer Inc. as of December 31. Merchandise inventory, goodwill and equipment (net)

Exhibit 15.1
Comparative Income Statements Based on Different Accounting
Policies for the Year Ending December 31
(amounts in 000's, except for per-share amounts)

	Conservative Limited		High Flyer Inc.	
	Financial Statement	Tax Return	Financial Statement	Tax Return
Sales Revenue	$42,000.0	$42,000.0	$42,000.0	$42,000.0
Less: Cost of Goods Sold	26,970.0[b]	26,130.0[b]	26,130.0	26,130.0
Gross Profit	$15,030.0	$15,870.0	$15,870.0	$15,870.0
Less: Expenses				
Depreciation on Equipment	$ 2,800.0	$ 2,800.0	$ 1,400.0[c]	$ 2,800.0[c]
Goodwill Amortized	800.0[d]	200.0[d]	100.0[d]	200.0[d]
Other Selling and Administrative . .	7,100.0	7,100.0	7,100.0	7,100.0
Total Expenses	$10,700.0	$10,100.0	$ 8,600.0	$10,100.0
Net Income before Income Tax	$ 4,330.0	$ 5,770.0	$ 7,270.0	$ 5,770.0
Income Tax Expense:				
Currently Payable	$ 2,654.2		$ 2,654.2	
Future[e]	(478.4)		713.0	
Total[a]	$ 2,175.8		$ 3,367.2	
Net Income	$ 2,154.2		$ 3,902.8	
Earnings per Share (2,000,000 shares outstanding)	$ 1.08		$ 1.95	

[a] Computation of Income Tax Expense:

Net Income Before Income Tax . . .	$ 4,330.0	$ 5,770.0	$ 7,270.0	$ 5,770.0
Plus: Permanent Timing Difference, Goodwill Amortization:				
(.5 × $800)	400.0			
(.5 × $100)			50.0	
Total	$ 4,730.0	$ 5,770.0	$ 7,320.0	$ 5,770.0
Income Tax on Current Income (at 46 percent)	$ 2,175.8		$ 3,367.2	
Income Tax Currently Payable (at 46 percent)		$ 2,654.2		$ 2,654.2
Income Taxes Deferred by Timing Differences:				
[b] For Cost of Goods Sold [.46 × ($26,130 − $26,970)] . . .	$ (386.4)			
[c] For Depreciation [.46 × ($2,800 − $1,400)]			$ 644.0	
[d] For Goodwill Amortization {.46 × [$200 − (.5 × $800)]}	(92.0)			
{.46 × [$200 − (.5 × $100)]}			69.0	
[e] Total Future Income Taxes	$ (478.4)		$ 713.0	

as well as total assets of Conservative Limited are stated at lower amounts than those of High Flyer Inc. There is no real difference between the economic positions of the two companies. They each hold identical assets and owe identical amounts. One apparent difference is shown in the balances of future income taxes. This difference arises

Exhibit 15.2
Comparative Balance Sheets Based on Alternative
Accounting Policies, December 31
(amounts in 000's)

	Conservative Limited	High Flyer Inc.
Assets		
Cash	$ 1,875.8	$ 1,875.8
Merchandise Inventory	8,400.0	9,240.0
Future Income Taxes (current)	386.4	—
Equipment	14,000.0	14,000.0
Less: Accumulated Depreciation	(2,800.0)	(1,400.0)
Goodwill	3,200.0	3,900.0
Future Income Taxes (noncurrent)	92.0	—
Total Assets	$25,154.2	$27,615.8
Equities		
Future Income Taxes	$ —	$ 713.0
Common Stock	23,000.0	23,000.0
Retained Earnings	2,154.2	3,902.8
Total Equities	$25,154.2	$27,615.8

not as a result of different current or future income tax payments but because of differences in reported income.

The differences in the amounts at which merchandise inventory, equipment (net) and goodwill are stated result from the different accounting methods used by the two companies. The amounts shown for Conservative Limited are smaller than the corresponding amounts for High Flyer Inc. because a larger portion of the costs incurred during the period by Conservative Limited has been recognized as an expense.

In the assets section of the balance sheet, Conservative Limited also shows debit balances of Future Income Taxes of $386.4 and $92 arising from differences in cost of sales and goodwill amortization respectively, for financial and tax reporting. High Flyer Inc. also reports future income taxes on the balance sheet resulting from differences in the timing of depreciation on equipment in the financial statements and income tax return.

Note the effect of using alternative accounting policies on the ratio, rate of return on total assets (= net income/total assets). Conservative Limited reports a smaller amount of net income but also a smaller amount of total assets. One might expect, then, the rate of return on total assets of the two firms to approximate each other more closely than either net income or total assets individually. Significant differences in the ratio for the two firms are still observable, however, in this illustration. The rate of return on total assets of Conservative Limited is 8.9 percent [= $2,154,200/($23,000,000 + $25,154,200)/2] and of High Flyer Inc. is 15.4 percent [= $3,902,800/($23,000,000 + $27,615,800)/2].

Comparative Statements of Changes in Financial Position

Exhibit 15.3 presents comparative statements of changes in financial position for Conservative Limited and High Flyer Inc. Despite the differences in income between the two companies, they report the same amount of cash used in operations. Since the firms are alike in all respects except for their method of accounting, the amount of the cash flow from operations is a more valid report comparing the two companies than is the amount of net income.

Note that the differences in depreciation methods, inventory cost flow assumptions and goodwill amortization methods do not affect the cash used in operations. As long as these firms use the same methods for the above on their income tax returns, cash flows will be the same. Thus, the statement of changes in financial position tends to be affected much less by alternative generally accepted accounting policies than are the balance sheet and the income statement.

Exhibit 15.3
Comparative Statements of Changes
in Financial Position for the Year Ending December 31
(amounts in 000's)

	Conservative Limited	High Flyer Inc.
Cash Provided by		
Financing Activities		
Issue of common shares	23,000.0	23,000.0
Cash Applied to		
Operations		
Net Income	2,154.2	3,902.8
Add (deduct)		
Depreciation expense	2,800.0	1,400.0
Goodwill amortization	800.0	100.0
Future Income Taxes	(478.4)	713.0
Increase in merchandise inventory	(8,400.0)	(9,240.0)
	($3,124.2)	($3,124.2)
Investment Activities		
Acquisition of subsidiary	(18,000.0)	(18,000.0)
	(21,124.2)	(21,124.2)
Net Increase in Cash[a] Position	$ 1,875.80	$ 1,875.80

[a]In this illustration there are no cash equivalents or bank indebtedness, so cash position is equivalent to cash alone.

Moral of the Illustration

In order to interpret published financial statements, you must be aware of which accounting policies from the set of alternative generally accepted accounting policies are used. When reports of several companies are compared, the amounts shown should be adjusted where possible for the different accounting methods used. The techniques for making some of these adjustments were illustrated in previous chapters (for example, LIFO to FIFO cost flow assumption, equity method to consolidated statements). The notes to the financial statements will disclose the accounting policies used, but not necessarily the data required to make appropriate adjustments.

How readable are our annual reports?

*T*he annual report is the main formal medium for the messages corporations wish to convey to their shareholders and other interested parties each year. Although newspapers often pre-empt the report as a timely source of information, it contains a comprehensive, credible database prepared and issued by the company involved.

Recipients review the report for guidance on many aspects related to the company's past, present and future behaviour. But communications of this guidance will be effective only if the readers understand the messages the preparers of the report intended to convey.

Studies have shown that, although the rest of the report receives some attention, shareholders spend most of the review time reading the chairman's address because of its general overview and less technical orientation. To ensure effective communication, therefore, companies should pay particular attention to the content, organization and readability of this address.

One way for report preparers to gauge communication effectiveness is to use readability formulas. These are quantitative methods for predicting whether certain text material is likely to be understood by a target audience.

Although there are more than five dozen variations of readability formulas, a simple two-variable (a word variable and a sentence variable), general-purpose formula is usually sufficient. It is believed that the length of a word is related to a reader's speed of recognition and that sentence length is related to memory span. While neither variable necessarily causes reading difficulty, each has been found to be a good index of such difficulty.

One popular formulas used in accounting studies is the Flesch reading ease measurement. This formula is equal to the constant number 206.835 less .846 times the word length (the number of syllables per 100 words of sampled prose) and then less 1.015 times sentence length (the average sentence length in the sampled passage).

The result of the equation is a reading ease score ranging from zero to 100—the closer the score to zero, the more incomprehensible the writing.

Validated comprehension tests have shown that prose scoring between 0-30 is very difficult to read—equivalent to scientific writing—and the reader needs to have a postgraduate degree to understand it. A score of 30-50 means the passage is still difficult—equivalent to academic literature—and requires at least an undergraduate education on the part of the reader. A score above 50 makes the message comprehensible to the majority of the readers.

To determine whether the annual report can be easily read and understood, several sample passages of 100 words should be selected at random. Count the number of sentences and words in each passage and calculate the average sentence length across all passages. Next, count the number of syllables in each passage and average it across the sample passages. Finally, insert the two results into the formula to yield the measure of reading ease.

I have conducted a series of studies on readability levels for Canadian annual reports for the years 1982, 1983 and 1984. I randomly selected 100-word prose passages from the chairman's address of 46 different year-end 1982 reports, 96 1983 reports and 65 1984 reports.

What I found was surprising. Contrary to expectations, the chairman's address was not easy to read. For all three years, the over-all average reading ease score for this section bordered on difficult to very difficult, with a score of 31.17. Only seven of 207 reports scored more than 50—96% of the sampled chairman's addresses were written on a level akin to scientific and academic writing! Fully 42% of the addresses seem to require readers to have postgraduate degrees to understand them.

But do most annual report recipients have the educational background to easily understand the chairman's address? If we look at the education of the adult Canadian population, based on 1981 census statistics, the chairman's address appears to be beyond the comprehension of 92% of the population.

It doesn't look quite so bad if we use the education levels of the Canadian investor population (as reported by the Toronto Stock Exchange's 1984 Shareholder Profile Study): 44% of shareholders have at least part of a university education. They should, therefore, be able to understand most of the intended messages.

Although readability formulas are based on two fundamental variables, they don't examine important matters, such as reader interest, and design format, such as length of type line, hyphenated words, long paragraphs, confusing punctuation, full pages of type, style and size of typeface, illustration and colour. Nor do they measure word frequency, concept density and level of abstraction, or whether there is logical organization, coherence and flow of ideas.

But the formulas are a quick way for those responsible for annual report preparation to get some indication of how easy it is to read their reports. If the reports fail the test, chances are that many readers will fail to get the message.

By John Courtis.
Reprinted with permission of *The Bottom Line*, June 1986.

Assessing the Effects of Alternative Accounting Policies on Investment Decisions

Previous sections of this chapter emphasized the flexibility that firms have in selecting accounting procedures and the possible effects of using different accounting procedures on the financial statements. We now focus briefly on a related and important question: do investors accept financial statement information as presented, or do they somehow filter out all or most of the differences in the financial statements of various firms resulting from differences in the methods of accounting employed? If investors accept financial statement information as presented, without adjustments for the methods of accounting used, then two firms, otherwise identical except for the accounting procedures employed, might receive a disproportionate amount of capital funds. Thus, the use of alternative accounting policies could lead to a misallocation of resources in the economy. On the other hand, if investors make adjustments for the different accounting procedures in analyzing the financial statements of various firms, perhaps the policy maker need not be concerned over the variety of acceptable accounting policies. If investors do make such adjustments, then increased disclosure of the procedures followed may be more important than greater uniformity in accounting policies.

The question as to the effect of alternative accounting policies on investment decisions has been the subject of extensive debate among public accountants, academicians, personnel in government agencies, and financial statement users.

Those who believe that investors can be misled point to examples where the market price of particular firms' shares have decreased dramatically after the effects of using specific accounting procedures have been carefully analyzed and reported in the financial press.[4] In these examples it is often difficult, however, to judge if the price change is attributable to the disclosure of the effects of using particular accounting procedures or to other, more temporary factors affecting the specific firm, its industry, or all firms in the economy. Also, it is difficult to generalize on the effects of using alternative accounting policies on investment decisions from isolated and anecdotal examples.

An expanding number of empirical research studies, on the other hand, have provided support for the view that investors at the aggregate market level are rarely misled by the accounting methods employed. This research has developed from the theory and empirical evidence that the stock market is efficient, in the sense that market prices adjust quickly and in an unbiased manner to new information.[5] Unlike the examples supporting the view that investors are misled, these empirical studies have been based on data for a large number of firms over long time periods. Also, an effort is made in these studies to control for the effects of economy-wide and industry effects on market price changes.

Several studies have shown that changes in earnings and changes in market prices are associated and, therefore, indicate that information contained in the financial statements is used by investors in making their resource allocation decisions.[6] Several studies have examined the effects of *changes* in the methods of accounting on market prices,[7] and a third group of studies looked at *differences* in the methods of accounting across firms.[8] The results of these last two groups of studies have been mixed, with several studies supporting the position that investors are misled and several studies supporting the position that they are not misled. The methodology

[4]For several examples, see Abraham J. Briloff, *More Debits Than Credits* (New York: Harper & Row, 1976). For an analysis of these examples see George Foster, "Briloff and the Capital Market," *Journal of Accounting Research* (Spring 1979): 262–274.

[5]See Eugene F. Fama, "Efficient Capital Markets: A Review of Theory and Empirical Work," *Journal of Finance* (May 1970): 383–417.

[6]See, for example, Ray Ball and Philip Brown, "An Empirical Evaluation of Accounting Income Numbers," *Journal of Accounting Research* (Autumn 1968): 159–178; William H. Beaver, "The Information Content of Annual Earnings Announcements," *Empirical Research in Accounting: Selected Studies, 1968*, Supplement to Vol. 6, *Journal of Accounting Research* (Autumn 1968): 67–92; Robert G. May, "The Influence of Quarterly Earnings Announcements on Investor Decisions as Reflected in Common Stock Price Changes," *Empirical Research in Accounting: Selected Studies, 1971*, Supplement to Vol. 9, *Journal of Accounting Research:* 119–163.

[7]See, for example, Ray Ball, "Changes in Accounting Techniques and Stock Prices," *Empirical Research in Accounting: Selected Studies, 1972*, Supplement to Vol. 10, *Journal of Accounting Research* (Autumn 1968): 1–38; Robert S. Kaplan and Richard Roll, "Investor Evaluation of Accounting Information: Some Empirical Evidence," *Journal of Business* (April 1972): 225–257; Shyam Sunder, "Relationships Between Accounting Changes and Stock Prices: Problems of Measurement and Some Empirical Evidence," *Empirical Research in Accounting: Selected Studies, 1973*, Supplement to Vol. 11, *Journal of Accounting Research:* 1–45.

[8]See, for example, Robert E. Jensen, "An Experimental Design for Study of Effects of Accounting Variations in Decision Making," *Journal of Accounting Research* (Autumn 1966): 224–238; Thomas R. Dyckman, "On the Investment Decision," *The Accounting Review* (April 1964): 285–295; John L. O'Donnell, "Relationships Between Reported Earnings and Stock Prices in the Electric Utility Industry," *The Accounting Review* (January 1965): 135–143.

employed in many of these studies has been extensively criticized, so the full implications are not clear.[9]

Research into the question regarding the effects of alternative accounting policies on investment decisions has not progressed sufficiently for any consensus to have been reached. The research that has been conducted has been described here briefly to emphasize an important point. It is not obvious, as it might first appear, that the current flexibility permitted firms in selecting accounting policies necessarily misleads investors and results in a misallocation of resources.[10]

Development of Accounting Principles

Chapter 7 indicated that the development of "generally accepted accounting principles" is essentially a political process. Various persons or groups have power or authority in the decision process, including the federal and provincial legislatures and the provincial securities commissions, the courts, professional accounting organizations and their members, business firms, and financial statement users. Although parliament has the ultimate authority to specify acceptable accounting methods for federally incorporated companies, it has delegated that authority to the Accounting Standards Committee of the CICA. The majority of the provincial securities commissions have similarly delegated their authority to the AcSC. In the United States and the United Kingdom, the legislatures have occasionally determined accounting principles. In those countries the role of the private sector *versus* the public sector in setting accounting policies and regulating professional accounting practice continues to be the subject of extensive public debate. In Canada, on the other hand, governments have not publicly influenced accounting principles and consequently the controversy has not arisen.

Summary

The structure of accounting policies might be depicted as shown in Figure 15.1. The *universe* of possible accounting policies is encircled by a dashed line because of the difficulty in defining the relative size, or boundaries, of circle A. The process of specifying the policies designated as *generally acceptable* (the subset of policies from circle A represented by circle B) is political in nature. The federal and provincial

---

[9]For a review of these studies, see Ray Ball and George Foster, "Corporate Financial Reporting: A Methodological Review of Empirical Research," *Studies in Current Methodologies in Accounting: A Critical Evaluation*, Supplement to Vol. 20 (1982), *Journal of Accounting Research*, pp. 117–148; Baruch Lev and James A. Ohlson, "Market-Based Empirical Research: A Review, Interpretation, and Extension," *Ibid.*, pp. 249–322.

[10]For a description of the theoretical framework and a summary of the empirical work behind this position, see Nicholas J. Gonedes and Nicholas Dopuch, "Capital Market Equilibrium, Information-Production, and Selecting Accounting Techniques: Theoretical Framework and Review of Empirical Work," *Studies on Financial Accounting Objectives: 1974*, Supplement to Vol. 12, *Journal of Accounting Research* (Autumn 1968): 48–129: and Robert S. Kaplan, "Information Content of Financial Accounting Numbers: A Survey of Empirical Evidence," in: *Symposium of Impact of Accounting Research in Financial Accounting and Disclosure on Accounting Practice*, ed. by T. Keller and R. Abdel-khalik (Durham: Duke University Press, 1978).

legislatures have the legal authority to make the selection, but most of the responsibility for doing so has, in effect, been delegated to the Accounting Standards Committee. The individual firm's selection of accounting policies (the subset of policies from circle B represented by circle C) might be based on a criterion of accurate presentation. However, because benefits received and services consumed are seldom observable events and are therefore difficult to measure, reaching consensus on which generally accepted accounting policies provide an accurate or fair presentation is difficult. This chapter suggests that a firm might pursue a specific reporting objective, such as conservatism, profit maximization, or income smoothing, in selecting its accounting policies.

Before we can know whether circle B should be widened or narrowed, we must learn whether investors accept financial statement information as presented or whether investors make adjustments to recognize the effects of using alternative accounting policies. This question has been, and continues to be, the subject of extensive research.

Master Review Problem for Self-Study

Presented below is a set of financial statements for Carter Corporation, including a consolidated income statement (Exhibit 15.4) and a consolidated statement of changes in financial position (Exhibit 15.6) for Year 2, and a comparative consolidated balance sheet (Exhibit 15.5) on December 31, Year 1 and Year 2. Following the financial statements is a series of notes providing additional information on certain items in the financial statements. Respond to each of the questions listed, using information from the financial statements and notes. It is suggested that you study the statements and notes carefully before attempting to respond to the questions.

a. Temporary investments costing $180,000 were sold during Year 2. Ascertain the price at which these securities were sold.

b. Refer to (**a**). Compute the cost of temporary investments purchased during Year 2.

Figure 15.1
Structure of Accounting Policies

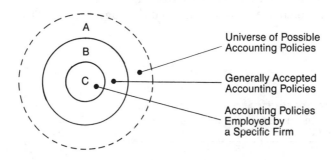

c. What was the amount of specific customers' accounts written off as uncollectible during Year 2?

d. Assume that all sales are made on account. Compute the amount of cash collected from customers during the year.

e. Compute the cost of units completed and transferred to the finished goods storeroom during Year 2.

f. Direct labour and overhead costs incurred in manufacturing during the year totaled $4,500,000. Determine the cost of raw materials purchased during Year 2.

g. What would cost of goods sold have been if current cost rather than weighted-average cost had been used?

h. Prepare an analysis that explains the causes of the changes in each of the three intercorporate investment accounts.

i. Assume that Eckel Credit Corporation has been consolidated with Carter Corporation instead of being treated as an unconsolidated subsidiary. Prepare a condensed consolidated balance sheet on December 31, Year 2 and a condensed consolidated income statement for Year 2 for Carter Corporation and Eckel Credit Corporation.

j. Prepare an analysis that explains the change in each of the following four accounts during Year 2: Land, Building, Equipment, and Accumulated Depreciation.

k. Give the journal entry made on Carter Corporation's books on January 2, Year 1, when it acquired Scott Corporation.

l. Compute the book value of the net assets of Scott Corporation on January 2, Year 1.

m. Compute the total amount of dividends declared by Scott Corporation during Year 2.

n. The four percent bonds payable were initially priced to yield six percent compounded semiannually. The ten percent bonds were initially priced to yield eight percent compounded semiannually. The eight percent bonds were issued at par. Using the appropriate present value tables at the back of the book, demonstrate that $208,640 was the correct balance for the bond premium less discount at December 31, Year 1.

o. Calculate the amount of interest expense and any change in the bond discount or premium for Year 2 on each of the three long-term bond issues.

p. Compute the amount of income taxes actually paid during Year 2.

q. Prepare an analysis explaining the change during Year 2 in each of the following accounts: Contributed Surplus, Retained Earnings, Treasury Shares.

Exhibit 15.4
CARTER CORPORATION
Consolidated Income Statement for Year 2
(amounts in 000's)

Sales	$12,000
Less: Cost of Goods Sold	7,200
Gross Profit	$ 4,800

Less: Operating Expenses		
Selling and Administrative	$2,689	
Loss on Sale of Equipment	80	2,769
Operating Profit		$ 2,031
Less: Financial Expenses		
Interest Expense (Notes 7 & 8)	561	
Unrealized Loss from Price Decline Of:		
Temporary Investments	20	
Portfolio Investments	15	
	$ 596	
Financial Income:		
Equity in Income of Unconsolidated Affiliates:		
Eckel Credit Corporation	$ 160	
Johnson Corporation	140	
Total	$ 300	
Dividend Revenue	20	
Gain on Sale of Temporary Investments	30	
	$ 350	246
Net Income before Income Taxes and Minority Interest		$ 1,785
Income Tax Expense		720
Net Income before Minority Interest		$ 1,065
Minority Interest in Earnings of Scott Corporation		40
Net Income		$ 1,025

Exhibit 15.5
CARTER CORPORATION
Consolidated Balance Sheets
December 31, Year 1 and Year 2
(amounts in 000's)

	December 31, Year 2	December 31, Year 1
Assets		
Current Assets:		
Cash	$ 2,739	$ 1,470
Temporary Investments (Note 2)	550	450
Accounts Receivable (net; Note 3)	2,850	2,300
Inventories (Note 4)	3,110	2,590
Prepayments	970	800
Total Current Assets	$10,219	$ 7,610
Investments (Note 5):		
Investment in Maher Corporation (10 percent)	$ 185	$ 200
Investment in Johnson Corporation (30 percent)	410	310
Investment in Eckel Credit Corporation (100 percent)	930	800
Total Investments	$ 1,525	$ 1,310

Property, Plant, and Equipment:

Land	$ 500	$ 400
Buildings	940	800
Equipment	3,800	3,300
Total Cost	$ 5,240	$ 4,500
Less: Accumulated Depreciation	(930)	(1,200)
Net Property, Plant, and Equipment	$ 4,310	$ 3,300
Goodwill (Note 6)	80	90
Total Assets	$16,134	$12,310

Liabilities and Shareholders' Equity

Current Liabilities:

Note Payable (Note 7)	$ 1,000	$ —
Accounts Payable	2,425	1,070
Salaries Payable	600	800
Interest Payable	400	300
Income Taxes Payable	375	250
Total Current Liabilities	$ 4,800	$ 2,420

Long-Term Liabilities:

Bonds Payable (Note 8)	$ 6,000	$ 6,000
Premium less Discount on Bonds Payable	209	209
Total Long-Term Liabilities	$ 6,209	$ 6,209
Future Income Taxes	$ 940	$ 820
Minority Interest	$ 214	$ 180

Shareholders' Equity:

Common Shares (no par value)	$ 1,800	$ 1,300
Contributed Surplus	5	—
Retained Earnings	2,186	1,411
Total	$ 3,991	$ 2,711
Less: Treasury Shares (at cost)	(20)	(30)
Total Shareholders' Equity	$ 3,971	$ 2,681
Total Liabilities and Shareholders' Equity	$16,134	$12,310

Exhibit 15.6
CARTER CORPORATION
Consolidated Statement of Changes in Financial Position for Year 2
(amounts in 000's)

Cash[a] Provided by
Operations

Net Income	$1,025

[a]Cash is defined for purposes of this statement as cash plus cash equivalents net of short-term
bank indebtedness.

Additions:

Depreciation	560	
Future Income Taxes	120	
Loss on Sale of Equipment	80	
Minority Interest in Undistributed Earnings of Consolidated Subsidiaries	34	
Unrealized Loss from Price Decline of Portfolio Investments	15	
Amortization of Discount on Bonds	28	
Amortization of Goodwill	10	
Increase in Notes Payable	1,000	
Increase in Accounts Payable	1,355	
Increase in Interest Payable	100	
Increase in Income Taxes Payable	125	

Subtractions:

Equity in Earnings of Affiliates and Subsidiaries in Excess of Dividends Received	(180)	
Amortization of Premium on Bonds	(28)	
Increase in Accounts Receivable	(550)	
Increase in Inventories	(520)	
Increase in Prepayments	(170)	
Decrease in Salaries Payable	(200)	
Cash Provided by Operations		$2,804

Financing Activities

Common Shares Issued	$ 500	
Treasury Shares Sold	15	
Investing Activities		515
Sale of Equipment		150
Total Sources of Cash		$3,469

Cash Applied to

Dividends		$ 250

Investing Activities

Acquisition of Assets:

Investment in Johnson Corporation	$ 50	
Land	100	
Building	300	
Equipment	1,400	
Net Increase in Cash Position		$1,369
Cash Position Beginning of Year		$1,920
Cash Position End of Year		$3,289

Note 1: Summary of Accounting Policies

Basis of Consolidation The financial statements of Carter Corporation are consolidated with Scott Corporation, an 80-percent-owned subsidiary acquired on January 2, Year 1. Eckel Credit Corporation, a wholly owned finance subsidiary, is excluded from the consolidation, since the inclusion would not provide more informative presentation to the shareholders. The investment is accounted for on an equity basis and condensed financial statements are presented in Note 5.

Temporary Investments Temporary investments are stated at the lower of acquisition cost and market.

Accounts Receivable Doubtful accounts of customers are accounted for using the allowance method.

Inventories Inventories are valued at the lower of weighted-average cost and replacement cost.

Investments Investments of less than 20 percent of the outstanding common shares of other companies are accounted for using the cost method. Investments of greater than or equal to 20 percent of the outstanding common shares of unconsolidated affiliates and subsidiaries are accounted for using the equity method.

Buildings and Equipment Depreciation for financial reporting purposes is calculated using the straight-line method. For income tax purposes, the maximum capital cost allowance is claimed.

Goodwill Goodwill is amortized over a period of ten years.

Interest on Long-Term Debt Interest expense on bonds payable is recognized using the effective-interest method.

Future Income Taxes Future income taxes are provided for timing differences between book income and taxable income.

Note 2: Temporary investments are shown net of an allowance for market price declines below acquisition cost of $50,000 on December 31, Year 1, and $70,000 on December 31, Year 2.

Note 3: Accounts receivable are shown net of an allowance for doubtful accounts of $200,000 on December 31, Year 1, and $250,000 on December 31, Year 2. Bad debts expense of $120,000 is included in Selling and Administrative expenses.

Note 4: Inventories consist of the following:

	December 31, Year 2	December 31, Year 1
Raw Materials	$ 380,000	$ 330,000
Work in Process	530,000	460,000
Finished Goods	2,200,000	1,800,000
Total	$3,110,000	$2,590,000

The current cost of inventories exceeded the amounts determined on a weighted-average basis by $420,000 on December 31, Year 1, and $730,000 on December 31, Year 2.

Note 5: Condensed financial statements for Eckel Credit Corporation, a wholly owned, unconsolidated subsidiary, are shown below.

Note 6: On January 2, Year 1, Carter Corporation acquired 80 percent of the outstanding common shares of Scott Corporation by issuing 20,000 shares of Carter Corporation. The Carter Corporation shares were selling on January 2, Year 1, for $40 a share. Any difference between the acquisition price and the book value of the net assets acquired was considered goodwill and is being amortized over a period of ten years from the date of acquisition.

Note 7: The note payable included under current liabilities is a one-year note due on January 2, Year 3. The note requires annual interest payments on December 31 of each year. The interest expense on this note for Year 2 was $101,000.

Note 8: Bonds payable are the following:

	December 31, Year 2	December 31, Year 1
4-percent bonds due December 31, Year 7, with interest payable semiannually	$2,000,000	$2,000,000
10-percent bonds due December 31, Year 11, with interest payable semiannually	3,000,000	3,000,000
8-percent bonds due on December 31, Year 17, with interest payable semiannually	1,000,000	1,000,000
Total	$6,000,000	$6,000,000

The interest expense of the bonds payable for Year 2 was $460,000.

ECKEL CREDIT CORPORATION
(Note 5) (amounts in 000's)

	December 31, Year 2	December 31, Year 1
Balance Sheet		
Cash and Temporary Investments	$ 840	$ 760
Accounts Receivable (net)	7,400	6,590
Other Assets	1,260	1,050
Total Assets	$9,500	$8,400
Notes Payable Due within 1 Year	$4,300	$3,900
Long-Term Note Payable	3,100	2,620
Other Liabilities	1,170	1,080
Common Stock	100	100
Contributed Surplus	300	300
Retained Earnings	530	400
Total Equities	$9,500	$8,400

Statement of Income and Retained Earnings

	Year 2
Revenues	$680
Expenses	520
Net Income	$160
Less: Dividends	(30)
Retained Earnings, December 31, Year 1	400
Retained Earnings, December 31, Year 2	$530

Note 9: The change in issued share capital during the year was as follows:

	Number of Shares	Amount
December 31, Year 1	50,000	$1,300,000
Issued for Cash	10,000	500,000
December 31, Year 2	60,000	$1,800,000

Suggested Solution

(The source of the data is shown in brackets as follows: Balance Sheet — BS; Income Statement — IS; Statement of Changes — SC; Question — Q; Answer — A; Note — N)

a.	Cost of Temporary Investments Sold (Q, A)	$180,000
	Gain on Sale (IS)	30,000
	Selling Price	$210,000

b.	Temporary Investments at Cost on December 31, Year 1 ($450,000 + $50,000) (BS)	$500,000
	Plus: Purchases	?
	Less: Cost of Temporary Investments Sold (Q, A)	(180,000)
	Temporary Investments at Cost on December 31, Year 2 ($550,000 + $70,000) (BS)	$620,000

The cost of temporary investments purchased during Year 2 was $300,000.

c.	Allowance for Doubtful Accounts, December 31, Year 1 (N, 2)	$200,000
	Plus: Bad Debts Expense during Year 2 (N, 2)	120,000
	Less: Specific Customers' Accounts Written Off as Uncollectible during Year 1	(?)
	Allowance for Doubtful Accounts, December 31, Year 2 (N, 2)	$250,000

Specific customers' accounts written off as uncollectible during Year 2 totaled $70,000.

d.

Gross Accounts Receivable December 31, Year 1[a]	$ 2,500
Plus: Sales during the Year (IS)	12,000
Less: Gross Accounts Receivable December 31, Year 2[b]	(3,100)
Accounts Collected or Written Off	$11,400
Less: Write-Offs (A, c)	(70)
Cash Collected during Year	$11,330

[a]$2,300 + $200. (BS + N, 2)
[b]$2,850 + $250. (BS + N, 2)

e.

Finished Goods Inventory, December 31, Year 1 (N, 4)	$1,800,000
Plus: Cost of Units Completed during the Year	?
Less: Cost of Units Sold during the Year (IS)	(7,200,000)
Finished Goods Inventory, December 31, Year 2 (N, 4)	$2,200,000

The cost of units completed was $7,600,000.

f.

Work-in-Process Inventory, December 31, Year 1 (N, 4)	$ 460,000
Plus: Cost of Raw Materials Used	?
Plus: Direct Labour and Manufacturing Overhead Costs Incurred (Q, f) . .	4,500,000
Less: Cost of Units Completed (A, e)	(7,600,000)
Work-in-Process Inventory, December 31, Year 2 (N, 4)	$ 530,000

The cost of raw materials used during Year 2 was $3,170,000.

Raw Materials Inventory, December 31, Year 1 (N, 4)	$ 330,000
Plus: Cost of Raw Materials Purchased	?
Less: Cost of Raw Materials Used (A, f)	(3,170,000)
Raw Materials Inventory, December 31, Year 2 (N, 4)	$ 380,000

The cost of raw materials purchased was $3,220,000.

	Weighted-Average	Difference	Current Cost
g. Inventory, December 31, Year 1	$ 2,590,000[1]	$420,000[3]	$ 3,010,000
Purchases Plus Costs Incurred	7,720,000[2]	—	7,720,000
Goods Available	$10,310,000	$420,000	$10,730,000
Less: Inventory, December 31, Year 2	3,110,000[1]	730,000[3]	3,840,000
Cost of Goods Sold	$ 7,200,000	($310,000)	$ 6,890,000

[1](BS).
[2]{$3,220,000 [(A, f) + $4,500,000 (Q, f)]}
[3]N, 4.

Cost of goods sold under Current Cost would have been $6,890,000.

h. **Investment in Maher Corporation (cost method)**

Balance, December 31, Year 1 (BS)	$200,000
Plus: Additional Investments (SC)	—
Less: Sales of Investments (SC)	—
Less: Increase in Unrealized Loss on Valuation of Investments (SC)	(15,000)
Balance, December 31, Year 2 (BS)	$185,000

Investment in Johnson Corporation (equity method)

Balance, December 31, Year 1 (BS)	$310,000
Plus: Additional Investments (SC)	50,000
Plus: Equity in Earnings (IS)	140,000
Less: Sale of Investments (SC)	—
Less: Dividend Received (plug)	(90,000)
Balance, December 31, Year 2 (BS)	$410,000

Investment in Eckel Credit Corporation (equity method)

Balance, December 31, Year 1 (BS)	$800,000
Plus: Additional Investments (SC)	—
Plus: Equity in Earnings (IS)	160,000
Less: Sale of Investments (SC)	—
Less: Dividends Received (plug)	(30,000)
Balance, December 31, Year 2 (BS)	$930,000

i.

Balance Sheet	Carter Corp.	Eckel Credit Corp.	Eliminations	Consolidated
Cash and Temporary Investments	$ 3,289	$ 840		$ 4,129
Accounts Receivable	2,850	7,400		10,250
Investment in Eckel Credit Corporation	930	—	$(930)	—
Other Assets	9,065	1,260		10,325
Total Assets	$16,134	$9,500	$(930)	$24,704
Notes Payable:				
Due within 1 Year	$ 1,000	$4,300		$ 5,300
Long-Term	6,209	3,100		9,309
Other Liabilities	3,800	1,170		4,970
Future Income Taxes	940	—		940
Minority Interest	214			214
Common Shares	1,800	100	$(100)	1,800
Contributed Surplus	5	300	(300)	5
Retained Earnings	2,186	530	(530)	2,186
Treasury Shares	(20)	—		(20)
Total Equities	$16,134	$9,500	$(930)	$24,704

Income Statement

Revenues	$12,000	$ 680		$12,680
Equity in Earnings of Unconsolidated Affiliates	300	—	$(160a)	140
Expenses	(11,275)	(520)		(11,795)
Net Income	$ 1,025	$ 160	$(160)	$ 1,025

aThe credit entry for $160 would be made to the Investment account in Eckel Credit Corporation. Because the entry above—to eliminate the investment account—was made to *post-closing* trial balance data, this $160 debit is implicitly included in the debit of $530 made to the Retained Earnings account.

j. **Land**

Balance, December 31, Year 1 (BS)	$ 400,000
Plus: Acquisitions (SC)	100,000
Less: Disposals (SC)	—
Balance, December 31, Year 2 (BS)	$ 500,000

Building

Balance, December 31, Year 1 (BS)	$ 800,000
Plus: Acquisition (SC)	300,000
Less: Disposals (SC)	(160,000)
Balance, December 31, Year 2 (BS)	$ 940,000

Equipment

Balance, December 31, Year 1 (BS)	$3,300,000
Plus: Acquisitions (SC)	1,400,000
Less: Disposals (plug)	(900,000)
Balance, December 31, Year 2 (BS)	$3,800,000

Accumulated Depreciation

Balance, December 31, Year 1 (BS)	$1,200,000
Plus: Depreciation for Year 2 (SC)	560,000
Less: Accumulated Depreciation on Building (plug)	(160,000)
Less: Accumulated Depreciation on Equipment Sold (see below)	(670,000)
Balance, December 31, Year 2 (BS)	$ 930,000

Selling Price of Equipment Sold (SC)	$ 150,000
Loss on Sale of Equipment (SC)	80,000
Book Value of Equipment Sold	$ 230,000

Cost of Equipment Sold (above)	$ 900,000
Less: Accumulated Depreciation on Equipment Sold (plug)	(670,000)
Book Value of Equipment Sold (above)	$ 230,000

k. Investment in Scott Corporation (N, 6) $800,000

     Common Shares (20,000 × $40) (N, 6) $800,000

l. Cost of Investment in Scott Corporation (A, k) .... $ 800,000

     Goodwill $80,000 + (2 × $10,000) (BS + SC) ....   (100,000)

     Book Value of Net Assets Acquired .... $ 700,000

80 percent acquired (N, 6); therefore, book value of Scott on date of acquisition is $700,000/.80 = $875,000.

m. Minority Interest in Scott Corporation, January 2, Year 2 (BS) $180,000

     Plus: Minority Interest in Earnings of Scott Corporation (IS)   40,000

     Less: Minority Interest in Dividends of Scott Corporation (plug) ....   (6,000)

     Minority Interest in Scott Corporation, December 31, Year 2, (BS) $214,000

Total dividends declared were $30,000 (= $6,000/.20).

n. **10-Percent Bond Issue**

Discounted Present Value[a] at December 31, Year 1:

     Interest payments for 10 years (= $150,000 × 13.59033)

     (N, 8) $2,038,550

     Par value at end of 10 years (= $3,000,000 × .45639)

     (N, 8)   1,369,170

     Total $3,407,720

Less: Par Value (N, 8)   3,000,000

Premium .... $ 407,720

4-Percent Bond Issue

Discounted Present Value[b] at December 31, Year 1:

     Interest payments for 6 years (= $40,000 × 9.9540)

     (N, 8) .... $ 398,160

     Par value at end of 6 years (= $2,000,000 × .70138)

     (N, 8)   1,402,760

     Total $1,800,920

Less: Par Value (N, 8)   2,000,000

Discount ....   (199,080)

Net Bond Premium at December 31, Year 1 .... $ 208,640

[a]At 8 percent compounded semiannually.

[b]At 6 percent compounded semiannually.

o. 4-Percent Bond Issue	Net Liability Beginning of the Period	Market Interest Rate	Interest Expense	Interest Payable	Bond Premium or Discount	
					Reduction during Period	Balance End of Period
January 1, Year 2	$1,800,920[2]	.03[1]	$ 54,028	$ 40,000	$14,028	$185,052
July 1, Year 2	1,814,948	.03[1]	54,448	40,000	14,448	170,604
Total			$108,476	$ 80,000	$28,476	
10-Percent Bond Issue						
January 1, Year 2	3,407,720[2]	.04[1]	$136,309	$150,000	$13,691	$394,029
July 1, Year 2	3,394,029	.04[1]	135,761	150,000	14,239	379,790
Total			$272,070	$300,000	$27,930	
8-Percent Bond Issue						
January 1, Year 2	1,000,000[1]	.04[1]	$ 40,000	$ 40,000	$ -0-	$ -0-
July 1, Year 2	1,000,000	.04[1]	40,000	40,000	$ -0-	$ -0-
Total			$ 80,000	$ 80,000	$ -0-	

[1](Q, 4)
[2](A, n)

p. Income Taxes Payable, December 31, Year 1 (BS) $250,000
Plus: Current Income Tax Expense for Year 2 (see below) 600,000
Less: Cash Payment during Year 2 . . . . ?
Income Taxes Payable, December 31, Year 2 (BS) $375,000

Total Income Tax Expense (IS) $720,000
Less: Increase in Future Income Taxes ($940 − $820)(BS) . . . . (120,000)
Current Income Tax Expense $600,000

Cash payments for income taxes totaled $475,000 during Year 2.

	Contributed Surplus	Retained Earnings	Treasury Shares
q. Balance, December 31, Year 1 (BS)	—	$1,411,000	$30,000
Treasury Shares Sold	$5,000[2]	—	(10,000)[1]
Net Income (IS)	—	$1,025,000	—
Dividends (SC)	—	(250,000)	—
Balance, December 31, Year 2 (BS)	$5,000	$2,186,000	$20,000

[1](plug).
[2][$15,000 (SC) − $10,000].

Questions, Exercises, Problems and Cases

Questions

1. Review the meaning of the following concepts or terms discussed in this chapter.
- **a.** Generally accepted accounting policies
- **b.** Accurate presentation
- **c.** Fair presentation
- **d.** Conservatism
- **e.** Profit maximization
- **f.** Income smoothing
- **g.** Least and latest rule
- **h.** Statement of accounting policies
- **i.** Development of accounting principles is a political process

2. A critic of accounting stated: ''The financial statements are virtually useless because firms have too much latitude in selecting from among generally accepted accounting methods.'' Another critic of accounting reacted: ''I agree that the financial statements are useless, but it is because there is too little latitude in the way certain transactions are accounted for under generally accepted accounting principles.'' Respond to these statements.

3. ''The controversy over alternative generally accepted accounting policies could be solved by requiring all firms to use the same methods of accounting in their financial statements that they use in their tax return.'' Respond to this proposal.

4. If net income over long enough time periods is equal to cash-in minus cash-out, why not allow the timing of cash flows to dictate revenue and expense recognition and eliminate alternative generally accepted accounting policies?

5. ''The total reported net income over long enough time periods will be the same regardless of whether a firm follows a conservative strategy or a profit-maximizing strategy in selecting its accounting methods.'' Explain.

6. ''The statement of changes in financial position is affected less by the use of alternative accounting policies than the balance sheet and income statement.'' Explain.

7. If capital markets react quickly and in an unbiased manner to the release of information, including information contained in the financial statements, what is the benefit of analyzing a set of financial statements?

Exercises

8. *Identifying generally accepted accounting policies.* Indicate the generally accepted accounting policy, or method, described in each of the following statements. Explain your reasoning.
- **a.** This inventory cost-flow assumption results in reporting the largest net income during periods of rising prices.
- **b.** This method of accounting for doubtful accounts recognizes the implied income reduction in the period of sale.
- **c.** This method of accounting for long-term investments in the securities of unconsolidated subsidiaries or other corporations usually requires an adjust-

ment to net income to calculate cash provided by operations in the statement of changes in financial position.

d. This method of accounting for long-term leases by the lessee gives rise to a noncurrent liability.

e. This inventory cost-flow assumption results in approximately the same balance sheet amount as the FIFO flow assumption.

f. This method of recognizing interest expense on bonds provides a uniform annual rate of interest expense over the life of the bond.

g. During periods of rising prices, this inventory valuation basis produces approximately the same results as the acquisition-cost valuation basis.

h. When specific customers' accounts are deemed uncollectible and written off, this method of accounting results in a decrease in the current ratio.

i. This method of depreciation generally provides the largest amounts of depreciation expense during the first several years of an asset's life.

j. This method of recognizing income from long-term contracts generally results in the least fluctuation in earnings over several periods.

k. When specific customers' accounts are deemed uncollectible and are written off, this method of accounting has no effect on working capital.

l. Under this method of accounting for long-term leases of equipment by the lessor, an amount for depreciation expense on the leased equipment will appear on the income statement.

m. This method of recognizing interest expense on bonds provides a uniform annual amount of interest expense over the life of the bonds.

9. *Identifying generally accepted accounting policies.* Indicate the accounting policy, or procedure, apparently being used to record each of the following independent transactions. Indicate your reasoning.

a. Bad Debt Expense	X	
Accounts Receivable		X
b. Cash	X	
Dividend Income		X
c. Income Taxes Payable — Current	X	
Deferred Investment Tax Credits		X
d. Unrealized Loss from Price Declines in Temporary Investments	X	
Allowance to Reduce Temporary Investments to Market		X
e. Cash	X	
Investment in Unconsolidated Subsidiary		X
Dividend declared and received from unconsolidated subsidiary.		
f. Bad Debt Expense	X	
Allowance for Doubtful Accounts		X

10. *Identifying generally accepted accounting policies.* Indicate the accounting policy, or procedure, apparently being used to record each of the following independent transactions. Give your reasoning.

		X	
a. Rent Expense (for Lease Contract)		X	
Cash			X
b. Advertising Expense		X	
Deferred Advertising Costs			X
c. Investment in Unconsolidated Subsidiary		X	
Equity in Earnings of Unconsolidated Subsidiary			X
d. Allowance for Doubtful Accounts		X	
Accounts Receivable			X
e. Loss from Price Decline for Inventories		X	
Merchandise Inventories			X
f. Liability Under Long-Term Lease		X	
Interest Expense		X	
Cash			X

11. *Identifying effects of generally accepted accounting policies on reported income.* Indicate the accounting policy that provides the smallest amount of earnings in each of the following cases.

a. FIFO, LIFO, or weighted-average cost flow assumption for inventories during periods of rising prices.

b. FIFO, LIFO, or weighted-average cost flow assumption for inventories during periods of declining prices.

c. Cost or equity method of accounting for minority investments in the securities of unconsolidated subsidiaries where dividends declared by the subsidiary are less than its earnings.

d. Declining-balance or straight-line depreciation method during the first one-third of an asset's life.

e. Declining-balance or straight-line depreciation method during the last one-third of an asset's life.

f. Percentage-of-completion or installment method of revenue recognition.

g. The valuation of inventories at acquisition cost or lower of cost and market.

h. Cost or equity method of accounting for long-term investments in the securities of unconsolidated subsidiaries where the investee realizes net losses and does not pay dividends.

i. Effective interest or straight-line method of recognizing interest expense on bonds in the first year that bonds originally issued at a discount are outstanding.

j. Effective interest or straight-line method of recognizing interest expense on bonds in the last year that bonds originally issued at a discount are outstanding.

Problems and Cases

12. *Impact of capitalizing and amortizing versus expensing when incurred.* South Co. Ltd. and North Corp. incur $50,000 of advertising costs each year. South Co. Ltd. expenses these costs immediately, whereas North Corp. capitalizes the costs and amortizes them over five years.

    a. Compute the amount of advertising expense and deferred advertising costs each firm would report beginning in the first year that advertising costs are incurred and continuing for six years.

b. For this part, assume that the amount of advertising costs incurred by each firm increases by $10,000 each year. Repeat part (**a**).

c. Comment on the differences noted in parts (**a**) and (**b**).

13. *Impact of alternative accounting policies on two firms.* On January 1, Year 1, two corporations are formed to operate merchandising businesses. The firms are alike in all respects except for their methods of accounting. Ruzicka Limited chooses the accounting policies that will minimize its reported net income. Murphy Inc. chooses the accounting policies that will maximize its reported net income but, where different procedures are permitted, will use accounting methods that minimize its taxable income. The following events occur during Year 1.

(1) Both companies issue 500,000 no-par-value common shares for $6 per share on January 2, Year 1.

(2) Both firms acquire equipment on January 2, Year 1, for $1,650,000 cash. The equipment is estimated to have a ten-year life and zero salvage value.

(3) Both firms engage in extensive sales promotion activities during 1982, incurring costs of $400,000.

(4) The two firms make the following purchases of merchandise inventory.

Date	Units Purchased	Unit Price	Cost of Purchase
January 2	50,000	$6.00	$ 300,000
April 1	60,000	6.20	372,000
August 15	40,000	6.25	250,000
November 30	50,000	6.50	325,000
Total	200,000		$1,247,000

(5) During the year, both firms sell 140,000 units at an average price of $15 each.

(6) Selling, general, and administrative expenses, other than advertising, total $100,000 during the year.

Ruzicka Limited uses the following accounting methods (for both book and tax purposes): weighted-average inventory cost-flow assumption, declining-balance depreciation method, with a rate of 20 percent, immediate expensing of the costs of sales promotion.

Murphy Inc. uses the following accounting methods: FIFO inventory cost-flow assumption for both book and tax purposes, the straight-line depreciation method for book and the declining-balance method for tax purposes with a rate of 20 percent, capitalization and amortization of the costs of the sales promotion campaign over four years for book and immediate expensing for tax purposes.

a. Prepare comparative income statements for the two firms for Year 1. Include separate computations of income tax expense. The income tax rate is 40 percent.

b. Prepare comparative balance sheets for the two firms as of December 31, Year 1. Both firms have $1 million of outstanding accounts receivable on this date and a single current liability for income taxes payable for the year.

c. Prepare comparative statements of changes in financial position for the two firms for Year 1, defining funds as cash.

14. *Impact of two sets of alternative accounting principles on net income and cash flows.* The Langston Corporation is formed on January 2, Year 1, with the issuance at par of 100,000 $10-par-value common shares for cash. During Year 1, the following transactions occur.

(1) The assets of the Dee's Department Store are acquired on January 2, Year 1, for $800,000 cash. The market values of the identifiable assets received are as follows: accounts receivable, $200,000; merchandise inventory, $400,000 (200,000 units); store equipment, $150,000; goodwill, $50,000.

(2) Merchandise inventory is purchased during Year 1 as follows:

Date	Units Purchased	Unit Price	Cost of Purchase
April 1	30,000	$2.10	$ 63,000
August 1	20,000	2.20	44,000
October 1	50,000	2.40	120,000
Total	100,000		$227,000

(3) During the year, 210,000 units are sold at an average price of $3.20.

(4) Extensive training programs are held during the year to acquaint previous employees of Dee's Department Store with the merchandising policies and procedures of Langston Corporation. The costs incurred in the training programs total $50,000.

(5) Selling, general, and administrative costs incurred and recognized as an expense during Year 1 are $80,000.

(6) The store equipment is estimated to have a five-year useful life and zero salvage value.

(7) The income tax rate is 40 percent. Ten percent of half of the goodwill arising from a corporate acquisition is deductible in computing taxable income and the remaining 50 percent is a permanent difference, not a timing difference. Ignore investment tax credit provisions in this problem.

The management of Langston Corporation is uncertain about the accounting methods that should be used in preparing its financial statements. The choice has been narrowed to two sets of accounting methods, and you have been asked to determine net income for Year 1 using each set.

Set A consists of the following accounting methods (for book and tax purposes): weighted-average inventory cost-flow assumption, declining-balance depreciation method at double the straight-line rate, immediate expensing of the costs of the training program, and amortization of goodwill over ten years.

Set B consists of the following accounting methods: FIFO inventory-costing assumption, straight-line depreciation for book and declining-balance for tax purposes, capitalization and amortization of the costs of the training program over five years for book and immediate expensing for tax purposes, and amortization of goodwill over 40 years.

a. Calculate net income for Year 1 under each set of accounting methods.

b. Calculate cash flow from operations under each set of accounting methods. Assume that accounts receivable at year end total $160,000.

15. *Impact of alternative accounting principles on net income, Year 2.* Net income of Miller Corporation for the year ending December 31, Year 2 is $600,000 based on the accounting methods actually used by the firm. You have been asked to determine the amount of net income that would have been reported under several alternative accounting methods. The income tax rate is 40 percent, and the same accounting methods are used for financial reporting and income tax purposes unless otherwise indicated. Each of the following questions should be considered independently.

a. Miller Corporation acquired a machine costing $300,000 on January 1, Year 2. The machine was depreciated during Year 2 using the straight-line method based on a five-year useful life and zero salvage value. What would net income have been if the declining-balance depreciation method, with a rate of 40 percent, had been used? Ignore the investment tax credit.

b. Miller Corporation used the cost method of accounting for its 18-percent investment in the common shares of General Tools Corporation. During Year 2, General Tools Corporation earned $200,000 and paid dividends of $50,000. The market value of General Tools Corporation was the same at the end of Year 2 as it was at the beginning of Year 2. What would net income have been during Year 2 if Miller Corporation used the equity method for financial reporting purposes? Ignore income tax.

c. Miller Corporation used the FIFO inventory cost-flow assumption. Under FIFO, the January 1, Year 2 inventory was $300,000, and the December 31, Year 2 inventory was $320,000. Under LIFO, the January 1, Year 2 inventory would have been $240,000 and the December 31, Year 2 inventory would have been $230,000. What would net income have been if the LIFO inventory costing assumption had been used?

16. *Computation of cash provided by operations.* The income statement of Garrett Corporation for Year 2 appears in Exhibit 15.7.

Current income tax expense has been reduced by $40,000 for amortization of deferred investment tax credits. The investment credit realized during Year 2 and added to the Deferred Investment Tax Credit account on the balance sheet is $60,000.

Determine the amount of cash provided by operations for Garrett Corporations during Year 2. Your analysis should begin with net income of $630,000.

Note 1: Depreciation charges of $200,000 and $100,000 are included in Cost of Goods Sold and Operating Expenses, respectively.

Note 2: Garrett Corporation owns 30 percent of the outstanding common shares of Knowles Corporation. During Year 2, Knowles Corporation earned $1,000,000 and declared dividends of $400,000.

Note 3: Garret Corporation owns ten percent of the outstanding common shares of Williams Corporation. During Year 2, Williams Corporation earned $2,000,000 and declared dividends of $600,000.

Note 4: Income Tax Expense is composed of the following:

Current	$500,000
Future	200,000
Total	$700,000

Exhibit 15.7
GARRETT CORPORATION
Income Statement
for the Year Ended
December 31, Year 2

Sales Revenue		$5,000,000
Less: Cost of Goods Sold (Note 1)		3,000,000
Gross Profit		$2,000,000
Operating Expenses (Note 1)		800,000
Net Operating Income		$1,200,000
Equity in Earnings of Unconsolidated Affiliate (Note 2)		300,000
		$1,500,000
Financial Expense:		
Interest Expense	$200,000	
Less: Interest Income	130,000	
	$ 70,000	
Dividend Income (Note 3)	60,000	$10,000
Income before Income Tax and Minority Interest		$1,490,000
Income Tax Expense (Note 4)		700,000
Income before Minority Interest		$ 790,000
Minority Interest in Income of Consolidated Subsidiary		160,000
Net Income		$ 630,000

Analysis of Changes
in Working Capital Accounts

Increase (Decrease) in Current Assets:	
Cash	$ 70,000
Marketable Securities	30,000
Accounts Receivable	430,000
Merchandise Inventories	370,000
Decrease (Increase) in Current Liabilities	
Accounts Payable	(320,000)
Income Taxes Payable	(120,000)
Increase in Working Capital	$460,000

17. *Preparation of financial statements from comprehensive data.* The data in Exhibit 15.8 are taken from the adjusted trial balances of the Hickory Merchandising Co. Ltd. as of December 31, Year 1 and Year 2. The brackets indicate amounts to be found in the solution of the problem.

Exhibit 15.8
HICKORY MERCHANDISING CO. LTD.
Adjusted Trial Balance
(Problem 17)

	December 31, Year 2		December 31, Year 1	
Accounts Payable		$ 98,715		$ 97,320
Accounts Receivable — Net	$ 617,530		$ 580,335	
Accruals and Withholdings Payable		99,700		99,800
Administrative Expenses	447,260		449,160	
Bonds Payable (6%)		277,000		275,000
Cash	149,485		114,080	
Common Shares		[ ]		100,000
Contributed Surplus		[ ]		700,000
Cost of Goods Sold	3,220,390		3,207,840	
Depreciation Expense	48,825		45,710	
Dividends on Common Shares — Cash and Stock	[ ]		50,000	
Dividends on Preferred Shares — Cash	6,000		6,000	
Dividends Payable		[ ]		—
Gain on Sale of Plant		[ ]		—
Income Tax Expense	122,675		104,975	
Income Tax Payable		111,675		104,975
Interest Expense on Bonds	[ ]		20,000	
Interest Expense on Notes	3,100		2,900	
Interest and Dividend Revenue		18,070		16,010
Inventories	633,690		616,120	
Investments in Subsidiaries	162,000		162,000	
Notes Payable		53,400		51,500
Notes Receivable	68,400		65,600	
Plant and Equipment — Net	[ ]		391,880	
Preferred Shares		100,000		100,000
Prepaid Insurance	7,640		8,240	
Retained Earnings		[ ]		[ ]
Royalties Revenue		44,285		37,020
Sales		4,605,275		4,552,320
Selling Expenses	656,230		642,530	
	$6,739,860	$6,739,860	$6,467,370	$6,467,370

Additional data:

(1) Preferred shares: six-percent, cumulative, $100-par value; 2,000 shares authorized.

(2) Common shares: $1-par value; 150,000 shares authorized.

(3) On January 10, Year 2, a ten-percent stock dividend was declared on common shares, issuable in common shares. The market price per share was $10 and the dividend was capitalized at $10 per share.

(4) On March 31 and September 30, Year 2, dividends of 25 cents per share were declared. The dividends were payable on April 20 and October 20, Year 2, respectively. On December 31, Year 2, an extra dividend of 12½ cents per

share was declared payable on January 20, Year 3. Note that all dividends, in cash and in shares, have been debited to Dividends accounts, not to Retained Earnings.

(5) Plant and equipment items having a cost of $39,240 and accumulated depreciation of $32,570 were retired and sold for $15,000. Acquisitions during Year 2 amounted to $71,500.

(6) The bonds are 30-year bonds and mature on June 30, Year 14. All bonds issued remain outstanding; straight-line amortization is used.

   a. Prepare a well-organized comparative statement of income and retained earnings.

   b. Prepare a well-organized comparative balance sheet.

   c. Prepare a well-organized statement of changes in financial position defining funds as cash.

18. *Preparation of three principal financial statements from comprehensive data.* The data in Exhibit 15.9 are taken from the records of the Barr Sales Inc.

Additional information:

(1) During the year the company retired fully depreciated fixtures that had cost $2,000. These were the only dispositions of furniture and fixtures.

(2) Furniture and fixtures acquired on May 10, Year 2, were financed one-third down, one-third due May 10, Year 3, and one-third due May 10, Year 4.

(3) On December 9, Year 2, the company sold a parcel of land it had purchased on January 14, Year 2, at a cost of $8,000.

Exhibit 15.9
BARR SALES INC.
Trial Balance Data

	December 31	
	Year 2 Adjusted Trial Balance	**Year 1 Post-closing Trial Balance**
Accounts Payable—Merchandise	$ 8,400	$ 9,160
Accounts Receivable	25,100	25,900
Accumulated Depreciation	4,600	5,600
Allowance for Doubtful Accounts	400	430
Cash	27,802	21,810
Common Shares (no par value)	59,500	54,000
Cost of Goods Sold	155,000	
Deposits by Customers	420	
Depreciation	1,000	
Dividends on Common Shares (both in cash and in shares)	8,125	
Dividends Payable	2,750	2,500
Furniture and Fixtures	21,000	20,000
Gain on Sale of Land	1,500	
Income Tax Expense	3,600	
Income Tax Payable	3,600	2,400

Installment Contracts Payable	2,000	
Interest Expense on Mortgage	482	
Interest Revenue on Investments	500	
Interest Payable on Mortgage	50	
Interest Receivable	50	30
Investments	14,000	15,000
Loss on Sales of Investments	300	
Merchandise Inventory	33,450	31,150
Mortgage Payable (5 percent)	10,122	10,140
Other Expenses	27,093	
Prepaid Rent	300	
Rent Expense	3,600	
Retained Earnings	28,860	28,860
Sales	210,000	
Sales Commissions	12,400	
Sales Commissions Payable	600	800

(4) On June 15, Year 2, the company purchased additional investments at a cost of $3,200. This was the only acquisition during the year. All investments are shown at cost, since market value exceeds cost.

(5) Merchandise was delivered during the year on customers' deposits in the amount of $1,200. All other deliveries were on account.

(6) On January 2, Year 2, the board of directors declared a five-percent stock dividend, capitalized at $11 per share. On January 2, Year 2, there were 5,000 shares outstanding, and 15,000 shares authorized.

(7) On June 20, Year 2, and December 20, Year 2, the board of directors declared the regular semiannual cash dividend of $.50 per share.

(8) On June 30, Year 2, the company issued 250 shares for cash.

(9) Note that all dividends, both in cash and in shares, were debited to Dividends on Common Shares, not to Retained Earnings.

    a. Prepare a well-organized statement of income and retained earnings for Year 2.

    b. Prepare a well-organized comparative balance sheet.

    c. Prepare a well-organized statement of changes in financial position for Year 2, defining funds as cash.

19. *Impact of alternative accounting principles on debt ratio.* Two conventional calculations of the debt ratio were introduced in Chapter 6. In this problem we focus on the following definition:

$$\text{Debt Ratio} = \frac{\text{Total Long-Term External Financing}}{\text{Owners' Equity}}$$

Many analysts use this ratio to assess the risk in the financial structure of a corporation. The higher the debt ratio, other things being equal, the greater the risk. Many analysts construct ratios from the conventional, historical-cost financial statements without adjustment. This problem illustrates how the assessment of the relative risk of companies can change as more sophisticated analysis of the financial statements is undertaken. In this problem, various adjustments to the conventional financial statements are made and new versions of the debt ratio are compared.

The problem may be worked all at once at the end of the course as a review, or it may be worked part by part as the various topics in the course are covered. Each part contains guidance as to when in the course the reader should be ready to work that part.

Data for four companies are presented in Exhibit 15.10. The methods are illustrated with the data for General Products Limited (from Appendix A). The reader is to prepare answers for the three other companies. All data are taken from the financial statements of the various companies for the same year. All dollar amounts are in millions. Income tax effects are ignored, except where noted.

Exhibit 15.10
(Dollar amounts in millions)
(Problem 19)

	General Products Limited	Bell Canada Enterprises Inc.	Consolidated-Bathurst Inc.	John Labatt Limited
1. Long-Term Debt	$1,000	$4,418	$546	$289
2. Deferred Tax Credits (Balance sheet)	1,242	1,819	223	88
3. Owners' Equity	8,200	5,731	626	449
4. Excess of Current Value over Book Value of:				
Inventory	2,358	(1)	4	2
Plant & Equipment	3,017	4,604	363	325
5. Pension Costs Not Recorded	2,046	—	—	10

    a. (After Chapter 6.) Compute the debt ratio for each of the companies. Include future income taxes with long-term financing in the numerator. For General Products Limited the debt ratio is:

$$= \frac{\$1,000 + \$1,242}{\$8,200}$$
$$= 27.3\%$$

Which companies appear to be significantly different from the others in terms of financial structure and risk? Discuss.

    b. (After Chapter 11.) Chapter 11 suggests that certain items shown as liabilities should not be, whereas certain other items not shown as liabilities should be. These two "errors" do not necessarily cancel each other out.

    (i) First, note that in most cases Future Income Taxes are not likely even to be paid and ought, in our opinion, to be reclassified as owners' equity. We can reflect this reclassification in the financial statements by making the following entry:

Future Income Taxes (Balance Sheet) $1,242
    Owners' Equity $1,242
Amount is that shown in line 2 of Exhibit 15.10.

After adjusting for future income taxes only, General Products Limited's debt ratio is:

$$\frac{\$1,000}{\$8,200 + \$1,242} = \frac{\$1,000}{\$9,442} = 10.6\%$$

Case-by-case analysis might be required in practice to find out if some of the companies' timing differences are likely to reverse in the foreseeable future. Our analysis of these companies' items does not reveal any such significant potential reversals.

(ii) The unrecognized prior service cost for pension plans meets all of the criteria to be a (long-term) liability, but is not shown as such. The amount is merely disclosed in the notes. To bring this number onto the balance sheet, the financial statements are adjusted with the following entry, which ignores income tax effects:

Owners' Equity	$2,046	
Pension Liability		$2,046

$2,046 million is the amount shown in General Products Limited's notes to the financial statements for unamortized prior-service costs.

After adjusting for the pension liability only, General Products Limited's debt ratio is:

$$\frac{\$1,000 + \$1,242 + \$2,046}{\$8,200 - \$2,046} = \frac{\$4,288}{\$6,154} = 69.7\%$$

Make the adjustments suggested above and recompute the debt ratio for each of the other three companies. Compute the ratios on a cumulative and non-cumulative basis; that is, compute the debt ratio after making each individual adjustment to the ratios computed in (a), and then after taking all the adjustments together, compute the percentage change in the ratio for each company. On which of the companies did each of these adjustments have the most impact?

c. (After Appendix D.) Appendix D illustrated the limitations of historical cost in making comparisons between companies. The two major balance sheet items of most companies that are affected by changing prices are inventories, and plant and equipment. To adjust the balance sheet values of inventory and of plant and equipment to current prices the following entries can be made for General Products Limited.

Inventories	$2,358	
Plant and Equipment	3,017	
Owners' Equity		$5,375

$2,358 million and $3,017 million are the excess of current cost over the historical cost amounts shown in General Products Limited balance sheet for inventory and for plant and equipment, respectively. See supplementary information following the notes to the financial statements.

After adjusting for changing prices only, General Products Limited debt-equity ratio is:

$$\frac{\$1,000 + \$1,242}{\$8,200 + \$2,358 + \$3,017} = \frac{\$2,242}{\$13,575} = 16.5\%$$

If all adjustments in (a), (b), and (c) are made, General Products Limited's debt ratio is:

$$\frac{\$1,000 + \$2,046}{\$8,200 + \$1,242 - \$2,046 + \$2,358 + \$3,017} = \frac{\$3,046}{\$12,771} = 23.9\%$$

Make the adjustments suggested above and recompute the debt ratio for each of the other three companies. Compute the ratios on cumulative and noncumulative bases: that is, compute the debt ratio after making each individual adjustment to the ratio computed in (a); then, after taking all the adjustments together, compute the percentage change in the ratio for each company. On which of the companies did each of these adjustments have the most impact?

d. What can you infer from this exercise about the debt ratio computed from published financial statements?

Exhibit 15.11
CALMES CORPORATION
Consolidated Statement of Income and Retained Earnings for the Year Ended December 31, Year 2
(Problem 20)

Sales Revenue		$6,000,000
Less: Cost of Goods Sold		2,500,000
Gross Profit		$3,500,000
Income from Completed Contracts		960,000
		$4,460,000
Less: Operating Expenses		
Employee Payroll	$1,500,000	
Depreciation on Plant and Equipment and Amortization of Leased Property Rights	500,000	
Amortization of Intangibles	100,000	
Bad Debts	60,000	
General Corporate Expenses	100,000	2,260,000
Operating Income		$2,200,000
Other Income:		
Equity in Earnings of Unconsolidated Subsidiaries and Affiliates:		
Calmes Finance Corporation	900,000	
Richardson Ltd.	50,000	
Anthony Inc.	50,000	
	$1,000,000	
Gain on Sale of Machinery and Equipment	100,000	1,100,000
		$3,300,000
Less: Interest Expense		300,000
Income before Income Tax		$3,000,000

Income Tax:

Current	$ 700,000	
Future	100,000	800,000
Income before Minority Interest		$2,200,000
Minority Interest in Earnings		200,000
Net Income		$2,000,000
Less: Dividends on Preferred Shares		60,000
Dividends on Common Shares		840,000
Increase in Retained Earnings		$1,100,000
Retained Earnings, January 1, Year 2		1,400,000
Retained Earnings, December 31, Year 2		$2,500,000
Basic Earnings per Common Share (based on 1,000,000 average shares outstanding)		$1.94
Fully Diluted Earnings per Share (assuming conversion of preferred shares)		$1.25

Exhibit 15.12
CALMES CORPORATION
Consolidated Balance Sheets
December 31
(Problem 20)

	Year 2	Year 1
Assets		
Current Assets:		
Cash	$ 50,000	$ 100,000
Temporary Investments at Lower of Cost and Market (market value, $160,000)	150,000	—
Accounts Receivable	300,000	250,000
Merchandise Inventory	700,000	600,000
Accumulated Costs under Contracts in Process in Excess of Progress Billings	200,000	150,000
Prepayments	100,000	100,000
Total Current Assets	$ 1,500,000	$1,200,000
Investments (at equity):		
Calmes Finance Corporation (100% owned)	$ 2,000,000	$1,100,000
Richardson Ltd. (50% owned)	500,000	450,000
Anthony Inc. (25% owned)	100,000	50,000
Total Investments	$ 2,600,000	$1,600,000
Property, Plant, and Equipment:		
Land	250,000	$ 200,000
Building	2,000,000	2,000,000
Machinery and Equipment	4,000,000	3,650,000
Property Rights Acquired under Lease	750,000	750,000
Total	$ 7,000,000	$6,600,000
Less: Accumulated Depreciation and Amortization	(2,000,000)	(1,900,000)
Total Property, Plant, and Equipment	$ 5,000,000	$4,700,000

Intangibles (at net book value):

	Year 2	Year 1
Discount on Bonds Payable	$ 176,000	$ 200,000
Patent	200,000	250,000
Goodwill	700,000	750,000
Total Intangibles	$ 1,076,000	$1,200,000
Total Assets	$10,176,000	$8,700,000

	Year 2	Year 1
Liabilities and Shareholders' Equity		
Current Liabilities:		
Notes Payable	$ 250,000	$ 200,000
Accounts Payable	350,000	330,000
Salaries Payable	150,000	120,000
Income Taxes Payable	200,000	150,000
Rent Received in Advance	50,000	—
Other Current Liabilities	200,000	100,000
Total Current Liabilities	$ 1,200,000	$ 900,000
Long-Term Debt:		
Bonds Payable	$ 2,000,000	$2,000,000
Equipment Mortgage Indebtedness	176,000	650,000
Obligation under Capital Lease	500,000	550,000
Future Income Taxes	$ 800,000	$ 700,000
Total Long-Term Debt	$ 3,476,000	$3,900,000
Minority Interest in Subsidiary	$ 500,000	$ 300,000
Shareholders' Equity:		
Convertible Preferred Shares	$ 1,000,000	$1,000,000
Common Shares	1,000,000	1,000,000
Contributed Surplus	1,000,000	900,000
Retained Earnings	2,500,000	1,400,000
Total	$ 5,500,000	$4,300,000
Less: Cost of Treasury Shares	(500,000)	(700,000)
Total Shareholders' Equity	$ 5,000,000	$3,600,000
Total Liabilities and Shareholders' Equity	$10,176,000	$8,700,000

20. *Comprehensive review problem.* The principal objective of this book has been to help you develop a sufficient understanding of the accounting process that generates financial statements for external users so that the resulting statements can then be (1) interpreted, (2) analyzed, and (3) evaluated. This problem has been designed partly as a review of the material covered in the book and partly as a means of assessing your progress toward this objective. A partial set of financial statements of Calmes Corporation for Year 2, including consolidated comparative balance sheets at December 31, Year 1, and Year 2, and a consolidated statement of income and retained earnings for the year Year 2 is presented in Exhibits 15.11 and 15.12. A series of discussion questions and short problems relating to the financial statements of Calmes Corporation is presented on pages 747 through 750. It is suggested that you study the financial statements before repsonding to these questions and problems.

Part I — Financial Statement Interpretation

For each of the accounts or items listed below and appearing on the consolidated balance sheets and income statement of the Calmes Corporation, describe **(1)** the nature of the account or item (that is, the transaction or conditions that resulted in its recognition) and **(2)** the valuation method used in determining its amount. Respond in descriptive terms rather than using specific numbers from the financial statements of the Calmes Corporation. The first one is provided as an example.

Additional information:
The balance of the allowance for doubtful accounts was $80,000 at December 31, Year 1 and $50,000 at December 31, Year 0.

a. Accumulated Costs under Contracts in Progress in Excess of Progress Billings—
The Calmes Corporation is providing services of some type to specific customers under contract. All costs incurred under the contracts are accumulated in this current asset account. When customers are billed periodically for a portion of the contract price, this account is credited. The account, therefore, reflects the excess of costs incurred to date on uncompleted contracts over the amounts billed to customers. Since the account does not include any income or profit from the contracts (that is, "accumulated costs"), the firm is apparently using the completed-contract method rather than the percentage-of-completion method of recognizing revenues.

b. Investment in Calmes Finance Corporation

c. Property Rights Acquired under Lease

d. Goodwill

e. Rent Received in Advance

f. Future Income Taxes (Balance Sheet)

g. Minority Interest in Subsidiary (Balance Sheet)

h. Treasury Shares

i. Bad Debts Expense (Income Statement)

Part II — Financial Statement Analysis

a. The Calmes Corporation used the LIFO cost-flow assumption in determining its cost of goods sold and beginning and ending merchandise inventory amounts. If the FIFO cost-flow assumption had been used, the beginning inventory would have been $900,000 and the ending inventory would have been $850,000. Compute the actual gross profit of the Calmes Corporation for Year 2 if FIFO had been used (ignore income tax effects). Calmes Corporation used the periodic inventory method.

b. Refer to **(a)**. What can be said about the quantity of merchandise inventory at the beginning and end of Year 2 and the direction of price changes during Year 2? Explain.

c. The Calmes Corporation accounts for its three intercorporate investments in unconsolidated subsidiaries under the equity method. The shares in each of these companies were acquired at book value at the time of acquisition. What were the total dividends declared by these three companies during Year 2? How can you tell?

d. The Calmes Corporation accounts for its three intercorporate investments in unconsolidated subsidiaries under the equity method. The shares in each of these companies were acquired at book value at the time of acquisition. Give the journal entry (entries) that was (were) made during Year 2 in applying the equity method.

e. The building was acquired on January 1, Year 1. It was estimated to have a 40-year useful life and zero salvage value at that time. Determine the amount of depreciation expense on this building for Year 2, assuming that the declining-balance method is used.

f. Machinery and equipment costing $500,000, and with a book value of $100,000, were sold for cash during Year 2. Give the journal entry to record the disposition.

g. The bonds payable carry six-percent annual coupons. Interest is paid on December 31 of each year. Give the journal entry made on December 31, Year 2 to recognize interest expense for Year 2, assuming that Calmes Corporation uses the effective-interest method.

h. Refer to (g). What was the effective or market interest rate on these bonds on the date they were issued? Explain.

i. The only timing difference between net income and taxable income during Year 2 was in the amount of depreciation expense. If the income tax rate was 40 percent, determine the difference between the depreciation deduction reported on the tax return and the depreciation expense reported on the income statement.

j. Give the journal entry that explains the change in the treasury shares account assuming that there were no other transactions affecting common or preferred shares during Year 2.

k. If the original amount of the patent acquired was $500,000, and the patent is being amortized on a straight-line basis, when was the patent acquired?

l. The shares of Anthony Inc. were acquired on December 31, Year 1. If the same amount of shares in Anthony Inc. were held during the year, but the amount represented only *15-percent* ownership of Anthony Inc., how would the financial statements have differed? Disregard income tax effects.

m. During Year 2, Calmes paid $85,000 to the lessor of property represented on the balance sheet by "Property Rights Acquired under Lease." Property rights acquired under lease have a ten-year life and are being amortized on a straight-line basis. What was the total expense reported by Calmes Corporation during Year 2 from using the leased property?

n. How would the financial statements have differed if the Calmes Corporation accounted for temporary investments on the lower-of-cost-and-market basis and the market value of these securities had been $130,000 instead of $160,000 at the end of Year 2? Disregard income tax effects.

o. If the Minority Interest in Subsidiary represents a 20-percent interest in Calmes Corporation's only consolidated subsidiary, what was the *total* amount of dividends declared by this subsidiary during Year 2? How can you tell?

p. Refer to the earnings-per-share amounts in the income statement of Calmes Corporation. How many common shares would be issued if all of the outstanding preferred shares were converted into common shares?

q. Insert the missing items of information numbered (3)–(27) in the statement of changes in financial position of the Calmes Corporation in Exhibit 15.13. Be sure to include both descriptions of the missing items and their amounts. Provide supporting calculations for each of the missing items in the statement.

r. On January 2, Year 3, the Calmes Corporation requested its bank to grant a six-month loan for $300,000. If approved, the loan would be granted on January 10, Year 3. As the bank's senior credit analyst, you have been asked to assess the liquidity of the Calmes Corporation and present a memorandum summarizing your conclusions. Include any ratios and any other information from the financial statements that you consider relevant. Also include a summary of information not disclosed in the financial statements that you think the loan officer should consider before making a final decision.

Exhibit 15.13
CALMES CORPORATION
Consolidated Statement of Changes in Financial
Position for the Year Ended December 31, Year 2

Cash Provided by

Operations:

(3)_____ ..... $_____

Add Expenses and Deductions Not Using Cash:

(4)_____ ..... _____

(5)_____ ..... _____

(6)_____ ..... _____

(7)_____ ..... _____

(8)_____ ..... _____

Add Credit Changes in Operating Current Asset and Current Liability Accounts:

(9)_____ ..... _____

(10)_____ ..... _____

(11)_____ ..... _____

(12)_____ ..... _____

(13)_____ ..... _____

(14)_____ ..... _____

Subtract Revenues and Additions Not Providing Cash:

(15)_____ ..... _____

(16)_____ ..... _____

Subtract Debit Changes in Operating Current Asset and Current Liability Accounts:

(17)_____ ..... _____

(18)_____ ..... _____

(19)_____ ..... _____

(20)_____ ..... _____

Cash Provided by Operations $1,774,000

New Financing:

(21)_____ ..... _____

(22)_____ ..... _____

Total Sources of Cash $2,274,000

Cash Applied to

Reduction in Financing:

(23)_____ ..... _____

(24)_____ ..... _____

(25)_____ ..... _____

Acquisition of Assets:

(26)_____	.....	_____
(27)_____	.....	_____
Total Uses of Cash		$2,324,000
Decrease in Cash		$ 50,000

Part III — Financial Statement Evaluation

a. The treasurer of the Calmes Corporation recently remarked. ''The value or worth of our company on December 31, Year 2, is $5,000,000, as measured by total shareholders' equity.'' Describe briefly at least three reasons why the difference between recorded total assets and recorded total liabilities on the balance sheet does not represent the firm's value or worth.

b. The accounting profession has been criticized for permitting several ''generally accepted accounting policies'' for the same or similar transactions. What are the major arguments for **(1)** narrowing the range of acceptable policies and **(2)** continuing the present system of permitting business firms some degree of flexibility in selecting their accounting methods?

21. *Comprehensive review problem.* Partial financial statements of Tuck Corporation for Year 2 are presented in Exhibit 15.14 (consolidated statement of income and retained earnings), and Exhibit 15.15 (consolidated balance sheet). Also shown are a statement of accounting policies and a set of notes to the financial statements. After studying these financial statements and notes, respond to each of the following questions.

a. Prepare an analysis that explains the change in Temporary Investments account during Year 2.

b. Calculate the proceeds from sales of temporary investments during Year 2.

c. Calculate the amount of the provision for doubtful accounts made during Year 2.

d. Give the journal entry(s) to account for the change in the Investments in Thayer Corporation — Net account during Year 2.

e. Calculate the amount of income or loss from the Investment in Thayer Corporation during Year 2.

f. Give the journal entry(s) to account for the change in the Investment in Tuck Credit Corporation account during Year 2.

g. Assume that Tuck Credit Corporation had been consolidated with Tuck Corporation on December 31, Year 2. Calculate the amount of (1) Total Assets, (2) Total Liabilities, and (3) Net Income.

h. Prepare an analysis that identifies the factors and the amounts that explain the change in the Minority Interest in Subsidiary account on the balance sheet.

i. Calculate the balance in the Investment in Harvard Corporation account on Tuck Corporation's books on December 31, Year 2, assuming that the equity method had been used.

j. Calculate the amount of cash received during Year 2 for rental fees.

k. Calculate the actual cost of goods and services required to service customers' warranties during Year 2.

l. Refer to Note 7. Calculate the amount of interest expense on the $1 million, six-percent bonds for Year 2.

m. Give the journal entry(s) that accounts for the change in the Mortgage Payable account during Year 2.

n. The income tax rate is 40 percent. Calculate the capital cost allowance claimed for income tax purposes for Year 2.

o. Give the journal entry made on July 1, Year 2 upon conversion of the preferred shares.

p. Give the journal entry(s) to account for the change in the Treasury Shares account during Year 2.

q. Prepare a T-account work sheet for the preparation of a statement of changes in financial position, defining *funds* as *cash*.

Exhibit 15.14
TUCK CORPORATION
Consolidated Statement of Income and Retained Earnings
for the Year Ended December 31, Year 2
(Problem 21)

Sales		$4,000,000
Less: Cost of Goods Sold (Note 1)		2,530,000
Gross Profit		$1,470,000
Less: Operating Expenses		
Selling & Administrative (Note 1)	$1,092,205	
Warranty Expense	46,800	
	$1,139,005	
Less: Gain on Sale of Equipment	3,000	$1,136,005
Operating Profit		$ 333,995
Plus: Financial Income (net)		
Rental Revenue	$ 240,000	
Dividend Revenue	8,000	
Equity in Income of Unconsolidated Subsidiary and Affiliate	102,000	
	$ 350,000	
Less: Financial Expenses:		
Interest	165,995	
Loss on Sale of Temporary Investments	8,000	
Unrealized Loss on Portfolio Investment	5,000	
	$ 178,995	171,005
Income before the Undernoted		$ 505,000
Income Tax Expense		200,000
Income before Minority Interest		$ 305,000
Minority Interest in Income of Consolidated Subsidiary		10,000
Consolidated Net Income		$ 295,000
Less: Dividends Declared		(120,000)
Increase in Retained Earnings for Year 2		$ 175,000
Retained Earnings, December 31, Year 1		204,000
Retained Earnings, December 31, Year 2		$ 379,000

Exhibit 15.15
TUCK CORPORATION
Consolidated Comparative Balance Sheets
(Problem 21)

	December 31, Year 2	December 31, Year 1
Assets:		
Current Assets:		
Cash	$ 280,000	$ 240,000
Temporary Investments (Note 2)........................	141,000	125,000
Accounts Receivable — Net (Note 3)	1,509,600	1,431,200
Inventories	1,525,315	1,257,261
Prepayments	32,000	28,000
Total Current Assets	$3,487,915	$3,081,461
Investments: (Note 4)		
Investment in Thayer Corporation — Net (15 percent owned) ...	$ 87,000	$ 92,000
Investment in Hitchcock Corporation (30 percent owned)	135,000	120,000
Investment in Tuck Credit Corporation (100 percent owned)	298,000	215,000
Total Investments	$ 520,000	$ 427,000
Property, Plant, and Equipment: (Note 5)		
Land	$ 82,000	$ 82,000
Building	843,000	843,000
Equipment	1,848,418	497,818
Leasehold	98,182	98,182
Total Plant Assets at Cost	$2,871,600	$1,521,000
Less: Accumulated Depreciation and Amortization	(413,000)	(376,000)
Total Plant Assets—Net	$2,458,600	$1,145,000
Intangibles:		
Discount on 8-percent Bonds Payable	$ 168,680	—
Goodwill — Net	$ 34,000	$ 36,000
Total Assets	$6,669,195	$4,689,461

	Year 2	Year 1
Liabilities and Shareholders' Equity		
Current Liabilities:		
Note Payable (Note 6)	$ 200,000	$ 100,000
Accounts Payable	723,700	666,100
Rental Fees Received in Advance	58,000	46,000
Estimated Warranty Liability	78,600	75,200
Interest Payable on Notes	2,000	1,500
Dividends Payable	30,000	25,000
Income Taxes Payable — Current	160,000	140,000
Total Current Liabilities	$1,252,300	$1,053,800

Noncurrent Liabilities:

Bonds Payable (Note 7)	$2,000,000	$1,000,000
Mortgage Payable (Note 8)	280,943	299,947
Obligation under Capital Lease (Note 9)	56,229	62,064
Premium on 6-percent Bonds Payable	99,823	104,650
Future Income Taxes	145,000	130,000
Total Noncurrent Liabilities	$2,581,995	$1,596,661
Total Liabilities	$3,834,295	$2,650,461
Minority Interest in Subsidiary	$ 36,500	$ 32,000

Shareholders' Equity:

Convertible Preferred Shares, $100-par Value (Note 10)	200,000	700,000
Common Shares, $10-par Value (Note 11)	1,650,000	1,000,000
Contributed Surplus	583,600	130,000
Retained Earnings	379,000	204,000
Total	$2,812,600	$2,034,000
Less: Cost of Treasury Shares (Note 12)	(14,200)	(27,000)
Total Shareholders' Equity	$2,798,400	$2,007,000
Total Liabilities and Shareholders' Equity	$6,669,195	$4,689,461

Statement of Accounting Policies

Basis of Consolidation The financial statements of Tuck Corporation are consolidated with Harvard Corporation, a 90-percent-owned subsidiary acquired on January 2, Year 0.

Temporary Investments Temporary Investments are stated at lower of acquisition cost and market.

Accounts Receivable Doubtful accounts of customers are accounted for using the allowance method.

Inventories Inventories are measured using a last-in, first-out cost-flow assumption.

Investments Investments of less than 20 percent of the outstanding common shares of other companies are accounted for using the cost method. Investments of greater than or equal to 20 percent of the outstanding common shares of unconsolidated affiliates and subsidiaries are accounted for using the equity method.

Building, Equipment, and Leaseholds Depreciation for financial reporting purposes is calculated using the straight-line method. For income tax purposes, the company claims the maximum capital cost allowance.

Goodwill Goodwill arising from investments in Harvard Corporation is amortized over a period of 20 years.

Interest Expense on Long-Term Debt Interest expense on long-term debt is recognized using the effective-interest method.

Future Income Taxes Future income taxes are provided for timing differences between book and taxable income. All timing differences relate to depreciation.

Notes to the Financial Statements

Note 1: Cost of goods sold and selling and administrative expenses include depreciation and amortization of $56,000.

Note 2: Temporary Investments costing $35,000 were sold during Year 2. No dividends were received from temporary investments during Year 2.

Note 3: Accounts receivable are shown net of an allowance for doubtful accounts of $128,800 on December 31, Year 1 and $210,400 on December 31, Year 2. A total of $63,000 of accounts were written off as uncollectible during Year 2.

Note 4: Condensed balance sheet data for Tuck Credit Corporation, a wholly owned, unconsolidated credit subsidiary, are shown below:

	December 31, Year 2	December 31, Year 1
Total Assets	$478,000	$375,000
Total Liabilities	$180,000	$160,000
Shareholders' Equity	$298,000	$215,000

Net income of Tuck Credit Corporation for Year 2 was $87,000. Dividends declared and paid during Year 2 totaled $24,000.

Note 5: Equipment with a cost of $23,000 and a book value of $4,000 was sold during Year 2. This was the only disposition of property, plant, or equipment during the year.

Note 6: A 90-day, 9-percent note with a face amount of $100,000 was paid with interest at maturity on January 30, Year 2. On December 1, Year 2, Tuck Corporation borrowed $200,000 from its local bank, promising to repay the principal plus interest at 12 percent in six months.

Note 7: Bonds Payable on the balance sheet is composed of the following:

	December 31, Year 2	December 31, Year 1
$1,000,000, 6-percent, semiannual coupon bonds, due December 31, Year 16, priced at $1,125,510 to yield 5 percent, compounded semiannually, at the time of issue	$1,000,000	$1,000,000
$1,000,000, 8-percent, semiannual coupon bonds, due December 31, Year 21, priced at $828,409 to yield 10 percent, compounded semiannually, at the time of issue	$1,000,000	—
Total	$2,000,000	$1,000,000

Note 8: Mortgage Payable represents a mortgage on buildings requiring equal installment payments of $40,000 on December 31 of each year. The loan underlying the mortgage bears interest of seven percent, compounded annually. The final installment payment is due on December 31, Year 12.

Note 9: The Obligation under Capital Lease represents a 20-year, noncancelable lease on certain equipment. The lease requires annual payments in advance of $10,000 on January 2 of each year. The last lease payment will be made on January 2, Year 8. The lease is capitalized at the lessee's borrowing rate (at the inception of the lease) of eight percent.

Note 10: Each preferred share is convertible into five common shares. On July 1, Year 2, holders of 5,000 preferred shares exercised their options. The conversion was recorded using book values.

Note 11: On October 1, Year 2, 40,000 common shares were issued on the open market for $15 per share.

Note 12: Treasury Shares are composed of the following:

December 31, Year 1: 2,250 shares at $12 per share	$27,000
December 31, Year 2: 450 shares at $12 per share	$ 5,400
550 shares at $16 per share	8,800
	$14,200

22. *Selecting accounting methods.* Champion Clothiers, Inc. owns and operates 80 retailing establishments throughout Quebec and the Maritimes, specializing in quality men's and women's clothing. The company was established many years ago by Jean-Pierre Champion and has been run by a member of the Champion family ever since. Currently, Roger Champion, grandson of the founder, is president and chief executive officer. The company's shares are held by members of the Champion family.

The setting for this case is March of 1988. The following conversation takes place between Roger Champion and the company's accountant, Tom Morrissey.

Champion (President): "Tom, you said on the telephone that the financial statements for 1987 were now complete. How much did we earn last year?"

Morrissey (Accountant): "Net income was $800,000, with earnings per share at $1.60. With the $1.20 per share earned in 1985 and $1.38 earned in 1986, we have maintained our 15 percent growth rate in profits."

Champion: "That sounds great! Tom, at our board meeting next week I am going to announce that the Champion family has decided to take the company public. We will be issuing shares equal to a 40 percent stake in the company early in 1989. It is important that our earnings for 1988 continue to reflect the growth rate we have been experiencing. By my calculations, we need an earnings per share for 1988 in the neighborhood of $1.84. Does this seem likely?"

Morrissey: "I'm afraid not. Our current projections indicate an earnings per share around $1.65 for this year. Major unexpected style changes earlier this year have left us with obsolete inventory that will have to be written off. In addition, increased competition in several of our major markets is putting a squeeze on margins. Even the acquisition of Green Trucking Limited in June of this year will not help earnings that much."

Champion: "I know you accountants have all kinds of games you can play to doctor up the numbers. There must be something we can do to increase earnings to the desired level. What about our use of LIFO for inventories?"

Morrissey: "We have been using LIFO in the past because it reduces income during a period of rising prices. The more recent, higher acquisition costs of inventory items are used in computing cost of goods sold in the income statement. The older, lower acquisition prices are used in the valuation of inventory on the balance sheet. We could switch to FIFO for 1988. That would add about $.21 to earnings per share. Since LIFO is not allowed for tax purposes, there would be no additional taxes to pay. However, income tax expense would be increased by about $50,000, and an offsetting increase in deferred income tax would be recorded.

Champion: FIFO certainly more closely approximates the physical flow of our goods. If we decide to stay on LIFO, is there anything we can do in applying the LIFO method that would prop up earnings?"

Morrissey: "We now classify our inventory very broadly into two LIFO groups, or pools: one for men's clothing and one for women's clothing. We do this to minimize the possibility of dipping into an old LIFO layer. As you will recall, if we sell more than we purchase during a given period, we dip into an old LIFO layer. These LIFO layers are valued using acquisition costs of the year the layer was added. Some of these layers reflect costs of the mid-50s. When we dip into one of these layers, we have to use these old, lower costs in figuring cost of goods sold and net income. By defining our LIFO pools broadly to include our dollar investment in men's clothing and our dollar investment in women's clothing, we minimize the probability of liquidating an old LIFO layer. We could define our LIFO pools more narrowly to increase the possibility of dipping. We could then let the inventory of particular items run down at the end of the year, dip into the LIFO layer to increase earnings, and then rebuild the inventory early in the next year. I suspect we could add about $.02 a share to 1988 earnings if we went with narrower pools."

Champion: "We own all of our store buildings and display counters. Is there anything we can do with depreciation expense?"

Morrissey: "We now depreciate these items using the fastest write-off permitted by tax law. However we do not have to calculate depreciation for financial reporting the same as we do for tax reporting. We could depreciate these items over the expected economic life of each asset. That should add about $.04 to earnings per share for 1985. We could also use the straight-line depreciation method for financial reporting. While our depreciable assets probably decrease in value faster than the straight-line method would indicate, we would be using the depreciation method that most of our competitors use for financial reporting. The use of straight-line depreciation would add another $.08."

Champion: "Now you're talking. What else can we do?"

Morrissey: "In previous years we have charged all interest accrued to expense. We could capitalize a portion of this interest as a cost of the plant under construction. For 1988 this would add another $.10 per share. There is also one thing we can do very easily with our pension plan to improve earnings. When we adopted the pension plan two years ago, we gave all employees credit for their service prior to adoption. This created an immediate obligation for past service. We are amortizing this obligation as a charge against earnings over a five-year period. Generally accepted accounting practice permits us to use 15 years, the average remaining work life of our employees, instead of five years as the amortization period; that switch would increase earnings per share by $.05 for 1988."

Champion: "All of the things you have suggested deal with the selection or application of accounting methods. Can we do anything with the timing of expenditures to help 1988 earnings?"

Morrissey: "Well, painting and other maintenance of our stores scheduled for the last quarter of this year could be postponed until the first quarter of next year. That would add $.02 to earnings per share. In addition, we anticipate running a major advertising campaign just after Christmas. While the advertising expenditure will be made in 1988 and will reduce earnings per share by $.07, all of the benefits of the campaign will be realized in greater sales early in 1989."

Champion: "I hadn't realized how much flexibility we had for managing our earnings. Before we decide which choices to make, can you think of any other avenues open to us?"

Morrissey: "We could always sell off assets on which we have potential gain. For example, we hold some temporary investments that we purchased last year. Selling those securities would net us an additional $.02 in earnings per share. In addition, we own two parcels of land that we hope to use some day for new stores. These parcels could be sold at a gain of $.04 per share."

Champion: "It strikes me that these alternatives could increase earnings per share for 1988 to the $2.00-plus range. This level is a lot more appealing than the $1.65 per share anticipated for the year. Will we have to do anything to earnings per share for prior years if we adopt any of these alternatives?"

Morrissey: "I have set out in Exhibit 15.16 the impact of each of the choices on earnings per share for 1988, as well as any retroactive adjustment required for prior years. This summary should be helpful as we decide our strategy."

How much do you think Champion Clothiers should report as earnings per share for 1988?

Exhibit 15.16
CHAMPION CLOTHIERS, INC.
Alternative Strategies for Managing Earnings per Share
(Problem 22)

	Impact on Earnings per Share			
Alternative	**1988**	**1987**	**1986**	**1985**
Actual or Anticipated	$1.65	$1.60	$1.38	$1.20
Adoption of FIFO	+.21	+.20	+.17	+.15
Use of Narrower LIFO Pools	+.02	+.02	+.03	+.02
Use of Longer Depreciable Lives	+.04	—	—	—
Adoption of Straight-Line Depreciation	+.08	+.07	+.06	+.05
Capitalizing Interest on Construction in Progress	+.10	+.06	+.04	+.02
Amortization of Pension Obligation over 15 Years	+.05	—	—	—
Deferral of Maintenance	+.02	—	—	—
Deferral of Advertising	+.07	—	—	—
Sale of Temporary Investments	+.02	—	—	—
Sale of Land	+.04	—	—	—

23. *Preparation of financial statements requiring assumptions by student.* The Coffee Mill is a retail business specializing in gourmet teas and coffees which are imported through a broker. The owner began the business on January 1, 1988, when she contributed $50,000 of personal savings to the business. The Coffee Mill is a private corporation. The owner and sole shareholder holds 100 shares with no par value.

Sales receipts for the past year totalled $65,000 including $2,400 received for gift certificates yet to be redeemed at the Coffee Mill. Purchases in the past year were made in three lots and were as follows:

Lot #	Date	Coffee Quantity (kg)	Coffee Cost ($/kg)	Tea Quantity (kg)	Tea Cost ($/kg)
1	January 1	1,000	$1.65	500	$1.24
2	April 15	2,500	1.85	700	1.45
3	November 15	3,400	2.05	900	1.62

The prices on these products are subject to many different variables in the international market. Ending inventory consists of 1,500 kg of coffee and 230 kg of tea.

The Coffee Mill is located in 800 square feet of retail space in a small shopping centre. It had signed a five-year lease at $20 per square foot. As an incentive, the landlord has offered the business the first year's rent free. Coffee Mill would be responsible for its share of the operating costs incurred by the Mall Merchants' Association which total $6.50 per square foot. Both the rent and the operating costs are expressed in annual terms. One twelfth of this total is payable monthly to the landlord.

During 1988, the owner of the Coffee Mill received a monthly salary of $2,000. The owner's husband and daughter each spent about twenty hours per week assisting in the store and running errands. As the owner had been very concerned with conserving cash, no payment had been made for this help. Extra personnel had been hired over the Christmas season at a cost of $1,600, based on a rate of $5 per hour. Promotion and advertising costs amounted to $6,400. Supplies costing $1,500 had been purchased on account.

The Coffee Mill has been in operation for exactly one year. The owner is considering opening a second shop which would require a bank loan.

a. The bank manager has requested that you prepare a balance sheet and an income statement for the Coffee Mill's first year of operations. He also wishes to have your comments regarding any accounting problems encountered and the assumptions you have made in preparing the above statements.

Adapted with the permission of the Society of Management Accountants of Canada.

Appendix A Corporate Financial Statements Illustrated and Annotated

This appendix illustrates current financial reporting with a comprehensive set of corporate financial statements prepared in accordance with generally accepted accounting principles.

The financial statements for the General Products Limited (GP), shown here, are adapted from those of the General Electric Company. The disclosure in these statements exceeds the minimum requirements of the *CICA Handbook*, but is not greater than that provided by a cross-section of Canadian companies.

This appendix is organized as follows. We have split the annual report of General Products Limited into four exhibits, numbered Exhibit A.1 to A.4. These exhibits are followed by notes to the financial statements, plus industry segment data and other information. Numerical footnotes refer to author's comments that explain various features of the accounting appearing in the financial statements. These authors' comments are contained in a separate section towards the end of the appendix, followed by questions and problems.

Exhibit A.1

GENERAL PRODUCTS LIMITED

Consolidated statement of income and retained earnings

For the years ended December 31 (In millions)		1988	1987	1986
Sales	Sales of products and services to customers	$24,959	$22,461	$19,654
Operating expenses (notes 1 and 2)	Cost of goods sold	17,751	15,991	13,915
	Gross profit	7,208	6,470	5,739
	Less: selling, general, and administrative expenses	4,965	4,340	3,781
	Operating profit	2,243	2,130	1,958
	Other income (note 3)	564	519	419
	Interest and other financial charges (note 4)	(314)	(258)	(224)
Income	Net income before income taxes and minority interest	2,493	2,391	2,153
	Income tax expense (note 5)[1]	(958)	(953)	(894)
	Minority interest in income of consolidated subsidiaries[2]	(21)	(29)	(29)
	Net income	$ 1,514	$ 1,409	$ 1,230
	Earnings per common share (in dollars) (note 6)[3]	$6.65	$6.20	$5.39
	Dividends declared per common share (in dollars)	$2.95	$2.75	$2.50
	Operating profit as a percentage of sales	9.0%	9.5%	10.0%
	Net income as a percentage of sales	6.1%	6.3%	6.3%

For the years ended December 31 (In millions)		1988	1987	1986
Retained Earnings	Balance January 1	$ 6,307	$ 5,522	$ 4,862
	Net income[4]	1,514	1,409	1,230
	Dividends declared on common shares	(670)	(624)	(570)
	Balance December 31	$ 7,151	$ 6,307	$ 5,522

The information in the notes is an integral part of these statements.

Auditors' report[5]

To Shareholders of General Products Limited

We have examined the consolidated balance sheet of General Products Limited as at December 31, 1988, and 1987, and the statements of income, retained earnings, and changes in financial position for each of the three years in the period ended December 31, 1988. Our examinations were made in accordance with generally accepted auditing standards, and accordingly included such tests and other procedures as we considered necessary in the circumstances.

In our opinion, these financial statements present fairly the financial position of General Products Limited as at December 31, 1988 and 1987, and the results of their operations and the changes in their financial position for each of the three years in the period ended December 31, 1988, in conformity with generally accepted accounting principles applied on a basis consistent with that of the preceding years.

Stuckey, Wells & Co.
Toronto, Canada

February 22, 1989

Exhibit A.2
GENERAL PRODUCTS LIMITED
Consolidated balance sheet

At December 31 (In millions)	1988	1987
Assets Cash (note 7)	$ 1,601	$ 1,904
Temporary investments (note 7)	600	672
Current receivables (note 8)	4,339	3,647
Inventories (note 9)	3,343	3,161
Current assets	9,883	9,384
Property, plant, and equipment — net (note 10)	5,780	4,613
Investments (note 11)	1,820	1,691
Other assets (note 12)	1,028	956
Total assets	$18,511	$16,644
Liabilities Short-term borrowings (note 13)	$ 1,093	$ 871
and equity Accounts payable (note 14)	1,671	1,477
Progress collections and price adjustments accrued[6] ..	2,084	1,957
Dividends payable	170	159
Income taxes payable	628	655
Other payables (note 15)	1,946	1,753
Current liabilities	7,592	6,872
Long-term borrowings (note 16)	1,000	947
Other liabilities	323	178
Future income taxes (note 5)[7]	1,242	1,133
Total liabilities	10,157	9,130
Minority interest in equity of consolidated subsidiaries[8] .	154	152
Preferred shares (no par value; 2,000,000 shares authorized; none issued)	—	—
Common shares (no par value; 251,500,000 shares authorized; 231,463,949 shares issued 1988 and 1987)	579	579
Contributed surplus	659	656
Retained earnings	7,151	6,307
	8,389	7,542
Deduct common shares held in treasury[9]	(189)	(180)
Total shareholders' equity (notes 17, 18, and 19)	8,200	7,362
Total liabilities and equity	$18,511	$16,644
Commitments and contingent liabilities (note 20)		

The information in the notes is an integral part of this statement.

Exhibit A.3
GENERAL PRODUCTS LIMITED
Consolidated Statement of changes in financial position[10]
For the years ended December 31 (in millions)

	1988	1987	1986
Cash[11] Provided by			
Operations[12]	$ 1,963	$ 2,322	$ 1,742
Financing Activities			
Issue of long-term debt	122	50	96
Issue of common shares (including shares held in the			
treasury)	136	148	193
Investing Activities			
Sale of long-term investments	—	—	24
Sale of[13] other long-term assets	143	102	149
	2,364	2,622	2,204
Cash Applied[14] to			
Financing Activities			
Reduction of long-term debt	69	97	386
Purchase of treasury shares	145	156	196
Investing Activities			
Additions to property, plant, and equipment	1,948	1,262	1,055
Acquisition of investments	129	281	—
Dividends[15]	670	624	570
	2,961	2,420	2,207
Increase (Decrease) in Cash Position (Cash + Cash			
Equivalents − Bank Indebtedness)	(597)	202	(3)
Cash Position at Beginning of Year	1,705	1,503	1,506
Cash Position at End of Year	$ 1,108	$ 1,705	$ 1,503
Cash Provided from Operations	**1988**	**1987**	**1986**
Net Income	$ 1,514	$ 1,409	$ 1,230
Add (deduct) noncash items			
Depreciation, depletion, and amortization[16]	707	624	576
Investment tax credit deferred—net[17]	56	45	25
Income tax timing differences[18]	63	(37)	32
Earnings retained by nonconsolidated finance subsidiary[19]	(22)	(18)	(15)
Minority interest in earnings of consolidated subsidiaries[20]	21	29	29
	2,339	2,052	1,877
Working Capital Accounts[21]			
Cash provided by net reduction (increase) in accounts			
receivable and inventory	(874)	(516)	(705)
Cash provided by net income (reduction) in current			
liabilities other than short-term borrowings	498	786	570
	(376)	270	(135)
	$ 1,963	$ 2,322	$ 1,742

The information in the notes is an integral part of this statement.

Exhibit A.4
Summary of significant
accounting policies[22]

Basis of consolidation[23]

The financial statements consolidate the accounts of the parent General Products Limited and those of all majority-owned ("subsidiary companies"), except the finance company whose operations are not similar to those of the consolidated group.[24] All significant items relating to transactions among the parent and subsidiary companies are eliminated from the consolidated statements.[25]

The nonconsolidated finance company is included in the balance sheet under investments and is valued at equity plus advances.[26] In addition, companies in which GP and/or its consolidated subsidiaries own 20% to 50% of the voting shares ("associated companies") are included under investments, valued at the appropriate share of equity plus advances. Aftertax earnings of nonconsolidated finance companies and associated companies are included in the income statement under other income.

Sales[27]

The Company and its consolidated subsidiaries record a transaction as a sale only when title to products passes to the customer.

Vacation expense[28]

Most employees earn credits during the current year for vacations to be taken in the following year. The expense for this liability is accrued during the year vacations are earned rather than in the year vacations are taken.

Pensions[29]

Investments of the General Products Pension Trust, which funds the obligations of the General Products Pension Plan, are carried at amortized cost plus programmed appreciation in the common share portfolio. The funding program and Company cost determination for the Pension Plan use 6% as the estimated rate of future Trust income. Trust income includes recognition of appreciation in the common share portfolio on a systematic basis which does not give undue weight to short-term market fluctuations. Programmed appreciation will not be recognized if average carrying value exceeds average market value, calculated on a moving basis over a multiyear period.

Changes in accrued actuarial obligation for prior services are amortized over 20 years. Net actuarial gains and losses are amortized over 15 years.

Costs of separate, supplementary pension plan, primarily affecting long-service professional and managerial employees, are not funded. Current service costs and amortization of actuarial liabilities for prior service over a period of 20 years are being charged to operating expenses currently.

Investment tax credit[30]

The investment tax credit is recorded by the "cost reduction approach" and is amortized as a reduction of the provision for taxes over the lives of the facilities to which the credit applies, rather than being "flowed through" to income in the year the asset is acquired.

Inventories

Substantially all manufacturing inventories are valued on a first-in, first-out, or FIFO, basis. Valuations are based on the cost of material, direct labour and manufacturing overhead, and do not exceed replacement cost or net realizable values.[31] Certain indirect manufacturing expenses are charged directly to operating costs during the period incurred, rather than being inventoried.[32]

Mining inventories, which include principally mined ore and coal, metal concentrates and mining supplies, are stated at the lower of average cost or net realizable value. The cost of mining inventories includes both direct and indirect costs consisting of labor, purchased supplies and services, and depreciation, depletion and amortization of property, plant, and equipment.

Property, plant and equipment

Manufacturing plant and equipment includes the original cost of land, buildings and equipment less accumulated depreciation, which is the estimated cost consumed by wear and obsolescence. Most manufacturing plant and equipment is depreciated on a straight-line basis. If manufacturing plant and equipment is subject to abnormal economic conditions or obsolescence, additional depreciation is provided. Expenditures for maintenance and repairs of manufacturing plant and equipment are charged to operations as incurred.

The cost of mining properties includes initial expenditures and cost of major rebuilding projects that substantially increase the useful lives of existing assets. The cost of mining properties is depreciated, depleted or amortized over the useful lives of the related assets by use of unit-of-production, straight-line or declining-balance methods.

Exhibit A.4 *cont'd*

Mining exploration costs are expensed until it is determined that the development of a mineral deposit is likely to be economically feasible. After this determination is made, all costs related to a further development are capitalized. Amortization of such costs begins upon commencement of production and is over ten years or the productive life of the property, whichever is less.
Oil and gas properties are accounted for by use of the full-cost method.[33]
Intangible assets are amortized over periods not exceeding 20 years.[34]

Notes to financial statements

1 Operating expenses

Operating costs by major categories are shown below:

(In millions)	1988	1987	1986
Employee compensation, including benefits	$ 9,196	$ 8,286	$ 7,401
Materials, supplies, services and other costs	12,696	11,320	9,867
Depreciation, depletion and amortization	707	624	576
Taxes, except income taxes	299	259	251
Increase in inventories during the year[35]	(182)	(158)	(399)
Operating expenses	$22,716	$20,331	$17,696

Supplemental details are as follows:

(In millions)	1988	1987	1986
Maintenance and repairs	$784	$775	$672
Company-funded research and development[36]	760	640	521
Advertising	315	282	247
Mineral royalties and export duties	80	82	79

2 Pensions

Total pension costs of General Products and consolidated subsidiaries were $478 million in 1988, $413 million in 1987, and $381 million in 1986. General Products and its subsidiaries have a number of pension plans. The most significant of these plans is the General Products Pension Plan (the "Plan"), in which substantially all employees are participating. Approximately 80,800 persons were receiving benefits at year-end 1988 (75,700 and 72,100 at year-end 1987 and 1986 respectively).

Pension benefits under the Plan are funded through the General Products Pension Trust. Earnings of the Trust, including the programmed recognition of common share appreciation, as a percentage of the carrying value of the portfolio, were 8.4% for 1988 and 1987, and 7.8% for 1986. The limitation on recognition of programmed appreciation of common shares was not exceeded in any year.

Condensed information for the General Products Pension Trust follows.

General Products Pension Trust

Change in net assets at current value

(In millions) For the year	1988	1987	1986
Net assets at January 1	$4,968	$4,202	$3,734
Company contributions	404	341	317
Employee contributions	86	94	83
Investment income	435	383	312
Pensions paid	(254)	(225)	(201)
Unrecognized portion of change in current value[37]	779	173	(43)
Net assets at December 31	$6,418	$4,968	$4,202

Net assets at current value (In millions) December 31	1988	1987	1986
Canadian government obligations and guarantees	$ 44	$ 118	$ 93
Corporate bonds and notes	727	496	340
Real estate and mortgages	825	713	725
Common shares and other equity securities	4,181	3,193	2,726
	5,777	4,520	3,884
Cash and short-term investments	553	371	240
Other assets — net	88	77	78
Current value of net assets	$6,418	$4,968	$4,202
Carrying value of net assets	$5,593	$4,922	$4,329

The actuarial present value of accumulated plan benefits for the General Products Pension Plan and the supplementary pension plan together represent over 90% of accumulated pension plan benefits for General Products and its consolidated subsidiaries. These present values have been calculated using a 6% interest rate assumption as of December 31 for each of the years in the table below. The table also sets forth the total of the current value of Pension Trust assets and the relevant accruals in the Company's accounts.

General Products Pension Plan and Supplementary Pension Plan (In millions) December 31	1988	1987	1986
Estimated actuarial present value of accumulated plan benefits:			
Vested benefits	$6,027	$5,426	$4,732
Nonvested benefits	1,355	624	352
Total benefits	$7,382	$6,050	$5,084
Current value of trust assets	$6,418	$4,968	$4,202

For pension plans not included above, there was no significant difference between accumulated benefits and the relevant fund assets plus accruals.

3 Other income

(In millions)	1988	1987	1986
Net income of General Products Credit Corporation[38]	$115	$ 90	$ 77
Income from:			
Temporary investments and bank deposits	229	229	140
Customer financing[39]	72	70	49
Royalty and technical agreements	52	50	44
Associated companies and nonconsolidated uranium mining subsidiary	22	11	34
Other investments:			
Interest	21	20	19
Dividends	13	11	10
Other sundry items	40	38	46
	$564	$519	$419

4 Interest and other financial charges[40]

Interest capitalized on major property, plant and equipment projects was $21 million, $18 million, and $15 million in 1988, 1987, and 1986, respectively.

5 Income tax expense[41]

(In millions)	1988	1987	1986
Canadian income taxes:			
Estimated amount currently payable	$849	$945	$837
Effect of timing differences[42]	53	(37)	32
Investment credit tax deferred—net[43]	56	45	25
Income tax expense	$958	$953	$894

Investment tax credit amounted to $92 million in 1988, compared with $76 million in 1987 and $51 million in 1986.[44] In 1988, $36 million were included in net earnings, compared with $31 million in 1987 and $26 million in 1986. At the end of 1988 the amount still deferred and to be included in net earnings in future years was $262 million, in 1987 the amount was $206 million and in 1986 the amount was $161 million.

Effect of timing differences on income taxes[45]
(In millions)

Increase (decrease) in provision for income taxes	1988	1987	1986
Tax over book depreciation[46]	$116	$ 15	$ 79
Margin on installment sales[47]	1	(10)	(10)
Provision for warranties[48]	(46)	(36)	(31)
Other — net	(18)	(6)	(6)
Total	$ 53	$(37)	$ 32

The cumulative net effect of timing differences has resulted in a future tax credit of $982 million at the end of 1988, $926 million at the end of 1987, and $964 million at the end of 1986.[49]

Reconciliation from statutory to effective income tax rates

	1988	1987	1986
Statutory rate	46.0%	46.0%	46.0%
Reduction in taxes resulting from:			
Manufacturing and processing tax rate reduction	(3.1)	(2.9)	(1.9)
Inventory rate reduction	(1.6)	(0.4)	(0.5)
Inclusion of earnings of the Credit Corporation in pretax			
income on an aftertax basis	(2.1)	(1.7)	(1.5)
Investment tax credit	(1.5)	(1.3)	(1.2)
Income tax at capital gains rate	(0.1)	—	(0.6)
Other — net	0.8	0.2	1.2
Effective tax rate	38.4%	39.9%	41.5%

6 Earnings per common share[50]

Earnings per share are based on the average number of shares outstanding. Any dilution that would result from the potential exercise or conversion of such items as stock options or convertible debt outstanding is not materially dilutive (less than 1% in 1988, 1987, and 1986).

7 Cash and temporary investments

Temporary investments are carried at the lower of amortized cost or market value. Carrying value was substantially the same as market value at year-end 1988 and 1987.[51]

8 Current receivables

(In millions) December 31	1988	1987
Customers' accounts and notes	$3,713	$3,165
Associated companies	25	36
Nonconsolidated subsidiary	17	7
Other	584	439
	$4,339	$3,647

9 Inventories

(In millions) December 31	1988	1987
Raw materials and work in process	$2,082	$1,943
Finished goods	961	966
Unbilled shipments	300	252
	$3,343	$3,161

10 Property, plant, and equipment

(In millions)	1988	1987
Major classes at December 31:		
Manufacturing plant and equipment		
Land and improvements	$ 139	$ 125
Buildings, structures and related equipment	2,329	2,098
Machinery and equipment	6,197	5,324
Leasehold costs and manufacturing plant under construction	453	372
Mineral property, plant and equipment	1,917	1,446
	$11,035	$9,365
Cost at January 1	$ 9,365	$8,328
Additions	1,948	1,262
Disposals	(278)	(225)
Cost at December 31	$11,035	$9,365
Accumulated depreciation, depletion, and amortization		
Balance at January 1	$ 4,752	$4,305
Current-year provision	707	624
Disposals	(214)	(188)
Other changes	10	11
Balance at December 31	$ 5,255	$4,752
Property, plant, and equipment less depreciation, depletion, and amortization at December 31	$ 5,780	$4,613

11 Investments

(In millions) December 31	1988	1987
Nonconsolidated finance subsidiary	$ 931	$ 817
Nonconsolidated uranium mining subsidiary	188	157
Portfolio investments (at cost):		
Government and government guaranteed securities	187	233
Other	187	199
	374	432
Associated companies	342	301
Less: Allowance for losses	(15)	(16)
	$1,820	$1,691

Condensed consolidated financial statements for the nonconsolidated finance subsidiary, General Products Credit Corporation (GPCC), follow. During the normal course of business, (GPCC) has transactions with the parent General Products Limited and certain of its subsidiaries. However, virtually all products financed by GPCC are manufactured by companies other than General Products.

General Products Credit Corporation
Income and retained earnings statement

(In millions) for the year	1988	1987	1986
Earned income	$1,389	$1,102	$813
Expenses:			
Interest and discount	719	528	337
Operating and administrative	451	396	315
Provision for losses			
— receivables	75	69	56
— other assets	3	(2)	8
Total expenses	1,248	991	716
Net income before income tax	141	111	97
Income tax expense	26	21	20
Net income	115	90	77
Less: Dividends[52]	(93)	(72)	(62)
Retained earnings at January 1	239	221	206
Retained earnings at December 31	$ 261	$ 239	$221

General Products Credit Corporation
Balance sheet

(In millions) December 31	1988	1987
Cash and temporary investments	$ 531	$ 374
Receivables:		
Time sales and loans	8,159	7,480
Deferred income	(1,380)	(1,124)
	6,779	6,356
Investment in leases	1,643	1,207
Sundry receivables	197	141
Total receivables	8,619	7,704
Allowance for losses	(249)	(231)
Net receivables	8,370	7,473
Other assets	443	321
Total assets[53]	$9,344	$8,168

Notes payable:

Due within one year	$4,425	$3,921
Long-term — senior	1,984	1,743
— subordinated	400	325
Other liabilities	707	631
Total liabilities	7,516	6,620
Future income taxes	876	718
Deferred investment tax credit	21	13
Share capital[52]	658	566
Contributed surplus	12	12
Retained earnings	261	239
Total shareholders' equity	931	817
Total liabilities and shareholders' equity	$9,344	$8,168

The nonconsolidated uranium mining company is valued at lower of cost or equity, plus advances.

The estimated realizable value of portfolio investments was $331 million at December 31, 1988 ($394 million at December 31, 1987).[54]

Investments in nonconsolidated subsidiary and associated companies included advances of $180 million at December 31, 1988 ($123 million at December 31, 1987).

12 Other assets

(In millions) December 31	1988	1987
Long-term receivables	$ 340	$307
Deferred charges	198	145
Real estate development projects	132	81
Recoverable engineering costs on government contracts	113	121
Customer financing	103	107
Licenses and other intangibles — net[55]	75	52
Other	67	143
	$1,028	$956

Licenses and other intangibles are being amortized over periods not exceeding 20 years.

13 Short-term borrowings

The average balance of short-term borrowing, excluding the current portion of long-term borrowings, was $822 million during 1988 (calculated by averaging all month-end balances for the year) compared with an average balance of $705 million in 1987. The maximum balance included in these calculations was $962 million and $727 million at the end of October 1988 and March 1987, respectively. The average effective interest rate for the year 1988 was 18.9%, and for 1987 was 17.6%. These average rates represent total short-term interest incurred divided by the average balance outstanding. A summary of short-term borrowings and the applicable interest rates is shown on the following page.

Short-term borrowings (In millions) December 31	1988		1987	
	Amount	Average rate at Dec. 31	Amount	Average rate at Dec. 31
Parent notes with trust departments	$ 353	15.05%	$290	12.62%
Consolidated subsidiary bank borrowings . . .	539	30.83	389	27.10
Other, including current portion of long-term borrowings	201		192	
	$1,093		$871	

Although the total unused credit available to the Company through banks and commercial credit markets is not readily quantifiable, informal credit lines in excess of $1 billion had been extended by Canadian banks at year-end.

14 Accounts Payable

(In millions) December 31	1988	1987
Trade accounts	$1,402	$1,259
Collected for the account of others	203	172
Nonconsolidated subsidiary[56]	66	46
	$1,671	$1,477

15 Other payables

The balances at year-end 1988 and 1987 included compensation and benefit cost accrued of $703 million and $641 million, respectively.

16 Long-term borrowings

(In millions) Outstanding December 31	1988	1987	Due date	Sinking fund prepayment period
General Products Limited:				
5¾% Notes	$ 62	$ 69	1993	1974-92
5.30% Debentures	70	80	1994	1975-93
7½% Debentures	135	149	1998	1979-97
8½% Debentures	288	295	2006	1987-2003
Coal International Inc.:				
Notes with banks	37	5	1995	1983-95
8% Guaranteed Sinking Fund Debentures	15	17	1989	1979-89
7.6% Notes	28	32	1990	1976-90
Other	32	25		
General Products Capital Corporation:				
4¼% Bonds	23	24	1994	1978-86
4¼% Debentures	50	50	1993	None
Other	43	45		
All other	217	156		
	$1,000	$947		

The amounts shown above are after deduction of the face value of securities held in treasury as follows.

Face value of long-term borrowings in treasury

(In millions) December 31	1988	1987
General Products Limited:		
5.30% Debentures	$50	$50
7½% Debentures	35	29
8½% Debentures	12	5
General Products Capital Corporation:		
4¼% Bonds	6	7

Coal International Inc. notes with banks were subject to average interest rates at year-end 1988 and 1987 of 11.3% and 7.9%, respectively.

Borrowings of General Products Capital Corporation are unconditionally guaranteed by General Products as to payment of principal, premium if any, and interest. This Corporation primarily assists in financing capital requirements of companies in which General Products has an equity interest, as well as financing certain customer purchases.

Borrowings include 4¼% Guaranteed Debentures due in 1993, which are convertible into General Products common shares at $80.75 a share. During 1988 and 1987, General Products Overseas Capital Corporation 4¼% Guaranteed Bonds having a face value and a reacquired cost of $2 million were retired in accordance with sinking fund provisions.

All other long-term borrowings were largely by real estate development subsidiaries with various interest rates and maturities and included amounts due to nonconsolidated subsidiary of $7 million in 1988 and 1987.

Long-term borrowing maturities during the next five years,[57] including the portion classified as current, are $91 million in 1989, $130 million in 1990, $62 million in 1991, $42 million in 1992, and $68 million in 1993. These amounts are after deducting reacquired debentures held in treasury for sinking fund requirements.

17 Common shares[58]

At December 31, 1988 and December 31, 1987, respectively, 227,765,000 and 227,839,000 common shares were outstanding. Common shares held in treasury at December 31, 1988, included 1,921,706 shares for the deferred compensation provisions of incentive compensation plans (1,785,656 shares at December 31, 1987). These shares are carried at market value at the time of allotment, which amounted to $96 million and $88 million at December 31, 1988 and 1987, respectively. The liability is recorded under other liabilities.

Other common shares in treasury, which is carried at cost, aggregated 1,777,382 and 1,839,762 shares at December 31, 1988 and 1987, respectively. These shares are held for future corporate requirements, including distributions under employee savings plans, incentive compensation awards and possible conversion of General Products Capital Corporation convertible indebtedness. The maximum number of shares required for conversions was 736,079 at December 3, 1988 (737,725 at December 31, 1987). Corporate requirements of shares for benefit plans and conversions may be met either from unissued shares or from shares in treasury.

	1988	1987	1988	1987
	(In millions)		(Thousands of shares)	
Common shares issued				
Balance January 1 and December 31	$579	$579	231,464	231,464
Contributed surplus				
Balance January 1	$656	$658		
Gain/(loss) on disposition of treasury shares[59] . . .	3	(2)		
Balance December 31	$659	$656		
Common shares held in treasury				
Balance January 1	$180	$172	3,625	3,428
Purchases	145	156	2,684	3,155

Dispositions:

Employee savings plans	(99)	(124)	(1,879)	(2,492)
Employee share ownership plan	(16)	(11)	(296)	(213)
Incentive compensation plans	(7)	(8)	(158)	(152)
Stock options and appreciation rights	(14)	(5)	(277)	(101)
Balance December 31	$189	$180	3,699	3,625

18 Retained earnings

Retained earnings at year-end 1988 included approximately $251 million ($246 million at December 31, 1987), representing the excess of earnings of nonconsolidated subsidiary and associates over dividends received since their formation.[60] In addition, retained earnings have been increased by $10 million ($5 million reduction at December 31, 1987), which represents the change in equity in these companies since acquisition.

19 Stock option information[61]

Stock option plans, appreciation rights, and performance units are described in the Company's current Proxy Statement. A summary of stock option transactions during the last two years follows.

Stock options		Average per share	
	Shares subject to option	Option price	Market price
Balance at January 1, 1987	4,088,853	$51.37	$47.13
Options granted	1,023,122	46.25	46.25
Options exercised	(98,145)	40.63	50.14
Options surrendered on exercise of appreciation rights	(68,834)	40.52	49.17
Options terminated	(186,068)	50.77	—
Balance at December 31, 1987	4,758,928	50.67	50.63
Options granted	98,100	61.50	61.50
Options exercised	(273,193)	44.13	56.16
Options surrendered on exercise of appreciation rights	(123,350)	41.93	54.92
Options terminated	(157,163)	51.02	—
Balance at December 31, 1988	4,303,322	51.56	61.25

The number of shares available for granting additional options at the end of 1988 was 1,862,756 (1,831,456 at the end of 1987).

20 Commitments and contingent liabilities

Lease commitments and contingent liabilities, consisting of guarantees, pending litigation, taxes, and other claims, in the opinion of management, are not considered to be material in relation to the Company's financial position.[62]

Industry segment information[63]

Consumer Products and Services consists of major appliances, air conditioning equipment, lighting products, housewares and audio products, television receivers, and broadcasting and cablevision services. It also includes service operations for major appliances, air conditioners, TV receivers, and housewares and audio products.

General Products Credit Corporation, a wholly owned nonconsolidated finance subsidiary, engages primarily in consumer, commercial, and industrial financing. It also participates, to a lesser degree, in life insurance and fire and casualty insurance activities. Products of companies other than GP constitute virtually all products financed by GPCC.

Industrial Products and Components includes components (appliance controls, small motors, and electronic components); industrial capital equipment (construction, automation, and transportation); maintenance, inspection, repair and rebuilding of electric, electronic and mechanical apparatus; and a network of supply houses offering products of General Products and other manufacturers.

Power Systems includes steam turbine-generators, gas turbines, nuclear power reactors and nuclear fuel assemblies, transformers, switchgear, meters, and installation and maintenance engineering services.

Technical Systems and Materials consists of jet engines for aircraft, industrial and marine applications; electronic and other high-technology products and services primarily for aerospace applications and defense; materials (engineered plastics, silicones, industrial cutting materials, laminated and insulating materials, and batteries); medical and communications equipment; and time sharing, computing, and remote data processing.

Natural Resources includes the mining of coking coal, uranium, steam coal, iron, and copper. In addition, it includes oil and natural gas production, ocean shipping (primarily in support of mining operations), and land acquisition and development.

(In millions)	**Revenues** For the years ended December 31								
	Total revenues			**Intersegment sales**			**External sales and other income**		
	1988	1987	1986	1988	1987	1986	1988	1987	1986
Consumer products and services	$ 8,833	$ 8,259	$ 7,555	$ 276	$ 263	$ 243	$ 8,557	$ 7,996	$ 7,312
Net earnings of GP Credit Corp.	115	90	77	—	—	—	115	90	77
Total consumer products and services	8,948	8,349	7,632	276	263	243	$ 8,672	$ 8,086	$ 7,389
Industrial products and components	5,157	4,803	4,124	565	508	468	4,592	4,295	3,656
Power systems	4,023	3,564	3,486	175	210	174	3,848	3,354	3,312
Technical systems and materials	7,128	6,061	4,745	258	255	190	6,870	5,806	4,555
Natural resources	1,374	1,260	1,032	—	—	—	1,374	1,260	1,032
Corporate items and eliminations	(1,107)	(1,057)	(946)	(1,274)	(1,236)	(1,075)	167	179	129
Total	$25,523	$22,980	$20,073	$ —	$ —	$ —	$25,523	$22,980	$20,073

	Operating profit For the years ended December 31			**Net earnings[64]** For the years ended December 31		
	1988	1987	1986	1988	1987	1986
Consumer products and services	$ 843	$ 809	$ 819	$ 360	$ 376	$ 376
Net earnings of GP Credit Corp.	115	90	77	115	90	77
Total consumer products and services	958	899	896	475	466	453
Industrial products and components . . .	568	485	426	315	272	223
Power systems	194	174	196	141	114	93
Technical systems and materials	774	672	545	373	356	278
Natural resources	404	431	372	224	208	180
Total segment operating profit	2,898	2,661	2,435			
Interest and other financial charges	(314)	(258)	(224)			
Corporate items and eliminations	(91)	(12)	(58)	(14)	(7)	3
Total	$2,493	$2,391	$2,153	$1,514	$1,409	$1,230

| | Assets At December 31 | | | Property, plant and equipment For the years ended December 31 | | | | | |
| | | | | Additions | | | Depreciation, depletion and amortization | | |
	1988	1987	1986	1988	1987	1986	1988	1987	1986
Consumer products and services	$ 4,889	$ 4,416	$ 4,118	$ 399	$ 317	$ 288	$199	$176	$168
Investment in GP Credit Corp.	931	817	677	—	—	—	—	—	—
Total consumer products and services	5,820	5,233	4,795	399	317	288	199	176	168
Industrial products and components	2,595	2,329	2,125	224	176	166	109	106	91
Power systems	2,289	2,135	2,105	129	101	84	91	84	79
Technical systems and materials	4,475	3,422	2,683	693	444	289	200	163	150
Natural resources	2,109	1,679	1,489	446	201	212	94	83	77
Corporate items and eliminations	1,223	1,846	1,839	57	23	16	14	12	11
Total	$18,511	$16,644	$15,036	$1,948	$1,262	$1,055	$707	$624	$576

Net earnings for industry segments[65] include allocation of corporate interest income, expense, and other financial charges to parent company components based on change in individual component average nonfixed investment. Interest and other financial charges of subsidiary companies recognize that such companies generally service their own debt.

General corporate expenses are allocated principally on the basis of cost of operations, with certain exceptions and reductions which recognize the varying degrees to which subsidiary companies maintain their own corporate structures.

In addition, income tax expense ($958 million in 1988, $953 million in 1987, and $894 million in 1986) is allocated based on the total corporate effective tax rate, except for GPCC and Natural Resources, whose income taxes are calculated separately.

Minority interest ($21 million in 1988 and $29 million in both 1987 and 1986) is allocated to operating components having responsibility for investments in consolidated subsidiaries.

In general, it is GP's policy to price internal sales as nearly as practicable to equivalent commercial selling prices.

Six-year summary (a)[66]
Selected financial data

(Dollar amounts in millions; per-share amounts in dollars)	1988	1987	1986	1985	1984	1983
Summary of operations						
Sales of products and services to customers . . .	$24,959	$22,461	$19,654	$17,519	$15,697	$14,105
Cost of goods sold	17,751	15,991	13,915	12,288	11,048	10,210
Selling, general, and administrative expense	4,258	3,716	3,205	3,011	2,635	2,238
Depreciation, depletion, and amortization	707	624	576	522	486	470
Operating costs	22,716	20,331	17,696	15,821	14,169	12,918
Operating profit	2,243	2,130	1,958	1,698	1,528	1,187
Other income	564	519	419	390	274	174
Interest and other financial charges	(314)	(258)	(224)	(199)	(175)	(187)
Earnings before income taxes and minority interest	2,493	2,391	2,153	1,889	1,627	1,174
Income tax expense	(958)	(953)	(894)	(773)	(668)	(460)
Minority interest	(21)	(29)	(29)	(28)	(28)	(26)
Net earnings	$ 1,514	$ 1,409	$ 1,230	$ 1,088	$ 931	$ 688
Earnings per common share (h)	$ 6.65	$ 6.20	$ 5.39	$ 4.79	$ 4.12	$ 3.07
Dividends declared per common share (c) . . .	$ 2.95	$ 2.75	$ 2.50	$ 2.10	$ 1.70	$ 1.60
Earnings as a percentage of sales	6.1%	6.3%	6.3%	6.2%	5.9%	4.9%
Earned on average shareholders' equity	19.5%	20.2%	19.6%	19.4%	18.9%	15.7%

(Dollar amounts in millions; per-share amounts in dollars)	1988	1987	1986	1985	1984	1983
Dividends — General Products	$ 670	$ 624	$ 570	$ 477	$ 333	$ 293
Dividends — Coal International Inc. (d)	—	—	—	—	$ 28	$ 33
Shares outstanding — average (in thousands) (e) .	227,541	227,173	227,985	227,154	225,791	224,262
Shareholders' accounts — average	524,000	540,000	552,000	553,000	566,000	582,000
Market price range per share (c)	63-44	$55\frac{1}{8}$-45	$57\frac{5}{8}$-$43\frac{5}{8}$	$57\frac{1}{4}$-$47\frac{3}{8}$	$59\frac{1}{4}$-46	$52\frac{7}{8}$-$32\frac{3}{8}$
Price/earnings ratio change (c)	9-7	9-7	11-8	12-10	14-11	17-10
Current assets	$ 9,883	$ 9,384	$ 8,755	$ 7,865	$ 6,685	$ 5,750
Current liabilities	7,592	6,872	6,175	5,417	4,605	4,163
Working capital	$ 2,291	$ 2,512	$ 2,580	$ 2,448	$ 2,080	$ 1,587
Short-term borrowings	$ 1,093	$ 871	$ 960	$ 772	$ 611	$ 667
Long-term borrowings	1,000	947	994	1,284	1,322	1,239
Minority interest in equity of consolidated affiliates	154	152	151	132	119	105
Shareholders' equity	8,200	7,362	6,587	5,943	5,253	4,617
Total capital invested	$10,447	$ 9,332	$ 8,692	$ 8,131	$ 7,305	$ 6,628
Earned on average total capital invested	17.3%	17.6%	16.3%	15.8%	15.1%	12.5%
Shareholders' equity per common share — year-end (b)	$ 36.00	$ 32.31	$ 28.88	$ 26.05	$ 23.18	$ 20.49
Total assets	$18,511	$16,644	$15,036	$13,697	$12,050	$10,741
Property, plant, and equipment additions	$ 1,948	$ 1,262	$ 1,055	$ 823	$ 740	$ 588
Employees — average worldwide	402,000	405,000	401,000	384,000	380,000	380,000

(a) Unless specifically noted, all years are adjusted to include Coal International Inc., which became a wholly owned subsidiary of General Products on December 20, 1984, through the exchange of 41,002,034 General Products common shares for all of the outstanding shares of Coal.
(b) Computed using outstanding shares as described in note (e).
(c) For General Products common shares as reported in the years shown.
(d) Reflects transactions prior to merger date.
(e) Includes General Products outstanding average shares or year-end shares as appropriate, plus, in 1984 and prior years, outstanding shares previously reported by Coal multiplied by 1.3. Adjustments have been made for the two-for-one Coal stock split effected in the form of share dividends in 1981.

Other information (unaudited)

Quarterly dividend and stock market information

	Dividends declared		Common shares market price range	
	1988	1987	1988	1987
First quarter	70¢	65¢	$57\frac{1}{2}$-$44\frac{3}{8}$	$50\frac{3}{8}$-$45\frac{1}{2}$
Second quarter	75	70	52 - $44\frac{1}{2}$	$51\frac{5}{8}$- $46\frac{7}{8}$
Third quarter	75	70	$58\frac{1}{8}$- $51\frac{1}{8}$	$55\frac{1}{8}$- $49\frac{1}{8}$
Fourth quarter	75	70	63 - $51\frac{1}{2}$	$52\frac{1}{4}$- 45

The Toronto Stock Exchange is the principal market on which GP common shares are traded and, as of December 8, 1988, there were approximately 512,282 shareholders of record.

Operations by quarter for 1988 and 1987[67] (Dollar amounts in millions; per share amounts in dollars)	First quarter	Second quarter	Third quarter	Fourth quarter
1988				
Sales of products and services to customers	$5,881	$6,197	$5,963	$6,918
Operating profit	527	556	513	647
Net income	342	403	358	411
Net income per common share	1.50	1.77	1.58	1.80
1987				
Sales of products and services to customers	$5,082	$5,642	$5,609	$6,128
Operating profit	470	598	511	551
Net Income	303	382	341	383
Net income per common share	1.33	1.69	1.50	1.68

Accounting for the effects of inflation (unaudited)[68]

During periods of inflation, historical financial statements do not properly measure the erosion in a company's overall purchasing power, its ability to fund the replacement of its operating capacity and real distribution of earnings through dividends. Although the rate of inflation in North America has declined recently, the need for inflation accounting still remains. The historical dollar values of inventory and property, plant and equipment are usually lower than their current replacement cost resulting in an understatement of the real cost of sales and depreciation expense.

Supplementary inflation adjusted data has been prepared, for the most part in accordance with the Canadian Institute of Chartered Accountants (CICA) recommendations, and is displayed in the tables on the following page.[69]

Current cost of inventories and property, plant and equipment[70] represent the lower of the amount that would be needed to produce or purchase assets of equivalent operating capability at the balance sheet date or the discounted value of the net amount recoverable from the use or sale of the assets. All other assets and liabilities are of a monetary nature and are stated at their historic amounts.

Property has been valued based either on previous appraisals adjusted by indexing or estimated current market prices. Plant and equipment values have been determined by indexing prior years' engineering appraisals and the results have been adjusted to reflect changes in technology and economies of scale. Depreciation has been restated by writing off the current value of the assets' unexpired service potential evenly over their estimated remaining lives resulting in additional depreciation of $385 million ($392 million in 1987).

Inventories are valued at the lower of current cost and net realizable value with current cost being based on current prices for raw materials, labour and other processing costs. The cost of sales adjustment of $141 million ($145 million in 1987) provides for the additional cost of replacing inventories sold during the year.

The net monetary working capital adjustment[71] of $161 million ($236 million in 1987) represents the estimated loss in purchasing power of the funds invested in cash, temporary investments and accounts receivable net of the financing provided by short term creditors.

To determine current cost earnings (loss) attributable to common shareholders[71] it is necessary to make a financing adjustment which recognizes that the funds required to maintain a company's invested capital are obtained partly from creditors. The financing adjustment of $74 million ($69 million in 1987) reflects mainly the extent to which the current year's movement in the current cost amounts of inventory and property, plant and equipment are financed by net monetary liabilities, primarily long-term debt. The adjustment represents a notional benefit to shareholders in that they did not have to finance the entire effect of the specific price increases during the year for operating assets, as a portion of these price changes were financed by creditors. As a going concern, a company must continue to replace its invested capital which, in turn, prevents the distribution of the financing adjustment to shareholders.

The general purchasing power gain on net monetary liabilities represents the benefit to the shareholder from the decline in the purchasing power of the net amounts owed. During periods of inflation, gains are recognized from holding long-term debt and other monetary liabilities since they will be repaid in dollars having less purchasing power. General Products Limited has a net benefit since monetary liabilities exceed monetary assets. The general purchasing power gain of $361 million ($336 million in 1987) can be considered a hedge against the erosion in the value of the dollar and a positive factor in preserving the general purchasing power of shareholders' equity. This theoretical benefit does not provide immediate funds to the company and any distribution of this gain would impair the company's operating capital.

No adjustment has been made to reflect the effects of inflation on the provision for income taxes.[72] Canadian government tax regulations have not yet been adjusted in any material way to recognize the continuing erosion of a company's capital base and earnings due to inflation. In 1988, the income tax provision on historical earnings represented an effective tax rate of 38.4%, but in real terms the company incurred an income tax expense of $958 million on an inflation adjusted income before taxes of $1,806 million.

Dividends on General Products Limited's common shares of $670 million in 1988 represent 44% of historical net earnings attributable to common shareholders,[73] In current cost terms they represent 74% of current cost net earnings.

Pre-tax return on average capital employed (net working capital and total operating fixed assets before deducting accumulated depreciation) in 1988 was 15% on an inflation adjusted basis compared to 42% in historic terms.

While the effects of inflation are a matter of serious concern, it should be noted that the higher current cost values of inventory, property, plant and equipment are reflected in common shareholders' equity. With this increase in net asset value, the book value of General Products Limited's common shares on a current cost basis is substantially higher ($58.75) than when measured in historical terms ($35.42). The long-term debt/equity ratio is also significantly lower when measured in current cost dollars (8:92) than when measured in historical dollars (12:88).

The following tables compare selected supplementary financial data adjusted for the effects of changing prices. To facilitate the year-to-year comparison the 1987 figures have been restated in 1988 dollars using the Gross National Expenditure Implicit Price Deflator.

Reconciliation of historical cost earnings to current cost earnings

(Millions of dollars)		1988		1987 restated
Historical cost earnings before interest and income taxes[74]		$2,807		$ 3,063
Current cost adjustments				
Depreciation	$ 385		$ 372	
Cost of sales	141		145	
Net monetary working capital	161	687	236	773
		$2,120		$ 2,290
Interest expense		314		298
Current cost earnings before following items		$1,806		$ 1,992
Income taxes — current	$(849)		$ (1,093)	
future	(109)	(958)	(9)	(1,102)
Minority interest		(21)		(34)
Current cost earnings (loss)		$ 827		$ 856
Financing adjustment		74		69
Current cost earnings (loss) attributable to common shareholders		$ 901		$ 925
Current cost earnings (loss) per common share (dollars)		$ 3.96		$ 4.07

*Before extraordinary items.

Selected data for changing prices

(Millions of dollars)	Historical Cost 1988	Current Cost 1988	Current Cost 1987 restated
Inventories	$3,343	$ 5,701	$ 3,858
Property, plant and equipment less accumulated depreciation including oil and gas assets and land under development	$5,780	$ 8,797	$ 7,873
Common shareholders' equity	$8,200	$13,575	$12,659
General purchasing power gain on net monetary liabilities		$ 361	$ 336
Increase in current cost amounts of inventory, and property, plant and equipment based on: General inflation		$ 469	$ 947
Specific prices		396	819
Difference		$ 73	$ 128
Financing adjustment based on realized current cost adjustments to earnings		$ 106	$ 131

Authors' Comments

[1]This balance does not necessarily represent the amount of income taxes currently payable. See GP's note 5.

[2]GP does not own all the shares in all of its consolidated subsidiaries. Some of the shares belong to outsiders, called the *minority interest*. The minority interest's share of the earnings of the subsidiary companies does not belong to GP's shareholders. Hence, in deriving income to GP's shareholders, the minority interest's share earnings is subtracted from consolidated income. Note, however, that this reduction in income uses no cash or other funds, so that there is an adjustment on the Statement of Changes in Financial Position for this charge against income. See authors' comment 16.

[3]This is basic earnings per share, as called for by *CICA Handbook*, section 3500. See GP's note 6 for a discussion of fully diluted earnings per share. Fully diluted earnings per share is not separately shown here because the amount is within 1 percent of the basic earnings per share amount and is not considered materially dilutive.

[4]Generally accepted accounting principles call for a reconciliation of changes in all of the shareholders' equity accounts during the year. The only major changes in GP's retained earnings account are caused by the earning of income and the declaration of dividends. GP's note 17 explains other changes in shareholders' equity.

[5]This auditors' report is unqualified. The first paragraph of the auditors' report is the scope paragraph—telling the work done—and the last paragraph is the opinion. An unqualified opinion provides some assurance to readers of these financial statements that they present fairly the financial position of the company and are based on the application of generally accepted accounting principles.

[6]GP uses the completed contract method of recognizing revenue from long-term construction contracts; see GP's Summary of Significant Accounting Policies at "Sales." As GP incurs costs on these contracts it makes journal entries such as:

Work-in-Process Inventory for Long-Term Contracts	X	
Various Assets and Liabilities		X
To record cost of construction activity.		

Some of GP's long-term construction contracts provide that the customer shall make progress payments to GP as the work is done. GP does not recognize revenue until the work is completed, so the journal entry made at the time cash is received is one such as:

Cash	Y	
Advances from Customers on Long-Term Contracts		Y
To record cash received and to set up the corresponding liability.		

When the balance sheet is prepared, the amounts in the inventory accounts, X (debit balance), are netted against the amounts in the liability accounts, Y (credit balance). If there is a net credit balance, as here, with Y greater than X, then the difference, Y − X, is recorded as a liability. GP shows this liability under the title "Progress collections and price adjustments accrued." On contracts where the amounts in the inventory account exceed the cash collections, then the difference, X − Y, is shown as an asset under a title such as "Costs Incurred on Long-Term Contracts in Excess of Billings."

On many of GP's contracts the only cash collected before completion of construction is for engineering costs incurred in preparation to undertake construction. GP expenses these engineering costs, rather than accumulating them in Work-in-Process inventory accounts. Thus, there is no asset account to net against the liability. The "Progress collections" title is appropriate because it tends to represent gross "advances from customers," rather than a netting of work-in-process inventory against advances from customers.

[7]Refer to authors' comments 42 to 49 explaining the reasons for the cumulative effect of the deferral of income tax payments resulting from timing differences and the adoption of the cost reduction method for the investment tax credits.

[8](Refer to authors' comment 2 for a description of "minority interest" on the income statement.) This account represents the equity of the minority shareholders in the consolidated subsidiaries. From the point of view of GP's shareholders, this equity belonging to the minority is a liability. From the point of view of the consolidated entity, the minority shareholders' interest is part of total shareholders' equity. Thus whether one believes that minority interest is a liability or an item of shareholders' equity depends upon whether one views the financial statements as being prepared for the shareholders of GP (the proprietorship theory) or for all potential readers (the entity theory). Note that the accounting profession in Canada avoids the issue by not classifying "minority interest" either with liabilities or with shareholders' equity.

[9]GP uses the cost method of accounting for treasury shares and shows the cost of its own shares acquired on the market as contra to all of shareholders' equity. Refer to authors' comment 59.

[10]Before the CICA recommended this title, the statement used to be called Statement of Sources and Applications of Funds. The choice of this new title is somewhat curious since the *CICA Handbook* does not officially define what financial position is. This makes it somewhat difficult to visualize what is being changed. The title makes more sense if one realizes that the profession attempted (unsuccessfully) to change the title ''Balance Sheet'' to ''Statement of Financial Position.'' The statement of changes in financial position explains then how the company got from last year's financial position to this year's, i.e., it explains *how* the changes in the balance sheet were caused.

The USA has adopted a different title—Statement of Cash Flows, which has some appeal since cash flow is what the financial statement readers are really interested in. The *CICA Handbook* allows the use of this title.

[11]The word cash is technically incorrect since the *CICA Handbook* says the statement should report changes in cash and cash equivalents net of short-term borrowings. This broader concept is used because what is really important is not the current bank balance, but rather how much liquidity could be marshalled in a day or so if the need arose. Perhaps a new term should be coined to avoid confusion.

[12]As indicated in Chapters 5 and 14, companies have a great deal of latitude in the format selected for this statement. The essential requirement is to show the respective contribution of operating, financing, and investing activities to cash flow.

[13]This does not reconcile to the change in the balance sheet account. The actual financial statements from which these are adapted reported this merely as ''Other-net'' which is inadequate disclosure for an item generating $143,000,000 of cash flow. An assumption has been made that assets have been sold.

[14]Since the new operating/financing/investing format was adopted for the statement of changes in financial position some companies have stopped having separate sections of the statements for sources and for applications. Instead, under the respective headings of operations, financing, and investing the use or non-use of brackets indicates whether the item is a source or use of cash. This is punitive to the reader especially since the use of brackets reverses for some of the working capital accounts. For clarity, the authors strongly recommend that sources and applications be grouped into distinct sections on the statement.

[15]Dividends is the most contentious item in the statement in terms of where to classify it. The most common placement in practice is as a financing activity but the rationale supporting this is weak. Placing dividends in a separate category altogether avoids this problem.

[16]Depreciation is *not* a source of funds. Rather, it is an expense that reduces net income without using any funds. The funds were used some time in the past when the depreciable assets were acquired.

[17]See authors' comment 44. GP earns investment tax credits in the year it acquires new qualifying assets. Because it uses the conservative cost reduction approach for

investment credits, it recognizes the effect on income over the lives of the assets acquired. More funds are provided by the tax investment credit than are recognized in income in the year of acquisition. On the other hand, income is increased somewhat because of the effect of amounts deferred in prior years that are used to reduce reported tax expense in the current year. The net difference is added to net income in deriving funds provided by operations.

[18]In 1988 and 1986, income tax expense for the year exceeded the amount of income taxes payable. See the discussion at GP's note 5 and authors' comments 45–48. Because fewer funds were used for income taxes than were reported as income tax expense, there has to be an addition for the amount of expense not using funds in deriving funds from operations. The results for 1987 show that taxes payable exceeded tax expense.

[19]All earnings of the GP Credit Corporation ($115 million in 1988) are included in income under the equity method. See "Other income," GP's note 3. Only $93 million of dividends were declared by the Credit Corporation; see the "Current and retained earnings statement" of the Credit Company in GP's note 11. The difference, $22 (= $115 − $93) million, provided no funds to GP and must be subtracted from net income to derive GP's funds from operations. That is, the entire $115 million is included in the $1,514 million shown as net earnings by GP, but dividend declarations of the Credit Corporation provided funds of only $93 million.

[20]See authors' comment 2. The charge on the income statement for the minority's interest in earnings (of $21 million in 1986) reduces the income reported to GP's shareholders, but does not reduce the amount of funds provided by operations of the consolidated entity. Thus, there is an addback to net income for $21 million in 1986 in deriving funds produced by operations.

[21]Conceptually, one of the most difficult things for students to visualize is how changes in working capital accounts affect cash from operations (see page 233). If cash from operations was presented in terms of actual cash flows instead of a reconciliation to net income it would be much easier to understand in the following format:

Cash Flow From Operating Activity
Cash Received from Customers
Cash Disbursed for Operating Activities
   —to suppliers
   —to employees
   —for taxes
   —etc.

---

[22]Section 1505 of the *CICA Handbook* recommends that all financial statements include a summary of significant accounting principles used so that the reader can know which accounting alternatives have been chosen by the company.

[23]A parent, such as GP, usually consolidates a subsidiary when all four of the following criteria are met:

   (i) The parent owns more than 50 percent of the voting shares of the subsidiary.

(ii) There are no important restrictions on the ability of the parent to exercise effec-tive control of the subsidiary.

(iii) The asset and equity structure of the subsidiary is not significantly different from that of the parent.

(iv) There are no legal restrictions prohibiting the consolidation of certain sub-sidiaries.

[24]GP tells us here that it consolidates all ''majority-owned'' (greater than 50 percent) and ''controlled'' companies except the finance company, which is not similar to the others in the consolidated group. Instead, the finance subsidiary is accounted for under the equity method. As can be seen from GP Credit Corporation's balance sheet in note 11, most (90 percent at year-end 1988) of the Credit Corporation's assets are receivables and most (80 percent) of its equities are debt, rather than owner's equity. In this sense, the operations of the finance subsidiary ''are not similar to those of the consolidated group.'' As authors' comment 53 points out, the non-consolidation of the finance company makes GP's balance sheet differ substantially from its appear-ance if the finance subsidiary were consolidated. Although there is no effect on final net income, the components of income are affected.

[25]Consolidated financial statements present information about a group of affiliated companies as if the group were one economic entity. Consequently, gains or losses on sales of assets between companies in the consolidated group must be eliminated from reported financial statements. The recognition of such gains or losses is post-poned until the assets are sold by one company of the consolidated group to a buyer outside of the consolidated group.

[26]GP tells us that it uses the equity method for the nonconsolidated finance subsidiary. See authors' comment 19.

[27]GP uses the completed contract method of recognizing revenue on long-term con-struction projects. See authors' comment 6.

[28]GP tells us that it charges vacation pay to expense (or product cost) accounts as employees earn vacations, rather than charging income when employees take their vacations.

[29]That is, in computing future values of pension fund investments and interest on unfunded obligations for prior service costs, a 6-percent rate is used. GP's note 2 indicates that the rate earned in 1988 was 8.4 percent.

[30]See authors' comment 44 for a discussion of the investment tax credit and the effect of GP's using the conservative cost reduction approach.

[31]Most governments (except the U.S.) do not allow LIFO for tax purposes, so GP uses a method acceptable for tax purposes.

[32]GP tells us it will not show an item of inventory on the balance sheet at an amount greater than replacement cost or net realizable value; we can deduce that it must be using a lower-of-cost-and-market valuation basis.

[33]GP uses ''full cost'' accounting for its oil and gas operations. See the Glossary at *reserve recognition accounting* for discussion of the options. GP's reported income

is probably slightly larger because it uses full cost accounting rather than successful efforts accounting.

[34]The *CICA Handbook*, section 1505, recommends the disclosure of the accounting policy adopted on amortization of intangibles.

[35]All manufacturing costs incurred during the year are shown as components of operating costs. If inventories have increased (ending inventory > beginning inventory), then some of those costs have not expired and are not expenses. Hence, the increase in inventories is deducted from total operating costs to derive operating *expenses*.

[36]Section 3450 of the *CICA Handbook* recommends the expensing of all research and most development costs, and the disclosure, such as GP's here, of the costs incurred during the year for R & D. The *CICA Handbook* allows the capitalizing of R & D costs that are incurred under contract and that are reimbursable. GP is making clear that these costs ($760 million in 1988) do not qualify for capitalization.

[37]The "unrecognized portion of changes in current value" is analogous to unrealized holding gains.

[38]GP uses the equity method of accounting for its 100-percent ownership of the GP Credit Corporation. Hence it shows 100 percent of the earnings of the Credit Corporation as "Other income." See authors' comments 19 and 52.

[39]"Customer financing" is interest on receivables held by GP arising from some of its sales.

[40]GP follows the policy of capitalizing interest into plant under construction. See the discussion in Chapter 9.

[41]This first schedule shows the details of income tax expense. The bottom line of the first schedule is the total expense reported on the income statement. The income tax expense amounts are derived in essentially two steps: first is shown the amount of taxes payable; then there is an adjustment for timing differences. GP also shows the effect of the investment tax credit, which is discussed below in authors' comment 44.

[42]In 1986 income expenses exceeded income taxes payable because of timing differences. The details of the Canadian timing differences are shown in the next schedule.

[43]GP uses the cost reduction approach of accounting for the investment tax credit; see authors' comment 44 and Chapter 9.

[44]GP uses the cost reduction approach of accounting for the investment tax credit, rather than the less conservative flow through approach. (Most Canadian corporations used the flow through method until 1984. Commencing in 1985 they are required by section 3805 of the *CICA Handbook* to use the cost reduction approach.) GP earned $92 million of investment tax credits during 1988. A portion (which cannot be computed from the published data) of this $92 million reduced reported tax expense in 1988, the remainder is shown as a deferred investment credit on the balance sheet (under "Future income taxes"). A portion of previous years' investment credits, which had been deferred, also served to reduce 1988 reported tax expense. The total of these two reductions of reported tax expense in 1988 was $36 million. If GP had

adopted the flow through approach, income tax expense would have been reduced by an additional $56 (= $92 − $36) million and 1988 net income would have been $56 million larger. Under the flow through approach, retained earnings at the end of 1988 would have been $262 million larger. Total deferred investment tax credits of $262 million are part of "Future income taxes" on the balance sheet.

[45]This schedule shows the components of the timing differences on income taxes.

[46]Capital cost allowance (CCA) claimed on the tax return exceeded the amount of depreciation included in cost of goods sold and other expenses on the financial statements. For most companies, CCA claimed exceeds book depreciation. We can compute the excess of CCA claimed over the book depreciation expense reported in the financial statements by using the $77 million timing difference shown here for 1988. If income tax expense exceeds income taxes payable by $77 million because of depreciation timing differences and if the marginal income tax rate is 46 percent of pretax income, then depreciation on the tax return must have exceeded depreciation on the financial statements by x where

$$.46x = \$77 \text{ million or}$$
$$x = \$77 \text{ million}/.46, \text{ or}$$
$$x = \$167 \text{ million}.$$

[47]GP makes sales on credit, with cash payments from the customer to GP spread over time. Such sales are called "installment sales." GP recognizes the revenue from installment sales in the period of sale. For tax purposes, GP recognizes revenue when the cash payments are collected. Thus, a timing difference is created. The amount shown here for GP is relatively small because GP tends not to have large percentages of its sales on the installment method.

[48]Estimated warranty expense recognized by the "allowance method" does not qualify as a tax deduction. GP uses the "allowance method" of recognizing warranty expense for financial reporting. As products carrying warranties are sold, GP makes the following entry recognizing the estimated liability for future repairs and replacements:

Estimated Warranty Expense (Provision)	X	
Estimated Warranty Liability		X
Entry made in the period of sale for expected warranty costs.		

Later, when repairs are made, and warranty costs are incurred, the entry is:

Estimated Warranty Liability	Y	
Assets Used and Liabilities Incurred		Y
To recognize cost of actual repairs and replacements.		

The repair and, therefore, the second entry often occur in a year subsequent to the year of sale. The cost of providing the warranty service does not become a tax deduction until the repair is actually made. Thus timing differences are created: an expense is subtracted on the financial statements in one year but is deducted on the tax return in a later year. We can make the following statements about all three years reported on. The provision for warranties (the estimated expense) results in income taxes payable being larger than income tax expense. Therefore, it must be true that the estimated expense of rendering warranty service in future years for sales in the current year is greater than the actual costs of warranty repairs made in current years, most of which related to sales of earlier years.

[49]Primarily because of the accounting for depreciation and warranties (explained above), GP's cumulative income tax expense reported in the financial statements has exceeded GP's income tax payments. The total income tax deferred due to timing differences and to the investment tax credit, at the end of 1988 was $1,242 million (= $980 + $262) and at the end of 1986 was $1,125 million (= $964 + $161).

[50]GP reports only basic earnings per share. Because it has so few dilutive securities outstanding, the result is not considered materially dilutive and the *CICA Handbook* exempts the company from disclosing fully diluted earnings per share.

[51]*CICA Handbook*, section 3010, requires disclosure of aggregate cost and aggregate market value of these temporary investments.

[52]Note that the following two events both occurred during 1988:
 (i) GP required GPCC to declare dividends (payable to GP) in the amount of $93 million, and
 (ii) GP invested an additional $92 (= $658 − $566) million in GPCC through the purchase of "Share capital."
One might wonder why the parent bothers to have the subsidiary declare dividends and then turn right around and reinvest that cash in the same subsidiary. The executive compensation plan for the top managers of GP contains bonus clauses tying total pay to the reported income of the parent company as computed with a special formula. In that formula, the income from the Credit Company is based on accounting using the cost method, not the equity method. (One of the questions at the end of this Appendix explores why this fact might explain the otherwise-puzzling phenomenon.)

[53]If the Credit Corporation were consolidated, rather than accounted for on the equity method, all these assets, liabilities, and deferred credits would be shown on GP's balance sheet. GP's consolidated retained earnings would be no different, however, because the equity method records income of unconsolidated subsidiaries as earned. The $931 (= $9,344 − $7,516 − $876 − 21) million of net assets added to GP's balance sheet would be offset with the elimination of $931 shown on the balance sheet and detailed in GP's note 11.

If GP were to consolidate GP Credit Corporation, the results would be as shown in Exhibit A.5 on page 786. It shows the income statement and balance sheet as reported and as they would appear if GP Credit Corporation were consolidated. We also show two key financial ratios, as they would be calculated from year-end account balances. The consolidation policy with respect to GP Credit Corporation affects the appearance of the financial statements.

[54]The disclosure of both historical cost and current market values follows the recommendation of *CICA Handbook*, section 3050. The net realizable value of these secu-

rities at year-end 1988 is $331 million; the cost (see GP's note 11) was $374 million. Thus, GP has an unrealized holding loss on these securities of $43 (= $331 value − $374 cost) million at year-end 1988. At year-end 1987, the unrealized holding loss was $38 (= $432 − $394) million. Thus, the unrealized holding loss increased during the year by $5 million, from $38 million to $43 million. GP therefore had unrealized holding loss during 1988 of $5 million on these securities.

[55]See authors' comment 34.

[56]*CICA Handbook*, section 1510, recommends that amounts due to subsidiaries not consolidated be shown separately.

[57]GP's note 13 gives the details of its short-term borrowings. GP's note 16 gives the details of its long-term borrowings. This paragraph helps the analyst to understand GP's intermediate-term borrowings. From these data, the analyst can estimate cash requirements for debt retirement over the next several years.

[58]*CICA Handbook*, section 3240, recommends the disclosure of changes in share capital accounts. The schedule in note 17 shows the sources of the changes in the other owners' equity accounts.

Exhibit A.5
GENERAL PRODUCTS and GP CREDIT CORPORATION, 1988
(for Authors' Comment 53)

Income Statement	Equity Method (as Reported)	Adjustment Debit	Adjustment Credit	Consol- idated
Revenues (other than from Credit Corporation)[a]	$25,408	$	$ 1,389 (1)	$26,797
Equity Method Revenues from Credit Corporation	115	115 (1)		
Total Revenues[b]	$25,523			
Total Expenses[c]	24,009	1,274 (1)		25,283
Net Income	$ 1,514			$ 1,514
Balance Sheet				
All Assets Except Investment in Credit Corporation	$17,580	9,344 (2)		$26,924
Investment in Credit Corporation	931		931 (2)	
Total Assets	$18,511			$26,924
Liabilities (including Minority Interest)	$10,311		8,413[d] (2)	$18,724
Owners' Equity	8,200			8,200
Total Equities	$18,511	$10,733	$10,733	$26,924

Rate of Return on Assets:

$$\frac{\$1,514 + \$21^e + (.54 \times \$314^f)}{\$18,511} \qquad \frac{\$1,514 + \$21^e + .54 \times (\$314^f + \$719^g)}{\$26,924}$$

Debt-Equity Ratio:

$$= \frac{\$1,705}{\$18,511} = 9.2\% \qquad\qquad = \frac{\$2,093}{\$26,924} = 7.8\%$$

$$\frac{\$10,311}{\$18,511} = 56\% \qquad\qquad \frac{\$18,724}{\$26,924} = 70\%$$

a$24,959 + $564 − $115.
b$24,959 shown as sales in Exhibit A.1 plus $564 of Other income.
c$17,751 + $4,965 (operating expense) + $314 (interest) + $958 (income taxes) + $21 (minority interest).
dGP Credit's "liabilities" ($7,516) plus "deferred income taxes" ($876) plus "deferred investment credit" ($21).
eMinority interest in net income from income statement.
fGP's interest expense. Multiply by 0.54 to present on aftertax basis.
gGP Credit's interest expense. Multiply by 0.54 to present on aftertax basis.

Adjusting entry (1) adds the revenues and expenses of the Credit Corporation to the consolidated totals, while removing the equity method revenue reported by GP.

Adjusting entry (2) adds the assets and liabilities of the Credit Corporation to the consolidated totals, while removing GP's net investment from the asset account for Investments.

[59]Neither gain nor loss can be recognized on transactions by a company in its own shares (called *treasury shares*). GP's accounting is correct, but the use of the terms *gain* and *loss* may be misleading. When GP reissues previously acquired treasury shares, the adjustment to achieve equal debits and credits is not to a gain or loss account (to appear on the income statement), but to the account "Contributed surplus or retained earnings." If treasury shares are acquired for an outlay of $1,000 and then are reissued for $1,200, then the entries would be:

Common Shares Held in Treasury	$1,000	
Cash		$1,000
To record acquisition of treasury shares.		
Cash	$1,200	
Common Shares Held in Treasury		$1,000
Contributed Surplus (not Gain on Disposition of Treasury Shares)		200
To record reissue of treasury shares for an amount greater than outlay to acquire them.		

[60]Associated companies are those companies over which GP can exercise significant influence, which in this case are 20-percent to 50-percent owned by GP. *CICA Handbook*, section 3050, recommends GP use the equity method for its investment in those companies.

[61]*CICA Handbook*, section 3240, recommends the disclosure of the details of stock option plans and of the currently outstanding options. At the end of 1988, the market price of GP common shares was $61.25. The average price of the 4,303,322 options exercisable at the end of 1988 was $51.56. Thus, if all the options were exercised, the present owners' equity would be diluted by approximately $42 million [= ($61.25 − $51.56) × 4,303,322 shares] in comparison to the issue of new shares at the current market price.

[62]The *CICA Handbook*, section 3065, recommends disclosure of material commitments under operating leases. GP has no such material commitments. In general, the disclosures must include the effects on both the income statement and the balance

sheet of capitalizing such leases. If GP had contracted for the use of facilities under capital leases, section 3065 of the *CICA Handbook* requires the asset and related liability be recorded in the balance sheet with depreciation and interest expense recorded in the income statement. GP has no material capital leases.

[63]The *CICA Handbook*, section 1700, recommends disclosure of segment data. Segments are required to be defined both by industry (consumer products, industrial power) and by geographic location. Since GP operates primarily in Canada, no segregation of operations by geographic location is required. See pages 773 and 774.

[64]Earnings of the individual segments total an amount larger than net income for 1988 of $1,514 by $14 million. Assets of the individual segments sum to an amount smaller than total assets by $1,223 million. Hence rates of return computed for individual segments will overstate true rate of return. If a "true" rate of return for the company as a whole is defined to be net income over total assets, then GP's rate of return is 8.2 percent (= $1,514/$18,511). The incomes of the individual segments total $1,528 million and the sum of the segments assets is $17,288 (= $18,511 − $1,223) million. If one were computing rates of return for individual segments, then the aggregate rate of return might be computed as 8.8 percent (= $1,528/$17,288). For GP, the resulting overstatement of the combined segment rates of return is not as dramatic as it is for some other companies. Some who criticize segment reporting have in mind the misleading inferences the unwary analyst (or politician or government regulator) might draw from computing rates of return for individual segments. Note that the difference between the sum of the individual segments is reconciled with the total shown on the GP financial statements by entries for "corporate items and eliminations" and "interest and other finance charges."

[65]The major difficulty in constructing meaningful and useful segment reports is the allocation of these "corporate items" to the major categories. They are truly common or joint costs of running the entire corporation but must be allocated to the various segments in order to present subtotals for segment earnings that add up to the total earnings, $1,514 million for 1988.

[66]The detail shown here by GP shows six years of data so that one can construct time series analysis for at least five years in all cases. Note that if only five columns are shown, then growth rates for items like sales can be computed for only four years.

[67]During the year, GP (and most other public companies) are required by regulatory authorities to send quarterly (interim) financial statements to shareholders.

[68]Section 4510 of the *CICA Handbook* recommends that companies explain the need to supply supplementary information on the effect of changing prices on financial statements.

[69]Since the *CICA Handbook* recommends that the supplementary information on accounting for the effects of changing prices be outside the scope of the auditor's examination, a company may exclude this information without causing a reservation in the auditor's report. Partly as a result of this factor many companies have excluded any reference to the problem and solution of accounting for changing prices.

[70]The *CICA Handbook* recommends that the bases and methods used to determine cost be disclosed. The characteristics of the company and its environment, and the management's view of the relevance of the information, will influence the methods adopted.

[71]GP has restricted the purchasing power (monetary) loss to the monetary loss resulting from holding net monetary working capital assets during the year. $161,000,000 must be retained by the company during 1988 in order to finance the cash, receivables and other current monetary assets and liabilities at higher prices. The financing adjustment is based on the remaining (non current) net monetary assets and measures the increased cost of maintaining productive capacity born by the long-term creditors.

[72]There is disagreement on the treatment of future income tax and the related expense. In conformity with the *CICA Handbook* recommendation both of these items are considered as non-monetary.

[73]The impact of accounting for changing price levels is reflected in these two paragraphs. Many companies have shown that the dividends paid exceed the current cost income reported, and that income tax expense exceeds reported current cost income before income tax.

[74]Note that the current cost earnings for 1987 have been converted to dollars of constant purchasing power at the end of 1988. Consequently the amounts reported in the 1988 statement will differ from those reported in the supplementary information presented in the previous year.

Questions and Problems

1. Review the meaning of the following concepts or terms discussed in this appendix.
  a. Central corporate expenses and central corporate assets hinder measures of segment rates of return.
  b. Consolidated financial statements.
  c. Future income tax debit.
  d. Installment sales.
  e. Minority interest on income statement *vs* minority interest on balance sheet.
  f. Progress billings.
  g. Statutory *vs* effective income tax rate.

2. Assume that all sales of General Products Limited and consolidated subsidiaries for the year 1988 were made on account. How much cash was collected from customers?

3. What amount of cash was disbursed during 1988 by GP for dividends?

4. Refer to note 8 of the GP annual report. Observe there receivables labeled "Associated companies" and "Nonconsolidated subsidiary." Are these receivables more likely to represent amounts owed to GP by these "Associated companies" and "Nonconsolidated subsidiary" or are they amounts owed by customers to "Associated companies" and "Nonconsolidated subsidiary"? Explain your reasoning.

5. Refer to the data in GP's note 14 on accounts payable. Are the amounts shown for ''nonconsolidated subsidiary'' more likely amounts owed by GP to this ''nonconsolidated subsidiary'' or amounts owed by it to others? Explain your reasoning.

6. Refer to the data in GP's note 13 on short-term borrowings. Compute the dollar amount of interest expense on these borrowings for 1988.

7. Assume that GP prepared the statement of changes in financial position using funds defined as working capital, rather than as cash plus temporary investments less short-term borrowings. Prepare an analysis of changes in funds for the year 1988.

8. Refer to GP's note 18 on retained earnings. What are the retained earnings of the nonconsolidated subsidiaries and associates *other* than those of GP Credit Corporation at the end of 1988?

9. Assuming a marginal income tax rate of 46 percent, by what amount did depreciation claimed on the tax return for 1987 differ from the depreciation expense reported in the financial statements for 1987?

10. Refer to author's comment 52. Explain why the compensation agreement described there might help one understand the simultaneous dividend declaration and common share issue of GP Credit Corporation.

11. Assume that GP Credit Corporation was consolidated, rather than accounted for on the equity method.

    a. By how much would GP's consolidated revenue and other income for 1987 differ from the amounts reported?

    b. By how much would GP's consolidated expenses for 1987 differ from the amounts reported?

    c. By how much would GP's consolidated income for 1987 differ from the amount reported?

    d. By how much would GP's consolidated assets differ from the amount reported?

    e. By how much would GP's consolidated shareholders' equity differ from the amount reported?

Appendix B Compound Interest Concepts and Applications

Money is a scarce resource, which its owner can use to command other resources. Like owners of other scarce resources, owners of money can permit borrowers to rent the use of their money for a period of time. Payment for the use of money differs little from other rental payments, such as those made to a landlord for the use of property or to a car rental agency for the use of a car. Payment for the use of money is called *interest*. Accounting is concerned with interest because it must record transactions in which the use of money is bought and sold.

Accountants and managers are concerned with interest calculations for another, equally important, reason. Expenditures for an asset most often do not occur at the same time as the receipts for services produced by that asset. Money received sooner is more valuable than money received later. The difference in timing can affect whether or not acquiring an asset is profitable. Amounts of money received at different times are different commodities. Managers use interest calculations to make amounts of money to be paid or received at different times comparable. For example, an analyst might compare two amounts to be received at two different times by using interest calculations to find the equivalent value of one amount at the time the other is due.

Contracts involving a series of money payments over time, such as bonds, mortgages, notes, and leases, are evaluated by finding the *present value* of the stream of payments. The present value of a stream of payments is a single amount of money at the present time that is the economic equivalent of the entire stream.

Compound Interest Concepts

The quotation of interest "cost" is typically specified as a percentage of the amount borrowed per unit of time. Examples are 12 percent per year and one percent per month, which are not the same. Another example occurs in the context of discounts on purchases. The terms of sale "2/10, net/30" is equivalent to two percent for 20 days because, if the discount is not taken, payment can be delayed and the money can be used for up to an extra 20 (= 30 − 10) days.

The amount borrowed or loaned is called the *principal*. To *compound* interest means that the amount of interest earned during a period is added to the principal and the principal for the next interest period is larger.

For example, if you deposit $1,000 in a savings account that pays compound interest at the rate of six percent per year, you will earn $60 by the end of one year. If you do not withdraw the $60, then $1,060 will be earning interest during the second year. During the second year your principal of $1,060 will earn $63.60 interest, $60 on the initial deposit of $1,000 and $3.60 on the $60 earned the first year. By the end of the second year, you will have $1,123.60.

When only the original principal earns interest during the entire life of the loan, the interest due at the time the loan is repaid is called *simple* interest. In simple interest calculations, interest on previously earned interest is ignored.[1] The use of simple interest calculations in accounting arises in the following way. If you borrow $10,000 at a rate of 12 percent per year, but compute interest for any month as $100 ($= \$10,000 \times .12 \times \frac{1}{12}$), then you are using a simple interest calculation. Nearly all economic calculations involve compound interest.

The ''force,'' or effect, of compound interest is more substantial than many people realize. For example, compounded annually at eight percent, money ''doubles itself'' in less than nine years. Put another way, if you invest $100 at eight percent compounded annually, you will have $200 in 9 years.

Problems involving compound interest generally fall into two groups with respect to time: first, there are the problems for which we want to know the future value of money invested or loaned today; second, there are the problems for which we want to know the present value, or today's value, of money to be received or paid at later dates. In addition, the accountant must sometimes compute the interest rate implicit in certain payment streams, and determine identical combined payments of principal and interest to repay a debt over a specified period.

Future Value

When $1.00 is invested today at 12 percent compounded annually, it will grow to $1.12000 at the end of 1 year, $1.25440 at the end of 2 years, $1.40493 at the end of 3 years, and so on according to the formula

$$F_n = P(1 + r)^n$$

where
F_n represents the accumulation or future value,
P represents the one-time investment today,
r is the interest rate per period, and
n is the number of periods from today.

The amount F_n is the future value of the present payment, P, compounded at r percent per period for n periods. Table C.1, page 814, shows the future values of $P = \$1$ for various numbers of periods and for various interest rates. Extracts from that table are shown here in Table B.1.

Table B.1 (Excerpt from Table C.1)
Future value of $1 at 6 percent and 12 percent per period
$F_n = P(1 + r)^n$

Number of Periods = n	Rate = r	
	6%	12%
1	1.06000	1.12000
2	1.12360	1.25440
3	1.19102	1.40493
10	1.79085	3.10585
20	3.20714	9.64629

---

[1]If interest earned may be withdrawn, then compounded interest techniques are relevant. The withdrawn interest can be invested elsewhere to earn additional interest.

Sample Problems in Computing Future Value

Example 1 How much will $1,000 deposited today at six percent compounded annually be worth ten years from now?

One dollar deposited today at six percent will grow to $1.79085; therefore, $1,000 will grow to $1,000(1.06)^{10} = $1,000 \times 1.79085 = $1,790.85$.

Example 2 Macaulay Corporation deposits $10,000 in an expansion fund today. The fund will earn 12 percent per year. How much will the $10,000 grow to in 20 years if the entire fund and all interest earned on it are left on deposit in the fund?

One dollar deposited today at 12 percent will grow to $9.64629 in 20 years. Therefore, $10,000 will grow to $96,463 (= $10,000 \times 9.64629) in 20 years.

Present Value

The preceding section developed the tools for computing the future value, F_n, of a sum of money, P, deposited or invested today. P is known; F_n is calculated. This section deals with the problems of calculating how much principal, P, has to be invested today in order to have a specified amount, F_n, at the end of n periods. The future amount, F_n, the interest rate, r, and the number of periods, n, are known; P is to be found. In order to have $1 one year from today when interest is earned at six percent, P of $.94340 must be invested today. That is, $F^1 = P(1.06)^1$ or $1 = $.94340 \times 1.06$. Because $F_n = P(1 + r)^n$, dividing both sides of the equation by $(1 + r)^n$ yields

$$\frac{F_n}{(1 + r)^n} = P$$

or

$$P = \frac{F_n}{(1 + r)^n} = F_n(1 + r)^{-n}.$$

Present Value Terminology

The number $(1 + r)^{-n}$ is the present value of $1 to be received after n periods when interest is earned at r percent per period. The term *discount* is used in this context as follows: The *discounted* present value of $1 to be received n periods in the future is $(1 + r)^{-n}$ when the *discount* rate is r percent per period for n periods. The number r is the discount *rate* and the number $(1 + r)^{-n}$ is the discount *factor* for n periods. A discount factor $(1 + r)^{-n}$ is merely the reciprocal, or inverse, of a number, $(1 + r)^n$, in Table B.1. Therefore, tables of discount factors are not necessary for present-value calculations if tables of future values are at hand, and vice versa. But present value calculations are so frequently needed that tables of discount factors are as widely available as tables of future values. Portions of Table C.2 (page 815), which shows discount factors or, equivalently, present values of $1 for various numbers of periods, appear in Table B.2.

Table B.2 (Excerpt from Table C.2)
Present value of $1 at 6 percent and 12 percent per period
$$P = F_n(1 + r)^{-n}$$

Number of Periods = n	Rate = r	
	6%	12%
1	.94340	.89286
2	.89000	.79719
3	.83962	.71178
10	.55839	.32197
20	.31180	.10367

Sample Problems in Determining Present Values

Example 3 What is the present value of $1 due ten years from now if the interest (equivalently, the discount) rate r is six percent per year?

From Table B.2, six-percent column, 10-period row, the present value of $1 to be received ten periods hence at six percent is $.55839.

Example 4 (This example is used in Chapter 11.) You issue a noninterest-bearing note that promises to pay $16,000 three years from today in exchange for used equipment. How much is that promise worth today if the discount rate appropriate for such notes is 12 percent per period?

One dollar received three years hence discounted at 12 percent has a present value of $.71178. Thus, the promise is worth $16,000 × .71178 = $11,388.

Changing the Compounding Period: Nominal and Effective Rates

"Twelve percent, compounded annually" is the price for a loan; this means that interest is added to or *converted* into principal once a year at the rate of 12 percent. Often, however, the price for a loan states that compounding is to take place more than once a year. A bank may advertise that it pays six percent, compounded quarterly. This means that at the end of each quarter the bank credits savings accounts with interest calculated at the rate 1.5 percent (= 6 percent/4). The interest payment can be withdrawn or left on deposit to earn more interest.

If $10,000 is invested today at 12 percent compounded annually, its future value one year later is $11,200. If the rate of interest is stated as 12 percent compounded semiannually, then six percent interest is added to the principal every six months. At the end of the first six months, $10,000 will have grown to $10,600, so that the accumulation will be $10,600 × 1.06 = $11,236 by the end of the year. Notice that 12 percent compounded *semiannually* is equivalent to 12.36 percent compounded *annually*.

Suppose that the price is quoted as 12 percent, compounded quarterly. Then an additional three percent of the principal will be added to, or converted into, principal every three months. By the end of the year, $10,000 will grow to $10,000 × $(1.03)^4$ = $10,000 × 1.12551 = $11,255. Twelve percent compounded quarterly is equivalent to 12.55 percent compounded annually. If 12 percent is compounded monthly, then $1 will grow to $1 × $(1.01)^{12}$ = $1.12683 and $10,000 will grow to $11,268. Thus, 12 percent compounded monthly is equivalent to 12.68 percent compounded annually.

For a given *nominal* rate, such as the 12 percent in the examples above, the more often interest is compounded or converted into principal, the higher the *effective* rate of interest paid. If a nominal rate, r, is compounded m times per year, then the effective rate is $1 + r/m)^m - 1$.

In practice, to solve problems that require computation of interest quoted at a nominal rate of r percent per period compounded m times per period for n periods, merely use the tables for the rate r/m and $m \times n$ periods. For example, 12 percent compounded quarterly for five years is equivalent to the rate found in the interest tables for $r = 12/4 = 3$ percent for $m \times n = 4 \times 5 = 20$ periods.

Some banks advertise that they compound interest daily or even continuously. The mathematics of calculus provides a mechanism for finding the effective rate when interest is compounded continuously. If interest is compounded continuously at nominal rate r per year, then the effective annual interest rate is $e^r - 1$, where e is the base of the natural logarithms. Tables of values of e^r are widely available.[2] Six percent per year compounded continuously is equivalent to 6.1837 percent compounded annually; 12 percent per year compounded continuously is equivalent to 12.75 percent compounded annually. Do not confuse the compounding period with the payment period. Some banks, for example, compound interest daily but pay interest quarterly.

Sample Problems in Changing the Compounding Period

Example 5 What is the future value five years hence of $600 invested at 12 percent compounded semiannually?

Twelve percent compounded two times per year for five years is equivalent to six percent per period compounded for ten periods. Table B.1 shows the value of F_{10} = $(1.06)^{10}$ to be 1.79085. Six hundred dollars, then, would grow to $600 × 1.79085 = $1,074.51.

Example 6 How much money must be invested today at 12 percent compounded semiannually in order to have $10,000 ten years from today?

Twelve percent compounded two times a year for ten years is equivalent to six percent per period compounded for 20 periods. The *present* value, Table B.2, of $1 received 20 periods hence at six percent per period is $.31180. That is, $.31180

---

[2]See, for example, *Handbook of Modern Accounting*, 3rd ed. edited by Sidney Davidson and Roman L. Weil, McGraw-Hill Book Company, New York, 1983, chap. 9, Exhibit 1.

invested today for 20 periods at an interest rate of six percent per period will grow to $1. To have $10,000 in 20 periods (ten years), $3,118 (= $10,000 × $.31180) must be invested today.

Example 7 A local department store offers its customers credit and advertises its interest rate at 18 percent per year, compounded monthly at the rate of 1½ percent per month. What is the effective annual interest rate?

One-and-one-half percent per month for 12 months is equivalent to $(1.015)^{12} - 1 = 19.562$ percent per year. See Table 1, 12-period row, 1½ percent column where the factor is 1.19562.

Example 8 If prices increased at the rate of six percent during each of two consecutive six-month periods, how much did prices increase during the entire year?

If a price index is 100.00 at the start of the year, it will be $100.00 \times (1.06)^2 = 112.36$ at the end of the year. The price change for the entire year is $(112.36/100.00) - 1 = 12.36$ percent.

Annuities

An *annuity* is a series of equal payments made at the beginning or end of equal periods of time. Examples of annuities include monthly rental payments, semiannual corporate bond coupon (or interest) payments, and annual payments to a lessor under a lease contract. Armed with an understanding of the tables for future and present values, you can solve any annuity problem. Annuities arise so often, however, and their solution is so tedious without special tables that annuity problems warrant special study and the use of special tables.

Terminology for Annuities

The terminology used for annuities can be confusing because not all writers use the same terms. Definitions of the terms used in this text follow.

An annuity whose payments occur at the *end* of each period is called an *ordinary annuity* or an *annuity in arrears*. Semiannual corporate bond coupon payments are usually paid in arrears, that is, the first payment does not occur until after the bond has been outstanding for six months.

An annuity whose payments occur at the *beginning* of each period is called an *annuity due* or an *annuity in advance*. Rent is usually paid in advance, so that a series of rental payments is an annuity due.

A *deferred* annuity is one whose first payment is at some time later than the end of the first period.

Annuities can be paid forever. Such annuities are called *perpetuities*. A perpetuity can be in arrears or in advance. The only difference between the two is the timing of the first payment.

Annuities can be confusing. Their study is made easier with a *time line* such as the one shown below.

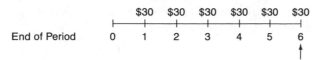

A time line marks the end of each period, numbers the periods, shows the payments to be received or paid, and shows the time at which the annuity is valued. The time line above represents an ordinary annuity (in arrears) for six periods of $30 to be valued at the end of period 6. The end of period 0 is "now." The first payment is to be received or paid one period from now.

Ordinary Annuities (Annuities in Arrears)

The future values of ordinary annuities are shown in the back of the book in Table C.3, portions of which Table B.3 reproduces.

Table B.3 (Excerpt from Table C.3)
Future value of an ordinary annuity of $1 at 6 percent and 12 percent

$$F_A = \frac{[(1 + r)^n - 1]}{r}$$

Number of Periods = n	Rate = r	
	6%	12%
1	1.00000	1.00000
2	2.06000	2.12000
3	3.18360	3.37440
5	5.63709	6.35285
10	13.18079	17.54874
20	36.78559	72.05244

Consider an ordinary annuity for three periods at six percent. The time line for the future value of such an annuity is

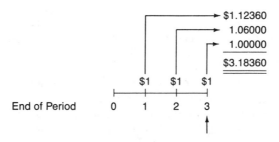

The $1 received at the end of the first period earns interest for two periods, so it is worth $1.2360 at the end of period 3. (See Table B.1.) The $1 received at the end of the second period grows to $1.06 by the end of period 3, and the $1 received at the end of period 3 is, of course, worth $1 at the end of period 3. The entire annuity is worth $3.18360 at the end of period 3. This is the amount shown in Table B.3 for the future value of an ordinary annuity for three periods at six percent. The future value of an ordinary annuity is calculated as follows:

$$\begin{matrix} \text{Future Value of} \\ \text{Ordinary Annuity} \end{matrix} = \begin{matrix} \text{Periodic} \\ \text{Payment} \end{matrix} \times \begin{matrix} \text{Factor for the Future} \\ \text{Value of an Ordinary} \\ \text{Annuity of \$1} \end{matrix}$$

Thus,

$$\$3.18360 = \$1 \times 3.18360$$

Table C.4 at the end of this Appendix shows the present value of ordinary annuities. Table B.4 reproduces excerpts from Table C.4.

Table B.4 (Excerpt from Table C.4)
Present value of an ordinary annuity of $1 per period at 6 percent and 12 percent

$$P_A = \frac{[1 - (1 + r)^{-n}]}{r}$$

Number of	Rate = r	
Periods = n	6%	12%
1	.94340	.89286
2	1.83339	1.69005
3	2.67301	2.40183
5	4.21236	3.60478
10	7.36009	5.65022
20	11.46992	7.46944

The time line for the present value of an ordinary annuity of $1 per period for three periods, discounted at six percent, is

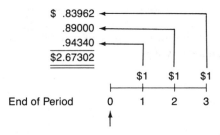

The $1 to be received at the end of period 1 has a present value of $.94340, the $1 to be received at the end of period 2 has a present value of $.89000, and the dollar to be received at the end of the third period has a present value of $.83962. Each of these numbers comes from Table B.2. The present value of the annuity is the sum of these individual present values, $2.67302, shown in Table B.4 as 2.67301 (our calculation differs because of roundings).

The present value of an ordinary annuity for n periods is the sum of the present value of $1 received one period from now plus the present value of $1 received two periods from now, and so on until we add on the present value of $1 received n periods from now. The present value of an ordinary annuity is calculated as follows:

Present Value of an Ordinary Annuity = Periodic Payment × Factor for the Present Value of an Ordinary Annuity of $1

Thus,

$2.67302 = $1 × 2.67302

Sample Problems Involving Ordinary Annuities

Example 9 An individual plans to invest $1,000 at the end of each of the next ten years in a savings account. The savings account accumulates interest of 12 percent compounded annually. What will be the balance in the savings account at the end of ten years?

The time line for this problem is

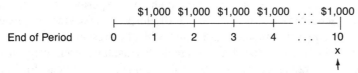

The symbol x denotes the amount to be calculated. Table B.3 indicates that the factor for the future value of an annuity at 12 percent for ten periods is 17.54874. Thus,

Future Value of an Ordinary Annuity = Periodic Payment × Factor for the Future Value of an Ordinary Annuity of $1

x = $1,000 × 17.54874

x = $17,549.

Example 10 An individual wishes to receive $60 every six months, starting six months hence, for the next five years. How much must be invested today in a savings account if the interest rate on the savings account is 12 percent compounded semiannually?

The time line is

The factor from Table B.4 for the present value of an annuity at six percent (= 12 percent per year/2 semiannual periods per year) for 10 (= 2 periods per year × 5 years) periods is 7.36009. Thus,

Present Value of an Ordinary Annuity = Periodic Payment × Factor for the Present Value of an Ordinary Annuity of $1

x = $60 × 7.36009

x = $441.61

If $441.61 is invested today, the principal plus interest compounded on the principal will provide sufficient funds so that $60 can be withdrawn every six months for the next five years.

Example 11 (Western Co. Ltd. mortgage example, from Chapter 10.) A company borrows $125,000 from a bank. The interest rate on the loan is 12 percent compounded semiannually. The company agrees to repay the loan in equal semiannual installments over the next five years. The first payment is to be made six months from now. What is the amount of the required semiannual payment?

The time line is

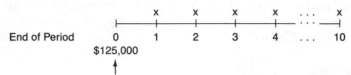

This problem is similar to Example 10 because both involve periodic payments in the future that are discounted to today. In Example 10, the periodic payments were given and the present value was computed. In Example 11, the present value is given and the periodic payment is computed. Table B.4 indicates that the present value of annuity at six percent (= 12 percent per year/2 semiannual periods per year) for 10 (= 2 periods per year × 5 years) periods is 7.36009. Thus,

$$
\begin{array}{llcl}
\text{Present Value} & & & \text{Factor for the} \\
\text{of an} & = & \text{Periodic} \times & \text{Present Value of an} \\
\text{Ordinary Annuity} & & \text{Payment} & \text{Ordinary Annuity of \$1} \\
\$125,000 & = & x \quad \times & 7.36009 \\
x & = & \dfrac{\$125,000}{7.36009} & \\
x & = & \$16,983 &
\end{array}
$$

Because the periodic payment is being calculated, the present value amount of $125,000 must be divided by the present value factor. (You may wish to turn to Exhibit 10.1 page 499 to study the amortization table for this loan. The amount of each semiannual payment shown here is $17,000 rather than $16,983, but the last payment is less than $17,000.)

Example 12 (Myers Inc. lease example, from Chapter 11.) A company signs a lease acquiring the right to use property for three years. Lease payments of $19,709 are to be made annually at the end of this and the next two years. The discount, or interest, rate is 15 percent per year. What is the present value of the lease payments?

The time line is

		$19,709	$19,709	$19,709
End of Period	0	1	2	3
	x			

The factor from Table C.4 for the present value of an annuity at 15 percent for three periods is 2.28323. Thus,

$$
\begin{array}{ccc}
\text{Present Value} & & \text{Factor for the} \\
\text{of an} & = \text{Periodic} \times & \text{Present Value} \\
\text{Ordinary Annuity} & \text{Payment} & \text{of an Ordinary} \\
& & \text{Annuity of \$1}
\end{array}
$$

$$x = \$19,709 \times 2.28323$$

$$x = \$45,000$$

In the Myers Inc. example in Chapter 11, the cost of the equipment is given at $45,000 and the periodic rental payment is computed with an annuity factor. Thus,

$$
\begin{array}{ccc}
\text{Present Value} & & \text{Factor for the} \\
\text{of an} & = \text{Periodic} \times & \text{Present Value of} \\
\text{Ordinary Annuity} & \text{Payment} & \text{an Annuity of \$1}
\end{array}
$$

$$\$45,000 = x \times 2.28323$$

$$x = \frac{\$45,000}{2.28323}$$

$$x = \$19,709$$

Example 13 (Pension funding example.) A company is obligated to make annual payments to a pension fund at the end of the next 30 years. The present value of those payments is to be $100,000. What must the annual payment be if the fund is projected to earn interest at the rate of eight percent per year?

The time line is

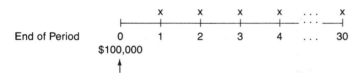

Table C.4 indicates that the factor for the present value of $1 paid at the end of the next 30 periods at eight percent per period is 11.25778. Thus,

$$
\begin{array}{ccc}
\text{Present Value} & & \text{Factor for the} \\
\text{of an} & = \text{Periodic} \times & \text{Present Value of an} \\
\text{Ordinary Annuity} & \text{Payment} & \text{Ordinary Annuity of \$1}
\end{array}
$$

$$\$100,000 = x \times 11.25778$$

$$x = \frac{\$100,000}{11.25778}$$

$$x = \$8,883$$

Example 14 Mr. Mason is 62 years old. He wishes to invest equal amounts on his sixty-third, sixty-fourth, and sixty-fifth birthdays so that starting on his sixty-sixth birthday he can withdraw $5,000 on each birthday for ten years. His investments will earn eight percent per year. How much should be invested on the sixty-third through sixty-fifth birthdays?

The time line for this problem is

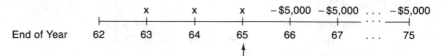

On his sixty-fifth birthday, Mr. Mason needs to have accumulated a fund equal to the present value of an annuity of $5,000 per period for ten periods, discounted at eight percent per period. The factor from Table C.4 for eight percent and ten periods is 6.71008. Thus,

$$
\begin{array}{ccc}
\text{Present Value} & & \text{Factor for the} \\
\text{of an} & = \text{Periodic} \times & \text{Present Value of an} \\
\text{Ordinary Annuity} & \text{Payment} & \text{Ordinary Annuity of \$1} \\
x & = \$5,000 \times & 6.71008 \\
x & = \$33,550 &
\end{array}
$$

The time line now appears as follows:

The question now becomes: How much must be invested on Mr. Mason's sixty-third, sixty-fourth, and sixty-fifth birthdays to accumulate to a fund of $33,550 on his sixty-fifth birthday? The factor for the future value of an annuity for three periods at eight percent is 3.24640. Thus,

$$
\begin{array}{ccc}
\text{Future Value} & & \text{Factor for the} \\
\text{of an} & = \text{Periodic} \times & \text{Future Value of an} \\
\text{Ordinary Annuity} & \text{Payment} & \text{Ordinary Annuity of \$1} \\
\$33,550 & = \quad x \quad \times & 3.24640 \\
x & = \dfrac{\$33,550}{3.24640} & \\
x & = \$10,335 &
\end{array}
$$

In the solution above, all calculations are expressed in terms of equivalent amounts on Mr. Mason's sixty-fifth birthday. That is, the present value of an annuity of $5,000 per period for ten periods at eight percent is equal to the future value of an annuity of $10,335 per period for three periods at eight percent and both of these amounts are equal to $33,550. The problem could have been worked by selecting any specific date between Mr. Mason's sixty-second and seventy-fifth birthdays.

One possibility would be to express all calculations in terms of equivalent amounts on Mr. Mason's sixty-second birthday. To solve the problem in this way, first find the present value on Mr. Mason's *sixty-fifth* birthday of an annuity of $5,000 per period for ten periods ($33,550 = $5,000 × 6.71008). Discount $33,550 back three periods using Table C.2 for the present value of $1 ($26,633 = $33,550 × .79383). The result is the present value of the payments to be made to Mr. Mason *measured as of his sixty-second birthday.* Then find the amounts that must be invested by Mr. Mason on his sixty-third, sixty-fourth, and sixty-fifth birthdays that have a *present value* on his sixty-second birthday equal to $26,633. The calculation is as follows:

Present Value of an Ordinary Annuity		Periodic Payment		Factor for the Present Value of an Ordinary Annuity of $1
$26,633	=	x	×	2.57710
x	=	$10,335		

The amount $10,335 is the same as that found above.

Perpetuities

A periodic payment to be received forever is called a *perpetuity*. Future values of perpetuities are undefined. If $1 is to be received at the end of every period and the discount rate is r percent, then the present value of the perpetuity is $1/r$. This expression can be derived with algebra or by observing what happens in the expression for the present value of an ordinary annuity of A per payment as n, the number of payments, approaches infinity:

$$P_A = \frac{A[1 - (1 + r)^{-n}]}{r}$$

As n approaches infinity, $(1 + r)^{-n}$ approaches zero, so that P_A approaches $A(1/r)$. If the first payment of the perpetuity occurs now, the present value is $A[1 + 1/r]$.

Examples of Perpetuities

Example 15 The Canadian government offers to pay $30 every six months forever in the form of a perpetual bond. What is that bond worth if the discount rate is 15 percent compounded semiannually?

Fifteen percent compounded semiannually is equivalent to 7.5 percent per six-month period. If the first payment occurs six months from now, the present value is $30/.075 = $400. If the first payment occurs today, the present value is $30 + $400 = $430.

Example 16 Every two years, Ms. Young gives $10,000 to a university to provide a scholarship for an entering student in a two-year business administration course. If the university credits six percent per year to its investment accounts, how much must Ms. Young give to the university to provide such a scholarship every two years forever, starting two years hence?

A perpetuity in arrears assumes one payment at the end of each period. Here, the period is two years; six percent compounded once a year over two years is equivalent to a rate of $(1.06)^2 - 1 = .12360$ or 12.36 percent compounded once per two-year period. Consequently, the present value of the perpetuity paid in arrears every two years is $80,906 (= $10,000/.12360). A gift of $80,906 will be sufficient to provide a $10,000 scholarship forever. If the first scholarship is to be awarded now, the gift must be $90,906 (= $80,906 + $10,000).

Implicit Interest Rates: Finding Internal Rates of Return

In the preceding examples, given the interest rate and stated cash payments, a future value or a present value was computed. Or the required payments were computed given their known future value or their known present value. In some calculations, the present or future value and the periodic payments are known; the implicit interest rate is to be found. For example, Chapter 11 illustrates a case in which the cash price of some equipment is known to be $10,500 and the asset was acquired using a note. The note is non-interest-bearing, has a face value of $16,000, and matures in three years. In order to compute interest expense over the three-year period, the implicit interest rate must be found. The time line for this problem is

$$+\$10,500 \quad\quad 0 \quad\quad\quad 0 \quad\quad -\$16,000$$

| End of Year | 0 | 1 | 2 | 3 |

The implicit interest rate is r, such that

(I)
$$\$10,500 = \frac{\$16,000}{(1 + r)^3}$$

(II)
$$0 = \$10,500 - \frac{\$16,000}{(1 + r)^3}$$

That is, the present value of $16,000 discounted three periods at r percent per period is $10,500. The present value of all current and future cash flows nets to zero when future flows are discounted at r per period. In general, the only way to find such an r is a trial-and-error procedure. In case where r appears only in one term, as here, r can be found analytically. Here, $r = (\$16,000/\$10,500)^{1/3} - 1 = .1507 = 15.1$ percent.

The general procedure is called "finding the internal rate of return" or "finding the implicit interest rate" of a series of cash flows. The *internal rate of return* of a series of cash flows is the discount rate that equates the net present value of that series of cash flows to zero. The steps in finding the internal rate of return are as follows:

1. Make an educated guess, called the "trial rate," at the internal rate of return. If you have no idea what to guess, try zero.
2. Calculate the present value of all the cash flows (including the one at the end of year 0).
3. If the present value of the cash flows is zero, stop. The current trial rate is the internal rate of return.
4. If the amount found in step 2 is less than zero, try a larger interest rate as the trial rate and go back to step 2.
5. If the amount found in step 2 is greater than zero, try a smaller interest rate as the new trial rate and go back to step 2.

The iterations below illustrate the process for the example in equation (II).

Iteration Number	Trial Rate = r	Net Present Value: Right-Hand Side of (II)
1	0.0%	($5,500)
2	10.0	(1,521)
3	15.0	(20)
4	15.5	116
5	15.2	34
6	15.1	7

With a trial rate of 15.1 percent, the right-hand side is close enough to zero so that 15.1 percent can be used as the implicit interest rate. Continued iterations would find trial rates even closer to the true rate, which is about 15.0739 percent.

Finding the internal rate of return for a series of cash flows can be tedious and should not be attepted unless one has at least a calculator. An exponential feature, the feature that allows the computation of $(1 + r)$ raised to various powers, helps.[3]

Sample Problem Involving Implicit Interest Rates

Example 17 The Alexis Co. Inc. acquires a machine with a cash price of $10,500. It pays for the machine by giving a note promising to make payments equal to seven percent of the face value, $840, at the end of each of the next three years and a single payment of $12,000 in three years. What is the implicit interest rate in the loan?

The time line for this problem is

	$10,500	– $840	– $840	– $12,840
End of Period	0	1	2	3

The implicit interest rate is r, such that[4]

$$(\text{III}) \qquad \$10,500 = \frac{\$840}{(1 + r)} + \frac{\$840}{(1 + r)^2} + \frac{\$12,840}{(1 + r)^3}$$

The internal rate of return is found to the nearest tenth of 1 percent to be 12.2 percent:

---

[3]There are ways to guess the trial rate that will approximate the true rate in fewer iterations than the method described here. If you want to find internal rates of return efficiently with successive trial rates, then refer to a mathematical reference book to learn about the "Newton search" method, sometimes called the "method of false position."

[4]Compare this formulation to that in equation (I), above. Note that the left-hand side is zero in one case but not in the other. The left-hand side can be either a nonzero number or zero, depending on what seems convenient for the particular context.

Iteration Number	Trial Rate	Right-Hand Side of (III)
1	7.0%	$12,000
2	15.0	9,808
3	11.0	10,827
4	13.0	10,300
5	12.0	10,559
6	12.5	10,428
7	12.3	10,480
8	12.2	10,506
9	12.1	10,532

Summary

Accountants typically deal with four kinds of compound interest problems: those involving the present or future value of a single payment or of a series of payments. In working annuity problems, you will find drawing a time line helpful in deciding which particular kind of annuity is involved.

Questions, Exercises, Problems and Cases

Questions

1. Review the following concepts or terms discussed in this appendix.
   a. Compound interest
   b. Principal
   c. Simple interest
   d. Future value
   e. Present value
   f. Discounted value
   g. Discount factor
   h. Discount rate
   i. Ordinary annuity (annuity in arrears)
   j. Perpetuity
   k. Implicit interest rate (internal rate of return)

2. What is interest?

3. Distinguish between simple and compound interest.

4. Distinguish between the discounted present value of a stream of future payments and their net present value. If there is no distinction, then so state.

5. Distinguish between an annuity due and an ordinary annuity.

6. Describe the "implicit interest rate" for a series of cash flows and a procedure for finding it.

7. Does the present value of a given amount to be paid in ten years increase or decrease if the interest rate increases? Suppose that the amount were due in five years? 20

years? Does the present value of an annuity to be paid for ten years increase or decrease if the discount rate decreases? Suppose that the annuity were for five years? 20 years?

8. Rather than pay you $100 a month for the next 20 years, the person who injured you in an automobile accident is willing to pay a single amount now to settle your claim for injuries. Would you rather an interest rate of six percent or twelve percent be used in computing the present value of the lump-sum settlement? Comment or explain.

Exercises

9. *Effective interest rates.* State the rate per period and the number of periods, in each of the following:
   a. 12 percent per annum, for five years, compounded annually.
   b. 12 percent per annum, for five years, commpounded semiannually.
   c. 12 percent per annum, for five years, compounded quarterly.
   d. 12 percent per annum, for five years, compounded monthly.

10. Compute the future value of:
   a. $100 invested for five years at four percent compounded annually.
   b. $500 invested for 15 periods at two percent compounded once per period.
   c. $200 invested for eight years at three percent compounded semiannually.
   d. $2,500 invested for 14 years at eight percent compounded quarterly.
   e. $600 invested for three years at 12 percent compounded monthly.

11. Compute the present value of:
   a. $100 due in 30 years at four percent compounded annually.
   b. $250 due in eight years at eight percent compounded quarterly.
   c. $1,000 due in two years at 12 percent compounded monthly.

12. Compute the amount (future value) of an ordinary annuity (an annuity in arrears) of:
   a. 13 rents of $100 at 1½ percent per period.
   b. 8 rents of $850 at six percent per period.
   c. 28 rents of $400 at four percent per period.

13. Mr. Adams has $500 to invest. He wishes to know how much it will amount to if he invests it at
   a. 6 percent per year for 21 years.
   b. 8 percent per year for 33 years.

14. Ms. Black wishes to have $15,000 at the end of eight years. How much must she invest today to accomplish this purpose if the interest rate is
   a. 6 percent per year?
   b. 8 percent per year?

15. Mr. Case plans to sct aside $4,000 each year, the first payment to be made on January 1, 1986, and the last on January 1, 1991. How much will he have accumulated by January 1, 1991 if the interest rate is
   a. 6 percent per year?
   b. 8 percent per year?

16. Ms. David wants to have $450,000 on her sixty-fifth birthday. How much must she deposit on each birthday from her fifty-eighth to sixty-fifth, inclusive, in order to receive this amount? Assume an interest rate of

    a. 8 percent per year.

    b. 12 percent per year.

17. If Mr. Edwards invests $900 on June 1 of each year from 1986 to 1996, inclusive, how much will he have accumulated on June 1, 1997 (note that one year elapses after last payment) if the interest rate is

    a. 5 percent per year?

    b. 10 percent per year?

18. Mr. Frank has $145,000 with which he purchases an annuity on February 1, 1986. The annuity consists of six annual payments, the first to be made on February 1, 1987. How much will he receive in each payment? Assume an interest rate of

    a. 8 percent per year.

    b. 12 percent per year.

19. In the preceding Exercises 10–18, you have been asked to compute a number. First you must decide what factor from the tables is appropriate and then you use that factor in the appropriate calculation. Notice that the last step could be omitted. You could write an arithmetic expression showing the factor you want to use without actually copying down the number and doing the arithmetic. For example, define the following notation: $T(i, p, r)$ means Table i (C.1, 2, 3, or 4), row p (periods 1 to 20, 22, 24, . . . , 40, 45, 50, 100), and column r (interest rates from ½ percent up to 20 percent). Thus, $T(3, 16, 12)$ would be the factor in Table C.3 for 16 periods and an interest rate of 12 percent per period, which is 42.75328. Using this notation, you can write an expression for any compound interest problem. Any clerk can evaluate the expression.

You can check that you understand this notation by observing that the following are true statements:

$T(C.1, 20, 8)$ = 4.66096
$T(C.2, 12, 5)$ = 0.55684
$T(C.3, 16, 12)$ = 42.75328
$T(C.4, 10, 20)$ = 4.19247.

In the following questions, write an expression for the correct answer using the notation introduced here, but do not attempt to evaluate the expression.

    a. Work the (**a**) parts of Exercises 10–14.

    b. Work the (**b**) parts of Exercises 15–18.

    c. How might the use of this notation make it easier for your instructor to write examination questions on compound interest?

20. Ms. Grady agrees to lease a certain property for 10 years, at the following annual rentals, payable in advance:

Years 1 and 2 — $1,000 per year.

Years 3 to 6 — $2,000 per year.

Years 7 to 10 — $2,500 per year.

What single immediate sum will pay all of these rents if they are discounted at
  a. 6 percent per year?
  b. 8 percent per year?
  c. 10 percent per year?

21. In order to establish a fund that will provide a scholarship of $3,000 a year indefinitely, with the first award to occur now, how much must be deposited if the fund earns:
  a. 6 percent per period?
  b. 8 percent per period?

22. Consider the scholarship fund in the preceding question. Suppose that the first scholarship is not to be awarded until one year from now. How much should be deposited if the fund earns:
  a. 6 percent per period?
  b. 8 percent per period?

  Suppose that the first scholarship is not to be awarded until five years from now. How much should be deposited if the fund earns:
  c. 6 percent per year?
  d. 8 percent per year?

23. The province helps a rural county maintain a bridge and has agreed to pay $6,000 now and every two years thereafter forever toward the expenses. The province wishes to discharge its obligation by paying a single sum to the county now in lieu of the payment due and all future payments. How much should the province pay the county if the discount rate is
  a. 8 percent per year?
  b. 12 percent per year?

24. Find the interest rate implicit in a loan of $100,000 that is discharged with the two annual installments of $55,307 each paid at the ends of Years 1 and 2.

25. A single-payment note has a face value of $140,493, to be paid in three years. The note is exchanged for equipment having a fair market value of $100,000 three years before the maturity date on the note.
  What interest rate will be imputed in accounting for the single-payment note?

26. A single-payment note has a face value of $67,280, due on maturity of the note. The note is exchanged for land with a fair market value of $50,000 two years before the maturity date on the note.
  a. What interest rate will be imputed in accounting for this single-payment note?
  b. Construct an amortization schedule for the note using the interest rate imputed. Show book value of the note at the start of each year, interest for each year, amount reducing or increasing book value each year, and book value at the end of the year.

27. *Finding implicit interest rates; constructing amortization schedules.* Berman Limited purchased a plot of land for possible future development. The land had fair market value of $86,000. Berman Limited gave a three-year interest-bearing note. The note had face value of $100,000 and provided for interest at a stated rate of eight percent — payments of $8,000 were due at the end of each of three years, the last payment coinciding with the maturity of the note's face value of $100,000.

    a. What is the interest rate implicit in the note accurate to the nearest tenth of one percent?

    b. Construct an amortization schedule for the note for each year, showing the book value of the note at the start of the year, interest for the year, payment for the year, amount reducing or increasing the book value of the note for each payment, and the book value of the note at the end of each year. Use the interest rate found in part (**a**). See Exhibit 10.1, page 499 for an example of an amortization schedule.

28. The terms of sale "2/10, net/30" mean that a discount of two percent from gross invoice price can be taken if the invoice is paid within ten days and that otherwise the full amount is due within 30 days.

    a. Write an expression for the implied annual rate of interest being offered, if the entire discount is viewed as being interest for funds received sooner rather than later. (Note that 98 percent of the gross invoice price is being borrowed for 20 days.)

    b. The tables at the back of the book do not permit the exact evaluation of the expression derived in part (**a**). The rate of interest implied is 44.59 percent per year. Use the tables to convince yourself that this astounding (to some) answer must be close to correct.

Problems and Cases

29. *Present value of a perpetuity.* An oil-drilling company figures that $300 must be spent for an initial supply of drill bits and that $100 must be spent every month to replace the worn-out bits. What is the present value of the cost of the bits if the company plans to be in business indefinitely and discounts payments at one percent per month?

The following problems involve using future value and present value techniques to solve a variety of realistic problems. No hints as to the specific calculation are given with the problems.

30. If you promise to leave $35,000 on deposit at the Quarter Bank for four years, the bank will give you a new car today in lieu of interest and your $35,000 back at the end of four years. How much are you, in effect, paying today for the car if the bank pays eight percent interest compounded quarterly (two percent paid four times per year)?

31. When Mr. Shafer died, his estate after taxes amounted to $300,000. His will provided that Mrs. Shafer would receive $24,000 per year starting immediately from the principal of the estate and that the balance of the principal would pass to the Shafers' children upon Mrs. Shafer's death. The law governing this estate provided for a *dower* option. If Mrs. Shafer elects the dower option, she renounces the will and can have one-third of the estate in cash now. The remainder will then pass immediately to their children. Mrs. Shafer wants to maximize the present value of her

bequest. Should she take the annuity or elect the dower option if she will receive five payments and discounts payments at:
  a. 8 percent per year?
  b. 12 percent per year?

32. Mrs. Heileman occasionally drinks beer. She consumes one case in 20 weeks. She can buy beer in disposable bottles for $12.60 per case or for $12.00 a case of returnable bottles if a $1.50 refundable deposit is paid at the time of purchase. If her discount rate is ¼ percent per week, how much in present value dollars does she save by buying the returnables and thereby losing the use of the $1.50 deposit for 20 weeks?

33. When the General Electric Company first introduced the Lucalox ceramic, screw-in light bulb, the bulb cost three-and-one-half times as much as an ordinary bulb but lasted five times as long. An ordinary bulb cost $.50 and lasted about eight months. If a firm has a discount rate of 12 percent compounded three times a year, how much would it save in present value dollars by using one Lucalox bulb?

34. The Roberts Dairy Company switched from delivery trucks with regular gasoline engines to ones with diesel engines. The diesel trucks cost $2,000 more than the ordinary gasoline trucks, but $600 per year less to operate. Assume that the operating costs are saved at the end of each month. If Roberts Dairy uses a discount rate of one percent per month, approximately how many months, at a minimum, must the diesel truck remain in service for the switch to save money?

35. On January 1, Year 1, Outergarments, Inc., opened a new textile plant for the production of synthetic fabrics. The plant is on leased land; 20 years remain on the nonrenewable lease.

   The cost of the plant was $2 million. Net cash flow to be derived from the project is estimated to be $300,000 per year. The company does not normally invest in such projects unless the anticipated yield is at least 12 percent.

   On December 31, Year 1, the company finds cash flows from the plant to be $280,000 for the year. On the same day, farm experts predict cotton production to be unusually low for the next two years. Outergarments estimates the resulting increase in demand for synthetic fabrics to boost cash flows to $350,000 for each of the next two years. Subsequent years' estimates remain unchanged. Ignore tax considerations.
   a. Calculate the present value of the future expected cash flows from the plant when it was opened.
   b. What is the present value of the plant on January 1, Year 2, immediately after the reestimation of future incomes?
   c. On January 2, Year 2, the day following the cotton production news release, Overalls Corp. announces plans to build a synthetic fabrics plant to be opened in three years. Outergarments, Inc., keeps its Year 2–Year 4 estimates, but reduces the estimated annual cash flows for subsequent years to $200,000. What is the value of the Outergarments' present plant on January 1, Year 2, after the new projections?
   d. On January 2, Year 2, an investor contacts Outergarments about purchasing a 20 percent share of the plant. If the investor expects to earn at least a 12 percent annual return on the investment, what is the maximum amount that

the investor can pay? Assume that the investor and Outergarments, Inc., both know all relevant information and use the same estimates of annual cash flows.

36. *Finding implicit interest rates (truth-in-lending laws reduce the type of deception suggested by this problem).* The Friendly Loan Company Inc. advertises that it is willing to lend money for five years at the low rate of eight percent per year. A potential borrower discovers that a five-year, $10,000 loan requires that the eight percent interest be paid in advance, with interest deducted from the loan proceeds. The borrower will collect $6,000 [= $10,000 − (5 × .08 × $10,000)] cash and must repay the ''$10,000'' loan in five annual installments of $2,000, one each at the end of the next five years.

Compute the effective interest rate implied by these loan terms.

37. *Deriving net present value of cash flows for decision to dispose of asset.* The Wisher Washer Co. Ltd. purchased a made-to-order machine tool for grinding washing machine parts. The machine cost $100,000 and was installed yesterday. Today, a machine tool is offered that will do exactly the same work but costs only $50,000. Assume that the discount rate is 12 percent, that both machines will last for five years, that both machines will be depreciated on a straight-line basis for tax purposes with no salvage value, that thc income tax rate is and will continue to be 40 percent, and that Wisher Washer Co. Ltd. earns sufficient income that any loss from disposing of or depreciating the ''old'' machine can be used to offset other taxable income. Ignore the investment tax credit.

How much, at a minimum, must the ''old'' machine fetch on resale at this time to make purchasing the new machine worthwhile?

38. *Computation of present value of cash flows; untaxed acquisition, no change in tax basis of assets.* The balance sheet of Lynch Limited shows assets of $1,000,000, net, and owners' equity of $1,000,000. The assets are all depreciable assets with remaining lives of 20 years. The income statement for the year shows revenues of $700,000, depreciation of $50,000 (= $1,000,000/20 years), no other expenses, income taxes of $260,000 (40 percent of pretax income of $650,000), and net income of $390,000.

Zeff Incorporated is considering purchasing all of the stock of Lynch Limited. It is willing to pay an amount equal to the present value of the cash flows from operations for the next 20 years discounted at a rate of ten percent per year.

The transaction will not be taxable; that is, after the purchase, the tax basis of the assets of Lynch Limited will remain unchanged, so that depreciation charges will remain at $50,000 per year and income taxes will remain at $260,000 per year. Revenues will be $700,000 per year for the next 20 years.

    a. Compute the annual cash flows produced by Lynch Incorporated.

    b. Compute the maximum amount Zeff Incorporated should be willing to pay.

39. *Computation of present value of cash flows; taxable acquisition, changing tax basis of assets.* Refer to the data in the preceding problem. Assume now that the acquisition is taxable, so that the tax basis of the assets acquired changes after the purchase. If the purchase price is $V, then depreciation charges will be $V/20 per year for 20 years. Income taxes will be 40 percent of pretax income.

What is the maximum Zeff Incorporated should be willing to pay for Lynch Limited?

Appendix C Compound Interest, Annuity, and Bond Tables

Table C.1
Future Value of $1

$$F_n = P(1 + r)^n$$

r = interest rate; n = number of periods until valuation; $P = \$1$

Periods = n	½%	1%	1½%	2%	3%	4%	5%	6%	7%	8%	10%	12%	15%	20%	25%
1	1.00500	1.01000	1.01500	1.02000	1.03000	1.04000	1.05000	1.06000	1.07000	1.08000	1.10000	1.12000	1.15000	1.20000	1.25000
2	1.01003	1.02010	1.03023	1.04040	1.06090	1.08160	1.10250	1.12360	1.14490	1.16640	1.21000	1.25440	1.32250	1.44000	1.56250
3	1.01508	1.03030	1.04568	1.06121	1.09273	1.12486	1.15763	1.19102	1.22504	1.25971	1.33100	1.40493	1.52088	1.72800	1.95313
4	1.02015	1.04060	1.06136	1.08243	1.12551	1.16986	1.21551	1.26248	1.31080	1.36049	1.46410	1.57352	1.74901	2.07360	2.44141
5	1.02525	1.05101	1.07728	1.10408	1.15927	1.21665	1.27628	1.33823	1.40255	1.46933	1.61051	1.76234	2.01136	2.48832	3.05176
6	1.03038	1.06152	1.09344	1.12616	1.19405	1.26532	1.34010	1.41852	1.50073	1.58687	1.77156	1.97382	2.31306	2.98598	3.81470
7	1.03553	1.07214	1.10984	1.14869	1.22987	1.31593	1.40710	1.50363	1.60578	1.71382	1.94872	2.21068	2.66002	3.58318	4.76837
8	1.04071	1.08286	1.12649	1.17166	1.26677	1.36857	1.47746	1.59385	1.71819	1.85093	2.14359	2.47596	3.05902	4.29982	5.96046
9	1.04591	1.09369	1.14339	1.19509	1.30477	1.42331	1.55133	1.68948	1.83846	1.99900	2.35795	2.77308	3.51788	5.15978	7.45058
10	1.05114	1.10462	1.16054	1.21899	1.34392	1.48024	1.62889	1.79085	1.96715	2.15892	2.59374	3.10585	4.04556	6.19174	9.31323
11	1.05640	1.11567	1.17795	1.24337	1.38423	1.53945	1.71034	1.89830	2.10485	2.33164	2.85312	3.47855	4.65239	7.43008	11.64153
12	1.06168	1.12683	1.19562	1.26824	1.42576	1.60103	1.79586	2.01220	2.25219	2.51817	3.13843	3.89598	5.35025	8.91610	14.55192
13	1.06699	1.13809	1.21355	1.29361	1.46853	1.66507	1.88565	2.13293	2.40985	2.71962	3.45227	4.36349	6.15279	10.69932	18.18989
14	1.07232	1.14947	1.23176	1.31948	1.51259	1.73168	1.97993	2.26090	2.57853	2.93750	3.79750	4.88711	7.07571	12.83918	22.73737
15	1.07768	1.16097	1.25023	1.34587	1.55797	1.80094	2.07893	2.39656	2.75903	3.17217	4.17725	5.47357	8.13706	15.40702	28.42171
16	1.08307	1.17258	1.26899	1.37279	1.60471	1.87298	2.18287	2.54035	2.95216	3.42594	4.59497	6.13039	9.35762	18.48843	35.52714
17	1.08849	1.18430	1.28802	1.40024	1.65285	1.94790	2.29202	2.69277	3.15882	3.70002	5.05447	6.86604	10.76126	22.18611	44.40892
18	1.09393	1.19615	1.30734	1.42825	1.70243	2.02582	2.40662	2.85434	3.37993	3.99602	5.55992	7.68997	12.37545	26.62333	55.51115
19	1.09940	1.20811	1.32695	1.45681	1.75351	2.10685	2.52695	3.02560	3.61653	4.31570	6.11591	8.61276	14.23177	31.94800	69.38894
20	1.10490	1.22019	1.34686	1.48595	1.80611	2.19112	2.65330	3.20714	3.86968	4.66096	6.72750	9.64629	16.36654	38.33760	86.73617
22	1.11597	1.24472	1.38756	1.54598	1.91610	2.36992	2.92526	3.60354	4.43040	5.43654	8.14027	12.10031	21.64475	55.20614	135.5253
24	1.12716	1.26973	1.42950	1.60844	2.03279	2.56330	3.22510	4.04893	5.07237	6.34118	9.84973	15.17863	28.62518	79.49685	211.7582
26	1.13846	1.29526	1.47271	1.67342	2.15659	2.77247	3.55567	4.54938	5.80735	7.39635	11.91818	19.04007	37.85680	114.4755	330.8722
28	1.14987	1.32129	1.51722	1.74102	2.28793	2.99870	3.92013	5.11169	6.64884	8.62711	14.42099	23.88387	50.06561	164.8447	516.9879
30	1.16140	1.34785	1.56308	1.81136	2.42726	3.24340	4.32194	5.74349	7.61226	10.06266	17.44940	29.95992	66.21177	237.3763	807.7936
32	1.17304	1.37304	1.61032	1.88454	2.57508	3.50806	4.76494	6.45339	8.71527	11.73708	21.11378	37.58173	87.56507	341.8219	1262.177
34	1.18480	1.40258	1.65900	1.96068	2.73191	3.79432	5.25335	7.25103	9.97811	13.69013	25.54767	47.14252	115.80480	492.2235	1972.152
36	1.19668	1.43077	1.70914	2.03989	2.89828	4.10393	5.79182	8.14725	11.42394	15.96817	30.91268	59.13557	153.15185	708.8019	3081.488
38	1.20868	1.45953	1.76080	2.12230	3.07478	4.43881	6.38548	9.15425	13.07927	18.62528	37.40434	74.17966	202.54332	1020.675	4814.825
40	1.22079	1.48886	1.81402	2.20804	3.26204	4.80102	7.03999	10.28572	14.97446	21.72452	45.25926	93.05097	267.86355	1469.772	7523.164
45	1.25162	1.56481	1.95421	2.43785	3.78160	5.84118	8.98501	13.76461	21.00245	31.92045	72.89048	163.9876	538.76927	3657.262	22958.87
50	1.26323	1.64463	2.10524	2.69159	4.38391	7.10668	11.46740	18.42015	29.45703	46.90161	117.3909	289.0022	1083.65744	9100.438	70064.92
100	1.64667	2.70481	4.43205	7.24465	19.21863	50.50495	131.5013	339.3021	867.7163	2199.761	13780.61	83522.27	117×10^{4}	828×10^{5}	491×10^{7}

Table C.2
Present Value of $1

$$P = F_n(1 + r)^{-n}$$

r = discount rate; n = number of periods until payment; $F_n = \$1$

Periods = n	½%	1%	1½%	2%	3%	4%	5%	6%	7%	8%	10%	12%	15%	20%	25%
1	.99502	.99010	.98522	.98039	.97087	.96154	.95238	.94340	.93458	.92593	.90909	.89286	.86957	.83333	.80000
2	.99007	.98030	.97066	.96117	.94260	.92456	.90703	.89000	.87344	.85734	.82645	.79719	.75614	.69444	.64000
3	.98515	.97059	.95632	.94232	.91514	.88900	.86384	.83962	.81630	.79383	.75131	.71178	.65752	.57870	.51200
4	.98025	.96098	.94218	.92385	.88849	.85480	.82270	.79209	.76290	.73503	.68301	.63552	.57175	.48225	.40960
5	.97537	.95147	.92826	.90573	.86261	.82193	.78353	.74726	.71299	.68058	.62092	.56743	.49718	.40188	.32768
6	.97052	.94205	.91454	.88797	.83748	.79031	.74622	.70496	.66634	.63017	.56447	.50663	.43233	.33490	.26214
7	.96569	.93272	.90103	.87056	.81309	.75992	.71068	.66506	.62275	.58349	.51316	.45235	.37594	.27908	.20972
8	.96089	.92348	.88771	.85349	.78941	.73069	.67684	.62741	.58201	.54027	.46651	.40388	.32690	.23257	.16777
9	.95610	.91434	.87459	.83676	.76642	.70259	.64461	.59190	.54393	.50025	.42410	.36061	.28426	.19381	.13422
10	.95135	.90529	.86167	.82035	.74409	.67556	.61391	.55839	.50835	.46319	.38554	.32197	.24718	.16151	.10737
11	.94661	.89632	.84893	.80426	.72242	.64958	.58468	.52679	.47509	.42888	.35049	.28748	.21494	.13459	.08590
12	.94191	.88745	.83639	.78849	.70138	.62460	.55684	.49697	.44401	.39711	.31863	.25668	.18691	.11216	.06872
13	.93722	.87866	.82403	.77303	.68095	.60057	.53032	.46884	.41496	.36770	.28966	.22917	.16253	.09346	.05498
14	.93256	.86996	.81185	.75788	.66112	.57748	.50507	.44230	.38782	.34046	.26333	.20462	.14133	.07789	.04398
15	.92792	.86135	.79985	.74301	.64186	.55526	.48102	.41727	.36245	.31524	.23939	.18270	.12289	.06491	.03518
16	.92330	.85282	.78803	.72845	.62317	.53391	.45811	.39365	.33873	.29189	.21763	.16312	.10686	.05409	.02815
17	.91871	.84438	.77639	.71416	.60502	.51337	.43630	.37136	.31657	.27027	.19784	.14564	.09293	.04507	.02252
18	.91414	.83602	.76491	.70016	.58739	.49363	.41552	.35034	.29586	.25025	.17986	.13004	.08081	.03756	.01801
19	.90959	.82774	.75361	.68643	.57029	.47464	.39573	.33051	.27651	.23171	.16351	.11611	.07027	.03130	.01441
20	.90506	.81954	.74247	.67297	.55368	.45639	.37689	.31180	.25842	.21455	.14864	.10367	.06110	.02608	.01153
22	.89608	.80340	.72069	.64684	.52189	.42196	.34185	.27751	.22571	.18394	.12285	.08264	.04620	.01811	.00738
24	.88719	.78757	.69954	.62172	.49193	.39012	.31007	.24698	.19715	.15770	.10153	.06588	.03493	.01258	.00472
26	.87838	.77205	.67902	.59758	.46369	.36069	.28124	.21981	.17220	.13520	.08391	.05252	.02642	.00874	.00302
28	.86966	.75684	.65910	.57437	.43708	.33348	.25509	.19563	.15040	.11591	.06934	.04187	.01997	.00607	.00193
30	.86103	.74192	.63976	.55207	.41199	.30832	.23138	.17411	.13137	.09938	.05731	.03338	.01510	.00421	.00124
32	.85248	.72730	.62099	.53063	.38834	.28506	.20987	.15496	.11474	.08520	.04736	.02661	.01142	.00293	.00079
34	.84402	.71297	.60277	.51003	.36604	.26355	.19035	.13791	.10022	.07305	.03914	.02121	.00864	.00203	.00051
36	.83564	.69892	.58509	.49022	.34503	.24367	.17266	.12274	.08754	.06262	.03235	.01691	.00653	.00141	.00032
38	.82735	.68515	.56792	.47119	.32523	.22529	.15661	.10924	.07646	.05369	.02673	.01348	.00494	.00098	.00021
40	.81914	.67165	.55126	.45289	.30656	.20829	.14205	.09722	.06678	.04603	.02209	.01075	.00373	.00068	.00013
45	.79896	.63905	.51171	.41020	.26444	.17120	.11130	.07265	.04761	.03133	.01372	.00610	.00186	.00027	.00004
50	.77929	.60804	.47500	.37153	.22811	.14071	.08720	.05429	.03395	.02132	.00852	.00346	.00092	.00011	.00001
100	.60729	.36971	.22563	.13803	.05203	.01980	.00760	.00295	.00115	.00045	.00007	.00001	.00000	.00000	.00000

Table C.3
Future Value of Annuity of $1 in Arrears

$$F = \frac{(1+r)^n - 1}{r}$$

r = interest rate; n = number of payments

No. of Payments $= n$	1%	2%	3%	4%	5%	6%	7%	8%	10%	12%	14%	15%	16%	18%	20%	25%
1	1.00000	1.00000	1.00000	1.00000	1.00000	1.00000	1.00000	1.00000	1.00000	1.00000	1.00000	1.00000	1.00000	1.00000	1.00000	1.00000
2	2.01000	2.02000	2.03000	2.04000	2.05000	2.06000	2.07000	2.08000	2.10000	2.12000	2.14000	2.15000	2.16000	2.18000	2.20000	2.25000
3	3.03010	3.06040	3.09090	3.12160	3.15250	3.18360	3.21490	3.24640	3.31000	3.37440	3.43960	3.47250	3.50560	3.57240	3.64000	3.81250
4	4.06040	4.12161	4.18363	4.24646	4.31013	4.37462	4.43994	4.50611	4.64100	4.77933	4.92114	4.99338	5.06650	5.21543	5.36800	5.76563
5	5.10101	5.20404	5.30914	5.41632	5.52563	5.63709	5.75074	5.86660	6.10510	6.35285	6.61010	6.74238	6.87714	7.15421	7.44160	8.20703
6	6.15202	6.30812	6.46841	6.63298	6.80191	6.97532	7.15329	7.33593	7.71561	8.11519	8.53552	8.75374	8.97748	9.44197	9.92992	11.25879
7	7.21354	7.43428	7.66246	7.89829	8.14201	8.39384	8.65402	8.92280	9.48717	10.08901	10.73049	11.06680	11.41387	12.14152	12.91590	15.07349
8	8.28567	8.58297	8.89234	9.21423	9.54911	9.89747	10.25980	10.63663	11.43589	12.29969	13.23276	13.72682	14.24009	15.32700	16.49908	19.84186
9	9.36853	9.75463	10.15911	10.58280	11.02656	11.49132	11.97799	12.48756	13.57948	14.77566	16.08535	16.78584	17.51851	19.08585	20.79890	25.80232
10	10.46221	10.94972	11.46388	12.00611	12.57789	13.18079	13.81645	14.48656	15.93742	17.54874	19.33730	20.30372	21.32147	23.52131	25.95868	33.25290
11	11.56683	12.16872	12.80780	13.48635	14.20679	14.97164	15.78360	16.64549	18.53117	20.65458	23.04452	24.34928	25.73290	28.75514	32.15042	42.56613
12	12.68250	13.41209	14.19203	15.02581	15.91713	16.86994	17.88845	18.97713	21.38428	24.13313	27.27075	29.00167	30.85017	34.93107	39.58050	54.20766
13	13.80933	14.68033	15.61779	16.62684	17.71298	18.88214	20.14064	21.49530	24.55271	28.02911	32.08865	34.35192	36.78620	42.21866	48.49660	68.75958
14	14.94742	15.97394	17.08632	18.29191	19.59863	21.01507	22.55049	24.21492	27.97498	32.39260	37.58107	40.50471	43.67199	50.81802	59.19592	86.94947
15	16.09690	17.29342	18.59891	20.02359	21.57856	23.27597	25.12902	27.15211	31.77248	37.27971	43.84241	47.58041	51.65951	60.96527	72.03511	109.6868
16	17.25786	18.63929	20.15688	21.82453	23.65749	25.67253	27.88805	30.32428	35.94973	42.75328	50.98035	55.71747	60.92503	72.93901	87.44213	138.1086
17	18.43044	20.01207	21.76159	23.69751	25.84037	28.21288	30.84022	33.75023	40.54470	48.88367	59.11760	65.07509	71.67303	87.06804	105.9306	173.6357
18	19.61475	21.41231	23.41444	25.64541	28.13238	30.90565	33.99903	37.45024	45.59917	55.74971	68.39407	75.83636	84.14072	103.7403	128.1167	218.0446
19	20.81090	22.84056	25.11687	27.67123	30.53900	33.75999	37.37896	41.44626	51.15909	63.43968	78.96923	88.21181	98.60323	123.4135	154.7400	273.5558
20	22.01900	24.29737	26.87037	29.77808	33.06595	36.78559	40.99549	45.76196	57.27500	72.05244	91.02493	102.44358	115.3798	146.6280	186.6880	342.947
22	24.47159	27.29898	30.53678	34.24797	38.50521	43.39229	49.00574	55.45676	71.40275	92.50258	120.4360	137.63164	157.4150	206.3448	271.0307	538.1011
24	26.97346	30.42186	34.42647	39.08260	44.50200	50.81558	58.17667	66.76476	88.49733	118.1552	158.6586	184.16784	213.9776	289.4945	392.4842	843.0330
26	29.52563	33.67091	38.55304	44.31174	51.11345	59.15638	68.67647	79.95442	109.1818	150.3339	208.3327	245.71197	290.0883	405.2721	567.3773	1319.489
28	32.12910	37.05121	42.93092	49.96758	58.40258	68.52811	80.69769	95.33883	134.2099	190.6989	272.2892	327.10408	392.5028	566.4809	819.2233	2063.952
30	34.78489	40.56808	47.57542	56.08494	66.43885	79.05819	94.46079	113.2832	164.4940	241.3327	356.7869	434.74515	530.3117	790.9480	1181.881	3227.174
32	37.49407	44.22703	52.50276	62.70147	75.29883	90.88978	110.2181	134.2135	201.1378	304.8477	465.8202	577.10046	715.7475	1103.496	1704.109	5044.710
34	40.25770	48.03380	57.73018	69.85791	85.06696	104.1838	128.2588	158.6267	245.4767	384.5210	607.5199	765.36535	965.2698	1538.688	2456.118	7884.609
36	43.07688	51.99437	63.27594	77.59831	95.83632	119.1209	148.9135	189.1268	299.1268	484.4631	791.6729	1014.34568	1301.027	2144.649	3539.009	12321.95
38	45.95272	56.11494	69.15945	85.97034	107.7095	135.9042	172.5610	220.3159	364.0434	609.3305	1030.998	1343.62216	1752.822	2988.389	5098.373	19255.30
40	48.88637	60.40198	75.40126	95.02552	120.7998	154.7620	199.6351	259.0565	442.5926	767.0914	1342.025	1779.09031	2360.757	4163.213	7343.858	30088.66
45	56.48107	71.89271	92.71986	121.0294	159.7002	212.7435	285.7493	386.5056	718.9048	1358.230	2590.565	3585.12846	4965.274	9531.577	18281.31	91831.50
50	64.46318	84.57940	112.7969	152.6671	209.3480	290.3359	406.5289	573.7702	1163.909	2400.018	4994.521	7217.71628	10435.65	21813.09	45497.19	280255.7
100	170.4814	312.2323	607.2877	1237.624	2610.025	5638.368	1238.166	27484.52	137796.1	696010.5	9502323	783×10^4	174×10^5	857×10^5	414×10^6	196×10^6

Note: To convert from this table to values of an annuity in advance, determine the annuity in arrears above for one more period and subtract 1.00000.

Table C.4
Present Value of Annuity of $1 in Arrears

$$P_A = \frac{1 - (1+r)^{-n}}{r}$$

r = discount rate; n = number of payments

No. of Payments = n	½%	1%	1½%	2%	3%	4%	5%	6%	7%	8%	10%	12%	15%	20%	25%
1	.99502	.99010	.98522	.98039	.97087	.96154	.95238	.94340	.93458	.92593	.90909	.89286	.86957	.83333	.80000
2	1.98510	1.97040	1.95588	1.94156	1.91347	1.88609	1.85941	1.83339	1.80802	1.78326	1.73554	1.69005	1.62571	1.52778	1.44000
3	2.97025	2.94099	2.91220	2.88388	2.82861	2.77509	2.72325	2.67301	2.62432	2.57710	2.48685	2.40183	2.28323	2.10648	1.95200
4	3.95050	3.90197	3.85438	3.80773	3.71710	3.62990	3.54595	3.46511	3.38721	3.31213	3.16987	3.03735	2.85498	2.58873	2.36160
5	4.92587	4.85343	4.78264	4.71346	4.57971	4.45182	4.32948	4.21236	4.10020	3.99271	3.79079	3.60478	3.35216	2.99061	2.68928
6	5.89638	5.79548	5.69719	5.60143	5.41719	5.24212	5.07569	4.91732	4.76654	4.62288	4.35526	4.11141	3.78448	3.32551	2.95142
7	6.86207	6.72819	6.59821	6.47199	6.23028	6.00205	5.78637	5.58238	5.38929	5.20637	4.86842	4.56376	4.16042	3.60459	3.16114
8	7.82296	7.65168	7.48593	7.32548	7.01969	6.73274	6.46321	6.20979	5.97130	5.74664	5.33493	4.96764	4.48732	3.83716	3.32891
9	8.77906	8.56602	8.36052	8.16224	7.78611	7.43533	7.10782	6.80169	6.51523	6.24689	5.75902	5.32825	4.77158	4.03097	3.46313
10	9.73041	9.47130	9.22218	8.98259	8.53020	8.11090	7.72173	7.36009	7.02358	6.71008	6.14457	5.65022	5.01877	4.19247	3.57050
11	10.67703	10.36763	10.07112	9.78685	9.25262	8.76048	8.30641	7.88687	7.49867	7.13896	6.49506	5.93770	5.23371	4.32706	3.65640
12	11.61893	11.25508	10.90751	10.57534	9.95400	9.38507	8.86325	8.38384	7.94269	7.53608	6.81369	6.19437	5.42062	4.43922	3.72512
13	12.55615	12.13374	11.73153	11.34837	10.63496	9.98565	9.39357	8.85268	8.35765	7.90378	7.10336	6.42355	5.58315	4.53268	3.78010
14	13.48871	13.00370	12.54338	12.10625	11.29607	10.56312	9.89864	9.29498	8.74547	8.24424	7.36669	6.62817	5.72448	4.61057	3.82408
15	14.41662	13.86505	13.34323	12.84926	11.93794	11.11839	10.37966	9.71225	9.10791	8.55948	7.60608	6.81086	5.84737	4.67547	3.85926
16	15.33993	14.71787	14.13126	13.57771	12.56110	11.65230	10.83777	10.10590	9.44665	8.85137	7.82371	6.97399	5.95423	4.72956	3.88741
17	16.25863	15.56225	14.90765	14.29187	13.16612	12.16567	11.27407	10.47726	9.76322	9.12164	8.02155	7.11963	6.04716	4.77463	3.90993
18	17.17277	16.39827	15.67256	14.99203	13.75351	12.65930	11.68959	10.82760	10.05909	9.37189	8.20141	7.24967	6.12797	4.81219	3.92794
19	18.08236	17.22601	16.42617	15.67846	14.32380	13.13394	12.08532	11.15812	10.33560	9.60360	8.36492	7.36578	6.19823	4.84350	3.94235
20	18.98742	18.04555	17.16864	16.35143	14.87747	13.59033	12.46221	11.46992	10.59401	9.81815	8.51356	7.46944	6.25933	4.86958	3.95388
22	20.78406	19.66038	18.62082	17.65805	15.93692	14.45112	13.16300	12.04158	11.06124	10.20074	8.77154	7.64465	6.35866	4.90943	3.97049
24	22.56287	21.24339	20.03041	18.91393	16.93554	15.24696	13.79864	12.55036	11.46933	10.52876	8.98474	7.78432	6.43377	4.93710	3.98111
26	24.32402	22.79520	21.39863	20.12104	17.87684	15.98277	14.37519	13.00317	11.82578	10.80998	9.16095	7.89566	6.49056	4.95632	3.98791
28	26.06769	24.31644	22.72672	21.28127	18.76411	16.66306	14.89813	13.40616	12.13711	11.05108	9.30657	7.98442	6.53351	4.96967	3.99226
30	27.79405	25.80771	24.01584	22.39646	19.60044	17.29203	15.37245	13.76483	12.40904	11.25778	9.42691	8.05518	6.56598	4.97894	3.99505
32	29.50328	27.26959	25.26714	23.46833	20.38877	17.87355	15.80268	14.08404	12.64656	11.43500	9.52638	8.11159	6.59053	4.98537	3.99683
34	31.19555	28.70267	26.48173	24.49859	21.13184	18.41120	16.19290	14.36814	12.85401	11.58693	9.60857	8.15656	6.60910	4.98984	3.99797
36	32.87102	30.10751	27.66068	25.48884	21.83225	18.90828	16.54685	14.62099	13.03521	11.71719	9.67651	8.19241	6.62314	4.99295	3.99870
38	34.52985	31.48466	28.80505	26.44064	22.49246	19.36786	16.86789	14.84602	13.19347	11.82887	9.73265	8.22099	6.63375	4.99510	3.99917
40	36.17223	32.83469	29.91585	27.35548	23.11477	19.79277	17.15909	15.04630	13.33171	11.92461	9.77905	8.24378	6.64178	4.99660	3.99947
45	40.20720	36.09451	32.55234	29.49016	24.51871	20.72004	17.77407	15.45583	13.60552	12.10840	9.86281	8.28252	6.65429	4.99863	3.99983
50	44.14279	39.19612	34.99969	31.42361	25.72976	21.48216	18.25593	15.76186	13.80075	12.23348	9.91481	8.30450	6.66051	4.99945	3.99994
100	78.54264	63.02888	51.62470	43.09835	31.59891	24.50500	19.84791	16.61755	14.26925	12.49432	9.99927	8.33323	6.66666	5.00000	4.00000

Note: To convert from this table to values of an annuity in advance, determine the annuity in arrears above for one less period and add 1.00000.

Table C.5
Bond Values in Percent of Par:
10-Percent Semiannual Coupons

Bond value $= 10/r + (100 - 10/r)(1 + r/2)^{-2n}$
r = yield to maturity; n = years to maturity

Market Yield Percent per Year Compounded Semiannually

Years to Maturity	8.0	9.0	9.5	10.0	10.5	11.0	12.0	13.0	14.0	15.0	20.0
0.5	100.9615	100.4785	100.2387	100.0	99.7625	99.5261	99.0566	98.5915	98.1308	97.6744	95.4545
1.0	101.8861	100.9363	100.4665	100.0	99.5368	99.0768	98.1666	97.2691	96.3840	95.5111	91.3223
1.5	102.7751	101.3745	100.6840	100.0	99.3224	98.6510	97.3270	96.0273	94.7514	93.4987	87.5657
2.0	103.6299	101.7938	100.8917	100.0	99.1186	98.2474	96.5349	94.8613	93.2256	91.6267	84.1507
2.5	104.4518	102.1950	101.0899	100.0	98.9251	97.8649	95.7876	93.7665	91.7996	89.8853	81.0461
5.0	108.1109	103.9564	101.9541	100.0	98.0928	96.2312	92.6399	89.2168	85.9528	82.8398	69.2772
9.0	112.6593	106.0800	102.9803	100.0	97.1339	94.3770	89.1724	84.3513	79.8818	75.7350	58.9929
9.5	113.1339	106.2966	103.0838	100.0	97.0393	94.1962	88.8419	83.8979	79.3288	75.1023	58.1754
10.0	113.5903	106.5040	103.1827	100.0	96.9494	94.0248	88.5301	83.4722	78.8120	74.5138	57.4322
15.0	117.2920	108.1444	103.9551	100.0	96.2640	92.7331	86.2352	80.4120	75.1819	70.4740	52.8654
19.0	119.3679	109.0250	104.3608	100.0	95.9194	92.0976	85.1540	79.0312	73.6131	68.8015	51.3367
19.5	119.5845	109.1148	104.4017	100.0	95.8854	92.0357	85.0509	78.9025	73.4701	68.6525	51.2152
20.0	119.7928	109.2008	104.4408	100.0	95.8531	91.9769	84.9537	78.7817	73.3366	68.5140	51.1047
25.0	121.4822	109.8810	104.7461	100.0	95.6068	91.5342	84.2381	77.9132	72.3985	67.5630	50.4259
30.0	122.6235	110.3190	104.9381	100.0	95.4591	91.2751	83.8386	77.4506	71.9216	67.1015	50.1642
40.0	123.9154	110.7827	105.1347	100.0	95.3175	91.0345	83.4909	77.0728	71.5560	66.7690	50.0244
50.0	124.5050	110.9749	105.2124	100.0	95.2666	90.9521	83.3825	76.9656	71.4615	66.6908	50.0036

Table C.6
Bond Values in Percent of Par:
12-Percent Semiannual Coupons

$$\text{Bond value} = 12/r + (100 - 12/r)(1 + r/2)^{-2n}$$

r = yield to maturity; n = years to maturity

Years to Maturity	Market Yield Percent per Year Compounded Semiannually										
	8.0	9.0	10.0	11.0	11.5	12.0	12.5	13.0	14.0	15.0	20.0
0.5	101.9231	101.4354	100.9524	100.4739	100.2364	100.0	99.7647	99.5305	99.0654	98.6047	96.3636
1.0	103.7722	102.8090	101.8594	100.9232	100.4600	100.0	99.5433	99.0897	98.1920	97.3067	93.0579
1.5	105.5502	104.1234	102.7232	101.3490	100.6714	100.0	99.3348	98.6758	97.3757	96.0992	90.0526
2.0	107.2598	105.3813	103.5459	101.7526	100.8713	100.0	99.1387	98.2871	96.6128	94.9760	87.3205
2.5	108.9036	106.5850	104.3295	102.1351	101.0603	100.0	98.9540	97.9222	95.8998	93.9312	84.8369
5.0	116.2218	111.8691	107.7217	103.7688	101.8620	100.0	98.1816	96.4056	92.9764	89.7039	75.4217
9.0	125.3186	118.2400	111.6896	105.6230	102.7585	100.0	97.3432	94.7838	89.9409	85.4410	67.1944
9.5	126.2679	118.8899	112.0853	105.8038	102.8449	100.0	97.2642	94.6326	89.6644	85.0614	66.5403
10.0	127.1807	119.5119	112.4622	105.9752	102.9266	100.0	97.1898	94.4907	89.4060	84.7083	65.9457
15.0	134.5841	124.4333	115.3724	107.2669	103.5353	100.0	96.6489	93.4707	87.5910	82.2844	62.2923
19.0	138.7357	127.0750	116.8679	107.9024	103.8283	100.0	96.3995	93.0104	86.8065	81.2809	61.0694
19.5	139.1690	127.3445	117.0170	107.9643	103.8565	100.0	96.3760	92.9675	86.7351	81.1915	60.9722
20.0	139.5855	127.6024	117.1591	108.0231	103.8832	100.0	96.3539	92.9272	86.6663	81.1084	60.8838
25.0	142.9644	129.6430	118.2559	108.4658	104.0822	100.0	96.1930	92.6377	86.1993	80.5378	60.3407
30.0	145.2470	130.9570	118.9293	108.7249	104.1960	100.0	96.1053	92.4835	85.9608	80.2609	60.1314
40.0	147.8308	132.3480	119.5965	108.9655	104.2982	100.0	96.0313	92.3576	85.7780	80.0614	60.0195
50.0	149.0100	132.9248	119.8479	109.0479	104.3316	100.0	96.0093	92.3219	85.7307	80.0145	60.0029

Appendix D Accounting for the Effects of Changing Prices

One of the most persistent and significant criticisms of the conventional accounting model based on historical costs is that it ignores the economic facts of life. Throughout the world, a steady and rapid upward movement in prices has been occurring during the last decade. Yet, until recently, this important economic phenomenon largely went unrecognized by accounting standard-setting bodies. Motivated by the increased inflation rate in the 1970s, accounting standard-setting bodies in many countries, including Canada, initiated studies on accounting for the effects of changing prices. These reports failed to agree on the solution, and the acceptance by the standard-setting bodies varied. In 1974 the Accounting Research Committee of the CICA issued an accounting guideline, "Accounting for the Effects of Changes in the Purchasing Power of Money," which presented the principles of general price level restatement and illustrated their application. The guideline was intended to be incorporated as a recommendation in the *Handbook*, but never achieved this status and was withdrawn in 1982 when superseded by section 4510, "Reporting the Effects of Changing Prices." During this eight-year period the ARC issued a number of studies and proposals on accounting for changing prices, including an exposure draft (in 1979) and a reexposure draft (in 1981) of a proposed addition to the *CICA Handbook*. This *Handbook* addition was eventually issued in December 1982 by the renamed Accounting Standards Committee.

Standard-setting bodies in Canada and in many other countries, including the United Kingdom and the United States, have recommended supplementary disclosure of selected accounting data adjusted for specific price changes. This chapter discusses the accounting problems associated with changing prices and illustrates techniques for dealing with them.

Impact of Changing Prices on Conventional Financial Statements

The accounting problems associated with changing prices might be separated into those related to *changes in general price levels* and those associated with *changes in prices of specific goods and services*. This distinction might be grasped most easily by considering the manner in which a price index is constructed.

Nature and Construction of Price Indices

A *price index* is a measure of the prices of a group, or "basket," of goods and services between two dates. For example, assume that we wish to construct a price index for food to measure the change in overall prices between January 1 and December 31 of a particular year. We begin by constructing a typical market basket of food items. To keep the illustration simple, suppose we specify that a typical market basket includes meat, starch, vegetable, beverage, and bread. We ascertain the price of a specific commodity in each of these food groupings at the beginning and end of a year. The prices of the individual commodities at each date are summed to obtain the aggregate market price of the basket of goods. The aggregate market price at one date is then compared to the aggregate price at the other date to obtain a price index. Exhibit D.1 illustrates the construction of such a price index.[1]

Exhibit D.1
Illustration of the Construction of a Price Index

Commodity	December 31	January 1	Percentage Change in Market Price of Individual Commodities
Sirloin Steak (kilogram)	$ 6.60	$ 6.00	+ 10%
Rice (32 grams)	2.20	2.40	− 8
Frozen Vegetables (package) . . .	1.38	1.20	+ 15
Beer (six-pack)	4.64	3.80	+ 22
Bread (loaf)	1.24	1.20	+ 3
Total	$16.06	$14.60	
Price index, where January 1 prices equal 100	110	100	(= $16.06/$14.60)

Prices for this group of commodities increased an average of ten percent between the beginning and end of the year. The prices of the individual commodities, however, changed at different rates. The price of bread remained relatively stable, while the price of rice decreased. The prices of sirloin steak, frozen vegetables, and beer increased significantly, but only that of the frozen vegetables and the beer increased more than the average ten percent for the group.

Price indices are constructed by the federal government for many different groupings, or baskets, of commodities. Some of these indices are based on a wide assortment of goods and services and are intended as measures of price changes in general. The two most important *general price indices* are the Gross National Expenditure Implicit Price Deflator (issued quarterly) and the Consumer Price Index for Canada (issued monthly). Other price indices are constructed for many specific groupings of goods and services, such as dairy products, household furniture, motor vehicles, and clothing. Even these more *specific price indices*, however, contain an assortment of

---

[1]A price series is a set of index numbers, such as 100 and 110 in Exhibit D.1, that represent the price levels at different times. The absolute numbers are not important. The percentage change in the numbers from one period to the next provides the information about the change in relative prices. Thus, a price index series of 50 and 55 represents the same price increase, of 10 percent, as does a price index series of 100 and 110. Similarly a price index series of 200 and 220 represents a price increase of 10 percent. By convention, the time period for which the price index is 100 is called the "base period" of a given price series.

goods of various qualities, dimensions, and styles within the particular product category.

Accounting Problems Associated with General Price Changes

The conventional accounting model uses as a measuring unit the *actual*, or *nominal*, dollars expended or received over time in recording transactions or events in the accounts. Implicit in the use of nominal dollars is the assumption that the dollar represents a constant, or uniform, measuring unit over time. That is, the measuring unit (the dollar) used in recording the acquisition of a machine costing $10,000 five years ago is assumed to have the same economic significance as the measuring unit used in recording the acquisition of merchandise inventory one week ago for $10,000.

As general price levels change, however, the purchasing power of the dollar, or its command over goods and services, changes. The general purchasing power sacrificed to acquire the machine five years ago is not equivalent to the purchasing power sacrificed last week to acquire the merchandise inventory. In terms of general purchasing power, therefore, the dollar does not represent a constant, or uniform, measuring unit through time.

Because the conventional financial statements do not recognize the changing purchasing power of the dollar, the amounts assigned to individual assets in the balance sheet cannot be meaningfully summed to measure the total purchasing power sacrificed to acquire assets. Likewise, the dollars sacrificed to acquire the various assets consumed as expenses differ in purchasing power from the dollars generated by the revenues of the period. The income statement therefore matches dollar amounts measured in different purchasing powers.

Accounting Problems Associated with Specific Price Changes

The conventional accounting model also rests on *historical cost valuations*. Increases in the market prices of individual assets are not reflected in the valuation of assets on the balance sheet or as gains in measuring net income until the assets are sold. Only at the time of sale is the measurement of the gain considered to be sufficiently objective to warrant recognition in the accounts.

Management, however, bases many decisions on information about changes in the prices of individual assets and liabilities. In pricing decisions, management considers the current cost of replacing the goods and services sold. In plant asset replacement decisions, management considers the current market values of individual assets held relative to the acquisition prices of assets with similar operating characteristics. In refinancing decisions, management considers the current market value of outstanding debt relative to the cost of issuing new debt. By using historical cost valuations and the realization convention, the conventional financial statements fail to reflect properly the results of management's decisions in the firm's current economic environment.

Official Pronouncement on Accounting for Changing Prices

Recognizing the deficiencies of the conventional accounting model based on nominal dollars and historical-cost valuations, AcSC requires large, publicly held firms to report certain supplementary information about the impact of changing prices.[2] The types of information that may be required to be disclosed are described and illustrated in the remaining sections of the chapter under the following headings:

1. Historical cost/constant dollar accounting — Conventional financial statement data are restated to a constant dollar basis to obtain a uniform measuring unit.
2. Current cost/nominal dollar accounting — Historical cost valuations are replaced with current cost valuations.
3. Current cost/constant dollar accounting — Current cost valuations are restated to a constant dollar basis.

The illustrations in this chapter present complete balance sheets and income statements under each of these three approaches to accounting for changing prices. The AcSC, however, requires only that certain financial data prepared under these three approaches be reported. The committee's reasoning is that the disclosures are sufficiently new and complex that a period of education and experimentation is required. After studying the uses made of the various supplemental disclosures, the AcSC expects to issue another pronouncement that will narrow somewhat the type of information reported. The illustrations in this chapter should provide sufficient conceptual background for understanding both current supplemental disclosures and any new reporting formats the AcSC may subsequently require.

The illustrations of the three approaches to accounting for changing prices are based on data for Hanna Corporation for the current year. The following transactions and events take place.

1. January 2. The firm is organized by issuing common shares for $400 cash. The Consumer Price Index (CPI), a measure of the general price level, is 200 on this date.
2. January 2, Hanna Corporation purchases two widgets for $100 each and equipment with a 5-year life for $100 (CPI = 200).
3. January 2 to June 30. The CPI increases 5 percent during the 6-month period, from 200 to 210.
4. June 30. The firm sells one widget for $240. It replaces it with a new widget costing $115. It also pays other operating expenses of $100 (CPI = 210).
5. July 1 to December 31. The CPI increases 10 percent during this 6-month period, from 210 to 231.
6. December 31. At the end of the year, the current cost of replacing one widget is $140, and the current cost of replacing the equipment in new condition is $120 (CPI = 231).
   Exhibit D.2 summarizes these data.

---

[2] *CICA Handbook*, section 4510.

Exhibit D.2
Data for Inflation Accounting Illustration — Hana Corporation

Balance Sheet as of January 2
Cash: $400   Share Capital: $400

	January 2	June 30	December 31
Consumer Price Index (CPI)	200	210[a]	231[b]
Cost of One Widget	$100	$115	$140
Cost of Equipment	$100	$110	$120
Transactions	1) Buy 2 widgets at $100 each, $200.	1) Sell 1 widget for $240; replace widget at $115.	1) Close books and prepare statements.
	2) Purchase equipment (5-year life) for $100.	2) Pay other expenses of $100	

[a] 5% increase from January 2.
[b] 10% increase from June 30.

Historical Cost/ Constant Dollar Accounting

Objective of Historical Cost/ Constant Dollar Accounting

The objective of historical cost/constant dollar accounting is to state all financial statement amounts in dollars of uniform general purchasing power, thereby obtaining a constant, or uniform, measuring unit. The general approach is to convert the actual, or nominal, dollars received or expended over time to an equivalent number of dollars on some constant-dollar date. For example, consider the equipment acquired on January 2 by Hanna Corporation for $100. This acquisition cost amount represents a sacrifice of 100 January 2 dollars. That sacrifice in purchasing power can be stated in several different ways, as illustrated next.

1. The purchasing power of $100 on January 2 is equal to the purchasing power of $50 base-year (when index was 100) because

$$\$100 \times 100/200 = \$50$$

2. The purchasing power of $100 on January 2 is equal to the purchasing power of 105 June 30 dollars because

$$\$100 \times 210/200 = \$105$$

3. The purchasing power of $100 on January 2 is equal to the purchasing power of 115.50 December 31 dollars because

$$\$100 \times 231/200 = \$115.50$$

In words, 100 dollars of January 2 purchasing power have 50 dollars of base-year purchasing power or 105 dollars of June 30 purchasing power or 115.50 dollars of December 31 purchasing power.

Using the constant dollar notation, we can write

$$C\$_{1/2} \ 100.00 \ = \ C\$_{Base} \ 50.00 \ = \ C\$_{6/30} \ 105.00 \ = \ C\$_{12/31} \ 115.50$$

These four amounts are economically equivalent because they represent equal amounts of general purchasing power. The notation "C\$" denotes that constant, instead of nominal, dollars underlie the measurements made.[3]

The constant-dollar date used for restating financial statement amounts is an arbitrary choice. Some have suggested that the date ought to be the base year of the price index used for restatement. Others have suggested using the end of the current year. Still others, including the AcSC for certain disclosures, advocate mid-year dollars of the most recent year being reported. The restatement procedures are analogous, whatever date is used. In the illustrations in this chapter, constant dollars of December 31 purchasing power are used.

It should be noted that the historical cost/constant dollar amounts do not equal the market prices of individual assets. The market price of the equipment of Hanna Corporation, for example, could have changed in an entirely different direction and pattern from that of the general price change (just as the prices of the individual food items in Exhibit D.1 changed at a different rate than the average of ten percent for the group). Historical cost/constant dollar accounting makes the measuring unit used in acquisition cost-based accounting systems more comparable over time. It is not intended as a technique for reflecting current market prices of individual assets and equities.

Restatement of Monetary and Nonmonetary Items

An important distinction is made in the constant dollar restatement procedure between monetary items and nonmonetary items.

Monetary Items A *monetary item* is a claim receivable or payable in a specified number of dollars, regardless of changes in the general purchasing power of the dollar. Examples of monetary items are cash; accounts, notes, and interest receivable; accounts, notes, and interest payable; income taxes payable; and bonds. In preparing a constant-dollar restated balance sheet, the valuation of monetary items at the number of dollars due on the date of the balance sheet automatically states them in terms of the general purchasing power of the dollar at that time. No restatement is therefore

---

[3]In principle, the notation "C\$" is incomplete. To be completely unambiguous, there should be a subscript indicating which date's purchasing power is being used. Because the constant dollar date is fixed for a given set of financial statements, the typical accounting disclosure indicates the constant dollar date in units of December 31 purchasing power. In the paragraph above, however, the subscripts on the C\$ notation have been used to indicate the different dates that might be used in stating the purchasing power given up to acquire the asset.

necessary and the conventionally reported and restated amounts are the same. For example, Hanna Corporation has $125 of cash on December 31. On the conventionally prepared balance sheet, this item would be stated at $125, the amount of cash on hand. On the constant dollar-restated balance sheet, this item would also be reported at C$125, representing $125 of December 31 general purchasing power.

Because monetary items are receivable or payable in a specified number of dollars rather than in terms of a given amount of general purchasing power, holding monetary items over time while the general purchasing power of the dollar changes gives rise to *purchasing power gains and losses*. During a period of inflation, holders of monetary assets lose general purchasing power. For example, a firm with outstanding notes receivable incurs a purchasing-power loss, because the dollars loaned out are worth more in terms of general purchasing power than the dollars to be received when the account is collected. Likewise, a holder of monetary liabilities gains in general purchasing power during periods of inflation, because the dollars required to repay the debt represent less purchasing power than the dollars originally borrowed.[4] The gain or loss from holding monetary items is reported as an element of constant dollar net income but is not included in conventionally reported nominal dollar net income.

Nonmonetary Items A *nonmonetary item* is an asset or equity that does not represent a claim to or for a specified number of dollars. That is, if an item is not a monetary item, then it must be nonmonetary. Examples of nonmonetary items are inventory, land, buildings, equipment, share capital, revenues, and expenses. In conventionally prepared financial statements, nonmonetary items are stated in terms of varying amounts of general purchasing power depending on the date the nonmonetary assets were acquired and nonmonetary equities arose. These conventionally reported amounts must be restated to an equivalent number of dollars as of the constant dollar restatement date. The amount of this restatement does not represent a gain or loss to be included in net income, but is merely an adjustment to equalize the measuring unit being used.

Illustration of the Restatement Procedure

Column (1) of Exhibit D.3 presents an income statement for the year and a balance sheet on December 31 for Hanna Corporation as conventionally reported, based on historical cost/nominal dollars. Column (2) presents the multiplier used to convert the historical cost/nominal dollar amounts to the historical cost amounts related to constant dollars of December 31 purchasing power shown in column (3). The data included in columns (4), (5) and (6) will be considered later.

---

[4]The purchasing power gain on long-term debt is conceptually an offset to interest expense. In setting an interest rate on long-term borrowing, lenders recognize that the dollars to be received when the debt is repaid will be worth less in terms of general purchasing power than the dollars loaned out. Lenders will, therefore, set a higher interest rate to compensate for this expected purchasing power loss. To the borrower, the purchasing power gain has effectively been "paid for" as part of the higher interest cost on the debt. As long as the actual rate of inflation coincides with that anticipated in setting the interest rate, the borrower is not better off as a result of reporting a purchasing power gain. The borrower is better (worse) off only if the actual rate of inflation is greater (less) than the anticipated rate.

Exhibit D.3
HANNA CORPORATION
Financial Statements Reflecting Accounting for Changing Prices

	(1) Historical Cost/ Nominal Dollars	(2) Ratio	(3) Historical Cost/ Constant Dollars	(4) Current Cost/ Nominal Dollars	(5) Ratio	(6) Current Cost/ Constant Dollars
Income Statement						
Sales	$240	231/210	C$264.0	$240	231/210	C$264.0
Cost of Goods Sold	100	231/200	115.5	115	231/210	126.5
Gross Profit	$140		C$148.5	$125		C$137.5
Depreciation	$ 20	a	C$ 23.1[c]	$ 22[d]	231/220	C$ 24.2
Other Expenses	100	231/210	110.0[d]	100	231/210	110.0
Operating Income	$ 20		C$ 15.4	$ 3		C$ 3.3
Accrued Holding Gains:						
Realized:						
Goods Sold	—		—	15[e]		11.0[i]
Depreciable Assets Used	—		—	2[f]		1.1[j]
Unrealized:						
Inventory	—		—	65[g]		38.0[k]
Depreciable Assets	—		—	16[h]		3.6[l]
Purchasing Power Loss	—		(18.0)[m]	—		(18.0)[m]
Net Income	$ 20		C$ (2.6)	$101		C$ 39.0
Balance Sheet						
Cash	$125	231/231	C$125.0	$125	231/231	C$125
Inventory	215	b	242.0	280	231/231	280
Equipment	$100	231/200	C$115.5	$120	231/231	C$120
Accumulated Depreciation	(20)	231/200	(23.1)	(24)[n]	231/231	(24)[n]
Total Assets	$420		C$459.4	$501		C$501
Share Capital	$400	231/200	C$462.0	$400	231/200	C$462
Retained Earnings	20		(2.6)	101		39
Total Equities	$420		C$459.4	$501		C$501

Notes for Exhibit D.3 appear on page 828.

Notes to Exhibit D.3
[a]$20 × (231/200) = C$23.1
[b]$100 × (231/200) + $115 × (231/210) = C$242.
[c]See page 830.
[d]($100 + $120)/2 = $110; $110/5 = $22.
[e]$115 − $100 = $15 see page 833.
[f]$22 − $20 = $2 see page 833.
[g]$280 − $215 = $65.
[h]$96 − $80 = $16.
[i]C$126.5 − $115.5 = C$11.
[j]C$24.2 − $23.1 = C$1.1.
[k]C$280 − $242 = C$38.
[l]C$96 − $92.4 = $C3.6.
[m]See page 829.
[n]The amount shown for accumulated depreciation differs from the amount shown for depreciation expense at the end of Hanna Corporation's first year of operations. The difference arises because depreciation expense is measured in terms of *average* current cost and accumulated depreciation is measured in terms of *end-of-year* current cost.

Income Statement

Consider first the income statement. The sale of the widget for $240 occurred on June 30 when the CPI was 210. The equivalent number of constant December 31 dollars is C$264 (= $240 × 231/210). The widget that was sold had a historical cost in nominal dollars of $100 on January 2 when the CPI was 200. The equivalent number of constant December 31 dollars is C$115.50 (= $100 × 231/200). The restatement of depreciation and other operating expenses likewise reflects the cumulative change in the CPI between the date the original historical-cost measurements were made (January 2 and June 30 respectively) and the end of the year.

Operating income measured in constant dollars will typically be less than operating income measured in nominal dollars, as is the case for Hanna Corporation. Sales and operating expenses will typically be restated for approximately six months of general price change. Cost of goods sold will usually reflect either somewhat less (LIFO cost-flow assumption) or somewhat more (FIFO cost flow assumption) than six months of price change. Depreciation expense, however, will reflect cumulative inflation since the depreciable assets were acquired. The restatement of depreciation expense for Hanna Corporation for the current year reflects only one year of general price change. The restatement of depreciation expense on the equipment for next year will reflect changes in the general price level for both this year and next year. In later years, still more cumulative inflation will be reflected in the restatements. Firms with relatively large amounts of old depreciable assets find that depreciation expense stated in constant dollars is much larger than depreciation expense stated in nominal dollars.

Also shown in column (3) is the purchasing power loss for the year. Hanna Corporation held cash during the year, its only monetary item, and incurred a loss in general purchasing power of C$18. The calculation of this loss appears in Exhibit D.4.

The first column in Exhibit D.4 shows the sources and uses of net monetary assets measured in nominal dollars. In the third column, these nominal dollar amounts are restated to equivalent December 31 dollars. In order for Hanna Corporation to have maintained the purchasing power of its net monetary assets, a net monetary asset position of $143 would be required at year end. Because the actual net monetary

Exhibit D.4
Calculation of Purchasing Power Gain or Loss for Hanna Corporation

	Historical Cost/ Nominal Dollars	Restatement	Historical Cost/ Constant Dollars
Net Monetary Asset Position, Jan. 1	—		—
Increases in Net Monetary Assets:			
Issue of Common Stock for Cash	$400	231/200	C$462.00
Sale of Widget	240	231/210	264.00
Decreases in Net Monetary Assets:			
Purchase of 2 Widgets on Jan. 1	(200)	231/200	(231.00)
Purchase of Equipment	(100)	231/200	(115.50)
Purchase of 1 Widget on June 30	(115)	231/210	(126.50)
Payment of Operating Expenses	(100)	231/210	(110.00)
Net Monetary Asset Position, Dec. 31	$125		C$143.00

Purchasing Power Loss: $125 − C$143 = C$18.

asset position is only $125, Hanna Corporation has lost $18 of purchasing power during the year.

An alternative method of determining the gain or loss from holding monetary assets is to determine the balance of monetary assets held for various periods during a year and for each period determine the gain or loss. The calculation of the loss from holding monetary assets for Hanna Corporation for the year follows:

Purchasing Power Loss on $100 (= $400 − $200 − $100) held during first 6 months when CPI increased 5 percent; $100 × 10/200 = $5. Restatement of purchasing power loss to constant December 31 dollars; $5 × 231/210	C$ 5.50
Purchasing Power Loss on $125 (= $100 + $240 − $115 − $100) held during second 6 months when CPI increased 10 percent; $125 × 21/210	12.50
Total Purchasing Power Loss	C$18.00

Most publicly held firms are in a net monetary liability position because of outstanding long-term debt. Therefore, they experience purchasing power gains instead of losses during periods of inflation. These purchasing power gains sometimes more than offset the lower operating income resulting from the restatement of depreciation.

Balance Sheet Column (3) of Exhibit D.3 also shows the restatement of the balance sheet to a constant-dollar basis. Cash is the only monetary item. It is shown at C$125, the same amount as in the nominal-dollar balance sheet. Ending inventory is composed of two units, one purchased for $100 on January 2, and the other purchased for $115 on June 30. The December 31 constant dollar equivalent of these amounts is:

January 2 Purchase: $100 × 231/200	C$115.50
June 30 Purchase: $115 × 231/210	126.50
Total	C$242.00

The cost of the equipment purchased for $100 on January 31 is restated to C$115.50 December 31 dollars (= $100 × 231/200). Accumulated depreciation is equal to one-fifth of the constant dollar cost, or C$23.10. Share capital is likewise restated for one year of general price change; $400 × 231/200 = C$462. Constant dollar retained earnings is equal to the constant-dollar net loss for the year.

Summary of Constant Dollar Restatement Procedure The constant dollar restatement procedure can be summarized as follows:

1. Select the constant dollar date to which all financial statement items will be restated.
2. Restate revenues and expenses on the income statement from the nominal dollars underlying their measurement in the conventional income statement to dollars of the desired constant general purchasing power. The numerator of the restatement factor is the Consumer Price Index on the desired constant dollar date. The denominator is the Consumer Price Index on the date of the underlying nominal dollar measurements.
3. Calculate the purchasing power gain or loss. Begin with a listing of the sources and uses of net monetary items during the period. This listing of inflows and outflows should fully account for the change in the net monetary position between the beginning and end of the period. Then restate the beginning net monetary position and all sources and uses of net monetary items from the price level in which the monetary item is measured in nominal dollars to the price level on the constant dollar date. The difference between the actual and constant dollar net monetary position at the end of the period is the purchasing power gain or loss for the period. The purchasing power gain or loss will be reported in the income statement.
4. Restate each balance sheet item to its constant-dollar equivalent. If dollars of end-of-the-year purchasing power are selected as the constant dollar, monetary items are automatically stated in year-end dollars, and no restatement is required. Nonmonetary items must be restated from the nominal dollars underlying their measurement in the conventional financial statements to the equivalent number of constant dollars.

Evaluation of Historical Cost/Constant-Dollar Accounting

The procedures for restating financial statements to a constant-dollar basis can be traced back to before 1920.[5] Yet it was not until 1974 that an accounting *Guideline* was issued by the Accounting Research Committee of the CICA that presented the techniques of general price level restatement of historical cost financial statements. This *Guideline* avoided expressing an opinion on the appropriateness of this method of accounting for the effects of changing prices and did not include any disclosure requirements. This *Guideline* was withdrawn when section 4510 of the *Handbook*, "Reporting the Effects of Changing Prices," was issued in 1983. The usefulness of constant-dollar information has been, and continues to be, controversial.

The Case for Constant Dollar Accounting Proponents of constant dollar accounting offer the following arguments:

1. Constant dollar accounting makes the results of arithmetic operations more meaningful. If the measuring unit (the dollar) varies over times because of changes in the general purchasing power of the dollar, then additions and subtractions of recorded amounts cannot be made meaningfully.
2. Constant dollar accounting makes interperiod comparisons more meaningful. Changes in the amount of an item (sales, cost of goods sold) are difficult to interpret if the measuring unit used is not the same over time.
3. Constant dollar accounting improves the meaning and measurement of net income. Revenues and expenses are matched in terms of a constant measuring unit. Also, a gain or loss is explicitly recognized for the change in the general purchasing power of monetary assets and liabilities held. Income before the purchasing power gain or loss must exceed any loss of purchasing power of monetary assets and equities if the purchasing power of the monetary, or financial, capital of the firm is to be maintained.
4. Constant dollar accounting is relatively objective in that government-prepared price indices are used to restate audited historical cost amounts.

The Case against Constant Dollar Accounting Opponents of constant dollar accounting argue that it fails to measure the economically significant effects of changing prices on a firm. They argue as follows:

1. With respect to nonmonetary items, the strategies that firms follow in coping with inflation focus on changes in the prices of the specific goods and services that the firm normally acquires and not on changes in the prices of a broad market basket of consumer goods and services. Raw materials are purchased early in anticipation of increased acquisition costs. A capital intensive plant is constructed in anticipation of increased labor costs. Yet, under constant dollar accounting, the results of these decisions are judged against a standard based on changes in the general purchasing power of the dollar which may be significantly different from results based on changes in specific prices.
2. With respect to monetary items, the purchasing power gain or loss is based on an

---

[5]See Livingston Middleditch, Jr., "Should Accounts Reflect the Changing Value of the Dollar?" *Journal of Accountancy* (February 1918): 114–120. This article was "rediscovered" and reprinted by Stephen A. Zeff (ed.) in *Asset Appreciation, Business Income and Price-Level Accounting: 1918–1935* (New York: Arno Press, 1976). Generally, however, the credit for developing constant-dollar accounting is given to Henry W. Sweeney for his *Stabilized Accounting* (New York: Harper & Brothers, 1936).

inappropriate index of purchasing power. Users of financial statements are interested in a firm's ability to maintain the purchasing power of its monetary assets for the particular kinds of goods and services that it normally purchases.

Current Cost/Nominal Dollar Accounting

Objective of Current Cost/Nominal Dollar Accounting

The objective of current cost/nominal dollar accounting is to report the effects of specific price changes on the operating performance and financial position of a firm.[6] Current cost is generally defined as the amount a firm would have to pay currently to replace the service potential embodied in its specific assets. It takes into account the inherent technological capabilities and levels of obsolescence of the existing assets. For example, if a firm owned a two-year-old automobile, it would base its current replacement cost valuation on the prices of similar two-year-old automobiles in the used car market. If replacement cost amounts for identical, used assets are not available, then the replacement cost of new assets with similar service potential would be used. The replacement cost of the new asset would be adjusted downward, however, for both the used condition of the existing asset and any technological changes that have occurred.

Measuring Current-Cost Amounts

There are several sources of information that might be consulted in ascertaining the current cost of a particular asset.

1. Used Asset Market For automobiles, furniture, office machines, and similar items, active used-asset markets exist that can help to measure the current cost of such assets.

2. Suppliers Catalogues For inventories of raw materials, supplies, and standardized equipment, suppliers catalogues can be consulted.

3. Appraisals The current cost of land and building might be determined from real estate appraisers.

4. Specific Price Indices The federal government prepares specific price indices for a wide assortment of goods and services. These price indices indicate the change

---

[6]Several alternative approaches to reflecting changes in specific prices have been suggested by various writers. These include:

1. *Current reproduction cost* — The cost of material, labor, and overhead that would be required currently to reproduce an asset identical to that now owned.
2. *Current replacement cost* — The cost of acquiring an asset that has the same service potential or operating capacity as an asset now owned.
3. *Net realizable value* — The net amount that would be received if an asset were sold currently.
4. *Present value of future cash flows* — The present value of the future cash inflows and cash outflows expected from an asset.

The arguments for and against each of these alternative valuation bases are beyond the scope of this book, but are considered in intermediate accounting texts.

over time in the price of particular classes of items. These indices typically indicate the current cost of items in new condition. To use the price indices to measure the current cost of existing assets, some recognition must be given to their used condition.

Illustration of Current Cost/Nominal Dollar Accounting

Column (4) of Exhibit D.3 on page 827 shows the income statement and balance sheet of Hanna Corporation on a current cost/nominal dollar basis.

Income Statement Sales revenue is stated at the amount of cash received (or expected to be received) from the sale of inventory items; the amount is the same as in the conventional financial statements. Matched against sales revenue is the current cost of inventory sold, equipment services used, and other goods and services consumed. When the widget was sold on June 30 it had a replacement cost of $115. The current cost of goods sold is, therefore, stated at this amount. The equipment of Hanna Corporation had an average current cost of $110 during the year. Based on a five-year life and the straight-line depreciation method, depreciation expense on a current-cost basis is $22 (= $110/5). Other expenses incurred during the year are already stated in terms of current cost.

Operating income indicates the extent to which selling prices were set sufficiently high to cover the current cost of replacing goods and services sold or consumed during the period. If a firm is to maintain its operating capacity, it must be able to replace assets as they are used up. Cash generated from sales is the primary means for doing so. Thus, operating income on a current cost basis indicates the extent to which a firm has maintained its operating capacity during the period.

The income statement also shows holding gains and losses on nonmonetary assets accrued during 1985. Some of these gains are realized through disposal[7] of the assets whereas gains accrued on assets held at the balance sheet date are considered unrealized. Recall from the discussion of inventories in Chapter 8 that a holding gain arises when an asset is held while its current cost increases. Consider, for example, the widget purchased on January 1 for $100 and sold on June 30 for $240. The current cost of replacing the widget on June 30 was $115. While the widget was held, its current cost increased $15 (= $115 − $100). Because this widget was sold during the year, the holding gain has been realized. The conventional gross profit on the sale of $140 in column (1) is separated in column (4) into a gross profit of $125, and a realized holding gain of $15 (= current cost of goods sold − historical cost of goods sold = $115 − $100). There is also a realized holding gain of $2 on the equipment used. The gain is equal to the difference between the current cost of the equipment's services used during the year of $22 and the historical cost of those services of $20. Note that operating income plus realized holding gains on a current cost/nominal dollar basis are equal to net income in the conventional financial statements: $3 + $15 + $2 = $20.

The income statement in column (4) also includes unrealized holding gains on inventory and equipment not yet sold or used. The current cost of replacing the two

---

[7]In subsequent years, gains accrued but unrealized in previous years may be realized in the current year.

widgets at the end of the year is $280 (= $140 × 2). The historical cost of these widgets is $215 (= $110 + $115). Thus, the unrealized holding gain is $65 (= $280 − $215). Similarly, the current cost of replacing the equipment in new condition at the end of 1982 is $120. If the equipment has a five-year life, the current cost of replacing the equipment in its existing one-year-old condition is $96 (= $\frac{4}{5}$ × $120). The difference between the current cost of the equipment of $96 and the historical cost of the same service potential of $80 (= $\frac{4}{5}$ × $100) is an unrealized holding gain.

Net income on a current cost/nominal dollar basis, adopting the financial capital maintenance concept,[8] is composed of operating income, realized holding gains and losses, and unrealized holding gains and losses.

Balance Sheet Cash is stated at its face amount in the current cost balance sheet. If Aliber Corporation had other monetary items (accounts receivable, accounts payable, bonds payable), they should, at least theoretically, also be revalued to a current cost basis. The approach is to ascertain the current interest rate appropriate to the monetary item. The future cash flows associated with the monetary item should be discounted to their present value using the current interest rate. As a practical matter, probably only *long-term* receivables and *long-term* debt would be revalued.

The inventory and equipment, both nonmonetary items, are stated at their current cost on December 31. Share capital is stated at its historical cost/nominal dollar amount, because it is not feasible to measure the current cost of such share capital at the end of the year. The current market value of the share capital might appear to be an appropriate basis for such a current-cost valuation. However, this market value is for the firm's entire net assets (share capital plus retained earnings), not just the share capital portion. Retained earnings for Hanna Corporation is equal to current-cost net income for the year.

Evaluation of Current Cost/Nominal Dollar Accounting

Current cost/nominal dollar accounting continues to be controversial.

The Case for Current Cost/Nominal Dollar Accounting Advocates of current cost/ nominal dollar accounting offer the following arguments.

1. Management's actions to cope with changing prices are based on expected changes in the prices of the particular goods and services normally acquired by a firm. Current cost financial statements provide a consistent basis on which to evaluate management's actions and performance.

2. Current cost income is separated into operating profit and holding gains and losses, permitting statement users to assess the impact of changing prices on the profitability of the firm.

---

[8]Considerable controversy exists in accounting as to whether holding gains and losses, both realized and unrealized, should be included in net income. Advocates of a *financial capital maintenance* viewpoint argue that they should be included, whereas advocates of a *physical capital maintenance* viewpoint argue that they should not be included. The issues involved in this controversy are beyond the scope of this book.

3. Current cost balance sheets provide a more realistic indication of the current economic value of assets and liabilities than do the balance sheets based on historical costs.

The Case against Current Cost/Nominal Dollar Accounting Opponents of current cost/nominal dollar accounting offer the following arguments.

1. Current cost amounts are often difficult to calculate, particularly for specialized used assets, raising questions about the reliability and comparability of current cost data between firms.
2. Current cost net income which includes holding gains and losses, must be interpreted cautiously. Unrealized holding gains do not produce cash or claims to cash. Basing dividends on current cost net income may result in impairing the operating capacity of the firm.[9]
3. Current cost accounting in nominal dollars fails to recognize that the measuring unit used to calculate current cost amounts is not of the same dimension over time. Changes in the general purchasing power of the dollar make current cost amounts on the balance sheet at the beginning and end of the period noncomparable. Likewise, net income amounts over time, using current costs, are not based on a constant measuring unit.
4. Changes in current costs relative to changes in the general price level are not considered in measuring holding gains and losses under current cost/nominal dollar accounting. A holding gain of eight percent on a tract of land on a current cost basis has one meaning when the general price level increases six percent and another meaning when general prices increase by ten percent.
5. Current-cost accounting fails to recognize purchasing power, or inflation, gains or losses on monetary items. As discussed earlier in this chapter, monetary items gain or lose purchasing power as they are held over time. These gains and losses are often equally as important as holding gains and losses on inventories, depreciable assets, and similar items.

Current Cost/Constant Dollar Accounting

Objective of Current Cost/Constant Dollar Accounting

The objective of current cost/constant dollar accounting is to report in a constant measuring unit the effects of specific price changes on the operating performance and financial position of a firm. Because constant dollar accounting deals with the measuring unit and current cost accounting deals with the valuation basis, there are no theoretical obstacles to combining the two approaches.

---

[9]For this reason, advocates of a physical capital maintenance concept of income would exclude holding gains and losses. See footnote 8.

Illustration of Current Cost/Constant Dollar Accounting

Column (6) of Exhibit D.3 on page 827 shows the income statement and balance sheet of Hanna Corporation on a current cost/constant dollar basis. The constant dollar date is December 31.

Income Statement Sales revenue, cost of goods sold, depreciation, and other expenses are stated in column (4) at their current cost on June 30 measured in terms of June 30 dollars. To measure them in terms of December 31 dollars requires that they be restated using the factor 231/210.

The realized holding gains must be recomputed to reflect a constant measuring unit. Recall that the realized holding gain on the widget sold in column (4) is equal to the current cost of the widget on June 30 of $115 less the historical cost on January 1 of $100. These two amounts are expressed in different measuring units. Both amounts must be restated to constant December 31 dollars as follows:

Current Cost of Widget Sold: $115 × 231/210	C$126.50
Historical Cost of Widget Sold: $100 × 231/200	115.50
Realized Holding Gain on Inventory Sold[10]	C$ 11.00

Similarly, the realized holding gain on depreciable assets used in column (4) is the difference between the average current cost of the services used during the year of $22 and the historical cost of the services of $20. Both amounts must be expressed in constant December 31 dollars as follows:

Current Cost of Depreciable Assets Used: $22 × 231/210	C$24.2
Historical Cost of Depreciable Assets Used: $20 × 231/200	23.1
Realized Holding Gain on Depreciable Assets Used	C$ 1.1

The unrealized holding gains must also be recalculated to place all measurements in terms of constant December 31 dollars.

Current cost/constant dollar net income is composed of operating income, realized and unrealized holding gains and losses on nonmonetary items, and purchasing power gains and losses on monetary items.

Balance Sheet The amounts on the asset side of the balance sheet in column (4) reflect current costs on December 31. Because these amounts are already stated in terms of December 31 dollars, no restatement is necessary. Share capital is restated from January 1 to December 31 dollars using the factor 231/200.

---

[10]Alternatively, the realized holding gain to the date of sale could be calculated in nominal dollars and converted to constant dollars at the statement date. In this case [$115 − ($100 × 210/200)] × 231/210 = $11.

Evaluation of Current Cost/Constant Dollar Accounting

A careful reading of the arguments for and against historical cost/constant dollar accounting and current cost/nominal dollar accounting reveals that most of the criticisms of these two approaches are overcome by combining them. An added difficulty arises, however. The computations may be so complex that readers of the financial statements will be unable to understand and interpret the disclosures made. An educational effort is required to inform statement readers as to the kinds of interpretations that should and should not be made.

Required Disclosures under the CICA Handbook

The AcSC recognizes that opinions vary widely on the usefulness of information generated by each of the three approaches to accounting for changing prices discussed in this chapter (that is, the information of columns (3), (4) and (6) of Exhibit D.3). Rather than require that a full set of supplemental financial statements be prepared under only one of these three approaches, the *CICA Handbook* requires certain minimum disclosures using each of the three approaches. This approach provides statement users with time to educate themselves as to the nature of the disclosures made and to assess their relative usefulness. The AcSC will continually monitor the reporting process to determine if the required disclosures should be altered.

The minimum disclosures are required by enterprises having publicly traded debt or equity securities, as well as either (a) inventories and property, plant and equipment (before deducting accumulated depreciation, depletion and amortization), totalling $50 million or more; or (b) total assets (after deducting accumulated depreciation, depletion and amortization) of $350 million or more at the beginning of the fiscal year for which the financial statements are being prepared. The following disclosures are required:

1. The current cost amounts of cost of goods sold and of depreciation, depletion and amortization of property, plant and equipment or the current cost adjustments for these items. These amounts are included in column (4) or (6) of Exhibit D.3 depending on whether Hanna Corporation chooses to report in December 31 dollars or average year dollars.
2. The current and deferred amounts of income tax expense. To simplify, income taxes have been excluded from the Hanna Corporation illustration.
3. Income before extraordinary items, after reflecting items (1) and (2). This is reported as Operating Income in column (4) or (6) of Exhibit D.3 depending on the measuring unit selected.
4. The amount of the changes during the reporting period in the current cost amounts of inventory and property, plant and equipment. This is the total Accrued Holding Gain presented in column (4) or (6) of Exhibit D.3 depending on the measuring unit selected. In a more realistic example the realized holding gains would be reduced by the unrealized holding gains at the end of the previous year.

5. The carrying value of inventory and property, plant and equipment on a current cost basis at the end of the reporting period. These amounts are included in columns (4) and (6) of Exhibit D.3. Other assets and equities need not be stated at current cost.

6. Net assets after restating inventory and property, plant and equipment on a current cost basis at the end of the reporting period. This amount is included in columns (4) and (6) of Exhibit D.3. Since there are no liabilities, either Total Assets or Total Shareholders' Equity can be selected.

7. The amount of the financing adjustment. The financing adjustment was excluded from the Hanna Corporation illustration. It is the amount of changes during the year in the current cost of a corporation's assets that, on the basis of the existing relationship between debt and equity, do not need to be charged against revenues to provide for the common shareholders' proportionate interest in the operating capability of the corporation. It is a replacement for the Purchasing Power Gain or Loss. further discussion of the Financing Adjustment is left to intermediate accounting texts.

8. The amount of changes during the reporting period in the current cost amounts of inventory and property, plant and equipment that is attributed to general inflation. This amount is not presented directly in Exhibit D.3, but may be calculated for each of the two groups of assets by deducting the amounts in column (6) from comparable amounts in column (3).

9. The amount of the gain or loss in general purchasing power that results from holding net monetary items during the year. This amount is called the Purchasing Power Loss from holding monetary assets in the Hanna Corporation illustration and is shown in both columns (3) and (6) in Exhibit D.3. This amount is also called the monetary gain or loss.

All of this information would be reported for both the current and the immediately preceding reporting period. To improve comparability of information between periods, dollar amounts for the immediately preceding period would be restated for the change in the general purchasing power of the Canadian dollar. The index used to measure changes in the purchasing power of the Canadian dollar would be either the Consumer Price Index for Canada or the Gross National Expenditure Implicit Price Deflator, published by Statistics Canada.

The recommendations emphasize that the numerical data alone cannot convey the full significance of the effects of changing prices on enterprise activities. For this reason, the management of an enterprise is to provide an explanation of the information disclosed, a description of the basis and methods used in its preparation, and a narrative discussion of its significance. This narrative discussion might include an identification of and commentary on significant items that have not been adjusted for the effects of changing prices, such as interest and income taxes, and an explanation of how the supplementary financial data can be used as a basis for assessing maintenance of operating capability financed by common shareholders and maintenance of general purchasing power of capital.

The recommendations do not apply to income-producing real estate assets and banks, trust companies, and insurance companies.

Changing Prices and the Statement of Changes in Financial Position

Of the three principal financial statements, the statement of changes in financial position is the least affected by changing prices. Most transactions affecting the flow of funds occur during the period being reported. Any adjustment of these amounts for either general or specific price changes would reflect price changes for approximately one year or less.

As is the case in preparing the statement of changes in financial position in historical cost/nominal dollars, the restated statement reflecting either general or specific price changes can be most easily prepared after the balance sheet and income statement have been restated for price changes. The amounts included in the restated statement of changes in financial position can usually be obtained from either the restated balance sheet or the restated income statement.

Summary

Accounting for changing prices is currently in a period of transition and experimentation. Financial statement preparers and users have recognized for many years that changing prices, either in general or for specific goods and services, bring to question the validity and meaningfulness of conventional financial statements based on historical cost and nominal dollars. The pronouncement by the Accounting Standards Committee allows firms considerable flexibility in the way changing prices are accounted for and disclosed. Whether constant dollar accounting, current cost accounting, or some other approach replaces or regularly supplements the historical cost/nominal dollars, financial statements will depend on the benefits of the disclosures as perceived by users, relative to the cost of generating the necessary data. It is, as yet, too early to evaluate effectively these benefits and costs.

Problem for Self-Study

The Vachon Corporation was formed on January 2 to conduct an office rental business. Listed below are various transactions and other events of the firm during the year. The assumed values of the Consumer Price Index (CPI) are shown in parentheses.

(1) January 2 (CPI = 200): No par value common shares are issued for $1,000,000.

(2) January 2 (CPI = 200): Land costing $100,000 and a building costing $1,500,000 are acquired. A cash payment of $900,000 is made for the land and building with a long-term, ten-percent note signed for the remainder of the purchase price. Interest on the note is payable on December 31 of each year, and the principal is repayable in ten years.

(3) January 2 to December 31 (average CPI = 212): Rentals totaling $300,000 for the year are collected in cash.

(4) January 2 to December 31 (average CPI = 212): Operating costs incurred evenly over the year total $60,000, of which $40,000 are paid in cash and the remainder are on account. All of these costs are expenses of the current year.

(5) January 2 to December 31 (average CPI = 212): Interest costs are accrued monthly on the mortgage payable and are paid on December 31.

(6) December 31 (CPI = 224): Depreciation on the building is calculated using the straight-line method, a 30-year life, and zero salvage value.

(7) December 31 (CPI = 224): A cash dividend of $75,000 is declared and paid.

On December 31 the land had a current cost of $150,000. A similar new office building had a current cost in new condition of $1,560,000, while a similar one-year-old office building had a current cost of $1,508,000. The amounts reported as operating and interest expenses in the conventional financial statements closely approximate their average current costs during the year.

Prepare an income statement for the current year and a balance sheet as of December 31 for Vachon Corporation under each of the following (round all amounts to the nearest dollar).

    a. Historical cost/nominal dollars.

    b. Historical cost/constant dollars of December 31 purchasing power.

    c. Current cost/nominal dollars.

    d. Current cost/constant dollars of December 31 purchasing power.

Suggested Solution

Exhibit D.5 presents income statements and balance sheets for Vachon Corporation for the current year. The computations are shown in Exhibit D.5 below and in the notes to Exhibit D.6 (page 841).

Exhibit D.5
VACHON CORPORATION
Calculation of Purchasing Power Gain or Loss
for the Current year

	Historical-Cost/ Nominal Dollars	Restatement	Historical-Cost/ Constant Dollars
Net Monetary Position, January 1	—	—	—
Increases in Net Monetary Assets:			
Issue of Common Shares for Cash	$1,000,000	224/200	C$1,120,000
Accrual of Rent Receivable	300,000	224/212	316,981
Decreases in Net Monetary Assets:			
Disbursement of Cash in Acquisition of Land and Building	(900,000)	224/200	(1,008,000)

Issuance of Note Payable in
  Acquisition of Land and
    Building ....
	(700,000)	224/200	(784,000)

Accrual of Operating Costs	(60,000)	224/212	(63,396)
Accrual of Interest Costs	(70,000)	224/212	(73,962)
Declaration of Dividend	(75,000)	224/224	(75,000)
Net Monetary Liability Position, December 31	$(505,000)		C $(567,377)

Purchasing Power Gain: C$567,377 − $505,000 = C$62,377.

Exhibit D.6
VACHON CORPORATION
Financial Statements Reflecting Accounting for Changing Prices

	Historical-Cost/ Nominal Dollars	Ratio	Historical-Cost/ Constant Dollars	Current-Cost/ Nominal Dollars	Ratio	Current-Cost/ Constant Dollars
Income Statement						
Rent Revenue	$ 300,000	224/212	C$ 316,981	$ 300,000	224/212	C$ 316,981
Depreciation Expense	(50,000)	224/200	(56,000)	(51,000)[b]	224/212	(53,887)
Operating Expenses	(60,000)	224/212	(63,396)	(60,000)	224/212	(63,396)
Interest Expense	(70,000)	224/212	(73,962)	(70,000)	224/212	(73,962)
Operating Income	$ 120,000		C$ 123,623	$ 119,000		C$ 125,736
Realized Holding Gain:						
Building	—		—	1,000[c]		(2,113)[g]
Unrealized Holding Gain:						
Land	—		—	50,000[d]		38,000[h]
Building	—		—	58,000[e]		(116,000)[i]
Purchasing Power Gain	—		62,377[a]	—		62,377[a]
Net Income	$ 120,000		C$ 186,000	$ 228,000		C$ 108,000
Less: Dividends Declared	(75,000)		(75,000)	(75,000)		(75,000)
Retained Earnings, December 31	$ 45,000		C$ 111,000	$ 153,000		C$ 33,000
Balance Sheet						
Assets:						
Cash	$ 215,000	224/224	C$ 215,000	$ 215,000	224/224	C$ 215,000
Land	100,000	224/200	112,000	150,000	224/224	150,000
Building—Cost	1,500,000	224/200	1,680,000	1,560,000	224/224	1,560,000
Less: Accumulated Depreciation	(50,000)	224/200	(56,000)	(52,000)[f]	224/224	(52,000)
Total Assets	$1,765,000		C$1,951,000	$1,873,000		C$1,873,000
Liabilities and Shareholders' Equity:						
Accounts Payable	$ 20,000	224/224	C$ 20,000	$ 20,000	224/224	C$ 20,000
Note Payable	700,000	224/224	700,000	700,000	224/224	700,000
Common Shares	1,000,000	224/200	1,120,000	1,000,000	224/200	1,120,000
Retained Earnings	45,000		111,000	153,000		33,000
Total Equities	$1,765,000		C$1,951,000	$1,873,000		C$1,873,000

[a]See Exhibit D.5.
[b]($1,500,000 + $1,560,000)/2 = $1,530,000; $1,530,000/30 = $51,000.
[c]$51,000 − $50,000 = $1,000.
[d]$150,000 − $100,000 = $50,000.
[e]($1,560,000 − $52,000) − ($1,500,000 − $50,000) = $1,508,000 − $1,450,000 = $58,000.

[f]$1,560,000/30 = $52,000.
[g]($51,000 × 224/212) − ($50,000 × 224/200) = C$53,887 − C$56,000 = C$(2,113).
[h]$150,000 − ($100,000 × 224/200) = C$150,000 − C$112,000 = C$38,000.
[i]$1,508,000 − C$1,624,000 = C$(116,000).

Questions, Exercises, Problems and Cases

Questions

1. Review the meaning of the following concepts or terms discussed in this chapter.
   - a. General price level changes
   - b. Specific price changes
   - c. Price index
   - d. Nominal dollars
   - e. Constant dollars
   - f. Acquisition cost
   - g. Current cost
   - h. Constant dollar date
   - i. Monetary item
   - j. Nonmonetary item
   - k. Purchasing power gain or loss on monetary items
   - l. Realized holding gain or loss on nonmonetary items
   - m. Unrealized holding gain or loss on nonmonetary items
   - n. Holding gains and losses net of inflation

2. Refer to the income statements and balance sheets of Hanna Corporation in Exhibit D.3 in the chapter.
   - a. Under what conditions will the amounts in column (1) (historical cost/nominal dollars) and column (3) (current cost/nominal dollars) be the same?
   - b. Under what conditions will the amounts in column (2) (historical cost/constant dollars) and column (4) (current cost/constant dollars) be the same?
   - c. Under what conditions will the amounts in column (2) (historical cost/constant dollars) and column (3) (current cost/nominal dollars) be the same?

3. When historical cost/constant dollar financial statements are prepared, under what conditions will a firm incur:
   - a. A purchasing power gain?
   - b. A purchasing power loss?
   - c. Neither a purchasing power gain nor a purchasing power loss?

4. Why is there no purchasing power gain or loss on nonmonetary items in historical cost/constant dollar financial statements?

5. "Financial statements prepared under the conventional accounting model reflect dollars of mixed purchasing power." Explain the meaning of this statement in relation to the balance sheet, income statement, and statement of changes in financial position.

6. For which types of asset and equity structures would you expect:
   - a. Significant differences between net income as conventionally reported and as restated to a constant dollar basis (including the purchasing power gain or loss)?
   - b. Insignificant differences between the two earnings measures?

7. "The amount of income for any given year on a historical cost/constant dollar basis will differ depending on which constant dollar date is selected." Explain.

8. "Operating income on a current cost/nominal dollar basis indicates the extent to which a firm has maintained its operating capacity during a period." Explain.

9. "All realized holding gains or losses were once unrealized holding gains or losses." Do you agree? Why or why not?

10. A firm reports a realized holding gain on land in its current cost/nominal dollar income statement but a realized holding loss in its current cost/constant dollar income statement. What is the likely explanation for this difference?

11. "The LIFO cost flow assumption for inventories and accelerated depreciation methods for plant and equipment are only partial solutions to the accounting problems associated with specific price changes." Explain.

Exercises

12. *Calculating the gain on sale of land under various approaches to accounting for changing prices*. Rockness Corporation acquired a parcel of land on January 2 for $50,000. The parcel was sold on July 1 of the same year for $65,000. An index of the general price level and the current cost of the land on various dates are as follows:

	General Price Index	Current Cost
January 2	160	$50,000
July 1	185	65,000
December 31	200	75,000

Calculate the amount of income or loss relating to this land for the year under each of the following bases (round amounts to the nearest dollar).
  a. Historical cost/nominal dollars.
  b. Historical cost/constant dollars of December 31 purchasing power.
  c. Current cost/nominal dollars.
  d. Current cost/constant dollars of December 31 purchasing power.

13. *Disaggregating the gross margin into operating margin and holding gains*. The merchandise inventory of Scoggin's Appliance Store on January 1 consists of 1,000 units acquired for $250 each. During the year, 2,500 units are purchased at a unit price of $300, while 2,400 units are sold for $400 each. The average current cost per unit during the year is $300, whereas the current cost on December 31 is $360 per unit.
  a. Using historical cost and nominal dollars, calculate the gross profit (sales minus cost of goods sold) for the year using the FIFO and the LIFO cost flow assumptions.
  b. Using current cost and nominal dollars, disaggregate the gross profit in part (a) into the operating profit and realized holding gain. Compute unrealized holding gains and the source of operating profit plus all holding gains.

14. *Restating equipment and depreciation to a constant dollar basis*. Sunder Equipment Corporation depreciates its machinery using the straight-line method over a ten-year life with zero estimated salvage value. A full year's depreciation is taken in the year of acquisition and none in the year of disposal. Acquisitions, which took place evenly over the appropriate years, were as follows: Year 1, $400,000; Year 2, $200,000; Year 3, $300,000. An index of the average general price level during Year 1 was 180, during Year 2 was 220, and during Year 3 was 240. The general price index on December 31, Year 3, is 250.

a. Calculate the amount of depreciation expense for Year 3 and the book value of the machinery on December 31, Year 3, using the historical costs and nominal dollars.

b. Repeat part (a) using the historical costs and constant dollars of December 31, Year 3, purchasing power. Round all amounts to the nearest dollar.

15. *Calculating the purchasing power gain or loss*. The Cunningham Drug Store Ltd. had a net monetary asset position of $300,000 on January 1, at which time an index of the general price level was 200. Transactions during the year and associated indices of the general price level (GPI) are listed below.

(1) Purchases, all on account, totaled $400,000 (GPI = 210).
(2) Sales, all on account, totaled $600,000 (GPI = 210).
(3) Collections from customers for sales on account, $450,000 (GPI = 215).
(4) Payments to suppliers for purchases on account, $300,000 (GPI = 215).
(5) Declaration of a $200,000 dividend, payable during January of next year (GPI = 250). The general price index on December 31 is 230.

a. Calculate the amount of the purchasing power gain or loss for the year stated in terms of constant December 31 dollars. Round all amounts to the nearest dollar.

b. Repeat part (a) assuming a net monetary liability position of $300,000 on January 1.

16. *Calculating the purchasing power gain or loss*. On January 1 the Langston family had $800 in its chequing account and $4,000 in a savings account. The unpaid balance for the mortgage on their home totaled $25,000, and unpaid bills relating to purchases during December of last year amounted to $600. An index of the general price level on January 1 was 210. During the current year, the following transactions occurred (general price index is shown in parentheses):

(1) Bill Langston's take-home salary was $25,000 (average GPI = 225).
(2) The unpaid bills of $600 on January 1 were paid (GPI = 213).
(3) Principal repayments of $2,000 were made on the home mortgage loan (average GPI = 225).
(4) Food, clothing, interest, and other costs incurred by the family totaled $20,500 of which $19,700 was paid in cash (average GPI = 225).
(5) Interest earned and added to the savings account totaled $300 (average GPI = 225).
(6) In addition to the interest earned in (5), $1,500 was transferred from the chequing to the savings account (GPI = 158). The general price index on December 31 is 240.

Calculate the purchasing power gain or loss for the year for the family stated in terms of constant December 31 dollars.

17. *Preparing income statement and balance sheet under four measurement and valuation approaches*. Straus Corporation is organized on January 2 with the issuance of common shares for $200. The following transactions occur during the year.

(1) January 2. Two widgets are purchased for $50 each.

(2) January 2. Furniture with a five-year life and zero estimated salvage value is acquired for $50. The straight-line depreciation method is used.

(3) June 30. One widget is sold for $120.

(4) June 30. One new widget is purchased for $80.

(5) June 30. Other expenses of $50 are paid in cash.

An index of the general price level was 100 on January 1, 120 on June 30, and 132 on December 31. On December 31, the current cost of a widget was $90. On this same date, the current cost of replacing the furniture in new condition was $60.

    a. Prepare a four-column income statement and balance sheet as of December 31 for Straus Corporation using the following headings:

        (1) Historical cost/nominal dollars.

        (2) Historical cost/constant dollars of December 31 purchasing power.

        (3) Current cost/nominal dollars.

        (4) Current cost/constant dollars of December 31 purchasing power.

    b. How successful was Straus Corporation in coping with inflation during the year?

18. *Graphical illustration of changing prices relationships.* The Bulova Corporation acquired two tables on January 1. One of these tables was sold on June 30. The other table was still in inventory on December 31. Figure D.1 depicts various selling price and cost relationships relating to these tables during the year. Point A is the acquisition cost of each table. Using the letters shown in Figure D.1 indicate the computation of the following items.

    a. Gross profit on sale in historical cost/nominal dollars.

    b. Gross profit on sale in historical cost/constant dollars of June 30 purchasing power.

Figure D.1 Selling Price and Cost Relationships for Bulova Corporation

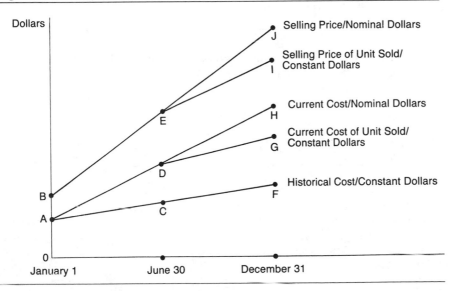

    c. Gross profit on sale in historical cost/constant dollars of December 31 purchasing power.

    d. Operating profit before holding gains and losses in current cost/nominal dollars.

    e. Realized holding gain in current cost/nominal dollars.

    f. Unrealized holding gain in current cost/nominal dollars.

    g. Operating profit before holding gains and losses in current cost/nominal dollars of June 30 purchasing power.

    h. Operating profit before holding gains and losses in current cost/constant dollars of December 31 purchasing power.

    i. Realized holding gain or loss in current cost/constant dollars of June 30 purchasing power.

    j. Realized holding gain or loss in current cost/constant dollars of December 31 purchasing power.

    k. Unrealized holding gain or loss in current cost/constant dollars of December 31 purchasing power.

Problems and Cases

19. *Preparing historical cost/constant dollar financial statements—Year 1.* The financial statements of the Hargrave Corporation for Year 1, its first year of operations, are presented in Exhibits D.7 and D.8.

    Indices of the general price level on various dates were as follows (round dollar amounts to the nearest dollar).

(1) On January 1, Year 1, when common shares were issued	200
(2) When store equipment was acquired	205
(3) When merchandise inventory was acquired	210
(4) When sales were made	220
(5) When selling and administrative costs were incurred	215
(6) When income taxes were incurred	220
(7) On December 31, Year 1	240

    a. Restate the balance sheet on December 31, Year 1, to the general purchasing power of the dollar on December 31, Year 1.

Exhibit D.7
HARGRAVE CORPORATION
Balance Sheet
December 31, Year 1

Assets

Cash	$ 70,000
Accounts Receivable	200,000
Merchandise Inventory	350,000
Store Equipment	400,000
Less: Accumulated Depreciation	(40,000)
Total Assets	$980,000

Equities

Accounts Payable	$480,000
Common Shares	250,000
Contributed Surplus	50,000
Retained Earnings	200,000
Total Equities	$980,000

Exhibit D.8
HARGRAVE CORPORATION
Income Statement
for Year 1

Sales Revenue		$930,000
Less: Cost of Goods Sold		450,000
Gross Profit		$480,000
Less: Operating Expenses		
Depreciation	$ 40,000	
Selling and Administrative	110,000	150,000
Net Income before Income Tax		$330,000
Less: Income Tax		130,000
Net Income		$200,000

    b. Restate the income statement for Year 1 to the general purchasing power of the dollar on December 31, Year 1. Include a separate calculation of the monetary gain or loss.

20. *Preparing current cost financial statement in nominal and constant dollars.* Refer to the data for Hargrave Corporation in Problem (**19**). Assuming the following additional information about current cost for Year 1:

	December 31, Year 1
Merchandise Inventory	$410,000
Store Equipment (net)	396,000

	For Year 1
Cost of Goods Sold	$490,000
Depreciation Expense	42,000

    a. Prepare an income statement for Year 1 and a balance sheet as of December 31, Year 1, for Hargrave Corporation in terms of current cost and nominal dollars.

    b. Repeat part (**a**), but state all amounts in terms of constant December 31, Year 1, dollars. Assume that sales were made evenly over the year.

21. *Preparing historical cost/constant dollar financial statements — Year 2.* The financial statements of the Hargrave Corporation [see Problem (**19**)] for Year 2, its second year of operations, are presented in Exhibits D.9 and D.10.

Exhibit D.9
HARGRAVE CORPORATION
Balance Sheet
December 31, Year 2

Assets

Cash	$ 110,000
Accounts Receivable	210,000
Merchandise Inventory (based on FIFO)	500,000
Store Equipment	400,000
Less: Accumulated Depreciation	(80,000)
Total Assets	$1,140,000

Equities

Accounts Payable	$ 490,000
Common Shares	250,000
Contributed Surplus	50,000
Retained Earnings	350,000
Total Equities	$1,140,000

Exhibit D.10
HARGARVE CORPORATION
Income Statement for Year 2

Sales Revenue		$1,170,000
Less: Cost of Goods Sold		550,000
Gross Profit		$ 620,000
Less: Operating Expenses		
Depreciation	$ 40,000	
Selling and Administrative	150,000	$ 190,000
Net Income before Income Tax		$ 430,000
Less: Income Tax		170,000
Net Income		$ 260,000

Indices of the general price level on various dates during Year 2 were as follows (round conversion factors to two decimal places; for example, $225/200 = 1.13$).

(1) On January 1, Year 2	240
(2) When merchandise inventory was acquired	245
(3) When sales were made	260
(4) When selling and administrative costs were incurred	255
(5) When dividend was declared and paid	280
(6) When income taxes were incurred	220
(7) On December 31, Year 2	280

    a. Restate the balance sheet on December 31, Year 2, in terms of constant dollars of December 31, Year 2, purchasing power.

b. Restate the income statement for the year ending December 31, Year 2, in terms of constant dollars of December 31, Year 2, purchasing power. Include a separate calculation of the purchasing power gain or loss.

c. Prepare an analysis of changes in retained earnings for the year ending December 31, Year 2, before and after restatement to a constant dollar basis. The January 1, Year 2, balance in retained earnings, restated to constant dollars of December 31, Year 2, purchasing power is C$293,375.

22. *Interpreting income statements restated for changing prices.* Exhibit D.1 presents a skeleton four-column income statement under four accounting valuation and measurement bases. Various lines of these income statements are denoted by letter. Using these letters, identify the line or lines on the income statement being described in each of the following cases.

a. A firm wishes to know whether its selling prices are sufficiently high to cover the cost of replacing goods and services consumed during the period.

b. A firm wishes to know how much of its conventional net income is due to operating advantages in the markets it serves and how much is due to acquiring assets prior to increases in their replacement cost.

Exhibit D.11

	Historical Cost/ Nominal Dollars (1)	Historical Cost/ Constant Dollars (2)	Current Cost/ Nominal Dollars (3)	Current Cost/ Constant Dollars (4)
Sales	A	E	J	P
Expenses	B	F	K	Q
Operating Income	C	G	L	R
Realized Holding Gains and Losses	—	—	M	S
Unrealized Holding Gains and Losses	—	—	N	T
Purchasing Power Gain or Loss	—	H	—	U
Net Income	D	I	O	V

c. A firm wishes to know whether the costs of replacing its inventory and depreciable assets have increased faster or slower during the current period than changes in the general price level.

d. A firm's dividend policy is to pay out the maximum dividend without impairing operating capacity. Which item in Exhibit D.11 should form the basis for this firm's dividend decisions?

e. When there have been no changes in either specific or general prices, these net income amounts will be the same.

f. When specific prices have changed at the same rate as the general price level, these measures of operating income will be the same.

g. When specific prices of inventory, property, plant, and equipment have increased at a faster rate than the general price level, what will be the relation between M and S?

h. Respond to part (**g**), assuming that specific prices have increased at a slower rate than the general price level.

i. Respond to part (**g**), assuming that specific prices have increased at the same rate as the general price level.

j. If sales and cost incurrences occur evenly over the year and the constant dollar date is mid-year dollars, what should be the relation between L and R?

k. If sales and cost incurrences occur evenly over the year and the constant dollar date is year-end dollars, what should be the relation between L and R assuming both are positive?

l. During inflation, a firm with a relatively large net debt-equity ratio will find this item to be a positive amount.

23. *Interpreting financial statements restated for changing prices.* Refer to the supplementary information on the impact of changing prices presented for General Products Limited in Appendix A. Respond to each of the following questions.

a. Was General Products Limited likely to have been in a net monetary asset position or a net monetary liability position during 1988? Explain.

b. How much of the conventional income before income taxes, as reported in historical cost/nominal dollars of $2,493 million for 1988, is composed of realized holding gains on inventory items sold and depreciable assets used?

c. During 1988, did the general price level increase at a faster or a slower rate than the specific prices of depreciable assets and inventory? Explain.

d. What is the amount of unrealized holding gain or loss at December 31, 1988. on inventory and on property, plant, and equipment?

Glossary[1]

A

AAA. *American Accounting Association.*

Abacus. A scholarly journal containing articles on theoretical aspects of accounting. Published twice a year by the Sydney University Press, Sydney, Australia.

abatement. The reduction of an *expenditure*. The deduction of minor *revenues* incidental to an operation in calculating the cost of the operation. A tax reduction provided for under statute.

abnormal spoilage. Actual spoilage exceeding that expected to occur if operations are normally efficient. Usual practice treats this cost as an *expense* of the period rather than as a *product cost*. Contrast with *normal spoilage*.

aboriginal cost. In public utility accounting, the *acquisition cost* of an *asset* incurred by the first *entity* devoting that asset to public use. Most public utility regulation is based on aboriginal cost. If it were not, then public utilities could exchange assets among themselves at ever-increasing prices in order to raise the rate base and, then, prices based thereon.

absorbed overhead. *Overhead* costs allocated to individual products at some *overhead rate*. See *applied overhead*.

absorption costing. The generally accepted method of *costing* that assigns all types of *manufacturing costs* (direct material and labour as well as fixed and variable overhead) to units produced. Sometimes called "full costing." Contrast with *direct costing*.

accelerated depreciation. Any method of calculating *depreciation* charges where the charges become progressively smaller each period. An example is the *declining balance* method.

acceptance. A written promise to pay that is equivalent to a promissory *note*.

acceptance sampling. The use of a sampling technique whereby an entire population is accepted if and only if the sample contains less than a specified number of disparities.

account. A formal record of an *asset, liability, proprietorship, revenue*, or *expense*, in which the effects of operations or transactions are indicated in terms of money or some other unit of measurement. A statement setting out a summary of the operations or transactions in terms of money between individuals and/or organizations for a stated period.

account form. The form of *balance sheet* where *assets* are shown on the left and *equities* are shown on the right. Contrast with *report form*. See *T-account*.

account payable. A *liability* representing an amount owed to a *creditor*, usually arising from purchase of *merchandise* or materials and supplies; not necessarily due or past due. Normally, a *current liability*.

account receivable. A claim against a *debtor* usually arising from sales or services rendered; not necessarily due or past due. Normally, a *current asset*.

accountability centre. See *responsibility centre*.

accountancy. Accounting theory and practice as a whole. The accounting profession. The British word for *accounting*.

accountant. A person skilled in accounting. Often used to refer to *public accountant* (colloq.).

Accountants' Index. A publication of the *AICPA* that indexes, in detail, the accounting literature of the period.

accounting. An *information system* conveying information about a specific *entity*. The information is in financial terms and is restricted to information that can be made reasonably precise.

[1]The *italicized* words or terms, or variants of them, are themselves explained elsewhere in the Glossary. This Glossary defines some terms that are not included in text.

accounting changes. A change in (1) an *accounting policy* (such as a switch from the ''taxes payable'' to the ''tax allocation'' basis of accounting for income taxes), (2) an accounting estimate (such as estimated useful lives or salvage value of depreciable assets and estimates of *warranty* costs or *uncollectible accounts*), and (3) the reporting *entity*. Changes of type (1) should be disclosed. The cumulative effect of the change on *retained earnings* at the start of the period during which the change was made should be included as reported earnings for the period of change. Changes of type (2) should be treated as affecting only the period of change and, if necessary, future periods. The reasons for changes of type (3) should be disclosed and, in statements reporting on operations of the period of the change, the effect of the change on all other periods reported on for comparative purposes should also be shown. Changes of type (1) are treated like changes of type (3). That is, for these changes all statements shown for prior periods must be restated to show the effect of adopting the change for those periods as well. See *all-inclusive concept* and *accounting errors*.

accounting concepts. The basic assumptions derived from the economic and social environment including the uses to which accounting information is put, which underlie the development of accounting principles.

accounting control. The *accounting procedures* used as a check on the reliability of the information contained in accounting records, e.g., the use of a *control* to balance the total of the accounts in a *subsidiary ledger*.

accounting conventions. A phrase of vague meaning encompassing *accounting postulates, accounting principles* and/or *accounting procedures*.

accounting cycle. The sequence of accounting procedures starting with *journal entries* for various transactions and events and ending with the *financial statements* or, perhaps, the *post-closing trial balance*.

accounting deficiency. A failure to adhere to generally accepted *accounting principles* or to disclose essential information in *financial statements*. (Compare *auditing deficiency*.)

accounting entity. See *entity*.

accounting equation. *Assets = Equities. Assets = Liabilities + Owners' Equity.*

accounting errors. Arithmetic errors and misapplications of *accounting* policies in previously published financial statements that are corrected in the current period with direct *debits* or *credits* to *retained earnings*. In this regard, they are treated like *prior-period adjustments*. See *accounting changes* and contrast with changes in accounting estimates as described there.

accounting event. Any occurrence that is recorded as a transaction in the accounting records.

accounting income. In accounting for income taxes, the

amount on which the total income tax expense is based. The amount is calculated by taking income before income taxes and extraordinary items, adding or deducting extraordinary items before related income taxes, and then adjusting for any permanent differences between accounting and taxable income. (Compare *taxable income*.)

accounting manual. A detailed description of the accounting policies followed by an organization, usually including a description of the official procedures, forms and responsibilities.

accounting methods. *Accounting principles*. Procedures for carrying out accounting policies.

accounting period. The time period for which *financial statements* that measure *flows*, such as the *income statement* and the *statement of changes in financial position*, are prepared. Should be clearly identified on the financial statements. See *interim statements*.

accounting policies. The specific accounting principles and the methods used in their application that are selected by an enterprise as being the most appropriate in the circumstances.

accounting postulates. The basic assumptions derived from observations of the economic and social environment, including the uses to which accounting information is put, which are pertinent to the development of accounting principles.

accounting principle(s). The rules which give guidance in the measurement, classification and interpretation of economic information and communication of the results through the medium of financial statements. A rule accepted as the only accounting rule to be followed in given circumstances, as opposed to an accounting practice which may be one of several alternatives.

accounting procedures. See *accounting principles*, but usually this term refers to the methods required to implement accounting principles.

accounting rate of return. Income for a period divided by average investment during the period. Based on income rather than discounted cash flows and, hence, is a poor decision-making aid or tool. See *ratio*.

accounting records. The formal books of account and supporting documentary evidence.

The Accounting Review. Scholarly publication of the *American Accounting Association*, which appears four times a year.

accounting standards. *Accounting principles*.

accounting system. The procedures for collecting and summarizing financial data in a firm.

Accounting Trends and Techniques. An annual publication of the *AICPA* that surveys the reporting practices of

600 large corporations. It presents tabulations of specific practices, terminology, and disclosures along with illustrations taken from individual annual reports.

accounting unit. An organization, or a department, section, or branch for which a separate set of accounts is maintained.

accounts receivable turnover. *Net sales* on account for a period divided by the average balance of net accounts receivable. See *ratio*.

accretion. Increase in economic worth through physical change, usually said of a natural resource such as an orchard, caused by natural growth. Contrast with *appreciation*.

accrual. Recognition of an *expense* (or *revenue*) and the related *liability* (or *asset*) that is caused by an *accounting event*, frequently by the passage of time, and that is not signaled by an explicit cash transaction. For example, the recognition of interest expense or revenue (or wages, salaries, or rent) at the end of a period even though no explicit cash transaction is made at that time. Cash flow occurs after accounting recognition; contrast with *deferral*.

accrual basis of accounting. The method of recognizing *revenues* as *goods* are sold (or delivered) and as *services* are rendered, independent of the time when cash is received. *Expenses* are recognized in the period when the related revenue is recognized independent of the time when when cash is paid out. Contrast with the *cash basis of accounting*. See *accrual* and *deferral*. The basis would more correctly be called "accural/deferral" accounting.

accrued. Said of a *revenue* (*expense*) that has been earned (recognized) even though the related *receivable* (*payable*) is not yet due. This adjective should not be used as part of an account title. Thus, we prefer to use Interest Receivable (Payable) as the account title, rather than Accrued Interest Receivable (Payable). See *matching convention*. See *accrual*.

accrued actuarial obligation. The portion of the actuarial present value of pension plan benefits not provided for by future normal costs.

accrued asset. A developing but not yet enforceable claim against another person which is accumulating with the passage of time or the rendering of service. It arises from the sale of services (including the use of money) which at the date of accounting have been only partly performed, are not yet billable and have not been paid for.

accrued expense. An expense which has been incurred in an accounting period but for which there is no enforceable claim in that accounting period by the person who rendered the service. It arises from the purchase of services (including the use of money) which at the date of accounting have been only partly performed, are not yet billable and have not been paid for.

accrued liability. A developing but not yet enforceable claim by another person, which is accumulating with the passage of time or the receipt of service. It arises from the purchase of services (including the use of money) which at the date of accounting have been only partly performed, are not yet billable and have not been paid for.

accrued payable. A *payable* usually resulting from the passage of time. For example, *salaries* and *interest* accrue as time passes. See *accrued*.

accrued receivable. A *receivable* usually resulting from the passage of time. See *accrued*.

accrued revenue. Revenue which has been earned in an accounting period but for which there is no enforceable claim in that accounting period against the person for whom the service was rendered. It arises from the sale of services (including the use of money) which at the date of accounting have been only partly performed, are not yet billable, and have not been paid for.

accumulated depletion. The total to date of the periodic depletion charges relating to wasting assets since the assets were placed in use.

accumulated depreciation. A preferred title for the *contra-asset* account that shows the sum of *depreciation* charges on an asset since it was acquired.

accurate presentation. The qualitative accounting objective suggesting that information reported in financial statements should correspond as precisely as possible with the economic effects underlying transactions and events. See *fair presentation* and *full disclosure*.

acid test ratio. Sum of (*cash, current marketable securities*, and *receivables*) divided by *current liabilities*. Some nonliquid receivables may be excluded from the numerator. Often called the *quick ratio*. See *ratio*.

acquired share. A share purchased by the issuing company and available for resale by that company. Compare *cancelled share*.

acquisition cost. Of an *asset*, the net *invoice* price plus all *expenditures* to place and ready the asset for its intended use. The other expenditures might include legal fees, transportation charges, and installation costs.

acquisition equation. An equation reflecting a business combination, in which the net assets brought into the combination represent one side of the equation and the consideration given represents the other side.

AcSC. Accounting Standards Committee of the *CICA*. Formerly, the Accounting Research Committee.

activity accounting. *Responsibility accounting*.

activity-based depreciation. *Production method of depreciation*.

actual cost (basis). *Acquisition* or *historical cost*. Contrast with *standard cost*.

actual costing. Method of allocating costs to products using actual *direct materials,* actual *direct labor,* and actual *factory overhead.* Contrast with *normal costing* and *standard cost system.*

actuarial. Usually said of computations or analyses that involve both *compound interest* and probabilities, such as the computation of the *present value* of a life-contingent annuity. Sometimes the term is used if only one of the two is involved.

actuarial assumption. An assumption as to the occurrence of future events that may affect pension or insurance costs, such as: mortality, withdrawal, disablement and retirement; rates of investment earnings and asset appreciation or loss; changes in levels of compensation and of social security benefits.

actuarial cost methods. Methods used by actuaries for allocating costs to particular periods. Such methods include computations involving *compound interest*, retirement, and mortality estimates.

actuarial valuation. A periodic assessment of a pension plan consisting of: a valuation of assets held, an estimate of the actuarial present value of benefits to be paid, experience gain (loss) and an estimate of the required future contributions.

adequate disclosure. *Fair presentation* of *financial statements* requires *disclosure* of *material* items. This *auditing standard* does not, however, require publicizing all information detrimental to a company. For example, the company may be threatened with a lawsuit and disclosure might seem to require a *debit* to a *loss* account and a *credit* to an *estimated liability.* But the mere making of this entry might adversely affect the actual outcome of the suit. Such entries need not be made, although impending suits should be disclosed.

adjunct account. An *account* that accumulates additions to another account. For example, Premium on Bonds Payable is adjunct to the liability Bonds Payable; the effective liability is the sum of the two account balances at a given date. Contrast with *contra account.*

adjusted acquisition (historical) cost. Cost adjusted to a *constant dollar amount* to reflect *general price level changes.* See also *book value.*

adjusted bank balance of cash. The *balance* shown on the statement from the bank plus or minus amounts, such as for unrecorded deposits or outstanding cheques, to reconcile the bank's balance with the correct cash balance. See *adjusted book balance of cash.*

adjusted basis. The *basis* used to compute gain or loss for tax purposes on disposition of an *asset.* Also, see *book value.*

adjusted book balance of cash. The *balance* shown in the firm's account for cash in bank plus or minus amounts, such as for *notes* collected by the bank or bank service charges, to reconcile the account balance with the correct cash balance. See *adjusted bank balance of cash.*

adjusted trial balance. *Trial balance* taken after *adjusting entries* but before *closing entries.* Contrast with *pre-* and *post-closing trail balance.* See *unadjusted trial balance* and *work sheet.*

adjusting entry. An entry made at the end of an *accounting period* to record a *transaction* or other *accounting event,* which for some reason has not been recorded or has been improperly recorded during the accounting period. An entry to update the accounts. See *work sheet.*

adjustment. A change in an *account* produced by an *adjusting* entry. Sometimes the term is used to refer to the process of restating *financial statement* amounts to *constant dollars.*

administrative expense. An *expense* related to the enterprise as a whole as contrasted to expenses related to more specific functions such as manufacturing or selling.

admission of partner. Legally, when a new partner joins a *partnership*, the old partnership is dissolved and a new partnership comes into being. In practice, however, the old accounting records may be kept in use and the accounting entries reflect the manner in which the new partner joined the firm. If the new partner merely purchases the interest of another partner, the only accounting is to change the name for one capital amount. If the new partner contributes *assets* and *liabilities* to the partnership, then the new assets must be recognized with debits and the liabilities and other source of capital, with credits. See *bonus method.*

ad valorem. A method of levying a tax or duty on goods by using their estimated value as the tax base.

advances from (by) customers. A preferred term for the *liability* account representing *receipts* of *cash* in advance of delivering the *goods* or rendering the *service* (that will cause *revenue* to be recognized). Sometimes called "deferred revenue" or "deferred income."

advances to affiliates. *Loans* by one *associated company* to another. Frequently combined with "investment in subsidiary" as "investments and advances to subsidiary" and shown as a *noncurrent asset* on the parent *balance sheet.* These advances are eliminated in *consolidated financial statements.*

advances to suppliers. A preferred term for *disbursements* of cash in advance of receiving *assets* or *services.*

adverse opinion. An *auditor's opinion* stating that the financial statements are not fair or are not in accord with *GAAP.*

affiliated company. A company that directly or indirectly, through one or more intermediaries, controls or is controlled by or is under common control with, another company. Syn. for *associated company.* A company related to another company in a manner defined by legislation for particular purposes.

after closing. *Post closing*; said of a *trial balance* at the end of the period.

aftercost. Said of *expenditures* to be made subsequent to *revenue* recognition. For example, *expenditures* for *repairs* under warranty are aftercosts. Proper recognition of aftercosts involves a debit to expense at the time of the sale and a credit to an *estimated liability*. When the liability is discharged, the debit is to the estimated liability and the credit is to the assets consumed.

agency fund. An account for *assets* received by governmental units in the capacity of trustee or agent.

agency theory. A branch of economics relating the behavior of principals (such as owner nonmanagers or bosses) and their *agents* (such as nonowner managers or subordinates). The principal assigns responsibility and authority to the agent, but the agent has his or her own risks and preferences different from those of the principal. The principal is unable to observe all activities of the agent. Thus the principal must be careful about the kinds of observations of or reports sought from the agent, perhaps through an independent *auditor*, and the sorts of incentive contracts that the principal makes with the agent.

agent. One authorized to transact business, including executing contracts, for another.

aging accounts receivable. The process of classifying *accounts receivable* by the time elapsed since the claim came into existence for the purpose of estimating the amount of uncollectible accounts receivable as of a given date. See *sales, estimated uncollectible accounts* and *allowance for doubtful accounts.*

aging schedule. A listing of *accounts receivable,* classified by age, used in *aging account receivable.*

AICPA. American Institute of Certified Public Accountants. The national organization that represents CPAs. It oversees the writing and grading of the Uniform CPA Examination. Each state, however, sets its own requirements for becoming a CPA in that state. See *certified public accountant.*

all capital earnings rate. *Rate of return on assets.*

all financial resources. All *assets* less all *liabilities*. Sometimes the *statement of changes in financial position* explains the changes in all financial resources rather than only the changes in *working capital.*

all-financial-resources concept. The view that a statement of changes in financial position is more informative and useful when it reports all additions of financial resources to the entity and all distribution of resources as well as changes in the composition of resources. See *statement of changes in financial position.*

all-inclusive (income) concept. Under this concept, no distinction is drawn between *operating* and *nonoperating revenues* and *expenses*; thus the only entries to retained earnings are for *net income* and *dividends*. Under this concept all income, *gains* and *losses* are reported in the *income statement*; thus, events reported as *prior-period adjustments* and as *corrections of errors* are included in net income.

all-inclusive income statement. A form of financial statement in which all transactions affecting the net increase or decrease in *owner's equity* during the period, except capital transactions, are shown in the *income statement*. (Compare *current operating performance concept.*)

allocate. To spread a *cost* from one *account* to several accounts, to several products, or activities, or to several periods.

allocation of income taxes. See *deferred income tax.*

allotted share. A share for which a subscription has been received and accepted by the directors.

allowance. A balance sheet *contra account* generally used for *receivables* and depreciable assets. See *sales (or purchase) allowance* for another use of this term.

allowance for doubtful accounts. See *allowance for uncollectibles.*

allowance for funds used during construction. One principle of public utility regulation and rate setting is that customers should pay the full costs of producing the services (e.g., electricity) that they use — nothing more and nothing less. Thus a public utility is even more careful than other businesses to capitalize into an *asset account* the full costs, but no more, of producing a new electric power generating plant. One of the costs of building a new plant is the *interest* cost on money tied up during construction. If *funds* are explicitly borrowed by an ordinary business, the journal entry for interest of $1,000 is typically:

Interest Expense	$1,000	
Interest Payable		$1,000

Interest expense for the period.

If the firm is a public utility constructing a new plant (or one of a group of ordinary businesses that for whatever reason follows the same practice in constructing new plants), then another entry would be made:

Construction Work in progress	$750	
Interest Expense		$750

Capitalize relevant portion of interest relating to construction work in progress into the asset account.

The cost of the *plant asset* is increased; when the plant is used, *depreciation* is charged; the interest will become an expense through the depreciation process in the later period of use, not currently as the interest is paid. Thus the full cost of the electricity generated during a given period is reported as expense in that period.

But suppose, as is common, that the electric utility does not explicitly borrow the funds, but uses some of its own funds, including funds raised from shares as well as from debt. Even though there is no explicit interest expense, there is the *opportunity cost* of the funds. Put another way, the cost of the plant under construction is not less in an economic sense just because the firm used its own cash, rather than borrow. The public utility using its own funds, on which $750 of interest would be payable if the funds had been explicitly borrowed, will make the following entry:

Construction Work in progress	$750
Allowance for Funds Used During Construction	$750
Recognition of interest, an opportunity cost on own funds used.	

The allowance account is a form of *revenue*, to appear on the income statement, and will be closed to Retained Earnings, increasing it. On the *funds statement*, it is an income or revenue item not producing funds and so must be subtracted from net income in deriving *funds provided by operations*.

allowance for uncollectibles (accounts receivable). A *contra* to Accounts Receivable that shows the estimated amount of *accounts receivable* that will not be collected. When such an allowance is used, the actual *write-off* of specific accounts receivable (debit allowance, *credit* specific account) does not affect *revenue* or *expense* at the time of the write-off. The revenue reduction is recognized when the allowance is credited; the amount of the credit to the allowance may be based on a percentage of sales on account for a period of time or determined from *aging accounts receivable*. This contra account enables an estimate to be shown of the amount of receivables that will be collected without identifying specific uncollectible accounts. See *allowance method*.

allowance method. A method of attempting to *match* all *expenses* of a transaction with its associated *revenues*. Usually involves a debit to expense and credit to an *estimated liability*, such as for estimated warranty expenditures, or a debit to a revenue (*contra*) account and a credit to an asset (*contra*) account, such as for uncollectible accounts. See *allowance for uncollectibles* for further explanation. When the allowance method is used for *sales discounts,* sales are recorded at *gross invoice* prices (not reduced by the amounts of discounts made available). An estimate of the amount of discounts to be taken is debited to a *revenue contra account* and *credited* to an allowance account, shown contra to *accounts receivable*.

American Accounting Association (AAA). An organization primarily for academic accountants, but open to all interested in accounting. It publishes *The Accounting Review*.

American Institute of Certified Public Accountants. See *AICPA*.

amortization. Strictly speaking, the process of liquidating or extinguishing ("bringing to death") a *debt* with a series of payments to the *creditor* (or to a *sinking fund*). From that usage has evolved a related use involving the accounting for the payments themselves: "amortization schedule" for a mortgage which is a table showing the allocation between *interest* and *principal*. The term has come to mean writing off ("liquidating") the cost of an asset. In this context it means the general process of *allocating acquisition cost* of an asset to either the periods of benefit as *expenses* or to *inventory* accounts as *product costs*. Called *depreciation* for *plant assets*, *depletion* for *wasting assets* (natural resources), and "amortization" for *intangibles*.

amortized cost. The original cost of an asset less any portion amortized or treated as an expense or loss.

amortized value. The value at which an asset has been recorded in the books less any portion amortized or treated as an expense or loss.

analysis of changes in working capital accounts. The *statement of changes in financial position*, with *funds* defined as *working capital*, explains the causes of the changes in *working capital* during a period. This part of the statement, which may appear in footnotes, shows the net changes in the specific working capital accounts that have been explained in the main section of the statement.

analysis of variances. See *variance analysis*.

analytical auditing. An auditing technique aimed at assessing the adequacy of an organization's accounting systems and internal control, through the use of flow charts and in-depth testing of a limited number of transactions.

annual report. A report for shareholders and other interested parties prepared once a year; includes a *balance sheet*, an *income statement*, a *statement of changes in financial position*, a reconciliation of changes in *owner's equity* accounts, a *summary of significant accounting principles*, other explanatory notes, the *auditor's report*, and, perhaps, comment from management about the year's events. See *financial statements*.

annuitant. One who receives an *annuity*.

annuity. A series of payments, usually made at equally spaced time intervals.

annuity certain. An *annuity* payable for a definite number of periods. Contrast with *contingent annuity*.

annuity due. An *annuity* whose first payment is made at the start of period 1 (or at the end of period 0). Contrast with *annuity in arrears*.

annuity in advance. An *annuity due*.

annuity in arrears. An *ordinary annuity* whose first payment occurs at the end of the first period.

annuity method of depreciation. See *compound interest depreciation.*

antidilutive. Said of a *potentially dilutive security* that will increase *earnings per share* if it is *exercised* or *converted* into common stock. In computing *basic* and *fully diluted earnings per share*, antidilutive securities may not be assumed to be exercised or converted and hence do not affect reported earnings per share in a given period.

application of funds. Any transaction that reduces *funds* (however "funds" is defined). A *use of funds.* Since the *CICA Handbook* defined funds as cash and cash equivalents instead of working capital, this term is seldom used anymore. Similarly, the term funds statement has given way to statement of changes in financial position or cash-flow statement.

applied cost. A *cost* that has been *allocated* to a department, product, or activity; need not be based on actual costs incurred.

applied overhead. *Overhead costs* charged to departments, products, or activities. See *absorbed overhead.*

appraisal. The process of obtaining a valuation for an *asset* or *liability* that involves expert opinion rather than evaluation of explicit market transactions.

appraisal method of depreciation. The periodic *depreciation* charge is the difference between the beginning and end-of-period appraised value of the *asset* if that difference is positive. If negative, there is no charge. Not generally accepted.

appraisal increase credit, appraisal increment. The credit resulting from an increase in the recorded value of *fixed assets* arising from an *appraisal*. A suitable designation for an appraisal increase would be "Excess of appraised value of fixed assets over cost" (or "over depreciated cost," if that is the case).

appraisal surplus. (*obs.*) Syn. for *appraisal increase credit.*

appreciation. An increase in economic worth caused by rising market prices for an *asset*. Contrast with *accretion.*

appropriated retained earnings. See *retained earnings, appropriated.*

appropriation. In governmental accounting, an *expenditure* authorized for a specific amount, purpose, and time.

appropriation account. In governmental accounting, an account set up to record specific authorizations to spend; it is credited with appropriation amounts. *Expenditures* during the period and *encumbrances* outstanding at the end of the period are closed (debited) to this account at the end of the period.

arbitrage. Strictly speaking, the simultaneous purchase in one market and sale in another of a *security* or commodity in hope of making a *profit* on price differences in the different markets. Often this term is loosely used when the item sold is somewhat different from the item purchased; for example, the sale of *common shares* and the simultaneous purchase of a *convertible bond* that is convertible into identical common shares.

ARC. See AcSC.

arithmetic mean. The total value of a series of items, divided by the number of items in the series.

arm's length. Said of a transaction negotiated by unrelated parties, each acting in his or her own self interest; the basis for a *fair market value* determination. Under income tax legislation, the term has a special meaning.

arrears. Said of *cumulative preferred share dividends* that have not been declared up to the current date. See *annuity in arrears* for another context.

ARS. Accounting Research Study.

articles of association. The internal regulations of a *limited company* incorporated by registration; analogous to the by-laws of a limited company incorporated by letters patent. See *by-laws.*

articles of incorporation. See *instrument of incorporation.*

articulate. Said of the relationship between any operating statement (for example, *income statement* or *statement of changes in financial position*) and *comparative balance sheets,* where the operating statement explains (or reconciles) the change in some major balance sheet category (for example, *retained earnings* or *working capital*).

assess. To value property for the purpose of property taxation; the assessment is determined by the taxing authority. To levy a change on the owner of property for improvements thereto, such as for sewers or sidewalks.

assessed valuation. A dollar amount for real estate or other property used by a government as a basis for levying taxes. The amount may or may not bear some relation to *market value.*

asset. A probable future economic benefit obtained or controlled by a particular entity as a result of past transactions. An asset has three essential characteristics: (a) it embodies a probable future benefit that involves a capacity, singly or in combination with other assets, to contribute directly or indirectly to future net cash inflows, (b) a particular enterprise can obtain the benefit and control others' access to it, and (c) the transaction or other event giving rise to the enterprise's right to or control of the benefit has already occurred. The word "probable" means that which can be reasonably expected or believed but is neither certain nor proved. May be *tangible* or *intangible, short-term* (current) or *long-term* (noncurrent).

asset turnover. Ratio of net sales to average assets. See *ratio.*

assignment of accounts receivable. Transfer of the legal ownership of an *account receivable* through its sale. Contrast with *pledging* accounts receivable where the receivables serve as *collateral* for a *loan*.

associated company. A company operating either wholly or partially in cooperation with another by reason of common control, contract or agreement. (Compare *affiliated company*.) A company related to another company in a manner defined by legislation for particular purposes.

at par. Said of a *bond* or *preferred share* issued or selling at its *face amount*.

attachment. The laying claim to the *assets* of a borrower or debtor by a lender or creditor when the borrower has failed to pay debts on time.

attest function. The expression of a professional opinion on *financial statements* by an independent *public accountant*.

attribute measured. When making physical measurements, such as of a person, one needs to decide the units with which to measure, such as inches or centimetres or pounds or grams. One chooses the attribute — height or weight — independently of the measuring unit — English or metric. In conventional accounting the attribute measured is *historical cost* and the measuring unit is *nominal dollars*. Some theorists argue that accounting is more useful when the attribute measured is *current cost*. Others argue that accounting is more useful when the measuring unit is *constant dollars*. Some, including us, think both changes from conventional accounting should be made. The attribute historical cost can be measured in nominal dollars or in constant dollars. The attribute current cost can also be measured in nominal dollars or constant dollars. Choosing between two attributes and two measuring units implies four different accounting systems. Each of these four has its uses.

attribute(s) sampling. The use of a sampling technique in which each item selected is assessed on the basis of whether it has a particular qualitative characteristic in order to determine the rate of occurrence of this characteristic in the population. See also *estimation sampling*. Compare *variables sampling*.

audit. An examination of evidential matter to determine the reliability of a record or assertion or to evaluate compliance with rules or policies or with conditions of an agreement. In connection with financial statements or other financial information, an examination of accounting records and other supporting evidence for the purpose of expressing an opinion as to whether such statements or information are presented fairly in accordance with generally accepted accounting principles. See *auditor's report*.

audit committee. A committee of directors of a *corporation* whose specific responsibility is to review the annual *financial statements* before submission to the board of directors. The committee generally acts as liaison between the *auditor* and the board of directors and its activities may include the review of nomination of the auditors, overall scope of the audit, results of the audit, internal financial controls and financial information for publication.

audit evidence. The source documents, accounting records and all other information that an auditor uses in forming a professional opinion.

audit program. The procedures followed by the *auditors* in carrying out the *audit*.

audit software. Computer programs used as an audit tool.

audit trail. A reference accompanying an *entry*, or *posting*, to an underlying source or document. A good audit trail is essential for efficiently checking the accuracy of accounting entries and is an important part of a system of internal control. If adequate audit trails exist, every amount in the financial statements should be able to be traced back to the source transactions and every transaction should be able to be traced to its ultimate disposition in a financial statement balance. See *cross-reference*.

auditing deficiency. Anything that precludes the issue of an unqualified auditor's report on the financial statements. The deficiency may be a problem with GAAP on an inability of the auditor to gather all the necessary evidence to formulate a conclusion.

auditing standards. A set of eight standards promulgated by the *CICA*, including one general standard, three standards of field work, and four standards of reporting. According to the *CICA*, these standards "relate to the quality of the work to be performed, to the objectives to be attained by the use of the procedures undertaken, and to the suitability of the auditor's report," rather than to specific auditing procedures.

auditing techniques. The methods of obtaining *audit evidence*, e.g. confirmation, observation and analysis.

auditor. One who checks the accuracy, fairness, and general acceptability of accounting records and statements and then *attests* to them.

auditor's opinion. *Auditor's report*.

auditor's report. The formal document in which an auditor expresses an opinion as to whether *financial statements* of the organization present fairly its position as at a given date and the results of its operations for the period ended on that date in accordance with generally accepted accounting principles. Any report by an auditor in accordance with the terms of his or her appointment.

authorized capital stock. The number of *shares* of stock that can be issued by a company.

average. The arithmetic mean of a set of numbers; obtained by summing the items and dividing by the number of items.

average collection period of receivables. See *ratio*.

average-cost flow assumption. An *inventory flow assumption* where the cost of units is the *weighted average* cost of the *beginning inventory* and purchases. See *inventory equation*.

average tax rate. The rate found by dividing *income tax expense* by *net income* before taxes. Contrast with *marginal tax rate, statutory tax rate*.

average yield. The average return from a number of investments. The average return from an investment over a period of time. See *yield to maturity*.

averaging. A concept under income tax legislation which mitigates the tax impact of large increases in income received by a taxpayer in a particular year. **General averaging** permits a taxpayer, where income in a taxation year exceeds a defined threshold amount, to calculate the tax or the excess over this amount in a special manner. **Forward averaging** permits a taxpayer to spread certain types of income over a number of future years through the purchase of a special income-averaging annuity contract.

avoidable cost. An *incremental* or *variable cost*. See *programmed cost*.

B

backlog depreciation. In *current cost accounting*, a problem arising from the *accumulated depreciation* on *plant assets*. Consider an *asset* costing $10,000 with a 10-year life depreciated with the *straight-line method*. Assume that a similar asset has a current cost of $10,000 at the end of the first year but $12,000 at the end of the second year. Assume that the depreciation charge is based on the average current cost during the year, $10,000 for the first year and $11,000 for the second. The depreciation charge for the first year is $1,000 and for the second is $1,100 (= .10 × $11,000), so the *accumulated depreciation account* is $2,100 after 2 years. Note that at the end of the second year, 20 percent of the asset's future benefits have been used, so the accounting records based on current costs must show a *net book value* of $9,600 (= .80 × $12,000), which would result if accumulated depreciation of $2,400 were subtracted from a current cost of $12,000. But the sum of the depreciation charges has been only $2,100. The *journal entry* to increase the accumulated depreciation account requires a *credit* to that account of $300. The question arises, what account is to be debited? That is the problem of backlog depreciation. Some theorists would *debit* an *income* account and others would *debit* a *balance sheet owners' equity* account without reducing current-period earnings. The answer to the question of what to do with the debit is closely tied to the problem of how *holding gains* are recorded. When the asset account is debited for $2,000 to increase the recorded amount from $10,000 to $12,000, a holding gain or $2,000 must be recorded with a credit. Many theorists believe that whatever account is credited for the holding gains is the same account that should be debited for backlog depreciation. Sometimes called "catch-up depreciation."

bad debt. An *uncollectible account receivable*; see *sales, uncollectible accounts adjustment*.

bad debt expense. See *sales, uncollectible accounts adjustment*.

bad debt recovery. Collection, perhaps partial, of a spe-

cific account receivable previously written off as uncollectible. If the *allowance method* is used, the *credit* is usually to the *allowance* account. If the direct write-off method is used, the credit is to a *revenue account*.

balance. The sum of *debit* entries minus the sum of *credit* entries in an *account*. If positive, the difference is called a debit balance; if negative, a credit balance.

balance sheet. A concise statement of financial position showing *assets, liabilities,* and *owners' equity* in a classified manner and as at a particular moment of time. The balance sheet is a statement of current resources, unexpired costs, liabilities to be met and sources of ownership funds, rather than a statement of economic worth.

balance sheet account. An account that can appear on a balance sheet. A *permanent account*; contrast with *temporary account*.

balance sheet audit. An audit sufficient to provide the basis for an expression of opinion as to whether the balance sheet presents fairly the financial position of the organization, usually without implying any extensive examination of the records of transactions for the period; an examination of position rather than of transactions.

bank balance. The amount of the balance in a chequing account shown on the *bank statement*. Compare with *adjusted bank balance* and *bank reconciliation schedule*.

bank confirmation. A statement obtained by an auditor from the client's banker reporting the position, at a stated date, of the client's bank accounts, loans and other liabilities, security held against liabilities and other matters.

bank discount. The amount deducted by a bank from the face amount or maturity value of a note, representing interest paid in advance.

bank prime rate. See *prime rate*.

bank reconciliation. A schedule that shows how the difference between the book balance of the cash in bank account and the bank's statement can be explained. Takes into account the amount of such items as cheques issued that have not cleared or deposits that have not been recorded by the bank as well as errors made by the bank or the firm.

bank statement. A statement sent by the bank to a chequing account customer showing deposits, cheques cleared, and service charges for a period, usually one month.

bankrupt. The legal status of a person who has made an assignment in bankruptcy or against whom a receiving order has been made.

bargain purchase option. A provision of a lease allowing the lessee, at its option, to purchase a leased property for a price which is sufficiently lower than the expected fair value of the property, at the date the option becomes exercisable, that exercise of the option appears, at the inception of the lease, to be reasonably assured.

bargain renewal option. A provision of a lease allowing the lessee, at its option, to renew the lease for a rental which is sufficiently lower than the expected fair rental of the property, at the date the option becomes exercisable, that exercise of the option appears, at the inception of the lease, to be reasonably assured.

barter transaction. An exchange of goods or services for other goods or services rather than for cash.

base stock method. A method of inventory valuation that assumes that there is a minimum normal or base stock of goods that must be kept on hand at all times for effective continuity of operations. This base quantity is valued at *acquisition cost* of the inventory on hand in the earliest period when inventory was on hand.

basic earnings per share. The amount of current earnings attributable to each *common share* outstanding during the period.

basis. *Acquisition cost*, or some substitute therefore, of an asset used in computing gain or loss on disposition or retirement. *Attribute measured*.

basket purchase. Purchase of a group of assets for a single price; *costs* must be assigned to each of the assets so that the individual item can be recorded in the *accounts*.

batch processing. A technique whereby similar items are collected into groups (batches) for processing by a computer. Compare *real-time processing*.

bear. One who believes that security prices will fall. A ''bear market'' refers to a time when stock prices are generally declining. Contrast with *bull*.

bearer bond. See *registered bond* for contrast and definition.

beginning inventory. Valuation of *inventory* on hand at the beginning of the accounting period.

beneficial owner. The real owner of an asset, usually a security, title to which is registered in the name of a trustee. Compare *nominal owner*.

benefit based (pension) plan. *Defined benefit (pension) plan*.

best efforts offering. An arrangement between an issuer of securities and an investment dealer, whereby the latter, acting as an agent rather than an underwriter, undertakes to sell as many of the securities as he can on a commission basis. See *underwriter*.

betterment. An *improvement*, usually *capitalized*.

bias. As used in measurement, the tendency of a measure to fall more often on one side than the other of what it represents. Bias in accounting measures means a tendency to be consistently too high or too low.

bid. An offer to purchase, or the amount of the offer.

big bath. A *write-off* of a substantial amount of costs previously treated as *assets*. Usually caused when a corporation drops a line of business that required a large investment but that proved to be unprofitable. Sometimes used to describe a situation where a corporation takes a large write-off in one period in order to free later periods of gradual write-offs of those amounts. In this sense it frequently occurs when there is a change in top management.

bill. An *invoice* of charges and *terms of sale* for *goods* and *services*. Also, a piece of currency.

bill of exchange. An unconditional order in writing, addressed by one person to another, signed by the person giving it, requiring the person to whom it is addressed to pay, on demand or at a fixed or determinable future time, a sum certain in money to or to the order of a specified person, or to bearer.

bill of lading. A memorandum given by a carrier acknowledging the receipt of consigned goods and which serves as a document of title to the goods.

bill of materials. A specification of the quantities of *direct materials* expected to be used to produce a given job or quantity of output.

blocked currency. Currency that by law cannot be withdrawn from the issuing country or exchanged for the currency of another country.

blue chip stock. Shares in a well-established company, normally with a long and satisfactory divided record and other attributes of a safe investment.

board of directors. The governing body of a company elected by the shareholders.

bond. A certificate to show evidence of debt. The term usually implies the assets have been pledged as security. The *par value* is the *principal* or face amount of the bond payable at maturity. The *coupon rate* is the amount of interest payable in one year divided by the principal amount. Coupon bonds have attached to them coupons that can be redeemed at stated dates for interest payments. Normally, bonds carry semiannual coupons.

bond conversion. The act of exchanging *convertible bonds* for *preferred* or *common shares*.

bond discount. From the standpoint of the issuer of a *bond* at the issue date, the excess of the *par value* of a bond over its initial sales price; at later dates the excess of par over the sum of the initial issue price plus the portion of discount already amortized. From the standpoint of a bondholder, the difference between par value and selling price when the bond sells below par.

bond indenture. The contract between an issuer of *bonds* and the bondholders.

bond issue expense. The cost incurred when issuing bonds, including legal fees, cost of pledging security, advertising, selling and printing costs.

bond premium. Exactly parallel to *bond discount* except that the issue price (or current selling price) is higher than *par value*.

bond ratings. Ratings of corporate and *municipal bond* issues by Moody's Investors Service and by Standard & Poor's Corporation, based on the issuer's existing *debt* level, its previous record of payment, the *coupon rate* on the bonds, and the safety of the *assets or revenues* that are committed to paying off *principal* and *interest*. Moody's top rating is Aaa; Standard & Poor's is AAA.

bond redemption. Retirement of *bonds*. A *corporation* acquires its *bonds* from the bondholders. Bonds can be retired at *maturity* or before, either by paying *cash*, exchanging *shares* of *stock* (if the bond is *convertible*), by serial retirement (for *serial bonds*), by setting up a *sinking fund*, or by replacing one bond issue with another (*bond refunding*).

bond refunding. To incur *debt*, usually through the issue of new *bonds*, intending to use the proceeds to retire an *outstanding* bond *issue*.

bond sinking fund. See *sinking fund*.

bond table. A table showing the current price of a *bond* as a function of the *coupon rate*, years to *maturity*, and effective *yield to maturity* (or *effective rate*).

bonus. Premium over normal *wage* or *salary*, paid usually for meritorious performance.

bonus method. When a new partner is admitted to a *partnership* and the new partner is to be credited with *capital* in excess proportion to the amount of *tangible* assets he or she contributes, two methods may be used to recognize this excess, say $10,000. First, $10,000 may be transferred from the old partners to the new one. This is the bonus method. Second, goodwill in the amount of $10,000 may be recognized as an asset with the credit to the new partner's capital account. This is the *goodwill method*. (Notice that the new partner's percentage of total ownership is *not* the same under the two methods.) If the new partner is to be credited with capital in smaller proportion than the amount of contribution, then there will be bonus or goodwill for the old partners.

book. As a verb, to record a transaction. As a noun, usually plural, the *journals* and *ledgers*. As an adjective, see *book value*.

book inventory. An *inventory* amount that results, not from physical count, but from the amount of initial inventory plus *invoice* amounts of purchases less invoice amounts of *requisitions* or withdrawals; implies a perpetual method.

book of original entry. A book of account in which individual operations and transactions are recorded preparatory to summarization and/or posting to ledger accounts. See *journal*.

book value. The amount shown in the books or in the

accounts for any *asset, liability*, or *owners' equity* item. Generally used to refer to the net amount of an asset or group of assets shown in the accounts that record the asset and reductions, such as for *amortization*, in its cost. Of a firm, the excess of total assets over total liabilities. *Net assets*.

book value per share of common shares. Common *shareholders' equity* divided by the number of *common shares outstanding*. See *ratio*.

bookkeeping. The process of analyzing and recording transactions in the accounting records.

boot. The additional money paid or received along with a used item in a trade-in or exchange transaction for another item. See *trade-in transaction*.

borrower. See *loan*.

branch. A sales office or other unit of an enterprise physically separated from the home office of the enterprise but not organized as a legally separate *subsidiary*. The term is rarely used to refer to manufacturing units.

branch accounting. An accounting procedure that enables the financial position and operations of each *branch* to be reported separately but later combined for published statements.

breakeven analysis. See *breakeven chart*.

breakeven chart. Two kinds of breakeven charts are shown here. The charts are based on the information for a month shown below. Revenue is $30 per unit.

Cost Classification	Variable Cost, per Unit	Fixed Cost per Month
Manufacturing costs:		
Direct material	$ 4	—
Direct labour.	9	—
Overhead	4	$3,060
Total manufacturing costs	$17	$3,060
Selling, general, and administrative costs	5	1,740
Total cost	$22	$4,800

The cost-volume-profit graph presents the relationship of changes in volume to the amount of *profit*, or *income*. On such a graph, total *revenue* and total *costs* for each volume level are indicated and profit or loss at any volume can be read directly from the chart. The profit-volume graph does not show revenues and costs but more readily indicates profit (or loss) at various output levels.

Two caveats should be kept in mind about these graphs. Although the curve depicting *variable cost* and total cost is shown as being a straight line for its entire length, it is likely that at very low or very high levels of output, variable cost would probably be different from $22 per unit. The variable cost figure was probably established by studies of operations at some broad central area of production, called the *relevant range*. For very low (or very high) levels of activity, the chart may not be applicable. For this reason, the total cost and profit-loss curves are sometimes shown as dotted lines at lower (or higher) volume levels. Second, this chart is simplified because it assumes a single-product firm. For a multiproduct firm, the horizontal axis would have to be stated in dollars rather than in physical units of output. Breakeven charts for multiproduct firms necessarily assume that constant proportions of the several products are sold, and changes in this mixture as well as in costs or selling prices would invalidate such a chart.

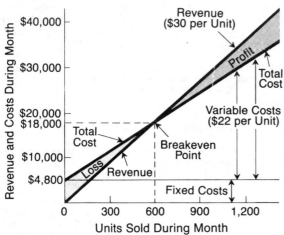

A. Cost-Volume-Profit Graph

B. Profit-Volume Graph

breakeven point. The volume of sales required so that total *revenues* and total *costs* are equal. May be expressed in units (*fixed costs/contribution per unit*) or in sales dollars [selling price per unit × (fixed costs/contribution per unit)].

budget. A financial plan used to estimate the results of future operations. Frequently used to help control future operations.

budget variance. The difference between the total overhead incurred and the total budgeted overhead based on standard volume for work done. See *variance*.

budgetary accounts. In governmental accounting, the accounts that reflect estimated operations and financial condition, as affected by estimated *revenues*, *appropriations*, and *encumbrances*. Contrast to *proprietary accounts*, which record the transactions.

budgetary control. Management of governmental (nongovernmental) unit in accordance with an official (approved) *budget* in order to keep total expenditures within authorized (planned) limits.

budgeted cost. See *standard cost* for definition and contrast.

budgeted statements. *Pro forma* statements prepared before the event or period occurs.

bull. One who believes that security prices will rise. A "bull market" refers to a time when stock prices are generally rising. Contrast with *bear*.

burden. See *overhead costs*.

business combination. Any transaction whereby one economic unit unites with or obtains control over another economic unit, regardless of the legal avenue by which such control is obtained and regardless of the resultant form of the economic unit emerging from the transaction. A conglomerate business combination involves economic units operating in widely different industries. A horizontal business combination involves economic units whose products are similar. A vertical business combination involves economic units where the output can be used as input for the other.

business corporation. A term defined in legislation; broadly, a commercial corporation with share capital, usually excluding a financial and similar institution. See *limited company*.

business entity. *Entity. Accounting entity.*

business interruption insurance. Insurance against continuing expenses and loss of earnings resulting from interruption of business caused by fire or other insured peril.

buyer's market. A condition within an industry or geographic area where the supply of a product or service exceeds the demand; hence trading conditions favour the buyer. Compare *seller's market*.

bylaws. The rules adopted by the shareholders of a company that specify the general methods for carrying out the functions of the corporation.

by-product. A *joint product* whose sales value is so small relative to the sales value of the other joint product(s) that it does not receive normal accounting treatment. The costs assigned to by-products reduce the costs of the main product(s). By-products are allocated a share of joint costs such that the expected gain or loss upon their sale is zero. Thus, by-products are shown in the *accounts* at *net realizable value*.

C

CA. *Chartered Accountant*. Professional designation given to individuals who qualify for membership in the Canadian Institute of Chartered Accountants. A national qualifying set of exams (the UFEs) must be passed and a university degree is required. Members must abide by a professional code of ethics. CAs work as independent auditors in public practice, government, and industry.

call. A right to buy *shares* of a publicly traded corporation at a fixed price during a fixed time span. Contrast with *put*.

call option. The right to buy a specific number of *shares* of a publicly traded corporation during a fixed time span.

call premium. See *callable bond*.

call price. See *callable bond*.

callable bond. A *bond* for which the issuer reserves the right to pay a specific amount, the call price, to retire the obligation before *maturity* date. If the issuer agrees to pay more than the *face amount* of the bond when called, the excess of the payment over the face amount is the call premium.

Canada Pension Plan. A national (except Quebec) federal government retirement plan financed by employee and employer contributions.

Canadian Institute of Chartered Accountants. The national organization that represents *Chartered Accountants* in Canada.

cancelable lease. See *lease*.

canceled share. A share purchased by the issuing company and subsequently cancelled. Compare *acquired share*.

capacity. Stated in units of product, the amount that can be produced per unit of time. Stated in units of input, such as *direct labour* hours, the amount of input that can be used in production per unit of time. This measure of output or input is used in allocating *fixed costs* if the amounts producible are normal, rather than maximum, amounts.

capacity costs. A *fixed cost* incurred to provide a firm with the capability to produce or to sell. Consists of *standby costs* and *enabling costs*. Contrast with *programmed costs*.

capacity variance. Standard fixed *overhead* rate per unit of normal *capacity* (or base activity) times (units of base activity budgeted or planned for a period minus actual units of base activity worked or assigned to product during the period). Often called a "volume variance."

capital. *Owner's equity* in a business. Often used, equally correctly, to mean the total assets of a business. Sometimes used to mean *capital assets*. Sometimes used to mean *cash* or *funds*.

capital asset. An *asset*, whether tangible or intangible, intended for long-term use and held as such. (Compare *fixed asset*.) Any asset of the capital fund (*government accounting*).

capital budget. Plan of proposed outlays for acquiring long-term *assets* and the means of *financing* the acquisition.

capital budgeting. The process of choosing *investment* projects for an enterprise by considering the *present value* of cash flows and deciding how to raise the funds required by the investment.

capital consumption allowance. The term used for *depreciation expense* in national income accounting and the reporting of flows of funds in the economy.

capital contributed in excess of par (or stated) value. A title for the account that shows the amount received by the issuer for *capital stock* in excess of *par* (or *stated*) value. See *contributed surplus*.

capital cost allowance. A deduction, akin to *depreciation*, allowed in computing income for income tax purposes.

capital expenditure (outlay). An *expenditure* to acquire long-term *assets*.

capital gain. Profit on the sale or disposition of a *capital asset*. A gain resulting from a scaling down of business debts as in a reorganization, an arrangement with creditors, or a purchase of the company's own bonds at a discount. Under income tax legislation, the term has a special meaning.

capital lease. A lease that, from the point of view of the lessee, transfers substantially all the benefits and risks incident to ownership of property to the lessee. It is treated by the lessee as both the borrowing of funds and the acquisition of an asset to be amortized. Contrast with *operating lease*.

capital loss. A negative capital gain; see *capital gain*.

capital maintenance concept. A concept for determining income of an enterprise based on the premise that income can only be recognized if capital has been kept intact.

capital rationing. In a *capital budgeting* context, the imposing of constraints on the amounts of total capital expenditures in each period.

capital stock. The ownership interest in a *limited company* authorized by its *instrument of incorporation*. See also *share capital*.

capital structure. The composition of a corporation's equities; the relative proportions of *short-term debt, long-term debt*, and *owners' equity*.

capital surplus. Under certain corporations legislation, the statutory designation used to describe retained earnings appropriated in connection with the redemption of preferred shares under certain circumstances. Obsolete term. See *reserve*. Premium on shares issued. See *contributed surplus*.

capitalization of a corporation. A term used by investment analysts to indicate *shareholders' equity* plus *bonds outstanding*.

capitalization of earnings. The process of estimating the economic worth of a firm by computing the *net present value* of the predicted *net income* (not *cash flows*) of the firm for the future.

capitalization rate. An *interest rate* used to convert a series of payments or receipts or earnings into a single *present value*.

capitalize. To record an *expenditure* that may benefit a future period as an *asset* rather than to treat the expenditure as an *expense* of the period of its occurrence.

career-average pay formula. A formula whereby pension benefits are related to the employee's compensation over the period of service with the employer.

carryback, carryforward, carryover. The use of losses or tax credits in one period to reduce income taxes payable in other periods.

carrying cost. Costs (such as property taxes and insurance) of holding, or storing, *inventory* from the time of purchase until the time of sale or use.

carrying value (amount). *Book value*.

cash. Currency and coins, negotiable cheques, and balances in bank accounts.

cash basis of accounting. In contrast to the *accrual basis of accounting*, a system of accounting in which *revenues* are recognized when *cash* is received and *expenses* are recognized as *disbursements* are made. No attempt is made to *match revenues* and *expenses* in determining *income*. See *modified cash basis*.

cash book. A book of original entry for recording cash received and/or paid out.

cash budget. A schedule of expected cash *receipts* and *disbursements*.

cash collection basis. The *installment method* for recognizing *revenue*. Not to be confused with the *cash basis of accounting*.

cash cycle. The period of time that elapses during which *cash* is converted into *inventories*, inventories are converted into *accounts receivable*, and receivables are converted back into cash. *Earnings cycle*.

cash disbursements journal. A specialized *journal* used to record *expenditures* by *cash* and by *cheque*. If a *cheque register* is also used, a cash disbursements journal records only expenditures of currency and coins.

cash discount. A reduction in sales or purchase price allowed for prompt payment.

cash dividend. See *dividened*.

cash equivalent value. A term used to describe the amount for which an *asset* could be sold. *Market value. Fair market price (value)*.

cash flow. Cash *receipts* minus *disbursements* from a given *asset*, or group of assets, for a given period.

cash flow per share. The cash flow for a particular period of time divided by the number of *common shares* outstanding.

cash flow statement. A statement similar to the typical *statement of changes in financial position* where the flows of cash, rather than of *working capital*, are explained.

cash receipts journal. A specialized *journal* used to record all *receipts of cash*.

cash (surrender) value of life insurance. An amount equal, not to the face value of the policy to be paid in event of death, but to the amount that could be realized if the policy were immediately canceled and traded with the insurance company for cash. If a firm owns a life insurance policy, the policy is reported as an asset at an amount equal to this value.

cash yield. See *yield*.

cashier's cheque. A bank's own *cheque* drawn on itself and signed by the cashier or other authorized official. It is a direct obligation of the bank. Compare with *certified cheque*.

catch-up depreciation. *Backlog depreciation*.

CCA. *Capital cost allowance*. A deduction from income to derive taxable income under the Income Tax Act, replacing accounting depreciation and amortization.

central corporate expenses. General *overhead expenses* incurred in running the corporate headquarters and related supporting activities of a corporation. These expenses are treated as *period expenses*. Contrast with *manufacturing* *overhead*. A major problem in *segment reporting* is the treatment of these expenses.

central processing unit (CPU). The component of a computer system where the arithmetic, logic and data transfer control is carried out.

certificate. The document that is the physical embodiment of a *bond* or a *share*. A term sometimes used for the *auditor's report*.

certified cheque. The *cheque* of a depositor drawn on a bank on the face of which the bank has inserted the words "accepted" or "certified" with the date and signature of a bank official. The cheque then becomes an obligation of the bank.

certified internal auditor. See *CIA*.

Certified Public Accountant (CPA). The title used in the United States for an accountant who has satisfied the statutory and administrative requirements of his or her jurisdiction to be registered or licensed as a public accountant.

CGA. Certified General Accountant. An accountant who has satisfied the experience, education, and examination requirements of the *Certified General Accountants' Association of Canada*.

chain discount. A series of *discount* percentages; for example, if a chain discount of 10 and 5 percent is quoted, then the actual, or *invoice*, price is the nominal, or list, price times .90 times .95, or 85.5% of invoice price.

change fund. Coins and currency issued to cashiers, delivery drivers, and so on.

changes, accounting. See *accounting changes*.

changes in financial position. See *statement of changes in financial position*.

charge. As a noun, a *debit* to an account; as a verb, to debit.

charge off. To treat as a *loss* or *expense* an amount originally recorded as an *asset*; usually the term is used when the charge is not in accord with original expectations.

chart of accounts. A list of names and numbers of *accounts* systematically organized.

charter. The letters patent, special Act or other *instrument of incorporation*.

chattel mortgage. A mortgage on personal property as contrasted with real estate.

cheque. Legally a cheque is defined as "a bill of exchange drawn on a bank, payable on demand."

cheque register. A book of original entry in which cheques issued are recorded.

CIA. Certified Internal Auditor. One who has satisfied certain requirements of the *Institute of Internal Auditors* including experience, ethics, education, and examinations.

CICA. *Canadian Institute of Chartered Accountants*.

CIF. A term used in contracts along with the name of a given port to indicate that the quoted price includes insurance, handling, and freight charges up to delivery by the seller at the given port.

class action. A legal suit where one or more persons sue as representatives of a group (class) having a common claim.

clean surplus concept. The notion that the only entries to the *retained earnings* account are to record net earnings and dividends. See *comprehensive income*. Contrast with *current operating performance concept*.

clearing account. An account containing amounts to be transferred to another account(s) before the end of the *accounting period*. Examples are the *income summary* account (whose balance is transferred to retained earnings) and the purchases account (whose balance is transferred to *inventory* or to *cost of goods sold*).

clearing house. An organization that facilitates transfer transactions among members of an industry, profession or other group; e.g., a bank clearing house allows daily settlements to be made among banks for cheques drawn and deposits transferred.

close. As a verb, to transfer the *balance* of a *temporary* or *contra* or *adjunct* account to the main account to which it relates; for example, to transfer *revenue* and *expense* accounts directly, or through the *income summary* account, to an *owner's equity* account, or to transfer *purchase discounts* to purchases.

closed account. An account with equal debits and credits, usually as a result of a closing entry. See *ruling an account*.

closed end. Relating to the *capital structure* of an organization where *shares* or units of participation once issued are transferable but cannot be cancelled or redeemed except by resolution of the shareholders or unit holders or under regulation or legislation.

closely-held corporation. A corporation in which the *shares* are held by a small number of *shareholders*.

closing entries. The entries that accomplish the transfer of balances in temporary accounts to the related balance sheet accounts. See *work sheet*.

closing inventory. *Ending inventory*.

CMA. *Certified Management Accountant*. Professional accounting designation offered by Society of Management Accountants of Canada. CMAs are most commonly employed in industry.

CoCoA. *Continuously contemporary accounting*.

COD. Cash on delivery. A condition of sale where the purchaser is required to pay the purchase price in cash immediately upon delivery of goods.

coding of accounts. The numbering of *accounts*, as for a *chart of accounts*, which is particularly necessary for computerized accounting.

coinsurance. Insurance policies that protect against hazards such as fire or water damage often specify that the owner of the property may not collect the full amount of insurance for a loss unless the insurance policy covers at least some specified percentage, usually about 80 percent, of the *replacement cost* of the property. Coinsurance clauses induce the owner to carry full, or nearly full, coverage.

COLA. Cost of living adjustment. See *indexation*.

collateral. Assets pledged by a *borrower* that will be given up if the *loan* is not paid.

collateral security. *Security* which is given in addition to the principal security and only to be resorted to after the principal security has been realized upon.

collectible. Capable of being converted into cash; now, if due; later, otherwise.

combination. See *business combination*.

combined financial statement. A composite financial statement comprising the accounts of two or more companies which are usually related. Compare consolidated financial statements.

comfort letter. A letter by which an auditor conveys negative assurance as to unaudited financial statements in a prospectus or draft financial statements included in a preliminary prospectus.

commercial paper. *Short-term notes* issued by corporate borrowers.

commission. Remuneration, usually expressed as a percentage, to employees based on an activity rate, such as sales.

committed costs. *Capacity costs*.

common cost. *Cost* resulting from use of *raw materials*, a facility (for example, plant or machines), or a service (for example, fire insurance) that benefits several products or departments and must be allocated to those products or departments. Common costs result when multiple products are produced together although they could be produced separately; joint costs occur when multiple products are of necessity produced together. Many writers use common costs and *joint costs* synonymously. See *joint costs, indirect costs,* and *overhead*.

common dollar accounting. *Constant dollar accounting*.

common monetary measuring unit. For Canadian companies, the dollar. See also *stable monetary unit assumption* and *constant dollar accounting*.

common revenue. Revenue which is not directly traceable to specific parts of the organization.

common shares. *Shares* representing the class of owners who have residual claims on the assets and earnings of a company after all debt and preferred shareholders' claims have been met.

common-size statement. A financial statement in which the components are expressed as a percentage of a specific item included in the statement; in the case of the balance sheet, the total *assets* and the total *liabilities* and *owners' equities* respectively, and in the case of the income statement, the *net sales*.

common stock equivalent. (*U.S.*) A security which, because of its terms and the circumstances under which it was issued, is regarded as equivalent to a common share for purposes of calculating the earnings per share.

company. Any association, whether incorporated or unincorporated, of persons who are joined in a common interest, generally for the purpose of carrying on a business undertaking; used commonly to refer to a limited company. (Compare *corporation*; *limited company*.)

company-wide control. See *control system*.

comparability. The quality of information that enables users to identify similarities in and differences between two sets of economic phenomena.

comparative (financial) statements. Financial statements showing information for the same company for different times, usually two successive years. Nearly all published financial statements are in this form. See the annual report for General Products Limited in Appendix A. Contrast with *historical summary*.

compensating balance. When a bank lends funds to a customer, it often requires that the customer keep on deposit in his or her chequing account an amount equal to some percentage, say 20 percent of the loan. The amount required to be left on deposit is the compensating balance. Such amounts effectively increase the *interest rate*. The amounts of such balances must be disclosed in *notes* to the *financial statements*.

completed-contract method. Recognizing *revenues* and *expenses* for a job or order only when it is finished, except that when a loss on the contract is expected, revenues and expenses are recognized in the period when the loss is first forecast. This term is generally used only for long-term contracts. It is otherwise equivalent to the *sales basis* of *revenue recognition*.

completed-sales basis. See *sales basis of revenue recognition*.

completeness. The inclusion in reported information of everything material that is necessary for faithful representation of the relevant phenomena.

compliance audit. Objectively obtaining and evaluating evidence regarding assertions, actions, and events to ascertain the degree of correspondence between them and established performance criteria.

compliance procedure. An *audit* procedure used to gain evidence as to whether the prescribed internal controls are operating effectively.

composite depreciation. *Group depreciation* of dissimilar items.

composite life method. *Group depreciation* for items of unlike kind. The term may be used when a single item, such as a crane, which consists of separate units with differing service lives, such as the chassis, the motor, the lifting mechanism, and so on, is depreciated as a whole rather than treating each of the components separately.

compound entry. A *journal entry* with more than one *debit* or more than one *credit*, or both. See *trade-in transaction* for an example.

compound interest. *Interest* calculated on *principal* plus previously undistributed interest.

compound interest depreciation. A method designed to hold the *rate of return* on an asset constant. First find the *internal rate of return* on the cash inflows and outflows of the asset. The periodic depreciation charge is the cash flow for the period less the internal rate of return multiplied by the asset's book value at the beginning of the period. When the cash flows from the asset are constant over time, the method is sometimes called the ''annuity method'' of depreciation.

compounding period. The time period for which *interest* is calculated. At the end of the period, the interest may be paid to the lender or added (that it, converted) to principal for the next interest-earning period, which is usually a year or some portion of a year.

comprehensive budget. *Master budget*.

comprehensive income. The change in equity (net assets) of an entity during a period from transactions and other events and circumstances from nonowner sources. It includes all changes in equity during a period except those resulting from investments by owners and distributions to owners. In this definition, ''equity'' means *owners' equity*.

comptroller. Same meaning and pronunciation as *controller*.

computer language. Symbolic representation of instructions in a form such that they can be acted upon by a computer.

computer log. A chronological record of the activity of a computer system, including work performed and malfunctions.

conceptual framework. A coherent system of interrelated objectives and fundamentals, promulgated by the *FASB* primarily through its *SFAC* publications, expected to lead to consistent standards for *financial accounting* and reporting.

condensed financial statement. A financial statement in which less important detail is combined for the purpose of providing a readily comprehensible financial picture.

conditional discharge. The release of a bankrupt debtor from claims provable in bankruptcy subject to the fulfillment of certain specified conditions.

confidence level. The measure of probability that the actual characteristics of the population lie within the stated precision of the estimate derived from a sampling process. A sample estimate may be expressed in the following terms: ''Based on the sample, we are 95% sure [confidence level] that the true population value is within the range of X to Y [precision]''. See *precision*.

confirmation. A formal memorandum delivered by the customers or suppliers of a company to its independent *auditor* verifying the amounts shown as receivable or payable. The confirmation document is originally sent by the auditor to the customer. If the auditor asks that the document be returned whether the *balance* is correct or incorrect, then it is called a ''positive confirmation.'' If the auditor asks that the document be returned only if there is an error, it is called a ''negative confirmation.''

conglomerate. *Holding company*. This term is used when the owned companies are in dissimilar lines of business.

conservatism. A *reporting objective* that calls for anticipation of all *losses* and *expenses* but defers recognition of *gains* or *profits* until they are *realized* in *arm's-lenth* transactions. In the absence of certainty, events are to be reported in a way that tends to minimize cumulative income. A prudent reaction to uncertainty is to try to ensure that uncertainty and risks inherent in business situations are adequately considered.

consignee. See *on consignment*.

consignment. See *on consignment*.

consignor. See *on consignment*.

consistency. Treatment of like *transactions* in the same way on consecutive periods so that financial statements will be more comparable than otherwise. The reporting policy implying that procedures, once adopted, should be followed from period to period by a reporting *entity*. See *accounting changes* for the treatment of inconsistencies.

consolidated financial statements. Statements issued by legally separate companies that show financial position and income as they would appear if the companies were one legal *entity*. Such statements reflect an economic, rather than a legal, concept of the *entity*.

consolidated goodwill. The excess of cost of the shares to an acquiring corporation over the amounts assigned to its equity in the fair value of the identifiable net assets of the acquired corporation at the date of acquisition. (Compare *purchase discrepancy*.)

consolidation of shares. Reduction in the number of shares of a class of capital stock, with no change in the total dollar amount of the class, but with a converse increase in the par or stated value of the shares. This is achieved by issuing one new share in exchange for a specified number of old shares. Compare *stock split*.

constant dollar. A unit of constant general purchasing power used to measure financial statement items in terms of the general purchasing power of the dollar at a specified date.

constant dollar accounting. Accounting where items are measured in *constant dollars*. See *historical-cost/constant-dollar accounting* and *current-cost/constant-dollar accounting*.

constant dollar date. The time at which the *general purchasing power* of one *constant dollar* is exactly equal to the *general purchasing power* of one *nominal dollar*, that is, the date when C\$1 = \$1. When the constant dollar date is mid-period, then the nominal amounts of *revenues* and *expenses* spread evenly throughout the period are equal to their constant dollar amounts, but end-of-period *balance sheet* amounts measured in constant mid-period dollars differ from their nominal dollar amounts. When the constant dollar date is at the end of the period, then the constant dollar and nominal dollar amounts on a balance sheet for that date are identical.

constrained share company. A public company whose *instrument of incorporation* specifies that at least a certain prescribed percentage of the shares must be beneficially owned by persons who are Canadian citizens or who are corporations resident in Canada.

consumer price index (CPI). An index measuring changes in prices of retail goods and services purchased by the public.

Contemporary Accounting Research Scholarly publication of the Canadian Academic Accounting Association, published quarterly.

contingency. An existing condition or situation involving uncertainty as to possible gain or loss to an enterprise that ultimately will be resolved when one or more future events occur or fail to occur. If some possibility exists that a material contingent loss could occur, then footnote disclosure of this contingency is appropriate. If the likelihood is probable then the loss and associated liability should be formally set up in the accounts. Gain contingencies, however, applying the rule of conservatism, are not recognized unless there is virtual certainty as to the outcome.

contingency fund. Cash or investments set aside or reserved for unforeseen expenditures.

contingent annuity. An *annuity* whose number of payments depends on the outcome of an event whose timing is uncertain at the time the annuity is set up; for example, an annuity payable for the life of the *annuitant*. Contrast with *annuity certain*.

contingent asset. Something of potential value depending on the resolution of a contingency.

contingent issue (securities). Securities issuable to specific individuals upon the occurrence of some event, such as the firm's attaining a specified level of earnings.

contingent rental. A rental based on a factor other than the passage of time.

continuance. The process under corporations legislation which enables a corporation to transfer from one governing act to another.

continuing operations. See *income from continuing operations*.

continuity of operations. The assumption in accounting that the business *entity* will continue to operate long enough for current plans to be carried out. The *going-concern assumption*.

continuous audit. Any audit the various phases of which are performed continuously or at short intervals during the accounting period.

continuous budget. A *budget* that perpetually adds a month in the future as the month just ended is dropped.

continuous compounding. *Compound interest* where the *compounding period* is every instant of time. See *e* for the computation of the equivalent annual or periodic rate.

continuous process auditing. Automatic selection during live computer data processing of transactions for subsequent review by an auditor.

continuously contemporary accounting (CoCoA). A name coined by the Australian theorist, Raymond J. Chambers, to indicate a combination of current-value accounting where amounts are measured in *constant dollars* and based on *exit values*.

contra account. An *account*, such as *accumulated depreciation*, that accumulates subtractions from another account, such as machinery. Contrast with *adjunct account*.

contract. An agreement, intended to give rise to legal obligations, entered into between two or more persons to do or abstain from doing something.

contributed capital. The sum of the balances in *capital* *stock* accounts plus *capital contributed in excess of par (or stated) value* accounts. Contrast with *donated capital*.

contributed surplus. Surplus contributed by shareholders, being the premium received on the issue of *par value* shares, the portion of proceeds of issue of *no par* value shares that has been allocated to surplus, the proceeds of sale of donated shares, profit on forfeited shares, credits resulting from redemption or conversion of shares at less than the amount set up as *share capital*, or any other contribution in excess of *stated value* of shares made by shareholders as such. Capital donations from sources other than shareholders.

contribution approach. Method of preparing *income statements* that separates *variable costs* from *fixed costs* in order to emphasize the importance of cost behaviour patterns for purposes of planning and control.

contribution margin. *Revenue* from *sales* less all variable *expenses*.

contribution per unit. Selling price less *variable costs* per unit.

contributory. Said of a *pension plan* where employees, as well as employers, make payments to a pension *fund*. Note that the provisions for *vesting* are applicable to the employer's payments. Whatever the degree of vesting of the employer's payments, the employee typically gets back his or her payments, with interest, in case of death, or other cessation of employment, before retirement.

control (controlling) account. A summary *account* with totals equal to those of entries and balances that appear in individual accounts in a *subsidiary ledger*. Accounts Receivable is a control account backed up with accounts for each customer. The balance in a control account should not be changed unless a corresponding change is made in the subsidiary accounts.

control system. A device for ensuring that actions are carried out according to plan or for safeguarding *assets*. A system for ensuring that actions are carried out according to plan can be designed for a single function within the firm, called "operational control," for autonomous segments within the firm that generally have responsibility for both revenues and costs, called "divisional control," or for activities of the firm as a whole, called "company-wide control." Systems designed for safeguarding *assets* are called "internal control" systems.

controllable cost. A *cost* whose amount can be influenced by the way in which operations are carried out, such as advertising costs. These costs can be *fixed* or *variable*. See *programmed costs* and *managed costs*.

controlled company. A company, a majority of whose voting shares are held by an individual or corporation. Effective control can sometimes be exercised when less than 50 percent of the stock is owned.

controller. The title often used for the chief accountant of an organization. Sometimes spelled *comptroller*.

controlling interest. The ability possessed by anyone, or any group, to elect the majority of the company's directors.

controlling shareholder. A *shareholder* who has the power to elect at least a majority of the board of directors.

conversion. The act of exchanging a convertible security for another security.

conversion audit. An examination of change-over procedures, and new accounting procedures and files, that takes place when there has been a significant change in the accounting system (e.g. a change from a manual to a computerized system or a change of computers).

conversion cost. Direct *labour* costs plus factory *overhead* costs incurred in producing a product. That is, the cost to convert raw materials to finished products. *Manufacturing cost*.

conversion of foreign currency. The act of exchanging the currency of one country for the currency of another country. Compare *translation of foreign currency*.

conversion period. *Compounding period*. Period during which a *convertible bond* or *preferred shares* can be converted into *common shares*.

convertible bond. A *bond* that may be converted into a specified number of shares of *capital stock* during the *conversion period*.

convertible preferred shares. *Preferred shares* that may be converted into a specified number of shares of *common shares*.

co-operative. An incorporated organization formed for the benefit of its members (owners) who are either producers or consumers in order to acquire for them profits or savings which would otherwise accrue to middlemen. Control is exercised by the members on the basis of one vote per member.

co-product. A product sharing production facilities with another product. For example, if an apparel manufacturer produces shirts and jeans on the same line, these are co-products. Co-products are distinguished from *joint products* and *by-products* which, by their very nature, must be produced together, such as the various grades of wood produced in a lumber factory.

copyright. Exclusive right granted by the government to an individual author, composer, playwright, and the like for the life of the individual plus 50 years. The *economic life* of a *copyright* may be considerably less than the *legal life* as, for example, the *copyright* of this book.

corporate joint venture. A joint venture entered into by the parties through the vehicle of a corporation.

corporation. A legal entity, with or without *share capital*, separate and distinct from its owners or persons who constitute it, which has all the rights and responsibilities of a person except those rights which only a natural person can exercise. (Compare *company; limited company*).

correcting entry. An *adjusting entry* where an improperly recorded *transaction* is properly recorded. Not to be confused with entries that correct *accounting errors*.

correction of errors. See *accounting errors*.

correlation analysis. The measurement of the degree of relationship, if any, between two variables.

cost. The sacrifice, measured by the *price* paid or required to be paid, to acquire *goods* or *services*. See *acquisition cost* and *replacement cost*. The term "cost" is often used when referring to the valuation of a good or service acquired. When "cost" is used in this sense, a cost is an *asset*. When the benefits of the acquisition (the goods or services acquired) expire, the cost becomes an expense or *loss*. Some writers, however, use cost and expense as synonyms. Contrast with *expense*.

cost accounting. Classifying, summarizing, recording, reporting, and allocating current or predicted *costs*. A subset of *managerial accounting*.

cost accumulation. Bringing together, usually in a single *account*, all *costs* of a specified activity. Contrast with *cost allocation*.

cost allocation. Assuming *costs* to individual products or time periods. Contrast with *cost accumulation*.

cost and market, whichever is lower. See *lower of cost and market*.

cost based (pension) plan. See *defined contribution (pension) plan*.

cost behaviour. The functional relation between changes in activity and changes in *cost*. For example, *fixed* versus *variable costs*; *linear* versus *curvilinear cost*.

cost/benefit analysis. The evaluation of the profits, income, output or other benefits anticipated under a project or service against the costs of obtaining them.

cost centre. A unit of activity for which *expenditures* and *expenses* are accumulated.

cost effective. Among alternatives, the one whose benefit, or payoff, divided by cost is highest. Sometimes said of an action whose expected benefits exceed expected costs whether or not there are other alternatives with larger benefit/cost ratios.

cost estimation. The process of measuring the functional relation between changes in activity levels and changes in cost.

cost-flow assumption. See *flow assumption*.

cost flows. Costs passing through various classifications within an entry. See *flow of costs* for a diagram.

cost method (for investment). Accounting for an investment in the *capital stock* of another company where the investment is shown at *acquisition cost*, and only *dividends* declared are treated as *revenue*.

cost method (for treasury shares). The method of showing *treasury shares* as a *contra* to all items of *shareholders' equity* in an amount equal to that paid to reacquire the shares.

cost of capital. *Opportunity* cost of funds invested in a business. The rate of return required to be earned on an asset before the rational owner will devote that asset to a particular purpose. Sometimes measured as the average rate per year a company must pay for its *equities*. In efficient capital markets, the *discount rate* that equates the expected *present value* of all future cash flows to common shareholders with the market value of common stock at a given time.

cost of goods manufactured. The sum of all costs allocated to products completed during a period; includes materials, labour, and *overhead*.

cost of goods purchased. Net purchase price of goods acquired plus costs of storage and delivery to the place where the items can be productively used.

cost of goods sold. Inventoriable *costs* that are expensed because the units are sold; equals beginning inventory plus *cost of goods purchased* or *manufactured* minus *ending inventory*.

cost of sales. Generally refers to *cost of goods sold*; occasionally, to *selling expenses*.

cost percentage. One less *markup percentage*. *Cost* of *goods available for sale* divided by selling prices of goods available for sale (when *FIFO* is used). With LIFO, *cost* of *purchases* divided by selling price of purchases. See *markup* for further detail on inclusions in calculation of cost percentage.

cost-plus contract. A contract under which the contractor is to recover the costs incurred in performing the contract plus an agreed markup or fee. (Compare *fixed-price contract*.)

cost pool. *Indirect cost pool*.

cost principle. The *principle* that requires reporting *assets* at *historical* or *acquisition cost*, less accumulated *amortization*. This principle is based on the assumption that cost is equal to *fair market value* at the date of acquisition and subsequent changes are not likely to be significant.

cost-recovery-first method. A method of *revenue* recognition that *credits inventory* as collections are received until all costs are recovered. Only after costs are completely recovered is *income* recognized. To be used in financial reporting only when the total amount of collections is highly uncertain. Can never be used in income tax reporting. Contrast with the *installment method*, where constant proportions of each collection are credited both to cost and to income.

cost sheet. Statement that shows all the elements comprising the total cost of an item.

cost terminology. The word "cost" appears in many accounting terms. The exhibit (pp. 872–874) classifies some of these by the distinctions the terms are used to make. Joel Dean was, to our knowledge, the first to attempt such distinctions; we have used some of his ideas here. Some terms have more detailed discussion under their own listings.

cost-volume-profit analysis. The study of the effect on profits of changes in fixed costs, variable costs, sales quantities, sales prices and/or sales mix.

cost-volume-profit graph (chart). A graph that shows the relation between *fixed costs, contribution per unit, break-even point,* and *sales.* See *breakeven chart.*

costing. The process of determining the cost of activities, products, or services. The British word for *cost accounting.*

coupon. That portion of a *bond* document redeemable at a specified date for *interest* payments. Its physical form is much like a ticket; each coupon is dated and is deposited at a bank, just like a cheque, for collection or is mailed to the issuer's agent for collection.

coupon rate. Of a *bond,* the amount of annual coupons divided by par value. Contrast with *effective rate.*

covenant. A promise with legal validity.

CPA. See *certified public accountant.* The *AICPA* suggests that no periods be shown in the abbreviation.

CPI. *Consumer price index.*

CPP. Current purchasing power; usually used as an adjective modifying the word "accounting" to mean the accounting that produces *constant dollar adjusted statements. Canada Pension Plan.*

CPU. Abbreviation for *central processing unit.*

Cr. Abbreviation for *credit.*

credit. As a noun, an entry on the right-hand side of an *account.* As a verb, to make an entry on the right-hand side of an account. Records increases in *liabilities, owners' equity, revenues,* and *gains;* records decreases in *assets* and *expenses.* See *debit and credit conventions.* Also the ability or right to buy or borrow in return for a promise to pay later.

credit bureau. An organization which gathers and evalu-

ates data on the ability of a person to meet financial obligations and sells this information to clients.

credit loss. The amount of *accounts receivable* that is, or is expected to become, *uncollectible.*

credit memorandum. A document used by a seller to inform a buyer that the buyer's *account receivable* is being credited (reduced) because of *errors, returns,* or *allowances.* Also, the document provided by a bank to a depositor to indicate that the depositor's balance is being increased because of some event other than a deposit, such as the collection by the bank of the depositor's *note receivable.*

credit report. A report issued by a credit bureau giving factual information about an individual or corporation which may bear on a decision to grant credit to that individual or corporation.

credit union. A savings and loan institution organized on a co-operative basis to provide savings and loan services to and for the benefit of its members (owners).

creditor. One who lends.

Critical Path Method. A method of *network analysis* in which normal duration time is estimated for each activity within a project. The critical path identifies the shortest completion period based on the most time-consuming sequence of activities from the beginning to the end of the network. Compare *PERT.*

cross-reference (index). A number placed by each *account* in a *journal entry* indicating the *ledger* account to which the entry is posted and placing in the ledger the page number of the journal where the entry was made. Used to link the *debit* and *credit* parts of an entry in the ledger accounts back to the original entry in the journal. See *audit trail.*

cross-section analysis. Analysis of *financial statements* of various firms for a single period of time, as opposed to time series analysis where statements of a given firm are analyzed over several periods of time.

Crown corporation. A corporation that is ultimately accountable through a Minister of the Crown to Parliament or a legislature for the conduct of its affairs.

cum div. or cum dividend. The condition of shares whose quoted market price includes a declared but unpaid dividend. This condition pertains between the declaration date of the dividend and the record date. Compare *ex div.* or *ex dividend.*

cum rights. The condition of securities whose quoted market price includes the right to purchase new securities. (Compare *ex rights.*)

cumulative dividend. Preferred share *dividends* that, if not paid, accrue as a commitment that must be paid before dividends to common shareholders can be declared.

cumulative preferred shares. *Preferred shares* with *cumulative dividend* rights.

Cost Terminology: Distinctions among Terms Containing the Word "Cost"

Terms (Synonyms Given in Parentheses)			Distinctions and Comments
			1. The following pairs of terms distinguish the "attribute" or "basis" measured in accounting.
Historical Cost (Acquisition Cost)	vs	Current Cost	A distinction used in financial accounting. Current cost can be used more specifically to mean replacement cost, net realizable value, or present value of cash flows. "Current cost" is often used narrowly to mean replacement cost.
Historical Cost (Actual Cost)	vs	Standard Cost	The distinction between historical and standard costs arises in product costing for inventory valuation. Some systems record actual costs while others record the standard costs.
			2. The following pairs of terms denote various distinctions among historical costs. For each pair of terms, the sum of the two kinds of costs equals total historical cost used in financial reporting.
Variable Cost	vs	Fixed Cost (Constant Cost)	Distinction used in breakeven analysis and in designing cost accounting systems, particularly for product costing. See (4), below, for a further subdivision of fixed costs and (5), below, for an economic distinction closely paralleling this one.
Traceable Cost	vs	Common Cost (Joint Cost)	Distinction arises in allocating manufacturing costs to product. Common costs are allocated to product, but the allocations are more-or-less arbitrary. The distinction also arises in segment reporting and in separating manufacturing from nonmanufacturing costs.
Direct Cost	vs	Indirect Cost	Distinction arises in designing cost accounting systems and in product costing. The distinction generally applies only to manufacturing costs.
Out-of-Pocket Cost (Outlay Cost; Cash Cost)	vs	Book Cost	Virtually all costs recorded in financial statements require a cash outlay at one time or another. The distinction here separates expenditures to occur in the future from those already made and is used in making decisions. Book costs, such as for depreciation, reduce income without requiring a future outlay of cash. The cash has already been spent. See future vs past costs in (5), below.
Incremental Cost (Marginal Cost) (Differential Cost)	vs	Sunk Cost	Distinction used in making decisions. Incremental costs will be incurred (or saved) if a decision is made to go ahead (or to stop) some activity, but not otherwise. Sunk costs will be reported in financial statements whether the decision is made to go ahead or not, because cash has already been spent or committed. Not all sunk costs are book costs, as, for example, a salary promised but not yet earned, that will be paid even if a no-go decision is made.
			The economist restricts the term marginal cost to the cost of producing one more unit. Thus the next unit has a marginal cost; the next week's output has an incremental cost. If a firm produces and sells a new product the related new costs would properly be called incremental, not marginal. If a factory is closed, the costs saved are incremental, not marginal.
Escapable Cost	vs	Inescapable Cost (Unavoidable Cost)	Same distinction as incremental vs sunk costs, but this pair is used only when the decision maker is considering stopping something — ceasing to produce a product, closing a factory, or the like. See next pair.
Avoidable Cost	vs	Unavoidable Cost	A distinction sometimes used in discussing the merits of variable and absorption costing. Avoidable costs are treated as product cost and unavoidable costs are treated as period expenses under variable costing.

Cost Terminology: Distinction among Terms Containing the Word "Cost"

Terms (Synonyms Given in Parentheses)			Distinctions and Comments
Controllable Cost	vs	Uncontrollable Cost	The distinction here is used in allocating responsibility and in setting bonus or incentive plans. All costs can be affected by someone in the entity; those who design incentive schemes attempt to hold a person responsible for a cost only if that person can influence the amount of the cost.
			3. In each of the following pairs, used in historical cost accounting, the word "cost" appears in one of the terms where "expense" is meant.
Expired Cost	vs	Unexpired Cost	The distinction is between *expense* and *asset*.
Product Cost	vs	Period Cost	The terms distinguish product cost from period expense. When a given asset is used, is its cost converted into work in process and then finished goods on the balance sheet until the goods are sold or is it an expense shown on this period's income statement? Product costs appear on the income statement as part of cost of goods sold in the period when the goods are sold. Period expenses appear on the income statement with an appropriate caption for the item in the period when the cost is incurred or recognized.
			4. The following subdivisions of fixed (historical) costs are used in analyzing operations.
Capacity Cost	vs	Programmed Cost	Capacity costs give a firm the capability to produce or to sell. Programmed costs, such as for advertising or research and development, may not be essential, but once a decision to incur them is made, they become fixed costs.
Standby Cost	vs	Enabling Cost	Standby costs will be incurred whether capacity, once acquired, is used or not, such as property taxes and depreciation on a factory. Enabling costs, such as for security force, can be avoided if the capacity is unused.
Semifixed Cost	vs	Semivariable Cost	A cost fixed over a wide range but that can change at various levels is a semifixed cost or "step cost." An example is the cost of rail lines from the factory to the main rail line where fixed cost depends on whether there are one or two parallel lines, but are independent of the number of trains run per day. Semivariable costs combine a strictly fixed component cost plus a variable component. Telephone charges usually have a fixed monthly component plus a charge related to usage.
			5. The following pairs of terms distinguish among economic uses or decision making uses or regulatory uses of cost terms.
Fully Absorbed Cost (Full Cost)	vs	Variable Cost (Direct Cost)	Fully absorbed costs refer to costs where fixed costs have been allocated to units or departments as required by generally accepted accounting principles. Variable costs, in contrast, may be more relevant for making decisions, such as in setting prices.
Opportunity Cost	vs	Outlay Cost (Out-of-Pocket Cost)	Opportunity cost refers to the economic benefit foregone by using a resource for one purpose instead of for another. The outlay cost of the resource will be recorded in financial records. The distinction arises because a resource is already in the possession of the entity with a recorded historical cost. Its economic value to the firm, opportunity cost, generally differs from the historical cost; it can be either larger or smaller.

Cost Terminology: Distinctions among Terms Containing the Word "Cost"

Terms (Synonyms given in Parentheses)			Distinctions and Comments
Future Costs	vs	Past Cost	Effective decision making analyzes only the present; the future outlay costs, out-of-pocket costs, opportunity costs, are relevant for profit maximizing. Past costs are used in financial reporting.
Short-Run Cost	vs	Long-Run Cost	Short-run costs vary as output is varied for a given configuration of plant and equipment. Long-run costs can be incurred to change that configuration. This pair of terms is the economic analog of the accounting pair, see (2) above, variable and fixed costs. The analogy is not perfect because some short-run costs are fixed, such as property taxes on the factory, from the point of view of breakeven analysis.
Imputed Cost	vs	Book Cost	In a regulatory setting some costs, for example the cost of owner's equity capital, are calculated and used for various purposes. Imputed costs are not recorded in the historical cost accounting records for financial reporting. Book costs are recorded.
Average Cost	vs	Marginal Cost	The economic distinction equivalent to fully absorbed cost of product and direct cost of product. Average cost is total cost divided by number of units. Marginal cost is the cost to produce the next unit (or the last unit).

cumulative voting. A method of electing a board of directors whereby the owner of any one *share* is allowed as many votes as there are directors to be elected; the votes may then be allocated by the *shareholder* to one or more candidates at his or her discretion. Compare *majority rule voting*.

current account. A running account with a person or organization. A bank current account is usually a chequing account as contrasted with a savings account; a partner's current account is a record of drawings and the portion of profits available for withdrawal, as contrasted with the partner's investment in the business which is reflected in the capital account.

current asset. *Cash* and other *assets* that are ordinarily realizable within one year from the date of the balance sheet or within the normal operating cycle, where that is longer than a year. Current assets include *cash*, *temporary investments*, *receivables*, *inventory*, and *current prepayments*.

current cost. The amount of cash or other consideration that would be needed currently to acquire an asset having the same service potential as embodied by the asset owned. Depending on the extent of technological change, it would be determined by reference to either current reproduction cost or current replacement cost.

current-cost/nominal-dollar accounting. Accounting based on *current cost* valuations measured in *nominal dollars*. Components of *income* include an *operating margin* and *holding gains and losses*.

current fund. In governmental accounting, a synonym for *general fund*.

current funds. *Cash* and other assets readily convertible into cash.

current (gross) margin. See *operating margin* (*based on replacement costs*).

current liability. A debt or other obligation that must be discharged within one year from the date of the balance sheet or within the normal operating cycle, where this is longer than a year (the normal operating cycle should correspond with that used for current assets).

current maturities. The portion of long-term obligations to be retired during the ensuing twelve months, normally classified as a current liability.

current operating performance concept. The notion that reported *income* for a period ought to reflect only ordinary, normal, and recurring operations of that period. A consequence is that *extraordinary* and nonrecurring items are entered directly in the Retained Earnings account. Contrast with *clean surplus concept*. This concept is no longer acceptable.

current rate method. A method of translation which translates assets, liabilities, revenues and expenses in a manner that retains their bases of measurement in terms of the foreign currency (i.e., it uses the foreign currency as the unit of measure. In particular assets and liabilities are translated at the rate of exchange in effect at the balance sheet date and revenue and expense items (including depreciation and amortization) are translated at the rate of exchange in effect on the dates on which such items are recognized in income during the period.

current ratio. Sum of *current assets* divided by sum of *current liabilities*. See *ratio*.

current replacement cost. The amount of cash or other consideration that would be needed currently to acquire the best available asset to undertake the function of the asset owned, adjusted for depreciation or amortization if appropriate. Current cost may be determined by reference to current replacement cost when the function performed by the asset has been subject to significant technological change.

current reproduction cost. The amount of cash or other consideration that would be needed currently to acquire a used asset of the same age, in the same location and in the same condition as that owned or the amount of cash or other consideration that would be needed currently to acquire a new asset that has the same service potential as the existing asset had when it was new, adjusted for depreciation or amortization. Current reproduction cost is generally an appropriate measurement of current cost when the function performed by the asset has not been subject to significant technological change.

current selling price. The amount for which an *asset* could be sold as of a given time in an *arm's-length* transaction, rather than in a forced sale.

current service. Service recognized for pension purposes that is not *past service*.

current-value accounting. The form of accounting where all assets are shown at *current replacement cost (entry value)* or *current selling price* or *net realizable value (exit value)* and all *liabilities* are shown at *present value*. Entry and exit values may be quite different from each other, so there is no general agreement on the precise meaning of current-value accounting.

current yield. Of a *bond*, the annual amount of *interest coupons* divided by current market price of the bond. Contrast with *yield to maturity*.

currently attainable standard cost. *Normal standard cost.*

curvilinear (variable) cost. A continuous, but not necessarily linear (straight-line), functional relation between activity levels and *costs*.

customer's ledger. The *ledger* that shows accounts receivable of individual customers. It is the *subsidiary ledger* for the *controlling account*, Accounts Receivable.

cut-off. A notional break in the continuity of the recording of the flow of transactions or in the physical flow of goods, assumed at the end of an accounting period, in order to establish a proper segregation of income and expense items between that accounting period and the next.

cycle billing. A method of billing customers by specific groups throughout the accounting period so that all customers are billed once in each period. This method contrasts with billing all customers at one particular date.

D

data bank. An organized file of information, such as customer name and address file, used in and kept up to date by a processing system.

data base. A comprehensive collection of interrelated information stored together in computerized form to serve several applications.

data base management system. Generalized software programs used to handle physical storage and manipulation of data bases.

data centre. A data processing installation that provides services to several users.

dated retained earnings. *Retained earnings* of a corporation accumulated from the date of a *reorganization* or *quasi-reorganization*.

days of average inventory on hand. See *ratio*.

days of grace. The days allowed by law for payment of a debt after its due date.

DCF. *Discounted cash flow.*

DDB. *Double-declining-balance depreciation.*

debenture bond. A *bond* not secured with *collateral*.

debit. As a noun, an entry on the left-hand side of an *account*. As a verb, to make an entry on the left-hand side of an account. Records increases in *assets* and *expenses*; records decreases in *liabilities, owner's equity,* and *revenues*. See *debit and credit conventions*.

debit and credit conventions. The equality of the two sides of the *accounting equation* is maintained by recording equal amounts of *debits* and *credits* for each *transaction*. The conventional use of the *T-account* form and the rules for debit and credit in *balance sheet accounts* are summarized as follows:

Any Asset Account

Opening Balance Increase + Dr. Ending Balance	Decrease − Cr.

Any Liability Account

Decrease − Dr.	Opening Balance Increase + Cr. Ending Balance

Any Owners' Equity Account

Decrease – Dr.	Opening Balance Increase + Cr. Ending Balance

Revenue and expense accounts belong to the owner's equity group. The relationship and the rules for debit and credit in these accounts can be expressed as follows.

Owners' Equity

Decrease – Dr. Expenses		Increase + Cr. Revenues	
Dr. + *	Cr. –	Dr. –	Cr. + *

* Normal balance prior to closing.

debit memorandum. A document used by a seller to inform a buyer that the seller is debiting (increasing) the amount of the buyer's *account receivable*. Also, the document provided by a bank to a depositor to indicate that the depositor's *balance* is being decreased because of some event other than payment for a *cheque*, such as monthly service charges or the printing of cheques.

debt. An amount owed. The general name for *notes, bonds, mortgages*, and the like that are evidence of amounts owed and have definite payment dates.

debt capital. *Noncurrent liabilities.* See *debt financing* and contrast with *equity financing*.

debt-equity ratio. Total *liabilities* divided by total *equities*. See *ratio*. Sometimes the denominator is merely total *shareholders' equity*. Sometimes the numerator is restricted to *noncurrent debt*.

debt financing. Raising *funds* by issuing *bonds, mortgages*, or *notes*. Contrast with *equity financing*. *Leverage*.

debt guarantee. See *guarantee*.

debt ratio. *Debt-equity ratio.*

debt service requirement. The amount of cash required for payments of *interest*, current maturities of *principal* on outstanding *debt*, and payments to *sinking funds* (corporations).

debtor. One who borrows.

declaration date. Time when a *dividend* is declared by the *board of directors*.

declining-balance depreciation. The method of calculating the periodic *depreciation* charge by multiplying the *book value* at the start of the period by a constant percentage. In pure declining balance depreciation the constant percentage is $1 - n\sqrt{s/c}$ where n is the *depreciable life*, s is *salvage value*, and c is *acquisition cost*. See *double-declining-balance depreciation*.

deduction at source. A deduction made by a payer from amounts paid to the payee and remitted by the payer to a third party under the terms of a statute or private agreement.

deep discount bonds. Said of *bonds* selling much below (exactly how much is not clear) *par value*.

defalcation. Embezzlement.

default. Failure to pay *interest* or *principal* on a *debt* when due.

defensive interval. A financial *ratio* equal to the number of days of normal cash *expenditures* covered by *quick assets*. It is defined as

$$\frac{\text{quick assets}}{\text{(all expenses except amortization and others not using funds/365)}}$$

The denominator of the ratio is the cash expenditure per day. This ratio has been found useful in predicting *bankruptcy*.

deferral. The accounting process concerned with past *cash receipts* and *payments*; in contrast to *accrual*. Recognizing a liability resulting from a current cash receipt (as for magazines to be delivered) or recognizing an asset from a current cash payment (as for prepaid insurance or a long-term depreciable asset).

deferral method. The process of apportioning income taxes among periods.

deferred annuity. An *annuity* whose first payment is made sometime after the end of the first period.

deferred asset. *Deferred charge.*

deferred charge. *Expenditure* not recognized as an *expense* of the period when made but carried forward as an *asset* to be *written off* in future periods, such as for advance rent payments or insurance premiums. See *deferral*.

deferred compensation plan. A plan by which payment for services rendered by employees is deferred until some specified future time.

deferred cost. *Deferred charge.*

deferred credit. Sometimes used to indicate *advances from* *customers.* Also sometimes used to describe the *deferred income tax liability.*

deferred debit. *Deferred charge.*

deferred expense. *Deferred charge.*

deferred gross margin. *Unrealized gross margin.*

deferred income. *Advances from customers.*

deferred performance liability. *Estimated liability* that arises under product *warranty.* Sometimes used to mean *advances from customers.*

deferred revenue. Sometimes used to indicate *advances from customers.*

deficit. A *debit balance* in the Retained Earnings account; presented on the balance sheet as a *contra* to shareholders' equity. Sometimes used to mean negative *net income* for a period.

defined benefit plan. A *pension plan* where the employer promises specific benefits to each eligible employee. The amounts usually depend on a formula that takes into account such things as the employee's earnings, years of employment, and age. The employer's cash contributions and pension expense are adjusted in relation to *actuarial* experience in the eligible employee group and investment performance of the pension *fund.* Sometimes called a "fixed-benefit" pension plan. Contrast with *money purchase plan.*

defined contribution plan. A *money purchase (pension) plan* or other arrangement, based on formula or discretion, where the employer makes cash contributions to eligible individual employee *accounts* under the terms of a written plan document.

deflation. A period of declining *general price changes.*

demand deposit. A deposit in a bank or other financial institution that may be withdrawn on demand. (Compare *time deposit.*)

demand loan. See *term loan* for definition and contrast.

denial of opinion. The statement by an *auditor* that, for reasons which arose from his or her *audit,* he or she is unable to express an opinion whether the *financial statements* provide *fair presentation.*

denominator volume. Capacity measured in expected number of units to be produced this period; divided into *budgeted fixed costs* to obtain fixed costs applied per unit of product.

depletion. Exhaustion or *amortization* of a *wasting asset,* or natural resource. Also see *percentage depletion.*

depletion allowance. See *percentage depletion.*

deposit certificate. A certificate showing that a deposit of a specified amount has been made at a bank or trust company for a specified period of time, usually less than five years, and at a specified rate of interest. The certificate may be redeemable before maturity at the option of the holder, subject to an interest penalty. (Compare *guaranteed investment certificate.*)

deposit method (of revenue recognition). This method of *revenue* recognition is not distinct from the *completed sale* or *completed contract method.* In some contexts such as retail land sales, the customer must make substantial payments while still having the right to back out of the deal and receive a refund. When there is uncertainty about whether the deal will be completed but a cash collection is made by the seller, the seller must *credit* deposits, a *liability account,* rather than *revenue.* (In this regard, the accounting differs from the completed contract method where the account credited is offset against the *work in process inventory* account.) When the *sale* becomes complete, a revenue account is credited and the deposit account is *debited.*

deposit, sinking-fund. Payments made to a *sinking fund.*

deposits (by customers). A *liability* arising upon receipt of *cash* (as in a bank, or in a grocery store when the customer pays cash for sodapop bottles to be repaid when the bottles are returned).

deposits in transit. Deposits made by a firm but not yet reflected on the *bank statement.*

depreciable cost. That part of the *cost* of an asset, usually *acquisition cost* less *salvage value,* that is to be charged off over the life of the asset through the process of *depreciation.*

depreciable life. For an *asset,* the time period or units of activity (such as miles driven for a truck) over which *depreciable cost* is to be allocated. For tax returns, depreciable life may be shorter than estimated *service life.*

depreciation. *Amortization* of *plant assets*; the process of allocating the cost of an asset to the periods of benefit—the *depreciable life.* Classified as a *production cost* or a *period expense,* depending on the asset and whether *absorption* or *variable costing* is used. Depreciation methods described in this glossary include the *annuity method, appraisal method, composite method, compound interest method, declining-balance method, double-declining-balance method, production method, replacement method, retirement method, straight-line method, sinking-fund method,* and *sum-of-the-years'-digits method.*

depreciation accounting. An accounting procedure in which the cost or other recorded value of a fixed asset less estimated residual value (if any) is distributed over its estimated useful life in a systematic and rational manner. It is a process of allocation, not valuation. Compare *renewal accounting; retirement method of depreciation.*

depreciation rate. A percentage which when applied to the depreciation base (or, in the case of the diminishing balance method, the depreciation base less accumulated depreciation) will produce the depreciation expense for the period.

depreciation reserve. An inferior term for *accumulated depreciation*. See *reserve*. Do not confuse with a replacement *fund*.

Descartes' rule of signs. In a *capital budgeting* context, the rule says that a series of cash flows will have a nonnegative number of *internal rates of return*. The number is equal to the number of variations in the sign of the cash flow series or is less than that number by an even integer. Consider the following series of cash flows, the first occurring now and the others at subsequent yearly intervals: -100, -100, $+50$, $+175$, -50, $+100$. The internal rates of return are the numbers for r that satisfy the equation

$$-100 - \frac{100}{(1 + r)} + \frac{50}{(1 + r)^2} + \frac{175}{(1 + r)^3} - \frac{50}{(1 + r)^4} + \frac{100}{(1 + r)^5} = 0$$

The series of cash flows has three variations in sign: a change from minus to plus, a change from plus to minus, and a change from minus to plus. The rule says that this series must have either one or three internal rates of return; in fact, it has only one, about 12 percent. But see also *reinvestment rate*.

designated surplus. A term in income tax legislation; broadly, the *retained earnings* on hand in a corporation at the time when control is acquired by another corporation.

detective controls. Internal controls designed to detect, or maximize the chance of detection of, errors and other irregularities. Compare *preventive controls*.

determination. See *determine*.

determine The verb "determine" and the noun "determination" are often used by accountants and those who describe the accounting process. A leading dictionary associates the following meanings with the verb "determine": settle, decide, conclude, ascertain, cause, affect, control, impel, terminate, and decide upon. In addition, accounting writers can mean any one of the following: measure, allocate, report, calculate, compute, observe, choose, and legislate. In accounting, there are two distinct sets of meanings —those encompassed by the synonym "cause or legislate" and those encompassed by the synonym "measure." The first set of uses conveys the active notion of causing something to happen and the second set of uses conveys the more passive notion of observing something that someone else has caused to happen. An accountant who writes of cost or income "determination" generally means measurement or observation, not causation; management and economic conditions cause costs or income to be what they are. To one who writes of accounting principles "determination" can mean choosing or applying (as in "determining depreciation charges" from an allowable set) or causing to be acceptable. In the long run, income is cash in less cash out, so management and economic conditions "determine" (cause) income to be what it is. In the short run, reported income is a function of accounting policies chosen and applied, so the accountant "determines" (measures) income.

development. The translation of research findings or other knowledge into a plan or design for new or substantially improved materials, devices, products, processes, systems or services prior to the commencement of commercial production or use. See *research*.

development-stage enterprise. A firm whose planned principal *operations* have not commenced or, having commenced, have not generated significant *revenue*. Such enterprises should be so identified, but no special *accounting principles* apply to them.

differential analysis. Analysis of *incremental costs*.

differential cost. *Incremental cost*.

digital computer. A computer that operates by performing arithmetical and logical operations on data represented in digital form.

dilution. A potential reduction in *earnings per share* or *book value* per share by the potential *conversion* of securities or by the potential exercise of *warrants* or *options*.

dilutive. Said of a *security* that would reduce *earnings per share* if it were exchanged for *common shares*.

dipping into LIFO layers. See *LIFO inventory layer*.

diminishing balance method. The method in which the periodic charge is computed as a constant fraction of the depreciated cost so that the depreciation base is written off by the estimated date of retirement.

direct access. Access to computer storage where information can be located directly, regardless of its position in the storage file. Compare *sequential access*.

direct cost. Cost of *direct material* and *direct labour* incurred in producing a product. See *prime cost*. In some accounting literature, this term is used to mean the same thing as *variable cost*.

direct costing. The method of allocating costs that assigns only *variable manufacturing costs* to product and treats *fixed manufacturing costs as period expenses*. A better term for this concept is "variable costing." Contrast with *absorption costing*.

direct financing lease. A lease that, from the point of view of the lessor, transfers substantially all the benefits and risks incident to ownership of property to the lessee and, at the inception of the lease, the fair value of leased property is the same as its carrying amount.

direct labour (material) cost. Cost of labour (material) applied and assigned directly to a product; contrast with *indirect labour (material)*.

direct posting. A method of bookkeeping where *entries* are made directly in *ledger accounts*, without the use of a *journal*.

direct write-off method. See *write-off method.*

directors' circular. Under securities legislation, a document issued to shareholders by the board of directors of a corporation in response to a takeover bid.

disbursement. Payment by *cash* or by a *cheque.* See *expenditure.*

discharge. The legal effect of the repayment of a debt or the performance of an obligation or the release of a person from an obligation (e.g. the release of a bankrupt from claims provable in bankruptcy upon completion of the processes of bankruptcy).

disclaimer. A written communication accompanying financial statements prepared by, or with the assistance of, a public accountant setting out that, since the terms of the engagement did not call for an expression of opinion on the financial statements, he or she has not performed an audit and consequently no opinion is being expressed. (Compare *auditor's opinion—denial of opinion.*)

disclosure. The showing of facts in *financial statements, notes* thereto, or the *auditor's report.*

discount. In the context of *compound interest, bonds,* and *notes,* the difference between *face* or *future value* and *present value* of a payment. In the context of *sales* and *purchases,* a reduction in price granted for prompt payment. See also *chain discount, quality discount,* and *trade discount.*

discount factor. The reciprocal of one plus the *discount rate.* If the discount rate is 10 percent per period, the discount factor for three periods is $(1 + 10)^{13} = 0.75131.$

discount rate. *Interest rate* used to convert future payments to *present value.*

discounted bailout period. In a *capital budgeting* context, the total time that must elapse before discounted value of net accumulated cash flows from a project, including potential *salvage value* at various times of assets, equals or exceeds the *present value* of net accumulated cash outflows. Contrast with *discounted payback period.*

discounted cash flow (DCF). Using either the *net present value* or the *internal rate of return* in an analysis to measure the value of future expected cash *expenditures* and *receipts* at a common date.

discounted payback period. Amount of time over which the discounted present value of cash inflows from a project, excluding potential *salvage value* at various times of assets, equals the discounted *present value* of the cash outflows.

discounting a note. See *note receivable discounted* and *factoring.*

discounts lapsed (lost). The sum of *discounts* offered for prompt payment that were not taken (or allowed) because of expiration of the discount period. See *terms of sale.*

discovery sampling. Acceptance sampling whereby an entire population is accepted if and only if the sample contains no disparities.

discovery value accounting. See *reserve recognition accounting.*

dishonored note. A *promissory note* whose maker does not repay the loan at *maturity* for a *term loan,* or on demand, for a *demand loan.*

distributable income. The portion of conventional accounting net income that can be distributed to owners (usually in the form of *dividends*) without impairing the physical capacity of the firm to continue operations at current levels. Pretax distributable income is conventional pretax income less the excess of *current cost* of goods sold and *depreciation* charges based on the replacement cost of *productive capacity* over cost of goods sold and depreciation on an *acquisition cost basis.* Contrast with *sustainable income.* See *inventory profit.*

distributable surplus. The statutory designation under certain corporations legislation to describe the portion of the proceeds of the issue of shares without *par value* not allocated to *share capital.*

distributed processing. Processing in a complex computer information network, in which data relevant only to individual locations is processed locally, while information required elsewhere is transmitted either to the central computer or to another local computer for further processing.

distribution. Disposition of the assets of a business or estate upon winding up. In a partnership, allocations or payments to partners relating to operating profits.

distribution expense. *Expense* of selling, advertising, and delivery activities.

diversified company. A company that is engaged in several distinctly different lines of business directly or through subsidiaries.

dividend. A distribution of *assets* generated by *earnings* to owners of a corporation; it may be paid in cash (cash dividend), with shares (stock dividend), with property, or with other securities (dividend in kind). Dividends, except stock dividends, become a legal liability of the corporation when they are declared. Hence, the owner of shares ordinarily recognizes *revenue* when a dividend, other than a stock dividend, is declared. See also *liquidating dividend* and *stock dividend.*

dividend yield. *Dividends* declared for the year divided by market price of the shares as of a given time of the year.

dividends in arrears. Dividends on *cumulative preferred shares* that have not been declared in accordance with the preferred share contract. Such arrearages must usually be cleared before dividends on *common shares* can be declared.

dividends in kind. See *dividend.*

divisional control. See *control system.*

divisional reporting. *Line-of-business reporting.*

dollar-sign rules. In presenting accounting statements or schedules, place a dollar sign beside the first figure in each column and beside any figure below a horizontal line drawn under the preceding figure.

dollar-value LIFO method. A form of *LIFO* inventory accounting with inventory quantities (*layers*) measured in dollar, rather than physical, terms. Adjustments to account for changing prices are made by use of a specific price index appropriate for the kinds of items in the inventory.

donated capital. A *shareholder's equity* account credited when contributions, such as land or buildings, are freely given to the company. Do not confuse with *contributed capital.*

donated surplus. The value of gifts of assets to a corporation from shareholders or others; a form of *contributed surplus.*

double-declining-balance depreciation (DDB). *Declining-balance-depreciation,* where the constant percentage used to multiply by book value in determining the depreciation charge for the year is 2/*n* and *n* is the *depreciable life* in periods. *Salvage value* is omitted from the depreciable amount. Thus if the asset cost $100 and has a depreciable life of 5 years, the depreciation in the first year would be $40 = 2/5 × $100, in the second would be $24 = 2/5 × ($100 − $40), and in the third year would be $14.40 = 2/5 × ($100 − $40 − $24).

double entry. The system of recording transactions that maintains the equality of the accounting equation; each entry results in recording equal amounts of *debits* and *credits.*

double T-account. *T-account* with an extra horizontal line showing a change in the account balance to be explained by the subsequent entries into the account, such as:

Plant

42,000	

This account shows an increase in the asset account, plant, of $42,000 to be explained. Such accounts are useful in preparing the *statement of changes in financial position*; they are not a part of the formal record keeping process.

double taxation. Corporate income is subject to the corporate income tax and the aftertax income, when distributed to owners, is subject to the personal income tax.

doubtful accounts. *Accounts receivable* estimated to be *uncollectible.*

downpayment. A part payment of the purchase price made at the time the contract is entered into.

Dr. The abbreviation for *debit.*

draft. A written order by the first party, called the drawer, instructing a second party, called the drawee (such as a bank), to pay a third party, called the payee. See also *cheque, cashier's cheque, certified cheque, sight draft,* and *trade acceptance.*

draw-down. A charge againts a deferred income tax credit account arising from an excess of the current liability for income taxes over the income tax expense for the year computed on an interperiod tax allocation basis. This process applies also to deferred income tax debit balances.

drawee. See *draft.*

drawer. See *draft.*

drawing account. A *temporary account* used in *sole proprietorships* and *partnerships* to record payments to owners or partners during a period. At the end of the period, the drawing account is closed by crediting it and debiting the owner's or partner's share of income or perhaps his or her capital account.

drawings. Payments made to a *sole proprietor* or to a *partner* during a period. See *drawing account.*

drilling fund. An investment vehicle, usually in the form of a limited partnership, in which funds are provided for oil and gas exploration. This method of investing may provide the investor with income tax advantages.

dry-hole accounting. See *reserve recognition accounting.*

dual transactions assumption (fiction). In presenting the *statement of changes in financial position,* some transactions not involving *working capital* accounts are reported as though working capital was generated and then used. For example, the issue of *capital stock* in return for the *asset,* land, is reported in the statement of changes in financial position as though stock were issued for *cash* and cash were used to acquire land. Other examples of transactions that require the dual transaction fiction are the issue of the *mortgage* in return for a noncurrent asset and the issue of stock to bondholders on *conversion* of their *convertible bonds.*

duality. The axiom of *double-entry* record keeping that every *transaction* is broken down into equal *debit* and *credit* amounts.

E

e. The base of natural logarithms; 2.71828182846 . . . . If *interest* is compounded continuously during a period at a started rate of *r* per period, then the effective *interest rate* is equivalent to interest compounded once per period at rate *i*, where $i = e^r - 1$. Tables of e^r are widely available. If 12 percent annual interest is compounded continuously, the effective rate is $e^{.12} - 1 = 12.75$ percent.

earned income. A term used in income tax legislation; broadly, income from personal services rendered, the carrying on of business or rental income.

earned surplus. A term once used, but no longer considered proper, for *retained earnings*.

earning power. The ability of an entity or security to generate income. The term usually refers to the present value of estimated future earnings.

earnings. *Income*, or sometimes *profit*.

earnings cycle. The period of time that elapses for a given firm, or the series of transactions, during which *cash* is converted into *goods* and *services*, goods and services are sold to customers, and customers pay for their purchases with cash. *Cash cycle*.

earnings forecast. An estimate of the most probable results of operations of an organization for one or more future periods.

earnings per (common) share. *Net income* to common shareholders (net income minus *preferred dividends*) divided by the average number of *common shares* outstanding; see also *basic earnings per share* and *fully diluted earnings per share*. See *ratio*.

earnings per (preferred) share. *Net income* divided by the average number of *preferred shares* outstanding during the period. This ratio indicates how well the preferred dividends are covered or protected; it does not indicate a legal share of *earnings*. See *ratio*.

earnings, retained. See *retained earnings*.

earnings statement. *Income investment*.

earn-out. An agreement between two merging firms under which the amount of payment by the acquiring firm to the acquired firm's shareholders depends on the future earnings of the *consolidated entity*.

easement. The acquired right or privilege of one person to use, or have access to, certain property of another. For example, a public utility's right to lay pipes or lines under property of another and to service those facilities.

economic entity. See *entity*.

economic depreciation. Decline in *current cost* of an *asset* during a period.

economic life. The time span over which the benefits of an *asset* are expected to be received. The economic life of a *patent*, *copyright*, or *franchise* may be less than the legal life. *Service life*.

economic order quantity. In mathematical *inventory* analysis, the optimal amount of stock to order when inventory is reduced to a level called the "reorder point." If A represents the *incremental cost* of placing a single order, D represents the total demand for a period of time in units, and H represents the incremental holding cost during the period per unit of inventory, then the economic order quantity $Q = \sqrt{2AD/H}$. Q is sometimes called the "optimal lot size."

economic unit. Any person, or group of persons with a common purpose, who engages in business transactions with others. A group of business enterprises operating under common control where the financial statements could be consolidated.

ED. *Exposure Draft*.

edit. A computer input control technique used to detect and correct data which are inaccurate, incomplete or unreasonable.

EDP. Abbreviation for *electronic data processing*.

effective interest method. A systematic method for computing *interest expense* (or *revenue*) that makes the interest expense for each period divided by the amount of the net *liability* (*asset*) at the beginning of the period equal to the *yield rate* on the bond at the time of issue (acquisition). Interest for a period is the yield rate (at time of issue) multiplied by the net liability (asset) at the start of the period. The *amortization* of discount or premium is the *plug* to give equal *debits* and *credits*. (Interest expense is a debit and the amount of coupon payments is a credit.)

effective (interest) rate. Of a bond, the *internal rate of return* or *yield to maturity* at the time of issue. Contrast with *coupon rate*. If the bond is issued for a price below *par*, the effective rate is higher than the coupon rate; if it is issued for a price greater than par, then the effective rate is lower than the coupon rate. In the context of *compound interest*, when the *compounding period* on a *loan* is different from 1 year, such as a nominal interest rate of 12 percent compounded monthly, then the single rate that could be applied at the end of a year to the beginning balance is economically equivalent to the series of compound interest calculations. If 12 percent per year is compounded monthly, the effective interest rate is 12.683 percent. In general, if the nominal rate is r percent per year and is compounded m times per year, then the effective rate is $(1 + r/m)^m - 1$.

effectively controlled company. A corporation which is under the control of another corporation or person by some means other than through the ownership of a majority of the voting shares.

efficiency variance. A term used for the *quantity variance* for labour or *variable overhead* in a *standard cost system*.

efficient market hypothesis. The supposition in finance that securities' prices reflect all available information and react nearly instantaneously and in an unbiased fashion to new information.

eligible. Under income tax legislation, a term which restricts or otherwise alters the meaning of another tax or accounting term, generally to signify that the related assets or operations are entitled to specified tax treatment.

eliminations. *Work sheet* entries to prepare *consolidated statements* that are made to avoid duplicating the amounts of *assets, liabilities, owner's equity, revenues,* and *expenses* of the consolidated *entity* when the accounts of the *parent* and *subsidiaries* are summed.

embezzlement. Misappropriation of assets in one's custody. Embezzlement restricted to cash is usually referred to as defalcation.

employee stock option. See *stock option.*

employer, employee payroll taxes. See *payroll taxes.*

enabling costs. A type of *capacity cost* that will stop being incurred if operations are shut down completely but must be incurred in full if operations are carried out at any level. Costs of a security force or of a quality control inspector for an assembly line might be examples. Contrast with *standby costs.*

ending inventory. The *cost* of *inventory* on hand at the end of the *accounting period*, often called "closing inventory." The dollar amount of inventory to be carried to the subsequent period.

endorsee. See *endorser.*

endorsement. See *draft.* The *payee* signs the draft and transfers it to a fourth party, such as the payee's bank.

endorser. The *payee* of a *note* or *draft* signs it, after writing "Pay to the order of X," transfers the note to person X, and presumably receives some benefit, such as cash, in return. The payee who signs over the note is called the endorser and person X is called the endorsee. The endorsee then has the rights of the payee and may in turn become an endorser by endorsing the note to another endorsee.

endowment fund. Property (often in the form of cash or investments acquired by gift or bequest) of a charitable, religious, educational or other non-profit institution, the income from which is used for specified purposes and the principal of which must be maintained intact or applied to the purposes of the fund.

engagement letter. A letter from a public accountant to a client outlining the scope of the accountant's responsibilities and the arrangements agreed upon with respect to an engagement.

enterprise. Any business organization, usually defining the accounting *entity.*

entity. A person, *partnership, corporation,* or other organization. The *accounting entity* for which accounting statements are prepared may not be the same as the entity defined by law. For example, a *sole proprietorship* is an accounting entity but the individual's combined business and personal assets are the legal entity in most jurisdictions.

Several affiliated corporations may be separate legal entities while *consolidated financial statements* are prepared for the group of companies operating as a single economic entity.

entity theory. The view of the corporation that emphasizes the form of the *accounting equation* that says *assets = equities.* Contrast with *proprietorship theory.* The entity theory is less concerned with a distinct line between *liabilities* and *shareholders' equity* than is the proprietorship theory. Rather, all equities are provided to the corporation by outsiders who merely have claims of differing legal standings.

entity value (of asset). The value of an asset to the particular entity owning the asset as compared to the value of the asset to an outsider.

entry value. The current *cost* of acquiring an asset or service at a *fair-market price. Replacement cost.*

EOQ. *Economic order quantity.*

EPS. *Earnings per share.*

EPVI. *Excess present value index.*

equalization reserve. An inferior title for the allowance account when the *allowance method* is used for such things as maintenance expenses. Periodically, maintenance *expense* is debited and the allowance is credited. As maintenance *expenditures* are actually incurred, the allowance is debited and cash or the other asset expended is credited.

equities. *Liabilities* plus *owners' equity.*

equity. A claim to *assets*; a source of assets. The residual interest in the assets of an entity that remains after deducting its liabilities. Usage may be changing so that "equity" will exclude liabilities. We prefer to keep the broader definition, including liabilities, because there is no other single word that serves this useful purpose.

equity financing. Raising *funds* by issuance of *share capital.* Contrast with *debt financing.*

equity method. A method of accounting for an *investment* in the shares of another company in which the proportionate share of the earnings of the other company is debited to the investment account and credited to a *revenue* account as earned. When *dividends* are received, *cash* is debited and the investment account is credited. Used in reporting when the investor effectively controls an unconsolidated company. One of the few instances where revenue is recognized without a change in *working capital.*

equity ratio. *Shareholders' equity* divided by total *assets.* See *ratio.*

equivalent production. *Equivalent units.*

equivalent units (of work). The number of units of completed output that would require the same costs as were actually incurred for production of completed and partially completed units during a period. Used primarily in *process costing* calculations to measure in uniform terms the output of a continuous process.

error. An unintentional mistake such as (1) arithmetical or clerical mistake affecting the financial statements, (2) unintentional misapplication of accounting principles, and (3) the oversight or misinterpretation of facts. Compare *fraud*.

error accounting. See *accounting errors*.

escalator clause. A clause inserted in a purchase or rental contract which permits, under specified conditions, upward adjustments of price or allowances.

escrow. An agreement whereby a deed, money or other property is deposited with a trustee to be held until certain conditions are fulfilled.

estate planning. The arrangement of an individual's affairs to facilitate the passage of assets to beneficiaries and to minimize taxes upon death.

estimated cost system. A costing method in which the recorded costs of production are initially based on estimated costs and adjusted later for any differences between estimated and actual.

estimated expenses. See *after cost*.

estimated liability. The preferred terminology for estimated costs to be incurred for such uncertain things as repairs under *warranty*. An estimated liability is shown in the *balance sheet*. Contrast with *contingency*.

estimated revenue. A term used in governmental accounting to designate revenue expected to accrue during a period whether or not it will be collected during the period. A *budgetary account* usually established at the beginning of the budget period.

estimated salvage value. Synonymous with *salvage value* of an *asset* before its retirement.

estimates, changes in. See *accounting changes*.

estimation sampling. The use of a sampling technique whereby a qualitative or quantitative characteristic of the population is inferred from the occurrence of that characteristic in the sample drawn. See *attribute(s) sampling*; *variables sampling*.

examination standards. Generally accepted auditing standards that prescribe planning and supervision of an audit engagement, studying and evaluating internal controls and obtaining audit evidence.

except for. Qualification in *auditor's report*, usually caused by a change, approved by the auditor, from one acceptable accounting policy or procedure to another.

excess present value. In a *capital budgeting* context, *present value* of anticipated net cash inflows minus cash outflows, including initial cash outflow for a project. See *net present value*.

excess present value index. *Present value* of future *cash* inflows divided by initial cash outlay.

exchange. The generic term for a transaction (or more technically, a reciprocal transfer) between one entity and another. In another context, the name for a market, such as the Toronto Stock Exchange.

exchange gain or loss. The phrase used for *foreign exchange gain or loss*.

exchange rate. The *price* of one country's currency in terms of another country's currency. For example, the British pound might be worth $1.80 at a given time. The exchange rate would be stated as "one pound is worth one dollar and eighty cents" or "one dollar is worth .5556 (= £1/$1.80) pounds."

excise tax. Tax on the manufacture, sale, or consumption of a commodity.

ex-dividend. Said of a share at the time when the declared *dividend* becomes the property of the person who owned the share on the *record date*. The payment date follows the ex-dividend date.

executor. A person appointed by a testator to give effect to his or her will after death.

executory contract. An agreement providing for payment by a payor to a payee upon the performance of an act or service by the payee, such as a labor contract. Obligations under such contracts generally are not recognized as *liabilities*. Some contracts are partially executory; these give rise to an *asset* or *liability* to the extent of partial performance. An example is the downpayment on a purchase.

executory costs. Costs related to the operation of a leased property such as insurance, maintenance costs, and property taxes.

exemption. A term used for various amounts subtracted from gross income to determine taxable income. Not all such subtractions are called "exemptions." See *tax deduction*.

exercise. When the owner of an *option* or *warrant* purchases the security that the option entitles him or her to purchase, he or she has exercised the option or warrant.

exercise price. See *option*.

exit value. The proceeds that would be received if assets were disposed of in an *arm's-length transaction*. *Current selling price*. *Net realizable value*.

expected value. The mean or arithmetic *average* of a statistical distribution or series of numbers.

expenditure. Payment of *cash* for goods or services received. Payment may be made either at the time the goods or services are received or at a later time. Virtually synonymous with *disbursement* except that disbursement is a broader term and includes all payments for goods or services. Contrast with *expense*.

expense. As a noun, a decrease in *owners' equity* caused by the using up of *assets* in producing *revenue* or carrying out other activities that are part of the entity's *operations*. A "gone" asset; an expired cost. The amount is the *cost* of the assets used up. Do not confuse with *expenditure* or *disbursement*, which may occur before, when, or after the related expense is recognized. Use the word "cost" to refer to an item that still has service potential and is an asset. Use the word "expense" after the asset's service potential has been used. As a verb, to designate a past or current expenditure as a current expense.

expense account. An *account* to accumulate *expenses*; such accounts are closed at the end of the accounting period. A *temporary owners' equity* account. Also used to describe a listing of expenses by an employee submitted to the employer for reimbursement.

expense centre. *Cost centre.*

experience rating. A term used in insurance to denote changes from ordinary rates to reflect extraordinarily large or small amounts of claims over time by the insured.

expired cost. An *expense* or a *loss*.

Exposure Draft. A preliminary statement of the *CICA Standards Committees* that shows the contents of a pronouncement the Committee is considering making effective.

ex rights. The condition of securities whose quoted market price no longer includes the right to purchase new securities, such rights having expired or been retained by the vendor. Compare *cum rights*.

extendible bond. A bond which, *at the option of the holder* may be extended beyond the stated maturity date or exchanged for a bond of the same issuer maturing at a later date. Compare *retractable bond*.

external audit. An audit performed by a person independent of the organization subject to audit, usually a public accountant. Compare *internal audit*.

external reporting. Reporting to shareholders and the public, as opposed to internal reporting for management's benefit. See *financial accounting* and contrast with *managerial accounting*.

extra dividend. A dividend paid in addition to a regular dividend.

extraordinary item. Gains, losses and provisions for losses which result from occurrences the underlying nature of which is not typical of the normal business activities of the enterprise, are not expected to occur regularly over a period of years, and are not considered as recurring factors in any evaluation of the ordinary operations of the business.

F

face amount (value). The nominal amount due at *maturity* from a *bond* or *note* not including contractual interest that may also be due on the same date. The corresponding amount of a share certificate is best called the *par* or *stated value*, whichever is applicable.

factoring. The process of buying *notes* or *accounts receivable* at a *discount* from the holder to whom the debt is owed; from the holder's point of view, the selling of such notes or accounts. When a single note is involved, the process is called "discounting a note."

factory. Used synonymously with *manufacturing* as an adjective.

factory cost. *Manufacturing cost.*

factory expense. Manufacturing *overhead. Expense* is a poor term in this context because the item is a *product cost*.

factory overhead. Usually an item of *manufacturing cost* other than *direct labour* or *direct materials*.

fair-market price (value). Price (value) determined at *arm's length* between a willing buyer and a willing seller, each acting rationally in his or her own self-interest. May be estimated in the absence of a monetary transaction.

fair presentation (fairness). When the *auditor's report* says that the *financial statements* "present fairly . . .," the auditor means that the accounting alternatives used by the entity are all in accordance with *GAAP*. In rare cases, a disclosed basis of accounting other than GAAP is deemed to present fairly.

FASB. Financial Accounting Standards Board. An independent board responsible, since 1973, for establishing *generally accepted accounting principles*. Its official pronouncements are called *Statements of Financial Accounting Concepts* (*SFAC*), *Statements of Financial Accounting Standards* (*SFAS*), and *Interpretations of Financial Accounting Standards*.

feedback. The process of informing employees about how their actual performance compares with the expected or desired level of performance in the hope that the information will reinforce desired behaviour and reduce unproductive behaviour.

FEI. *Financial Executives Institute.*

fiduciary. Someone responsible for the custody or administration of property belonging to another, such as an executor (of an estate), agent, receiver (in *bankruptcy*), or trustee (of a trust).

field. An area established in a computer record or on a punched card to provide for the storage or collection of a unit of information for processing (e.g. a customer name or inventory quantity); or a set of one or more characters recorded in such area.

field work. Work carried out by an auditor outside of his office. All work performed by an auditor in planning and supervising an audit engagement, studying and evaluating internal controls and obtaining audit evidence.

FIFO. First-in, first-out; an *inventory-flow assumption* by which *ending inventory* cost is determined from most recent purchases and *cost of goods sold* is determined from oldest purchases including beginning inventory. See *LISH*. Contrast with *LIFO*.

file dump. The listing of large sections of, or complete, electronic files in written form for visual editing.

finance. As a verb, to supply with *funds* through the *issue* of shares, bonds, notes, or mortgages, or through the retention of earnings.

financial accounting. The accounting for *assets*, *equities*, *revenues*, and *expenses* of a business. Concerned primarily with the historical reporting of the *financial position* and operations of an *entity* to external users on a regular, periodic basis. Contrast with *managerial accounting*.

Financial Accounting Standards Board. *FASB*.

financial capital maintenance concept. A concept of capital maintenance under which the capital to be maintained is the amount of the net assets (historical or current cost), measured in either nominal or constant dollars.

Financial Executives Institute. An organization of financial executives, such as chief accountants, *controllers*, and treasurers, of large businesses.

financial expense. An *expense* incurred in rising or managing *funds*.

financial forecast. An estimate of the most probable results of operations, and the most probable financial position and changes in financial position of an organization for one or more future periods.

financial institution. A generic term used to describe an organization, usually of substantial size, which as a primary activity deals in money or investment funds as contrasted with the production of goods or services, e.g. bank, trust company, life insurance company. Under securities regulations, the term has a special meaning.

financial position (condition). Statement of the *assets* and *equities* of a firm displayed on the *balance sheet* statement.

financial position form. A form where current liabilities are deducted from current assets to show working capital to which is added either long-term assets or long-term assets less long-term liabilities which are then equal to either long-term liabilities plus shareholders' equity or shareholders' equity.

financial ratio. See *ratio*.

Financial Reporting in Canada. An annual publication of the CICA that surveys the financial reporting practices of 300 Canadian public companies. Other than the *CICA Handbook* itself, this book is the most important and comprehensive source of information on what are generally accepted accounting practices in Canada.

financial reporting objectives. FASB *Statement of Financial Accounting Concepts No. 1* sets out the broad objectives of financial reporting that are intended to guide the development of specific *accounting standards*.

financial statements. The *balance sheet*, *income statement*, *statement of retained earnings*, *statement of changes in financial position*, *statement of changes in owners' equity accounts*, and *notes* thereto.

financial structure. *Capital structure*.

financial year. The term for *fiscal year* in Australia and Britain.

financing adjustment. The term used to describe the amount of changes during a reporting period in the current cost of assets held by an enterprise that, on the basis of the existing relationship between debt and equity, do not need to be charged against present and future revenues to provide for maintenance of the common shareholders' proportionate interest in the operating capability of the enterprise. The amount of the adjustment can be determined by applying (a) the proportion of net monetary liabilities on a historical cost basis to the aggregate of common shareholders' equity on a current cost basis and the net monetary liabilities to (b) the amount of the changes during the reporting period in the current cost amounts of inventory and property, plant and equipment.

financing lease. *Capital lease*.

finished goods. Manufactured product ready for sale; a *current asset* (*inventory*) *account*.

firm. Informally, any business entity. (Strictly speaking, a firm is a *partnership*.)

first-in, first-out. See *FIFO*.

first mortgage. A mortgage having priority over all other mortgages on a property.

fiscal year. A period of 12 consecutive months chosen by a business as the *accounting period* for annual reports. May or may not be a *natural business year* or a calendar year.

FISH. An acronym, conceived by George H. Sorter, for *first-in, still-here*. FISH is the same cost-flow assumption as *LIFO*. Many readers of accounting statements find it easier to think about inventory questions in terms of items still on hand. Think of LIFO in connection with *cost of goods sold* but FISH in connection with *ending inventory*. See *LISH*.

fixed assets. *Plant assets*.

fixed assets turnover. *Sales* divided by average total *fixed assets*.

fixed-benefit plan. A *defined-benefit (pension) plan*.

fixed budget. A plan that provides for specified amounts of *expenditures* and *receipts* that do not vary with activity levels. Sometimes called a ''static budget.'' Contrast with *flexible budget*.

fixed charges earned (coverage) ratio. *Income* before *interest expense* and *income tax expense* divided by interest expense.

fixed cost (expense). An *expenditure* or *expense* that does not vary with volume of activity, at least in the short run. See *capacity costs*, which include *enabling costs* and *standby costs*, and *programmed costs* for various subdivisions of fixed costs. See *cost terminology*.

fixed interval sampling. A method of choosing a sample in which the first item is selected from the population randomly, with the remaining sample items drawn at equally spaced intervals. (Compare variable interval sampling.)

fixed liability. *Long-term* liability.

fixed manufacturing overhead applied. The portion of *mixed manufacturing overhead cost* allocated to units produced during a period.

fixed-price contract. A contract under which the contractor is to receive as payment a fixed amount stipulated in the contract. (Compare *cost-plus contract*.)

fixture. A part of fixed assets usually consisting of machinery or equipment attached to or forming a normal part of a building.

flexible budget. *Budget* that projects receipts and expenditures as a function of activity levels. Contrast with *fixed budget*.

flexible budget allowance. With respect to manufacturing overhead, the total cost that should have been incurred at the level of activity actually experienced during the period.

float. *Cheques* that have been added to the depositor's bank account, but not yet subtracted from the *drawer's* bank account.

floating charge. A general claim on the assets of a corporation, given as debt security, without attachment to specific assets.

flow. The change in the amount of an item over time. Contrast with *stock*.

flow assumption. When a *withdrawal* is made from *inventory*, the cost of the withdrawal must be computed by a flow assumption if *specific identification* of units is not used. The usual flow assumptions are *FIFO*, *LIFO*, and *weighted-average*.

flow chart. A graphic presentation of the movement in operational sequence of goods, documents or work flow.

flow of costs. *Costs* passing through various classifications within an *entity*. See the diagram (page 889) for a summary of *product* and *period cost* flows.

flow-through basis. See *taxes payable basis*.

FOB. Free on board at some location (for example, FOB shipping point; FOB destination); the *invoice* price includes delivery at seller's expense to that location. Title to goods usually passes from seller to buyer at the FOB location.

folio. A page number or other identifying reference used in posting to indicate the source of an entry.

footing. Adding a column of figures.

footnotes. More detailed information than that provided in the *income statement*, *balance sheet*, *statement of retained earnings*, and *statement of changes in financial position*; these are considered an integral part of the statements and are covered by the *auditor's report*. Sometimes called ''notes.''

forecast. See *financial forecast*.

foreclosure. The revocation by a lender of a borrower's right to redeem his or her property as a consequence of the borrower's failure to remit required payments (as on a *mortgage*). Assume that the lender sells the property but the proceeds of sale are insufficient to cover the outstanding balance on the loan at the time of foreclosure. Under the terms of most mortgages, the lender becomes an unsecured creditor of the borrower for the still-unrecovered balance of the loan.

foreign business corporation. An income tax term; broadly, a corporation incorporated in Canada which carries on its business operations and has its assets situated outside Canada.

foreign currency. For *financial statements* prepared in a given currency, any other currency.

foreign currency transactions. Transactions of the reporting enterprise whose terms are denominated in a currency other than its reporting currency.

foreign exchange gain or loss. Gain or loss from holding *net* foreign *monetary items* during a period when the *exchange rate* changes.

foreign operation. A subsidiary, division, branch, joint venture, or similar type of entity which undertakes and/or records its economic activites in a currency other than the reporting currency of the reporting enterprise. Foreign operations are divided into two categories: (a) integrated foreign operations and (b) self-sustaining foreign operations. In some cases, a foreign entity may contain several distinct operations, some of which are integrated and some of which are self-sustaining.

forfeited share. A share to which a subscriber has lost title because of nonpayment of a *call*.

forward exchange contract. An agreement to exchange at a specified future date currencies of different countries at a specified rate called the "forward rate."

forward price. The price of a commodity for delivery at a specified future date. Compare *spot price*.

franchise. A privilege granted or sold, such as to use a name or to sell products or services.

fraud. A deliberate act or deception or manipulation with the specific intent of cheating or injuring another person or organization and providing illegitimate personal gains.

free on board. *FOB*.

freight-in. The *cost* of freight or shipping in acquiring *inventory*, preferably treated as a part of the cost of *inventory*. Often shown temporarily in an *adjunct account* that is closed at the end of the period with other purchase accounts to the inventory account by the acquirer.

freight-out. The *cost* of freight or shipping incurred in selling *inventory*, treated by the seller as a selling *expense* in the period of sale.

frequency distribution. An array of numbers showing the actual number of items or occurrences in each class of various states of a variable, arranged in the order of the classes.

full absorption costing. *Absorption costing*; the "full" is not necessary, but it often used for emphasis. See *reserve recognition accounting* for another definition in the context of accounting for natural resources.

full disclosure. The reporting policy requiring that all significant or *material* information is to be presented in the financial statements. See *fair presentation*.

fully diluted earnings per share. Smallest *earnings per share* figure on *common shares* that can be obtained by computing an earnings per share for all possible combinations of assumed *exercise* or *conversion* of *potentially dilutive securities*. Must be reported on the *income statement*.

fully funded (pension) plan. A pension plan for which the fund is sufficient to provide for the pension benefits accrued to date. Compare *partially funded (pension) plan*; *unfunded (pension) plan*.

fully vested. Said of a *pension plan* when an employee (or his or her estate) has rights to all the benefits purchased with the employer's contributions to the plan even if the employee is not employed by this employer at the time of retirement.

function. In governmental accounting, said of a group of related activities for accomplishing a service or regulatory program for which the governmental unit is responsible. In mathematics, a rule for associating a number, called the dependent variable, with another number or numbers, called independent variable(s).

functional classification. *Income statement* reporting form in which *expenses* are reported by functions, that is, cost of goods sold, administrative expenses, financing expenses, selling expenses; contrast with *natural classification*.

fund. An *asset* or group of assets set aside for a specific purpose. See also *fund accounting*.

fund accounting. The accounting for resources, obligations, and *capital* balances, usually of a not-for-profit or governmental *entity*, which have been segregated into *accounts* representing logical groupings based on legal, donor, or administrative restrictions or requirements. The groupings are described as "funds." The accounts of each fund are *self-balancing* and from them a *balance sheet* and an operating statement for each fund can be prepared. See *fund* and *fund balance*.

fund balance. In governmental accounting, the excess of assets of a *fund* over its liabilities and reserves; the not-for-profit equivalent of *owners' equity*.

funded. Said of a *pension plan* or other obligation when *funds* have been set aside for meeting the obligation when it becomes due.

funded debt. Outstanding bonds, debentures and long-term notes.

funding. Replacing *short-term* liabilities with *long-term* debt.

funds. Generally *cash* or cash and *temporary investments*. Sometimes used to refer to *working capital*, current assets less current liabilities.

funds provided by operations. An important subtotal in the *statement of changes in financial position*. This amount is the total of revenues producing *funds* less *expenses* requiring funds. Often, the amount is shown as *net income* plus expenses not requiring funds (such as depreciation charges) minus revenues not producing funds (such as revenues recognized under the *equity method* of accounting for a long-term investment).

funds statement. An informal name often used for the *statement of changes in financial position*.

future value. The value at a specific future date of a payment or series of payments calculated at an appropriate *interest rate*.

futures. Contracts to purchase or sell commodites, traded on an organized exchange, for future delivery.

G

GAAP. *Generally accepted accounting principles*. A plural noun.

GAAS. *Generally accepted auditing standards*.

gain. Increase in *owners' equity* caused by a transaction not part of a firm's typical, day-to-day operations and not part of owners' *investment* or *withdrawals*. The term "gain" (or "*loss*") is distinguished in two separate ways from related terms. First, gains (and losses) are generally used for nonoperating, incidental, peripheral, or nonroutine transactions: gain on sale of land in contrast to *gross profit* on *sale* of *inventory*. Second, gains and losses are *net* concepts, not gross concepts: gain or loss results from subtracting some measure of *cost* from the measure of inflow. *Revenues* and *expenses*, on the other hand, are gross concepts; their difference is a net concept. Gain is nonroutine and net, *profit* or *margin* is routine and net; revenue is routine and gross. Loss is net but can be either routine ("loss on sale of inventory") or not ("loss on disposal of segment of business").

gain contingency. See *contingency*.

gearing. British term for *financial leverage*.

gearing adjustment. Consider a firm, part of whose assets are *noncurrent liabilities* and who has experienced *holding gains* on its *assets* during a period. All of the increase in wealth caused by the holding gains belongs to the owners; none typically belongs to the lenders. Some British accounting authorities believe that published *income statements* should show the part of the holding gain as financed with debt in *income* for the period. That part is called the "gearing adjustment."

general expenses. *Operating expenses* other than those specifically assigned to cost of goods sold, selling, and administration.

general insurance. Insurance other than life insurance; e.g. fire, accident, medical, business interruption.

general fixed asset (group of accounts). Accounts showing those long-term assets of a governmental unit not accounted for in *enterprise*, *trust*, or intragovernmental service funds.

general fund. Assets and liabilities of a nonprofit entity not specifically earmarked for other purposes; the primary operting fund of a governmental unit.

general journal. The formal record where transactions, or summaries of similar transactions, are recorded in *journal entry* form as they occur. Use of the adjective "general" usually implies only two columns for cash amounts or that there are also various *special journals*, such as a *cheque register* or *sales journal*, in use.

general ledger. The name for the formal *ledger* containing all of the financial statement accounts. Some of the accounts in the general ledger may be *controlling accounts*, supported by details contained in *subsidiary ledgers*.

general partner. Member of *partnership* personally liable for all debts of the parternship; contrast with *limited partner*.

general price index. A measure of the aggregate prices of a wide range of goods and services in the economy at one time relative to the prices during a base period. See *consumer price index* and *GNE implicit price index*. Contrast with *specific price index*.

general price level adjusted statements. See *constant dollar accounting*.

general price level changes. Changes in the aggregate prices of a wide range of goods and services in the economy. These price changes are measured using a *general price index*. Contrast with *specific price changes*.

general purchasing power. The command of the dollar over a wide range of goods and services in the economy. The general purchasing power of the dollar is inversely related to changes in a general price index. See *general price index*.

general purchasing power accounting. See *constant dollar accounting*.

generally accepted accounting principles (GAAP). The conventions, rules, and procedures necessary to define accepted accounting practice at a particular time; includes both broad guidelines and relatively detailed practices and procedures.

generally accepted auditing standards. The standards, as opposed to particular procedures, promulgated by the *CICA Auditing Standards Committee* that concern "the auditor's professional qualities" and "the judgement exercised

Flow of Costs (and Sales Revenue)

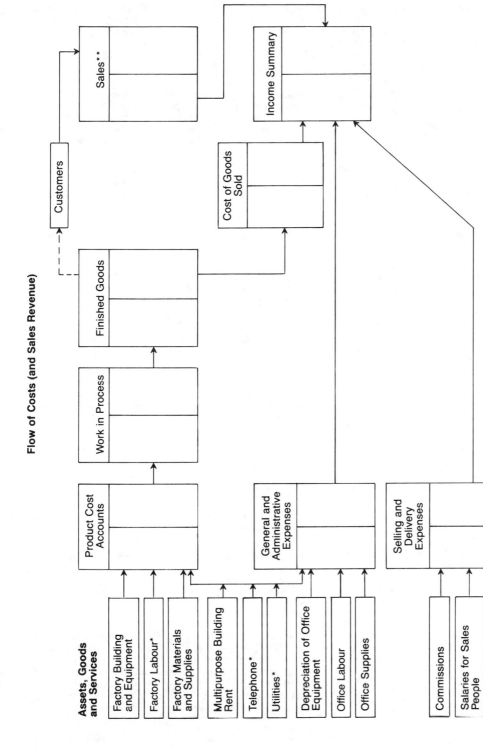

by him in the performance of his examination and in his report.'' Currently, there are eight standards: one general one (concerned with proficiency, independence, and degree of care to be exercised), three standards of field work, and four standards of reporting. The first standard of reporting requires that the *auditor's report* state whether or not the *financial statements* are prepared in accordance with *generally accepted accounting principles*. Thus the typical auditor's report says that the examination was conducted in accordance with generally accepted auditing standards and that the statements are prepared in accordance with generally accepted accounting principles. See *auditor's report*.

geographic segment. A single operation or a group of operations located in a particular geographic area, that generate revenue, incur costs and have assets employed in or associated with generating such revenue.

geometric mean. The nth root of the product of n values.

GNE implicit price index. Gross national expenditure implicit price index. An index measuring changes in prices for all final expenditures on goods and services produced in the domestic economy.

going-concern assumption. For accounting purposes a business is assumed to remain in operation long enough for all its current plans to be carried out. This assumption is part of the justification for the *acquisition cost* basis, rather than a *liquidation* or *exit value* basis, of accounting.

going concern value. The value of an asset or of net assets based on the going concern assumption. Compare *liquidation value*; *market value*.

going public. Said of a business when its *shares* become widely traded, rather than being closely held by relatively few *shareholders*. Issuing shares to the general investing public.

goods. Items of merchandise, supplies, raw materials, or finished goods. Sometimes the meaning of ''goods'' is extended to include all *tangible* items, as in the phrase ''goods and services.''

goods available for sale. The sum of *beginning inventory* plus all acquisitions, or purchases, of merchandise or finished goods during an *accounting period*.

goods in process. *Work in process*.

goodwill. The excess of cost of an acquired firm (or operating unit) over the current or *fair market value* of the separately identifiable *net assets* of the acquired unit. Before goodwill is recognized, all identifiable assets, whether or not on the books of the acquired unit, must be given a *fair market value*. For example, a firm has developed a *patent* that is not recognized on its books. If another company

acquires the firm, the acquirer will recognize the patent at an amount equal to its estimated fair market value. Informally, the term is used to indicate the value of good customer relations, high employee morale, a well-respected business name, and so on, that are expected to result in greater than normal earning power.

goodwill method. A method of accounting for the *admission* of a new partner to a *partnership* when the new partner is to be credited with a portion of capital different from the value of the *tangible* assets contributed as a fraction of tangible assets of the partnership. See *bonus method* for a description and contrast.

GPL. General price level; usually used as an adjective modifying the word ''accounting'' to mean *constant dollar accounting*.

GPLA. General price level-adjusted accounting; *constant dollar accounting*.

GPP. General purchasing power; usually used as an adjective modifying the word ''accounting'' to mean *constant dollar accounting*.

graded vesting. Said of a *pension plan* where not all employee benefits are currently *vested*. By law, the benefits must become vested according to one of several formulas as time passes.

grandfather clause. An exemption in new accounting *pronouncements* exempting transactions that occurred before a given date from the new accounting treatment.

gross. Not adjusted or reduced by deductions or subtractions. Contrast with *net*.

gross margin. *Gross profit*.

gross margin percentage. $100 \times (1 - cost\ of\ goods\ sold/net\ sales) = 100 \times (gross\ margin/net\ sales)$.

gross national product (GNP). The market value within a nation for a year of all goods and services produced as measured by final sales of goods and services to individuals, corporations, and governments plus the excess of exports over imports.

gross price method (of recording purchase or sales discounts). The *purchase* (or *sale*) is recorded at its *invoice price*, not deducting the amounts of *discounts* available. Discounts taken are recorded in a *contra* account to purchases (or sales). Information on discounts lapsed is not made available, and for this reason, most firms prefer the *net-price method* of recording purchase discounts.

gross profit. *Net sales* minus *cost of goods sold*.

gross profit method. A method of estimating *ending inventory* amounts. *Cost of goods sold* is measured as some fraction of sales; the *inventory equation* is then used to value *ending inventory*.

gross profit ratio. *Gross profit* divided by *net sales*.

gross profit test. A test of the validity of the closing inventory figure(s) by comparing the *gross profit ratio* for the period with those of prior periods taking into consideration known changes in selling prices and costs of production.

gross sales. All *sales* at *invoice* prices, not reduced by *discounts*, *allowances*, *returns* or other adjustments.

group accounts. The financial statements covering the business of a holding company and its subsidiary companies; the "group accounts" take the form of one or several sets of *consolidated statements* or a set consisting of the financial statements of each company in the group. British terminology.

group depreciation. A method of calculating *depreciation* charges where similar assets are combined, rather than depreciated separately. No gain or loss is recognized on retirement of items from the group until the last item in the group is sold or retired. See *composite life method.*

guarantee. A promise to answer for payment of debt or performance of some obligation if the person liable for the debt or obligation fails to perform. A guarantee is a *contingency* of the *entity* making the promise. Often, the words "guarantee" and "warranty" are used to mean the same thing. In precise usage, however, "guarantee" means a promise to fulfill the promise of some person to perform a contractual obligation, such as to pay a sum of money, whereas "warranty" is most often used to refer to promises about pieces of machinery or other products. See *warranty.*

guaranteed investment certificate. A certificate showing that a deposit of a specified amount has been made at a trust company for a specified period of time, generally five years, and at a specified rate of interest. In ordinary circumstances, the certificate is not redeemable before maturity. (Compare *deposit certificate*.)

guarantor. A person who gives a guarantee.

H

hardware. The physical equipment or devices forming a computer and peripheral equipment.

hash total. A control used to establish accuracy of processing, whereby a total of data is made by adding values which would not normally be added together (e.g. the sum of a list of part numbers) and subsequently compared to a computer-generated total of the same values.

hedge. To buy or sell commodity, foreign exchange or interest rate futures for the specific purpose of eliminating or restricting the risk involved in price or rate fluctuations.

hidden reserve. The term refers to an amount by which *owners' equity* has been understated, perhaps deliberately. The understatement arises from an undervaluation of *assets* or overvaluation of *liabilities*. By undervaluing assets on this period's *balance sheet*, *net income* in some future period can be made to look artificially high by disposing of the asset: actual *revenues* less artificially low cost of assets sold yields artificially high net income. There is no *account* that has this title.

hire-purchase agreement. A lease containing a purchase option.

histogram. A bar chart of a frequency distribution, in which the width of each band is the same and is equal to the class interval in the distribution and has a common boundary with the next band.

historical cost. *Acquisition cost*; *original cost*; a *sunk cost*.

historical-cost/constant-dollar accounting. Accounting based on *historical cost* valuations measured in *constant dollars*. *Nonmonetary items* are restated to reflect changes in the *general purchasing power* of the dollar since the time the specific *assets* were acquired or *liabilities* were incurred. A *gain* or *loss* is recognized on *monetary items* as they are held over time periods when the general purchasing power of the dollar changes.

historical summary. A part of the *annual report* to shareholders that shows important items, such as *net income*, *revenues*, *expenses*, *asset* and *equity* totals, *earnings per share*, and the like, for 5 or 10 periods including the current one. Usually not as much detail is shown in the historical summary as in *comparative statements*, which typically report as much detail for the year immediately preceding as for the current year. Annual reports may contain both comparative statements and a historical summary.

holdback. A portion of the progress payments called for under the terms of a contract which is not payable until the contract has been completed and the contractor has fulfilled his or her own financial obligations to subcontractors.

holding company. A company that confines its activities to owning *shares* in, and supervising management of, other companies. A holding company usually owns a controlling interest, that is more than 50 percent of the voting shares, in the companies whose shares it holds. In British usage the term refers to any company with controlling interest in another company.

holding gain or loss. Difference between end-of-period price and beginning-of-period price of an asset held during the period. Realized holding gains and losses are not ordinarily separately reported in financial statements. Unrealizied gains are not usually reflected in income at all. Some unrealized losses, such as on inventory or temporary investments, are reflected in income or *owners' equity* as the losses occur; see *lower of cost and market*. See *inventory profit* for further refinement, including *gains* on *assets* sold during the period. See also *backlog depreciation*.

holding gain or loss net of inflation. Increase or decrease in the *current cost* of an asset while it is held measured in units of *constant dollars*.

holding period. The time between acquisition and disposition of an *asset*. The length of the holding period can affect the tax rate applied to the *gain* or *loss* upon sale.

horizontal analysis. *Time-series analysis*.

horizontal integration. The extension of activity by an organization in the same general line of business or expansion into supplementary, complementary or compatible products. (Compare *vertical integration*.)

house account. An account with a customer where the usual sales commission is not paid. A member's account with his private club for use of the club's facilities and services as opposed to his membership fees.

human resource accounting. A term used to describe a variety of proposals that seek to report and emphasize the importance of human resources—knowledgeable, trained, and loyal employees—in a company's earning process and total assets.

hurdle rate. Required rate of return in a *discounted cash flow* analysis.

hybrid security. *Security*, such as a *convertible bond*, containing elements of both *debt* and *owners' equity*.

hypothecation. The *pledging* of property, without transfer of title or possession, to secure a loan.

I

ideal or theoretical capacity. The maximum level of production of which a resource or organizational unit is capable, making no allowance for interruptions.

ideal standard costs. *Standard costs* set equal to those that would be incurred under the best possible conditions.

identifiable assets. All tangible and intangible assets attributable to a segment, including the portion of those used jointly by two or more segments that can be allocated on a reasonable basis. Advances or loans to, or investments in, another segment are not included in identifiable assets of a segment unless its operations are primarily of a financial nature and such items are similar to those arising from transactions with customers outside the enterprise. In computing the amount of a segment's identifiable assets, allowances such as allowance for doubtful accounts and accumulated depreciation would be taken into account.

idle capacity. The portion of capacity that is not used due to lack of product demand, errors in planning or similar causes.

idle time. Time lost by labour or machinery because of lack of business, material shortages, machine breakdowns, retooling or similar causes. Compare *down time*.

IIA. *Institute of Internal Auditors*.

implicit interest. *Interest* not explicitly paid or received. See *interest*, *imputed*. All transactions involving the deferred payment or receipt of cash involve interest, whether explicitly mentioned or not. The implicit interest on a single-payment *note* is the difference between the amount collected at maturity less the amount lent at the start of the loan. The implicit *interest rate* per year can be computed from

$$\frac{\text{Cash Received at Maturity}}{\text{Cash Lent}^{(1/t)}} - 1$$

where t is the term of the loan in years; t need not be an integer.

imprest fund. A fund kept under the *imprest system*, e.g., imprest petty cash fund.

imprest system. A system for handling disbursements wherein a specified amount of cash or a bank balance is entrusted to an individual. The cash or bank balance is reimbursed from time to time for the exact amount of the disbursements from it on the basis of the vouchers covering the disbursements. At any time, the cash on hand or the bank balance plus the disbursement vouchers not reimbursed should equal the amount of the fund.

improvement. An *expenditure* to extend the useful life of an *asset* or to improve its performance (rate of output, cost) over that of the original asset. Such expenditures are *capitalized* as part of the asset's cost. Contrast with *maintenance* and *repair*.

imputed cost. A cost that does not appear in accounting records, such as the *interest* that could be earned on cash spent to acquire inventories rather than, say, government bonds. Or, consider the firm that owns the buildings it occupies. This firm has an imputed cost for rent in an amount equal to what it would have to pay to use similar buildings owned by another.

imputed interest. See *interest imputed*.

in the black (red). Operating at a profit (loss).

income. *Excess of revenues* and *gains* over *expenses* and *losses* for a period; *net income*. Sometimes used with an appropriate modifier to refer to the various intermediate amounts shown in a *multiple-step income statement*. Sometimes used to refer to revenues, as in "rental income." See *comprehensive income*.

income accounts. *Revenues* and *expense accounts*.

income before taxes. On the *income statement*, the difference between all *revenues* and *expenses* except *income tax* expense. Contrast with *net income* and *taxable income*.

income determination. See *determine*.

income distribution account. *Temporary account* sometimes debited when *dividends* are declared; closed to *retained earnings*.

income from continuing operations. All *revenues* less all *expenses* except for the following: results of operations, including income tax effects, that have been or will be discontinued; *gains* or *losses*, including income tax effects, on disposal of segments of the business; gains or losses, including income tax effects, from *extraordinary items*; and the cumulative effect of *accounting changes*.

income (revenue) bond. A bond on which the payment of interest depends on the level of the issuer's earnings.

income smoothing. A method of timing business *transactions* or choosing *accounting principles* so that variations in reported *income* from year to year are reduced from what they would otherwise be. Although income smoothing is an objective of some managements, it is not an official *accounting principle* or *reporting objective*.

income statement. The statement of *revenues*, *expenses*, *gains*, and *losses* for the period ending with *net income* for the period. The *earnings per share* amount is usually shown on the income statement; the *reconciliation* of beginning and ending balances of *retained earnings* may also be shown in a combined statement of income and retained earnings. See *extraordinary items*, *multiple-step*, *single-step*.

income summary. An *account* used in problem solving that serves as a surrogate for the *income statement*. All *revenues* are closed to the Income Summary as *credits*; all *expenses*, as *debits*. The *balance* in the account, after all other *closing entries* are made, is then closed to the retained earnings or other *owners' equity* account and represents *net income* for the period.

income tax. An annual tax levied by the federal and provincial governments on the income of an entity. An *expense*; if not yet paid, a *liability*.

income tax allocation. See *deferred tax liability* and *tax allocation*; *intrastatement*.

incorporation. The legal process of bringing a corporation into existence.

incremental. An adjective used to describe the change in *cost*, *expense*, *investment*, *cash flow*, *revenue*, *profit*, and the like if one or more units are produced or sold or if an activity is undertaken.

indenture. See *bond indenture*.

independence. The mental attitude required of the public accountant in performing the *attest* function. It implies impartiality and that the members of the auditing firm own no shares in the company being audited.

independent accountant. The *CA* who performs the *attest* function for a firm.

indeterminate-term liability. A *liability* lacking the criterion of being due at a definite time. This term is our own coinage to encompass the *deferred income tax liability* and *minority interest*.

indexation. An attempt by lawmakers or parties to a contract to cope with the effects of *inflation*. Amounts fixed in law or contracts are "indexed" when these amounts change as a given measure of price changes. For example, a so-called escalator clause (*COLA*) in a labour contract might provide that hourly wages will be increased as the *consumer price index* increases.

indexed bond. A bond on which the amount of interest and/or principal is linked to a specified index (generally an index related to the rate of inflation).

indirect cost pool. Any grouping of individual costs that are not identified with a *cost objective*.

indirect costs. Costs of production not easily associated with the production of specific goods and services; *overhead costs*. May be *allocated* on some arbitrary basis to specific products or departments.

indirect labour (material) cost. An *indirect cost* for labour (material) such as for supervision (supplies).

individual proprietorship. *Sole proprietorship*.

industry segment. A distinguishable component of an enterprise engaged in providing a product or service, or a group of related products or services, primarily to customers outside the enterprise.

inflation. A time of generally rising prices.

inflation accounting. Strictly speaking, *constant dollar accounting*. Some writers use the term, incorrectly, to mean *current cost accounting*.

information circular. Under corporations and securities legislation, a document, accompanying the notice of a shareholders' meeting, prepared in connection with the solicitation of proxies by or on behalf of the management of the corporation. It contains information concerning the persons making the solicitation, election of directors, appointment of auditors and other particulars of matters to be acted upon at the meeting.

information system. A system, sometimes formal and sometimes informal, for collecting, processing, and communicating data that are useful for the managerial functions of decision making, planning, and control, and for financial reporting under the *attest* requirement.

initial direct costs. In accounting for leases, the costs incurred by the lessor that are directly associated with negotiating and executing a specific leasing transaction, e.g. commissions, legal fees.

inner reserve. In financial institutions, a provision which is not separately disclosed in the balance sheet because it has been either applied against an asset or grouped with liabilities in whose transfer from or to income accounts are not disclosed in the income statement.

input. The quantity of goods or services entering the production process. Information introduced into a data processing system. To introduce information into a data processing system.

input/output analysis. A summary, usually in matrix form, of the transactions between all economic units involved, which shows the resources consumed or utilized by an economic unit and the resulting product of that unit.

insider. A person, as defined by corporate and securities legislation, who could be expected to be privy to information with respect to a corporation, e.g., directors, officers and major shareholders.

insolvent. Unable to pay debts when due. Said of a company even though *assets* exceed *liabilities*.

inspection. An auditing technique consisting of looking at records and documents or at assets having physical substance. It encompasses techniques of varying degrees of thoroughness such as examining, perusing, reading, reviewing, scanning and scrutinizing. Compare *observation*. See *practice inspection*.

inspector. A person appointed under corporations legislation to investigate the affairs and management of a corporation. One of a number of persons appointed by creditors of a bankrupt to guide the trustee and to supervise the administration of the estate.

installment. Partial payment of a debt or collection of a receivable, usually according to a contract.

installment contracts receivable. The name used for *accounts receivable* when the *installment method* of recognizing revenue is used. Its *contra, unrealized gross margin*, is shown on the balance sheet as a substraction from the amount receivable.

installment sales. Sales on account where the buyer promises to pay in several separate payments, called *installments*. Sometimes are, but need not be, accounted for on the *install-*

ment method. If installment sales are accounted for with the sales *basis of revenue recognition* for financial reporting but with the installment method for income tax returns, then a *deferred income tax liability* arises.

installment (sales) method. Recognizing *revenue* and *expense* (or *gross margin*) from a sales transaction in proportion to the fraction of the selling price collected during a period. Allowed for income tax reporting, but acceptable in *GAAP* only when cash collections are reasonably uncertain. See *unrealized* (and *realized*) *gross margin*.

Institute of Internal Auditors. The international association of accountants who are engaged in internal auditing and are employed by business firms. Administers a comprehensive professional examination; those who pass qualify to be designated CIA, certified internal auditor.

instrument of incorporation. The document by which a body corporate is created. Depending on the Canadian jurisdiction, it may be articles of incorporation, letters patent or memorandum of association.

insurable interest. A person's interest in property or in another person's life of such a nature as to expose him or her to pecuniary loss or liability in the event of damage or destruction to the property or injury or death of that other person.

insurance. A contract for reimbursement of specific losses; purchased with insurance premiums. Self-insurance is not insurance but merely the willingness to assume risk of incurring losses while saving the premium.

insurance fund. A fund of cash or investments set aside for self-insurance.

insured pension plan. A pension plan in which all benefits are purchased from and guaranteed by an insurance company as contributions are received. A pension plan for which the pension fund is held by an insurance company.

intangible asset. A nonphysical, *noncurrent* right that gives a firm an exclusive or preferred position in the marketplace. Examples are a *copyright*, *patent*, *trademark*, *goodwill*, *organization costs*, *capitalized* advertising cost, computer programs, licenses for any of the preceding, government licenses (e.g., broadcasting or the right to sell liquor), *leases*, *franchises*, mailing lists, exploration permits, import and export permits, construction permits, and marketing quotas.

integrated foreign operation. A foreign operation which is financially *or* operationally interdependent with the reporting enterprise such that the exposure to exchange rate changes is similar to the exposure which would exist had the transactions and activities of the foreign operation been undertaken by the reporting enterprise.

interactive. The capability of an on-line computer system to generate an immediate response to input or to a query entered from a user terminal.

intercompany elimination. See *eliminations*.

intercompany profit. If one *affiliated company* sells to another, and the goods remain in the second company's *inventory* at the end of the period, then the first company's *profit* has not been realized by a sale to an outsider. That profit is called "intercompany profit" and is eliminated from net *income* in *consolidated income statements* or when the *equity method* is used.

intercompany transaction. *Transaction* between *parent company* and *subsidiary* or between subsidiaries in a *consolidated entity* whose effects are eliminated in preparing *consolidated financial satements*. See *intercompany profit*.

intercorporate investment. A given *corporation* owns *shares* or *debt* issued by another.

interest. The charge or cost for using money; the earnings from lending money; expressed as a rate per period, usually 1 year, called the interest rate. See *effective interest rate* and *nominal interest rate*.

interest, imputed. If a borrower merely promises to pay a single amount, sometime later than the present, then the present value (computed at a *fair-market* interest rate, called the "imputed interest rate") of the promise is less than the *face amount* to be paid at *maturity*. The difference between the face amount and the present value of a promise is called imputed interest. See also *imputed cost*.

interest factor. One plus the *interest* rate.

interest method. See *effective-interest method*.

interest rate. See *interest*.

interfund accounts. In governmental accounting, the accounts that show transactions between funds, especially interfund receivables and payables.

interim certificate. A provisional certificate of shares, bonds, or other securities issued pending preparation of a formal certificate or payment in full on installment issues.

interim statements. Statements issued for periods less than the regular, annual *accounting period*. Most companies are required to issue interim statements on a quarterly basis. The basic issue in preparing interim reports is whether their purpose is to report on the interim period (1) as a self-contained accounting period, or (2) as an integral part of the year of which they are a part so that forecasts of annual performance can be made.

internal audit. An *audit* conducted by employees to ascertain whether or not *internal control* procedures are working, as opposed to an external audit.

internal check. A system of allocation of responsibility, division of work and methods of recording transactions whereby the work of an employee or group of employees is checked continuously by having to be in agreement with the work of others or by being correlated with the work of other employees. An essential feature is that no one employee or group of employees has exclusive control over any transactions or group of transactions. (Compare *internal control*.)

internal control. The plan of organization and all the coordinated methods and measures adopted by management to safeguard assets, ensure the accuracy and reliability of accounting data, promote operational efficiency and maintain adherence to prescribed policies.

internal control letter. A written communication from a public accountant, usually to client management, containing observations on internal control arising from the performance of his engagement. Compare *management letter*.

internal control questionnaire. As set of questions to identify controls and procedures in effect and to identify any weaknesses that exist in the system of internal control.

internal rate of return. The discount rate that equates the net *present value* of a stream of cash outflows and inflows to zero.

internal reporting. Reporting for management's use in planning and control; contrast with *external reporting* for financial statement users.

International Accounting Standards Committee. An organization that promotes the establishment of international accounting standards.

interperiod tax allocation. *Income tax expense* is assigned to the period when *income* is earned for *financial reporting* purposes rather than to the period when an obligation to pay *income taxes* is generated. This process is sometimes called "normalization" of income tax expense. See *deferred income tax liability*.

interpolation. The estimation of an unknown number intermediate between two (or more) known numbers.

intestate. A person who dies without leaving a will.

intrastatement tax allocation. See *tax allocation: intrastatement*.

inventoriable costs. *Costs* incurred that are added to the cost of manufactured products. *Product costs* (*assets*) as opposed to *period expenses*.

inventory. As a noun, the *balance* in an asset *account* such as raw materials, supplies, work in process, and finished goods. As a verb, to calculate the *cost* of goods on hand at given time or to physically count items on hand.

inventory control. The control of stock-in-trade by means of accounting controls, such as perpetual inventory records, and by means of physical controls, such as proper methods of buying, storing, issuing and periodic or continuous counting of inventories on hand.

inventory equation. *Beginning inventory + net additions − withdrawals = ending inventory*. Ordinarily, additions are net purchases and withdrawals are *cost of goods* *sold*. Notice that ending inventory, to be shown on the balance sheet, and cost of goods sold, to be shown on the income statement, are not independent of each other. The larger is one, the smaller must be the other. In valuing inventories, beginning inventory and net purchase are usually known. In some inventory methods (for example, some applications of the *retail inventory method*), cost of goods sold is measured and the equation is used to find the cost of ending inventory. In most methods, cost of ending inventory is measured and the equation is used to find the cost of goods sold (withdrawals). In *current cost* (in contrast to *historical cost*) accounting, *additions* (in the equation) include holding gains, whether realized or not. Thus the current cost inventory equation is Beginning Inventory (at Current Cost) + Purchases (where Current Cost is Historical Cost) + Holding Gains (whether Realized or not) − Ending Inventory (at Current Cost) = Cost of Goods Sold (Current Cost).

inventory certificate. A letter of representation obtained by the auditor from the client, covering the method of taking inventory, the basis of valuation and the ownership of goods included in the inventory.

inventory flow assumption. *Flow assumption* for measuring *inventory* and *cost of goods sold*.

inventory holding gains. See *inventory profit*.

inventory layer. See *LIFO inventory layer*.

inventory profit. This term has several possible meanings. Consider the data in the accompanying illustration. The *historical cost* data are derived in the conventional manner; the firm uses a *FIFO cost flow assumption*. The *current cost* data are assumed, but are of the kind that the *CICA Handbook* requires in section 4510.

Inventory Profit Illustration

	(Historical) Acquisition Cost Assuming FIFO	Current Cost
Assumed Data		
Inventory, 1/1/86	$ 900	$1,100
Inventory, 12/31/86	1,160	1,550
Cost of Goods Sold for 1986 . .	4,740	4,850
Sales for 1986	$5,200	$5,200
Income Statement for 1986		
Sales	$5,200	$5,200
Cost of Goods Sold	4,740	4,850
(1) Operating Income		$ 350
Realized Holding Gains		110[a]
(2) Realized Income = Conventional Net Income (under FIFO)	$ 460	460
Unrealized Holding Gain		190[b]
(3) Economic income		$ 650

[a]Realized holding gain during a period is current cost of goods sold less

historical cost of goods sold; for 1986 the realized holding gain under FIFO is $110 = $4,850 − $4,740. Some refer to this as "inventory profit."
[b]The total unrealized holding gain at any time is current cost of inventory on hand at that time less historical cost of that inventory. The unrealized holding gain during a period is unrealized holding gain at the end of the period less the unrealized holding gain at the beginning of the period. Unrealized holding gain prior to 1986 is $200 = $1,100 − $900. Unrealized holding gain during 1986 = ($1,500 − $1,160) − ($1,100 − $900) = $390 − $200 = $190.

The term "inventory profit" refers to the realized holding gain, $110 in the illustration. The amount of inventory profit will usually be material when FIFO is used and prices are rising.

Others, including us, prefer to use the term "inventory profit" to refer to the total *holding gains*, $330 (= $110 + $190, both realized and unrealized), but this appears to be a lost cause.

In periods of rising prices and increasing inventories, the realized holding gains under a FIFO cost-flow assumption will be substantially larger than under LIFO. In the illustration, for example, assume under LIFO that the historical cost of goods sold is $4,800, that historical LIFO cost of beginning inventory is $600, and that historical LIFO cost of ending inventory is $800. Then operating income, based on current costs, remains $350 (= $5,200 − $4,850), realized holding gains are $50 (= $4,850 − $4,800), realized income is $400 (= $350 + $50), the unrealized holding gain for the year is $250 (= ($1,500 − $800) − ($1,100 − $650)), and economic income is $650 (= $350 + $50 + $250). Because the only real effect of the cost flow assumption is to split the total holding gain into realized and unrealized portions, economic income is the same, independent of the cost-flow assumption. The total of holding gains is $300 in the illustration. The choice of cost flow assumption merely determines the portion reported as realized.

inventory turnover. Number of times the average *inventory* has been sold during a period; *cost of goods sold* for a period divided by average inventory for the period. See *ratio*.

invested capital. *Contributed capital*.

investee. A company whose shares are owned by another.

investigation. A special examination conducted for a particular purpose. It may be more or less extensive than the regular annual audit. Examples are an examination of operating results over a term of years for a prospective purchase or in connection with an issue of securities; an examination of books, vouchers, etc., in connection with fraud; an examination on behalf of a bank, finance company or prospective investor.

investment. An *expenditure* to acquire property or other assets in order to produce *revenue*; the *asset* so acquired; hence a *current* expenditure made in anticipation of future income. Said of *securities* of other companies held for the long term and shown in a separate section of the *balance sheet*; in this context, contrast with *temporary investments*.

investment tax credit. A reduction in income tax liability granted by the federal government to firms that buy new equipment. This item is a credit, in that it is deducted from the tax bill, not from pretax income. The tax credit has been a given percentage of the purchase price of certain assets purchased. The actual rules and rates have changed over the years. Section 3805 of the *CICA Handbook* recommends that the cost reduction approach be used. See *cost reduction approach* and *flow through basis*.

invoice. A document showing the details of a sale or purchase transaction.

I.O.U. (*colloq.*) An informal document acknowledging a debt, setting out the amount of the debt and signed by the debtor.

IRR. *Internal rate of return.*

issue. When a company exchanges its shares (or bonds) for cash or other assets, the company is said to issue, not sell, those shares (or bonds). Also used in the context of withdrawing supplies or materials from inventory for use in operations and drawing of a *cheque*.

issued shares. Those shares of *authorized capital stock* of a company that have been distributed to the shareholders. See *issue*. *Treasury shares* are legally issued but are not considered to be *outstanding* for the purpose of voting, *dividend declarations*, and *earnings-per-share* calculations.

J

job cost sheet. A schedule showing actual or budgeted inputs for a special order.

job-order costing. Accumulation of *costs* for a particular identifiable batch of product, known as a job, as it moves through production.

joint account. A bank account that may be drawn upon individually by two or more persons. An account or statement of a joint venture.

joint cost. Cost of simultaneously producing or otherwise acquiring two or more products, called joint products, that must, by the nature of the process, be produced or acquired together, such as the cost of the beef and hides of cattle. Generally, the joint costs of production are allocated to the individual products in proportion to their respective sales value at the *splitoff point*. Other examples include central *corporate expenses*, *overhead* of a department when several products are manufactured, and *basket purchases*. See *common cost*.

joint product. One of two or more outputs from a process that must be produced or acquired simultaneously. See *by-product* and *joint cost*.

joint venture. A business undertaking entered into by two or more parties, which terminates upon completion of the specified project.

journal. The place where transactions are recorded as they occur. The book of original entry.

journal entry. A recording in a *journal*, of equal *debits* and *credits*, with an explanation of the *transaction*, if necessary.

Journal of Accounting Research. Scholarly journal containing articles on theoretical and empirical aspects of accounting. Published three times a year by the Graduate School of Business of The University of Chicago.

journal voucher. A *voucher* documenting (and sometimes authorizing) a transaction, leading to an entry in the *journal*.

journalize. To make an entry in a *journal*.

judgment(al) sampling. A method of choosing a sample in which the selection of items to be examined is determined subjectively, as contrasted to selection by statistical methods. Compare *random sampling*.

junior security. A security that has a lower priority of claims on assets and/or income than certain other securities. Compare *senior security*.

K

K. Two to the tenth power (2^{10} or 1,024), when referring to computer storage capacity. It is derived from the prefix "kilo" which represents 1,000 in decimal notation.

kiting. This term means slightly different things in banking and auditing contexts. In both, however, it refers to the wrongful practice of taking advantage of the *float*, the time that elapses between the deposition of a *cheque* in one bank and its collection at another. In the banking context, an individual deposits in Bank A a cheque written on Bank B. He (or she) then writes cheques against the deposit created in Bank A. Several days later, he deposits in Bank B a cheque written on Bank A, to cover the original cheque written on Bank B. Still later, he deposits in Bank A a cheque written on Bank B. The process of covering the deposit in Bank A with a cheque written on Bank B and vice versa is continued until an actual deposit of cash can be arranged. In the auditing context, kiting refers to a form of *window dressing* where the amount of the account Cash in Bank is made to appear larger than it actually is by depositing in Bank A a cheque written on Bank B without recording the cheque written on Bank B in the *cheque register* until after the close of the *accounting period*.

know-how. Technical or business information of the type defined under *trade secret*, but that is not maintained as a secret. The rules of accounting for this asset are the same as for other *intangibles*.

L

labour. The cost of services and employees performing physical or mechanical tasks, usually paid as wages rather than salaries.

labour variances. The *price* (or rate) and *quantity* (or *usage*) *variances* for *direct labour* inputs in a *standard cost system*.

laid-down cost. The sum of all direct costs incurred for procurement of goods up to the time of physical receipt, such as invoice cost plus customs and excise duties, freight and cartage.

land. An *asset shown at acquisition cost* plus the *cost* of any nondepreciable *improvements*. In accounting, implies use as a plant or office site, rather than as a *natural resource* such as timberland or farm land.

land improvements. Expenditures incurred in the process of putting land into a usable condition, e.g. clearing, grading, landscaping, paving and installing utility services.

lapping (accounts receivable). The theft, by an employee, of cash sent in by a customer to discharge the latter's *payable*. The theft from the first customer is concealed by using cash received from a second customer. The theft from the second customer is concealed by using the cash received from a third customer, and so on. The process is continued until the thief returns the funds or can make the theft permanent by creating a fictitious *expense* or receivable write-off, or until the fraud is discovered.

lapse. To expire; said of, for example, an insurance policy or discounts made available for prompt payment that are not taken.

last-in, first-out. See *LIFO*.

layer. See *LIFO inventory layer*.

lead time. The time that elapses between order placing and receipt of the ordered *goods* or *services*.

learning curve. A mechanical expression of the phenomenon that incremental unit costs to produce decrease as managers and labour gain experience from practice.

lease. A contract calling for the lessee (user) to pay the lessor (owner) for the use of an asset. A cancelable lease is one the lessee can cancel at any time. A noncancelable lease requires payments from the lessee for the life of the lease and usually has many of the economic characteristics of *debt financing*. Most long-term noncancelable leases meet the usual criteria to be classified as a *liability*, but some leases entered into before 1979 need not be shown as a liability. The *CICA Handbook* requires disclosure in notes to the financial statements of the commitments for long-term noncancelable leases. See *capital lease* and *operating lease*.

leasehold. The *asset* representing the right of the *lessee* to used leased property. See *lease* and *leasehold improvement*.

leasehold improvement. An *improvement* to leased property. Should be *amortized* over *service life* or the life of the lease, whichever is shorter.

lease-option agreement. A lease which gives the lessee the option to purchase the property at a specified date for a stipulated price.

least and latest rule. Pay the least amount of taxes as late as possible within the law to minimize the *present value* of tax payments for a given set of operations.

ledger. A book of accounts. See *general ledger* and *subsidiary ledger*; contrast with *journal*.

legal capital. *Par* or *stated value* of issued *capital stock*. The amount of *contributed capital* that must remain permanently in the firm as protection for creditors.

legal entity. See *entity*.

lender. See *loan*.

lessee. See *lease*.

lessor. See *lease*.

letter of consent. A letter to a securities commission in which an auditor gives his or her consent to the publication of his or her report upon the financial statements contained in a prospectus.

letter of credit. A letter or document issued by a bank on behalf of a customer authorizing the person named therein to draw money to a specified amount from its branches or correspondents when the conditions set out in the document have been met.

letter of representation. A written declaration in which a client represents to the auditor that the information contained in the financial statements and other information provided to the auditor during the course of the audit are accurate and complete.

leverage. "Operating leverage" refers to the tendency of *net income* to rise at a faster rate than sales when there are *fixed costs*. A doubling of sales, for example, usually implies a more than doubling of net income. "Financial leverage" (or "capital leverage") refers to the increased rate of return on *owners' equity* (see *ratio*) when an investment earns a return larger than the *interest rate* paid for *debt* financing. Because the interest charges on debt are usually fixed, any *incremental* income benefits owners and none explicitly benefits debtors. When "leverage" is used without a qualifying adjective, it usually refers to financial leverage and means the use of *long-term* debt in securing *funds* for the *entity*.

leveraged lease. A special form of lease involving three parties—a *lender*, a *lessor*, and a *lessee*. The lender, such as a bank or insurance company, lends a portion, say 80 percent, of the cash required for acquiring the *asset*. The lessor puts out the remainder, 20 percent, of the cash required. The lessor acquires the asset with the cash, using the asset as security for the loan and leases it to the lessee on a *noncancelable* basis. The lessee makes periodic lease payments to the lessor, who in turn makes payment on the loan to the lender. Typically, the lessor has no obligation for the debt to the lender other than transferring a portion of the receipts from the lessee. If the lessee should default on required lease payments, then the lender can repossess the leased asset. The lessor is usually entitled to deductions for tax purposes for depreciation on the asset and for interest expense on the loan from the lender. The lease is leveraged in the sense that the lessor, who enjoys most of the risks and rewards of ownership, usually borrows most of the funds needed to acquire the asset. See *leverage*.

liability. Usually, a legal obligation to pay a definite or reasonably certain amount at a certain time in return for a current benefit. Some of the criteria are not met by items classified as liabilities where there are special circumstances. Examples are *pension* liabilities, estimates of future *warranty* expenditures, and *deferred tax liabilities*. See *indeterminate-term liability*. Other items meet the criteria to be a liability but are not shown as such, for example, noncancelable leases, which are sometimes disclosed only in footnotes; see *lease*.

liability certificate. A letter of representation obtained by the auditor from the client covering the client's actual and contingent liabilities, commitments, and assets pledged as security for debts.

lien. The right given by law or contract to a person to have a debt or duty satisfied out of the property belonging to the person owing the debt or duty.

life annuity. A *contingent annuity* in which payments cease at death of a specified person(s), usually the *annuitant(s)*.

life assurance. Insurance in which the amount specified in the contract is payable on the death of the person covered by the contract.

LIFO (last in first out). An *inventory-flow* assumption where the *cost of goods sold* is the cost of the most recently acquired units and the *ending inventory cost* is determined from costs of the oldest units: contrast with *FIFO*. In periods of rising prices and increasing inventories, *LIFO* leads to higher reported expenses and therefore lower reported income and lower balance sheet inventories than does FIFO. See *FISH* and *inventory profit*.

LIFO, dollar-value method. See *dollar-value LIFO method*.

LIFO inventory layer. The *ending inventory* for a period is likely to be larger than the *beginning inventory*. Under a *LIFO cost-flow assumption*, this increase in physical quantities is given a value determined by the prices of the earliest purchases during the year. The LIFO inventory then consists of layers, sometimes called "slices," which typically consist of relatively small amounts of physical quantities from each of the past several years. Each layer carries the prices from near the beginning of the period when it was acquired. The earliest layers will typically (in periods of rising prices) have prices very much less than current prices. If inventory quantities should decline in a subsequent period, the latest layers enter cost of goods sold first.

limited company. A corporation with share capital in which the liability of shareholders for debts of the corporation is limited to the amount of the capital for which they have subscribed. (Compare *company*; *corporation*.)

limited liability. Shareholders of corporations are not personally liable for debts of the company.

limited partner. Member of a *partnership* not personally liable for debts of the partnership; every partnership must have at least one *general partner* who is fully liable.

line-of-business reporting. See *segment reporting*.

line of credit. An agreement with a bank or set of banks for short-term borrowings on demand.

liquid. Said of a business with a substantial amount (the amount is unspecified) of *working capital*, especially *quick assets*.

liquid assets. *Cash*, *current marketable securities*, and, sometimes, *current receivables*.

liquidating dividend. *Dividend* declared in the winding up of a business to distribute the assets of the company to the shareholders. Usually treated by recipient as a return of *investment*, not as *revenue*.

liquidation. Payment of a debt. Sale of assets in closing down a business or a segment thereof.

liquidation value per share. The amount each *share* of stock will receive if the company is dissolved. For *preferred shares* with a *liquidation preference*, a stated amount per share.

liquidity. Refers to the availability of *cash*, or near-cash resources, for meeting a firm's obligations.

LISH. An acronym, conceived by George H. Sorter, for *last-in, still-here*. LISH is the same cost-flow assumption as *FIFO*. Many readers of accounting statements find it easier to think about inventory questions in terms of items still on hand. Think of FIFO in connection with *cost of goods sold* but of LISH in connection with *ending inventory*. See *FISH*.

list price. The published or nominally quoted price for goods.

list price method. See *trade-in transaction*.

listed security. A security that has been admitted to trading privileges on a stock exchange.

loading. An amount included in an instalment contract to cover administrative and selling costs, interest, risk and other factors. Sometimes referred to as finance charges.

loan. An arrangement where the owner of property, called the lender, allows someone else, called the borrower, the use of the property for a period of time that is usually specified in the agreement setting up the loan. The borrower promises to return the property to the lender and, often, to make a payment for use of the property. Generally used when the property is *cash* and the payment for its use is *interest*.

long-form report. A report, prepared by a public accountant at the conclusion of an engagement, containing such items as details of the items in the financial statements, statistical data, explanatory comments, recommendations to management or a description of the scope of the examination more detailed than the description found in the usual short-form report. The long-form report may or may not include an audit opinion. (Compare *short-form report*.)

long-lived (term) asset. An asset whose benefits are expected to be received over several years. A *noncurrent* asset; usually includes *investments*, *plant assets*, and *intangibles*.

long position. The condition of a person who owns securities or commodities carried on his account by a broker; such person is said to be "long" on those securities or commodities in the broker's accounts. The designations "long" and "short" are used in accounting for quantities of securities and commodities in the same way as the designations "debit" and "credit" are used in accounting for monetary values. Compare *short position*.

long-term (construction) contract accounting. The *percentage-of-completion* or *completed contract methods of revenue* recognition. Sometimes used to mean the *completed contract method*.

long-term liability. A liability which, in the ordinary course of business, will not be liquidated within one year or within the normal operating cycle where that is longer than a year.

loss. Excess of *cost* over net proceeds for a single transaction; negative *income* for a period. A cost expiration that produced no *revenue*. See *gain* for a discussion related and contrasting terms.

loss contingency. See *contingency*.

loss leader. An item which is sold at a very low price in order to attract customers with the hope that they will also buy other more profitable items.

loss ratio. (*insurance*) The ratio of claims allowed to premiums earned in a period for a particular type of risk.

lower of cost and market. A method of valuing items of inventory or temporary investments, under which losses inherent in declines of market prices below cost are recognized in the period in which such losses become apparent.

lump-sum acquisition. *Basket purchase*.

M

machine language. A computer language used in the internal operations of a computer. Compare *program(ming) language*.

maintenance. *Expenditures* undertaken to preserve an *asset's* service potential for its originally intended life; these expenditures are treated as *period expenses* or *product costs*; contrast with *improvement*. See *repair*.

majority rule voting. A method of electing a board of directors whereby the owner of any one share is allowed as many votes as there are directors to be elected but only one vote may be cast for a particular candidate. Compare *cumulative voting*.

make-or-buy decision. A managerial decision about whether the firm should produce a product internally or purchase it from others. Proper make-or-buy decisions in the short run result only when *opportunity costs* are the only costs considered in decision making.

maker (of note) (of cheque). One who signs a *note* to borrow. One who signs a *cheque*; in this context, synonymous with drawer; see *draft*.

management. Executive authority that operates a business.

management (managerial) accounting. Reporting designed to enhance the ability of management to do its job of decision making, planning, and control; contrast with *financial accounting*.

management audit. An audit conducted to determine whether the objectives, policies, and procedures for a firm or one of its operating units are properly carried out. Generally applies only to activities for which qualitative standards can be specified. See *audit* and *internal audit*.

management by exception. A principle of management where attention is focused only on performance that is significantly different from that expected.

management by objective. A management approach designed to focus on the definition and attainment of overall and individual objectives with the participation of all levels of management.

management consultant. A person who advises management of an organization concerning the conduct of its operations.

management information system. A system designed to provide all levels of management with timely and reliable information required for planning, control and evaluation of performance.

management letter. A written communication from a public accountant to client management containing observations on control and other matters arising from the performance of his engagement, together with recommendations for improvement. See also *long-form report*. Compare *internal control letter*.

managerial accounting. See *management accounting*.

manufacturing cost. Costs of producing goods, usually in a factory.

manufacturing expense. An imprecise, and generally incorrect, alternative title for *manufacturing overhead*.

manufacturing overhead. General manufacturing *costs* incurred in providing a capacity to carry on productive activities but that are not directly associated with identifiable units of product. *Fixed* manufacturing overhead costs are treated as a *product cost* under *absorption costing* but as an *expense* of the period under *direct costing*.

manufacturing statement. A financial statement showing particulars of the cost of the goods manufactured. See *cost of goods sold*.

margin. *Revenue* less specified expenses. See *contribution margin*, *gross margin*, and *current margin*.

margin of safety. Excess of actual, or budgeted, sales over *breakeven* sales. Usually expressed in dollars; may be expressed in units of product or as a *ratio*.

marginal cost. The *incremental cost* or *differential cost* of the last unit added to production or the first unit subtracted from production. See *cost terminology*.

marginal costing. *Direct costing*.

marginal revenue. The increment in *revenue* from sale of one additional unit of product.

marginal tax rate. The tax imposed on the next dollar of taxable income generated; contrast with *statutory tax rate* and *average tax rate*.

mark sense. To record electrically conductive marks manually on a punch card for later input into the data processing system.

markdown. See *markup* for definition and contrast.

markdown cancellation. See *markup* for definition and contrast.

market price. See *fair market price*.

market rate. The rate of *interest* a company must pay to borrow *funds* currently. See *effective rate*.

marketable securities. *Shares* and *bonds* of other companies held that can be readily sold on stock exchanges or over-the-counter markets and that the company plans to sell as cash is needed. Classified as *current* assets and as part of *working capital*. The same securities held for *long-term* purposes would be classified as *noncurrent assets*.

markon. See *markup* for definition and contrast.

markup. When a retailer acquires items for *inventory*, the items are given a selling price. The difference between the original selling price and cost is most precisely called

"markon," although many business people use the term "markup," and because of confusion of this use of "markup" with its precise definition (see below), "original markup" is sometimes used. If the originally established retail price is increased, the precise term for the amount of price increase is "markup," although "additional markup" is sometimes used. If a selling price is lowered, the terms "markdown" and "markup cancellation" are used. "Markup cancellation" refers to reduction in price following "additional markups" and can, by definition, be no more than the amount of the additional markup; "cancellation of additional markup," although not used, is descriptive. "Markdown" refers to price reductions from the original retail price. A price increase after a markdown is a "markdown cancellation." If original cost is $12 and original selling price is $20, then markon (original markup) is $8; if the price is later increased to $24, the $4 increase is markup (additional markup); if the price is later lowered to $21, the $3 reduction is markup cancellation; if price is lowered further to $17, the $4 reduction is $1 markup cancellation and $3 markdown; if price is later increased to $22, the $5 increase is $3 of markdown cancellation and $2 of markup (additional markup). Markup cancellations and markdowns are separately counted because the former are deducted (while the latter are not) in computing the selling prices of goods available for sale for the denominator of the *cost percentage* used in the conventional *retail inventory method*.

markup cancellation. See *markup* for definition and contrast.

markup percentage. *Markup* divided by (acquisition cost plus *markup*).

master budget. A *budget* projecting all *financial statements* and their components.

master file. A file of semi-permanent reference information that is used frequently or for more than one purpose in data processing.

matching convention. The concept of recognizing cost expirations (*expenses*) in the same accounting period when the related *revenues* are recognized. Combining or simultaneously recognizing the revenues and expenses that jointly result from the same *transactions* or other events.

material. As an adjective, it means relatively important. See *materiality*. Currently, no operational definition exists. As a noun, *raw material*.

material variances. *Price* and *quantity variances* for *direct materials* in *standard cost systems*. Sometimes used to mean variances that are significant; see *materiality*.

materiality. Significance. As a general rule, in the context of financial statements, matcriality may be judged in relation to the reasonable prospect of an item's significance in the making of decisions by users.

matrix. A rectangular array of numbers or mathematical symbols.

matrix inverse. For a given *square matrix* $\mathbf{A}$, the square matrix inverse is the matrix, $\mathbf{A}^{-1}$, such that $\mathbf{A}\mathbf{A}^{-1} = \mathbf{A}^{-1}\mathbf{A} = \mathbf{I}$, the *identity matrix*. Not all square matrices have inverses. Those that do not are called singular; those that do are nonsingular.

maturity. The date at which an obligation, such as the *principal* of a *bond* or a *note*, becomes due.

maturity value. The amount expected to be collected when a loan reaches *maturity*. Depending on the context, the amount may be *principal* or principal and *interest*.

MBO. Abbreviation for *management by objective*.

measuring unit. See *attribute measured* for definition and contrast.

median. The position in an array of numbers where there are an equal number of items or occurrences on each side.

memorandum entry. An explanatory notation in a book of account which does not change the balance in any account.

merchandise. *Finished goods* bought by a retailer or wholesaler for resale; contrast with finished goods of a manufacturing business.

merchandise turnover. *Inventory turnover* for merchandise; see *ratio*.

merchandising business. As opposed to a manufacturing or service business, one that purchases (rather than manufactures) *finished goods* for resale.

merger. The joining of two or more businesses into a single *economic entity*. See *holding company*.

mineral rights. The right to take minerals, oil or gas from under the surface of land or sea.

minority interest. A *balance sheet account* on *consolidated statements* showing the *equity* in a less-than-100-percent-owned *subsidiary* company allocable to those who are not part of the controlling (majority) interest. May be classified either as shareholders' equity or as a liability of *indeterminate term* on the consolidated balance sheet. On the *income statement*, the minority's interest in the current period's income of the less-than-100-percent-owned subsidiary must be substracted to arrive at consolidated *net income* for the period.

minority investment. A holding of less than 50 percent of the *voting shares* in another company. Accounted for with the *cost method* when it is not effectively controlled, and with the *equity method* otherwise.

minutes book. A record of all actions authorized at corporate *board of directors'* or shareholders' meetings.

MIS. Abbreviation for *management information system*.

mode. The most frequently occurring numerical value in a group of items.

modified cash basis. The *cash basis of accounting* with long-term assets accounted for with the *accrual basis of accounting*. Most uses of the term "cash basis of accounting" actually mean "modified cash basis."

monetary assets, liabilities. See *monetary items*.

monetary gain or loss. The *gain* or *loss* in general purchasing power as a result of holding *monetary assets* or liabilities during a period when the *general purchasing power of the dollar* changes. During periods of *inflation*, holders of net monetary assets lose, and holders of net monetary liabilities gain, general purchasing power. During periods of *deflation*, holders of net monetary assets gain, and holders of net monetary liabilities lose, general purchasing power. Explicitly reported in *constant dollar accounting*.

monetary items. Money and claims to money the value of which, in terms of the monetary unit, whether foreign or domestic, is fixed by contract or otherwise. Deferred income taxes are classified as non-monetary.

monetary unit sampling. A sampling technique in which the items in the population are defined in terms of individual monetary units (e.g. dollars) with each item having an equal chance of selection. (Compare *physical unit sampling*.)

money. A word seldom used with precision in accounting, at least in part because economists have not yet agreed on its definition. Economists use the term to refer to both a medium of exchange and a unit of value. See *cash* and *monetary items*.

money-purchase plan. A *pension plan* where the employer contributes a specified amount of cash each year to each employee's pension fund. Benefits ultimately received by the employee are not specifically defined but depend on the rate of return on the cash invested. Sometimes called a "defined-contribution" pension plan; contrast with *defined-benefit plan*. As of the mid-1970s most corporate pension plans were defined-benefit plans because both the law and *generally accepted accounting principles* for pensions made defined-benefit plans more attractive than money-purchase plans.

mortality table. Data on life expectancies or probabilities of death for persons of specified ages and sex.

mortgage. A claim given by the borrower (mortgagor) to the lender (mortgagee) against the borrower's property in return for a loan. See *chattel mortgage, first mortgage*.

mortgage bond. A bond secured by a mortgage.

moving average. An *average* computed on observations over time. As a new observation becomes available, the oldest one is dropped so that the average is always computed for the same number of observations and only the most recent ones. Sometimes, however, this term is inaccurately used synonymously with *weighted average*.

moving average method. *Weighted-average method.*

multinational company. A business enterprise with activities and invested capital in several countries.

multiple-step. Said of an *income* statement where various classes of *expenses* and *losses* are subtracted from *revenues* to show intermediate items such as *operating income*, income of the enterprise (operating plus *interest* income), income to investors (income of the enterprise less *income taxes*), net income to shareholders (income to investors less interest charges), and income retained (income to shareholders less dividends). See *entity theory*, *single step*.

municipal bond. A *bond* issued by a village, town, city, county, province, or other public body.

mutual fund. An investment company that issues its own shares to the public and uses the proceeds to invest in securities of other companies. A mutual fund usually owns less than 5 or 10 percent of the shares of any one company and accounts for its investments using current *market values*; contrast with *holding company*.

mutually exclusive projects. Competing investing projects, where accepting one project eliminates the possibility of undertaking the remaining projects.

N

national income accounting. The preparation and interpretation of overall economic statistics of a nation in financial statement form, measuring the total earnings of labour and property from the production of goods and services.

natural business year. A 12-month period chosen as the reporting period so that the end of the period coincides with a low point in activity or inventories. See *ratio* for a discussion of analyses of financial statements of companies using a natural business year.

natural classification. *Income statement* reporting form in which *expenses* are classified by nature of items as acquired, that is, materials, wages, salaries, insurance, and taxes, as well as depreciation; contrast with *functional classification*.

natural growth asset. An asset whose value will increase through natural growth, e.g., a stand of timber, a herd of cattle.

natural resources. Timberland, oil and gas wells, ore deposits, and other products of nature that have economic value. The cost of natural resources is subject to *depletion*. Natural resources are "nonrenewable" (for example, oil, coal, gas, ore deposits) or "renewable" (timber land, sod fields); the former are often called "wasting assets." See also *reserve recognition accounting* and *percentage depletion*.

NBV. Abbreviation for *net book value*.

negative assurance. A statement by an accountant or auditor to the effect that nothing has come to his attention in the course of his work which would give him reason to believe that the matters under consideration do not meet a given standard.

negative confirmation. See *confirmation*.

negative goodwill. Refer to *goodwill*. When the purchase price of the company acquired is less than the sum of the *fair value* of the *net assets* acquired, the *CICA Handbook* requires that the valuation of noncurrent assets (except *investments* in *marketable securities*) acquired be reduced until the purchase price equals the adjusted valuation of the fair market value of net assets acquired. If after the adjusted valuation of noncurrent assets is reduced to zero and the purchase price is still less than the net assets acquired, then the difference is shown as a credit balance in the balance sheet as negative goodwill and is amortized to income over a period not to exceed 40 years. For negative goodwill to exist, someone must be willing to sell a company for less than the fair market value of net current assets and marketable securities. Because such a bargain purchase is rare, negative goodwill is rarely found in the financial statements; when it does appear, it generally signals unrecorded obligations, such as for *pensions*.

negotiable. Legally capable of being transferred by endorsement. Usually said of *cheque* and *notes* and sometimes of *shares* and *bearer bonds*.

net. Reduced by all relevant deductions.

net assets. *Owners' equity*; total *assets* minus total *liabilities*.

net book value. The unexpired cost of an asset carried on the financial records of an organization, equal to *cost* less *accumulated depreciation*.

net current asset value (per share). *Working capital* divided by the number of common shares outstanding. Many security analysts think that when a common share trades in the market for an amount less than net current asset value, then the shares are undervalued and should be purchased. We find this view naive because it ignores the efficiency of capital markets generally and, specifically, unrecorded obligations such as for *pension plans*, not currently reported as liabilities in the *balance sheet* under *GAAP*.

net current assets. *Working capital = current assets − current liabilities*.

net income. The excess of all *revenues* and *gains* for a period over all *expenses* and *losses* of the period. See *comprehensive income*.

net loss. The excess of all *expenses* and *losses* for a period over all *revenues* and *gains* of the period. Negative *net income*.

net markup. In the context of *retail inventory methods*, *markups* less markup cancellations; a figure that usually ignores *markdowns* and markdown cancellations.

net of tax method. A nonsanctioned method for dealing with the problem of income tax allocation. Deferred tax credit items are subtracted from specific asset amounts rather than being shown as a deferred credit or liability.

net of tax reporting. Reporting, such as for *extraordinary items* and *prior-period adjustments*, where the amounts presented in *financial statements* have been adjusted for all income tax effects. For example, if an extraordinary loss amounted to $10,000 and the marginal tax rate were 40 percent, then the extraordinary item would be reported "net of taxes" as a $6,000 loss. Hence, all income taxes may not be reported on one line of the income statement. The taxes will be allocated to extraordinary items, cumulative effects of an *accounting change*, and prior-period adjustments.

net present value. Discounted or *present value* of all cash inflows and outflows of a project or from an *investment* at a given *discount rate*. See *excess present value*.

net present value method. A method of project evaluation based on the net present value of the expected cash outflows and inflows, usually using the cost of capital as the *discount rate*. See *excess present value*.

net price method (of recording purchase or sales discounts). The *purchase* (or *sale*) is recorded at its *invoice* price less all *discounts* made available under the assumption that nearly all discounts will be taken. Discounts lapsed through failure to pay promptly are recorded in an *adjunct account* to purchases (or sales) or in the purchasing context, to an *expense* account. For purchases, management usually prefers to know about the amount of discounts lost because of inefficient operations, not the amounts taken, so that most managers prefer the net price method to the *gross price method*.

net realizable value. The estimated selling price of an asset in the ordinary course of business less reasonably predictable costs of completion and disposal.

net sales. Sales (at gross invoice amount) less *returns*, *allowances*, freight paid for customers, and *discounts* taken.

net working capital. *Working capital*; the "net" is redundant in accounting. Financial analysts sometimes mean *current* assets when they speak of working capital, so for them the "net" is not redundant.

net worth. A misleading term, to be avoided, that means the same as *owners' equity*.

network analysis. A method of planning and scheduling a project, usually displayed in diagrammatic form, in order to identify the interrelated sequences that must be accomplished to complete the project.

neutrality. In accounting information, the absence of *bias* intended to attain a predetermined result or to induce a particular form of behaviour.

new entity method. A business combination in which the ownership interests of two or more companies are joined together through an exchange of voting shares and in which none of the parties can be identified as an acquirer.

next-in, first-out. See *NIFO*.

NIFO. *Next-in, first-out.* In making decisions, many managers consider *replacement costs* (rather than *historical costs*) and refer to them as NIFO costs.

no par. Said of *shares* without a *par value*.

no par value shares. Shares of capital stock which have no nominal or par value.

nominal accounts. *Temporary accounts* as opposed to *balance sheet accounts*. All nominal accounts are *closed* at the end of each *accounting period*.

nominal amount (value). An amount stated in dollars, in contrast to an amount stated in *constant dollars*. Contrast with *real amount (value)*.

nominal dollars. Actual money amounts used to measure financial statement items without adjustment for the fact that the general purchasing power of the dollar varies over time.

nominal interest rate. A rate specified on a *debt* instrument, which usually differs from the market or *effective rate*. Also, a rate of *interest* quoted for a year. If the interest is compounded more often than annually, then the *effective interest rate* is higher than the nominal rate.

nominal owner. The person who holds title to an asset, usually a security, on behalf of the beneficial owner. (Compare *beneficial owner*.)

non-arm's length. Converse of *arm's length*.

noncancelable. See *lease*.

nonconsolidated subsidiary. An *intercorporate investment* where more than 50 percent of the shares of the *subsidiary* are owned but the investment is accounted for with the *equity method* or, in some rare circumstances, the *cost method*.

noncontributory. Said of a *pension plan* where only the employer makes payments to a pension *fund*; contrast with *contributory*.

non-cumulative share. A share of non-cumulative stock.

non-cumulative stock. A class of preferred capital stock in which the right to a dividend lapses if not paid within a specified period, usually annually.

noncurrent. Due more than 1 year (or more than one *operating cycle*) hence.

noninterest-bearing note. A *note* that bears no explicit interest. The *present value* of such a note at any time before *maturity* is less than the *face value* so long as *interest rates* are positive.

nonmanufacturing costs. All *costs* incurred other than those to produce goods.

nonmonetary items. All items that are not monetary; see *monetary items*.

nonoperating. In the *income statement* context, said of revenues and expenses arising from transactions incidental to the company's main line(s) of business. In the *statement of changes in financial position* context, said of all sources or uses of *working capital* other than working capital provided by operations.

nonprofit organization. An incorporated *entity*, such as a hospital, with no owners who share in the earnings. It usually emphasizes providing services rather than maximizing income.

nonrecurring. Said of an event that is not expected to happen often for a given firm. The effects of such events should be disclosed separately, but as part of *ordinary* items unless the event is also unusual. See *extraordinary* item.

normal capacity. The maximum level of production of a resource or organizational unit under normal circumstances.

normal cost. *Pension plan expenses* incurred during an *accounting period* for employment services performed during that period; contrast with accrued actuarial obligation.

normal costing. Method of charging costs to products using actual *direct materials*, actual *direct labour*, and predetermined *factory overhead* rates.

normal curve. The graphic representation of a normal distribution. See also *bell-shaped curve*.

normal distribution. A frequency distribution where the behaviour of frequencies or magnitudes is subject only to chance or random forces. Such a distribution is symmetrical and continuous.

normal spoilage. Costs incurred because of ordinary amounts of spoilage; such costs should be prorated to units produced as *product costs*; contrast with *abnormal spoilage*.

normal standard cost. The *cost* expected to be incurred under reasonably efficient operating conditions with adequate provision for an average amount of rework, spoilage, and the like.

normal volume. The level of production over a time span, usually one year, that will satisfy demand by purchasers.

note. An unconditional written promise by the maker (borrower) to pay a certain amount on demand or at a certain future time. See *footnotes* for another context.

note receivable discounted. A *note* assigned by the holder to another. If the note is assigned with recourse, it is the

contingent liability of the assignor until the debt is paid. See *factoring*.

note to financial statements. Explanatory or supplementary information appended to and forming an integral part of financial statements.

nothings. (colloq.) An income tax term; broadly, intangible assets such as goodwill.

NSF cheque. Not sufficient funds. A cheque that is not honoured due to lack of funds in the account on which it is drawn.

number of days sales in inventory (or receivables). Days of average inventory on hand (or average collection period for receivables). See *ratio*.

O

objective. See *reporting objective* and *objectivity*.

objectivity. The reporting policy implying that formal recognition will not be given to an event in financial statements until the magnitude of the events can be measured with reasonable accuracy and is subject to independent verification.

observation. An auditing technique consisting of looking at a process or procedure being performed by others. Compare *inspection*.

obsolescence. A decline in *market value* of an *asset* caused by improved alternatives becoming available that will be more *cost-effective*; the decline in market value is unrelated to physical changes in the asset itself. See *partial obsolescence*.

off-balance-sheet financing. A description often used for a *long-term*, *noncancelable lease* accounted for as an *operating lease* and other means of borrowing that do not qualify as *liabilities*.

officer. Any person in a corporation on whom executive authority has been conferred by legislation, by-law or resolution of the board of directors.

offset. To reduce by applying opposites against each other, e.g., an account payable can be offset against an account receivable from the same person.

on consignment. Said of goods delivered by the owner (the consignor) to another (the consignee) to be sold by the consignee; the owner is entitled to the return of the property or payment of an amount agreed upon in advance. The goods are assets of the consignor.

on-line. Pertaining to equipment or devices under the control of the central processing unit.

on-line processing. Processing by a computer system which permits immediate and direct access to the central processing unit for input or output.

on (open) account. Said of a *purchase* or *sale* when payment is expected sometime after delivery and no *note* evidencing the *debt* is given or received. When a sale (purchase) is made on open account, *accounts receivable* (*payable*) is *debited* (*credited*).

one-write system. A system of bookkeeping in which several records, including original documents, are produced in one operation by the use of reproductive paper and special equipment which provides for proper alignment of the documents being processed.

open account. Any *account* with a nonzero debit or credit *balance*.

open-end. Relating to the capital structure of an organization where shares or units of participation are not transferable and may be redeemed at the sole option of the shareholder or unitholder. (Compare *closed-end*.)

open item file. A file of source documents serving as a ledger; open items, at any time, represent the account balance, e.g. a file of unpaid sales invoices serving as an accounts receivable ledger.

opening entry. An entry or one of a series of entries in the books, setting up assets, liabilities and capital, e.g. on the formation of an organization.

opening inventory. Inventory on hand at the beginning of an accounting period.

operating. An adjective used to refer to *revenue* and *expense* items relating to the company's main line(s) of business. See *operations*.

operating accounts. *Revenue*, *expense*, and *production cost accounts*; contrast with *balance sheet accounts*.

operating capability capital maintenance concept. A concept of capital maintenance under which the capital to be maintained represents the productive capacity of the monetary and physical assets measured in either nominal or constant dollars.

operating cycle. The time period between the acquisition of raw materials or merchandise and the recovery of cash from the related sale.

operating expenses. *Expenses* incurred in the course of *ordinary* activities of an *entity*. Frequently, a classification including only *selling*, *general*, and *administrative expenses*, thereby excluding *cost of goods sold*, *interest*, and *income tax* expenses.

operating lease. A lease in which the lessor does not transfer substantially all the benefits and risks incident to ownership of property.

operating leverage. Usually said of a firm with a large proportion of *fixed costs* in its *total costs*. Consider a book publisher or a railroad; the *incremental costs* of producing another book or transporting another freight car are much less than *average cost*, so the *gross margin* upon sale of the unit is relatively large. Contrast, for example, a grocery store, where the *cost of goods sold* is usually more than 95 percent of the selling price. For firms with equal profitability, however defined, the one with the larger percentage increase in income from a given percentage increase in unit sales is said to have the larger operating leverage. See *leverage* for contrast of this term with "financial leverage." See *cost terminology* for definition of terms involving the word "cost."

operating margin (based on current costs). *Revenues* from *sales* minus *current cost* of goods sold. A measure of operating efficiency that is independent of the *cost-flow assumption* for *inventory*. Sometimes called "current (gross) margin." See *inventory profit* for example computations.

operating ratio. See *ratio*.

operating statement. Syn. for *income statement*. A financial statement summarizing items of operating income. See also *operating*.

operating system. Software designed to facilitate scheduling, controlling and obtaining maximum efficiency of a computer and peripheral equipment by the user.

operational control. See *control system*.

operations. A word not precisely defined in *accounting*. Generally, operating activities (producing and selling *goods* or *services*) are distinguished from financing activities (raising funds). Acquiring goods on account and then paying them in one month, though generally classified as an operating activity, has the characteristics of a financing activity. Or consider the transaction of selling plant assets for a price in excess of book value. On the *income statement*, the gain is part of income from operations (continuing operations or discontinued operations, depending on the circumstances) but on the *statement of changes in financial position*, all the funds received on disposition are reported below the "funds for operations" section, as a nonoperating source of funds, disposition of noncurrent assets.

operations research. The scientific analysis of an organization's operations and the application of scientific techniques, often in the form of mathematical formulas or models, to solving operating problems or improving operating efficiency.

opinion. The *auditor*'s *report* containing an attestation or lack thereof.

opinion paragraph. Section of *auditor's report*, generally following the *scope paragraph*, giving the auditor's conclusion that the *financial statements* are (rarely, are not) in accordance with *GAAP* and present fairly the *financial position*, changes in financial position, and the results of *operations*.

opportunity cost. The *present value* of the *income* (or *costs*) that could be earned (or saved) from using an *asset* at its best alternative use to the one being considered.

option. The legal right to buy something during a specified period at a specified price, called the *exercise* price. Employee stock options should not be confused with put and call options traded in various public markets.

ordinary annuity. An *annuity in arrears*.

ordinary creditor. A person who, by statute, is entitled to satisfaction of his proven claim against the estate of a bankrupt only after the claims of all other classes of creditors have been satisfied. An unsecured creditor.

ordinary income. For income tax purposes, reportable *income* not qualifying as *capital gains*.

organization chart. A graphic presentation of the functional and procedural relationships, the lines of authority and responsibility, within an organization.

organization costs. The *costs* incurred in planning and establishing an *entity*; example of an *intangible* asset. Often, since the amounts are not *material*, the costs are treated as *expenses* in the period incurred even though the *expenditures* clearly provide future benefits and should be treated as *assets*.

original cost. *Acquisition cost*. In public utility accounting, the acquisition cost to the *entity* first devoting the asset to public use.

original entry. The first accounting record of a transaction.

outlay. The amount of an *expenditure*.

out-of-pocket. Said of an *expenditure* usually paid for with cash. An *incremental* cost.

out-of-pocket cost. An expense incurred for a third party and for which reimbursement may be sought. (Compare *allowance*.) That portion of the total cost of a particular project which must be met through the outlay of cash, as opposed to imputed cost.

out-of-stock cost. The estimated decrease in future *profit* as a result of losing customers because insufficient quantities of *inventory* are currently on hand to meet customers' demands.

output. Physical quantity or monetary measurement of *goods* and *services* produced.

outside director. A member of a board of directors who is not a company officer and does not participate in the company's day-to-day management.

outstanding. Unpaid or uncollected. When said of *shares*, the shares issued less *treasury shares*. When said of cheques, it means a cheque issued that did not clear the *drawer's* bank.

over-and-short. Title for an *expense account* used to account for small differences between book balances of cash and actual cash and vouchers or receipts in *petty cash* or *change funds*.

overapplied (overabsorbed) overhead. An excess of costs applied, or *charged*, to product for a period over actual *overhead* costs during the period. A *credit balance* in an overhead account after overhead is assigned to product.

overdraft. The excess of withdrawals over the amount available in an account such as a bank account or an appropriation account.

overflow. The situation arising when a computer program generates a numerical result larger than the space provided for its storage.

overhead costs. Any *cost* not associated directly with the production or sale of identifiable goods and services. Sometimes called "burden" or "indirect costs" and, in Britain, "oncosts." Frequently limited to manufacturing overhead. See *central corporate expenses* and *manufacturing overhead*.

overhead rate. Standard, or other predetermined, rate at which *overhead costs* are applied to products or to services.

over-the-counter. Said of a *security* traded in a negotiated transaction; rather than in an auctioned one on an organized stock exchange, such as the *Toronto Stock Exchange*.

owner of record. The person in whose name securities are registered in the books of a corporation.

owners' equity. *Proprietorship*; *assets* minus *liabilities*; *paid-in capital* plus *retained earnings* of a company; partners' capital accounts in a *partnership*; owner's capital account in a *sole proprietorship*.

P

P & L. Profit and loss statement; *income statement*.

package. A generic term referring to any group of detailed computer programs necessary to achieve a general objective, e.g. "accounts receivable package" would include all programs necessary to record transactions in customers' accounts, produce customers' statements, aged trial balances, etc.

paid-up capital. That part of issued capital for which settlement has been received. Under income tax legislation, the term has a special meaning.

paper profit. A *gain* not yet realized through a *transaction*. An *unrealized holding gain*.

par. See *at par* and *face amount*.

par value method. The method of accounting for *treasury shares* that *debits* a common share account with the *par value* of the shares reacquired and allocates the remaining debits between the *contributed surplus* and *retained earnings* accounts; contrast with *cost method*.

parent company. A corporation which controls one or more other corporations through ownership of a majority of the shares carrying the right to elect at least a majority of the members of the board of directors. Use of the term usually restricted to cases where the controlling corporation is a limited company.

partial obsolescence. As technology improves, the economic value of existing *assets* declines. In many cases, however, it will not pay a firm to replace the existing asset with a new one even though the new type, rather than the old, would be acquired if the acquisition were to be made currently. In these cases, the accountant should theoretically recognize a loss from partial obsolescence from the firm's owning an old, out-of-date asset, but *GAAP* do not permit recognition of partial obsolescence. The old asset will be carried at *cost* less *accumulated depreciation* until it is retired from service. See *obsolescence*.

partially funded. Said of a *pension plan* where not all earned benefits have been funded. See *funded* for funding requirements.

partially vested. Said of a *pension plan* where not all employee benefits are *vested*. See *graded vesting*.

participating dividend. *Dividend* paid to preferred shareholders in addition to the minimum preferred dividends when the *preferred share* contract allows such sharing in earnings. Usually applies after dividends on *common shares* have reached a certain level.

participating preferred shares. *Preferred shares* with rights to *participating dividends*.

partner's drawing. A payment to a partner to be charged against his or her share of income or capital. The name of a *temporary account* to record such payments.

partnership. Contractual arrangement between individuals to share resources and operations in a jointly run business. See *general* and *limited partner*.

passed dividend. The non-declaration of a dividend which would normally have been paid in accordance with the corporation's established dividend policy or with the requirements of a particular class of stock.

past service cost. *Present value* at a given time of a *pension plan's* unrecognized, and usually unfunded, benefits assigned to employees for their service before the inception of the plan. A part of *accrued actuarial obligation*. See *accrued actuarial obligation* for disclosure rules. See *funded*; contrast with *normal cost*.

patent. A right granted for up to 17 years by the federal government to exclude others from manufacturing, using or selling a claimed design, product, or plant (e.g., a new breed of rose) or from using a claimed process or method of manufacture. An asset if acquired by purchase. If developed internally, the research costs are *expensed* when incurred under current *GAAP*.

patronage dividend, patronage refund, patronage return. A distribution paid to customers, based on the vol-

ume of business done with each customer over a period.

pay as you go. Said of an *income tax* scheme where periodic payments of income taxes are made during the period when the income to be taxed is being earned; in contrast to a scheme where no payments are due until the end of, or after, the period whose income is being taxed. (Called PAYE — pay as you earn — in Britain.) Sometimes this phrase is used to describe an *unfunded pension plan*, where payments to pension plan beneficiaries are made from general corporate funds, not from cash previously contributed to a pension fund. Not acceptable as a method of accounting for pension plans.

payable. Unpaid but not necessarily due or past due.

payback period. Amount of time that must elapse before the cash inflows from a project equal the cash outflows.

payback reciprocal. One divided by the *payback period*. This number approximates the *internal rate of return* on a project when the project life is more than twice the payback period and the cash inflows are identical in every period after the initial investment.

PAYE. See *pay as you go*.

payee. The person or entity to whom a cash payment is made or who will receive the stated amount of money on a cheque. See *draft*.

payout ratio. *Common share dividends* declared for a year divided by net *income* to common shares for the year. A term used by financial analysts; contrast with *dividend yield*.

payroll. The book, sheet, or other record on which are listed the names of employees and the amounts payable to them as salaries or wages at a given time, with particulars as to rate of pay and deductions. The total amount payable to employees at a given time or for a given period.

payroll taxes. Taxes levied because salaries or wages are paid; for example, *CPP* and unemployment insurance taxes. Typically, the employer pays a portion and withholds part of the employee's wages for the other portion.

P/E ratio. *Price-earnings ratio*.

pension benefits. The pensions and any other payments to which employees or their beneficiaries may be entitled under a pension plan.

pension fund. *Fund*, the assets of which are to be paid to retired ex-employees, usually as a *life annuity*. Usually held by an independent trustee and thus is not an *asset* of the firm.

pension plan. Details or provisions of employer's contract with employees for paying retirement *annuities* or other benefits. See *(non) contributory, fully (partially, un-) funded, insured, funded, vested, normal cost, past service cost, prior service cost, money-purchase plan*, and *defined-benefit plan, defined contribution*.

per books. An expression used to refer to the *book value* of an item at a specific time.

percent. Any number, expressed as a decimal, multiplied by 100.

percentage depletion (allowance). Deductible *expense* allowed in some cases by the federal *income tax* regulations; computed as a percentage of gross income from a *natural resource* independent of the unamortized cost of the asset. Because the amount of the total deductions for tax purposes is usually greater than the cost of the asset being *depleted*, many people think the deduction is an unfair tax advantage or "loophole."

percentage-of-completion method. Recognizing *revenues* and *expenses* on a job, order, or contract (a) in proportion to the *costs* incurred for the period divided by total costs expected to be incurred for the job or order, or (b) in proportion to engineers' estimates of the incremental degree of completion of the job, order, or contract during the period. Contrast with *completed-contract method.*

percentage statement. A statement containing, in addition to *(or instead of)* dollar amounts, ratios of dollar amounts to some base. In a percentage *income statement*, the base is usually either *net sales* or total *revenues* and in a percentage *balance sheet*, the base is usually total *assets*. See *common size* statement.

period. *Accounting period.*

period cost. An inferior term for *period expense.*

period expense (charge). *Expenditure*, usually based on the passage of time, charged to operations of the accounting period rather than *capitalized* as an asset; contrast with *product cost.*

periodic inventory. A method of recording *inventory* that uses data on beginning inventory, additions to inventories, and ending inventory in order to find the cost of withdrawals from inventory.

periodic procedures. The process of making *adjusting entries, closing entries,* and preparing the *financial statements,* usually by use of *trial balances* and *work sheets.*

permanent account. An account that appears on the *balance sheet;* contrast with *temporary account.*

permanent capital. The portion of owners' equity that, by statute or agreement, is not to be withdrawn or distributed in the ordinary course of events.

permanent difference. Difference between reported income and taxable income that will never be reversed and, hence, requires no entry in the *deferred income tax (liability)* account. Contrast with *timing difference* and see *deferred income tax liability.*

permanent file. The file of working papers prepared by a public accountant containing information required for reference in successive professional engagements for a particular organization, as distinguished from working papers applicable only to a particular engagement.

perpetual annuity. *Perpetuity.*

perpetual inventory. Records on quantities and amounts of *inventory* that are changed or made current with each physical addition to or withdrawal from the stock of goods; an inventory so recorded. The records will show the physical quantities and, frequently, the dollar valuations that should be on hand at any time. Because *cost of goods sold* is computed explicitly, the *inventory equation* can be used to compute *ending inventory.* The computed amount of ending inventory can be compared to the actual amount of ending inventory as a *control* device. Contrast with *periodic inventory.*

perpetuity. An *annuity* whose payments continue forever. The *present value* of a perpetuity in *arrears* is p/r, where p is the periodic payment and r is the *interest rate* per period.

personal account. *Drawing account.*

personal financial statements. Financial statements of an individual or family, frequently limited to a statement of assets and liabilities.

personal property. Any asset, whether tangible or intangible, that is not real estate.

PERT. Program evaluation and review technique. A method of network analysis in which three time estimates are made for each activity — the optimistic time, the most likely time and the pessimistic time — and which gives an expected completion date for the project within a probability range.

PERT/cost. The integration of cost estimates on a *PERT* network.

petition. (bankruptcy). A request to the court by a creditor or group of creditors that the debtor be declared bankrupt.

petty cash. Cash kept on hand or in a special bank account as a convenience for making small payments.

physical capital maintenance concept. A concept of capital maintenance under which the capital to be maintained represents the physical assets or productive capacity of those assets measured in either nominal or constant dollars.

physical life. The period of time in which a fixed asset is capable of providing a service irrespective of obsolescence and excessive maintenance costs. (Compare *economic life.*)

physical unit sampling. A sampling technique in which items in a population are defined in terms of the physical or discrete units (e.g. invoices, items of inventory) with each item having an equal chance of selection. Compare *monetary unit sampling.*

physical verification. *Verification*, by an *auditor*, performed by actually inspecting items in *inventory, plant assets,* and the like; may be based on statistical sampling procedures; contrasted with mere checking of written records.

piecemeal opinion. An opinion where the auditor, while giving an adverse opinion or a denial of opinion with respect to the financial statements taken as a whole, expresses an unqualified opinion on certain specific items in the financial statements.

plant. *plant assets.*

plant assets. Buildings, machinery, equipment, land, and natural resources. The phrase "property, plant, and equipment" is, therefore, a redundancy. In this context, "plant" means buildings.

plant asset turnover. Number of dollars of *sales* generated per dollar of *plant assets.* Equal to sales divided by average *plant assets.*

pledging. The borrower assigns *assets* as security or *collateral* for repayment of a loan.

pledging of receivables. The process of using expected collections on amounts receivable as *collateral* for a loan. The borrower remains responsible for collecting the receivable but promises to use the proceeds for repaying the debt.

plow back. To retain assets generated by earnings for continued investment in the business.

plug. For any *account,* beginning balance + additions − deductions = ending balance; if any three of the four items are known, the fourth can be found by plugging. In making a *journal entry,* often all *debits* are known, as are all but one of the *credits* (or vice versa). Because *double-entry* bookkeeping requires equal debits and credits, the unknown quantity can be determined by subtracting the sum of the known credits from the sum of all the debits (or vice versa). This process is also known as plugging. The unknown found is called the plug. For example, if a *discount* on *bonds payable* is being *amortized* with the *straightline method,* then *interest expense* is a plug: interest expense = interest payable + discount amortization. See *trade-in transaction* for an example.

pooling-of-interests method. Accounting for a *business combination* by merely adding together the *book value* of the assets and *equities* of the combined firms. Contrast with *purchase method.* Generally leads to a higher reported *net income* for the combined firms than would be reported had the business combination been accounted for as a purchase, because the *market values* of the merged assets are generally larger than their book values.

population. The entire field of numbers or items which is to be the subject of sampling or other analysis.

portfolio investments. All long-term investments in companies which are not subsidiaries, effectively controlled companies or corporate joint ventures.

positive confirmation. See *confirmation.*

post. To record entries in an *account* in a *ledger;* usually the entries are transferred from a *journal.*

post-closing trial balance. *Trial balance* taken after all *temporary accounts* have been closed.

post-statement events. Events with *material* impact that occur between the end of the *accounting period* and the formal publication of the *financial statements.* Such events must be disclosed in notes for the auditor to give a *clean opinion,* even though the events are subsequent to the period being reported on. Commonly termed *subsequent events.*

potentially dilutive. A *security* that may be converted into, or exchanged for, common shares and thereby reduce reported *earnings per share; options, warrants, convertible bonds,* and *convertible preferred shares.*

PPBS. Planning, programming and budgeting system. (Used chiefly in government.) A management system concerned with the planning and control of resources in an organization to ensure that they are employed effectively to meet the organization's objectives. It emphasizes the definition of organizational objectives, selection of optimum programs for meeting these objectives, translation of planning and programming decisions into resource requirements and measurement of results (benefits) against resources used.

practical capacity. The maximum level at which the plant or department can realistically operate most efficiently, i.e. ideal capacity less allowances for unavoidable operating interruptions.

precision. The degree of accuracy with which the estimate derived from a sampling process is stated, usually expressed as a range of values around the estimate. A sample estimate may be expressed in the following terms: " Based on the sample, we are 95% sure [confidence level] that the true population value is within the range of X to Y [precision]". See *confidence level.*

pre-closing trial balance. *Trial balance* taken at the end of the period before *closing entries.* In this sense, an *adjusted trial balance.* Sometimes taken before *adjusting entries* and then is synonymous with *unadjusted trial balance.*

predetermined (factory) overhead rate. Rate used in applying *overhead* to products or departments developed at the start of a period by dividing estimated overhead cost by the estimated number of units of the overhead allocation base (or *denominator volume*) activity.

predictive value. The quality of information that helps users to increase the likelihood of correctly forecasting the outcome of events.

preemptive right. The privilege of a shareholder to maintain a proportionate share of ownership by purchasing a proportionate share of any new share issues.

preference as to assets. The rights of *preferred share-*

holders to receive certain payments in case of dissolution before common shareholders receive payments.

preferred creditor. A person who, by statute, is entitled to full satisfaction of his proven claim against the estate of a bankrupt before other unsecured creditors receive anything.

preferred shares. *Capital stock* with a claim to income or assets after bondholders but before *common shares*. *Dividends* on preferred shares are income distributions, not expenses. See *cumulative preferred shares*.

preliminary expense. Organization expense. More broadly, a general term for organization, development, and other preproduction expenses. Obsolete.

preliminary prospectus. A document filed with a securities commission in advance of a final prospectus, the information in which is incomplete or subject to amendment.

premium. The excess of issue (or market) price over *par value*. For a different context, see *insurance*.

prepaid expense. An *expenditure* that leads to a *deferred charge* or *prepayment*; strictly speaking, a contradiction in terms for an *expense* is a gone asset and this title refers to past *expenditures*, such as for rent or insurance premiums, that still have future benefits and thus are *assets*.

prepaid income. An inferior alternative title for *advances from customers*. An item should not be called *revenue* or *income* until earned, when goods are delivered or services are rendered.

prepayments. *Deferred charges*. *Assets* representing *expenditures* for future benefits. Rent and insurance premiums paid in advance are usually classified as *current* prepayments.

present value. Value today of an amount or amounts to be paid or received later, discounted at some *interest* or *discount rate*.

preventive controls. Internal controls designed to prevent, or minimize the chance of occurrence of, errors and other irregularities. Compare *detective controls*.

price. The quantity of one *good* or *service*, usually *cash*, asked in return for a unit of another good or service. See *fair market price*.

price-earnings ratio. At a given time, the market value of a company's *common shares*, per share, divided by the *earnings per* common *share* for the past year. See *ratio*.

price index. A series of numbers, one for each period, that purports to represent some *average* of prices for a series of periods, relative to a base period.

price level. The number from a *price index* series for a given period or date.

price maintenance. The action of a manufacturer, wholesaler or jobber who induces his or her retailers to sell his or her products to the public at not less than a specified price.

price variance. In accounting for *standard costs* (actual cost per unit — standard cost per unit) times quantity purchased.

primary distribution. The original distribution to the public of securities issued by a corporation. Compare *secondary distribution*.

primary issue. An issue of securities being offered in primary distribution.

prime cost. Sum of *direct materials* plus *direct labour* costs assigned to product.

prime rate. The rate for loans charged by banks to their most preferred risks.

principal. An amount on which *interest* is charged or earned.

principle. See *generally accepted accounting principles*.

prior-period adjustment. A gain or loss specifically identified with and directly related to the business activities of particular prior periods, not attributable to economic events occurring subsequent to the date of the financial statements for such prior periods, depending primarily on decisions or determinations by persons other than management or owners, and not reasonably estimable prior to such decisions or determinations. (Compare *accounting errors*.)

prior service cost. Accrued actuarial obligation.

private company. A limited company classified as a private company by virtue of the provisions of corporate legislation and its instrument of incorporation. (*colloq.*) A limited company whose shares are not listed on a recognized stock exchange or otherwise available to the public investor.

pro-forma statements. Hypothetical statements. Financial statements as they would appear if some event, such as a *merger* or increased production and sales, had occurred or were to occur. Pro forma is often spelled as one word.

proceeds. The *funds* received from disposition of assets or from the issue of securities.

process costing. A method of *cost accounting* based on average costs (total cost divided by the *equivalent units* of work done in a period). Typically used for assembly lines or for products that are produced in a series of steps that are more continuous than discrete.

product. *Goods* or *services* produced.

product cost. Any *manufacturing cost* that can be inventoried. See *flow of costs* for example and contrast with *period expenses*.

production cost. *Manufacturing cost.*

production cost account. A *temporary account* for collecting *manufacturing costs* during a period.

production department. A department producing salable *goods* or *services*; contrast with *service department*.

production method (depreciation). The depreciable asset is given a *depreciable life* measured, not in elapsed time, but in units of output or perhaps in units of time of expected use. Then the *depreciation* charge for a period is a portion of depreciable cost equal to a fraction computed by dividing the actual output produced during the period by the expected total output to be produced over the life of the asset. Sometimes called the "units-of-production (or output) method."

production method (revenue recognition). *Percentage-of-completion method* for recognizing *revenue*.

productive capacity. In computing *replacement costs* of *long-term assets*, we are interested in the cost of reproducing the productive capacity (for example, the ability to manufacture 1 million units a year), not the cost of reproducing the actual physical assets currently used (see *reproduction cost*). Replacement cost of productive capacity will be the same as reproduction cost of assets only in the unusual case when there has been no technological improvement in production processes and the relative prices of goods and services used in production have remained approximately the same as when the currently used ones were acquired.

productive capacity capital maintenance concept. See *operating capability capital maintenance concept.*

profit. Excess of *revenues* over *expenses* for a *transaction*; sometimes used synonymously with *net income* for the period.

profit and loss account. The ledger account to which the balances of the revenue, income, expense, and loss accounts at the end of an accounting period are transferred, to show the net differences as the net income or net loss for the period.

profit-and-loss sharing ratio. The fraction of *net income* or loss allocable to a partner in a *partnership*. Need not be the same fraction as the partner's share of capital.

profit-and-loss statement. *Income statement.*

profit centre. A unit of activity for which both *revenue* and *expenses* are accumulated; contrast with *cost centre*.

profit margin. Sales minus all expenses as a single amount. Frequently used to mean the ratio of sales minus all *operating* expenses divided by sales.

profit maximization. The doctrine that a given set of operations should be accounted for so as to make reported *net income* as large as possible; contrast with *conservatism*. This concept in accounting is slightly different from the profit maximizing concept in economics where the doctrine states that businesses should be run to maximize the present value of the firm's wealth, generally by equating *marginal costs* and *marginal revenues*.

profit-sharing plan. A plan under which an employer makes available to employees special current or deferred sums, based on the net income of the business, in addition to normal remuneration. Under income tax legislation, the term has a special meaning.

profit-volume graph. See *breakeven chart*.

profit-volume ratio. *Net income* divided by net sales in dollars. Also used to refer to *contribution margin* divided by *sales*.

profitability accounting. Responsibility accounting.

pro-forma. A term applied to a financial statement drawn up after giving effect to stated assumptions, which may include contractual commitments that have not yet been fulfilled.

pro-forma earnings per share. The amount of earnings per share reflecting transactions occurring subsequent to the end of the period involving the issue of common shares.

program. A definite plan to be followed in carrying out a procedure. The complete sequence of machine instructions necessary to carry out a task on a computer.

program budgeting. Specification and analysis of inputs, outputs, costs, and alternatives that link plans to *budgets*.

program(ming) language. A computer language used for the preparation of programs prior to their conversion by the computer into machine language. Compare *machine language*.

programmed costs. A *fixed cost* not essential for carrying out operations. Research and development and advertising designed to generate new business are controllable, but once a commitment is made to incur them, they become fixed costs. Sometimes called *managed costs* or *discretionary costs*; contrast with *capacity costs*.

progress billing. An interim billing based upon partial completion of a contract.

progress payment. An interim payment based upon partial completion of a contract.

progressive tax. Tax for which the rate increases as the taxed base, such as income, increases; contrast with *regressive tax*.

project financing arrangement. The financing of an investment project in which the lender looks principally to the *cash flows* and *earnings* of the project as the source of funds for repayment and to the *assets* of the project as *collateral* for the loan. The general *credit* of the project entity is usually not a significant factor, either because the entity is a *corporation* without other assets or because the financing is without direct *recourse* to the entity's owners.

projected financial statement. *Pro-forma* financial statement.

projection. An estimate of future events or conditions based on the present position and recent trends. For purposes of public reporting, management's estimate of results for a specified period of time in the future but based on stated assumptions which may not be the most likely. Compare *forecast*.

promissory note. An unconditional written promise to pay a specified sum of money on demand or at a specified date.

proof of journal. The process of checking arithmetic accuracy of *journal entries* by testing for the equality of all *debits* with all *credits* since the last previous proof.

property dividend. A *dividend in kind*.

proportionate consolidation. A presentation of the financial statements of any investor-investment relationship, whereby the investor's pro rata share of each asset, liability, income item and expense item is reflected in the financial statements of the investor under the various balance sheet and income statement headings.

proposal (bankruptcy). A scheme for extension of time and/or reduction or rearrangement of debt put forward to creditors by a debtor.

proprietorship. *Assets* minus *liabilities* of an *entity*; equals *contributed capital* plus *retained earnings*.

proprietorship theory. The view of the corporation that emphasizes the form of the *accounting equation* that says *assets − liabilities = owners' equity*; contrast with *equity theory*. The major implication of a choice between these theories deals with the treatment of *subsidiaries*. For example, the view that *minority interest* is an *indeterminate-term liability* is based on the proprietorship theory. The proprietorship theory implies using a *single-step income statement*.

prorate. To *allocate* in proportion to some base; for example, to allocate *service department* costs in proportion to hours of service used by the benefited departments.

prospectus. Under corporations and securities legislation, a document issued by a corporation in connection with an issue of securities. It contains information concerning the securities, a description of the corporation's business, names of its officers and directors, financial data and other pertinent facts.

protective covenant. A clause in a bond indenture placing restrictions on the operations of the borrower for the safeguarding of the lenders' interests.

provision. Often the exact amount of an *expense* is uncertain, but must be recognized currently anyway. The entry for the estimated expense, such as for *income taxes* or

expected costs under *warranty*, is

Expense (Estimated) X	
Liability (Estimated)	X

The term "provision" is often used in the expense account title of the above entry. Thus, Provision for Income Taxes is used to mean the estimate of income tax expense. (In British usage, the term "provision" is used in the title for the estimated liability of the above entry, so that Provision for Income Taxes is a balance sheet account.)

proxy. Written authorization given by one person to another so that the second person can act for the first, such as to vote shares of stock.

public accountant. Generally, this term is synonymous with *chartered accountant*. In some jurisdictions individuals have been licensed as public accountants without being CAs.

public accounting. That portion of accounting primarily involving the *attest* function, culminating in the *auditor's report*.

public company. A limited company which is not a private company. (*colloq.*) A limited company whose shares are available to the public investor.

public corporation. A term in income tax legislation, broadly, a public company.

PuPU. An acronym for *pu*rchasing *p*ower *u*nit, conceived by John C. Burton, former Chief Accountant of the *SEC*. Those who think *general price level adjusted* accounting is not particularly useful, poke fun at it by calling it "PuPU accounting."

purchase allowance. A reduction in sales *invoice price* usually granted because the *goods* received by the purchaser were not exactly as ordered. The goods are not returned to the seller, but are purchased at a price lower than originally agreed upon.

purchase discount. A reduction in purchase *invoice price* granted for prompt payment. See *sales discount* and *terms of sale*.

purchase discrepancy. The difference between the cost of the shares to an acquiring corporation and its *equity* in the *net assets* of the acquired corporation at the date of acquisition. (Compare *consolidated goodwill*.)

purchase journal. The book of original entry in which purchases are recorded.

purchase investigation. An investigation of the financial affairs of a company for the purpose of disclosing matters that may influence the terms or conclusion of a potential acquisition.

purchase method. Accounting for a *business combination* by adding the acquired company's assets at the price paid for them to the acquiring company's assets. Contrast with *pooling-of-interests method.* The acquired assets are put on the books at current, rather than original costs, the *amortization expenses* are usually larger (and reported income, smaller) than for the same business combination accounted for as a pooling of interests. The purchase method is required unless all criteria to be a pooling are met.

purchase order. Document authorizing a seller to deliver goods with payment to be made later.

purchasing power gain or loss. *Monetary gain or loss.*

put. An option to sell *shares* of a publicly-traded corporation at a fixed price during a fixed time span. Contrast with *call.*

put option. The right to make delivery within a specified time of a particular stock or commodity at a specified price and in specified amounts.

Q

qualification. A statement in an auditor's report setting forth a limitation or modification of his or her opinion.

qualified report (opinion). *Auditor's report* containing a statement that the auditor was unable to complete a satisfactory examination of all things considered relevant or that the auditor has doubts about the financial impact of some material item reported in the financial statements. See *except for* and *subject to.*

qualifying share. A share held by an individual to qualify as a director in the company.

quantity discount. A reduction in purchase price as quantity purchased increases. Not to be confused with *purchase discount.*

quantity variance. In *standard cost* systems, the standard price per unit times (actual quantity used minus standard quantity that should be used).

quasi-reorganization. A *reorganization* where no new company is formed or no court has intervened, as would happen in *bankruptcy.* The primary purpose is to absorb a *deficit* and get a ''fresh start.''

quick assets. *Assets* readily convertible into *cash*; includes cash, *current marketable securities* and *current receivables.*

quick ratio. Sum of (*cash, temporary investments*, and *receivables*) divided by *current liabilities.* Some nonliquid receivables may be excluded from the numerator. Often called the ''acid test ratio.'' See *ratio.*

quoted market price. The closing quotation for commodities, currency or securities on an established exchange.

R

R & D. See *research and development.*

random access. See *direct access.*

random number sampling. A method of choosing a sample in which the items to be selected from the population are determined by use of a random number table or generator.

random sampling. A method of choosing a sample in which all items in the population have an equal chance of being selected. Compare *judgment(al) sampling.*

rate of exchange. The price at which the currency of one country may be bought or sold in the currency of another country.

rate of return on assets. *Net income* plus aftertax *interest charges* plus *minority interest* in income divided by average total *assets.* Perhaps the single most useful ratio for assessing management's overall operating performance. See *ratio.*

rate of return on common stock equity. See *ratio.*

rate of return on shareholders' equity. See *ratio.*

rate of return (on total capital). See *ratio* and *rate of return on assets.*

rate variance. *Price variance*, usually for *direct labour costs.*

ratio. The number resulting when one number is divided by another. Ratios are generally used to assess aspects of profitability, solvency, and liquidity. The commonly used financial ratios are of three kinds:

1. Those that summarize some aspect of *operations* for a period, usually a year.
2. Those that summarize some aspect of *financial position* at a given moment — the moment for which a balance sheet has been prepared.
3. Those that relate some aspect of operations to some aspect of financial position.

Exhibit 6.11 on page 289 lists the most common financial ratios and shows separately both the numerator and denominator used to calculate the ratio.

For all ratios that require an average balance during the period, the average is most often derived as one-half the sum of the beginning and ending balances. Sophisticated analysts recognize, however, that when companies use a fiscal year different from the calendar year, this averaging of beginning and ending balances may be misleading. Consider, for example, the *all-capital earnings rate* of Hudson's Bay Co. Ltd., whose fiscal year ends on January 31. The ''Bay'' chooses a January 31 closing date at least in part because inventories are at a low level and are therefore easy to count — the Christmas merchandise has been sold and the Easter merchandise has not yet all been received. Furthermore, by January 31, most Christmas sales have been collected or returned, so receivable amounts are not unusually large. Thus at January 31, the amount of total assets is lower than at many other times during the year. Consequently, the denominator of the all-capital earnings rate, total assets, for the "Bay" is more likely to represent the smallest amount of total assets on hand during the year than the average amount. The all-capital earnings rate for the "Bay" and other companies who choose a fiscal year-end to coincide with low points in the inventory cycle is likely to be larger than if a more accurate estimate of the average amounts of total assets were used.

raw material. Goods purchased for use in manufacturing a product that are in the same condition as when they were purchased.

reacquired shares. *Treasury shares.*

real accounts. *Balance sheet accounts*; as opposed to *nominal accounts*. See *permanent accounts*.

real amount (value). An amount stated in *constant dollars*. For example, if an investment costing $100 is sold for $130 after a period of 10 percent general *inflation*, the *nominal amount* of *gain* is $30 (= $130 − $100) but the real amount of gain is C$ 20 (= $130 − 1.10 × $100), where "C$" denotes constant dollars of purchasing power on the date of sale.

real estate. *Land* and its *improvements*, such as landscaping and roads but not buildings.

real estate investment trust (REIT). An unincorporated trust, created under a trust deed, to operate as a mortgage and real estate financing intermediary.

realizable value. *Market value* or, sometimes, *net realizable value*.

realization account. An account sometimes used in the liquidation of an estate or business, in which the amounts realized on sale of the assets are offset against the book values of the assets, thus showing the profit or loss on realization.

realization convention. The accounting practice of delaying the recognition of *gains* and *losses* from changes in the market price of *assets* until the assets are sold. However, unrealized losses on *inventory* and *marketable securities* classified as *current assets* are recognized prior to sale when the *lower-of-cost-and-market* valuation basis is used.

realize. To convert into *funds*. When applied to a *gain* or *loss*, implies that an *arm's-length transaction* has taken place. Contrast with *recognize*; a loss (as for example on *marketable securities*) may be recognized in the financial statements even though it has not yet been realized in a transaction.

realized. An adjective generally used to describe a reve-

nue, profit, gain or loss on a completed transaction which has produced an increase or decrease in a monetary asset or in a liability, or in a more restricted sense, an increase or decrease in a liquid asset.

realized exchange gain/loss. A gain or loss resulting from the settlement of foreign currency receivables or payables, or from the conversion of currency, at rates which differ from those at which such items were originally recorded. (Compare *unrealized exchange gain/loss*.)

realized gain (or loss) on marketable equity securities. An income statement account title for the difference between the proceeds of disposition and the *original cost* of *marketable securities*.

realized holding gain. See *inventory profit* for definition and an example.

real-time processing. On-line processing in which an item is processed quickly enough to produce output which can be used in directing or controlling a process as it is occurring. Compare *batch processing*.

rearrangement costs. *Costs* of re-installing assets, perhaps in a different location. May be *capitalized* as part of the assets' cost, just as is original installation cost.

rebate. A price allowance or price reduction.

recapitalization. *Reorganization*.

recapture. Various provisions of the *income tax* rules require refund by the taxpayer (recapture by the government) of various tax advantages under certain conditions.

receipt. Acquisition of *cash*.

receivable. Any *collectible* whether or not it is currently due.

receivables turnover. See *ratio*.

receiver. A person appointed by a court or by a creditor to take charge of property pending final disposition of the matter before the court or payment in full of the debt owed to the creditor.

receivership. The legal status of a debtor for whom a *receiver* has been appointed.

receiving order. (bankruptcy) A court order, issued following a successful petition by a creditor or creditors, declaring that the debtor is bankrupt.

reciprocal holdings. Company A owns stock of Company B and Company B owns stock of Company A.

recognize. To enter a transaction in the accounts. Not synonymous with *realize*.

reconciliation. A calculation that shows how one balance or figure is derived systematically from another, such as a *reconciliation of retained earnings* or a *bank reconciliation*. See *articulate*.

record date. *Dividends* are paid on payment date to those who own shares on the record date.

recourse. See *note receivable discounted*.

recoverable amount. The current worth of the net amount of cash expected to be recovered from the use or sale of an asset, being value in use and net realizable value, respectively.

redeemable share. A share of redeemable stock. See *captial stock*.

redeemable stock. A class of *capital stock* callable for redemption at the option of the company in accordance with conditions determined by the instrument of incorporation.

redemption. Retirement by the issuer, usually by a purchase or *call*, of *shares* or *bonds*.

redemption premium. Call *premium*.

redemption value. The price to be paid by a company to retire *bonds* or *preferred shares* if called before *maturity*.

refinancing. An adjustment in the *capital structure* of a *corporation*, involving changes in the nature and amounts of the various classes of debt and, in some cases, capital as well as other components of shareholders' equity; asset carrying values in the accounts remain unchanged. (Compare *quasi-reorganization; recapitalization; reorganization.*)

refundable taxes. Income taxes payable by specific corporations recoverable in the future upon compliance with certain conditions.

refunding bond issue. Said of a *bond* issue whose proceeds are used to retire bonds already *outstanding*.

register. Collection of consecutive entries, or other information, in chronological order, such as a cheque register or an insurance register, which lists all insurance policies owned. If entries are recorded, it may serve as a *journal*.

registered bond. *Principal* of such a *bond* and *interest*, if registered as to interest, is paid to the owner listed on the books of the issuer. As opposed to a bearer bond, where the possessor of the bond is entitled to interest and principal.

registrar. An *agent*, usually a bank or trust company, appointed by a company to keep track of the names of shareholders and distributions of earnings.

regression analysis. A method of *cost estimates* based on statistical techniques for fitting a line (or its equivalent in higher mathematical dimensions) to an observed series of data points, usually by minimizing the sum of squared deviations of the observed data from the fitted line.

regressive tax. Tax for which the rate decreases as the taxed base, such as income, increases. Contrast with *progressive tax*.

rehabilitation. The improving of a used *asset* via an extensive repair. Ordinary *repairs* and *maintenance* restore or maintain expected *service potential* of an asset and are treated as *expenses*. A rehabilitation improves the asset beyond its current service potential, restoring the service potential to a significantly higher level than before the rehabilitation. Once rehabilitated, the asset may be better, but need not be, than it was when new. *Expenditures* for rehabilitation, like those for *betterments* and *improvements*, are *capitalized*.

reinsurance. A contract between insurers whereby one assumes part or all of the risk on an insurance contract issued by the other.

reinvestment rate. In a *capital budgeting* context, the rate at which cash inflows from a project occurring before the project's completion are invested. Once such a rate is assumed, there will never be multiple *internal rates of return*. See *Descartes' rule of signs*.

related parties. Two or more parties, where one party has the ability to exercise, directly or indirectly, control or significant influence over the operating and financial decisions of the others, or when they are subject to common control or significant influence.

relative sales value method. A method for *allocating joint costs* in proportion to *net realizable values* of the joint products. For example, joint products A and B together cost $100 and A sells for $60 whereas B sells for $90. Then A would be allocated ($60/$150) × $100 = .40 × $100 = $40 of cost, whereas B would be allocated ($90/$150) × $100 = $60 of cost.

relevance. The capacity of information to make a difference in a decision by helping users to form predictions about the outcome of events or to confirm or correct past expectations.

relevant range. Activity levels over which costs are linear or for which *flexible budget* estimates and *breakeven charts* will remain valid.

reliability. The quality of information that assures its reasonable freedom from error and bias and faithfully represents what it purports to represent.

remainderman. A person who is entitled to the remaining interest in a property after a life tenancy expires. Compare with *life tenant*.

remittance advice. Information on a *cheque* stub, or on a document attached to a cheque by the *drawer*, which tells the *payee* why a payment is being made.

remote access. Access to computer facilities by means of a terminal situation at a location different from that of the main facility.

renewal accounting. An accounting procedure in which no charge for expense is made for a *fixed asset* until replacement occurs, the cost of the replacement rather than the cost of the original asset then being charged to expense. (Compare *depreciation; retirement method.*)

rent. A charge for the use of land, buildings, or other assets.

reorganization. A major change in the *capital structure* of a company that leads to changes in the rights, interests and implied ownership of the various security owners. Usually results from a *merger* or agreement by senior security holders to take action to forestall *bankruptcy*.

repair. An *expenditure* to restore an *asset's* service potential after damage or after prolonged use. In the second sense, after prolonged use, the difference between repairs and maintenance is one of degree and not of kind. Treated as an *expense* of the period when incurred. Because repairs and maintenance are treated similarly in this regard, the distinction is not important. A repair helps to maintain capacity intact at levels planned when the *asset* was acquired; contrast with *improvement*.

replacement cost. For an asset, the current fair market price to purchase another, similar asset (with the same future benefit or service potential). *Current cost.* See *reproduction cost* and *productive capacity.* See also *distributable income* and *inventory profit*.

replacement-cost method of depreciation. The original-cost *depreciation* charge is augmented by an amount based on a portion of the difference between the *current replacement cost* of the asset and its *original cost*.

replacement system of depreciation. See *retirement method of depreciation* for definition and contrast.

replacement value accounting. The Dutch term for *current cost accounting*.

report. *Financial statement; auditor's report.*

report form. This form of *balance sheet* typically shows *assets* minus *liabilities* as one total. Then, below that it shows the components of *owner's equity* summing to the same total. Often, the top section shows *current* assets less current liabilities before *noncurrent* assets less noncurrent liabilities. Contrast with *account form*.

reporting objectives (policies). The general doctrines underlying accounting. These include *full disclosure, objectivity, consistency, conservatism*, the assumption of *continuity of operations*, and *materiality*.

reporting standards. Criteria for evaluating the fairness of financial statement presentation.

representational faithfulness. Correspondence or agreement between a measure or description of a phenomenon that it purports to represent (sometimes called "validity").

representative item sampling. Sampling where the sample selected is believed to be typical of the entire population from which it is drawn. Compare *specific item sampling*.

reproduction cost. The *cost* necessary to acquire an *asset* similar in all physical respects to another asset for which a *current value* is wanted. See *replacement cost* and *productive capacity* for further contrast.

required rate of return. The opportunity *cost of capital*.

requisition. A formal written order or request, such as for withdrawal of supplies from the storeroom.

resale value. *Exit value. Net realizable value*.

research. Planned investigation undertaken with the hope of gaining new scientific or technical knowledge and understanding. See *development*.

reserve. When properly used in accounting, the term refers to an account that appropriates *retained earnings* and restricts dividend declarations. Appropriating retained earnings is itself a poor and slowly vanishing practice, so the word should seldom be used in accounting. In addition, used in the past to indicate an asset *contra* (for example, "reserve for depreciation") or an *estimated liability* (for example "reserve for warranty costs"). *In any case, reserve accounts have credit balances and are not pools of funds* as the unwary reader might infer. If a company has set aside a pool of *cash* (or *marketable securities*), then that cash will be called a *fund*.

No other word in accounting is so misunderstood and misused by laymen and "experts" who should know better. A leading unabridged dictionary defines *reserve* as "Cash, or assets readily convertible into cash, held aside, as by a corporation, bank, state or national government, etc., to meet expected or unexpected demands." This definition is absolutely wrong in accounting. Reserves are not funds. For example, a contingency fund of $10,000 is created by depositing cash in a fund and this entry is made:

Dr. Contingency Fund	$10,000	
Cr. Cash		$10,000

The following entry may accompany this entry, if retained earnings are to be appropriated:

Dr. Retained Earnings	$10,000	
Cr. Reserve for Contingencies		$10,000

The transaction leading to the first entry is an event of economic significance. The second entry has little economic impact for most firms. The problem with the word "reserves" arises because the second entry can be made without the first—a company can create a reserve, that is appropriate retained earnings, without creating a fund. The problem is at least in part caused by the fact that in common usage, "reserve" means a pool of assets, as in the phrase "oil reserves."

reserve fund. A pool of designated assets, usually cash and investment securities, earmarked for a specified purpose, e.g., sinking fund for bond redemption.

reserve recognition accounting. In exploration for natural resources, there is the problem of what to do with the expenditures for exploration. Suppose that $10 million is spent to drill 10 holes ($1 million each) and that nine of them are dry whereas one is a gusher containing oil with a *net realizable value* of $40 million. Dry-hole, or *successful-efforts*, accounting would *expense* $9 million and *capitalize* $1 million to be *depleted* as the oil was lifted from the ground. *Full costing* would expense nothing but capitalize the $10 million of drilling costs to be depleted as the oil is lifted from the single productive well. Reserve-recognition accounting would capitalize $40 million to be depleted as the oil is lifted, with a $30 million *credit to income* or *contributed capital*. The *balance sheet* shows the *net realizable value* of proven oil and gas reserves. The *income statement* has three sorts of items: (1) current income resulting from production or "lifting profit," which is the *revenue* from sales of oil and gas less the expense based on the current valuation amount at which these items had been carried on the balance sheet, (2) profit or loss from exploration efforts where the current value of new discoveries is revenue and all the exploration cost is expense, and (3) gain or loss on changes in current value during the year, which is in other contexts called a *holding gain or loss*.

residual income. In an external reporting context, this term refers to *net income to common shares* = net income less *preferred share dividends*. In *managerial accounting*, this term refers to the excess of income for a division or *segment* of a company over the product of the *cost of capital* for the company multiplied by the average amount of capital invested in the division during the period over which the income was earned.

residual security. A *potentially dilutive security. Options, warrants, convertible bonds*, and *convertible preferred shares*.

residual value. At any time, the estimated or actual, *net realizable value* (that is, proceeds less removal costs) of an *asset*, usually a depreciable *plant asset*. In the context of depreciation accounting, this term is equivalent to *salvage value* and is preferable to *scrap value*, because the asset need not be scrapped. Sometimes used to mean *book value*. In the context of a *noncancelable* lease, the estimated value of the leased asset at the end of the lease period. See *lease*.

responsibility accounting. Accounting for a business by considering various units as separate entities, or *profit centres*, giving management of each unit responsibility for the unit's *revenues* and *expenses*. Sometimes called "activity accounting." See *transfer price*.

responsibility centre. Part or *segment* of an organization that is accountable for a specified set of activities. Also called "*accountability centre*."

restricted assets. Governmental resources restricted by legal or contractual requirements for specific purposes.

restricted retained earnings. That part of *retained earnings* not legally available for *dividends*. See *retained earnings, appropriated. Bond indentures* and other loan contracts can curtail the legal ability of the company to declare dividends without formally requiring a retained earnings appropriation, but disclosure is required.

retail inventory method. Ascertaining *inventory* amounts for financial statements by using ratios of cost to selling price. That is, *cost of sales* = (1 − *markup percentage*) × *sales*; and *ending inventory* = (1 − *markup percentages*) × *ending inventory* at retail prices.

retained earnings. Net *income* over the life of a company less all dividends (including capitalization through stock dividends); *owners' equity* less *contributed capital*.

retained earnings, appropriated. An *account* set up by crediting it and debiting *retained earnings*. Used to indicate that a portion of retained earnings is not available for dividends. The practice of appropriating retained earnings is misleading unless all capital is earmarked with its use, which is not practical. Use of formal retained earnings appropriations is declining.

retained earnings statement. *Generally accepted accounting principles* require that whenever *comparative balance sheets* and an *income statement* are presented, there must also be presented a *reconciliation* of the beginning and ending balances in the *retained earnings account*. This reconciliation can appear in a separate statement, in a combined statement of income and retained earnings or in the balance sheet.

retirement method of depreciation. No entry is recorded for *depreciation expense* until an *asset* is retired from service. Then, an entry is made *debiting* depreciation expense and *crediting* the asset account for the cost of the asset retired. If the retired asset has a *salvage value*, the amount of the debit to depreciation expense is reduced by the amount of salvage value with a corresponding debit to cash, receivables, or salvaged materials. The "replacement system of depreciation" is similar, except that the debit to depreciation expense equals the cost of the new asset less the salvage value, if any, of the old asset. These methods were used by some public utilities. For example, if ten telephone poles are acquired in Year 1 for $60 each and are replaced in Year 10 for $100 each when the salvage value of the old poles is $5 each, then the accounting would be as follows:

Retirement Method

Plant Assets	$600	
Cash		$600
To acquire assets in Year 1.		
Depreciation Expense	$550	
Salvage Receivable	50	
Plant Assets		$600
To record retirement and depreciation in Year 10.		

Plant Assets	$1,000	
Cash		$1,000

To record acquisition of new
assets in Year 10.

Replacement Method

Plant Assets	$600	
Cash		$600

To acquire assets in Year 1.

Depreciation Expense	$950	
Salvage Receivable	50	
Cash		$1,000

To record depreciation on old
asset in amount quantified by
net cost of replacement asset in
Year 10.

The retirement method is like *FIFO*, in that the cost of the first assets is recorded as depreciation and the cost of the second assets is put on the balance sheet. The replacement method is like *LIFO* in that the cost of the second assets determines the depreciation expense and the cost of the first assets remains on the balance sheet.

retirement plan. *Pension plan*.

return. A schedule of information required by governmental bodies such as the tax return required by the Income Tax Act. Also the physical return of merchandise. See also *return on investment*.

return on investment, return on capital. *Income* (before distributions to suppliers of capital) for a period. As a rate, this amount divided by average total assets. *Interest*, net of tax effects, should be added back to *net income* for the numerator. See *ratio*.

revenue. The increase in *owners' equity* caused by a service rendered or the sale of goods. The monetary measure of a service rendered. *Sales* of products, merchandise, and services, and earnings from *interest, dividends*, rents, and the like. The amount of revenue is the expected *net present value* of the *net assets* received. Do not confuse with *receipt of funds*, which may occur before, when, or after revenue is recognized. Contrast with *gain* and *income*. See also *holding gain*. Some writers use the term *gross income* synonymously with *revenue*; such usage is to be avoided.

revenue centre. A *responsibility centre* within a firm that has control only over revenue generated; contrast with *cost centre*. See *profit centre*.

revenue-cost graph. See *breakeven chart*.

revenue expenditure. A phrase sometimes used to mean an *expense* in contrast to a capital *expenditure* to acquire an *asset* or to discharge a *liability*. Avoid using this phrase; use *period expense* instead.

revenue received in advance. An inferior term for *advances from customers*.

reversal (reversing) entry. An *entry* in which all *debits* and *credits* are the credits and debits, respectively, of another entry, and in the same amounts. It is usually made on the first day of an *accounting period* to reverse a previous *adjusting entry*, usually an *accrual*. The purpose of such entries is to make the bookkeeper's tasks easier. Suppose that salaries are paid every other Friday, with paycheques compensating employees for the 2 weeks just ended. Total salaries accrue at the rate of $5,000 per 5-day work week. The bookkeeper is accustomed to making the following entry every other Friday:

(1) Salary Expense	$10,000	
Cash		$10,000

To record salary expense
and salary payments.

If paycheques are delivered to employees on Friday, June 25, then the *adjusting entry* made on June 30 (or, perhaps, later) to record accrued salaries for June 28, 29, and 30 would be

(2) Salary Expense	$3,000	
Salaries Payable		$3,000

To charge second-quarter
operations with all salaries
earned in second quarter.

The Salary Expense account would be closed as part of the June 30 *closing entries*. On the next payday, July 9, the salary entry would have to be

(3) Salary Expense	$7,000	
Salaries Payable	$3,000	
Cash		$10,000

To record salary payments
split between expense for
the third quarter (7 days) and
liability carried over from the
second quarter.

To make entry (3), the bookkeeper must look back into the records to see how much of the debit is to Salaries Payable accrued from the previous quarter so that total debits are properly split between third-quarter expense and the liability carried over from the second quarter. Notice that this entry forces the bookkeeper both (a) to refer to balances in old accounts and (b) to make an entry different from the one customarily made, entry (1).

The reversing entry, made just after the books have been closed for the second quarter, makes the salary entry for July 9 the same as that made on all other Friday paydays. The reversing entry merely *reverses* the adjusting entry (2):

(4) Salaries Payable	$3,000	
Salary Expense		$3,000
To reverse the adjusting entry.		

This entry results in a zero balance in the Salaries Payable account and a *credit* balance in the Salary Expense account. If entry (4) is made just after the books are closed for the second quarter, then the entry on July 9 will be the customary entry (1). Entries (4) and (1) together have exactly the same effect as entry (3).

The procedure for using reversal entries is as follows: The required adjustment to record an accrual (*payable* or *receivable*) is made at the end of an *accounting period*; the closing entry is made as usual; as of the first day of the following period, an entry is made reversing the adjusting entry; when a payment is made (or received), the entry is recorded as though no adjusting entry had been recorded. Whether or not reversal entries are used affects the record-keeping procedures, but not the financial statements.

Also used to describe the entry reversing an incorrect entry before recording the correct entry.

reverse stock split. A stock split in which the number of shares *outstanding* is decreased. See *stock split*.

Review Engagement Report. A report issued by a public accountant at the conclusion of a review engagement. As with an audit, the purpose of the engagement is to render independent professional opinion on whether the financial statements of a company are fairly presented in accordance with GAAP. Since a review is more superficial than an audit the amount of assurance provided by the public accountant is *much* lower than is provided by an audit report.

revolving fund. A *fund* whose amounts are continually expended and then replenished; for example, a *petty cash fund*.

revolving loan. A *loan* that is expected to be renewed at *maturity*.

RIA. Registered Industrial Accountant. A formally qualified member of the *SMAC*. Designation is only used in British Columbia. In other provinces it is CMA (Certified Management Accountant).

right. The privilege to subscribe to new *share* issues or to purchase shares. Usually, rights are contained in securities called *warrants* and the warrants may be sold to others. See also *preemptive right*.

risk. A measure of the variability of the *return on investment*. For a given expected amount of return, most people prefer less risk to more risk. Therefore, in rational markets, investments with more risk usually promise, or are expected to yield, a higher rate of return than investments with lower risk. Most people use "risk" and "uncertainty" as synonyms. In technical language, however, these terms have different meanings. "Risk" is used when the probabilities attached to the various outcomes are known, such

as the probabilities of heads or tails in the flip of a fair coin. "Uncertainty" refers to an event where the probabilities of the outcomes, such as winning or losing a lawsuit, can only be estimated.

risk-adjusted discount rate. In a *capital budgeting* context, a decision maker compares projects by comparing their *net present values* for a given *interest rate*, usually the *cost of capital*. If a given project's outcome is considered to be much more or much less risky than the normal undertakings of the company, then the interest rate will be increased (if the project is more risky) or decreased (if less risky) and the rate used is said to be risk-adjusted.

risk premium. Extra compensation paid to an employee or extra interest paid to a lender, over amounts usually considered normal, in return for their undertaking to engage in activities more risky than normal.

ROI. *Return on investment*, but usually to refer to a single project and expressed as a ratio: *income* divided by average *cost of assets* devoted to the project.

roll-over. A term in income tax legislation; broadly, a tax-free transfer of property which would otherwise have given rise to *income* or *capital gain*.

routine. A subdivision of a computer program consisting of two or more instructions that are functionally related.

royalty. Compensation for the use of property, usually a patent, copyrighted material, or natural resources. The amount is often expressed as a percentage of receipts from using the property or as an amount per unit produced.

RRA. See *Reserve recognition accounting*.

RRSP. Registered retirement savings plan. A specific type of savings plan as provided for under income tax legislation.

rule of 69. An amount of money invested at *r* percent per period will double in $69/r + .35$ periods. This approximation is accurate to one-tenth of a period for interest rates between 1/4 and 100 percent per period. For example, at 10 percent per period the rule says that a given sum will double in $69/10 + .35 = 7.25$ periods. At 10 percent per period, a given sum doubles in $7.27 +$ periods.

rule of 72. An amount of money invested at *r* percent per period will double in $72/r$ periods. A reasonable approximation but not nearly as accurate as the *rule of 69*. For example, at 10 percent per period, the rule says a given sum will double in $72/10 = 7.2$ periods.

rule of 78. The rule followed by many finance companies for allocating earnings on *loans* among the months of a year on the sum-of-the-months'-digits-basis when equal monthly payments from the borrower are to be received. The sum of the digits from 1 through 12 is 78, so 12/78 of the year's earnings are allocated to the first month, 11/78 to the second month, and so on. See *sum-of-the-years'-digits depreciation*.

ruling (and balancing) an account. The process of summarizing a series of entries in an *account* by computing a new *balance* and drawing double lines to indicate the information above the double lines has been summarized in the new balance. The process is illustrated below. The steps are as follows. (1) Compute the sum of all *debit* entries including opening debit balance, if any — $1,464.16. (2) Compute the sum of all credit entries including opening credit balance, if any — $413.57. (3) If the amount in (1) is larger than the amount in (2), then write the excess as a credit with a check mark — $1,464.16 − $413.57 = $1,050.59. (4) Add both debit and credit columns, which should now both sum to the same amount, and show that identical total at the foot of both columns. (5) Draw double lines under those numbers and write the excess of debits over credits as the new debit balance with a check mark. (6) If the amount in (2) is larger than the amount in (1), then write the excess as a debit with a check mark. (7) Do steps (4) and (5) except that the excess becomes the new credit balance. (8) If the amount in (1) is equal to the amount in (2), then the balance is zero and only the totals with the double lines beneath them need be shown.

This process is illustrated below.

S

salary. Compensation earned by managers, administrators, professionals, not based on an hourly rate. Contrast with *wage*.

sale. A *revenue* transaction where *goods* or *services* are delivered to a customer in return for cash or a contractual obligation to pay.

sale and leaseback. Phrase used to describe a *financing* transaction where property is sold but is taken back for use on a long-term *lease*. Such transactions often have advantageous income tax effects, but usually have no effect on *financial statement income*.

sales. The periodical total proceeds from disposition of stock-in-trade or by extension, from the rendering of services, net of returns and allowances. The terms "gross sales" and "net sales" are sometimes used to distinguish the sales aggregate before and after deduction of returns and allowances.

sales allowance. A reduction in sales *invoice* price usually given because the goods received by the buyer are not exactly what was ordered. The amounts of such adjustments are often accumulated by the seller in a temporary *revenue contra account* having this, or a similar, title. See *sales discount*.

sales basis of revenue recognition. *Revenue* is recognized, not as goods are produced nor as orders are received, but only when the sale (delivery) has been consummated and cash or a legal receivable obtained. Most revenue is recognized on this basis. Compare with the *percentage-of-completion method* and the *installment method*. Identical with the *completed-contract method* but this latter term is ordinarily used only for *long-term* construction projects.

sales discount. Reduction in sales *invoice* price usually offered for prompt payment. See *terms of sale* and *2/10, n/30*.

sales return. The physical return of merchandise; the amounts of such returns are often accumulated by the seller in a temporary *revenue contra account*.

sales-type lease. A lease that, from the point of view of the lessor, transfers substantially all the benefits and risks incident to ownership of property to the lessee and, at the inception of the lease, the fair value of the leased property is greater or less than its carrying amount, thus giving rise to a profit or loss to the lessor (usually a manufacturer or dealer).

An Open Account, Ruled and Balanced

(Steps indicated in parentheses correspond to steps described in "ruling an account.")

	Date 1985	Explanation	Ref.	Debit (1)		Date 1985	Explanation	Ref.	Credit (2)	
	Jan. 1	Balance	✓	100	00					
	Jan. 13		VR	121	37	Sept. 15		J		42
	Mar. 20		VR	56	42	Nov. 12		J	413	15
	June 5		J	1,138	09	Dec. 31	Balance	✓	1,050	59	(3)
	Aug. 18		J	1	21					
	Nov. 20		VR	38	43					
	Dec. 7		VR	8	64					
(4)				1,464	16				1,464	16	(4)
	1986					**1986**				
(5)	Jan. 1	Balance	✓	1,050	59					

sales value method. *Relative sales value method.*

salvage value. Actual or estimated selling price, net of removal or disposal costs, of a used *plant asset* to be sold or otherwise retired. See *residual value.*

sampling. The examination of a selection of items from a larger number of similar items, with the objective of judging the quality of the whole on the basis of the sample. See *acceptance sampling, attribute sampling, discovery sampling, dollar unit sampling, estimation sampling, fixed interval sampling, judgment sampling, monetary unit sampling, physical unit sampling, random number sampling, representative item sampling, specific item sampling, statistical sampling, stratified sampling, systematic sampling, variable interval sampling, variables sampling.*

scan. (auditing) To review data in order to locate significant items which may require further study. Compare *scrutinize.*

scatter diagram. A graphic representation of the relationship between two or more variables within a population, achieved by plotting each magnitude or item against the co-ordinates provided.

schedule. Supporting set of calculations that show how figures in a statement or tax return are derived.

scientific method. *Effective-interest method of amortizing bond discount or premium.*

scope paragraph. A paragraph in the audit report setting out the scope of the audit and the procedures followed in carrying out the engagement.

scrap value. *Salvage value* assuming item is to be junked. A *net realizable value. Residual value.*

scrutinize. *(auditing)* To review data searchingly in order to locate significant items which may require further study. Compare *scan.*

SEC. Securities and Exchange Commission, an agency authorized by the U.S. Congress to regulate, among other things, the financial reporting practices of most public corporations.

secondary distribution. The redistribution to the public of a significant block of securities of a corporation that have previously been distributed to the public.

secret reserve. *Hidden reserve.*

secured creditor. A person whose claim against a debtor is supported by certain assets which have been pledged to the creditor or upon which the creditor has a lien.

secured liability. A debt or other obligation supported by certain assets upon which the creditor or person to whom the obligation is owed has a *lien* or which have been pledged to the creditor or person to whom the obligation is owed.

security. Document that indicates ownership or indebtedness or potential ownership, such as an *option* or *warrant.*

Securities and Exchange Commission. *SEC.*

segment (of a business). A component of an *entity* whose activities represent a separate major line of business or class of customer. It may be a *subsidiary*, a division, or a department, provided that its *assets*, results of *operations*, and activities can be clearly distinguished, physically and operationally for financial reporting purposes, from the other assets, results of operations, and activities of the entity.

segment expense. An expense that is directly attributable to a segment or the relevant portion of an expense that can be allocated on a reasonable basis to the segments for whose benefit the expense was incurred. The following are excluded from segment expense because they either do not relate to segments or cannot always be allocated to segments: general corporate expenses; losses from investments accounted for on an equity basis; interest expense when the segment's operations are not primarily of a financial nature; income taxes; extraordinary charges; and minority interest.

segment operating profit or loss. The difference between segment revenue and segment expense.

segment reporting. Reporting of *sales, income*, and *assets* by *segments of a business*, usually classified by nature of products sold but sometimes by geographic area where goods are produced or sold, or by type of customers. Sometimes called "line-of-business reporting." *Central corporate expenses* are not allocated to the segments.

segment revenue. Revenue, directly attributable to a segment, derived from sales to customers outside the enterprise and from inter-segment sales or transfers of products and services.

Interest earned on advances or loans to other segments would normally not be included in segment revenue unless the segment's operations are primarily of a financial nature. The following are excluded from segment revenue because they either do not relate to segments or cannot always be allocated to segments: revenue earned at the head office or corporate level and not derived from operations of any segment; income from investments accounted for on an equity basis; interest and dividend income other than that earned on an asset included in the segment's identifiable assets; and extraordinary gains. Inter-segment billings for the cost of shared facilities or other jointly incurred costs do not represent inter-segment sales or transfers for purposes of this definition but represent a cost recovery that should form part of segment expense.

self-balancing. A set of records with equal *debits* and *credits* such as the *ledger* (but not individual accounts), the *balance sheet*, and a *fund* in nonprofit accounting.

self-checking digit. A digit forming part of an account or code number, normally the last digit of the number, which is mathematically derived from the other numbers of the code and is used to detect errors in transcribing the code number.

self-insurance. The assumption by a person of a risk that otherwise might have been covered by insurance.

self-sustaining foreign operation. A foreign operation which is financially and operationally independent of the reporting enterprise such that the exposure to exchange rate changes is limited to the reporting enterprise's net investment in the foreign operation.

sellers' market. A condition within an industry or geographic area where the demand for a product or service exceeds the supply; hence trading conditions favour the seller.

selling and administrative expenses. *Expenses* not specifically identifiable with, nor assigned to, production.

semifixed costs. *Costs* that increase with activity as a step function.

semivariable costs. *Costs* that increase strictly linearly with activity but that are positive at zero activity level. Royalty fees of 2 percent of sales are variable; royalty fees of $1,000 per year plus 2 percent of sales are semivariable.

senior securities. *Bonds* as opposed to *preferred shares*; *preferred shares* as opposed to *common shares*. The senior security has a claim against *earnings* or *assets* that must be met before the claim of less senior securities.

sensitivity analysis. The measurement of the degree of change in one variable in response to a given change in another variable.

sequential access. Access to computer storage where information can be located only by a sequential search of the storage file. Compare *direct access*.

serial bonds. An *issue of bonds* that mature in part at one date, another part on another date, and so on; the various maturity dates usually are equally spaced; contrast with *term bonds*.

service basis of depreciation. *Production method.*

service bureau. A commercial data centre providing service to various customers.

service department. A department, such as the personnel or computer department, that provides services to other departments, rather than direct work on a salable product; contrast with *production department*. Costs of service departments whose services benefit manufacturing operations must be *allocated* to *product costs* under *absorption costing*.

service life. Period of expected usefulness of an asset; may not coincide with *depreciable life* or income tax purposes.

service potential. Used to describe the output or service capacity of an *asset* and is normally determined by reference to the attributes of the asset owned, i.e., physical output capacity, associated operating costs, service life and quality of output.

services. Useful work done by a person, a machine, or an organization. See *goods and services*.

setup. The time or costs required to prepare production equipment for doing a job.

share. A unit of *stock* representing ownership in a company.

share capital. Synonymous with *capital stock*.

share certificate. The formal document issued by a limited company as evidence of ownership of *shares* in its *capital stock*.

share issue expense. The costs incurred when issuing *shares*, including legal fees, advertising, selling and printing costs.

share purchase warrant. A certificate, usually attached initially to *preferred shares* or *bonds* of a *limited company*, which gives its owner the right to purchase a specified number of shares of the company's *capital stock* at a stated price and normally within a stated period of time. Compare *share right*.

share right. A right granted by a shareholder on the occasion of a new issue of *capital stock*, which entitles him to purchase his or her pro rata share of the issue at the stated price and within a stated period of time.

shareholder. The legal owner of *shares* of a *limited company*.

shareholder of record. A *shareholder* in whose name *shares* are registered in the books of a *limited company*.

shareholders' deficiency. The excess of the *book value* of *liabilities* of a *limited company* over the book value of its *assets*; negative shareholders' equity.

shareholders' equity. *Proprietorship* or *owners' equity* of a *limited company*. The term stockholders' equity is usually used by American writers.

shipping order. A form conveying instructions for the shipment of specified goods.

short-form report. An audit report the substance of which contains only two elements: a statement of the scope of the examination and an opinion on the financial statements. (Compare *long-form report*.)

short position. The condition of a person who owes securities or commodities to a broker; such person is said to be ''short'' those securities or commodities in the broker's accounts. The designations ''long'' and ''short'' are used in accounting for quantities of securities and commodities in the same way as the designations ''debit'' and ''credit'' are used in accounting for monetary values. Compare *long position*.

short sale. The sale of a security or commodity not owned by the seller in the hope that the security or commodity can subsequently be purchased at a lower price before the settlement date. See also *short position*.

short-term. Current; ordinarily, due within one year.

shrinkage. An excess of *inventory* shown on the *books* over actual physical quantities on hand. Can result from theft or shoplifting as well as from evaporation or general wear and tear.

shutdown cost. Those fixed costs which continue to be incurred after production has ceased. The costs of closing down a particular production facility.

sight draft. A demand for payment drawn by a person to whom money is owed. The *draft* is presented to the borrower's (the debtor's) bank in expectation that the borrower will authorize its banks to disburse the funds. Such drafts are often used when a seller sells goods to a new customer in a different city. The seller is not sure whether the buyer will pay the bill. The seller sends the *bill of lading*, or other evidence of ownership of the goods, along with a sight draft to the buyer's bank. Before the goods can be released to the buyer, the buyer must instruct its bank to honour the sight draft by withdrawing funds from the buyers' account. Once the sight draft is honoured, the bill of lading or other document evidencing ownership is handed over to the buyer and the goods become the property of the buyer.

signing officer. An officer authorized to sign certain documents on behalf of an organization. In a restricted sense, the individual who signs cheques or bills of exchange on behalf of an organization.

simple interest. *Interest* calculated on *principal* where interest earned during periods before maturity of the loan is neither added to the principal nor paid to the lender. *Interest = principal × interest rate × time.* Seldom used in economic calculations except for periods less than 1 year; contrast with *compound interest*.

single-entry accounting. Accounting that is neither *self-balancing* nor *articulated*; that is, it does not rely on equal *debits* and *credits*. No journal entries are made. *Plugging* is required to derive *owners' equity* for the *balance sheet*.

single proprietorship. *Sole proprietorship*.

single step. Said of an *income statement* where all *ordinary revenue* and *gain* terms are shown first and totalled. Then all ordinary *expenses* and *losses* are totalled. Their difference, plus the effect of *extraordinary items,* is shown as *net income*; contrast with *multiple-step* and see *proprietorship theory*.

sinking fund. *Assets* and their earnings earmarked for the retirement of bonds or other long-term obligations. Earnings of sinking-fund investments are taxable income of the company.

sinking-fund method of depreciation. The periodic charge is an amount so that when the charges are considered to be

an *annuity*, the value of the annuity at the end of depreciable life is equal to the *acquisition cost* of the asset. In theory, the charge for a period ought also to include interest on the accumulated depreciation at the start of the period as well. A *fund* of cash is not necessarily, or even usually, accumulated. This method is rarely used.

sinking fund reserve. A portion of *retained earnings* appropriated for the purposes of a *sinking fund*.

skeleton account. *T-account*.

skewness. The degree of asymmetry of a frequency distribution.

SMAC. The Society of Management Accountants of Canada. The national association of accountants whose provincial associations engage in industrial and governmental accounting. The association undertakes research and administers an educational program and comprehensive examinations; those who pass qualify to be designated *CMA*s.

small business deduction. An income tax term; broadly, a tax reduction allowed to certain small businesses.

soak-up method. The *equity method*.

social accounting. The identification, measurement and reporting of social costs and benefits of economic activity. It is concerned with the positive or negative impact (social benefit or social cost) of an organization's activities upon the financial, physical or emotional well-being of those who are directly associated with the organization (such as investors, employees, beneficiaries of services, suppliers, customers or clients) and of those who are affected by the organization's activities by reason of geographic proximity or otherwise.

social costs. The loss to society resulting from action or inaction in particular circumstances. Such costs are often not readily measurable in monetary terms.

software. The programming aids, such as compilers, sort and report programs, and generators, which extend the capabilities of and simplify the use of the computer, as well as certain operating systems and other control programs. (Compare *hardware*.)

sole proprietorship. An unincorporated business in which all *owner's equity* belongs to one person.

solvent. Able to meet debts when due.

source document. An original record or evidence of a transaction.

source of funds. Any *transaction* that increases *working capital*.

sources and uses statement. *Statements of changes in financial position*.

special contribution. A payment to a pension plan to pay interest on and to amortize an unfunded actuarial liability. Special contributions arise from experience losses or the provision of benefits for past service. Compare *normal actuarial cost.*

special journal. A *journal,* such as a sales journal or cash disbursements journal, to record *transactions* of a similar nature that occur frequently.

specific identification method. Method for valuing *ending inventory* and *cost of goods sold* by identifying actual units sold and in inventory and summing the actual costs of those individual units. Usually used for items with large unit value, such as jewelry, automobiles, and fur coats.

specific item sampling. Sampling where particular items are selected because of their nature, value or method of recording. Compare *representative item sampling.*

specific price changes. Changes in the market prices of specific *goods* and *services*; contrast with *general price level changes.*

specific price index. A measure of the price of a specific good or service, or a small group of similar goods or services, at one time relative to the price during a base period; contrast with *general price index.* See *dollar-value LIFO method.*

spending variance. The equivalent of price and quantity variances for overhead costs.

split. *Stock split.* Sometimes called "splitup".

splitoff point. The point where all costs are no longer *joint costs* but can be identified with individual products or perhaps with a smaller number of *joint products.*

spoilage. See *abnormal spoilage* and *normal spoilage.*

spot price. The price of a commodity for immediate delivery. (Compare *forward price.*)

spot rate. The exchange rate available for the immediate exchange of two currencies.

spread. In financial institutions, the difference between the interest rate on amounts borrowed and on amounts loaned. The difference between the bid and asked price of a security or commodity.

spread sheet. A *work sheet* organized like a *matrix* that provides a two-way classification of accounting data. The rows and columns are both labelled with *account* titles. An entry in a row represents a *debit,* whereas an entry in a column represents a *credit.* Thus, the number "100" in the "cash" row and the "accounts receivable" column records an entry debiting cash and crediting accounts receivable for $100. A given row total indicates all debit entries to the account represented by that row and a given column total indicates the sum of all credit entries to the account represented by that column.

stable monetary unit assumption. In spite of *inflation* that appears to be a way of life, the assumption that underlies *historical cost/nominal dollar accounting* — namely, that current dollars and dollars of previous years can be meaningfully added together. No specific recognition is given to changing values of the dollar in the usual *financial statements.* See *constant dollar accounting.*

stale-dated cheque. A cheque which has not been presented to the bank on which it is drawn for payment within a reasonable time of its date (generally six months in Canada by the custom of bankers) and which may therefore be dishonoured by the bank without any breach of the banker-customer contract.

standard cost. Anticipated *cost* of producing a unit of output; a predetermined cost to be assigned to products produced. Standard cost implies a norm: what costs should be. Budgeted cost implies a forecast: something likely, but not necessarily a "should," as implied by a norm. Standard costs are used as the benchmark for gauging good and bad performance. While a budget may be used similarly, it need not be. A budget may be simply a planning document, subject to changes whenever plans change, whereas standard costs are usually not changed until technology changes or costs of labour and materials change.

standard cost system. *Product costing* using *standard costs* rather than actual costs. May be based on either *absorption* or *direct costing* principles.

standard deviation. A measure of the dispersion from the mean of the distribution. It is obtained by squaring the deviations of all values from the mean, summing them, taking the average, and then taking the square root of this average.

standard manufacturing overhead. *Overhead costs* expected to be incurred per unit of time and per unit produced.

standard price (rate). Unit price established for materials or labour used in *standard cost systems.*

standard quantity allowed. The quantity of direct material or direct labour (inputs) that should have been used if the units of output had been produced in accordance with preset *standards.*

standby costs. A type of *capacity cost,* such as property taxes, incurred even if operations are shut down completely. Contrast with *enabling costs.*

start-up costs. The aggregate of the costs, excluding acquisition costs, incurred to bring a new unit into production.

stated capital. A term used in corporate legislation to designate the aggregate consideration received by a corporation on the issue of each class of *share capital*.

stated value. A term sometimes used for the *face amount* of *capital stock*, when no *par value* is indicated. Where there is a stated value per share, it may be set by the directors (in which case, *contributed surplus* may come into being).

statement of affairs. A *balance sheet* showing immediate *liquidation* amounts, rather than *historical costs*, usually prepared when *insolvency* or *bankruptcy* is imminent. The *going concern assumption* is not used.

statement of changes in financial position. A statement that explains the changes in *working capital* (or cash) balances during a period and shows the changes in the working capital (or cash) accounts themselves. Sometimes called the "funds statement." See *dual-transactions assumption* and *all financial resources*.

statement of changes in net assets. A *statement of changes in financial position* adapted for investment companies. The details provided include a reconciliation of the *net assets* at the beginning and end of the period with emphasis on transactions and fluctuations in market value affecting the investment portfolio.

statement of charge and discharge. A financial statement as to *capital* or *income*, drawn up by an executor or administrator to account for receipts and dispositions of cash and/or other assets in an estate or trust.

statement of financial position. *Balance sheet.*

statement of material facts. Under securities legislation, a document filed by a corporation with a securities commission relating to a proposed *primary distribution* of securities exempt from prospectus requirements. It contains information concerning the securities, circumstances relating to their offering, names of the corporation's officers and directors, financial data and other pertinent facts.

statement of realization and liquidation. A financial statement drawn up by a trustee or liquidator to account for the winding-up of a business, showing the amounts realized on disposition of the assets and the amounts disbursed to liquidate the liabilities.

statement of receipts and disbursements. A financial statement summarizing the cash receipts and disbursements for a stated period, frequently showing the opening and closing balances of cash on hand and in bank. Compare *cash flow statement*.

statement of retained earnings (income). A statement that reconciles the beginning-of-period and end-of-period balances in the *retained earnings* account. It shows the effects of *earnings*, *dividend declarations*, and *prior-period adjustments*.

statement of revenue and expenditure. A financial state-ment summarizing the items of revenue and expenditure for a stated period. It is mainly used by government and non-profit organizations. Compare *income statement*.

statement of source and application of funds. A statement of changes in financial position which takes into account only those activities which have an effect on the amount of working capital. Compare *cash flow statement*; *statement of changes in financial position*.

static budget. *Fixed budget.*

statistical sampling. Any method of sampling that uses mathematical methods, based on laws of probability, to determine sample size, to select items for examination and to evaluate results.

statutory audit. An audit carried out under the provisions of a statute, such as a Corporations Act, *The Bank Act*, a Municipal Act.

statutory tax rate. The tax rate specified in the *income tax* law for each type of income (for example, *ordinary income*, *capital gain* or *loss*).

step-by-by-step purchase. The acquisition of shares in a company where the investment position has been reached as the result of two or more purchases.

step cost. *Semifixed cost.*

step-down method. The method for *allocating service department* costs that starts by allocating one service department's costs to *production departments* and to all other service departments. Then a second service department's costs, including costs allocated from the first, are allocated to production departments and to all other service departments except the first one. In this fashion, the costs of all service departments, including previous allocations, are allocated to production departments and to those service departments whose costs have not yet been allocated.

sterilized allocation. Optimal decisions result from considering *incremental costs* only. *Allocations* of *joint* or *common costs* are never required for optimal decisions. An allocation of these costs that causes the optimal decision choice not to differ from the one that occurs when joint or common costs are unallocated is "sterilized" with respect to that decision. The term was first used in this context by Arthur L. Thomas. Because *absorption costing* requires that all manufacturing costs be allocated to product, and because some allocations can lead to bad decisions, Thomas (and we) advocate that the allocation scheme chosen lead to sterilized allocations that do not alter the otherwise optimal decision. There is, however, no single allocation scheme that is always sterilized with respect to all decisions. Thus, Thomas (and we) advocate that decisions be made on the basis of incremental costs before any allocations.

stock. *Inventory. Capital stock.* A measure of the amount of something on hand at a specific time; in this sense, contrast with *flow*.

stock appreciation rights. The employer promises to pay to the employee an amount of *cash* on a certain future date. The amount of cash is the difference between the *market value* of a certain number of *shares* of *stock* in the employer's company on a given future date and the market value on the date the rights are granted. This is a form of compensation used because both changes in tax laws in recent years and stock market performance have made *stock options* relatively less attractive. *GAAP* do not allow any entry to be made when such rights are granted. Only when (and if) the cash is eventually paid is there an entry made recognizing *expense*.

stock dividend. A so-called *dividend* where additional *shares* of *capital stock* are distributed, without cash payments, to existing shareholders. It results in a *debit* to *retained earnings* in the amount of the market value of the shares issued and a *credit* to *capital stock* accounts. It is ordinarily used to indicate that earnings retained have been permanently reinvested in the business; contrast with a *stock split*, which requires no entry in the capital stock accounts other than a notation that the *par* or *stated value* per share has been changed.

stock option. The right granted by a *limited company* to purchase a specified number of shares of *stock* for a specified price at specified times, usually granted to employees; contrast with *warrant*.

stock purchase warrant. A certificate giving the owner of *preferred shares* or *bonds* of a *limited company* the right to purchase a specified number of shares of the company's *capital stock* at a stated price within a stated period of time. (Compare *share right*.)

stock split. Increase in the number of common shares to existing shareholders without additional capital contributions by them. Does not increase the total *par* (or *stated*) *value of common shares* outstanding because par (or stated) value per share is reduced in inverse proportion. A three-for-one stock split reduces par (or stated) value per share to one-third of its former amount. Stock splits are usually limited to distributions that increase the number of shares outstanding by 20 percent or more; compare with *stock dividend*.

stock subscriptions. See *subscription* and *subscribed stock*.

stock warrant. See *warrant*.

stockholders' equity. See *shareholders' equity*.

stop payment. An order by the drawer of a cheque to the bank on which it is drawn not to pay the cheque.

stores. *Raw materials*, parts, and supplies.

straight debt value. An estimate of what the *market value* of a *convertible bond* would be if the bond did not contain a conversion privilege.

straight-line depreciation. If the *depreciable life* is n periods, then the periodic *depreciation* charge is 1/n of the *depre-*

ciable cost.. Results in equal periodic charges and is sometimes called "straight-time depreciation."

stratified sampling. A method of choosing a sample in which the entire population is divided first into relatively homogeneous sub groups (strata), from which random samples are then selected.

street security. A stock certificate in immediately transferable form, most commonly because it is registered in the name of a broker and endorsed in blank. See also *bearer security*.

subordinated. Said of *debt* whose claim on income or assets is junior to, or comes after, claims of other debt.

subscribed stock. A *shareholders' equity* account showing the capital that will be contributed as soon as the subscription price is collected. A subscription is a legal contract so that an entry is made debiting a receivable and crediting subscribed stock as soon as the shares are subscribed.

subscription. Agreement to buy a *security*, or to purchase periodicals such as magazines.

subsequent events. *Post-statement events*.

subsidiary. Said of a company more than 50 percent of whose voting shares are owned by another.

subsidiary (ledger) accounts. The *accounts* in a *subsidiary ledger*.

subsidiary ledger. The *ledger* that contains the detailed accounts whose total is shown in a *controlling account* of the *general ledger*.

substantive test. An audit procedure used to gain evidence as to the validity of financial statement balances. Compare *compliance procedure*.

successful-efforts accounting. In petroleum accounting, the *capitalization* of the drilling costs of only those wells that contain oil. See *discovery-value accounting* for an example.

sufficiency. In auditing the term refers to the quantity of audit evidence obtained in a particular situation. Compare *appropriateness*.

summary of significant accounting policies. The *CICA Handbook* requires that every *annual report* summarize the significant *accounting* policies used in compiling the annual report. This summary may be a separate exhibit or the first *note* to the financial statements.

sum-of-the-years'-digits depreciation. An *accelerated depreciation* method for an asset with *depreciable life* of n years where the charge in period i (i = 1, . . ., n) is the fraction $n/[n(n + 1)/2]$ of the *depreciable cost*. If an asset has a depreciable cost of \$15,000 and a 5-year depreciable life, for example, the depreciation charges would be \$5,000 (= 5/15 × \$15,000) in the first year, \$4,000 in the second,

$3,000 in the third, $2,000 in the fourth, and $1,000 in the fifth.

sunk cost. *Costs* incurred in the past that are not affected by, and hence irrelevant for, current decisions, aside from *income tax* effects; contrast with *incremental costs* and *imputed costs*. For example, the *acquisition cost* of machinery is irrelevant to a decision of whether or not to scrap the machinery. The current *exit value* of the machine is the imputed cost of continuing to own it and the cost of, say, electricity to run the machine is an incremental cost of its operation. Sunk costs become relevant for decision making when *income taxes* (gain or *loss* on disposal of asset) are taken into account because the cash payment for income taxes depends on the tax basis of the asset.

supplemental actuarial value. Actuarial accrued liability.

supplies. Materials which are consumed in the operations of a business but do not become part of the physical content of any finished product.

supplementary statements (schedules). Statements (schedules) in addition to the four basic *financial statements* (including the retained earnings reconciliation as a basic statement).

surplus. A word once used but now considered poor terminology; prefaced by ''earned'' to mean *retained earnings*.

surplus reserves. Of all the words in accounting, *reserve* is the most objectionable and *surplus* is the second most objectionable. This phrase, then, has nothing to recommend it. It means, simply, *appropriated retained earnings*.

suspense account. A *temporary account* used to record part of a transaction prior to final analysis of that transaction. For example, if a business regularly classifies all sales into a dozen or more different categories but wants to deposit the proceeds of cash sales every day, it may credit a sales suspense account pending detailed classification of all sales into sales, type 1; sales, type 2; and so on.

sustainable income. The part of *distributable income* (computed from *replacement cost* data) that the firm can be expected to earn in the next accounting period if operations are continued at the same levels as during the current period. *Income from discontinued operations*, for example, may be distributable but not sustainable.

syndicate. A group of *underwriters*, who have joined together to market a particular *issue* of *securities*.

systematic sampling. Fixed interval sampling.

systems design. The specification of an organizational set-up of the procedures and methods to be used in carrying out an activity.

T

T-account. Account form shaped like the letter T with the title above the horizontal line. *Debits* are shown to the left of the vertical line, *credits* to the right.

take-or-pay contract. An agreement between a purchaser and a seller that provides for the purchaser to pay specified amounts periodically in return for products or services. The purchaser must make specified minimum payments even if it does not take delivery of the contracted products or services.

take-home pay. The amount of a paycheque; earned wages or *salary* reduced by deductions for *income taxes*, *Canada Pension Plan*, contributions to fringe benefit plans, union dues, and so on. Take-home pay might be as little as 60 percent of earned compensation.

takeover bid. A bid to purchase shares of a *limited company* with a view to gaining control.

takeover bid circular. Under securities legislation, the offering document issued by a prospective purchaser making a takeover bid.

tangible. Having physical form. Accounting has never satisfactorily defined the distinction between tangible and *intangible assets*. Typically, intangibles are defined by giving an exhaustive list and everything not on the list is defined as tangible.

target cost. *Standard cost.*

tax. A nonpenal, but compulsory, charge levied by a government on income, consumption, wealth, or other bases for the benefit of all those governed. The term does not include fines or specific charges for benefits accruing only to those paying the charges, such as licenses, permits, special assessments, admission fees, and tolls.

tax allocation: interperiod. See *deferred income tax liability*.

tax allocation: intrastatement. The showing of income tax effects on *extraordinary items* and *prior-period adjustments* along with these items, separately from income taxes on other income. See net-of-tax reporting.

tax avoidance. See *tax shelter*.

tax credit. A subtraction from taxes otherwise payable: contrast with *tax deduction*.

tax deduction. A subtraction from *revenues* and *gains* to arrive at taxable income. Tax deductions are technically different from tax *exemptions*, but the effect of both is to reduce gross income in computing taxable income. Both are different from *tax credits*, which are subtracted from the computed tax itself in determining taxes payable. If the tax rate is t percent of pretax income, then a *tax credit* of $1 is worth $1/t$ of *tax deductions*.

tax equity. A term in income tax legislation; broadly, the *net assets* of a corporation.

tax evasion. The fraudulent understatement of taxable income or overstatement of deductions and expenses or both; contrast with tax shelter.

tax haven. A political jurisdiction that levies significantly lower taxes than would otherwise be payable in other jurisdictions on similar income.

tax lien. An encumbrance placed upon a taxpayer's property as security for unpaid taxes.

tax shelter. The legal avoidance of, or reduction in, *income taxes* resulting from a careful reading of the complex income tax regulations and the subsequent rearrangement of financial affairs to take advantage of the regulations. Often the term is used pejoratively, but the courts have long held that an individual or company has no obligation to pay taxes any larger than the legal minimum. If the public concludes that a given tax shelter is "unfair," then the laws and regulations can be changed. Sometimes used to refer to the investment that permits tax avoidance.

tax shield. The amount of an *expense* that reduces taxable income but does not require *working capital*, such as *depreciation*. Sometimes this term is expanded to include expenses that reduce taxable income and use working capital. A depreciation deduction (or *R&D expense* in the expanded sense) of $10,000 provides a tax shield of $4,800 when the marginal tax rate is 48 percent.

taxable income. Income for a period, subject to taxation, as computed in accordance with income tax legislation. (Compare *accounting income*.)

taxes payable basis. A basis used in accounting for corporate income taxes where there are timing differences between *accounting income* and *taxable income*. The charge for income taxes is the estimated amount that will actually be levied for the period. (Compare *tax allocation* — interperiod.)

technology. The sum of a firm's technical *trade secrets* and *know-how*, as distinct from its *patents*.

temporal method (of foreign currency). A method of translation which translates assets, liabilities, revenues and expenses in a manner that retains their bases of measurement in terms of the Canadian dollar (i.e., it uses the Canadian dollar as the unit of measure). In particular: monetary items are translated at the rate of exchange in effect at the balance sheet date; non-monetary items are translated at historical exchange rates, unless such items are carried at market, in which case they are translated at the rate of exchange in effect at the balance sheet date; revenue and expense items are translated at the rate of exchange in effect on the dates they occur; depreciation or amortization of assets translated at historical exchange rates are translated at the same exchange rates as the assets to which they relate.

temporary account. *Account* that does not appear on the *balance sheet*. *Revenue* and *expense* accounts, their *adjuncts* and *contras*, *production cost accounts*, *income distribution accounts*, and purchases-related accounts (which are closed

to the various inventories). Sometimes called a "nominal account."

temporary difference. See *timing difference*.

temporary investments. Investments in *marketable securities* that the owner intends to sell within a short time, usually 1 year, and hence classified as *current assets*.

term bonds. A *bond issue* whose component bonds all mature at the same time; contrast with *serial bonds*.

term deposit. A deposit in a bank or other financial institution for a specific minimum period of time. Compare *demand deposit*.

term loan. A loan with a *maturity* date, as opposed to a demand loan which is due whenever the lender requests payment. In practice bankers and auditors use this phrase only for loans for a year or more.

term preferred share. A preferred share which has the legal form of an equity security but attributes of a debt security, e.g. a stipulated maturity or conditions for redemption which are not solely within the control of the issuer.

terminal. An input/output device connected to a computer.

terms of sale. The conditions governing payment for a sale. For example, the terms *2/10, n(et)/30* mean that if payment is made within 10 days of the invoice date, a *discount* of 2 percent from *invoice* price can be taken; the invoice amount must be paid, in any event, within 30 days or it becomes overdue.

test audit. An audit which is carried out by examining selected samples of transactions and accounting operations. Compare *detailed audit*.

test deck. A series of simulated transactions created for processing through a computer system for comparison with predetermined results.

thin capitalization. A state of having a high *debt* to *equity ratio*. Under income tax legislation, the term has a special meaning.

throughput contract. An agreement between a shipper (processor) and the owner of a transportation facility (such as an oil or natural gas pipeline or a ship) or a manufacturing facility that provides for the shipper (processor) to pay specified amounts periodically in return for the transportation (processing) of a product. The shipper (processor) is obligated to make cash payments even if it does not ship (process) the contracted quantities.

tickler file. A collection of vouchers or other memorandums arranged chronologically to remind the person in charge of certain duties to make payments (or to do other tasks) as scheduled.

time-adjusted rate of return. *Internal rate of return*.

time cost. *Period cost.*

time deposit. Cash in a bank earning interest; contrast with *demand deposit.*

time-period concept. The accounting concept that recognizes the need to subdivide the life of an enterprise into convenient time periods for accounting purposes. For management purposes, the time period is usually one month and for external reporting purposes the period is one year.

time-series analysis. See *cross-section analysis* for definition and contrast.

time sharing. The concurrent use of the same computer by several users.

timeliness. Having information available to a decision maker before it loses its capacity to influence decisions.

times-interest earned. Ratio of pretax *income* plus *interest* charges to interest charges. See *ratio.*

timing difference. A difference between taxable income and pretax income reported to shareholders that will be reversed in a subsequent period. It requires an entry in the *future income tax* account. For example, the use of *accelerated depreciation* for tax returns and *straight-line depreciation* for financial reporting. Contrast with *permanent difference.*

Toronto Stock Exchange (TSE). A public market where various corporate securities are traded.

total assets turnover. *Sales* divided by average total *assets.*

total overhead variance. Difference between total *overhead* costs and *absorbed overhead.*

trade acceptance. A *draft* drawn by a seller which is presented for signature (acceptance) to the buyer at the time goods are purchased and which then becomes the equivalent of a *note receivable* of the seller and the *note payable* of the buyer.

trade account payable. A debt for goods or services purchased in the ordinary course of business. See also *account payable.*

trade account receivable. An amount claimed against a customer for goods or services sold to him or to her in the ordinary course of business. See also *account receivable.*

trade credit. One business allows another to buy from it in return for a promise to pay later. As contrasted with consumer credit, where a business extends the privilege of paying later to a retail customer.

trade discount. A *discount* from *list price* offered to all customers of a given type; contrast with a *discount* offered for prompt payment and *quantity discount.*

trade payables (receivables). *Payables (receivables)* aris-ing in the ordinary course of business transactions. Most accounts payable (receivable) are of this kind.

trade secret. Technical or business information such as formulas, recipes, computer programs, and marketing data not generally known by competitors and maintained by the firm as a secret. A famous example is the secret formula for *Coca Cola* (a registered *trademark* of the company). Compare with *know-how.* Theoretically capable of having an infinite life, this intangible asset is capitalized only if purchased and then amortized. If it is developed internally, then no assets will be shown.

trade-in. Acquiring a new *asset* in exchange for a used one and perhaps additional cash. See *boot* and *trade-in transaction.*

trade-in transaction. The accounting for a trade-in depends on whether or not the asset received is "similar" to the asset traded in and whether the accounting is for *financial statements* or for *income tax* returns. Assume that an old asset cost $5,000, has $3,000 of *accumulated depreciation* (after recording depreciation to the date of the trade-in), and hence has a *book value* of $2,000. The old asset appears to have a market value of $1,500, according to price quotations in used-asset markets. The old asset is traded-in on a new asset with a list price of $10,000. The old asset and $5,500 cash (*boot*) are given for the new asset. The generic entry for the trade-in transaction is

New Asset	A		
Accumulated Depreciation (Old Asset)	3,000		
Adjustment on Exchange of Asset	B	or	B
Old Asset			5,000
Cash			5,500

(1) The *list price* method of accounting for trade-ins rests on the assumption that the list price of the new asset closely approximates its market value. The new asset is recorded at its list price (A = $10,000 in the example); B is a *plug* (= $2,500 credit in the example). If B requires a *debit* plug, the Adjustment on Exchange of Asset is a *loss*; if a *credit* plug is required (as in the example), the adjustment is a *gain.*

(2) Another theoretically sound method of accounting for trade-ins rests on the assumption that the price quotation from used-asset markets gives a more reliable measure of the market value of the old asset than is the list price a reliable measure of the market value of the new asset. This method uses the *fair market value* of the old asset, $1,500 in the example, to determine B (= $2,000 book value − $1,500 assumed proceeds on disposition = $500 debit or loss). The exchange results in a loss if the book value of the old asset exceeds its market value and in a gain if the market value exceeds the book value. The new asset is recorded on the books by plugging for A (= $7,000 in the example.)

(3) For income tax reporting, no gain or loss may be recognized on the trade-in. Thus the new asset is recorded on the books by assuming B is zero and plugging for A (= $7,500 in the example).

	Old Asset Compared with New Asset	
More Reliable Information As To Fair Market Value	**Similar**	**Not Similar**
New Asset List Price	A = $7,500	A = $10,000
	B = 0	B = 2,500 gain
Old Asset Market Price	A = $7,000	A = $ 7,000
	B = 500 loss	B = 500 loss

trademark. A distinctive word or symbol affixed to a product, its package or dispenser, which uniquely identifies the firm's products and services. See *trademark right*.

trademark right. The right to exclude competitors in sales or advertising from using words or symbols that may be confusingly similar to the firm's *trademarks*. Trademark rights last as long as the firm continues to use the trademarks in question. In Canada, trademark rights arise from use and not from government registration. They therefore have a legal life independent of the life of a registration. Registrations last 20 years and are renewable as long as the trademark is being used. Thus, as an asset, purchased trademark rights might, like land, not be subject to amortization if management believes that the life of the trademark is indefinite. In practice, accountants usually amortize a trademark right over some estimate of its life.

trading on the equity. Said of a firm engaging in *debt financing*; frequently said of a firm doing so to a degree considered abnormal for a firm of its kind. *Leverage*.

transaction. An exchange between the accounting *entity* and another party, or parties.

transfer agent. Usually a trust company *designated* by a company to make legal transfers of *shares* (*bonds*) and, perhaps, to pay *dividends* (*coupons*).

transfer price. A substitute for a *market*, or *arm's-length*, *price* used in *profit centre*, or *responsibility, accounting* when one segment of the business "sells" to another segment. Incentives of profit centre managers will not coincide with the best interests of the entire business unless transfer prices are properly set.

translation of foreign currency. The process of expressing financial statements derived from a set of accounts maintained in the currency of one country in terms of the currency of another country, or of expressing *monetary items* which are stated in one currency in equivalent terms of another currency. See *temporal method*, *current rate method*.

translation gain (or loss). *Foreign exchange gain (or loss)*.

transportation-in. *Freight-in*.

transposition error. An error in record keeping resulting from reversing the order of digits in a number, such as recording "32" for "23." If an error of this sort has been made in a number added in a total, then the incorrect total will differ from the correct total by a number divisible by nine. Thus if *trial balance* sums differ by a number divisible by nine, one might search for a transposition error.

treasury bill. A short-term government security issued at a discount in lieu of interest.

treasury bond. A bond issued by a company and then reacquired; such bonds are treated as retired when reacquired and an *extraordinary gain* or *loss* on reacquisition is recognized.

treasury shares. *Capital stock* issued and then reacquired by the company. Such reacquisitions result in a reduction of *shareholders' equity*, and are usually shown on the balance sheet as *contra* to shareholders' equity. Neither *gain* nor *loss* is recognized on transactions involving treasury shares. Any difference between the amounts paid and received for treasury share transactions is debited (if positive) or credited (if negative) to *contributed surplus*. See *cost method* and *par value method*.

trial balance. A listing of *account balances*; all accounts with *debit* balances are totaled separately from accounts with *credit* balances. The two totals should be equal. Trial balances are taken as a partial check of the arithmetic accuracy of the entries previously made. See *adjusted, pre-closing, post-closing, unadjusted trial balance*.

trust. A relationship between two persons by virtue of which one (the trustee) holds title to property for the benefit of, and stands in a fiduciary relationship to, the other (the beneficiary).

trustee. A person who holds title to property for the benefit of another.

trustee in bankruptcy. A person appointed by the court to administer the estate of a bankrupt and distribute available assets to creditors.

TSE. *Toronto Stock Exchange*.

turnover. The number of times that *assets*, such as *inventory* or *accounts receivable*, are replaced on average during the period. Accounts receivable turnover, for example, is total sales on account for a period divided by average accounts receivable balance for the period. See *ratio*.

turnover of plant and equipment. See *ratio*.

two-T-account method. A method for computing either (1) *foreign exchange gains and losses* or (2) *monetary gains* or *losses* for *general price level adjusted statements*. The left-hand *T-account* shows how actual net balances of *monetary items* and the right-hand T-account shows implied (*common*) *dollar* amounts.

2/10, n(et)/30. See *terms of sale*.

U

UCC. Undepreciated capital cost. Cost less accumulated capital cost allowance.

unadjusted trial balance. *Trial balance* before *adjusting* and *closing entries* are made at the end of the period.

unappropriated retained earnings. *Retained earnings* not appropriated and therefore against which *dividends* can be charged in the absence of retained earnings restrictions. See *restricted retained earnings*.

uncertainty. See *risk* for definition and contrast.

uncollectible account. An *account receivable* that will not be paid by the *debtor*. If the preferable *allowance method* is used, the entry on judging a specific account to be uncollectible is to *debit* the Allowance for Uncollectibles account and to *credit* the specific account receivable.

unconsolidated subsidiary. A *subsidiary* not consolidated and, hence, accounted for on the *equity method*. See *nonconsolidated subsidiary*.

uncontrollable cost. The opposite of *controllable cost*.

underabsorb. To charge to production estimated overhead which is less than actual overhead. Compare *overabsorb*.

underapplied (underabsorbed) overhead. An excess of actual *overhead costs* for a period over costs applied, or charged, to products produced during the period. A *debit balance* remaining in an overhead account after overhead is assigned to product.

underlying document. The record, memorandum, *voucher*, or other signal that is the authority for making an *entry* into a *journal*.

underwriter. One who agrees to purchase an entire *security issue* for a specified price, usually for resale to others.

undistributed income. A term in income tax legislation; broadly, *retained earnings* of a corporation.

unearned income (revenue). *Advances from customers*; strictly speaking, a contradiction in terms.

unexpired cost. An *asset*.

unfavourable variance. In *standard cost* accounting, an excess of actual cost over standard cost assigned to product.

unfunded. Not *funded*. An obligation or *liability*, usually for *pension costs*, exists but no *funds* have been set aside to discharge the obligation or liability.

unincorporated business. A business organization which is not a legal entity separate from its owners or members.

unissued capital stock. *Stock* authorized but not yet issued.

unit. One of the equal parts into which the ownership of a mutual fund or real estate investment trust is divided. A package of two or more securities of different classes of a corporation offered for sale.

unit cost. The cost of a unit of product or service, found by dividing the total applied costs for a given period or for a given operation by the number of units produced in that period or operation.

unit-of-measure concept. The accounting concept that asserts that accounting measures and reports the results of the economic activities in terms of a stable monetary unit.

units of production method. The *production method of depreciation*.

unlimited liability. The liability of *general partners* or a sole proprietor for all debts of the *partnership* or *sole proprietorship*.

unlisted security. A security which is not listed on a stock exchange and is traded over-the-counter.

unqualified opinion. See *auditor's report*.

unrealized. An adjective generally used to describe a profit, gain or loss on assets not yet converted into liquid assets or on liabilities not yet liquidated.

unrealized appreciation. An *unrealized holding gain*; frequently used in the context of *marketable securities*.

unrealized exchange gain/loss. An exchange adjustment which results from the translation of monetary assets and liabilities relating to foreign currency transactions and from the translation of foreign currency financial statements. Compare *realized exchange gain/loss*.

unrealized gross margin (profit). A *contra* account to *installment accounts receivable* used with the *installment method* of revenue recognition. Shows the amount of profit that will eventually be realized when the receivable is collected. Some accountants show this account as a *liability*.

unrealized holding gain. See *inventory profit* for definition and an example.

unrecovered cost. *Book value* of an asset.

unsecured account. An account receivable or payable, for which no collateral has been given.

usage variance. *Quantity variance*.

use of funds. Any transaction that reduces funds (however funds is defined).

useful life. Service life.

utility program. A computer program used for standard routines such as sorting, adding, printing, copying and tracing.

V

V Day. *Valuation Day*.

valuation account. A *contra account*. When *inventories* or *marketable securities* are shown at *cost* and the *lower-of-cost-or-market* valuation basis is to be used, often any declines in market value below cost will be credited to a valuation account. In this way, the acquisition cost and the amounts of price declines below cost can both be shown.

Valuation Day. The dates specified in Federal income tax legislation at which values for securities (December 22, 1971) and other assets (December 31, 1971) were determined on the introduction of capital gains tax.

value. Monetary worth; the term is usually so subjective that it ought not to be used without a modifying adjective unless most people would agree on the amount; not to be confused with *cost*. See *fair market value*, *entry value*, *exit value*.

value added. *Cost* of a product or *work in process*, minus the cost of the materials purchased for the product or work in process.

value added tax (VAT). A tax levied at each stage in the production and distribution chain on the basis of the value that is added to the goods or services passing through that stage.

value in use. The present value of future net cash flows expected to result from the use of an asset by the enterprise and from its ultimate disposition.

variable annuity. An *annuity* whose periodic payments depend on some uncertain outcome, such as stock market prices.

variable budget. *Flexible budget*.

variable costing. *Direct costing*. Contrast with *absorption costing*.

variable costs. *Costs* that change as activity levels change. Strictly speaking, variable costs are zero when the activity level is zero. See *semivariable costs*. In accounting, this term most often means the sum of *direct costs* and *variable overhead*.

variable interval sampling. A method of choosing a sample in which the intervals between items selected from the population are not equal but average to the desired sampling interval. Compare *fixed interval sampling*.

variables sampling. The use of a sampling technique whereby a particular quantitative characteristic of an entire population is inferred from a sample, e.g. money value. See also *estimation sampling*. Compare *attribute(s) sampling*.

variance. Difference between actual and *standard costs* or between *budgeted* and actual *expenditures* or, sometimes, *expenses*. In accounting, the word has a completely different meaning from its meaning in statistics, where it is a measure of dispersion of a distribution.

variance analysis. The calculation of *variances* in a *standard cost system*. This term has a different meaning in statistics.

variation analysis. Analysis of the causes of changes in items of interest in financial statements such as net *income* or *gross margin*.

VAT. *Value added tax*.

vendor. A seller. Sometimes spelled ''vender.''

venture accounting. The method of accounting for a specific business undertaking, in which all costs and revenues are carried forward as a net figure in the balance sheet of the venturer and the results are not determined until the venture is completed.

venture capital. A term of imprecise meaning often used to describe equity investment in corporations whose securities are not publicly traded, by persons (venture capitalists) not directly managing the business.

verifiability. The ability through consensus among measurers to ensure that information represents what it purports to represent or that the chosen method of measurement has been used without error or *bias*.

verifiable. A qualitative *objective* of financial reporting specifying that items in *financial statements* can be checked by tracing back to supporting *invoices*, canceled *cheques*, and other physical pieces of evidence.

verification. The auditor's act of reviewing or checking items in *financial statements* by tracing back to supporting *invoices*, canceled *cheques*, and other business documents, or sending out *confirmations* to be returned. Compare with *physical verification*.

vertical analysis. Analysis of *the financial statements* of a single firm as of a given date, as opposed to *horizontal* or *time series analysis* where items are compared over time or across firms.

vertical integration. The extension of activity by an organization into businesses directly related to the production or distribution of the organization's end products. Although products may be sold to others at various stages, a substantial proportion of the output at each stage is devoted to the production of the end products. Compare *horizontal integration*.

vested. Said of *pension plan* benefits that are not contingent on the employee continuing to work for the employer.

vesting. The irrevocable passing over to an employee of rights either to pension benefits or to withdrawal privileges as regards employer contribution.

volume variance. The difference between applied fixed overhead and budgeted fixed overhead.

voting trust. An agreement among security holders of a corporation whereby their votes are to be cast by a trustee on behalf of the group.

vouch. To verify by examination of supporting documents.

voucher. A document that serves to recognize a *liability* and authorize the disbursement of cash. Sometimes used to refer to the written evidence documenting an *accounting entry*, as in the term *journal voucher*.

voucher register. A book of original entry for expenditures which combines the functions of a cash disbursements book and a subsidiary record of vouchers payable.

voucher system. A method for controlling *cash* that requires each *cheque* to be authorized with an approved *voucher*. No cash *disbursements* are made except from *petty cash funds*.

W

wage. Compensation of employees based on time worked or output of product for manual labour. But see *take-home pay*.

warehouse receipt. Documentary evidence issued by the operator of a public warehouse that goods are being held in storage on behalf of their owner.

warrant. A certificate entitling the owner to buy a spec-

ified number of shares at a specified time(s) for a specified price. Differs from a *stock option* only in that options are granted to employees and warrants are issued to the public. See *right*.

warranty. A promise by a seller to correct deficiencies in products sold. When warranties are given, proper accounting practice recognizes an estimate of warranty *expense* and an *estimated liability* at the time of sale. See *guarantee* for contrast in proper usage.

warranty repairs. Repairs to goods sold under warranty, the cost being borne by the vendor or manufacturer.

waste. Residue of material from manufacturing operations with no sale value. Frequently, it has negative value because additional costs must be incurred for disposal.

wasting asset. A *natural resource* having a limited *useful life* and, hence, subject to *amortization* called *depletion*. Examples are timberland, oil and gas wells, and ore deposits.

watered stock. *Shares* issued for *assets* with *fair market value* less than *par value*. The assets are put onto the books at the overstated values. In the law, for shares to be considered watered, the *board of directors* must have acted in bad faith or fraudulently in issuing the shares under these circumstances. The term originated from a former practice of cattlemen who fed cattle (''stock'') large quantities of salt to make them thirsty. The cattle then drank a lot of water before being taken to market. This was done to make the cattle heavier and appear more valuable than otherwise.

wear and tear. Physical deterioration of a *capital asset* through use or exposure to the elements.

weighted average. An average computed by counting each occurrence of each value, not merely a single occurrence of each value. For example, if one unit is purchased for \$1 and two units are purchased for \$2 each, then the simple average of the purchase prices is \$1.50 but the weighted average price per unit is \$5/3 = \$1.67. Contrast with *moving average*.

weighted-average inventory method. Valuing either *withdrawals* or *ending inventory* at the *weighted average* purchase price of all units on hand at the time of withdrawal or of computing ending inventory. The *inventory equation* is used to calculate the other quantity. If the *perpetual inventory* method is in use, often inaccurately called the ''moving-average method.''

wholesale price index. An index measuring changes in prices of commodities sold by producers and distributors to retailers.

wind up. To bring to an end, such as the life of a corporation. This is accomplished either by following the winding-up provisions of applicable statutes, surrendering the charter or following bankruptcy proceedings. See also *liquidation*.

window dressing. The attempt to make financial statements show *operating* results, or *financial position*, more favourable than would be otherwise shown.

with recourse. See *note receivable discounted*.

withdrawals. *Assets* distributed to an owner. *Partner's drawings*. See *inventory equation* for another context.

withholding. Deductions from *salaries* or *wages*, usually for *income taxes*, to be remitted by the employer, in the employee's name, to the taxing authority.

without recourse. See *note receivable discounted*.

work in process (work in progress). Partly-finished goods, services or contracts which are in the process of manufacture or completion; an *asset* that is classified as *inventory*.

work order. Written instructions for the execution of specified work usually with specifications for the materials to be issued and the labour to be employed.

work sheet. A tabular schedule for convenient summary of *adjusting* and *closing entries*. The work sheet usually begins with an *unadjusted trial balance*. Adjusting entries are shown in the next two columns, one for *debits* and one for *credits*. The horizontal sum of each line is then carried to the right into either the *income statement* or *balance sheet* columns, as appropriate. The *plug* to equate the income statement column totals is the income, if a debit plug is required, or loss, if a credit plug is required, for the period. That income will be closed to retained earnings on the balance sheet. The income statement credit columns are the revenues for the period and the debit columns are the expenses (and revenue *contras*) to be shown on the income statement.

Work sheet is also used to refer to *schedules* for determining other items appearing on the *financial statements* that require adjustment or compilation.

working capital. *Current assets* minus *current liabilities*. The *statement of changes in financial position* usually explains the changes in working capital for a period.

working capital equation. The *balance sheet* states that *Assets = Equities*. The information in comparative balance sheets from the start and end of a period can be restated as:

$$\text{Change in Assets} = \text{Change in Equities}.$$

This equation can be further broken down to say that

| Change in Current Assets Plus Change in Noncurrent Assets | = | Change in Current Liabilities Plus Change in Noncurrent Equities |

which is equivalent to

| Change in Current Assets Less Change in Current Liabilities | = | Change in Noncurrent Equities Less Change in Noncurrent Assets |

The left-hand side of this equation is the change in *working capital* for the period. The items on the right-hand side cause the change in working capital during the period. The *statement of changes in financial position* typically shows the causes of the changes (right-hand side of the equation) at the top of the statement and the way working capital has changed (left-hand side of the equation) at the bottom of the statement.

working-capital provided by operations. See *funds provided by operations*.

working papers. The schedules and analyses prepared by the *auditor* in carrying out investigations prior to issuing an *opinion* on *financial statements*.

worth. *Value*. See *net worth*.

worth-debt ratio. Reciprocal of the *debt-equity ratio*. See *ratio*.

write down. *Write off*, except that not all the asset's cost is charged to expense or *loss*. Generally used for nonrecurring items.

write off. *Charge* an *asset* to *expense* or *loss*; that is, *debit* expense (or loss) and *credit* asset.

write-off method. A method for treating *uncollectible accounts* that charges *bad debt expense* and credits accounts receivable of specific customers as uncollectible amounts are identified. May not be used when uncollectible amounts are significant and can be estimated. See *sales* and *allowance method* for contrast.

write up. To increase the recorded *cost* of an *asset* with no corresponding *disbursement* of *funds*; that is, *debit* asset and *credit* revenue or, perhaps, *owners' equity*. Seldom done because currently accepted accounting principles are based on actual transactions.

Y

yield. *Internal rate of return* on a stream of cash flows Cash yield is cash flow divided by book value. See also *dividend yield*.

yield to maturity. At a given time, the *internal rate of return* of a series of cash flows, usually said of a *bond*. Sometimes called the "effective rate."

Z

zero-base(d) budgeting (ZBB). In preparing an ordinary *budget* for the next period, a manager starts with the budget for the current period and makes adjustments as seem necessary, because of changed conditions, for the next period. Since most managers like to increase the scope of the activities managed and since most prices increase most of the time, amounts in budgets prepared in the ordinary, incremental way seem to increase period after period. The authority approving the budget assumes operations will be carried out in the same way as in the past and that next period's expenditures will have to be at least as large as the current period's. Thus, this authority tends to study only the increments to the current period's budget. In ZBB, the authority questions the process for carrying out a program and the entire budget for the next period; every dollar in the budget is studied, not just the dollars incremental to the previous period's amounts. The advocates of ZBB claim that in this way: (1) programs or divisions of marginal benefit to the business or governmental unit will more likely be deleted from the program, rather than being continued with costs at least as large as the present ones, and (2) alternative, more cost-effective, ways of carrying out programs are more likely to be discovered and implemented. ZBB implies questioning the existence of programs, and the fundamental nature of the way they are carried out, not merely the amounts used to fund them. Experts appear to be evenly divided as to whether the middle word should be "base" or "based."

Index

To the Owner of this Book:

We are interested in your reaction to the fourth edition of *Financial Accounting: An Introduction to Concepts, Methods, and Uses.* Through feedback from you, we can improve this book in future editions.

1. What was your reason for using this book?

    _____University Course   _____Continuing Education

    _____College Course   _____Other (specify _____)

2. If you used this book for a course, what is the name of the school you attend?

    _____

3. Approximately how much of the book did you use?

    _____ ¼   _____ ½   _____ ¾   _____ all

4. Which chapters or sections were omitted from your course?

5. Have you any suggestions for improvement?

Fold here

- -

POSTAGE WILL BE PAID BY

DAVID COLLINGE
Publisher
College Editorial Department
**HOLT, RINEHART AND WINSTON
OF CANADA, LIMITED
55 HORNER AVENUE
TORONTO, ONTARIO
M8Z 9Z9**

Tape shut

CHAPTER 12

9.31(d) Credit to Deferred ICA Year 7 = $910
9.33(a) Rate of Return Year 4 = 18.33%
   (b) Rate of Return Year 4 = 15.67%
9.35(a) Net Income Year 4 = $32,000
   (b) Net Income Year 4 = $32,000
9.36(b) Loss = $28,000
9.38 Income Rises By = 53%
9.39 UCC's 12/31/Yr2 = 0; $54,700; 32,360; 15,200;
         6,750; 6300
9.43(a) Year 4 R of R = 15.8%
   (b) Year 4 R of R = 5.5%
9.44 Total CCA   = $8,792
     Tax on Excess   = $ 604
     PV of Advantage = $ 110 @10%
9.47(b) Difference (3 Years) = $10,040.63
DP9.1 Depreciation Year 40   = $86,916
       Accounting R01 Year 40 = 20%

CHAPTER 10

10.16(b) Total Expense = $240,800
10.17 Vacation Pay = $6,480
10.18(b) Balance End of Year 2 = $27,000
10.20(e) Expense = $64,695
10.22(a) Difference = $2,765
10.24 Balance January 2 = $23,561
10.25 Balance Month 4 = $108,684
10.26(b) Expense October 1, Year 2 = $49,257
10.27(c) Difference = $322
10.28(d) Expense, Third Payment = $50,224
10.29(d) Expense, Third Payment = $59,776
10.30 Correct Sales = $802,200
10.31 Sales = $105,000,000
10.34(a) Expenses = $5,545
   (b) Liability = $6,630
10.35(a) Contract Revenues 6/30 = $127,500
   (b) Account Balance 12/31 = $150,000
10.37(b) Loss = $231,667
10.39 Total Sources = $396,000
10.41(c) Ratio = 37.75%
10.42 PV = $2,563, 903
DP10.1 Proforma EPS, Feltham   = $2.05
        Proforma EPS, Mattesich = $1.14

CHAPTER 11

11.19(b) Income = $252,500
11.21 Expense = $234,500
11.22(b) Expense = $190,000
11.24(c) Total Expense = $150,000
11.25(c) Exact Rate = .72%
11.29(a) Ratio = 47.6%
   (b) PV = $21.1 billion
   (c) Ratio = 82.6%
   (d) Ratio = 96.3%
DP11.1 Aftertax Cost of Lease Alternative = $7,278/yr

CHAPTER 12

12.17 Correct Net Income = $120,000
12.18 Net Income = $304,000
12.31(c) Difference = $62.1 million
12.32(a) Loss = $11,500,000
12.34(b) BV after Conversion = 15^1/_3$ per share
         EPS after Conversion = $2.40
12.35(b) PV of Loan Repayment = $855,812
12.38(b) EPS = $3.276
   (c) EPS = $4.524
   (d) EPS = $3.429
   (e) EPS = $3.077
12.39 New Stated Capital = $80,000
12.40(c) Total Shareholders' Equity = $1,764,000
12.42(a) Dividends = $1,000,000
   (e) EPS   = $3.95
IP(P+11) Shareholders' Equity = $510,300

CHAPTER 13

13.8(d) Maximum = $14,500
13.10 Amortization Expense = $7,500
13.11(a) Amortization Expense = $ 9,250
   (b) Credit to Investment − $1,428,000
13.12(b) Income from Subsidiaries = $223,000
   (c) MI if Consolidated   = $ 53,000
13.14(b) Credit to Investment = $523,200
13.15(a)(8) Amortization Expense = $ 2,100
   (b) Credit to Investment = $335,700
13.16 Consolidated Gross Profit = $150,000
13.17(b) Fraction = 62.5%
13.18(c) Fraction = 85%
13.19(b) Assets = $500,000
13.22 Total Adjustments Column = $95
13.23(a) Credit to Investment = $108,000
13.24(a) Total Adjustments Column = $329.5
     Total MI   = $35.5
   (b) Total Assets   = $1,226,500
13.25 Total Adjustments Column = $93.7
13.26 Total Adjustments Column = $320.65
13.27 Total Assets = $1,067,000
13.28(a) Total Assets   = $450,000
   (b) Consolidated Retained Earnings = $125,000
   (c) Consolidated Retained Earnings = $124,500
13.30(a) Total Eliminations   = $51,800
     Goodwill June 30, Year 8 = $10,700
   (b) Total Assets   = $507,000
13.31 Consolidated Retained Earnings Case C =
       $112,000
13.32(a)(5) Goodwill 12/31 Year 7 = $27,000
   (b) Income Year 7   = $ 7,500
13.33 Difference = $4.9
13.34 Difference = $6.9
13.35 Difference = $8.1
13.37 Total Sources = $397,300

5.16	Total Sources = $117,000	
5.18	Total Sources = $79,000	
5.19	Total Sources = $64,000	
5.20	Total Sources = $655,000	
5.21	Working Capital Provided by Operations = $629,000	
5.22	Total Sources of Working Capital = $660,000	
5.23	Total Sources = $114,000	
5.24	Total Sources = $93,000	
5.25(a)	Total Sources = $259,000	
(b)	Total Sources = $375,000	
5.26	Total Assets = $925	
5.27	Total Sources Year 5 = $46.4	
	Total Sources Year 6 = $ 5.0	
DP5.1	Total Sources = $483	
IP5.1	Net Income = $ 370	
	Total Assets = $62,370	
	Total Sources = $49,140	

CHAPTER 6

6.20	Rate of Return on Assets = 6.8%, 5.6%, 5.1%
6.22	Other Expenses = $550
	Interest Expense = $250
6.23(c)	Required Earnings = $6,500,000
(d)	Level of Earnings = $4,500,000
6.27(b)	Cash From Operations = $257,400

CHAPTER 7

7.16	Total Cash = $80,378
7.17	Adjusted Balance = $6,713
7.18	Adjusted Balance = $938
7.19	Adjusted Balance = $5,050
7.31	Adjusted Balance = $3,605
7.32	LCM Holding Loss 12/12 Year 2 = $5,000
	ACM Holding Loss 12/12 Year 2 = $2,000
	Mkt Holding Gain 12/12 Year 2 = $4,000
7.34	Aggregate LCM Holding Loss Year 2 = $1,000
	Market Holding Gain Year 2 = $2,200
7.39	Percentage Uncollectible = 10%
7.43	Total Sources = $145,000
7.45	Net Income = $36,000
7.46	Individual LCM Holding Loss Reported = $20,000
	Aggregate LCM Holding Loss Reported = $ 5,000
DP7.1	Incomes = $28,200, $20,937, $26,162, $24,720

CHAPTER 8

8.15	Total Income FIFO = $288,000
	Total Income LIFO = $288,000
8.16	LCM Gross Profit Year 3 = $115,000
	Acquisition Cost Gross Profit Year 3 = $100,000

8.17	FIFO Gross Profit = $50,000	
	Minimum Gross Profit = $45,000	
	Maximum Gross Profit = $55,000	
8.18(a)	FIFO Periodic = $50,000	
(b)	Weighted Average Periodic = $50,720	
(c)	LIFO Periodic = $52,000	
(d)	FIFO Perpetual = $12,000	
(e)	Weighted Average Perpetual = $11,750	
(f)	LIFO Perpetual = $11,000	
8.21(a)	Pretax Income = $110	
(b)	Pretax Income = $ 50	
(c)	Pretax Income = $ 85	
8.23(c)	FIFO Gross Profit = $840,000	
	LIFO Gross Profit = $690,000	
(d)	FIFO Profit with Holding Gains = $1,020,000	
	LIFO Profit with Holding Gains = $1,020,000	
8.24	Year 1 Net Income = $100,000	
	Year 2 Net Income = $104,000	
8.29(a)	Ending Inventory = $50,000	
8.31(g)	After Tax Difference − $1,575	
8.32(a)	FIFO Profit with Holding Gain = $15,200	
	LIFO Profit with Holding Gain = $15,200	
	Wt. Ave. Profit with Holding Gain = $15,200	
8.32(b)	FIFO Profit with Holding Gain = $13,700	
	LIFO Profit with Holding Gain = $13,700	
	Wt. Ave. Profit with Holding Gain = $13,700	
8.34(a)	Net Income = $120,000	
(b)	Net Income = $144,000	
(c)	Net Income = $132,000	
8.38(a)	HC Current Ratio = 1.3	
	CC Current Ratio = 1.6	
	HC Inventory Turnover = 5.5	
	CC Inventory Turnover = 3.7	
	HC Rate of Return = 19%	
	CC Rate of Return = 10%	
8.42	Average Markup on Cost = 86.9%	
	Holding Gain = $51,875	
DP8.1	Cost of Inventory Affected by Fire = $403,700	

CHAPTER 9

9.7	Accumulated Depreciation = $31,850
9.9(d)	Accumulated Depreciation = $26,278
9.10(b)	Age of Building = 183 months
9.11(a)	Gain on Disposal = $165
9.13	Factory Building Total = $385,000
9.16(a)	Capitalized Interest = $500,000
9.19(b)	Loss on Retirement = $900
9.20(b)	Loss = $320
(c)	Gain/Loss = 0
9.21	Total Sources = $59,400
9.22	Total Sources = $62,000
9.25	Proceeds = $7,000
9.27(a)	Costs to be Capitalized = $54,550
(c)	NBV 12/31 Year 10 = $ 5,857
9.30	Total Sources = $435,000